INCA ORIGINS

Autobiographical Note:

Graeme R. Kearsley is an architect who has maintained a life-long interest in archaeology. He was born in New South Wales in Australia and began his architectural training at the University of New South Wales in Sydney. After five years he travelled to the U.K. and after some years recommenced his architectural studies at Thames Polytechnic (Greenwich University) where he graduated in 1977 with first class honours.

Front Cover Illustration:

A section of a tapestry band reflecting Tiahaunacan imagery of the winged Staff God from Cahuachi on the Nazca Plain in South Peru inherited by the Early Huari and dating to 800-1000 A.D.

ISBN 0-9541158-2-1

E-mail: mayangenesis@btinternet.com

Web Page: **www.mayan-genesis.com**

First published in the United Kingdom by the Yelsraek Publishing in the year 2003 A.D.

Printed and bound by    www.dd.com.pl

INCA ORIGINS

ASIAN INFLUENCES in EARLY SOUTH AMERICA in MYTH, MIGRATION and HISTORY

GRAEME R. KEARSLEY

PHOTOGRAPHIC SOURCES AND COPYRIGHT

Where possible throughout this work the original and earliest photographs available have been used since they are often the only source of many cultural aspects and iconographic elements which reflect the original context in which the ceramics, supporting panels, monoliths and walls supporting the elements of iconography of interest had been found. Some reflect crafts or social contexts that are no longer found.

The owners of the copyright of those photographs which have been incorporated which are still within that copyright have been notified where necessary depending on the varying regulations applicable at the time of publication. Because many of the photographs utilised have appeared in publications longer than seventy years ago or longer attempts to trace the origins, or contact those who might still have right of copyright have not always succeeded. Continuing attempts to contact such owners are still being undertaken and will be negotiated when that right has been established.

Old photographs have a charm of their own but their broad inclusion in this work, as for all photographic, sketch and graphic aspects, is to illustrate elements of iconography which are similar in India, Indonesia and Mesoamerica and associated cultural regions. The problem with early photographs is they often lack clarity of detail, but, for the most part, only those which depict related elements of iconography illustrated reasonably clearly has been included. Comparisons for the most part are achieved by juxtaposition where possible but since many illustrations depict more than one pertinent element of iconography the major element takes precedence in the photographic arrangement.

CONTENTS

INTRODUCTION

The origin of the Incas has for centuries been a subject of some interest, from the Spanish who came in contact with them at the time of the Conquest, and for later scholars. Many of the historians and the first anthropologists in the Victorian era, and from that time, were at first in general agreement that there was evidence for Asian influences, not only in the culture and records of the Incas but many of the earlier cultures that were beginning to be uncovered from one and a half centuries ago. Their view was less cluttered and they perceived the obvious and they were generally known later as the Diffusionists. However, emerging at this same time was a group of researchers who adamantly denied that there was any possibility of contact with the Old World, either Europe or Asia, and it is this movement, generally known as the Americanists, who gained the ascendancy from the mid-20th., century to the present day.

Although marginalized the pro-Diffusionists who support cultural transfer, either primary or secondary, from the Old World to the New have not completely died out. Some are in fact well-known authorities in their fields supporting either irregular or sporadic contacts between Asia and the Americas, or over a more protracted period. These include David H. Kelley, Michael D. Coe, Paul Tolstoy, Alice Kehoe and from an earlier generation, Gordon R. Willey, Gordon F. Ekholm, Robert Heine-Geldern, Clifford Evans and Betty J. Meggers. It is interesting to note that the Latin American historians and archaeologists have largely tended to support the idea of cross-Pacific influences into the Americas. A generation ago in Mexico Miguel Covarrubias was well-known for such views and earlier still in South America Emilio Estrada supported cross-Pacific contacts in Ecuador and his work influenced the next generation of archaeologists in Ecuador, most notably Meggers and Evans.

When seeking a reader for his book the present author approached the then curator of the Department of American Archaeology at the British Museum and after meeting the curator, but before presenting this request, was given a current review he had written for a well-known magazine while he went to retrieve other material. The subject of the review was a book on Ancient metallurgy in West Mexico and the curator in his opening sentences dismisses "trans-Pacific diffusion" as "fanciful notions"[1] without including justification for such comments. However, he also refers in this review to the South American connections extending back 2000 years evidenced in shaft tombs in Colombia and ceramics similar to those of Ecuador found in Western Mexico to indicate possible origins of metallurgy with South America. This assertion however, always supported by Diffusionists, was propounded by Covarrubias among others, was fiercely contested by Americanists. It is only in the last decade, with the more extensive excavations and interest in Western Mexico, that the connections with South America have become irrefutable. Behind such denials was always the problem that if South Americans reached such a great distance against the sea currents flowing along the respective Pacific coasts of the American continents then they were also capable of flowing with, and navigating these same currents as they swept away westward toward Polynesia and onward to Asia. The lack of suitable ocean-going craft and therefore navigational skills has always been the backbone of the pro-Americanist, isolationist or indigenous development theory.

Having largely completed the present book in draft the author came across at the last moment two books by the former American ambassador to Peru (1923-8), Miles Poindexter. These books were entitled the "The Ayar Incas" and "Peruvian Pharaohs" and clearly derive from his own interest and researches into the history of Peru as well as including references to other authorities of that time. His books deal with the apparent origins of the Incas and particularly to the title they arrogated to themselves - "Ayar". This term he claimed derived from an Aryan heritage and from that of the Brahman Aryans of India in particular and his extensive researches into racial and linguistic heritage are still of considerable interest to those who are willing to study these works. However, whatever his personal views of the events unfolding in Europe at the time may have been, the release of his books regarding Aryan heritage in the 1930's, one of the most inauspicious moments in Aryan history in Europe and the history of the West, was unfortunate to say the least. The Aryan lineal descent Poindexter considered to be the most likely for the Incas was the Aryan tribes of India. The Aryan Vedas are the most ancient and sacred books of India from before the middle of the first millennium, B.C. when they were first recorded in the form known into the present time. All of the high-status tribes and castes of India claim descent from the Aryan tribes that swept into the Subcontinent in the early first millennium, B.C. and they are exceptionally proud of that heritage. Even into our time this pride is reflected in the retention of the titles Ayya, Ayar, Airya, Aryana and others deriving from Aryan or Irian (Iran). The claims of this descent are based on 3,000 years of oral and written traditions and modern archaeology only confirms the veracity of most of these claims. If the subject of Nazi Aryanism ever occurs in India it is simply dealt with by denial that it has anything to do with them or their heritage, and correctly so, and in this vein the possibility, or probability, that the Incas descended from them a millennia or more before the present day must be adopted.

Because many of the traditions are recorded either from non-written sources or translated from non-Indo-European languages there are frequently more than one way of spelling or pronouncing certain words or deity names and where quoted the original has been retained. This is particularly evident where there is a very long tradition of regional dialects and languages expressing the same deity or place names and particularly so in the countryside of India. In the succeeding Vedic, Brahmanic and its two offspring, Buddhism and Hinduism, deities inherited and absorbed, or rejected elements, over many centuries modified and affected the original concepts and this becomes apparent in any study of deities or place names in India. There is therefore a multi-levelled stratification through the millennia and cultural epochs reflected in any one of the traditional deities in India and some such as Rudra have accreted and assimilated aspects that are in themselves evidential. In Peru and Bolivia it is particularly notable among the Andean gods that they lack these millennia of accretions assimilated from previous deities and philosophic constructs and are more loosely associated than those of India appearing to reflect associations through importation.

In India, in the dispersed communities in the countryside many of the tribes reflect a Hinduism that is permeated by pre-Aryan deities who are readily discernable. It would be expected that in the Andes, where communities are more widely isolated by high ranges separating the inhabited valleys, the same principle might apply. In fact the regional variations in the religious beliefs before the Conquest are still preserved in spite of "cleansing" by intensive missions imposing Christianisation by the Spanish, and are the subject of several interesting studies in the last few decades. But there is an unexplained lack of pre-Inca religious belief systems notable even in the works of the first Spanish missionaries that might have been expected to have survived since the Inca only extended control to its final boundaries a generation or two before the Conquest. This might further suggest that the religion(s) of Andean Peru were in fact a reflection of those imported by mariners that reinforced those of earlier imported beliefs by the same means and with similar origins. This might particularly be so since the myths and legends, such as they are, were in fact related to sea heroes, such as Viracocha, and the same might be said for other prominent deities and these will be of some note in this work.

In considering contacts between the Pacific Islands and South America none can be more controversial than the propositions linking Easter Island and Ancient Peru. There are many studies undertaken more readily accessible and Thor Heyerdahl in his works has shown that there are many parallels in the sculpture and iconography of Easter Island and the Andes. Recent research has shown that the most prominent genetic marker for the Polynesian people has been found in the bone analysis from early skeletons on Easter Island. However, there has never been a denial that the Polynesians formed the broad racial basis for migrations onto Easter Island and that they were not other than from the nearby Society Islands or the Tuamotu Archipelago or perhaps New Zealand. This important island indicates in fact a general principle in cross-Pacific contacts from Asia to South America.

The Polynesian were in part from Northern East Asia and also from the Malay Archipelago and they readily reflect that heritage. However, they are in many respects closely allied to Caucasians and were in many studies considered as such, and this racial heritage is still obvious in many islands in Eastern Polynesia as it was to the first European explorers. These migrations followed the same pattern as land migrations in that the male migrants, or mariners, traded, bought or captured marriage partners from coastal or island peoples thereby producing mixed race descendants. Therefore variable racial inheritance is clearly evident throughout the islands of the Pacific that is as true of Melanesia, Indonesia and Micronesia as it was, and is for Polynesia.

Jacob Roggeveen was the first European captain to discover Easter Island and his journal notes that the inhabitants approached the ship in canoes but also noted that they came out on reed floats. These were of totora reed, the exact same as that found in Peru and around the shores of Lake Titicaca and used in the same manner[2]. Noted also on this voyage was that these people readily wish to trade "... a large quantity of sugar-cane, fowls, yams and bananas" belying the recent belief that these people suffered starvation over several centuries after deforestation. A fellow mariner on the same voyage, Bouman, recorded that the fields of the Easter Islanders were "neatly divided into squares by furrows" and that they had coconut trees and, as in other parts of Polynesia, there were plantations of the sweet potato - a South American tuber[3]. The raised fields system appears identical to that of the Tiahuanacans around Lake Titicaca and this along with the fact that the same reed was also found on Easter Island along with many parallels in sculptural form, iconography, and cyclopean stonework at Vinapu, suggests that there must have been contacts, from at least one or more occasional voyages with South America.

In almost all of the reports by the first Europeans there are references to the variable skin colouring of Polynesian on different islands, but also within the people of one island. Roggeveen notes that the Easter Islanders were light-skinned, and were "pale yellow or sallow"[4] and they extended their ear lobes in the same way as the Andean peoples. Other observers have noted that the Miru clan were lighter and a different physical type to those of the general Polynesian people while Bauman recorded that there were many who appeared to be Indians of the Americas. Other Europeans have been quite specific in describing certain peoples among the Polynesian on some islands, usually revered, who were of the "Jewish " type and wore turbans and not least among these was Captain Cook. The evidence as recorded indicates that there were traders from Asia but also from South America, as well as the Polynesians themselves, who linked Asia across through the myriad islands of the Pacific to South America. It is these indomitable people as mariners who were responsible for introducing many aspects from the higher cultures that instigated major cultural changes that are evident to a lesser degree in the islands but obvious in South America and almost invariably evident on the Pacific Coast. Easter Island, along with all of the Pacific Coast of Peru, is connected by ocean currents that clearly indicate that these were used as marine highways and that the settlement of Easter Island and later contacts with the rest of Polynesia, albeit occasional, particularly Moriori and Maori New Zealand as well as Peru, were as a result of these ocean currents.

It will be shown in this work that the Incas are clearly the descendants of the fire-worshiping peoples not only of the Indian Vedas but also from Iran and the Ancient Middle East. The textual along with iconographical references and the artefactual elements available are often limited, since they were transferred by mariners who travelled light out of necessity. However, the surviving evidence will clearly indicate that there must have been cultural transfer across the Pacific from Asia, and India and the Ancient Middle East in particular, into South America. It will also be shown that the earlier traditions in South America, before the Incas, are also very probably the result of influences of the high culture epochs in the Ancient Middle East and that there were probably at least a few cultural transfers or contacts from South America across the Pacific as a counter-flow back to Asia. In these return voyages it is likely that the Andean and Peruvian cultures greatly influenced the Polynesians, and that the Maoris are likely to have been the result of at least one major stream from Peru merging with other influences from India and Ancient Iran.

The first section of this work is a general review of some of the researches undertaken by the first Europeans who entered the Pacific and who readily perceived as contacts and cultural connections between Asia and Australia, South America, and even Africa. The central chapters of this book reviews the archaeology and associated references in South America with parallels included where appropriate from Asia and more usually with the Ancient Middle East. This section concentrates more on the Inca Origin myths as well as the many references in myth and legend showing that there must have been mariner contacts between Asia and South America probably over 5000 years before the arrival of Europeans. The middle to last chapters deal with the many parallel cultural aspects that are reflected in the Ancient Middle East that most likely to be the result of this cross-Pacific transfer through Oceania to South America that appear in the available archaeological and iconographical record as well as the evidence preserved in the local oral traditions in myths and legends where applicable.

Many of the references and myths included in this work are less easily obtained or rarely noted by recent authors, and are therefore, when quoted, included more extensively for the interest and edification of the interested reader. Comparisons in cultural beliefs and rituals is rarely undertaken when paralleling Old and New World practices or beliefs and certainly almost never by recent authors on South American (or North American) history except derogatorily. This has facilitated the general belief that there was no cultural transfer from the Old to the New World. If no mentioned or no comparisons are presented then a conditioning of belief by default ensues that the high cultures of the Americas evolved from fundamentally indigenous cultural developments in both North and South America and this fiction can be utilised and maintained by those who propound the Isolationist theories. This work therefore extends the quotes and references to many aspects not considered in depth elsewhere that will indicate that even in the most basic elements of cultural life from the Incas, and evident also among their forebears, there is clear evidence that cultural transfer from Asia initiated major cultural changes in South America for five millennia before the Spanish Conquest.

CHAPTER 1

ANCIENT TRADE and MIGRATION
from INDIA to AUSTRALIA

Traces of the Most Ancient Cultural Transfers into the Pacific

It is at this time, from the middle of the last (20th.) century until today, that the notion of cross-Pacific voyages from the Old World of South, South East and East Asia to the Americas before the pre-European Colonial period has been considered historically impossible by the vocal majority of historians and archaeologists. This was not always the case since the largest number of the first European explorers, from first contact with the New World, perceived the apparent close similarities in the development of architecture, iconography and also in the surviving myths and those of Asia. During the eclipse of the cross-Pacific theory in the last fifty years a few have retained the view that there must have been contacts because so many cultural elements occurring in both Asia and the New World show too great a similarity to be coincidental. Barkcloth, and the bark-beaters used to produce it, are virtually identical throughout the Pacific Region[1] from Central and South America in the east through to South East Asia in the far west and beyond in India where barkcloth was a sacred cloth produced from the revered banyan[2]. Botanically another element of evidence for man-conveyed distribution by oceanic voyages is evident in the sweet potato. This tuber is a native of South America and can only be propagated by hand but is found distributed across the Pacific Islands to the Western Pacific in New Guinea. The so-called "kumara line" is determined from the route and appears as it is found along the line from South America into Eastern Polynesia through the Marquesas Islands, Society Islands, the Cook Islands and beyond to New Guinea - the furthest west in Melanesia. From Eastern Polynesia, the sweet potato, or kumara as it is known there, dispersed further to the north to Hawaii and South East to Easter Island, but most remarkably to New Zealand where many varieties were developed and cultivated. It is believed by recent researchers that these outer Polynesian Islands were "colonised by a people who already had the options of the sweet potato as a staple"[3] implying that they were possibly traders or colonisers from South America. The archaeology of Melanesia is a story of slow problematic processes due to difficult political and economic as well as topographical difficulties. In the highlands of New Guinea it is now known that cultivation beds and channels were developed 9000 years ago in the Wahgi area and the possibility that taro and the sweet potato had been introduced in this or subsequent periods is under investigation. Other cultivation fields are known from the Lapita period dating from about 3-4,000 years ago, and in the following millennia irrigated, wet and dry cultivation fields have been recorded in the Fijian Islands. In the Cook Islands the sweet potato has been identified as the first positive cultivation of this South America tuber dating at the oldest Carbon 14 analysis to about 1000 A.D.[4]. This date is an interesting one since it corresponds to the fall of Tiahuanaco and the sudden appearance of large forms of megalithic ruins of the Tiahuanaco type in the Eastern Polynesian Islands. This is also the time band of the settlement of New Zealand where the largest number of sweet potato varieties are found outside Peru suggesting a long association and understanding of the growth cycle necessary in raising this tuber.

Ancient Maori tradition notes that about 1150 A.D. an expedition under the Ariki Toi, consisting of two large canoes of men, set out from the ancestral homeland in Central Polynesia called Hawaiki for New Zealand. It is conjectured that it was this expedition that introduced the sweet potato into New Zealand[5] and may actually have been meant to represent the voyages of the first Polynesians to settle New Zealand, the Morioris. However, it is more likely that New Zealand was known for some time before the first settlement since migrants or venturers rarely set out for an unknown place. This was more probably so since there were many known islands to the west that would more likely to have been the sites for settlement as their Polynesian influences extended through the islands of Melanesia to New Guinea. Other Maori myths specifically state that there was a return voyage to Hawaiki for the specific intention of fetching the seed tubers of the sweet potato by a descendant of Toi, and these were successfully introduced in the main Fleet of settlers who returned with them in about 1350 A.D.[6]. The sweet potato or kumara, was in other versions said to have been introduced as nine seed tubers from the belt of the god Rongo, the deity of horticulture, and taro was believed to have been introduced at the same time. In the New Zealand region of the Aotea, probably named after the god Atea, the sweet potato was called Tatua o Rongorongo or "Belt of Rongorongo"[7]. Atea has an apparent special connection with the Ancient Middle East and will be broached later but it is notable that in another myth it is stated that the original homeland was Irihia and this, undoubtedly, was more likely Iran (Arya), also identified by early British researchers as Ancient Aryan India. In this Maori myth, or more likely legend of origin, the adjacent land to Irihia was Uru corresponding to Iran and Uru, another name for Sumeru, or Sumeria in the Ancient Middle East. This may or may not be coincidence but will be of more interest in later chapters. In the Irihia legend it is noted that sun-dried kumara was included in the provisions of their mariners, the Maori ancestors, or at least in one of their intrusive migrations. This tends to confirm the main theme of this book that there were many if not regular voyages from West, South and East Asia to South America and that they utilised the resources along the way, and the return journey, to provision themselves.

There is a curious anomaly in this myth since it states that the Irihia mariners had this dried sweet potato among their provisions but that this occurred before the kumara could have been diffused from South America to New Zealand. This curious assertion, recorded by the Maori chroniclers, indicates that the genealogies referring to the chiefs who introduced cultural advances and food plants in New Zealand, the Irihia Arikis, or canoe masters, commenced long before those of the first voyages of Toi and the First Fleet in 1150 and 1350 A.D. This implies that these Irihia mariners were crossing the Pacific Ocean from Asia to Central and South

1.001 : Barkbeaters from the Americas identical to those in Polynesia, Melanesia and Indonesia. c2000 B.C. - 1500 A.D.

1.004 : Typical bark-cloth patterns and block traditional in Polynesia for at least 1500-2500 years and probably introduced in the Lapita period. Samoa, Central Polynesia, Early 20th., century, A.D.

1.003 : Bark-beaters, typical of Polynesia, Melanesia and Indonesia through to South America. Marquesas Islands, Eastern Polynesia, Early 20th., century, A.D.

1.002 : A group of typical bark-beaters virtually identical in form and use throughout the island groups of Indonesia, Melanesia, Polynesia and Central and South America. Samoan Islands, Polynesia, Early 20th., century, A.D.

1.005 : Cloth patterns usually applied by carved blocks similar to those in far distant Melanesia and Polynesia. Shan Tribes, Northern Burma, Early-mid 20th., century, A.D.

1.006 : Finishing a tapa cloth, with typical geometric patterns. Fiji, Melanesia, Early 20th., century, A.D.

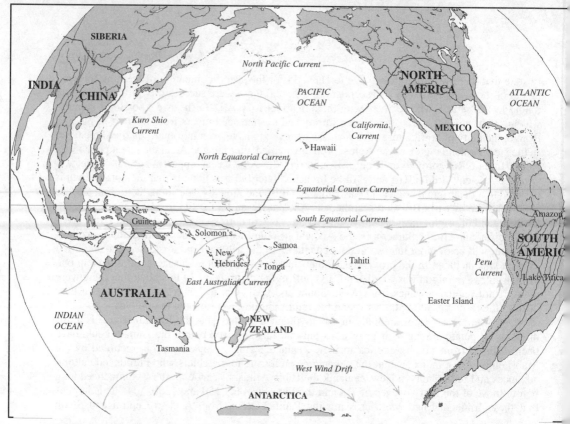

1.007 : The light coloured arrows indicate the ocean currents assisting mariners to traverse the open sea from island to island or between one continent and another. The overall Pacific distribution of these currents indicates that any mariners setting off from the Western Pacific were certain to land somewhere on the American shores - North or South. The distribution of myths from Asia to the Americas is determined by Joseph Campbell and others and is believed to centre on Samoa. This distribution is reflected not only in myths but corresponds to the dispersion of cultural aspects such as jointmarks, star clubs, panpipes, the blowpipe and many other aspects and references and is directed to the high culture regions of North, Central and South America clearly indicating transfer of culture by mariners from Asia to the Americas, and to Peru and Bolivia in particular in this case. It is clear also from the sea currents flowing to and circulating from the South American Coast why Easter Island was located and contacted from Tiahuanaco and Peru and its cyclopean architecture, cukltural elements, and botany relflects that of the Andes.

America long before the 12th;, to 14th., centuries and had learnt that the sweet potato could be dried and rehydrated when required and also that it could be planted as a tuber rather than seed derived from the long experience of the Peruvians. The belief in much more ancient voyages preserved in Polynesian myths concurs with the central theme of this work and is further confirmed in the iconography, shared imagery, and Aryan language terms found commonly in Asia and South America.

Another, long known inter-cultural element among many is joint-marking, clearly related from one island to another and distributed along the Pacific Rims of Asia and the Americas. This is demonstrated in iconography extending from South East Asia across the Pacific Islands to both the continents of North and South America. These are only a few cultural elements transferred by mariners via the marine highways that are the oceanic currents connecting these disparate regions.

In considering the many common cultural references throughout the Pacific it is particularly of note that all relate directly in their demography or distribution to the oceanic currents that have been essential in the migrations of the Micronesian, Polynesian and Melanesian peoples over millennia (*1.007*). These currents form a coherent pattern of marine highways for distribution of cultural and technological ideas and advances. This is confirmed by the fact that the earliest mariners clearly utilised them for trade and migration into more recent millennia and notable in the archaeological record from the second millennium B.C. known as the Lapita. Earlier migrations, probably trade based, show in the available evidence of pottery distribution similarities with early Jomon in Japan and the contemporary Chinese culture, broadly called the Neolithic, into the Yangshao, extending to New Guinea that was receiving influences from these Asian countries as early as 5000 B.C.[8].

As noted above the sweet potato may have been cultivated in the Waghi District in the Highlands of New Guinea, the third largest island in the world, from about 2000 B.C. This very large Melanesian island is not only the closest of the Pacific Island cultures to Indonesia, and therefore directly affected by Asian influences, but because of the early cultivation of the sweet potato provides the most direct contact between South America and Asia - a Melanesian crossover centre for disparate cultures. It should hardly need mentioning, therefore, that there is a direct oceanic current connecting the "high-culture" coast of Peru with South East Asia and Indonesia in particular that washes the full length of the south coast of New Guinea. This is known as the South Equatorial Current developing from the Peru Current (the Humboldt) that flows north along the South American Coast from the South. The Humboldt in its turn is the northern extension of the West Wind Drift Current, or Antarctic Ocean, circling from West to East south of Australia and Africa washing the shores of the Antarctic continent in the far south. The South Equatorial Current does not flow only to New Guinea from South America between this island and the north of Australia but a branch flows from the south of this great conveyor southwest from mid-Pacific to break upon the Australian Coast, as the East Australian Current, before curling north along the west coast of New Zealand and then flowing eastward distributing in part to the South Polynesian Islands. This includes Easter Island, but this East Australia Current after curling away from Australia mostly forms the north section, from West to East, of the West Wind Drift back to South America. This great oceanic system will be of greater interest in the later sections of this book and is critical to its theme.

To the north of New Guinea a lesser, but not least important, oceanic conveyor flows as a counter flow to both the South Equatorial Current and the North Equatorial Current, these two flowing from east to west. The Equatorial Counter Current therefore flows from west to east along the whole, and a little to the north, of the Equator itself. This forms a direct link between the South East Asian islands and New Guinea to Central and the North West Coast of South America (*1.007*). It is quite clear in the available demographic maps relating to cultural distribution that these three oceanic currents have played the most critical part in the distribution of cultural influences and from Asia and South America. In terms of assisting mariners to negotiate these great conveyors the prevailing winds must be of great importance. The North and South Equatorial Currents are both assisted by prevailing winds that are vital for those who use these currents to travel from east to west since on both sides of the Equator the winds blow in the same direction as these currents from east to west. The central Equatorial Current flanked by these two great conveyors is more moderate in its flow and the fact that the prevailing winds are head-on to mariners who wish to travel from west to east impedes their progress for most of the year noted by Captain Cook while in Polynesia[9]. However, it is clear that the Polynesians must have used tacking skills to overcome any such adversity to utilise the flow of this central and other adverse currents since they have distributed to all the islands in the Eastern Pacific from Asia. It is incorrect to believe that the prevailing winds

1.008 : The Sumerian sea god Enki depicted in his "water" house at the right. Akkad Dynasty, Mesopotamia, Late 3rd., millennium, B.C.

1.009 : Animal-headed demons, called Pee Pok-ka-long, were characteristic of Tibetan and Himalayan foothill peoples' iconography. Shan, North Burma, Pre-19th., century, A.D.

1.010 : Unfortunate soul being disciplined in hell but showing the joints emitting the fire of their own souls or the assigned part of the human soul. Shan, North Burma, Pre-19th., century, A.D.

1.012 : Seated figure in a posture found in Ancient Indonesia indicating a continuity of tradition of marking the joint-marks from Asia through the Pacific Ocean and into the Americas. Santa Cruz del Quiche, Guatemala, Late-Post Classic.

1.013 : Fine engraving of a Polynesian warrior with tattoo designs including faces drawn on the skin surface over the patella of the knee. Note also the conch shell found as a sacred instrument in Ancient South America and India. Marquesas Islands, Eastern Polynesia, 1813, A.D.

1.014 : Ruler or priest with characteristic brow band and deity faceplates adorning his knee joints as found also in India (*1.015*). Muisca, Colombia, 1000-1500 A.D.

1.015 : Joints of the human body were often considered as having special deities or aspects of the soul associated with them. Sometimes these were exaggerated and were adornerd with deity faces. This Jangam wears traditional plates of this type and a lion's head hangs between. South India, Early 20th., century, A.D.

1.011 : Tiger showing soul flames emerging from the shoulder joints, a common belief of fire being associated with the joints and in essence deriving from fire. Shan, North Burma, Pre-19th., century, A.D.

blew the whole of the time since usually they dropped in intensity in the evening and overnight. These marine adversities were moderated for a period of about 3 months at the end of the year through to the beginning of the first months of the next since the wind dropped at this time to allow daytime sailing as well as in the night. This was navigational knowledge was duly recorded by Captain Cook when given in the advice he received from the chief and priest, Tupou, when he visited Tahiti in the late 18th., century[10].

It is of particular interest that the central Equatorial Current flowed directly from the East Indonesian islands, across North New Guinea, through the north of Melanesia, to Micronesia, Polynesia and wash the coasts of Central America. Its southern branch splits off from the main current and flows south to South America along the Pacific Coast of Colombia to Ecuador. The earliest known pottery on coastal Ecuador appears closely related, and in a similar time frame, with the Jomon of Japan again providing a possible link for further investigation. It is important to remember that Jomon style pottery, and that of the Yangshao of Coastal China earlier noted, has been recovered in New Guinea where the South American sweet potato has been found emphasising the distribution of both elements by the major oceanic currents in the Central Pacific[11].

These ocean currents have not only assisted in a broad cultural diffusion from Asia through the Pacific to the Americas over at least the last three millennia but have been the routes along which coastal and perhaps the more fortunate of some inland populations, have escaped from periods of political strife, invasions, and perhaps above all the long years, or decades, of famine and climatic catastrophes. Many of these periods of major social disruption appear to have been caused largely by volcanic eruptions and other seismic related changes beside tribal and intercultural strife. These caused great climatic reversals and are now being more thoroughly investigated through the more recent science of dendrochronology - the study of tree ring data, and glacial ice core research - one being used to corroborate the other. The research data so far produced confirms that the major, dated upheavals that are known to have occurred in the high cultures of Asia and Europe concur with the known eruptions of Thera in the Greek islands in 1628 B.C., Hekla in 1289 B.C., and more recently the immense eruption of Krakatoa between the major Indonesian islands of Java and Sumatra in 537 A.D. The exact date of these catastrophes have been determined by cross-referencing with the available tree ring and ice core data.

Of particular interest are the oceanic links via sea currents from India and the Middle East through Indonesia and either north of Australia, or around it to the south into the Pacific proper. These also connect directly as extensions to the west with the Middle East and East Africa and the Red Sea. The ancient land connections between India and the Middle East have long been known, and confirmed ever more conclusively, and date back for a longer period in time with each generation of archaeological research, but the connections by sea have only been more widely recognised and confirmed in more recent decades. At the present it is known that the Indus civilisation in what is now Pakistan traded with Sumer and Akkad from the third millennium B.C. and had at least what appears to be a trading base in Bahrain. These known sea routes and their connection with India through to Indonesia and ultimately the Pacific provide the arteries along which cultural diffusion, probably both primary and secondary stimulus that can be determined from their origins and are essential in the theme of this book.

The diffusion of culture from India into South East and East Asia through trade, migration and cultural proselytisation from the late first millennium B.C. has been the subject of many learned publications particularly from the nineteenth century on, and need not been proven here. However, what is less well known is that there was an early intrusion of Austronesian peoples into the South India from the earliest times before this period linking a broad spread of these peoples with a common language from the west Pacific islands, Indonesia and Australia. This could only have been achieved by sea and over an extended period of time and survives as a recognisable language group in India.

These people moved north into Central India and traces are of interest in the very regions which show close apparent links with Indonesia, Australia and the Pacific in more historic times, probably up until the Spanish Conquest of the Americas in the 16th., century. It can be argued that these Austronesian peoples may have been as a retro-flow in response to the Lapita intrusions in the Pacific from the 2nd., millennium B.C. from South East Asia that was in turn stimulated by copper traders from the Middle East from at least as early as the 3rd., millennium B.C. Some of these arguments will be broached in later sections of this book, and it will be shown that these retro-flows of peoples and cultures continued into quite recent times probably terminating in the mid-second millennium A.D. as European Colonial powers began to dominate.

With the diffusion of peoples, most of whom would have been traders and other venturers rather than major population migrations, some distribution of botanical elements occurred. It would soon have become apparent to these people that food and medicinal plants could have been successfully transplanted to new environments or the extended period that these various species and climates could survive out of their natural habitat to assist in bridging the gap from one suitable clime to another. Some of these elements will be considered in the appropriate section later but of some interest is the fact that there are many myths in India indicating that some of the more common useful cultigens such as bamboo and grains were imported from abroad. More particularly of interest is that these myths frequently note that some deity or hero introduced these from either the depths of the ocean or across the sea. It is virtually impossible to determine from these myths to pinpoint a place of origin and indicators recorded are open to personal interpretation anyway. However, the overall gist encapsulated in the myths seems to indicate that cultivated plants did not all come overland from the Middle East or more locally the Indus or Ganges regions. This is particularly so with flora that has a worldwide distribution and of particular note along the land masses, large and small, in or adjacent to the major oceanic currents. Just such a plant is the bamboo that has a wide distribution in South and South East Asia but is also found throughout the Central Pacific Ocean region through to the tropical zones of the Americas. An excursion into some of the myths related to the origin of bamboo indicates a possible Pacific Rim origin for this exotic grass form emphasised by the critical part it plays in the myths and legends of many of the Indonesian and Oceanic peoples through to the Americas[12].

Sea Traders and Ancient Sea Voyages from the Middle East

In the most ancient references preserved in myths and legends of the Ancient Middle and Near East of Western Asia sea voyages were undertaken or were noted of intrusive peoples who were clearly mariners from lands far away, transferring major influences on the culture of Ancient Ur, Sumeria and Akkad, in the third millennium B.C., establishing the foundation for the succeeding kingdoms from Babylonia and Assyria through to the Assyrians, Archaemenids, Parthians and Sassanids in later millenniums. The great water god of Sumeria and Akkad, Enki (*1.008*), is recorded as being from, and residing in the ocean outside of the cultural zone of influence and possibly from outside the Middle East region and who is noted as being associated with those of the "south wind"[13]. These were probably mariners originally from the Indian Ocean region, or Enki himself as a personification of a mariner king or kingdom undertaking sea journeys as part of the unfolding of creation[14]. A great hero is also recorded as undertaking great ventures is named Adapa and he is driven by the "South Wind" to the middle of the sea even though Enki complained that this "wind" sent his "brothers against him"[15]. These ancient people set the foundation for great sea voyages, noted particularly in the Gilgamesh myth cycle, where the hero travels over great distances "and crossed to and fro all seas" to lands described in the myths that appear not to match those of the Ancient Middle or Near East[16].

These mariner peoples are sometimes described as sea monsters and probably because they were originally enemies of the ruling elite, and in one celebrated myth they and Enki's servant Isimud follow the "Queen of Heaven" in her canoe, Innana (Ishtar). She is recorded undertaking this journey to the Abzu or the centre of the watery dwelling where Enki resides[17] determined to confront him. Enki's shrine, located in the celebrated ancient city of Eridu, was even for those times, when the myth was written down about 2000 B.C., within easy distance of those cities dedicated to the other great gods of Sumer and Akkad. This canoe journey to Enki's residence in the centre of the great Abzu, or sea, or watery abyss, is clearly relating a cosmic journey rather than a lesser earthly journey from one shrine in Mesopotamia in another. The greatest gods were considered to have their own sky canoes and to traverse heaven more or less corresponding to the planetary orbits of the bodies with which they were identified. The canoe conveying Innana to visit Enki was the "Boat of Heaven" and on its journey it was seized by the sea monsters but was saved by Ninshubur, and repeatedly occurred at each of the seven shrines along the journey's route until it reached Enki's residence. This relation clearly represents the identification of ancient myths, mariner voyages, and migrations with cosmology where their record had been subsumed overall from the mists of time into this Sumerian myth. It is probably from these early, and later voyages, that these Ancient kings laid claim to be the rulers of the "Four Quarters" - nothing less than the whole world.

In the great king lists of Sumer it is recorded that the monarchs were claimed to have remained on their thrones for very long reigns. These lists were recorded from epochs even more ancient than the Sumerian dynasties and were frequently associated in some way with the sea or sea travel. In the reign of Mes-kiag-gasher, son of Utu, who reigned, it is recorded, for 324 years went into the sea "and came out (from it) to the mountains" several generations (possibly four over 1720 years - probably intended to mean dynasties) before the fabled Gilgamesh[18]. Records left by the kings in their reigns claim that Lugal-zaggisi, king of Erech, conquered the lands from the sea, here meaning the Mediterranean, his kingdom covering the Tigris and Euphrates that already included these rivers to their deltas in the Persian Gulf - from the "lower sea" (the Persian Gulf, where the "upper sea" was the Mediterranean)[19]. The great Akkadian king, Sargon, in the late third millennium B.C. is recorded to have conquered a distant country covered in mountains and forests, believed to have been Anatolia, centuries before the rise of the Hittites[20]. He and his successors, Amar-Sin, Gimil-Sin and Ibi-Sin all regaled themselves with the title of "King of the Four Quarters of the World"[21]. The term "Sin" refers to their tutelary deity the male Moon god named Sin, a deity that will recur throughout this work.

An abiding myth of great importance throughout the Ancient Near and Middle East is that of the rising and dying Sun relating to the seasonal variation of the Sun's yearly cycle and linked to crop sowing and reaping. This myth is best known preserved in the Ancient Egyptian myth cycle of Osiris but is prefigured in the more ancient Mesopotamian myths surviving in the Sumerian deity Dumu-Zi and later recoded in the Semitic dynasties as Tammuz. In later periods this deity is considered the lover of Ishtar, usually associated with the planet Venus, but in the earliest form the name of this Sun god is also written Ta-mu-zu, Du-'u-zu, Du-u-zu - all variations on Dumu-Zi meaning "true or faithful son". Another extended form of the name is Dumi-Zi-Ab-Zu meaning "faithful son of the deep" and is, as Albert Clay notes, "the picture of the sun rising out of the ocean"[22]. Nowhere is it considered odd that a supposedly land-locked people, whose eastern and western boundaries are bounded by vast regions of arid land and plateau, should adopt a deity rising out of the ocean. Logically it would indicate that at a very early time this imagery may have been introduced with migrations from shores where the Sun rising over the sea might have been usual. In the Ancient Andes, in Inca and Aymara myths, the Sun was considered to have arisen from Lake Titicaca and particularly noted as first doing so in the Creation period. This is logical since the great sacred city of Tiahuanaco, where so many of the Inca traditions originated was sited on the Lake's shores so that the Sun appeared to rise from the Lake itself. In both the Tiahuanaco period and the later Inca Dynasty the territory of influence extended to the west, to the shore of the Pacific Ocean, so these people were well aware that the Sun set over the ocean in the far west. Since the rising Sun, as the initiator of the Sun cycle, is more important in the philosophical speculations of these ancient times, as it was among the later Vedic Brahmans in India, it is unlikely that the knowledge or extension of the early empire in the Ancient Middle East to the Mediterranean shore in the west initiated the beliefs in a rising Sun from the ocean but derived from as earlier introduction.

In Ancient Mediterranean sea power was of great importance and well developed technically. In the first dynasty of Egypt, in the middle of the third millennium B.C., orders for full length beams of cedar to roof the great mastaba tombs of the first kings are recorded and sea going barges were dispatched to Lebanon to obtain these materials. In the second millennium B.C sea power was critical and not only for the well-recorded trading links but for the infamous Sea Peoples who threatened all the Eastern Mediterranean countries in the 12th., century B.C. This particular threat was probably initiated by the disastrous eruption of Hekla in 1159 B.C. resulting in great famine lasting for years in Europe and forcing large numbers of people to migrate south in an attempt to find new lands on the warmer Mediterranean shores and threatening even Egypt in North East Africa. This period saw the sudden, catastrophic end of the Hittite kingdom and these Sea Peoples have been cited as the cause[23]. It is more likely, however, that migrations from the Caucasus and Russia to the north were in fact the true cause of the fall of these empires during this long period of cold and resulting crop failures.

The Hittites were a maritime people occupying, with their subject states, most of Anatolia in the extreme North-East Mediterranean. Their language, with that of the Mitanni who occupied the region along the southern Caucasus foothills in the headwater region of the Tigris and Euphrates now known as Kurdistan, was known to be closely related to Sanskrit, the language of Aryans of Vedic India[24]. The great Vedic deities, Indra the storm god and Varuna, the sea gods are the same gods who are first recorded in Anatolia over 1500 miles (2250 kilometres) to the north west of the Indus and found many centuries later in North India. In the Hittite myths the same anomaly of a Sun god arising from the sea occurs and in one of the Hittite texts he is referred to as having a fishes' head and known as the "Sun-god in the water"[25]. This suggests a relocation or introduction from a people who once inhabited a seashore facing the east or a mariner people. This tends to be confirmed in Hittite texts and inscriptions relating that the god Kumarbi, probably the equivalent of the Greek Uranos or Zeus, conspired against his son Teshub, the storm god, and to achieve his aim, he married the daughter of the Sea to produce a hero named Ullikummi who grew up in the middle of the sea[26]. This might indicate that the union of Hittites with other peoples beyond their shore, reachable only be sea produced a distant people whose later generations would return to create havoc among the Hittites. These myths and legends were current in the second half of the second millennium B.C. and indicate that there was little hindrance technically or socially in travel by sea in either the Mediterranean or the Persian Gulf in these early millennia.

Apart from myth the importance and development of sea trade is well-known in the Mediterranean[27] and it is now known that sea trade was early developed between the first rank nations over millennia in the Persian Gulf and India with land incursions, migrations and trade extending back to at least the 6th., millennium, B.C. In the reign of a king of Lagash in 2520 B.C. ships are recorded as transporting large constructional timbers from Dilmun[28]. Geoffrey Bibby, whose famous book "Looking for Dilmun" places Dilmun on the island of Bahrein, also records the doubts of other authors as to its location and the objections to this identification. Ancient texts placed Dilmun to the east of Sumeria not the south as it would be if it was Bahrein. The Assyrian records note that the god Nabu ruled Dilmun and that he lived in an abode "like that of a fish" in the "midst of the sea of the rising Sun" referring again to the east not the south[29].

The argument of the exact location of Dilmun, the ancient ancestral land and paradise of the ancient Sumerians and Akkadians through to the Assyrians of the middle of the first millennium B.C. two millennia later, will run and run. From Bahrein it is now known that the island was a half way house in the sea trade between the Akkadian dynasty and later succeeding kingdoms, and the Indus from at least as early third and second millennium B.C. This is proven by archaeology even though no mention of this sea trade is recorded in the contemporary surviving texts in the Mesopotamian region[30]. This is perhaps not unexpected since trade routes were highly secretively maintained and guarded by the great powers of the time and records were never normally kept in case they were discovered by, or betrayed to competitors - trade was power!!! The most important element for this work, however, is that the location of Dilmun near or in the distant sea to the east and associations with sea gods and mariners from the earliest period indicates that sea travel was an important element in their myths as it was in their daily life from the most ancient times. After 2100 B.C. in the post-Akkadian phase in the Gulf region there is a remarkable increase of trade from the Indus region, already noticed in Bahrein, but extending into mainland Arabia in what is modern Oman and Iran to the east. This expansion of trade included not only the Indus Valley but also aspects related to the Ganges Plains in the Subcontinent and was clearly a period of great importance not suspected until the researches and excavations of recent decades[31].

India and Cultural Dispersion by Sea

The connections between the Ancient Middle East and India have been referred to at length in earlier works[32] and the importance of the Mandaeans[33], the islands of Sri Lanka[34] and the peoples of the East and South Coast of India repeatedly noted[35]. Undoubtedly many of these contacts were under the aegis of the ruling dynasty of the time in the Ancient Middle East and this was undoubtedly true in the Assyrian period from about the 10th., century to the 7th., century, B.C. Near the Ganges Delta in Orissa there are many references and indications of sea trade with South East Asia and China[36] and undoubtedly the Americas. Equally there are references to intrusive mariners causing havoc and disruption in a similar way noted much earlier in the Ancient Middle Eastern texts indicating that mariners were an even present force that extended trade[37] and influence but also had a down side being paralleled by sea pirates and bandits who were every bit as skilled as their legitimate counterparts[38]. Shipwreck was an ever present hazard[39] but this is no way prevented many people taking to the sea, as a living or for adventure,, to migrate and for setting up colonies and trading posts far from their own homeland.

Eminent scholars have recognised that most of the influences in the stone-built architecture from the Mauryan Dynasty in the 3rd., century, B.C. in North India were in fact introduced as a result of migration after the collapse of the Achaemenid dynasty in Iran[40] - this being a result of the vandalism of Alexander the Great at Persepolis in particular. Asoka, the great ruler of the Mauryan Dynasty, extended this architectural influence and style throughout his empire and over later centuries it was gradually modified with indigenous aspects through imagery and local styles. This was particularly true of Orissa on the North East Coast of India fronting the Bay of Bengal, a little to the south of the Ganges Delta. Here the influences that were transferred by the silpins, the architects and artisans who travelled the extent of India to construct palaces and temples[41], met the local influences that were arriving by sea from South East Asia and beyond but also from the Middle East. Here also Tantric influences from Tibet and the Nagas hills in Bengal merged with local and the temple styles from Northern India. With so many aspects present in both the Aboriginal tribes and the later Aryan Buddhist, Jain and Hindu cultures deriving originally from Ancient Iran it is not surprising that some of the rulers of Orissa after the mid-first millennium A.D. were noted for boasting that they were Maharja Adhiraja Tri-Kaling Adhipati, that is "emperor, king of kings, lord of the three Kalingas", and often also that they had conquered the whole world[42].

The Kois, Koyis or Koyas, a tribe related to the Gonds in India a once powerful mixed Aryan and Aboriginal race, called themselves Bhumi Razulu, or "Kings of the Earth"[43]. Ancestor worship was particularly important among them and they are noted for carrying around at festivals velpus, these being large three-cornered red cloths with figures representing particular ancestors in different colours, blue, yellow, green or white, stitched to the main cloth[44]. These people, and particularly the Gonds, will be of more interest in later chapters.

In Gond myths there are many references to sea journeys across the ocean and in several there are references to their great heroes, the Panior brothers, some of whom are said to have journeyed across the sea to fetch their gods[45]. There are references that may have derived from contacts with the golden shrines of Burma or perhaps Oc Eo, known as the "golden city" located in what was a flourishing region of the lower Mekong River of Cambodia and Vietnam in the last millennium B.C. to the early first millennium A.D. There are other references in Gond myths indicating that they received corn, a crop from Central America, from across the sea that may be an early reference before its later reintroduction in European times[46]. These Gond myths woven around their Corn Queen seem too old to have been elaborated after the European colonial period. In the most ancient Vedic traditions in India the deity Varuna, god of the west, was a sea god and derived from the Hittites and the contemporary Hatti and Mitanni, a millennium before is a deity was particularly associated with sea trade and mariners. In other traditions the serpent worshippers of early India claim descent from heroes or ancestors who were half-serpents and some myths and legends they were called "sea born"[47].

In the Ancient Middle East, in the marshes of Iraq, the Mandaeans appear to have been connected with ancient sea voyages and boat building[48]. It is recorded in their myths that they originated in Sri Lanka suggesting an ancient pre-Hindu link with the Indian Subcontinent and references of temple building with the construction of the Mandaean shrine hut along with rites similar to those of the Ashipu priests of Babylonia[49]. The term Manda is also found among the Assyrians as Umman-Manda suggesting that they and the Mandaeans had a common origin or that one was influenced by the other[50].

As a sample of similar practices of customs and traditions that are too similar to be coincidental a few preliminary examples can be given before the more detailed comparisons of Aryan cultural transfers from India to South America in later chapters. The common link is not only in the rituals or deity names but also the reigning dynasties or power complexes operating in political and trading structures associated in the contemporary periods that will be of note in due course.

One of the most unusual marriage practises found, or surviving in India into the last century was that found among the Nayadis in South India. A large pandal, a marriage hut, was constructed and the bride placed in it. All the young men and women gathered around the hut in the form of a ring. The girl's father or nearest male relative sat a short distance from the people with a drum and commenced to beat the drum and lead a chant taken up by those present translated as follows:

> "Take a stick, my sweetest daughter,
> Now seize the stick, my dearest love,
> Should you not capture the husband you wish for,
> Remember, 'tis fate decides whom you shall have."

All the young men are eligible for marriage and they take a bamboo stick each and begin to dance around the hut. After dancing for an hour or so they each thrust their stick through the leafy cladding of the hut. The girl takes one of the sticks and thereby chooses its owner as her future husband. When this part of the ceremony completed it is then followed by feasting leading to the consummation of the marriage[51]. The same ceremony is found among the Ulladans and before the arrival of the British these people were considered the property of the hill temples or great landowners. The Ulladans were also known to sell their services to the Nayars (Nairs), Syrian Christians and others on the South Coast of India[52].

The Tobas of the Gran Chaco in Central South America, east of the Andes, retained into the twentieth century a tradition where, when a young man had considered that he had achieved sufficient respect in his community he set about seeking the hand of the girl he wished to marry. He approached her parents and it was required, if they considered that he might be suitable, that they build a hut and their daughter placed within it from which she does not emerge until the test required of the prospective husband is concluded. This trial is undertaken by the young man for as long as it takes and he begins by seating himself outside and commencing to drum while wearing a girdle made up of the bones of animals he has killed. During the drumming he moves himself from side to side so as to make the bones rattle and this performance may last for up to eight days. This ritual among others was recorded by Rafael Karsten 3 generations ago and resembles that of the Ulladans of India too closely not to be connected, and this could only have been by sea.

Origin legends in Melanesia bear striking resemblances either to those of India in the far west or to those of Polynesia and South America in the East and far east. This is due to the fact that the islands, including New Guinea were on the main east to west oceanic equatorial current flowing directly from South America through their islands to Asia. Among the Motu tribe, a people with marked Polynesian traditions, an origin myth states that the Kotari and Kirimaikape people came down to earth with one female dog. The men had relations with the dog and their issue was first a son, then a daughter. When these children grew up they married and had fourteen children and two of them went inland and formed the Koriari tribe and the others went along the coast to the Laronge River and formed the Koitapu tribe[53]. This resembles closely similar myths in India but more completely myths widely spreads in South America and also Central America and clearly indicate contact and some of these will be of interest later in this work.

The Kula and the Art of Beauty Magic in the Sea Trade Rituals of Melanesia
A favourite theme in more recent decades for film producers catering for a made-for-T.V. series is camera witness documentaries in searches for hidden forest tribes, particularly those that might shock and perhaps thrill the audiences, aimed at an increase in viewing numbers by billing them as cannibals. For those in earlier centuries of European exploration in the Southern hemisphere this danger in contact with such tribes, if not cannibals then certainly headhunters and sacrificers of humans, was all too real. In more recent times these expeditions have been largely confined to the vastness of the Amazon rain forests and to the rugged terrain of the third largest island in the world, New Guinea. There are many reliable reports of traders and missionaries in more recent centuries being killed upon entering islands that were hostile to intruders. Even if there was no material benefit to be gained in maintaining contact or pursuing further contact these missionaries, and even traders, were immediately replaced and not discouraged through fear of premature death.

In more ancient times the human spirit was no less adventurous than today although perhaps more superstitious and more religiously orientated. This spirit of discovery coupled with state demands for prestige goods and the resulting rewards spurred the ancient explorers, prospectors and adventurers to take to the sea regardless of the risks. The known reports from the high civilisations that had developed a writing system records the problems faced by the traders and venturers in their wider contacts with often fierce-some tribes on the periphery of their territories or far beyond. The Ancient Egyptians record that ventures were sent far into Africa and also recorded similar problems of tribes that were hostile and threatening on their known frontiers. The Ancient Sumerians through to the Ancient Greeks all record troublesome tribes in lands far from their own country and this undoubtedly occurred also in the experience of peoples who had left no record or had not the script to do so.

Most of these more highly developed societies placed themselves under the patronage of certain deities whom they believed would assist them in their endeavours when abroad and records exist of the individual ceremonies and rites performed when seeking their aid. The Greeks recorded some of these and the same was true from the time of the much earlier Sumerians. In later India, after records began in the first millennium B.C. and sea trade was long developed, the God Varuna, and in some regions that deity was Tara[54], who was particularly associated with sea travel and sea traders. These sea ventures form the theme of this book and are essentially that of the cultural transfer from the Ancient Middle East, India and Tibet to Ancient South America but these achievements first entailed the travail of many centuries of sea traders in their island-hopping explorations through Indonesia into the Pacific Ocean.

The first evidence of deliberate transfer of culture along a specific sea route is that of the Lapita dating from about 2000 B.C. arriving from the Asian Mainland either from South China[55], Vietnam, or through the Indonesian Islands across to the islands off the north coast of New Guinea called the Bismark Archipelago. From here this identifiable culture was transferred into the island groups to the east in Melanesia and into Central Polynesia evident in Samoa and Tonga by about 1500 B.C.[56]. Certain elements of the Lapita culture are believed to have reached as Far East as Easter Island in the early-mid first millennium, A.D.[57].

From the comparisons of early South American culture it is evident that the spread of Asian culture to South America took place much earlier than the Lapita period but left little material evidence in the Pacific Islands. It may be that these mariners took the sea route around the Pacific Rim of North America after skirting the Mexican coast thence on to South America. Such journeys were always highly risky since the long periods on stormy or even becalmed seas were always a threat and frequently resulted in shipwreck and loss of life. Yet, although well apprised of the dangers there appeared never to have been a period when mariners were not ready to put out to sea and often into the unknown. It was not only the weather conditions that they had to be wary of for in many of the islands, particularly those of Melanesia there was real danger that they would not survive an encounter with the local tribes and to face such threats rituals were believed necessary in an attempt to seek special guidance and support from the mariner's guiding deities. These religious undertakings, religious or superstitious, were usually observed with the prescribed rituals performed before departure and in some case, as among the Polynesians, priests were taken on board in an effort to ensure the support of the gods and ancestors. There can be little doubt that many of these rituals and beliefs were derived from India and there are references that still appear among the coastal tribes of the Sub-continent that find their echoes in the islands of Melanesia but must have extended to the shores of Central and South America at one time.

Aspects Related to the Kula in India
The term Kula is one that is found as the name for the clan division of the Badagas, a tribe linked to the Todas residing in the Nilgiri Hills in South India, and who will be of more interest in later chapters. The origin of the term is not determined but may derive from the fact that these people have retained into the twentieth centuries aspects of Middle Eastern culture including that associated with sacred stones or kals. These were erected in every village with a raised platform called a Suththu Kallu, and one called a Mandhe Kallu as a sitting place appearing to relate to the Dahu of the Nagas of Assam considered in a later chapter[58]. The terms Kallu and Mande appear to confirm the link to the Ancient Middle East where Kallu related to the sacred stone altar[59] and Mandhe is a reference to the religious aspects of the Manda, the ritual hut of the Mandaeans. The Okkiliya are a large caste of Canarese farmers and include a division called Hatti and the headman is called Patta-Karan, terms that will be of interest in due course. Their clan divisions are also called Kula[60].

Among the Satani tribe in Kerala in the far South West coastal India these people retain a division including one called the Kula-sekhara who claimed descent from the kings of that region[61]. The Sondi were Oriya palm-wine sellers whose clans were also called Kula but who retained caste myths and legends closely similar to those found in the Gilbert Islands where the supreme deity created the first man, god, or the world from his brow[62]. They also are known for their ground designs[63] that have in other researches have been considered to be one of the prototypes of those in the New Hebrides.

On the Eastern Coast of India the Kalingis were the servant caste of the Kalinga kings. The maintained priests who were called Kula-Razus and here the term Kula appears to relate to the priestly function of these coastal people[64]. Kula and Kal for both priest and stone, or the priest who presides at the stone altar derives directly from that of the Ancient Middle East. In the South of India there was a system of extortion initiated by a tribal section of the Kallans to gain payment from the owners for the return of their stolen cattle called Tuppu-Kuli. This form of payment appears to derive from the payment to priest for petitioners to the gods at the Kallu or Kula.

The term kula is of importance in Ancient India since it is stated in the ancient texts that the concept of the Panca-Tathagatas or the Five Transcendant Buddhas who guarded the cardinal points of the world, North, South, East and West plus the central World Axis, had a specific relation to the Aryan clans from whom the first worshippers and the Buddha himself were descended. Appointed to each of the Aryan clans was a bodhisattva and called the Kulesa, that is Sire or Lord, of that family and this title derives from the term for family - Kula[65]. This is undoubtedly the first recorded origin for the clan divisional name of kula. In many tribes and castes in India the headman was originally also the priest, and titles, although the functions were later separated and the original title remained as a tradition. Among the Meda, Medara or Medara-Karan, an example of this was that the headman was called the Kula-Pedda, where pedda means "big" in the sense of status[66].

Associated also with religion in Ancient India is the term Agni-Kula[67] or the "fire-races", those believed to be descended from the hallowed peoples who formed the tribes and castes of the Vedic Aryans who invaded India in the early first millennium B.C. In South India these people are particularly identified with the Pallis or Pallavas and these are known in their dynastic period in the middle of the first millennium A.D. to have extended their influence to Sumatra and Java in Indonesia and probably beyond with the later and probably earlier, Cholas from the same region of South India. Myths and legends surround their rituals to the Sun and horse sacrifices while other beliefs focused on the wind deity Vayu[68]. The deity Vayu will be of considerable interest in later chapters since the wind deity was of such importance for mariners and their long distance craft with sails. Another South Indian caste, the Vada, a fisherman caste, also retain the name Kula-Raju for their caste headman - raju deriving from raja or "ruler". They are particularly known for their pot shrines found also among the Gond tribes of Central India[69]. The long history of conflict between the various tribes and religions in India have made the interface through contact dependent on prescribed rituals developed by long and weary custom through necessity. In India also the rituals from childbirth to marriage and finally death are all subject to similarly developed need for celebration and ritual and each persons allocated place within the ceremonies evolved over millennia. For death rites the ceremonies are particularly onerous since it was considered a great stain to touch or even be associated with the lifeless corpse that engendered pollution. To wash away the pollution that clings to each participant at the interment ceremonies rituals were, and are scrupulously carried out at the funerals according to the long established rules of each caste. One of the most interesting is that of the Pula-Kuli of the Tiyans, a people who will be of more interest in later chapters, and their pollution rituals will be considered in due course since pollution ceremonies were also undertaken in Ancient Peru.

In each case, kula as a term, relates to family, clan and ritual interfaces associated with other clans and transition and protection from one state to another particularly where death was concerned, or threatened, as well as to rulers as heads of clans and also in a sense domination of others. Of special note in these terms considered is that the Gonds, a tribe of great importance in this work, preserved a greeting dance into the present day called the Man Kola or the Sar Kola. This was formed by many tribal members in a typical line that "opens and closes" and these dances include movements to the four cardinal points suggesting the importance of direction with probable cosmological undertones[70].

The kula, therefore, can be perceived as a ritualised form of social rites that are required to be performed to gain acceptance or absolve or defuse possible perceived pollution, reaction or rejection in formalised relationships with others. It is from these various aspects, long attested as traditional in India, that it is recognisable in ritualised mariner's approaches to Island peoples.

The Kula and Melanesia

One of the most interesting rituals performances recognised throughout the islands was located off the eastern end of New Guinea and part of its mainland known as the Kula. This was a ceremonial perambulation by trading canoes along a recognised sequence of islands and a section of the New Guinea mainland undertaken by the local chiefs and traders. These islands included parts of the Louisades, the Trobriand Archipelago, the d'Entrecasteaux Islands, and Woodlark Island and are all notable for being the islands groups that show clear connections along with the Eastern section of the New Guinea coast known as exhibiting influences from Polynesia and possibly Central and South America. The islands between these groups and Polynesia, the Solomon's and New Hebrides (Vanuatu) in Melanesia, also show clear evidence, long recognised from Polynesia but more controversially from South America.

The influences from Polynesia follow the natural flow of the South Equatorial current direct from Coastal Peru through Polynesia to Melanesia. This leads directly to the islands associated with the Kula where this current flows from here through the only passage from the east supported by the prevailing winds from the Southern Pacific to Indonesia and India between New Guinea and Cape York Peninsula in Northern Australia. The Kula appears to have been associated with long forgotten rituals of long distance sea trade carried on over far greater distances than generally accepted but that has become localised as the traders' authority, territorial ambitions and power bases became more contracted or were superseded by others. Bronislaw Malinowski, who reported through research and observation in the islands in 1915 and 1916, wrote of the Kula: "It looms paramount in the tribal life of those natives who live within its circuit, and its importance is fully realised by the tribesmen themselves, whose ideas, ambitions, desires and vanities are very much bound up with the Kula"[71]. He includes a map showing the canoe circuit as maintained in the years of his residence among the peoples who participated in them[72].

Before these ritual undertakings over long distances by canoe there were the religious, mystical and of particular note certain important mortuary ceremonies to be performed reminiscent of those recorded among the Pula-Kuli of the Tiyans in South India. Most important of these rituals were the preparations of taboos and magical protection ceremonies before setting out and the notifications associated with the trading circuit[73]. Paramount also was the beauty magic considered necessary to charm the trading partners on the other islands.

The perambulations or ritual sea-trading circuits undertaken by the islanders are in two opposite directions, one trades only in necklaces made up of soulava, or red Spondylus shell, and other exchanges only in white shell bracelets called Mwali. On their way round the circuit at specified island stops one type of item is exchanged for the other type where transactions are

1.016 :
Armshells brought from Kitava to Omarakana as part of the ritual exchange in the Kula of 1915. Trobriand Islands, Papua New Guinea.

1.017 : Ceremonial canoe setting off with its ritual exchange shells shown strung off the back on poles from the canoe. New Guinea, Early 20th., century, A.D.

1.018 : A sacred enclosure dedicated to ancestral rites and sea mariners deities with conch shell trumpets in line with images of the revered crocodile. Torres Straits, Melanesia, Pre-20th., century, A.D.

1.019 : Skulls and shell trumpets laid with sacred stones under trees dedicated to the ancestors. Melanesia, Early 20th., century, A.D.

1.020 : Conch shell traditional in the rites and ceremonies in both Melanesia and Polynesia as well as in India and South America. Marquesas Islands, Eastern Polynesia, Pre or early 20th., century, A.D.

fixed by long established rules and regulations and elaborate magical, social and greeting rituals[74]. The villages on this circuit are fixed in a definite sequence so that in the one cycle shell necklaces will be exchanged with shell bracelets and the converse for the bracelets[75]. On each of the islands men who have exchanged their items for the incoming complimentary ones, retain them for a set period of time before passing them on in the ritual exchange system. Once a man comes into possession of these items, either Soulava - red Spondylus shell necklaces, or Mwali - white shell bracelets, he cannot opt out, but must always trade repeatedly from that time on and the relations established between the two men performing the trade is always permanent and they are considered as complimentary partners. As Malinowski comments, "once in the Kula, always in the Kula"!!!.[76].

The important point of the Kula is that it was ceremonial and one based on the ceremonies, mystical performances, and social greeting rituals rather than for actual gain, and it is unlikely to be an accident that the shells used, particularly the red shells were the highly prized and mystically valued Spondylus is found anciently on the Pacific coast of South America. The principle was that of regulation to establish trust and alliances through ceremonial gift exchange at the level of equal partnership that was repaid by an equivalent value counter-gift[77]. Clearly this is based on the approaches by traders centuries probably millennia ago in attempting to establish peaceful trading exchanges and are typical in the annals of all peoples with a written record or oral traditions from the earliest times. Apart from these rituals involving the exchange of the highly prized shells of the Soulava and Mwali items other, separate barter trade took place but this was based on commercial value and was undertaken at the same time but considered apart from that of the Kula proper. The natives themselves consciously distinguished the Kula from barter since the Kula was an ritual exchange involving ceremonies and exchanges that could extend over some time while ordinary trade or barter was called gimwali and exchanges were immediate[78]. These ritual shell necklaces and bracelets were generally called vaygu'a, as a collective term for the Kula valuables, and were held only by certain individuals who have the right to retain and trade them. These men would have a few recognised counterparts on other islands with whom he could trade exchange them in the prescribed manner. A chief on the other hand, had hundreds of men he could exchange with indicating that title and rank were as important in the exchange as they were in each of the island social structures[79]. This relationship, often inherited, provides a special relationship between two men on different islands and their tribes since they are seen as hosts as well as allies providing mutual assistance. Clearly this type of relationship, out of which neither actually benefits in terms of immediate material gain, since each exchanges an equivalent shell object, either necklace or bracelet, based on creating goodwill and allies in very dangerous situations in foreign islands where death was ever present for intruders. A similar parallel to the Kula exchange could be drawn in the present day attempts by anthropologists over the last couple of generations hanging out goods, usually beads and brightly coloured objects, to make contact with tribes long hidden in the dark forests of Amazonia and New Guinea. This is a contact technique that has long been attempted from the earliest explorers and undoubtedly used to some effect alluded to by the Ancient Egyptians in their famous expeditions abroad to the more extensively recorded attempts in the European colonial period and in later anthropological expeditions.

In the Kula region and beyond in the rest of Melanesia a chief was expected to share whatever he had accumulated regardless of whether a person was a friend, strangers or pauper from outside the village. These rituals have been found in similar exchanges in South America and have been paralleled in more recent researches on the subject of trade and ritual exchange in the extensive studies recorded by Claude Levi-Strauss.

Canoe Magic in the Kula

The canoe in the islands participating in the Kula was called the waga, similar to the Polynesian term waka, these in turn derive from the Sanskrit term vaha - a vehicle, and the Kula canoe had its own special name of masawa - "sea-going canoe"[80]. The construction of a canoe was surrounded with ceremony and magical rituals and this extended to all aspects to be faced in the life of a canoe. This included its inception, construction, sails and sailing, wreckage and salvage and the operations it played in inter-island trade as well as the diving for the Conus and Spondylus shell[81]. No canoe could be constructed without magic and no man with the authority involved in the Kula would allow one to be constructed without it since his belief in the efficaciousness of the associated rituals was absolute. In Fiji similar rituals included endowing the war canoe with guardian souls by it being launched over live slaves used as rollers so that their souls as they died entered the boat to protect it[82]. It is likely that something of the same rituals were followed in Western Melanesia but had ceased through lack of sufficient slaves or substitution of pigs for humans known elsewhere.

In the construction of the masawa, or sea-going canoe, the first section of magic spells and ritual was called Tokway, and this relates to the "flying canoe cycle" undoubtedly associated with ancient myth cycles attached to the orbits of the Sun and Moon and more explicitly preserved in the sky canoe myths in the Solomon Islands to the north east. The tokway is actually the spirit of the tree that is selected for the canoe's construction and similar respect is shown for the tree's inhabiting soul by the Maori. In the Maori and Kula rites the dismissal of the tree's resident spirit in cutting the tree down is of some importance since it is believed to be able to cast a malevolent spell upon the canoe[83]. In this first section of rites the carved canoe prow-boards are shaped[84] for fitting and it is now recognised that their style and construction is related to that of the Maori in New Zealand, the Sepik of South New Guinea, and South Chinese traditions. The second stage is related to the actual fitting together of the separate elements and accompanied by the appropriate spells and rituals. Exorcisms were of special importance and spells were performed for the lashings made from selected creepers called the wayugo[85]. Every stage therefore from the construction to waterproofing by caulking, and the launching was attended by their own associated spells and magical performances and generally called mwasila or the Kula magic[86].

1.021 : Polynesian sacred bundle wrapped in barkcloth. Marquesas Islands, Late 19th., century, A.D.

1.022 : Old God or Pauahtun paddling in his skin covered canoe or coracle with a sacred bundle and a bird as guide that probably signifies navigation by bird migration routes at sea. Codex Dresden, Mexico, Pre-post Conquest.

1.023 : Animal sacrifices, here a llama, offered to the ancestral mountain gods and a sacred bundle offered by another priest with a lunar crescent on his turban similar to Saivite images in India. Poma de Ayala; Inca Peru, 16th., century, A.D.

1.024 : Kula canoe setting off with a crew of 18 men. Papau-New Guinea, early 20th., century, A.D.

The magic spells themselves were called either megwa or yopa[87], terms possibly associated with the sacrificial post of the Brahmans in India called the Yupa. Important also is the axe or adze used for cutting the mooring rope from the canoe to the shore and this was called the ligogu and was subject to its own magical rites and was considered among the primary rites essential to the canoe along with the dismissal of the tokway (tree spirit), the ritual cutting of the pulling rope, the lashing creeper, the caulking and painting of the hull black[88]. In its launching, red ochre daubing and a cowrie shell are placed at each end before in its final protective ceremonies among other festivities[89].

Aboard the masawa, or trading sea-going canoe, are four classes of men, the toliwaga the ship master or owner, the usagelu - crewmen or mariners, the silasila or helpers who look after the sails, and the boys who are trainees for later Kula expeditions[90]. Essential also on these voyages was the betel nut, a form of light narcotic still chewed in the islands of Indonesia and Melanesia, and from Micronesia through to India. It was undoubtedly an essential element in reducing the pangs of hunger and thirst on long sea voyages and became an essential ritual item in the Kula and subject to its own spells and usage in exchange. The peaks of mountains on the various islands were more easily seen at sea that the shores and were used as guides in navigation. In the betel nut spells references to mountains are made which appear to have more significance than purely for navigation and the name of the mountain, koya, suggests that it may have mythical or cosmological attributes[91]. These mountains, particularly associated with the Amphlett and d'Entrecasteaux Islands, are believed to be the homes of witches and fierce demons and were seen as a constant threat for the mariners. One of these islands and a main desitnation in the Kula was Dobu and these people were also considered dangerous with a reputation for having a partiality for human flesh[92].

The myths associated with the Kula are many but vary from island to island and in some case the landing sites associated with the trading circuit a century ago appear not to have preserved any traditions into more recent times. The myths do not yield any special insights into why these ceremonials exchanges were initiated and this, with the fact that there are no traditions preserved in some of the ports of call, suggests that this whole tradition has been a contraction of earlier trading expeditions that perhaps covered the whole Pacific. The interesting references to the Kula being a double circuit including very specific landing places suggests that this may have developed from the routes undertaken in cross-Pacific voyages utilising the Equatorial Current to travel from South East Asia through Micronesia, Polynesia and to the Central and South American shores. The voyages utilising the South Equatorial Current may reflect the complementary trading route to return to Asia from South America through Central and Southern Polynesia to Melanesia and New Guinea back to Indonesia and South East Asia. The myths are such that they do not record any real historical information and the native Melanesians were rarely inclined to record or remember accurate historical information since their cultures did not require its use or accord any importance to such records unlike the Polynesians. The myths as far as they go usually attribute the beginning of the Kula to ancient heroes but in one of the myths a hero is named as Tokosikuna and he brings Spondylus necklaces to trade and other men collect arm shells in a form of the Kula. There are references in these myths to these men intending to drowning Tokosikuna in the deep sea - in Pilolu, certainly a form of the Polynesian underworld Pulotu[93]. In the first part of this myth the hero appears as a badly pocked marked man of poor stature but through magic acquired in his trip in Northern regions he assumes the shape of a young, very handsome man of fine stature and appearance. This magic thus acquired eulogises his great success and popularity particularly with women and this engenders the envy of his own people against him hence their attempt to drown him.

The Kula myths do indicate that there is likely to be considerable gain through undertaking the more ancient versions of the Kula expedition. Since there is little to be gained in the exchange of the shell necklaces and shell bracelets, since the demand is that this should be matched in return, it is the barter that is carried on beside the Kula rituals that provides other commercial opportunities. However, this success is considered due to the magic spells and rituals that are performed before setting out on these expeditions, before landing at each destination, and those also performed before leaving a port and those for the ultimate return journey that receive the credit for such success. These rites therefore include the magical rituals for the canoe, for the weather, for appeasement before landing and similar rituals for all other occasions and for the essential constructional items in the construction of the canoe.

1.025 : A Pahuatun, or Old God, being greeted by a young Mayan lord hiding a ritual sacrificial knife behind his back who is depicted on the other side of the vessel and identical to that shown in *1.026* - see also colour version *1.116* . Both have applied face paint and their red lips are particularly prominent as part of the beauty magic rituals. Chama, Guatemala, 600-900 A.D.

1.026 : A young Mayan lord hiding a ritual sacrificial knife behind his back as he greets the Pahuatun, or Old God that is depicted on the other side of the vessel and identical to that shown in *1.025* - see also colour version *1.114* . Both have applied face paint and their red lips are particularly prominent as part the beauty magic rituals. Chama, Guatemala, 600- A.D.

The Lilava - the Sacred Magic Bundle in Kula Ritual

An essential item taken aboard the masara, or sea-going canoe, without which it could not depart for the Kula, was the lilava or sacred bundle. A few of the items sacred to the Kula and the trade associated with the greeting rituals, such as a bunch of betel-nut, a lime pot, a comb and a plaited armlet are placed on a newly woven mat and then folded while the appropriate magical spell is recited to form the sacred bundle. This inner bundle is then placed on another mat, or perhaps two, and folded again to ensure that the contents are secure within, all the while magical spells are being intoned, and there appeared to be a belief that it was endowed with a "magical portent" called kariyala. It was said that whenever the sacred bundle was opened rain, thunder and lightning would result. Malinowski believed that this might have something to do with

1.030 : Bronze Tumi or ritual sacrificial knife with ornamentation of a priest or ruler being carried on a litter by two men . Moche, North Coast Peru, 200-600 A.D.

027 : Palanquin with leaf parasol-type ...nopy more typical of Ancient India. Note ...e cross decoration similar to the Jama-...aque on Coastal Ecuador but more so of ...ncient India. Poma de Ayala; Inca Peru, ...th., century, A.D.

1.029 : Ruler being carried in a traditional litter - a type often used in high-status marriage. Jain, Chola Dynasty, Tirupati-Kundram, South India, 14th., century, A.D.

1.028 : Grafitti sketch of the typical elite palanquin among the Maya 1500 years ago. Tikal, Guatemala, 400-600 A.D.

1.031 : Palanquin of a type suspended from the palanki, poles carrying the frames carriage called a "dooli", similar in principle to that of the Mayan (*1.032*). Chota Nagpore, East Central India, Early 20th., century, A.D.

1.033 : Clay ceramic model of two men carrying a litter. Note the Indonesian style caps and the plaits or braided hair hanging down in front of the ears in traditional Ancient Middle Eastern fashion. Chan Chan, Chimu, North Coast Peru, 900-1350 A.D.

.032 : Mayan lord being transported in a woven basket litter accompanied by guards carrying ceremonial paddle possibly ...ferring to mariner contacts. All appear to have adorned themselves with beauty products particularly evident in the reddened ...s. This scene appears to relate to those depicted in *1.1025* and *1.026*. Chama, Guatemala, 600-900 A.D.

1.034 : Carved stela, here referring to Nebuchadnezzar 1, from a tradition known for millennia in the Ancient Middle East. The Supreme deity was the Moon god Sin represented by the crescent Moon centrally placed in the highest register . Assyria, 6th., century, A.D.

1.035 : Coconuts used on a carrying pole or yolk were biodegradable and did not last from ancient times but were common for long distance voyages throughout the Pacific Ocean. Samoa, Central Polynesia, Early 20th., century, A.D.

the fact that in the tropics there was almost guaranteed to be thunder and lightning daily in the afternoons in the monsoon season followed by rain and this climatic reality had become attached to the sacred bundle. This might be an indicator that the most ancient voyages took place in the monsoon season and had became attached to the sacred bundle as the main repository of the absolute belief in the magical portents and luck associated with it on the voyage. The bundle had its own special place at the centre of the deck of the canoe clearly indicating its central importance in the purpose of the ceremonial voyages and was not opened for the first time until reaching Dobu[94]. This, as earlier noted, was a place renown and feared by those on the Kula since the Dobuans were reputedly cannibals in the days before the effective British Administration in the first years of the twentieth century.

Malinowski records the magical spell associated with the lilava bundle and he notes that repetition forms the central structure in their recitation. This recalls the Ancient Sumerian myths and texts that utilise similar metrical repetitions. There are references in the myth to a small coral island conveniently placed when winds are contrary or bad weather sets in and was considered a place of refuge for those exposed in the Kula. This island is particularly noted as a place where turtles lay their eggs and these sea-going animals are particularly revered in Melanesia, Indonesia to the west and from the Ancient Middle East, India and in the Americas. There are references also to the rainbow and in this myth it was said to "stand up" on the top of Koyatabu, this being the name for the main mountain on several of the islands[95]. Koya was noted earlier as the term for mountains associated with witches and female demons while tabu probably derives from the Polynesian taboo, originally tapu, the term for a special sanction placed on a person, ritual, object or festival.

In the long poles that connect the canoe hull to the outrigger there are compartments, numbering 10, 11 or 12, called liku. Nearest the canoe hull is the compartment that always hold the conch, a necessary element for the Kula since this is required during religious and social ceremonies and used in announcing the Kula canoe before it enters port or ties up on the beach. The young boys, as trainees, sit in the hull near this compartment and it is they who blow the conch when required. In the fourth compartment the baler is always kept and many of these have survived, particularly noted among the Maori if New Zealand, and are considered great works or art. In the third water containers made from coconuts have their place[96] (*1.035*).

The Kula and the Application and Efficacy of Beauty Magic

Having set out on their voyage regaled with all the magical spells and rituals so long beyond memory traditionally applied to the canoe, the ritual objects and all who were allowed on board, the Kula undertook the first leg of the planned voyage. In principle each leg was fundamentally a repetition of the first and for the canoe that set out from Sinaketa the first stop was the most feared - Dobu. However, the name Sina-keta is of interest since the great hero in the adjacent island archipelago - the Solomons, was named Sina Kwao, or "Shining Bright". Sina is repeatedly found throughout both the Melanesian and Polynesian islands of the Pacific and refers as a proper name for the Moon and all related references in some form such as "bright". This term clearly derives from the name of the Ancient Akkadian name for their Moon god Sin, and found also as the Moon god Si on the coast Peru. The name appears to be evidence for ancient traders who appear to have reached the Pacific millennia before from the Ancient Middle East and considered elsewhere in this work. The hero name in one of the most important Kula myths, Toko-Sikuna probably has a similar or common origin with Sina Kwao.

In the most ancient days it was estimated that the Kula could have easily been made up from canoes from all the participating islands numbering in all about one hundred canoes. In 1918 Malinowski journeyed aboard the Kula and recorded that the Sinaketan canoes were joined by sixty canoes from Dobu, twelve from the Amphlett Islands and the same number from Vakuta[97]. This was considered a large one for its day and some had joined up out of curiosity having heard of Malinowski's interest in the Kula.

When a group of canoes nears its destination the expedition stops, the sails are furled, the masts taken down and the canoes moored. Most Melanesian villages were not constructed near the shore unless they housed fishermen and those with occupations dependent on the sea and in sea estuaries the houses were often constructed on piles that were easier to defend. A safe distance from the nearest settlement and therefore themselves less likely to be attacked from the land the boys aboard swim ashore and collected leaves to bring them back to the canoes. Here the

1.039 : Face tattoos in principle similar to those of Polynesia and similarly applied to women and for the same reasons. Gran Chaco, Late 19th., - early 20th., century, A.D.

36 : A carved and tattooed arm model found on [Nort]h Coastal Peru featuring typical Moche motifs. Such [exam]ples are virtually identical in principle to similar [one]s in the Marquesas Islands. Note the projecting mid-[f]inger that appears to be representative of the five [sacre]d mountain peaks. Moche, North Coast Peru, 200-[...]A.D.

1.037 : Face tattoo or Moko traditional among the Maori but also found among the Tahitians. Maori Culture, New Zealand, Mid-19th., century, A.D.

1.041 : Ainu woman with mouth tattoo that is identical to those depicted in Ancient Central America and similar to those in the Amazon Basin - see also Remojadas tattoo (*12.093*). Ainu, North Japan, Late 19th., century, A.D.

1.038 : Typical body tattoos depicted on this carved wooden female figure. Maori Culture, New Zealand, 19th., century, A.D. or earlier.

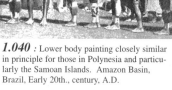

1.040 : Lower body painting closely similar in principle for those in Polynesia and particularly the Samoan Islands. Amazon Basin, Brazil, Early 20th., century, A.D.

1.042 : Finely designed geometric leg tattoos similar to those also applied anciently in Polynesia to parts of the body with patterns similar to the Gond in India and with Tiahuanacan references. Marquesas Islands, Eastern Polynesia, Late 19th., century, A.D.

older men and the toliwaga, or canoe master, recited magical spells over the leaves and all washed themselves in seawater and then rubbed themselves all over with the magically impregnated leaves to transfer the efficacy to their own beings. This was followed by coconuts being broken, scraped of their contents, and the meat then "medicated", and this greasy mixture was then rubbed on the skin giving it a high sheen.

The next stage in the beauty magic ritual was the chanting over a comb and the hair was then teased out with it. Betel nuts were then crushed and mixed with lime and the red paste was used to draw ornamental designs on their faces and sayyaku, a resinous aromatic substance, was used to draw black designs on their backs. Aromatic mint, preserved in coconut oil, that had been subject to magical spells before setting out on the Kula was then inserted into the armlets and a few drops of the oil smeared on the body, over the sacred bundle, the lilava, and over the pari - the trade goods. At all times, every act was accompanied by recitations and protective invocations, all related to the mwasila - the beauty magic specially associated with the Kula[98].

The whole purpose of these lengthy and careful preparations and intonated spells was to dazzle the trading partners on the island about to be entered so that the recipients of the ceremonial exchange items, the Soulava and Mwali, are overwhelmed by the allurements of their collective and individual beauty and the status of their trade goods and are willing to exchange and guarantee their safety while on their island.

The myth of Tokosiketa, the Kula hero, implies that the most handsome and virile of men were successful in love and were therefore considered to also attract status as well as the most valuable trade goods and each performance upon reaching the islands in the Kula was in fact an attempt by sympathetic magic to emulate Tokosikuna's success. However, behind this façade was the menacing problem of safety, as other of the myths and legends associated with the Kula attest, and prompted by the ever-present danger that strangers risked when visiting the islands and mainland territories of other tribes in the circuit. Traders and mariners were not always welcome and frequently ended up being massacred either in whole or part, those being caught sometimes ending up as part of the local food supply, a factor so noted of the Solomon Islands into the earlier twentieth century. It is most likely, in fact, that the Tokosikuna myth relates to ancient trading journeys that took on relief crews from the islands and who returned much rewarded, at least in local terms, for their long periods spent at sea lasting many months or perhaps years. The first European ships regularly took on replacement crews from the islands and Indonesia and it is likely that the Tokosikuna myth derives from substance and references from earlier experiences.

The magical spells and beauty magic probably derives from the extremely superstitious trading people who plied the Pacific long before the Europeans. The more recent Pacific Islanders in the Kula who emulated the believed efficacious means of protection known to them such as tattooing their faces or at least covering them with protective designs and colours, usually red, believed that they provided protection from danger. Face and body designs and tattooing for protection are known from India to the Ainu of Japan, the Indonesians, Melanesians and Polynesians and found identically in Ancient Mexico, Central America and South America. The mouth was considered especially vulnerable and this was subject to reddening with the urucu juice in South America, and betel in the Western Pacific as noted above and tattooed black identically among the Ainu[99] of Japan (*1.041*) and Mexico (*12.093*).

Clearly the art of beauty magic is actually aimed by mariners at providing their own protection against the many dangers of peoples were only occasionally visited and the prescribed protective magical spells and rites performed before contact were meant to elicit supernatural assistance in what must have on many occasions appeared fearsome island peoples. And yet the traders and venturers were never discouraged and unlikely to have been so in centuries and millennia before the development of the Kula. This is exemplified in more recent centuries in the Pacific where the recorded deaths of traders, and missionaries[100], at the hands of the island peoples particularly in Melanesia, number in the hundreds, but although well-known to those who succeeded them did not prevent them repeatedly attempting contact.

In the islands of Melanesia and Polynesia the myths and legends surrounding the Poea, or beautiful boy, have long been noted and are of interest since the pursuit of beauty and the allurement of the beautiful person is a characteristic among Pacific Islanders. There are legends recording that Polynesians have landed on cannibal islands but have been saved because their beauty has allured the flesh-eaters and saved their lives resulting in them being treated with great respect as demi-gods[101]. The connections with Polynesia and the islands frequented by the Kula has long been established and this leads to another curious parallel in the Kula rituals that appears to have some connection with the Marquesas Islands far to the East and the nearest group to Central America. In the rites of beauty magic there are lines in the oral tradition recitations that Malinowski was unable to elicit an explanation but encapsulated as a passage from the magical spells the whole of the mwasila and these are recorded as follows:

"Here we are ugly; we eat bad fish, bad food; our faces remain ugly. We want to sail to Dobu; we keep taboos, we don't eat bad food. We go to Sarubwoyna; we wash; we charm the leaves of silasila; we charm the coco-nut; we putuma; we make our red paint and black paint; we put in our fine-smelling vana; we arrive in Dobu beautiful looking. Our partner looks at us, sees our faces are beautiful; he throws the vaygu'a to us."[102].

The putuma is the anointing of the body noted above and the vana is the herbal sprig ointment placed in the armlets while the vaygu'a are the trade goods. The beauty magic is clearly aimed at not becoming beautiful originally as recorded in the Tokosikuna myth but as traders attempting to charm by allurement the island people. This by extension includes any other peoples they come into contact with in the wider sense so that they would be willing to trade, as noted in the last line of this ritual recitation, and not a little aimed at avoiding the cannibalism with the reference to the Dobuans. The first line, however, is unusual as Malinowski notes and the traders on the Kula were unable to enlighten him as to the meaning engendered in the references to eating fish. It is very likely that this in fact is an obscure reference to the victims of conflict and probably a likely fate of some island traders in the Marquesas Islands since the dead victim of warfare or the sacrificial victim for rites involving cannibalism were called "fish"[103]. The beauty magic of the Kula was aimed at pacifying the islanders and others on the New Guinea mainland and establish the friendliest of conditions so that the potential trading partners would appear as the myth notes, that they would just throw the trade goods to them so astounded were they by their beauty. When the Europeans entered the Pacific all the various people in both Polynesia and Melanesia considered them to be the ancestral gods returning to claim their earthly kingdoms and frequently were regaled with benefits they would not have otherwise been accorded. This belief is exemplified by Captain Cook's visit to Hawaii where he was considered the incarnation of the god Lono or Rongo, a misperception that ultimately cost him his life.

The references to the fish in the spell of the Kula beauty magic seems therefore to be an oblique reference to the Dobuan appetite for human flesh and any others who may have similar tastes but that derived from the much wider trading routes in earlier millennia when the trade "circuit" extended to the Marquesas Islands and when it was probably in the control of the mariners from India or their descendants in Polynesia and the Maoris in particular. This extension and transference of culture by long distance mariners will be of more interest in later chapters but as indicated in earlier works[104] there are many aspects of culture that connect the Marquesas Islanders to Central America and the Maya in particular and the coastal cultures of South America.

The Kula may have extended to South Eastern Australia originally where the term for "man" was Kulin as well as a tribe of the same name[105]. This term was possibly confused with the deity, Koen or Koin, but since this area is particularly noted for its Polynesian cultural references these contacts will be of note later in this work.

In South America the term for the Inca throne or stool as it actually was the duho[106], this is identical to the chief's stool among the Nagas of Assam[107], daho and tehuba - burial platform[108], were the sacred sitting place on the New Guinea coast was the dubu[109] and where the sacred dancing ground among the Marquesans was the tohua[110], considered to be related to that of the tehuba in Naga Assam. It is likely that the tribe called the Dobu in New Guinea had some special relation to the Assamese and may have been their mariners descendants in the paternal line. Among the Maya the thrones and seats used for people of status resemble those of Indonesia, Burma and early India, and their term for their wind gods was Pauahtun[111], the identical name for the wind god in the Ganges Delta. This term is also similarly found in Assam to the North, and East Coast of India facing the Bay of Bengal, where the wind deity was Pawa, and the people called themselves Pawan-ban, "Children of the Wind"[112].

In some of the finely painted and very descriptive vase decorations often representing mythical or legendry scenes the Pauahtun, emerging from his shell, clearly represents a mariner or sea deity, requiring the wind, Pawa, for his sails, shown being greeted by a Mayan ruler or official who is hiding a flint sacrificial knife behind his back. The greetings are deliberately displayed as false! In one Chama ceramic illustration, one of several almost identical vessels designs, the Mayan ruler is shown beckoning the Pauahtun to approach while holding a flint knife hidden behind his back with the other hand (*1.026*). In a more elaborate example it shows him unequivocally grasping the hand of the Pauahtun with the intention of sacrificing him with the raised flint knife (*6.116*). Of special interest is that the lips of the Mayan ruler are clearly, brightly rouged or painted red in an exaggerated manner and pouted to deflect the Pauahtun's attention. His face more than usually reflects the intention of a "beauteous" appearance probably due to some make-up preparation similar to that greeting and, or trading rituals similar to that of the Kula. Clearly both scenes are intended to represent some recognised greeting ritual involving special emphasis on facial preparations and seemingly to indicate that the Kula extended in the ancient times to the Americas, at least from the middle of the first millennium A.D., and probably before that time. Traders prepared carefully, and were at risk of their lives, in the West of the Pacific in extending their contacts from Asia to the Americas, as depicted on these ceramics illustrations, and into more recent centuries and surviving in the rare contacted and encapsulated rituals of the Kula.

The whole purpose of presenting in this work the rites of the Kula in Melanesia, more or less centrally situated between Asia and South America, is to set the scene for considering the evidence and many surviving and recorded references that indicate that the extraordinary courage and sense of adventure exited and established contact with the Americas and maintained that contact over millennia. Clearly this contact from the Ancient Middle East has left evidence in India on the coasts where this stopping area and staging post was long a major centre of trade. From India the references to the Kula appear in status and clan relationships with links to maritime activities and appears to be the origins for the ritual trading circuit surviving in Melanesia. The Kula appears to be a later contraction to a microcosm in Melanesia of a Pacific-wide sea trade carried on from the most ancient times, extending from South, South East and East Asia through to the Americas. The sacred bundle - the lilava, in the Kula, has its equivalent in the sacred bundle, so well known in the far east of Polynesia in the Marquesas and recorded among the Maya. In surviving Mayan illustrations the sacred bundle is depicted in the canoe of a Pauahtun connected with the wind deity and the sea in Mayan texts, and an eagle's head clearly indicating long distance sea trade (*1.022*). Mariner's observed these fixed migration routes of birds across the oceans as a navigational aid on long sea voyages so famously preserved in the myths, and iconography, of Melanesian but particularly Polynesian mariners.

Aspects of Continuity from Melanesia to Polynesia and South America

Further to the east in Polynesia the many references to the great, fair-skinned ancestors alluded to in the myths and legends in Melanesia are found to be more likely to be substantially based in the claims of the Polynesian to white, fair-haired or red-haired ancestry[113] derived from Central Asian or early Vedic Aryan inhabitants of India. There are clear indications that they descend from early Caucasian intruders into the Pacific and blood analysis indicates that they have descent from those Caucasians in Central Asia[114] through Korea and the Ainu of Japan into the Pacific but also from the Malaysian region of South East Asia where their language and cultural ties have been clearly identified.

The Gran Chaco and Amazonian tribes show many aspects of South East Asian culture and traditions detected by earlier researchers. One of many examples indicates that imagery and myths could only be transferred from the opposite of the world by mariners just as the blowgun if found so similarly in Borneo and South East Asia as well as in the Amazon forests. Other aspects are also shared in myths and a few examples give a general flavour before later references included in this work.

Menstruation is considered a period of great threat for a woman since it was considered by the Toba that women were particularly liable to attack in this part of their monthly cycle from evil spirits. To obviate this problem seclusion with protective rites were undertaken and this included the woman painting her face with the red of the urucu fruit and was subject to restrictions in her diet. Fish was particularly prohibited since it was believed that if she ate fish she would go mad and if her husband brought a parrot home after a day's hunting she would snatch it and eat its head raw. The woman would then turn into a "tiger" and turn on her own family[115]. In a myth from the Angami Nagas, a people noted for the continuing devotion to the traditional erection of megaliths, myths preserved about female ogres appear in modern analysis to refer to the menstrual state in woman known generally as PMT when the less rational state predominates in the monthly cycle and in an Angami myth it is stated that a female ogre was responsible for biting off the heads of birds in the snared hunt of two small boys[116]. This appears to have close similarities to the Toba myth and along with many other aspects of apparent shared aspects of culture this myth motif seems to militate in favour of probable contact between Assam and South America. As with the Nagas of Assam most of the tribes of the Pilcomayo River region in the Gran Chaco leading from the Parana to the highlands of Bolivia were scalp and head-hunters[117].

Protective rites, in attempting to deter the attack from evil spirits that women were believed to be particularly vulnerable, were largely directed to the face, beside the lower openings in the body, since it was in the head that the eyes, ears and mouth that most of the openings were located[118]. Success in warding off these demon attacks was believed to be achievable by tattooing and in the Ancient ceramics of the Nazca Plains and in Mexico the genitals and face were tattooed. In some cases these mouth tattoos were identically to those of the Ainu of Japan and for the same reasons and found similarly also in India, Indonesia and Melanesia.

These few examples in the foregoing are only indicators in the possible, or probable transfer of Asian culture to the Americas, but also there is likely to have been a conterflow that should not be ignored. It is necessary to consider, albeit briefly, some aspects of cultural transfer from Ancient Asia, to Australia, as a staging post from the Western Pacific into the Pacific Islands where the ocean currents lead directly to South America.

Elements of Cultural Transfer from India to Aboriginal Australia

The implications of the abundant myths legends and folklore from India referring to long distance sea travel is confirmed by the spread of the cultures from the Sub-continent into South East Asia. As has been noted Austronesian speaking peoples penetrated into South India from very ancient times and appear to have left their imprint on the "aboriginal" peoples with whom they integrated. Such intrusions and associations are confirmed not only in the surviving myths, legends and linguistic studies but in the archaeology, as far as it has been examined, since it is known that the so-called teri artefacts found on the south east coast near Madras appear identical in type and manufactured technique to those found in Sri Lanka and the Andaman Islands before the Iron Age in the early first millennium B.C.[119].

The manufacture of flaked blades is interesting since the special method of splitting the quartz used in the Andaman Islands is found in the coastal sites of this teri culture indicating that these islands 900 miles (1350 km) from either the Madras coast of India or Sri Lanka was in contact by sea that appeared to have presented no problem of accessibility to apparently proven maritime venturers at such an early date. This implies that venturing further east would probably not have been a problem particularly as the Burmese coast was much not far distant from India with landfalls beyond to assist in island hopping.

Early contact with the Andamans, located in the middle of the Bay of Bengal between India and Burma, appears to be confirmed in some of the myths and customs of the Andamanese with India. Contact is noted in an interesting example of traditional myth where the death of a child is effected by enclosing it in a tree[120]. This extraordinary act is related in many myths in India as well as through the Pacific region to the Americas where it was believed that humanity, or heroes or deities in particular, emerged from trees. The act of immuring the child is undoubtedly a symbolic act of returning its body and spirit to the original source and is found in myths, legends and traditions from India into the Pacific region.

Of particular interest is that the Andaman Islands, along with the Nicobars, appears to have had a close relationship not only with the pre- Aryan tribes of Sri Lanka and Aboriginal India - in the South and on the East Coast especially, but to have been linked in the broader flow of traders and venturers to the ancient island continent of Australia. This relationship was clearly seen by some of the early Victorian researchers in India and indigenous scholars such as Sarat Chandra Roy[121], but also those among the early settlers in Australia who were interested in the indigenous Aboriginal culture[122]. More direct associations through myths legends and later cultural and artefactual cross-references were clear for those who wished to see them and were perceived as originating in India and diffused into Aboriginal Australia.

As noted one of the most important of the Aboriginal tribes of India were the Gonds (also Konds or Khonds), who appear to have been the masters of large parts of Central India into the 16-17th centuries A.D. Although now much reduced in material culture and social status they were noted by the early British researchers as being once of some importance. W. V. Grigson, whose studies in the Gond language are still of importance, quotes R. V. Russell: "Gond rules of exogamy appear to preserve traces of the system found in Australia, by

1.043 : tattoos char tic of South but found a identically Caroline Is Nazca Cult South Coas 200-600 A.

1.044 : Tattooed genital region illustrated on this ment sculpture but identical to those found in Ancie Coast Peru. Caroline Islands, Micronesia, 19th., cen A.D. or before.

1.045: Kurnai man in a possum cape similar to those worn by the Maoris of New Zealand and the Ona of Tierra del Fuego. South East Australia, Late 19th., century, A.D.

1.046: Maori chief wearing a native dog-skin cape and dual feather headdress identical to that of the Incas. Maori, New Zealand, Late 19th., century, A.D.

1.047: Kurnai man with spotted shield design typical of many of the Pacific cultures but also of the coastal Peruvians in South America. South East Australia, Mid 19th., century, A.D.

which the whole tribe is split into two or four main divisions, and every man in one or two of them must marry a woman in the other one or two ..."[123]. In terms of Aboriginal clan structures several of the early British-Australian and -Melanesian researchers pick up on the same relationships and perceived the close similarities not only with India but also to certain tribes in Ethiopia and China which will be of special interest in later sections.

1.048: Gond Palace of Garha-Mandla. Ramnagar, Central India, 13-16th., century A.D.

The clan structure is certainly not the only cultural cross-reference but related elements of the ritual to celebrating courtship and marriage yield very interesting parallels. Grigson noted that when a girl has remained unmarried for longer than expected the parents arranged a form of marriage-capture called poyse'ottur where the first-cousin will carry her off to be his wife. Related to the Gonds are the Bison Horn Maria clan who retained also into the last century aspects of sham or mock fighting associated with the marriage capture where the male relatives of the girl staged a form of resistance to the prospective bridegroom to abduct her[124]. This ritual appears to have developed from actual attacks upon the Aboriginal peoples either by related clans or by marauding males seeking wives from outside the tribal boundaries who had too few women within their own tribes to accommodate their requirements. This shortage of suitable girls of marriageable age undoubtedly resulted from polygamy where the higher status males and especially the chiefs had prior selection rights and sociably acceptable multiple marriage privileges. Those males who had been dispossessed, due to invasion and escape after defeat in war, would probably also resort to such tactics to set up new clans in more distant retreats.

Not least of those for whom this form of marriage would become traditional are those who travelled by sea and settled temporarily or permanently in new lands so that bride capture or barter was essential. Since clan rules were usually binding, often excluding marriage outside the few or many clans who made up the tribe in its geographic boundaries, and the only possibility for many males would be to resort to bride-capture, wherever they came from. The history of India is one of many invasions from the North West - the Iranian plateau, but also by sea, and therefore the system of bride-capture appears to have become sanctified by time and necessity even when not strictly required. Undoubtedly this form of liaison, along with much of their cultural achievement were exported by sea-going peoples in India and transferred far beyond the shores where the culture of the Gonds and their related peoples are particularly notable in Australia but, as will be also noted, even found in the Americas. The link to Australia is emphasised not only in clan structure and sham fighting in marriage capture but the related names among the Gond tribes of India, reflected in the name Kurnai that is that of a major tribe of interest in the southeast of Australia.

.

The Kurnai - Culture and Traditions

The Kurni in India were a caste in India and of some interest was the fact that they had a sept or clan division called Banni or Vanni[125]. The name Kurni appears to have been a mutation of the terms kuri (sheep) and vanni (wool) since the caste were originally weavers of wool and this factor will be of greater note later. Into last century they had moved into weaving cotton and silk which they also cultivated along with the weaving of wool - all related to status products[126]. One of the clan subdivisions of this caste was known as Vanki, meaning an armlet, this being an object that was more than ornamentation but had religious significance. The term Vanni, Banni, or Vanki has probably developed from Van that is already associated with the Kurni and will be shown to be a term of some importance later in this work[127]. The clan division names often describe the exact vocation of that section, such as Sara meaning thread, and their duties were specifically related to the preparation and spinning of the thread[128]. An occupational term applied to them as weavers was Nese[129]. One of the clan subdivisions or gotras was called Nellu relating to paddy or unhusked rice and associated with them were a ploughmen subdivision called Ulava ("the ploughman")[130]. Many of the castes had extended duties or occupations and one gotra of the Kurni were called Sinddhu or drummers. This suggests that at one time they had associations with the sacred temple drums and that their origins in part were in Sind in North West India[131] - a region which prominent in diffusion in West and South India by sea.

Of some interest is that consonant with the custom of many of the castes in India the Kurni were divided into two sections, a dual social structure, one being called Hire ("big") the other Chikka ("small") - this dual organisation will be of some importance in later chapters. One of the elevated clan divisions was called Kuru-hina Settis suggesting contacts with Oceania where the tern kuru meant red and associated with ruling lineages and hina the name of the Moon and a goddess but certainly, originally, from the male Moon deity Sin in the ancient Middle East. It is of some interest that one of the clan divisions was named Banaju which meant "painted or trade wooden toys" considering the distribution of clay toys of the same type in Central America where it is that they are noted to be virtually identical to the prototypes in India[132]. Most of the Kurni were worshippers of the deity Siva and wore the lingayat or phallic representation of this deity as a pendant around their necks[133]. One of the synonyms of the Kurni was Jada or Jandra which meant "great men" - a term found also among the Devangas[134] who will also be mentioned later.

The theory of the possibility of transfer of culture from one place to another remote from it has become almost anathema for many researchers but their dictates and those for whom they lend support rarely provide scholarly investigations to justify these opinions. For the most prominent Victorians writers who visited or settled in Australia from the beginning of the 19th., century, it became quickly apparent that there were too many similarities in the cultures of the Australian Aborigines with Asia, and India in particular, for there not to have been sustained contact over centuries or millennia between these disparate regions of the globe. Of special note are the researches of A.W. Howitt whose several works include one specifically recording the customs and myths of the tribes of South East Australia and relating to the Kurnai in particular.

The dress of the Kurnai was simple but more sophisticated than some of the other tribes who eschewed clothing completely. It consisted only of a cape made from opossum skin furs but sometimes they wore several of these capes and at other times discarded them completely[135]. This type of clothing is highly reminiscent of the Maori cape that was also the only form of dress originally apart from a conical fur cap. In the latter case it no doubt reflected the lack of need for clothing in the torrid homelands of their ancestral Polynesian home near the Equator, but assumed the cape when approaching the southern, cooler latitudes, in their oceanic migrations. In similar latitudes in South America the Ona and other Indian tribes wore almost identical capes and fur caps to those of the Maoris and this will be of further interest later.

Interestingly the Kunai were divided into five clans[136] suggesting the fundamental division noted frequently in India and that was, and is also a sacred division among the Huichol of Western Mexico and the Incas of Peru. These clans spoke dialects that were virtually unintelligible to each other suggesting a long evolution from the mother tongue. It is also probable that they had been influenced and diverged by being merged in one or more sections with local foreign tribes or possibly absorbing or being dominated by intrusions from outside causing premature deviations in the common tongue - possibly by sea migrations.

Theories of intrusive peoples occur regularly in the Australian Aboriginal myths and it is quite apparent that marriage capture was a recognised form of acquiring a bride. The Kurnai and the other local tribes in South East Australia were local to the seashore in the region around to the east, north and west now occupied by the city of Melbourne, a modern port on the extreme south coast of Australia north of the island state of Tasmania. They would have been subject to either trade or attack from the sea, and there is evidence that the Maoris at least had contact with this part of the island continent. The extreme isolation of this part of Australia and this continent from other landmasses meant that any mariners would have had to have been at sea for many weeks or months from mainland Asia to have reached it. In most cases they would have been absent from home for much longer, and therefore any port of call would have been seen as an opportunity to have temporary or semi-permanent relationships with the local women by whatever means.

Howitt notes what appears to be a deep-seated form of resentment between the male and female members of the Kurnai tribe that appears to have developed into a 'battle-of-the-sexes' noting: "In the Kurnai tribe sometimes ill-feeling arose between the men and the women, and then some of the latter went out and killed one of the men's brothers to spite them. On their return to the camps with the victim, the men attacked them with their clubs, and they defended themselves with their digging-sticks. Or the men might go out and kill a woman's 'sister' whereupon the women would attack them".

"But the most remarkable feature of these fights over the killing of the man's brother or the woman's sister, was when they were young women who were marriageable, but not mated, and when the eligible bachelors were backward. In this tribe, as I have explained in the chapter on Marriage, there was no practice of betrothal, the cases thereof being so rare as to prove the rule. Marriage was by elopement, and therefore the young woman had the power to refuse, unless constrained by the incantations of the Bunjil-yenjin". ….. "In this fight it was only those young men who had been made Jeraeil (initiated), and who were now allowed by the old men to marry, who took part in these affrays ….." As a result of these "affrays" it appears that the available young men met the equally available young women and this led to the elopement. The deity Bunjil will be of importance in due course. Howitt continues: "Fights between the sexes on account of the killing of the brother or sister totem occurred in a great number of tribes, and probably in all the tribes now referred to, but it is only in the Kurnai tribe that I have met with the sex-totems as instrumental in promoting marriage"[137]. It appears most likely that the Kurnai were in fact a branch of the Kurni of India and that the male traders among them had reached Southern Australia either directly down the West Coast from the Indonesian islands or from further East down the East coast of Australia from Melanesia. In reaching this most Southern part of the continent they set up their own clan groups by capturing, or at least attempting to capture less than willing recruits to create new dynasties in this very foreign land. The fact that these real battles remained as part of their tradition suggests that this was long a means of acquiring women although the later elopements suggest that it became a custom rather than a necessity. It is interesting to note that a similar tradition survived among the Ona of South America similar to that of the Kurnai but with perhaps less fierce battles taking place, and to be of note later.

The custom of bride-capture alone hardly constitutes incontrovertible evidence of contact between India and the most distant region of Australia. Other aspects are of particular note that cannot so easily be denied. Sexual licence was allowable to those who were Jeraeil (initiated) between their wives and their sisters who were swapped between these initiates under certain circumstances as Howitt records: "...the sexual licence occurred in this tribe beyond this, except when the Aurora Australis was seen, when they thought it to be Mungan's fire, which might burn them up. The old men then told them to exchange wives for the same day, and the Bret (the dried hand of their dead kinfolk) was swung backwards and forwards with cries of 'Send it away'"[138]. Of particular note here is the reference to the important deity Mungan who is no other than the Tamil (South India) god Murrugan. This deity is also known as Mugan and Daramulen in Australia, and in India and among the Nagas of Assam, as Murukan and reappears as the god Dumagid in the Philippines.

In the extensive records of the boys' initiation Howitt also relates the origin of the deity Mungan as follows: "Long ago there was a Great Being, called Mungan-Ngaua, who lived on earth, and who taught the Kurnai of that time to make implements, nets, canoes, weapons, in fact, all the arts they know. He also gave them the personal names they bear, such as Tulaba. Mungan-Ngaua had a son named Tundan, who was married, and who is the direct ancestor - (the Wehntwin or father's father) - of the Kurnai. Mungan-Ngaua instituted the Jeraeil, which was conducted by Tundan, who made the instruments which bear the names of himself and his wife". "Some tribal traitor once impiously revealed the secrets of the Jeraeil to women, and thereby brought down the anger of Mungan upon the Kurnai. He sent fire (the Aurora Australia), which killed the whole space between earth and sky. Men went mad with fear, and speared one another, fathers killing their children, husbands their wives, and brethren each other. Then sea rushed over the land, and nearly all mankind were drowned. Those who survived became the ancestors of the Kurnai. Some of them turned into animals, birds, reptiles, fishes; and Tundan and his wife became porpoises. Mungan left the earth, and ascended to the sky, where he still remains"[139]. As an interesting extension of this theme bull-roarers were said to be the "paddle belonging to Tundan" since the bark paddle used in the Kurnai canoes resembled in shape that of this sacred object[140].

The affix Ngaua make have developed from the Kurnai's special reverence for the crow named Ngarugal but which is said to answer their questions with the affirmative Ngaa. The bird was essentially associated with the sky and appears particularly to relate to Mungan as the sky deity and the term Mungan-Ngaua means "Father of us all", Mungan alone meaning "Father". As such he is considered headman in the sky country analogous to a headman or chief on earth[141]. The Flood myth is truly an extraordinary one since it implies that there was a period of great volcanic activity or perhaps a meteorite that devastated the land of the ancient ancestral Kurnai homeland. This may have caused a giant tidal wave - the type that has received much media attention along with other natural disasters such as El Nino in recent years. However it is unlikely that anything that may have become identified with the flame-like Aurora Borealis could have been anything other than one or other of these events which tends to indicate that this was an ancient memory imported with the Kurnai men from India or perhaps from those who had contact with the "Ring-of-Fire" around the Pacific Rim. The fact that Tundan in one myth became a porpoise (similar to a dolphin) along with his wife and in another that he paddled away suggests that the ancestors he represented were sea travellers or mariners. Bullroarers noted in the myth were not exclusive to Australia and were found also across the Pacific into South America.

In Arnhem Land in the far north coast region of Central Australia the Aborigines believed that during the wet season hailstones were sent from the sky by a deity called

Munguguan. This hail was considered to be the "seed" of the cycads the fruit of which was of great importance in their subsistence diet[142]. In the same region the "lightning-man" was named Mamaragan and stone axes were considered to be his thunderbolts[143] - a belief held widely throughout the Pacific into Asia but extending also to Africa and the Americas. The Kurnai believed the Aurora to be "Mungan's fire"[144]. In Central Australia, where cultural and racial influences from this northern region were early apparent, among the Warramunga tribe it is recorded in a myth that a black Kakan (Eagle-Hawk man) made fire by rubbing two sticks together. He attempted to retain this fire for his deity Murungan but set the landscape alight instead[145]. The more complete myth will be of interest later but it is sufficient to note that the deity Murugan was spread widely throughout Aboriginal Australia.

In India, Murugan, or Murukan, derives from the Tamil meaning "young man" which is the appellation of the "divine youth" in ancient tradition of this South Indian people[146]. In South India also the god who ensured sunshine and good weather was called Mullan and this appears to have had a common origin with Murugan and is possibly the origin of Dara-mullen, identified with Murugan in Australia[147]. Of some note is the tradition of constructing a near life-size earth figure representing Daramulen about 12" high (300mm) was constructed with an exaggerated phallus[148] in a manner that was also a simple, if crude way of representing Siva in India. It is of interest therefore to record that in India Murugan (Mungan) was identified with both ithyphallic Siva and his prototype whom he assimilated, Rudra, and was also known as the "Red One"[149]. Mungan is clearly identical to Daramulen and this will be further interest in due course.

The Aboriginal Deity Named Daramulen

Daramulen was a deity particularly associated in South East Australia with the Coast Murring tribe[150], but also the Theddora, Wolgal and Ngarigo[151] - the Yuin believed that the thunder was the voice of Daramulen[152]. The Theodora sometimes pronounced this deity's name as Tharamulen but also called him Papang meaning "father"[153]. It was specifically from this deity, and his equivalent among other tribes, that the "medicine man" was believed to have received his powers. It was also believed that the medicine man, known as the Birraak, was able to climb up to the sky to consult with Daramulen, by a rope which they threw up, or was let down by him. Interestingly it was also believed that the medicine man could blow out a spider's web-like cord from his mouth and to be able to climb up by this to the sky[154]. Such references have close parallels in Melanesia and are also found in the Americas and these themes or motifs have no doubt been distributed by the Oceanic sea routes that connect them[155]. It is of some interest that it was necessary for the Birrack to wear his Gumbart - his nose peg, since it was said that by this the Mrarts, or spirits in the bush, conveyed him on his spiritual journey through the clouds. Some of the early tribal informants reported that another means of conveying the Birraak was by the Marrangrang that was a rope or a seat on which he sat. When he reached the sky world the Mrarts placed a "rug" over his lead and lead him to a place where he could see the people there. There the men in the sky world danced and the women beat rugs and from them the Birraack learnt new songs and some of the dances (Gunyeru) that he later taught to the Kurnai[156]. The whole episode suggests in fact that this is an ancient memory of either abduction or voluntary voyages where certain of the males with status were taken to foreign lands and that the nose peg may originally have been a method of securing the person to prevent escape or adopted from them. It is of interest that closely similar nose pegs are prominent in some of the surviving murals and reliefs of the Maya. The covering of the head may have been part of this memory where the abductees were covered to concur with caste rules in India where those without caste status were considered unclean or secured in the holds of a boat. The relation of the women beating rugs could readily apply to India along with the males dancing. However, these elements may be an addition

through retelling or part of the original story of some contact instead with Samoa and Polynesia where women wove the rugs and cloth made from bark was beaten with bark-beaters. Bark-cloth was early known in India, Indonesia and through the Pacific to both North and South America and manufactured in exactly the same way with virtually identical bark-beaters. Once the Birraack had undertaken this first journey to the sky it was believed that he could return at will calling on the Mrarts or bush spirits. He was able to travel either by the Marrangrang, the sky cord, or along the Wau-Unga-Nurt which was the track to the sky along which the Yambo spirit travels after death[157]. This was probably meant to be the Milky Way but the term Yambo is of interest since this may well have derived from the name of the god of the Underworld in India called Yama who will be of some interest later.

1.049 : An earth image of the deity known as Daramulen. Note the dual feather headdress characteristic of imagery from India through the Pacific Islands to South America. Mid-19th., century, A.D.

In a creation myth among the Yuin in South East Australia Howitt recorded their perception of the primal world and the flood as follows. "Long ago Daramulen lived on the earth with his mother Ngalabal. Originally the earth was bare and 'like the sky, as hard as stone', and the land extended far out where the sea is now. There were no men or women, but only animals, birds, and reptiles. He placed trees on the earth. After Kaboka, the thrush, had caused a great flood on the earth, which covered all the coast country, there were no people left, except-ing some who crawled out of the water on to Mount Dromedary. Then Daramulen went up to the sky, where he lives and watches the actions of men. It was he who first made the Kuringal and the bull-roarer, the sound of which represents his voice. He told the Yuin what to do, and he gave them the laws that the old people have handed down from father to son to this time. He gives the Gommeras their power to use the Joias, and other magic. When a man dies and his Tungal (spirit) goes away, it is Daramulen who meets it and takes care of it. It is a man's shadow which goes up to Daramulem."

The mother of Daramulen was in some cases said to be Ngalabal where Ngalal was the sinew at the back of the knee[158] but in other myths she was the emu[159]. In this concept of the most ancient of times the idea of land covering the sea is not unusual, occurring among other Aboriginal tribes, and bears a striking resemblance to some of the scientific theories being pre-sented at this time. It does suggest, however, that this may have been an import with migrant peoples from Central Asia who had no contact with the sea until arriving at the coastal shoreline since the oceans have existed for much longer than humanity has occupied the Australian conti-nent. Also of interest is the notion that the thrush was the cause of the flood is found similarly among the Coast Salish on the North West Coast of North America[160]. This belief, among others, extended from the Yuin's territory in the South East corner of Australia for about 500 miles (800km) north along the east coast.

Baiame - A Deity as a Reflection of Buddha or Brahma

An important deity, who appears to be interchangeable to some extent, or at least on par with Mungan and Daramulen, was Baiame. Howitt notes: "The belief in Daramulen, the 'Father', and Biamban, or 'master', is common to all of the tribes who attend the Yuin Kuringal"[161]. This Biamban is another version of Baiame and Howitt quotes Ridley: "He says that Baiame is the name of the Kamilaroi of the maker (from Biai, 'to make or build') who created and preserves all things. Generally invisible, he has, they believe, appeared in human form, and has bestowed on their race various gifts"[162]. The Kamilaroi are prominent in the records of these early anthropol-ogists and their name may have derived from Tamil - the people noted already in the South of India, and the Arioi, Areoi or Aeroi whose are well know "magicians" leaning towards the black arts in Polynesia who will be of note later. Howitt particularly notes that he believed these Southern tribes may have been influenced from the North and that some of the northern tribes may have descended by the Darling-Murray Rivers drainage system originating in the mountains along the Queensland coast into the southern regions. The close similarities of the Polynesian Bora and Melanesian Nanga initiation ceremonials to those along the East Coast of Australia suggests that Howitt and others were probably correct, at least in part. This is particularly likely since some of the coastal ceremonials of the Eastern Australian Aboriginals were also called the Bora. Other myths suggest that Baiame came from Central Australia to the East with his two wives to Golarinbri where he was said to have spent a few days before travelling toward the east coast. As most of the myths and legends refer to migrations in ancient times these may have been references to a return to their point of origin or to a separate hero who had become identified with Baiame[163]. The relationship of the tribes-people and the Mungan-kurnai, or "Great Men", in particular to their deity as being their "Father" in the religious sense is identical to that of these other deities as Howitt notes: "Now this is precisely the position in which tribespeople stand to Bunjil, Daramulen, Baiame, and Mungan-ngaua, who are all spoken of as 'father'; while the last has no other name than ' "Father of all of us'"[164].

Among the tribes-people of Botany Bay (Sydney), on the East Coast of Australia, Baiame was known as Be-anna[165] while among the Yuin he was known as Biamban who was identified there with Gommera[166]. Crystals are very prominent in the magical arts of the Australian Aborigines and these were intimately connected with Baiame. It was believed that an initiate, medicine man, or the spirit after death would travel up to the sky and see "... Baiame sitting in his camp. He was a very great old man with a long beard. He sat with his legs under him and from his shoulders extended two great quartz crystals to the sky above him. There were also numbers of the boys of Baiame and his people, who are birds and beasts ..."[167]. Others reports by James Manning between 1844-5 are recorded as: "...they (the natives from North and south of the east Murray River region including around Canberra) believe in a supreme Being called Boyma (also Baiame), who dwells in the north-east, in a heaven of beautiful appearance. He is represented as seated on a throne of transparent crystal, with beautiful pillars of crystal on each side. Grogorally is his son, who watches over the actions of mankind. He leads the souls of the dead to Boyma. The first man made by Boyma was called Moodgegally, who lives near the heaven of Boyma. He lives on the earth and has the power of visiting Boyma, whose place he reaches by a winding path, round a mountain, whence he ascends by a ladder or flight of steps. There he received laws from Boyma"[168]. The concept of pillars of stone, crystal or turquoise supporting the sky, as would appear the intent, indicated here is found in Buddhism in particular but also similarly among the Navaho in South West United States[169], an area shown in the author's book, "Mayan Genesis", to be greatly influenced from the Pacific region[170]. Sky Pillars as such are widely noted in Polynesian mythology through to India providing a pattern of diffusion from Asia. Remarkably also in the second version associated with Boyma it is noted that this deity is approached by a "winding path", "stair", or "round a mountain" and extraordinarily the Buddhist stupa represent the divine mound or mountain upon which the parasol on top represented the Axis Mundae or World Tree - the World axis pointing at the Pole Star.

The greatest of the existing stupas incorporated a winding stair around the outside of the dome of the stupa from the ground to the observation-ceremonial platform at the top. The ceremonial circumambulation of the stupa or sacred mountains still survives in Buddhist rituals to this day and occurs also in the Hindu practices focused on Mount Kailas, the Mount Meru of the Buddhists, in Tibet that will be of special interest in later chapters. The finest example is the stupa at Sanchi in North Central India dating from the 3rd., century B.C. It is therefore not surprising that some of the early researchers in Australia perceived a derivation of Baiame from the Buddha himself or his missionaries. Howitt, commenting on Manning's record stated: "In these statements I easily recognise, although in a distorted form, the familiar features of Baiame and his son Daramulen, Bunjil and his son Binbeal, or Mungan-ngaua and his son Tundan. The first man who ascends to the sky-land is typical of the medicine-man who says that he can ascend to the sky and commune with the 'great master'"[171].

A missionary named Rev John Mathew wrote a book called "Eaglehawk and Crow" relating the myths, legends and customs of the tribes who held these two avians in great respect. Mathew wrote: "Buddai, or as it is pronounced by the aborigines towards the mountains in the Moreton Bay (Brisbane), Budjah (quasi Buddah), they regard as a common ancestor of their race and describe an old man of great stature, who has been asleep for ages. The question may be reasonably asked is this Buddai not as likely to refer to Daibaitah of the Marsden, the same deity is known as 'Wat', the first and third syllables of the name being lopped off. And further may it not be possible that Baiame, of New South Wales, and Punjil, of Victoria, refer to the same supernatural being? Baiame, indeed, may be a local equivalent of Barma, another Sumatran deity"[172]. The broad classical education received by the Victorians is clearly seen as a valuable aid against which other aspects and streams of culture can be assessed and analysed. The more recent trends toward specialization have lead to isolationism and dissociation in analysis and cultural assessment. As suggested by Mathew the stepping-stones of cross fertilisation of culture lead back to India even if that route includes a Sumatran variant. He has also seen the connection between Buddhism and Wat that is the name of a temple in India and Cambodia but also relates in Indonesia to bat, bethel, baetyl and its variants wat and wato meaning a stone. This term will be of some importance in due course.

Buddhism is closely connected with ancient stone worship but of particular note is the World Tree that forms the Axis Mundae in their philosophic speculations. The initiation ceremonies of the Wiradjuri tribe are therefore of some interest in these terms noted by Howitt: "The ceremonies are marked off into various stages by particular representations. For instance, the men strip off from a tree near the Gumbu (fire-place) a spiral piece of bark round the bole, from the limbs to the ground, which represents the path from the sky to the earth, and they cut on the ground the figure of Daramulen, who is not the Supernatural Being of the Yuin beliefs, but the 'boy' or son of Baiame. He is always represented as having only one leg, the other terminating in a sharp point of bone. There is also figured on the ground the tomahawk which Daramulen let fall as he slipped down from the tree before mentioned to the ground; then two footprints of an emu a little distance from each other, made when trying to escape from Daramulen. Finally there is the figure of the emu where it fell when he killed it"[173].

The "spiral" bark stripped from the tree appears to reflect the spiral staircase of the Buddhist stupa as noted above where the tree represented the World Tree or Axis Mundae. The bole of the tree in this case represents the mound or stupa on which the World Tree was planted. The footprints are a symbol well known where in Buddhism when it was forbidden to represent the Buddha figuratively He was represented by the footprints he left when on earth. Of special note is the inclusion of a description of this Daramulen being one-legged with a bone in place of the other which was pointed and sharpened. This extraordinary reference is also found almost identically in myths in the Amazon basin. It is sufficient to note here that Daramulen is already identified with Mungen who in turn is clearly Siva in his one-legged aspect known as Ekapada - common in Orissa in India[174]. The association of this myth with the fireplace suggests a probably confusion between Buddhist principles with the Vedic fire rituals of India possibly originally occurring in India itself. In South India sacrificial ceremonies were undertaken in worshipping the tree with oblations to Agni, the god of fire, where the tree itself is called Bharma (Brahma) which seems to be the more likely origin of the name Baiame. Edgar Thurston quotes a mantram associated with this ritual[175]:

"I adore Bharma in the roots;
Vishnu who is the trunk;
Rudra (Mahadev) pervading the branches
And the Devas in every leaf".

It has already been noted that Rudra is Siva and identified as the "Red One" paralleling Mungan or Murugan associated with the Tamils of South India. Brahma is the supreme deity of the Vedas of India and Vishnu is the Sky Deity in Hinduism, an extension of Vedic Aryanism that developed from Vedic Brahmanism and the Devas of both religions are the equivalent of the Christian angels.

In Melanesia, in the Torres Straits islands, a mask worn by initiates was called the Bomai and probably derives from sea travellers who had intimate contact with the Australian East Coast more or less due south[176]. In nearby places names appear also to reflect this deity such as Boianai on the New Guinea coast[177], associated with the Bomai-Malu cult[178] - a place known for its spirals designs on stones[179]. The Bomai can be traced to Tuger in New Guinea before its adherents took refuge on the Torres Islands[180]. A myth recorded among the people of this coastal region relates that an enormous pig in ancient times ate humans and the people were forced to migrate to other islands. A woman who was expectant with a child dug a hole out in the bole of a hollow tree stump and closeted herself inside. After she had given birth to a son, and when he had reached manhood, he killed the pig and plucked off some of its bristles and sent them off on a raft to the lands of the exiles. When they saw the raft the exiled people realised that the pig had been killed and returned to their homeland[181]. The myth contains the bole of the tree that appears to be of importance in the Australian myth, particularly as it is linked with the name Baiame, but the myth itself is very common in many guises throughout Melanesia and usually features a giant or ogre rather than a pig. The fierce pig appears to have close associations with that of Hawaii known as Puaka[182] and therefore transferred from Polynesia by sea migrations or traders.

The Hero-God named Kwoim; Kohin or Coen

Closely associated with the Bomai-Malu cults is the deity known as Kwoiam. He is known for his journeys to many of the islands and reputedly slayed the whole population of some of them. From these forays he is said to have returned home with a boatload of trophy heads[183]. It is said that after being defeated by a group of Mao and Badu men he retired to a hill where the victors piled up a cairn over his body, with the head pointing south, having heaped up their weapons on his body overlooking the island of Pulu[184]. The cairn was said to still exist into the early 20th., century and that old shell trumpets were traditionally laid on it[185]. One of the exploits remembered of Kwoiam was that he drove his spear into a rock, after he had turned thirty, and water gushed out and continued to flow from that day[186]. This suggests that there was some Biblical derivation from Moses striking the rock with his rod. This may not have necessarily have been a result of later European contact since there were obvious connections with the Middle East throughout Oceania from millennia ago. The shell trumpet was widely associated with sea travel from India through Indonesia to Melanesia and Polynesia to South America and will be of interest later.

In New Guinea, at Iatmul, a "beautiful" hero was called Mwaim-Nangur and who was said to have introduced the extraction process for sago[187]. The prefix is almost certainly derived from Kwoiam but the suffix appears to derive from Nanga - a term known in India and the same for the sacred megalithic rites in Fiji. Among the people of Iatmul the dancing ground was known as Agehu that is probably a derivation of the Assamese Naga Daho and Tahua, and Polynesian Tehuba, Tohua or Tahua[188]. In the Trans-Fly District of New Guinea the hero who released the Gambadi people in their origin myth from a tree at Kwavaru was named Takweri and his son was called Gwam[189]. In the tribal groups of the Gambadi or Keraki, Gwam was the broth-er of Muri - the latter a common name among the tribes of the Australian Aborigines. Gwam was considered to be either red or white while Muri was black - a frequent association of broth-ers or heroes in myths to skin-colour and racial types[190]. In a myth from Mabuig Island - a name for Adolphus Island, Kwoiam was said to have lived with his mother who belonged to the Muri. As a great fighting hero his weapons were the throwing stick and the javelin. He is said to have killed his mother and decapitated her and then went to Baka Reef where he went on the rampage killing many people and collecting their heads for trophies. He went to Saibai and Danan but did not fight these people. His canoe is said to be a stone at Gebar. After his death on the hill called Kwoiam-Antra the Maibuiag threw his javelin and throwing stick towards Australia[191]. The term Kwoiam is clearly the Gwam or Mwaim in nearby regions of Melanesia and it must be signifi-cant that this region is due north of the North East extending to the South-East Coast of Australia where the hero name Coen, Kohin or Lohan is found adjacent to the tribal lands of the Kurnai.

It has been noted that the neighbours of the Kurnai in South East Australia were the Yuin whose thunder deity was Daramulen. Among the Gringai people the recognisably same god was called Coen or Koen[192]. The tribes around Port Stephens on the Central New South Wales coast believed in an "evil being" named Coen who could take the form of birds and animals and was said to be responsible for "strange noises" during the night. A thunderstorm was believed to be Coen becoming active and at this time the Aborigines believed that he had the power to "steal them away" if they fell asleep in the bush. This figure was said to be black but painted with pipe clay and carried a fire-torch. Howitt draws the close parallel between this deity with Daramulen and Baiame and saw all three representing the same deity and probably deriving from the same origin. This is also confirmed by the report that Howitt had been told by the old men of the Yuin that their ceremonials extended up along the East Coast to modern day Newcastle where these deities are widely known[193]. It is significant that even earlier researchers in Tasmania noted that Koen not only represented the thunder, but in some tribes was the Sun who killed her husband the Moon Taorong every month[194]. James Bonwick wrote on the correspondences on the Australian mainland relating to this deity who appeared to resemble also the Egyptian lunar deity Kron or Khun (Khon) but it may be no coincidence that the Sun in early South America was also called Con and this reference will be of interest in due course.

Among the tribes of Queensland in North East Australia around modern Maryborough a deity named Birral was known and along the Herbert River a "supernatural" named Kohin. Birral appears to be Kohin who was believed to inhabit the Milky Way - the Kuling, but who roamed the earth at night killing those who were unfortunate enough to cross his path. Kohin is known as the thunder god in this region and was said to have come down from the Milky Way long ago as a carpet snake. This deity was said to be greatly offended by those who do not keep tribal rules especially those who wish to take a wife from the prohibited sub-class. It was declared that Kohin came from a "good" land that was full of "splendid" fish[195].

Not only does this Kohin equate to the deity of the Yuin far to the south but he provides a link to the Kwoiam in the Torres Strait and New Guinea. The confusion as to whether he came from the Milky Way or from a "good land" full of fish is common and the whole suggests that he personified migrants from a distant land. Clearly serpent worship is associated as a fundamen-tal with this hero but the reference to strict social rules suggests the caste system of India where marriages between castes retained among Aboriginal tribes there is regulated within marriage clans, gotras or septs and were strictly applied under threat of caste or clan expulsion.

Kohin was not just a wrathful deity but was said to have presented the Herbert River tribal men with two Tikovinas, these being flat thin pieces of soft wood cut from north Queensland fig-tree. Of particular note is the fact that the designs applied to the surface are

closely similar to the sacred textile designs found in India and Indonesia through to the A
This pattern was painted in red and black with human blood and clay. The Tikovinas were au
12 inches long (300 mm) and about 4 inches wide (100 mm) and the top was supposed to be
carved as a representation of a human face. It was believed that those who were favoured with
possession of these precious objects could fly from tree to tree and eventually to fly up to the
Milky Way and back[196]. In combat they were believed to endow the possessor with unassailable
skill and accuracy in delivery. In assessing the attributes and distribution of Kohin or Coen
Howitt wrote: It seems quite clear that Nurrendere, Nurelli, Bunjil, Murugan-ngaua, Daramulen,
and Baiame all represent the same being under different names. To this may be reasonably added
Koin of the Lake Macquarie tribes, Maamba, Birral, and Kohin of those of the Herbert River,
thus extending the range of this belief certainly over the whole of Victoria and of New South
Wales, up to the eastern boundaries of the tribes of the Darling River. If the Queensland coast
tribes are included, then the western bounds might be indicated by a line drawn from the mouth
of the Murray River to Cardwell, including the Great Dividing Range, with some of the fall
inland in New South Wales"[197].

Coen, Koen or Kohin is also called Lohan and in Tasmania the Aboriginals around
Oyster Bay related a myth about two "black men" who were said to be the personification of the
twin stars Castor and Pollux. Two mythical women associated with them in this story were
known as Lowanna, a name clearly derived from Lohan of the South East Australian natives[198].
Among the Wurunjeri it was said that long ago Loan, "a non-natural man", travelled following
the migrating swans along the Yarra River on which modern day Melbourne is situated. He settled near Wilson's Promontory at the most southern part of the coast of mainland Australia. This
was well within the Kurnai territory and they too had a similar legend stating also that he had a
wife called Loan-tuka[199]. He was considered by them as their protector his territory covered their
tribal lands that extended from the lower Murray River to eastern Gippsland in South East
Victoria[200]. Interestingly the Kurnai named the first European settlers after this legendary man -
Lohan, but also as Mrart[201]. Howitt records that when he was being informed of the Kurnai's
impressions of the first white men they saw they cried "Loan! Loan!", but he also notes that the
boy who was describing this averted his eyes each time[202]. This is reminiscent of the ancient
Ethiopian practice of averting the eyes before the deity or a superior of rank and there are many
indicators in the clan systems of Australia and Melanesia linking them to India, and Ethiopia, and
related elements will be considered later in this work.

Among the Besisi division of the Jakun of Malaya it was believed that a mythical giant
named Bohal emerged through the "hole of Gubin" in a bamboo to become the founder of their
race and he was particularly associated with their chiefs. The Victorian naturalist William W.
Skeat notes: "A further explanation was that 'Gubin' meant a dog, as indeed it does in the Blandas
dialect of Selangor, and that the passage therefore meant 'The Dog's Hole in the Ancestral
Bamboo' in which case the explanation doubtless rests upon the traditions which connect the dog
with the mythical ancestor..."[203]. The giant Bohan undoubtedly relates to the migrating Lohan
of the Kurnai, the Wurunjeri and the Tasmanians but the association of the dog will be of particular note in other Australian myths in due course, but is also found in Melanesia. In India the
wrathful Tantric deity Bhairava in Hinduism was almost always depicted with his dog and in the
Malayan myth it would appear that there was at least a partial assimilation of the Indian deity.
The emergence of the first person or people from either a tree or bamboo will be considered separately but is widely spread along the sea currents from Asia through the Pacific to the Americas.

In considering the name Lohan and his relationship or identification with the other
deities or heroes in the South East half of Australia it must be remembered that some of these
deities such as Baiame are clearly derived from Buddhism or Brahmanism. In Buddhism the

appellation of Lohan is applied to Buddha himself since he is considered the highest of the Lohan - that is sainthood of the highest standing[204]. In a remarkable ritual, perhaps a percolation of later Tantric rites into Buddhism, it was believed that the achievement of the status of Lohan could be "short-circuited" in three stages. This may have been originally intended to be, and practised as a symbolic rite, but is recorded as if it was actually by a dubious form of "self-immolation". The three stages of "becoming" were: 1) a saint; 2) an Anagaim; 3) a Lohan, these claimed to be the three stages of "cutting the throat"[205]. It does not take much imagination to realise that if such a ritual was transferred or known to a less developed people that they might well take it literally and emulate the practice. In ancient India some of the Aboriginal peoples were well known for their blood-rites and the stages of becoming appears modest in the face of some of these. That Buddhism an offshoot of Vedic Brahmanism, should have developed such practices seems more difficult to accept since they had long eschewed such practices. In the regions in which Tantric practices were notable such as Bengal and Orissa between and flanking the Bay of Bengal and Tibet such rituals and ceremonies seemed to be permeated and inflamed by the association of these Aryan religions of India with ancient rites of the Bon-po of Tibet. Such mutations led to the development of the blood-rites of Bhairava and Heruka that in some cases extended beyond this region, particularly those of Bhairava who was seen as an aspect of Siva and is still revered and associated with his dog to this day (*1.050*).

The Eagle-Hawk as the Sky God Bunjil or Punjal

Among the Kurnai, the title Bunjil was applied to men of mature age[206] whereas for the Wurunjeri Bunjil was the equivalent of Daramulen, the storm god of the Coast Murring and others[207]. Howitt notes that the "Wurunjerri used a curious 'aide memoire' for Bunjil and his 'boys'. The little finger of the left hand is Tadjeri, the ring-finger Dantun, the thumb Thara, and the thumb of the right hand is Jurt-jurt"[208]. Bunjil is the name among them for the eagle-hawk that was the supreme representative of the sky totems in South East Australia. The aggressive aspect of the eagle-hawk's prowess at pin-pointing its prey from a great height was seen as essential in some of the magical rituals as Howitt notes among the Kurnai: "The Kurnai fastened some personal object belonging to the intended victim to a spear-thrower, together with some eagle-hawk's

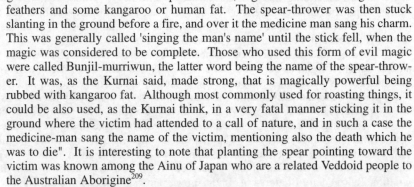

feathers and some kangaroo or human fat. The spear-thrower was then stuck slanting in the ground before a fire, and over it the medicine man sang his charm. This was generally called 'singing the man's name' until the stick fell, when the magic was considered to be complete. Those who used this form of evil magic were called Bunjil-murriwun, the latter word being the name of the spear-throw-er. It was, as the Kurnai said, made strong, that is magically powerful being rubbed with kangaroo fat. Although most commonly used for roasting things, it could be also used, as the Kurnai think, in a very fatal manner sticking it in the ground where the victim had attended to a call of nature, and in such a case the medicine-man sang the name of the victim, mentioning also the death which he was to die". It is interesting to note that planting the spear pointing toward the victim was known among the Ainu of Japan who are a related Veddoid people to the Australian Aborigine[209].

The association of Bunjil with ritual magic in the Bunjil-barn which is intended to kill an enemy or victim is noted further by Howitt: "They chose a young He-oak, lopped the branches and pointed the stem, then drawing the out-line (Yambog-inni) of a man as if the tree-stump grew out of his chest, they also cleared the ground for a space round the tree, making a sort of magical circle. Then they stripped themselves naked, rubbed themselves over with charcoal and grease, a common garb of magic, and danced and chanted the Barn song". The purpose of the initial ceremonies is to "mesmerise" the intended victim who would then be drawn to the magic dancing circle in a trance. Howitt continues: "When the victim entered the magic circle the Bunjil-barn would throw small pieces of He-oak wood, shaped like the Gulwils before mentioned, at him. When he fell to the ground they would cut out his tongue, or rather, as the Bunjil-barn explained to me, would have pulled out a great length of it, cutting it free at each side as it was protruded, and so sent him home to die"[210]. No indication is given as to whether these rituals were successful or purely symbolic but it is of note that blackening the body in such a way corresponds to those in the Amazon where black body-paint was always used in conflict. Red was always avoided since, through sympathetic magic, like was believed to attract like and therefore the subject was likely to have his own red blood spilt. Black was always preferred since this indicated the night when it made the subject very difficult to see, and some believed that it made them invisible.

Among the Wurunjerri shining white bones were associated with Bunjil[211] and many of the rituals among the Australian Aborigines appear to have close similarities not only with the Tantric sects of North East India and Tibet, but also the Zapotecs of Southern Mexico. The association of Bunjil with lands beyond Australia is noted in its interchangeability with the other tribal deities such as Daramulen and Baiame. The sky world of the Wurunjerri was called Tharangalk-bek - the gum tree country. It was recorded in tribal legends that Bunjil descended from there with all his people in a whirlwind. The Kurnai called their sky land Blinte-da-nurk translated as "bright sky of the cloud" and Bring a-nurt that meant "bone of the cloud". The Theddora, Wolgal and Ngarigo tribes called their sky country Kulumbi and related that there was another country that was covered in trees and rivers[212]. Distant memories of similar lands beyond their own suggest that these "sky" countries were in fact located across the seas rather than in the heavens. In Polynesia there are myths that indicate that the Polynesians believed that the sky and sea were not separate but were an extension and that deities from the upper world descended through an opening by lifting up the horizon. Many of the Melanesian as well as Polynesian peoples believed that the first Europeans were in fact papalangi or "sky-bursters"[213] who entered their world in this way so it is equally likely that the same was true for earlier intrusions from Asia. This would probably explain why the local indigenous people did not differentiate between mythical lands and the Sky. While most of the tribes believed that Bunjil descended from the sky most also believed that he later returned or migrated away. The Wotjobaluk knew of Bunjil as a great man who once lived on earth but returned to the sky[214] but this tribe did not have initiation ceremonies of the Bora type and the name prefix, Wotjo, will be of interest in due course[215].

The most remarkable aspects of the hero or deity known as Bunjal or Punjel is that he is particularly associated with certain stars in the night sky. Howitt notes: "According to the Wurunjerri, the Pleiades are a group of young women, the Karat-goruk, about whom there is a legend which recounts that they were digging up ant's eggs with their yam-sticks, at the ends of which they had coals of fire, which Waang, the crow, stole from them by a stratagem. They were ultimately swept up into the sky, when Bellin-Bellin, the musk-crow, let the whirlwind out of his bag, at the command of Bunjil, and remained there as the Pleiades, still carrying fire on the ends of their yam-sticks"[216].

Among some of the Australian tribes many of the stars are named and constellations or star clusters were also recognised including the sons of Bunjil among these[217]. Many also believed that the sky was a "hard vault" while the earth was a flat surface[218]. It is not surprising therefore that some considered that the dark patches were in fact holes in the sky although this idea appears to run in parallel with the stars as living beings who observed mankind's every move and were able to descend to earth at will. Both of these concepts parallels philosophic speculations among the peoples of both North and South America and will be considered in a later chapter. The Wurunjeri believed that their medicine man was carried by ghosts, while in a trance state, through a hole in the sky to visit Bunjil himself[219]. The Wotjobaluk considered Bunjil as the "great man" and was a star that was pointed out by them to Howitt and one he recognised as Fomalhaut, while his brother Djurt was said to be a star nearby, but not identified[220]. However, among the Kulin, also in Victoria, this star was identified as Altair[221].

In another myth from Victoria in the South East of Australia it is said that the legendary heroes called Toordt and Trrar came from the sky to reveal to the people where the crow had hidden fire and then returned. Punjel (Bunjil) changed Toordt into the planet Mars for his good deeds[222]. One the most interesting associations with Bunjil, who in this tribe called the Chepara, is identified as earlier noted with Maamba, is with the Bora initiation rites. Howitt notes: "In the middle of the cleared space in which the ceremonies take place, a small tree is taken up and placed with its roots in the air, and around it saplings, peeled of their bark, are placed, the whole being tied together with strips of bark, thus making a sort of small enclosure. The saplings are painted with ochre. On this structure one of the medicine men stands with a cord hanging out of his mouth. He is said to represent a supernatural being called Maamba. The medicine men are called Bujeram, and the one just spoken of is the principal one of the tribe, and is believed to ascend at night to the sky to consult Maamba about the welfare of the tribes-people. During this part of the ceremonies the initiated men sit round the upturned tree and chant a song in low tones, which is only used at this time, and which is forbidden for the women to hear. A woman who was found to have listened to this would be killed" …. "At one part of the ceremonies the men, while the Kippers (boys to be initiated) are lying down, make a long and narrow fire, on one side of which they sit, while the boys, who have been roused up, sit on the other in a sleepy state. The men pretend that it is a stormy, and that it rains, making noises to represent the wind. Then a number of the men hop about and croak like frogs. Finally the men all dance and then extinguish the fire by jumping on it with their feet" …. "Besides these representations of animated creatures there are others. For instance, the men twist ropes of grass and make disguises of them. Mounds of grass are also built up in the centre of the cleared space, round which the men dance. Another is that the men stand in a row with fire-sticks in their hands, and wave them about. The Kippers are told that the whole country is on fire"[223]. This initiation ceremony appears to have several elements that connect it to India. The final section noted above appears to be imitating the Vedic fire rituals where the sacred grass covers the altar and around which the participants who circumambulate it. Clearly the fire torches being "waved" are similar in intent to that of the Vedic and later Hindu fire rituals that can been seen in India to this day. The upturned tree is highly reminiscent to myth motifs in India through Indonesia into the Pacific Islands and to North America where at Izapa representations of the "upside-down-tree" have been included in an earlier work[224]. The name of the medicine men - Bujeram, appears to have derived from the name Bunjil itself.

Other references to Punjel are included in flood myths in Victoria indicating that he became angry with mankind when he discovered that they were "bad" and very numerous so that he caused great whirlwinds which caused catastrophe. He then proceeded to dismember the humans although they did not die and each piece of flesh moved like "worms". These were carried to the clouds and scattered over the earth[225]. This relation is reminiscent of the Sumerian and Aboriginal versions in India where mankind was expunged because they became too noisy and forgot the gods as their progenitors. The resultant "worms" in the Australian version is also similar to some versions in Polynesian myths[226].

A myth from the Gadaju people in the Northern Territory near Darwin in the far north of Australia notes a hero called Bandjal who was a "Dreaming Man". This indicates that he was an ancient ancestor in the form of a tortoise who had transformed into a young spirit man who stole fire for three other Dreaming people[227]. Since the Tortoise man is clearly derived from Bunjil or Punjal the tribe, located on the northern coast of Australia immediately adjacent the sea routes from Melanesia to Indonesia and India, he provides another link between those of South East Australia and Borneo.

In North Borneo a myth at Samalong relating the origin of death among humans, records that, at the end of this relation, a large rock that had been hacked down fell and became the great cliff known as Batu Punggul[228]. The reference to a great phalliform hill standing beside the river suggests a sky that is reached or is being penetrated that would be particularly evocative in periods of low cloud or mist. The name Batu is simply the local name for sacred stone or rock throughout Borneo and adjacent islands but Punggul is clearly related to Punjel of Australia especially so since another reference to this deity name is recorded in the above oral tradition from this part of Indonesia. However, of particular note is the fact that references that have probably given rise to this name are found in North India and Tibet.

In the 7th., century A.D. the rulers of Tibet invited Buddhist teachers to enter the kingdom initiating commenced the conversion of a large part of the people and rulers to this religion. However, many regions retained their original worship of wrathful deities in the Bon-po religion that still exists in the more isolated regions and especially in the east of that land. The Buddhist faith in this remote, elevated, Himalayan massif became permeated to varying degrees by the original Bon-po to form a hybrid that would not have been recognisable to its founder Gautama Sakyamuni - the Buddha. In the ancient religion of Tibet a belief in the sky descent of deities or heroes was endemic. In the history of Sum-pa Khen-po, who lived in the eighteenth century, the origin of kingship indicates the belief that the King of Vatsala, Udayana, descended from the sky[229]. The Bon-po magicians stated that this king came from the land of Mu and descended from the "land of the Gods" in the Sky by the "Mu-cord" landing on the peak of the holy mountain called "Enchantment peak" in the Himalayas[230]. The ancient name of Tibet appears to have been Pu, and the rulers were called Pugyel - "Sovereign of Pu"[231].

In the inscription dated 821-2 A.D. a treaty between the Tibetans and Chinese refer to the reigning king Ral-pa-cen who is identified with his mythical ancestor O-de-pu-gyel[232]. Interestingly, for reasons long lost in the mist of time, he is called "Neck-Enthroned". Considering that the many depictions of Naga deities in North India show cobras emerging from the neck or shoulders from at least the second half of the first millennium B.C. it is clear that there must have been a connection, particularly as the first king had an Indian name - Udayama. It is unlikely to be a coincidence therefore that the crystals, especially associated with Buddhism, are said to have emerged from the shoulders of Baiame - an Australian Aboriginal deity already identified with Buddha, and these were said to support the sky[233].

It would therefore appear that the North Bornean version described as Batu Punggul must have been perceived as a microcosm of the Himalayas with Tibet located in what appeared to them to be the "celestial" region. It must be noted that the many of the people of Borneo and other islands in Indonesia exhibit long recognised close cultural affinities with the Assamese Nagas. These Naga tribes are located immediately to the north of the Ganges/Brahmaputra River Delta in the most travelled, and nearest southern approach to Tibet in the foothills of the Himalayas.

Pu-gyel was identified as the ancient ancestor hero of Tibet as well as the original name of the country[234]. It is interesting to note that both the Bon-pa and its permeation into the Buddhist faith in Tibet retained the wrathful deities of the former and these appear to derive from the mythical period "when a black demon held sway". In the following period a belief is still retained that in Tibet there was a period when the people were descended from a hermit and an ogress who produced red-faced offspring and were cannibals - a conceptual mutation, perhaps, of animal and spirit. The third period corresponds a time when serpents with "powers" held sway and grain appeared which was active in waters (rice?). This was followed by the time of the nine brethren, or "Unclean Ones", and combat weapons appeared as the fourth period. In the fifth period a being called the Za-ram, who it was said to have had six lives, ruled the country and horse riding and earrings appeared. This time was called that of the "eighteen brigades". Following this the twelve petty kingdoms evolved resulting in "good manners" and "polite speech" - the land being called "eight frontier posts". In the seventh period Pu-gyel the Mighty ruled and the country was known as the "Tibet of the four divisions" (Ru-bzhi)[235] reminiscent of Tahuantinsuyu - the Inca's Land of the Four Quarters.

In an earlier work[236] the close apparent contacts between the Assamese Nagas, Oceania and the Americas was highlighted throughout. The connection between the Australian deities such as Punjil or Pungel and those of Borneo appears to indicate that the Nagas were in fact sea traders who contacted not only these distant Pacific lands but were responsible also for continuing from the Bay of Bengal into Tibet via their homeland in Assam. It is known that there were close contacts between the Assamese Nagas and the Gond tribes along with the Bhuiyas and there are many references to their association with megalithic cultural forms that existed into last century and to be of note later in this work. The proposal that Tibet may have been in contact with Oceania and the Americas direct or through intermediaries is a highly contentious one at this time but in fact a century ago it would have been considered quite reasonable and will be of some importance in later chapters of this book. It is sufficient to note at this time that the ascent or descent from the sky by heroes or deities and other aspects of early Tibetan culture are found similarly in India and Australia through to the Americas. Other elements such as fierce-some giant ogres or ogresses are also found widely throughout the Aboriginal tribes of Australia as they are in Tibet and the conversion of the original name of both ancient hero and country into a deity named Punjil is perhaps too great to be a coincidence.

The Extension of Bunjil as Boorn and the Sun God Boran

It has been earlier noted that Bunjil, Punjel or Pundyil is identified with Baiame in New South Wales and Buddha in India and Barma of Sumatra[237]. Of special note is the fact that Bunjil or Punjel is considered a creator deity. John Mathew notes: "The Melbourne blacks say that Punjel made of clay two males. He took stringey bark from the tree, made hair of it, and placed it on their heads, on one straight hair and on the other curled hair. The man with the straight hair he called Ber-rook Boorn, the man with the curled hair Koo-kin Berook"[238]. The Kurnai, however, have a most important record noted by Howitt: "There is a legend that the first Kurnai man marched across the country from the north-west, bearing on his head a bark canoe in which his wife Tuk, that is Musk-duck, he being Borun, the Pelican"[239]. He further notes another Kurnai myth as follows: "There was a great flood which covered the land, and drowned the people, excepting a man and two women. Bunjil Borun, the Pelican, came by in his canoe, and took the man across to the mainland, then one women, leaving the better-looking to the last. She, being frightened, swam over to the land, having placed a log rolled up in her rug by the fire as if she were asleep. Bunjil Borun discovering this, when he returned, became very much enraged and began to paint himself ready for fighting with the man whose wife had played him this trick. While he was doing this another pelican came up, and seeing a queer-looking creature, half-black and half-white, struck at it with his beak and killed Bunjil Borun"[240]. In this myth Bunjil is associated with Borun - the Pelican. In the previous myth but one the first created men was prefixed Boorn which is clearly an inflexion of Borun. In the last two myths the canoe no doubt denotes coast or sea migrations and primal ancestors or important cultural incursions. It is of great importance therefore that a similar deity is to be found in Borneo that has clearly derived from India.

The Sea Dyaks of Borneo retained a myth which notes that the "demon" Batu Burung Endan is able to assist the manang, or healer, to reach the spirit world - Sabayan, to find and recover the diseased soul to return it to his body[241]. This has close similarities with the assistance given to the Australian Aboriginal medicine men to reach the hole in the sky to converse with, and receive instructions from Bunjil. In the example from Borneo Endan means pelican and Burung is clearly Boran or Boorn as in Australia. Batu means a stone and it has been seen that there are many associations on magic stones with medicine and spirit flying which will be of interest later. The term Sabayan suggests the Saba or Savaras, an Aboriginal tribe in India related to the Bhuiyas and associated geographically with the Gonds all of whom will be of further note.

In India it is to the Aboriginal tribes and the Gonds in particular, again, that references to the deity known as Boran are found. As in Australia where Bunjil was said to four sons so among the Bhuiyas, a Munda tribe, there are four deities who, originally, probably represented the cardinal points. Edward Tutte Dalton, whose researches among the Bhuiyas a century and a half ago in Central India are of critical importance in an earlier work[242], notes: "They have their own priests called deoris (deo = god), and their sacred groves called "Deota Sara", dedicated to four deities, Dasum Pat, Bamoni Pat, Koisar Pat, and Boram. The first three are brethren, but there was some difference of opinion as to whether Bamoni was male or female. Boram is the sun, also worshipped under the name of Dharm Deota, but Boram has no representation. Boram, as the first and greatest of gods and as creator, is invoked at the growing season with the offering of a white cock"[243]. He further notes of the Bhuiyas in the Keonjhur Hills: "The religion appears to be much the same as that of the Bonai Bhuiyas. They worship the sun as Dharam, and pay attention to Boram, who is also called 'Bir', that is Vira or Mahabir Hanuman; but their private and most frequent devotions are paid to a blood-thirsty tutelary goddess called Thakurani something, generally 'Thakurani Maie', in all probability the origin of the Hindu Kali .."[244]. The term Bir will be of interest later but it is sufficient to note here that one of the prominent southeastern tribes was called the Wira-juri and probably derives their name originally from Vira. This connection with India is particularly of note since it is associated with the Bhuiyas who were of such note in connections with the Maya noted in an earlier work[245] and the term relates to the wind and the sea and no doubt migrations - to be of further note later.

Boram among the Hill Bhuiyas is propitiated in times of epidemic[246] and was identified by the broader population grouping of Aboriginal tribes in India - the Mundas, with the Sun. He is also identified among some groups as noted above with Dharam-deota and associated with the serpent goddess Basuki-mata that is probably a corruption of Basumati - the Earth[247]. The tribal name of Bhuiya means "Earth-born"[248]. A creation story of the Hill Bhuiyas is of interest and Sarat Chandra Roy recorded a version a century ago noting: "In the beginning there existed only God or Dharma whose visible representation was the Sun with the Moon. Then there appeared an ocean of water of the depth of seven times the height of a man with upraised hands (sat-tar pani); and out of depths of the ocean up came a mass of mud to a height of fourteen times the height of a man with upraised hands (chowdatar-panka). Then Dharma on this mud bank created a man and a woman known respectively as Parihar Burha and Barmani Burhi. The mud-bank (earth) began to shake and tremble (talmal hala). God saw from heaven that such an earth was not fit for human habitation. Then He made clay figures of a tiger and tigress (Rai Bagh and Rai Baghini), infused life into them, and ordered them - 'Go, kill the human couple - and put their blood and flesh on the four corners of the Earth so as to make it firm'. The tiger and tigress did as they were ordered. The blood and flesh of the original human couple settled down in the four corners of the earth as iron-pillars supporting the earth; and the earth became hardened like stone.

Then God created another couple who became, in due time, parents of seven sons and seven daughters. From these seven couples descended the different peoples of the earth. And Parihar Burha and Baramani Burhi became the gods Baram and Baramni or Burha-burhi ..."[249].

The sacred tree of the Naga tribe of Assam was the ficus indica, a species broadly including the sacred banyan. The suckers usual for this tree were trained to create a tree house in which the stones used in war were kept[250]. In Naga myth the great primal tree was cut down to allow the Sun to shine on the world[251] and hence seem to have close references to the Australian myths noted above. The name Bor usually relates in mythology to the grandson of the primeval cow Audumla, his father being Buri, in ancient Europe and noted by the early researchers in India in the Younger Edda and the giant Ymir who was killed by the sons of the god Bor[252]. The name Bor, in terms of the European myth, means literally to be "born" and it is interesting to note that, within the Tukano tribe of Amazonian Colombia in North West South America, the mythical progenitors are called Bareka-pora. Bareka is derived from Bore meaning "to be born"[253]. The initiation ceremonies already noted in Australia and found also in Melanesia are clearly related to spiritual rebirth rituals of tribal boys as their entry into manhood and are directly related in origin to the term Boran or Boram. It should be of interest therefore that Colombia is connected directly by the Equatorial Currents that connects South America with South East Asia and these Tukano people will be of greater interest in later chapters.

Many early researchers were fascinated by the apparent references to ancient Egyptian culture both in India and Australia and this Hill Bhuiya myth is just one such case. The emergence of the primal hill from the cosmic waters from whence came the first man, particularly with references to a figure with upraised arms similar to the god Ka, certainly is closely similar in principle to the creation myths in India noted above. This is exacerbated by the motifs utilised in the myth said to stabilise the Earth by the creation of pillars - here of iron, at the four corners or cardinal points, having its exact parallel in Egypt. In this Bhuiya version the Baram is identical with Boram who in other myths is clearly the Sun. It has already been noted that Boran in Australia is linked to the sky as stars or identified with the Pleiades and it is of interest therefore that the flat earth supported by pillars is also a mythical concept known among some of the Australian Aboriginal tribes and will be considered in a later chapter.

Ara-Wotya; Wotjo and Wat Relating to Sacred Stones

In ancient India, Indonesia and Melanesia the term wat or watu is the equivalent of bat and batu already noted earlier and still widely common in the later. The term is usually a reference to a sacred stone and particularly used for monoliths marking a particular site or as a reference to heroes, deities, or sea-going migrants who introduced a stone-using culture. Among the Australian Aborigines Wotjo or Wotya or similar terms are found as part of some of the tribal names and clearly must have derived from incursions from Asia.

Among early Australians of European descent were educated explorers who formed the early spearhead of modern anthropologists and were often noted for their acute observational powers. One in particular was of special note - George Grey, later knighted, whose reports were of such note in his time that he was later made governor in the colony of South Australia (1841). This was followed by a period as the Governor of New Zealand (1845-53) and South Africa Cape Colony (1854) and his written work has prove to be of interest to all serious researchers. In his book resulting from his expeditions to West and North West Australia in 1837-9 he notes: "The natives of South-western Australia likewise pay a respect, almost amounting to veneration, to shining stones or pieces of crystal, which they call 'Teyl'. None but their sorcerers or priests are allowed to touch these, and no bribe can induce an unqualified native to lay his hand on them." "The accordance of this word in sound and signification with the Baetyli mentioned in the following extract from Burder's Oriental Customs, (vol. I page 16) is remarkable."

"And Jacob rose up early in the morning, and took the stone that he had put for his pillow, and set it up for a pillar, and poured oil upon the top of it, and he called the name of that place Bethel."

"From this conduct of Jacob and this Hebrew appellation, the learned Bochart, with great ingenuity and reason, insists that the name and veneration of the sacred stones called Baetyli, so celebrated in all Pagan antiquity, were derived."

"These Bae-tyli were stones of a round form, they were supposed to be animated by means of magical incantations, with a portion of the Deity; they were consulted on occasions of great and pressing emergency as a kind of divine oracle, and were suspended either round the neck or some other part of the body."[254].

Grey further records that he was able to persuade one of the owners of these crystals to show it to him and he notes: "After unrolling many yards of woollen cord made from the fur of the opossum, the contents proved to be a quartz-like substance of the size of a pigeon's egg, he allowed me to break it and retain a part. It is transparent like white sugar-candy; they swallow the small crystalline particle which crumble off as a preventative of sickness" .... "A third specimen contains a portion of cornelian, partially crystallized, a fragment of chalcedony, and a fragment of a crystal of white quartz."[255]. In a reference to his illustrious predecessor Grey further records: "And again in Mitchell's Expeditions into Australia, vol. 2. P. 338: - 'In these girdles the men especially their coradjes or priests. Frequently carry crystals or other shining stones, which they hold in high estimation, and very unwillingly show to any one; invariably taking care, when they do unfold them, that no woman shall see them'".[256].

These references indicate the close parallels between the names and uses of sacred stones from Eurasia into Australia suggesting not just ancient contact but in retaining names that have not become almost unrecognisable with time and therefore confirming contacts into more recent times. The great advantages of the broad Classical education of the Victorians can be immediately seen again since even with minimal contact with the native cultures they were able to assess their possible influences sufficiently to provide avenues for future reference and research. Of particular interest is the term for priest - coradje, which must surely be a reference to the Toradja of Celebes in North Central Indonesia and who will be of interest in following chapters. It is of critical interest to note that there are recognised contacts between the Early Toalian cultures in South Celebes, who appeared to be peoples entering from the north, and Australia dating from 2000 B.C.[257]. These contacts are evidenced in cave paintings, stencils and other elements of that culture in caves a thousand miles (1600km) from Celebes and clearly indicates that the people responsible must have been transferred by, or were themselves skilled mariners able to negotiate such a distance at that early date. If it was possible at that time then it is certainly probable that later peoples infiltrated into the Australian continent after that date and these contacts were reflected in the languages of the Aborigines in the northwest.

Among the Sea Dyaks of Borneo the medicine chest of the priest, called the Manang, was called a lufong that contained many charms including, among other things, pebbles and fragments of quartz. A century ago Edwin Gomez noted: "One important and necessary charm is the Batu Ilau ('stone of light') - a bit of quartz crystal which many manang possesses"[258]. Clearly the term Batu means here a stone and closely relates in practice to those used by the priests or medicine men in Australia. The "sacred bundle" or chest also included boar's tusks and these were of ritual significance from India through Indonesia to Melanesia along the sea routes connecting them on to the Australian continent. Recorded also by Gomes from Hose and McDougal's famous work on the peoples of Borneo is that Batu Bintang - "star stone", was a transparent stone and the badge of authority; Batu Lintar was a dark coloured stone representing the thunderbolt but also another one called Batu Nitar - a small crystal; Batu Kran Jiranan which was a petrified ginger root; Batu Ilau which was a "sparkling stone" also called Batu Kras - a six-sided crystal[259]. Also of note is that rounded stones were called Batu Tuloi[260] and stone spheres similar to those found in Costa Rica in Central America are also found in the Indonesian Islands. Hose and McDougall noted that: "Peculiar adjuncts of the altar-posts of the Kenyahs are the Dracaena plant (whose deep red leaves are generally to be seen growing in a clump not far from them) and a number of large spherical stones, Batu tuloi. These are perpetual possessions of the house. Their history is unknown, they are supposed to grow larger and to move spontaneously when danger threatens the house …etc."[261]. The Dyaks celebrated a feast known as the Gawai Batu or "stone feast"[262] and among these Dyaks was a belief that anything, including people, could be turned to stone as a result of the wrath of the gods[263].

Gomes recorded briefly the ritual associated with the Stone Festival: "This feast takes place before the farming operations begin, and is in honour of Pulang Gana, the god of the land, who lives in the bowels of the earth, and has the power to make the land fruitful or unfruitful. In this feast invocations are made to this god, and he is asked to give them a good harvest. The whetstones and farming implements are placed in a heap in the veranda of the Dyak house, and offerings are made to the whetstones with a request that they may sharpen their tools and thus lighten their labours. After the feast is over the whetstones are taken to the different farms, and the work of cutting down the jungle planting begins"[264].

The deity Pulang Gana as earth god is the same noted in an earlier work[265] where part of a long myth recording a version of the "woodchip myth" which was virtually identical to a section in the Popol Vuh of the Quiche-Maya in Guatemala[266]. The terms and uses of the stones are closely similar to those Australia as well as the perceived rituals associated with implements, whether for farming or weapons. The term Batu is derived, as the Australian examples noted by George Grey, from the Middle Eastern "Baetyl", the Biblical "Bethel" and reflect these terms in the most basic form as bat, batu or wat and watu. The term Batu Punggul has already been noted from the same region as probably connecting with Tibet and refers to a mythical mountain[267] and the term batu is frequently found in the names of sacred sites. Owen Rutter, who recorded the myth of Batu Punggul, notes also that: "A few miles below Tenom, the headquarters of the Interior Residency, the Padas River narrows into a deep gorge, at the head of which stands a great rock, known as Batu Penotal, the centre of many a legend. The Temoguns say that in olden days the Padas had no outlet here, but formed into lake and that Batu Penotal (which is not to be confused with Penotal Hill in the Tagul country), was a towering wall of rock that marked the end of the world, where earth met sky. There are several stories to account for the break through of the river. One is that a giant used to wash his sago in the lake, but he was so tall that he kept bumping his head against the sky, and finally, in fury, he aimed a mighty kick at the rock, which was shattered to pieces and so allowed the Padas to break through."[268].

The myth motif of a giant hitting head against the sky is found throughout Indonesia and he is often found as the prime mover in separating the earth from the sky but the association with the ancestors, sacred sites or topographical features is further confirmed and need not be pursued further. More intimately Batu is found in Borneo as a boy's name and was considered by Europeans to be the equivalent of their "Peter" - the Semitic derivative from the name for a stone[269]. The giant is usually found in relation to creation myths or floods but one from North Celebes, the large island to the east of Borneo relates a more unusual flood myth but associating the sacred mountain of refuge in the flood with the term Batu. This records that; "A rock called Batu Ijan is to be seen between Bolaang Mongondon and Bolaang Uki in North Celebes in a place near the former village of Todonga, the inhabitants of which were punished by the gods by means of a flood. The only survivor of this disaster was a man called Ijan, who escaped by boat.

He clambered on to a stone that stuck up out of the water. He then called upon the gods to allow him to sink into it, and his request was granted. His descendants put offerings upon this stone in time of epidemics"[270]. This association of stone propitiation with epidemics and disease is found widely in India and Australia since it was believed that the gods could be contacted directly through the stone, which is also known in the ancient Near East but also in South America.

In Java, a ritual that apparently had an ancient history, was that where a stone was thrown over a large pyramidal mound. The ritual commenced with a perambulation three times around the pyramid before throwing the stone that was meant to clear the top of the construction[271]. The ritual is remarkably reminiscent of the Polynesian game of Tika that may have developed from this ancient Javan ritual. In the Polynesian version a dart, arrow or spear was thrown at a mound, known as teka or sika, and in this form is found not only in Polynesia but also in North and South America, both directly connected by the sea currents of the Pacific Ocean to Indonesia[272].

Of some interest are the Batu Islands in Indonesia that are noted for their megalithic culture - hence the name. The statues are phalliform and known as adjuadju and there appears to be cultural connections with the Mentawei Islands off the north coast of Sumatra[273]. These are clearly an extension of those on other Indonesian islands and originate in their cultural expression from Asia.

In Melanesia, and the New Hebrides in particular, the term "bat" is found as John Layard notes: "… other culture-heroes, many of whose names begin with the syllable 'Bat' meaning stone, are said to have been coral blocks capable of detaching themselves from the surrounding reef and travelling to and fro between Atchin and certain islands whence their descendents are said to have come"[274]. The term is also found more widely spread in Polynesia. One of the ancestors of the Gilbert Islanders was said to be Bat-i-ku the Skull and his brother Kanii. They were believed to have dwelt beneath the Tree of Samoa, and their "food" was reputed to be the heads of the first born[275]. This myth sounds remarkably similar to the sacrifice of the first born thought to have existed among the Phoenicians in the first millennium B.C. and in this central Pacific location they may also have had connections with the child sacrifice ceremonies known in the Andes cultures of South America. The possible connections with Asia, India in particular and South America will be of interest in due course but it is of interest that in Asia and other Pacific Islands trophy heads were hung on, or at the foot of sacred trees and were clearly related to stones also laid in at or among their roots. Similar practices appears to have occurred also among the Mayans where the Popol Vuh records that the head of Hun-Hunaphu was attached to an Underworld tree by the Lords of Xibalba[276].

In Melanesia the references to watu relating to sacred stones or stone-using people are many. The Tami in the New Hebrides have a great hero known as Kalo-Watu and the various peoples of these islands are known for their megalithic cultures and for the myths and legends of sea-going heroes and migrants who introduced them[277]. Clearly Watu refers to stone but Kalu is a name associated in the Middle East and India with priests and rituals focused on a stone altar. In the Solomon Islands there is an island called Olo-watu that is entirely artificial[278]. These islands were constructed of stone and were inhabited into the beginning of the last century - therefore Watu was entirely applicable in the constructional sense. The term Olo appears to relate to hero names in Micronesia that may indicate the origin of those who built them. Olo is also a prefix found among the Cuna of Panama in Central America[279]. In the D'Entrcasteaux islands a myth, about twin ogre slaying heroes, names their mother as Inela-wata and who were associated with stone-using migrants known throughout Melanesia[280]. She is also associated with caring for a giant serpent in a cave that had one large tooth and this will be of more interest later.

The Abelham tribe reside in the interior of New Guinea and it is significant that their dancing ground, the focal centre for the tribe, is called Amei appears to derive from the Polynesian Marae. The main feature of this dancing ground was the Mbabmu-Matu or "moon stone" around which the various ritual ceremonies were performed. The spirits called the "Wale" correspond to the "Wagan" of Iatmul, a people already noted, who in turn appear to correspond to the Pawan wind deities of India[281]. One of their heroes associated with the Wale is Kaua-Mbuangga where Kaua is a deity name found both in Polynesia and India where New Guinea is a mid-point in the sea journey between the two regions. One of the straits along the sea journey was called Kadim-Watu, because it was guarded by prominent, mythically important rocks flanking the Kula ceremonial trading circuit, noted earlier[282]. A magical spell had the name of Bora'i that originally had been associated with the Bora initiation ceremonies found in Melanesia and East and South East Australia and appears to be particularly associated with the Kadim-Watu rocks[283]. At the island of Manu-Watu shells are collected that are called "Water of Manuwatu" and are used for ceremonial armbands[284].

On Malekula, the most important island in the New Hebrides group for megalithic sites, it has been noted that the ancient ancestors were regaled with the title of Am-bat, Ka-bat or Ham-bat. The significance of their association with these megalithic sites is clearly implied in their title and they were said to be white-skinned, stone-using migrants. It is also of interest that one of the titles given to the sisters of the important descendant clans from the Ambat and his brothers was in fact wato simply confirming their lineage from these ancestors[285].

1.051 : Incised rock designs associated with rainmaking in Aboriginal Central Australia. Arunta Tribe, Central Australia, Pre - 19th., century, A.D.

In the extensive researches of Abraham Fornander he perceived a century and a half ago the association of the Middle Eastern term for stone and its correspondences among the Polynesians. He wrote: "That these sacrificial stones were closely connected with the Phoenician Boetylia, dedicated to the same purposes, and indicative of a similarity of creeds and symbols, may be shown from the name itself, 'Boetylia', is evidently a composite word, but may not, as some lexicographers indicate, be of Semitic-Hebrew extraction. The thing and its name must be older than the adoption of a Semitic dialect by the

1.052 : Churingas or sacred carved wooden objects or rocks considered the essential extension of the individual and group soul among the Aborigines in Central Australia. Arunta, Central Australia, Late 19th., century, A.D.

1.053 : A tikovina or sacred object similar to a churinga typical of the Herbert River tribes. Southern Australia, Late 19th., century, A.D.

1.054 : Sacred rocks and objects usually designated as churingas similar to those revered in Ancient India and Peru. Central Australia, 19th., century, A.D.

1.055 : Sacred rocks identified with the ancestors Dreamtime in Aboriginal Australia. Urabunna Tribe Pigeon Rocks, South Central Australia, Late 19th., ry, A.D.

Phoenicians. But, as often happens in transition periods, the term 'Boetylia' may be a compromise between the older Cushite and later Semitic languages spoken by the Phoenicians. I consider, therefore, the word as composed of Batu and Il, Illu, or El. The latter term is evidently Semitic, and, through all dialects, signifies God, the God. The former, however, I take to be a Cushite word. It certainly has no Arian connections. But in nearly all the Polynesian cogeners we find this word retaining both its primary and derivative sense, both 'Stone' and 'God' or Lord. In the ancient Madura dialect 'Batu' means a stone. At Pulo Nias 'Batu' is used as a name for the deity who has charge of the earth, and is called Batu-Da-Danau. The expression Battala, used by the pre-Malay Battas in Sumatra, and Bitara of the Bali Islanders, for their deities, may reasonably be referred to the same origin. In the Polynesian dialects proper, we find Patu amd Patapatu, 'stone', in New Zealand; Fatu in Tahiti and Marquesas signifying 'Lord', 'Master', also 'Stone'; Haku in the Hawaiian means 'Lord', 'Master', while with the intensive prefix po it becomes Pohaku, 'a stone'."[286].

Fornander's researches are full of interest and useful information for the present although they are largely ignored by modern archaeologists. He clearly shows that the term batu derived from the ancient Middle or Near East and that baetyl was also a term used in the same sense by the Greeks[287] and that this term among the Pacific Islanders must have been imported by traders or migrants from that distant region. He did not relate the term to the Australian Aborigines but it is clear that their term originates in their cultures from Indonesia and possibly also from Southern China. Fornander's analysis of the mutation of Batu with Il, Illu or El is of great import and will be of major interest in a later chapter. In India, the term batu forms part of the caste names of several sections, but among the Tellugus of South India the Karna-Battu are a weaving caste and will be among those who will be of interest in due course[288]. Also in India there are many references to the term Hatu that will be of interest among, inevitably, the Gonds, and the Asurs who appear to have derived this term also from the Middle East or Anatolia and these references will be considered later.

Returning to Indonesia again, on the island of Bali at the temple in Tenganan, a low wall of piled-up stones surrounding a great banyan tree was the centre of religious ritual. Sacred stones were known as Batu Menurun and were considered fragments of a mythical horse of the hero Outje Seraya[289]. The banyan is of course the sacred tree of India and is found as far as Eastern Polynesia, undoubtedly planted on the various Pacific islands by the traders, or migrants from India. Of particular note is the hero name Outje which is a local variation of Wotje that also relates to stone and is probably the origin of the Aboriginal Wotjo-Baluk and others.

While researching mainly in Minahassa in North Celebes a century and a half ago the English naturalist Sydney Hickson noted also many cultural traits, myths and legends. He wrote that "... the island (Manado) is from time to time visited by the canoes of those strange, gipsy-like people, the Wadjorese, who wander from place to place, subsisting alone on the fish they catch to eat or barter, and seem to known no home but their frail little outrigger canoes ..."[290]. The term Wadjo was undoubtedly developed from an association with Wad, Wat or Watu but here has taken this local form relating to that of the Balinese hero. Hickson further notes that the Minahassers call the prehistoric celts, grubbed up in cultivation or surface found, Watu-ing Kilat[291]. This follows exactly the pattern of claim in Australia and elsewhere in Indonesia, India, Asia and indeed worldwide that they were lightning stones. Characteristically the local peoples denied all knowledge as to who the manufacturers were although Hickson simply deflects attention to this problem by attributing this to forgetfulness.

In a Minahassa myth it is stated that a coconut was cast up on to the island and from it a tree grew which is called Maha-Watu and from this emerged the first man called Wangi[292]. Clearly this tree represents the World Tree but the prefix of the name is clearly derived from

Maha that is literally "great" in the myths of India such as Maha-Deo - Great God, and Watu means a stone. This would indicate that the myth had been imported by megalithic people into the district where it had become adapted to existing myths. The term Wangi is probably the same as the Sky god, Rangi, often associated with the first people, and identical to that of Polynesia.

Minahassa is a fruitful area for sea-going myths and another relates that a hero called Maengkom during his travels created an island out of a peninsula that was then called Tinulap. While he rested on this island he chewed betel-nut and when he spat out the residue his saliva stained the rocks red. This place became known as Watu merah[293]. It is no coincidence that a sacred mountain and its spirits in Minahassa should be called Kla-bat[294], clearly related to the stone-using ancestors in Malekula and that Minahassa in North Celebes should be a half way point between that part of Melanesia and North East India where Ka-bat was a ritual official[295]. In fact Celebes is known for its megalithic culture of some import which some have paralleled with or derived from that of Easter Island.

In Central Celebes, around Lake Poso, it is believed that this region was the homeland of the Toradja tribe. These people have already been noted as probably having given their name to the priest/medicine-men of North West Australia as recorded by Grey. They will prove to have a much greater role in the theme of this work but around Lake Poso they are thought to have been responsible for placing stone monoliths in groups representing ancestral heroes or deities[296]. These stones are called watoe mpoga and other stones are believed to be the petrified forms of ancestral figures. The term watoe means of course a stone but it follows the more local form and pronunciation relating to watje and outje.

In Melanesia, in Buka in theNorth West Solomon Islands, an initiation ceremony for boys was known as Wat-awuts. During the ceremony the boys, having allowed their hair to grow long over the previous twelve months, climbed a tree planted in front of the ceremonial house. A boy, as he descended from the tree, had to step on a sacrificial pig to make it squeal[297]. Although eyewitnesses have described the cutting-down of the trees for this ceremony and their erection in front of the house there is no mention of a stone being associated with either the pole or sacrificial pig. The name of the ceremony must originally have entailed a stone either at the base of the tree as a foundation or as a sacrificial altar for the sacrifice which at one time was certainly a human, probably a captive warrior consonant with the traditions on other Melanesian islands. The term wat betrays the origin of this ceremony with originally the sacrificial stone and while a similar ceremony was known on San Cristoval known as Kurtachi. Associated with this ceremony was a ritual involving the burning of trees on a stone platform[298]. Trees planted on or ritually associated with stone platforms or mounds in known from the Middle East, India through Indonesia to Melanesia, Polynesia to the Americas and with the Maya in particular. The term Kurtachi is undoubtedly related to similar terms in Melanesia and Australia and probably relates to the Kurdaichi in Central Australia.

In other islands of Melanesia a similar ritual to the Wat-awuts is found where pigs were tied to mango trees and "sacrificed slowly" to ensure that the longest and loudest squealing was achieved[299]. Among the Mafulu highland people of New Guinea ceremonies that are highly reminiscent of Asia are found such as those for the first-born. Williamson noted of one of these ceremonies a century ago: "Each of the pigs is killed by the pig-killer under a chief's (raised) platform grave, or if no such platform then exists, upon the site of one, and is cut up. Before the cutting-up, however, the child in each case stands upon the body of the pig, and whilst he stands he is dressed with a feather ornament put over his head…"[300]. Since pigs were usually admitted to be substitutes for human sacrifice and that the latter were still being sought up until a century ago in parts of Melanesia it is clear that the pig itself was only a later substitute for the human male. Of importance in this section is the sacrifice for not only initiation but for almost all ritual ceremonies and sacred buildings. This was in most cases a sacrificial stone - wat or bat, on which the victim was sacrificed or on which the sacred buildings or sites were constructed.

In considering the direct transfer of Australian Aboriginal cultural elements to Tierra del Fuego in Southern South America it is interesting to note that the neighbours of the Ona preserve a term that may also have derived from the Western Pacific. The neighbouring tribe is the Yaghan and their Supreme deity is called Wat-a-uineiwa, who was said not to have a physical form[301] and resembles the name for the sacred initiation ceremony in the Solomon Islands.

The Gonds of India are fundamental to the theme of this book in the cultural transfer from India to Australia and through to the Americas. Of particular interest is that they exhibited into last century the remnants of a megalithic culture. It is significant therefore that the legendary Gond homeland was called Watan. This may have become corrupted into Matang - an elephant deity and also as Matangi the "vehicle" of the fierce smallpox deity Sitala - a form of Durga. In Tongan myth Matangi the wind married "calm" and their children were twin albinos[302]. Matang was also the homeland of the Gilbert Islanders along with Buru suggesting that the deity of the allied Santal people in India Maran Buru was connected[303].

It is interesting to note that Ganesa, as the elephant headed god of Hinduism, is reflected among the Maya in Central America associated with the stone pillar or World Tree in the form of some of the depictions in India emerging from the shoulders of Vishnu, or among the Maya the ruler. This iconography of the elephant exhibited in Central America and at Copan in particular is dealt with elsewhere[304] but a vase from Yalloch in Guatemala (*6.109*) shows also the anthropomorphic form known as Ganesa in India. The extension and merging of symbolism is very complex in India but elephants sculptured in stone and emerging from stone, as at Angkor Wat in Cambodia, are many and convey this animal as the cosmic "foundation". This concept is extended by the divine elephant in Buddhism replacing the cow in Brahmanism and representing the cosmic male spirit or demiurge which impregnated Maya who later gave birth to Gautama who became the Buddha. The term "wad", however, extends throughout many castes in India and appears in many cases to reflect their inheritance as intrusive, for the most part, from the Middle East region.

Many rituals of Gonds take place around the central dancing ground or ceremonial space. Usually monolithic stones representing the deities are found underneath the sacred clan tree, adjacent or nearby. It is not surprising therefore that the clan priest among the Hill Maria Gonds who performs most of the rituals and oblations at this (or these) stones is called the Modul-Waddai[305]. Among these people in particular the dancing shields or disks with long peacock "tails" or extensions hanging from them placed in the small of the back, called moghi[306] (*7.062*), are virtually identical with those depicted in ancient sculptures, ceramics and codices in Mexico[307] (*7.064*). Among other Bison Horn Maria Gonds the term for the priest was Pen-Waddai where Pen was a collective term for the clan gods and the clan temple was called Pen-Rawar. One of the Pen was the Village Mother who was represented as a cairn or as a bamboo net full of stones or a low table-stone at the foot of the sacred clan tree. Often associated with the Gond villages and their gods was the sacred grove which could never be cut down called Ma Olai or Danteshwari Mai - Ma and Mai both referring to the ancient earth goddess of India[308]. Of some interest is the fact that the clan god was also known as the Anga[309] and Verrier Elwin suggests that the Anga cult may have originated with divination from a corpse[310]. It is particularly significant that the megalithically associated Nanga rites in Melanesia, and Fiji in particular, resembles that of the Gonds and will be considered in due course.

One of the important rituals associated with the Pen stones performed by the Pen-Waddai was offering an egg after the winnowing of the first harvest and during this period of ritual the men were sworn to celibacy[311]. Hunting forays were governed by strict protocol and from

1.056 : Stone dolmens were common on the smaller Indonesian islands along the central sea route from the Pacific to South East Asia. Sumba, Central Indonesia, Pre - 20th., century, A.D.

1.057 : Massi dolmen near Maram in Manipur in the Naga region of Himalayan foothills. Manipur, North East India, Pre - 20th., century, A.D.

1.058 : Dolmen of the type found in Eurasia and in the Melanesian Islands. Peru, Early-mid first millennium, A.D.

1.059 : Stone dolmen of the type found in Eurasia and South America. Melanesia, Pre-20th., century, A.D.

1.061 : Shaft and chamber burials and dolmens, called heo, similar to those in Ecuador and Peru. Tawatana, Arosi, Solomon Islands, Pre-20th., century, A.D.

1.060 : Stone dolmen near Lake Titicaca similar to those of Melanesia and South Asia. Aymara, Bolivia, 1st., millennium, A.D.

the kill the Waddai's portion was usually the liver and this he offered to the Bison Horn Maria Pen deities[312]. The Bison Horn Marias' clan god, Pen, was usually centred on one of the five groups of clans or phratries called Tarr or Rutmam. For the Hill Maria Gonds each large clan had for the area it occupied its own clan god centre or temple and their Modul-Waddai, clan priest, was exclusively associated with his own large clan known as Pari or Katta[313].

Besides the sacred stones representing the clan gods there were menhir sites that were erected as memorials to departed ancestors and was a current practice up until a century ago. These were called Koto-kal or memorial ground or cemetery also known as Uras-kal[314]. The term kal as suffix related to the stone itself but also the priest and undoubtedly derives from the ritual known as the Kallu in the Ancient Middle East. This term will be of more interest in due course but it is of interest to note that the Gonds believed that the spirit of the departed went to a world called Pogho Bhum - Bhum meaning the Earth, hence the name of the earth god Bhumi. Pogho appears to be related to spirit or a deity ruling that world and it is interesting to note that a term for the stone-using migrants in the New Hebrides was Nogho and Nommo[315]. The Gonds have a Young Mens' house as part of their traditional social structure called the Ghotul and this is almost certainly the model for the same institution in the New Hebrides called the Ghamal or Amal[316].

The Waddai acts not only as ceremonial clan priest but also as oracle and a myth records that the name came from the first Maria Gond man to discover honey[317]. He waits until he is possessed, by the deity to be consulted, or who presides over a particular ceremonial which is described as "the god comes upon him" or "sits on him"[318]. This may have developed from the

Middle Eastern ritual of sitting on, or at leaning against the stones forming a stone circle in the expectation that the gods or ancestor associated with each stone respectively would inspire and, or possess the supplicant. The priest was also the healer and used a spray of the Amaltus (Cassia fistula) in various magical rituals. "Waddai" was also the name for magic and black magic was also called Pangan[319].

Megalithic forms, such as cromlechs or dolmens, were constructed up into last centre in the form shown in (*1.057*) a large flat stone slab is supported on four boulders and this type of construction was known in India as a "Danya-Kal"[320]. These stones were much too large to be surface found and were in fact quarried suggesting an age-old tradition that was still readily seen up until two generations ago in India. These megalithic structures, or monoliths, were usually associated with memorials to tribal elders or heroes. If, however, a person died unnaturally such as being murdered or drowned he was covered with stones and a cairn built up over some years as those passing by threw more stones over him[321]. These cairns were known as Punji-Paknar among the Halbi tribe[322]. This appears to have some relation with the souls of the dead or medicine-men being taken to the sky to see Punjil in Australian myths particularly as the Gond people will be shown to have close affinities with Tibetan culture anciently. Some of the initiation ceremonies and dances also appear to have common origins. Large menhirs were also erected and from the same quarries and it cannot be other that they were in a major way associated with the dispersion of megalithic cultures in centuries past into Indonesia and the Pacific region.

Among the Bison Horn Maria Gonds, where a death was caused by smallpox or a woman died in pregnancy or child-birth, the victims were buried but not in the usual cremation ground. Before the burial it was necessary for the Waddai, sometimes also called Gunia, to ensure that the malignant spirit of the person could not escape from its body. He drove nails into her knees and elbows and after the burial menhirs were allowed to be erected[323]. This custom may well have a connection with the "jointmarks" found so widely throughout the Pacific region and its Rim (*1.009-15*). It was believed by some peoples that the human spirit was made up by smaller souls centred in the joints; in the head and in the hair, as well as in the finger and toe-nails. The priest name guna may be the origin of the Aboriginal Australian term for priest, gom-mera, earlier noted.

In other castes in India the term Wad or Wat in its many variations are found among very interesting peoples. The Gollars or Golabas as a caste are of some interest since they show a possible connection with the Zapotecs noted in an earlier work[324]. One of their clan subdivisions is called Woddar or Ode[325]. Their clan structure has septs, gotras or clans called Inti-Peru and one of the unusual features of the worship of their clan deities is that in their ritual chest they include three of four whip like ropes made of cotton or agave. These are called Vira-Thadlu or "heroes ropes". Their ancestors are called Vira-Lu and the name affix usually referring to ancestral descent is ayya, referring to Aryan descent[326]. Cowries are also revered objects and relate to ancient sea travel and they practice rituals that include ground designs linking them to South India and the New Hebrides.

Some of the castes have long lost their fundamental megalithic associations but obvious hints are to be found among their deities. One such caste is the Rellis whose deities are represented in historic times by wooden dolls[327]. However, the name for the chief deity is Odda Polamma where the term Odda relates to the sacred stone by which she was represented by other South Indian peoples. A caste known as the Oddars was known to pan for gold in rivers, watercourses and drains near goldsmiths[328]. The Koravas are a widespread caste who have four main divisions two of which are named Pattu-Pu and Odde (Wad)[329]. The Korava priests are called Gadde which is highly reminiscent of Gadu which is a name associated with the Phoenicians and whom Herodotus notes as having probably originating in India[330]. Coupled with this possible

1.062:
Uruskal stones
erected as memo-
rial stones to
ancestors contin-
uing a long
megalithic tradi-
tion in Central
and South India
from 500 B.C.
Gond Culture,
Dantewara,
Central India,
Early 20th., cen-
tury, A.D.

Middle Eastern connection is the fact that they call their villages "Ur", which has similar ancient connections with Ancient Sumeria and Akkad.

The Koravas will be of more interest when considering clan structures around the Pacific region but also of interest are the Koyas or Kois and their priests who are called Oddis - a term that has clearly developed from the original connection with stone worship[331]. In Mysore in South Central India the Wod-eyars ruled from 1399-1610 A.D. and the name indicates that they had probably been stone-worshippers although they were also called Udaiyan connecting them with the Kashmir region[332]. Among the Oddes caste, who are earth-workers, have a sub-division called Manti probably originating from a Mandaean connection[333].

In Polynesia Abraham Fornander recorded that Oahu in Hawaii was the equivalent of Ouahou in Central and South East Borneo, among the Dyaks, and in Central Celebes among the Buguis it was Ouadju[334]. The term clearly relates to those noted as occurring in similar guises in India and Fornander presented abundant evidence that these and other terms derived from further west in South Arabia or among the Cushites of Southern Egypt and the Sudan. An altar with inscriptions in Minaean and Greek is known on the island of Delos in Greece recorded as provided by two merchants from Ma'in in Southern Arabia in honour of their god Wadd[335]. In the Temple of Wad an altar was a truncated pyramid with cuboid top that was hollowed out for offerings[336]. In Ancient Ethiopia and in Anatolia a similar construction for the altar was known and associated with the Moon. In Ma'in the national god Wadd was interpreted as "love", and Wadd'ab meant "Wadd is Father"[337]. It is important to note that there were close connections between the South Arabian states and Mesopotamia since Sin was also the Moon god of Hadramaut[338]. An ancient place in South Arabia was called An-Wadm where rocks were covered with inscriptions and were of great ceremonial significance for the king and people of Shabwa[339]. This town was the capital of Hadramauwt and it would appear that these rocks anciently gave the name to the Moon god of the adjacent state of Ma'in or Marin - perhaps originally a territory belonging to them or from which they migrated or were ejected.

In considering South Arabia it is essential to note the far distant sea contacts that these kingdoms maintained and with India itself since the Subcontinent appears also to have been well within their orbit. There can be little doubt that they travelled much further east than India into South East Asia, Australia and into the Pacific as Fornander long ago perceived. It is interesting to note that "power objects", usually stones, were called Waqanquis in Peru sounding as if this term has developed from wat or wad[340].

Wat, Wad and the Tradition of Stone Worship in Aboriginal Australia
More recent research among the surviving Aboriginal peoples of Australia in the last part of last century indicates that the derivation and preservation of the Middle Eastern associations, along with the traditions of India, of the stone and the Moon with the term Wad. Among the Mara speaking people in Arnhem Land in the far North of Australia, located near the sea route to Indonesia and India from Melanesia and Polynesia, a tradition identifies two mythical men with the goanna - a monitor type lizard, who were known jointly as the Wadi Gudjara[341]. They were often associated in these myths with the Mamu who were said to be spirits who came and went

and who were usually considered to be cannibals. Another Mara myth notes that Wadi Bira was the name for the mythical Moon man[342]. Interestingly he was also called Galga that sounds as if it was derived from Galla - a name associated with Halmahera also known as Gilolo in the eastern Indonesian spice islands and traceable to South Arabia and the Galla of Ethiopia. The Galla will be of more interest in a future planned publication.

Among the Gugadju, located south of the Kimberleys in North West Australia, a mythical "'white" Snake Man was called Wadi Liru which indicates the terms forming the name being associated with reptiles as above and besides rocks[343]. Another myth from the Mara notes the mythical giant named Wadi Nurai, and his wife Minma. It will be of interest in a later chapter that many of the Aboriginal myths note that the mythical peoples who migrated across their landscape were in fact giants. It is sufficient to note here, however, that the name is associated by the Aborigines themselves with a separate people. This myth tells of Wadi Nurai building a dancing ground for himself and part of this ritual performance is the display of his "enormous", erect penis[344]. This is highly reminiscent of the dancing Siva in India called Nataraja, and where this deity is often depicted with his phallus erect (*3.041*). Siva as one the Hindu triad is one of the oldest deities in India and was absorbed into Hinduism perhaps two millennia after seals in the Indus civilisation show him seated in a characteristic seated "lotus" posture. With so many of the subjected castes, the Hindu peoples along with the Aboriginal peoples of India, were devoted to the god Siva. Among them were a number that indicate origins of stone worship and connections with the Middle East, reflecting names derived from Wat or Wad, it can be of little surprise, therefore, to find allied names and rituals reminiscent of India in Australia.

The Man-gunda-speaking people retain a myth which is similar to the Gugadja but located in south west South Australia and refers to the two Wadi Gudjara, "Two Men", who had came upon the hole of a Rainbow Snake. The snake had left and travelled westward so the Wadi Gudjara walked on to the Wilirung-gana waterhole. There was located a sand ridge called the Bira - Moon, where Bira the Moon Man had dug a hole in which he rested. Bira had two dogs that guarded him but he made friends with the Two Men. After travelling west and then east, perhaps describing his orbit around the earth, Bira the Moon Man left wad-inga stone implements that were used in circumcision rites[345]. Circumcision is associated with the Semitic peoples of the Middle East and references have already been included with the terms used by the Aborigines for stones and crystals. In the most ancient records the Middle Eastern god Sin, the moon god, was also known in South Arabia, and the prefix wad to the term for the circumcision implement of stone appears far too great a coincidence for there not to have been contacts. Later contacts with the Muslims of Malaya and Indonesia probably reinforced such customs. But is also of note that the link of similar terms in Melanesia extends much further south to Maori New Zealand where the term whatu for sacred stone is also found[346], and that will be shown to be closely linked to South East Australia.

It has been noted above that the term vira, also wira is widely known in South India, a title assumed by the Chola dynasty, and meant "hero". It is very likely therefore that tribal names such as Wira-djuri were in fact derived from these terms particularly as they are associated with the South East Australian cultures who exhibit such close cross-references to those in India. The same is likely to be true of appellations for heroes, mythical people or tribes such Ara-Wotya and the Wotjo-baluk. Howitt records that in the legends and myths of the Dieri there was a belief that beyond the sky was another land. Ara-Wotya, said to dwell in the sky, was said to let down a long cord made of hair and by this means pulled up the Mura-mura Ankuritcha and all those who were with him[347]. These Mura-mura play an important role in the Australian Aboriginal myths and will be referred to in a later chapter and are noted also in the following Dieri reference. This myth relates that the fossil remains found around Lake Eyre in Central Australia, called by them

Kadimarkara, had been creatures which in the age of the Mura-muras in ancient times climbed down from the sky by the huge Eucalytus trees that grew on the western side of this lake[348]. In a similar Wotjo-baluk myth a pine-tree extended up through the sky (Wurra-wurra) to the land or abode beyond of Mamen-gorak - literally "father-ours"[349]. The term for a sky deity named Ara-Wotya suggests that this was a deity related to stone originally. If it was an imported deity then any memory of the traditional wotya or wat connection might soon be lost unless reinforced by other contacts. Ara or arya is a term specifically associated with the descendants of the Aryans in India and prefixed frequently to their individual and caste names.

The Wotjobaluk tribe was in historic time occupiers of territory in North West Victoria and into South Eastern Australia. The prefix Wotjo means "man" and Baluk means "people" and the term Woto[350] was seen by Howitt as a possible link to Africa[351]. A totem list is of interest since it shows elements that are likely to be reflected in divisions of incursive peoples:

Ngungul	the Sea	Wanyip	Fire
Ngaui	the Sun	Barewun	Cave
Mitjen	the Moon	Ngungul	the Sea
Bunjil	Fomalhault	Munya	Yam

The importance of the Sun, Moon and at least one major star with the Sea suggest mariners who used the sky by day and night for sea migrations or trade and the importance of the star Fomalhault as Bunjil has already been noted. Found among the Wotjo are ghosts called the Bir-racks[352] suggesting that the term many have derived from the wind and forest deities known as Bir in Viras in South India. It is interesting to note that the Wotjobaluk shared with the other two major tribes who exhibit major incursive traits from Asia, the Kurnai and Wurunjerri, a ball-game where one side kept the ball as long as possible by throwing it from one to another[353] probably derived from those of India and South East Asia.

The association of the shaman/medicine-man with stones is found throughout Australia and the training of the Wotjo-baluk was of interest. Howitt records this process: ".... if it became known that a boy could see his mother's ghost (Nungim) sitting by her grave, a medicine-man would take him for the purpose of making him a Lanyingel, or medicine-man. Part of the process of making a boy a Lanyingel was to smoke him with the leaves of the native cherry (Exocarpus cupressiformis) and anoint him with red ochre and grease. These were public acts ....". Howitt further notes: "The Wotjobaluk believed that a man became a Bangal by being met by a super-natural being called by them Ngatya, who is said to live in hollows in the ground, in the mallee scrubs. They think that the Ngatya opens the man's side and inserts in it such things as quartz crystals, by which he obtains his power. From that time on he can, as they say, 'pull things out of himself and others, such as quartz, wood, charcoal, etc., and also out of his arms something like feathers, which are considered to have healing properties. In the case quoted elsewhere, these feathers are spoken of in connection with a medicine-man of the Jupagalk tribe, which belongs to the Wotjobaluk nation".
"In the Jajaurung tribe the office of doctor is alleged to be obtained by the individual visiting the world of spirits while in a trance of two or three days' duration, and there receive the necessary initiation."
"The Wurunjerri believed that their medicine men became such by being carried by the ghosts through a hole in the sky to Bunjil, from whom they received magical powers"[354].

It has been shown that Bunjil is related through Australia, Indonesia to India and even Tibet that may have been the origin of this sky deity. The term Bangal for an initiate may derive from Bangla - the native name for Bengal covering the Ganges and Brahmaputra. The insertion of crystals in the side of the initiate suggests an inversion of the Buddhist myth of His being born through the side of the mother. It has been noted earlier that crystals are intimately associated with magic and healing powers in India among the Hindu and Aboriginal tribes of India as well as in Buddhist cosmology.

The cosmology of the Wotjo-Baluk and others will be further explored but in considering certain other aspects it is interesting to note that among the Wotjobaluk the native cat named Boamberik was said to be forever chasing the Pleiades and was represented by a star in the sky[355]. Howitt notes the native cat was called Dasyurus and that this Wotjo name was constructed of boam or "tail" and berik - "stinking". The actual name is one which is almost identical to the Vedic Aryan name for the dark-skinned Aboriginal and "Untouchable" people in India - the Dasus or Dasyus ("unclean" or "dirty"), while boam and berik in their translation clearly indicate the social level and unclean state which was believed of them. The star assigned to be this animal was thought by Howitt to be Aldebaran.

When the first white people entered Australia two centuries ago it was recorded of the natives in all regions that they thought the Europeans were the spirits of their ancestors returning. Returning spirits were not always welcome except under the control of the shaman or medicine-man since otherwise they were consider unruly and troublesome bringing disease and misfortune. This was also the case in India among many less advanced peoples. The term used for a spirit that had departed for the sky world was animadiate meaning "He is gone to be made a white man"[356]. Other references to a similar term applied to the white man were found among the Jajaurung tribe, Amydeet and the Witowurung, Amerjig. Among Wotjo people it was the practice to roast them and eat the skin of the "thigh" and sides of those who were killed by them - a ritual called Amidiat[357]. Howitt believed that this association of the skin colour into white changing from the natural dark brown or black skin colour when the body was "roasted" gave rise to this association with the belief that the origin of the white man was a returning spirit. Howtitt noted that this same custom was found among the Kurnai[358]. A similar theory has been applied in more recent times to explain the many myths that record pre-Colombian contacts with white people in the Amazon region of South America that will be of interest in due course. The Amidiat appears to have developed from a cremation ritual where the body was placed on a fire heap to be deliberately burnt to ash and the symbol of the person's vocation or occupation planted where the head was on the pyre after[359]. Cremation was the hallmark of Hindu burials and among some of the Aboriginal peoples the planting of their occupational symbol was certainly known among some of them.

In examining the mythology and legends of the Australian Aborigines it is clear that there had to have at least occasional contacts with Indonesia, India and the Middle East that are more likely to have given rise to the association of white people with ancestral spirits. This is particularly so since whites were also identified as their ancestors or with megalithic peoples in Melanesia and Polynesia and not least of all in the Americas. It is certainly significant that the tribes of South East Australia in particular make this claim. So many other mythical or legendary heroes, terms or cosmological constructs are so closely similar to those of Asia that it is unlikely that the discoloration to white during the roasting process was anything other than a notable, perceived, significant coincidence to the natives themselves reminding them of their "divine" ancestry. The Australian Aboriginal has long been recognised as a southern section of the early Caucasoid races related to the Veddahs of India, Sri Lanka, and certain parts of Indonesia. They are particularly related to the Ainu - the Caucasian occupiers of Japan all of whom originated in Central Asia (*1.041*).

The modes of burial, and the various customs, are a subject of enormity and cannot be attempted here except to record one or two references that shows striking parallels to reinforce cultural-cross-references already noted. One of these is that noted by Howitt found in the South East of Australia and he wrote; "...on the Maranoa the graves are nearly always boomerang shaped, with the convex side towards the west. The body is tied up in a sheet of bark immediately after death, the toes, being tied together, as are the hands also. Occasionally a vessel containing water is suspended near the grave lest the deceased should want a drink. Not infrequently, however, the body is dried and carried about for a long time - even as in one case, for three years. Such a body is dried by being placed on a stage under which the women keep a slow fire constantly burning. The fat which exudes from it collected in vessels and the young men rub it over their bodies to impart the good qualities of the deceased to themselves". Etc.[360]. Tying the toes and hands (more usually the thumbs of the hands) together is the identical practice found in India among the Brahmans and adopted widely by the many castes influenced by them. In the most ancient records from the Vedic period in India it is implied that the big toes relate to lightning with which the enemies of the gods can be crushed (by the big toes) and this facility appears also be the same for thumbs[361]. Lightning appears early to relate to the divine spark believed to separate off from the primal flame to form the human spirit and which saw the god of fire, Agni, as its parent. It was thought that this custom was initiated in the belief that tying the thumbs and toes prevented the spirit re-entering the body or to prevent it from using the spirit of lightning to re-animate the thumbs or toes to cause damage or destruction should that spirit be malignant in death[362]. In the burial customs of the Karen of Burma (Myanmar) the thumbs and toes of the deceased are also tied being undoubtedly influenced from India. Also associated with these funeral rites is the provision of a duck meant to form the food for the deceased but its spirit is intended to guide the deceased to the spirit world. Harry I. Marshall, recording this ceremony a century ago noted; "…. The beak, wings, and legs of the duck are dried a little by the fire and laid by the corpse, the following words expressing their purpose in so doing:

> Let the beak become a canoe for him.
> Let the wings become his sail
> And the legs, his paddles."

"Placing two bits of liver on the eyes of the corpse, they utter the wish: 'May these become bright eyes for you, to see clearly your way as you go back'"[363].

The Karen ceremony not only reflects those of India but introduces the boat with sails and paddle usually associated with sea-travellers or mariners suggesting that this element was introduced into Burma from the sea and includes the bird as soul or accompanying it to the spirit world. If these aspects of burial customs alone were similar to those in India it would have been possible to consider it a coincidence, but with the many other references it must surely indicate that there had to have been cultural incursions from there into Australia. The mummification process is highly reminiscent of traditions found not only in Melanesia but also in Central and South America and will be referred to in due course.

It is of interest in the context of possible connections with initiation rites such as the Bora, so clearly influenced from Melanesia and found distributed in the region displaying so many elements of Asian customs in the South East, that the Wotjo-Baluk did not have an equivalent. The initiated shaman or medicine man retained their secret rituals and beliefs that were never shared but this was true also of those tribes who had initiation rites. In other respects they resemble the broad traditions seemingly to have derived from South Asia and found also in the adjacent regions of Melanesia and Polynesia. It may have been that they were stone-worshipping migrants or mariners who came from Asia either before or after those who brought the Bora ceremonies from the North East in Melanesia. It may also be they were a tribe who resulted from intermarriage with travelling migrants who did not stay long enough with their captured women to pass on their rituals to their sons until the age of initiation at about twelve years - similar to that in the Middle East. The creation of clans of this type are apparent throughout sea routes in the Indian and Pacific Oceans and are typical particularly of those associated with mariners.

Inheritance is usually through the female line by necessity and it may not be coincidence that this was a common form in the islands of Indonesia associated with sea travel and whose mythical gods and other references relate to Polynesia in pre-Muslim communities and among those peoples who have retained their earlier beliefs systems.

The association of the soul as, or with a bird in Australian myth is widespread and often identified with the totemic opposites, eagle-hawk or crow, and among the Sema Naga located in the Assamese hills the soul was said to sometimes take the form of a particular hawk. This was said to fly to the Hill of the Dead at Wokha - undoubtedly originally related to a stone, monolith or rock outcrop[364]. It was believed that the soul ascended Wokha mountain by what appeared to the Sema as a winding path to the summit which were in fact stratifications exposed by erosion and called by them "Dead-man's Path". At the very top there was said to be a tower containing a ladder that was used by the soul to reach the sky world[365]. The ladder imagery appears closely similar to that shown on boulder reliefs on the Guatemalan coast at Bilbao and on the stela from Piedras Negras[366]. Wokha Hill was also approached from the Lhota Naga villages by a route known similarly as "dead man's road" - Etchhilan. This road was flanked by memorials to the dead where offerings were placed and bamboo erections "...showing the prowess in war and hunting of those recently deceased"[367]. The Naga deities, customs and rituals will be of interest in later chapters.

In South West China near the border with Tibet there are references to ancient associations and probably through trade if not migrations from India but also the Middle East. In what were the Chiaring States one was called Wassu where the men were unusually tall and robust and the adjacent state was called Wotje who were racially related[368]. Mani stones, that is, ancient stones carved with Buddhist prayers, were common in Wotje state[369] and may have given it its name from a pre-Buddhist period - the Buddhist texts being probably intended to exorcise these sacred stones. It is clear from early myths and legends that these states were in contact with the Nagas of Assam from a very early period. Contacts with the ancient Buddhists also occurred since there are references to an historical patriarch named P'u known in the Western Dynasty of Ts'in from 265-317 A.D. in South West China[370].

The most notable elements among cosmology of the Australian Aborigines are the forms of tree worship and stone worship. The Middle Eastern term wad or wat has been noted as being incursive along with related terms developed or residual from bat or batu - the shortened forms of baetyl - a (sacred) stone. The associated myths with heroes and deities are so very many and are so closely related to those traditions in India to the North West and Melanesia, Polynesia and South and Central America that they will be considered as two separate chapters. Another element that appears peculiar to the Australians is that of the "incomplete humans" who required "cutting" to be made complete.

Increase Rituals - Incomplete Humans - The Inapertwa
The "incomplete humans" among the Aborigines were said to come into existence by the emergence of "eggs" from sacred stones that were usually "found" or placed at the foot of trees or at the base of rock outcrops or faces in Central Australia. The Witchetty Grub people of the Arunta tribe exemplify the tradition belief that child spirits emerge from stones and whom the Alcheringa, or mythical people of the Dreamtime, were said to carry in their bodies. Spencer and Gillan recorded the myths one of which states: "The Alcheringa Udnerringita (Witchetty Grub) people, both men and women, are supposed to have been full of eggs, which are now represented by rounded water-worn stones" ... "...a gaunt old gum tree, with a large projecting bole about the middle of the trunk, indicates the exact spot where an Alcheringa man, who was very full of eggs, arose when he transformed out of a witchetty grub ..."[371]. These Witchetty grub men in the

mythic age were said to be able to perform "increase" rituals in a cave called the Ilthura oknira, or the great Ilthura. During these rites he (Intwailinka Alcheringa head of the Witchetties) performed the ceremony called Intichiuma, the object of which was then, as at the present day, to increase the number of the Udnirrigita grub on which he and his companions fed[372]. These "eggs" were believed to develop into incomplete humans without a laval stage in some cases. Those of the Fire Totem had a myth where the Inapertwa creatures developed from sparks as noted: "In the Alcheringa a spark of fire (urinchitha) ascended into the sky at Ura-puncha (Inca Punchao = spark = Sun - see later in this work), the place of fire, which was far away in the north, and was blown by the north wind to a spot, and by a large mountain also called Urapuncha, or Mount Hay. Here it fell to earth and a great fire sprang up which by and by subsided, and from the ashes came out some Inapertwa creatures - the ancestors of the people of the fire totem."[373]. Some of these Inapertwa were said to have been born locally as incomplete creatures but in other cases they migrated into the territories of the various tribes[374]. Among the Kaitish tribes these incomplete humans were called "inter-intera" and in one of their myths two boys (eaglehawks) were born out of eggs and who grew up migrating to the north. The deity Atnatu, a "black-faced" deity without an anus sent down from the sky a large stone knife - a "leilira", with which they could circumcise themselves "to make themselves men"[375].

The identification of eaglehawks as mythical tribal heroes will be of interest later but the point of interest in these myths is that increase rituals were associated with the production not only of game and other food animals but also of human kind. The use of sacred stones for increase rituals is usual among the Australian Aborigines because it is believed that the sacred rocks themselves were the place at which the ancestor of the animal they were trying to increase was the final form it took as it sank into the ground for the last time. By rubbing or pulverising chips from these stones it was believed that an increase in the descendants of these animals would take place. By rubbing certain of the corresponding stones it was also believed possible to increase kurunba, more or less equivalent to the Melanesian mana, and the Jarapiri mythical serpent would fly into the air[376]. Stones were not the only focus of increase rituals - the rituals associated with water increase or rain-making were critical in the woodlands and dry interior of Australia and took many forms, one of which Howitt notes: "There is a spot at Lake Victoria, in the Narrinyeri country, where when the water is, at long intervals, exceptionally low, it causes a tree-stump to become visible. This is in the charge of a family, and it is the duty of one of the men to anoint it with grease and red ochre. The reason for this is that they believe that if it is not done the lake would dry up and the supply of fish be lessened. This duty is hereditary from father to son."[377]. Many stones including the sacred churingas were anointed by grease and red ochre and similar rituals are found widely outside of Australia, particularly in Aboriginal India.

Among the Mara tribe of North Central Australia Spencer and Gillan note their ritual; "...they can, if they care to do so, secure the increase by means of magic. The Mara tribe have certain ceremonies for this purpose which they call gunlungun-paiatjula. On the banks of the Baramundi Creek, close to the Limmen River, there is a large heavy stone representing a very big honey bag, which was carried about by the old ancestor of the totem, and left there on the spot where he finally went down into the ground. The Murungan and Mumabli men, who form the half of the tribe to which the honey-bag totem belongs, can increase the number of the bees and therefore of the honey supplies by striking off the stone and blowing it about in all directions: this scattered powder gives rise to bees."[378]. The name of the Murungun men sounds as if it has associated with Murrugan or Mungan already noted and apparently derived from the Tamil god of South India.

In India, inevitably among the Gonds, increase rituals were also found into last century. To increase the produce from an agricultural plot, after the land was cleared, at the foot of the

Saja tree, a stone was set up against it root and an egg placed upright on its top. The priest squatted before the stone with the egg to the right of it and the headman to the left. The men put their hands together palm to palm, touched the ground below the egg with them then raised them to their foreheads while uttering a mantram or sacred formula[379]. It should be remembered that one of the increase rituals above noted in Australia involved eggs and rituals of this Gond type, for fertility or agricultural increase were common throughout Indonesia.

The breadth of the Classical education received these early researchers gave them great advantages in India were they quickly perceived the close parallels in the local customs and beliefs systems to those in Eurasia - the same was true for early Australia. Among the Aboriginal tribes of India R.V. Russell records of the increase rituals: "Before sowing the crops, a common practice is to sow small quantities of grain in baskets or pots in rich soil, so that it will sprout and grow up quickly, the idea being to ensure that the real crop will have a similarly successful growth. These baskets are the well-known Gardens of Adonis fully described in the Golden Bough. They are grown for nine days, and on the tenth day are taken in procession by the women and deposited in a river. The women may be seen carrying the baskets of wheat to the river after nine days fasts of Chait and Kunwar (March and September) in many towns of the Central Provinces, as the Athenian women carried the Gardens of Adonis to the sea on the day the expedition under Nicias set sail for Syracuse. The fire kindled at the Holi festival in spring is meant," ....., "to increase the power of the sun for the growth of vegetation. By the production of fire the quantity and strength of the heavenly fire is increased. He (Sir James Frazer) remarks: - 'The red powder thrown over everybody at the Holi is said to represent the seed of life ...'"[380].

It will be obvious from the above myths that baskets and net bags are also of importance in these rituals and are accounted for among the stones necessary to produce increase in both India and Australia. Red ochre is therefore a critical factor in many of the customs of the Aboriginals of India but also the Hindu Aryans whose ancestors entered India early in the first millennium B.C. The red ochre is of equal importance to the Australian Aborigines in their increase rituals as indicated by rubbing the exposed tree stump for water but particularly so for their most sacred of stones - the churingas.

The Sacred Churingas of Aboriginal Central Australia

The marriage and clan laws of the Australian Aborigines were usually strictly enforced and inheritance was more often through the female line than not. In Central Australia a man may inherit his sacred stone or churinga through his deceased elder sister but never the younger one[381], in other cases it is handed from father to son[382]. When a child was born it was the mother who named the place where the child "germ" or spirit entered her and it was here that a brother, father or other close male relative searched for the child's personal stone. It was believed absolutely that at conception the child's spirit dropped a stone at this place and it was believed to exist there regardless of whether it could be found or not. If not found a wooden one with sacred designs was substituted and this was made from the Mulga or other hardwood nearest to the Nanja as the conception location was called[383]. The churinga was kept in the clan storehouse and should the owner fall ill a scrapping was taken from it and mixed with dust and water as a curative potion[384]. Some of the smaller wooden churingas had holes bored through them to act as bullroarers, but the stone ones that have been bored are never used in this way[385]. The churingas are periodically rubbed and polished with grease and red ochre but a myth from the Binbunga people indicate it was obtained in the Alcheringa, or mythical time, but the tradition was more probably imported by migrant peoples. Spencer and Gillan record this belief: "In the Bibinga tribe the origin of the Churinga is attributed to two Dingo men of the Alcheringa, who also first introduced the use of a stone knife at circumcision. They used to carry sacred sticks, which they called 'watu-murra' under their arms during the day, but placed them on their heads at night."[386]. The term watu has been noted before as deriving from the stone traditions of Indonesia; India and the Middle East and where it is also noted as being occasionally transferred to wooden substitutes as here. The name murra relates to another widely used term for spirit and will be of interest later.

Alphonse Riesenfeld noted the close similarities of the culture of the Australian Aborigines to that of New Caledonia[387]. Riesenfeld quotes Sarasin who indicated that the designs exhibited in the petroglyphs of New Caledonia "…seem related to the drawings and carvings on the Australian stone churingas"[388]. The hero or deity name of Atnatu above related to the "eagle-hawk" boys and their stone knife is found widely in the Pacific Ocean as Anute; Anutu, Anuto, Anu-tuat all derived from or closely related to the term Atua in Polynesia and Fiji[389]. The last deity name - Anu-tuat combines two names for the sky and underworld, Anu for the sky in the ancient Middle East and Tuat as the Underworld in ancient Egypt. Other names such as Sina, the Moon god in Sumeria and Akkad and "Ra" as the ancient Sun god of Egypt and Samoa suggest that Fornander was correct in tracing them back from Polynesia to Western Asia and the Nile regions. There are many cross-cultural references between Melanesia, Polynesia and Central America and it is sufficient to note here that the churingas being stored in a separate clan house seems to be paralleled to a degree by sacred stones called Chichic, Huanca or Chacrayoc in the rafters of houses in Peru noted by Father Pablo Arriaga in the 16th., century and stones and trees will be subjects of interest in due course in a separate chapter[390].

Linguistic Influences in Aboriginal Australia

It was clear to the Victorian researchers, mostly self-motivated interested parties, from the beginning of the nineteenth century - two centuries ago, that there had been incursions from Indonesia into in the north west half of Australia and that there were close cross-cultural elements from Melanesia and Polynesia permeating that of the south eastern half. The hero and deity names have clearly indicated this to be so throughout this chapter and this is true also as recorded by the same authors in extensive writings recording that the native languages in both halves reflected those influences. More recent researchers have played down or denied cultural incursions insisting that the culture of the Aborigines was entirely indigenous but this is a romantic fiction that was generated to justify their own preconceptions, although such denials are not entirely modern[391]. Some of the earliest researchers in fact took the comparisons much further than South East Asia and Melanesia-Polynesia. James Bonwick quoting J. R. Logan in 1870 stated: " 'The first person, I, is rendered: Chinese ngo; West Australian, nga-nag and nga-nya; New South Wales, nga-toa; Adelaide, ngaityo; Encounter Bay, nga-pe; Port Lincoln, ngai; Murray, ngappo; Murrumbidgee, naddo; Lower Murray, Ngapa; Hunter's River, ngatoa; Khond of India, na-na; Malayan, nga-n; Tamil, ya-na; Santal, inge; Sunda, aing; Timor, ani; Sumba, ngu-nga; Formosa, ina; Thibet, nga; Burmese, ngai; Korea, nai; Sioux, ne; Shoshone, of West America, ni; and Chinook Indian, nai."[392]. It is interesting to note that Khond (Gond), Tamil and Santal are all in India and Santal is one of the Aboriginal tribes along with the Khond who are of such importance to this study along with the Tibetan and Burmese peoples nearby and long in contact with them.

Bonwick further records Logan quoting him directly recording that: " 'In Australia', continues Mr. Logan, 'the pronominal roots are compounded with definitives, singular and plural, with the numeral 'two' to form duals, with masculine and feminine definitives in the third person, and in all the three persons with each other; thus producing not only absolute and relative plurals of the first person, but several other complex plurals'. It is singular that the Hottentot should also, have a double plural, one common and one particular, and a double first person plural. Mr. Logan connects the language saying: 'The Draviro-Australian or Archaic Indo-Asonesian pronomalous system, with its numerous distinct elements and combinations, appears to be more ancient, or less impaire, than most of the systems of other Harmonic formations of the Old World. From its general structure it must be considered as cognate with proto-Scythic, or Scythico-American. It is richer than Scythic, which has neither sexual forms, nor any plurals save the ordinary generic ones.'"

" ' .... The Draviro-Australian is not, however, derived from the Tibeto-Ultraindian, but each had an independent connexion with an archaic Midasiatic system - Chinese in roots, and Scythic in form, etc. ....'"[393].

From the beginning of contact with the Australian Aborigines scholars such as Logan soon "broke the code" since there were recognisable parallels that were obvious in other languages and could be categorised into known systems. In the history of India the Scythic peoples were known intruders and some castes claimed descent from them into last century, although their intrusions had occurred two thousand years or more ago. This had left an imprint along with others in the various languages of India and, as noted, it is significant that there are also links to the Gonds. Another element is the connection with the Hottentots of Southern Africa since a belief that there were Negroid elements in the Australian Aboriginal population occurs a number of times among these researchers. It is also of interest that the very specific element of genital mutilation at the marriage of a young man - the removal of a testicle, is found in Ethiopia/Somalia, probably anciently in India, and in the Caroline Islands into last century[394]. It is such an unusual form of initiation that it could only have been conveyed by mariners travelling over half the latitudes of the Earth to establish it in those Micronesian islands. The geographical distance from Southern Africa, and the island of Madagascar in particular, is a very much shorter sea journey assisted from West to East by very strong sea currents and prevailing winds, the Roaring Forties, and would seem entirely feasible to such mariners (*2.004*).

Howitt quotes Dr. R. M. Latham who concluded in 1882 that: " '...the Tasmanian language had affinities with both the Australian and New Caledonian languages, but in a stronger degree with the latter'. This, he considered, will at once explain the points of physical contrast between the Tasmanian tribes and those of Australia, and will indicate that the stream of population for Van Dieman's Land ran round Australia rather than across it.'"[395]. Others noted that there were connections between the South Australian natives and those of Tasmania[396] and from South Australia with extreme Western Australia[397]. If these connections are correct then Latham's perceptions would appear to be justified. Researches into language and anthropometry in those early days saw Tasmanians as being related to the broad distribution of "Oceanic Negritoes". Of particular note is that they were related to the Andaman Islanders, who also red-ochred their hair along with the Tasmanians, as well as to the Semang of Malaya and the extinct Kalangs of Java[398]. The connections in this most extremely isolated region of Australia with a wider field of contact is noted by Dr. Codrington, whose researches into Melanesia culture are still useful to this day, whom Howitt quotes: "Dr. Codrington conclusively shows that the elements which are common to them and the Malay have not been derived from the latter, but are common to all the ocean languages, from the Malagasy in the west to the Hawaiian in the east and the Maori in the south. He says, further, that this indicates an original oceanic stock language from which the Polynesian, Melanesian, and Malay tongues have derived their common elements, which is now extinct and of which the Malay is one of the younger descendants. The presence of certain words in the ancient ocean languages testifies that the speakers made canoes, built houses, cultivated gardens, before the time when their posterity branched off on their way to Madagascar and Fiji."[399]. This substratum of a primal oceanic language may not be acceptable to all authorities but the broader cultural affinities are recognised from even this early time between the northerly and easterly extremes of Polynesia to Madagascar off the east coast of Africa. There may have been, therefore, mariner-based traders who transferred populations, possibly in large numbers as workers or slaves from the east coast of Africa to Australia or perhaps more likely to Polynesia or Melanesia via the considerably shorter crossing to Southern Australia.

The Australians may then have been an admixture of an indigenous or naturalised veddoid or negrito population, Africans, Melanesians and Polynesians, along with Tamils and Gonds from India. Howitt suggests that the Tasmanians were in fact the original indigenous or naturalised inhabitants of Australia and then mixed with, or were expunged by a later people. He notes: "The occupation of the continent by the Australians who, it may be reasonably held, were in a somewhat higher state of culture and who were better armed than the Tasmanians, must have resulted in the amalgamation of the two races, either by the subjection of the latter, or, what is more likely from what we know of the Australians of the present day, by the extermination of the former inhabitants, at least so far as regarded the males, and the absorption of the females into conquering tribes."

"At any rate, whatever the process may have been, the result of a strong negroid cross in the Australians may be accepted"[400]. This agrees in principle with others at the time such as E.M. Curr and Mr. Hyde Clarke[401], while either such as Professor Huxley and Dr. Topinard perceived a close connection with the Deccan in South Central India as a result of migrations[402]. Others such as Reverend John Mathews recognised the view that the languages of the North West half of Australia reflected influences from the Malays but one of the main purposes of his book, "Eaglehawk and Crow", was to show "conclusively" that, "… the main stream of population entered Australia on the north-east and crossed in a south-westerly direction"[403].

This southern route direct from the Red Sea and Ethiopian region and West Asia via Madagascar or direct seems to be confirmed by the reed canoes found in these areas being similar to those of Tasmania and New Zealand but none were found around the coast of mainland Australia. The identical reed canoes appear to be the prototypes of those found on Lake Titicaca and the Peruvian Coast and complete the round-the-world linkage by being transferred from there to New Zealand and the Maoris were clearly in contact with Tasmania (*2.025; 2.028*). Washthrough rafts called Keleks along with wash-through canoes used similar principles in punts to carry cargo across rivers and appear to be the prototypes of those found in New Zealand among the Morioris and in South America, as well as on the coast of India as the catamaran.

In considering the opinions and research results above noted it would certainly suggest that there are connections from Africa and Madagascar by the sea route to the South West corner of Australia and then to the South Australian coast to Victoria and Tasmania. But is almost certainly true that there are also the other, perhaps more importantly, routes by which Australia was subjected from outside to its shores from India, the South East Asia mainland, the Indonesian islands, Melanesia and Polynesia. It must also be considered as to whom the mariners were who enabling these voyages and populations, large or small, to travel between islands and continents over vast distances and periods of time, and their destinations.

CHAPTER 2

MARINERS and MIGRATIONS from AUSTRALIA to SOUTH AMERICA via SOUTH POLYNESIA

Ancient Contacts Between Aboriginal Australia and New Zealand

For any of the islands of the Pacific Ocean to be inhabited the mariners must have been skilled in navigation and boat-building to have crossed from the continental masses of Asia and between the islands themselves, many being hundreds of miles apart. For the routes from the south east of the Australian continent to New Zealand to be connected the mariners must have been the equal to those in modern times but using less developed techniques in navigation and construction. The distance from South East Australia to New Zealand is over one thousand miles (1600km) of often-turbulent ocean. In examining the ocean currents it becomes clear why the cultural influences were so clearly detected by the early Victorians between the Australian Aborigines in South East Australia and the Maoris. Because the British settlements were naturally located in the most fertile regions for agriculture since these were the areas with highest rainfall. The most fertile land occurs along the east coast but particularly in the temperate south-east and along the eastern half of the south coast from the Great Australian Bight along with Tasmania. A relatively small area in the southwest tip of Western Australia had a Mediterranean climate and it was not long before this too was settled by the British. The south-eastern regions received much more attention in terms of cross-Pacific contacts as a result of these settlements and accessibility and their aspect to the Pacific region became more accentuated - this interest in the Pacific region being retained into the present day.

The South Equatorial current sweeps across the Central Pacific Ocean from the Peruvian coast of South America directly through Southern Polynesia, Melanesia and washes the North East Australian coast (*2.004*). Part of this current forces its way through the Torres Straits between the north tip of the Australian state of Queensland and the south coast of New Guinea. The Melanesians therefore have a broad, clearly defined sea route from all of their islands to the North East Australian coast and tends to support claims for cultural and linguistic filtration from there. However a substantial southern section of the South Equatorial Current splits of and takes an oblique route further to the south and connects the southern Polynesian islands with the south east coast of Australia and this is called the East Australian current. This powerful current sweeps the east coast of the continent southward before being forcibly confronted by the enormity of the West Wind Drift of the Antarctic Ocean and then more or less ricochets up in a loop washing both the west coast and east coasts of the main islands of New Zealand. Should any fisherman-mariner in a sea-worthy canoe have drifted away from the coast of South East Australia or Tasmania he would end up in most cases on the coast of New Zealand. For Polynesians to have reached New Zealand from their main tropical islands to the north east they would have had to have crossed, or tacked, the main East Australian Current on its return journey to Polynesia including Easter Island - there is no direct current to this island except from South America. It becomes clear why the early Victorian researchers noted so many cultural cross-references between New Caledonia, Fiji with those of the East Coast of Australia and the island of Tasmania since this current provided a conveyor as a direct marine highway from these islands to this long eastern coast of Australia.

This point is of some interest since the Maori people of New Zealand and their predecessors as occupiers of those islands reflect in their physical make-up and, or in their myths, legends and cultural influences certain aspects suggesting that these southern sea currents have played a very major part in Oceanic history[1]. The long accepted principle behind direct voyages in canoes from Central Polynesia, or in their legends, Hawaiiki - the Polynesian homeland, becomes less mythical and more legendary and historical in considering the reality of these ocean currents. It has long been accepted that there are elements of the Melanesian in the physical con-

2.001 : Child with naturally red-hair characteristic of many parts of Melanesia. For others limed hair emulated the fair-haired legendary ancestors. Bungi Island, New Guinea, Melanesia, Early 20th., century, A.D.

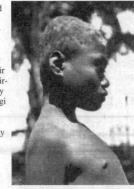

2.002 : Fair and straight hair is common in children among many of the Australian Aboriginal tribes indicating a Caucasian descent and known to be related to the Ainu of Japan. Central Australia, Late 19th., century, A.D.

stitution of the Maori beside the fundamental Polynesian but it is also known that there are aspects of the Sepik region of New Guinea that reflects strongly in Maori art and these in turn appear to be a diffusion from Southern China. To this might then be added Australian contacts or infusions, perhaps only limited, but with the South East Australians such as the Kurnai and Yuin in particular since there are distinct aspects of cultural traits reflective of the Polynesian among them.

In Maori legends the islands making up New Zealand were said to be occupied by more than one "fair-skinned" race when they first arrived around a thousand years ago. A people called by them pakepakeha were said to exist there as well as the blond-haired Turehu, who lived in the Urewera mountains. It is said that the Turehu subdued the former possessors of the South Island called the Tutumaiao who before them had subjected the Kui. These last were said to have been granted the land by Maui the great Polynesian volcanic deity said to have "fished-up" the islands. Another of these fair-haired, fair-skinned people was called the Karitehe who were driven out into the forests and caves but who intermarried with the newcomers and disappeared as an independent people[2]. It is from the term pakepakeha that the term pakeha is derived and was, and is usually now applied by the Moaris to denote the white Europeans settlers from when they first appeared in the islands a century and a half ago. This is consistent with the many traditions of white mariners, traders and migrants in Polynesia, Melanesia and Australia who are recognisably white people in earlier eras among them and the inhabitants of those regions were able to apply existing terms when the Europeans arrived. This belies attempts to identify such terms with whites, particularly in Australia, and in the Amazon, with the white flesh of broiled bodies human carcases in Aboriginal rituals earlier mentioned, or among the Melanesians or even among the Maoris themselves who were noted celebrating similar practices.

The people called the Patu-Paiarehe are the focus of some of the most interesting myths and legends in Maori New Zealand. It is said that they had fair or blond hair and that they only emerged from the gloom of the forests and caves where they were said to hide. They were credited with the construction of hill forts and occupied the larger part of the North Island. The stature of these Patu-Paiarehe was likened to that of giants, and even in one legend a giantess, named Kurangaituku, carried off a Moari man called Hatu-Patu - a name that will be of interest later. Of particular note are the references to the fact that they were not only white-skinned and blond-haired but also wore white cloth. It was believed by some that these people had albino fathers and, it is significant therefore, that one of their tribes was called Ngati-korako or "the children of the albino"[3].

In considering Maori ancestry it is notable that they recognised the special descent of those who had their own traditional designation - Uru-Kehu, who were those who were considered fortunate in being born with the colour hair identified with the ancient, revered ancestors - that is blond,

2.003 : A Maori family showing full-blooded parents with their Uru-Kehu son reflecting the fair or red hair of their legendary ancestors. New Zealand, Late 19th., century, A.D.

2.004 : An unusual view of the world called the Zenith projection but ideal for showing the circular west-to-east flow of the West Wind Drift - or Roaring Forties as they are more usually known, indicated by the lighter coloured arrows. This more clearly indicates the probable use of this ocean current being a considerably shorter distance between the southern tips of three continents - Africa, Australia and South America. This could be used as a "fast track conveyor" between these continents and nearby islands and would account for such close similarities in cultural expression between the Australian Aborigine and the Ona of South America facilitated by the Maoris and perhaps others. The darker arrows indicate the mariners' routes utilising the ocean currents to assist them in spanning the oceans and why Madagacsar is found to reflect aspects of the cultures of the Ancient Middel East, India, Indonesia and Polynesia and the dispersion of some aspects of African culture into West Australia. The highest route follows the Equator using the Equatorial Counter Current across the Pacific giving direct access from Asia to Central America to Ecuador.

light brown or red. This corresponds to the Maori adage - "Red Hair - Chief's Hair"[4]. Clearly the many references and the reflection of physical hereditary in the present-day people of light-skin, particularly at birth and in their hair colour, cannot be accidental and must indicate contact with Caucasian races who entered Oceania before the Europeans and mixed with those peoples already in the islands. It should also be considered that the Maoris were themselves the mariners, whether they commenced on the Asian mainland or not, and proceeded into the Pacific, cohabiting along the way with these many and various island peoples. Typically the mariner fathers departed but often returned, perhaps years later, to collect their mixed race sons to accompany them in their further peregrinations before settling in New Zealand. There is much to suggest that this was the age-old principle that had existed between Asia and Oceania for millennia, at least from the Lapita time up until a century or two before the Europeans entered the Pacific region.

In South West Australia there are elements suggesting contact with Madagascar and East Africa from early times and this influence is notable along the South Australian coast to Victoria in South East Australia. From the delta of the Murray, Murrumbidgee and Darling River system eastwards the Polynesian influences become more apparent along with elements clearly linked to India. The most logical connection considering the ocean currents and prevailing winds from the west, is that mariners or traders operated, if only occasionally, from South Asia via Madagascar. This large island off the East Coast of Africa has strong cross-cultural references with the Ancient Middle East and India but also Polynesia (*2.004*). Mariners returning from Madagascar via the West Wind Drift to the South West corner of Western Australia, sail off the southern coast to South East Australia before entering the Pacific. This is a distance of less than

2000 miles (3200km), being no more than the direct journey across the Indian Ocean probably undertaken from Indonesia to Madagascar, and the East Coast of Africa, assisted by the direction of the sea currents and prevailing winds (the "Roaring Forties"). From South Western Australia there was little problem in coastal hopping to the relative calm of the South Australian harbours before sailing further east to the Kurnai territory around Port Philip Bay and the Yarra River. The journey to Cape Howe, the most south-easterly point in Australia would present little problem for seasoned mariners before enduring the excitement of the East Australian Current as it veers dramatically eastward after its journey south along the East Coast of Australia toward New Zealand. This undertaking, for mariners entering the Pacific from South East Australia, usually means being buffeted for all the thousand miles by the West Wind Drift and the westerlies of the Roaring Forties before reaching New Zealand.

The First New Zealanders - the Moriori; Maruini; Maruiwi or Maiaurli

The first peoples known for certain to have inhabited the New Zealand islands were the Moriori, a Polynesian people, and therefore related to, and predating the Maoris in this southern land. The Maoris themselves were believed to have come from Tahiti, and on entering New Zealand or Aeteoroa (Land of the Long White Cloud) as they called it, were confronted, as their traditions relate, not with a people who resembled themselves, that is another Polynesian people - the Moriois, but "...black, and that their culture was extremely primitive"[5]. The early British researchers in New Zealand saw clearly ·from first contact with the surviving Moriori in the Chatham Islands that their culture "...was not in any way more primitive than that of the Maoris. And since a series of investigations in Moriori craniology had shown that the Morioris were in no degree less Polynesian than the Maoris, it became evident that Maori traditional account, was not in consonance with the facts, and that an examination of all other lines of evidence was called for"[6]. Another traditional version, written down by a Maori named T. Whatahoro notes; "In the Maori version the Moriori are stated to be a fugitive section of the original inhabitants of New Zealand, to whom the name Maruiwi is usually applied. The country of their origin, which was larger than New Zealand, lay to the southwest of it. Their ancestors, while out fishing in canoes, had been caught by a storm and driven before it till they reached New Zealand"[7].

Whatahoro's accounts stimulated some discussion and controversy and Skinner notes: " 'But the difficulties presented by these points are small compared with those raised by the physical characteristics of Maruiwi. One authority, quoting Whatahoro's material says; 'They were very dark-skinned folk of repulsive appearance, tall, spare, and spindle-shanked, having flat noses, with turned-up nostrils: in some cases the nostrils seemed to be all the nose. They had flat faces and overhanging eyebrows. They were big-boned people, and they had curious eyes, like those of a lizard. An idle folk and a chilly, who felt the cold much, and slept anyhow: they were of a treacherous disposition. They did not preserve their traditions as we do'"[8]. It is of interest therefore to note that these Morioris actually buried their dead facing due west towards the ancient homeland and this would tend to suggest that they had come in the last leg of their journey from South East Australia and that the description in fact was of Australian Aborigines rather than the Moriori themselves. This view tends to be reflected in those who were interested in the Moriois and their origins since it is clear that the Maruiwi, where even the name appears antecedent to their later name given to them by the Maoris, is found in Australia.

The Maoris have described the Morioris as a "fugitive" section and indicates a known trait among the Polynesians that, when defeated in battle or in some other way rejected by the society or rulers of their homeland, were banished - if they were lucky. The most common fate was that all opponents in battle were massacred to the last man and if a battle threatened it was usual for canoes to be set by for the express purpose of a judicious escape. Equally they may

2.005 : Traditional river raft characteristic in India from the earliest times into the twentieth century. Abor tribe, Dihang River, India, Early 20th., century, A.D.

2.006 : Ocean-going sail boat typical of early India from the late first millennium B.C. Cave 2, Ajanta, West Central India, 5-6th., century, A.D.

2.007 : Double hull canoe traditional for many centuries on the Godavari and Kistna Rivers in South Central East India similar to those found in Polynesia and on the North West Coast of North America. Central East India, Early 20th., century, A.D.

2.008 : Double hull canoe structure supporting a platform between the canoes with a hut providing a working platform but unsuitable for ocean-going travel and restricted to riverine transport. Yalu River, Korea, Late 19th., century, A.D.

2.010 : Treble-hull canoes traditional in the East Central Coast of India and closely similar to those of the Indians of North West Coast of North America. Godavari River, East Central India, Early 20th., century, A.D.

have been the sea-going venturers who travelled from island group to island group and perhaps were in some way involved in sailing to Madagascar in the most ancient times. It is known that there had been Polynesian contact with Madagascar from Tahiti since terms found there are more related to the Tahitian language than those of other Polynesian groups are found there.

2.009 : Fine Burmese State Canoe almost certainly the model for the Polynesian funerary and ceremonial canoes. Pegu, Burma, 19th., century, A.D.

It has been recognised that some of the origins still recognisable in the Maori language have been added to the largely Malayo-Polynesian linguistic family. Nigel Heseltine noted, regarding the Maori language that; "Other ethnic and cultural elements have been supplied by immigrants from Africa and Arabia, but these are all subordinated to a Malayo-Polynesian cultural and linguistic unity"[9]. This would seem to augment the linguistic evidence found in Madagascar for Tahitian origins and support the view that these Polynesian mariners crossed to South West Australia, then to South East Australia to enter the Pacific to reach New Zealand. He further notes that the Polynesian term for a woman, vahine, is found in Madagascar among other cultural intrusions[10]. The Polynesians were great mariners and the sea was in their blood and during the three months that Captain James Cook spent in Tahiti observing the transit of Venus he recorded in his journal that he was approached every day by young Tahitian men begging to be allowed to sail with him[11]. In the event one did, a not so young priest named Tupua and his servants, since he was very much out of favour with the king and Cook had little doubt that he would not survive long after his expedition had left the island. This resembles one of the personal escapes that was traditional in war as noted but must have applied also to individuals and fami-

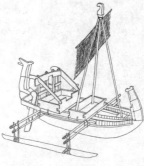

2.012 : Model of a single hul with reed sail and outrigger and upturned prows characteristic of Ancient Middle East and the ree canoes of the Moche. Moluccas Indonesia, Mid-19th., century, A

2.015 : Stick navigation chart acteristically used in ancient time throughout Polynesia and Micro Marshall Islands, North Central Polynesia, Late 19th., century, A

2.011 : Fine ocean-going ceremonial canoes with priest in ritual robes similar to those found among South Indian "devil-dancers". Tahiti, Eastern Polynesia, Late 18th., century, A.D.

2.013 : Large ocean-going war canoe - "waka taua", with traditional raised prow probably evolved from early India or the Ancient Middle East illustrated during Captain Cook's voyage to New Zealand. Maori, New Zealand, 1769 A.D.

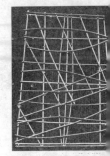

2.014 : One of several types ditional Samoan double hull car showing the elevated viewing p form reserved for the Ariki or s captain. Manu'a, Central Polyn Late 19th., century, A.D.

ly groups. There are numerous myths relating these escapes but for this purpose it is only important to note that the Morioris were considered fugitive and it was probable that they had arrived from the west after some lengthy contact, perhaps some generations, on the Australian mainland.

The Morioris, even if as fugitives, may have arrived on the Australian coast via the Madagascar route, perhaps on trading or even slaving missions to East Africa, or perhaps this was a known "fast track" return route to Polynesia from that distant continent after visiting India. It is a viable return journey even from West Asia to return to Polynesia by this route and there appears to have references in their myths and legends to confirm this to be noted later. The most acceptable cultural incursions into Australia by some mariners would be that from Tahiti and it is possible also that the Morioris reached Australia by the most direct means and that was by the East Australian Current flowing from South Polynesia through southern Melanesia to the East Australian coast. This is feasible since the broad background of cultural influences including the initiation ceremonies in Australia such as the Bora and Nanga clearly took this route. Having landed they spread out from the northern east coast inland along the Bowen, Darling and its tributary rivers down to the Murray River where they were directed south into Victoria and toward the South East corner of South Australia to the Murray delta.

Whether the Morioris took this inland route or followed the coast down to the southeast corner that exhibits many more of the Polynesian influences than other regions may never be known. It may be that if they had taken this option on one of their sea expeditions they met up with those already with some Polynesian descent in that cooler region who had come from Madagascar at an earlier period. What is more certain is that their influence, either by the Indian Ocean route around the bottom of the island continent to South East Australia from the west or the more obvious route direct to the east coast, left possible markers among the Australian Aborigines surviving for the Victorian researchers to record, albeit unknowingly.

In Australian Aboriginal myth associated with the ancestral people in the Alcheringa (Ularaka) mythical times, among the Urabunna people in Central Australia, there were two mythical snakes called Kurnwara. At a place called Mura-murara they left spirit children called Mai-aurli who were eventually born. The Kurnwara created all the mounds and springs during their wanderings giving the country its own peculiar topography[12]. It was also said that in the beginning half-human people lived in the Alcheringa or Ularaka and no one knows where they came from. These ancient semi-humans accompanied the Urabunna in their "walkabouts" in the territories occupied by them performing sacred ceremonies. The Ularaka men deposited spirit children, the mai-aurli, in rocks and other sacred places and these emerged to become men and women who formed the first totem groups among them[13].

Among the Yuin who occupied territory to the east of the Kurnai in South East Victoria the "incomplete beings" were called "Mura-urai"[14] and appear closely related to the spirit children of the Urabunna. It would also appear that the term Kurnwara probably derives or originates from Kurnai and corresponds to some of the myths earlier noted indicating that at least one of their migrations extended into the continent from the coast, or had common origins. In this region the Kulin greenstone quarries were a centre of production and distribution of materials for traditional axes. Considering the availability of the wide range of suitable materials for such a utilitarian implement it is clear that the greenstone was required more for ceremonial axes rather than for practical function[15]. It is of interest that they are a dual organisation tribe through a patrilineal descent and this will be of interest in a later section. It is probably no coincidence that greenstone was greatly revered throughout Polynesia, Melanesia through to the Americas and

2.017 : Fine sight of a double sail inter-island trading canoe constructed as a platform supported on a double canoe hull construction. New Guinea, Melanesia, Late 19th., century, A.D.

2.016 : Raft-like platforms extended across two canoes to for double-hull ocean-going vessels with sails were common in Polynesia. Samoa, Central Polynesia, 18th., century, A.D.

.018 : Log raft characteristic of traditional types found om the Indus civilisation into the twentieth century. Indus iver, Pakistan, Early 20th., century, A.D.

2.019 : Alia type traditional ocean-going Samoan double hull canoe. The elevated platform above the hut built on the crossbeam platform is for land and bird migration route spotting and scanning the horizon for land. Central Polynesian, Late 19th., century, A.D.

2.020 : Three views of a wash-through reed canoes, the Waka Puhara, characteristic of the Moriori people in New Zealand similar in principle to those of India and South America. Moriori, Chatham Islands, New Zealand, Late 19th., century, A.D.

probably derives from the same tradition.

In Rockingham Bay on the North East Australian coast it was early reported that ground ovens (umu) similar to those in Tahiti were discovered. Some were also found in Glenelg in modern-day Queensland and hundreds were found in Victoria[16]. In one place a mound 79 yards round were created with ovens in the centre that were later used for burial[17]. Of special interest is that the Victorians recorded that some of the South East Australians were noted making fire from the pith of the tree and the Fuegians of South America were known to use the same technique and this geographical distribution will be of interest in due course[18]. Interestingly also is that they also used a possum cape as their only clothing with a hole in the centre for the head exactly similar to a Andean poncho[19]. Known also to both Tasmanians and Fuegians was the deliberate sitting posture with the foot or heal concealing the individual's genitals[20].

Characteristically the Kurnai were a people with so many reflections of Polynesia and Howitt noted their first contacts with the first settlers in Port Philip in 1803. He records: "... A party who were surveying 'at the north-west point of the bay' were met by a number of natives, who, on a shot being fired over their heads, ran away a small distance, but soon approached again with the king, who wore a very elegant turban crown and was always carried upon the shoulders of the men. Whenever he desired them to halt, or to approach, they did it immediately"[21]. Howitt suggests that this may mean no more than that the king was unable to walk which is surprisingly for such an author since similar customs were known in Africa, Asia, Polynesia and South America. In Polynesia the Reverend William Ellis provides an illustration of a king being carried in the traditional manner reflecting that of the Kurnai (*2.033*).

2.021 : Men crossing a river on animal-skin floats traditional for thousands of years in the Ancient Middle East. Assyria, Early first millennium, B.C.

Among the Kulin (or Kurnai) the term for the bright colour of the sunset was Karalk and was said to be caused by the spirits of the dead going in and out of Ngamat. This was believed to be the receptacle of the Sun just beyond the edge of the earth[22]. It is of interest therefore that the Moriori term for the Sky World was Rangimat and was the region of heroes suggesting that the term Ngamat is simply a variation of the Moriori confirming their contacts with South East Australia[23]. It was believed by the Wurunjerri that the human spirit or ghost was called Ku-it-gil and among the Jajaurung was identified by them as Murup[24]. The term muru or mura is widely found relating to spirits and heroes in the mythical times and who were believed by the

2.023 : Gufa of the type from the long tradition known for over 6000 years in Mesopotamia. Iraq, Early 20th., century, A.D.

2.022 : Traditional skin-covered framed coracle typical of the Tsang Po, (Upper Brahmaputra). Tibet, Late 19th., century, A.D.

2.024 : Inflated animal skin floats characteristic on Asian rivers for millennia and also in Peru. Sutlej River, North India, Early 20th., century, A.D.

2.025 : Group of typical reed floats, one with reed sail, identical to those found in Maori New Zealand (2.028). Lake Titicaca, Bolivia, Early 20th., century, A.D.

2.026 : Assyrian conquest in Babylonia in the Tigris-Euphrates delta marshes. Note the tradtional reed boats identical to those in South America. Bas-relief, Ninevah, Assyria, 9-7th., century, A.D.

2.028 : Traditional Maori reed canoe identical to that of the Ancient Bolivian cultures located around Lake Titicaca reflecting the built-up form of the float called the Mokihi. New Zealand, Early 20th., century, A.D.

2.027 : Simplest form of the reed float, or Mohiki, found among the Maori and closely similar to that of Coastal Peru used from the most ancient times into the present day. New Zealand, Late 19th., century, A.D.

2.029 : Bound bark float identical in form and type as those of Maoris in New Zealand and in Bolivia. Tasmania, Southern Australia, Mid-19th., century, A.D.

2.030 : Reed float called a Mokihi with upturned prow characteristic of Polynesian designs and also found in South America. Maori, New Zealand, Early 20th., century, A.D.

Aborigines to have survived into recent centuries and this term will be of considerable interest in later chapters.

The Moari traditions states that when they entered New Zealand they defeated the resident Morioris and the last they saw of them were six canoes loaded with refugees fleeing in the direction of the South Island. Some of their descendants form a part of the Ngati-Mamoe tribe in the south of the South Island. Others settled in the Chatham Islands 600 miles to the east[25]. The very south of the South Island of New Zealand is the most likely first landfalls for those who sailed from South East Australia and suggests that these refugees who did not leave for the Chatham Islands in fact retired to a region already known and occupied by their kinsmen. Descriptions of their physical stature vary since, as a race, they became extinct in the late 19th., century. Among them, according to eyewitness accounts, were the Uru-Kehu, already noted of the Maoris with blonde hair or of a reddish tint[26]. Skinner quotes Hunt on their appearance who stated that they were "… somewhat akin to the Maoris in manners, customs, and language, but totally devoid of their energy, intelligence and ferocity, they are a people of middle stature, with almond shaped eyes and hooked noses: indeed they bear a most remarkable resemblance to the Jewish race"[27]. Skinner, writing in the early 20th., century, wrote: "The evidence as to Moriori physical characteristics which I was able to collect from settlers of the group (Chatham Islands) is as follows: 'Mr. Odman, of Waitangi, told me that when he came to the group in the 'sixties (1860's) there were a number of Morioris alive, and although rarely tall they were, on average, extremely big people. He could remember only one who would weigh less than 14 stone (196 pounds). His impression of unusual size was confirmed by other settlers. Mr. R. McClurg told me that most of the Morioris he remembered were like Maoris, but that there were some he could scarcely distinguish in features from old, smoke-dried Irishmen. Many years ago the late Alexander Shand told me that the Moriori men were broad-shouldered, deep-chested, and of great physical strength,..." etc.,[28].

A more detailed description of the Moriori is that of Baucke quoted by Skinner: "The distinctive physical appearance of the men of this type was the large head; coarse, inclined to close-curly hair; pent simian eyebrows, with rather protruding brown eyes; flat, or depressed nose bridge with bulbous lobes; wide mouth - in some, seeming to extend across the face; thick out-curved lips; short columnar neck; abnormal width across the shoulders; long body to the hips, with buttocks prominent; short thick thighs; out-curved globular knees, short legs with enormous calves and wide in-curved feet; not observably long arms, but fleshy, yet well-contoured; large forceful thick fingered hands - the whole giving the impression of slow power, but great endurance; presenting the appearance that the body upward of the hips seemed extraordinarily the longer half ..."

"The other, the northern type, included in their territory the remaining area; that is, the western round to the eastern shores of Te Wanga lake, and thence touching the irregular boundary of the southern tribe. This northern section of the race differed from the other in the predominating narrow Aztec face; the pinched high-ridged down-curving nose; the less pented eyebrows; the straighter finer, occasionally lighter hair; the taller less massive body-trunk; the less pronounced muscle bulge of the arms and calves - in some, especially the women, appearing as taperless cylindrical props; the feet, still incurved, sickle-shaped, but narrow; also physically robust, shown by the prevalent cough, indicating pthysis and pulmonary affliction; the disposition of the men morose, giving the impression of decaying vitality, of frustrated endeavour and careless of the consequence ..." etc.[29].

2.031 : Canoe carved relief illustrating the flood myth from the Ancient Vedic Aryan myths. Sanchi, North Central India, 200 B.C. - 200 A.D.

These descriptions of the Moriois are largely from eyewitness accounts of a people long defeated by the Maoris and for the most part living in exile in the Chatham Islands - a place of limited opportunities. For the most part they appear to have many common features - that they were stocky, often tall, and yet at once an impressive people. Interestingly Baucke's description suggests that the variations in physical type was a result of a Semitic, Jewish, or even as he suggests an Aztec element incursive into the main stock and similar suggestions are made of the Maoris themselves and evident in the numerous sketches and photos available from the 19-20th., century. The possible link with an American people is also interesting since there are elements in the Moriois culture that suggests contacts from South America with Easter Island as a "stepping stone".

Some observers have seen negroid traits among the Polynesians, more particularly among the Hawaiians but Skinner notes that there was an apparent lack of infusion from negroid sources[30]. In the craniology and osteology of the skeletons studied it was noted that Polynesian strains among the Moriori was predominant but Dr. H. Poll reported elements in the skulls indicating a relation to "Tasmanian stock"[31]. The Tasmanian connection, and the fact that the people in the extreme south of the island where the East Australian

2.032 : Carrying a highborn clan chief or ruler on the shoulders was a tradition found in Polynesia and South East ·Australia as well as widely in Asia and also in Central America. Basalt, Barriles, Chiriqui, Panama, 300 B.C.- 300 A.D.

2.033 : The first Europeans in Polynesia noted that those of highest status were shouldered as a mark or respect - the same tradition in South East Australia and parts of Asia and Central America. Tahiti, First half of the 19th., century, A.D.

Current washes directly from South East Australia and Tasmania onto that region of New Zealand occupied by the Moriori suggests that some Australian Aboriginal racial infusion took place confirming the craniological researches. This also confirms the legends stating the Maruiwi homeland was indeed, in part, in the west in South East Australia after migrating there from Polynesia. This tends to be confirmed in Moriori legend where it was noted that they had come from a larger land than New Zealand[32]. This could not have been any of the other Polynesian or Melanesian islands since they are all much smaller except for New Guinea to the far northwest. It is therefore also notable that the Moriori kept stones wrapped in a mat much as some of the Australian Aboriginals did with their sacred stones - the Churingas[33] (*1.053*).

The term Australian term Ngau may relate to the New Zealand name Ngati prefixing the tribal name Ngati-Mamoe who were a tribe among the Moriori, and among the Wotjo-Baluk of South Eastern Australia the Ngaui clan had a second name - Ngau-na-guli meaning "Men of the Sun"[34]. Among early researchers in the early 20th., century there were several prominent members who supported the diffusion of the Egyptian and Middle Eastern solar cults into the Pacific Islands and the Moriori could well have qualified for one of their standard bearers. It has been shown in the previous chapter that there are many related forms of this prefix, and also its derivatives and applications, throughout Australia but extending from East Africa though South Asia, Indonesia and into the Pacific region. The Maori author, Sir Peter Buck - Te Rangi Hiroa, noted in his recorded traditions that one of the leading tribes in Mangaia, in Central Polynesia, was the Ngati Mana'une who were probably the Hawaiian Menehune and Tahitian Manahune whom Fornander identifies as probably from the Nile region in Ancient Egypt. He further suggests that the legendary tangata whenua in New Zealand were probably descended from them[35]. It should not be surprising therefore to find that the Moriori considered themselves as Men of the Sun.

The Sun was central to Moriori cosmology and of particular interest is that their term preserved the old form of Polynesian name - Ra, the name of the Sun in ancient Egypt. The Supreme deities were:

> Wai-o-Rangi - father of the Tami-te-Ra - the Sun god
> Ra's wives - Hine-ate (morning),
> Hine-aotea (noon),
> Hina-ahiahi (evening)[36].

Rangi was the sky god throughout Polynesia while Ra as the Sun was still extant in Samoa with submerged references elsewhere. Hine, or Hina, usually relates to the Moon with Sina is found as the alternative in Samoa, and where Sina is also the name of the Moon god in the ancient Middle East. The term is also found among hero names such as Sina Kwao in the Solomon Islands where this title means "shining bright" relating to the Moon also. This hero is probably the Polynesian hero or god Sina-Loa and where the same name is found on the coast of Western Pacific Coast Mexico later adopted as a state name. The references to the Sun in Moriori culture were focused through the final rites in death where a dying man's head was cradled by a person who points to the Sun and says:

> "Ascend direct above.
> To the beams of the sun,
> To the rays of the morning,
> Thou, O son, grandchild of Waiorangi;
> Ascend direct, ascend direct above
> To Hikurangi, to Rarotonga,
> To the source, to the sun,
> To Whangamatata, the gate of Rangiriri;
> Ascend direct, ascend direct thither.
> To the cold, to the cold, to the cold,
> Ascend direct, ascend direct thither.
> Thou art severed, thou art separated,
> Ascend direct, ascend direct above.
> To the first heaven, to the second heaven,
> Ascend direct, ascend direct above.
> To the third heaven, to the fourth heaven,
> Ascend direct, ascend direct above.
> To the fourth heaven, to the fifth heaven,
> Ascend direct, ascend direct above.
> To the seventh heaven, to the eighth heaven,
> Ascend direct, ascend direct above.
> To the heaven which has never been reached - O spirit of heaven,
> Ascend direct, ascend direct above."

The chant records the belief not only that the Moriori considered the Sun as the origin of life but also gives their ancestral origin that was believed to be Rarotonga in Central Polynesia near the Tongan Islands. This is identified also as Hiku-Rangi where Rangi is the personification of the sky but in nearby Tonga myth relating to the demi-god name Hikuleo are of importance and noted in and earlier work[37] as probably an element of contact between the Huichols of North West Mexico and Polynesia. Whanga-matata means "heaven-opening" and appears to be an extension of a widely held belief in Australia and Oceania that there were openings or "holes" in the sky through which deities and spirits could, and did descend and through which priests and the spirits of the dead could ascend and similar beliefs are found in South America. Wairu-Rangi was the "Spirit of Heaven"[38]. Characteristically of Pacific peoples the first European contacts and later settlers were considered to be related to ancestral spirits returning to visit them and the Moriori were no exception. Skinner quotes some of the earliest records of first contact and notes: "They seemed a cheerful race, our conversation frequently exciting violent bursts of laughter among them. On our first landing their surprise and exclamations can hardly be imagined; they pointed to the sun and then to us, as if to ask whether we had come from thence ..."[39]. The pale skin and a range of light-coloured hair exhibited by the first Europeans always fascinated the Pacific peoples since their legends recorded that their ancestors were of the same varying type. Among some of the people such as the Polynesians some "throw-backs" were clearly visible to them and even given the specific name of "Uru-Kehu", and these were shown as evidence of a believed common descent.

The main object of focus in the Moriori tradition is obviously the Sun and its "beams" and "rays" here of note are highly reminiscent of the Akhenatun and his Sun worship as the deified Sun disk, Atun - a revisionism which was considered a heresy by the long established priesthood in Ancient Egypt. It is therefore not unexpected that other references that could have derived from Egypt are apparent. The Moriori male considered himself "a very sacred chap" and believed that if he infracted these self-imposed laws of tchap or "holiness" he would die[40]. The Moriori believed that they were "Tchakat Henu" which was no longer understood as a phrase but was derived from a canoe myth which Skinner records as given by the Morioris verbatim: "The Moriori is a 'Tchakat henu'. We do not know from whence he came. Arrived one day a canoe from Hawaiiki. Kahu was the Arik (Canoe Captain). He went away. Our people woken up by this intrusion went to sleep again. Came one day another canoe, how long after Kahu no one knows. The name was Rangimat. The people settled among us and took our girls for wives. Children and children were born and grew many clans. 'Ko Dauru-Kah' ('Rauru the strong') they called themselves, and fought with Wheteina and other clans; sometimes to be beaten, but mostly to win. Some think our ancestors were 'tchakat henu', some think not. That is all we know."[41]. The myth records the canoe name Rangi-Mat that is probably the origin of the Australian Ngamat earlier noted since sacred canoes were often noted as conveying the spirits of the captains and chiefs to the Sky world, particularly notable in myths in the Solomon Islands and the Ancient Middle East.

The term Tachakat Henu however is of great interest since it would appear the phrase derives directly from Ancient Egypt. The Hennu was the sacred boat associated with the deity Seker but for earlier epochs, after the earliest record, this deity in perhaps the oldest known representation is associated with Osiris and is found in his shrine[42]. Of special interest is the fact that it is believed by scholars that the Hennu boat was placed on a sledge and towed around the shrine at dawn to imitate the course of the Sun[43]. It is recorded in the papyrus of Mes-em-neter that a rubric to Chapter 64 in the Book of the Dead was found in the foundations of the shrine of the divine Hennu boat at the time of the First Dynasty king Semti. The vignette illustrating the Papyrus of Nebseni from which the chapter is taken shows the deceased adoring a Sun atop a sycamore tree - a mythical image which would be recognisable in many local beliefs from India through South East Asia to the Pacific Islands and Australia[44].

The Tchatcha in Egypt were the "heads" or "chiefs" and when related to the rituals of Osiris they were his four attendants[45]. They were sometimes called the "Children of Osiris" or the "Children of Horus" who were the guardians or gods of the four cardinal points. Kestha appeared with the head of a man; Hapi with the head of an ape; Tuamutef with the head of a jackel and the fourth, Qebhsennuf with the head of a hawk[46]. Osiris was renown in myths for having travelled in his solar boat and it would appear therefore that the Moriori expression, Tchakat Henu, had a remarkable, preserved derivation from Ancient Egypt meaning mariners and, or traders who travelled with the Sun or even were delegated by the Pharaohs to trade or explore the

Moriori Genealogical Dates:

Ancestor	Generations to 1900 A.D.	Total Years	Date
Toi	167	4,175	2275 B.C.
Rongomai-whenua	127 (129)	3,175	1275 B.C.
Kahuti (Of Kahu)	101 (101)	2,525	625 A.D.
Rongo Papa (Of Rangimata canoe)	28 (31)	700	1200 A.D.

2.034: Akimbo guardian figure carved on rim of ceremonial platter. Tiahuanaco, Bolivia, 600-900 A.D.

2.035: Akimbo figure atop a Melanesian Canoe panel with a design type known to derive from contacts with South China, Sepik region of New Guinea and the Maori. Melanesia, 19th., century, A.D.

2.036: Akimbo pose displayed by a Gana or the equivalent of the Mayan Pauahtun or wind god. Khandagiri, Bhubanesvar, Orissa, India, 2-3rd., century, A. D.

2.037: Earth goddess named Adya-Sakti in characteristic birth posture but found also on the Ecuador as the akimbo goddess on several stelae - *4.071*; *4.073*. Alampur, Central South India, 11th., century, A.D.

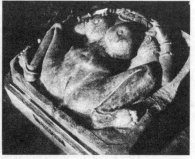

2.038: Akimbo pose, Gana supporting deity with Siva mendicant hairstyle as a base of a stupa shrine. Si Djoreng, Belangah, Padamg Lawas, Indonesia, 8-9th., century, A.D.

2.039: Akimbo figure carved atop a spatula an image found frequently in Melanesia. New Guinea, Early 20th., century, A.D.

world. The Hennu was the boat of Seker, where sek meant "to pull along" and seker meaning "he who is confined"[47]. This would seem appropriate considering mariners are confined to their boat for long periods and are "pulled along" by the wind in its sails. Another aspect the Morioris may have inherited is the fact that they reflected every deity with his female equivalent[48], a feature known from the earliest Egyptian religions.

In considering possible routes that any Egyptians who may have sailed from the Red Sea into the Indian Ocean took it should be apparent, therefore, that one or more groups may have sailed down the east coast of Africa to Madagascar. From there they could have taken the southern route to Southern Australia before the short, but very rough, "fast track" hop to New Zealand. In the famous Papyrus of Nu the supplicant is shown kneeling before the Hennu boat of Seker imploring him to assist his soul rising from the body to sit in the radiance of the "God of Light" - Khu[49]. The name Ku is recognisably that of another deity found not only throughout Oceania but among the Maya in Central America. Since Ku, along with Ra among the Egyptian references, are some of the supreme deities of Polynesia it would seem, therefore, that the Ancient Egyptians not only penetrated the Pacific by this possible southern route but also to Melanesia to Polynesia. Abraham Fornander's researches indicated that the ancient Egyptians formed one of the earliest detectable influences in the Pacific but further research is projected on this probability to be considered in a later publication.

The genealogical oral histories of the Moriori supplied by Tamahiwai in 1868 A.D.

notes 183 generations to that time. The history commences with the mythical deified heroes Tu, Rongo, Tane and Tangaroa down to Rongomai-whenua (the first inhabitant), and ends with Tawahiwai, one of the last Morioris[50]. This includes the period of ancestral descent in their original homeland, said to be Raratonga and results in the following dates allowing 25 years per generation:

The dates are of some interest since the first of these corresponds to about the initial incursions of the Lapita people into Melanesia and Polynesia although this is usually determined as some centuries later in some count-backs and may indicate the departure date from their original homeland. There was a second florescence of the Lapita, noted in Tonga until about 500 A.D., conveniently linking to the second last date. Certain elements of Lapita were noted in Easter Island some centuries later[51] and it may be the record of a dispersion from Tonga at about 1000 A.D. is that noted in the Maoris legends. Since the Morioris preceded the Maoris into New Zealand it is possible that at least one branch were either expelled, as fugitives as noted, or migrated to other lands and ended up for perhaps a few generations as suggested earlier in Australia before migrating to New Zealand corresponding to 625 A.D. The date of 1200 A.D. is

2.042 : Akimbo pose at the apex of the torana or sky arch at the top of the relief carving. Nanda Temple, Burma, Second half first millennium, A.D.

2.040 : Akimbo pose derived from the iconography of India. Sukuh, Java, Indonesia, 15th., century, A.D.

2.043 : Akimbo figure found frequently in Chatham Island imagery from the Moriori traditions. New Zealand, Pre-19th.,., century, A.D.

2.041 : Akimbo pose characteristic in many example as Melanesian imagery. Malangganen, Bismark Archipelago, Melanesia, 19th., century, A.D. or earlier.

2.044 : Akimbo design found on shields representing guardian spirits painted also on barkcloth ponchos and capes. Dyak, Borneo, Early or pre-20th., century, A.D.

2.045 : Shell carvings virtually identical to gold foil cut-outs found in the cenote in the Yucatan, but with motifs and techniques similar to South America. Rubiana, Solomon Islands, 19th., century, A.D. or before.

2.046 : Seated Deity, in ithyphallic pose characteristic of India. Veracruz, East Coast Mexico, 1st., millennium B.C.

2.047 : Akimbo posed carved on portion of column. Central Peru, 1st., millennium, A.D.

reasonably accurate in terms of the Maoris entering New Zealand and gives some credence to the whole.

The influences recorded in the available Moriori oral records through myths and legends do not end with migrations from Central Polynesia with other possible earlier influences from the Nile and Ancient Middle East. It is of note that the petroglyphs on the cliffs in the Chatham Islands were there when they first settled the islands. These cliff designs appear to relate to the earliest artefacts known in the islands of New Zealand that perhaps date to the mid-second half of the first millennium A.D.52.

2.048 :
Maori raised platform, a "fighting tower", look-outs typical of those found on the North West Coast of North America and through to Indonesia and the Nagas of Assam. Maori, New Zealand, 19th., century, A.D.

This suggests that other earlier people recorded in the Maori myths did inhabit these islands or at least visited them on a semi-permanent basis. As already noted the East Australian current flowed from Central Polynesia south west to the east coast of Australia before looping, as a result of contact with the West Wind Drift, to wash both sides other islands of New Zealand. The current then disperses to the east toward Southern Polynesia and joins the descending flow that have dispersed from the main branch of the South Equatorial Current toward the Austral Islands (Tubuai), the Tuamotu Archipelago, Pitcairn Island, and Easter Island. In an earlier work[53] it is noted that rats in India were generally considered unclean but for mariners it is likely that they were, as stowaways, on many voyages looked upon as lifesavers from starvation. When burial took place frequently an obolos was placed in the mouth to sustain the soul on its journey to the spirit land. In some belief systems it was payment to the guardian who prevented the unworthy from entering the next world or to pay the ferryman across the river thought to separate that world from the living. It was of particular note that among the Moriori they were

2.049 : Maori fort or Pa indicating the hill-shaping characteristic of such constructions and common in the core of the stepped pyramids and platforms in Ancient Peru. Maori, New Zealand, Late 18th., century A.D. or earlier.

2.050 : A typical scene of Maori village life a century and a half ago. Note the palisade protecting Putiki village in the background. Whanganui, New Zealand, Mid-19th., century, A.D.

2.051 : Maori palisaded fort with pillar sculptures of a similar type found on the North West Coast of North America and Melanesia. New Zealand, Late 19th., century, A.D. or earlier.

known to place a rat in the mouth of the deceased[54] and remarkably this was the identical practice known on Easter Island[55]. In India one of the trading castes was known to consider the rat or mouse lucky since they fattened themselves on the large grain stores that were a sign of wealth for their owners. It is very likely, since these people were involved in the growing of betel or areca nut used so widely as a moderate narcotic, that they were involved in sea trading[56]. This tends to be confirmed by the fact that betel and the areca nut is found from India to Micronesia north of New Guinea. The belief that the rat was lucky probably entered by this route and descended into adjacent Polynesia in times when the animal was used as obolos before other customs took its place. In view of this, and judging from the linking sea routes, it was much probable that this practice was established among the Moriori first before being transferred to Easter Island.

2.052 : Spear used as memorial post at the head of a warrior's grave. Ainu, Hokkaido, Japan, Late 19th., century, A.D.

2.053 : Maori boy wearing the two feathers indicating status characteristic also of the Inca. The mixed Maori heritage is reflected in Melanesian traits in his features in an otherwise Polynesian descent. New Zealand, Early 20th., century, A.D.

One of the most interesting aspects of deities related to cross-cultural transfer from India to Peru and Bolivia are the attributes of Rudra, the Lord of Tears. Another aspect is the reference to this deity being associated with the mole or rat. In the Satapatha Brahmana, the oldest recorded of the Vedas, it is said that the priest in his propitiation provides an additional sacrifice as a mole or rat in a molehill after a five-fold lustration. It is said that Rudra on accepting this offering "puts it in his mouth"[57]. Considering that this element appears as an obolos in Moriori New Zealand and Easter Island both en-route to South America it would appear that this ritual has been anciently an aspect of the mariners belief system and heritage deriving from India.

Several forms of burial were known to the Moriorís including among them in bone-boxes known as hakana. These were usually found in dense scrub-land along with bundles of votive spears that were fighting spears, eight or nine feet long, known as tao. The term hakana does not appear to relate that that of the Maori but apparently derived from or shared a common origin with that in the Marquesas Islands that referred to a burial cave[58]. It is also likely that the form of bone burial known on San Cristoval as hakana is related to that of the Moriori where they placed the bones in a bowl of that name[59]. San Cristoval will also be of interest later since it had a mound culture that was considered by the early solar cult enthusiasts to be a centre of the spread from the high cultures of West Asia and Egypt. The various forms of burial tend to be associated with particular clans suggesting that they were originally migrants from a different region who imported their traditions retained either exclusively or adopted more generally over a long period of time. Cremation was practiced only by one section of the Moriori called the Te Harua[60]. This form of burial was favoured by them since there was no way the spirit could return to trouble the living. Such minority forms of burial suggest that the Te Harua were a separate people who settled among the Moriorís retaining some of their original customs. Cremation was, and still is a major form of burial in India and since many other aspects of Polynesian culture appear to derive from there it is likely that this form of burial had common origins from there.

2.054 : A Maori chief exhibiting the Caucasian features, characteristic of many of the Polynesians, probably derived from mariners from India or the Ancient Middle East. The textile cape pattern is closely similar to that of Indonesia and Ancient Peru. Maori, New Zealand, Early 20th., century, A.D.

2.055 : Maori warrior with a face tattoo or moko performing a form of the haka with a patu - the symbol of chieftainship and displaying leg tattoos. Maori, New Zealand, Early 20th., century, A.D.

Cremation was only one of seven forms of inhumation including tree, partial burial sitting, complete burial sitting, burial in coffins, launching at sea and mummi-fication. Tree burial and sitting burials of all types were also well known in India and "launch-ing at sea" clearly indicates a tradition common among a sea-going people where the body is placed in a canoe and sent off in the direction from whence the ancestors had arrived. The most common form of burial was sitting burial as Skinner notes: "The most common mode, howev-er, was this: when a person conceived the approach of death to be near, he would select a long piece of the heart of 'hake-hake', about the thickness of a man's wrist and sharpened at one end. Upon the top he would rudely carve the figure of a bird or fish. He would then go to a particu-lar spot and kindle a fire with brushwood. Where the fire had died out he would stick in the hake-hake, and that would be the place of his sepulchre. When dead the arms were forced forward against the chest, and securely bound there with plaited green flax ropes; the hands were bound together and drawn over the knees, and a stick was inserted between the arms and knees. This was the orthodox method" …. "The dead was enveloped in plaited flax matting, and interred as far as the knees, the upper portion of the body being invariably above the soil,…" etc.[61]. This form of burial was noted as being found also in the New Hebrides but the wrapping of the body in this way suggests a possible derivation from those of Peru where the flax matting was substi-tuted for fine textiles and where the digging of shaft and bottle tombs had become too difficult or discarded through generations of migration. The New Hebrides will be of note in due course as being an island group that exhibited numerous important cross-cultural references with South America. Further connection between the Moriois and the other Polynesians is noted as Skinner records that the Marquesan Islanders, "…understand the process of embalming, and practice it with such success that the bodies of their great chiefs are frequently preserved for many years in the very houses in which they died. I saw three of these in my visit to the Bay of Tior. One was involved in immense folds of Tapa, with only the face exposed, and hung erect against the side of the dwelling" …. "The heads of enemies slain in the battle are invariably preserved and hung up as trophies.". Among the Moriori Skinner notes; "The children of Dei took the head of their eldest brother and returned in a canoe to their home, where it was shown to relatives," etc.[62]. The practice of embalming and mummification is a further reminder of probable cultural connections with Peru, of which there will be shown to be many in due course, from the Marquesas Islanders to the Moriois but head-hunting was clearly also a feature of all three. Of interest is that the leg-endary return of the head of the eldest brother by the children of Dei since Deo is the name for God among the Aboriginal tribes of India such as in "Maha Deo - "Great God", and parallels that of the alternative among the Polynesians generally - "Io". The driving of the hake-hake into the ground has apparent connection with similar grave locations among the Ainu of Japan and the Aboriginal tribes in India where among the Gonds their deities were represented as spears driv-en into the ground called Sale[63]. The food of the formative deified ancestors among the Samoans was said to be the "heads of the first-born" and this apparent related Moriori tradition indicates a common origin.

In considering the connections between the Moriois and South America it should be noted that in Tasmania, also linked with the Moriois, the form of canoe they built was clearly similar to that of the peoples who lived around Lake Titicaca in modern day Bolivia (*2.025*; *2.028*). The Moriori called their canoe the waka and was said to carry between 60-70 people. Of particular interest is the reference in Skinner's report: "The Moriori have many things which dif-ferentiate them from the Maoris. They have wash-through canoes (waka-patu) for fishing: they sit with face to stern as in rowing; they have in their phonology the consonant ch which appears in no other Polynesian dialect except Tongan. I have always thought they came from a group dif-ferent from the Maoris. Their waka-patu remind me of the balsas or buoyant rafts of the Peruvian coast. On Lake Titicaca, I saw canoes made of reeds of much the same type (i.e. wash-through) as the Moriori, and their attitude in propelling stands alone in Oceania, except in new Caledonia, where they had double canoe rafts with holes in the decking through which they punted their craft"[64]. Such eyewitness accounts and related claims have been made for connections between South America and Easter Island and these will be considered in due course.

The Moriois had a elementary calendar based on the laying season of birds that the early authorities associated with Easter Island[65]. It was recorded, however, that there was an older calendar that was said to have been obtained. "...by ancestral heroes from Irea, in which the year began with the rising of the star (Rigel), and was divided into twelve months. The days were reckoned by the nights of the moon, and there was a separate name for each to the thirty-first"[66]. The land of Irea was believed by some early Europeans to be India and many aspects of Polynesian culture seems to support at least partial incursions from there, and will be a major point of interest in later chapters. Certainly India had a well-developed lunar calendar that could be the common origin for the Polynesian calendars as a whole since counting by nights was known widely in the islands in the Central and Eastern Pacific but also in Nias in Indonesia[67]. The counting by nights in Polynesia probably developed from their sea-going venturers when navigation by the night sky was much more reliable than during the day and Rigel was a main point of reference in navigation. It is interesting to note the Easter Island connection since it was recorded also by W. Travers of the Moriori: "They had no hereditary chiefs; the most successful bird-catcher, or fisherman, or any member of the tribe distinguished by extraordinary stature or by any useful quality, being looked upon as recognised leader"[68]. The landscape of the Chatham Islands resembled that of Easter Island with no large trees and their dependence on the birds supplying them with eggs beside sea food appears to have either developed in parallel with Easter Island or as a result of contact.

The Moriori arrived in the Chatham Islands in their own reckoning 28 generations back from 1900 A.D. making there occupation dating from about 1200 A.D. using a generation of 25 years, but this might be earlier. The first discovery of the European explorers occurred in 1791 A.D. but their settlement by the British did not occur until after the Maori invaded the islands in 1835 A.D. The first contact with Europeans apparently was without any hostility worth reporting and the Moriois themselves appear to have received them with wonderment but hospitably. The death knoll however, was already sounding for the last of these people since, before British settlement nearly two generations later, an expeditionary force of Maoris arrived from New Zealand in 1835 A.D. and subjected them into a state of wretchedness. A little before this Maori invasion a census was carried out that recorded all the names of the 1,673 Moriori survivors, and of these it was later discovered 216 had been cannibalised by the Maoris[69]. The Maoris cannot be considered to have been acting in anything other than a manner that was consonant with Oceanic traditions, regardless of present day "morality", since in the Moriori traditions there are those that relate that they too were of a warlike disposition in earlier days. Their own oral histories record that they used flint knives to dismember the bodies of the slain in their wars with associated cannibal feasts and that they retained the warriors' heads as trophies[70]. The Moriois were unable to sustain themselves and by the time of the first British settlement they were already clearly heading for extinction.

Terraced Forts in Miconesia from Ponape to Peru
The terraces on the island of Palau, in Micronesia, appear to have been commenced in the 5th., century, A.D. reaching a peak about 1000-1400 A.D. It is thought that they are not related to those of the Maori, but have been considered reminiscent of those of Monk's Mound at Cahokia, Etowah and Moundville in Eastern U.S.A.[71]. The Palauan terraces are particularly seen as being similar to those serving as the base for the Temple of the Sun at Pachacamac on the Pacific Coast

of Peru[72]. It is undoubtedly no coincidence that these islands in Micronesia are on the direct route formed by the North Equatorial Current from the South East Asia to Ecuador and North Peru.

Among the Nagas of Assam lookouts were constructed, some in stone and other with logs, as watch towers to detect the approach of enemies (*2.048*). Among the Angami Nagas they were found on all the higher prominences in the villages and were constructed of undressed logs and sometimes rose to a height of 30 feet (9 m.). In some cases these were raised platforms made of planks rather than towers and often did double-duty as official seating platforms or viewing platforms for parading[73]. In western Indonesia the type of fortification found among the Assamese Nagas was also found in Sumatra and was known by the Sanskrit derived name "Pa", a term also for those in New Zealand of the Maori and which resemble those of Sumatra[74] in name and form.

The Maoris - Second Wave in New Zealand Originating in Peru, India and South China

In Maori legend it was said that Maui, the volcanic god, who stowed away in his brother's canoe, emerged from his hiding place and forced his brothers to steer for the south away from their homeland in Polynesia[75]. Ultimately, far to the south, he is said to have used his grandmother's jawbone as a fishhook and drew up the North Island of New Zealand from the deep and called it Te Ika a Maui or "The Fish of Maui". The South Island in some traditions is called Te Waka o Maui or "The Canoe of Maui". In another myth the South Island was said to have fallen off the sacred mountain - Mount Hiku-rangi, and drifted to its present position. The Ngati Porou tribe retained a belief that Maui's canoe was still to be found in a petrified state high up on the top of this mountain[76]. The term Hiku-rangi has already been met with since Hiku undoubtedly relates to the Tongan demi-gods' named Hikuleo who appears to have connections with the Huichols in Western Mexico. Rangi is the name for the sky god throughout Polynesia.

Maui was said to have been born prematurely and kept wrapped for protection in his mother's topknot. He was the youngest of five brothers and as such seems to be an extension of the many myths of brother hero mariners throughout Polynesia and Melanesia. That he was kept in his mother's topknot is an anomaly since this form of hairstyle was in fact that dedicated to the male exclusively. His mother was also called by the name of her husband and it would appear that this is a not uncommon gender reversal pointing to this myth being adopted and adapted by the Polynesians from another source. This tends to be confirmed by the fact that Maui is a late-comer in the myths of Polynesia since he does not appear among the early deities. His full name was Maui-tiki-tiki and there are references that suggest that he may have developed from con-tacts with South America[77]. In one myth Percy Smith notes that Maui overcomes a sea monster and that on this voyage he visited U-peru, which he suggests may have been Peru itself[78].

The first hero who was said to have reached New Zealand first in both Moriori legends and those of the Maori, was Kupe while other genealogies suggest that there may have been two mariners by that name fifteen generations apart. Percy Smith over a century ago studied the Maori lineages and came to the conclusion that averaging out the genealogies to 39 generations settled on an approximate date for 925 A.D. as the discovery date of New Zealand by the first Kupe[79]. Several traditions note that Kupe discovered the islands and saw only birds then returned to his homeland to inform them of his find and to return with immigrants. The Aotea tribe note that Kupe gave directions to their ancestor Turi who set out with a fleet, but on reaching New Zealand the legend states that the land was full of people, conflicting with Kupe's report. Another myth notes that it was believed that a giant octopus lured Kupe, his wife and five children and sixty crew to the islands of New Zealand[80].

The Moari traditions record that there were wars and strife in their homeland called Hawaiki and the location of this land has been the subject of much debate over the last two hundred years and has yet to be resolved. The expeditions of Kupe were in response to these troubles and it would appear that those who arrived from Hawaiki were in fact the escapees or defeated tribes in these conflicts[81]. In Samoa, a centre of diffusion for several branches of the Polynesians, an island called Savaiki is thought by some to be that Hawaiki, although, because of the similarity of names, Hawaii is also a popular candidate. In an earlier work it is noted that Samoa is probably the Tamoa of note among the Mixtec traditions in Mexico[82]. It is of interest is that Abraham Fornander, in researching the Hawaiian branch of the Polynesian languages believed that "Hawa" as both the prefix to Hawaii and Hawaiki and a previous name for Java might be at the root of the Polynesian myth and that in turn it had connections with India and the Middle East.

Although Hawaiki is considered the semi-divine homeland other researchers indicate convincingly that the Maori in fact came from the islands of Tonga. J. Kerry-Nichols over a century ago considered the above locations of Hawaiki as too distant requiring long voyages over many months not only to reach New Zealand but also the same for the return journey seemingly not concurring with the Kupe legends. He notes: "Turning again to the Tonga Islands, not only do the Maoris bear a marked physical resemblance to the natives of that group, but many of their manners and customs are very similar to those of the islanders. There is also a very remarkable affinity between the Maori and Tongan languages - so much so, in fact, that the natives of the two countries find little difficulty in conversing when brought in contact with each other. It is likewise worthy of remark that the word 'Tonga' is of frequent occurrence in the Maori language."
"Thus, tonga, a southern region, he hau tonga, a south wind; tonga, a blemish on the skin; tonga-ko, to fester; tonga-kotara-tara and tongama-uru, south-west wind; tonga-mimi, a bladder; tonga-nga, uncooked, raw, broken; tonga rerewa, an ornament for the ear, a word of endearment, a treasure; Tonga-riro, the active volcano held sacred by the Maoris; Matua-a-Tonga, literally 'Father of Tonga', the name of the stone idol said to have been brought in the Arawa canoe from Hawaiki; Paratetai-tonga, the name of the south end of Mount Ruapehu, also whaka-tonga, to keep one's-self quiet, to restrain one's feelings, to entertain feelings which one does not show outwardly; whaka-tonga-tia, to be murmured at, be found fault with secretly. The name of the principal island in the Tonga group is Tonga-tabu, literally 'Sacred Tonga'; Hunga-tonga and Rara-tonga are also adjacent islands. Thus each of these proper names is compounded of Maori words, very common in that language at the present day. Hence in tabu, or taboo, as it is sometimes written, may be traced the tapu of the Maoris, both words in the respective languages having the same signification, i.e., to render sacred; hunga signifies in Maori a company of persons, while rara is a frequent term of various significations. Again, as showing the affinity of many of the native names of the islands with those of Maori words of the present day, it may be remarked that a short distance to the east of the Tonga group there are three islands which geographically form part of the same group, named respectively Aitu-taki, Manga-ia, and Oheteroa. In the Maori language the signification of these names may be transplanted as follows:- Aitu denotes a spiritual deity; taki signifies to take to one side, take out of the way, to tow with a line from the shore; Manga is equivalent to the branch of a tree or river; and ia implies a current, a sound made by rushing water; while in Ohe-te-roa there is a remarkable resemblance to the word Aotea-roa, the Maori name, ..., for the North Island of New Zealand"[83].

Since the Tonga Islands are the nearest group to New Zealand, about one thousand miles to the north, it is a more feasible location for at least some of the traditions to be the ancestral location. It is of importance to note that there are varying traditions and more recent research clearly indicates that beside the predominant Polynesian strains there are elements of Melanesian, Malay and possibly also from South China. The varying Maori traditions indicates that there were more than one migration into New Zealand after the first explorer Kupe and it is likely that

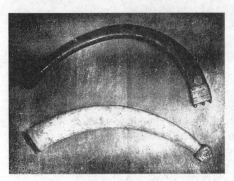

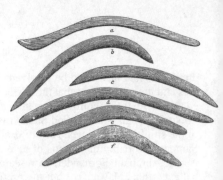

2.056 : Ceremonial boomerangs of a type found in South India and sharing the same origin with those of Aboriginal Australia. South India, Pre-20th., century.

2.057 : Traditional boomerangs from tribes in South Eastern Australia and similar to those found in South India. Mid-19th., century, A.D.

they came from very different parts of Polynesia and Melanesia. Undoubtedly the most powerful tribes imposed their own traditions, where possible, through dominance and these became the "official" version(s). The Tongan connection is of particular importance since there are apparent reflections of the megalithic traditions of South America and to the particular developments in Tiahuanaco in present-day Bolivia and these will be of interest in later chapters.

The direct voyage more or less due south from Tonga meant cutting across the East Australian Current separating this group from New Zealand. It is clear from known contacts between the other island groups that the Polynesians were well able to manoeuvre their canoes by tacking and undoubtedly this journey presented little out of the ordinary for them once they had set their destination. Peter Buck suggests that there were three main phases in the populating of New Zealand as he records: "The Moari people who were in occupation of New Zealand at the time of European contact were the descendants of the intermixture of the three successive groups of immigrants: the moa hunters and the early tangata whenua (Moriori) who came with the Maruiwi, the two crews under Toi and Whatonga, and the settlers from the fleet of 1350 A.D."[84]. He also records other arrivals but on a lesser scale but the contemporary studies of skeletal material indicates infusions, besides recognisable Polynesians, early Melanesians, Tasmanians, Ainu of Japan and Fuegians of South America[85]. The confirmation not only in Tasmanian links with the Fuegians of South America but also here in the skeletal analysis indicates that direct contacts must have taken place to be recognisable[86]. On arriving in New Zealand the first Maori warriors were unlikely to have been accorded a warm welcome, reflected in myths and ultimately, in the retreat of the Morioris, many of the Moriori women would have been captured and been reserved as the wives, concubines and slaves to begin the first native clans in New Zealand.

The Transfer of the Sweet Potato or Kumara from Peru to Polynesia and New Zealand

Other aspects associated with South America also contribute further evidence the contacts not only between that continent and New Zealand but much of the rest of Polynesia. The most interesting is that among the first legendary voyages during the period when the "kumara" or sweet potato was introduced. This tuber had its own deity called Rongo-maraeroa, also known simply as Rongo, the god of horticulture. It was said that these were introduced as the nine seed potatoes in the double belt of Rongo-rongo and the honorific name given it in their clan territory was Tahua o Rongrongo - "Belt of Rongorongo"[87].

Sir Peter Buck quotes a legend from the Matorohanga tradition relating that the original Maori homeland was named Irihia and he notes that Percy Smith, an earlier researcher into the myths and legends of Hawaiki, considered this to be another name for India, corresponding with the Moriori Iria earlier noted. This legend notes that the adjacent land was called Uru, some researchers perceiving this as a connection to Ur of the Chaldees, who came into conflict with the people of Irihia (Arya, Iran or India) and as a result some of its peoples set out in canoes with sun-dried sweet potato (kumara) among their provisions[88]. This interesting legend refers to the sweet potato only in passing but with important implications. As a native of South America, the sweet potato, which can only be cultivated outside of its native region by human transfer of the tuber itself, must have been transferred by sea voyagers from the South American coast into the Pacific region. The indicators in this myth suggest that Irhia is not India but located in South America, and critically, one of the first known Andean peoples in the Central Andes near Lake Titicaca was the Uru. The implication is that Irhia was probably somewhere adjacent to this Lake famous for its megalithic ruins of Tiahuanaco and the great stone structures here relate to the Tongan megalithic constructions on the island of Tonga-Tapu. It can be no coincidence that the South Equatorial Current flows from the coast of Peru directly towards the Southern Polynesian islands where the Tonga Islands are situated. The southern branch of this oceanic current, the East Australian Current, flows onwards past the south of Tonga to the East Coast of Australia and New Zealand.

However convincing the association of elements with the term Irihia or Iria might be with South America there is little to immediately associate this term with other known references to locales there. A compromise might be suggested which is pertinent to the theme of this book. The Polynesians always laid their dead to rest facing west or northwest suggesting that they retained the memory of their ancestral provenance even though its exact location became confused with time. This would not necessarily negate contacts with South America since, as will be shown, trade voyages or missions have left an indelible imprint upon the history contacts from that direction and Colombia, Ecuador and Peru. It appears therefore that in retaining the memory of Irhia, probably India or Iran, they are recording that this was at least in one, or several migrations into the Pacific their homeland retained in their memory over centuries and possibly millennia. The references to the kumara or sweet potato are events and experiences along the routes these mariners travelled, and the kumara was an important provision on which their lives depended during their voyages away from that continent whether via the Marquesas or Tahiti and all have become compressed into the one, or a few myths. This will be seen as a basic principle of the Bue myths to be considered in a later chapter. In considering some of the Amazonian myths it will be seen that the various elements composing any body of myths have been merged with other elements that are clearly inconsistent with other, apparently unrelated myths containing one or several of the same elements - such are common in all myths throughout the world.

In considering the Maori oral traditions and the location of Irhia it is worth considering the view of earlier researchers into Polynesian history, Percy Smith, whose work was held in high esteem even by Maoris such as Sir Peter Buck. He wrote a century ago, when the myths and legends were still fresh in the minds of the older generations of Polynesian men who were alive after the first contacts with Europeans: "I would make the following suggestion as a possible confirmation regarding Tawhiti-nui (in Maori myths) as a sacred mountain in India. It is well-known to all Polynesian scholars that Miru is the goddess of Hades, or the 'Po'; the place where departed spirits all go before arriving at Hui-te-rangiora, or Paradise. Now it may be that Miru = Meru, or Mount Meru in India, the high Kailasa, the heaven of the Saivites, the first great mountain (deity) of India." ..... "According to the Krishna Purana, the ocean fell on this Meru, and coursing down it, and four times round it, formed the four rivers of Paradise."[89]. The suggestion is an interesting one and it will be shown that the sacred mountain of Kailasa is of critical importance in the theme of this work in the connection between the North Indian Himalayas, Tibet and Tiahuanaco in Bolivia in following chapters.

It need only be mentioned here that the Maori tradition of this sacred mountain given by Smith notes: "Hawaiki-nui was a mainland (tua-whenua) with vast plains towards the sea and a high range of snowy mountains on the island side; through this country ran the river Tohinga". He notes further; "The Deluge stories of the Maoris are connected with the river Tohinga, showing how ancient Hawaiki is" .... "These mountains are mentioned in another legend referring to the father-land in which it is named Te Paparoa-I-Hawaiki or the 'Great extending Hawaiki', and again indicating a continent."[90]. The information on this continent, or "Great Extending Land" was that the place ... "was the growth or origin of man, and they spread from there, spreading from the Paparoa-I-Hawaiki, spreading the great ocean and dwelling there"[91].

The descriptions given in both versions could apply to the Himalayas or the Andes, although the plains on the "island side" in front of the mountains are much more limited in South America. Certainly the final references in stipulating that mankind originated on the plain would militate conclusively for the Ganges as the location of tua-whenua and the sacred mountain of Hui-te-rangiora. It is interesting to note that the terms Rangi, the name of the Sky god in Polynesia, also occurs in some references preserved in India among the Nagas of Assam and con-sidered elsewhere. This would confirm Percy Smith's belief that this mountain was in fact Meru, the Buddhist name of Kailasa - the sacred mountain in the Himalayas and preserved in the god-dess name of Miru.

The Polynesian name of the sweet potato is usually Kumara or variations on it and the link between India and South America as suggested might be found in the name of the Hindu deity in India - Kumara. Smith suggested that the name Irihia or Iria was in fact a corruption of the name of the Hindu storm deity Indra. This deity was inherited in India from ancient Iran, but originally from Anatolia, and although reduced in status under Hinduism, was actually was a major deity in the Vedic period in India in the first millennium B.C. The myth surrounding Kumara's origin recorded that the gods, headed by Indra, were being tormented by an "anti-god" named Taraka and decided to seek a remedy for the situation. They went to Siva, the great Yogi, but he was in deep meditation and Kama, the god of "lust" or love, attempted to interrupt his ecstatic state but, being irritated by this intrusion, Siva opened his "third eye" and his glance reduced Kama to ashes. One of the female deities - Parvati, then began to practice "austerities" which eventually attracted Siva's attention, and he became aroused and his seed fell into the mouth of Agni, the god of fire, and afterwards flowed into the Ganges. Eventually the seed deposited in a thicket of kasa grass called the "Forest-of-Arrows" and gave birth to Skanda, an aspect of the Sun god, who was also known as Kumara - the "Chaste-Adolescent". The kasa grass links this deity to the sacred city of Kasi or Benares[92]. He was considered not to have been born of woman but was raised by the six Pleiades or Krttikas and is therefore called the "Son of the Pleiades". Kumara was appointed to be the secret chief of God's army and was therefore lord of war. It is of interest that the term for secret-chief is guha that may well have been the origin of Guna and other titles found in Australia and Oceania.

Of particular interest is that Kumara had very great strength and in a parallel to the English myth of the sword Excalibur in the Arthurian legends he was said to thrust his spear into the ground in a challenge to all-comers to extract it or even shake it. His spear was said never to miss its mark and to return to him boomerang-like, from which this weapon was probably devel-oped since his cult is a very ancient one. Of special interest is that in South India he was identi-fied with Boy, Murugan, already noted as a deity whose derivatives occur widely in Australia[93]. Another reference associated with him is the fact that women were forbidden to worship him[94]. As a more general term it relates to sons where groups of youths or princes are called kumara[95].

It must be of great interest that, throughout Oceania and also in the Americas the boy who had miraculous strength is found in many myths and these will be considered later. It must be of importance that Kumara as a deity is identified with Murugan since this gives him another connection far beyond South India in Australia already noted. The fact that woman are not asso-ciated with his worship and that those associated with him are males always separated from women suggests that mariners had special allegiance to him and would account for the distribu-tion of the miraculous boy or youth myths so widely noted in Oceania. This detachment from

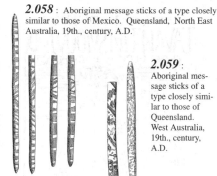

2.058 : Aboriginal message sticks of a type closely similar to those of Mexico. Queensland, North East Australia, 19th., century, A.D.

2.059 : Aboriginal message sticks of a type closely similar to those of Queensland. West Australia, 19th., century, A.D.

2.060 : Message sticks from the Tongaranka, Narranga, Mundain-Bura and Yukunbura Aboriginal tribes. Southern Australia, 19th., century, A.D.

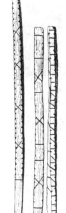

2.061 : Message sticks similar to those found in Aboriginal Australia. Tepehuane, North West Mexico, 19th., century, A.D.

2.062 : Message sticks characteristic of the Wurunjeri, Narrinyeri, Gournditch-Mara and Wotjo-Baluk Aboriginal tribes. Victoria, South East Australia, 19th., century, A.D.

2.063 : Carved and ornamented sticks possibly intended as message sticks. Note the circle and dot ornamentation characteristic of South India through the Pacific Islands to Ancient South America. Pachacamac, Peru, 500-1000 A.D.

2.064 : Message sticks from Aboriginal tribes from Queensland. North East Australia, 19th., century, A.D.

2.065 : Carved and ornamented sticks possibly intended as message sticks. Note the circle and dot ornamentation characteristic of South India through the Pacific Islands to Ancient South America. Pachacamac, Peru, 500-1000 A.D.

2.066 : Human bones notched as message sticks. Huichol, Western Mexico, Late 19th., century, A.D.

the female in nature would be appropriate for those at sea for very long periods - years or perhaps never to return to their homeland and a natural focus therefore for mariners. This may be the basis for many of the strictly held tribal regulations against women being in any way involved in religious worship and any customs imported by mariners' ancestors and their canoes. It is unlikely, therefore, be a coincidence that the deity Kumara is so closely connected with the Pleiades - always associated with the agricultural calendar rites in Oceania and the Americas. It follows, therefore, that Kumara could feasibly give his name to the sweet potato after it had been transferred from South America into the Pacific on the return journey by those who revered him and who remembered their homeland of India, or Irihia. It appears by the time he reached New Zealand perhaps via Rarotonga, Tahiti or the Marquesas he had been identified, or became, the "horticultural" deity of Polynesia and known among the Maori as Rongo-maraeroa.

The destruction or atomisation of the deity Kama - the god of love, desire or lust, who was the catalyst who eventually inspired Siva to lust after Parvati in the above myth is therefore vital to the generation of Kumara as the magical child. From the residue of the bones of Kama, or sublimated essence of lust, the Moon was said to have been made. Soma, the ambrosia of immortality consumed by the gods, was believed to be provided or in the charge of the Moon. The Moon was said to be divided into 16 parts or "digits" and each day the gods consumed one digit. The belief was that the Sun consumed the last digit as the Moon approached it in its orbit, but to achieve immortality the demon serpent Rahu, disguised as a god, attempted to swallow the Sun resulting in the eclipse[96]. This is one version of the cause of the eclipse of the Sun by the Moon and such myths are known from the Vedic period in India from the early first millennium B.C.

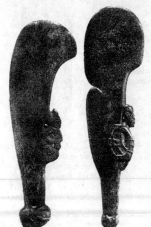

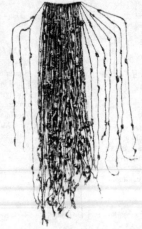

2.069 : A camayoc holding a quipu typical in Ancient Peru before the Incas until the Conquest. Poma de Ayala; Inca Peru, 16th., century, A.D.

2.067 : Two ceremonial patus, or clubs, of the wahaika type. Maori; New Zealand, 19th., century, A.D.

2.068 : Typical Ancient Peruvian quipu but not an exclusive method of counting and recording and found in the Pacific Islands, India and China. Peru, 1350-1521 A.D.

The deity Kama as god of Love was of course visualised as the most beautiful of young men and his association with the name of Kumara was reflected as the "beautiful youth" - the Poea, so revered and widespread in Polynesian legend. It is not a surprise therefore to find that, along with the importation of Kumara and the "beautiful youth" myths, the eclipse demon Rahu, relating to the Moon's North Node, is found widely throughout Oceania but more particularly identifiably in Mexico and Central America. In one version of the ancient Vedic texts it is noted that the Moon occupied the lowest of the upper world[97] construct and this is the identical proposition in the Marquesas Islands[98].

It is feasible therefore that mariners from India could have undertaken voyages to South America - achievable in one year, and returned with the kumara and any other food plants into the Pacific. The Maori myths note that the taro[99] - another tuber, or cultigen, probably originally from South America, was also brought with the kumara, along with yams but the latter failed in New Zealand, but the sweet potato has been found recently in archaeological digs in the Cook Islands dated to 1052 (+/-70 years) A.D.[100]. This corresponds with the first migrations of the Maori to New Zealand but much earlier traces of this tuber may have been found in the highlands of New Guinea where cultivation trenches are found in the Whagi Valley from 7000 years ago[101]. Although dateable material is not yet available the Cook Islands researches indicate that the Whagi Valley probably had introduced tubers of the sweet potato from at least as early as those of Eastern Polynesia. There are recorded to be over thirty varieties of the sweet potato cultivated in New Zealand as variants from those in South America suggesting a long period of evolution in cultivation to allow for such development[102]. These may have been augmented by other introductions in later voyages rather than an extension of the one type, but all apparently have evolved from the species type Ipomoea batatas[103].

The Quipu or Knotted Cord in Oceania

The quipu is forever identified with the Inca of South America but it is less well known that many island peoples in Oceania actually utilised this form of communication. In Tahitian traditions the island of Ra-iatea was believed to anciently be the Polynesian homeland of Hawaiki, and is located a little over 100 miles from Tahiti itself[104]. In one of the myths it is recoded that the grandson of Toi, Whatonga, who was part of the crew of a race between Tahiti and Ra-iatea, send back messages by a knotted string to Tahiti indicating their progress[105].

The Maori historian Sir Peter Buck noted that the Marquesans used a mnemonic device known as ta'o mate made of sennit. This recorded genealogies with a knot for each generation but among the Maoris a variation occurred where a stick - rakau whakapapa, had the generations recorded on it by string knots[106]. This form of device appears to be a halfway house between the knotted string or quipu and the message stick. The message stick known in Australia is another element which links them with the Maoris, and probably introduced by their predecessors the Morioris, from Australia to the Pacific Islands where a variety of message sticks are known through to the Americas (2.058-66).

In Hawaii the local taxes were assessed and recorded by tying various sizes and colours of knots, tufts and loops to a cord. These devices were usually an "aide memoire" assisting in recording these imposed demands to be paid in dogs, pigs and the like but although they appear to lack the sophistication of those of the Incas they are in principle devised for the same purpose, and probably share the same origin. It should also be noted that similar cords were used in China and India and it is likely that as an easily transportable type of "abacus" it was conveyed by mariners from India through to China and then into the Pacific Islands and the continental rim and will be considered more widely in a later section.

Ceremonial Clubs Known as the Patu

The throwing stick was called the kotaha in New Zealand and was known as a weapon in the rest of Polynesia, Australia and South America. This was used also in the game called teka found throughout Polynesia, but also in North West America and South America[107]. Spears or lances were also used in New Zealand as elsewhere in Polynesia but of particular note among the Maoris and Morioris were the clubs used both in war and ceremonials. Two types of patu, or short club, used by the Maori appear to have been developed by the Moriori since they had been found in the Chatham Islands[108]. The patu is found widely in Polynesia and also among the Indians of the North West Coast of North America who exhibit many cultural connections with the Maoris in particular. Numerous other cross-cultural elements will be considered in the following sections.

Cosmological Myths of the Maoris

Percy Smith, one of the most perceptive of the early researchers into Polynesian history, wrote: "If the hypothesis is right to the effect that the Polynesians are a branch of the ancient Gangetic race, it is obvious from the above table that they must have had several centuries of communication with the Sanskrit speaking race, from the period when the latter occupied the mid-Ganges in B.C. 800, down to the probable time of the Polynesians leaving India about the fourth or fifth century B.C., which is the date we arrived at by the aid of the Raratongan traditions"[109] (Cook Islands). Even a century ago the cultural cross-references with the great cultures of South Asia and the Polynesians were obvious and of particular interest also were aspects of Naga culture in the hills adjacent to the Ganges Delta were also seen as having close contacts as Smith notes: "... the tattoo marks on the face of the Sema divisions is apparently just like the old Maori moko-kuri, whilst the description of the ceremonies connected with tattooing and the tools used, might be taken as descriptive of those of the Polynesians today"[110]. The associations between the Naga tribes and the Pacific extends not only to the Polynesians but all the way to South America and will be of critical interest in later chapters.

It is of little surprise therefore that many of the cosmological speculations of the Maoris are reminiscent of those of India and the ancient Middle East. The first great gods of the Maori are recognised as having been brought by them from Tahiti to New Zealand. This conflicts with an apparent migration from Tonga with its closer linguistic references but since these deities are found throughout Polynesia it is clear that they all originated either in Tahiti or were naturalised there after being imported from elsewhere. These earliest gods are Tane, Tu, Rongo and Tangaroa but as a local variant the Maoris make them the sons of Rangi - the sky god and Papa - the earth goddess[111].

The oldest myth of creation among the Polynesians appears to be that recording that the deity Rangi, the Sky, was separated from the embrace with his wife Papa, the Earth by the god Ru standing on his head and using his feet to force Rangi upwards[112]. To ensure that they remained apart he placed props between them and these were the prototypical sky pillars found throughout Oceania and from India to the Americas. Among the Maori the later version noted that it was Tane instead of Ru who forced apart the Sky and Earth and this version was current throughout New Zealand suggesting that this developed after the separation of the first migrations from Central Polynesia[113]. Tane became the supreme deity among the Maoris and he appears similarly prominent in Hawaii suggesting a closer period of contact, at least in one epoch. In some versions of earliest stories relating to this separation myth it is notably the volcanic gods who are associated with a period of darkness or gloom. It was said that after the separation of "Father-heaven" and "Mother-earth" they continually wept and the "avenues of light" were clouded or "closed" with the mists that arose from their tears[114]. This suggests a period of major volcanic activity that may again indicate ancestors from Hawaii where the volcanic lava flows causing just such local misting during an eruption.

In Indonesia on the island of Borneo it was believed that the sky was very close to the earth. One day when a giant named Usai was working sago with a wooden mallet he struck the sky and it raised itself far beyond the reach of man[115]. On the island of Roti it was said that anciently the sky was so close to the earth that it was possible for men to ascend into the sky and return again, particularly seeking fire, and for the people up there to descend to earth and return to their sky world. In distant times it was believed that a very tall man called Liahaiwak could only walk stooped to avoid hitting his head on the sky and the birds had difficulty in flying any distance. He requested the sky to move a little further from the earth so that he could walk upright. The sky became angry and raised itself far from the earth and the giant was able to stand upright. The myth notes that he then began to step on the adjacent islands and in eventually travelling "he went round the earth" never returning to Roti[116]. This is clearly a localised version of the legends recorded of the giant Bhima of India who is recorded also to have travelled all over the earth.

Among the Marquesans it is recorded that the god Tane was in fact known but played a much less important role in their pantheon. He is associated with the adze and is perceived as the ancestor of the white race[117]. When Papa Una, above, was separated from Papa A'o, under, were thrust apart in Marquesas myths 19 deities proceeded to emerge - among them Tane and Tea[118]. In the Marquesas "Tea" means "white", and therefore also the deity Atea means the white god, but plays little part in those islands mythology and is the same as Wakea in the Hawaii and Vatea in the Cook Islands where this deity is of greater importance[119]. Tane being the god who separated the heaven from earth in New Zealand is therefore also found in the Marquesas shown to have the adze as his special implement. The connections with India have been noted but many of these are clearly derived from the ancient Middle East. The Polynesians, and those noted particularly in New Zealand, have elements recording clearly derived from there. In ancient Sumerian mythology cuneiform tablets are preserved recording that Enlil "... Took care to move away heaven from earth. In order to make grow the creature that came forth,...". Of particular interest is the fact that this myth records only two lines noting that he brought the pickaxe into existence and that he made it "exalted", of "gold" with a head of "lapis lazuli". It is particularly emphasised in this poem that this pickaxe is the symbol of his "black-headed people" - the Sumerians - the name they called themselves[120]. In a line in the myth it is also stated that the pickaxe is the "tooth" of its "lapis lazuli head". This association of a "tooth" with axes; pickaxes and adzes is found widely along the sea routes that are of interest to this study, and will be of further interest later. The separation of heaven and earth noted in the Sumerian myth is clearly the originator of the Polynesian variations particularly as the Marquesan notes that the adze or pickaxe is associated with the god Tane - the separator of Heaven and Earth among the Maori. Such connections will be extended in later chapters.

In a flood myth derived from the Ngaitahu clan among the Maori it was recorded in an oral tradition that in ancient times many tribes forgot the worship of their supreme god, Tane, and wrongdoing became the norm. One family however, did continue to revere Tane, a man named Parawhenuamea and his father were named but were despised by the other people. They felled two trees named the totora and kahikatea and the heroes built from them a raft (moki). They placed on it fern root, sweet potato and dogs and then prayed to Tane for rain to demonstrate their faith to other people. Their wish was granted and it then rained for four or five days and, as the waters rose, the raft floated away along the river Tohinga and away for about eight months before the waters subsided. All the tribes who had so despised the man and his father were drowned included all the women and children[121]. Interestingly Para-whenua mea means "old", a surprising appellation for the son rather than the father, but it is of note that Noah was called the "old man" and appears to be the origin for this myth. In fact a Biblical link is unlikely since many other myths of this type are found throughout Melanesia, and Polynesia. The motif of the deity becoming dissatisfied with the lack of adoration from human-kind and attempting to destroy them by a flood is well-known in the much earlier Sumerian mythology and this myth motif found its way into the Aboriginal myths in India.

In India it is the Aboriginal tribes who preserve element this aspect of the ancient Middle Eastern mythology suggesting that they had become incursive before the Aryan invasions in the first millennium B.C. A Gond myth relates that the sky and the earth were at one time very close together and one day an old woman who was sweeping knocked her head against the sky and in a fit of temper she thrust it upwards to its present position[122]. In a similar myth it is stated that a Birhor woman was husking rice and hit the sky by accident with her pestle[123]. In the Andaman Islands it was believed that originally the sky was so close to the earth that it only just cleared the trees and one day a giant made a bow and lifted it using the bow to prop it up[124]. Several of the clearly related myths in other tribes in India have been recorded where even the instruments utilised for pushing up the sky have either been borrowed through contact or have a common origin. These myths are clearly related to the references of the mallet, the substitute for the broom or pestle, and giant in the Bornean myths above noted in Indonesia that have clearly been derived from these models in India.

It is notable that it is among the Gonds that there are versions of this myth where the sky had at one time been close to the earth myth. This tribal group in India will be of increasing importance in the theme of this book but it is sufficient to note at this time that the myths of separation of the sky and the earth in Asia, so similar in principle to those of the Polynesians and the Maori in particular, can hardly be considered a coincidence. This myth has clearly travelled from the ancient Middle East to India, through Indonesia and Melanesia before reaching Polynesia. In Melanesia a myth from Rossel Island notes that the creator heroes named Mbasi and Konjini became stones on a beach after they had created an egg between them from which human-kind emerged. This beach was located in a sacred place called Yaba and it is of interest that Mbasi as the main hero was associated with the outrigger canoe and before the creation of the egg he had arrived in his canoe with the Sun, Moon, and a dog. After Mbasi and Konjini turned into stones the Sun and Moon flew up into the sky but the Moon found the Sun heat too hot, and the Sun considered the Moon too cold. The hero Wonaja decided that the Sun should appear by day and the Moon at night to resolve their differences then raised the whole of the sky to its present position[125].

This Melanesian example is a condensed version of many notable myths found in Oceania and contains elements of cosmology integrated with creation myths that originally formed entirely separate myths, some having been considered in an earlier work[126]. The hero Mbasi in another version was said to be darker-skinned and Konjini a fair-skinned woman suggesting that the whole indicates migrations of one physically distinct people into the region of another - a classic clash of cultures. Mbasi was one of the "snake-people" as was Wonajo who unsuccessfully courted Konjini[127]. Mbasi was associated with the outrigger while Wonajo and two of his "snake" friends travelled to Sudest on a "wooden dish" since they knew nothing of canoes. The wooden dish may have been a raft but the whole myth suggests that there might have been two migrations of the same people termed "snakes" - a similar racial origin, or serpent worshippers from two different regions - one of which possessed the outrigger, while the other utilised the raft.

In a myth from the traditions of the Wotjo-baluk in South Eastern Australia it is recorded that the sky in the most ancient times rested upon the earth and prevented the Sun from moving. Eventually the magpie (a black and white bird) propped up the sky with a long stick and since then the Sun has moved around the earth[128]. The Wotjo-baluk have been noted prominently in the preceding chapter and it cannot be a surprise therefore that they should also retain a memory of a myth found along the sea routes that link the Australian continent with India, Indonesia, Melanesia and Polynesia. It is of interest therefore that sky-raising traditions are noted in Central America where Ehecatl, probably a deity originating from mariners, also known as "9 Wind" among the Zapotecs, is said to have been responsible for such feats[129].

The ancient connections with India appear to be confirmed by the most traditional belief that the world of the dead lay in the west for many Polynesians and this is usually the direction from where the first ancestors came from. In New Zealand far to the south of all of the other Polynesian islands it was believed that the spirits of the deceased travelled north before then travelling west to their ancestral home[130]. Interestingly the tradition notes that there was a leaping-off point from a cliff at the northerly part of New Zealand corresponding to such "spirit leaps" in Assam among the Nagas[131] and in South America also[132] and noted also in the Quiche-Mayan Popol Vuh[133]. It is clear therefore, along with their very long, memorised genealogies and lineages the Polynesians generally retained their traditions faithfully over many centuries. Although the Polynesians retained these traditions, apparently reasonably accurately, other aspects that more clearly relate to the Eastern Polynesian island groups of the Marquesas, Tahiti and also to South America seem not to have completely clouded the memory of their most ancient homeland.

Tane as the supreme deity of the Maori had special responsibility for trees and before cutting a tree down rituals were performed to him. In Hawaii, Tane was called Kane and was considered one of the most important gods and tree-cutting rites were sacred undoubtedly because, as with the Maoris, trees were used for canoes and sea migration was an essential element in the population of the Pacific[134]. In Mangaia in Central Polynesia woodsmen paid special homage to Tane and called him Tane-mata-ariki or "Tane-of-the-Regal-Face" while in Tahiti craftsmen offered him the first chip cut from the trunk of a tree in commencing the felling. In a series of related myths called the "Woodchip Myths" it is noted that in the felling of certain trees they were unable to be cut down since the chips returned to their original positions and healed to wholeness, often overnight, due to magical forces[135]. One of the most prominent of these comes from Samoa involving the demigod Rata[136] while other clearly related myths in Melanesia note that only in concealing or burning the first chip was the mission to chop the tree down successful[137]. Closely similar myths are found among the Cuna of Panama[138] and the Naga of Assam[139] in North East India all of which are connected by the direct sea currents of the Pacific Ocean. It would appear therefore that the Tahitian custom of offering the first woodchip to Tane derived from a similar origin with the Woodchip Myth. This myth has been shown to extend not only from Central America to India through Polynesia and Melanesia but also from Western Mexico and will be shown to have also penetrated into South America.

The Nagas will be of repeated interest in this work and it is significant that the term Ao is of some importance among them. The term appears to be similar or correspond in origin to Au, Hau, Sau, Chau, and Ahau being applied to elevated of chiefly status among the Polynesians in particular, the Micronesians, sometimes among the Melanesians and among the Maya of Central America and in South America. The Maoris retained this term, Ao, meaning "the world"[140], and this may have derived from intermediate influences in Melanesia.

Maui and Noosing the Sun

One of the most interesting aspects of Polynesian myths preserved in Maori cosmology is the belief that the Sun could be slowed in its course or even stopped. The Maori version states that because the Sun moved so quickly in its orbit that mankind was unable to hunt and farm for long enough each day to be successful. It was believed that the Sun emerged from a hole in the east after setting each night and continuing under the earth, sometimes thought to be confined in a tunnel, to rise again each day. It was said that Maui laid "rope snares" around this opening and he and his brothers waited until the Sun's head and shoulders had emerged above the nose before tightening the noose so that his arms were "pinioned" against his sides. Maui then beat the Sun with the jawbone of his grandmother - Muriranga-whenua (Great Son of the Sun - where Muriranga is probably Murugan - the Son of the Sun in Tamil India and Australia), an element also noted earlier in this work - one of his titles. Having been clubbed by Maui in such a manner the Sun moved more slowly in his course thus allowing mankind more time to farm and hunt for their food[141].

Versions of this myth are known elsewhere in Polynesia and will be considered in due course[142]. Of some importance, however, is the fact that the among the Incas, and perhaps their predecessors, ceremonies were held at the Intihuatana, or Hitching Post of the Sun, specifically in the belief, and with the intent, that the Sun could be controlled and regulated in its course. This Maori myth forms one of a body of cultural elements that can clearly be traced to contacts with South America - and with India.

The phallic associations of Maui are also highly reminiscent of India where the Dentata Vagina myths are found, and not only there, but also on the West, Pacific coast of Mexico and the North West coast of North America. Many of these are clearly related and are noted in an earlier work[143] but in the New Zealand myths their term tiki was used to denote the spiritual essence of the male member personified by the deity Tane[144]. The divine or spiritual essence of Maui came from the tiki or male member in its physical form, which ultimately died, and was derived from the female element personified by Hineahuone - the first woman made from the earth. The broad principle of the Vagina Dentata myths appears to be indicated by the fact that Maui, at the end of his existence, died through strangulation by the female organ of Hinenuitepo during his quest for immortality. This act is said to have instituted death among mankind and the female organ as a result was referred to as te whare o Aitu or "the House of Death"[145].

Heroes; Demi-Gods; Priests and Maui the Fire God

Maui was, as deified hero, he who appears to have assimilated elements and attributes of other creator gods. The idea that Maui could die tends to indicate that he was a great hero who even-

2.070 : A finely carved high relief stone panel depicting an unknown subject in this jataka, or didactic plaque. The boy hanging upside down is virtually identical to similar representations in South America. Sirkap, Taxila, North West India, 100-200 A.D.

2.071 : A section of a textile design depicting a deity appearing to give birth to a child but more possibly a local version of the Buddhist representation (2.070(11.085). Pachacamac, South Coast Peru, 500-1000 B.C.

2.072 : A magical design long tional in Tibet and inherited into Buddhism from the Bon Po. The upside deity is characteristic and p bly related to earlier images in Buddhism and found far into the I Ocean to South America. Daba, Khorsum, Tibet, Early 20th., cent A..D.

2.073 : A carved wooden pillar depicting a deity with an inverted head and upper body possibly being intended to represent a defeated enemy but also similar to others in India and South America. Maori, New Zealand, 19th., century, A.D. or earlier.

2.074 : Inverted figure appearing to hang or descend from the main warrior, hero or deity closely reflecting imagery found in India, Polynesia and Colombia. Spiro Mound culture, Ohio, 800-1350 A.D.

2.075 : A remarkable stela about 5-6 metres high depicting a wrathful deity holding a child upside down and an inverted deity of victim at the base identical to similar iconographical motifs among the Maori and the Gandharans and others in North West India. San Agustin, Southern Colombia, 50 B.C. - 800 A.D.

2.076 : The close similarity to iconography in India of the figure of a child hanging upside down is unlikely to coincidental. The horned feature above the centre of the brow is identical to those found among the Nagas of Assam but more particularly among the Sidamo on the East Coast of Africa. Comala, Colima, Western Mexico, 300 B.C. - 300 A.D.

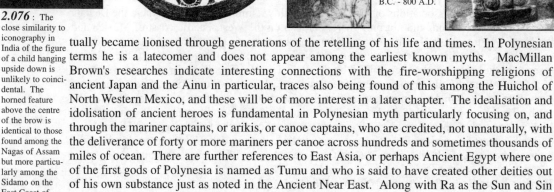

tually became lionised through generations of the retelling of his life and times. In Polynesian terms he is a latecomer and does not appear among the earliest known myths. MacMillan Brown's researches indicate interesting connections with the fire-worshipping religions of ancient Japan and the Ainu in particular, traces also being found of this among the Huichol of North Western Mexico, and these will be of more interest in a later chapter. The idealisation and idolisation of ancient heroes is fundamental in Polynesian myth particularly focusing on, and through the mariner captains, or arikis, or canoe captains, who are credited, not unnaturally, with the deliverance of forty or more mariners per canoe across hundreds and sometimes thousands of miles of ocean. There are further references to East Asia, or perhaps Ancient Egypt where one of the first gods of Polynesia is named as Tumu and who is said to have created other deities out of his own substance just as noted in the Ancient Near East. Along with Ra as the Sun and Sin as the Moon, Tum or Tumu of Egypt appears to have been transferred by mariners into the Pacific along with other traces of their ancient culture. There are connections, however, with the name Tumu as mythical chief in the traditions of the No Su in South West China and it has been shown that these people have very close ties with the Maya in Guatemala and the Huichol in Mexico anciently[146]. This region of South China may have been a halfway house on the Asian mainland before some of these venturers from Egypt or the Middle East travelled into the Pacific Ocean as Fornander detected over a century ago. These mariners would have diffused their myths and deities throughout the islands becoming corrupted by assimilation to other incursive or indigenous traditions - the Maui traditions being evidence of this among them.

One of the Polynesian heroes to be deified is the great chief Tangiia of Raratonga (Cook Islands) and was deified (by Oceanic standards) in nearby Mangaia in Central Polynesia. An unusual form of deification has been recorded of him indicating that when Tangiia died his spirit was "loath" to quit his body. The spirit hovered above Mount Ikurangi and there it was joined by the gods Tangaroa and Tonga-iti who, after some consultation, swallowed it in turn and spat it out. Tangiia's spirit was "invited" to do likewise with their spirits and the three went on to the house of Rongomatane. There Tangiaa's spirit was served as a relish (ono) with the sacred beverage of the assembled gods kava, and each of these deities present swallowed him and "spat", "vomited" or "disgorged" him. Rongomatane then directed Tonga-iti and Tangaroa to take Tangiia's deified spirit and locate a human medium through which he could communicate[147].

The whole episode centres around swallowing and disgorging and this appears to have a clear relation to the first gods of Egypt being "vomited" forth or disgorged by Tum or Tumu, Temu or Atum[148] the identical name found as creator deity in Polynesia. However there are also clear references in both the surviving iconography and mythology of India indicating that the rituals associated with the Egyptian myth may have been preserved there before entering the Pacific. The disgorging motif is reflected in the Makara images of the Ganges region in North India that are such an important element in the cultural connections between India, Indonesia and the Maya and Mexico and may have contributed to the retention of this myth motif in Polynesia. Of interest also in the Tangiia myth is the mention of the human medium since this person is termed pura-pura (a term alluding to white men) and the ancient spirits in Aboriginal Australia were term the mura-mura[149]. This same term, and with the Australian meaning linking to ancestral spirits in Peru also called mura-mura[150]. It is unlikely that this could be a coincidence and therefore probably derived from cross-cultural contact. Also of interest is the fact that the human medium found for Tangiia's spirit was named Ruru[151]. Ru was the sea god in Polynesia and related terms are known also in India. Doubled or "diminished" as Ru-ru and associated forms of the name are found throughout Polynesia and as the term or prefix found in Peru for an Inca ruler or official, and these terms will be considered further in due course[152].

It is sufficient at this stage to note that it was believed that without a human medium the gods could die and such a medium was termed waka atua or "canoe of the gods" - waka = canoe and atua = gods[153]. The consistent theme of oceanic associations is obvious throughout Maori, and Polynesian, histories and logical since they were a sea-going immigrant people whose priests travelled in their canoes along with the warriors mariners who populated New Zealand. The names for priests throughout Polynesia are usually variants derived from the same root but perhaps being influenced also by outside terms. In the Cook Islands (Raratonga) the priest was called ta'unga; the Society Islands (Tahiti) "Tahu'a"; the Marquesas he was the tuhuna and in Hawaii kahuna. In these islands also the same, or a similar term meant a skilled craftsman. In the other main Polynesian islands, such as the Tuamotus and Mangareva, the same terms for priest are found with the minimal variant of tauta being found in Samoa and Tonga[154]. This last term being found in Tonga in particular suggests another connection, beside its megalithic culture, with Peru since the Incan term for the priest, who specialised in the preservation and ᵣecitation of traditions, was the Amauta and indicates another direct connection with South America. The act of a medium being taken possession by the god was called uru - umu being a term for a priest in Peru, and along with the term Ruru and others will be considered later.

The Origin of the Foetus in Maori Ritual and Sacrifice

In considering connections between the Maori and Peru it is of interest that the human foetus in most cultures was rarely considered to be of special ritual or spiritual significance before birth. In many cultures a child who died before a set period of days was not considered to have developed a soul or that it was so insignificant in its development that it was not of great importance and accorded little or no burial rites. It is of some interest therefore that among the Maoris sometimes considered the foetus after abortion to be worthy of attention in their myths. It was believed that the spirit of such a foetus was taken by the spirit of a deceased relative to the Underworld, "Po", where it was raised to adulthood, as it would have been in a physical body. In myths about these spirits it was believed that they were endowed with human and spiritual qualities and could become heroes also, as they might have done on the physical plane had they lived, and that they possessed magical qualities. It is significant that the hero Maui noted above was said to have developed from a discarded foetus. These minor, or lowest grade deities, said to have developed from foetuses were usually confined to the families from which the foetus had come either by miscarriage or abortion. They were more properly called atua kahu or atua kahukahu from the term for the enveloping membrane of the embryo - kahu[155]. This use of the "doubled" form of a term to indicate diminishment, used so appropriately here for an undeveloped human form, is utilised throughout Polynesia in this descriptive form and is an element found also in South America (*11.086*) and Indonesia.

Thor Heyerdahl's theories, backed up with excavational material, have not always been accepted by the Establishment, but there is little doubt that many of his arguments are well-thought out and supported by artefactual evidence. He notes the very wide reverence across the whole of Polynesia that the hero-deity Maui has in folklore and myth but makes the controversial assertion that he is a hero deriving from South America. It is generally accepted that Maui is a later introduction into Polynesian myths and his link to the term tiki or tiki-tiki and its variations led Heyerdahl to suggest that this was a Peruvian hero. Abraham Fornander suggested that this name is to be found in the West, in Asia or the Ancient Middle East, although Heyerdahl disagrees and there is no doubt that it is the appended term of tiki to Maui's name that he considers to be Peruvian[156].

Maui has been derived from Mauri, a term that will be of greater interest in a projected future publication, and can be found in both the Ancient Middle East and South America. Heyerdahl links Tiki to Ticci or Tiki Viracocha, the great Creator/hero-deity of the Andes and Coastal Peru, who will be of some interest later in this work. Heyerdahl's work is still worthy of consideration at length but cannot by further included here except to note that his work was in support of the American Indian populations' entry as migrants across the Pacific Islands while that of Fornander's was aimed at from Asia, particularly West Asian, incursions into the Pacific. Both are worthy of further consideration in future researches.

In Peru the human foetus was not so revered as that of the Maori as far as is known or recorded, but of note are the many child and foetus mummies found there from earlier than the Inca Dynasty and the special rituals and magical qualities associated with the llama foetus before, during and after the Inca dynasty in Andean Peru were clearly of ritual importance. The rituals and ceremonials of the Maoris related to the foetus may have been a transfer of the llama foetus rituals to the human foetus in islands that did not have similar animals and could have acted as substitutes for those known in the Andes after at least one stream of their forebears had left that region far to the east. Such an extraordinary focus for rituals will be considered in a later chapter but it is of further interest that there are other connections indicating that there were originally similar traditions along the sea routes of the Pacific leading back to India that may provide connections.

The lowest rank of the gods among the Maoris were those worshipped within the family and these were usually made up of the souls of miscarriages and foetuses and termed atua kahu or atua kahukahu from the membrane or cowl that enveloped the embryo[157]. In Mangareva, in Central Polynesia the foetuses from abortions or miscarriages were said to be collected by Underworld spirits and raised there to maturity and thereby acquiring both human and spiritual qualities[158]. It is proposed by earlier researchers that the Maori were closely linked with India and in this work also with Iran. In a Gond myth from India it is stated that the Great God (Maha-Deo, a form of Siva) was requested by his wife Parvati to create trees and flowers. Maha-Deo acceded to this wish and the perfume from the flowers entered Parvati and she became pregnant. After three months she miscarried and threw the foetus into the river where it became a god-fish named Banasmar Marra Deo. This fish entered each of the daughters of Jalandar Guru when they swam in the river and each contracted an illness or suffered in some way[159]. Fish are often associated with, or a euphemism for mariners in many myths and it is elsewhere suggested that the Maoris and other mariners entered the Pacific from India and the Ancient Middle East and the association of the foetus with the gods noted in this and other stories may indicate the reverence or fear in which it was held in the Pacific region. Deo relates to Deus, God, and the Polynesian Io, and the term Marra may possibly have some origin references to Maori or Maui.

In the Ancient Middle East the Greek sign for Omega was that related to the womb as an inverted "U" from the third millennium, B.C. through to the Old Babylonian and Neo-Babylonian epochs. In this long period of time, two thousand years, the Omega sign was believed to represent to womb, and also swaddling clothes, and in these terms associated with the mother goddess Ninhursaga. This may have some relation with the depictions on textiles in Peru where the child is depicted emerging from the womb (*2.071; 11.085*). The omega symbol is also associated in script with the curved horns of oxen and a wig. In the Old Babylonian period foetus forms inscribed on clay tablets under the omega symbol have been found. It is known that there was a form of foetus worship for the so-called kubu-demons in those periods and these depictions suggest again that these were the still-born, miscarriages or abortions identified with them. On the upper Euphrates a cylinder seal has preserved a lunar deity, probably Nanna-Suen (Sin), standing in his sky canoe holding the crescent Moon and in the other an Omega symbol[160].

It is noted several times in this work that the Moon god Sin from ancient Mesopotamia appears to be the same lunar god with the same name found also in Melanesia, Polynesia and of particular interest on the coast of Peru. The Moon has long associated with the womb and the Moon-related menstrual cycle and childbirth and therefore also with the foetus and it being an object of fear or veneration. It is likely therefore that such references were transferred into India and then onward into the Pacific islands from the Ancient Middle East eventually being intro-

77 :
nd Oven
e type
d among
Maori and
North
rican
ns. Maria
d, Central
, Early
, century,

2.078 : The traditional ground oven called the umu also found anciently on the coast of Chile. New Zealand, Early 20th., century, A.D.

duced into the North Coast cultures of Peru.

Journey of the Soul to the Underworld among the Maori and Polynesians

The journey of the soul was a well-developed belief in Maori and other Polynesian cultures and these almost invariably indicated the direction from which the main migrations had come into their respective islands since the deceased spirit was believed to head back to the land of his ancestors. The most important rites associated with burial are those of the chiefs. As with many related traditions along major sea routes from the Ancient Middle East one or more slaves were dispatched to accompany and serve the chief's departing spirit[161]. In the region north of the present day city of Auckland "... slaves were killed, cooked, and placed on a stage near the dead chief..." since it was believed that they were the provisions the chief's spirit required on his journey otherwise known as o matenga[162]. The spirit world was called Reinga and was believed among the Maori not actually to be the ancestral homeland but located close to it. This suggests that wherever their ancestral roots had been they were in fact the descendants of a country that had itself been colonised by the original ancestral people at least in part. If the original people had been Middle Eastern then that colony may have been in India, and if from India itself then an extended colony may have been located in Java or one of the other Indonesian islands and this would certainly appear to have been one of the points of departure earlier noted.

Having left his tribe with his servant(s) the chief's soul then travelled to the North Island of New Zealand to a place called Te Rerengawairua or "The Spirit's Leap". This is a rock promontory in the extreme north of the island and it was recorded in more detail in the myths of the Maoris of the north part of the island that the spirit climbed the highest hill there called Taumataihaumu. Before reaching this point he gathered certain leaves and bracken and planted one of the leaves in the middle of the ninety-mile beach in a sand dune. This is clearly a remembrance of the place at which early migrations had landed on the North Island. Similarly in Melanesia, Indonesia and India the leaf represented the soul and suggests that this was a location marker or "touchstone" for the spirit to return to advise his people through the services of a human medium when required as earlier noted above.

One of the remarkably consistent cultural references found along the marine highways from Asia to South America, and the return, is the reference to the soul after death making its way back to the land of the ancestors. The frequency of myths indicating that the soul must leaf off a cliff, mountain or promontory, leaves little doubt that these beliefs are all connected with the transfer evident in artefactual, legendary and mythological evidence from common origins. Such leaping-off points are found among the Nagas of Assam[163] and the Gond of India[164]. From India this motif is found in Fiji in Melanesia[165], the Marquesas Islands[166] in Polynesia, as well as among the Ona[167], already noted. Not surprisingly such a belief in a leaping-off point in the first stages of the journey of the soul is found n the Quiche-Maya sacred book - the Popol Vuh[168].

Having "leapt" from the promontory some traditions suggest that the soul took to the sea either above or below it and travelled north. Others indicate that he descended from the hill and carried on along a small path that crossed a small stream called Te Waioraropo or "The Water-of-the-Underworld". The spirit is advised not to drink its waters since there is no way to return if he was ill at the time of his death. The spirit's thirst always compels him to drink and he then passes on to the beach called Te Oneirehia that is generally interpreted as "twighlight". The spirit crosses the beach and ascends "rising ground" and must cross another stream that is noted for its "gurgling" sound as it courses through the flanking rocks. The spirit's path leads out onto the promontory projecting out into the "Great-Ocean-of-Kiwa".

The first researchers into the Maori culture could not help but notice the close parallels between many elements of Polynesian myths and those of Eurasia. The journey-of-the-soul in

2.079 : Typical Angami Naga house similar to those found widely throughout the Pacific Rim and Islands. Assam, North East India, Early 20th., century, A.D.

2.081 : Assamese type of house found also in India. Similar buildings, derived from the same South Asian tradition, are found widely in the Pacific Islands. New Hebrides, Melanesia, Late 19th., century, A.D.

2.080 : Kota house, the neighbouring tribe to the Todas in the Nilgiri Hills, typical of many similar traditional buildings among the Aboriginal and Nagas peoples and in Oceania. South India, Early 20th., century, A.D.

this Maori version clearly has much in common with those known in traditional European cultures and particularly that of Greece. The believed loss of memory in drinking the waters of the stream called Te Waioraropo is identical to the motif of the Greek "Waters of Lethe" and the crossing of the streams parallels the River of the Styx. The "leaping-off" point has particular parallels in the Toba myths of South India and these people will be interest later. In the spirit reaching the "Great-Ocean-of-Kiwa" it must surely be a memory of connections with ancient India where Siwa, Siva or Shiva is the great Hindu god of time and life cycles and particularly associated with the beginning of life and its ending in death. This almost certainly also forms a connection, not necessarily directly, with the Americas where Cihua as the prefix to the god Cihuacoatl (Coatl = snake) is pronounced in the identical way to Siwa, a serpent god, and is undoubtedly derived also from the same deity. It is notable also that Greek influences penetrated in historic times from the conquests of Alexander the Great into the Indus Valley in the third century B.C. into India. In fact there are almost certainly earlier influences from Greece and the Western Mediterranean and particularly so from Anatolia where the original prototypical Vedic gods of India are recorded in the second half of the second millennium B.C.[169]. These Greek mythical influences into India would account for their being dispersed from there into the Pacific and ultimately those elements found among the Maoris.

Of special note is an alternate version of the journey of the soul following the above noted scenario to the first stream known as Te Waiorata. The name indicates that the colour of the water was rusty red and receives its name from the red flower called "rata". Having crossed the stream the spirit proceeds to Rerengawairua - the promontory, where at the edge of the cliff the pohutukawa tree grew that was said to have an "exposed root" extending down to a platform below. The spirits of the dead from all tribes were said to descend from the promontory down the root of the tree that was known as Akakite-reinga or "Root-to-the-Underworld". The Maori historian Sir Peter Buck noted a similar version in the Cook Islands (Raratonga) where the dead gathered "…and went direct to the Underworld, like a mechanical lift"[170]. The descent by, or to the root of a tree, bears striking parallels to the Mayan version in Central America as depicted on Pacal's slab at Palenque and has elements similar to other versions along the island routes from the Americas to India (see author's "Pacal's Portal to Paradise at Palenque").

It is significant therefore, that in this Maori version the spirit, having arrived at the platform, waited for a wave hitting the edge of the platform by the sea to recede since it exposed the entrance hole to a tunnel leading northward to Ohau. On this island the spirit there climbed a hill to gaze one final time on the land he was departing from and then he departed on the "western trail of the setting sun" that leads to the spirit land of the ancestors"[171]. This Maori version has in common with most Polynesian versions that the land of spirits was in fact towards the setting Sun and this follows the South Equatorial Currents of the Pacific Ocean flowing due east and to the west. In fact these traditional routes using these currents and consonant with Polynesian traditions points at either Indonesia or India as the most likely locations of the ancestral lands. This does not, however, preclude other lesser-known traditions that indicate other incursive migrations and influences from the east. These are apparent among the Maori, as already noted in part, and will be of interest in later sections of this work in other parts of Polynesia.

Cultural Transfer in Melanesia and Polynesia

In Melanesia the earth-oven known so widely throughout Polynesia and found also in South East Australia, earlier noted, is widely found in Melanesia and more so ion the islands known to have been contacted and settled by the Polynesians. Among the Maori the term used by them for this oven is kopa[172] but also umu as various types of ceremonial hearths and where the ritual fire-walking pit was called umu ti[173]. In the New Hebrides some myths have close resemblances to those of Maori suggesting that there must have been contact through, or with these Melanesian islands by the Maoris themselves or via the other Polynesian islands. In a Nguna myth from the New Hebrides it is said that the heroes shot an arrow into the sky and it stuck in heaven. They then shot another arrow which stuck in the end of the first and after they had shot ten arrows one into the other in this way they climbed up to heaven to see their blind grandmother. Their intent in seeking her out was to find out where their father and mother were and while they were there they took a piece of sugarcane and cut open the closed eyelids of their grandmother so that she could see[174]. Another well-known researcher a century ago, Capell, notes close similarities of this myth with those of the Maori: "The story has its counterpart in Maori legend, where Karihi and his brother Tawhaki try to ascend into heaven, but in this case Karihi fails, and only Tawhaki reaches the dwelling of his blind grandmother Matakerepo. Tawhaki restored her sight to her"[175].

Other authors have noted close similarities with the great myth cycle of Qat, and the Ambat of Malekula, noted in part in the author's book "Mayan Genesis", to Maori traditions. Layard, whose great work on the New Hebrides traditions three generations ago remains unsurpassed, notes that in the Mangaian traditions the heroes were said to have been the fair-haired children of Tangaloa. He compares these traditions to those of the sea-going Ambat where similar claims were made and the Maori, whose traditions state that the atua - or ancestral gods, called the Pakehakeha were said to be white in complexion, lived on the sea[176]. The Ambat are of special interest since their name denotes megalithic or stone-using people who were widely known throughout Melanesia. There is considerable evidence that the probable connection of these people with the Maoris extends further to the western extremes of Melanesia in the Sepik region of Southern New Guinea. Here similarities in the designs of the estuary region to those of the Malekulan Ambat are clear but also with those of the Maoris. It was early noted that physical appearance of these Sepik people was clearly different from other tribal groups since they were taller and fairer-skinned[177].

On the South Eastern New Guinea coast, washed by the South Equatorial Current leading from Polynesia through Melanesia to Indonesia, the Lakatoi warriors, when having killed another in war were considered taboo in the Polynesian manner and they could not be approached by women and had to be fed with a fork[178]. This tradition was well known in Maori custom for tabooed persons but was also known in India when a cleansing ritual for a man requiring purification was performed[179]. Greenstone was highly prized by Polynesians and contacts with New Caledonia where their supplies of this material was found must have meant that at least occa-

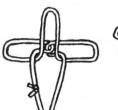

2.082 : Cat's cradle were common all along the marine highways throughout the Pacific Ocean Islands. Bukaua, Bismark Archipelago, Papua-New Guinea, Late 19th., century, A.D.

2.083 : Cat's cradle found among the Maya. Lacadon, Yucatan, Guatemala, Late 19th., century, A.D.

2.084 : Cat's cradle representing a canoe with two masts. Torres Straits, Melanesia, Pre-20th., century, A.D.

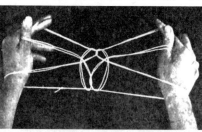

2.085 : Cat's cradle typical of Melanesia shown against black background. Early 20th., century; A.D.

2.087 : Cat's Cradle representing the setting closely similar to identical traditions found in Oceania and the Maya of Central America. Torres Straits, Melanesia, Early 20th., century, A.D.

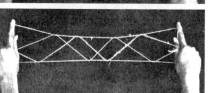

086 : Cat's cradle typical of Melanesia shown against ack background. Early 20th., century; A.D.

2.088 : Maori cat's cradle known as "whai". New Zealand, Early 20th., century, A.D.

sional contacts were made by canoe long after the Maoris had settled in New Zealand and did not remain isolated as some believe[180]. This belies the tradition that the Maori were a homogeneous people who arrived from the same island groups by canoe in two or three migrations. Some authors have considered that the Maoris now known were not the first in New Zealand as earlier noted but that another group, perhaps the Morioris, or perhaps a later people known as the Maui worshippers arrived and were responsible for building the many forts, or "Pa's", and earthworks attributed to the Maori (2.049) and that the Maori adopted their traditions. They are also believed to have been the people who were attracted to greenstone and who used it for their ritual implements[181]. In light of the probable connection already broadly accepted that the Maoris were connected with some of the Sepik people it is not difficult to accept also the assertions that there are origins for this tradition in Southern China. The Chinese are well known for their millennia-old fascination for nephritic stones of all colours particularly jade and other greenstones.

In traditions from the same source it is said that the exceptional woodcarving skills of the Maoris were introduced by a "fierce maritime people" called the Ponaturi. These various incursions of peoples with different skills suggests that they came in to New Zealand from many different areas of the Pacific region, or accessible to it, not just from Polynesia, and the similarities of the customs to other island groups suggests the validity of this proposition. This tends to be confirmed by the fact that Maori craft-skills were largely localised where one region produced elements that were not necessarily found in another - the war canoes as a speciality were found on the east coast of the North Island of New Zealand being given as a case in point[182]. Boat building types in other regions of the Pacific Rim suggest contact focusing particularly on those found traditionally in China, Japan and North West America having elements and in some of these similarly the drum is also used to assist in maintaining the rhythm of the oar stroke[183]. Thor Heyerdahl has provided extensive evidence of constructional, decorative and cultural connections between the house building types of the Maori and those of the Indians of the North West coast of North America[184]. Although these regions reflect traditions closely similar to those of the Maori but they are also similar to those of the Nagas of Assam[185] (*2.079-81*) and these tribes will be of more interest in due course.

The connections between the Maoris, or their predecessors the Morioris, and China repeatedly occurs and it is of interest that the Morioris noted that their ancient land was called Matan and in Southern China[186] an important gorge was called Matan suggesting that this may have been the name of an ancient ancestral region. This would make sense if the pre-Maori people noted above were in fact part of, or assimilated to, the Morioris giving them a greenstone link also to China. The Matan gorge is in the land of the Lolos or No-Su who are so closely linked to the Maya and Huichols iconographically in ancient Mexico[187]. Matang is associated with the Santals in India but further inland in Southern China and Tibet in the Man Tzu country is the region called Batang[188] suggesting that this may be the origin of, or have links to the Gilbert Islander's homeland of Matang. It is in this region that the state of Wotje is found, a name earlier noted to probably have stone associations with the Indonesian islands, Australia, New Zealand and through to the Middle East[189].

During the naturalist, Ernest Wilson's exploration in Southern China a century ago he wrote: "The Chinese flora is largely peculiar to the country itself, the number of endemic species being remarkable even when the size of the country is given due consideration. Yet in spite of its generally local character, the Chinese flora presents many interesting problems in plant distribution. Not the least interesting is to account for the presence of a species of Libiocedrus (L. macrolepis); seeing that the other members of this genus are found in California, Chili, and New Zealand. Another noteworthy feature is a species of Osteomeles (O. Schwerinae), which occurs in the far west of China, the other members of this family being found scattered through the islands of the Pacific Ocean. But perhaps the most extraordinary fact in this connection is the presence on Mount Omei of a species of Uetera (U. sinensis), the other members of this family being purely insular and confined to the Southern Hemisphere"[190].

This remarkable record clearly indicates that these species of flora travelled not as seeds in birds' wings to be propagated in far off places, as contemporary "wisdom" would have it, but clearly along the sea routes by human hands from their locations indicated throughout the Pacific Rim islands and Oceania. The distribution of these trees, particularly Libiocedrus, suggests that this had much to do with Chinese contacts resulting in ornamental designs along with the tree itself being transferred to these distant parts since they tend to correspond with known or suggested contacts in areas associated with the Maoris. This may also be the case with the Uetera found on Mount Omei - a tree found almost exclusively in the Southern Hemisphere, the domain of the Maori. MacMillan Brown long ago traced the name of the deity Maui to Japan[191] and this most sacred mountain in China, Omei, appears to be another form of Maui or perhaps even its origin. The third tree, from the far west of China, again suggests deliberate transfer to the Pacific islands since it is from the highland region near the Tibetan border that many cultural affinities between those people - the No Su, and the Maori are evident as are also iconographical references to the Maya in Central America. Robert Heine-Geldern's work on comparisons between Chinese designs and those found in the Sepik region of New Guinea, the Pacific islands and the Maori in particular are now accepted broadly indicating the vast distances that mariners transferred cultural elements from one region to another[192].

The Moriori , the Maori and the Tangi - the Weeping Greeting

A custom known to the Maori as Tangi - a form of "weeping greeting", was known also in the Andaman Islands and this is an island group that preserved many cultural cross-references as already noted to Australia and Oceania. In the Amazon basin, among the Tupinamba, exactly the same form of greeting was recorded a century ago[193]. This custom is epitomised in a myth recorded from the Ge traditions among the Shavante tribe in the Amazon Basin and it is of interest that this tradition notes the search for the "white men" by women and in that search they came across the mythical or legendary people called the Tsimihopari and they were regaled with the "weeping" greeting[194]. It is perhaps not a coincidence that the Polynesians considered their ancestors also to be "fair-skinned" with red or blond hair. In this Ge myth the term Tsimi-Hopari suggests another people exhibiting many cultural references in their traditions with India and the Eastern Polynesians - the Hopi of Western Mexico[195].

In India the Aboriginal tribes retained into the 20th., century customs that appeared to be closely linked with those of the Polynesians and the Maoris in particular. The Bhil tribes-men danced before battles that were part of ceremonials aimed at generating bravery and fearlessness in the warriors[196]. Of particular interest are certain of the reduced status Rajput castes from Marwar. Some were called Marori - a corruption of the regional occupant, Marwari[197] that could be the original derivation for both Moriori and Maori, these latter possibly representing two migrations separated by generations or centuries. They were considered lesser status probably because they married Sudra or low caste brides that for some was a necessity since higher caste women were often in short supply as a result of polygamous marriages among the headmen and rulers. The Todas are one of the most interesting peoples of India and among them the "leaping-off" place so notable among the Melanesian and Polynesians in the journey of the soul is also found among them. Similarly it was noted by at least one researcher that the men were much the better-looking of the sexes making the comparison with the Maoris of New Zealand similarly indicated as the "fairer" sex[198].

In later chapters of this work the connections between India and the Gilbert Islands will be broached but Sir Arthur Grimble, the Islands' governor early in the twentieth century, noted the similarities of some of their creation myths to those of the Maori considering the "rugged beauty" of the Maori myths the more evocative[199]. This suggests that the Gilbert Island versions had "travelled" further from their common origin in time if not in distance. The histories of the Gilbert Islanders claim descent from the "Tree-of-Samoa" where their forebears lived until their dispersal when dissention broke out and many were forced to flee to their present islands homes in the northwest. Such dispersals appear frequent from at least the beginning of the second mil-

2.089 : Crying greeting traditional of the Andaman Islanders and the Maori and known also among a few tribes in the Amazon Basin. Andaman Islands, Bay of Bengal, Late 19th., century, A.D.

lennium A.D. in Polynesia and Percy Smith detected that about 1250 A.D. the Samoans gained supremacy over the "Tongan-Fijians" who were the same people as the "Maori-Raratongans". This period was considered by him to correspond with the great Maori heroes of their sagas, Karika and Tangiia. Karika's double canoe was called Te-au-ki-Tonga confirming his close connection with that group, and during the island wars, before venturing to New Zealand, he was said to have made eight journeys between the Central Polynesian island groups[200].

Percy Smith considered in his research on the legendary homeland of the Polynesians, Hawaiki, that it was in the time of the Maori hero Tawhaki, that contact with cannibalism is implied in myths and legends retained by the Maoris. He suggests from working back through the preserved genealogies that in about the

2.090 : Group of Ona men in ceremonial body paint with bold striping similar to the Australian Aborigines and fur cap similar to those traditional of the Maori men. Tierra del Fuego, Chile, Early 20th., century, A.D.

2.091 : Striped body paint similar to that found among the Ona along with other aspects of apparently shared culture. Central North Australia, Early 20th., century, A.D.

8th., century A.D. this controversial element was introduced from contact with Melanesia[201]. The "Tongan-Fijians", identifying with the "Maori-Raratongans", these having colonised parts of Fiji, and he notes: "...it was in Fiji and Samoa in which they lived; and one of the Maori stories says that Tawhaki ascended a mountain called Whiti-haua, in which Whiti is the Maori pronunciation for Rarotongan Iti - Fiji. Connected with these heroes are the names Whiti, Matuku and Peka, all given, at different times, as the names of fierce semi-human monsters. In them I see the names of islands, used metaphorically for the people of these islands. Peka is the Tongan name for Bengga, a Fiji Group, and Matuku is also a well-known name of one of the Fiji islands. In one of the same series of stories is mentioned a place called Muri-wai-o-ata, and this is the name of a stream on the south coast of Upolo,..."[202]. Smith further notes; "In the Maori story the tribes defeated by Tawhaki on his ascent of the mountain are called Te Tini-o-te-Makahua and Te Papaka-wheoro; with reference to the last name, Papaka means a crab, and in Rarotonga and Nuie, the words for crab (unga and tupa) are always applied to slaves, meaning Melanesian slaves."[203]. The special connection with Raratonga is again confirmed with the preservation of the myths relating to an ancestress named Apakura. The Raratongan version state that there were seven generations between her and Tangiia dating to about 875 A.D. - 39 generations before 1900 A.D. These myths and legends are known only there and among the Maori, who record that she burnt down the temple of Te Uru-o-Manono in Raratonga, but not mentioned in the myths of her homeland[204]. The burning of the temple was in revenge for the death of her son Tu-ranga-taua renown for his "beauty and skill"[205]. Interestingly the term tupua in Maori meant "odd, out-lan-dish, demon, weird-one" and is frequently found in their chants and traditions[206]. This appears to be another form of tupa meaning Melanesian slave but in other islands this name refers to a Peruvian hero and will be considered in due course.

The connections with Raratonga indicate an intimacy reflecting that they were one of the main ancestral island groups for the Maori clearly established in legend and myth. However, it is also clear from the Raratongan histories that they were closely allied in racial origins with the Marquesas Islands and although they were known blood relations they were also "bitter ene-mies"[207]. Other lines through the hero Tangiia-nui and his immediate ancestors appeared to have originated from Tahiti[208]. Smith deduced from the genealogies that Hawaii was first settled by 650 A.D. from Fiji. More recent archaeologically based studies has pushed that date back several centuries while connections with the Cook Islands (Raratonga) appear to be confirmed at the date suggested by Smith[209]. From Smith's standpoint, using the analysis of these tribal histories, he may be broadly correct in considering that from the central island groups he was studying and that migrations did take place at that time. It is thought that Hawaii remained isolated from Central Polynesia from that time until about 1150 A.D. but appearing to be connected to the Raratongans and Maoris[210]. This connection between Raratonga and the Maori with Hawaii may in fact have been in the opposite direction since Thor Heyerdahl presents a strong case for con-nections between the Indians of the North West Coast of British Colombia and Alaska and the

Polynesians of Hawaii, and the Maori[211]. Interestingly a tradition from Old Queen Charlotte Islands stating that their ancestors arrived in "six boatloads" who sailed "out of the foam" or sea is largely the tradition and exact number recorded by the Maori in their origin legends[212].

Thor Heyerdahl in extending the connections between these American Indians on the Pacific Coast of North West America into Polynesia refers to an unusual form of foot-drum that was placed in a hole in the ground and stamped on with the foot[213]. This same type was found also in Hawaii and Easter Island and appears similar to that known among the Andaman Islanders in the Bay of Bengal, a people who appeared to have connections with other Oceanic people and Tasmanians. However, other cultural artefacts such as gourd rattles recorded during Captain James Cook's voyage to the coast of Alaska are closely similar to those of Mexico and Peru[214]. Of particular interest are the feather cloaks so very similar among the Polynesians (*5.146*) and these natives on the Pacific Coast of Alaska and British Colombia, Mexico and Peru[215]. Those of the Inca and Maori bear strikingly similar designs these are only a few cultural elements suggesting again that there were close contacts between the Americas and Eastern and Central Pacific Islands (*5.140/1; 5.144*).

The mariner links to the Maoris extend also across the Central Pacific and far across the to the west into the Indian Ocean where the large African island of Madagascar exhibited the famous "Maori greeting" of touching or rubbing noses. This connection was recognised a century and a half ago when recorded by the Reverend William Ellis who proselytised in Polynesia and later in Madagascar. He notes that the terms used to describe this custom was called "Hogni" in New Zealand (but also tangi earlier noted), Honi in Hawaii, and Hoi among the Tahitians[216]. Connections between the Polynesians with Madagascar are numerous and have already been noted in part and indicate the vast distances that the Oceanic peoples travelled in their ocean-going canoes.

Such vast distances to Madagascar from Tahiti - 10,000 miles via Indonesia, and from New Zealand - 4000 miles by the most direct route along the Southern Australian coast, indicates that the journey to the South American continent from the island group of New Zealand at about 4-5000 miles, would have presented little problem. Of particular interest are the voyages noted indicating that the Maori sailed not only south from Central Polynesia to New Zealand but in at least a few voyages actually must have reached the Antarctic Circle and returned to tell the tale. The references to at least one voyage is related in an edited, abridged version of the adventures of the great Maori hero named Tangiia already noted in part. Percy Smith, in attempting to plot the voyages of this hero who sailed to Avaiki-te-varinga, usually located by him in Central

2.095 : Nurtunja headdress representing a horizontal form of the sacred totem staff. Central Australia, Late 19th., century, A.D.

2.092 : Conical headdress of the Central Australian tribes closely similar to the Ona in the far south of South America. Central Australia, Late 19th., century, A.D.

2.093 : Bold black and white body painting an conical mask closely similar to examples of tribal ceremonial designs in Aboriginal Australia. Tierra del Fuego, Early 20th., century, A.D.

2.094 : Highly geometric design body paint design with a ceremonial rod headdress similar to the Nurtunja of the Aboriginal Australians. Ona tribe, Tierra del Fuego, Chile, Early 20th., century, A.D.

117

Polynesia but in this epic clearly not anywhere near it, suggests that he may have reached Indonesia - about 6000 miles to the west[217]. In considering this along with the connections with Madagascar much further to the South West of Indonesia it would certainly not seem that this was an impossible destination.

In the great Polynesian sailing epics there are references indicating the characteristic ethnological problems in facing those who wish to unravel the historic lineages of any people emphasised in maritime history - not least among the Maori. It is noted in Tangiia's voyages that his lineage derives from Tahiti in Eastern Polynesia. It is related that he had travelled to Avaiki before returning eastwards to Polynesia where he arrived at Raratonga (Tumu-te-varo-varo)[218], to the west of Tahiti and east of Tonga. He discovered that two brothers of Apakura, the ancestress noted in Maori legends, had settled there after killing all the men but retaining the women[219]. This is an extreme case where all the males are killed in a take-over but frequently this is a strategy born out of necessity in the survival of migrant, exiled, or even marginalized or vagrant males seeking a more permanent place to occupy. They form the lineages from intermarriage with the local woman resulting in a hybrid race(s)[220]. This is recorded of Tangaii on Raratonga and is characteristic of customs throughout the sea routes of the world and is clearly relevant to the pre-European history of New Zealand. It is clear that in the later, Maori incursions that the Moriori were defeated and the males were massacred or fled to safe havens such as into the mountain retreats or the Chatham Islands. The Moriori women were then apportioned to the victors and new mixed race lineages evolved. References to mariners indicates that they are almost entirely male although in a few minor traditions incursions are noted with women. This would inevitably result in a broad unity of resultant offspring through women of the home peoples but who also exhibited varying traits and physical characteristics from the backgrounds of their father's peoples resulting in controversies of their apparently disparate origins[221].

In returning to Tangaia's voyages, the long sea journeys undertaken by this hero, and probably others, are highlighted by the reference that in one of them he was away for so long that his sons had grown up into manhood before he had returned from the Western Pacific[222]. This has parallels in the myths of the Indians of the North West Pacific Coast of North America, particularly the Kwakiutl, who state in several records that all the hair on the hero's head had fallen out by the time of his return and was sometimes old indicating the elapse of a long time period[223]. Before finally arriving at Raratonga he visited Fiji to the north west and has many adventures that delay and threaten him but he finally meets up with his people again later in Fiji where they number four hundred - a magical figure (e rau rau)[224]. In a confrontation with another hero at sea, Karika, Tangiia obtains the ascendancy and learns from him the course to navigate for Raratonga. In setting sail he misses the island group and eventually arrives at a "...part of the ocean where great currents meet, and Tangiia concludes he has reached the 'mountainous waves' of the south referred to in tradition, in which he is sup-ported by finding the sea quite cold"[225]. This suggests that he was actually swept by the East Australian Current past Raratonga, the Tongan group, and along the wide band of this current to where it is buffeted and deflected by the West Wind Drift south of the Australian mainland. It is said in the legends that he realised then that he had missed his target and turned around and eventually reached his destination, Raratonga. This outward journey to the south would have meant a journey of 3000 miles and the same again on the return to Raratonga - a distance that seems inconceivable for his fleet to have survived without extra supplies. It is likely that this legend, as with so many others, is probably an actual voyage but one that has become overlaid and mutated with others but nonetheless reflects knowledge through experience of the cold southern region south of Australia and New Zealand. When read with the earlier noted connections between the southern coastal peoples of Australia and the Maori and Moriori it is clear that the Polynesians must originally have sailed those southern regions on more than one occasion. This is emphasised by the fact that Tangiia's voyage is said to have confirmed the earlier traditions of his people that a cold region did exist far to the south. This region was particularly determined by the cold sea currents, a factor that must have been of special note to these professional mariners, and is found only south of Australia and New Zealand. This current flows across the south of the globe from the South Atlantic to South America as the notorious West Wind Drift in the region of the Roaring Forties (*2.004*).

The hero Tangiia and his voyages have greatly inspired many generations of Polynesians and particularly the Raratongans and Maoris. For them his ignominious defeat and eviction in flight after a period of great strife in Tahiti was a great stain in their history and genealogy. For the hero himself a poem attributed to him sums up much of the great sorrow and loss caused to those who survived this strife to flee and fight another day as they left their island homes, and for most never to return:

> "Great is my love for my own dear land -
> For Tahiti that I'm leaving.
> Great is my love for my sacred temple -
> For Pure-ora that I'm leaving.
> Great is my love for the drinking spring -
> For Vai-kura-a-mata, that I am leaving;
> For my bathing streams, for Vai-iria,
> For Vai-te-pa, that I am leaving;
> For my own old homes, for Puna-auia.
> For Papa-ete, that I am leaving;
> For my loved mountains, for Tika-kura-marumaru,
> For Ao-rangi, that I am leaving.
> And alas ! for my beloved children,
> For Pou-te-anaunua and Motoro now dead.
> Alas, my grief ! my beloved children,
> My children ! O ! my grief.
> O Pou-te-anuanua. Alas ! Alas !
> O Motoro ! Alas ! O Motoro !"[226].

In this poem the term for sacred water Vai is the Hai found elsewhere in Polynesia but is a term found also similarly in Central America and probably derives from the Mandaean Hai as noted in an earlier work[227]. The myths and legends as oral history should not be ignored in the assessment of a peoples' history but the care necessary in using them as fact is highlighted by the fact that Tangiia's son Motoro, here lamented as deceased victim of war in this poem, in another legend is considered an ancestor of the Mangaians[228] - an island near Raratonga. The name of the sacred mountain, Ao-rangi, in Tahiti in this poem is also the Maori name of Mount Cook in New Zealand indicating the transfer of identity common in the migrations in many peoples and tends to indicate that there is the kernel of truth in these myths.

In the great epics surrounding the hero Tangaii it is also noted that in the preparation to occupy Raratonga while he was in Fiji he requests that his ally, Iro (Whiro in Tahiti), appoint his son name Tai-te-ariki to be the ariki or canoe captain for this expedition. The young man, however, was said to be in Rapa-nui, Easter Island, and Tangiia then sets out on this voyage of some 4200 miles to fetch him - "...a voyage dead against the trade wind"[229]. Since many of the Polynesian islands must have been populated by sailing against the trade winds this voyage would have presented no special problems. It is certain that he must have called in at many of the islands on the way but these are not mentioned in the myths. On reaching Rapa-nui the young chief joined Tangiia and they proceeded to Morea, an island near Tahiti. Tangiia meets up with his estranged sister on the way to Raratonga to whom he explains his mission and reveals Iro's son to be the substitute for the sons that he has lost in battle lamented in the poem. Smith's record of this confrontation is worth repeating here: "…I cannot remain; I must go. There is an island named Tumu-te-varo-varo (Rarotonga) which was disclosed to me by Tonga-iti." "What land is that?" "What land, indeed! I have never seen it. I shall go there to live and die, and set up Iro's son as an ariki over my people." He then names the clans over which Tai-te-ariki is to rule, including the Manuane and others already referred to and the sister then gives Tai-te-ariki a new name, Te-ariki-upoko-tini (the many-headed ariki), referring doubtless to the many clans he was to govern[230]. This ariki along with Tangii were to loom large in the history of the Maoris where the descendants of Tai-te-ariki were known into recent times in New Zealand.

The myth indicates the close connection between Easter Island, Tahiti, Raratonga and Maori New Zealand, in spite of the fact that recent researchers in Easter Island history have determined that after initial settlement Rapa-nui, Easter Island, apparently received little or no contact from the outer world. It has already been noted that burial traditions show connections, e.g. the rat obolos in the mouth, between the Moriori of the Chatham Islands and Easter Island are very likely from a connected tradition. Dating, resulting from archaeological research, tends to indicate that Easter Island was populated some centuries before New Zealand and even Hawaii[231] perhaps commencing in about 300 A.D., but this would not conflict with the Tangiia legends. It is of interest therefore that any person who was considered an expert in any profession on Easter Island was called maori, although the original term was tufunga[232]. In the records of Easter Island, one particular hero, Hotua Matua, is of special note. It was noted by Thor Heyerdahl from Thomsen's records that he came from where the Sun rose[233], but other traditions collected by Kathleen Scoresby Routledge on the island nearly a century ago indicate that he came from the south east[234]. This latter record clearly indicates that the warm north section of the West Wind Drift current flowing directly from New Zealand to Southern Polynesia, and Easter Island, would point to his having come from the Maoris, and the term for renown craftsmanship may have replaced the original name with their own in time. If a hero named Tangiia had indeed been able to sail to Easter Island and fetch his son as ariki and later populate New Zealand, even by default after not succeeding in Raratonga, then the knowledge of Rapa-nui and its location was probably sufficient for it to be known and located before and by their descendants generations later.

The Physical Stature of the Maori in Early European Records

The connections of Rapa-nui, or Easter Island, with the South American mainland will be of more interest later, but one more element of the Maori, and the Polynesians in general, is of interest, and that is their physical stature. J. Kerry-Nicholls considered the Maoris "…as the finest aboriginal race of the Pacific. In their physical characteristics they are well built, well-shaped, and erect in figure, with broad chests and massive rounded limbs, which usually display great muscular development. The average height of the men is about 5 feet 6 1/2 inches, but there are many who exceed that standard." And he further states; "As a rule, the chiefs with the Maoris are tall, display a martial and independent air, and move about with a bold and dignified carriage. The tallest native who came under my observation was Mohi, a chief of the Ngatimoharetoa tribe of Taupo. He was a man of herculean build, standing barefooted over 6 feet 4 inches. The next largest man was Wahanui, chief of the Ngatimaniapoto tribe, who, with a height of over 6 feet, was besides remarkable for the great size of his head, the fine physical development of his limbs, and the extraordinary breadth of his chest and shoulders."[235].

The descriptions recorded by other noted authors tends to reflect similar impressions but

2.097 : Wrestling was traditional at social occasions and religious festivals and here Gond men participate at one of these gatherings at Koilibera. Central India, Early 20th., century, A.D.

2.099 : Ona wrestlers, who normally only wore an animal skin cape dropped when any activity was required. The staged bout shows one of the men wearing his cap similar to that of the Maori. Tierro del Fuego, Chile, Early 20th., century, A.D.

2.096 : Wrestling was an combat rite associated with important festivals and was probably related to similar rites in Indonesia, Polynesia and South America. Kitike, Sema Naga, Assam, North East India, Early 20th., century, A.D.

2.098 : Wrestling was a common activity seriously pursued by many of the islands peoples in Indonesia, and similarly in India, Polynesia and South America. Dyak, Borneo, Early 20th., century, A.D.

of particular interest is that at the time Kerry-Nicholls was writing in the second half of the nineteenth century when a mixed Maori and European people was evolving: He wrote: "The intercourse between the European and Maori has given rise to an intermediate class of individuals, which now forms a connecting link between the two races. The half-castes are not only remarkable for their fine, well-formed persons, but also for their intellectual powers." ... "Although possessing as fine a physique, the half-castes are not equal in stamina to the pure bred Maoris, while they age much faster than other members of the race."[236]. Although Kerry-Nicholls refers to the "pure-bred" Maori, there was in fact no such thing. The reference to the "half-caste" or mixed race is of particular interest since this is exactly the repetition of events which occurred when the first immigrant "Maoris" arrived, epitomised by the canoes of Tangiia many centuries earlier. For those allied to the incomers women were given by the local chiefs to confirm their alliance, but if in opposition, the women would be captured or captive after defeat of the earlier Moriori tribes creating a new hybrid people. This was clearly the pattern for later immigrants or mariners arriving in New Zealand but was also the usual pattern throughout the Pacific.

It was almost exclusively the males who travelled in their canoes either as professional mariners and traders or escapees from wars. To ensure progeny it was necessary to obtain women by treaty, trade or capture or invasion of the territory of other islands' chiefdoms and their offspring were therefore almost invariably of mixed race and the many references to such practices in the myths and legends only confirms the basic truth of the oral traditions. Kerry-Nicholls confirms this pattern: "It is worthy of remark that alliances are usually brought about between the two races by a European marrying a Maori woman, an event which in the early days of the colony was a frequent occurrence, and even at the present day unions of this nature are not infrequent. Individually, I never came across an instance where a Maori had taken unto himself a European wife."[237]. The same principle is as ancient as time and is found along all the migration routes both on land and sea throughout all the continents and islands of the world.

In Polynesia the imposing physical stature of the men in particular was of special note among European explorers and missionaries. Although Kerry-Nicholls considered the Maori the finest he notes that not only have they a "very remarkable affinity" with the Tongan language but the "...Maoris bear a remarkable physical resemblance to the natives of that group."[238]. In earlier noted legends the Maori have clear ancestral connections also to Tahiti and it was noted by a pre-Victorian missionary, William Ellis, that the chiefs were taller than the average stature of the other men in the islands although a few were of similar height[239]. He describes the king of Tahiti as follows: "In person, Pomare, like most of the chiefs of the South Sea Islands, was tall and stout, in stature he was six feet four inches high, his limbs active and well-proportioned, and his whole form and gait imposing ..."[240]. Ellis notes that his first impression of this king at their first meeting as of "gigantic appearance" and aged about 40 years of age[241]. After several years in Tahiti Ellis was sent on to Hawaii and noted: "The natives are in general rather above middle stature, well-formed, with fine muscular limbs, open countenances, and features frequently resembling those of Europeans." "...The chiefs in particular are tall and stout, and their personal appearance is so much superior to that of the common people, that some have imagined them a distinct race. This, however, is not the fact; the great care taken of them in childhood, and their better living, have probably occasioned the difference."[242]. The descriptions of these Polynesian peoples is almost identical and Ellis's comments regarding the chiefs as a better cared for section of their communities is a principle which has been seized upon by more recent anthropologists and archaeological researchers. However, in applying this comment to Polynesians it is in conflict with the many legends that indicates foreign extraction for many of the royal houses in the islands kingdoms and chiefdoms. This element will be of more interest in later chapters but it is sufficient here to note that the Maoris were clearly related in stature and descent from these Central and Eastern Polynesian people of great stature. They were, and are exemplars of the roving, trading, and refugee mariners forming separate clans and chiefdoms with the local women as the matrix giving them partial identity with other peoples of the same island group, and this mixing in turn modified their obvious differences in the racial origin of the male ancestors. The remarkable stature of the Polynesians has often been seen as one block to any relationship with the Mongoloid derived peoples of South America - the Amerindians. However there is one group known as the Ona, or Selkhnam, located in the far south of South America who were unusually tall and statuesque and who have been considered as a result of possible incursions of Polynesians into that Continent and who are therefore of special interest.

Transferred Iconography from Australia and New Zealand in Southern South America

Their are many references recorded from the surviving Moriori myths and legends that link New Zealand to South East Australia to their obvious descent in the main from Polynesian ancestry. The ultimate assimilation of elements imported by mariners into the mainland Maori population confirms the occupation of New Zealand as having been directly related to the flow and direction of the ocean currents and the lands that these connected. Even Easter Island, Rapa-nui, is shown to be connected by sea currents as well as in legend to New Zealand and from Central Polynesia. The major sea current flowing from South America forming the South Equatorial Current will be of some interest in later chapters, but the extraordinary history of the Maori and their ancestors recording the fact of the cold currents in the far south from Polynesia suggests that they, anciently, before the record of settlement in New Zealand, utilised this current to reach South America.

The Ona People of Tierra del Fuego in Myth and Ritual

The Ona, now more usually called the Selkhnam, were a people who were distinct from their neighbouring tribes and were particularly noted for their great stature. The earliest reports from explorers and mariners travelling through the straits of Magellan between the mainland of South America and Tierra del Fuego reported that they had sighted, traded, or had contact with giants. Thomas Falkner, one of the more clear-headed and reliable early writers in his "Description of Patagonia" compiled the reports known up until his time. The probably related groups of peoples to the Ona were all said to have greater than average stature even when compared to Europeans in the Patagonian region. Undoubtedly rumours exaggerated the height of these people until reports of physical descriptions of impossibly large people were being circulated. Faulkner commented: "... that gigantic race, which others have mentioned. Anthropologists class the Tehuelches with the tallest groups of the world, and men over six feet tall were common, while a height of seven feet was not rare. Their stature was impressive, but Antonio Pigafetta, who accompanied Magellan on his voyage around Cape Horn and the author of the first account of the Patagonians, established them as unnatural giants when he wrote that while the ship was in the bay of San Julian a native appeared who was 'so tall that the tallest of us only came up to his waist'. As Magellan undoubtedly had one man six feet tall in his crew, the native has an implied height of ten or twelve feet. However, Pigafetta is known to have exaggerated on occasion, and is probable that if he were placed under oath he might reduce the height somewhat"[243]. From his book published in 1774 A.D. he further quotes Thomas Pennant; " '...let it be observed that out of the fifteen first voyagers who passed through the Magellanic streights, not fewer than nine are undeniable witnesses to the existence of giants'"[244]. In considering these earlier reports Faulkner reviews the Spanish accounts and notes that of the Cacique (chief) Cangapol: "His figure and dress are represented on the map, and those of his wife Huennee. This Chief who was called by the Spaniards the Cacique Bravo, was tall and well-proportioned. He must have been seven feet and some inches in height; because, on tiptoe, I could not reach to the top of his head" .... "His brother, Sausimain, was about six feet high. The Patagonians, or Puelches, are a large bodied people; but I have never heard of that gigantic race, which others have mentioned ..."[245]. Faulkner further notes that there were many bones of exceptional size found, some of those he saw he considered may have been human[246], but it is more likely that these may have been extinct animals. Of the surviving Indians he saw in Eastern Patagonia he notes that the Puelches "... were a large race of people, and several of them near seven feet six inches high ..."[247]. Among these people of greater stature the Moluches or Mapuche will be of further interest in due course.

It is of some interest that the burial customs noted of these southern Indians was that of secondary burial where the flesh was removed from the skeleton and the bones interred in pits near the sea[248]. This suggests that these tribes were at least in part descended from a mariner people who arrived on the sea shore and therefore required that they should be returned to their ancestors at death at the point, or as near in principle, to the landing point. This is a common form of burial found with or without coffins among the peoples of the Pacific Ocean and South and South East Asia. It is also of interest that the male "wizards" - shamans, dressed as females and is reflective of a custom known in Central America and particularly in India[249].

In the nineteenth and early twentieth centuries the Ona lived on the island of Tierra del Fuego at the very southern tip of South America. They shared the island with another people of lesser stature called the Yaghan but who called themselves the Yamana, and the Acaloof. The Eastern or Etalum Ona called themselves Aush while the main body called themselves Shelknam or Selkhnam[250]. The climate is one of the most difficult to be found on Earth and being so near the Antarctic continent is influenced by the extremity of a severe cold climate. To the immediate north of the island, above the Straits of Magellan, the vast open steppe grasslands attracted European sheep farmers, many among them being the British. Tierra del Fuego is about the size of Newfoundland or Ireland and is also sheep country and in 1871 A.D. a British missionary family arrived to replace the first missionaries to survive among the Yaghan (Yamana) in Tierra del Fuego. Their son, E. Lucas Bridges, grew up among them and was to write authoratively about the tribes of this most remote region on earth. With the extinction of the Ona by the mid-twentieth century Bridges interest, observations and record of them is of critical importance. He was one of the few to penetrate their religious rituals and was himself initiated into their rites acquiring a more intimate knowledge of these people besides that of general day-to-day contact with a neighbouring people[251]. His interest in these people grew for the most part from employing them as sheep-herders in the hills away from home where he would spend extended periods among them listening to their stories and myths.

Bridges believed that the Ona and Aush were in fact a southern extension of the Tehuelches of southern Patagonia north of the straits of Magellan. The Aush appeared to have preceded the Ona by some time so that when the Ona arrived in Tierra del Fuego their respective languages had changed so much that communication was difficult. He believed that at one time the Aush had occupied the whole of the island but were eventually pushed into the eastern corner as their place names, that have no meaning in the language of the other incoming tribes, appears to confirm[252]. The intrusion of these peoples must have been so long ago that there are no myths or legends that Bridges could retrieve from them although he admits that he did not spend sufficient time with the Aush to be certain of their traditions in depth. However, the origin of such extraordinarily large people inhabiting this southern region of South America cannot be explained by diet and living conditions alone since their food supplies resembled those of the physically smaller Amerindians who were also long term neighbours to the Ona, Aush and Teheulches.

The separate origin of the Ona appears in a number of cultural traits and not least in the weapons critical for their survival. They utilised only the bow and arrow and were much feared by the adjacent tribes[253] and Bridges noted that: "... I have never seen - either in those places (Paraguay and Brazil) or anywhere else - an aboriginal weapon to compare in workmanship with the Ona bow and arrow"[254]. Interestingly a ritual for settling a feud was that of having five arrows fired at the man as he ran towards the marksman having to dodge each as it came at him[255]. This same ritual was also part of a peace ceremony between warring factions except the "victim" was a youth who was pelted with small pebbles as a preparation[256]. As in Central America, among the Huichol in particular, and India the number five is of importance and seems to have been imported along with other related aspects such as the Hain.

The Hain was the sacred initiation lodge for the young men or youths and no aspect of its construction or the rites that took place could be imparted to woman under threat of death[257]. The lodge was the very heart of the religious and ceremonial life of the male Ona and at its centre was a ridgepole called the "Black Shag", or Kiayeshk, that was the focus of their rituals[258].

The Ona Myth of the Hain

The myth of the origins of the Hain are of interest and Lucas Bridges recorded it as follows: "In the days when all the forest was evergreen, before Kerrhprrh the parakeet painted the autumn leaves red with the colour of his breast, before the giants Kwonyipe and Chashkilchesh wandered through the woods with their heads above the tree-tops; in the days when Krren (= the Sun, as Kon or Con?) and Kreeh (the Moon = Si?) walked the earth as man and wife, and many of the great sleeping mountains were human beings: in those far-off days witchcraft was known only by the women of Ona-land. They kept their own particular lodge, which no man dared approach. The girls, nearing womanhood were instructed in the magic arts, learning how to bring sickness and even death to all those who displeased them."

"The men lived in abject fear and subjection. Certainly they had bows and arrows with which to supply the camp with meat, yet they asked, what use were such weapons against witchcraft and sickness? This tyranny of women grew from bad to worse until it occurred to the men that a dead witch was less dangerous than a live one. They conspired together to kill off all the women; and there ensued a great massacre, from which not one woman escaped in human form."

"Even the young girls only just beginning their studies in witchcraft were killed with the rest, so the men now found themselves without wives. For these they must wait until the little girls grew into women. Meanwhile the great question arose: How could men keep the upper hand now they had got it? One day, when these girl children reached maturity, they might band together and retain their old ascendancy. To forestall this, the men inaugurated a secret society of their own and banished forever the women's lodge in which so many wicked plots had been hatched against them. No woman was allowed to come near the Hain, under penalty of death. To make quite certain that this decree was respected by their womenfolk, the men invented a new branch of Ona demonology - a collection of strange beings - drawn partly from their own imaginations and partly from folk-lore and ancient legends - who would take visible shape by being impersonated by members of the Lodge and thus scare the woman away from the secret councils of the Hain. It was given out that these creatures hated women, but were well disposed towards men, even supplying them with mysterious food during the often very protracted proceedings of the Lodge. Sometimes, however, these beings were short-tempered and hasty. Their irritability was manifested to the women of the encampment by the shouts and uncanny cries arising from the Hain, and, it might be, the scratched faces and bleeding noses with which the men returned home when some especially exciting session was over"[259].

The Hain, or Lodge, was usually located about half a mile from the village and faced away from it so that none could peer in and preferably near a clump of trees used to screen the open entrance and was constructed as a "wigwam". Of interest is that the situation was chosen out of respect for the west wind (from the Pacific Ocean) that was considered favourable by the Ona[260]. Bridges informant on the rites and traditions of the Hain revealed some remarkable myths or legends associated with the Lodge and he notes; "Aneki told me during that first discourse that, from the fire in the centre of the Hain, an imaginary chasm of untold depth, and with a flaming inferno at the bottom of it, ran through the door and away eastward into the distance. Ages ago, when the Hain was new, this chasm had really existed and anyone trying to cross it had fallen in and been lost. Its presence now was only assumed, yet it was still not without its perils when a meeting was in session. Any man treading, however inadvertently, on the place where it was supposed to be would be thrown on the fire - though, added Aneki, he would not be held down there …".

"This hypothetical chasm had another purpose. It divided the Lodge into two groups, according to parentage or place of birth. The men from the north sat to the south of the fissure, and the men from the south to the north."

"… There, half-way along (inside the Hain), was Kiayeshk, which meant Black Shag and was the name of the pole darkened by burning "…."At the end of the meetings all these restraints were lifted and we could leave the Hain in any way we liked" ….."When not in use as a Lodge, the wigwam served as sleeping-quarters and living-house for the bachelors, … widowers … and kloten (youths) who had passed their entrance examination. The boys who did not know the secret had to sleep in the encampment"[261].

The report based on long experience between the Ona and the author E. Lucas Bridges, as an initiate among them, has resulted in one of the few authentic reports of the Hain and its mysteries. Although he himself, as a practising Christian and brother-in-law to the missionary Barbrooke Grubb who ministered for some time among the Lengua in the Gran Chaco, dismisses the rites and beliefs of the Ona as "ludicrous"[262] he did at least record them for posterity. His brother-in-law also produced a classic on the Lengua and will be of note later but their example was not followed by many missionaries whose only intent was to eliminate all traces of the original culture and belief systems of their subjects.

The Ona term for their Lodge is of some interest since the root Hai is found widely

2.100 : Ona man with a fur cap similar to the traditional Maori cap and face paint extending from the nose to the ears on both side of the face. Similar face paint is widely found in the Pacific Island culture and in South America. Tierra del Fuego, Chile, Early 20th., century, A.D.

2.101 : Maori chief wearing the fur cap that appears to be the model for those of the Ona in South America. He wears also the feather cape indicating chiefly status and identical to those of Polynesia and Peru. New Zealand, Early 20th., century, A.D.

2.102 : Ona hunter, also known as Selknam, with conical fur cap and usually an animal fur cape closely similar to those of the Maori. Tierra del Fuego, Chile, Early 20th., century, A.D.

throughout the Pacific Ocean and its Rim. The Huichol were of great interest in establishing connections between them in the north west of Mexico and India and their cave, from which the haino - a bird from the Pacific coast resided, sacred to the fire god, that was called the Hain-otega[263]. This cave was considered the birthplace of the fire god where it was believed that he came forth as a spark. The temple at this place faces west - towards the Pacific Ocean and undoubtedly represents the origin of the incursions of mariners from that direction so noted in their mythology and recorded in part in an earlier work[264]. Carl Lumholtz noted a century ago that a statue of the god standing on a disk was the centre of adoration in this most sacred place in the Huichol country called Te-Akata and when this is removed it revealed a hole two feet deep (600mm) in which stood another statue on a miniature chair[265]. He also notes: "This figure is ancient, and is more sacred to the Huichols than the larger one, because volcanic fire represents the god more directly and forcibly. The god above the ground talks to the sun in the daytime, while the one underneath talks to him at night, while the sun is travelling underground."[266].

The Huichol prefix for their fire god, Hain-otega, is surely related to the Ona "Hain" both relating to fire and volcanic deities or rites involving pits and hearths. Of particular interest is that the Hain probably relates to the Ain-u of Japan who were fire-worshippers whose name derives from Huchi, Huichi or Fuichi hence Fuji the volcano. The Ainu term huchi is a derivative of uhui (= to burn) and is a word for fire and where the Ainu goddess is named Kamui Huchi linked in principle to the fire god Maui of Polynesia[267]. Kamui is a deity prefix found also among the Huichol[268]. Huichi is probably therefore the name of the Huich-ol that appears to have been adopted at a later date from one or several incursions from across the other side of the Pacific Ocean, the original probably being from India. Lumholtz notes further on the Huichol sacred fire temple: "The locality, the most sacred in the entire Huichol country derives its name from Te-akata, from the cavity (te-aka) underneath this little temple. The word te-aka designates the hole in the ground in which deer-meat and mescal-hearts are cooked between hot stones under cover of an earth mound. The name, therefore, means the place where there is the te-aka par excellence, and gives one an insight into the original conception of the principal god of the Huichols as the one who cooks the food dearest to the tribe, on which in ancient times they no doubt mainly subsisted."[269]. It is also interesting to note that the statues are renewed every five years a number that repeats throughout most of the Huichols rituals, and is a number noted among the Ona far to the south[270]. It is of interest that among the Yamana of Tierra del Fuego a flood myth records that there are said to have been five mountain retreats[271]. This appears to concur with that of the Navaho where there was one in the centre and four at the cardinal points that appears to repeat the Buddhist and Hindu cosmologies. There are five sacred peaks in the Himalayas in Buddhist and Hindu mythology, from which the sacred rivers flow, and these would appear to have been the origin of such myths[272].

The clouds in the sky were of some importance to the Ona, but among the Huichols, the Goddess of the Western Clouds was associated with Te-Akata, the temple of the fire god[273]. Lumholtz notes the importance of the hunters and their associations with clouds: "Deer-hunters after death become crystals and accompany the sun on its travels. They live where the sun rises, which place they call Hai Tonolipa ("clouds liberating themselves"). In that region are believed to be many clouds, which spread themselves out like plumes. Indeed, clouds are sometimes conceived of as plumes"[274].

The Patagonians widely believed that some of the more important people after death returned to the "divine" ancestral caves reflecting those they occupied in life and believed that the stars of the Milky Way were in fact old Indians. They were said to hunt the celestial ostriches and that the two celestial clouds of the Milky Way seen in the Southern Hemisphere were the feathers of these ostriches that they had killed[275]. The importance of clouds, feathers or plumes parallels, among the Ona, the beliefs of the Huichol and their identification of plumes with clouds apparently reflects another aspect of cultural exchange either directly or from a third group of influences.

It is remarkable to note that the focus of the Huichol fire temple was in fact a statue standing on a disk that covered a hole meant to access the underworld of fire since this is almost identical to the imagery conjured up by the Ona in the hearth of their Hain noted above. This can hardly be coincidence since they share reflections of the same name related to fire. The door of the Huichol temple faced west toward the Pacific Ocean, undoubtedly the region of the ancestors, but the Ona Hain also faced west - ostensibly for the favourable wind. Such a wind appears to have no real advantage to the Ona except that it is a vague memory of the enormity of the great prevailing southern winds driving the West Wind Drift Current direct from Southern Australia and Tasmania as well as from New Zealand. It is of interest that Bridges notes that there are virtually no memories of migrations among the Ona into their territory, a truly extraordinary admission, since the ancestral origins of most peoples are usually the most sacred and jealously retained. Those that do exist are lacking in indicators of origins or descent.

The Huichol term Hai-Tonolipa, a cloud deity, suggests another Polynesian connection among many[276] and Hei is the god of wisdom among the Maori[277]. Hai or Haii is found widely in Polynesia meaning sacred water and therefore relates clearly to the Huichol deity associated with clouds. Although there appears to be connections with the Ainu of Japan it is perhaps more likely, in the far south of South America, that these influences entered with the Maoris who are known to have close cultural influences that derived from China which they introduced to the south of New Guinea and New Zealand. Whether first contact with South America was achieved by the first Maoris or their predecessors the Morioris is debatable but it is most likely that either or both introduced not only these associations with the fire deity but much which has already been noted as being closely connected with Tasmania and mainland Australia.

The references that early Victorian researchers have perceived indicate close connections between the Tasmanians and mainland Australian Aborigines with the Fuegians of Tierra del Fuego at the southern tip of South America have been noted earlier in this chapter. There are fewer indicators from researches based of those more interested in that of the Patagonians who have perceived parallels with the Australian Aborigines, or indeed, the Maoris that contact took place. This is probably because the region has attracted very few professional anthropologists or archaeologists until much more recent times and that those who settled the region were in fact only successful from the late nineteenth century. This region was a frontier until only half a century ago although some consider it so today only the reports of interested educated missionaries or settlers for the first two generations of the 20th., century.

It was noted that the Ona used red ochre to "impregnate" their hair[278], a custom found also in the Amazon basin far to the north but also noted of the Tasmanian Aborigines. Burial customs of the Patagonians generally have been noted already but of particular interest among them was that the Ona and Aush gashed themselves in mourning. This follows the exact custom among the Australian Aborigines and Pacific Islands in mourning rituals and the wrapping of body in skins was also known among them as the usual for the Ona[279]. It is not surprising that Andrew Lang and Father Schmidt considered the gods of the Ona -the Selk"nam (Selkhnam), similar to those of the Kurnai of South East Australia and this appears to be confirmed by the important work recorded among these people by Father Martin Gusinde dating from 1919 to 1923[280]. The Kurnai exhibited the greatest similarities to the New Zealanders and it is clear that there must have been contact between them, probably initiated by the Morioris or at least one of the racial strands that formed them, and no doubt extended by the Maoris to the Ona after them. It is of some interest therefore that the sole element of clothing the Ona males retained was that of the guanaco pelt (chohn k-oli) and equates to the possum skin cape of the Tasmanians. That of the Maori was clearly related although they were more elaborate and extended to include ceremonial types and enhanced by decorative designs and techniques. Of particular note is the ceremonial "cap" (goochilh or kochel) worn by the Ona (*2.100*; *2.102*) since this clearly has been derived from that of the Maori and is the counterpart of the "close-feathered" framed headdress or crown, the pare-kure. In Ona myth this cap, or kochel, was said to have been made by the giant ogre Chaskels from the pubic triangle of women[281]. Fine early portraits of the Ona and Maori show that not only their clothing and ceremonial caps are similar but the physical features of the overall stature and face are closely similar (*2.101*).

Ona Creation Myths of the First Man who Travelled All Over the World
Among the most interesting of the myths to have survived from the Ona and their Yaghan or Yamana neighbours are those dealing with their ancestral origins but lacking in-depth information that might refer to ancient migrations or origins. These are somewhat truncated and no more than a basic structure but enough has survived to draw parallels and inferences indicating that there had been intrusions of foreigners who had settled among them from time to time. It is clear that these relate more to incursive males as demi-heroes or ogres and who exhibit familiar roles in myths that are in many cases reminiscent of those in the Pacific islands - a similar situation found far to the north in the Amazon Basin.

Of the creation of the world and the first people there are some examples that are basic but are of interest for comparative purposes. It was said by the Ona that the first being was Kenos who was the only one on earth in the beginning who had been designated the task by Tamaukel ("Someone up There") to create order in the world. He was said to be the "Son of the South and the Heavens" and he wandered all over the earth. Eventually he returned to Tierra del Fuego to a "swampy place" and dug up some earth mixed with grass tufts and roots and shaped a male phallus with it and placed it on the ground. From another lump of earth he sculpted the female organ and placed it beside that of the male and left. During the night the male and female members joined and the first Ancestor emerged who was similar to a human. During subsequent nights the male and female organs re-united producing other human-like people and their numbers began to grow[282]. This myth could have been taken from the enormous body of Aboriginal myths in India where the giant Bhima and other heroes, considered primal ancestors, were said to have "travelled over the world". Equally the vague memory of people who in some way were like them having visited them earlier and then returned suggests a migrant or trading people. The fact that this and other of the Ona myths indicate a "giant" people or person suggests that these were a race of much greater physical stature compared to themselves. The copulating of the male and female genital organs uniting as if independent is a motif found in India and also among the Indians of the coast of Alaska and British Colombia suggesting contact by sea[283].

The Polynesians were undoubtedly those mariners whose myths and legends connect so closely with those of India, to be of further interest in due course, and the North West Coast of North America. In another Ona myth it was said the Kenos, already noted as the Son of the South and Heaven - a title that has close parallels to those of the Polynesian heroes and deities, who pushed the heaven apart from the earth[284]. Kenos was believed to have arisen into the heavens after this act to become a star but the motifs of the sky being at one time close to the earth and being pushed up by a god or hero is identical to those of Polynesia already noted and found through Melanesia to Indonesia. These motifs can be traced ultimately to India where among others many representations of Krishna raising the sky are known which are closely similar to those depicted in Mesoamerica[285].

The Pacific peoples most likely to have been in contact with the South American coast relating to the far south are the Polynesians and judging from the flow of the ocean currents, this would point to the Maoris in particular. The first Ancestor, Kenos suggests that this may have derived from Kanem, or Tane of the Maori, their supreme hero-god, or Koen (Con?) from Australia. The Ona Sky deity, Tamau-kel, appears to have derived from Tumu, also one of the first gods in the Polynesian pantheon and a name found among the ancient Egyptians. This name is that of a chieftain among the No-su of Southern China - a people believed to have been connected to the Maori, and found also as Tume or Zume in Colombia in the North West of South America.

In another myth cycle it was said that a giant or ogre named Chaskels lived in a great ravine near Rio MacLean and this was known as his "hut". He was greatly skilled with the sling and all lived in great fear of him and his fierce dogs that could track any one down and pursue them relentlessly until caught. Chaskels was particularly partial to pregnant women whom he consumed with relish after roasting them. Babies he was said to have stacked behind his cap or kochel, while the larger children he hung from his belt as his larder. His cloak was believed to have been made from human skins and his cloak, as noted earlier, was from the pubic triangle of women. In one day's foray he seized the two young nephews of Kwonyipe and hung them on his belt but kept them alive for the moment to force them to clean out the intestines from the bodies of those he had already killed and to fetch the firewood to cook them. Having discovered the abduction Kwonyipe set out to rescue his nephews, and while the ogre sat beside the fire he made a sign to the boys from a hiding place pointing out where he would await for them when they had the opportunity to escape. When the moment arrived the boys took off in the direction indicated and arrived at a riverbank that Kwonyipe had joined to allow them to cross. When the boys were safe Kwonyipe separated and destabilised the banks so that the pursuing giant, Chaskels the Cannibal, slipped down the bank and collapsed at the bottom face down. Kwonyipe broke the spine of the cannibal with a stamping of his foot and the ogre died. As it was now safe the boys flung two stones in their slings at the ogre's eyes, bursting them and from each of them came an insect "buzzing loudly". His body then turned to stone where it was said by the Ona to still be seen on the bank of the broad Rio Grande of Tierra del Fuego.

The myth has several remarkable aspects and the first of these is that the motif of the children defeating a devouring giant is well-known in Melanesia[286] in particular and probably deriving from the giant, cannibalistic Danos, Danavas, or Rakshas in the myths of India. It will be noted repeatedly in this work that other researchers in Andean studies and particularly those reporting on the Amazon Basin cultures, indicate close parallels with Melanesia in particular. The Melanesian myths are themed around two boys or youths who kill the giant in revenge for the long period of tyranny and cannibalisation of their people and in at least one case the two

2.103 : Breastband customary among the Toba Indians in the Gran Chaco of Peru. Toba tribe, Gran Chaco, Paraguay, South America, Late 19th., century, A.D.

2.105 : Breastband similar to that found in India and also in South America and Melanesia. Remojadas, Veracruz, East Coast Mexico, 6-900 A.D.

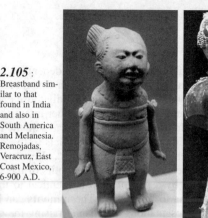

2.104 : Breastband customary in New Caledonia but here substituting a Western belt and buckle. New Caledonia, Melanesia, Early 20th., century, A.D.

2.106 : One breastband of several types found in ancient India into more recent times. Ganga, Pala Dynsaty, East India, 8-9th., century, A.D.

boys, as here, are made to serve the giant first. In Ona myths in Japan it is notable that a bridge that collapses with the evildoer falling into the river below that is highly reminiscent of the Cinvat Bridge in the Ancient Middle East, a motif found also in India, Indonesia, and Melanesia through to the Americas[287]. This appears to be fundamental in the rescue of the two children and despatch of the ogre. This bridge is a motif that is essential in the journey of the soul of those who have already died and is a trial faced by the soul whereby, if it has been exemplary during its time on earth, it will cross the bridge without any problems, but if evil it will in someway fall off into the river or hell-hole below. Of special interest is that the eyes of the giant were "burst" by the boys' slingshots since the eyes were a special offering in the defeat of Polynesian enemies and were usually given to the victor's ruler or priest to swallow or bight symbolically. From each eye it was said that a "buzzing insect" emerged and this is remarkably similar to the motif of insects emerging from the fallen bodies of the giant Usai in Borneo[288], the Ainu in Japan[289], and the Kwakiutl of Pacific Coast of British Colombia[290]. The final motif of the giant's body, or that of some other malevolent being or demi-god, turning to stone is found further to the north in the classic late cultures of Peru and is found widely distributed along the sea routes from the Americas to India and will be considered in due course.

It is clear, therefore, that the Ona myth of Chaskels the Cannibal is a merging of many aspects of myths imported by mariners along the sea routes from South East Asia and Melanesia in particular and clearly indicating their origins from there. The name Chask-els may have developed from the Quichua name for star, Chas'ka, retained from the Incan period into the present day Indians in Peru. The Ona myths, and those associated with the Hain, or Initiation Lodge, also exhibit other motifs that are particularly related to those of India and Oceania.

Myths of the Ona Hain Deities

The spirits of the Hain were usually baleful and a threat to women - they might even be called the misogynist supernaturals. Lucas Bridges does not in fact include them as gods or deities and went so far as concluding that there were no gods or religious practices among the Ona and certainly not in the European sense of high celestial beings and associated rituals being perhaps more similar to folk plays[291]. The supernaturals who were said to visit the Hain were impersonated by the members themselves but of special interest is the fact that the body paint and decoration applied to the naked body with the appropriate mask were so closely, and strikingly similar to those of the Australian Aborigines (2.090-95). They used designs, colours and even bird's down in the same way as the Aborigines and is found no where else in even remotely the same way among their neighbours or the more northern Patagonians from whom they apparently sprung, in part, as the southernmost migration.

The most prominent supernaturals of the Hain were the "horned" Hachai, also known as Halahachish, and his two sisters Halpen and Tanu. Halpen was known as the "white" spirit who came from the white cumulus clouds and her sister Tanu came from the red clay and both shared a reputation for fearsome cruelty[292]. Hachai was said to have emerged from the lichen-covered rocks and was therefore reflected as grey. Some deities share the prefix of hal or hala before the female Hal-pen and male Hachai or Hala-hachish, Hachai clearly deriving from hachish, appears to derive from the term for deity or demon called Hala. This term is known not only among the Nagas of Assam and the Aboriginal tribes of India but found also in Indonesia, Polynesia and among the Huichol in North West Mexico[293]. The second sister being named Tanu suggests again a gender reversal of the Polynesian, and Maori Tane, not unknown in foreign, assimilated, forms. She was said to have come from red clay and this element is of interest relating to creation of deities and supernatural in Melanesia such as Hatuibwari who will be of interest in due course. The "horns" attributed to Hachai, however, are anomalous since horned animals that could have been a model are unknown in South America. This suggests an introduction from a very distant source whatever its meaning but it may actually be an interpretation of the dual feathers worn projecting vertically from a headband worn into last century by the Maoris and other Oceanic peoples (*6.059-76*). These may have also become adapted to horn shapes in ritual performances when contact with Spanish introduced cattle some centuries before these myths were recorded a century ago.

Hachai was impersonated by one of the men who were painted from head to toe with red and white patterns, with the latter being more dominant and since he was said to have emerged from the lichen-covered rocks the impersonator was also decorated with grey down to represent the lichen. A padded miniature bow was tied across his forehead and his head was then covered with a mask of white colour with red-rimmed holes for him to see through. Bridges describes the appearance of the finished mask as that of a "short-nosed cow" and in fact "snorting" and threats of "charging", was part of the performance[294]. He was convinced that this ceremonial performance had been performed for countless generations before he witnessed it and was not a recent introduction[295].

Reminiscent of Hachai but a more frequent "visitor" to the Hain than him was the spirit known as "Short" and unlike Hachai and his two sisters he was said also to rove away from the lodge into the forests. He was said to have been seen occasionally by women collecting berries who had reason to fear him since he was believed to "dangerous" to women and inclined to kill them. His impersonator was decorated in a similar manner to Hachai dressed only with a "whitish" parchment-like skin as a mask with the eyeholes and an opening for the mouth. The body-paint was variable and consisted of stripes of red and white with one or other of the limbs painted a solid colour. Grey down was also applied to represent the lichen found covering the rocks from which he too also emerged[296]. There appears to have been several spirits called Short, perhaps representing a multiple personality, but he was believed to have had a son named Kterren. This supernatural was more amenable to humankind and was even "kindly disposed" towards women and appeared as a small young man or youth. His impersonator too was decorated with elaborate designs and included grey bird down[297].

A further supernatural known was of interest and his name was Kmantah who was said to appear dressed in beech bark since he emerged from his mother, Kualchink - the beech tree, and to whom he returned[298]. The name of this deity, perhaps a variation of, or derivation from "Manta", suggests a connection with Ecuador and in that same region it was famous at the time of the Spanish Conquest for its legends of giants who arrived by rafts from the Pacific and known for barkcloth. The motif of emergence from a tree is found frequently in the myths of Asia and the Pacific Islands but the legends of giants is also found among the South American peoples and forms a part of many of the most important of their myth cycles. It is therefore of little surprise that the mountains in Ona-land were considered had been "human beings long ago" and should be treated with respect[299] and that the peoples of the altiplano in Bolivia and Peru also considered their peaks as gods or "grandfathers". These Peruvian mountain spirits will be of more interest later.

The myths of Kwonyipe (Kwon-yipe = Kon-i-raya?) are remarkable in that they seem to resemble those of the Ecuadorian giants. There are many references to indicate that the repeated hostility toward women not only characteristic of these giants but by almost all of the supernaturals. This suggests that they were the very ancient intrusive peoples, and probably mariners, who had for weeks and months been isolated at sea, sought out women to have their way with them and were therefore seen as threatening and life-endangering just as was reported of the giants of Ecuador. There are many references to woman attempting to escape the clutches of these legendary, and mythical males and it was believed that meteors were in fact heroes or demons in search of women[300]. This reference to meteors or night observations may be dim memories of navigation by the night sky that was an essential skill in Polynesian sea voyages. It has to be said that the direct association of ancient supernaturals or giants with the sea is rare in Ona myths and for the most part references to migrations of any type, by land or sea are missing but one particular legend is of interest. This is a brief legend of the origin of the crested vulture stating that he was a "strong ill-natured" medicine-man named Kwaweishen. It was said that he came from a country in the far south and since all the water in that place was always frozen he could find nothing to drink and this caused the marrow in his bones to dry up. Tierra del Fuego is the southernmost island of any size at the very south of the South American continent and the only land beyond is the Antarctic Continent. In conventional Isolationist theories the legend therefore it could only be that the medicine-man represented mariners who arrived at the most southern coast of the island is likely who had come from either the east or west coasts of South America further to the north. Such conventional theories would not explain why the medicine man should arrived from even further south and where the water was always frozen. The legend implies that mariners must have travelled near or to the Antarctic Continent and this may well have a common origin with the Maoris or other Polynesians who appeared to know of the bitter cold of the far south referred to earlier. It may well have been these Polynesians peoples who, by their ocean-going canoes, were delivered by the West Wind Drift from either Australia or New Zealand but suffered the cold being so far south in the latitude of Cape Horn at the very south of Tierra del Fuego. Certainly the remarkably close similarities in ritual body-paint designs of the Ona to those of the Australian Aborigines and the many other apparent connections and similarities besides that of dress and stature corresponding with the Maori suggests that there had to be more than a single contact between them.

The Mapuche of Central Chile in Myth and Recent Research

The Mapuche occupied anciently, before the Spanish Conquest, a large region of the Southern Andes and remain to this day a substantial presence in the racial make-up of southern Chile. They were usually considered, broadly, as part of the Araucanian peoples and only in more recent times have been singled out for study - although to a much lesser degree than those peoples of Bolivia and Peru much further to the north. Many of their ceremonials reflect elements of a broad tradition shared with the shamanistic Amerindian populations who spread from Siberia through into North America down into Central America and then ultimately to the very southern tip of South America to the island of Tierra del Fuego. Some of the ritual objects such as shamanistic drums have been retained in a recognisable form from their inheritance from the Siberians as well as their general physical stature and character traits[301]. This is true also of the Tierra del Fuegans such as the Ona, Yamana (Yaghan) and the Acaluf, but as with these same people they exhibited certain elements indicating likely incursions from Polynesia.

There has been limited in-depth archaeological research into the past of the Mapuche but what is known is that they appeared to have been organised into chiefdoms that numbered from about 500 to 8000 people[302]. The chief, or longko, appears to have derived his position from genealogical descent and through his ability to regulate distribution throughout the community and arrange marriage alliances[303]. The importance of marriage rites was related to inheritance since land passes with the woman, when, through marriage she takes it from the clan she was brought up in to that of her husband and therefore the size of the chiefdom can fluctuate along with its resources[304]. Marriage rules of this type tend to indicate that inheritance, in part or whole, through the women who were part of tribes who existed in a region and subject to transitory or incursive males who were of insufficient strength to be able to wrest the land from its tradition-al owners. Such males, if they were of insufficient number and strength, would usually be incor-porated into the tribe, but subjected perhaps to inferior status, where inheritance rules over a peri-od of time (of a number of such incursions) would establish the women as the inheritors of the land regardless of the number of incursions. Traditions existing previous to such incursions would tend to survive as a matrix for the society and if the males were incursive or stayed for only short periods - such as with mariners or traders, or the society was perpetually at war with one another - apparently the case in Tierra del Fuego, then it was essential that property be invest-ed with the females for continuity and survival of the families. This is the pattern repeatedly found along the sea routes in South East Asia and found also in tribal India and elsewhere where these similar conditions applied.

The most important surviving sites of the Mapuche are located along the narrow coastal strip fronting the Pacific Ocean with the backdrop of the Andes for its full length in what is now Chile. Significantly the Humboldt Current, also called the Peruvian Current, which is an exten-sion of the cold West Wind Drift current of the Antarctic Ocean, washes this shoreline and sweeps northward to the continuing extension of this coastline to Peru and Ecuador. It has been noted that the Ona culture in particular far to the south receives the same current from the west and exhibits aspects of ritual and ceremony that are most likely to have derived from New Zealand and Aboriginal Australia. Influences from the same region of Polynesia, more specifi-cally from the Maori, are found among the Mapuche.

Among the Maori the chief was considered identified with the sky heroes or gods and termed Ranga-tira - Ranga being the term for sky and where the alternative is Langa found more commonly in Indonesia. Also identified with the sky and among the first deities of Polynesia is Rongo with whom the Hawaiian mistakenly identified Captain Cook on his fatal visit to those islands. In a later section it will be noted that there may only be a word or two that appears to be imported to indicate foreign incursions and keeping this in mind it is particularly notable that the Mapuche term for chief - longko[305] is clearly a term which has derived from langa being confused with Rongo. Such merging of terms is found widely in culture regions that have had contact with Polynesia such as Melanesia and is undoubtedly the case here with the Mapuche. Another term probably derived from an Oceanic import is that for house - ruca[306] where the Polynesian word is ruma, a term found also in Indonesia and among the Nagas of Assam in North East India. The Mapuche for house construction is rucatun and the root ruca may have been derived from Polynesian influence either directly from the Maori onto the Chile coast or from Peru where influences from the north have clearly percolated through to the south either via migration through trade or military incursion. Confirming the connection with Oceania is that the religious altar of the Mapuche was called the langi-langi[307] this being not only the Polynesian name for sky but is doubled in precisely the manner customary among them to indicate a microcosmic or con- centrated form of the main term.

The Mapuche constructed ceremonial mounds and interestingly they also prepared dancing grounds at their bases corresponding with the typical layout of those in Polynesia. It is believed that there exists about 100-150 mounds in the Mapuche territory and these have sur- vived in clusters of about 8-12 mounds[308]. The types of burial indicate that there are many forms of cultural influence that were integrated into the Mapuche nation. Besides interment in earthen mounds, known types of burial are in urns, stone-slab coffins, log chambers, and not least of all canoe burial. Canoe burial usually indicates cultural influences introduced by seafarers and it should not be any surprise to find this form here. It is clear that many of these burial forms have been introduced from the north from Peru or Bolivia but the direct Polynesian influences in such prominent terms for chief, house and altar must indicate the importance of their influence. This region of the Pacific coast of South America receives more attention from Miles Poindexter than can be given here. He considers the term Arica, the town name on the North Chilean Coast, is descended from the place where the Polynesian Arikis arrived from their Pacific Islands. Among the Mapuche the most prominent chiefs and the priests alone were given mound burials[309] as they were in Polynesia although in certain of the islands special canoe rites were specially designat- ed. During the later rites, after burial associated with the shallow eltun grave, layers of earth were added over the grave every four to eight years as a "capping" and this was done by the chief's successor for the length of his office. A dancing ground was also laid out at its base for rituals associated with the grave and ancestral rites. Of particular interest was the fact that a hole was constructed in the side of the mound to the body itself to allow the blood of sacrifices to flow down to the deceased[310]. This is an almost identical practice to those found throughout Oceania and particularly in Melanesia[311], Indonesia[312] and in India[313].

Blood sacrifices were carried out from very ancient times, including human sacrifices, on these mounds and it was rumoured that these were being carried out late into the twentieth century[314]. Such reports of sacrifices were recorded by the early Spanish in the sixteenth centu- ry and in Chile it was said that after the conquest in 1575 A.D. another was made of a child after the earthquake of that year. In more recent times two miners searching for the fabled treasure of the Incas on Mount Plomo discovered the remains of an Inca burial of a child sacrifice - a capa- cocha, in February, 1954[315]. This sacrifice in later times, and no doubt anciently, was carried out by the priests or sorcerers called "Machi"[316]. In India the term Machi is applied to a branch of the Brahmans - a priestly caste of South India who were in fact not true Brahmans but who dis- placed the native peoples in the coastal region of Canara[317]. This region of South India is criti- cal to the theme of this work and will be considered at length in following chapters. This term Machi may also have links with the Maki rites involving human sacrifice in Melanesia[318] but deriving ultimately from Asia and will be of more interest in due course.

The Ancient Chinchorro in the Atacama Region of North Chile

From about 5000-3000 B.C. an early culture appeared on the North Chilean coast that has been named Chinchorro centred in some of the driest desert terrain imaginable. A millennia before this time the people of the central Peruvian coast, at La Paloma, preserved the body by salting it to arrest decay. It was notable that, although still a hunter-gatherer society, the Chinchorros began to practice burial rites that indicated a more sophisticated view of the after-life. In these rites the preservation of the body was either desirable or a necessity and was achieved by brac- ing the skeletons of the deceased with reeds[319]. This seems to reflect a broader view developing among the Andean peoples that for the spirit to be able to enter the ancestral afterlife the body needed to be preserved on earth suggesting ancestor worship as a fundamental societal belief. These rites appear to have lead by continuity to the later preservation of mummies so notable among the Incas culture and as in the earlier examples in the coastal cultures, these preserved remains were retained in accessible spaces apparently to receive propitiatory offerings from their relatives[320]. From about 2000 B.C. these funerary practices had developed to such an extent that they appeared to be out of proportion to the rest of the surviving material culture. The careful treatment of the body appeared to be paramount and extensive preservation techniques were applied to this end. In the most prestigious burials the brain and viscera were removed and replaced with many organic materials such as wood and sticks, herbs, vegetable fibres and even fragments of basketry and then bound together with a vegetable resin. Interestingly sticks were "inserted" along the limbs to maintain their final shape and placement and the muscles were padded out with materials such as grass, thread and other materials to retain a more realistic form in death. A wig of human hair was created for the head and a mask was placed over the face and finally covered with a thin layer of clay before being buried in an extended position in contrast to the flexed position of other Chilean and Peruvian burials. No explanation has yet been forthcoming for this unusual development in what appeared to be a culture little developed from the early hunter-gatherer stages a millennia before[321].

The later Chinchorro/Lancho cultures appear to have co-existed between 1000-500 B.C. in a state of decline[322]. They are perceived as highland cultures in Bolivia that had colonised the southern valleys of Azapa and Camarones at the mouth of the Loa River and also perhaps Iquique. Irrigation and the cultivation of maize, chili peppers sweet potatoes, along with the herding of camelids and possibly also guinea pigs, and undertaken it is presumed for export to the highlands. This culture appeared in the north of Chile but the textiles and elaborate designs of the Asuruni-Pajano in the highlands were reflected also in turbans and caps. Gold and copper metallurgy is evident in their ornaments including reptilian designs known in the highlands. This lowland culture also exhibits such practices as cranial deformation, rituals centred on trophy heads, and included ritual hallucinogenic snuffs and the boxes, tubes, spatulas and tablets associated with them[323].

After this epoch it is the Initial Period leading to the greatest of the Bolivian highland cultures that appears reflected in the designs and stone monuments extending from Pucara (Pukara) South East of Cuzco toward Puno through the highlands to the northern valleys of coastal Chile[324]. Burial mounds in this part of North Chile have revealed tapestries that have been woven in the Pucara style displaying characteristic designs including trophy heads, frogs and rayed feline heads. It has been suggested that Pucara may have maintained these coastal sites as satellites and is seen as an appropriate curtain-raiser for the great Classic age of Tiahuanaco (Tiwanaku) between 400-600 A.D. Others perceive the relationship of the highland with those of the coast as Kurakas (Curakas - clan chiefs) from Pucara and their entourage retaining a centre in the coastal settlements on a rotational basis, occasional or regular, as trading centres. Undoubtedly it was the marriage alliances formed that cemented their access to the local mineral rich coastal resources[325]. This is entirely consistent with the principle of itinerant males intermarrying all along the trade and sea routes of the world and particularly notable in the myths and legends of the Pacific Ocean islands and was applicable also to the Ona and other tribes in the far south of South America.

During the great age of Tiahuanacu the colonisation by them of the Azapa Valley in North Chile as well as the Cochabamba Valley in Eastern Bolivia and towards the west the Moquegua Valley gave direct access from the highlands to the Pacific Ocean proceeding from the second half of the first millennium B.C.[326]. The regions influenced by Tiahuanaco include the San Pedro de Atacama oasis in North Central Chile away from the coast and also the Quebrada de Humahuaca in the northwest of Argentina both regions producing notable cultural artefacts[327]. It is of interest to note that the Azapa Valley in the north of Chile was for so long of importance and it has long been assumed by more recent researchers that it was only for the local mineral resources that these settlements were made. It has been largely ignored that this coastal region was the ideal landing stage for those crossing the Pacific from Australia, South Eastern Polynesia, and even from Melanesia and ultimately from Indonesia and South East Asia. This is undoubtedly reflected in the contacts that appear to be obviously reflected in the cultures of Tierra del Fuega already noted of the Ona and Yamana. It should also be pointed out that this coast, for the full distance from the Chilean coast to Ecuador was also ideal for launching on the Peruvian Current (Humboldt) to Eastern Polynesia, Melanesia, Indonesia and South East Asia and this will soon be seen to be of importance.

The Diaguita or Santa Maria Culture of the Ava Chiriguanos

Among the more interesting of the lesser-known peoples in South Central South America are the Chiriguanos. They were considered a scourge by the Incas and in one particular attack in 1524 A.D. it was said that a Spaniard accompanied them named Alejo Garcia who had survived a ship-wreck during the Solis expedition on the Rio Plata in Eastern South America[328]. It is said that the Chiriguanos were intent on looting Inca gold and this suggests that this raid may have been instigated by the Spaniard. A native Quechua author who will be of some importance to the theme of this work, Pachacuti-Yamqui Salcamayhua, notes that the "Ynca Huayna Ccapac" was besieged by the Chiriguanos when suppressing other provinces of the empire. This is not con-

2.107 : Crosses and "Megalithic S" typical of Pacific Coast South America and similar also to those of Asia - *8.015, 8.020, 8.034, 8.036.* Calchaqui Valley, Santamaria, N.W. Argentina, 1000-1450 A.D.

nected by Salcamayhua with the 1524 A.D. raid but it is said that this Ynca despatched his most experienced captains and twenty thousand soldiers to suppress these invaders indicating that they may have been a greater force than is generally recognised[329]. It would appear that the Chiriguanos were an ever-present threat to the Incas and their surviving material culture suggest that they were much more than unruly backwater tribesmen. Rafael Karsten considered that they were, with the Guaranized Chave, a "special group" who exhibited many features specifically their own and these should not be considered as Chaco tribes proper. The Guarani tribes called themselves Ava meaning "men"[330].

The earliest reports of these people indicate that they were a lighter-skinned people than some of the other Guarani tribes whose homeland was believed to be that part of the Gran Chaco that lies within modern Paraguay[331]. The men of this tribe wore the reed tube through the lower lip - a trait they shared with the Chiancas. However they are more associated with the lip-plug, or tembeta, that was said to be given to the men by the fox-god named Agnaratunpa and this is considered the only true "baptism" into the struggle for existence that this god was said to aid[332]. It is particularly interesting to note that the miniature "arrows" placed into the lower lip of children was an equivalent of the Chinese acupuncture needles since they were said to "...kill or strike terror into the evil spirit in the blood"[333]. In fact this belief parallels more identically that of the Ainu of Japan who believed that tattooing the mouth of women was a necessity since it prevented the natural "bad blood" of women from venting itself upon the rest of humanity[334]. Identical tattoos to those of the Ainu are found among the peoples of ancient Veracruz suggesting an intimate connection and it may be that the "arrows" of the Amazon tribes are in fact meant to imitate the tattoo needles since other aspects of their culture appear among them (*1.037/8*).

Of particular note is the fact that a tribe from the same region as the

Chiriguanos - the Pilmaches, were said to have derived their name from the ballgame called pilma, believed to have come from the term pillota[335]. It cannot be a coincidence that patolli was the name for the ballgame in Central America[336] with a name so similar and known as ulama among the Mayans. It is of interest to note that there were many of the lower Amazonian tribes through to the Gran Chaco including the Chiriguano who were involved in the rubber trade and preparation of the balls for the ballgame[337]. It may have been that the demand for the rubber, an Amazonian product so well known into more recent times, perpetuated the contact over many centuries between Central America and the Amazonian Basin. It is likely that certain tribes had the monopoly in trading contacts with the far north and that they facilitated cultural dispersion from the north among them concentrating naturally on the coasts as transferrals by mariners[338]. Among these were the Tainos who appear later to invade from South America into the Caribbean Islands and this may have been a direct result of, and along the established trading channels for the rubber trade with Central America. They may have been one of the trading tribes or subject to the Omaguas whose central location on the Mid-Amazonian river junctions suggests a controlling interest. These people will be of more interest in a projected future publication. An earlier connection in concert with the rubber trade is the distribution of weaving techniques where the Chiriguano used the so-called Arawak loom[339] suggesting techniques distributed long before the Carib supremacy that was gaining momentum before the Spanish Conquest. Twilling techniques were anciently known in South America and were widely found from the most ancient on the Peruvian coast through into the forest tribes of the Amazon. This technique is also known among the Chiriguanos and has been found impressed upon some of their ancient ceramics[340]. More advanced weaving techniques are also known and displayed in their ponchos, blankets, tipoys and other decorative palettes[341].

Among the tribes of the South American pampas the sling is found among the Tehuelche and found also far to the south among the Ona and Yamana, as well as among a few of the Gran Chaco tribes. The Chiriguano were believed to have obtained the sling from their Quechua neighbours but is found as the favoured weapons all along the Andes through Peru (*5.028-34*) to Ecuador, and in Colombia where the Quimbaya were a people of note[342]. What is much less well-known is that the identical sling is found among the Marquesas Islanders who are the most likely distributors or receivers of influences to, or from South America in Eastern Polynesia and who will be of more interest in due course. Clubs also figure prominently in cross-Pacific cultural dispersion and those of the Chiriguano, or apparently related Diaguita on the central Chilean coast where they were made of stone being either a star shape[343] virtually identical to those surviving in Melanesia (*5.006-14*) or simple ring-shaped stones also found widely in the Pacific. Spear-throwers are also found among the Daiguita or Chiriguanos, in pre-pottery levels and these follow the Andean models[344], but it is also of note that spear-throwers were also used in Pacific Ocean countries and particularly notably of Australia. In the Amazon Basin itself the Tapirape tribe were noted for a game using the spear-thrower[345] that suggests that it developed from teka, the game using a dart or arrow known widely throughout Polynesia.

Into early last century ceremonies were being witnessed among the Aymara of the altiplano in Bolivia near Tiahuanaco that were processed by all-male dancers called Chunchu-Sicuri. The second set in the procession was called Chirihuanos suggesting an ancient alliance between these highland people and the Chiriguanos of the southern Andean slopes[346]. The pan-flute used by the musicians was called in its largest size (about as tall as a full-grown man) the zampona. There were several sizes of pan-flute and its smallest representative was known as the kena-kena that is a term oft the exact form of "doubled" diminution used to describe anything smaller of its type by the Polynesians. Interestingly these dancers did not allow women to dance with them, a tradition also highly reminiscent of the dancers of the sacred performers in Polynesia.

It appears that the Chiriguano were no ordinary tribe since they were said to have maintained control from Tarija in southern Bolivia, in the eastern upland of the Andes, to the Atlantic Ocean a thousand miles (1600km) to the east[347]. This included the La Plata - Rio Parana river systems that give direct access into the Gran Chaco from the Atlantic Coast and to their regions of origin in the upper Pilcamayo River in the Andean foothills. This seems to be confirmed by the ceramic tradition among the Chiriguanos being related to those of the Chilean north and central coast, North West Argentina, through to the eastern lowlands towards the Gran Chaco. This tradition extends for an unknown distance since less research has been focused on this region than the notable high cultures of the Andes. There are probable relationships between them and the later Araucanians but the most expressive of these traditions is that known as the Santa Maria from North West Argentina. The highly decorated burial urns are of particular note (*2.107*) and their decoration seems to indicate links to the more ancient Ancon-Supe tradition on the Central Peruvian coast[348]. They were also mound-builders[349] and may have had an ancestral relationship with later historic peoples further to the south such as the Mapuche. The Chiriguano were also noted for having been road-builders but this region is within the sphere of influence of the Incas and their predecessors and this may therefore have been as a result of their empire-building strategies[350].

It is interesting to note that among other local tribes the Chiriguanos were later associated with white men as a Toba myth notes. An edited version relates that in ancient times almost all the people of the world were destroyed by a great fire except the Toba themselves who survived by hiding deep in the trench in one of their own earthworks. After three days a small boy was sent out to determine whether the earth was safe to walk upon and he returned to say that it was. The Toba survivors had to climb out of the pit with a cloth tied around their eyes on the threat of being turned into an animal if they disobeyed. It was said that that after this catastrophe the culture-hero Peritnalik began to recreate the world. It was at this time it was believed the Chiriguanos came down from heaven with the Christians (white men) and fruit and vegetable seeds were sent e later. Some of this seed, it was said, was stolen by the Toba for themselves[351].

The fact that the Chiriguanos were apparently identified as outsiders and believed to originate from the same place as the white men that suggests that they were originally not from the Gran Chaco, at least in the male line. This would also explain their paler skin than was apparent among some of the other indigenous people. The Chiriguanos were perceived as culture-bearers and in another myth about them the Toba it was said that they had hidden fire away so that no others could use it, but a Toba man spied on them and managed to steal it while they were away gathering food[352]. There are many motifs among these Gran Chaco/Amazonian people that are highly reminiscent of Oceanic myths and those of India and the stealing of fire is a well known motif in Indo-European myths. The Toba themselves exhibit traits that are not entirely indigenous and will be of more interest in due course.

The reports of other white or fairer-skinned than the majority of Gran Chaco people near or among the Chiriguanos were not unusual. Giovanni Pelleschi more than a century ago wrote that he repeatedly heard of white Indians who lived in the interior of the forest in Central South America. He notes of one of these tribes; "...the Chirionossos are said to be troglodytes or dwellers in caves, fair, extremely fierce, with blue eyes; their women, too, have crooked feet turned inwards, so as to be hidden when they are seated. Both men and women are always naked. I have never seen them myself, but such is the universal account of these people" ... "A Chiriguano, who assured me he had seen them and fought them, told me that their knees were turned backwards like ostriches"[353]. The references to fair-skinned, blue-eyed tribes are not unusual among the forest tribes of South America and some researchers have dismissed these as later reports of Europeans but this is a too narrow view as will be shown. The report of people with their "legs turned backward" or "reversed" will be shown later to have parallels in India along with other elements of Amazon and Gran Chaco cultures. Noted of these people also is the belief that an eclipse of the Sun or the Moon was caused by a "fabulous green tiger" (jaguar), named Yagurogui that pursued them and attempted to swallow them[354]. This is the exact same motif, substituting the jaguar for the tiger among the Nagas of Assam[355], and is in turn identical to the Rahu myth of ancient India where the serpent Rahu was the Moon's Node[356]. In material culture, of particular note, were the pellet bows in South America which were found among the Chiriguano and Yurucare among others but which is considered to be remarkably similar to those used anciently in India. So alike are these that it has been suggested that they have been introduced after the Spanish Conquest[357]. With the many other parallels between ancient South America and India this is unlikely and beside the Chiriguanos the Yurucares will also be of further interest.

Tree burial has already been noted in Australia and is found in various forms across the Pacific to South East Asia and India. The fact that these elements are reported by, or from people near or associated with the Chiriguano is significant. It must also be remembered that these tribes in the Amazon Basin and Gran Chaco remained almost without contact with the outside world except for rare exploratory incursion by explorers and missionaries until a century ago. These burial practices of these Gran Chaco people were as recorded: "Some Indians, among whom are the Cherionossos (Chiriguanos), dwelling on the borders of Bolivia and Brazil, bury the dead among trees. To this end they seek the thickest part of the forest, and having pitched upon a ginccian tree - the trunk of which is shaped like a jar, and is of cork-like texture - they empty it and place the body inside the cavity, covering it up securely that vultures may not disturb or devour it …"[358]. The Chiriguanos, or Avas, believed that the departed spirit went to a place called Ihuoca where they lead a happy life consuming copious quantities of maize beer and partook of great feasts. After a prolonged stay there the soul was then said to transmigrate into a fox, and after its death it went through other transformations. The body was also preserved after death to facilitate the rebirth of the soul[359].

Of particular note was the fact that it was believed by some of those Gan Chaco tribes that the woman could conceive without the male by the use of "bina-charms". Rafael Karsten, one of the most prominent researches among these peoples noted; "The Bina-charm harbours the embroyonal beginning which in ordinary cases is transferred to the woman by man at the sexual act, but the soul, which has associated itself with the body of the child to be born, is evidently one of those human souls which, according to Dr. Roth, emanating from a corpse, have found a temporary resting-place in waters or in the forest and bush, and are therefore called respectively Water and Forest or Bush Spirits"[360]. The interesting report records the close similarities of the belief that child spirits or souls could be introduced into the woman through charms or stones and reflects closely that of the Australian Aborigines already noted as having cultural parallels with the Ona far to the south of the Gran Chaco. These were particularly associated with stones which were believed to be found at the base of trees and tree burial was known also among the Australian Aborigines and among the Morioris of New Zealand referred to earlier. Of special note must be the fact that the Gran Chaco charm is called bina that must surely be the bindu of India that represents the seed soul as the "divine spark" forming the soul. This and the previous eclipse myth among other cultural references are so very similar that there is little chance of coincidence with those of India and other parallels will be noted in due course.

CHAPTER 3

SOUTH PACIFIC COAST, HIGHLANDS, AND GRAN CHACO THROUGH TO THE PRE-CERAMIC IN PERU

Influences from India and Polynesia among the Tobas of Paraguay

The Gran Chaco was said to be the Spanish aggrandisement for the Inca term Chacu meaning "hunting" or "chase". Of the Gran Chaco tribes the Tobas form a separate group with their own language and character and vary from the others such as the Mataco, Choroti and Ashluslay, anthropologically . The Tobas called themselves Pilagas or Pitilagas and some groups called themselves Toba-Michi or "the little Tobas" while others use the term takshik[2]. It has been considered that the Tobas originated in the far south of Patagonia since their legends note destruction of the world by snow and ice[3]. This again suggests that there had been contacts with tribes such as the Yamana and Ona of Tierra del Fuego who retained cultural elements indicating relations with peoples in the Patagonian north, Gran Chaco and even the Amazon basin. The impressive physical stature of the Ona was considered among the largest of the human race then existing a century ago and has already been of note because they appear to be relate to that of the Polynesians. The Toba were considered to be the tallest of the South American Indians and in this respect Rafael Karsten considered them related to the ancient Patagonians and the Ona in particular[4].

The neighbouring tribes, the Mataco and Choroti, were apparently related since they showed the same affinity in physical stature as they did in language. The Mataco were a little taller than the Choroti but they exhibited the broader stature more noted of the mountain Indians and it was believed that they were in fact most likely a mix of the Incan Quechua men with indigenous women. Of some interest is the fact that among both these tribes face tattooing was known, particularly among the women who displayed more complex designs, while among the men it was only occasionally done and then in less complex designs[5].

The Toba, Mataco and Choroti exhibited similar dress codes utilising minimal cover. Among all three the cotton waist cloth or girdle was the most important element of clothing with, for the Toba, a small apron of skin or other material to cover the genitals, otherwise clothing was eschewed. For the Mataco and Choroti the belt was of broad leather with a fringe that covered the genital region. For cold weather and for festivals the men wore large woollen blankets that featured interweave patterns and was sometimes worn with a belt so that it could hang in a fold when not required[6]. The women wore a short cotton apron to below the knees made of deer or nutria skins sewn together, otherwise no other clothing was worn. During hunting, or when fighting, a tiger's skin breastplate was worn by the men and leggings crudely made of deer or tapir skin were worn[7]. These in turn resemble the leggings exhibited on the reliefs at Xelha in the Mayan Yucatan and these are closely similar to those known in China in the same time frame. It was of note to the early researchers that only the Tobas actually used dogs for hunting and as watchdogs. Other tribal groups did not feed them or care for them in any way suggesting that the Tobas in fact were the remnants of a people with a long tradition that had cultivated the dog as a useful domestic ally[8].

Only among the Tobas was there a clan chief, called the Alynek, and he seemed to wield authority more prominently during periods of conflict and war. The Tobas were not considered a warlike race in the same way as the Chiriguanos but were known for their aggressive response when considered necessary[9]. Of some note was the practice of depilation of the forehead back to the crown of the head among the Guaycaru, or Toba tribes so that this area of the head was completely bald. This ritual was said to have magical significance and was called nalemra and was made to cover a larger area in the case of the chief[10]. It is interesting to note that among many early painting in India the high born or Brahman men were depicted shaved in this manner and this was carried out with special ceremonies and adopted more widely from their tradition among the other tribes and castes.

Among the Toba there was a Council of Elders who had the power to remove a chief when considered necessary to do so. This Council was constituted by the eldest men from each sub-tribe and was called Eakachi - "The Old Ones"[11]. In Central America the deity associated with the Pochteca or trader was called Ek Chauk, and this may be a reference to a common ancestral incursion linked with traders. Other common references will be noted in due course but the prefix Ek in Mexico[12], and perhaps here among the Tobas of South America, has been linked to the Orissa region of India where the deities names Ekadasa, Ekamasa are prominent and linked to the sea trade in the Bay of Bengal. Ekapada is the "one-legged" Siva whose image appears in South America (*3.041*). The Toba Councils, or Eakachi, were held under an algoraba tree at the time of the New Moon[13] and it is interesting to note that Ekadasa in India is another name for Siva, who was often shown with the Moon symbol attached to his topknot. It is not surprising to discover therefore that many of the religious rituals of the main religions of India were centred on the sacred village tree.

Characteristic of the Gran Chaco region, descent was through the female line, and a child was therefore considered to belong to the mother's clan and not that of the father. Female "right" or descent is usually found along the trading routes, both on land and at sea, where the males are itinerant and who may be away from home for long periods or only be transient, perhaps spending only days, weeks or months in one place before moving on perhaps never to return. Inevitably liaisons with local women occurred and the mother's clan by necessity brought up the surviving children - there usually being no father's clan locally or within the same country or island group. There are many legends recording sons who have suddenly appeared after many years searching for their fathers throughout the islands of the Pacific and elsewhere where such itinerant journeys undertaken by males were frequent. This undoubtedly is the origin of inheritance through the female line and in India this is recorded more explicitly in legend and myth and is no doubt the reason for such inheritance rules among the Toba and other tribes in South America. Almost invariably such practices of marriage by capture and proof of eligibility of the courting male by the bride's parents are characteristics of the system, indicating that the incursive males are outsiders and have not the numbers to create their own separate patrilineal clans.

The interrelationships the Bolivian Tobas had with the other important cultural groups considered here is highlighted by the fact that, although they grew limited areas of maize, they in fact traded dried fish for the bulk of their requirements along with this important staple cereal with the Chiriguano (Ava)[14]. In the time of Inca domination over the Chaco the local Indians were employed as drivers in the chase, but it is believed that the most densely forested central regions were unknown to the Incas themselves[15]. The Mataco are believed in part to be a people with some Inca blood, or more likely that of the Quichua, but largely that of the indigenous Indians[16]. However the term Chiriguano was not used by that tribe themselves since it was a term of derision meaning guano-seekers - "guano" meaning the excrement of birds usually associated with the coast of North Chile. The Chiriguano called themselves Ava or "men" and this will be a point of interest later[17] but they and the Toba in their contacts with the Pacific coast itself seem to have filtered deep into the heart of South America and from the earliest time from the Chinchorro period.

Gods and Demons of the Toba; Choroti and Mataco

It is of particular interest that some of the researchers in South America often noted that among many of the Indian tribes they retained the idea of a supreme being such as a creator god in the Western sense but was missing, as noted by Lucas Bridges, of the Ona among a few others. The creator in these cases was often an ancestor who had been mystically elevated to fill that role and generally such identifications with storm, wind or other gods was assigned to those "spirits" who were often considered to once have been men[18]. Old men among the Choroti were revered in life but after death were believed to be able to wreak havoc among the tribal survivors on earth and were thought of as malevolent spirits called Ayieu or Aittah[19]. It might be conjectured that the term Ayieu and Aittah are a localised form of Atua - the name for ancestral spirits in Polynesia. In fact so feared were the old men among them that they were never allowed to die a natural death but as they grew weak and sickly the clan determined to end their life by an arrow shot through the heart. After this they were immediately burnt with all their property, instead of according them the usual burial, to prevent the spirit from returning to seek its own body or its possessions to become sorcerers after death[20]. Among the Choroti magical power was believed to increase with age and deep fear of its use for evil was widespread[21].

Spirits or demons were called peyak by the Toba, Ayieu, aittah or nahut by the Mataco, mohsek by the Choroti, and it is significant therefore that they took, in general, the form of old withered men. These "demons" or spirits were considered also to have wings to allow them to fly through the air to attack their victims and because of their bird-like appearance were also called ahuena - "the birds"[22]. These demons were believed to attack the living and even to enter their homes, particularly at night, for which the rattle or pelite was much used to scare them away. The spirits or ghosts of the dead were believed to constitute the broad population of these offenders and those of the recently dead were called yal[23].

In South American myths the sky people or demons are usually considered to be intimately concerned with the matters of humankind and in many there are references to them descending to crossbreed with humans to produce tribes and clans. They are usually considered evil and therefore demons since they were believed to force their attentions upon often unwilling tribes or their fated members and besides these the natural characteristics were deemed personalised and antagonistic to people. The rain demons were of great importance and others were responsible for thunderstorms that ravaged the landscape and destroyed the crops. The flash of the lightning and the thunder itself were considered by the Choroti to be a great many mohsek who speed through the atmosphere and targeted their villages in an outburst of malice. These were the demons that the Indians referred to as ahuena - the birds, already noted, but the proper Choroti name for them was Suntini[24]. When a thunderstorm approached the Indians started shouting in that direction in an attempt to scare away the immanent danger to their crops and huts. Spirits, mohsek, were also considered to inhabit and animate trees and plants and these people believed that the whole of their world was composed of competing levels of occasionally mutually beneficent spirits but more usually antagonistic life energies.

The Tobas considered the equivalent of the Choroti mohsek, or demon spirits, to assume the shape of small boys, the peyak or more commonly the natolik, but although they usually were perceived as human in form they often were thought to take the form of birds. In bird form these took for the most part the shape of an "ostrich" or native South America rhea. Only the priests or medicine men actually could see and able to describe them and were normally therefore invisible to the common man[25]. Apart from this aspect of their appearance these spirit demons reflected the broad opinion of the malevolent character attributed to them by the other neighbouring tribes and those generally in the forest regions or the Gran Chaco and Amazon Basin in South America.

The Mataco Indians reflected similar cultural development in their supernatural construct to that of the Choroti but appeared to also reflect some of that of the Toba as well as being similar to the latter in their material life. They called their spirits or demons aittah along with the other Indian peoples but as with the Toba divided their pantheon into two levels - the greater and lesser demons. They were both called aittah but the lesser level was appended with the term slamisa or slasha meaning "small". Unlike the Choroti, however, who conceived their demons, as a whole, as old wizened men the Mataco thought of these smaller beings as having the appearance of young boys called natses. This corresponds with the belief of the Toba peyak, or natolik who also appeared in this form and who were likewise considered to have wings so that they could fly rapidly on the wind from one place to another. The Mataco also considered these boy demons to be malevolent in disposition - in their case termed taua-kai, and they were active at night and were dispelled by the appropriate ritual dances[26].

On the second level of Mataco demons existed the most evil or malevolent of all called the nahit. These were thought of, and depicted, as the shadows of dead men who arise from the grave. For the most part they remain attached to their final plot and live within the earth but sometimes wander from the cemetery and are then a cause for great alarm. Death is the most feared event and all that surrounds it is perceived as perilous for the living Indians. These "shadows" are described as "thin", or skeletal replicas of the living person when alive and were often called nahut yil since yil was the Mataco term for death. As in many societies the most feared illness leading to death was smallpox and this nahit was called oto-ahtya[27]. This is probably another form developed from aittah.

The ahtya or aittah generated and controlled the greatest natural phenomena such as cyclones, whirlwinds, thunder and lightning, droughts and eclipses. The thunder and lightning was operated by the demons called more specifically by the Mataco aittah tavakai pahlai or "the thunder demons" who are airborne and penetrate the clouds. As with anything out of the usual eclipses of the Moon were greatly feared by the Amerindians and these were called by them aittah hayah, and personified as a demon that was said to prey upon the Moon[28]. Characteristically the Mataco attempted to frighten away this demon when an eclipse was in progress by shouting and beating their drums - a practice almost universal in the Americas and elsewhere such as in Aboriginal India.

The myths associated with the eclipse demon among the Mataco who was believed to be attempting to swallow the Moon as a motif is identical to that among the peoples of Central America considered in an earlier work[29], but also in the Western Pacific and the islands of Indonesia in particular. Many of the main Indonesian islands exhibit clear cultural contacts with Polynesia and South America and are particularly noted of Sumatra, Borneo and Celebes but also with the smaller island of Nias. These islands, however, were early considered, in the nineteenth century when anthropological research began in earnest, as

3.001 : Canoe transport across land from one river to another, and even across hills and mountains is found in most lands where riverine and marine traffic was traditional. Aneto tribe, Amazon Basin, 19th., century, A.D.

3.002 : Canoe transport from one riverhead to another characteristic of 19th., century exploration. Amazon Basin, Late 19th., - early 20th., century, A.D.

3.003 : Transport of long canoe across the land bridges from one river to another was a characteristic known in South East Asia and Amazonian South America. Luang Prabang, Laos, 19th., century, A.D.

3.004 : The map of South America shows the remarkable river system allowing riverine navigation that facilitates accessibility to almost every part of the continent. The lowest passes across the Andes, - the longest mountain chain in the world, were very early sought out and this appears to have been achieved by mariners and traders to allow access from the Pacific into the Amazon and Gran Chaco regions. The black arrows indicate the most notable of these and the highlands of Bolivia in the centre-west of the continent where Tiahuanaco is located, adjacent to the more northern of the two black-coloured lakes high on the Altiplano, also was placed to be accessible to the Pacific Coast and to several of the Amazon and Gran Chaco rivers headwaters. The light-coloured arrows indicate the flow of the West Wind Drift delivering directly from the Western Pacific including Australia and New Zealand. The Equatorial Counter Current in the far north delivers directly from Asia through Melanesia, Polynesia onto Pacific coast of Colombia and Ecuador. These two ocean currents then conjoin off the coast of Ecuador and flow westwards to Eastern Polynesia then through Melanesia to South East Asia and probably explains why the Inca Tupac set off with his fleet westwards from Ecuador.

being very closely connected culturally to the Nagas of Assam in modern North East India, north of the joint Ganges and Brahmaputra River deltas. This region will be of major importance in this work as it was in an earlier work by the same author. Of interest in this section is that the term for spirit or demon of particular note among the Nagas was, and is hala and appears to be the origin or derived from a common origin of the Mataco hayah. This term hala and similar variations are found in Indonesia, the Nagas of Assam, and is found also among the Huichol of North Western Mexico[30]. In Eastern India hala-hala was the name for a poison[31].

    If this term hayah was the sole connector to the Pacific and the Nagas in particular it could be genuinely relegated to coincidence. However, virtually all the terms recorded by early, and sometimes only researchers such as Rafael Karsten indicate clear references to Polynesia, India or the Nagas as noted. The term aittah, and ahtya above noted denoting spirits or demons must surely be identical to the aitu, or spirit heroes of the Polynesians and already noted among the Maori. Among the Mataco aittah is the thunder demon tayakai pahlai and pahlai suggests that this has developed from pillai or Pillan, the thunder god of the Araucanians. This term probably developed from an earlier Central Andean original but the description of this deity may have developed from the South Indian deity Pillai who will be of more interest in a following section. The Toba called their "boy demons" by the term payak, but it is critical to note that all these demons had wings and were said to fly - an essential function relating them to the wind. It is therefore of some interest that the name of the deity for the wind in the Ganges Delta region and Orissa in India was Pawa, a term linked to the ancient wind deity of India - Vayu, both terms found as Pauah-tun, Uay; Uayeb, and U-vayey-ab among the Maya[32]. Variations of this deity are found among the Melanesians and the Polynesians as Pawa and Paoa. Among the Mataco the term for a vast group of these demons flying through, either the wind or constituting the wind was vuh, again suggesting the derivation from India via Polynesia. The Mataco called their boy-demons natses that appears to relate to that of the Toba natolik. Interestingly the spirits and demons are called nats by the Burmese, both good and evil, and these people share links with their northern neighbours, the Nagas.

The Mataco group name for these demons is taua-kai that is, separated into its two constituent parts, is probably kaua, a Polynesian term and found also in Melanesia[33] and Orissa in India, a name for a hero-deity Kaua Bhandari, and the crow in myth[34], a deified bird in Melanesia and Aboriginal Australia. Kai is found widely in Polynesia and is a term that developed from hai, or sacred water among the Marquesans[35] and represents also a deity name, Haiy among the Mandaeans as a group of four great deities[36], where among the Maori the name is Hei[37]. The term noted for the general terms for demons or spirits was ahuena that appears to have derived from the merging of two Polynesian terms ahu and ina. The former relates to a sacred place and the latter to ceremonials or lunar (night) rituals since ina originates from Hina the deity for the Moon. The Mataco term ahuena referring to the "evil" spirits of old men appears interchangeable with another of their terms, ayieu. This latter is of interest since it surely has a common origin with the Polynesian "Io" which in turn appears to have originated with the name for god among the Aboriginals of India - Deo. The term ayieu may also have ancestral connotations since the Inca entitled themselves Ayar.

The residual elements of the influences of contacts with the Pacific permeate many of the tribes and peoples of South America. It is of particular note that in considering the Gran Chaco tribes, distant from the Pacific Coast, where among the Tobas the term for the creator deity was Kalo-ariak or the "Evil One"[38]. The Toba are among the few tribes to include a conception of a "high god" in their belief system and here the deity is considered evil and wreaking havoc and misfortune upon mankind reflecting the fatalistic mindset of the Tobas that the world was full of suffering and woe. In considering the name of their supreme deity it is immediately clear that this is a mutation of borrowed terms that did not originally apply to a major deity as such. The prefix of the name Kalo-ariak - kalo is found in Polynesia but more prominently in Melanesia where in Fiji a deity was named Kalu-vu[39]. This refers to a deity or priest and no doubt derives from many references to priests in Aboriginal India who were often called kalu particularly where stone or megalithic worship still existed (kal = sacred stone). Of particular note in Southern India were the Todas, who have long been of anthropological interest, where kal is the sacred stone and kalvol the special ritual pathways that approach a village[40]. It is probably not a coincidence that Toba and Toda are just an inflection in pronunciation and that there is likely to be a direct connection between the two. The Toda form in India in turn derives from the same term, Kallu, in the Ancient Middle East and this will be of more interest in a later section. The suffix, araik of Kalo-araik must surely be the Polynesian arik or ariki referring to a canoe captain and noted already among the Maoris. Miles Poindexter notes the probable connection with the Polynesian Ariki with Arica on the North Coast of Chile, earlier noted, a natural entreport for the Bolivian Highland and beyond to the river systems of the Gran Chaco.

The interest in sacred stones occurs universally among the Peruvian and other Andean peoples but this appears to be inverted because of their geological rarity in the central and eastern regions of the Gran Chaco. The forests and savannah of Paraguay are largely featureless alluvial plains that have built up over millennia by soils being washed down from the Andes in the west towards the east. Stones are therefore exceedingly rare and the extremely superstitious minds of the indigenous tribes have distorted their original sacredness into objects of dread. It was believed that stones were the homes of an evil spirits, the mohsek, and that they could invade the being of anyone who was foolish enough to wear even the most attractive of these objects bringing illness and ill-fortune. In working black magic it was thought that by throwing a stone at a victim he would fall ill and die. Magical spells could be imbued into, or embodied within these stones, as well as into other small bones, cactus thorns, certain insects etc. and in this respect the projection toward the victim resembles the "pointing-of-the-bone" among Australian Aborigines and some of the practices in Melanesia. As in these lands on the Western Pacific so among the Amerindians where illness and disease was always considered the result of sorcery or evil intent on the part of a plethora of malevolent spirits or demons. The medicine man or sorcerer was considered to some extent protected by his powerful spirits and was able to use his own special healing stones to draw out the evil spirit causing an illness in a patient and this is closely similar to beliefs and practices in Aboriginal Australia[41].

Of special interest in considering the Gran Chaco tribes, and also those on Tierra del Fuego, is the face tattooing that appears to have close parallels with that of Polynesia - called Moko by the Maori (*1.038*). Among the Choroti and the Mataco the technique was similar but applied for the most part to women but only occasionally to men. The painful application of the tattoos was carried on from the time of puberty until, and up to when a girl was married. It appears therefore that the purpose of the tattoo was associated with marriage and the fact that girls and women were considered to be particularly susceptible to the wicked designs and thraldom of evil spirits[42]. Female initiation rites were also aimed at drawing out and deflecting the attention of these spirits and it was said that as girls reached puberty they were particularly liable to succumb to the evil snake demon who was said to be able to enter her vagina and cause pregnancy. The men performed ritual dances with rattles and full paraphernalia to deter this demon and any other from attacking at this dangerous time[43]. This belief is extraordinary only in its concept since exactly the same belief is found among Aboriginal tribes in India and are generally considered among Vagina Dentata myths found also among the Huichols of North Western Mexico and dealt with to some degree in an earlier work[44]. The tattooing of the girls to prevent the attack of evil, however, has close parallels among the Ainu of Japan where women were considered to attract evil because of their naturally "bad blood", or as the absolute requirement for the soul to enter heaven, and also of some peoples in Indonesia[45] and Melanesia[46] including New Guinea[47] but also in India[48]. Face tattoos were of particular note among the Polynesians who developed this art to the highest form[49] known as moko in New Zealand[50]. Other peoples who exhibited face tattooing as a cultural expression were some of the tribes in the Indonesian Islands, and to a lesser degree the males among the Toba but for the most part the females of the Gran Chaco[51] - the only ones in South America who exhibited more than quite simple designs but who also practised ear lobe boring and extension better known of the Orejones in Incan Peru.

Several allusions to the Nagas of Assam have been noted in this work and whatever may be said about these people it can be used also as a reference to some degree relating to the Sumatran, Borneans and peoples of Celebes in Indonesia. It is of interest that some of the most notable of the non-Andean peoples of South America were headhunters and the Tobas were among the foremost of these. This custom was known to all the tribes along the Pilcomayo River that leads from Rio Parana up to the Andean foothills, and where in the custom the head was usually scalped and the skull retained. These trophies were fixed to long poles and planted at the entrances of villages and the Tobas of Tucuman in North West Argentina used Y-posts onto which the skull was fixed and used as boundary markers[52]. Karl Luckert, in his study of serpent worship and the distribution of Y-posts, suggested that those found in Central and North America appeared to be related to those found in closely similar traditions in Eastern Asia, Melanesia, Indonesia, Australia, and India through to Assam[53]. These examples from South America would also suggest contacts with the same regions and deserves more research. It is also of interest that in these same regions red ochre body paint and red head-bands[54] are found of special significance linking ancient sea mariners ancestors in Polynesia and Melanesia, and it would seem that these too were imported into the Gran Chaco region along with so many cultural aspects already noted.

There are many parallels in the various customs and traditions that are reflected between the Tobas of the Gran Chaco and the Nagas of Assam and there is one of interest showing the closeness of these parallels unlikely to be through independent development of an indigenous culture. The menstrual period of woman has been the subject of intensive restrictions and rites by many of the world's people and there are clearly some of these that have been imported from one cultural group to another. During the menstrual period of a Toba woman she will paint her face red with urucu juice as a protection against demons since the peyak or evil spirits were said to be "enraged" by this event. She is also subject to dietary restrictions since, if she ate fish during this dangerous time, she believed she would go mad. If she had eaten fish and her husband had been out hunting and brought home a parrot it is said that the woman is compelled to eat its head raw and turn into a "tiger", or jaguar. She was then thought to commit infanticide upon her own children[55]. Extraordinarily a very similar motif in principle existed among the Angami Nagas of Assam that can hardly be consigned to coincidence.

A century ago a myth was collected by one of the prominent early anthropologists named J.II. Hutton and it is fortunate for scholarship that he was one of researchers among the Nagas. An edited version of this myth is as follows: Two orphan boys lived by snaring birds since they had not been taught to till the fields. One morning they checked out their snares and found that the captured bird's heads had been eaten, and they secreted themselves to keep watch to discover the culprit. When an old ogress turned up to enjoy another clutch of birds' heads the boys challenged her to explain her actions. She convinced the boys to return with her to the Land of Cannibals, which was surrounded by a broad river, where she used a charm to enable them cross by parting the waters. The intention of the ogress was to eat them but she kept the younger with her and her husband who wished to fatten him while his brother was kept elsewhere. The younger brother pretended to be asleep and overheard their intentions and managed to warn his brother. He stole the magic charm and both escaped from the island and the ogress was unable therefore to cross the river in pursuit and they made their bid for freedom.

It is of interest to note that Hutton, in a footnote draws attention to the fact that the Ntlakapamux Indians in North America preserved a closely similar myth recorded by Teit in his "Traditions of the Thompson River Indians", dated 1898 A.D.[56]. The basic motif of women turning ogress due to menstrual madness among the Toba is clearly related to the Naga myth. Apart from the North American Indian parallels the section relating to the ogress and two boys being taken back to her house is found widely among the Melanesians in a variety of forms and clearly derives from the Naga prototype and probably shares a common origin with the Ona myth of Kwonyipe. There are many myths interrelating cannibal ogres or ogresses, tigers (halas or Choroti Hayak) with mythical heroes who free the lands from their blight and many of these are almost identical in Indonesia and Melanesia to those of South America - some of these will be of more interest in due course.

It is clear therefore that these many terms found among the Gran Chaco tribes have been as a result of Indonesian, Melanesian and Polynesian contacts on the Pacific Ocean coast of South America and the North Chile coast in particular. It would appear that perhaps some of the Polynesian crews attempted to find their way across the continent seeking the headwaters of the major rivers systems. Local beliefs among the lands draining to the eastern ocean would assist them to find the riverine routes far to the east opening into the Atlantic coast. In seeking these riverine highways the mariners left, all along the way, besides some of their cultural values and beliefs, their progeny.

The archaeological evidence available, as already noted, shows that the Diaguita culture of North to North Central Chile was spread across the Andean passes relating to that of the

Chiriguano and this in turn appears to be related to that of the Toba. In only a few places are their more direct routes giving access to the foothills of the mountain ranges in the south east of Ecuador, the mountain range being too high and too broad to be easily passable. This concurs with the Polynesian legends of there being a great wall of mountains far to the east "where the sun rises". These "Andean corridors" are hundreds of miles apart and appear to be critically sited where ancient cultures have developed in response to trade, and no doubt founded as a result of the strategic defence of these routes. For Polynesians landing on the Pacific Coast it is clear that it had to be by these "corridors" that any of their influences could be distributed beyond the coastal region to the Gran Chaco and Amazon Basin. It is clear that any Polynesian ariks guiding their canoe crews far to the east of Polynesia would prefer to land on a coast that is within milder or tropical climate latitudes unless driven south into the turbulent weather in the much colder regions of Southern Chile and Tierra del Fuego. Northern Chile and the Peruvian coast would appear the most likely entreports judging from the flow of the ocean currents and many must have landed on the coast occupied by the Diaguita, Mapuche and the long established high cultures of the Peru immediately to the north. They have clearly left evidence of their visits and related cultural references are there for all to research.

The Lengua of the Gran Chaco

There can be little doubt that the Gran Chaco Indians were greatly influenced by the high civilisations of the Andes and that the Incas themselves knew of a large part of it, utilising it for their hunting excursions, although these must have taken on the expeditionary nature of modern safaris. In the final days of their empire they must also have found refuge there just as is known to have occurred in less distant tropical hideouts where the last Incas availed and secreted themselves until they were finally eliminated as a power. Barbrooke Grubb notes from Padre Lozano's records of early missions in Paraguay that indicates that the Incas fled into the Gran Chaco ostensibly as a result of the Spanish Conquest and in great numbers[57]. Further to the north and east of the Tobas, Mataco and Choroti were a people with very different oral traditions but who also, ultimately, appeared to retain memories of an Andean origin that the other Indians of the Gran Chaco and Amazonia lacked. These were the Lengua, whose traditions were recorded by a British missionary with the unlikely name of W. Barbrooke Grubb, but who was the brother-in-law of E. Lucas Bridges already so noted in the recording of the traditions of the Ona far to the south in Tierra del Fuego.

This missionary, Barbrooke Grubb, noted the marked physical differences in stature and intelligence of the Lengua during his years in the forest region. This light-skinned people with fine features he attributed to the probable descent from the Incas. He also notes that among the Lenguas their custom was to distend their ears in the same way as the Inca orejones inserting plugs and regaling themselves with and similar headdresses to those known among the Incas themselves[58]. References to the fear or reverence of the rainbow was recorded of the Lengua, particularly on the event that it appeared in the west, when it was thought to be an omen of evil but their attitude to it reminded Barbrooke Grubb of the Incas mystical elevation of this natural phenomena[59]. In the context of possible origins for the Lenguas in the Andes it was recorded that they believed that the first leader or ruler remembered in their oral traditions was a woman who was the last of her line, or family. This family had arrived from the northwest, the direction of Peru, and was considered by them as "superior". Barbrooke Grubb notes that in that direction in his time a century ago that there were families living among tribes, and in some cases clans or whole tribes, who were "… of fairer skin, finer features, greater intelligence, and a more self-reliant and aggressive character"[60].

The tradition of racial origins for the Lengua far to the north west in Peru, or at least in

3.008 : Magician's apron subsumed from the Bon Po religion into Tibetan Buddhist rituals made of human bone and similar in design and application to those found among the Maya and Peru. Tibet, Pre-20th., century, A.D.

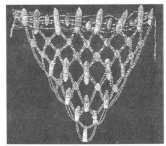

3.007 : Large ceremonial urn showing a simplified magician's apron closely reflected in those found in South America. Tuxtla Gutierrez, Southern Mexico, Late Classic.

3.005 : Mayan ruler identified with the World Tree and shown here wearing the apron or kilt identical to that of the magician's apron in Tibet - *3.006*. Copan, Honduras, 8th., century, A.D.

3.006 : Buddhist priest in full regalia and wearing the magic apron carved from human bone depicted in ancient paintings, and identical to those in Central America and South America. Talung Monastery, Sikkim, Early 20th., century, A.D.

3.010 : Beaded ceremonial belts reflecting stylistic similarities to those found among the Maya (*3.007*) but probably deriving from Tibet. Chuquitana, Peru, 1st., millennium, A.D.

3.009 : Beaded collar, with shell disk pendant, in the form of collar found depicted at Angkor Wat in Cambodia relating to imported regalia from Tibet. Ancon, Peru, 1st., millennium, A.D.

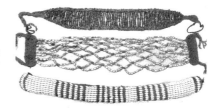

the Andean highlands, appears to be confirmed by their belief that the journey of the soul after death departed in that north-westerly direction to return to the land of the ancestors, or, as the Lengua called it - "the cities of the dead". These cities were said to be of "considerable size" with many houses made of solid material indicating from their description that it was brick that may have been intended. These houses were thought to have been built regularly along streets in an overall regular pattern. Barbrooke Grubb was bemused by these traditions and noted that the Lengua, to reach their present territory from the highlands, had to have travelled through the lands of a great number of hostile tribes, many of whom were mortal enemies, to reach the Andes. They expected in death that the soul by necessity had to traverse such a hostile terrain with unpleasant inhabiting denizens to reach their ancestral home that they could describe so reasonably accurately without having seen it for many generations - perhaps for at least 400 years there appeared to be some substance in an Andean origin. The fact that the Lengua had never constructed, let alone seen, any permanent dwelling in their own, or their immediate ancestors lifetimes, or those in the surrounding tribal territories amazed Barbrooke Grubb and he penned his final rhetorical bemusement on the subject as follows; "How, therefore, can we account for this belief, unless we assume that these Indians were at some remote period connected with the ancient cities of Peru and Bolivia, and that they have a distinct tradition of the land from which that they originally came?!!".

The use of brick was conjectural among the Lenguas since they only considered brickwork as a solid material without considering stone, but bricks suggest mud-bricks traditional in coastal Peru that is still consistent with Andean origins since coastal people moved very early into the highlands. That they may have originated from the Incas themselves has some references of interest in Lengua legends since they retained a memory of secreted treasure hidden in a long passage cut into the rock-face penetrating deep into the hillside. This place the Lengua said was located far distant from their own territory on the frontier in a land occupied by Indians whose name they did not know[61]. It is known that the bulk of the Inca treasure did in fact avoid the grasp of the Spanish Conquistadors and its final hiding place is one of the great mysteries of Andean history.

This possible origin in the Andean highlands has some further reinforcement since there is another tradition noting that there was a strange and wonderful people who would, it was predicted, arrive among them in the future. Barbrooke Grubb records a more specific version his informant had received from an "old wizard" in the far west nearer the Andes just before he died. Barbrooke Grubb arrived to minister to the Lenguas before his informant went on a visit to the Western Lenguas and after they were notified of the white mans' arrival he was questioned closely by the wizard·regarding this missionary stranger. The reason was that this tradition, passed onto the informant by the wizard, was that the headmen and priests of the Western Lenguas had believed over generations that "strange foreigners" would arrive among them who would reveal to them the mysteries of the spirit world and would make them a great people. A warning was included that if harm came to these people at the hands of the Indians then calamity would ensue and the tribes would cease to exist. These foreigners would speak the Lengua language and were called the Imlah but not of Lengua origin[62]. Needless to say Barbrooke Grubb saw the benefit in identifying himself with these expected "foreigners" particularly as he himself was in fact in the business of spreading his particular interpretation of the Christian beliefs in the world beyond. He also noted that the firm belief in this legend was undoubtedly the reason why he had received a "cautious" welcome among the Lengua instead of the usual hostility from many of the other tribes.

Some of the traditions recorded by Barbrooke Grubb will be of interest in a projected future volume since they are so unusual in the cultural environment of the dense forests of Central South America but are of some importance. Interestingly, few of their heroes, demons or spirits appear to have derived from a common origin with the Toba, Chorti or Mataco suggesting that there had been a separate incursion(s), who settled among the indigenous people to form a new input within the existing matrices of the Amazonian cultures. Others suggest that there are other incursions that are from further abroad because of parallels in other tribes who exhibit foreign elements. Just such a motif is that of the belief that the Lengua believed that to the north of their territory there lived a people whose knees were reversed[63], a motif already noted among the Chiriguanos and will again be noted in due course. Other traditions note that there was a race of pygmies and a race of giants to the west and in the comparisons of modern anthropology this can be considered true since in the Amazon region there were, or are some of the smallest people in the world (*11.041/2; 11.044*) and some of the tallest. Among the latter are Chavanne whose myths will be of interest in due course and whose men average close to 6 foot in height.

Remarkable among the Lengua myths is that they have a Creator deity that is a scarablike Beetle named Aksak[64]. Both Barbrooke Grubb and his brother-in-law Lucas Bridges both note the close similarity of this myth to that of the Egyptian and this will be considered in a projected future volume. For the present purpose it is of interest that the first people were formed from the clay Aksak threw up from his burrow but these turned out to be Siamese twins (*3.036*). On appeal from the twins the Beetle separated them and gave each the power of propagation[65]. The motif of a first ancestral pair being Siamese twins is unusual, and therefore notable, but a joined pair of twins is known in the Polynesian pantheon and as an aspect of the Vedic god of fire named Agni (*3.034*). It is also of note that Miguel Covarrubias, the noted Mexican archaeologist, considered the Siamese twins figurines found in Western Mexico as similar and probably related to those of Polynesia and he was convinced of cross-Pacific contacts with Asia[66]. Further connections between the Amazon Basin and Central America and Mexico in particular will be of more interest in later chapters.

The cosmology of the Lengua, as far as it had survived into the late nineteenth century appeared to have originated from a more complete, perhaps Andean system. The training of the "witch-doctors" was a severe one including extreme fasting and abstention from fluids to an extent that was thought to affect the nervous system and brain. As in Melanesia and other Western Pacific regions novices spent time in seclusion and herbs were used as one of the few items of sustenance. From this training the candidates apparently were believed to see spirits and ghosts as well as communicate with them through the trance state. Interestingly they were required to consume live toads and this concurs with more recent research into hallucinogenic toad secretions and particularly noted in Central America and coastal western South America. Close similarities between the myths of the Toba of the Gran Chaco and the Angamis Nagas has already been noted regarding bird's heads. It was believed by the Lenguas that the shamans swallowing "certain little birds" was supposed to endow the recipient with the power of whistling considered a special means of communication[67].

Barbrooke Grubb, in considering the Lengua's more elevated beliefs in a supernatural world more elevated than those of many of the other tribes exhibited itself, among other aspects in the recognition of a level of "angels", reminiscent of the Christian form, called kilyikhama[68]. This resulted in his attempt to "gloss" or identify the Indian form with that of the Christian much as was done in Central America by the early Spanish. Other aspects of the Lengua's beliefs and rituals that suggested origins from the Andes was reflected in the recognition or reflection of the cardinal points in their ceremonies, or rites, or social structures. A man who was judged guilty of murdering another of his own tribe was executed, but then also cremated and the ashes scattered ritually to the "four winds" or cardinal points. The damned spirit was then considered unable to assume a definite form in the afterworld and was therefore unrecognisable and unable to communicate with his deceased fellow tribesmen or ancestors. Souls of the departed were believed to take the form that they had in their former life so that if they were tall originally they would take a tall form in the afterlife and if short on earth were again short in the spirit world[69].

Among the Lengua there appeared to be three levels of spirit or divine worlds. The highest appeared to be that those already mentioned the "angels" or kilyikhama; the aphangak that are the souls of men; and the lowest was populated by the souls of the departed who form the lower creation. It was said that there was a "white kilyikhama" who was seen sailing across the waters and was considered malevolent. Another was that of a boy of about twelve years old with bright lights on both sides of his head[70]. Other denizens residing in this spirit strata were considered malevolent while some were thought to assist the Lengua in their hunting and agricultural pursuits. The most malevolent of all was a kilyakhama who was encountered on the peripherals of the forest who was said to be a giant "... of immense height, extremely thin, and with eyes flaming like balls of fire". To stumble across this spirit was said to cause instant death for the unlucky Indian[71]. Although the Lengua had no clear idea of their evolution these spirits were, it would seem, a foreign people who intruded from time to time into their forest domain and had become deified, and were probably in fact riverine mariners, or canoeists, who were thin with malnutrition from long weeks at sea. The motif of the "blood red eyes" is one than occurs continually throughout the Amazon Basin and is found also in the Pacific Ocean islands and will be of more interest in a later section.

The soul was called the aphangak and among the less developed Indians this was believed to wander "disconsolately" over the countryside with similar spirits of its type. Others considered that the soul dwelt in the earth at the burial site but was able to wander at night in the near environs. The more culturally advanced in the tribe maintained that the souls of their deceased clans went to the cities in the mountains in the far west already noted. It appears that these more advanced clans retained a belief that the whole human consisted of a threefold division, or union of three principles. This included a soul that could wander independently from the still living and functioning mental and physical forms. It was also thought that if the soul did wander it was in mortal danger since it was believed that if it emerged from the chest cavity in which it dwelt it could be seized by a kilyikhama[72]. During sleep it was feared that if the soul wandered during dreaming away from the body that there was immanent danger of a kilyikhama descending to seize control of the physical form since they were believed to be constantly on the lookout to manifest in a human form. This belief tended to confirm the vague assertion that these spirits or kilyakhama were once men or walked on the earth but as Barbrooke Grubb notes "…whether the Indian idea was originally that they were a distinct spiritual creation, or simply the souls of a prehistoric race, is not clear"[73].

The Milky Way was believed to be the path of these kilyikhama and it was said that the stones used in the burial rites of the Lengua flew up to this region of the sky[74]. Interestingly, commonly in burial rites, the sides of the body are cut open and heated stones, an armadillo's claw, a few dog bones, and occasionally red ants were inserted[75]. This custom is highly reminiscent of those in Aboriginal Australia and perhaps among the Indians of the North Coast of North America where the side of initiates were cut open and crystals sometimes inserted[76]. This is reminiscent of the burial of a child at Ancon in Peru where its heart was replaced by a crystal[77] and Huichols of North West Mexico who believed that deer-hunters became crystals after death and accompanied the Sun in its orbit[78]. The insertion of red ants suggest that they were associated with life force (red) and regeneration and in the Quetzalcoatl myths in Mexico it was to the mythical red ants that the deity recoursed to steal the sacred bones to regenerate humankind[79]. The Pleiades was another region of the sky to be of importance since this constellation heralded spring and was associated with agricultural rites as it was also widely in the Americas and the Pacific Islands. The Lengua considered the Pleiades to be the grandfather of the "devil" and reflects the ambivalence of the Lengua's attitude to the spirit world. This appeared to be able to swing from benevolence to threatening doom in the same breath and in which none could be fully trusted[80].

Of some interest in considering the Lengua cosmology is that they held festivals to celebrate the commencement of each of the seasons that was called the kyaiya. During these ceremonies only the men danced and games associated with it probably originally related to cosmic myths or stellar objects. During these dances a man was the centre of the circle formed by the participants and he repeatedly pointed to the cardinal points during the performance[81]. It is interesting to note that the Ona called the central post in their men's club or Hain, Kiayeshk meaning "Black Shag"[82], suggesting that this may originally have had a or common origin in their beliefs system with that of the Lengua. The Hain or Kloketen[83] was intimately associated with the initiation of boys and among the Lengua the ceremonies for the initiation of their youths was called the Wain-kya and is unlikely to be of coincidence[84].

The initiation for females was called the Yanmana[85], a term that has reflections of the Ona's neighbouring tribe called the Yamama (Yaghan) and although research is lacking it seems too great a coincidence that there should be such similarities. That the males were incursive into existing indigenous tribal people from whom they drew their female partners is evidenced by the fact that inheritance was traceable through the female line[86]. Early historians note repeatedly references to the Andean incursors or other foreign intruders and this appears to be confirmed in the selection of victims for infanticide. Twins were considered evil and always put to death and if the first-born child of a couple was female it was also killed. This tends to indicate that the first child was of some importance and reflects a right found also in the Pacific Islands and will be of note later. The lighter skin so noted by Barbrooke Grubb as probably indicating Andean descent and almost invariably associated with the more advanced Amazonian tribes is reflected in the custom of killing any child that is born with darker skin[87]. This suggests the custom among the Incan elite in their attempt to breed back to the original physical type reflective of the ancestors by the tradition of incest. The association of culture-bearers with white or fair skin is found wide-ly in the highlands and western coastal region of South America, and is evident in the surviving mummies of the earliest period through to the Incas, and these peoples will be of further note. This tradition appears to have been known also among other tribes and may have been the origin of the myth of killing the women among the Ona far to the south, already noted, in their attempt to regenerate their legendary ancestral physical appearance paralleling that of the Polynesians. The Ona considered the women of their tribe in ancient times to be evil and the men were hide-bound by the malevolence and thraldom of their witchcraft and in liberating themselves, accord-ing to their legends, they massacred all but the youngest. There appears to be a reflection and par-allel in the Ona legend with the sinister infanticide traditions among the Lengua since this form of infanticide was imposed and carried out by certain of the old women. Barbrooke Grubb's com-mented on this custom writing that "…infanticide is mainly perpetrated on female infants and by the old women, who, knowing that their comfort, influence and power depend upon there not being too many of them, make use of this means to limit the number of their own sex. The result is that every girl has a wide selection of partners, and consequently many men have to remain unmarried" … "The men resent this artificial means of destroying the balance of the sexes, but superstition is strong, and they are powerless to alter matters"[88]. This may well have been one of the reasons for the Ona men's action in culling, mythically, a whole generation of women to break this custom of infanticide amongst others. This again suggests that the men were intruders who were not a large enough group to be able to set up and sustain their own patrilineal clan structure in their traditional mould and were forced to adopt established local customs. Over generations they were undoubtedly weakened in time through repeated intermarriage within the same tribal groups compromising their own racial identity and traditions as indicated in the Lengua custom of infanticide.

Myths and Traditions of the Amazonian Tribes - Blood and Red Ochre

Throughout the tribal cultures of South America there are many constants that were clearly per-ceived by most of the early researchers. One of the most interesting was the use red ochre and the aspects of belief systems and myths surrounding its use and the parallels in the rites utilising real blood. Throughout South America, and already noted of the Ona, was the practice of smear-ing the hair of the head with red ochre or other substitutes. The geographical extent of this cus-tom from the Guianas on the north, Caribbean Coast to the very south in Tierra del Fuego indi-cates that it almost certainly originates from a common tradition[89]. In many tribes, particularly in the forested regions of the north and centre, the men extended the red ochre to cover the whole body with body paint of the same colour in the belief that it infused them with the life-force denoted by the colour as a form of sympathetic magic confined largely to ceremonials[90]. Such customs were noted among the Colorado (Red) Indians of Equador, who painted also their cloth-ing, or the minimum that passed as such[91]. Identification with the life force through the colour red extended beyond the body-paint to other objects and animals of the same colour and the Bororo identified particularly with the colour of red macaws[92].

Red ochre was not itself the only form of body paint used by the Indians and the juice of the urucu pod and blood itself were widely important for utilisation in decoration or protection. The Abipones (Toba) applied oxen blood to their hair but this was must have been a more recent substitute after the Spanish Conquest for red ochre[93]. The application of red ochre onto the hair of the head was believed to protect their soul thought to dwell there[94]. When a Carib child fell ill it was noted that the mother would prick her tongue and cover her child with the resultant flow. When complying with the custom of couvade a Carib father bled himself and smeared the blood on his child if born a "delicate" son[95]. In ceremonies appearing to have possible parallels among the Maya the Payaguas of Paraguay pricked their tongues and penes and smeared themselves with the blood emitted in the belief that it energised themselves in the anticipated battle or hunt[96]. In funerary ceremonies for the secondary burials the bones of the deceased were painted red and the jawbone often decorated with feathers[97]. The jawbone was of some symbolic, importance and a tradition also of importance in Melanesia in particular. Similar traditions were known among the Mexicans and Maya of Central America where the jawbone it was an important trophy cut out from the victims of war. The ritual application of red ochre is found identically in this form of secondary burial in the Western Pacific and Indonesia through into mainland Asia as well as more broadly in South America beyond the Amazon.

The application of black body paint was used during the night when attack from evil spirits seeking to enter their bodies was feared during sleep since humans were considered unprotected during that period of dark. It was believed that these denizens feared black as a colour and often the recently deceased were also painted black for the same purpose before their burial[98]. During couvade the husband lay on his bed in a form of imitation childbirth as his wife was giving birth where the Guarayi's body was also then painted black to prevent the attack of these same demons. The couvade is widely known outside South America and its origins have long been a subject of controversy. In some of the South American tribes it was believed that the "egg" from which the child developed originated in the father and the mother was only the incubator.
It may be that the husband, considered as the originator of the child's life, was therefore more vulnerable, but it may also be that this was a diversionary tactic. Throughout South America the woman was considered to be highly subject to the approach and attack of evil spirits and dances at the time of the first menstruation and other rites associated with her were usually designed to avert the attentions of these spirits. After her marriage, if her husband should decide to leave his family or was killed in battle or die from some disease, his wife would usually have his children put to death. This suggests that they considered the intimate spiritual bond to exist beyond the transfer of the "egg" from him to her long after childbirth. The couvade, therefore, may be a form of protection of his lineage but should he leave or die then the bond was broken or the children were returned to his ancestors in the spirit world.

The soul was believed to reside in the scalp lock and it was believed that in headhunting rituals the trophy head was believed to have entrapped in it the soul of the victim who then became a slave, albeit discarnate, to the victor. Because evil spirits were believed to enter through the apertures of the body particularly those of the head, these openings in trophy head, by the same logic, were blocked to prevent the soul escaping. It was also believed by some that there was some soul substance in all the other areas of hair on the body, the eyebrows, eyelashes, that above the upper lip and the chin, under the arms and around the genitals. Because the hair on the head appeared to house the most important element that constituted the soul it was rare to find a completely shaved head in the forests of South America. Part shaving, however, was frequent since it was in the scalp lock and not the whole of the head hair in which the soul resided[99]. Part-shaving was required of women in particular during mourning rituals since it was believed that if it was the husband who died he would be able to force her to follow him if he had a scalp-lock to hold onto[100]. Because the woman was considered the easy victim of evil and discarnate spirits shaving became another means of protection. Part-shaving or tonsuring the crown of the head was a particular feature[101], as it is to this day among some of the more remote tribes.

Among the Jivaros in the North East Andean region the men were noted to grow their hair and bind them into three pigtails. One pigtail hung either side from the temples and a larger one down the rear of the head. These were believed to give them strength and courage and without which he was not considered a real man[102]. It is of particular note that this type of pigtail arrangement was in fact typical either as braids or plaits, or ringlets, from the temples in India and the Ancient Middle East (*8.064-72*). The hair and nails on the human body grow quickly and this was as obvious to the Indians as it is to modern Westerners and when cut soon re-grow to a longer size. It is clear therefore that from the earliest times these elements were indicators of the continuing health of the life-force, within that flowed from the head and chest manifesting at the extremities. In cutting or trimming the nails or hair therefore, since they were still a part of the life force great care was perceived to be required in their disposal so that none could obtain them to gain access to and injure the individual's soul. To cut the hair or a nail was to also sever a part of the soul and it had to be done with the appropriate rituals for protection and disposal of, or secreted in the correct manner[103]. In many cultures it was incumbent to allow the hair to grow long particularly among the men, and if that was impracticable then it was usually necessary that the priest, who protected the community, allowed his to grow so that he operated at maximum spiritual strength.

The perceived need for protection of the soul of the Amerindian is clearly indicated in the foregoing and tattooing was also considered to provide that insurance, perhaps where red ochre supplies were less certain, against those mysterious demonic intruders who brought disease and death. The women's faces were more highly tattooed than those of the men since they were considered more vulnerable as already noted and not only did this custom survive into modern times but is preserved as being a very ancient tradition in the high cultures of the Pacific Coast of Peru[104]. For youths entering the world of men it was considered that to achieve the "keen sight" and strong arm muscles for shooting it was considered necessary that his face required scarring which was extended to the upper arms[105]. To rid the body of evil spirits from the physical body bleeding was prescribed and after scars were then applied as charms against the further attack of malevolent demons[106]. In a similar vein, but recognisably with references to the practices of the Australian Aboriginals, crystals were inserted into the bodies. The practice of the Amazonian Indians was that related to "venesection" performed on the arm. A crystal was attached to the arrowhead of a miniature bow and arrow and then pressed against the vein before being released. The crystal was believed to channel magical spirit healing powers and the intent in this act was as a charm against disease and death. Miniature bow and arrows are widely known in Melanesia and found in New Guinea[107] also as well as in South America. Crystals were also worn as charms and it has been reported of the Guahivos Indians of the Orinoco that one had been seen wearing a caiman's tooth inset with crystal. This charm was called guanare but it is reminiscent of the Mayan practice of insertion of jewels and crystals in the teeth of the elite but was a practice also found in South East Asia[108].

It is interesting to note in the possible comparisons between the Amazonian Indians and the Maya since they also practiced rituals that are found more closely similar, or identical to those found in the Western Pacific. Of particular note is the male ritual called by some "incision" while others consider it a moderate form of circumcision. In the Amazon only a few tribes performed these ceremonies and early reports by Fernandez de Souza recorded that upon the young initiates an almost "imperceptible" incision on the prepuce was cut[109]. Apart from the Maya, who also imposed the same form of incision, this form is known particularly in the New Hebrides. On the island Malekula, in particular, this custom was reported on at length by the notable researcher

3.011 : The Polynesian god Tangaroa showing the lesser deities said to be born from him and similar to those of Western Mexico (*3.011*). Rurutu, Tubai (Austral) Islands, South East Polynesia, Pre-19th., century, A.D.

3.012 : A clay figurine thought to represent a mother goddess but with a headdress similar to those found at San Austin in Southern Colombia. The many smaller figures, or babies, covering the body appear to duplicate the basic principle behind the Polynesian god Tangaroa who was said to have given birth to humanity from his own substance. Colima, Comala Phase, West Mexico, 200 B.C.-300 A.D.

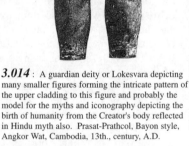

3.013 : The boar depicted as the Hindu Sky God Vishnu from whom mankind and all things emerged. This is indicated by the multitude of figures carved on the surface and probably the origin for such beliefs in Oceania. Varaha, Eran, Late Gupta Dynasty, North India, c490 A.D.

3.014 : A guardian deity or Lokesvara depicting many smaller figures forming the intricate pattern of the upper cladding to this figure and probably the model for the myths and iconography depicting the birth of humanity from the Creator's body reflected in Hindu myth also. Prasat-Prathcol, Bayon style, Angkor Wat, Cambodia, 13th., century, A.D.

John Layard almost three generations ago[110] - an island group that will be of some importance in later sections.

Since the apertures of the body were thought the most likely to be attacked to gain forced entry by an evil spirit into the subject's body the seven openings in the head were the most guarded and where the most complex protective designs were applied. In a woman the genital region was also considered a danger and elaborate tattoos have survived on ceramics that indicate close similarities with examples which have survived in more recent centuries in Micronesia and Melanesia but anciently found in Peru (*1.043/4*). It is of note that in many myths associated with women's vulnerability it is said that unless they are protected by shaving or some other form the fish they eat could allow a demon secreted in its belly to impregnate them or they would die[111]. It was also thought that the women were at risk from the spirit of the whirlwind since it was believed that, as in Aboriginal Australia, child spirits awaiting rebirth could enter them causing an unwanted pregnancy[112].

The soul is perceived to reside centred in the hair, but also extending from their into a continuous flow of life force to the extremities through to the nails on the ends of the hands and feet. The skin also was reverenced as constituting an element of the soul, possibly because it was observed that, as an envelope, it enclosed all parts of the being to be protected. As moisture was clearly related to the well-being the exudations of sweat, usually greatly revered in mythical thought along with spittle and considered creative substances in their own right, percolating from the body must have been of concern and awe for the Amerindian as it was for others. In the construction of sacred drums the skin of a male sacrificial victim was stretched across the opening since it was believed that the soul was trapped and doomed to "eternal torments" by being beaten for as long as the drum survived[113]. Armlets and other bands were also considered to be a protection for the limbs and arms in particular worn almost universally by Amerindian and other less developed peoples[114].

There are many parallels of Amazonian traditions with those of the Pacific, and indeed India, but there are several that are of particular note. Among the Ona one of the most remarkable was that of gashing of the body in mourning that so disfigured the thighs and was noted of the Aboriginal Australians but among the latter and found also in the Amazon is the custom of the amputation of finger joints as another ritual of mourning[115]. This custom was also found among the Melanesians but particularly recorded of the Polynesians and similarly with the same geographical distribution from India through the Pacific Islands to the Amazon is tooth evulsion and usually for similar reasons[116].

Among the Tupis the teeth of enemies, some collected on strings more than two metres long, were worn into battle against the tribes whose captives had been killed and cannibalised to taunt and intimidate them. The bones of the captives' bodies were also displayed in these skirmishes for the same purposes and among the Paraguayan tribes these bones were used as ritual girdles or belts[117]. Interestingly magician's aprons of human bones were worn in rituals among the Maya (*3.005; 3007*), and similar beaded relics have been recovered from Ancient Peru (*3.009/10*) and these appear to imitate identically those among the Tibetans (*3.006; 3.008*). The Paraguayan Indians also wore collars which included human bones along with stones and animals' teeth and it was the occupation of old female sorcerers to string these and no doubt imbue protection for the wearer against the malevolent emanations for their opponents[118]. In Peru captive victims' teeth, were also strung into necklaces and worn into battle but it is not surprising therefore to find that necklaces of teeth both human and animal, were also part of the combat adornment found among the Pacific Ocean peoples.

The mouth was an opening of the body which was considered to be under particular threat from evil spirits and to this end small piercing sticks similar to tattoo sticks were inserted around the mouth called "arrows"[119]. Karsten considered these "arrows" as the parallel of the Chinese acupuncture needles but thought that their use orientated entirely to dispel the evil spirits tainting the blood[120]. This certainly parallels the use of tattooing among the Ainu of Japan and may have direct or indirect origins with the East Asian practices. Eating was a time when evil spirits were especially feared since the repeated opening of the mouth meant that the evil spirits could slip in with the food undetected. So fearful were the Indians of this danger that at particular times, when the day or month attack was more likely, they fasted since the risk from ingestion of an evil spirit with the food was much too great. At any other time the Indians ate their food in silence and this was considered to assist in averting the attention of the discarnate demons on the prowl. Of particular note was that women ate separately from men, a custom well-known in Polynesia, and this no doubt was reinforced among the Amazonian tribes in the belief that women tended to attract these demons and were less able to resist their attentions[121].

These many parallels with Polynesian influences are unlikely to be coincidence and of particular interest is a myth found among the Tupari is of special note. It is recorded from their traditions that the creators of the first people were two sorcerers who lived in the air named Antaba and Koluba. Their bodies were covered with "little babies" no bigger than a human hand.

These "babies" exuded from the flesh of these two old men and they were said to cling to their skin and weep. During the night Antaba and Koluba come down to the Earth and when they perceived that a woman had had intercourse, by means of incantations they placed one of these babies spirits into her womb. It was believed that the human father was considered to take some part in the child's creation but it was thought not possible without the intervention of the old sorcerers[122]. The myth is an interesting one since there is a close parallel with a myth relating to Mollope on the Peruvian Pacific Coast but more particularly with the myths relating to Tangaroa in Polynesia as the Creator and these.

The myth of "Mollope the Lousy" appears to have originated at least from the Moche period on the North Coast of Peru and it is said that as her lice multiplied so humanity would multiply and flourish[123]. This supernatural is found depicted on ceramics along with scenes of cannibalism and sodomy, so frequently associated with mariner peoples where males are at sea for many weeks and months and with only enough food to cover a standard length of journey. Should there be delays, or they are swept away in a storm, or are becalmed for long periods, a common problem near the Equator, then cannibalism was an expedient perhaps not even as a last resort. The myth of Mollope is a likely adaption through suffering a gender reversal deriving from Tangaroa, the Polynesian high god, and mankind was said to have derived from the sweat of his body and believed to be depicted in numerous carved figures illustrating this creative act (*3.011*). Similar figures are depicted in Western Mexican ceramic figures of female deities probably having the same origin (*3.012*).

The broad but brief review of myths and gods apparently relating to and deriving from the mariner contacts from the Pacific extend far from the long Pacific Coast along the west of the South American continent through to the east into the Gran Chaco and Amazon. This more general review sets the scene for the more detailed considerations of the archaeology and traditions recorded in the cultures of the Andes and the Pacific Coast of Colombia, Ecuador Peru and Chile.

PRECERAMIC PERIOD in PERU and INDIA

The Rise to High Culture on the Pacific Coast and Andes in South America
When the Spanish first heard of the fabulous lands of gold far to the South when they entered Panama in Central America in 1511 A.D. it was several years before a group of venturers could be funded to undertake the necessary expeditions[124]. This was because the Spanish were so preoccupied with Mexico and the resulting insurrections, since the fall of the Aztecs, due to their extreme measures in imposing control over the land. The Spanish also had to cope with the attacks on their fleets from other European powers who were asserting themselves at sea and were particularly attracted to carving out for themselves a share of the booty that was exclusively in the hands of the Spanish.

Francisco Pizarro sailed from Darien in 1524 and was forced to return in 1525 without having reached Peru. His second voyage commenced in 1526 and he sailed as far as the extreme north coast of Peru before having to return in 1527. By 1531 Pizarro was in Coaque, in Ecuador, and on his third voyage and in sailing further south met, and captured Atahualpa at Cajamarca and later executed the Inca emperor in June or July, 1533 A.D. The confrontation with the nominal Inca, Atahaulpa, in Cajamarca and their march on Cuzco resulted in the tragic fall of the ruling dynasty of the Ayar Incas. The Spaniards met ocean-going rafts of Indians merchants off the coast of Ecuador who were terrified at the sight of their strange new ship and many threw themselves overboard and were drowned rather than be captured. On the island of Puna, opposite the Ecuadorian coast at Manta, the Spanish reported on the strange appearance of the people, their clothes, habits and ceremonials involving, so frequently, human sacrifice. Gold was lavishly used by native peoples in their temples for ritual objects including the elite ornaments worn by the priests and rulers, and along with the emeralds so frequently adorning their religious relics and idols. One idol of particular interest was that of Umina made, reputedly, entirely from a single large emerald. Such conspicuous display of precious metals and stones convinced the Spanish that they had reason to return for a much closer look among these people and to journey further south where they had been informed of a great empire of gold - that of the Incas.

The history of the Spanish Conquest of Peru has been told many times and need not be considered here in the detail that many more recent writings have been presented it. It is sufficient to indicate that the Spanish records at the time focused on all that was unusual in their eyes and so very different from their own homeland environment and culture. This was exacerbated by the search for gold and booty so that their focus on the remarkable achievements and history of the Incas and their forebears is much more scantily reported than it might have been. The great irrigations schemes and the vast areas covered by the irrigated terraces in coastal and Andean Peru, many of that had continuously been used for many centuries and probably millennia, were hardly mentioned even though thc sight of them brings expressions of surprise and praise even in the present day (6.108; 6.111/2). It is believed, however, that the name of the South American mountain chain, the longest in the world, the Andes, received its name from the Spanish from the native term for the terracing - "ardenes". These extensive, irrigated terraces have been called more recently the greatest monument to human endeavour[125].

The achievements in irrigation and agriculture were all the more extraordinary since the lands the Peruvians occupied were subject to great climatic extremes. The coastal strip, less that a few miles wide in some places but averaging about fifty, was then, and still is some of the driest desert in the World, frequently composed of sand dunes or near total aridity. Crossing these coastal strips were narrow bands of silted flats flanking the rivers that descended to the Pacific Ocean from the fertile valleys in the Andes themselves. The foothills through which the rivers made their way rose steeply from the barren coastal strip to the great heights of the Andes proper.

The Andes is a young, rising mountain chain and there are many volcanoes including some of the highest mountains in the length of the chain extending over two thousand miles. Some of these erupt with great force and the land is also subject to tectonic plate movements along the Pacific Coast and subsidence's have occurred where parts of the coast have disappeared overnight into the sea[126]. The seismic activity and eruptions have long been a part of the Andean way of life and in 1600 A.D., in the South of Peru the volcano Hauyna Putina erupted with such force that it destroyed itself in the explosion leaving only a gaping hole[127].

The great cyclical climatic change known as the El Nino, or literally "The Boy Child" as an allusion to the "Christ Child", has been newsworthy in these more environmentally aware times. It is associated with great catastrophes and with the believed nine-year cyclical event where the latest prognostications indicate that global warming may be resulting in more frequent cycles. As in Eurasia these major changes of climate, and those in South America caused by El Nino, resulted in periods of climatic change and correspond to the collapse of cultures and civilisations. In Ancient Peru and Bolivia the El Nino events most notable are those occurring between 500 A.D. and 1100 A.D. and these correspond with the end of the Moche period on the North Central Peruvian coast at the beginning of the 6th., century A.D. and the end of the Tiahuanacan Empire about the 11th., century A.D. There is a particular period of major change between 562-94 A.D. but this may have been due to the major climatic change resulting from aftermath of the massive eruption of Krakatoa in the Indonesian islands in 535 B.C., many times of greater force than that of the same volcano between the islands of Java and Sumatra in 1883

A.D. The 535 A.D. eruption was one of the greatest ever recorded and it is believed to have affected the climate for many decades after. It is now known that this event resulted in devastating disruption in the agricultural cycles causing great famines and the fall of many dynasties and empires contemporary with it. Clearly it must have been this eruption that caused the total disruption of all cultural levels evident throughout Ecuador, Peru and Bolivia corresponding so completely with this historical epoch. Although this catastrophe saw the ending of contemporary culture and it also resulted in regeneration decades later. Peru was a land of topographic and environmental extremes and therefore more greatly affected by the extremes in climate.

The natural heat reservoirs in the Pacific, affected by the El Nino should emphasise, however, by its direct flow across the Pacific Ocean following the Equatorial Currents both side of the Equator from Asia to South and Central America, that it was not only the intense climatic changes more usually centred on Indonesia and South East Asia that were transferred. The flow of the Equatorial currents so directly from West to East must also have tempted and encouraged mariners from the most ancient times to voyage to the limits of the known and beyond. This can be illustrated by the close similarities noted in the ceramic artefacts and designs surviving from the earliest ceramic period in South America, located in Ecuador and South East Asia. Ceramic evidence of cultural contact that could only have been achieved in transfer by sea between Southern Japan, East Coast China and New Guinea in Melanesia has been recognised for decades dating about 5,000 B.C. There is no reason that can be offered why mariners who travelled over thousands of miles between these distant regions in the Western Pacific would not have continued on eventually into the Melanesian and Polynesian islands further to the east and subsequently on to the Pacific Coast of South America.

Pre-Ceramic Period in Ancient South America

During the Ice Age, ending about 8,000 B.C., it must be realised that the sea level was about 100 metres (approx. 325 feet) lower than its present level[128]. Since food resources related to fishing and shell collection would have been one of the most sustainable many early hunter-gatherers would have congregated in their settlements around the coasts. However, evidence of these localised villages would have been lost as the warmer climate after the Ice Age ice caps began to cause the sea waters to rise through the melting of the extended Ice Caps at the North and South Poles and, as a result, the seas rose toward their present level. Because of the high mountains mass that formed a large part of South America the continent would have been heavily glaciated, but the eastern lowlands that were to become the Amazon basin and the seashore along the Pacific Coast allowed people to pass from North and Central America into the southern regions of the continent.

The Lithic Period in South America, initiated by hunter-gathers, began about 9-10,000 years ago and lasted until about 3000 B.C. This was a period when the sea levels were rising and therefore there must be evidence missing from that assessment of man's history along the seashores of the world that may never be determined. The Amerindians of South America were characteristically descended from the Siberian populations, of three known genetic types, who crossed over the land bridge connected to the North American continent[129]. The remnants of this island bridge from the Ice Age are now called the Aleutian Islands. Not all of these tribes reached South America and those who ventured south took several thousand years after crossing the land bridge south of mainland Alaska from Siberia. The very south of South America was reached by about 9,000 B.C. and these people were known for a very particular type of spearhead called "fluted points" and related examples are also found earlier in North America[130]. In this period, at the very end of the far south of South America, evidence for the diet of these first peoples includes the wild horse, guanaco and also the giant wild sloth[131].

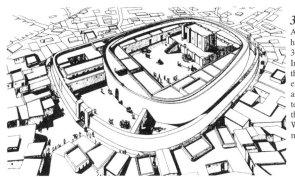

3.017 : Ancient Peruvian Andean ceremonial centres had curved corners in the 3-2nd., millennium B.C. In the Ancient Middle East the major towns also exhibited curved corners and found in more regional temple constructions into the first millennium A.D. Warka, Sumeria, Iraq, 3rd. millennium, B.C.

3.018 : The curved walls of the early Andean ceremonial sites follows and utilizes similar technical, constructional and design features from contemporary developments long utilized in Ancient Mesopotamia and this is also true for later epochs - see fire altar *8.039*. La Galgada, Pre-Post-ceramic Periods, 2300-1750 A.D.

Secondary burials were known on the Santa Elena Peninsula from about 8,000 to 4,600 B.C. and this indicates religious rites and beliefs regarding the soul after death were developed to some degree in these societies. These were very different from those developed in a similar time frame in the mountain regions. In the Zana and Lanbeyeque River zones from about 6,000 B.C., over about 500 years, small mounds are found at a place called Nanchoc that are lozenge shaped and that are wider on the southwest side than they are on the northeast side. These mounds are aligned about 15 metres apart and in three tiers to about 1.2 to 1.5 metres high and were faced with fitted stones. Radiocarbon dating from material in their base has defined dates of between 6,000 and 5,500 B.C. The mounds are built up of superimposed floors resting on layers of fill that have increased the height of the structures over time, a construction form found later in Andean platform construction. It is believed that these approximately parallel mounds reflect the beginnings of the U-shaped ceremonial mound tradition found through coastal and montane Peru in the following millennia. These occupied zones appear to be concentrated in residential areas of about 100 metres diameter, and there is evidence of hearths along with middens (rubbish mounds) and foodstuffs together with secondary burials[132].

From about 8,000 to 5,700 B.C. in the Chicama Valley on the Central Peruvian Coast grinding stones and human burials are known in a very localised region but extending towards the valley of Ica in the South. The earliest distribution of these cultural traits occurs in the later and larger civic monuments along the coastal strip and these were associated with a fishing culture along with evidence of hooks and nets[133].

In the far south of Peru, along the Moquegua River valley, rock-shelters and caves were utilised as habitations and cave paintings are to be found in some of them near Toquepala. These date to about 7,500 B.C. and in this Lithic Period the higher altitude shelters that appear to have been the most favoured were occupied from that early time until about 1,640 B.C. Small circular dwellings were evident from about 3,000 B.C. whose walls were constructed of perishable material such as animal skins, brush or reeds, or clay plastered over woven reeds or other material. These dwellings appear clustered around a ceremonial construction with a clay floor laid with care. These houses were of about 10 metres diameter and their single remaining feature appears to be a cairn that was probably the focus of religious devotion[134].

The Chinchorros in the Atacama of Chile

One of the most remarkable developments in South American culture was that found on the North Chilean Coastal region in the extremely barren deserts of the Atacama in possibly related in this location to take advantage of mariner influences from the Pacific. These people were known as the Chinchorros, some distance south of the Moquegua River region, were predominantly a fishing orientated people but supplementing their diet with hunting and gathering. Their industrious and inventive array of fishing tackle and equipment including hooks, nets and harpoons indicating that they were an advanced-for-their-time culture and who increased in numbers at the time they begin to exhibit tendencies that appear to express a higher ceremonial awareness evident more usually in advanced cultures. The belief system appears to be adapted and advanced in a spiritual belief in an afterlife the requirement of mummification after death. This is evident in a remarkable braced skeleton technique and the filling of the eviscerated body with herbs and plants as well as plastering the face. The resultant mask formed over the bone structure to obtain a life-like image was painted and these ritual processes are evident in development from 5000 B.C. until the end of the second millennium B.C.[135]. The close similarities with practises known among the Caucasian Tocharians in Central Asia, in the same or similar time frame, have been noted in recent works located around the far west of China's ancient sites called Urumqi[136]. It was at this time also that the Ancient Egyptians were developing their well-known mummification practises, but few "experts" would admit that there might be a connection between the far-distant culture. The close cultural similarities between the Western Pacific and South America earlier noted may explain why this unusual and apparently related preservation rituals and techniques appear in South America on the Pacific Coast.

Of particular interest among the Chinchorros funerary ceremonies was that wigs were also made to regale the completed mummy with its plaster-moulded face and its life-like painted finish. Further to the north religious beliefs had developed to a degree that required the preservation of the corpse as a mummy after death. At La Paloma, sited on the Central Peruvian Coast, the body was preserved by salting to preserve it from rapid deterioration a technique dating to about 4000 B.C.[137]. The preservation of the life-like mummy was of great importance in later Coastal and Andean cultures in North Western South America and reached its finality among the Incas themselves.

Lithic to Pre-ceramic in Andean and Coastal Peru

The period where change became more pronounced commences with an emphasis on the predominantly hunter-gatherer stage moving toward settled villages and focusing on a mixed economy of farming supplemented by hunting. The appearance of cotton at about 3000 B.C. on the North Coast of Peru has been utilised as a convenient time marker for a period of the emergence of Peru from the Lithic to the Pre-ceramic[138]. This remarkable pre-ceramic period is unique in that it covers a vast amount of time, about 1200 years in the developmental history of Ancient Peru without any appearance of pottery but featuring the construction of vast ceremonial complexes. This lack of the basic essential of pottery in a settled organised, society that was required to provide water and supplies

3.017 :
Stepped pyramid showing the rounded base platform usually formed by filling-in, or overbuilding the earlier occupations depicted in a carved relief, in the same manner to those in Peru. Konyundjik, Assyria, First half of the first millennium, B.C.

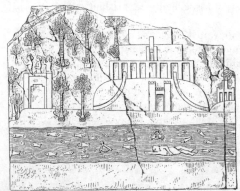

3.018 :
Building of mounds formed over previous epochs typical in the Ancient Middle East and found also at Kotosh and other sites in Ancient Peru in the same time band. Assyria, 9-7th., century, A.D.

3.019 : The fire god is seen rising between two long flags and generally paralleled with shutters in China as the sign for the rising Sun. Akkad Dynasty, Iraq, Late third millennium, B.C.

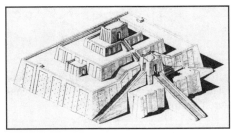

3.021 : Clay pots embedded into a brick construction and plaster finished wall surround. Warka, Uruk, Iraq, 4th., millennium, B.C.

3.020 : Sophisticated stepped pyramid, the result of many centuries of architectural construction and design with brick panelling and brick marks, reflected later among the Moche on the Peruvian coast. Great Ziggurat dedicated to the Moon God Sin, Ur, Mesopotamia, Mid-third millennium, B.C.

3.022 : An array of cone mosaics in various patterns typical of a period when clay cones were characteristic in the construction of the Ancient Middle East over two millennia. Warka, Uruk, Iraq, 4th., millennium, B.C.

3.023 : Characteristic clay cone from Ancient Iraq, in a time band when clay cones were also used with mud bricks on the Pacific Coast of Peru. Iraq, 3rd., millennium, B.C.

for regular labour over many years besides the necessities of daily domestic life has puzzled archaeologists and historians for decades. Pottery has been seen as an essential element in the evolution of social structures before they embark on such major civic projects[139].

Another remarkable fact about the evolution of cultures in Peru is that over the present land surface enclosed within its present boundaries only 2% of the land is considered suitable for agriculture, resulting in irrigation terraces that were more extensive in early millennia than they are now. This meant that cultivation was limited in the Pre-ceramic and early ceramic periods to the valley floors and coasts before evidence of terracing and by necessity this would mean isolation and division for its population. Such separation of population into widely dispersed communities would not be conducive for the evolution of extended social organisations drawing on large populations with a secure economic base with the cumulative resources necessary to support and construct the enormous ceremonial complexes characteristic of this early period (3.064). Isolation would also tend to preserve local traditions rather than provide access and dispersal for new ideas and beliefs or innovations and techniques. In other words the topography of Peru was very much against the likelihood of progress of the type found in Peru - it is perhaps the least likely place for the developments known to have taken place over the 6,000 years up until the fall of the Inca. Even the more conventional archaeologists and historians have recorded similar views[140]. The explanation must be found in other initiatives originating from elsewhere, and abroad in particular and these will be considered throughout this work.

The onset of a progressive pre-ceramic period commences about 3000 B.C. but there is no evidence that pottery was manufactured until it appears in Northern and Central Peru about 1800 B.C.[141]. It is largely agreed that this introduction probably occurs as a result of contact with Ecuador to the north, but in that region ceramics had been known from the beginning of the pre-ceramic in Peru - 3000 B.C.[142], predating its introduction into Peru by about 1200 years. This extraordinary anomaly also remains unexplained since other trade goods were found from Ecuador in the Peruvian ceremonial sites long before the advent of pottery and the reason as to why pottery was not also transferred remaining one of the great mysteries of World archaeology as noted. Once pottery is found first introduced into Peru this innovation takes another 400 years to travel via trade routes, long established, before it is found in the Lake Titicaca region, at about 1400 B.C., and this is also true of Northern Chile[143]. This suggests a population that is very conservative rather than progressive and adaptive and inured against innovation.

Aspero - U-shaped Ceremonial Platforms and the Emergence of the Peruvian Cultures

Many of the larger sites in Peru that have known for several generations and were considered to be of a later period than they are now known to be. With the recent dating techniques applied to the datable material from these sites a shock was to settle into South American archaeology from the results achieved. Many had considered Chavin de Huantar the first great Peruvian civilisation but the massive platform and pyramidal constructions on the coast have now been determined to predate the great Andean highland site by 2000 years.

The monumental coastal sites were characterised by the U-shaped constructions usually composed of a central, higher stepped pyramid and two flanking wings of similar shape and form but never exactly the same. In the later Initial Period the flanking platforms were of a much greater scale in relation to the central pyramid, while constructions or reconstructions of the central pyramid is overall much larger in proportion to the whole. The site layout focus is always on the central pyramid with its ceremonial staircase leading from the plaza, formed between the two wing platforms, up to the temples constructed on its summit. Between the Lurin and Chancay Valleys all the pyramid complexes are orientated to the northeast between 13 and 64 degrees. Remarkably the scale of these civic schemes in the earliest phases is greater than in the late Pre-ceramic constructions. In the later Initial Period constructions the U-shape layout is always fundamental to the ceremonial civic architecture and these are largerly a feature of the Central Peruvian Coast valley lowlands but sometimes found further inland and as far north as the Supe Valley. Up until the 1990's about 20 of the U-shaped pyramid-platform complexes from this period had been identified[144].

In the Lurin Valley, at the U-shaped ceremonial centre of Mina Perdida, there have been identified over 30 construction and rebuilding phases and there are four main staircases up to the central pyramid, one overbuilt upon the other still evident. The oldest of these was built of conical adobes and this was at a time contemporary with the use of clay cone construction in the Ancient Middle East[145]. In the second last staircase construction adobes of a cubical shape were utilised while in the final phase stone masonry was utilised. Hemispherical adobes (sun-dried mud bricks) were also used, reflecting in principle the "bun-shaped" mud bricks used in the Indus Valley, along with river cobbles. The constructional forms therefore appear to mirror the development of clay cone and mud brick forms used in the Ancient Middle East and Indus from about 4,000 B.C. through to the first millennium B.C. suggesting transfer of building construction tech-

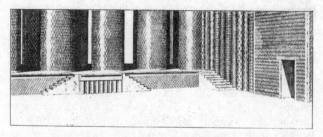

3.024 : Columned courtyard and arcades are a feature of the temples and civic buildings in the Ancient Near and Middle East and are a feature of temples in the Pre-ceramic and Post-ceramic periods in Ancient Peru in the same time band. Kish, Iraq, 4th., millennium, B.C.

3.025 : Massive circular columns with cone-shaped mosaic decoration contemporary with similar architectural features on coastal Peru. Warka, Uruk, Iraq, 4th., millennium, B.C.

niques from there to South America (*3.021/3*). This is likely to explain why massive platform and pyramid sites developed rapidly in the early period of Peruvian history and then diminished when there are cultural changes in the Ancient Middle East.

Building Construction in Ancient Sumer; Akkad and Elam

In the Ancient Middle East W.K. Loftus, in examining the ruins of Shushi in 1852, in what is now considered Elam but then generally called Mesopotamia, recorded among the mud bricks many clay clones[146]. These cones were frequently used as the structural insert into a column or wall where the cone base was coloured and fired as faience and these were utilised as mosaic surface claddings on many of the great pillars so notable in the architecture of that time. This site is dated to the 3rd., millennium, B.C. and this was in fact an epoch that was the result already of about 2-3 thousand years of development in building techniques and materials of that type as well as stone construction. The towns and villages had long chosen natural eminences where possible for defence and probably also to reserve the lower lying, less rocky, silted areas for agriculture and grazing.

The clay cones used for decorative display inserted into the surface clay mortar on the columns were undoubtedly themselves based on cruder forms at an earlier time that developed to form the basis of a decorative cladding support for the colourful mosaic finish. With these building techniques and decorations other elements of iconography and religious aspects of culture must have been transferred, although imperfectly, and it should not be surprising to find, therefore, contemporary building techniques in Ancient Andean and Coastal Peru reflect those of the Ancient Middle East from the 4th., millennium, B.C. and earlier.

As the Elamite, or Mesopotamian, villages grew and expanded gradually into smaller kingdoms, before and after being merged into Empires at each successive epoch, current archaeology notes that rebuilding took place over that of the earlier building clusters by filling in and levelling[147] - the exact form of constructional technique found in early Peru. Even interments into the platform and surrounding precincts are similar in principle to those found in Peru[148]. Such developments are typified by detailed studies at Susa, a major centre from the 5th., millennium, B.C. that was repeatedly rebuilt and reoccupied into the first millennium, B.C. The levelling of the natural eminence and being capped by a mud brick platform on which Susa A was built commenced in about 4395 B.C. and this phase of construction and development lasted until about 3955 B.C.[149]. The original eminence in this platform was levelled to form a truncated core and this seems to have been emulated both elsewhere in the surrounding region of West Asia and in the beginnings of the monumental phases in Coastal and Andean Peru and retained there as a principle for a couple of thousand years. Interestingly at Susa the residential and public buildings seem to have been deliberately finished rose-coloured[150] and this was a colour much favoured in the wall and surface finishes in both Central and South America.

In Susa B, the following phase, a stepped platform was erected over a midden of accumulated refuse as a result of an "indeterminable period of time". Both the stepped platform profile and the fact that it was built over a midden is reflected in the later ceremonial and Public structures in Coastal Peru. This great platform at Susa measured about 70 x 65 metres and is found to have stood on a larger base about 2 metres high and 80 metres on a side[151]. Because the construction of the whole site from truncated natural eminence to stepped platform is so similar in principle to that of the Apadana constructed by Darius at Persepolis (begun 518 B.C.) archaeologists now refer to such acropolii as an apadana[152] - a term that will be of some significance in due course in a later chapter.

The Susiana plain that constituted the main centre of Elam at this early time has revealed at least 40 settlements and is therefore more densely populated than any other known contempo-

3.026 : A sketch of a Tasmanian Aboriginal male with red ochred hair identical in principle to tribes in the Amazon Basin and Gran Chaco. He also wears a cape knotted over one shoulder similar to those of the Incas and the Nagas of the Assam. Tasmania, Southern Australia, Early 19th., century, A.D.

3.027 : A Tasmanian native named Woreddy ("Doctor") wearing a typical possum cape traditionally knotted, and red ochred hair. The Tasmanians crafted canoes that were virtually identical to those of the Maori and those of Peru and Lake Titicaca. Tasmania, South East Australia, Early 19th., century, A.D.

3.028 : Cape called Aghaopucho, knotted in the same way as the Tasmanian Aborigines and Ancient Peruvians. The term Aghao-pucho appears to relate directly to the Peruvian poncho. Sema Nagas, Assam, North East India, Early 20th., century, A.D.

3.029 : A sketch by Poma de Ayala of the early Inca ruler, Mayta Capac, showing the helmet type of Inca crown, star club, and the cape tied in the manner of the peoples of the Western Pacific and the Nagas of Assam. Post Conquest, Peru.

rary region. At this same period, from the 5-4th., millennium, B.C., Susa was unique as a centre of civilisation and it was here that clay seals make their first known appearance and were probably the model for those found a later in Ancient Peru and Ecuador[153]. In more remote regions of Elam, in the South West corner of Iran, there are extensive city wall constructions in mud brick at Tal-i Malyan, in Fars Province. These walls extend for about 5 km. and date from about 5500 B.C. and contemporary with Susa III period[154].

It is interesting to note that these phases are contemporary and appear to be connected with Luristan[155], renowned in later periods for its finely designed and manufactured bronze artefacts and this extends these interregional cultural transfers by land toward the Indus River and the India Subcontinent[156]. These bronzes preserved animal armorial designs (*5.149-51*) that have long been noted to be closely similar, and in some cases identical to those found in South America and at Tiahuanaco in particular (*5.154*).

In the adjacent independent city state of Uruk advances were also being made since it was here that the first writing has been found. It is probably significant that the first examples are related storage seals relating to accounts and by extension to trade[157]. In the Eastern Mediterranean it is known that trade routes were fiercely guarded and maintained in great secrecy since trade was power. It is likely therefore that traders, if literate, were forbidden to write any reference to any ports, routes or cargo that they carried or to keep any form of log that might be seized or stolen to give advantage to an enemy. This was certainly known of the Phoenicians and, as a result, their sites are usually only discovered by accident or rumour. As an example, it was long attested that the Phoenicians did not venture into the Atlantic until one of their sites on the Moroccan Coast at Mogador disproved this theory[158]. It is likely therefore that ensuring only the most trusted sea-trade captains, with crews who could not read or write, were employed was in fact the reason why no form of writing was developed in South America, references only appearing millennia later to some form of script that the Inca Pachacuti forbade in the first half of the 15th., century.

The cultural transfer by mariners from the Ancient Middle East, and later also India, may explain not only the lack of writing but the delayed development of any form of pottery or ceramics in Peru until about 1800 B.C. Mariners in Ancient Eurasia, although originating in potter-based cultures would still have used lightweight water-carriers where possible such as animals skins known into the present day in poorer regions of the world and for travel across deserts.

Long utilised at sea were disposable and renewable resources such as coconuts and bamboo joints and there are many illustrations of these being used in parallel in pottery-based societies or those who had ceased pottery production (*1.035*) such as the post-Lapita islands of Polynesia. In transfer by mariners imitation of construction techniques found along the coasts and in mariner societies in the Ancient Middle East would be less problematic since many would have been employed in these occupations out of season. It would also explain why the Peruvian ceremonial sites are reminiscent of those in the Ancient Middle East.

Similar building techniques to those of the Middle East occurred during renovation and rebuilding new walls in Peru that were constructed and faced with stone a little outside the existing constructions and then the space between was filled with rubble. Floors were superimposed and the outer surfaces were then surfaced with plaster, and murals and reliefs then applied. There is little apparent damage to the earlier phases in excavations suggesting that there was no great imperative from the destruction of war or revolution initiating these rebuilding and remodelling undertakings[159]. It is probable that these were related to calendrical, or agriculturally related cyclical phases or as change, as a result of a shift in emphasis in the belief systems held by these ancient peoples.

Aspero and the Supe Valley
One of the first monumental constructions in the Americas is a site in the Supe Valley known as Huaca de los Idolos and where C14 readings give the earliest date as 3001 B.C. Dating defines 2903 B.C. for the nearby Huaca de los Sacrificios as the earliest reading but averages of the C14 datings suggest a time band around 2750 B.C. for the site. These readings are not from the first levels of these constructions where it is believed that there were constructions from about 200 years earlier[160]. This extraordinary Peruvian complex is contemporary with the earliest pyramids of Ancient Egypt and Sumeria and far ahead of any other monumental complexes in North or South America[161]. Although the Aspero constructions are very large they are not true pyramids but are built as battered or sloping sided platforms banked against a natural rise typical in South America reflecting the basic principle earlier found in Elam.

These largest monuments in South America that were constructed in the 3rd., to 2nd., millennium BC. are located on the coast of Peru between the Chao and Chillon rivers. This is a very arid stretch of coast and was largely free of ceramics until the last phases of their occupation. There are a number of sites classified broadly in the Aspero tradition and these were distinguished by Public works on a grander scale than other coastal fishing settlements suggesting a governance and hierarchy able to command labour and resources capable of sustaining such vast expenditures of works over many centuries. The sites included in the apparently mutually influenced tradition are Rio Seco, Bundurria, Pierda Parada and Aspero in the Supe River region. This tradition is found also at the sites of Culebras and Huaynuna near Casma, and Salinas da Chao and Los Morteros near the Chao River. These vast mounds were flat-topped to provide platforms for ceremonial display to a wide audience who would have congregated around the mounds - the fundamental principal of their rites appeared therefore to be diametrically opposed to those of the mountain regions since they included public ceremonial display[162]. The largest of the Pre-ceramic constructions was that at El Paraiso 150 kilometres to the south near modern-day Lima. El Paraiso appears to be a variation in this time period and most of the sites have sufficient domestic occupational refuse to indicate a resident population who could have been mobilised in the construction of these works.

The site of Aspero itself reveals 6 mounds of larger size up to 4 to 10 metres in height and 11 smaller mounds between 1 and 2 metres high and their alignments vary by up to 20 degrees. Platform or terrace areas adjacent the mounds, some stone-faced, included areas of courts and paved areas and these in part may have been reserved as residential. The two larger mounds at Aspero have been the focus of investigation over some time and these are known as Huaca Idolos and Huaca de los Sacrificios. Huaca de los Sacrificios was constructed of basalt block rather than rounded large stones and, although the latest phases at the top of the platform yielded radio carbon dates of about 2900 B.C. while the earliest layers, not dated and must be several centuries earlier at least earlier noted. The construction of basalt standing stones and horizontal fill between reflects construction known in other later sites at Chavin de Huantar and Tiahuanaco, but also in the Polynesian Islands millennia later. The ceremonial stairway to the top of the pyramid was located on the east side and this gave access to a large walled court on the summit behind which was several chambers and courts. In the centre of the first court at the top of the stair, to the east of the ceremonial rooms and courts, a hemispherical fire pit was located and charcoal from this hearth produced a date of 2533 B.C. This would have corresponded to the last usage of this pit and the last days of occupation of the site[163]. The eastern facing location suggests that the fire-rituals at this hearth were orientated to the rising Sun at dawn.

In one of the chambers on the summit of Huaca de los Sacrificios two burials were found suggesting ritual sacrifice. The adult was perhaps a separate sacrifice, and appears poorly endowed with grave goods or was a slave intended to accompany the child who was more richly buried including a cap with 500 objects of shell, clay and plants beads. The child was placed on its right side facing west suggesting that it was intended to follow the setting Sun into the Underworld before rising for rebirth - a belief recorded millennia later even after the end of the Inca Empire. However, this may also indicate the direction from where the ancestors arrived across the Pacific onto the Peruvian Coast consonant with surviving Indian oral traditions.

Huaca de los Idolos was built against a small hill and the constructions on its summit cover an area of 30 by 20 metres and gains its name from the cache of figurines of unbaked clay found in a chamber in the summit constructions. The figurines appear to have been the work of a single artist and were found with twined baskets, mats, and other items. Other figurines are found from Rio Seco, Bandurria, El Paraiso and Kotosh and these are thought to have been used, then as later, in curing ceremonies.

By the end of the Pre-ceramic period of about 1800 B.C. the coastal traditions had coalesced around the three major ceremonial architectural features of the platform mound, the rectangular court and the sunken circular court. The site of Piedra Parada exemplifies that tradition and is located in the Supe Valley and its noted for its platforms - built extending from a naturally occurring hill or eminence. The site appears to correspond with the period of changeover from Pre-ceramic to an early Ceramic date[164].

At Casma on the Central Pacific Coast of Peru, at a place called Huaynuna, the ceremonial complex centred on a mound contained a chamber similar to that at Kotosh suggesting contacts between the coast and the inland region. This settlement reveals occupational dates of between 2250 and 1775 B.C. and appears to have been a centre of cultural interchange between coast and highland or a settlement instituted from the highland with the Pacific for trade or connections with the sea.

It has been conjectured in learned papers that only "coherent states" are capable of mobilising the resources necessary in constructing massive projects over many years[165], including frequent renovation and overbuilding in the following centuries. In the Peruvian projects, however, many of the sites appear to have been insufficient urban developments to support civic projects on such a massive scale. It has been suggested that farmers in the off-season troughs were mobilised to build these projects but this presupposes an established elite with a persuasive belief system or sufficient "muscle" to impose their demands upon the population. Both the power to organise and initiate, as well as a coercive military backing to motivate and pressure a

3.030 : Mazdean-Zoroastrian fire altars at Nakhsh-I-Rustam constructed on a stone platform that are the more elaborate form for state ceremonials. Iran, Mid-first millennium, B.C.

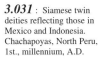

3.031 : Siamese twin deities reflecting those in Mexico and Indonesia. Chachapoyas, North Peru, 1st., millennium, A.D.

3.034 : The dual-headed fire god, Agni, often depicted as a Siamese twin as here. Siamese twin gods were also carved in Polynesia, West Mexico and Ancient Peru. South India, 10-13th., century, A.D.

3.033 : The Vedic fire god, Agni, displaying the rays of the fire extending from his body. Post Gupta Dynasty, Benisagar, Bihar, 6-7th., century, A.D.

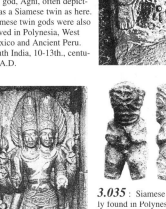

3.032 : Siamese twin figurine common in Ancient Mexico. Valley of Mexico, Second half of the first millennium, B.C.

3.035 : Siamese twins are widely found in Polynesian tradition but reflect similar carvings of Agni as a dual deity in India, and similarly found in Mexico and Peru. Marquesas Islands, Eastern Polynesia, 10-12 century, A.D.

3.036 : Siamese twin deities that appear to emulate the more sophisticated carvings of the fire god of India named Agni. Late Chavin, Tembladera, Jequetepeque Valley, North Peru, 700-400 B.C.

very conservative people are required even to begin such projects let alone maintain that impetus over many decades and possibly also the religious sanctions to instil fear as retribution beyond physical discipline would usually be required.

      The economy that supported the communities responsible for these exceptional ceremonial centres, requiring vast numbers of man-days in construction and labour-release organisations, was largely sustained through marine resources, such as shell fish, and coastal fishing including the use of nets, lines and spears so important over the millennia along Coastal Peru[166]. This is a minimal resource economy supporting an apparently highly sophisticated social system that appears entirely anomalous. Floodplain agriculture and long-distance trade were also factors in daily subsistence but these were not developed sufficiently to explain the necessity and capability to generate such massive building projects. Squash, beans and chilli peppers were also cultivated but were not the primary ingredients in the local economy and where agriculture is evident it was usually within convenient walking distance from the Pacific Coast shore[167].

      Overall the social development located in isolated valleys in the fourth millennium B.C. hardly explains the sudden impetus to undertake massive engineering projects unless that stimulus was initiated from outside Peru - a consideration that is anathema to all Americanists. The fact that fishing had little progressed from a primitive level and remained so much a part of the contemporary economies of the site and that even agriculture was bound to the coast suggests that this stimulus was from the sea. This appears to be confirmed by the fact that long distance sea trade was already evident in the exchange goods clearly derived from Ecuador a thousand miles north of the first great structures on the Central Coast of Peru. Pyro-engraved gourds have been found in a grave at Huaca Prieta have been considered to be imported from Ecuador[168]. Long distance trade by land was also a feature since obsidian from the nearest source on the coast, a little under 400 kilometres to the south[169], indicates that there was extensive communication by land and sea in coastal and Andean South America at that time.

Salt in Ancient Peru was also of importance and the largest site on the Peruvian Coast was located at Salinas de Chao where salt production is evident over a long period in the Pre-ceramic. This site is composed of terraced platforms built into a hillside and features a large partially sunken court and another circular one detached from the main construction[170]. At La Galgada a grave revealed a salt crystal that was placed under the head of a woman and in two later burials a bed of salt crystals was covered by charcoal[171]. It is known that occupations were divided between the sexes and it may have been that the women were associated with salt or certain aspects of the salt trade.

Cotton and gourds were introduced from the more humid valleys onto the drier and more arid coast[172]. Cotton was important for use in fishing nets and where gourds may have been used as substitutes for pottery but these were unlikely to be the sole answer for the lack of ceramics for so long. Cotton, however, was a necessity for the first developments in particular aspects of Peruvian textiles and these are first developed from twined thread and are frequently more like gauze or open-mesh fabrics although examples of finer textiles have been excavated[173].

It appears that all land was considered to be the property of the community and traditional land distribution extended from the rivers or valley floors vertically to the high pastures of the mountains extending through several ecological zones[174]. The right to own this land appears to have been invested in the clan ancestor who in some way had been born from a natural feature including in the boundaries of the land such as a river, stream, spring, cave or other special feature such as a large and, or unusual rock.

In the theme of this work it will be seen that there appears to have been a determination by mariners, traders and others from outside the Americas to deliberately seek the riverine highways of the Amazon Basin from the Pacific Ocean and vice versa. This drive from West to East across South America appears to reflect in the surviving archaeology in South America where deliberate seeking out of the mountain passes and openings available to them is apparent (*3.064*). The vertical structuring in the agricultural stratification preserved by the Peruvian and Bolivian Indians may reflect their perception of early mariners and traders attempting to scale the mountains from one side to the other. The slow progress imposed by altitude problems would have meant that the ascents were slow requiring, perhaps, long-term camps and at least some need for agriculture to sustain them and that these became more established over decades and centuries. It may also be that such undertakings resulted in alliances being formed between highland and coastal peoples, perhaps mariners, and the merging of Andean and lowland territories through clan intermarriage and inheritance.

The earliest textiles were mantles since cloth, cut or shaped into coats, shirts, or trousers in the Western sense were unknown. It is interesting to note that mariners used mantles in this simplest manner where the mantle was wrapped around the waist as broad girdle until needed, and when in use was then tied as a cape, often over one shoulder and under the arm to allow greater flexibility. Such girdles and capes became customary, retained as traditional elements of ceremonial status, and found as such among the Incas and the Nagas of Assam (*3.028/9*).

Further to the south there is evidence that there was conflict in at least one of the Pre-ceramic Peruvian sites, unusual for the period. At Asia, a settlement about 100 kilometres south of Lima, headless skeletons have been retrieved with few grave goods and this is considered as evidence of further violence. In a skull found here the facial skin had been torn off one and a hole punched in the brow of another so that a cord could be inserted to hang it as a trophy head. Weapons, including a wooden club with shark's teeth inserts, were also found at this site[175]. Evidence for war was common a couple of millennia later and this earlier outbreak may indicate incursions from mariners who had contacts with, or were the origin of such traditions.

Piedra Parada and El Paraiso

Located near Aspero, Piedra Parada is composed of large terraced platforms and a circular sunken plaza measuring about 20 metres in diameter, not unlike Salinas de Chao, but there are differences in orientation and the reasons for this have not yet been established[176]. The site of El Paraiso is the largest known in the Pre-ceramic period of Peru, and it is estimated that 100,000 tons of stone was required in its construction. Two of the largest structures are over 400 metres each in length and must have taken up to 2,000,000 man-days to complete and overall covers an area of 58 hectares[177]. The most common artefacts found at the site are grinding mortars covered with red ochre indicating the great importance of its use in the history of Peru in parallel with identical practices in the Old World. The orientation of the site is reasonably consistent suggesting that the angle 24 or 25 degrees was important. Excavations have revealed that rooms at the site were filled after a certain period of time to elevate the platform on which new constructions were undertaken - a practice identical to those contemporary in the Ancient Middle East.

Interestingly, in a few sections of flanking mounds, pilasters or engaged columns without an apparent function have been found. These appear to have been built as "ornaments" but may have symbolic portal functions not unlike similar structures in the Ancient Near and Middle East and India (3.024/5). These are particularly interesting in that portals and colonnades become more prominent in the architecture of Peru as the Pre-ceramic progresses to the Post-ceramic period. Coloured feathers of green, pink, blue and yellow suggest that they were associated with the cardinal points since these same colours are found corresponding in this way in Central America and in ancient traditions in Asia. Feathers have been found at the Rio Seco centre and on one of the Aspero mounds. Clay figurine fragments have also been found beside the El Paraiso platform at Rio Seco and Aspero[178].

El Paraiso and the Chillon Valley Tradition

Recent interest in the monuments of the Chillon Valley and those of El Paraiso in particular stem from the fact here is to be found the largest site construction in the Americas before 1800 B.C. Dating indicates that the site was occupied and under construction by 2000 B.C. and had expanded to about two-thirds its final size before pottery appeared about 1800 B.C.[179]. Nine complexes are known, constructed from stone quarried nearby, that cover 58 hectares in the Chillon Valley located about 2 km from the seashore and some groups of these constructions appear to have reached about 7 metres or more in height. The largest construction is that of a U-shaped complex where each wing was about 50 metres wide and 250 metres long and the main ceremonial staircase approached from the west. Between the flanking wings a plaza was located with other smaller ceremonial buildings. As noted at other sites the techniques of laying stone-filled mesh bags called shikras were laid to form structures with interconnecting courts, chambers and walls standing 2 metres or more high. Stones walls were plastered with adobe and then painted[180]. In a reception chamber behind the entry painted red was a sunken floor measuring 4.5 by 4.25 metres with the perimeter outside this floor at the higher level forming a bench around it. The floor was screeded with fine clay surfacing and at the corners were four circular fire pits 1 metre in diameter each pointing to one of the cardinal points from the focus at the centre of the chamber[181]. The fire rituals held here are perceived as being related to the traditions at Huaca de los Sacrificios, Aspero and Kotosh[182] and their local regions of influence. The Chillon Valley development is seen by some historians as being influenced through transfer by migrants, already expert in irrigation, into the dry zones of the coast and taking with them their traditions associated with their fire-religion. Other have seen this site as the precursor of the movement from the coast to dominate the highland sites transferring the U-shaped ceremonial site inland reaching its apogee at Chavin de Huantar a millennium later[183].

The Early Fire Religions of Peru

In returning to the known sites in this Tradition of this period, with reflections of the twin mound ceremonial sites at Kotosh, at La Galgada in the Central Peruvian Highlands were constructed twin mounds with chambers similar to Kotosh, under the platforms themselves. This site apparently witnesses a merging of the former independent traditions of fire-temples found in the Andean sites and the twin mound tradition long known on the Pacific coast of Peru. The chambers found here also reveal a duct system to ventilate the hearth and the split-level floor type. The La Galgada mounds are ovaloid and the larger of the two mounds was faced with fine quality masonry. There is a sunken court located at the front of it and the site overall is the most preserved of the earlier ceremonial centres[184]. Buildings located on these platforms were constructed of stone set in mud mortar and roofed with logs sealed on the upper surface with clay. Each of the rooms in this building was entered by a door facing west towards the front of the mound on which it stood.

Found in the rooms built on the platforms were deer antlers and feathers from tropical birds. Among other residue in the fire-pits were chilli-peppers and these were believed to have been deliberately added to ensure tears were shed by the participants and observers at these ceremonies - tears being anciently represented in the iconography of Ancient Peru and Bolivia[185]. In an interesting variation these rooms, after their original use was terminated, were used as burial chambers where both males and females were laid to rest together. In the late construction phases of this period burial galleries and house interments were of note and this corresponds to the introduction of feline motifs in slate and shell mosaic apparently connected with Chavin centuries later[186].

La Galgada is also significant since, in the last two periods of mound building and alteration at the site, ceramics make their first appearance and significantly correspond with the introduction of the heddle loom and innovations in architecture and design. Instead of several structures being built on top of the stepped mounds these were replaced by a single larger construction with a much larger fire pan or basin accommodating a larger number of people. This appears to signal a change from the small chambers, accommodating a family or a few priests, to more Publicly orientated ceremonies. The last phases also saw the U-shape platform mound construction around a central court but without a ceremonial hearth suggesting coastal influences, where the U-shape was long known, extending into the Andean highlands and valleys[187].

One of the most remarkable sites in Ancient Peru was that of Kotosh, located on the banks of the Higueros River, near Huanuco in the upland region of Central Peru. This river is a tributary of the Huallega River - itself a major tributary to the Amazon flowing away to the Atlantic on the east side of the Andes. Kotosh was constructed at a height of 2,000 meters, about 6,500 feet, and is composed of two large platform mounds with other smaller structures adjacent built on a river-side terrace. It has been suggested that the twin mounds are an example of the dual organisation system found traditionally throughout this region in later epochs and this will be of more interest in the following chapters. Perhaps characteristic also is the fact that one of the moieties of the dual organisation believed to have developed as the social structure from the earliest times was considered a higher status than the other. At Kotosh one of the twin mounds was larger than the other with a "footprint" diameter of almost 100 metres and a height of 8 metres.

Excavations have revealed that the final mounds had been overbuilt on earlier structures and reflected a long tradition of ceremonial use. Because of repeated rebuilding the mounds developed as stepped, multi-tiered truncated platforms, contained by stone revetments, on which the masonry fire-temple was built[188]. Interestingly, there is little evidence of agriculture or hunting at the site suggesting that it was a dedicated shrine or the complex was used for ceremonial purposes only[189]. The fact that Kotosh was situated on a critical access from the west of Peru, and ultimately the coast into the Amazon, suggests that this site was in some way connected with trade routes between the regions from west to east, Pacific to Amazon to the east, or vice versa. Stone axes from Kotosh appear to resemble those found on the Amazonian side of the Andean region confirming early passage from one lowland environmental zone in the east through these access gorges into the Andes valleys and then to the Pacific Coast.

The civic or ceremonial constructions in the highlands of Peru have been attributed to the mobilisation and belief system of the hill and valley farmers[190]. The early societies of Peru have been promoted as social organisations based on a broad equality supervised only by kurakas, or clan leaders, who wielded limited powers on behalf of the clan. Few have attempted to explain how such a society developed the initiative and structure to mobilise the whole of the clan system under the less than absolute power of these clan leaders. It is believed by some historians to have been a society lead by what is purported to have been a leadership only one step higher than all others, otherwise considered as equals. Usually the dual organisation system is invoked to indicate a possible explanation but this does not explain how the power to initiate supposedly equal status sections of a clan structure to undertake such massive projects and to maintain initiative over such long periods.

It is much more likely that advanced outsiders, and probably Asian mariners, intruded upon the primitive hunter-gathers of the South American coast, and later Andes, and were perceived as gods, much as the later Europeans were in many isolated societies. It was natural that mariners institutionalised the indigenous superstition and ultra-conservatism of the indigenous people and promoted this idolisation and existing social structures as they found them to maintain their own status and control and marshalled this power in the building of their ceremonial sites. As already noted in examples recorded by the missionary Barbrooke Grubb, while ministering to the Lengua, the first Christians were always ready to identify with mythical heroes or heroes that would give them sway and control, as well as increasing their own security, over the subject populace and this was also true of the Spaniards being identified with the Andean hero-deity, Viracocha.

The Kotosh Fire Temples
The temples or shrines associated with Kotosh religion appear to have been square or circular structures without apparent elaboration. In these ceremonial structures rituals associated with burnt animals sacrifices have been detected and these appear to resemble those recorded of the early Vedic Aryans in India but originating from the earlier fire rites in Ancient Iran. The Kotosh rites have been described as "mysterious"[191] but this is only because they have left no written or verbal record from 4,000 years ago when these rites were performed and the refusal by historians to compare them with the known Asian traditions. In more recent decades other ceremonial centres closely similar to those of Kotosh have been discovered and these are located at Shillacoto and Waira-jirca in the Huallega River Valley, Huaricoto in the Callejon de Huaylas, La Glagada in the Tablachaca Valley and Piruru in the Tantamayo Valley region[192].

The characteristic constructions of these similar sites are of a small freestanding temple with centrally located, stone-lined fire-pits. These buildings usually feature rounded corners (*3.016/7*) and appear to have wall niches incorporated probably for religious icons or effigies. The floor and walls were clay plastered and a bench was often a feature constructed against the wall. Several of these sites reveal identical temple structures that had a common wall revealing a dual chamber concept. As at other coastal sites these chambers were filled at a later date to provide a higher platform on which new constructions were erected[193]. Kotosh is best known for its relief of crossed hands located directly below a niche that was probably intended to house a portrait sculpture[194]. The "hands" appear to be those of the jaguar since similar iconography appears in South Arabia (*3.056/7*) where they represented the paws of a lion or leopard cape indicating high status identically found in South America.

The textual references to rituals record that the fire-god of India, Agni, was considered the fundamental element of life and all existence and perceived as the life force of the Sun. As the divine fire he was also to be found within the earth, that is, as volcanic fire in its earliest and fundamental form. Large public fire temples were almost unknown in Early India outside the major population centres and many of the middle and high status peoples maintained a family hut employing a Brahman priest to celebrate their own private rites on a regular basis. Clearly this allowed for many interpretations of the fire-temple, and on many different scales, focusing on the one essential function of the highly prescribed fire altar rites devolving upon the fire-pan on the altar at the centre of the rites. In transfer to another region or country it would be expected that such a fundamental arrangement would be adapted to the local conditions. The basic, even elementary architecture of the fire-temples found at La Galgada and Kotosh in Peru would suggest that the model for the fire temples was imported from Iran as it was into Vedic India and likewise adapted. The Vedic fire-huts were exactly that, modest framed structures, not at all the grand masonry structures from which it evolved in the main ceremonial centres of Iran (*3.030*) although there too many smaller shrines must have existed.

Animal sacrifices were an essential part of the ceremonies among the Iranian and Vedic Aryan sacrifices. Sacrificial rituals were often associated with the lunar, and later solar cycles and with the half-yearly and annual calendrical cycles enumerated among others[195]. Sacrificial offerings consisted of one of the five sacred, or "higher" animals offered to the deities by burning them at the end of the sacrifice in the traditional manner known for millennia in the Ancient Near and Middle East. Only unblemished male animals were permitted and originally, in the earliest records, these five highest sacrifices were defined as men, horse, oxen, sheep and goats[196]. The number five was, and still is a sacred number found throughout the religious myths, legends and rituals of the Ancient Middle East and India and the same is true in the Peruvian Coast and Andean cultures. In many lesser rites, such as for personal sacrifices, either to the ancestors, gods for agriculturally associated rites, or for retribution, lesser animals were permitted. Clearly in transfer to South America the necessity of the rites for suitable, available animals sacrifices was of little problem since the highest requirement for animals with pure white coats and for sheep-like attributes was clearly identifiable in the indigenous llamas. These of the camelid family were ideally suited particularly in that they provided for other colours in their fleece that would also correspond to the stipulations for certain rites recorded in the Vedic texts and to be considered in due course.

The Fire Temples at Huaricoto and Piruru

The ritual temples, probably dedicated to the worship of fire contemporary with Kotosh, have been found at Huaricoto, a construction situated on a terrace overlooking the valley of Callejon de Huaylas. The building of the temple itself was sited on a platform and was of perishable materials such as wattle and daub, and the floors of clay reflected the split-level floors found at other sites of this period and in the Kotosh tradition. Stone-lined fire-pits were of a simpler type constructed without the sophisticated under-floor vents from outside of the temple usually providing an air supply for the fire when in operation. The residues in the fire-pits revealed that meat products, shells and quartz were offered in these hearths.

On the banks of the River Tantamayo at Piriru, located at the highest level of agricultural cultivation, a ceremonial site in the Kotosh tradition has been located. Here three Pre-ceramic chambers (pre-1800 B.C.) with vented central hearths with flues have been revealed below 4-5 metres of later occupation with one of these being built with a split-level floor. The chambers were built on a low stone wall using this as a footing and above with wattle and daub construction[197].

La Galgada in the Early Fire Temple Tradition

La Galgada was another early site located in the Callejon de Huaylas in the Central Peruvian mountains on the east bank of the Tablachaca, a tributary of the Santa River flowing westward to the Pacific Ocean. The earliest dates are determined through C14 analysis at 2821 B.C. in La Galgada compared with 2796 B.C. at Huaricoto[198]. This valley is an important one in the historical development of Peru and its access to the Pacific Ocean is of great importance. The location of this site appears to be of some strategic value since it is located mid-way between the West, Pacific coast of Peru and the access to the Maranon River. This major tributary leads almost the whole length of Peru all the way from the Amazon southward through the valleys of the Inca and ultimately leading to the Tiahuanacan Empire in the Peruvian and Bolivian Highlands. La Galgada also consists of two ceremonial mounds but there are surrounding dwellings attached to this ceremonial site. The larger of the two mounds has yielded radiocarbon dates of between 2000 and 1200 B.C and from this time there is evidence that agriculture was pursued, assisted by irrigation channels, growing gourds, squash, beans, fruits and chilli-peppers and cotton. This mound reached a height of over 15 metres and was ultimately renovated with three terraced circular revetment walls and in one period had five or more chambers constructed asymmetrically on its summit. Examination of the residues in the hearths has found seeds of the chilli-peppers and it is known that burning these caused unpleasant smoke producing tears in those nearby[199]. It has been considered that these seeds were deliberately added to cause the "weeping" effect depicted on the faces of so many of these carvings and other representations of Andean deities in relief ceramics and textiles. Excavations reveal that this site was constructed well before the ceramic period but was still in use when the first pottery appeared at the site in about 1800 B.C.[200].

3.037 : Shell carving of a spider deity possibly related to Sky Spiders in myths in Melanesia and iconography found on the coast of Ecuador. Spiro Mound cultures, Eastern USA, 1200-1350, A.D.

At La Galgada objects interred with burials include objects, sometimes fashioned or carved, from shells traded from the Pacific Ocean coast and included ornaments made from bone along with feathers traded or obtained from the Amazon Basin. This site appears to have been an important crossroads for trade routes not only from east to west or the reverse from the Pacific Ocean to the Amazon Basin through the Andes valleys but from North to South

3.039 : Ancient spider designs of a type found also in the iconography of Ecuador but also in North America and Coastal Ecuador. Babylonian Period, Central Iran, c1200 B.C.

3.038 : Central spider shell design with a swastika depicted on the carapace. Spiro Mound Culture, Ohio, Eastern USA, 950-1200 A.D.

from Ecuador to Bolivia and Chile[201].

Recent studies have determined that the domestication of plants was evident from about 5000 B.C., and by 3000 B.C. the full range found in subsistence agriculture had been developed. Maize was grown in the highland region among others and this formed about 20% of the people's diet in the Pre-ceramic period. Other crops included potatoes, oca, ullucu and the native Andean cultigens of quinoa, legumes and lupines, and these provided an important supplement to hunted wild game still commonly pursued[202]. This wild game appears to have been largely deer meat rather than that of the llama where the wool and meat of the latter did not appear extensively used in the coastal regions until about 500 B.C.[203].

At this early time, before 1800 B.C., there is evidence that long distance trade was of importance to the ceremonial site of La Galgada. Spondylus shell has been noted in some of the earliest graves in Peru indicating trade with Ecuador hundreds of kilometres to the north. This was true also of the Chinchorro graves far to the south in North Chile and La Galgada and the Kotosh tradition were something of a mid-point between these extremes of north and south. However, as in so many cases, it is the east-west connection that is appears to be of importance since here at La Galgada in the central highland regions of Peru, as at so many of these early Pre-ceramic sites, shells and fish products from the Pacific are found together with feathers riverine and forest products from the torrid climate of the Amazon Basin to the east. The renowned razor sharp teeth of the piranha were used here as a engraving tool in the crafting of bone and wood[204]. La Galgada is unusual in that this is the only highland site at this time revealing a residential occupation and at the present time 50 houses of about 14 sq. km. have been located. These were round and made of unwrought fieldstones set in mortar with bare earth floor and although ash is found inside and out there are no constructed fire-pits[205]. Burial was in the lower chambers under the temple mounds that were no longer used from earlier periods and in galleries constructed between them as well as the revetments of the later renovations. Most of the burials appear to represent a cross-section of the population indicating perhaps that these were clan-related sites in life, worship and death. Most of the interments were between the ages of 4 and 40 years but about a quarter were over the age of 50. Grave goods increased in the late Pre-ceramic and these included textiles, cotton bags, Pacific shell beads and Spondylus shells from Ecuador[206]. At this same time large-scale monuments were constructed along the Peruvian coast where the available high-yield fishing and sea products allowed a rapid increase in population. Great monuments were erected in the Pre-ceramic and among these was that of La Paloma already referred to regarding the preservation of the dead.

In the highland sites as well as those of the coast it has been noted repeatedly by recent researchers and archaeologists that there is little evidence for a long period of transition between the establishment of stable agricultural settlements and the creation of large public works. This has generated speculation that the life of the Peruvian Indians was an idyll of associated clans and where equality ruled and social cooperation was the norm. The fact that so many of the massive projects in the Pre-ceramic were constructed without evidence of a developed agricultural economy flies in the face of all known principles of progressive development and evolution throughout the Old World.

Some have suggested that the principles developed in the New World and Peru in particular are radically different from those of the Old but do not explain how this could be possible[207]. To move from a hunter-gather people into monument builders in one step of some of the largest earth-moving structures known is unparalleled and leans toward the incoherent. It is necessary to have an established, regular and abundant food supply to begin the process of labour release, even if seasonal, to construct these works. But there must also be a priestly elite as well as architects and or engineers who are capable in conceiving these monuments and the techniques

3.041: Ithyphallic image of the Hindu deity Siva called Ekapada - "One-legged", and similar images are found in South America (*3.040*). Somesvara Temple, Mukhalingam, Orissa, 8th., century, A.D.

3.043 : Example of 8 "tikis" considered to be symbols of fertility. They probably originate in the lingas worn by the devotees of Siva in India. Maori, New Zealand, Late 19th., century, A.D.

3.040 : Ithyphallic mono-ith clearly in the tradition of Siva representations in coun-ryside India found under 42 eet (11 metres) of guano on he islets off the South Peruvian coast. Moche Period, 200-600 A.D.

3.042 : Phallic monolith with the deity face of Tow-hatu carved in relief identical to Siva lingas in India (*12.007*) and in Colombia (*12.006*; *12.009*). Moriori, New Zealand, Pre-19th., century, A.D.

3.044 : Carved monolith showing the protruding rib cage probably indicating mariner ancestors at sea for long periods of time suffering from malnutrition and similar in principle to those in Polynesia. Besoa, Central Celebes, Indonesia, Mid-first millennium, B.C.

3.045 : Carved ithyphallic figure that was probably derived from the deity Siva in India. Saloe Bihe, Bada, Central Celebes, Indonesia, Mid-first millennium, A.D.

and long evolving lessons of experience to build them. Certainly trial and error is a large part of any building process in the Old World and the New, but in Ancient Sumeria and Ancient Egypt, contemporary with the Peruvian initiatives that were commencing from almost no real prece-dents, they had millennia of earlier constructional experience on a lesser scale before progress-ing to the larger, but related, monumental scale on which to draw. It is more likely that these first, remarkable Peruvian monuments, both of the coastal and highland type, were initiated by those who were intruders from those Old World civilisations experienced in, or who retained the tradi-tions from West Asia and later India. This would explain why hunting, gathering and fishing was still the main occupations of the indigenous people with little settled cultivation at the time these monuments were initiated on the Peruvian coast.

It is more likely that the Aryan model in India was the same as that found originally on the Peruvian coast and whose intrusive people as mariners, traders and missions initiated the con-struction of these monuments by coercive labour. This was probably instigated by forming high status clans directing the indigenous peoples, categorised in traditional moiety models as the sec-ond and lower status of that dual organisation, when required. The introduction at the same time of an expanding irrigation system of settled agriculture, and sudden advances in later epoch where no previous development from evolutionary steps can be found, tends to confirm intrusive stimulus at this and later times.

The results of studies of so-called "equality-based" societies indicates that they degen-erated into stagnation since every decision is based on communal agreement and leads to long-term dissention by opposing factions and alliances. Frequently the "equal say" organisation also leads to total fragmentation since, at best, a result corresponding to the lowest common denom-

3.047 : Indonesian double crescent gold headdress with plume. The Incan neck pendants featured a similar cut down crescent that may have derived from this symbolism. Indonesia, Late 19th., century, A.D.

3.046 : Indonesian single crescent gold crown made from two "leaves" of gold "feathers" and a plume. Crescents were common in the headdresses of the Incas. Indonesia, Late 19th., century, A.D.

3.048 : The great deity of Hindu India named Siva was a lunar deity indicated by the large crescent sitting on his topknot. This is an exaggerated form of those found elsewhere in India but known also in Peru. Paharpur, Bengal, 8th., century, A.D.

EL CATORZE CAPITAN
MALLCO CASTILLA
PARI

3.049 : Lunar crescent on hat front similar to those shown on the Siva hairstyle. The neck ornament appears to be a truncated form of double crescent form found in Indonesia (*3.047*). Poma de Ayala; Inca Peru, 16th., century, A.D.

3.050 : Sun/Moon symbol surmounting the stepped crown of a king seated on his throne supported by carvings of addorsed, winged horses. Parthian Dynasty, Ancient Iran, Late first millennium, B.C.

inator has to be adopted that emasculates any decisive action towards a clear goal. Such processes have been encapsulated in a popular saying that a camel was the result of a committee designing a horse - that is the end product of constant compromise. Initiative and direct action are required to undertake such massive projects by those few, or a single ruler or priest-king, who had the power and authority to impose his will and vision and the resources at his command to carry it to fruition. In modern-day societies the right for all to have their say has lead, as an example, to repeated inaction in English town-planning and highway developments leading to huge wastages in resources and stagnation of planning and renewal developments. This is true of any society providing the right of dissent and equal say but this is not the model exhibited in early Peru.

In the normal evolution of advances in cultures necessary to the undertaking of the construction of great monuments the people who have little experience of vision beyond daily shelter and satiation of hunger and thirst at its minimum are unlikely to be the one initiating great structures. Inevitably it is the result of progressive or enforced Public initiatives instituted under great leaders over centuries since each is built on the success or failure of the previous development imposed upon them. These great leaders with the ability to create or utilise resources through absolute control of an empire are those who impose their concept of a patrimony for the future on an often less than willing populace. It is they who also direct their traders to obtain the necessary prestige items or control of raw materials necessary for ritual display and security of the state or empire and Asoka of Mauryan India is an appropriate example of this type. The long period of successive priest-kings, rulers, states and empires establish a hegemony that allows sufficient periods of stability and efflorescence to allow for sustained initiatives to be directed both overland and overseas far beyond their borders and these are recorded from at least the fourth millennium, B.C., in the Ancient Middle East. From these initiatives missions of culturally and technically more advanced people arrived over many centuries on the Pacific Coast of South America and established control, even if localised, over the existing social order, such as they were, much as they had done so also in India over millennia through trade and migration.

This model would seem to be the model found among the South American Indians generally, and surviving as references in myths and legends confirming the intrusion of culture-heroes from abroad and with special references to the West or the Pacific Ocean, and is certainly the model established in India. This is also true of the European settlements in the Colonial period where they established their own "clans" separating themselves socially from the indigenous peoples in all the continents they migrated into and settled. This "elite" ruling clan is exemplified by the Spanish on subjugating Peru where they intermarried with the existing Incas as the ruling clan and were recognised as separate and socially superior to the broad mass of people as indicated by Garcillasso de la Vega (Vol.2-532/3) where the Incas themselves he said recognised the issue of a Inca woman and a Spaniard as "children of their god, the Sun". It is likely that this was also the principle originating from the most ancient times in South America.

In the Pre-ceramic it has been suggested that the dual organisation resulting from marriage clans, so similar to those in Aboriginal Australia and Asia, were initiated from this time or may have been endemic in the indigenous tribal arrangements from the most ancient of times. However, any study of the clan systems of Aboriginal Australia, India and indeed those of Inca Peru will indicate that the dual organisation system was more usually a fundamental imposition from the incursions of a culturally more advanced people. These incursive peoples remained separate from the indigenous people associating only through intermediate marriage clans deriving from marriage arrangements that were critical to maintaining their own identity. The intrusive peoples, operating through their own high status clans, imposed control through the establishment of their own social organisations and ambitions on a captive, or less advanced labour force controlled through a clan system corresponding to a caste system. This was certainly the case with the Incas and was also true in Ancient Aryan India and will be of more interest in following chapters.

The Peruvian Pacific Coast Tradition of La Paloma

There is considerable variation in the traditions of the highlands, exemplified by Kotosh fire-chambers compared with that of the coast. The Kotosh tradition reveals several unique features and these temples were built as single-room temples and most likely private to the officiants and family or clan members only. Other special features are the split-level floors in some of the chambers and the fact that these chambers are usually independent and unconnected even if separated only by a wall. In the Coastal tradition the ceremonial site is characteristically a large complex of inter-connected rooms and appear to include elements of Public congregation and display. The developments on the coast in this period were prefigured by the developments at the great Pre-ceramic site of El Paraiso[208] but related to the widely distributed trading contacts running north and south on land and by sea, and where the traditional sea-orientated marine economy was largely replaced by settled irrigation farming. This is put down to population increase, but since the Peruvian waters are also among the most productive in the world, and recent analyses have shown that they could have supported a much larger population than that known in the

3.052 : Fish in nets were paralleled with references to trophy heads secured in the same way. This is overtly extended in many images in Nazcan iconography. Nazca, South Coast Peru, 100-300 A.D.

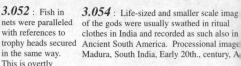

3.054 : Life-sized and smaller scale image of the gods were usually swathed in ritual clothes in India and recorded as such also in Ancient South America. Processional image Madura, South India, Early 20th., century, A

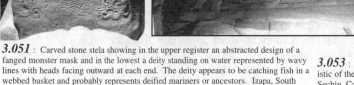

3.051 : Carved stone stela showing in the upper register an abstracted design of a fanged monster mask and in the lowest a deity standing on water represented by wavy lines with heads facing outward at each end. The deity appears to be catching fish in a webbed basket and probably represents deified mariners or ancestors. Izapa, South Pacific Coast Mexico, 100 B.C. - 200 A.D.

3.053 : Polychrome fish design with upturned mouth characteristic of the Makara or stylised Ganges crocodile in India. Cerro Sechin, Casma, Central Coast Peru, Late second millennium B.C.

Late Pre-ceramic, there is little agreement on the reasons for this change[209].

Near Bartolo Bay north of the Chilca River[210], the site of La Paloma has been noted for its three occupations periods between 4,500 B.C. and 3,000 B.C. These occupations were never large since evidence of residential accommodation uncovered cannot account for a larger population of more than about 35 people. These dwellings were circular in plan and were usually constructed above a lower than ground level floor, called pit-houses, using cane as the wall struts, and reeds and thatch to cover this and the roof. The final resting places for family members were in pits under the floor. Here they were placed in a seated posture with the legs drawn up under the chin and wrapped in twine-woven mats, after being salted to preserve them, and occasionally accompanied by grave goods[211]. This custom was seen by some as the beginnings of the tradition later instituted in Tiahuanaco, followed many centuries after by the Incas, where the ancestral mummies were kept in their houses and brought out during ceremonial festivities.

At La Paloma, from the recent analysis's of the diet of the inhabitants, the males appear to have been occupied in the fishing industry and sea orientated occupations much more than the females since osseous was pronounced among them caused by cold water immersion for long periods of time. Their diet was more protein rich than that of the females and suggests that they consumed a higher proportion of the fish protein although this difference diminished in time. As the population expanded the stature of the people also increased and there is evidence that there were attempts to control the rate of increase by instituting female infanticide after birth and delayed marriage[212].

Gourds, squash and beans were cultivated at La Paloma and this site was involved in the long distance trade since Spondylus shell from Ecuador, obsidian from the highlands and the remains of tropical monkeys from the Amazon forest were all found at this site. Between the Pre-ceramic period, 3000 to 1800 B.C., cotton was of the greatest importance all along the coast and its cultivation was expanded and was a factor that became of great importance as the population increased rapidly. Cotton was used in a rich fishing economy for nets and in the expansion of twill fabrics and later textiles found in many of these early sites. It is suggested that the deforestation and overexploitation of the natural resources throughout Peru forced the development of the agriculture industry away from the coast, so dependent on the over-fished oceans in later epochs, to the valleys in the mountain regions of the Andes[213].

Huaca Prieta in Peruvian Tradition
The first coastal agriculture appears to have been instituted by fishing peoples and one of the most famous sites in the history of Peruvian archaeology, Huaca Prieta, appears to have been, in conventional archaeology, a prime example in support of this belief. Crops were cultivated on the floodplains of the rivers flowing from the mountain valleys and when harvested were transported back to the fishing villages on the coast. Maize is first found in an isolated region between the Culebras and Supe Rivers[214] suggesting that it was the result of contact with Ecuador. On the Ecuadorian coast maize is first found in Pacific South America after being imported from Mexico in the 5-4th., millennium B.C. Maize from the coastal and inland sites of Central Peru may have been introduced by land traders either along the coastal strip connecting Ecuador with Peru or by the inland route along the eastern mountain region where the Amazon Basin rises to form the Eastern Cordillera, both regions appear to have been frequented in the Pre-ceramic Period. Equally possible is that coastal sea traders may have also introduced maize from Ecuador along with the Spondylus shell and other tropical products.

The Transition Phase from the Pre-ceramic to the Ceramic Period
Garagay is located on the outskirts of modern Lima, the capital of Peru. It is situated about 8 kilometres inland from the outflow of the River Rimac at the sea where modern Lima stands, and covers an area of about 16 square kilometres. This ceremonial centre was established in the middle of the Initial Period and is dated by the radiocarbon C14 process to between 1643 B.C. and 897 B.C. The basic U-shape plan of the ceremonial buildings can still be defined but is much eroded and the central stepped earthen mound was over 23 metres in height and faced with stone and plaster finish on its external face. Imagery associated with this temple, overbuilt on the earlier constructions, suggests that it predates Chavin de Huantar and was perhaps the forerunner to that great inland site[215]. Spondylus shell has also been found here and indicates that trade links with Ecuador were still being maintained from at least two-three millennia before.

　　The surviving clay relief friezes are of some interest, since they have been determined to represent a supernatural spider, and were painted in red, blue, black and yellow - the colours normally associated with the cardinal points in Central America and in Ancient India and China. It is noted in much later, Inca times that divination by spiders was a practice of those "sorcerers" who specialised in casting oracles from this creature. These diviners were called paccharicuc[216], referred to by the first Spanish who entered Peru, and the friezes at Garagay suggest that this practise was very ancient in Peru. Spines found associated with dressed figurines related to the spider imagery have been found to derive from the San Pedro cactus and this was used as a hallucinogenic in shamans' rituals. The spider deity is particularly linked with rainmaking and it is thought that the variable orientation of the contemporary ceremonial sites may be due to these centres being aligned with mountains associated with water and rainfall[217].

　　The mural imagery found on the walls of Garagay have shown fishermen with nets but instead of fish the have caught human heads as their catch[218]. This appears to indicate that there was an identification between fish and the human trophy head, and it is of interest, and probably no coincidence that the human warrior sacrifice in the Marquesas Islands was hung up with a hook in the mouth and called a "fish"[219]. In the Marquesas also the term tiki, noted elsewhere in this work is also that used for gods in the form of a fish indicating a sea borne influence[220]. The "one-legged" Tiki in the Marquesas[221] was in fact identical to the ithyphallic Siva in India (*3.041*), where tiki was a known expression for the phallic iconography of the pendant so well known among the Maori (*3.042; 3.045*). It cannot be a coincidence that the "fish", or the human sacrifice, was hung up on or near the Tohua[222], this being the exact named used for the sacred meeting place dedicated to the ancestors among the Nagas of Assam noted elsewhere in this work. This indicates again that many of the cultural elements found in Polynesia originated in India and that from here these influences extended to Central and South America. Although a tropical island group the Marquesas were subject to drought on occasions and it was believed that human sacrifice was necessary as a propitiation to the gods to bring rain[223]. Fishermen were particularly at risk as prey for those seeking a human sacrifice victim since fishing was frequently undertaken at night allowing predators to steal upon them unnoticed[224]. This would appear to reflect the symbolism in some of the iconography of both the Coast of Central America at Izapa where fish are thought to represent human sacrifices (*3.051*) and identically in a different style to depictions on the South Peruvian Coast (*3.052*). The Marquesas Islands are the nearest of the Eastern Polynesian Island groups to the Americas and here there are many cultural references shared with both Central America as well as South America.

In returning to Garagay the atrium where this mural was discovered is shown guarded, significantly, by a pair of warriors with shields and later overbuilt in another phase. It is notable that ritual forays by village or clan warriors upon others external to their own tribal kin groups to obtain heads, particularly related to seed sowing and soil fertility, was found into modern times among the island peoples of the Marquesas, Indonesia, particularly Borneo, and the Nagas of Assam in North West India. The later overbuild and remodelling appears to be as the result of a completely different belief system to that occurring earlier where human figures with bird-like features and attributes were prominent. Anthropomorphic faces with large upper protruding fangs suggests contacts with Chavin de Huantar and these elements of iconography at Garagay

3.055 : The fire god emerges from the sacred mountain (or altar mound) at dawn between two pennants or flag poles similar to those known for millennia in the Himalayas (*3.060-2*) and the Ancient Middle East and closely similar to those incised on monoliths at Cerro Sechin (*3.059*). Akkad Cylinder Seal Roll-out, Mesopotamia, Late 3rd., millennium, B.C.

are also found in those regaling the villages of Ancon and Curayacu. This could indicate a spread of ideas along the coast and regular contact or settlement by those whose belief system it illustrated[225] - probably associated with mariners.

More or less contemporary with Garagay was the U-shaped ceremonial centre of Cardal, 37 kilometres southeast, and 15 kilometres from the Pacific coast. A road was constructed along the axis of the ceremonial site from the northeast to the centre of the complex. This road passes between two vast rectangular enclosures and two sunken circular courts to reach the raised central ceremonial plaza. Across the plaza a "massive" 6 metres wide staircase rises to the summit of the central stepped pyramid. Here also four superimposed stair constructions have been located indicating four major rebuilding phases beside any intermediate renovations. On the summit there is an entrance from this stair through into the ceremonial forecourt and is decorated with large abstracted fanged mouth motifs as the main feature on a extended frieze flanking each side of the entrance in red and yellow pigments in low relief. Other motifs found at the site show that these sites were extracted or imported from a similar belief system, and were probably closely connected, but other elements including an additional architectural innovation in the form of a small chamber have no known parallel. There are eight circular sunken courts at Cardal and these have been noted as resembling those of the Hopi kivas in the South West United States[226].

The resources to construct these vast centres must have been readily available derived from a stable economy and government competent to mobilise the human labour necessary for such long term and labour intensive constructions. Apart from the conjectures already noted earlier the point has been made by some historians that large populations of subsistence farmers in Africa did not produce the initiatives and organisations, necessary to undertake such projects that occurred on the coast of Peru in a less promising environment. The Peruvian ceramic communities exhibited a high dependence upon non-preservable marine resources such as fish, and sea bird or animal meats such as pelican, cormorants and sea lions. This was supplemented by land hunting and gathering from wild deer and land snails requiring year round pursuit and collection but overall there appeared to be too few seasonal agricultural pursuits in proportion to provide the necessary releasable labour for these massive projects.

The ceremonial centres were located in this time band, for the most part, in valleys near the sea where little arable land was available and evidence shows that irrigation schemes were small scale and largely aimed at taking water from local springs or rivers although they greatly increased the production of the plots that were being cultivated. Calculations show, however, that even this increased productivity would have been far too little to provide for the labour release required, as well as in producing sufficient food, to allow for the construction of massive ceremonial centres in the ceramic period as for the Pre-ceramic. Necessary to consider in this calculation also is that the irrigation canals and associated system required annual out-of-season maintenance and this also would have reduced the labour available in off-peak seasonal troughs[277]. The cultivation of foodstuffs was supplemented by the introduction of ritual substances from other environmental zones such as the coca bush. The coca leaf was cultivated in the coastal valleys before 1000 B.C. in the mid-valley regions of Peru and appears to have been used as a form of exchange over a wide area and chewed with lime powder to relieve fatigue[228]. Maize also appears on the coast for the first time in the late Initial Period sites (1800-800 B.C.) but does not appear to have been intensively cultivated until later times when the population had increased dramatically and agriculture had become more established and surpluses produced[229].

The social organisations are therefore conjectural and certainly so the means and persuasive tactics used, apparently successfully, to build these complexes over millennia on the Peruvian coast. Some have suggested that elite clans were required to coerce the mass regardless of whether they were of a related tribe or kin-group established through a moiety system. Others have cited the Kogi model found among these people in North West Colombia and preserved in their social organisation to this day where the clan system is ruled by priests who drew their successors from the youth of kin groups within the tribe. Parallels with this system have been made with those of the theocracy of Tibet, and where earlier researchers in the first half of the twentieth century considered the many parallels between the Andean and Tibetan cultures to be too close and significant to be coincidence[230].

For the average person in coastal Peru in the Initial Period the end of life was finalised in a flexed burial on their side wrapped in a cloth, placed on a reed mat in a shallow grave and accompanied by a cooking or water vessel. Burial customs show generally that there was a gradual change in traditions between the Pre-ceramic and the Initial Period and widely traded goods appear in the graves of more elite persons. In a grave from Ancon a figurine made of chonta wood, found only in the Amazonian hot, humid forests, was recovered with articulated arms and inlaid shell eyes exemplifying the combination of widely traded materials to make this figure[231]. Another burial at Ancon illustrates possible mystic attributes of animals from the Amazon Basin area where a young man was interred with a cebus monkey. This monkey had been placed across the knees of the young man and covered with mica flakes, a substance found of some significance in Ancient Mexico[232]. A string of stone beads was placed around the young man's neck and another of feathers and iron pyrites placed on his brow. A fan of red, yellow and green feathers was included and he wore armbands and necklaces with a bowl beneath his head containing more feathers with a pestle and mortar revealing traces of red pigment together with a decorated bowl and spouted vessel[233]. It is likely that these grave goods were associated with the burial of a priest or monkey oracle since monkeys were often associated with mental acuity and believed to be messengers of the gods and the young man therefore may have been a shaman or religious mendicant.

In what is believed to be a dedicatory offering a child of about 3-5 years old was found buried beneath a subterranean structure before it had been built. It is thought that the interment under one of its corners was a dedication to the house god believed to preside over this construction. The eyes of the child had been removed and pieces of mica placed in the sockets and on its stomach a gourd had been placed with a quartz crystal placed over the heart. This appears to have been in accord with the long tradition noted of dedicatory burials found also at Ancon in the Pre-ceramic period and surviving into the twentieth century[234].

In Ancon Bay known ceremonial sites foreshadow the close of the Pre-ceramic where pottery and new cultigens were introduced about 1800 B.C. but the earliest pottery in coastal and highland Peru bears few similarities to that of Valdivia in Ecuador indicating little influence. Interestingly, baked clay figurines were found in a few notable pre-pottery sites, suggesting that the fundamental technology and understanding for the manufacture of ceramics was known but not utilised. The earliest pottery reflect imitations of gourds suggesting that gourds were not only the models for pottery but were one of the reasons why ceramics took so long to develop in Ancient Peru - the gourd being a native of South America. Although there are differences in decoration the first pottery from Huaca Negra in the Viru Valley in Northern Peru, Ancon and La Florida in the Rimac Valley in Central Peru, and Ica in Southern Peru show close similarities in manufacture[235]. Tubers - including the sweet potato, become more widely cultivated along with the beans, squash, chilli-peppers and guava fruit, among others, together with root crops. The desert valleys became more intensively farmed at this time and irrigation more evident with pottery appearing at these sites for the first time. Traditional fishing and farming began to diverge as separate ways of life[236].

In the period of transition from the Pre-ceramic to Ceramic, U-shaped centres occur less frequently north of Chancay where most of the centres draw their ceremonial traditions from the valleys of Pativilca, Huarmey, Supe and Casma[237]. At Rio Seco, 10 km north of the Chancay River in Central Peru, dual platforms up too 3 metres high appear to have developed from the earlier twin mound ceremonial sites[238]. Sites such as these imply rituals requiring a priestly hierarchy and therefore a society that is organised not only ceremonially but also in terms of daily life. Apportionment of labour and resources to undertake the essential cultivation of subsistence foodstuffs and raw materials and that necessary to be pledged to construct these civil and religious structures must have been established and enforced. The populace were buried both in their dwellings, as in earlier sites, and in cemeteries outside the settlements. Little attention was given to those who died young and they appear to have been disposed of in the refuse heaps or middens. The existence of higher male status appears to be indicated in the burial rites where men generally were given precedence at the Asia site in the Culebras drainage region. Male burials have been found to include human trophy heads wrapped in mats and endowed, also with textiles, averaging from two to four cloths, a few had many more, and other grave goods[239].

Graves from this region in the late pre-ceramic period included objects of stone, baked clay and wood but also shell, bone, basketry, fabrics and importantly, barkcloth. The fabrics and textiles were twined but were often of extensive and ornate types and various techniques and patterns have been determined from their structure[240]. It is an extraordinary realisation, however, that during this time, from the late Pre-ceramic into the Early Ceramic in Peru, the largest constructions in the whole of the Americas were being erected in a period that corresponds to the late Old Kingdom and its decline in Ancient Egypt

In the Pre-ceramic period the ceremonial sites appear to have utilised the twin pyramid layout, except for a few less usual sites. It is remarkable that many of these sites when uncovered revealed ceremonial floors lacking in debris suggesting that they had been regularly or ritually swept clean[241]. This appears to emulate other known sweeping rituals known also in the ceremonial sites in the fire religions in the Ancient Near and Middle East[242] and later in India[243] where these were inherited through transference by Ancient Middle Eastern migrants.

It is believed that the platforms and stepped mounds in Peru were meant to represent sacred mountains[244] and their central position clearly indicates that the communities associated with them were engaged in support and construction of communal works on an organised basis. Those mounds paired as twin mounds appear to represent dual organisations possibly set up on the moiety system known later in Peruvian and Bolivian history but also in the Ancient Near and Middle East and India. The mounds appear to represent the different status of these dual organisations and these appear to have been built based on an earlier system of ceremonial rooms perhaps forming an early type of fire temple over which the mounds and stepped pyramids were built into two separate constructions. It is also believed that the differentiation of platform sizes and number, where smaller constructions often attended the larger stepped pyramids, reflected the greater stratification into levels of status within that society[245].

Woven Reed Bag Rubble Construction - Shikras

Earlier mound construction appears to have been focused on middens that were built around and over them to create the desired platform or pyramid. A new form of construction is later noted after this period where stones roughly quarried into suitable sizes was contained in woven cane mesh bags called skikras and these would have weighed up to 26 kg when full of rubble. The shikra was then laid in sequence without emptying and it is thought that this allowed supervisors of the work to account for the volume of labour expended by labour gangs.

Contemporary with the Peruvian coastal developments were those in the Ancient Middle East and particularly of note in the context of constructional techniques are those recorded in the texts from that period. In an ancient Sumerian myth, in the construction of the irrigation canals and dykes, it is noted that reeds were "bound" to form the banks of canals with the excavated soil[246] and there appears to be in this reference echoes in a ritualised form in one of the most celebrated works of the period known as the Babylonian Epic of Creation. In a curious reference in a ritual dedicated to the god Marduk, identified with Bel or El, noted later in this work, reeds bundles are cast into the ritual fire with the bound gods, the Asaku[247]. This may have derived from ceremonies associated with reed reinforcement for the dykes and banks in canal construction, most of which would have been the focus of rites to ensure success in their final built form, and the appropriate sacrifices required at that time dedicated. This is likely to have included human sacrifices where the rituals were intended to "bind" their sacrificed souls to the canal as guardians - a belief known throughout the ancient Old World but also in South America and considered separately. From these bound sacrifices and reed construction, known to be included in mud brickwork, the Peruvian shikra may have developed.

An interesting variation in platform and pyramid construction occurred between the sites located on the Peruvian coast and those in the highlands and that was that the highland examples were rounded at the corners, leading eventually to oval shapes constructions, while those on the coast were not. In later Chavin de Huantar the ovaloid or rounded platform characteristic of the early Andes return to the formalised squared corners found on the coast.

Mounding into platforms was formed from freestanding eminences or by utilising a hill where the construction material was banked against it and the natural rise was incorporated into the ceremonial construction. The stonework was often tiered and laid in mud mortar to form stepped mounds or pyramids and plastered with adobe and painted in religious designs related to the worship of the deities associated with each particular construction[248].

Characteristic in the design of these platforms or stepped pyramid mounds was that many appeared to be constructed with centrally located staircases from ground level to the top on one or two (usually opposite) sides. The staircase and the platform summit were undoubtedly utilised for ritual display by priests and community leaders in agriculturally significant events related to the calendar. In the Pre-ceramic period a small circular sunken court was common in the front of the ceremonial platform, more usually centrally placed. Where the sunken courts are aligned with the platform or mound it is believed that they formed part of a sequential ritual processional way from the perimeter of the sacred precinct. This processional way extended through the sunken court and ascended the staircase to the top of the mound and that the opposite stair on the other side was used for ceremonial descent from the summit as the rituals drew to a close. This is a characteristic also of highland sites where the focus appears to cast this court as central in the ceremonial construction of the fire altars[249].

Some historians believe that the sunken courts were the result of propitiating the goddess of Mother Earth, Pacha Mama - this deity being of some importance where weather conditions had frequent devastating effects on the fertility of the soil throughout Peru. Other suggestions are that these sunken courts were associated with the rites of the many myths of clan and tribal origins of emergence from the earth found throughout the Andes and South America. This is also true of many peoples in Asia and found particularly in India, but it is much more likely

that these sunken courts relate to the fire religions of Central America and the Ancient Near and Middle East and in India. In the latter sunken courts and fire pits were centrally located in the courts and are still retained in the rituals of the Parsees and Zoroastrian devotees to this day and these must have resembled those of the Andean ceremonial centres and were current in the same time frames from at least the 4th., millennium, B.C.

The association of fertility and the earth with volcanic fire is found among the Olmecs of Mexico in Central America and found also in Asia. It may be that the sunken courts among the Peruvians were in fact a symbolic reference identifying their central hearth with the emergence of the volcanic fire as lava where the sunken court was a symbolic descent into the earth - into the region of these explosively unpredictable fires. The sunken court may have been seen also as a symbolic "burrowing" into Pacha Mama to initiate fertilisation between the male fire below to release it symbolically as the New Sun, the principle of fertilisation, into the sunken court as the womb of Pacha Mama, the earth itself. In ancient Iran, the agricultural rites celebrated in honour of the fire god, Ahura Mazda, are initiated by a purificator, the priest or other selected elder, and a purified man and the furrows are drawn by them in the soil to take the seed[250]. In ceremonies such as these the fire itself is worshipped and commentaries for the most appropriate ritual means of feeding it are prescribed in detail in surviving texts[251]. The fire-pan itself was intended to represent the universe and in traditional Ancient Middle Eastern and Aryan Vedic thought this is usually depicted, or represented in a circular form. In detailed cosmological principles the various elements associated with constructing the sacred fire altar and pan are recorded in the oldest of the Aryan Vedic texts, the Satapatha Brahmana and this includes describing the fire-pan, where the fire is contained on the altar, as the "womb" and the sacrificer or Vedic priest as the "seed"[252]. The Vedic fire-ceremonies were always conducted

3.056 : Bronze statue or a priest of nobleman with a lion pelt cape tied by crossing the paws around the neck. This appears to be reflected in Andean iconography where puma and jaguar pelts were utilized in the same way. Ma-adi Karib - Awwam Temple of Marib, South Arabia, 8-7th., century, A.D.

3.057 : The celebrated "crossed arms" relief below a niche, one of several, at Kotosh. It is believed that the niches held heads either trophy or carved and the crossed arms therefore probably represented the puma or jaguar cape - the sign of high status. Kotosh, Central Highland Peru, 2nd., millennium, B.C.

in the night preferably a little after midnight, to ensure catching the "rising" Sun of the coming day. The night corresponded to the darkness of the earth below as well as the universe and the fire as the New Sun was seen as emerging as a result of the prescribed fire rituals, by necessity, completed before the first glimmer of dawn.

Kotosh and Huaricoto from Pre-Ceramic to Post Ceramic Period in Central Peru
Related to Kotosh was the site of Huaricoto and the principle of wall niches and friezes found in their similar architecture from the Pre-ceramic period were still being incorporated through the many epochs of the Andes into Inca times[253]. Sunken courts were also evident across three millennia throughout the Andes culminating in the most elaborate of them all in the form of the Kalasaya at Tiahuanaco dating from about 200-550 A.D. Huaricoto was characteristic of many sites in the Central Andes where the simple form of one-chamber fire temples are found, similar in principle to those of Ancient Iran and later Vedic India. This site was occupied for two millennia where the one-chamber structures afforded single entry where the central hearth and a finely plastered floor first appeared about 2260 B.C. occurred at the height of the Mazdaean revision of the Zurvanite fire religions in Ancient Iran. It was from these Iranian people that the Vedic Aryans were soon to split off and immigrate into India about a century or so later.

The evidence interpreted by recent archaeologists in Peru suggests that these small temples were utilised by a single family or clan and research indicates that the fire-altars or hearths were intensively used. The fire-temples appear to have been the only building of importance in settlements that exhibit few large-scale works and indicates a total orientation to small-scale personalised devotion rather than tribal or regional deities. Of special interest is that the doors of these temples at Huaricoto could be "tightly closed"[254] and this suggests, or confirms their development from those of Ancient Iran where it was essential in the rites at the fire altar that they could be secured and "cleansed" both physically and ritually with spells and ceremonies before and during the ceremony. Any contamination, even if they were accidentally seen at a distance, required the ceremony to be stopped and re-cleansing ceremonies, often requiring hours, commenced again. These ceremonies are described in the Vedas[255] and also found among peoples still in the Middle East such as the Mandaeans in a modified form[256]. The sacred chamber was sealed when rites were in progress and ventilation for the ceremonial hearth was provided by a stone-lined duct passing under the benches from outside. Some of these chambers were constructed on a split level plan where it has been suggested that the upper level was some type of viewing gallery for those allowed to enter where the lower was for those performing the rituals at the altar[257].

The ancient traditions in the Near and Middle East provided also for divisions but these were for the males surrounding the altar while the women were confined to the outer gallery or reserved zone away from the altar proper. This arrangement still exists in the Middle East and was long ago adopted into both the early Christian and Moslem traditions in that region. This was also true in the Vedic Aryans from whom the Buddhist and Hindu religions developed from the Vedic religion proper where the fire-ceremony provided for special rites to purify the sacred fire hut. The women who were allowed to attend were ritually cleansed to "protect" the altar along with the regulation placement of the woman away from the sacred fire and altar behind the head of the household or clan - the husband or son.

Kotosh into Post Ceramic
At Huaricoto the personalised form of fire-altar and its hut or temple follow that of Iran in their correspondences and divergences from a standard pattern but they retain this recognised form into, and beyond the introduction of ceramics. Kotosh saw further development probably as a

result of contact with the Peruvian coast where twin terraced platforms were constructed over existing, elaborate chambers of the earlier tradition. Some of these niches retained a motif of crossed hands under the niches[258] (*3.057*) that probably held figurines of ancestors or deities and these apparently have some probable reference to crossed hands or arms reflected in carving in Central and South America. It is interesting to note that the niche, if it was intended to house a portrait head of a deity, ruler or hero would have imitated the personage wearing a revered lion or puma skin cape with the paws characteristically securing it around the neck identically to those shown depicted in the Ancient Middle East (*3.056*).

In the later phase these early fire-chambers were discontinued and restoration and extension of the platforms as they were immediately before the Post-ceramic was undertaken. Galleries in these new extensions were constructed for burial chambers and grave goods were included with these inhumations, including incised shells and mosaic applied to stone reflecting designs reminiscent of later Chavin de Huantar. These galleries are seen as forerunners of a tradition of private tombs built for the clan chiefs a millennium later and beyond[259].

The first appearance of ceramics at Kotosh is called the Waira-jirca phase and this pottery has similarities with that found in the so-called Owl cave less than 100 km away in the Amazon forest at only about 500 metres above sea level[260]. It has been suggested that this is as a result of mountain people descending in the annual agricultural cycle to cultivate in the lower regions, and this included Kotosh. But this might have occurred by disused or broken pottery being left as a result of trading parties either sheltering, or trading with mountain people. The centre appears to have changed its orientation in the traditional worship of their ancient fire-religion but other sites such as Huaricoto remained faithful to the original tradition with a very large fire-chamber being built not far distant at Shillacoto.

The early coastal ceramics of this early first introduction period are rarely decorated but in the highland examples at Kotosh and Waira-jirca they are elaborate and reflect that style of the Early and Late Tutishcainyo styles found in the Cave of the Owls. The decorative motifs include Amazonian inspired designs reflecting the jaguar, monkeys, spectacled owl and snakes[261] and appear overall to have been inspired from, or a traditional developed in the Amazon region that penetrated from the forest into the highlands. To complicate matters the earliest highland pottery appears above the pre-ceramic layers of Pandache near the important site of Pacopampa site in Northern Peru and these resemble those of contemporary Valdivia in Ecuador[262]. This suggests that there were few innovation centres in Peru but were subject to new influences introduced from abroad through trading and possible explorative ventures from more distant lands.

The Appearance of First Metals in Peru

In the Central South highlands around what is now Ayacucho, in the early Initial Period, the first ceramics show little contact with those further north and were sparsely decorated. The pottery type known as Wichqana is found here at a U-shaped ceremonial site with the interred skulls of decapitated women. In the Andahuaylas Valley in the same region at the Waywarka site, a stone bowl dated to about 1440 B.C. has yielded metalworking tools and pieces of gold beaten to a foil and is the earliest evidence of gold working in Peru or Bolivia[263]. Pottery also appears in the Cuzco valley at this time and some examples are decorated with metallic paint[264]. Pottery of the same period from Tiahuanaco beside Lake Titicaca is also found in the Cuzco Valley and this type is known as Qaluyu. After Qaluyu was occupied by the Pukara people in the first millennium B.C. it was abandoned but later they remodelled the mound at this site into the form of a catfish[265]. South of Tiahuanaco, near Lake Poopo, the walled villages of Wankarani exhibit the first evidence for metalworking in the Southern Andean region of Bolivia. Slags from copper smelting have been excavated at these sites and have been radiocarbon dated to between 1200

3.059 : Pennant attached to a flagpole in the manner of early Aryan and Buddhist pennants in Vedic India. Cerro Sechin, Casma Valley, Central Coast Peru, Late second millennium, B.C.

058 : Fine panorama of the Himalayan foothills showing the typical Buddhist pennants extending up a flag-ole. Donkia Pass, Tibet.

3.061 : Another type of Buddhist pennant hung from the pole top as a steamer but one of many type inherited from the Ancient Aryan migrants in the early first millennium B.C. Shan, Northern Burma, Early 20th., century, A.D.

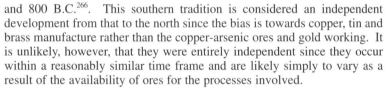

060 : Typical Buddhist pennants outside a monastery in the ...malayas. The flag type is traditionally attached on the long side as ...wn and known for several thousand years in India and the Ancient ...ddle East. Tachiding, Sikkim, Early 20th., century, A.D.

and 800 B.C.[266]. This southern tradition is considered an independent development from that to the north since the bias is towards copper, tin and brass manufacture rather than the copper-arsenic ores and gold working. It is unlikely, however, that they were entirely independent since they occur within a reasonably similar time frame and are likely simply to vary as a result of the availability of ores for the processes involved.

However, the caste system developed in concert with the dual social organisation or moieties has been argued by the most conservative of present day historians to have been endemic in the Andes and coastal Peru from the earliest times from about 3000 B.C. In India the same form of dual organisation developed through a caste system that was applied in India from the entry of the Vedic Aryans at least as early as the beginning of the first millennium B.C. In India this caste system was largely occupationally based and applied to the four, originally three, sacred divisions of the Aryan tribes, but which was overlaid onto the whole of the peoples of the Subcontinent, during the Hindu ascendancy, by the Brahmans and later Hindus. The metal-workers were separated into their own castes and those who worked at the forge were of lesser status that those who worked from the "purified" metal smelted from the ore. Those who sold the finished product were considered an even higher status caste than the other two since they did not need to dirty their hands. Purity and pollution were the keywords to the caste system as it was applied and tribes were classified in the same way as the traditional occupations to which they were confined for their life and the lives of their descendants. Iron working, or black-smithing, was considered to be among the lowest of the caste occupations in status classifications and for some of the Aryan and non-Aryan castes the blacksmith was an outcast and could not live among the villagers they served. This degradation among some of the metalworking castes

3.062 : Buddhist pennants of the traditional type fixed the length of the pole as found in the earliest example at Cerro Sechin. Tashiding Monastery, Sikkim, Late 19th., century, A.D.

affected their smelting and metalworking techniques since the lowest castes were extremely poor and had difficulty in affording the most basic equipment. In India, because metals were associated with the cardinal points as part of a philosophical classification in both Buddhist and Hindu speculations, gold was considered the most sacred and therefore was assigned the highest status corresponding to the wealthiest castes and those who worked in this metal were of the highest status and employed techniques neither allowed nor affordable for the smithies.

It is fundamental to the theme of this work that the caste and dual organisation system imposed from the earliest times in Peru was in fact imported from the Ancient Near and Middle East, Iran, and India in particular. The later contacts between Iran and India reinforced these social structures and corresponding metalworking castes and their techniques along with the strictures applied not only to the different metals but also to the smelting and working rituals and techniques for the same metal. This would account for the variations between those in Central Peru and those at Wankarani in Southern Bolivia after being imported from a land where such divisions in caste status and occupational divisions and techniques were endemic. Because they occur in the Andes rather abruptly the suggestion must be that they were imported from West and South Asia where a long period of development over several millennia occurred before smelting techniques were sufficiently efficient to be able to produce copper goods to the required standard. It also must be significant that these sudden developments occur at times of significant climatic change when peoples in Eurasia and probably South America also were forced from their traditional lands.

The eruption of Hekla in Iceland in 1159 B.C. was a major climatic event causing decades of severe cold and crop failure in Northern Europe and the resultant enforced migrations caused the collapse of kingdoms across Europe and Asia as the hungry hordes swept south to warmer climes. For those in their path they had only two choices, stay and fight for their homes and lands where the most likely outcome was that they would be killed, or flee wherever long-established trade routes afforded a means of escape. For most in Iran the only option was to flee to the southeast into Baluchistan and then into India, and this was the proven escape route for millennia in similar circumstances and was therefore well known. However, for others the only possibility would have been to take to the boats and escape either to India or further east to South East Asia and into the Pacific to the Americas.

India provides abundant evidence that it became a safe haven over millennia for people from Iran from at least 6-7000 B.C. onwards, but the sudden appearance of metal-working and later other techniques, unexplainable in South American history, points to Asians arriving as a result of these dark periods of climate change and social upheaval in their own lands. To set out for South America or intermediate lands can hardly have been a shot in the dark but were undertaken in the knowledge of sea routes that were well known to such distant regions. Such routes must have been frequented long before about 3100 B.C. when pottery suddenly appears on the coast of Ecuador at the exact place where the sea currents from Asia would wash ashore any mariners attempting the journey (*2.004*). It is unlikely therefore to be a coincidence that there was another massive eruption dating to 3195 B.C. recorded in the Irish Oak tree ring sequences and confirmed in the Greenland ice bores that corresponds to the appearance of the first ceramics. The second sudden appearance of new ceramic forms and technological advances in Peru, such as the heddle loom, date to a period placed at about 1800 B.C. +/- a century or two, and it may be no coincidence that the eruption of Thera in the Cyclades in Greece is dated to 1628 B.C. Other lesser eruptions and climate changes occurred and these also correspond to sudden advances in technology and cultural expansion and one of the most important of these occurred in the 6-7 th., century, B.C. 535 A.D. This resulted afterwards in similar expansions and rapid changes in the 7th., century, A.D. - a period of sudden advance that is recorded in Colombia,

Ecuador, Peru and Bolivia. This occurred as a result of one of the greatest eruptions known to have occurred for about 100,000 years, that of the volcano Krakatoa in Indonesia, that caused catastrophic climate changes throughout the world. This same time band saw the collapse of the some the greatest contemporary American cultures such as Teotihuacan in Mexico, the Moche in North Peru, and the Nazcan in South Peru as well as the first major Andean empire at Tiahuanaco.

The Casma Valley - Sechin Alto and Cerro Sechin

Sechin Alto, located above the Casma Valley extending inland from the Central Coast of Peru, had developed into the largest ancient monumental complex in the Americas by 1200 B.C. The ceremonial centre was focused on a U-shaped mound complex and appears to be directly associated with Cerro Sechin at the entrance to the Casma Valley. This critically located centre at the valley opening onto the Pacific Ocean coast was within sight below Sechin Alto to the west only a few kilometres from the seashore, this lower site being established about 1290 B.C. in its more developed form[267]. In the Initial Period at Sechin Alto there were two major sites each covering about 200 hectares among five or six important centres located in this valley. This is not unusual in this period since other important centres are found in the Rimac, Chillon and Chancay valleys[268]. Evidence is available for a settlement first established at Cerro Sechin from about 1700 B.C. and its final epoch ends about 500 B.C. appearing to coincide with a new phase of cultural influences in Ancient Peru. It appears that, generally, these sites on the coast where ceramics suddenly appear around 1800 B.C., were subject to, and the result of new incursive influences related also to agricultural advances through irrigation and technical initiatives supported by prodigious canal building. That these should occur on the coast should be significant since many of the myths and legends surviving into later millennia suggest that these were related to sea borne influences and therefore first appear on, and are distributed along the coast. This concurs with a sudden increase in inland centres and widespread irrigation schemes and associated ceremonial centres[269]. However there is an anomaly here since early pottery is found on the eastern foothills of the Andes at Tutishcainyo on the Ucayali River dating to 2000 B.C.[270]. The fact that this is earlier than that of coastal and highland Peru and whether this Andean site was the source for the sudden appearance of pottery elsewhere in Peru is unresolved since the style and type appear not to be directly related.

Cerro Sechin and the Casma Valley Cultures

This important ceremonial site is located near the confluence of the Sechin and Moxeke Rivers and is clearly associated with one of the largest sites in the Americas known, Sechin Alto, overlooking Cerro Sechin from a shoreline vantage point on a hill above the valley floor[271]. The ceremonial centre of Cerro Sechin is the best known in the Casma region because of the remarkable carved monoliths found embedded in the revetment facing the main platform. The site of Cerro Sechin is particularly interesting because of the iconography and surviving physical evidence of those who occupied the site. The murals preserve particular images of fish resembling those of the upturned mouth found among the peoples, including the Maya, of the Pacific coast of Central America (*3.053*). More particularly of interest are the depictions of flags bound by cord to a pole incised on a monolith placed each side of the ceremonial stair to the mound complex (*3.059*). This type of flag is identical to those used from early evidence in Asia and utilised into more recent times by Buddhist pilgrims and monasteries in the Himalayas and into Northern India (*3.058*; *3.060-2*). Of interest also are the footprints reserved from around the ceremonial precinct since they indicate an unusually large average foot size. This element of evidence is of note since the indigenous Mongoloid Amerindians are considered to have very small feet and perceived as such by early European writers[272]. These footprints may indicate contact on the coast by Asian and Polynesian peoples who brought with them traditions relating to textiles, bark cloth and the heddle loom as well as ceramics. The Polynesians themselves are unlikely to have brought these from their own traditions but it must be remembered that bark cloth and bark beaters found in the Pacific Coast of South America probably imported by the Polynesians or Indonesians. This tradition was probably the Lapita Culture dating from 2000 B.C. in the Western Pacific, and evident about 1500 B.C. in Western Polynesia or soon after, and may have been responsible for the initial introduction of the bark-beater and bark-cloth as a result of this penetration into the Pacific from Asia.

The three-tiered stepped platform at Cerro Sechin, orientated to the cardinal points, was flanked by two smaller constructions and it is thought that there was a sunken court located in the front open area where the ceremonial staircase rises in the front of the main stepped platform. The platform is stone faced and featured rounded corners but not that similar to those of the earlier Kotosh tradition. This outer wall to the platform has yielded about 400 stone carvings and are a special feature since retrieval of sculptures from other sites in Peru have produced nothing to compare with this number[273].

These low reliefs, for which Cerro Sechin is renown, are carved from very hard granite and these stones were set in the outer wall and are as pristine as they were three thousand years ago when first carved. It is believed that the many stones depictions form a sequence referring to mythological illustrations of some cosmological saga or a legendary battle. Decapitated human heads (about 70% of the depictions), often with tears, or blood streams from the eyes or gushing from the mouth, are frequent and figures severed at the waist and intestines hanging down are also to be found[274]. Various depictions of body parts are also frequent but in other full-height panels rulers, deities, or priests are depicted with sceptres apparently reflecting iconography related to cardinal points and cosmological references (*9.030*; *9.045*).

These images appear to represent ritual or occasional war parties and the results of skirmishes with other tribes that were possibly arranged on a ritual basis. The scenes depicted are considered not to appear to indicate that warfare was common since there is no evidence for palisades or masonry fortifications for another thousand years. The stone revetment was a late renovation since the site dates from the early Initial Period when three prior constructions developed around the original platform constructed of conical adobes laid in mortar measuring 34 metres on each side. These conical adobes had circular bases, tapering to a point[275], and appear to be based on those of the Ancient Middle Eastern civilisation who used similar and various other shaped mud brick shapes for millennia, so similar to those found widely in Ancient Peru as well as at Chavin de Huantar. Radiocarbon dates indicate that the site suffered a holocaust about 1519 B.C., shortly after the site with its stone revetment incorporating the granite relief carvings had been completed, but no precautions to protect the site appear to have been undertaken suggesting a one-off event[276].

The ceremonial chambers located on the summit of the Cerro Sechin platform were painted in pink and blue similar to the rest of the complex and imagery preserved in a mural is that of black felines with burnt orange coloured paws and white claws. The background plaster was painted yellow and this mural flanked the entrance to the main ritual room on the summit. These first buildings on the summit were extended with a second set in the next phase featuring ornamental, or perhaps more likely, symbolic pilasters. Clay friezes preserved the motif of a human figure turned upside-

3.063 :
Footprints preserved from the sacred precincts of Cerro Sechin. These footprints measure about 250-300 mm and are too large to have been made by indigenous Indians in Peru since their feet are typically Mongoloid and the smallest of the human groups. Cerro Sechin, Casma Valley, Central Peru, Late second or early first millennium, B.C.

down with the eyes closed and apparently blood streams illustrated streaming from the eyes. The style is earlier than that of the stone revetment granite carvings but appears to indicate that human sacrifice was central to the rituals on the platform summit[277]. In the third phase the platform base revealed a painted and incised frieze preserving the images of two large fish[278].

Sechin Alto as a Fortress Ceremonial Site in the Casma Valley
Sechin Alto is one of the larger complexes in Peru, centrally located on the coast, and is composed of several complex types including the U-shaped platform and its main pyramid rose to a height of about 30 metres. The site is culturally linked to the Las Llama-Moxeke complex 10 km distance and to the better-known Cerro Sechin at the entrance to the valley opening onto the Pacific shoreline and was one of the largest complexes ever created in the ancient world. In the second millennium B.C. it is believed to have been the largest ceremonial site in the New World at that time since the volume of constructional materials utilised was about double that of La Florida in the Rimac Valley near modern-day Lima. The core of the old structure is formed of conical adobes and there is evidence surviving of a coloured clay frieze from this formative platform. The extent of the plazas and platforms extended at their base for about a mile or 1.5 kilometres and include four extensive plazas each projecting linearly from the other commencing at the base of the main pyramid.

From radiocarbon dating trials it appears that the first buildings at the site were constructed during the early to mid-Initial Period and a date of about 1721 B.C. has been determined. In the last construction, built over the earlier reconstructions and extensions, the outer revetment was faced with granite blocks, some being of cyclopean proportions weighing over two tons. The use of granite in the outer revetments is reminiscent of the lower site of Cerro Sechin at the entrance to the valley, overlooked by Sechin Alto, and the sculpture is also similar to that of the lower site found at this higher-altitude complex[279].

Moxeke in the Casma - a Remarkable Ceremonial Site
Moxeke is culturally a regional development of the Casma River Valley tradition along with the contemporary complexes and shared cultural origins at Sechin Alto, and Cerro Sechin near the Pacific Coast. This site is particularly noted for the remarkable façade of the main mound composed of very large niches enclosing high reliefs and friezes painted in blue, red black and white. Two elaborately dressed figures face forward with one depicting the back of a bound prisoner in a manner found later among the Moche on the North Coast of Peru. These are included also with two human faces depicted on the larger platform[280]. The ceremonial site is built on an axis and this is determined at N41°E and along this axis is an extensive central terraced plaza with a large platform-pyramid at each end. It is interesting to note that this site formed a coherent whole from its beginning from the early Initial Period and included the lesser structures thought to be residential compounds to the east and west of the ceremonial complexes. The initial dates obtained so far suggest that this site was occupied between 1800 B.C. and 1400 B.C. - that is, from the beginning of the introduction of pottery into Peru[281].

There have been noted over 70 aligned platforms at this site, varying from 10 metres to 50 metres along the base and from 2 to 5 metres in height, along the east and west side of the plaza flanking the main ceremonial complex of the site of Moxeke[282]. The principal mound resembles Cerro Sechin in one particular aspect and that is that the main mound is stepped with rounded corners, a characteristic reminiscent of the Kotosh Fire-temple complexes. The pyramid is constructed in its core with conical adobes and in the last remodelling and enlargement it was surrounded with massive stone revetment walls incorporating finely polished and shaped stone ashlars[283].

Moxeke is now known for its remarkable clay high relief sculptures dating from the last renovation of the complex found on the outer face of the walls of the third tier of the main platform terrace. This wall was constructed with large recesses 3.9 metres wide and 1.7 metres deep but of unknown height, possibly 3 metres, since the sculptures and the backing walls only survive from the shoulders down. Incised lines were highlighted by black paint along with pink, blue and white used for the wall designs. The high relief sculptures depict large (up to 3 metres high) clay high relief priestly figures set in the recesses wearing a mantle over a tunic and short kilt measuring 3.2 metres in width. One of these figures was painted entirely in black and another adjacent figure wore a twisted cord belt and was depicted with upraised hands holding bicephalic-headed snakes with forked tongues[284].

The same building was built with recesses along the northwest face and featured reliefs representing massive heads. One of these exhibited a mask or face with bared clenched teeth, a characteristic of both Central and South America, and was painted emerald green with pink lines vertically down from its half-circular shaped black eyes. Another head has closed eyes and mouth reminiscent of the depictions of trophy heads at Cerro Sechin. These sculptures seem to be evidence that the stepped pyramid staircases and summits were used for ritual display since the figures and faces are meant to be seen from the surrounding Public areas forming the sacred precincts and were part of the ritual stage setting integral with the platform structures.

The large terraced platform at the north east of the main mound, is known as Huaca A, and it is of interest in that it was built upon by a complex of double faced rooms with walls of considerable thickness. These buildings cover the platform summit 140 metres square and 9 metres in height and are largely constructed with un-worked stones set in clay mortar rendered over with white plaster and included rows of niches set into the upper walls. The purpose of the maze of rooms formed within its perimeter is unknown and most of the rooms appear to have high thresholds and wooden bars to prevent entry.

In the residential buildings there are two identifiable groups and both include centrally located subterranean hearths. One of these groups is associated and aligned with the main pyramid and its contiguous structures and connected to these constructions. Their walls were built of quarried stone, plaster finished, and painted red and had storage rooms associated with them. This suggests that these were the residences of the elite rulers and priests and possibly reserved for the higher status clans in a social organisation system based on dual moiety marriage divisions known in South America but probably reflecting the Asian model. Interestingly, most of the stamp and cylinder seals known from this site were found in the elite houses suggesting an association of these with power and status. Both these types of seals were common in the Ancient Middle East in the same time band and the stone bowls used for grinding red pigment, found also in the elite residences at Moxeke, was traditional widely in Asia from the most ancient times into the present day in India. The other, clearly residential buildings do not align with the ceremonial constructions and were framed or were cane structures built on stone cobble wall foundations[285]. This suggests that the lower status common people were housed in this less elaborate form of accommodation and were probably under the direction of the elite clan(s) or their rulers and priests. The association of elite residences at Moxeke with the ceremonial buildings is found also at Cardal. This arrangement appears to undermine the theory held by historians that the social organisation in Peru were based on an unlikely egalitarian system earlier noted.

The building of Huaca A at Moxeke appears to date more precisely to 1500-1400 B.C. and is therefore contemporary with Cerro Sechin on the coast and probably interacted socially with it. In the centre of this development on the summit of the platform was a sunken courtyard and it has been suggested that this complex of rooms, halls and an enclosed court was for storage of ceremonial paraphernalia. This probably also included the foodstuffs and other elements of ritual display and festival supply and ritual exchange and considered similar to those used by the Warao[286], an Amazon forest tribe but also found among the Melanesians noted in the early works of Dr. George Brown, A.B. Brewster and others.

Moxeke was built on the tributary of the Casma and Cerro Sechin was sited beside the confluence of this and the main Casma River not far from the seashore. The low scale irrigation patterns are of interest in the Casma in that the labour required to construct, renovate and maintain such vast complexes as reflected in the contemporary centres of Moxeke itself, Cerro Sechin and Sechin Alto was a huge labour drain on limited resources. The irrigation engineering was extremely low tech by any standards being of the most elementary form of gravity feed and technically of the simplest type. Gravity feed systems were found widely for water supply in the Western Pacific through to the Himalayan foothills and the Nagas of Assam. One characteristic throughout South American history is that when an innovation appears (rarely develops or evolves), it is retained in the identical form for many generations or centuries after with little evolutionary development from that introduction. This first simplest form is retained until a more advanced form appears again without any apparent experimentation or logical progression. This is certainly true also of textiles and the associated techniques or technology from twine through to the more advanced technology of the heddle loom as was true for irrigation.

Comparisons between the irrigation systems of Mexico and South America were made over a century ago. European observers noted with apparent bemusement and frustration the ultra-conservatism of the indigenous peoples relating to the rejection or inability to re-utilise the simplest of the pre-Colombian agricultural works without coercion, and even then not successfully, so apparent even into the present day. Edward B. Tylor noted a century and a half ago of the indigenous Mexicans; "They carry pots of water to irrigate their ground with instead of digging trenches. This is the more curious as at the time of the Conquest irrigation was much practised by the Aztecs in the plains, and remains of water-canals still exist showing that they had carried the art to great perfection"[287].

In an earlier work by the present author it is recorded of Tylor that he further noted of the Indians that they loaded one panier on a side of the donkey with vegetables while counterbalancing it with the other panier filled with stones instead of filling both with vegetables thereby requiring only half the number of journeys. He reported that the Indians rejected advice suggesting the more efficient, rational method accusing him as a stranger who showed "... little understanding or decency who interfered in the established customs of the country"[288]. In addition the response these Amerindian peoples gave was that they had always imitated the traditions of their ancestors and this clearly illustrates a people unable to break free and progress where their long held, cherished beliefs restricted them to the simplest methods because they were attributed to the ancestors. It also illustrates the attitude fiercely preserved into the present day reflective in the vast areas of ancient terraces that stand idle and decaying without being used. This clearly illustrates the truth in the myths and legends that their culture-heroes who introduced these radical engineering feats originated from outside South America. Implied or stated is that when these culture-bearers and their descendants died out through repeated intermarriage or left to "cross the sea", the initiative and irrigation skills died out. Although it is not politically correct it is clear that these ultra-conservative peoples could not maintain the fundamental principles of irrigation and imported technology since it had not developed from within their own traditions or technological development but clearly relates to that of the Ancient Middle East, India and later in Indonesia, the Philippines, South China and Assam.

Complicating the distribution of labour in the Casma valley was the fact that Moxeke and Sechin Alto were at a higher level above the valley floor while most of the available agricultural land was in the narrow flanking strips of alluvial soil adjacent to the river on the valley floor[289]. The logistics of building and maintaining these ceremonial sites would appear beyond the resources available to the builders of these centres and human resources must have been stretched to the limit suggesting coercion rather than the principle of cooperation so promoted by more recent historians. Contact with fishing villages on the coast through Cerro Sechin at the lower valley level appears to have been maintained but no large population bases appear sufficiently large to draw upon to assist in the construction of the inland centres.

On the coast the only large site nearby to Moxeke, Sechin Alto and Cerro Sechin, to the north of the Casma River on the coast, was at Las Haldas where a central pyramid together with rectangular plazas and circular courts have been located. The older residential occupations relate to the last stages in the late Initial Period covers and extends to about 8 square hectares (1 hectare = 2.471 acres). The ceremonial architecture at this site is similar to that at Cerro Sechin and the dietary analysis at these sites suggests that they all formed a common cultural link by association, political control, or tribal or racial descent. The meat products consumed at Moxeke, Sechin Alto, Cerro Sechin and Las Haldas was largely marine, e.g. fish, and shell-fish, supplemented with deer meat along with non-protein products such as squash, beans, avocados, chilli-peppers, manioc, sweet potato, peanuts, etc.[290].

It has been suggested that each of these ceremonial centres maintained its own small territory supported by its own agricultural system and interlinked through moieties providing marriage links between these culturally similar centres. However, Sechin Alto appears to have been a stronghold suggesting that it may have been a retreat in times of war or possibly when under attack from irregular forays by mariners from the Pacific Ocean for all of the main centres in the Casma Valley. The clear cultural associations that each of these four sites reflects with the others and their apparent orientation to the coast suggests that they were formed by largely mariner peoples who established a foothold on the Central Coast of Peru.

The Central Coast Valleys of Nepena and Santa
To the north of the Casma Valley are the historically important valleys of Nepena and Santa. Nepena is less attractive to settlers since it only has half the arable to that of Casma and the same is true of Santa although the river itself carries a larger volume of water, because its base is much deeper than any other coastal valley. These valleys have few obvious ceremonial centres dating from the earliest period in Peruvian history and this has presented a puzzle for archaeologists. There is, however, a more recent interest in one of the Pre-ceramic sites known as Caral in the Santa Valley and two small ceremonial centres with sunken courts have been found at Condorcerro and Cerro Obrero.

Caral as an Early Coastal Site in Central Peru
Caral dates from about 3500 B.C. and from its inception there is little other development yet discovered that would suggest an expansion from this site since these two later sites date from about 2000 B.C.[291]. Caral has been known since its discovery in 1905 but because there has never been any pottery discovered at the site it has received much less attention from both hauqueros (graverobbers) and archaeologists. However, this monumental site has received a considerable amount of attention in the last year or so since recent dated material suggests that the very large and extensive platform mounds date from 2600-2000 B.C. The monuments include sunken circular plazas with fire pits and construction using the shikra, or woven reed bags, found at other Peruvian sites. It has even been suggested, in recent television presentations, that Caral may have been the birthplace of civilisation since many of the platforms are of a size more usually associated with those a millennium later.

Caral, however, is more likely to prove the point that this was an introduced culture along with constructional methods and that the lack of pottery indicates that these advances were introduced by mariners who did not use or require pottery. It is likely that the basic skills of agricultural and constructional labouring were a means for long seasonal periods when not at sea whereas skilled tradesmen would have been more fully occupied on an annual basis. This would have provided the mariners and traders who reached the South American coast to be able to erect platforms and mounds in the image of those long built in their own Asian traditions without the long associated developmental epochs. It would also explain the lack of pottery for so long lacking in these great monumental sites on the Peruvian coast and their mariner heritage would explain why they did not feel the need to import potters, exacerbated by the fact that coconut shells were readily available in the Pacific Islands or gourds on the South American coast for water storage. This mariner origin probably also explains why the Spondylus and Stombus shells, so noted of the Kula in the Western Pacific, were so revered from the earliest times in Ancient Peru. Such important cultural aspects are likely also to have been initiated long before Caral since this site is probably not the first settlement of these ocean-going people from Asia. This point is emphasised by the fact that Ecuador to the north had already been manufacturing pottery for half a millennia and this is believed influenced by the Jomon of Japan in Eastern Asia. The conservative nature of the indigenous people has already been noted and with successive generations of mariners using coconuts or gourds as water-carriers. It is probable that this aspect became revered and emulated by the Peruvians eschewing the use of pottery in favour of their ancestors' practical means of water storage in organic vessels.

Punkuri and the Nepena Valley

In the Nepena Valley, located 27 kilometres from the Pacific shore the ceremonial site of Punkuri covered an area of about 2 hectares where its mound measured about 45 metres on each side and rose to a height of about 10 metres. Excavations two generations ago revealed superimposed platforms where the oldest was built of fieldstones set in clay mortar and unusually orientated to N20°W differing from those in the Casma linked sites. Some of the platform surfaces displayed painted clay high relief sculptures and friezes but most the famous image is the sculpted, snarling head of a fanged feline together with its two front paws, larger than life, placed in the centre of the ceremonial staircase leading up to the second platform level. The head was painted green, with gums in the mouth coloured red and its crossed fangs painted white. The paws were separated by a central gap reminiscent of the staircase division at Cerro Sechin. In a sub-floor chamber, under the paws of the jaguar head, offerings of a decapitated woman has been recovered. A kilogram in weight of turquoise beads was placed on her pelvis and these were believed to have been the remains of a sequined garment worn by the sacrificial victim. This female sacrifice was accompanied by a Strombus shell, two Spondylus shells, and also a stone pestle and mortar following the overall traditions known of the Aspero site[292]. More recent interpretations of the construction, friezes and artefacts from this site are associated with the Moxeke tradition and include the use of conical adobes found at this contemporary period[293].

Initial Period in the Highland Centres

The developments on the coast were affected by contemporary advances in the agriculturally more favourable valleys of the North Central Andes in Peru. The ceremonial centres appeared to reflect similar cross-cultural influences in religious and social structures but lacked the surrounding urban development that might be expected to support the larger complexes. Agriculture did not require irrigation as was the case for the coastal regions and more reliable food supplies did not seems to affect particularly the construction of the sites in any radical sense. Important sites were scattered throughout the highlands with less developed and less populated regions between. The most advanced centres appear toward what is now Ecuador but interregional trade and cultural exchange seemed to have been maintained between the regions as a whole.

The population groups located in the lower eastern forests traded with the more advanced highland centres and supplied them with characteristic forest products, such as feathers, and animal skins found in so many sites as prestige ritual items. These trade patterns repeatedly emphasise the great importance of the east-west routes from the Pacific Coast through the Highlands to the Amazon tributaries in the east.

Pacopampa is located about 150 kilometres south of the modern border with Ecuador and located in one of the most isolated regions of the Peruvian highlands. Significantly the site is located about mid-way, 70 kilometres from each, between the Pacific Coast and the Maranon River, this being the major western tributary and extension of the Amazon River. In this part of the Andes the overall height of the long north-south mountain chain is lower and narrower than any other section in Peru and allows less restricted access from the Pacific Ocean to the Amazon Basin. Pacopampa is located above the lesser Chotano River that joins a sub-tributary of the Maranon itself called the Chambaya River. This allows direct access to the Maranon and thence to the Amazon proper[294]. This accessibility between the Pacific Ocean and the Amazon Basin would seem critical to the location of the great site of Pacopampa and others in the region and in principal to the location of many of the great ceremonial sites in early Peru (*3.064*).

The valleys around this site, located below the 2,140 metres elevation, were ideal for cultivation of tropical crops such as manioc, found widely in the Amazon Basin, and chirimoya as well as cotton. The camelids found in the higher Andes were not found in the early phases of excavations and deer were pursued in the hunt as the only large game food and agriculture as an occupation does not occur in this region before the Initial Period.

At the Pacopampa site the first occupation is found on a small mound within the temple site named Pandache and excavation has yielded a form of unknown pottery dating to the beginning of the Initial Period (1800 B.C.). The decoration on these ceramics appears to have preserved design motifs similar to contemporary types at Valdivia and Machalilla in Ecuador. In the middle of the Initial Period, in the second millennium B.C., the first temple buildings were established and on a scale much larger than those in other northern sites. Several centuries later the temple zone at Pacopampa covered 9 hectares and the natural hill where the first temple buildings were constructed was utilised as the core of a great rectangular stepped pyramid encompassing the conical hill. The stepped pyramid summit featured sunken courts and freestanding buildings and including a comprehensive drainage system with stone-lined conduits and ducts dating almost entirely from the Initial Period[295].

The site is noted for its many fragments of stone sculpture and one of the more complete examples features an animal with horns, or a double serpent with a single head similar to that found at Huaca A at Moxeke but only remotely related to imagery at Chavin de Huantar[296]. The Pacopampa example[297] feature the carved imprints of a pair of feet while at Moxeke the reverse side features a carved human hand suggesting some shared iconographical meaning. Such illustrations of hands and particularly feet were a feature later in Central America and in Asia in the Buddhist, Jain and later Hindu religions of India from the second half of the first millennium B.C. into the present day but probably developed from earlier traditions.

Ceramics appear to have played an important part in the rituals at Pacopampa and the styles and images are distinctive from those of other traditions in that time frame in Peru. Many of the smaller artefacts appear to be for ritual use and include a small stone spoon probably for inhaling hallucinogens, decorated in the Pacopampa style and a stone cup probably for the consumption of chichi (maize beer) at ceremonials[298]. Among ritual items shells are of some importance in the life of contemporary Pacopampa in the second millennium B.C. It has been suggested that they were introduced from the distant Pacific Coast not for food but for rainmaking ceremonies. However, it is just as likely, or more so, that they were a symbol of their paternal line as mariners from that shore. It is likely that they travelled inland seeking access to the riverine highways of the Amazon Basin where this east-west movement is repeatedly evident from the earliest sites in Peru and Southern Ecuador. This association with hereditary and the ancestors appears to be confirmed in the fact that shells are widely found in the graves from the earliest times into that of the Incas (*6.124*) where they are found hung around the neck like pendants and less likely to be connected with rain in the afterlife.

One of the most interesting discoveries at Pacopmapa are the unusual, large, hollow clay figurines about half a metre (1.5 feet) high and are thought to be males dressed in a long ceremonial tunic exhibiting an unusual hairstyle. Recovered also were other elementarily shaped figurines of felines, bears, dogs and viscachas. Among the largest number of ceramic vessels found in that period, including some from outside the cultural region, were roller and stamp seals of the Cupisnique type suggesting widespread trading connections[299]. This assemblage included one ceramic stamp with the "megalithic S" featured so widely in Tiahuanaco iconography two millennia later indicating the conservative retention of iconography and symbols after their introduction throughout South America but widespread also in Eurasia.

Studies on agriculture for this site have not been conclusive but animal foods such as deer meat has been determined as the main protein source and supplemented with dogs, guinea pigs and birds. Of special interest is the fact that among the food refuse is that human bones occur preserving the evidence that they were deliberately cut, gnawed, scraped and calcined and are found second only to the number of deer bones. This appears to be evidence for cannibalism either as a source of food or for ritual purposes although the number of human bones found suggests more than might be required for rituals.

Cajarmarca in the Central Peruvian Highlands

Cajarmarca River drains this large intermontane valley eastward to the Maranon, the major western tributary of the Amazon, and is located south of Pacopmapa. The main central settlement area for the valley is, however, conveniently situated less than ten kilometres from the headwaters of the Jequetepeque River flowing in the opposite direction westwards to the Pacific Ocean. Clearly it is this location on the access routes eastward to the Amazon Basin and westward to the Pacific that is once again the probable founding factor initiating the earlier settlements. Perhaps because of the less direct access from the Pacific shoreline there is little evidence for pre-ceramic settlements in this Cajamarca Valley and the earliest settlements date from the Initial Period early in the second millennium B.C.

The Initial Period sites in this valley have been divided into two phases called the Early Huacaloma Phase and the Late Huacaloma Phase named after the prime site in the valley. Because of repeated reuse of the sites the earlier is usually buried under the occupation levels of the later phase at Huacaloma sites. There are common characteristics that appear to link the early Huacaloma Phase with that of the Pandache phase at Pacopampa to the north and some consider them to be contemporary sites[300]. Game deer from the forest hunt appears to have been the primary protein source and it is likely that this meat supply was supplemented by agriculture but the extent of this is as yet to be determined.

At the deepest levels at Huacaloma a building constructed of a type of volcanic rock was plastered with thin layers of clay to both the interior and exterior walls and the floor. In the centre of the room was a semi-subterranean fire-pit and the surrounding floors had been scorched by the heat but kept swept[301]. It appears that this fire chamber related to the Kotosh Tradition where fire-pits were central to the religious rites carried out in them and where the floors exhibit the same characteristic swept condition. This chamber was later rebuilt by infill into the chamber and overbuilding in the form of a large, stepped platform 109 by 81 metres and featured friezes incorporating the iconography of felines and serpents.

A broad, centrally located stairway ascended the three-tiered stepped pyramid to the summit and this was roofed over with stone slabs and the internalised walls then plastered to form a subterranean staircase in the last phase of the Initial Period. On the summit stone-lined canals and stone buildings were constructed and this is reminiscent of drainage channels found at Pacopampa and found also on the summit and terraces of the largest site in the Cajarmarca regions at Layzon and Agua Papada. These last two are centres built on opposite sides of a narrow chasm at an altitude of 3,200 metres. At Layzon the pyramid is constructed in six tiers from the natural volcanic bedrock, or living stone, and with stone facing of the same material. The sites of Layzon and Agua Tapada appear to have been a single centre focused around the Cumbemayo canal[302].

The Cumbemayo Canal - From Pacific Ocean to the Amazon Basin

The Cumbemayo Canal is considered one of the most remarkable engineering feats in South America. The largely artificially constructed canal is narrow at about 12 to 18 inches (300 - 500 mm) wide and is of no great depth at about 12 inches (300 mm) to a little over two feet (600 mm). The canal begins at the foot of Cerro Cumbe on the Pacific Ocean, or western side, where it commences on its natural downward flowing course until it reaches the hill where Agua Tapada is sited and is then bored into the hill emerging on the other side in the form of a spring. Here the canal divides and one part flows along the southern perimeter of Agua Tapada while the other flows along the southern side of the Layzon site. Below the two ritual centres the canals rejoin and flow as a single artificial watercourse to the valley floor. This overall construction is perceived as an example of sacred geography and, since the canal is not large enough to transport significant amounts of water for irrigation, it is believed to have been constructed as a form of sympathetic magic utilised in associated, cyclical rituals in rainmaking ceremonies. The flow of the channel from west to east, that is symbolically from the Pacific side to the east, the mountain or Cordillera side and the Amazon Basin further east, reflects the belief found later in Inca religious myth that the ocean flowed under the land in rivers and thence up into the mountains and emerged as rain, streams and rivers to water the crops and fertilise the land[303]. It might also be mentioned that these myths, and others similar, indicate that they are intimately bound up with culture heroes who are themselves associated with arrival on the Pacific Ocean coast of Peru and later departing across the Ocean to the west.

Kuntur Wasi in the Jequetepeque Valley

The importance of the interrelation of the Cajarmarca Valley centres and those located nearby in the upper Jequetepeque Valley is illustrated by the primary site of Kuntar Wasi. Kuntar Wasi was first constructed in the Late Initial Period in the second half of the second millennium B.C., equating to the Late Huacaloma Phase in Cajarmarca and the ceramics found at this site are similar to those of contemporary Huacaloma. This site was constructed by levelling and transforming the peak of La Copa into a stepped platform of four terraces that covered an area of 13 hectares. The summit features a sunken court 24 metres square and reached by a very wide ceremonial staircase 11 metres wide. A subterranean stone-lined canal drain cut into the bedrock from the summit was constructed in the earliest phase.

The walls of the sunken court feature clay murals painted in red, orange black and white, and other sunken courts, platforms and structures were located elsewhere on the summit. A stone platform was constructed next to the court 2 metres high on the summit and this may have been where timber framed temples were constructed. From the summit stone sculpture has been recovered and some of these appear to be prototypes for the Chavin de Huantar epoch soon to follow Kuntar Wasi[304]. These fanged "monster-faced" figures have brow curls similar to those on the Lanzon monolith at Chavin but are reminiscent of the monoliths if the Olmecs in Central America. Interestingly this highland site appears to confirm the repeated importance of related coastal references confirmed a decade ago reflected in crown discovered with imagery "human heads dangling within two braided bands" and a gold image of a crab found at Chongoyape[305]. Only 2 kilometres from Kuntur Wasi, located on a low rise, is the site of Cerro Blanco where the first dates indicate that this centre may have been settled from before Kuntur Wasi, possibly as early as 1730 B.C., at the time of the first introduction of ceramics in Peru. The ceramic designs varied from those of Kuntur Wasi suggesting that this may have been due to ritual necessity or tradition. This site is particularly known for its shaft tomb cut into earlier occupation levels and at the bottom of this shaft the chamber was cut horizontally away from the shaft where the interment was covered with red pigment. The ceramics recovered from this tomb were of a Cupisnique style while others indicate contacts with the Pirua region of Northern Peru nearer the Ecuador border. The discovery of images of the crab fashioned in gold at Chongoyape[306] and other deep sea "monsters" emphasiscs the importance of sea related imagery that probably augments that of evidence for mariners and ocean-going contacts reflected in religious iconography over many generations near the coast of Peru (*5.091*; *5.094/5*).

The burial at Cerro Blanco also yielded a necklace of lapis lazuli, probably traded from Northern Chile, and the pectoral worn also contained this stone, turquoise and Spondylus shell from Ecuador. A Spondylus shell pendant displaying a North Peruvian type face design indicates that Spondylus was imported for the purpose of specialist crafts to suit the belief system of the local populations at these centres. Clearly these materials represented wealth and status and also the prestige of having incorporated such expensive elite products from long distances. This indicates also that trading was continuously undertaken over vast distances of Andean and Coastal North West South America at this time[307].

The Lambayeque and the Zana River Headwaters
In the Initial Period there are eight known sites in the occupation levels in the upper Zana Valley where one is known to have been established in the Pre-ceramic and continued in occupation through to the introduction of pottery and called Macauco. These sites are located generally on the crest of hills where they are terraced and rectangular in structure. The largest tiered mound at El Palmo measuring 180 metres square and 10-12 metres high and is located the intermediate zone between the warm yunga mid-valley drainage and the higher upper valley environmental zone called the quechua. As with the sites of Layzon and Agua Tapada in the Cajamarca Valley, the centres of La Toma and Uscundal face each other in the Zana across a deep escarpment. These Zana sites have suffered from lack of investigation and must remain for future researchers to report on, but a larger ceremonial site in the Lambeyeque Valley north of the Zana is of some interest.

At the headwaters of the Chancay River in the Lambeyeque Valley is located the site called Poro Poro or Udima where five built up areas cover 8 square kilometres. Within the few sections of the site investigated that of a terraced mound in a quadrangular form with an adjacent sunken plaza in front has been revealed. The stonework used to construct the plaza is notable for its high quality cut, dressed and polished dark stone masonry. Massive monoliths, 2.6 metres high, were set beside a broad stone staircase from the plaza to the platform summit. The platform includes a stone subterranean canal system and other massive carved stone blocks with a depression one side have been discovered and are defined as altars. The stonework at Poro Poro is considered to be of a similar exceptional standard as that at Chavin de Huantar, Cerro Sechin,

3.064 : The northwest corner of the South American continent that hosted some of the earliest civilisations of mankind since the last Ice Age. It is particularly notable that these are some of the most inhospitable coasts on any continent but are exactly where the direct ocean currents from the Western Pacific and Asia wash the coast.

    The narrow band of the Andes mountains is penetrable by several mountain passes where the earliest settlements occurred. It is clear from the archaeological record that there was contact between the Pacific Coast settlements and the Amazon rivers. It is likely that it was in fact Pacific mariners who reached across the Andes to the vast riverine highways that penetrate the vastness of the Amazon Basin, the Mato Grosso and through to the Gran Chaco.

    It is notable that Tiahuanaco to the south east of Lake Titicaca is readily accessible from the Pacific Coast but also it near the headwaters of several Amazon and Gran Chaco rivers. Cuzco was also accessible to the Amazon river system and took that route into the forests to escape the invading Conquistadors. The narrowest, and lowest section of the Northern Andes in Southern Ecuador was also long known and gave direct access into the Amazon River via the Maranon but that also derives from the Central Andes along which many of the earliest Pre-Colombian sites were located. The inter-Amazonian forest trade via the riverine system from Ecuador, Colombia and Venezuela into the high culture zones of Coastal Peru and the Andes is evident in the archeological record from at least 2-3000 B.C.

    The Equator is located a few degrees above Manta on the Ecuador Coast and it isin this region where ocean currents from Asia sweep the shore that the first civilisations of South America are found.

Huaricoto and Galgada and the alternating large standing monoliths with rows of smaller stones constituting infill panel walls are reminiscent of the constructional form found at Tiahuanaco. Ceramics retrieved from the summit indicate that these were from the late Initial Period and appear to have originated from other sites, perhaps as imported prestige goods, whereas ceramics used otherwise at the site relate to those of Pacopampa, Kuntar Wasi and Huacaloma[308].
One of the important aspects in the archaeology of Northern Peru is that the development is unexpectedly so unequal, in regarding ceramics especially[309]. This is as yet unexplained, particularly so since this region is not less suitable for settlement than any other but this might indicate that the more ancient routes from the Pacific coast to the Amazon Basin through the mountain passes are preferred. This may also have been due to the fact that these were more readily accessible and defensible, more likely perhaps in a land apparently so notoriously conservative where innovation is concerned.

Eastern Andean Slopes into the Amazon Basin
One of the most interesting elements that must have been of critical importance in historic devel-

opment in the Andean and Coastal cultures of Ecuador, Peru and Northern Chile is the immensity of the Amazon Basin and its effects culturally, climatically and environmentally. For the most part the remarkable uplift of the Andes blocks the ease of access from the Pacific Ocean through to the Amazon except where the mountain chain is a little lower and provides naturally warmer passes and routes avoiding the difficult altitude problems found in the Cordillera of South Peru and all of Bolivia.

The Amazon Basin rain forests have survived into the twentieth century as one of the great, almost impenetrable wildernesses. However, it appears that when the Spaniards first stumbled into the great riverine tributaries that fed the Amazon and then explored along its length they described it as being full of settlements, many so populous that they extended and covered long sections of the river banks. However on the eastern side these forests penetrated the Andes in deep cut valleys and provided a hot and humid lowland environment within the montane system from the eastern side. On the west the long river valleys also penetrated deep into the Andes tending to run east west toward the valleys that were penetrating from the east. In several critical cases there was reasonably easy access through low passes or interconnecting valleys to link the eastern valley system with that of the west. Some of the greatest centres from the earliest times have been erected in just such locations indicating their strategic location to monitor and protect trade routes between the Pacific Coast, Cordillera and Amazon Basin as well as for strategic defence against marauding tribes from the eastern forests.

Few of the archaeological sites that might exist within the lowland eastern mountain valleys and adjacent penetrating Amazon rain forest have been discovered so far and none of these are of any great size. On a tributary, the Manachaki River, to a tributary of the Huallega, itself an eastern tributary of the important Maranon leading to the Amazon River, a site named Cueva Manachaki has been located. This is a rock shelter site that reveals deep deposits of human occupational refuse from the Pre-ceramic into the Initial period revealed in the sequences of pottery deposits. It has been determined that the earliest ceramics are similar to those of Valdivia in Peru and Pandache at Pacopamapa suggesting that there was a rain forest trade route between these ancient centres from at least the 3rd., millennium, B.C.

At another site located, along the Utcubamba River at the foot of the Eastern Andes near the confluence of this river with the Maranon, is called Bagua and this has been studied. Small villages dispersed over the local region appear to have provided shelter for between 5 to 25 families and date from the Initial period after 2000 A.D. Deer meat and the cultivation of maize, manioc and sweet potatoes were evident in the foodstuffs deposits. It is clear that these settlements were actively associated with trading centres in Southern Ecuador, other parts of the Amazon Basin, and the contemporary sites in the highlands of Peru. Pottery, found at the bottom of deposits excavated at Bagua Grande, reflect that of Pandache at Pacopampa and Huacaloma in the Cajarmarca Valley. The sites at Bagua were, it appears, at the crossroads of trading routes that were active through the rain forests of the Eastern Andes and adjacent Western Amazon Basin from at least as early as 2000 B.C.[310]. It is these Peruvian Highland sites from this period that are of interest in the next section of this work.

CHAPTER 4

PRE-CERAMIC TO CERAMIC in
PRE-COLOMBIAN SOUTH AMERICA

The Huallega and the Callejon de Huaylas in the Initial Period

The Callejon de Huaylas is an important central valley system that links the headwaters of the Pacific Coast rivers with those of the Eastern valley slopes flowing to the Amazon River via the Maranon. This section of the central valleys is in effect an extension of the Santa River Valley near by existing to the Pacific Ocean, and accessible to the headwaters of the Mosna River where Chavin de Huantar is located. In the earliest period the Kotosh tradition flourished in this central region, no doubt deliberately sited to take advantage of the critical connections between these eastern and western valleys with the Callejon connecting both. This same region was also critical in the north-south trade routes between Northern Chile, Bolivia, Southern Peru, through to Ecuador far to the north. This strategic location continued to be of importance through from the Pre-ceramic into the early ceramic phases of the Initial Period and for long periods afterwards. With the sudden introduction of ceramics, so long delayed after the 1200 year continuous tradition on the coast of Ecuador to the north, this period in Peruvian history become the Initial Period dating from 1800 B.C. to about 900 B.C.

After the introduction of ceramics the Kotosh Tradition of fire temples did not perish but continued with the localised form of religious expression focused through the separate free-standing chambers as fire-temples. These older sites were maintained through into the Initial Period but evidence for the survival into the late Initial Period, about 1000 B.C., is not yet forthcoming. One of the largest of the later Kotosh Fire-temple tradition sites has been revealed at Shillacoto on a site near the confluence of the Huallega River and its tributary the Higueras - an Initial Period site covering an area about five times the ceremonial centre of Kotosh.

In Kotosh itself, building activity after the late Initial Period appears to reveal evidence for a shift in the belief system since the rebuilding of the fire temple in the late Initial Period was largely destroyed by a new construction. The sacrificial interment of three headless bodies under the late Initial Period floor seems to foreshadow a more difficult millennia to come where warfare, trophy heads, and the retreat to forts would become more apparent. A theme common in the iconography found at Kotosh and the eastern Andean foothill site of Waira-jirca is that of trophy heads and these are naturalistically depicted. A bottle modelled in the form of a trophy head has been recovered from a tomb at Shillacoto where the liquid was poured through the spout modelled as the extended human hairstyle and one actual trophy head was retrieved from a small stone cyst at Kotosh[1]. In the Initial Period, from Shillacoto, a fire-hardened human cranium was utilised as a ritual cup that is closely similar examples found of cut cranium at Chupicuaro in Western Mexico[2] and also found later in Tibet and Tantric North India where they are called kapala. Kapala were depicted frequently in the ancient symbolism preserved in the sculpture of India and Tibet and many actual examples are found in museums throughout the world either as drinking cups or as sections of hand drums or otherwise embellished that derived from earlier Ancient Middle Eastern tradition[3].

The remodelling that had taken place at Kotosh in the Initial Period indicates that the fire-pit had been shifted to the pyramid summit where the rituals being performed could be seen by a wider audience. This would seem to confirm that there had been an intrusion of the earlier coastal ideas into the highland sites. In the last remodelling at Kotosh the asymmetric arrangement of multiple fire-temples on the upper terrace of the pyramid was replaced by a symmetrical arrangement on the ground with an axially placed single fire-pit.

At Huaricoto the longest occupational sequence for any site in the Callejon de Huaylas is found and in the Initial Period this site featured central fire-pits enclosed centrally placed in small chambers located on top of narrow stone terraces. The Huaricoto fire chambers were all of small size and were most likely reserved for a few members of the elite or single families. The size and shape of these chambers suggested that status differentiation occurred at this site. The variations in the chambers built at Huaricoto, and those in other parts of the Callejon de Huaylas and the Upper Huallega at Tablachaca suggest that there were considerable differences developing in fire-worshipping tradition and evident in the social structure even though they clearly shared a similar belief system[4]. Coastal shells and quartz found in the fire-pits at Huaricoto have been considered evidence of rainmaking ceremonies. The imagery depicted on the surviving fragments of pottery depict animals from the Amazon Basin to the east that were important in their belief system, perhaps because they were associated with regular precipitation in the rain forests found there.

At Shillicoto and La Galgada interments in burial chambers and elaborate stone tombs has been excavated and rich burial arrangements have been exposed. One tomb built at Shillacoto was of a rectangular form of stone chamber measuring 3.7 x 3.2 metres and 2 metres high - the internal walls had been plastered and painted white with the lower section red. Gallery tombs were built at La Galgada in the Initial period between the old structures and the new revetments and these included multiple burials of all ages of men, women and children. These tombs display wealth that is of a higher degree and includes bone pins inlaid with turquoise and a drilled amber pendant beside Pacific shells, goods traded from afar, and of particular interest is the discovery of a piece of a meteorite[5].

Exceptional burials displaying unusual wealth and dedication caches are found at this time in the Initial Period at Shillacoto and La Galgada. This seemingly indicates that, since they sometimes occur as exceptional at one site but more common at others, they were wealthy merchants, traders or priests who travelled from the main centres to those further afield. It is likely that they remained there to found new settlements, or were representatives of a small ruling elite group, or were on their way from one centre to a remote destination. The iconography depicted on the many sherds, bones and shell carvings suggests that many items were traded from one centre to another and not a few from far distant regions. One of the more important of these participating sites was Chavin de Huantar from its early beginnings in the Initial Period and also reflected at Garagay. The trading routes embraced sites in the Amazon rain forest where parrot bones and Early Shakimu pottery were found[6]. Such Amazonian products emphasises the location of the sites of Kotosh, La Galgada, Shillacoto, Huaricoto and La Galgada in terms of their interrelationship in a region noted for nodal connections between Amazon rain forest and the Pacific Ocean.

In the Initial Period, camelid herding (mostly llamas) was increasing and, although deer meat was a principal food, that of the llama began to be utilised more frequently although llama-herding had been prominent in the highland areas for millennia before this time. Other camelids, forming a smaller part of the diet, were the vicuna, guanaco and other wild fauna. At Kotosh the guinea pig formed about a fifth of the meat protein consumed and this was a popular food item from earlier times into the present day[7].

Considering the vast number of sites known in this region, and to the north, that remain unexcavated the movement of peoples and religious belief systems cannot be determined with absolute certainty. The difficulties caused by the dense forest cover on the eastern slopes into the Amazon Basin makes such undertakings for known sites very difficult and the prospecting for new sites extremely arduous and expensive. It is likely that more certain information and analyses will be forthcoming in the immediate years ahead but will take decades for a more definitive overview to be formulated.

First Evidence of Metallurgy in South America

The first metallurgy appeared "unexpectedly" in excavations on an Initial Period site called Waywaka in Andahuaylas near modern Ayacucho in the Peruvian Southern Highlands already noted. This site exhibited early Muyu Moqo ceramics and dozens of tiny sheets of hammered thin gold foil have been recovered dating to between 1900-1450 B.C. Interestingly, nine of these tiny foil sheets of gold were placed in the hand of a male burial and another placed in his mouth. This clearly reflects the tradition of placing a gold obolos in the mouth and sometimes at the other openings of the body and in the hands found in China and other parts of Asia suggesting contact between Asia and South America, at least at this time. The goldsmith's tools have also been recovered and it is believed that the gold may have been panned as small nuggets from the bottom of a stream and worked into the tiny foil sheets. It is significant that no other examples of this craft have been found at Initial Period sites and therefore this technology was not adopted by, or spread to other centres and does not appear to have been reintroduced until a millennia later. Also of interest is that copper is usually being the first of the metals to be worked technology also does not appear at all until the late Initial Period about 1000 B.C.[8].

First Traditions in the Bolivian Highlands - Chiripa, Pukara and Tiahuanaco

Chiripa, situated on the shore of Lake Titicaca appears to have been settled since the middle of the second millennium, B.C. Up until that time pastoralism appears to have been the traditional occupation of nomadic herders of the llama for millennia before - and after. From 1400 B.C. the residues of fishing and the hunting of waterfowl and the domestic use of shore-side plants has been discovered and dated and this typifies the food supplies until about 850 B.C. Evident from this date the cultivation of quinoa and the sweet potato also occurs and the totora reeds on the Lake edges appear to have been used to construct their reeds canoes, floats and boats, a practice still preserved into the present day. Textiles were manufactured in the traditional manner and pottery appears to have been produced on the southern banks of the Lake at the site of Chiripa. The pottery featured incised designs of felines, animal heads and human faces and ceramic trumpets were first produced in the Andes at that time where vegetable matter was used as temper common to other pottery traditions[9].

The first mound at Chiripa was constructed about 1000 B.C., being stone-faced with a sunken court on the summit surrounded by small buildings and this site was later remodelled followed by abandonment on several occasions. A second period of remodelling between 600 and 100 B.C. featured carved stone plaques reflecting animal, serpent and human motifs relating more directly to the nearby Tiahuanaco tradition. The overall dimension of this main mound was about 55 metres square and 6 metres high with a sunken court measuring 23 metres square and 1.5 metres deep. A large monolith, probably carved, was centrally located in the court, and was possibly a form of Intihuatana or Sun obelisk. There were 16 buildings constructed symmetrically around the summit, three on each of the four sides, built away from the edge of the sunken court and one splayed at 45° at each of the corners, forming a type of octagon. It is believed that the principle of inset doorways fitted into a framed architrave opening characteristic of Tiahuanaco was initiated in the first examples at Chiripa and this architectural feature survived into the Inca Empire (*5.050*). The illustrations show however, that this doorway type was identical to the oldest known portals in the early Buddhist carvings, some dating back to 300 B.C. and into early Hindu cave and temple architecture (*5.048/9*). The stone carving and iconography at Chiripa appears to relate to that of the so-called Yaya-Mama Religious traditions in the Lake Titicaca Basin dating to about 500 B.C. and this in turn appears to have spawned that of Tiahuanaco.

The pottery traditions of Chiripa and Qaluyu are similar to those found at Wankarani beside Lake Poopo in Southern Bolivia, in the Moqegua Valley, and in the Azapa Drainage at Faldsas de Moro in Southern Peru. These two latter are probably as a result of transfer along the trade routes to the Pacific Coast and the former to contacts between Northern Chile and Argentina. At an intermediate level between the ocean and altiplano in Bolivia is a site called Huaricani dating from the first millennium B.C. Here irrigation channels and associated dwellings are found along with seated burials in stone-lined cylindrical pits in cemeteries near the settlements. This form of burial was characteristic of the chullpas in Lake Titicaca region confirming contact with the highlands and migration from there to the warmer regions nearer the Pacific shore[10].

The Chinchorros in North Chile were of interest earlier in this work and their culture appears precocious and unexplainable in terms of other developments in South America being so apparently so isolated from the other cultural "hot spots" developed far to the north on the Peruvian coast and Ecuador. As the North expanded those influences no doubt were transferred to the south and from the altiplano of Bolivia the developments at Chiripa appear to have influenced the long established Chinchoros. By 1200 B.C., pottery, textiles and irrigation appear to have been introduced along with cotton, squash and gourd cultivation from the North West Peruvian coastal traditions[11]. Many of the influences found among the Mapuche on the coast of Central Chile and other Southern South Americans reflect aspects and terms clearly derived from the Polynesians, including the Maoris of New Zealand, noted earlier, and this may have been a landfall from the Lapita period. The Morioris in New Zealand appear to reflect influences from before the Lapita expansion into Melanesia and Polynesia from Asia. As will be seen by the ocean currents of the Pacific the prevailing winds and sea currents deliver any mariner from Polynesia, and that particular route from Asia, directly onto the coast of South America in Central and North Chile. It would appear therefore that one of the ancient land trade routes would have extended from what is now Arica, the nearest point to the Bolivian highlands and Lake Titicaca, into the Altiplano and across the Andes to the Gran Chaco or the Amazon Basin tributaries to the North. Equally other trade routes would have long been established from Arica north east along the coast of Peru to Ecuador running parallel to trade routes in the same direction from Lake Titicaca through the Andes to Ecuador and Colombia.

The initial influences feeding in over long periods traditionally maintained in later centuries, and for millennia, are therefore accountable as influences brought by mariners or migrants across the Pacific and also confirm the reason why Polynesian traditions such as the "umu" or earth oven are found in Chile and not further north. Once the Lake Titicaca region had been settled and expanded from the ceremonial centres it was natural for them to re-establish contact with their sea origins, if they had become dissociated at all, becoming racially mixed with the indigenous peoples as they entered new regions.

The Truncated City State that was Pucara

The Yaya-Mama tradition centred near Lake Titcaca was more identifiable from about 400 B.C. and this culture appears to have been an early influence on both the rising initial period at Tiahuanaco as well as the Pucara (Pukara) located at opposite ends of the lakeside. The site of Pucara is known for its own style and is noted particularly for its carved stone sculptures and ceramic designs[12]. Examples of the sculptural art in the Pucaran style are found in the valley of Cuzco but too few survive to indicate political expansion from their Lake Titicaca highland base. The Pucaran influence is found also to the west towards the coast at Azapa and in the Moquegua valley[13]. Felines and human heads were often a subject for decoration in relief or on ceramics generally and the ceramic trumpets were also a feature of the potter's art. Human trophy heads were also an important iconographic part of the Pucara tradition and appear on textiles and feature in the low relief carvings from this site. The site is perhaps best known, however, for its civic architecture and featured large terraces constructed on hillsides faced with rock slabs and boulders and that included one on the summit of the largest of these, a sunken court reminiscent of Chiripa[14]. Pucara was a site spread over several kilometres and included agricultural development including ridged fields and small lakes or reservoirs where water for the irrigation was drawn into the water channels necessary for agriculture.

The carved stone traditions of the Yaya-Mama sites near Lake Titicaca appear to have given rise not only to Pucara but also to its other probably related site of Tiahuanaco at the opposite end of the Lake. Although neither centre appears in the first several hundred years of their existence to be dominant over the other it was not evident until about 100 B.C. that Pucara came to an end while Tiahuanco continued to expand. The first two phases at Tiahuanaco were dated from about 400 B.C. and lasted until about 2-100 B.C. marking two critical dates in South American history. The middle of the first millennium B.C. is a time when radical new influences make their sudden appearance in the Andean and coastal cultures. These innovative influences are likely to have been as a result of importation from abroad since the natural evolution and development processes associated with the introduction of new techniques and technologies are missing in the archaeological record. The great site of Tiahuanaco is reserved for later consideration in archaeology, myths and legends in this work.

Paracas and the South Central Coast of Peru

Paracas, located on a small peninsula 20 km south of Pisco, is an ancient funerary and ceremonial centre on the South Coast of Peru, and about 255 km south of modern-day Lima. It is more particularly known for its textiles retrieved from the large number of tombs in cemeteries but little of the ceremonial centre is known. The site of Paracas was perhaps only connected with the mortuary rites of this very sacred place since the Y-post constructions associated with it that may have given clues of temple or mortuary structures have long disappeared except for a few still left standing.

The Paracas period is divided into two reflecting the dates of the two cemetery sites, the first associated with Paracas Cavernas dating from 500-300 B.C., and the Paracas Necropolis dating from 300 B.C. to 100 A.D. Paracas Cavernas is so-called because this period featured a cemetery of bottle tombs - a circular bottle-shaped tomb being a structure that was dug deep into the ground, often to a depth of 6 metres, with the neck of the "bottle" extended to the surface at ground level to allow access. The inhumations appear to have been family groups or clan related and have provided archaeology with a large number of textile shrouds and art that are, in design, characteristic of the period. These interments were accompanied by grave goods including many representing high quality products of the potter's art. Among these were clay musical instruments and ceramics as well decorated gourds.

The Paracas Cavernas styles appear to reflect those of Pucara and Tiahuanaco and the iconography also appears to be reflected more broadly in South Coastal Peru at Pisco, Ica and Nazca. At Paracas, after 200 B.C., the influences of Tiahuanaco were apparent in continuing to be felt in this same region and apparent also at the later Paracas Cavernas cemetery dating from that period while Pucara ceased to be influential. The change of cultural influences appears reflected also in the tomb type where the Paracas Cavernas was a bottle-tomb while that of Paracas Necropolis was a masonry crypt. Although there are few monuments surviving from the period the Paracas Cavernas people were a sophisticated, advanced culture whose burial shrouds provide archaeology with some of the finest textiles ever recovered from an early civilisation. These shrouded mummy bundles, wrapped in their finest textiles, were laid to rest in their tombs seated in baskets - a form of burial known also in the Old World of Asia.

4.001 : Trephinned (or trepanned) skulls frequently discovered on the Southern Coast of Peru. Second half of the first millennium, B.C.

4.002 : Trepanned skull characteristic of many skulls found in the early coastal cultures of Southern Peru. Southern Peru, Eearly first millennium, A.D.

4.004 : Extreme example of deformed skull similar to those still being deformed in Melanesia into the twentieth century. Paracas Peninsula, Southern Coastal Peru, Second half of the first millennium, B.C.

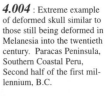

4.003 : Incised "fish" symbol inscribed on brow of skull similar to the same technique in Central America and Indonesia. Easter Island, Eastern Polynesia, Pre-18th., century, A.D.

4.005 + 4.006 : Frontal view and profile of a Kwakiutl woman with cranial deformation. North West Coast of North America, Late 19th., century, A.D.

4.007 : Adult with cranial deformation extending the forehead upward soon after birth to achieve this most desired final form. Almus, New Ireland, New Guinea, Melanesia, Early 20th., century, A.D.

4.008 : Trepanned skull, with trephinning instruments, found on coastal Peru. Trepanation is found also in Melanesia. Paracas Peninsula, Southern Coastal Peru, Second half of the first millennium B.C.

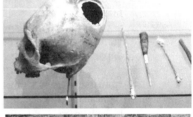

Among the Maori basket burial was traditional among the Arawa tribe[15], perhaps derived from Peru, and these people may be the Arawa referred to in the Solomon Islands traditions. In Ambryn, an island in the New Hebrides group, bones were wrapped in a basket as a secondary burial[16] and in New Guinea skulls were wrapped in a basket-work bundle[17].

It may have been that some of these people were in fact based elsewhere and utilised this peninsula because of its ancestral associations with the seashore and mariner ancestors. The Paracas Necropolis people also exhibited remarkable examples of trepanation where the skull is opened and an operation performed through the hole into the brain of the patient[18]. Closely similar traditions are noted also in the New Hebrides, and in parts of Polynesia, where the highly risky surgical intrusion of trepanation, or trephining, was also known and where many examples of cranial deformation, another widely maintained custom in South America was practised. Healing around these openings has shown that many survived such drastic surgery. The Asian and West Pacific associations with the cemeteries may be apparent from both periods on the coast of Peru since the Humboldt or Peruvian Current sweeps directly from the southern route from South and South East Asia, Melanesia and Polynesia onto the coast of Northern Chile and Peru (*1.007*). This suggests that the significance of the peninsula was that it was a point of departure for the soul to return the land of the ancestors. Death and mortuary ceremonies were usually undertaken by

4.009 : Extreme cranial deformation was a characteristic of the Mayan civilisation. Guatemala, 600-900 A.D.

4.010 : Adult with cranial deformation extending the forehead upward soon after birth to achieve this most desired final form. Murien Tribe, New Ireland, New Guinea, Melanesia, Early 20th., century, A.D.

4.012 : Amazonian mother with her baby exhibiting the headboard bindings to deform the skull to a desired altered shape. Chama, Brazil, Early 20th., century, A.D.

4.011 : Mother and her child with a bandage binding to achieve the profile so admired in past centuries corresponding to traditions in Central America and Peru. Moewe Haven, New Guinea, Melanesia, Early 20th., century, A.D.

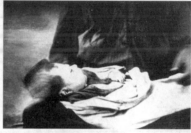

4.013 : The deformed skull of an Amazonian child after the deformation headboards had been removed. Chama, Brazil, Early 20th., century, A.D.

the priest at the traditional ritual and included the last reminder to the soul of the hazards likely to be met on the way during this journey to that land. Similar rituals occurred and were recorded of the Melanesians into the 20th., century. The Paracas people appear to have, believed, as so many did, that the soul cast off from a special location on a specific course to the land of the ancestors. The myths of culture-heroes such as Viracocha leaving the coast for the west tends to confirm this belief where those of a mariner origin, with roots in South or South East Asia, departed on their last journey to these ancestral lands across the sea to the west.

Along with textiles the ceramics that form a such feature of the South Coast cultures from the late first millennium B.C. appear to reflect in this earlier period contemporary with Paracas a sequence divided into a series of phases and denoted as Ocucaje[19]. This sequence reflects aspects of influence clearly derived from Chavin de Huantar in the Central Highlands of Peru. This suggests that the great highland cultures of Pucara, Tiahuanaco, and Chavin all converged upon this region of coast confirming that this Pacific seashore had some special significance and associations in Andean beliefs and traditions with the Pacific Ocean.

Chavin de Huantar and the Upland Tradition in the Central Peruvian Highlands

It is now believed that the founding of Chavin de Huantar, located in the Mosna River valley, at its confluence with its tributary the Huachesa River in the foothills of Cerro Blanco in the eastern slopes of the Andes, was instituted in the late Initial Period about 900 A.D. The original large temple varies from the Kotosh tradition in many ways and seems largely independent of it in its influences and orientation. In the earliest layout these variations occur in the planning, the form of masonry construction and in the architectural details, suggesting influences from another tradition merging with those of coastal Peru. Although not the largest centre it is believed by some archaeologists to have rivalled that of Pacopampa and Kuntar Wasi in the northern highlands, or Garagay and Huaca de los Reyes on the Peruvian Coast[20].

The location is of great importance since the ceremonial site lies about 6 days walk down to the Mosna River Valley where it merges with the Huari River to form the Pukcha before it reaches the Maranon River and onward to the Ceja de Selva region, more recognisably an Amazonian forest environment. In the opposite direction, to the west. past the headwaters of the Mosna and across the Cerro Blanco into the Callejon de Huaylas, there is another six days walk over the Cerro Negras into the coastal valley of the Casma emerging at Cerro Sechin near the

Pacific Coast. This emphasises what must have been seen, from more ancient times, a critical route and strategic location between the Pacific Coast and the Amazon River.

It was believed by the local Indians then living around the ruins of Chavin de Huantar after the Spanish Conquest that this complex was built by a race of giants and that it was dedicated to the god Huari[21]. In 1657 A.D. a Spanish Church representative stumbled on a priest in one of the passageways in the underground chambers who was burning black maize kernels and had masticated coca leaves performing rituals probably over 2000 years old. In these rituals the smoke from the brazier was believed to be an offering to Huari and to conduct the prayer of the priest to the deity and while this was being done a black spider that had been placed on the rim of the brazier, crawling around it, and it was said to divine for the priests the predictions for those who consulted it is an oracle[22]. The unique carvings and iconography that had inspired the people, but a century after the Conquest was feared by the them, still preserved in the temple complex, have long been a mystery since their origin from earlier precedents have not been found despite extensive searches in the region.

The valley of the Mosna is suited to a mixed farming economy and camelid herding and sufficient rainfall along with the snowmelt from the surrounding Cordillera ensures agricultural surpluses sufficient to support the great ceremonial centre. The valley environment, although good, is not exceptional compared to some of the adjacent valleys but it is the access to both the Pacific Ocean and the Amazon Basin that appears to have been the reason for the location of the major centre in this valley. This section of the Andean Cordillera known as Cerro Blanco extends as a spine along the centre of Peru with a restricted number of accessible passes across the mountains to the eastern foothills and the Amazon. Only ten occur along the 180 kilometre stretch in Central Peru below the snow line and therefore Chavin de Huantar, at the junction of two of these, is an important and obvious location for accessibility at these lowest of the passes[23].

The junction of two rivers was, and is still perceived by the Quechua Indians as the harmonious meeting place of two opposing forces and called tinkuy (Tay Pi)[24]. This in fact is also a fundamental of Ancient Vedic thought where the junction of the Jumna and Ganges Rivers in North India is considered one of the most sacred places in the world and the location of one of the holiest cities in Hinduism - Allahabad. This expression of tinkuy has its parallels in Tiahuanaco and will be of interest in later chapters.

The earliest temple complex at Chavin appears to have small scale residential accommodation built in the vicinity of the ceremonial complex and the maximum number of residential buildings at capacity housed about 500 people. It may have been that the local agricultural work force and the several known villages and settlements supported the religious complex and maintained the centre with a resident group of priests and hierarchic kurakas, or clan chiefs, located in this accommodation. Inter-communication at Chavin with other sites and long-distance trading is evident with the retrieval of the Spondylus shell, revered from the earliest pre-ceramic period up until the Spanish Conquest In Peru.

A section of the monumental building phase at Chavin de Huantar commenced about 800 B.C. but cultural transfer from the coastal sites only becomes evident about 400 B.C.[25]. This large and particularly important ceremonial site was one of the most influential in its time and its iconography and cultural advances spread widely. The shrine itself appears to have developed as a pilgrimage centre attracting devotees from throughout the Andean highlands, valleys and Peruvian coastal centres. This extension of Chavin influence appears on the South Coast where Chavin textiles have been found in a cache at Karwa on the Paracas Peninsula[26] and this may have been one of a number of satellites developed from Chavin itself. The term Karwa is an interesting one since it is the more recent name remembered from a pervious age and has been spelt Cahua but also Carawa and Corowa and illustrates a problem in determining the correct

4.014 : The great Lanzon at Chavin de Huantar representing a deity associated with the cardinal points. The fanged monster mask and brow curls are characteristic of Asian traditions. Central Highlands, Peru, 9-800 B.C.

4.015 : Full height depiction of the Lanzon in the Old Temple. Chavin de Huantar, Central Highland Peru, 9-800 B.C.

names remembered over long periods of time for a particular and their deviation from the original, in this case unknown[27]. The textiles of Chavin, however, appear to have been painted according to a strict canon[28] and this was also the case from the first millennium B.C. when canons were drawn up for architecture and all religious iconography in India and similar structures were applied also in contemporary China. These were probably inherited from the earlier Ancient Middle Eastern Cultures but in India they are still used to this day.

Chavin de Huantar Old Temple from 800 B.C.

The Old Temple, dating from this earlier Initial Period, reflected the U-shape ground plan characteristic of the Coastal Peruvian centres from the Pre-ceramic and Post-ceramic periods. This tends to confirm that this great ceremonial centre may have been initiated by coastal intrusions as a result of intercommunication by trade from the Pacific Coast through the interconnecting valleys to the Amazon Basin. The masonry structure is constructed with alternating rows of deep and shallow coursed stone blocks of limestone, sandstone and granite and slabs of fieldstone placed horizontally to reinforce the clay mortar used in the walls. Inserted into these walls, as carved stone tenons, were fanged masked deities or supernaturals (*4.016*). These were possibly to indicate the purpose of the structure or to impress and subdue the pilgrims.

Characteristic also of the coastal centres was the fact that one wing of the U-shape plan was larger than the other and, as at Chavin, the north was a little larger than that of the south. The defined approaches led the visitors or devotees to the towering west, north and south faces in turn before entering the ceremonial section of the site facing east and this may have been to impress them, and induce awe with the massiveness of the construction since the walls of the wings rise from 11 metres to 16 metres high[29]. The ceremonial precinct between the wings of the U-shaped structure faces the rising Sun and the Mosna River. It is believed that the two wings with the sunken court between them is a metaphor of the dual philosophy of opposing forces[30] to be found preserved into modern times among the Quechua and Aymara. This aspect of highland religious and philosophical constructs was recorded by some of the Spanish chroniclers soon after the Conquest and this will be of more importance in later chapters.

The wings have a circular sunken court between them, displaying some of the finest stone relief carving in Ancient South America, and this possibly reflects aspects from earlier highland traditions. The inclusion of a large fossilised gastropod (mollusc) in the floor of the sunken court was clearly of some significance since fossils of this type do not occur in this region and had to be imported[31] - this may indicate a coastal or a mariner origin. One of the most pristine of the carved relief panels lining the circular court depicts a supernatural or mythical fanged figure holding a San Pedro cactus as a staff[32] and this emphasises the importance of hallucinogens in the religious, probably shamanistic ceremonies focused in the court and in its many chamber and tunnels. It has been noted in an earlier work by the present author that the Hikuli or Peyote cactus in Mexico was probably sought

4.016 : Demon mask probably representing a deified ancestor. The head is also considered to represent the shamanistic state attained after taking hallucinogenic snuffs. Chavin de Huantar, Central Highland Peru, Early-first millenium, B.C.

4.017 : Masked stone carved head typical of many sculptures found at the pilgrimage site of Chavin de Huantar. Chavin de Huantar, Central Peru, 800-400 B.C.

4.018 : Stone-lined air vent-holes originally inside the primary mound at Chavin de Huantar. Elaborate water conduits and underground tunnels were constructed throughout the mound and unique in South America. Chavin de Huantar, Peru, 800-400 B.C.

4.019 : Portrait heads reflecting probable different racial origins, the right hand one of La Tolita style. The left-hand portrait shows the cheek bulges characteristic of coca quids used by Andean peoples to alleviate fatigue but probable here taken by long distance mariners to obviate hunger and thirst. Tumaco culture, Popoyan, Southern Colombia, 400 B.C. - 500 A.D.

4.020 : Masked figure reminiscent of similar depictions at Chavin de Huantar in the Central Peru. Coastal Guatemala, 200-700, A.D.

4.021 : Masked head showing mucus discharges from the nose characteristic of snuff reaction when used by shamans in hallucinogenically induced trances. Chavin de Huantar, Central Peru, 800-400 B.C.

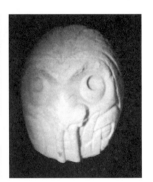

out by mariners, and that coca was probably used in links between Polynesia and South America to assuage hunger and thirst on long sea voyages[33].

The walls of the wings rise from 11 metres to 16 metres high[34] and the perambulations imposed by the processional approach appears to be a possible origin of, or related to those of the later Nazcans on the Nazca Plains that might have developed through the Chavin settlements and influence at Karwa. The ceremonial precinct between the arms faces the rising Sun and the Mosna River. This belief that the two wings with the sunken court between them is a metaphor of the dual philosophy of opposing forces[35] and found into modern times among the Quechua and Aymara is also indicated in Tiahuanaco and retained through into the Inca Dynasty two millennia later. This aspect of highland religious and philosophical constructs was recorded by some of the Spanish chroniclers soon after the Conquest and this will be of more importance in later chapters. Ritual religious processions around sacred precincts was, and still is part of traditional ceremonials in the temple precincts in Buddhist and Hindu India and Asia.

The Lanzon Monolith of Chavin de Huantar

Located on the east-west axis of the Old Temple site through the centre of the sunken court and the central mound the Lanzon is a large stone monolith 4.53 metres high and incised with low relief carvings depicting a fanged supernatural deity (*4.014/5*) located in an underground passage in the central mound. The incised relief figure displays the right hand raised while the left is rest-

4.023: Incised piece of obsidian showing a masked Mayan priest smoking a cigar emitting the dual smoke trails characteristic of mystical symbolism throughout Central and South America. Tepeu Culture, Guatemala, Late Classic.

4.022 : Lime was chewed with coca to facilitate the effects but lime gourds and spoons were also found across the Pacific particularly noted in Melanesia. This Waga Waga tribe lime gourd was called a faonga. New Guinea, Late 19th., century, A.D.

4.024 : Nose labrets that appear to simulate the nasal associations of hallucinogenic snuffs. Amnanga, Marind-anim, New Guinea, Early 20th., century, A.D.

4.025 : Nose labrets that appear to simulate the nasal associations of hallucinogenic snuffs. Amnanga, Marind-anim, New Guinea Highlands, Early 20th., century, A.D.

4.026 : A priest or chief with a lime spatula and pot similar to those used in South America. Note the hornbill beak headdress and braided hair similar in principle to those in Colombia. New Guinea, Melanesia, Early 20th., century, A.D.

ing normally at the side. The general belief is that this figure represents the Axis Mundi or World Axis and this appears to be supported by the fact that the top of the monolith penetrates the floor above and through which a libation or anointing process was ritually performed. The monolith stands in a cruciform gallery and this might also reflect the cardinal directions of the four compass points[36].

Excavations of the tunnels within the Old Temple reveal 233 human bones and it is believed that they included parts from males, females and children. The fact that they were in fragments and calcined suggests that ritual cannibalism was practised at this centre particularly as human bones are not found in the refuse deposits outside the building. Pottery found in one particular gallery, the Gallery of the Offerings, is unique and not found elsewhere in other galleries or among the other ceramics of the site indicating that they were manufactured exclusively for special rituals associated only with that gallery and with proscribed designs. In the other sections of the ceremonial site the ceramics found within the sacred precincts are not found in the surrounding settlement but have been imported from other regions suggesting special associations with other locations, these being perhaps those from where the priests were drawn. If this was the case it is probable that the priests and hierarchy of Chavin de Huantar were alien to the local peoples who were retained only as the servants of the temple and provided an underclass to support the temple. This in fact followed a similar model in India where the Aryan Hindus set up religious centres among the Dravidian or Aboriginal people in India by from 3,000 years ago. The Aryan Brahmanic and later Hindu priests and devotees allowed only their own few immigrant people and priests into the temples. However, only after an extended period of time were the local peoples (Sudras) Hinduised but even then they were allowed only to approach the temple to within a prescribed distance and no further[37]. Religious paraphernalia and ritual objects were acceptable only from the approved castes of Aryan craftsmen and no profane object was allowed to pollute the temple of the higher status Aryan Hindus and these strictures may well have their reflection at Chavin.

The remarkable drainage and ventilation system have been of note since the first discovery of the site in modern times over two generations ago. The region in which Chavin de Huantar is located is subject to high rainfall in some seasons and the internal conduit system is highly efficient in draining the excess water away form the centre. Recent studies of this drainage system indicate that the engineers who were responsible for the site displayed "a sophisticated empirical knowledge of hydraulic engineering as well as constructional skills"[38]. Through demonstration the noise created by the flow of the water from the platform summit through the internal channels appears to have been deliberately augmented. This is now believed to be associated with rain-making rituals and the imitation of the belief of a water cycle flowing from the top of the mountains (the summit of the main mound at Chavin) through internal channels representing streams and rivers into the river that flows ultimately to the ocean[39] and then return again under the land to the mountain. At Tiahuanaco a similar system appears to have been incorporated into some of the main structures and such beliefs were retained into post Conquest times.

It is now conjectured that the internal galleries and chambers may have been reserved for the closeting of acolytes training for the priesthood on the Kogi model found anciently and through into the present day in Northern Colombia. Among the Kogi selected youths who displayed aptitude were confined to inner sanctuaries in the day and allowed out only in the night. This was believed to develop their psychic and spiritual functions and the enforced training usually lasted for some years. Similar confinement systems for youths are found in Melanesia and probably derive from that known in Ancient India and Iran. Confinement of youths in this way may have originally related to ceremonials and shamanism associated with the Moon as the supreme deity and therefore night orientated.

In the most ancient belief systems of the Ancient Middle East and India the Moon god was held supreme and the associated lunar calendar was that followed in agriculture and civic ceremonies - the solar calendar only becoming more prominent at the end of the first millennium B.C. The training of selected youths for the priesthood in India were, and still arc also confined in monasteries or ashrams but it is not certain that this confinement originally was correspondingly directed to excluding day release in favour of the night as in the Kogi system. It is likely also that the exclusion of the common people and the insistence of a twenty-day fast before entering the sacred precinct to consult the oracle at Pachacamac[40] was probably an imitation of similar strictures imposed at Chavin de Huantar. It should be noted that this was the case originally also in India and the Middle East where fasting rituals were well-known and widely practised.

Chavin Design Style and Sculpture in the Central Highland Tradition

The large majority of sculptures found at Chavin de Huantar were carved from white granite or black limestone while the sandstone and quartzite found locally were less frequently used suggesting these stone had special associations. The most important sculptures appear to have been carved from granite, the hardest stone, including the Lanzon, suggesting that its durability was considered an important element of the sculptures and their meaning. The Lanzon itself appears to relate to the first major building of the Old Temple, or Phase A while the Tello Obelisk appears to relate to Phase C[41]. The quarrying and moving of these large blocks, up to two tons in weight must have been a major undertaking since there were no draught animals in South America that were suitable for the task, the llama being a light packed animal and the terrain rugged. The nearest quarries were not less than 15 km away and this must have tested the resolve of the priests'

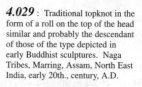

4.028 : Topknot of a type found in the earliest figurative carvings of the Buddhists from the late first millennium B.C. Late Chavin, Templadera, Jequetepeque Valley, North Cast Peru, 700-400 B.C.

4.029 : Traditional topknot in the form of a roll on the top of the head similar and probably the descendant of those of the type depicted in early Buddhist sculptures. Naga Tribes, Marring, Assam, North East India, early 20th., century, A.D.

4.030 : Topknot of the type found in early Buddhist India common in Ancient China but here displayed by a "northern barbarian". Han Dynasty, 200 B.C. - 200 A.D.

4.027 : Coiled head-cloth or turban of the type found anciently in Asia but also found among the Ancient Peruvians in South America. Note also the addorsed armorial animals in the bottom register found in the Andes. Katra, Mathura, c1st., century, A.D.

and clan leaders' organizational abilities to succeed in their projects. Their skill must have been of the highest order reflecting an imperative to create these centres in honour of strongly held beliefs and determined faith in their god. The carving pecking and polishing lavished upon these sculptures, after carving and shaping of the quarried stone, was prodigious and not surpassed in the cultures of South America[42]. This remarkable skill in carving was also extended to their planning and masonry skills in general and is a striking feature that the present day viewer cannot fail to appreciate even in the ruined form that has survived for nearly 3000 years. This was achieved without any metal tools and was such a prodigious feat that has added to its mystique and led to the question as to whether the ruling priest and clan leaders were actually from the Andes, or even from South America at all. The hairstyle and the particular turban depicted among the Chavin priests[43] is of particular interest and the few surviving portrait depictions in contemporary Cupisnique (*4.028*) in the lower valley of the Jequetepeque, show examples identical to those in the earliest sculptures of the Buddhists in Northern India in the 4th.,-1st., centuries B.C. (*4.027*) and preserved in those of the simpler from worn by Sikh boys to this day. The fine stonework continued into the relief carving panels of Chavin depicts headhunting, possibly originating in the Amazon Basin tribes, identical to similar traditions among the some of the peoples of Indonesia and the Nagas of Assam. A more detached study of the fine carvings and the iconography illustrated at Chavin is planned as a section in a projected future work and is too lengthy a subject to be considered here but only a few general references can be included here.

The stylised carvings of birds and animals is striking since these depictions emphasises their mysterious qualities and a particular repeated element is their "agnathic" form (from the Greek, gnathos), that is shown minus the jaw[44]. Throughout the Polynesian[45] and Melanesian Islands the removal of the jaw was part of the ritual of headhunting[46]. This custom appears traceable to very early references in Ancient South and East Asia[47] and India relating, in the earliest texts, to the tongue, jaws and teeth of a mythical serpent associated in their imagery to the cardinal points[48]. The interlocking, protruding canines is a characteristic of Chavin art and virtually the identical motif is found in more recent centuries preserved in Indonesia but earlier in India and other parts of South East Asia and reflected widely in the iconography beyond Chavin in South America. Attention to references to the parallels in Kogi thought and the underlying meanings of Chavin symbolism as visual metaphors has been made by recent archaeologists[49]. It will be shown in other chapters of this work relating to the myths and legends of the Kogi and the Desnana Tukano in Colombia that many aspects relate to those in Melanesia and Aboriginal Australia as well as South and South East Asia.

The crested eagle, probably the harpy eagle in the Amazon forests, other raptorials including the condor, and felines are prominent in the iconography of Chavin and one of the most prominent features in the design of these symbolic representations is that they are still coherent and meaningful whether viewed upright or turned in any of the other ways, 90 degrees left or right, or upside down. In fact some of the sculptures can only be considered the right way up from the position in which they were found and this is most famously exemplified by the Raimondi stone where its design upside down appears to have been as important and coherent as when considered upright (*4.126/7*). This shows an unparalleled sophistication in mental and religious acuity as in the intellectual dexterity of the designers who created and codified such depictions reflected through repetitive designs and a bilateral symmetry of certain motifs across a vertical axis. The feline imagery of the Lanzon, from the first phase of the Old Temple dating to 900-800 A.D. is considered to be based on the human form since it displays human hands with five fingers, including the thumb, and human feet, with the projecting fangs from the mouth and clenched teeth characteristic of many Ancient Peruvian depictions and found also in the Pacific Islands through to South East Asia and India already noted. An early 20th., century Peruvian archaeologist, Julio Tello, believed that the Lanzon represented the deity Wira-Kocha, who will be of more interest in later chapters. This sculpture known as the Lanzon, at Chavin, will be of more interest in a future, projected publication.

The Tello Obelisk - Depictions of the Supernatural Caiman of Chavin
Although apparently carved in a later phase of the Chavin Temple period the iconography and style of the Tello Obelisk (*4.031*) appears to indicate that the Lanzon and this monolith was reflective of an unchanged religious tradition regardless of the time difference between their respective carvings. The Tello Obelisk illustrates an iconography expressed through symbolism and the associations that reflects the mystical projection of the caiman, another aspect of Amazonian based imagery at Chavin. The prominent depictions of Amazonian birds and animals in Chavin iconography and the fact that this centre was located in one of the few convenient lower level passes between the Pacific coast, the highlands, and the eastern rain forests suggests that the eastern influences must have been of great importance to the priests of Chavin. This also indicates that there were overriding influences from the Amazon Basin of more importance than those of the long established iconography of the coast and that from the easterly direction the centre may have been founded, at least in part, by peoples or priests who came, or were influenced from that direction.

Myths associated with the giant caiman as the creator, who introduced food plants to the people, have been noted by some researchers in other parts of South America and considered apposite to Chavin de Hauntar[50]. The Tello Obelisk caiman is depicted carrying the food plants associated with warm tropical climes such as manioc, achira, the gourd, hot peppers and perhaps peanuts. This suggests the veracity of the myths and may therefore, in principle, be applied to Chavin, where these food plants were cultivated at a height of 3,150 metres above sea level outside of their natural environment[51]. Other archaeologists and historians have seen the close similarities of the Chavin Obelisk caiman with that of the reptilian deity Itzamna indicating that they considered it the same deity deriving from the same origin[52]. This early Mayan deity is frequently depicted in Mayan iconography and is especially prominent on stelae at Izapa on the Pacific Coast of Southern Mexico and shown elsewhere to have derived from the iconography of India[53]. Others have seen that the themes and deities of Izapa and Chavin are probably from an identical source but reflect the style of the local tradition[54] with those of the intermediate geographic locality of San Agustin in Southern Colombia participating in the same iconographic tradition[55]. These iconographical depictions parallel similar myth references in South East Asia and India where the Ganges crocodile is known as makara and whose imagery is identically found in

Central America among the Maya[56].

The Nazcan people on the southern coastal plains of Peru were seen as intimately connected with the later phases of Chavin and who perhaps provided their temple priests and rulers with privileged access to the Pacific Ocean. Although the Nazcans were the inheritors of some of the Chavin iconography the purity and strength of the Andean deities exhibiting the powerful numinosity of the dark Amazonian animal deities appears to have been diluted and the feline is seen as bearer of food-plants rather than the caiman. One author notes that the Nazcan iconography depicting their deities derived from the clarity and uncompromising iconography of the Chavin, showed that the greater desire for naturalism was "a growing preference for depicting the real world (that) pulled the Chavin gods from their throne, (and that) robbed them of their magic" and that this "often endowed them with a mundane, non-supernatural character"[57]. This suggests a loss of connection, or reduced contact with the Amazon Basin as the origin and revitalising force behind Chavin iconography.

Interestingly, however, if the hot climes of the Amazonian forest did supply the imagery and food plants, that the ceramics developed at the Old Temple site settlements called Urabarriu appeared little influenced from that easterly direction. The pottery found in the same period in the forested Amazon foothills of the Andes contemporary with this period, called late Tutishcainyo[58], had little in common with Chavin while this latter showed shared features with other highland sites and the Pacific Coast of Peru. Archaeologists who have considered this highly sophisticated pottery found at Tutishcainyo to be linked to the traditions of the lower Orinoco in Venezuela and arrived in the Ucayali River region of Peru through the riverine highways linked to the Amazon[59]. This stylistic tradition seemed to reserve an important place for ritual cups associated with chichi drinking that had common influences with Kotosh and Pacopampa. This suggests again that the priesthood at Chavin may have been intruders who set up their ceremonial site, and temple ceramic tradition and associated iconography, meaningful for them amongst the alien valley people who reflected the long held traditions of the other Andean Indians. These local Indians reflected subsistence agriculture going back a 1000 years before the construction of the Old Temple at Chavin and clearly reflects the long-established Andean traditions that continued in day to day life regardless of the presence or otherwise of temples near to, or far from them.

The iconography introduced from the earliest phases influenced from the Amazon Basin, seems to be at loggerheads with the fundamental ground plan of the Old Temple reflecting the U-shape of the Coastal Peruvian ceremonial centres and the sunken circular court found on the coast but also in parts of the highlands. This merging of traditions at Chavin may be further evidence of mariners travelling from the Pacific Coast to the Amazon basin across the land bridges connecting the headwaters beside other influences noted from Amazonian Venezuela. These mariners appeared to have undertaken for millennia and the inevitable merging of influences that must have taken place as a result reflected among the Andean peoples by the introduction of shamanistic beliefs and rituals from under the dark canopy of the Amazon forest. The iconography associated with hallucinogenic drugs found widely in use among the Amazonian shamans appears at Chavin[60]. The streaming mucus from the nose is illustrated in many carvings (*4.021*) and was the result of inhalation after the snuffs were ritually ground from the seeds of the vilca or epena[61]. In the many surviving examples of stone mortars found in the highlands as well as in and around Chavin the San Pedro cactus is clearly used for similar related purposes. Ritual usage of such narcotic snuffs is not exclusive to the Americas and is found also in Asia, but in some of the ritual ornaments among the people of New Guinea certain of their nose plugs and labrets suggest that they represent the nasal discharge depicted at Chavin

4.031 : The Tello Monolith clearly showing the incised relief of a caiman believed in myth to be the bringer of food plants into the Andes. Chavin de Huantar, Central Highlands Peru, 600-400 B.C.

(*4.024/5*) and noted of the Muisca Indians in Colombia by the friar Pedro Simon in the 17th., century[62]. The ritual consumption of lime from pouches and containers similar to those associated to facilitate the use of coca in South America id found also in Melanesia, and New Guinea and particular (*4.022; 4.026*).

Outside the Old Temple one of the best known features surviving from the Old Temple period was that of the so-called rumi chaka, the corbelled stone bridge across the Hauchesa River that flows to the north of the ceremonial site into the Mosna to the east. This survived until 1945 when an exceptionally large torrent swept it away and it had to be replaced by a temporary structure[63]. The engineering principles utilised in the construction of the bridge relate to those of the Old Temple period and therefore should be dated from about 900 B.C.

Six hundred metres south of the Old Temple, on the other side of the Huachesa River a section of a monolithic wall has survived and it is believed that this extended in each direction so as to form a barrier, perhaps with a tollgate, to those approaching from the direction of the Amazonian lowlands. Many of the rough hewn stones were over 2 metres high and 1 metres wide and weighed almost a ton, and the surviving length of this wall is only a fraction of its original length at about 160 metres[64]. In later times it is known that there was a wall built across the Vilcanota Valley[65] and this too had a gate to control entrance to traders and defence from marauding tribes before and during the Inca dynasty. Such toll gates located in wall for the same dual purposes were still in evidence in the early 20th., century in Tibet (*4.042*).

The Urabarriu Phase during the Old Temple period at Chavin de Huantar, lasted from about 1000 to 500 B.C. and was succeeded by the last phases at this great site that are divided into three named Chakinani, Janabarriu and Huaras ending about 200 B.C. While noted for fine ceramics, superior to those of the previous epochs, those of the Urubarriu phase were made in the town and associated with the Chakinani Phase. They are rarely found in the refuse in the Old

4.033 : Carved living rock similar to that found in Chavin de Huantar 2,000 years before and in Asia. The Intihuatana or "Hitching post of the Sun" is seen to the upper right. Inca period, Machu Picchu, 1350-1500 A.D.

4.032 : Carved natural rock outcrops sacred to the Buddhists characteristic of the Buddhists in India. Udaigiri/ Khandagiri, Bhubanesvar, Orissa, East Central India, 300 B.C. - 100 A.D.

4.034 : Ceremonial benches or altars carved in the living rock characteristic in Andean traditions for millennia. Machu Picchu, Peru, 15th., century, A.D.

4.035 : Carved steps into a sacred water tank where ritual bathing was traditional from the Ancient Indus civilisation. Nagarjunakonda, South East India, 3rd., century, A.D.

4.036 : Carved stair and sacred platforms adjacent cave shrines similar to those known in South America. Udaigiri/Kandagiri, Bhubanesvar, Orissa, India, 300 B.C. - 100 A.D.

4.037 : Carved natural stone platform with stair up to ceremonial platform similar to rock shrines and platforms in Orissa in India (*4.036*). Concancha, South Highlands Peru, 1300-1500 A.D.

4.038 : Natural outcrops carved into platforms, seats and altars similar to those found at Chavin de Huantar in the same time frame and later in Inca Peru. Petra, Jordan, Ancient Near East, c900-200 B.C.

4.039 : Stone outcrop with carved altar or ceremonial seats and access. Chavin de Huantar, Central Highland Peru, 900-800 B.C.

4.041 : Carved mountaintop and monoliths as altars and raised platforms similar in manner to those found at many Peruvian sites. Petra, Jordan, First half of the first millennium, B.C.

4.040 : Large rock caves extended and carved as hermitages and shrines. Udaigiri/Kandagiri, Bhubanesvar, Orissa, India, 300 B.C.-500 A.D.

Temple site suggesting again a division between elite of the temple and the common people who inhabited the town. This possibly indicates a social division that was also based on a tribal or racial basis. In this phase the high lustre finish of these Chakini ceramics was never surpassed in the valley with their high lustre and silvery-mirror-like finishes. Stirrup-spouted vessels also appear and elaborate incised designs cover the main body and extending to the stirrup itself[66].

Highland Irrigation and Agriculture in the Chavin de Huantar Epoch

The studies in the food-supply indicated in the early settlements in Chavin suggest that there was a local sufficiency existing in the valley before the rise of the Old Temple. Associated with the Old Temple period were extensive and sophisticated irrigation systems that required annual maintenance. A water supply system is known within the Old Temple precincts and the remains of a contemporary canal has been located 3 km from the site but the full extent of the overall system is unknown[67]. In the fallow months in the agricultural cycle festivals and cyclic celebrations associated with fertility and ancestor worship were a highlight of the year. These yearly markers were perceived as an integral part of the natural annual rhythm of seed sowing through to reaping.

After the Old temple period there is a major shift away from the more independent form of farming to that tied to the temple itself. Protein supply was developed away from that provided by the rabbit-like viscacha and camelid (llama, vicuna) meat where the major source from

042 : Sikkim-Tibet customs walled barrier constructed to restrict traffic for fence and toll charges but found similarly also at Chavin de Huantar and the ⏐lley of Vilcanota in Central and South Peru. Chumbi Valley, Sikkim/Tibet, Pre-⏐th., century, A.D.

4.043 : Finely carved ashlar masonry applied to rough coursed stonework similar to the Vinapu platform on Easter Island and for millennia in Mesopotamia. Ollantaytambo, Peru, 1350-1500 A.D.

4.044 : Finely constructed brick superstructure of Sargon's palace faced with finely carved ashlars similar to that found in Ancient Peru into the Inca dynasty. Khorsabad, Iran, early 2nd., millennium, B.C.

herding by breeding of llamas appears to be of importance. This is believed to be caused by the fact that herding in the highlands was producing dried llama meat for trade, called ch'arki, and this was exchanged at the lower altitudes with farmers for maize and other goods. There is a greater supply of fish and shell foods from the Pacific Ocean appearing to be a result of greater and more extensive trade along already long trodden routes[68]. Maize consumption increased little, where this and other grains were ground by the introduction of the rocker grinder, but potatoes (mashua; oca) remained the staple of the diet at this centre[69].

The Chakinani Phase lasted from about 500-400 B.C. and the following Janabarriu Phase extended from the end of this phase to about 200 B.C. that witnessed the increasing use of llamas as cargo animals appearing to be reflected in the increase of trade goods between distant regions. In the Chakini refuse there is evidence that obsidian was traded with the South Peruvian region known for producing that volcanic glass in Huancavelica at a place called Quispisisa. The period from 500 B.C. onwards is called the Early Horizon and initiates a new period of temple building and remodelling in Chavin.

The Early Horizon and the Janabarriu Phase at Chavin
Examination of the residential settlements around the Old Temple at Chavin de Huantar indicates that the population around the site may have reached about 3000 people constituting one of the largest urban areas in Peru at that time. The population spread along the valley floor was so large in this narrow valley that the slopes were terraced to supply the land required. Guinea pigs and Spondylus shell have been recovered in excavations as an ancient offering in the construction of one of these terraces[70]. Not only was the Spondylus used as an offering to the gods but also imported from Ecuador and crafted on site for prestige goods associated with the Temple[71].

It has been suggested that in this new phase, from 400 B.C., a more powerful priestly elite emerged and imposed control upon the Valley and its economy. These social changes in turn led to the emergence of a ruling class reflected in the increased demand for elite goods and resulting in apparent social divisions. The names of the priests and rulers, however, eludes the researchers since the lack of any surviving writing has probably forever consigned them to oblivion. The Old Temple was renovated and extended to reflect the new prosperity and the power base that created it. A massive extension was constructed to the Old Temple U-shaped mound on the south side producing an overall asymmetrical plan[72]. New galleries were constructed and extended from those already existing in the Old Temple and one of its galleries, the Chamber of the Ornamental Beams has unique carved roof beams and one of the carvings preserves two types of cross. These are said to represent Spondylus shells, with a carved fish[73] (*8.027*), that may connect to the iconography of Tiahuanaco. A ceremonial portal flanked by two columns fronting the east of the mound is reminiscent of the columned galleries on the Coast but more similar to those of the Old World in that the access to the mound is confined to a portal. Rising immediately behind the portal that gives access to the summit of the mound is the New Temple, and at ground level the portal connects to a rectangular plaza in front. The planned phases in this extension were never completed since some of the column sections lie about the site unfinished[74]. The sunken plaza and the cylindrical columns are unknown in the Old Temple architecture but are known at Huaca Lucia, Purulen and Huaca de los Reyes[75].

The overall imagery found in this period is in fact an extension of that from the earlier period, but more elaborately carved, loosing some of the power of projection exhibited by the earlier forms. The supreme deity is considered by some to express the androgyny of a god/goddess and is reminiscent of the much later serpent deities of Aztec period in Mexico. This god was depicted, by the carvers at Chavin, as a monster-faced fanged-deity with intertwined serpents instead of hair and a pair of double-headed serpent belts ands clawed hands and feet probably representing aspects of a bird deity. This deity holds a Strombus shell in the right hand and a Spondylus shell in the left and is considered a metaphor for the balance of opposing forces in the universe[76]. Interestingly the tradition among the archaeologists of Ecuador varies completely to that espoused by the Americanists of North America. These researchers and historians give more credence to the conclusions of those who suggest that the Chavin efflorescence was not autochthonous to Peru but had a common origin with that of the Olmec such as propounded by Dr. H. D. Disselhoff and evident in the archaeological sites of Sangay at the foot of the volcano of the same name in Central Ecuador. This follows Emilio Estrada's earlier conclusions that the Valdivian culture was influenced by mariners from the Jomon of Japan[77] and more recent archaeologists in Ecuador have tended to support this or a similar line on cultural incursions into South America[78].

Serpents and their symbolic association with hair were known in Ancient Greek myths and related iconography is particularly identified with the Medusa in the Perseus myth cycle. The two, twisted serpents probably represent the ringlets, plaits and braids, known so widely among many peoples in the Middle East and in India, from the most ancient times into the twentieth century. The long single, double or multiple plaits or braids known of Middle Eastern men and mariners (*8.064/5; 8.066; 8.069*) throughout the world derived in South America no doubt from contact with them and is probably the inspiration for the plaited braids of this Chavin deity. The fanged monster mask is found in ancient depictions in the Ancient Near and Middle East, Ancient Greece and Ancient India over millennia and the earrings indicated status and privilege and in tribes or clan in Asia as they appeared to have done in Central and South America. The twin, double-headed serpent belt appears to duplicate one of the oldest references in Ancient Middle Eastern myths where the waist cord or girdle represents the double-headed serpent known as Rahu who was identified with the Moon's Nodes. These nodes are depicted in Ancient Indian myths as the two heads of the ecliptic serpent that girdled the world, and in Ancient Buddhist ceremonial dress a twin, bound girdle was common since this symbolised the two halves of mankind in the symbolic sense. The upper half represented the spirit while the lower half the Earth corresponding to the opposing duality fundamental to Andean cosmology and religious myth. The clawed hands and feet refer to its relation to the sky god at Chavin and Rahu is a reference to the sky as the ecliptic and therefore the path of the Sun, Moon and planets, never fully defined outside of myth in the Ancient texts of India.

This duality of opposing forces is believed to be represented in the Raimondi stone found in the New Temple dating to the late period before 200 B.C. where this stela can be read in the opposite direction when located in the upright and the upside-down position[79]. It is thought that the deity depicted in the Raimondi stone is the same as that of the supreme deity who famously holds two shells, the Strombus used for blowing through as a trumpet, is male and the Spondylus is female since they are reminiscent and reflective of the female genitals. This corresponds closely with the symbolism of the male linga, or phallus in India and the right side or right hand, and the yoni, as the female form reflected in the conch or here the Spondylus and to the left side of left hand[80].

The monumental staircase leads down from the New Temple extension through the pillared portal to the monumental plaza in front and to the east of the temple complex at Chavin. The plaza is 105 metres by 85 metres and in the southwest corner of the plaza a large monolith of limestone has seven circular depressions carved into the upper surface. These marks are believed to represent the Pleiades, known in Peru as Collca (storehouse), a constellation widely observed in South America and the Pacific Islands in their rising and setting to indicate the beginning and end of the agricultural season and called there by a similar name, Maka-lii, found in the Ancient Near East as Makha-ili[81]. Stone altars of a similar type with such depressions are found in the late Initial sites of Poro-Poro at the head of the Zana Valley[82] in the Inca Dynasty and the Ancient Middle East.

The other best-known carved monolith found at Chavin de Huantar, the Tello Obelisk, depicts a caiman and its associated iconography with manioc, pepper and aspects of agriculture from the warmer and particularly with the Amazon Basin[83]. This imagery is linked to the carved stone monuments and iconography of Chavin and suggests an intrusive culture well versed in the highest skills of a long developmental tradition. The location of the ceremonial centre is clearly critical and strategically constructed in a narrow valley connecting the central Andes valleys and the Pacific Coast to the drainage flowing into the Amazon Basin to the east. The overall iconography of forest dwelling felines and influences suggest that there may have been intrusions from the Amazon tributaries flowing through this strategic access route from the east to the west. The elements of imagery were integrated with externally introduced artesnal traditions in stone carving and masonry.

As the ceremonial centre at Chavin expanded the traditional belief structure and social organisation is adjusted towards coastal influences in the U-shaped ceremonial centre and it appears that Chavin began to be perceived as the successor or the centre of stability in a dramatically changing social environment. These changes took place about 500 B.C. and appear to be the result of influences flowing into Peru and Bolivia along with new technologies and techniques particularly related to textiles and therefore weaving and metallurgy detectable a few centuries earlier. Some have considered the collapse of the U-shaped ceremonial tradition to be as a result of a natural disaster dating to about that period, possibly an El Nino event or a tsunami, since the long established sites in the Jequetepeque down to the Chillon Valleys from the North to the Central Coasts of Peru preserve evidence of dramatic erosion causing serious damage to the coastal sites in this epoch.

Although there are now numerous studies of climatic changes causing the collapse of civilisations throughout the world, it is more usual that damaged sites are replaced by rebuilding under new overlords reconstructing on the model of what had gone before rather than introducing new technologies and innovations. When new innovations and inventions suddenly occur it is invariably the result of an overrun of the original culture by newcomers or intruders who import their own traditions, inventions and technologies and this in fact is evident at Chavin and other centres in South America. The sudden appearance of "far-reaching technological changes" should alert any serious researchers or interested bystander that more than a natural development in social life has occurred. All progress is normally based on the experience but also initiate to create, innovate and resolve problems in the existing social and religious structure and agricultural framework and this by necessity must be based on what has gone before reflecting a natural process of developmental principles. A child must crawl before it stands, must toddle before it walks, and walks before it runs. It is not possible to run before any of these processes are mastered and the same is true for innovation and invention. There must be a logical, perceptible developmental process on which the final successful functioning invention or innovation is based for it to exist. This does not occur in the sudden appearance of metallurgy of, and in some of the inventions associated with the loom and weaving, among others, in the Peruvian, Coastal and Andean cultures at this time. It is clear that these developments suddenly introduced into South America were as a result of intrusion from abroad since the development sequence or basis for them did not exist anywhere in the Americas at that time.

Twining had been utilised as the technique to produce cloth in South America until the abrupt introduction of the heddle-loom in the first half of the first millennium B.C. This revolutionised textile production but none have been able to explain how this and other innovations came to be developed or the developmental bases on which these processes evolved. The remarkable aspect of such changes in South America is their consistency in being sudden and disconnected with previous techniques and technologies. Not only are there no developmental sequences leading up to the final working loom or other innovation but that introduced technology remains static and unchanged until a further introduction is evident, again without accountable developmental sequences. This clearly militates for a long history of contacts with the Old World, and Asia in particular introducing these new technologies and innovations into South America as working models. The developmental sequences can be traced in Europe or Asia but South America always appears as an extension or repository of the primary Eurasian cultures in any one time band and when this was accomplished these introductions are preserved and consolidated unchanged until the next infusion. Not only is this apparent in the sudden and rapid introduction of technologies and techniques into South America but also appears preserved in their myths and legends recording that the culture-bearers, often described as white and certainly foreign, introduced all their cultural advances. In these myths, and those relating to burial practises, it might be inferred that Paracas was one of these sacred sections of the coast where ancestral intrusions occurred. This is emphasised by the sea currents from Melanesia and Polynesia and ultimately South East Asia washing this part of the Peruvian coast. By frequent, or occasional landings, and consolidation by repetition of associations in myths and legends, it is likely that the landing stage at Paracas became revered in tradition as the place where the descendants of the culture-bearers left to rejoin their Asian ancestors. It will be seen that beside the introduction of the technology of the heddle-loom and the associated weaving techniques such as the continuous warps and tapestry, extending from it other textile arts such as painted textiles and Batik[84] also appear in the same unaccountable way. The technique of Batik is most famously associated with in Indonesia, a land of many islands, and of some interests in the theme of this book, and this techniques is abruptly found also in Peru at this same time in the middle of the first millennium B.C. This suggests also, among many other aspects, that this was a result of contact between India and South America, via Indonesia, to the coastal region of Peru and the

Andean highlands of South America.

Chavin Influence Extending from the Central Highlands of Peru

Some historians have proposed that the rise of Chavin was as a result of increased trade and cross-cultural fertilisation throughout the Central Andes from the second millennium B.C. This, they propose, resulted in the establishment and long-term survival of Chavin de Huantar as a ceremonial centre and then as a pilgrimage destination. However, the same historians will also note that there were "radical disruptions" occurring along the Central and North Peruvian Coast at the beginning of the first millennium, B.C.[85]. Such a theory of gradual expansion and reasonably smooth, even development over the millennia leading to a period of expansion and agricultural and material prosperity, belies such a theory and suggests that the disruption occurred because of something far more apocalyptic, imposed from outside or serious collapse from within.

The introduction of advanced technologies without any apparent previous development anywhere along the high culture regions such as the heddle loom and the technical advances metallurgy suggests that this disruption was caused from outside South America. That the sudden appearance of Chavin about 9-800 B.C. at a time when the great coastal ceremonial centres suddenly declined dramatically and ceased to function cannot be a coincidence[86]. Some of these sites, such as Cardal on the South Central Coast, were simply abandoned in an unfinished state suggesting that a major cause was at the root of these events. This "rupture" is particularly evident on the Central Coast in the Casma Valley where new constructions and renovations being undertaken ceased in the lower valley of Casma at Sechin Bajo, Sechin Alto and others[87]. This description is further emphasised by the fact that Chavin was founded at the pass in the Mosna Valley on a critical east-west trade route from the Amazon and the Pacific coast and also suggests that this was consistent with other major incursions from outside Peru notable in earlier periods of Andean history up to that time in Peru. This would appear to be illustrated by the fact that the large Early Horizon centres (from the middle of the first millennium B.C.) were "radically" different in their planning and architecture from the Initial Period that had just ceased to exist[88]. It would also appear therefore that there was a complete loss of confidence in the ancient gods and associated with them the ceremonial traditions and little appears to have been preserved from the old ways of expressing their former religious beliefs in the sacred and civic architecture built in this new period.

In the lower Casma Valley in the Early Horizon, contemporary with the Janabarriu phase at Chavin, large urban settlements were built and occupied but lacked the ceremonial and civic architecture found at the earlier Initial Period sites. The sites of Pampa Rosario and San Diego in the Casma Valley covered areas of 40 and 50 hectares but featured instead of pyramids and plazas a great number of small mounds surrounded by interconnecting rooms, corridors and courtyards. Only at Pampa Rosario is there a platform, possibly used for civic or religious occasions, from 1-3 metres high, located on the edge of the city[89]. This remarkable development suggests the return to a form of enclosed, personal religious ceremonies, possibly even of personal shrines, located in the individual houses or focussed on the small mounds found throughout these urban centres.

In the Viru Valley the ruins now to be found on the hill top residential areas from this time preserve a few low platforms within their precincts suggesting that labour could not be afforded upon expensive civic works. Extra effort and time appears to have been expended upon the daily travel to and from the agricultural fields on the valley floor and on defence. Many of these villages seem to have relied upon their strategic position on top of a ridge to fend off attacks rather than constructing labour intensive fortifications[90].

In other more northern valleys dense populations were living on hilltops and defensible

4.045 : Llama with his driver modelled as a fine black clay ceramic ceremonial vessel. Moche, Valle de Chicama, Peru, 200-600 A.D.

4.046 : Domestication of the camel is believed to have been achieved by the 2nd., mill. B.C. in Asia and this was followed in Peru in the 1st., mill. B.C. of the llama - itself a camelid. Note the Phrygian caps worn by the camel-masters. Babylonian Period, 1200-900 B.C.

4.048 : Llama typical of grave votive ornaments found throughout Bolivia and Peru. Island of the Sun, Lake Titicaca, Bolivia, 1350-1500 A.D.

4.049 : Llama typical of grave votive ornaments found throughout Bolivia and Peru. Island of the Sun, Lake Titicaca, Bolivia, 1350-1500 A

4.047 : Typical llama in front of the extensive "sawtooth" fort walls built of massive stone blocks forming the Sacsahuaman fort. Cuzco, South Central Peru, 1350-1500 A.D.

locations[91] suggesting a total breakdown of the old system of governance and religious beliefs. These settlements were supported by the construction of hilltop forts indicating the constant threat of attack from possible bands of bandits hiding in the adjacent rugged hills. The best known of the first fortifications of this type constructed at this time is that of Chankillo in the Casma Valley[92] (*5.016*). This fort is unusual in that it is constructed on the more recognisably Eurasian planning strategy of concentric elliptical walls with what appears to be centralised keeps and dating from the middle of the first millennium B.C.

Ceremonial Centres in the Andean Highlands Influenced from Chavin de Huantar

Public architecture was still being undertaken in the highland regions of Peru while the coastal regions were declining during this period of instability indicating that the greatest problems were occurring on the coast and probably originating with sea borne influences. This would also suggest that there were probable connections between the progressive and more stable highland sites and the new influences disturbing the coastal regions. At Pacopmapa a sunken rectangular plaza was constructed during the Early Horizon phase in the beginning to middle of the first millennium B.C. featuring polished stone and a central staircase flanked by cylindrical columns. Motifs similar to those of Chavin were also a feature of this site. At Kuntur Wasi the site appears to have reached its apogee in this period and the summit of the terraced hill was redeveloped with three platforms arranged around a sunken rectangular plaza. The staircase was adorned with relief carvings in stone clearly related to those at Chavin depicting the fanged head with "serpent hair" where both left and right hand sides of the face can be read also as a profile[93].

In the Early Horizon Kotosh was also expanded with constructions that surpassed those of the earlier phases and at La Pampa the three monumental phases date to this period and have little to suggest that this was a continuation from the earlier phases. At Huaricoto in the Callejon de Huaylas next to the Mosna Valley a break with tradition is noted and a circular sunken court was built possibly as a response to the circular court in the Old Temple at Chavin de Huantar. It is equally possible that this phase at Huaricoto was an extension of the fire rituals adapted to new influences modified by the new, rising religious establishment of Chavin.

There appears to have been shrines long established through the region of the Andes, along the coasts and laterally and longitudinally across the Andes and these were frequented by pilgrims, probably also traders and those who travelled with them over the centuries and millennia. This probably accounts for the survival and refurbishment of centres such as Huaricoto on the main valley trails providing also nodal points as markets and accommodation centres for those passing through on a short or long term basis. This would appear to follow the model in India where to this day there are sacred shrines scattered all across the Subcontinent supported in some cases by all three of the major religions but particularly noted of the Hindu. The pilgrims, no matter how poor, determine to travel to some or all of the sacred shrines scattered across a million square miles and consider it a life ambition and goal to visit at least the most holy among them. Many of these are in fact peripheral to Hinduism and not recognised by the strict, more orthodox Aryan Hindus since they have been adopted into the religion as Hinduism spread among the Aboriginal tribes. In principle many of these peripheral centres incorporating surviving shrines of what were once major religious movements or deity cults. These were abhorrent to the first Aryans when they first confronted them as they penetrated deeper into the Subcontinent from the northwest with the increasing pressure of their continuing migrations from Iran in the first millennium B.C. The Hindus were not a proselytising religion since the basis for being a devotee rested on their being one of the three recognised Aryan castes and this depended on being of, originally, Iranian Aryan descent. A fourth caste was added later to include the descendants of those who had intermarried with the indigenous or naturalised peoples of India and called the Sudras. It is likely that the radical changes and new religious beliefs with its related iconography brought into Peru to initiate the Early Horizon were of this type and spread only by advanced cultures and domination rather than proselytisation leaving the indigenous or naturalised belief systems intact in peripheral areas.

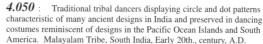

4.052 : Circle and dot design that may be intended to represent energy centres or cosmological patterns. Mohenjo Daro, Pakistan, 3rd., millennium B.C.

The coastal region in the first millennium B.C. was not immune to the influences from Chavin de

4.050 :   Traditional tribal dancers displaying circle and dot patterns characteristic of many ancient designs in India and preserved in dancing costumes reminiscent of designs in the Pacific Ocean Islands and South America. Malayalam Tribe, South India, Early 20th., century, A.D.

4.051 : Circle and centre dot was a characteristic design found in similar patterns from India through the Pacific Islands to South America similar to this carved block from the Indus Valley. Mohenjo Daro, Pakistan, 3rd., millennium B.C.

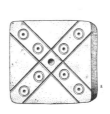

4.053 : Circle and dot designs incised on a carved stone block typical of Chinese gaming chips that spread throughout S.E. Asia. La Plata Island, Bahia Period, Ecuador Coast, 500 B.C.-300 A.D.

4.054 : Dish decorated with birds standing on a pillar characteristic of cosmological concepts found from Asia through the Pacific Islands to the Americas. Carabuco; Bolivia, 1st. Millennium, A.D.

4.056 : Cardinal points or four quarters with serpent enclosed iconography in each of the four lobes. The serpent heads resemble the Makara heads found ubiquitously in India through to Indonesia. Codex Borgia, Mexico, pre-post Conquest, 16th., century, A.D.

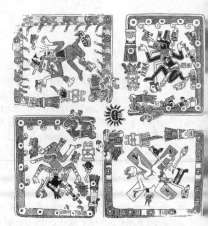

4.055 : Cardinal points focused on the face of the Sun god. Tiahuanaco, Bolivia, 300-1000 A.D.

4.057 : Cardinal points or the four corners are found in the myths and cosmology of Ancient Eurasia and the Americas. Similar designs depict this concept along with associated myths. Recuay, Central Peru, 200-800 A.D.

Huantar and one of the most interesting connections with the coast is found near the Paracas coast about 8 km south of the famous Necropolis site. The cemetery at Karwa preserved a tomb yielding an abundance of textiles with unmistakeable Chavin de Huantar designs along with Paracas ceramics. Over 200 fragments of cloth were retrieved and the iconography depicted upon them appears to relate clearly to the Janabarriu phase dating from 400-200 B.C. and is detectable in the Paracas ceramics of the time. The staff god is found also as a motif preserved on these textiles and is considered a modified form of that found also at Tiahuanaco at that time from the beginning of its foundation beside Lake Titicaca in the Bolivian Highlands[94] (*9.024*). Interestingly the staff god at Karwa has a female counterpart, a possibly fiercer form of the male, and is depicted with cotton bolls attached to her headdress[95], suggesting that this deity had become adapted to the fundamental concepts of duality indigenous along the Peru coast for millennia. Aspects of this, and other depictions of the female in Chavin iconography, suggests the vagina dentata myths so common in the Amazon Basin. This type of iconography is found also in the contemporary iconography of Pacopampa and the vagina dentata myths are found widely in Western Mexico and through the Pacific Ocean to India where there are many examples of this myth type preserved[96]. Other elements of the Karwa textiles preserve other non-Chavin elements suggesting a coastal adaption at Paracas rather than a cultural copy transported from the highland centre itself.

Some have claimed that there is little connection between Tiahuanaco and Chavin but this staff god, reappearing in the Bolivian Highlands and later in the Huari, would indicate otherwise. The fact that Karwa was found on the Paracas Peninsula, a region known to have cultural and trade ties with Tiahuanaco suggests that the staff god was imported into the Andes along with many of the other abrupt technological advances about 9-800 B.C. and was transferred into the Central Highlands of Peru to Chavin but also to the Bolivian Highlands. Connecting trade routes between and beyond these two great centres would indicate that they did not remain totally independent creations nor were the two centres unaware of the other's iconography.

Many of these Karwa textiles were so large that it has been doubted that they were originally burial shrouds but may have been wall hangings. One textile measured 4.2 metres wide by 2.7 metres high and many of the other textiles were of unusual size. Although the tomb is considered unique the textiles are not since, through grave-robbing activity of huaqueros, more textiles of a similar type are said to be from the coastal town of Collango in the Ica Valley have been retrieved[97].

4.058 : Animal-headed deities or demons derived from the Bon Po, the anterior indigenous devotee called "devil-worshippers", in Tibet before the advent of Buddhism and extending throughout the Himalayan kingdoms. Sikkim, late 19th., century, A.D. or earlier.

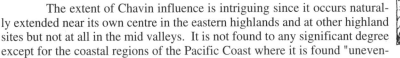

The extent of Chavin influence is intriguing since it occurs naturally extended near its own centre in the eastern highlands and at other highland sites but not at all in the mid valleys. It is not found to any significant degree except for the coastal regions of the Pacific Coast where it is found "unevenly" from the Ica Valley in the South to the Lambeyeque in the North. Pre-Chavin iconography, considered as prototypes for that of Chavin, are found at Moxeke and Cerro Sechin in the Casma Valley and these sites are considered themselves to have been the recipients of radical influences a millennia before, probably sea-borne, in the second millennium B.C. Other sites with Chavin-like elements have been found in the upper Lambeyque-La Leche drainage where a pair of carved columns, similar to those at Chavin, were found[98].

4.059 : A sketch of an agriculture worker guarding his fields. Note the animal pelt headdress identical to those depicted in Asia and India. Poma de Ayala; Inca Peru, 16th., century, A.D.

Chavin iconography and construction is largely associated with finely chiselled stonework but in the Nepena Valley Chavin style modelled clay decoration has been applied facing the adobe construction and is of exceptional design at the site of Cerro Blanco. The finely moulded clay design is modular and was painted white, black, greenish yellow, pink and orange. The site appears to have been abandoned after a short occupation at the beginning of the Early Horizon in the first half of the first millennium B.C. Cerro Blanco may have had contacts with another site in the Chicama Valley where one of the painted mud brick columns preserves an image of a bird motif similar to that found at Chavin[99].

Ritual Objects and Ceremonial Art in the Highlands of Peru Contemporary with Chavin

Conches similar in use to those of Central America and the Pacific Islands, have been found frequently in Peru along with Spondylus shells from Ecuador, and these were of the type strombus galeatus, otherwise called pututu or huayllaquepa[100]. The term pututu is an interesting since, as with so many terms and expressions in Ancient Peru, this has its parallel in Polynesia where the term putona for the same object is found in the Marquesas Islands in Eastern Polynesia[101] - the nearest inhabited island group to the Americas. It is unlikely to be a coincidence that the bamboo tube trumpet is called the phupphu by the Lhota Nagas of Assam and is probably derived from that of the Peruvian prototype[102]. Conch blowing is well known in Ancient Peruvian art and is found almost universally throughout the coastal and Andean excavations from Ecuador to Chile. It was also anciently known in the Near and Middle East as well as in India into the last century and was used at almost every Hindu shrine throughout India where the conch shell was called the Sank.

Chavin de Huantar - Camelids and Weaving

So many of the innovations appearing at Chavin have been the subject of debate since, as declared by one authority, in "… both metallurgy and textile production, numerous innovations appear suddenly and diffuse over an extensive area"[103]. These "innovations" appear to be associated with Chavin and their adoption throughout Ancient Peru appears to be directly as a result of diffusion from that centre. Some experts such as William Conklin stated that cloth techniques

4.061 : Animal masks and headdresses were anciently traditional in South East Asia similar to the Maya. Cambodia, Early 20th., century, A.D.

4.062 : Raft paddle head to handle depicting four figures with animal head-dresses, proba-bly representing llamas almost identical to simi-lar depictions in Central America. Ica, South Coast Peru, 500-1000, A.D.

4.063 : Carved stone monolith of a seated deity, ancestor or priest with an animal headdress. Pensacola Island, Lake Nicaragua, Nicaragua, Central America, 8-12th., century A.D.

4.064 : Carved basalt seated deity, ancestor or priest with a giant animal, probably caiman, headdress a motif found identically among the coastal cul-tures of Peru. Zapatero Island, Lake Nicaragua, Nicaragua, Central America, 8-12th., century A.D.

4.060 : Animal Masks were a feature of Mayan rituals and these appear to be too similar to those of S.E. Asia to be coincidence. Chama, Guatemala, 600-900 A.D.

and production were "revolutionised" at the time of the rise of Chavin and yet there was no evidence of a recognised developmental evolution to pro-duce these remarkable changes in both textiles and metallurgy. The achievements considered to have "suddenly" occurred include the use of camelid hair in textiles extending to dyeing of the hair and painting on tex-tiles. Innovative textile techniques included tie-dye and batik otherwise known as negative and resist techniques; textile weaves including tapestry from supplemental discontinuous warps, and the common adoption of sim-ilar techniques and design styles.

All of the new textile associated innovations suggest introduction from abroad and camelid hair retrieval was long known in Central and South Asia and probably introduced and into India from there and Iran by the Assyrians, Archaemenids and with later the Parthians and Kushans. The calendar in India appears regulated to that of Ancient Babylon[104] and was introduced from there in the early first millennium B.C. along with the other techniques mentioned such as textile-making and loom types were probably also transferred along with other cultural advances. There are so many parallels between the Assyrian constructional types and those of Peru that it seems likely that textile technology and that associated with metallurgy, well-advanced by that period were directly introduced into Ancient Peru along known sea routes long established. It may well have been that the boast of the Assyrian kings that they ruled the "Four Corners of the World" may have been nearly literal.

Metallurgy in Chavin de Huantar

Metallurgical advances that "suddenly" appeared in Chavin included the development of gold technology through hammering into large sheets and the joining by this method of two sheets into a larger "pre-shaped" tem-plate. From these sheets three-dimensional gold objects were made and both gold and silver forged and annealed ornaments along with designs illustrating hammered complex Chavin motifs and decorations that were characteristic[105]. Also otherwise unexplainable are the advanced tech-niques of soldering, sweat welding and repousse decoration in Chavin objects along with silver-gold alloys. Both the former well-known researchers in Chavin history, William Conklin and H. Lechtman, assert that there is a link between the Chavin culture and the introduction of this wave of new technology[106]. These recognised, unexplained advances are unlikely to have coincidently occurred without a natural development period and where each aspect of progress lacked a reasonable incremental spacing over a period of time for evolution as elsewhere in the world.

The high quality of the Chavin ornamentation and craftsmanship is so sophisticated and so profuse and complex in design that it has been proposed that it is the product of specialist full-time artisans. This would in fact follow the examples found in both Ancient Assyria in the same time band of the first half of the first millennium B.C. and of India later in that millennium. It should not be surprising that some of the pieces of Recuay gold-work (*12.087*) bear striking resemblances to that of Assyria through to the Sassanid Dynasty a millennia later in Iran (*9.105-7*) where a number of pieces of a winged deity resemble those of the Assyrian eagle and the Recuay culture in Peru and noted by authors in the early twentieth century.

It is interesting to note that the agricultural system remained unchanged, almost at a primitive level, and there appeared to be no advances introduced in farming at the time the new technologies were introduced in the early first millennium B.C.[107]. This less developed form of food production evident at this time was based on the traditional mixed agriculture largely of high altitude crops and llama herding[108]. This emphasises the likelihood that the new technologies in metallurgy and textiles was in fact due to the incursion of an elite and their retainers, that imposed themselves on an existing rural society. This society was comprised of predominantly, and extremely conservative, agricultural workers who formed the large indigenous population and who would have been retained by the new elite in their traditional roles as food producers. Such a scenario foreshadows that of all of the major Andean and Coastal cultures of Peru and partic-ularly those of Tiahuanaco and the Incas. It is further of interest to note that it was only during the Chavin period after 900-800 B.C., at the beginning of the so-called Early Horizon epoch, that camelids, and llamas in particular became more widely used outside of their natural high altitude zones and utilised as pack animals for interregional trading in long distance caravans over vast areas of the Andean region[109]. It is therefore not an unreasonable conjecture that this use of a camelid essential in long distance trade parallels exactly the developments long known in Asia where camels were used also as pack animals for the same purposes and possibly occurred due to Asian influences in Peru. This factor, therefore, along with the many of "sudden" advances imported along with the extension and commandeering of the domesticated llama in South America for such purposes, indicates that they were introduced by a people well-versed in the domestication and exploitation of the camelid as well as the corresponding advances in metal-lurgy and textile production.

Chongoyape and the Lambeyeque Valley

Social inequality is clearly perceived by some historians in the early Horizon period but also pre-figured in the Initial Period. Some believe that this later period was in contradistinction to the normal political and social developments and propound that a predominantly egalitarian society of cooperation existed that was a unique development of the Peruvian Coastal and Andean cul-tures. This differentiation in the social structure appears to have elevated a small minority over the vast majority since only a few high status graves have been located with the largest portion of the metals so highly prized in that society. Grave goods appear to have been focused on met-als, largely of gold, rather than on textiles, since the shrouds recovered were largely plain cotton textiles for even those reflecting the highest status. Particularly fine grave goods, many of gold, were found around the town of Chongoyape in the upper Lambeyeque Valley in Northern Peru. Other rich graves from around Kuntur Wasi have yielded ceramics and gold grave goods reflect-ing the iconography of Later Chavin[110]. In one grave at Pacopampa an individual was interred with a crystal obolos in his mouth and it has been suggested that this related to his life activities of a religious or healing occupation. Another who appears to have been a shaman interred at

Moro de Eten since he was buried with the carved rattle made from a deer bone inserted in his right leg. The sheath in the man's right calf was in fact created during his life while he was still alive and was well in use when he died at about the age of 60 years. An anthracite mirror was placed near this man's head, suggesting its possible use for scrying, and two bone spatulas probably for the inhalation of hallucinogenic snuffs associated with a shaman's vocation. Generally the elements making up the iconography of Kuntur Wasi were variants on the Chavin style with some elements indicating influences from the Cupisnique tradition on the North Coast of Peru.

Coastal Peru Influenced from Chavin de Huantar

In the regions influenced from Chavin the pottery shows decorations that closely resembles the circle with a central dot so frequently found in Assyria and later in Ancient India (*4.051/2*) through into the Pacific region[111] (*4.053*). Found also at this time in the more specific Janabarriu phase at Chavin is the decoration of the "megalithic S" on bowls[112] and other items and retained in the armoury of traditional styles throughout the pre-Conquest period. The more elaborate temple and civic ceramics are remarkable for their integrated resolution of numinous demonic or wrathful symbolic elements. This features abstracted human portraits and Amazon animal mask designs that extend away from the Amazon region into the coastal valleys, transferring towards Ecuador[113]. This style is exemplified by its restrained iconography reflecting clearly certain aspects, such as topknot turbans, clearly derived from Asia (*4.027-30*).

The Forest Site of Bagua and Amazonia

Among the Bagua sites on the eastern, Amazonian slopes was a settlement that appeared to be connected to the highland centres of Peru in the Initial Period. After that time the economic and cultural emphasis appears to dissociate and shift towards those forest societies of the Amazon Basin and the Orinoco. This dissociation is difficult to explain since it would be expected that the greatness of Chavin would bind the eastern Andean sites more closely economically and religiously since the Chavin iconography appears to derive so much from Amazonian influences. The new phase in this period at Bagua is called El Salado after the apparent influences from the Saladoid Tradition on the Orinoco River in Venezuela far to the north. Other sites in the Maranon River region do reflect influences into, and from the highland sites including at Huayarco where carved stone bowls, Strombus shells and marine shell necklaces have been retrieved from burials[114]. One of the most interesting Chavinoid sculptures has been recovered from one of the eastern Andes forest sites, known as Yauya this being a polished stela-type monolith with an incised disgorging head and its "cascading" fanged mouths[115] reminiscent of the Raimondi stone at Chavin.

The Yaya Mama and Chiripa on the Bolivian Altiplano

In the Bolivian Plateau around Late Titicaca the culture known as Yaya Mama established by 600 B.C., contemporary with Chavin de Huantar, shows little influence from there. The Yaya Mama features sunken courts in which are built low platforms with brightly painted storage buildings built on top of them. Central heads, with four rays as serpents or tails, perhaps intended to depict the Sun or the four cardinal points[116], are found carved on a stone relief panel and are similar to later Recuay (*4.054-7*) examples from Central Peru and is characteristic of the Chiripa around the Lake Titicaca region. Some have seen the emergence of Tiahuanaco in the Bolivian Highlands and Recuay in the Central Highlands of Peru as the legacy, at least in part, of Chavin from its gradual decline from about 300 B.C.[117]. This reference is particularly drawn when the iconography of the Staff God is considered since there can be little doubt that this central symbolic element of iconography at Tiahuanaco, and later Huari, iconography is first developed at Chavin[118].

These iconographical elements are extended from Chavin northwards onto the coast into the Moche culture emerging at this same time[119]. Elizabeth Benson notes the similarities of the Chavin derived symbolism in the Moche "God of the Mountains" and is reflected in the Pariaraca myth preserved into the Inca Dynasty over a millennia later and has parallels with the Staff God of Tiahuanaco[120]. This myth and the iconography of the Staff god will be of more interest in the following chapters. The early Chiripa and Yaya Mama cultures appear to have been the progenitors for both Tiahuanaco and Pucara emerging about the same time but the first of these were founded after 1100 B.C. at the time of the great climate change caused by the eruption of Hekla in 1159 B.C. This period corresponds with the fall of Babylon in the Ancient Middle East followed by the emergence of Assyria and the migration of the Vedic Aryans into India. These population movements indicate that there are so many sudden influences in Peru of the advances known in Asia that this catastrophic period in Asia appears to have initiated voyages abroad to as far as Peru where Chiripa and Chavin were beneficiaries. These migrants and culture-bearers into Peru formed the foundation and goal for others in later centuries who were traders or who needed to escape from the many centuries of tribulations that followed in Asia. The major periods of change in Asia are represented in the same time bands as periods of sudden advances in South America.

Although there are examples of ceramic designs from Chavin that may have influenced the Piura Valley region in North Coast Peru there is no evidence that Chavin was in contact with the contemporary Chorrera culture in Ecuador and no examples of Chavin metal work have been yet found in the north. Ecuadorian obsidian from the Cayambe region of North Ecuador was found in southern Ecuador, but at Pacopampa, a 1000 kilometres south of this Ecuadorian site, but nearer than the nearest other supply point 1325 kilometres to the south, the obsidian found was of the southern type. This, among other factors suggests that there was a decline in contact between the high cultures of Ecuador and Peru in that contemporary cultural epoch[121] although it did not cease altogether since Spondylus and Strombus shells were still traded across this border. In this same contemporary period in the first millennium B.C. it is a remarkable fact that Southern Ecuador, the nearest region to Peru further to the south but separated by the Sechura Desert - a semi-desert, the Chorrera emerged who were a very different civilisation. Large ceremonial centres were not constructed by the Chorrera and irrigation was of minimal development, and associated developments such as the rocker-grinder for reducing grain were unknown. Other metallurgical developments had not reached them to produce the gold and silver ornaments so expansively utilised at Chavin and extending through Peru particularly in the Northern uplands, valleys and coast[122]. As a result of an expansion of regionalism others have perceived a closer relationship extending from Chavin through to Ecuador because of the long established connections from the most ancient times evident two millennia earlier of the Spondylus and Strombus shells only obtainable from Ecuador[123]. It can be conjectured that this was a result of the fundamentally different effect of Asian influences in South America that were flowing from across the Pacific Ocean. The southern route, in the higher latitudes of the West Wind Drift from Melanesia and Australia, was clearly being utilised, predominantly, by South and West Asians who sailed on to the North Chile and South and Central Peruvian Coast. South East and East Asians including the Chinese, for the most part, utilised the Equatorial Current, flowing from the north of Indonesia and Melanesia, and they sailed onward to the coast of Ecuador. There seems almost to have been some proprietary interest or tentative agreement in these routes so clearly and separately defined are the cultural and developmental directions the two regions of Ecuador and Peru seems to have taken in their ancient history. The Ecuadorian intrusions seem largely related to those of Indonesia, China and the Jomon of Japan and reflect their development and cultural ornamentation, while the Peruvian almost entirely appears to reflect that of the Ancient

4.066 : Copper pectoral depicting censers also known in Ancient Iran as well as the Maltese crosses (*6.083*) and armorial animals similar to the La Aguada culture in N.W. Argentina. Tiahuanaco, Bolivia, 700-1000 A.D.

4.067 : Finely cast pectoral typical of the bronze work south of Bolivia with the characteristic armorial animals flanking the central figure known in Tiahuanaco, and on the coast of Peru but also in Luristan in Southern Iran. Catamarca, North West Argentina, 700-1350 A.D.

4.065 : Copper pectoral with Maltese crosses similar to those found in Assyria (*4.066/7; 6.083*). La Rioja, Northern Argentina, 1000-1450 A.D.

Middle East and India. Clearly, however, these interests and influences are not entirely exclusive since the Manta and Mantero cultures of Coastal Ecuador are clearly related to those of India and probably more specifically those of the Chalukyan Dynasty and Orissa in particular - a group of influences also clearly noted among the Maya in Central America[124]. It is from these South Indian dynasties that the terms of Chola, Colhua and Colla probably developed. It cannot be a coincidence that this "separateness" of Chavin de Huantar is also noted, being recognised by traditional archaeologists and historians and considered "fundamentally different"[125].

Recuay in the Central Peruvian Highlands

The expansion of Chavin and the devolved regionalism that followed, and perhaps as a result of its decline, is thought to have left an important legacy in the Callejon de Hauylas in the adjacent valley nearer the Pacific coast, in the florescence of the Recuay culture. This valley has been less studied than many of the coastal and highland sites so only general comments can be recorded but the traditions for very large stone built complexes, underground chambers and galleries appears to have their origins in the Chavin Tradition. The iconography expressed through the stone carvings and ceramic designs suggest that a hybrid culture emerged after the Chavin influence abated[126]. On the coast in the Moche and Chicama Valleys, the Gallinazo and Salinar traditions developed in parallel with Chavin and then took their own course when the great centre declined in the late first millennium B.C.[127]. Interestingly the U-shaped temple plans that formed the foundation of the Old Temple at Chavin de Huantar appear to indicate that symmetry was of a lesser interest for those who extended the arrangement in the second phase or New Temple. However, in the same time band the U-shaped temple structure appears to have been reborn in the foundation for the religious structures of the La Tolita people located in the extreme north on the Coast of Ecuador[128]. The later fierce felines preserved in their iconography may have derived some impetus from Chavin either by migration or through trading contacts.

One of the interesting propositions, more recently proposed, is that it was in the Recuay region that the dual social division originated, based on the marriage moiety system, and it is this that is believed to be the model for that in the Bolivian Highlands among the Uru and Aymara[129]. As noted in earlier sections of this work other authors have considered the dual system to have been endemic in Peru from the earliest temple constructions and evidenced by the dual wings of the U-shaped temple complexes. The dual organisation and caste systems evident in Peru will be of more interest in the following chapters.

Contacts between Chavin and Recuay in the Callejon de Huaylas in the Upper Santa

Valley are confirmed[130] but there also appears to be contacts between the highly megalithic monuments still surviving at San Agustin in Southern Colombia and Recuay where shared shamanistic mythical themes are apparent[131]. The display of the "overshadowing" protective animal deity is found also closely similar in Central America, particularly notable on Zapatero Island in Lake Nicaragua (*4.063/4*), and through into the South Peruvian coastal iconography (*4.062*). Star-related cosmology and the association of astronomy with the dark clouds constellations and their personification as animal deities related to mediation by shamanistic rituals survived among the inhabitants of the Callejon de Hauylas from the Recuay culture[132] long after its demise over a millennium ago.

Early Moche and the North Coast Tradition

In what is called the Initial Period after the introduction of ceramics three apparently independent centres supported by irrigation systems are established in the North of Peru. Nearer the river delta the large ceremonial site of Caballo Muerto features prominent platform construction and irrigation projects. The whole of the valley was to be held under the sway of the ceremonial sites focused on the Huaca del Sol and the associated Huaca del Luna near modern Trujillo on the coast (*5.018*). This was to be succeeded over a millennia later by the Chimu who were said to have arrived on the coast by rafts and settled on the coast to eventually establish their kingdom that lasted for about 4-5 centuries[133].

The vast irrigation works required to support the growing population and the hierarchy necessary to govern an expanding regional kingdom, are believed to have provided the finer quality silt preferred for manufacturing the enormous demand for mud bricks to alleviate the intensive demand for quarried stone evident at earlier sites. The mud brick types were in fact reminiscent of those in the Old World of Asia where mud brick production could be traced back for millennia to the first settlements in the Ancient Near and Middle East. Even the sugar-loaf form found utilised during the Moche epoch was similar in principle to those found in the Indus from the second millennium B.C. and brick-maker's marks were also a feature found here as well as on the coast of China and among the Moche themselves. Clay cones were a feature of early clay based construction among the Moche found in earlier Peruvian coastal epochs that probably developed from those of similar form found in the Ancient Near and Middle East from at least the third millennium to the first millennium B.C. (*3.023*; *3.025*) earlier noted.

It has been considered that the evidence surviving in the monumental centres on the north coast during this early ceramic phase points to local religious and social conditions being influenced to a lesser or greater degree by the major traditions of the Kotosh fire-chamber traditions and the U-shaped architectural monumental traditions and sunken courts. The influence of the early U-shaped traditions on those throughout Peru is difficult to understated since they appear across four millennia. However they appear at their grandest in the earlier monumental tradition in the second millennium B.C. In later phases at Chimor and among the Inca the U-shaped itself is reduced from the overall monumentality of the grand pyramid to localised elements within the later complexes[134].

The U-shaped monumental structure became reduced in form to a symbolic arrangement atop large platform structures in the Initial Period from the beginning of the Ceramic phase and of special note was the introduction of colonnades in the architectural layouts. Elements already long traditional such as the U-shaped monumental form were adapted in later expansions at sites such as at Huaca los Reyes where the vast overall U-shaped plan contains the older temple group, also based on the U-shape, and two smaller temple mounds, one on either side. The extensive remodelling and additional temple buildings are noted for their massive temple colonnades with square pillars and in time these elements became expanded and utilised as panels for friezes depicting large forward-facing figures of deities or ancestors[135].

It is a remarkable fact of New World history that there were at least ten centres in the Initial (Post-ceramic) Period in Peru where the sites were greater in extent, bulk of construction-al materials and labour in this earlier epoch than at Chavin de Huantar. It has been considered that these earlier centres are related in principle to the El Paraiso tradition[136]. These sites required populations of considerable size since the average person could not be released from essential sections of the agricultural year and the expenditure of labour alone must have been into million of man-days for each site. After the extraordinary ceremonial site conceptions and achievements of this early period spanning from the third to the first millennium B.C. the sites declined to being smaller in size and more ornate.

Cardal and the Lurin Valley

At Cardal, in the Lurin Valley, excavations have revealed a U-shaped structure with a circular sunken court in both of the wings and one in the courtyard between these. The court at Cardal has been estimated to be able to accommodate up to 65,000 people at the major festivals, and this was one of the smallest of the four in that valley. The cranium of a child's skull was found under one of the hearths and the floors around these fire-pans were kept swept clean. The central façade of the primary mound preserves a polychrome painted clay frieze exhibiting a giant mouth with interlocking teeth and prominent projecting canines about a metre long. This frieze was painted cream, yellow, rose and black and had been reworked at least four times[137]. This centre appears to have been used in association with other centres nearby at Manchay Bajo and Mina Perdida and it is suggested that these ceremonial centres may have been allocated or maintained by sep-arate clans or ayllu groups.

In the Chavin period there was a more discernable expansion of influence and popula-tion growth in the Southern Highlands of Peru. This region had been sparsely populated until the Early Horizon Period making the earlier, aberrant discovery of the small pieces of gold in the late Initial Period, hundreds of years before Chavin at Waywaka in the Andahuaylas, all the more unlikely as an indigenous development even if considered precocious. The lack of a firm, sup-portive, expansive and large population base with a progressive attitude from the grass roots upwards, is lacking at Waywarka and clearly lacking also in the Early Horizon at Chavin and yet these "sudden" developments, noted from the earliest times in Ancient Ecuador and Peru kept on coming. Having on one hand suggested that sudden advances of exceptional degree in Chavin, and earlier epochs in Peru, would have left traces of centuries of an evolutionary process any-where else in the world, the reader is regaled by historians with varying non-explanations as to the social, cultural and environmental conditions in South America that must have been com-bined in such way as to have made normal evolutionary processes redundant[138]. Others, having in their own work given vague suggestions (not reasons) as to why they think these sudden advances may have occurred then do not hesitate in another part of their work to record for the Early Horizon, with influences from Chavin, that the "new pan-regional economic and religious phenomena of the Early Horizon would not have transformed this pattern unless they also pro-voked a fundamental change at the household level. This continued popularity of local ceramic traditions in some regions of the Inca Empire illustrates the point"[139].

Huari or Wari - The Last Flight of the Staff God

It has been confirmed by archaeological research that the rugged highland region south of Lake Titicaca and bounded by the coastal lowlands of the Pacific Ocean were among the last to be set-tled to any degree in the more recent millennia of Peruvian history. After the great initial col-lapse of the Tiahuanaco Empire in the 6th., century, the various regions emerged independent

4.069 : Carved stone stela with a relief of a caiman and a bat emerging from its jaws. The skeletal vertebrae are seven in number, a sacred number in both the Old World and the New and flanked by nine dots on either side probably indicating the Moon Node's cycle of 18 years. Cerro Jaboncillo, Manta, Ecuador, 9-14th., century, A.D.

4.070 : Carved stone stela showing another representation of a caiman. The four-fold division of the carapace probably indicate the four cardinal directions. Cerro Jaboncillo, Manta, Ecuador, 9-14th., century, A.D.

4.068 : Carved stone stela showing a calendrical design around the head of the figure in the abstracted manner of those in India. The corners and ends of the design show square panels in the typical saltire in other panels found in Central America into South America. The centred panels between the saltire panels show a bar with four dots, two each side, that may indicate a Mayan number, perhaps representing in each case the number nine. Cerro Jaboncillo, Manteno, Ecuador, 9-14th., century, A.D.

4.071 : Standing female figure with rayed halo probably representing the sky arch. The flanking squares either side of the niche are characteristic of those in Central and South America, and probably derived from those of Ancient Iran (ILLUST). Manteno Culture, Cerro Jaboncillo, Ecuador, 9-14th., century, A.D.

4.073 : A further Akimbo goddess panel showing the step torana, sky arch, probably derived from India and found also among the Maya in Central America. The crocodile maw symbol is found at the top centre of the panel defining the sky arch. Mantano, Cerro Jaboncillo, Manabi, Ecuador, 9-14th., century, A.D.

4.072 : Akimbo female deity showing the stepped torana, or sky arch, characteristic of Ancient Buddhist iconography in the mid-first millennium A.D. The diagonal stepped divisions of the squares forming the torana appears to relate to astronomical divisions. The akimbo deity is almost certainly the Hindu Adya-Sakti ("Ultimate-Ground"), the "Genetrix of All Things". Mantano, Cerro Jaboncillo, Manabi, Ecuador, 850-1500 A.D.

from the weakened, centralised kingdom. This severe change in the weather was almost certainly the result of a catastrophic, long-term reversal in the climate due to the massive eruption of Krakatoa in 535 A.D. in Indonesia causing decades of disruption throughout the world. It is believed that this particular eruption was the greatest to have occurred in the world's history since the end of the last ice age 11,000 years ago and perhaps since long before that time.

Tiahuanaco survived in its own valley area that surrounds and extends from Lake Titicaca and regenerated in the following centuries to witness another great building period only to finally succumb to another period of devastation caused by climate change in the 11th., century, A.D. One of the regions to gain strength and emerged independent in the 6th., century, A.D. was the Huari who seem to have followed more closely that of the parent state judging from its iconography. The architecture, however, is not similar to that of Tiahuanaco and suggests form-

4.074: Incised plaque depicting a torana or sky arch with rulers or deities passing below. This example shows the lotus as a saltire cross in a square as a basic element in multiples as the symbolic decoration of the several arches similar to those in Ancient Iran and also found in South America. Begram, Andhra Style, 1st., century, A.D.

ative influences from another source insinuating earlier into the regional control of the mother culture. There can be little doubt that there were connections between Tiahuanaco and the Paracas and Nazca Coastal cultures and that the Huari were at the mid point between these geographical locations of Pacific Coast and Altiplano. What was Guamanga and is now called Ayacucho appears to have been the centre between these two disparate regions and from here the expansion of the Huari state moved North toward the contemporary Sican on the North Peruvian Coast. Expansion also occurred to the west towards the Pacific Coast influencing that nearer geographical regions after the collapse of the Nazca culture in the 6th., century, A.D.

On the North Coast the Huari influences are found immediately following Moche V, a period that followed the collapse during the 6th., century and that ended in the 7th., century. This corresponds to the expansion of Huari from Ayacucho in 7th., century, and it has been proposed that the Huari was responsible for terminating the final Moche phase between 700-750 A.D.[140]. The Nazca Phases 7-8 also show the same pattern and it is likely that the collapse and resulting political and social confusion caused by the long period of climatic disruption was seen as an opportunity by the Huari to expand into the coastal plain of Nazca and Ica in the same time band[141]. The contemporary influences south of Lima at Pachacamac appear to suggest that the Huari had close connections with the shrine but the styles were not identical. This may be because the deities revered at Pachacamac were too long established to adopt that of the staff god and the iconography that went with it that Huari adopted from Tiahuanaco. However, further south in Nazca and Ica this iconography had become readily assimilated[142] perhaps because of the earlier connections with Tiahuanaco in the first half of the first millennium A.D.

The Huari in their northern expansion appear on the Central coast north of Lima at Acari[143] and then move further northward. In the collapse of Tiahuanaco in the 6th., century, it is considered, reflected through the iconography that resulted, that there had been a loss of intensity and conviction compared to the direct expression and power of the earlier imagery imposed or borrowed from Tiahuanaco. The staff god from Tiahuanaco is clearly seen in the late Huari iconography[144] and the related regional iconography typified by a more geometric and cuboid style and appears more intellectual in colour, composition, design and linear rhythm[145]. It is this joint Tiahuanaco-Huari legacy that is clearly perceived as the basis of the succeeding Aymara, Inca and Central Coast socio-religious developments[146].

Interestingly, in preserved oral traditions, the first mention of the early peoples of Peru notes that they were so often called giants and the Huaris are recorded from the Indians themselves and noted by Arriaga, a reliable source, to have been giants also and were known as the first "populators" of the land. Huaman Poma de Ayala described the first men of Peru as the Wari-Wirakocharunas probably implying a connection with the Viracochas of Tiahuanaco and Lake Titicaca and the later Huaris who were their heirs[147]. Arriaga also notes that this Huari was also the "god of force" and was invoked when building houses and other constructions[148] and is possibly the direct descendent of the god Huari at Chavin. Interestingly huari among the Tupi of the Amazon forests is the sacred drum and used for communication[149]. The first quipus known are, from that period, the Huari Empire, but it is unknown whether they were introduced into this

Empire or were used in earlier times[150].

Aguada in the Southern Highlands Traditions

Succeeding the Cienaga and Condorhuasi cultures in North West Argentina, the Aguada was known for its striking geometric designs covering their ceramics. They were also known for their advanced metallurgical techniques and appear to be connected to the Atacama culture on the Chilean North Coast. The geometric patterns seem to illustrate what could be described as almost demonic aspects of felines and reptiles that they depicted in both monochrome and polychrome. These are thought to be connected with the much earlier forms of supernaturals found at Paracas and Coastal Chavin but with only limited reflection of Tiahuanaco iconography. This culture is best known for its bronze-making producing some of the most interesting pectorals found in South America[151]. Some of these pectorals exhibit the classic Ancient Middle Eastern armorial animals placed either side of a central figure and featuring the "Maltese" cross also found first, and for a long period, in the Ancient Near and Middle East, usually as decoration on incense burners. Crosses of this type are also found on incense burners in the Mexican codices. The location of the Aguada and its association with the contemporary Atacama culture on the coast, being less connected to Tiahuanaco, suggests that this may have been as the result of settlers arriving on the coast and travelled inland either from modern day Arica in North Chile or further south before settling in the North West region of Argentina.

Atacama and Auracania

In the North of Chile in the barren regions adjacent the Atacama Desert the inhabiting people located between the western side of the Andes and the Pacific Ocean appeared to have subsisted here to exploit the valuable mineral ores for their metallurgical requirements and skills and for exchange. They also practised intensified agriculture and at San Pedro de Atacama there is evidence that there were social stratifications evident in the burial practices where high status burials have been excavated. A few of these include, beside imported textiles and pottery, gold with Tiahuanaco influenced connections as well as gold diadems and pectorals[152].

South of the Atacama the Auracanian people in Central Chile appear to have settled in the region after about 500 A.D. and at a site near Temuco burial urns with model funerary canoes have been uncovered[153]. However there appears to have been no urn burial traditions among the Auracanian Mapuche although the tradition was common and widespread among their neighbouring tribes suggesting this tradition originated from a separate line of development or influence[154]. It has been earlier noted that the Mapuche preserve references to Polynesian culture including the umù, the Polynesian earth oven, not usual elsewhere on the South American coast and these influences can be seen to be obvious since the north section of the West Wind Drift Current flows directly from Southern Polynesia to the Chilean coast.

The Lowland Cultures of Llanos de Mojos in Eastern Bolivia

To the east of the Bolivian Andes the mountains decline precipitously in height to the hot lowland regions of the Gran Chaco - the southern zone extending from the Amazon rain forests. This lowland forms a large region of swampland from the eastern foothills into the undulating plains far to the east to the Parana River and located adjacent to the foothills is the wetlands called the Llanos de Mojos. This vast area has only been partially investigated but it is known that the region shows settlements located on artificial islands connected to other settlements and natural rises by causeways. These constructions and occupations date from the last century B.C. through to about 1100 A.D. Burial urns with elaborate decoration have been retrieved from the later stages of these occupations after the appearance of pottery about 500 A.D. Occupied sites in this region date from an earlier period, about 2000 B.C., thereafter being periodically abandoned in times of excessive dry when the water levels dropped, overall remaining occupied until about 1400 A.D. Burials were interred under the floors of the houses and reflect a high infant mortality and there were few grave goods included apart from personal ornaments[155].

CERAMIC PERIOD in ECUADOR; COLOMBIA and VENEZUELA

Early Ceramic Period in Ecuador

The sites of early Ecuador are famous throughout the world of American archaeology because they provide the earliest known examples of figurines in a ceramic tradition. At Loma Alta in Ecuador the Early Valdivia Phase assemblages were considered to be repositories for the spirits during shamanistic trances. Over five hundred figurines have been recovered in the various levels of occupational refuse and of these less than 100 have no deliberate damage inflicted upon them such as decapitation or facial defacement[156]. The fact that these figurines are so often scarred and unceremoniously dumped in the household refuse (*4.075*) suggests that the spirits believed to inhabit these figurines were not welcome among the people for any period of time or allowed to be permanently housed in the figurine. In curing rituals shamans were believed to be able to coax spirits thought to cause illness into the figurine during healing rituals and then the spirit is "disabled" by the defacement of the figurine or its decapitation.

The Loma Alta Phase, dating from 3000-2300 B.C., and the later Valdivian period dating from 2300-2000 B.C. in Ecuador appear to embody this tradition of decapitation and defacement since it is extended into both phases with stylistic references indicating continuity. The Valdivian Culture figurines continued recognisably to Phase 6, until 1700 B.C., and this time band sees a parallel phase at San Pablo clearly related and inspired from Valdivia. The figurines of the following Machalilla phase are simplified and abstracted and date from 1500-1000 B.C.[157]. Face or mask designs found on the ceramics from the Valdivian period in Ecuador are thought to be related to those found etched on gourd vessels from Huaca Prieta in Northern Peru indicating contact[158].

From c1300-300 B.C. the Chorrero cultural types and derivatives extend more widely in Ecuador and these are considered fine ceramics with high quality modelling that feature a variety of pottery shapes including bottles and whistles (ocarinas)[159]. This period reflects the continuity of ceramic traditions developed in Ecuador up until the beginning of this phase and the extension of this style into regions where they are not found before in this cultural zone. This tradition is noted for its use of iridescent and organic resist painting on their ceramics[160] and this has been considered as the possible origin for the same specialist technique found in Guatemala and Western Mexico. This tradition, known broadly as Chorreroid, covers also the Esmeraldas tradition so well known for its gold working tradition centred on La Tolita and extending a little to the north in Tumaco now in Southern Colombia[161]. The La Tolita tradition, and later the Mantero is noted for its artefacts and ceramics, have much in common in their iconography with motifs suggesting that they was influenced from India and Indonesia. It is thought that the tradition of building house mounds, so common in this tradition, commenced about 500 B.C. and lasted until about 500 A.D. and house models have survived showing thatched gabled houses[162] highly reminiscent of Melanesia and Indonesia (*4.079-84*).

The tomb types that developed in the North West of South America are of a greater variety than found in Andean and Bolivian Peru. In Ecuador there are shaft and chamber, stone-covered pits, circular pits, stone box graves and gallery graves. Of special interest are the above ground log coffins and grave huts in the forested regions[163] highly reminiscent of those in Melanesia, Indonesia and among the Maori of New Zealand. These types are more commonly

4.075 : ...gurines charac-
...ristic of the
...ldivia period in
...outhern Colombia
...d Ecuador but
...osely similar to
...ose of the Jomon
...Japan. Pasto,
...outhern
...olombia, 3-2nd.,
...illennium, B.C.

4.077 : Jomon mask of a closely similar type found in Colombia and Venezuela. Jomon, Japan, 1st., millennium, B.C.

4.078 : Masked face indicated by the eyes visible through the openings similar in principle to examples found in Chavin and other ceremonial sites. Jomon, Japan, 1st., millennium, B.C.

4.076 : Jomon masked seated figure of a similar type ...und widely in Colombia and Venezuela in South America. ...mon, Japan, 1st., millennium, B.C.

found in Colombia but to a more limited degree in the Peruvian Andes. The connections with the Western Pacific extend to spear-throwers and many hooks more associated with these Melanesian peoples have been found in Ecuador as well as other parts of South America[164]. Kwakiutl myths are closely similar to those of Polynesia and North West North America shamanism is closely similar to that of South America. The shamanistic rituals and rites in Ecuador have been noted to be similar to those of the Western Pacific islands and Aboriginal Australia[165].

The political economy of the most northern of the coastal regions of South America appears to have developed differently from those of the Peruvian Andes, Bolivia and through to Northern Argentina and Chile. The classic Andean model indicates that interregional traders were a feature but this appears more concentrated among those of the tribes of Ecuador and Colombia and it is known that these long-distance traders were called Mindalaes. It was these Mindalaes operating in Ecuador and along the coast in particular who informed the Inca Tupac Yupanqui, after his incursions and conquering thrust into Ecuador, of the lands of gold that existed far to the west across the Pacific Ocean.

The interregional trading platforms were apparently developed from the greater complexity of interrelationships found between the Caranqui and Cayambe tribes in the centre north of Ecuador in the later pre-Inca phases[166]. One of the archaeological features of these cultures is that the numerous clusters of house mounds are a usual feature of the Ecuadorian peoples rather than large ceremonial complexes at the settlement centres. These mounds are called tolas and this is the identical name found in India for burial mounds[167]. Some of these settlements contain over 60 mounds and are usually considered raised residential mounds[168]. On these were constructed several houses and possibly were intended to be compounds for clans or extended families. The houses constructed on these tolas known from the Valdivia period were probably flimsy and built of cane framing and with woven cane mat walls[169]. In many of the house mounds interments have been located in the mound itself under the houses or nearby[170].

In the later periods of Ecuador of special interest is the Jama-Coaque culture, considered a "long-lived" efflorescence located on the Pacific Coast. Over 150 sites have been located into the last decade and their history indicates that there was a progressive society reflected in growth and expansion outwards from their initial home location. Of some interest is that these sites appeared to have been subject at some time to volcanic catastrophes since these sites reveal ash covering them to a considerable depth[171]. These people were related to the Guangala and the Bahia cultures and these produced ceramics of a distinctive type including small jars associated with chewing coca. Metallurgy is well attested to in the form of copper implements and metal ornaments recovered from inhumations[172].

In the Quito region of Central Ecuador, on the western plateau of the Andes located almost directly under the Equator, shaft and chamber tombs at La Florida have been examined on the slopes of the Pinchincha volcano and revealed a number of seated burials and many ceramics dating to about 500 A.D. These rich tombs were clearly those of nobles and one woollen textile was retrieved with copper "spangles" sewn to it[173]. A number of rich shaft and chamber tombs have yielded metal work, left after looting, displaying influences from the Huari style from Southern Peru exhibited in the hammered gold and silver objects with characteristic angels and rayed heads[174].

On the sometimes-rugged coastal plains of Ecuador the Guangala culture changed and developed over time and entered another phase known as the Manteno. These cultures are of especial note since their influence extended down the coast from La Tolita on the border with Colombia to Machalilla with a centre at Salango and probably at the very large urban site of Agua Blanca nearby. Salango was noted into the Conquest period for merchants involved in the Spondylus shell trade[175] and was probably in the same location or region that the ancient trade with Peru and even Chile far to the south was organised from. Not only is this Manteno culture important from this coastal trading aspect but from the remarkable legacy of the stelae surviving from that period dating from 500 to 1000 A.D.

The Manteno stelae left to posterity are remarkable for the iconography depicting simplified versions of the Buddhist and later Hindu toranas, or sky arches. The individual squares or modules used in constructing these stepped arches are identical to several of the originally "squared" lotus forms found in Ancient India (*4.074*; *9.125*; *9.148*) but originally derived from Ancient Iran (*9.119*). Examples of the arches or circular borders or bandings are many in these ancient cultures of Asia (*9.120*) and found identically as such outside torana or sky arch forms in Central and South America (*9.117*; *9.121*; *9.130*; *9.133*). The stepped or sprung arch is found in India, most famously at the ancient Buddhist University of Nalanda (*7.078*), in Orissa in North East India, and also in Indonesia in Javan Buddhist architecture. This same form of stepped arch is found among the Maya in Central America and is clearly related to that depicted on the Manteno stelae (*7.082/3*). Also frequently depicted on the stela with the stepped sky arch surrounding the head or whole figure is the female deity seated with legs akimbo identical to the primal female earth goddess of India, known as Kali-Bija or Adyabija[176] and also Padmamunda whom the god Jambhala is sometimes depicted trampling[177]. Found also highly figured in the iconography of the Manteno is the caiman and this also appears to reflect the Ganges crocodile known in its mythical role as the makara associated with the cardinal points and the emergence of the World order (*4.069/70*). Similar vertically carved illustrations of the crocodile appears in the imagery of the Nagas of Assam, Indonesia and Melanesia. This later period after 500 A.D. in Ecuador appears to reflect also the same influences from India in Central America so frequently displayed by the Maya in the same time frame with the Chalukyan Dynasty. This period in South Central India is considered the nursery of Hindu stone built and carved architecture and its great expansionist influence is still found widely in the rest of India. The Chalukyan iconography is widely adopted in various regions from that time in India but importantly this influence seems also to extend abroad to the Americas but assimilated into the local styles where it was adopted. Identical stonework found at the Chalukyan sites is virtually identical to aspects of that built in the end of the corresponding period at Tiahuanaco (*8.016-20*).

The Legend of the Skyris (Scyris) and the Kingdom of Quito
The evidence for the Skyris and the establishment of their Kingdom at Quito in Ecuador are entirely due to the reports of one person, Jaun de Velasco, and his works have been considered a garbled version of historical facts with the references he uses somewhat lightweight[178]. He wrote

4.081 : A typical variation of an elevated hut found on Nias off Sumatra and these islands are closely connected culturally with Polynesia and the Nagas of Assam. Late 19th., century, A.D.

4.080 : A building that is probably intended to emulate a Buddhist stupa (9.023). The image inside however is closely similar to depictions of gods in South India. Jama-Coaque, Ecuador, 200-400 A.D.

4.079 : The aperture through which the god is seen represents the opening of the World Tree or Axis Mundae and appears to be the model for the example found on the Ecuador Coast (4.080). Lingodbhavamurti, Kailasanathasvamin Temple, Kanchipuram, South India, 7th.,-8th.,century, A.D.

4.082 : Architectural house type found widely in the Pacific Ocean and thought to be similar to those on the West Coast of Mexico and on the coast of Ecuador in the first millennium A.D. Bismark Archipelago, Northern New Guinea, Late 19th., century, A.D.

4.083 : Yam houses typical of traditional house construction and design with decorative motifs to gable roof ends similar to the Manta coast of Ecuador. Kiriwina, Bismark archipelago, Melanesia, Late 19th., century, A.D.

his account in some detail two and half centuries after the Conquest and there appears to have been little initiative in his work to separate fact from myth and legend. Since in many cases there is only myth or legend to go on this does not necessarily rule out his history and more recent archaeology may bear out something of the truth in his report.

Velasco records that in the years between 700 and 800 A.D. sailors under their leader Caran arrived on the coast of Ecuador. Here they and their descendants settled for about 200 years founding their capital at Caraquez. After a period of expansion these Cara began to move upriver to where Quito now stands and settled there in about 980 A.D. People who had long been settled in that region opposed the Skyri but were defeated by them and these outsiders founded the Cara empire, known as the Kingdom of Quito. They worshipped the Sun and Moon and erected a temple to the Sun at the site now called Panecillo near Quito that featured an eastern door where two large columns were placed for observing the solstices[179]. They also erected twelve columns to one side of temple and this is reminiscent of the pillars erected by the Incas at Cuzco centuries later.

4.084 : Characteristic West Mexican temple typical of Batak-Toba and other Indonesian and Melanesian Islands. Ixtlan del Rio, Nayarit, West Mexico, 300 B.C.-200 A.D.

This record preserved by Velasco may be seen as another instance of foreign influences arriving on the shores of South America consistent with so many others current among the Indians of South America - and the Inca. This Ecuadorian name, Skyri, is of interest since it appears to correspond to that of a type of priest, a skyri, in the Himalayan foothills of Tibet. There the term skyri might derive from that preserved by the Saka or Sakya from their descent from the Scythian tribes who migrated from Central Asia - the tribe of the Buddha who were the ruling Sakya clan in North India in the 6th., century, B.C. The early Buddhists were intimately involved in proselytisation throughout India and beyond and it has been proposed elsewhere that they were the initiators of trade and missions from India to Indonesia and then to the Americas[180]. This may not appear significant in terms of South American history except to note that Indian iconography is also evident on the coast of Ecuador noted above and there is certainly aspects of imagery that appear too closely similar to that of Tibet to be coincidence found elsewhere in Peru. At about the same time as the Cara incursions into Coastal Ecuador the Garuda bird appears in the imagery of Sican (*5.129-33*) on the North Coast of Peru and this may reflect a broader contact with Asia than might be accounted for by just a few boatloads of men. Even the term Cara appears to relate to the South Indian Canara, long known to be sea trade intermediaries and enablers throughout Asia, but as Miles Poindexter concludes Cara may also relate to Cari and the Polynesian Ari or Ariki[181], terms derived from Ancient India. It is also worth noting that the male Cari or Canari were recorded as wearing their hair long and tied up as a topknot and the most noble among them wore a "hoop" similar to a sieve through which their hair was rolled[182]. This description resemble the topknot so common in India and the hoop sounds remarkable similar to those of the Nagas of Assam and the Tibetans who specialised in hoop-like arrangements.

However, with the increasing knowledge and insight about the Inca state through greater credence now being given to eyewitness accounts after the Conquest, the report of erection of pillars at the Sun temple by the Skyri at about 980-1000 A.D. is reminiscent of those of the Incas several centuries later at Cuzco and suggests a common origin. Since some of the Inca Origin legends note that they came from the North originally it may be that the Cara were in part their ancestors and derived from them their traditions relating to cosmological pillars. One of the most celebrated passages in the history of the Incas is the march north from Pachacamac to overthrow the later Kingdom of Quito lead by Tupac, the son of the reigning Inca Yupanqui, and after achieving this victory he undertook his famed voyage across the Pacific to the west from Manta on the Ecuadorian coast. This conquest may in fact have been initiated by a desire to regain their traditional estate in the north since the later Incas built what was in effect a second capital at Tupibamba in Ecuador. The son of Tupac, Inca Hauyna Capac, married a local Ecuadorian princess and their son Atahualpa challenged for the throne and this may have been based on a joint inheritance claim by right of ancient ancestral descent from the Skyri. Tupac's voyage to the west across the Pacific may have been based on more than sea merchants' information but impelled by a desire to seek out the lands of their forefathers and this undertaking will be of further interest in later chapters.

4.085 :
Wooden ice-boards and a paddle for navigating balsa rafts along with ceremonial rods. Pisco, Southern Highlands Peru, 1300-1521 A.D.

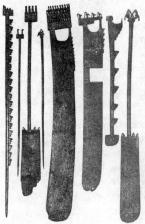

At about 700 A.D. changes in the coastal cultures are evident in recent archaeological research and it may well have been that it was the Skyri under Caran who were the culture-bearers who brought new influences from Asia. In the iconography of this and following periods the Mantero were of particular interest since their stelae clearly records iconography that is related to the Maya and Ancient India in that time band. This follows the path suggested by Poindexter that the Colhua and Quiche of Southern Mexico and Guatemala migrated to Peru and became the Colla (Aymara) and Quechua and this migration is likely also to have left its mark on Ecuador. However, the thesis of Poindexter was that the Ayar Incas were originally from Ancient India, the migration of the Colhuas and Quiche from Central Mexico being an intermediate step among others in their rise to power and their remembered descent was reflected in the retention of the title of great prestige - Ayar[183]. The Skyri may have been a party in that migration, or more likely were a direct trading expedition from Asia, as one of many who still had among them those who could

4.086 : Dual horns as one of the sacred symbols of Buddhism, here representing elephant's tusks, but also apparently found in the Jama-Coaque culture on coastal Ecuador and Western Mexico. Tibet, Late 19th., century, A.D.

4.087 : The Hindu elephant deity Ganesa traditionally holding one tusk that was broken off according to myth. Tusk horns were used traditionally for ritual potions and herbs. Kitching, Orissa, Eastern India, 8-9th., century, A.D.

4.088 : Priest or ruler with dual tusk pendants possibly used for herbs or hallucinogens. These possibly emulate the revered dual tusks found widely depicted in Tibetan Buddhist iconography. Jama-Coaque, Ecuador Coast, 200-400 A.D.

claim the title Ayar and this and other propositions will be of more interest in due course.

Ceramics - An Unsolved Mystery on the Coast of Ecuador

One of the great anomalies in South American history is the fact that among the quite basic and early forms of hunting and gathering equipment on the Ecuador coast there suddenly appears "completely made and beautifully decorated pottery"[184]. The hunter-gatherer artefacts from this and earlier periods are common not only to the coast of Ecuador but also Panama to the North and Peru and Chile to the south consisting of bones and shells, the later in large number being fashioned into fish hooks, with a lesser number utilised for dippers and scoops and some fashioned into pendants. Nothing suggests that these people had developed clay-working skills to produce pottery or figurines let alone producing well-considered technically competent pottery so closely similar to that produced on the other side of the world. This development only occurs on the Ecuadorian coast where the Equatorial Currents flows directly from Asia to Ecuador as the first viable stop in South America.

The first period of pottery was initialises from 3200-2300 B.C.[185] and is robustly made but of high quality of its type and include polished red-slipped ware as well as tetrapod vessels. About 2300 B.C. Phase B is indicated by the introduction of new techniques such as cord impression and incision decoration lasting into succeeding phases. From about 2000 B.C. the pottery in this Valdivia phase had changed and many of the earlier techniques and decorative methods of applications had disappeared. These are replaced by simpler techniques such as rib-and-rub appliqué and rocker stamping and after 1500 B.C. the pottery displays a thinner walled type and is less well polished than in the earlier phases[186]. The most famous product of the early archaeology in Ecuador are the clay figurines (4.075) so similar to those of the Jomon in Japan as indeed is the earlier first phases of pottery. These occur initially in Phase B, about 2300 B.C. but as so often in South American history the first introduction is the finest of the style and technique and there is a gradual descent into less competency and design achievement[187].

Unlike the archaeologists in other countries in South America those of Ecuador, both native and foreign, have been less reticent in recording comparisons with ceramics and figurative achievements in the Old World and Asia in particular. This may be because those of Ecuador and Asia are so similar that comparisons are difficult to deny. They have gone on record a number of times to express their belief that the many parallels between the first of the pottery and the slightly later phase introducing clay figurines showing a fully developed style without any trace of evolution are most likely to have been introduced from abroad and Japan in particular. Betty Meggers, a well-known archaeologist specialising in South American sites, notes the "abrupt" appearance of this fully developed pottery around 3200 B.C., now redated to about 3000 B.C. These first dates are based on Carbon 14 analysis and supports the conclusions of the Ecuadorian archaeologist Emilio Estrada that the "fully-fledged" techniques and style of this first pottery are too similar to that of the Jomon to be coincidental. This conclusion is based on the style and technique of pottery from the Jomon tradition in Kyushu in the same time band as that in Ecuador[188]. Such a conclusion tends to be supported by the fact that this Valdivia pottery and the later figurines appear fully developed and are not surpassed in that style or technique suggesting that it evolved in a tradition elsewhere that went through the various stages of development of technique and decorative design before being introduced into Ecuador. Since pottery was unknown in South America at that time the long period of development necessary to initiate clay products, usually sun dried at first, then fired, must have occurred abroad.

By Phase C, dated from about 2000 B.C., a new type of pottery appears on the Manabi coast of Ecuador and the resulting culture is named the Machalilla and this feature important pottery shapes that were to revolutionise the ceramics of South America including the stirrup spout types. This development was associated with a sea orientated society and saw the introduction of large sea hooks, possibly for deep-sea fishing in the early cultures of Japan and Korea that were particularly noted for their advanced hooks related to deep-sea fishing[189]. This period also witnesses the introduction of the "large, loaf-like" grinding stones and figurative pottery with eyes of the typical "coffee-bean"-shape similar to examples found in Asia and noses with a high ridge[190].

From Valdivia and Machalilla to Chorrero and Influences from Central America

From the Late Formative Period, dating from about 1500 B.C.[191], or a little later, there was a marked change in climate where the coastal mangroves dried out and wcre replaced by salt-flats. Maize and manioc became the staple crops and the more advanced coastal sites of Valdivia and Machalilla expanded inland and developed into the more innovative Chorrero Culture[192]. This new phase was focused on the Guayas River region suggesting an inward thrust from the sea toward the highlands but also toward the lowest section of the Andes giving access to the Napo and therefore the Amazon Rivers (*3.004*). This new Chorrera phase (1500-500 B.C.) witnesses the introduction of high quality thin-walled coiled pottery and lustre-ware finish[193] that links with a similar surface finish later known in Central America and Western Mexico. This period also sees the introduction of "napkin-ring" ear spools or cylinder tubes made of finely textured and highly polished ceramic clay probably associated with clan status[194]. The type of pottery and the ear-spools in particular suggest contact between Ecuador and the Ocos culture of Guatemala and Chalchuapa in Western El Salvador. In examinations of the Chorrera assemblages of pottery and other ceramic products such as the ear spools there are some antecedents in the pottery in the Machalilla phase in Ecuador that have become assimilated into the Chorrera. However, there are many aspects that are not found in earlier Ecuador but these all occur in the Ocos in Guatemala suggesting that this is an intrusive style deriving from Central America[195].

There are many who have long denied or doubted any contact between Central and South America but the contacts between the Chorrera of Ecuador and the Ocos of Guatemala are undeniable and these are later followed by mould produced figurines among many other aspects of cultural transfer. The problem that generated such insistence of lack of contact by these Americanist has it root in the fact that if sea travellers 2400 miles away from South America had the navigation and ship (raft)-building skills to successfully complete such distances then they would be able to reach the Eastern Polynesian islands without any problem. To reach either

Central America from South America or vice versa by sea meant long sections of the journey battling opposing sea currents that impeded mariners in their progress. Mariners, either intentionally or blown of course would drift according to the prevailing winds and the flow of the sea currents. These in fact favour journeys directly to the Eastern Polynesian Islands to the west and a study of the myths and legends of Coastal South America as well as their artefacts suggests that this occurred many times. An admission that mariners could navigate between the high cultural zones of Central America and South America therefore was also an admission that they could have as, or more easily have reached Polynesia, Melanesia, Indonesia and Asia.

In the microcosm of the Ecuadorian coast Meggers notes the assertion of Emilio Estrada that, as a weekend sailor himself as well as an archaeologist, he knew only to well that tacking was necessary for merchants mariners to sail their traditional rafts from the north coast of Ecuador down to the Guayas Delta[196]. This was because the powerful rip of the Humboldt Current flowing northward from Chile and Peru also flowed up the coast of Ecuador and then turned west into the Central South Pacific when it met the Equatorial Counter Current. This current flowed across from Asia to Central America where one branch flowed north up to Mexico and the other south to meet the Humboldt off Northern Ecuador before joining it in its westward flow. This tacking in a sailed raft was achieved by the South American sailors by the insertion of adjustable keel-boards inserted between the logs of the raft down into the water and raised or lowered to increase or reduce the resistance and deflect the direction as necessary[197]. These rafts were known among the Bahians on the Central Ecuador Coast and were probably based on those developed in earlier times since similar centre boards (sometimes called "ice-boards") are found in the excavated sites in Peru much further south (*4.085*). Meggers noted that similar rafts with centreboards were to be found in South East Asia[198]. It is clear that such ocean-going craft were used in trading all along the Chilean, Peruvian and Ecuadorian coasts and undoubtedly it was this ability to manoeuvre their rafts with centre- or keel- boards that allowed then to sail onward and return against contrary winds and currents to Central America and Western Mexico.

Meggers noted that at the time of the Jomon in Japan large sea craft capable of carrying 100 men and a 1000 metric tons were plying the China seas. These large craft would have taken into account not only supplies including water sufficient to complete their voyages but allowed a contingency for additional time for voyages in typhoons, common at certain times of the year when they were blown off course[199]. It is now known that ancient mariners sailed the seas before the Jomon period from Japan to the coast of China, and also to Thailand in the west and probably India, and as far east as New Guinea dating from the 5th., millennium, B.C.[200]. Clearly, if they were so capable of reaching so very far across thousands of miles of open and climatically dangerous ocean, it is unlikely that they would have stopped at New Guinea. It is unlikely also to be a coincidence that it was in this millennium that cultural advances were suddenly established on the Peruvian coast. It is simply not logical that some mariners would not have been adventurous enough to seek further in the Pacific Islands in the following millennia when the evidence for long distance oceanic sailing goes so far back in time.

The weight of evidence accumulating from archaeological excavations in Mexico and Guatemala, however, is progressing beyond the stage where denials that there were contacts between North and South America can be sustained. In recent research the Nayarit and other cultures of Western Mexico have produced so many identified aspects of South American iconography in Mexico that contact between the two distant regions cannot be any longer denied and is moving toward full acceptance. In a recent inclusion in a well-illustrated book Patricia Rieff Anawalt[201] records the progress in Ancient West Mexican excavations paralleling and linking them directly with those in Ecuador. This forms a radical shift away from the indigenous development theory so beloved of the politically correct late twentieth century generation.

The style of the many figurines found among the Nayarit and Ecuadorian figurines is clearly delineated and proven beyond doubt in the exact parallels in iconography reflected in textiles and decorative motifs and ritual objects. Anawalt notes of the Nayarit that there is no region in Mesoamerica whose "archaeology is so distinct from that of its neighbours" and this includes "shaft tombs, mortuary offerings, ceremonial architecture, ceramic vessel forms, and design motifs"[202]. These various elements are paralleled in examples such as shaft tombs known in Colombia, Ecuador and Peru and shared elements of culture extend to the Tarascans. These people were the neighbours of the Nayarit and their clothing is shown to have parallels also with South America[203]. Paralleled along with numerous other aspects are the similarities of Ecuadorian figurines including animals and hunched-back humans with those of Western Mexico and of particular note during the Jama-Coaque period in Ecuador (200-400 A.D.) were the dual tusk pendant common to both regions that is specifically noted in early Buddhist iconography (*4.088*). This would not be of note except that there are many other aspects of Jama-Coaque iconography that appears to have been introduced from India, the Himalayas but also Tibet (*4.086/7*). Other parallels now accepted due to mariner contact are axe-money and metallurgy and these are reflected in metal artefacts such as tweezers, bells, rings[204] and spirals that reflect the same artefacts and their designs also known in Indonesia and India.

Chorrero to Guangala in Ecuador
Succeeding the Chorrero phase was the Guangala, along with the Jambeli and this absorbed the iridescent speciality and ceramic forms from the Chorrero[205]. The Jambeli was located in the Guayas Deltas region and is known for its bark-beaters made from stone. Bark-beaters are known from Indonesia through Melanesia, Polynesia into Central and South America and appear as something of an anachronism in a society that was well-advanced in producing textiles. In Polynesia and Melanesia the bark-beater was an essential item since the loom never occurred in the former and only as a late introduction in the latter island group. Both loom and bark-beater existed together in parts of Indonesia since bark-cloth was anciently associated for the most part with deified mariner ancestors and was not supplanted by the later looms and cloth techniques such as painted and batik textiles. All of these techniques are first found in India and were transferred from there anciently into Indonesia but this was done only piecemeal to certain centres in Java and Sumatra before gradually being adopted in the more populous regions on the Indonesian Islands. Hence the first technique of bark beating was long adopted and associated with status before the introduction of the loom and retained as such from then on. At a considerably later date the loom was introduced and all of these techniques along with many aspects of cultural development were transferred from Java to South America and Ecuador in particular.

In considering cultural transfer Betty Meggers noted, and illustrated, the remarkable similarity of the gabled house of coastal Ecuador preserved in a number of examples of finely modelled clay and those of the Palau Islands in Micronesia. This is also reflected in some of the sloping bargeboards fascias to the gable and the decoration applied[206] and similar examples of the house type and decoration were still being constructed into the twentieth century. Many other aspects of this Jama-Coaque phase such as the crosses identical to the contemporary decorated crosses in India (*8.026*) and those of Peru and especially at Tiahuanaco in Bolivia are significant. This same culture in Ecuador reflects aspects of Tibetan iconography also found in Peru and are found also more widely in Melanesia and probably originating in Indonesia. These connections with the Pacific Islands, South East Asia, India, and with the Maya, are proved by the stelae iconography from Cerro Jaboncillo all displaying aspects of the calendrically related sky arch or torana of India (*4.068-74*).

In the more local Bahia phase in this period, surviving there into the early twentieth cen-

tury, a great number of platform mounds and large middens of occupation refuse were constructed. Many of the terraces had been faced with uncut stones and some of these constructions
were terraced in tiers of three or four steps. Ramps or staircases provided access to the summit
and depressions, thought to have been reservoirs, were located between these platforms measuring from 20-50 metres wide and 50-175 metres long. Unfortunately they were all destroyed after
the first modern survey in 1923 that resulted in a great loss for Ecuadorian history since this was
among the most populous and long occupied regions in coastal Ecuador[207].

The Coastal Bahia in Ecuador
In the Bahia phase also bark-beaters (*1.001-3*), headrests and stools are found closely similar to
those found in Oceania (*4.092-9*), and Asia and include gaming pieces with markings of a dot in
a circle so similar to those found in Asia[208]. Also considered by Meggers as influences from the
Pacific are the variety of feather headdress found among these Ecuadorian people identical to
those found in Oceania and Asia. Meggers notes of the figurative Bahia imagery surviving in the
ceramic assemblages that the "resemblance in sitting position between Asian and Bahia Phase
images might be dismissed as coincidence were it not for the presence of other Asiatic elements"
and this included the headrests and "saddle-roofed house models"[209]. Evident also, and probably
so in earlier phases, was the many examples surviving from this phase of nose ornaments identical to many found India (*10.022/3*), in Indonesia and Melanesia (*10.008*; *10.012/3*; *10.015*;
10.018)[210]. The mould-made figurines are also evident at this time and are closely similar to
mould-made figurines adapted to the cultures of Mexico[211] and Central America and it is of interest therefore that mould-made figurines were a speciality after about 6-700 A.D. in Burma and
earlier in Northern India.

The sea trade extended from South America to Mexico on log rafts, or balsas with sails
and keel-boards, this sailing technique already being note, and the arrival of these people in Bahia
has been suggested by Meggers as "best explained as the result of transpacific contact"[212]. The
Bahia people introduced radical changes, so many clearly so similar to those of the Old World
that natural development from the existing cultural levels before them was not sufficient to
explain the sudden changes that occurred. However, the opinion is that the Bahia people arrived
at an opportune moment in the development of Ecuador, such as it was, since there appeared to
be a sufficiently settled and stable agricultural base for these intrusive culture-bearers to be able

4.090 : Ruined stone throne with a coiled serpent design with four small coiled
serpents in each corner almost certainly representing the cardinal points identical to
some representations in India and Burma. Manteno culture, Mantra, Coastal
Ecuador, 9-14th., century, A.D.

4.089 : Ancient statuesque depiction of a ruler seated on his high status
stool that was probably the origin of similar stools from the Ancient
Middle East to India through the Pacific Islands to South America. Tello
Mound, Lagash, Sumeria, Mid-3rd., millennium, B.C.

4.091 : A ruler name seal or cartouche traditional in Mesopotamia is here depicted
supported on addorsed figures of bulls. This addorsed motif that was later transferred and utilized in India and found among the Maya and in the Andes. Akkad
Dynasty, Mesopotamia, Late 3rd., millennium, B.C.

4.092 : Stone-carved figure standing on a stool, or altar. The seat or altar top is supported by a integral crouching anthropoid puma featured in many surviving examples. Cerro de Jaboncillo, Manteno, Coastal Ecuador, 850-1450 A.D.

4.093 + 4.094 : Moulded clay stools similar in design to those of wood construction elsewhere in South America and in Polynesia. Ecuador Coast, 1st., millennium, A.D.

4.095 : Royal throne in the original form of a elaborate stool. Ninevah, Assyrian Period, 900-700 B.C.

4.096 : Wooden stool of an elliptical type but essentially similar in design and purpose to those in South America and Polynesia. Ancon, North Coast Peru.

4.097 : Long wooden stool typical of the Tukano Desana in Southern Colombia. Tuyuka, Rio Tiquie, South Eastern Colombia, Pre-20th., century, A.D.

4.098 : Stools of a Tukano type found in North West Amazonia. Tukano, Rio Tiquie, South East Colombia, Pre-20th., century, A.D.

4.099 : A fine example of the typical stone carved throne found on the coast of Ecuador. Manteno Culture, Manta, East Coast Ecuador, 9-14th., century, A.D.

to establish themselves without having to start from scratch.

From this period it was seen that, from the time of the Bahia phase, contact between Ecuador and Mexico was established on a more regular basis since the later cultural phases exhibit cross-cultural exchanges more comprehensively[213]. This would confirm theories in principle held by Miles Poindexter and others two generations and earlier ago that there were intrusions from Mexico that were to establish themselves among the native peoples of South America. This confirms the links between the Mexican Colhuas, Mayan Chols and Quiche-Mayans and the Collas (Aymaras) and Quechua in South America[214]. The fact that this Bahia phase continues with traditions of the Jambeli phase associated with the Western Pacific in architecture and the production of bark-cloth suggests that Poindexter's conclusions, postulated from the available evidence in his day, were correct in assuming that the myths and legends of culture-bearers arriving by sea from Asia to Mexico and then on to Ecuador without excluding direct contact[215].

Jama-Coaque after Bahia

The Jama-Coaque phase was another that developed on the coast of Ecuador and this evolved north of the Bahia, located on the Central Coast, but south of La Tolita. This phase continued the traditions already known for their shared artefactual types with Polynesia and Asia such as headrests, status stools, spindle whorls and clay stamps. From the Bahia phase, house models are found that continue the tradition into this phase and these also reflect the characteristic curvature of the ridge with front and rear gables so reminiscent of Western Pacific framed architecture. Not least of note are the gold nose plates found in Colombia as well as Ecuador but also in Melanesia and likely to have been introduced there from South America. In this period also fine designs applied by cylinder seals are also found and believed to have be used in stamping patterns for textiles and body decoration. This use of clay or wooden stamps and cylinder seals is shared from the earlier period with Peru and is highly reminiscent of India where the ancient tradition of carved flat stamps are still used into the modern day for textile printing. This technique originally derived from the Indus Valley civilisation from the 4 and 3rd., millennium B.C. and aspects of stamp and cylinder seals are similar to those of the Near and Ancient Middle East[216].

In this phase pipes were manufactured and these are believed to have been used, for the most part, for ritual tobacco smoking. This tradition of pipe smoking may have been instituted by mariners who used narcotic substances, and probably tobacco as well, to stave off hunger and thirst at sea by smoking or more often chewing it to dull the senses (*4.026*). Other researchers and historians believed that coca was used on long distance voyages between South America and Eastern Polynesia for precisely this reason. Myths and legends record that a particular leaf was chewed by mariners in Samoa in Central Polynesia to assist in alleviating hunger and thirst over long months at sea[217]. Many illustrations in ceramics and clay sculpture depicting portrait heads where coca quids are obviously being chewed since the bulge in the cheeks betrays this habit (*4.019*).

Betty Meggers observed that this culture also shared many aspects of its culture with Central America and that many of these appeared to have greater antiquity in Mexico and suggests therefore that this was due to sea contact from Mexico and Central America into Ecuador. This entry in fact appears to have been a "re-establishment" of contacts since there were earlier periods reflecting similar cultural exchanges[218]. In the Jama-Coaque phase the dress and ornamentation, including feathered headdresses, are similar to those of Mexico where the contemporary period was that of the apogee of Teotihuacan in Central Mexico. This Central American expansion of influence into Southern Mexico and among the Maya, particularly in the Guatemalan high lands near the Pacific Ocean Coast, is witnessed in the art and architecture of Santa Lucia Cotzumalguapa, Bilbao, and other coastal sites between 200-700 A.D. This region shares many aspects of contact not only with Ecuador but with Indonesia and India literally on the other side of the World[219].

From Jama-Coaque to Gold Rich La Tolita

In the extreme north of Coastal Ecuador the most famous of the Ecuadorian cultures was located at a river entrance called La Tolita. The nucleus of the site was centred over an area of one square kilometre in the phases to the last century B.C.[220] on an island in the Rio Santiago near Esmeraldas. The culture is known for over forty mounds but those on the island itself are the centre of the civilisation that saw one of the more abundant producers in gold ornamentation known. These mounds were more or less rectangular in shape and the highest reached 9 metres and covered an area of 20 by 45 metres. Some of the constructions appear to have been platforms where the largest was 82 by 25 metres but only 2 metres high. Besides rectangular mounds others are circular or ovoid and are between 1.5 and 7.5 meters high where the highest of these are situated around a plaza while others are located along the riverbank[221].

Early Tolita occurs from about 600 B.C. when first habitations are erected near the mouth of the Santiago River, a region known for its mangrove swamps in difficult waterlogged terrain. As the population expanded the small islands, and coastal strips

4.100 : Eunuchs were a common feature in Ancient Mesopotamia. This archer is considered typical of the beardless eunuch who were used as archers and courtiers but known also in Ancient South America. Assyrian relief, 900-700 B.C.

flanking the river, were occupied and figurines, utensils and vessels with decoration having references to the Machalilla (1800-1500 B.C.) and Chorrera (1500-300 B.C.) phases to the south in Coastal Ecuador are evident. From 400 B.C. significant changes are evident at La Tolita reflected in a steep rise in population and the attempts at land reclamation are undertaken to provide for this expansion contemporary with the first introduction of gold ornamentation[222].

The urbanisation of La Tolita was established by 200 B.C. and it reached its apogee in about 400 A.D. in the Classic Phase. Contacts with Western Mexico and Central America, and Colombia as an intermediate, are evident and recognised to have existed from earlier centuries by present-day Ecuadorian archaeologists. La Tolita is now seen as a ritual site where people from far outside the region gathered for festivals and the exchange of trade goods and ideas. The closest reflections that Ecuador has with Mexico are found among the probable prototypes in Vera Cruz region on the east coast of Mexico, the Valley of Mexico at Teotihuacan, and Oaxaca in Southern Mexico[223].

From the first century A.D. in the Classic phase the urban centre expanded to about 2 square kilometres and is thought to have housed about 5000 people[224]. In this Classic period the main ceremonial core was focused on a rectangular plaza about 190 metres wide with the most important mounds surrounding it on the perimeter, forming overall a U-shaped arrangement. Parallels have been drawn with the U-shaped ceremonial centres found far to the south in, or near the Casma Valley at Las Haldas and Moxeke dating to a millennium before La Tolita. The sacredness of the site as a pilgrimage centre appears to have been the focus of desire for people from the surrounding regions to consider it a suitable place for burial since it has an unusually high density of gravesites on this island centre. Many excavated burials have revealed great wealth and an abundance of gold ornaments, attracting the looters greed that has almost destroyed the site from early in the last century[225]. Gold occurs locally and this, along with readily accessible silver and copper supplies, was used for ornaments and ritual objects[226]. These ornaments were interred in graves in great numbers and included fine gold masks corresponding to those later known in Colombia and Peru but also known in the Old World in the same time band.

In agriculture, raised fields were also utilised in intensive agriculture and this took advantage of the swampy ground to create drainage channels that were open at the northeast end to remove excess water. The soil removed from the channels was heaped up the removed soil onto the crop area between them to raise the natural ground level higher not dissimilar in principle to the raised field systems at Tiahuanaco. In the final period of La Tolita, after 90 A.D to 400 A.D., some of the marshy shores of the island were reclaimed by infill to provide additional land for housing to accommodate the expanding population[227].

In the La Tolita phase many of the elements of material culture were shared with the contemporary Jama-Coaque further to the south, and their respective figurines and ocarinas modelled in anthropomorphic forms, along with flutes and panpipes are indistinguishable. Figurines are of particular note in La Tolita for, apart from those that are so often found mould-made[228], as in Central America, there are those that exhibit an individual style. These appear to have special votive functions, possibly representing aspects of divinity or cosmology, and much prized by collectors because of their ornate and expressive qualities.

Contemporary with La Tolita is the Atacames culture on the North Coast of Ecuador that featured mounds with chimney burials and other interments that were dug directly into the ground. Gold inlays in the incisor teeth occur here before they are found further south in the Guayas region and were also inserted into the skin for ornamental effect that dated to about 270 A.D.[229]. Such teeth ornaments are well known among the Maya but also the No-Su of South China and some of the Naga tribes of Assam[230].

Apart from La Tolita's connections to the Jama-Coaque there are other regional cultures that were initiated or progressed during the second half on the first millennium B.C. Some of these occur inland in the southern region of Ecuador such as the Chaullabamba Phase dating from about 600 B.C.[231]. Others occur inland along the western highlands of the Andes northward from Cuenca to the Colombian border, and beyond, but are too limited at this time in their archaeological investigation to be progressed further here. From the middle of the first millennium A.D. the expanding influence from the coastal cultures begins to change the character of these highland polities and the legends of the Canar expansion from the North Coast into the highlands appears to set the pattern of change for these smaller highland cultural units.

Integration Period from 700 A.D. in Ecuador

As the expanding coastal cultures began to influence, and perhaps control, the highland centres from about 700 A.D. there is a notable shift toward shaft and tomb interments in the archaeology resembling the traditions in Colombia and Peru but also including urn burials[232]. Notable also was the continuing tradition of copper axe-money and the first appearance of stone and copper mace heads perhaps arriving from the North Coast of Peru where the post-Moche Sican culture was establishing itself and expanding northward. Spear-throwers, lances, slings and wooden swords[233] found also in Peru make their appearance and artefacts such as copper tweezers are also found[234]. Overall, however, the quality of ceramics declines because of the increase in mass production and mould-made objects[235].

The Manteno Phase - Guayaquil to Bahia on Coastal Ecuador

The Manteno phase features a period of building wells where these were constructed by deep excavations in either soil or rock where the former were lined with rocks that were either surface found or worked. Reservoirs were also built and terraces, still used into the twentieth century, were constructed around the Cerro de Hojas for cultivations and house building. Particularly notable among the Manteno is the use of stone in the construction of the whole building, unusual before this time[236].

Low rectangular mounds were constructed between the houses and among these excavated graves, probably related to the adjacent family occupations, the few shaft and chamber tombs found appeared to have been reserved for the elite clans. Other forms of interment were also found direct into the earth and secondarily in a pot. In the north of Ecuador near the Colombian border there are references in Spanish chronicles to another form of ritual disposal after death and that including first the flaying the bodies. The skin was then subject to preservation processes and the body itself burned after which the skin was stuffed with straw and hung from the temple roof. The heads were subject to further processes where it was reduced in size to that not much larger than a man's fist and the same process was noted applied into historic times among the Jivaros in the Amazonian forest in Eastern Ecuador[237].

Stuffed Flayed Effigies of North West South America

The custom of flaying and stuffing the human skin appears to derive from Colombia, at least in terms of diffusive influences in South America. In more historic times, the exact date being uncertain, the Canelos Quechua Indians of the foothills of the Eastern Andes in the Amazon forest adopted the Colombian custom of smoking and stuffing the flayed skins of the vanquished enemies[238]. The Incas themselves also claimed to have flayed and stuffed the skins of their fierce, implacable enemies, the Chancas after their final defeat, with ashes and straw and displayed these to remind all of the fate of those who opposed the will of the Inca[239].

In transit through Colombia with his squadron of Spanish soldiers from the North of

Colombia Cieza de Leon recorded on the way to Ecuador, and then on to Peru, the customs of the peoples encountered, and while in Colombia he wrote of the custom of flaying and stuffing of victim's bodies. He recorded; "Near this valley (Cali) there was a village, the chief of which was the most powerful and respected of all the chiefs of the neighbourhood. His name was Petecuy. In the centre of his village there was a great and lofty round wooden house, with a door in the centre. In this dwelling the light was admitted by four windows in the upper part, and the roof was of straw. As one entered through the door, there was a long board stretching from one end of the house to the other, on which many human bodies were placed in rows, being those of men who had been defeated and taken in war. They were all cut open, and this is done with stone knives, after which they eat the flesh, stuff the skin with ashes, and place them on the board in such sort as to appear like living men. In the hands of some they placed lances, and in those of others darts and clubs. Besides these bodies, there is a great abundance of arms and legs collected together in the great house, insomuch that it was fearful to see them, thus" ..... "But these Indians gloried in the sight, saying that their fathers and ancestors taught them to act thus. Not content with natural food, they turned their bellies into the tombs of their neighbours ...."[240].

This eyewitness account recorded by Cieza de Leon is highly reminiscent of the body parts and death scenes of captives at Cerro Sechin in the Casma Valley far to the south in Central Peru. In Colombia and Peru these customs may well have been instituted by mariners who were forced to resort to, or were accustomed to cannibalism, due to extreme hunger and thirst on the last long leg of their ocean voyage from Eastern Polynesia to the American Pacific Coast. In Ecuador Cieza de Leon reported that, "In some villages of these Indians they have a great quantity of skins of men full of ashes, the appearance of which is frightful as those in the valley of Lile near the city of Cali ..."[241].

It s now known that the Chinchorro in the 4th millennium B.C. were actually preserving the outer form of the dead by a more sophisticated form of mummification but using herbs and sticks to fill the abdominal cavity. In the more northern version reported by Cieza de Leon it may have been a more poorly understood by the indigenous people and their version adopted or applied from contact or from a common source. Filling skins with straw is certainly not exclusive to South America and in Indonesia cloth imitations of elephants were filled with straw and placed on a grave as a monument into more recent centuries and a similar custom was known among the Nagas of Assam and in China[242]. In India a snakes skin was believed to be able to endow invisibility upon its owner and in an ancient text, Kautilya's Arthasastra, the skin of a snake was filled with the ashes of a man bitten by a snake and this was believed to cause animals to be invisible[243]. From about the second century A.D. after the collapse of the Hunno-Sarmatian, a Scthyian people in Siberia, clay masks appear in inhumations and apparently seen in kurgars from the 2nd century B.C. to 2nd century A.D.[244]. Effigies made from the sacks of the ashes of the cremated deceased and stuffed with straw were then endowed with the clay masks and clad in a fur coat[245]. It must be remembered that Professor Victor Maier, a specialist in that region, noted the close similarities of the local effigies and those of the Chinchorros on the other side of the world[246]. These comparisons along with other aspects of later Tiahuanacan iconography seem to be a little too similar to be coincidence. The Siberian examples have been paralleled with the most ancient examples known in the Egyptian rites where effigies of the god Osiris were stuffed with grain in the belief that they would ensure a good harvest[247]. This also links with the practise of human sacrifice at sowing time since Osiris was the sacrificed deity suffered to ensure the rebirth of mankind. It is likely therefore that the South American examples were the simplified versions of the Asian introductions probably from India and Indonesia, the intermediaries between the Ancient Near and Middle East and China with the Pacific.

Human sacrifice appears to have been a part of the calendrically defined agricultural rit-

4.101 : Prisoners of war in Assyria were often pegged out and flayed and frequently had their heads carried off as trophies reminiscent of Ancient North and South Coastal Peru in the first half of the first millennium A.D. Assyria, First half of the first millennium, B.C.

4.102 : Frame-tied prisoner but characteristic of framed burials in Melanesia. Moche, Chimbote, North Central Coast, Peru, 400-600 A.D.

4.103 : Frame-tied prisoner but characteristic of framed burials in Melanesia. Moche, Trujillo, North Central Coast, Peru, 400-600 A.D.

4.104 : Assyrian prisoners were pegged out and following their death eagles fed upon their bodies and carried off their entrails as depicted here. Moche prisoners on the Peruvian coast suffered similar fates. Assyrian Period relief, 900-700 B.C.

ual in South America as they were in Aboriginal India and in Indonesia. Cieza de Leon noted that the peoples of Ecuador offered the hearts of human sacrifices to their gods suggesting that the contacts with Mexico were still maintained into the Conquest era. After the heart was torn from the victim it was planted with the sowing of the seed in their fields, also on occasions when a chief fell ill, and these events were accompanied by the sound of drums, bells and the idols of the gods including feline images of the jaguar. The English archaeologist and historian G.H.S. Bushnell considered that these rites on the Manta coast were so different from those that had preceded it, including other cultural aspects such as the ceramic types of this period, that they had to have been introduced from abroad. Others have noted that the use of personal names corresponding to the date of birth, known in Mexico, and India; gold inlays in the teeth particularly known among the Maya in Central America, and among the Nagas of Assam and in Southern China; ceramic masks and pottery painted after firing, are among sixty-four elements common to both Mexico and Central America and Ecuador complied by Stephan de Bhorhegy[248].

Manta, Cerro de Hojas and the Stela de Jaboncillo

The U-shaped seats found inland from Manta on the Pacific shore, so celebrated as the most known elements of the Mantero culture in earlier generations have been conjectured to derive from South East Asian contacts. Because these finely carved stone seats were discovered in situ surrounded by stonewalls and similar constructions existed in Asia, this has been seen as evidence of trans-Pacific intrusions. The best known of these were discovered in a circle of at least thirty carved stone thrones at Cerro de Hojas in 1850 A.D. and one retained a statue standing on it (4.092) instigating the question as to whether these were intended to be seats or altars[249]. Other suggestions included the most likely alternative to thrones of priests and that was that these were intended to be spirit seats similar to those found among the Huichol in Western Mexico and in South East Asia and Melanesia (10.055/6). What is clear, however, is that the stelae at Cerro de Jaboncillo and so many of the aspects associated with the Mantero also show common origins not only in Mexico but in India and therefore appears to correspond to a period when there was a substantial movement of mariners, traders and possibly settlers from India to Central America and from Central America to Ecuador as well as from India directly to Ecuador. This also corresponds to the importations, or emphasise continuing contacts with Indonesia since so many of

4.105 : Framed, mummified tribal ancestors usually kept in the roof rafters after the rites and ritual drying of the corpse has been performed. Ugar (Stephen's Island), Melanesia, late 19th., century, A.D.

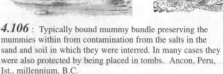

4.106 : Typically bound mummy bundle preserving the mummies within from contamination from the salts in the sand and soil in which they were interred. In many cases they were also protected by being placed in tombs. Ancon, Peru, Ist., millennium, B.C.

4.107 : The preserved heads of war victims whose decapitated heads were arrayed as in life. Note the dual feathers typical of Peruvian headdresses. Maori, New Zealand Early 19th., century, A.D.

4.108 : Typical mummy bundle from North Central Coast Peru with "soul nets" at the lower left identical to those produced in Western Mexico, among the No-Su of Southern China, the Nagas of Assam and the Gonds of India. Ancon, North Central Coast Peru, First millennium, B.C.

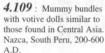

4.109 : Mummy bundles with votive dolls similar to those found in Central Asia. Nazca, South Peru, 200-600 A.D.

4.110 : Bound mummy in a region displayed influences from India and Polynesia. South Australia is on the ancient sea route from Madagascar to New Zealand and South America on the "fast track" utilising the Roaring Forties . Adelaide, South Australia, Early 19th., century, A.D. or earlier.

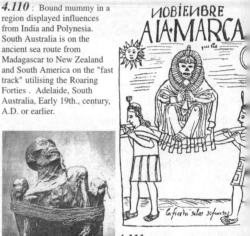

4.111 : Incas and those of high st were mummified and adored after d and attended festivals as if alive. P Ayala; Inca Peru, 16th., century, A.I

4.112 : Preserved body fixed to frames in a similar manner to those found on Coastal Peru. Darnley Island, South Australia, or Torres Straits, Papua-New Guinea, Melanesia Pre-19th., century, A.D.

these traits and traditions are recognisable there among the peoples of Celebes and Borneo.

A feature of the Manteno Phase was the manifest differentiation of levels of status in society reflected in the individual elite ornaments, burial grave goods and reflective of a society headed by an overall chief with sub-chiefs, and corresponding levels of status appears typically on the Manabi coast at their capital of Manta. The great chief was accompanied in processions by trumpeters and drummers and his house and harem were guarded by eunuchs whose nose and lips were cut off to disfigure them[250] (*4.100*). This would appear to reflect the contemporary style of the courts of India and Ancient Middle East contemporary with this period.

It is known that the Inca Atahualpa, before he was captured by the Conquistadors, had planned to have all the Spaniards killed except for the horse-handler, since he was considered useful in tapping for the knowledge of the training and care of the horses, and the Inca intended to have castrated. It is also recorded that there were several groups of priests in the Inca Empire

4.114 : Meriah sacrificial post used for strapping a human victim to it to be cut to pieces while alive in the belief that the body parts would bring fertility to the fields in which they were planted. Gond, Central India, Late 19th., century, A.D.

4.113 : Sketch of Meriah Sacrifice as witnessed at Goomsur - the sacrifice of a female is usual and may be a fanciful introduction to create sympathetic opposition to a long tradition of human sacrifice. Gond, Central India, Mid-19th., century, A.D.

4.115 : A group of Meriah victims rescued before sacrifice at the yupe or sacrificial post. Gond, Central India, Mid-19th., century, A.D.

excluding the High Priest, the Villca Humu, and the Hatun Villca, who were monks and who were largely eunuchs, known as Corasca[251], and the religious sections included nuns who were largely closeted. Bernabe Cobo notes that guards were provided at the nunneries and House of the Virgins to protect their "honour" and it is likely that they were also eunuchs although he does not mention it as a fact[252]. This follows the pattern in Ancient Near and Middle East and in India where in Iran the term for a court eunuch was kwaja sara where kwaja meant master or an honorific title and appears to be the origin for the Peruvian term.

In India the term Kirasani appears to derive from that of the Persian kwaja-sara. In South India this assistant of the caste priest of the Gadabas, of note in connection with Central America in an earlier publication[253], was known by this term of Kirasani. In the more ancient ceremonies associated with the village goddess in the hills the Kirasani acted as the priest when animal sacrifices were required. Near to the shrine of the village goddess was a ceremonial swing where thorns were attached to its upper surface and the presiding priest, or priestess if the male was not available, swings annually once a year and was said to be able to do so without harm in a ritual relating to agricultural rites. However, the male priest is only allowed to sit on the swing if he was a eunuch, since he was considered "lucky" for the village if this was the case[254]. This suggests that the thorns in fact originally, anciently, related to castration rites where the priest's blood was considered an essential element to be mixed with the sowing of the new grain in the annual sowing cycle and certainly would then derive from rites known in the Ancient Middle East. Many researchers have seen the parallels between these early rites and those of the galli or self-mutilating priests of Cybele known from West Asia through Greece into Rome and beyond into Central and North Europe[255]. This would appear to indicate that in more ancient times priests were often, or more usually eunuchs and this was transferred to Peru long before the Inca Dynasty.

The eunuch in India was called Hrija in Hindu tradition and Khoja in that deriving from the Muslim[256]. Khoja clearly derives from Kwaja earlier noted and was the term that in more recent times applied to deliberately castrated males while the term Hrija referred to those naturally or accidentally occurring[257]. In myth the personified element of the Sky, Dyaus, remained in material form as the eunuch Bhiksha[258] (*7.086*) suggesting that ritual castration was not necessarily considered a degradation, and expected of priests and court retainers, and this would appear to be the case also in Ancient Peru.

Meriah Sacrifice and the Blood Rituals in South America

The association of human blood to ensure a good harvest is known from the most ancient times in Eurasia. The first intimations occur in the Ancient Egyptian rituals related to Osiris and extended, and possibly derived from the Ancient Near and Middle East. These ritualised traditions are preserved in the myths and legends of the creation of mankind as the sacrifice of one of the gods whose blood was used mixed with clay or ground grain to create mankind. It is now known that major migrations extended repeatedly over many millennia long before the more famed Aryan migrations into the Indian Subcontinent in the early first millennium B.C. Undoubtedly these ancient myths and rituals were transferred with many others into the successive cultural layers of Aboriginal and pre-Aryan India and that this belief in human blood being required to "anoint" the new sown grain undoubtedly was transferred with them. The great myths of Merodach (Marduk, also called Kingu) being sacrificed, or perhaps more accurately this deity ordering another deity to suffer his fate, possibly an independent god named Kingu, and this myth appears to have been assimilated into India and have been dealt with in an earlier work[259]. In India, dissociated from the broader context of their original homeland, these myths were assimilated and adapted according to the emotional and religious needs and development of the many and various tribes indigenous and naturalised in the Subcontinent. Among many of the Aboriginal tribes and those later peoples who had become partially or wholly immured in them were the Gonds who retained the tradition of human sacrifice into the late 19th., and possibly early 20th., century, despite the concerted attempts by the British colonial administration to stamp it out. This form of sacrifice related to the season for sowing the seed in the fields, especially important of this agricultural people, was known as the Meriah Sacrifice. The Gonds have proved to be of importance in previous works in relation to Ancient Mexico and Central America[260] and their influence appears also to have extended to South America even if only via Central America.

In India, human sacrifices were long established in the belief that they would ensure the viability, safety and permanence of buildings and constructions such as bridges and forts much in the same tradition and beliefs associated with the same sacrifices that were performed in the Andes[261]. Human fat was anciently considered an efficacious ointment and that obtained from boys was considered especially useful in this preparation since they were allowed to roam further from the home and therefore more readily waylaid[262]. The most suitable man for a Meriah Sacrifice was one that had been purchased and the Lambadi caste was one that kidnapped suitable men and boys or bought them as slaves from the markets and sold them to the hill tribes for high prices[263]. This same caste was known for another sacrifice of placing a child at the entrance of a corral or road and driving cattle over it in the belief that it would haunt the place as a guardian spirit - a practice noted also in Madagascar[264].

Notes recorded by those who acted on reports of abductions and the sale of men for Meriah Sacrifice in the mid-19th., century (*4.113-5*) indicate the horrific nature of these sacrifices and a record of the sacrifice is given as follows after the description of the sacrificial post that consisted of, "… of a stout post, on which it is made to revolve. After the performance of the usual ceremonies, the intended victim is fastened to the proboscis of the elephant (a model), and amidst the shouts and yells of the exited multitude of Khonds, is rapidly whirled around, when, at a given signal by the officiating Zanee or priest (Zume of Colombia?), the crowd rush in, seize the Meriah, and with their knives cut the flesh off the shrieking wretch so long as life remains. He is then cut down, the skeleton burnt, and the horrid orgies are over. In several villages I counted as many as fourteen effigies of elephants, which had been used in former sacrifices. These I caused to be overthrown by the baggage elephants attached to my camp in the presence of the assembled Khonds (Gonds), to show them that these venerated objects had no power against the living animal, and to remove all vestiges of their bloody superstition." This report by Colonel Herbert Hope Risley includes the chant recorded from the Gonds and illustrates the long held belief in sympathetic magic at the root of such sacrifices and he also records that before and during the sacrifice the people are intoxicated and roused to fever pitch. An extract from this chant is translated and abridged as follows:

> "As the tears stream from thine eyes,
> So may the rain pour down in August,
> As the mucus trickles from thy nostrils,
> So may it drizzle at intervals;
> As the blood gushes forth,
> So may the vegetation sprout,
> As the gore falls in drops,
> So may the grains of rice form."[265].

The remarkable references to the need to see mucus and tears are highly reminiscent of South American iconography and the necessary blood is clearly intended for similar purposes as that in Peruvian and Bolivian rituals. In another variation of the Meriah Sacrifice Colonel John Campbell in the mid-19th., century noted that the victim was dragged by the "half-intoxicated" participants along the fields and while "shouting and screaming" they "rush upon him, and with their knives cut the flesh piecemeal from the bones, avoiding the head and bowels." The skeleton was then burnt and the ashes mixed with the grain to be sown to "protect it from insects". Edgar Thurston in quoting from Colonel Campbell records that, "It is", he says, "always succeeded by the sacrifice of three human beings, two to the sun in the east and west of the village, and one in the centre, with the usual barbarities of the Meriah. A stout wooden post about six feet long is firmly fixed in the ground, at the foot of it a narrow grave is dug, and to the top of the post the victim is firmly fastened by the long hair of his head. Four assistants hold his outstretched arms and legs, the body being suspended horizontally over the grave, with the face toward the earth. The officiating Junna or priest, standing on the right side, repeats the following invocation, at intervals hacking with his sacrificing knife the back of the shrieking victim's neck ...." It is not necessary to repeat the invocation here but it needs only be said that it is a plea for protection from the clan enemies and that they will be granted prosperity by their deity (in this case) Manicksoro[266].

In a census taken in Madras in 1901 there were twenty-five people who returned themselves as Meria or Meriah-Kaya because they were descendants of those sold for the Meriah Sacrifice but who were rescued before sacrifice in the 19th., century[267]. Gond myths note that the sacred hills and mountains who were the first gods were located in the Upper World and lived on blood and milk while men below lived on flesh and bones. This arrangement was said to have been made by their great god Mahaprabhu and from this direction the first boy and girl were born. This deity gave water to the first people and in return mankind gave the Meriah Sacrifice. It was believed by the Gonds that, since the British forbade the Meriah, the hills were angry and gave them "nothing but fever"[268]. Thurston notes that even as late as 1902 a British magistrate in Ganjam in South India received a petition asking for permission to perform a human sacrifice[269]. Even in the early part of the twentieth century bull sacrifices similar to the Meriah Sacrifice were still being performed in South India and these appear also to relate to the early bull sacrifices known in the Ancient Middle East[270]. In rituals at the installation of the local Rajah evidence of an earlier form of Meriah Sacrifice was still to be found in a symbolic form among the Hill Bhuiyas in Orissa. Here the neck of the clan chief, or Kabat, as a symbolic Meriah slave was offered as he knelt before the Rajah but was only touched by him as recognition of allegiance[271]. Reports from the hill tribes Nagas of Assam indicate a human sacrificial form possibly due to anciently held beliefs surrounding the Meriah Sacrifices[272], and other traditions were retained before the British Colonial period in the late 19th., century, A.D. Here reports of Meriah Sacrifice occur along with headhunting and the specific case of a boy being sacrificed were

4.116 :
Sacrificial figures
severed at the
waist descending
into the
Underworld - a
motif found in
India and at Cerro
Sechin in Peru.
Bac-T'ul Stela,
Guatemala, 199
A.D.

4.117 : Low
relief monolith
depicting a figure
severed at the
waist. Cerro
Sechin, Central
Coast Peru, Late
second millenni-
um, B.C.

recorded and these acts were considered beneficial for the crops and the community as a whole. These reports also record the decapitation of the human victims in these rites and the removal of the hands and feet[273]. This particular custom is remarkably similar to those known in Polynesia where hands and feet severed from the warrior victims of war were presented to the king as his "portion". Such sacrifices are also highly reminiscent of South America and in Peru and Bolivia in particular.

More generally it was believed in earlier agricultural societies that, when sacrificial food was prepared, a human being should be sacrificed as the substitute for the grain god and his flesh eaten in imitation of the ritual of his self-sacrifice known in the most ancient myths. In the Meriah Sacrifice of the Gonds it was believed that, for proper efficacy, the flesh to be sown with grain in the prepared fields must itself still be living. A dead sacrifice would not be suitable since the life force would have already departed. For the spirit of the victims to be successfully imparted into the seed, he must still remain alive and bleeding as the flesh cut from him, and as it was planted in the soil. The living victim was tied to the plough-shaped sacrificial post and after anointing by the Gond priest the people rushed at the victim and slashed pieces of flesh and then ran to their fields to bury their portion with the seed in their fields. Only the head, intestines and skeleton were left tied to the post and this was a tradition deeply embedded into the tribal soul of the Gonds who were loathed to desist from this long held custom. It is believed that in more ancient times portions of the flesh were also swallowed, thought to be a custom surviving from when the sacrificial victim was torn apart by the victorious group and the pieces of flesh eaten raw and the blood drunk, and this in turn probably derived from the pursuit of animal prey in very ancient times.

Many of the traditions found in Indonesia were transferred from Aboriginal India and closely linked to the Nagas of Assam, and among the various tribes of Dyaks in Borneo there was evidence that the Meriah Sacrifice was endemic among the population centuries before the advent of the Europeans. At the death of an influential chief a slave was purchased and secured in a cage for a week or so while friends of the chief's relatives from the region were invited to a feast as a send-off for the soul of the chief. On the day of this feast the crowd was incited by arrack, a strong palm-wine, and each in turn thrust a spear into the slave. None of the thrusts were allowed to be fatal until all had used their spears and then the slave was taken to the chief's grave, decapitated and while the body was placed in the grave the head was impaled on a pole by the grave. In some cases the guests were so frenzied that they cut pieces from the body and swallowed them[274]. Other similar customs considered very ancient were found among the Kenyah and Kayan in Borneo[275].

In Sumatra also the Meriah Sacrifice was tied to a stake and the chief cuts off pieces from the cheeks and forearm for himself as the choicest pieces. All the remaining men then slashed pieces from the victim and roasted and ate the pieces while other swallowed the pieces whole and uncooked[276]. Among the Pak-Pak people in Sumatra the hands and feet are cut off and hung up in the clan hut[277].

Similar Meriah practises survived in Melanesia on the sea route to South America from Asia. In Buka on the islands of Bougainville in the Solomon Islands, a captured victim was hung up in a tree and pieces were cut off his arms legs and shoulders in a ritual clearly derived from the Meriah Sacrifice of the Gonds in India[278]. A closely similar ritual was reported more than two generations ago from the Central Solomon Islands where a man wounded in battle was not killed on the spot but bound with "withes" - thin flexible branches. He was carried back to the village where he was eaten piece by piece with taro as a "relish", but the entrails were never touched, identical with the Gond tradition in India[279].

In Arabia similar sacrifices almost to the detail, were known into recent centuries in camel sacrifices, where one was tied to an altar and the flesh was cut from the body and swallowed "raw and bleeding"[280]. It may therefore be no coincidence that the exact same Meriah Sacrifice was preserved into more recent centuries from the most ancient times in both human and llama sacrifices in Ancient Bolivia and Peru[281], and in the most sacred rituals, llama fat[282], was considered an essential ingredient as human fat was in Aboriginal India to be referred to in a later chapter.

In Peru, in a remarkable passage, Garcilasso de la Vega, the son of a Spanish Conquistador and an Inca princess, recorded that the noble men of the enemies in pre-Conquest and pre-Inca time among the Antis, residing in the eastern region of the Empire, were carried back to the capital and there the victorious chiefs and their families would assemble. At the appointed time the restrained victim, while still alive, and fully conscious would have his flesh slashed away piece by piece and eaten by the participants. The women would "anoint their teats so that the infants may suck blood". De la Vega continued: "But, if, during the torture, the victim was firm, composed, and, fierce, after having eaten the flesh, with all the inside, they dried the bones and nerves in the sun, and placing them in a lofty part of the mountains, worshipped them as gods, and offered them sacrifices"[283]. De la Vega blamed this cruelty on influence from immigrant Mexicans and this interesting conclusion parallels the beliefs of Miles Poindexter that the Aymara (Colla) and the Quechua were immigrants from Central America.

In the attempts to extend their conquest south into Central Chile the Spanish were defeated by the Auracanians and one of their captains, Valdivia, was eaten piece by piece after being captured[284]. This extraordinary custom was still imposed in more recent times among the Indians of Chile where reports by modern investigators discovered that a man named Isani was collectively judged by a remote community, then hanged, and pieces of flesh were cut from his body and eaten[285]. These unusual sacrifices bear too close a comparison to those of the Meriah Sacrifice in India to be coincidence and particularly when considered together with the evidence of so many aspects of cultural transfer from Asia to South America.

Human Sacrifice and Y-posts as a Reflection of the Yupe
Horned posts or Y-posts are well known in the Ancient Americas and such forked posts are considered related to lunar cosmology in these ancient cultures of the New World. In the Old World interchangeability with menhirs is also noted particularly in the South East Asian arena where they are abundantly found deriving from the most ancient Asian cultures in the Middle East and India. In Central America Karl Luckert associated these Y-posts with the split tongue of the ser-

pent found so frequently in Mexican and Mayan iconography and these he asserts were used to attach the sacrificial animals in exactly the manner known in Ancient India and Middle East[286]. He further suggests that the form and use of this Y-post is too similar to that along the Western Pacific Rim, Australia and India to that on the Eastern side in Mexico not to be related and likely to be the result of diffusion[287]. He notes also the similarities of the Hopi and Navaho sand paintings in South West U.S.A. and those of Malekula in the New Hebrides (Vanuatu)[288] and these in turn have been shown by John Layard two generations ago to have derived from South India. He sees contacts between ridgepole alignments and other aspects of Western and Central Pacific culture too similar to those of Ancient Mexico and Central and North America not to be connected. Y-posts were also erected in the Marquesas Islands associated with childbirth and death but the origins initiating their use appear not to have been known or recorded[289]. Forked trunks and posts were also revered in Melanesia and many examples have been sighted and recorded by early Europeans in the Pacific290.

Y-posts are long known in South America particularly from their constructional function in supporting the ridgepole of a symbolic structure such as a ruler's pavilion or temple on the summit of a stepped pyramid or platform[291]. House posts of this type are common throughout the Pacific and have cosmological associations along with the ridgepole. Among the Gonds in India the first pole of the roof support system for a house is made from the sacred Saja tree and Y-posts were, and into the 20th., century still used three on each side of the highest beam known as the roof tree[292]. This is reminiscent of the "roof tree" made from an actual trunk with some of the roots still left attached among the Nagas of Assam[293]. Among them, as ridge beam, this tree represents the World Tree and the rest of the building originally identified with cosmological aspects of the sky that so clearly relates to similar beliefs in the ridgepole myths incorporated into temple building in Melanesia[294] Polynesia[295] and among the Tukano[296].

The Raj Gonds of Adilabad also preserved references to two-pointed pillars in their origin myths associated with the number eight, usually a reference to the cardinal points and the four intermediate directions, suggesting that this symbolic form is very ancient[297]. There are many cultural connections between the Gonds and the Nagas of Assam and among the Sema Nagas Y-posts are carved with the symbols of the Sun and Moon[298] indicating a cosmological relationship largely forgotten by the beginning of the twentieth century.

It was noticed by the British administrators in the early part of the twentieth century that the Naga tribes in Assam, who erected megaliths, usually also constructed terraces for cultivation. The foremost of these was the Angami whose living traditions were still flourishing and dominant in the region at that time. These traditions were followed by the Kacha (Nzemi) and Khoirao and less so by the Rengmas, Tangkuls and Maram Nagas, tribes who have been greatly influenced by the Angamis[299]. However there are variations to the general rule since the Rengmas and Lhotas Nagas erected megaliths but dud nor construct terraces. In the North and

4.118 : A small stone monolith dedicated to the local deity Potu-Razu with the yupe or sacrificial impaling post behind traditional in village India. South India, Early 20th., century, A.D.

East of the Naga territories monuments are erected as wooden pillars or Y-posts rather than stones, while others frequently erect them when no suitable stone is obtainable, although they clearly are utilised for the same purpose. There appears also to be some influences derived from previous occupants in the nearby ancient kingdoms as J.P. Mills notes that the Y-shaped posts of the Ao and Sema Nagas have rounded tops closely resembling the ancient stone monuments erected by the Kachari kings of Dimapur[300].

In Angami villages, in the Naga Hills, a tradition

was preserved noting that the "spirit of fertility" was encourage to perambulate the village at the time of the Lisu genna. This was represented by a Y-shaped post, symbolising the female power of generation, being dragged around the village by "chaste" boys, together with a wooden pillar symbolising the phallus, or linga, carried by a man[301]. In other Naga tribes the stone monoliths were often grouped in pairs on a stone platform representing, male and female (*9.018*), and similar groupings were known in Melanesia[302].

It has been noted by the several celebrated authors on the Naga cultures, T.C. Hodson, J.H. Hutton, J.P. Mills along with Colonel Gurdon and Colonel Playfair, that there were a great number of cultural traditions and artefacts along with myths and legends shared with the distant tribes of Borneo, the Philippines and Melanesia. These traditions and artefactual heritage appears to have been shared also with some the Aboriginal tribes of India such as the Bhuiyas and Gonds, and the Munda tribes generally. In many cases these parallels have been extended to North, Central and South America and have been mentioned elsewhere in this book, or in earlier works by the author, or are readily available in the existing text and footnotes in the books of these authors. It does appear however that these parallels are too many to be considered coincidence and require a specialist study in that cannot be included here.

The securing of the Meriah Sacrifice to a tree or imitation plough clearly has ancient roots associated with fertility of the earth and the grain crop following the sowing season. These are related to sacrificial posts originally imported as the focus of sacrificial ritual from the Ancient Middle East and here they utilised trees as substitutes for stone monoliths and both traditions found their way into India. Originally the highest sacrifice to be offered to the gods was the finest male warrior and there are references preserved in the Vedic texts that record that this is one of the five forms acceptable to the gods[303]. In the ancient Vedic texts, in records of what may have been the origins of the Meriah Sacrifice, are to be found in the Satapatha Brahmana, the oldest surviving Vedic text. Here the highest value sacrifices are delineated and on the sixth and "central" day of the Paurushamedhika ceremonies a man is considered the appropriate sacrifice. On the seventh day, all the sacrifices are seized including the sacrificial man and pieces of skin are cut off along with chopped sections of herbs and trees and all kinds of food[304]. The stake to which the human victim is tied is considered to symbolise the initial creator, Prajapati, and consists of eleven stakes, or sacrificial posts, in all and these are identified with the thunderbolt[305]. Interestingly the body is perceived as representing five layers from the feet to the head corresponding to the five sacred days of the festival, the five seasons, and the waist is considered the centre separating the upper body from the lower[306]. In other references the waist was perceived as the ecliptic and symbolically to separate the Earth from the Sky. The belt or girdle was considered sacred in this context and associated with special rituals in the Ancient Middle East[307] and in India[308] (*9.111-8*). The first forty-eight victims were tied to the central of the 11 stakes and the other ten stakes have 11 victims tied in turn to them. In this Purushamedha (Purusha = man; medha = sacrifice), this amounts to 158 victims while some records state that there were an additional 26 while others indicate that there were other additional sacrifices depending on caste[309].

In the Satapatha Brahmana, in a reference to the sacrificial post, it is noted that the Aryan intent in worshipping and sacrificing was to imitate the gods and to perform the necessary rituals to ensure that they would gain access to the region of the gods when the time to leave this earthly region arrived. In response to the victory of the Aryan tribes in entering the Subcontinent of India the priests say, " 'How may this (celestial regions) be made attainable by men?' They then sipped the sap of the sacrifice, as he would suck out honey; and having drained the sacrifice and effaced the traces of it with the (sacrificial) post, they concealed themselves: and because they effaced (the sacrifice) with it, therefore it is called yupa (sacrificial post) ..."[310].

The sacrificial post was imported by the Aryans into India at least as early as the beginning of the first millennium B.C. but probably earlier in previous migrations. This old section of the Satapatha Brahmana naming the sacrificial post leaves no doubt that this reference, among others, is to a human sacrifice and has close similarities noted elsewhere to the drinking of sacrificial blood in Tantric practices preserved in early Sumatra[311] more than a millennium later. The sacrificial post was also most famously used in the horse sacrifices known from Central Asia through into Ancient India and was particularly associated with Aryan heritage in India itself usually requiring twenty-one posts made of different sacred woods in groups of six and one of three[312].

Human Sacrifice - Severed at the Waist

Later laws instituted by the Brahmans include references to the penalties suffered by those who betrayed the words and laws of the Vedas to the ears of the unacceptable castes and tribes not included in the recognised descent from their Aryan forebears. It was forbidden to for a Brahman to relate any part of the Vedas to any other than the recognised caste members and if a Sudra, a member of one of the lowest social groups of castes recognised in India, should even accidentally hear these recitations he would be subjected to having his ears sealed with lac or lead. If he dared to recite them he was liable to be cut in two as a Brahmanic penalty[313]. There are many myths in India and Indonesia referring to half human heroes or deities and people being cut into two, probably deriving from the Brahmanic penalty across the waist. It is clear that this is a very ancient, corrupted, and adapted form of philosophic construct that perceived the separation on the upper body from the lower already noted from the Vedic texts. The upper half was symbolically related to the Upper World and spirit and the lower half to the Earth, and the act of cutting in two was, therefore, seen as deactivating the ensouled spirit and neutralising its effects upon mankind. This form of penalty is seen from the most ancient times in the traditions of warfare, religious sacrifices, in Ancient West and South Asia into the 18-19th., century, when this Brahman penalty was still said to operate.

In Central America the famous Mayan stela dedicated to the ruler Bac-T'ul dated to 199 A.D. depicts a Vision Serpent in the form of a staff curving over his head as a parasol undoubtedly derived from Ancient Buddhist iconography[314]. Remarkably the lower extension of the staff shows godlings or human souls, perhaps sacrificial victims, severed at the waist (*4.116*) highly reminiscent of those in Cerro Sechin (*4.117*) a millennium earlier on Coastal Peru. The dazante or so-called "dancers" incised carvings on monoliths at Monte Alban, in the Zapotec territory of South Mexico, appear similar to those of Cerro Sechin many centuries earlier. The term for the Zapotec temple was yohopee[315], virtually the same as the name for the Vedic Indian sacrificial post - Yupe. It may be that these traditions were retained and transferred from India to South America to Cerro Sechin and then to Mexico, but it is more likely that these were transferred on a number of occasions to each independently from the continuing, parent tradition in the Ancient Middle East and India from the second and first millennium B.C.

The Brahmanic penalty appears to have been adopted India either from the Brahmans or introduced earlier in migrations from the Ancient Middle East since some of the Sudras themselves and other peripheral Hindu people maintained similar practices assimilated over the centuries. The Canarese-speaking Gauda caste, on the third day after the cremation of a man, collected the ashes and moulded the shape of the man on the ground. As this was done this figure was cut into two at the waist and then covered over with a mound as a form of burial. Two planks were placed on the floor of the dead man's house and covered with cloths. On one of these a vessel of milk was placed and on the other a lamp, rice, coconut, pumpkin and other foods. Of special interest is the tradition associated with a man's brothers or agnates since these are often evidence of derivation from the Ancient Middle East. These agnates of the dead man with some boys perambulated around these planks three times taking some of the articles with them in a cloth. Three plantain leaves were placed in front of the mound and cooked foods, for the spirit of the deceased, placed on them. Four posts were set up around the mound and cloth stretched over them as a canopy, and around the side forming a type of tent. On the sixteenth day sixteen plantains were laid out in front of the burial mound with one of the leaves separated from the others. Various foods were placed in leaf cups on the leaves and one of the assembled agnates, usually the oldest, recited the traditional homily; "We have done everything as we should do, and so our ancestors who have died must take the man who is now dead to their regions. I put the leaf which is apart in the same row with the sixteen leaves"[316]. The tradition is an interesting one since it not only preserves the ancient custom of severing at the waist known in Vedic sacrifices and in war but relates it directly to separating the spirit from earthly ties after death. The number sixteen is common in the cosmology of India, this being a division of the four cardinal points or four notional quarters into four, and here identified with the land of the ancestors or heavenly state. As noted in Ancient Middle Eastern traditions the waist symbolically represented the ecliptic and was seen as the entrance into the earthly state at birth and its exit after death. This basic concept appears in India where this division is reflected in the upper and lower parts of the waist and the division of the Earth and Sky[317].

In another, perhaps older folk tradition reflecting at root similar beliefs is another report that a child was born to a Gauda woman who was extremely abnormal and the description of its appearance still survived to be recorded. Such freak births were, and still are considered the incarnation of some devil spirit and the clan members determined to kill it so that is could not wreak havoc upon its mother. It was believed that she, in particular, in her weakened state after childbirth, was particularly vulnerable, according to the traditional belief. A vessel was placed over half of the child and used as the guide for a large knife to cut the child into two halves at the waist according to the accepted custom[318]. Clearly this rite has its foundation in the assimilation of much more ancient traditions now long lost but probably has common origins with that of the Brahmanic penalty.

The foregoing is sufficient for the purpose of this work and no further expansion is necessary on this subject except to note that the Y-post, the sacrificial post, and the ancient megalith were utilised by both Asian and Old World people as sacrificial posts. These were used in various ways, apart for religious rites, in punishments and severing at the waist was one of these and reflected in closely similar traditions and no doubt with common origins with those in Mexico, and probably South America. These customs in India, in turn, are seen to have derived from the Ancient Middle East and many of the flaying (*4.101*), impaling (*11.051*) and spread-eagled tortures, including decapitation are seen commonly in Assyrian as well as earlier and later period carved relief's and are clearly those that had been utilised and applied in Coastal and Andean South America in a similar time frame (*4.102/3*). It is likely therefore that Karl Luckert is correct in suggesting that the similarities in traditions between the Americas and South East Asia and Australia are correct and worthy of further examination. This, if undertaken, is likely to show connections between Aboriginal India and the Nagas of Assam in particular that are too many to be considered coincidental with those of the coastal and Andean cultures of South America.

Early Textiles in Ancient Ecuador

In returning to the archaeology of Ecuador cotton was grown in Ecuador and textiles appear to be elaborate at an early stage evidenced by the presence of spindle whorls[319]. The earliest known evidence of textiles in Ecuador, apart from pictorial, is that of impressions on a fired lump of clay from Valdivia dated between 2150-1950 B.C.[320]. The discovery of dyed camelid fibres at the

4.119 : Patu (wooden club) shaped baton with woven sin-net outlining the figure of the Polynesian deity Oro, god of war, closely similar to the deities cast in gold in Colombia (*4.120*). Tahiti, Eastern Polynesia, 19th., century, A.D.

4.120 : A gold cast figure of a hero or deity holding a patu or Moari type scep-tre. This appears to have derived from the string figures applied to wooden palette sceptre typical of Tahiti in Polynesia. Colombia, 700-1450 A.D.

highland site of Pirincay indicates that influences from Peru had reached Ecuador in the first millennium B.C., possibly deriving from Chavin de Huantar. A tex-tile recovered from one of the tombs at this site using camelid hair occur in a later period royal tomb with copper "sequins" sewn to the fabric of a royal tunic[321]. This tunic appears to reflect aspects of ornamentation found further south in the same time frame of Moche and the following Sican cultures.

Early Settlements in the Amazon Drainage of Eastern Ecuador

The upper Maranon and regions of the Ucayali river drainage systems have yield-ed the earliest evidence among the Amazon tributaries for contact between the Pacific Coast and the Amazon. Then Bagua Phase dating from 1500-1200 B.C. appears to reflect influences and contacts with Kotosh and Pacopomapa predom-inantly in the Peruvian Highlands[322] and these show a probable trading contact with the contemporary cultures of Ecuador via the Amazonian tributaries. This period is more or less contemporary with the Tutishcainyo and later period ceramics from this site exhibit double spout and bridge vessels and with incised line decoration. After the end of Tutishcainyo a period known as Early Shakimu is found over this area and dated to about the 7th., century B.C.[323] and later Chavin influences are found occasionally in these forested valleys and settle-ments.

Contemporary with the Tutishcainyo but located on the Napo River fur-ther to the North than the Maranon and itself a major tributary via the Curucay River to the Amazon draining the eastern slopes of the Ecuadorian Andes, are the Yasuni sites. This style of pottery is found widely spread along the waterways of the Napo and its tributaries and indicating that the settlements along these rivers and streams had long been associated with the higher Andean cultures through long distance trade along the riverine highways of the eastern, Amazonian forests. The ceramics of the Yasuni culture are somewhat reminiscent of those of the Ananatuba deep in the Amazonian forests and featured sand and cariape tem-pered bell shaped bowls with crosshatch decoration[324]. The ease of navigation along the Amazon and its tributaries is evident when it is noted that steamers could navigate from the mouth of the Amazon into the Napo and to the eastern foothills of the Andes into modern times[325] and ancient canoes could, and cer-tainly did so. The Andes in Southern Ecuador narrows to only 70 kilometres width[326] and are considerably lower without major obstructions except the forest cover itself. Undoubtedly it is this fact and that navigable rivers are found on both side of the mountains that attracted the attention of ancient mariners in seek-ing more certain routes travelling from the Pacific seashore through into the vast navigable streams and rivers of the Amazon.

Ananatuba ceramics have been found on the large island of Marajo at the mouth of the Amazon in its delta with the Atlantic Ocean. This style has now been dated to its earliest site at about 980 B.C. and is still found being produced in a recognisable type on Marajo Island at about 700 A.D.[327]. This was succeed-ed by another pottery type known as Mangueiras but this island will be of more interest in a projected future publication. The fact that the island of Marajo is at one end of the Amazon and the River Napo drains the eastern Ecuadorian high-lands at the other should suggest that there was sustained riverine traffic over this distance of not less than 2000 miles for millennia suggesting that these were an extension of long distance voyages that were of some importance even if only for exchange and trade. But since the examples of Yasuni date back beyond that of Marajo it is clear that the movement from the eastern Andes to the Atlantic Ocean was earlier than that Marajo, so that the riverine traffic was from West to East, or Pacific to Atlantic, based on the available limited evidence at this time.

The archaeology and legends preserved in the highlands of Ecuador in the later periods in the first millennium A.D. indicate that powerful kingdoms and chiefdoms were the more usual form of social structure. Those located in the more southerly regions were the Canari and their occupational sites at Tomebamba near modern day Cuenca and Ingapirca (Hatun Canar) have yielded rich burials. These have yielded copper ornaments including headdresses, plumes, tumi knives, etc., along with human sacrifices to accompany the elite person entombed[328].

The Manteno culture developed into the Manteno-Huancavilca phase and appears to have formed several distinct social units or chiefdoms extending to include the Gulf of Guayaquil up to Manta and including also the Island of Puno, so important in the annals of the Spanish Conquest. These people were renown for constructing stone-enclosed precincts as ceremonial centres and in these they erected their stone stelae[329] depicting the stepped sky arches already described and the stone carved thrones also depicting the calendrical bands earlier noted so common in Ancient India, Assyria and Iran as well as in Central America. Closely related to the Manteno were the Milagro-Quesado people who occupied the inland regions in the Guayas Basin but whose mode of interment varied from the shaft and chambers utilised by the Mantero.

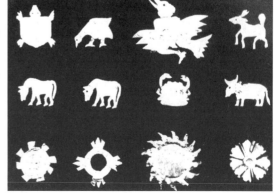

4.121 : Gold foil cut outs typical of early India. Piprawa Stupa, Gudivada, Masulipatam, North India, c3rd., century, B.C.

4.122 : Gold foil cut out objects similar to those found anciently in Indonesia and India. Peru; 1st., millennium, B.C.

4.123 : Cut gold foil objects mostly animals typical in Ancient Indonesia but similar to those found in Peru.

The Milagro Phase in the Uplands of Ecuador

In earlier periods the Daule and Tejar Phases occupied the region between the coast and the Andes and was noted for its cultivation of beans, sweet potatoes, manioc and other edible products. This phase has left hundreds of mounds and were more numerous in the Guayas River Basin in South Western Ecuador where there were regular inundations occur in the wet season. The Milagro buried their dead in "artificial platforms" but in a unique manner called "chimney burials". These "coffins" were formed by the bottoms of large urns being knocked out and then several of these placed one above the other into which the shrouded body was placed with a secondary burial placed in the lower-most pot[330]. This type of burial was also found in the north of Ecuador and the region between.

Found in these later tombs, and those in the highlands, is the copper "axe-money"[331] already noted for earlier periods so similar to that of Ancient China and Western Mexico reflecting its use as a form of currency further south in the Sican period on the North Peruvian Coast[332]. There can be little doubt that the people of Coastal Ecuador were merchants and the descendants of sea-going traders from the 4th., millennium B.C. through until the Spanish Conquest. This period also features textiles of Ikat and men's dress is depicted with a characteristic "tail" and both of these textile adaptions probably derives from Indonesia where similar techniques and dress modes occur. Mirrors, and copper tools and axes are more widely known at this period and nose ornaments are more common.

During the second millennium B.C., in India, double or multiple urns were joined at the base and knocked through as a type of coffin probably developing as a cheap form of clay coffin so long known in the Ancient Near and Middle East[333]. These double urn burials were usually used for secondary burials and this same custom appears to be identical to that noted above in the Milagro phase in Ecuador - probably transferred by later descendants of the form of burial that became widespread in India.

The Coastal Cara Phase and the Upland Tradition in Ecuador

In the Ibarra and Quito Basins at altitudes below about 3000 metres, circular earth mounds were constructed in groups and singularly. These large platforms measure up to about 120-150 to 75-95 metres on the sides with long ramps, usually from a riverside up to the summit on the long side. The larger mounds are thought to have been ceremonial while the smaller were used as house platforms and feature also under-floor pit interments. Common also were shafts cut into the side, and into the bottom of the side of the platforms and grave goods usually consisted of ceramics and occasionally metal objects[334]. One of the most interesting features of this culture is

4.124 : Very individual style of figurine found in the Indonesian Islands but closely similar to those found in Indonesia. Quimbaya, Colombia, 500-1000 A.D.

4.125 : Seated figures of the identical type found in Colombia in the La Tolita phase in Ecuador and Colombia. Sumba, Indonesia, Early 1st., millennium, A.D.

the development of star-shaped chambers from a common shaft to accommodate more interments in the one tomb. In an interesting development star-shaped mounds for house or ceremonial platforms have been excavated in Samoa[335]. Star-shaped clubs are also found and were also a symbol of Incan authority and found identically in Melanesia both earlier and later (*5.006/7; 5.009*).

This Cara Phase traditionally dates from about 700 A.D. and it is believed in legend that these people arrived on the coast and were there 200 years before migrating up to the valleys near modern Quito. These people in their later settlements in the uplands were believed to worship the sky and the snow-capped peaks[336] suggesting similar beliefs to those found on both the coasts and highland regions of Southern Peru. Similarities also occur in pilgrimages led to the mountain heights and shrines in the peaks to those known into Inca times in Southern Highland Peru. In the interments of their dead metals are less frequently found but copper star clubs are found and were possibly obtained by trade with the Guayas region. Star clubs also feature in the weapon assemblages in Melanesia and it may be that the lack of metals among the Caras was as a result of their lack of traditional use of this material because their origins, noted in their myths, identify them as mariners having arrived on the coast of Ecuador on rafts. These star clubs in Melanesia (*5.013/4*) are clustered in the islands flanking the only east to west access route supported by prevailing winds and ocean currents between New Guinea and the North of Australia. This sea route leads to Indonesia and South East Asia and India to the west suggesting that, in these islands of the Western Pacific, star-clubs were derived mariners returning from South America to Asia.

In the far south of Ecuador near Cuenca the Canari are possibly a related people to the Cara and here coca was raised in great quantities. In tombs at Sigsig and Ucur gold disks are found in large numbers in rich Canar tombs[337]. In the characteristic east-west layering of cultures in South America the connections between the Cara Phase in the highlands links more closely to the western coast of Ecuador than its does to the neighbouring Puruhua Phase contemporary with it to the south. The Puruhua were more closely connected also with the Pacific coast to the west than to the cultures north to south of their territory[338]. This emphasises the continuous drive from the coast inland toward the east and probably with the intention to find a passage through to the eastern Andean slopes and the Amazonian Basin river system and this same principle appears to be the initiating force in Ancient Peru and Northern Chile in the most ancient times.

Tradition, Archaeology and Monumental Iconography in Highland Colombia

San Agustin is one of the most mysterious of ceremonial sites in South America. It varies considerably from all others in being entirely a megalithic site almost unique in its stone-carved monoliths than any other in the North and South continents of the Americas. The first settlements appear to date from the first half of the first millennium B.C. and are named the Horqueta phase. These people were farmers who lived in scattered villages rather than in urban centres attached to ceremonial centres and they produced basic, dark coloured ceramics with incised decoration. Following these settlers a phase called the Primavera dates from about 500 B.C. From this phase wooden coffins appear to be the early models for the later stone sarcophagi so notable at this site and this period progressed to the next phase called the Isnos witnessing a considerable expansion in the population and residential settlements at the site. In this phase large earthworks were undertaken including embankments and possibly roads and works on mountain ridges. New pottery types appeared including double-spouted bottles, effigy urns and red-slipped ceramics with organic resist decoration. This phase also witnessed the introduction of metallurgy but many statues found at San Agustin wear ornaments more typical of other regions in Colombia. This gold work occurs locally but may indicate that the centre was also a pilgrimage centre where representations of priests or deities from other regions were assimilated or tolerated. The sudden changes in ceramics and the appearance of metallurgy suggests outside intervention or introduction towards the period of decline at Chavin far to the south in Central Peru and Gerrado Reichel-Dolmatoff believed that this was caused by immigrants who supplanted the Primavera people[339]. This period appears to chart the gradual northern movement of metallurgy from Peru to Ecuador and Colombia by the last centuries of the first millennium B.C. and then to Panama in Central America by c500 A.D. and Western Mexico by about 800 A.D.

San Agustin is above all else known for its remarkable carved stone monoliths now numbering over 300 and it is believed that they were erected in the Isnos period after about 50 B.C. The remarkable depictions are of demonic figures but more particularly they appear to relate directly to the megalithic phase after 500 B.C. in South India since so many of the depictions are closely similar to iconographic carvings and images of the linga, relating to phallus worship, surviving there. The Siva linga (*12.006-9*) or the phallic stones with a face carved on them is so reminiscent of the worship of Siva in India anciently and surviving into the present day that coincidence is extremely unlikely. Stone covered cyst tombs and large dolmens are also characteristic of India and some of these exhibit the "soul holes" found in the South Indian tombs[340] and also known around Tiahauanco and Ancient Peru.

In the region of Tierradentro statues of a similar type are found, and similar types of carved monoliths are found in Central America, often where elaborate shaft tombs are frequently found[341]. It might also be said that the monolithic figures occur in similar carved types in Eastern Polynesia and appear to take their original, inspiration from South India also. The Isnos people apparently retained their traditions until about 1200 A.D. when they suddenly cease carving or disappear and they were replaced by the Sambrillos people whose descendants claimed not to know who the former occupants were and did not erect stone monuments[342].

In Western Colombia the people once called the Early Calima are now known as the Llama. They are known for the quality of their modelled and incised decorated pottery. Inhumation was in shaft and chamber tombs and these people were largely maize farmers widely spread in that part of Colombia[343]. The Llama were succeeded by the more famous Quimbaya who were renowned as gold workers producing some of the most extraordinary of all artefacts in Ancient South America. Large containers, usually based on the naked human form, are finely modelled in gold and were intended to be used as lime containers, called poporo in Peru - the lime being taken to modify coca when it was chewed. Lime, being specially contained for ritual consumption, was also found on the opposite, western side of the Pacific, in Melanesia (*4.026*). Some of the iconographical details, such as the double spiral, associated with these Quimbaya figures depicted on this fine gold work are found in the symbolism of Indonesia, and through to India and the Ancient Middle East. Indonesia is also renown for its ancient gold work that included masks, pendants, beads and other of the items and also found among the Quimbaya. Not least similar are the many examples of gold sheet or foil cut-outs almost identical to those of India (*4.121*) Indonesia (*4.123*) found in Ancient Peru (*4.122*).

The Quimbaya built shaft and chamber tombs similar to the Llama people before them and these revealed many examples of finest gold work ever to be found. They include cinerary urns[344] suggesting an intrusive cremation culture possibly exclusive to the ruling clans, less usual in South America, suggesting connections with India and the Aryan traditions of some of the Vaishnavite Hindu sects. This would tally with other clearly Saivite Hindu iconography found in the phallic or linga aspects found at San Agustin in an earlier period. This gold-work was still being produced by the successors of the Quimbaya at the time of the Spanish Conquest in the 16th., century, A.D. and the influence reflected in their metallurgy, in technique and style, was found into Central America as far as Costa Rica.

This movement northward into Central America is noted generally of metallurgy but

4.126 + 4.127 : The Raimondi monolith with remarkably sophisticated carving of a Staff God that is also readable from the other way up. This feline deity is probably the prototype of the Tiahuanaco Staff God. Chavin de Huantar, Central Highland Peru, 800-600 B.C.

also the shaft and chamber burial system since these are found in West of Mexico among other influences. Long distance trade, undoubtedly by sea, is noted between the north of Chile, the Bolivian and Peruvian Highlands and the Calama of Colombia and also from the Amazonian forest to the south and east of the Colombian Andes long distance overland[345]. This trading system was part of a long established pattern that extended the cultural transfer not only of metallurgy and burial systems into Mexico from South America but also the specialised lustre-ware ceramic finishes found in Central America in the west of Mexico reflected also in a counterflow.

Clay trumpets were also a unique feature in this later time after 500 A.D. in the Narino culture[346] but may reflect influence from the far south where these were long manufactured in the Bolivian Highlands. In the later pre-Conquest period in Northern Colombia there were a people called the Sinu who were renowned goldsmiths and worked also in alloy called tumbaga. These ornaments were highly desirable and were found widely outside their own territory but although the means of distribution is not certain what is known is that such items were widely traded into Central America beside inside Colombia itself before the 12th., century A.D.[347].

The Sinu were a part of a larger movement in the Magdelena Valley in Colombia who formed politically defined kingdoms along the lower floodplains flanking the river system. Large civic and burial platforms were constructed relating to these and earlier states and one of these was at the time of the Conquest noted as being ruled by a woman. Their temples were replete with carved wooden figurative depictions of their deities covered with gold and these attracted pilgrims from both within and outside the Sinu kingdoms. Much of their gold ornamentation used in life as adornments was buried with their owners after death[348].

The Muisca Tradition of Central Highland Colombia
The Tairona, and their direct descendants the Kogi, appear to have continued the tradition of gold working in Northern Colombia[349] and their images are renown for the fine craftsmanship. Of special interest are the metal caps that many of their supernatural figurines wear being so similar to the metal ceremonial hat worn by the Tibetan monks (*9.096*). More centrally located in Colombia were the Muisca who were also fine gold workers and it was recorded that their chiefs were buried in selected tombs located under natural stone shelters or constructed of stone and covered with a slab. Because they were accessible these were looted by the Spanish but the Muisca were also known for their textiles and ceramics many depicting figures of warriors priests with high caps[350]. The Muisca textiles are of plain weave cotton painted with elaborate, decorative designs appearing to have little significance to religious beliefs or related iconography. It is also certain that there were stone monoliths found in their territory although it is not known

whether they were erected by the Muisca or their predecessors and it is possible that they related to the culture of a people called Herrera[351].

The Sun and Moon were worshipped by the Muisca and in the erection of the temple or chiefly residence, often the same thing, since the chiefs appear to have also been the priests, a child was placed in the postholes of the building frame and the pole driven down upon it[352]. Slaves were destined also to be sacrificed in the ceremonies of worship for the Sun and Moon and these rituals and traditions are highly reminiscent of those found in the Polynesia and the Western Pacific islands of Melanesia, Indonesia and through into South and South East Asia. Slaves were usually acquired as captives through war and this was not an infrequent occurrence in South America, no doubt a tradition inspired by the need for human sacrifices for the many ceremonies of dedication required in the annual ceremonial calendar.

Venezuela from the Pre-Ceramic to the Ceramic

The Orinoco drainage includes tributaries extending via the Casiquiare, Baria and Cauaburi to the River Negro a massive waterway running in parallel to the north and joining the Amazon mid-way in its course to the Atlantic. The Dabajuro tradition is largely a ceramic tradition that was continuous for the longest period in the north of South America in its history continuing from about 1800 B.C. into the 16 century, A.D. The first known examples occurred on the Maracaibo-Coro Coast extending into the Andes and along the coasts of the major islands off the Venezuelan coast. Clay griddles, characteristic also in the manioc traditions of the Central Amazon, are found here indicating that a stable agricultural tradition had developed by that time supplemented by hunting and fishing[353]. Maize was also developed and farmed early and many could be described as "corn farmers". Urn burials are found among these people in the western sites nearer the Andes while at the other sites burial in shell middens was the norm but only stone ornaments or amulets have been recovered from these interments.

Around the middle Orinoco a tradition known as the Saladero occurs where manioc culture was a year-round occupation. Ceramics of the La Gruta tradition are found here centred around Parmana and this tradition was replaced about 1600 B.C. by a ceramic style called the Ronquin and then by the Ronquin Sombra about 1100 B.C.[354]. The Ronquin Sombra was replaced by the very different Corozal phases commencing about 800 B.C. with quite distinctive ceramic decoration traditions suggesting radical influences. In the more lower and central reaches of the Orinoco, further to the east, the Barracoid culture flourished dating from about 1000 B.C. Stylistic similarities to those of the earliest ceramics yet found in South America at the coastal site of Puerto Hormigo have been considered by some to be the antecedent of this tradition[355].

At several sites along the Orinoco, during the Cano del Oro and La Betama phases, conical mounds and causeways were a feature. These mounds and causeways and raised paths appear to have been constructed to provide access during the wet season when the water levels rose and it may have been that the larger mounds supported framed temple constructions[356].

CHAPTER 5

MOCHE SPLENDOUR to the GREATNESS OF
TIAHUANACO through to the INCA ORIGIN MYTHS

Cupisnique and Epochs from Initial and Intermediate Periods to Monumental Decline

Following the decline of Chavin influence in Central Peru, ceramic analysis from cemeteries and inhumations during this Intermediate Period show five different influences related by trade and mutual religious and social elements. These ceramic sequences are named as Cupisnique, Transitory Cupisnique, Salinar, Viru or Galinazo, and Moche (Mochica). The iconography of Cupisnique reflects elements of imagery apparently derived from the Amazon Basin and considered a variant of that of Chavin de Huantar, then in wane, before assimilating maritime elements from the shore of the Pacific Ocean[1]. Cupisnique products were found traded in the Nepena, Santa and Lambeyeque Valleys but it is considered by some that its epicentre was in fact in the Chicama Valley[2].

Pottery stamps in bird forms and clay roller stamps are highly reminiscent of those known for millennia in the Ancient Middle East and India and those of the Cupisnique period were found in the Huaca Prieta burials in the Chicama Valley. Shell ornaments, and carved bone with shell and turquoise inlays were also recovered along with polished jet mirrors, and necklaces of beads made from Lapis lazuli, turquoise and clear quartz crystal were found in these oval irregular burial pits dug into the subsoil. The bodies were usually flexed and often covered with red hematite powder appearing to imitate the red-ochred skeletons in burials in earlier epochs, in Ancient India and throughout Asia. Stone carved artefacts are another feature of these burials and they are often mace heads considered distinctive to the North Coast[3] identical in form to those found in Melanesia (*5.006/7*; *5.009*) mainland Asia.

5.001 : Lump of clay with stamp impression. Mesopotamia, 3rd., millennium, B.C.

Intermediate Period -c200 B.C. - 600 A.D.

The first of these phases illustrates the breakdown of the social organisation that was until that time, apparently almost ubiquitous throughout Peru, along with the characteristic U-shaped platform ceremonial centres. The settlements initiated at the Cupisnique sites were contemporary with the high point at the Sechin Alto complex in Central Peru in the early first millennium, B.C.[4]. After this period, when the collapse of the U-shaped centres was clearly evident, the widely distributed motifs and designs illustrated in the ceramic assemblages in the coastal regions appear promiscuously adopted more widely. This apparently occurs through lack of an imposed set of religious beliefs supported by specific iconographical interrelationships. At Chankillo the ancient fort built in an ovoid form (*5.016*) about 900 B.C. is seen by some as a prototype for later defensive structures built in the Intermediate Period dating about 342-120 B.C. in defence of the valleys and agricultural lands in Central Coastal Peru[5].

During the period after 500 A.D. fortifications increased suggesting that intertribal or hostilities between neighbouring valleys was on the increase and was probably exacerbated by the demand for arable land for agriculture in arid valleys in the

5.003 : Incised clay cylinder. Mayan, Belize, 1st., millennium, A.D.

5.002 : Early clay cyclinders with incised seals. Mesopotamia, 3rd., millennium, B.C.

5.004 : Stela of the Assyrian king Sama-vul II showing him holding a club of the identical type found at Paracas, Peru, and into the Pacific Islands. Assyria, First half of the first millennium, B.C.

5.005 : A Samoan with a fluted club identical to those typical in the ancient depictions in reliefs known in India and probably the prototype for the Peruvian star clubs. Central Polynesia, Early 19th., century, A.D.

5.006 : A group of stone clubs with feathered plumes closely similar to those in Assam but also reflecting into recent centuries the star clubs of Ancient Peru. Collingwood Bay, Papua New Guinea, 19th., century, A.D.

5.007 : A large selection of stone clubs traditional in Melanesia and here from New Guinea. Melanesia, Late 19th., century, A.D.

5.008 : Sennacherib with bow and arrows referring to victory in war but also as ruler of the sky or the four corners. The lotus pattern on his mantle may be the model for star clubs later found among the Inca as signifier of rulership. Assyria, 6-7th., century, B.C.

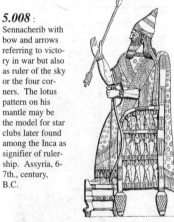

5.009 : Two types of stone star-club heads closely similar to those found in Ancient Peru. Torres Straits and Daudai, New Guinea area, Melanesia, Pre-19th., century, A.D.

5.010 : Peruvian bronze Tumis, and axe head and star clubs typical of weapons found in Melanesia and West Asia. Peru, 700-1500 A.D.

coastal zone. From the earliest part of this period ditches and moats were also used in integral defensive outer rings as part of the fortifications to protect the villages. Sling stones retrieved from these sites indicate that the sling was a popular weapon used in defence of these fortifications but long sieges were usually adverse for the inhabitants since water supply was rarely sufficient to stave off a prolonged, determined attack[6]. The Santa Valley in Central Coastal Peru has revealed the greatest number of forts numbering around forty[7].

This period of instability saw, toward the end of this Period, the emergence of Galinazo centred in the Viru Valley, and from their consolidation the Moche people in the neighbouring Moche valley eventually emerged as their successors to expand into an extensive coastal state from the North to Central Peru[8]. It is clear from the surviving imagery from this period that banditry and violence counteracted with militarism and war was a fundamental basis on which the foundation of the state was cemented and the Moche were the first empire to establish an extended territory beyond that of a city state in the North Central Coast of Peru.

Fundamental to the stability of an expanding state were the irrigation systems necessary in the difficult terrain with its broad sandy coastal strip relieved only by the floodplains of rich silt as the rivers flowed across this coastal strip to the Pacific Ocean. The river valleys extend-

5.011 : Double-headed stone club probably modelled on the metal axe heads of South and West Asia. Nicaragua, Central America, First millennium, A.D.

5.012 : Two bronze weapons including a star club with integral tumi closely similar to those of Melanesia. Peru, 700-1500 A.D.

5.013 : A group of star club heads all but one combined with a tumi as a halberd. Ecuador, Peru and Bolivia, 700-1500 A.D.

5.014 : A stone star-club from the front and side. Waghi-Tal, Central Highland New Guinea, Melanesia, 19th., century, A.D. or earlier.

ing inland were also arid and required extensive irrigation and the military prowess of the state was apparently utilised fully in protecting the agricultural wealth produced from them. Fortifications to protect their state and the agricultural workers associated with them appear particularly in the Viru, Moche and Chicama Valleys but extend south to Casma, already of note earlier.

In the Viru Valley metal-working has been detected with the residues of copper slag and related equipment and it appears that this production was controlled by the privileged position of the clan headman or Kuraka (curaka). The social organisation of the Moche state appears to have been a parallel with, or derived from those of the dual clan system long established in the Andes and is in Peru contemporary with similar developments in India. There the Laws of Manu instituting the caste system were said to have been formulated in about 800 B.C. By the time of the Moche Empire in Peru in the first half of the first millennium B.C., this caste system defined in these laws were merging and being assimilated locally in a less than totally integrated form with the dual organisation system of two moieties virtually identical to those of later Inca Peru. One of these moieties was formed by those who were descended from the Aryan tribes from Iran and the other formed by the categorization of the indigenous tribes of the Subcontinent.

5.015 : Ainu fluted club similar to those traditional in India, Melanesia, Polynesia and South America. Ainu, Hokkaido, North Japan, Pre-19th., century, A.D.

In India copper was associated with traders from the Ancient Middle East and the results of cultural incursions from millennia of prospecting and trading in this metal has been undertaken elsewhere[9]. In the Galinazo period the difference in status appears to reflect closely similar structures to those in India and where copper in some clans was also associated with status. In this part of Peru occupied by Galinazo it was the kurakas who appeared to maintain control of its production through its various stages. Their status was emphasised by the adobe houses they constructed for themselves since the general mass of the people were accommodated in small cane walls on stone footings[10].

Galinazo in the Peruvian North Coast Tradition

The Galinazo cultural region extended from the Santa River drainage to the Chicama drainage from North Central to Central Peru. By the first century B.C. their settlements were being transformed by dramatic expansion reflected in the irrigation works exemplified by surviving traces of their canal works associated with rapid population growth. The Galinazo period was particularly noted for its mud brick construction and this originally was always produced by hand and long known on coastal Peru. Soon, however, the shear size of their sites and ambitions of the Galinazo leaders required a greater volume and mass-produced bricks from moulds greatly increased the numbers of bricks expended on ever increasing civic projects. Mould-made bricks are a tradition long known in the Ancient Middle East and the Indus. It is thought the Galinazo capital may have been a large site below the peak called Huaca Tomoval in Viru Valley[11].

Their building methods, and the sudden appearance of a clan head, Kuraka (Curaka),

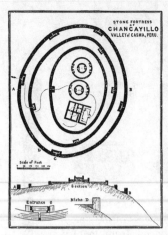

5.016 : Elliptical fort know known as Sechin Alto located high above the Casma Valley. Sechin Alto, Casma Valley, Cnetral Coast Peru, Early first millennium, B.C.

5.017 : Massive terraced fort of Paramonga with vast central temple complex. Paramonga, Central Coast Peru, Ist., millennium, B.C.

controlling the prestigious use of copper suggests introduction of similar traditions from the Ancient Middle East or India. It is likely that the Kurakas were descendants of mariners and migrants from Asia who formed their own clans and alliances with peoples in these North Coast valleys in Peru. Such a proposition would be consistent with the oral tradition for the introduction of culture heroes onto the coast arriving by sea.

The Splendour that was the Moche from 300 B.C. - 300 A.D.

The Moche are believed to have originated from the region around Cerro Blanco, a remarkably beautiful mountainous region accessible to Chavin de Huantar, but with access to the coast through Casma and other central valleys. This is the central region where Kotosh and La Galgada emerged millennia before and appeared to have thrived on the West-East contact from the Pacific Ocean shore through the Cerro Blanco region to the Amazon Basin. This suggests that, similar to those earlier epochs, and the sudden impulses they received without any apparent developmental period, they may have been the descendants of intruders from the Pacific Shores. It is likely that they would have headed for the earlier or contemporary sacred shrines and intermarried with indigenous or naturalised peoples and whose descendants, reinvigorated with new blood, struck out to carve a kingdom for themselves in a critical region on the Peruvian river drainages on the North Central Coast. This would be consistent with "sudden" unexplainable advances evident at every new epoch in Peruvian history and most likely to have occurred also at Chavin and Galinazo who were at their apogee or in decline at the initiating of the Moche period.

It is thought that the Moche as a people first gained control of the Moche Valley, either by conquest or alliances, and from here they emerged to take control of the Central North Coast of Peru. What is clear is that the Moche either adopted or extended the Galinazo traditions with their own iconographical tradition and this formed the basis of the highly individual style that has received worldwide attention and renown from the earliest days of archaeological research into South American history.

The site believed to be the capital of the early Moche state is now known as Cerro Blanco and this was founded, it would appear, after the independent valleys of Moche and Chicama formed a political unity. The site is remarkable since it is composed of two very large complexes and possibly reflects either the dual hegemony of the unified valleys or the imposition of the dual moiety social organisation so characteristic of the empire of the Inca a millennium later. Both of these complexes at the foot of Cerro Blanco were dominated respectively by the Huaca del Sol - the Pyramid of the Sun originally a cruciform shape, and Huaca del Luna or the Pyramid of the Moon[12] (*5.018*). The siting was not entirely auspicious since both complexes stood beside the river at the base of this hill and the lower pyramid, that of the Sun, suffered by extensive scouring erosion on several occasions as a result of flooding from the adjacent river. Little now remains of the vast and elaborate complexes that surrounded these two pyramids constructed from millions of mud bricks, with their characteristic makers' marks, similar in principle to those found in the Indus in Ancient North West India[13] and the Ancient Middle East as well as Coastal China[14]. Also of interest is that the brickwork was constructed in panels and this is another aspect also found in the Ancient Middle East (*5.019*). Here there were splendid residences for the clan rulers and the kurakas, workshops for the expansive metalworking and craft industries, and civic buildings besides the temples relating to the two pyramids. Associated also with the site were cemeteries where the kurakas and the nobility were interred[15].

The Huaca del Sol was the centre of government and where the ruler presided over the council of elders and other officials whereas the Huaca del Luna was the focus of the state religion and associated ceremonies, festivals and devotions. The Moon pyramid has preserved the largest area of Moche murals yet discovered and this huaca was also noted during excavations to have been kept swept clean since refuse was conspicuously absent. The same sweeping rites were associated with the ceremonial temples and centres in Ancient Iran and India and will be of note later.

Stirrup spouted ceramics were a feature of Moche art and have been found in abundance at both the Moche sites and in connected trade regions in interments as grave goods. These appear to have been largely made from multi-piece moulds but integrated in a masterly fashion and were clearly as prestigious in their appreciation abroad as they were in the Moche state itself (*5.027*). The form of this vessel was also associated with status and appears early in the Moche period and remained unchanged until the collapse of the state as a result of severe climate change the 6th., century A.D.[16]. It has been considered that the technology developed for such moulds was probably imported from Ecuador, and it is to be noted that stirrup vessels, although not mould-made have been found in a less well manufactured type in the Pacific Islands of Melanesia. This form of policy appears in the Western Pacific along with many aspects of South America high culture, including musical instruments such as the trumpet and panpipes, weaponry, cranial deformation, and trepanation[17]. The coast far to the South in Peru and further south still in Northern Chile connect directly with inflowing Pacific Ocean currents from Asia and Melanesia through Southern Polynesia. To the north, the Ecuador coast is directly accessible from Asia, Indonesia and Melanesia through Northern Polynesia onto the South America coast and thence to Northern Peru. The ocean currents sweep the Peruvian coast from the south and then flow directly westward across through Polynesia to Melanesia before flowing onward across the top of Australia through Indonesia to South Asia. Any cultural aspects found in Melanesia corresponding with those on coastal Peru should not, therefore, be a surprise.

5.019 : Massive mud brick walls long traditional in the Ancient Middle East showing the panelled form reflecting a similar tradition among the later Moche building techniques on the coast of Peru. Ur-Nammu Ziggurat, Iraq, Mid-third millennium, B.C.

5.018 : The Moche built with clay brick that were made with maker's marks as they were anciently in Mesopotamia and the Indus Valley. Pyramid of the Moon looking toward the Pyramid of the Sun, Trujillo, North Coast Peru, 200 B.C. - 200 A.D.

5.021 : A monk holds a kapala or cranium sectioned from a human skull before his altar similarly set out to those recorded in Peru. Note the image set on the highest level of the altar virtually identical to those found at Bolivia (*5.029*). Tibet, Early 20th., century, A.D.

5.020 : Bronze object with a facial depiction similar to those in Melanesia but more likely to have been a copy of the Tibetan altar images (*5.021*). Bolivia, 700-1450 A.D.

5.022 : Tantric altar table furnished with vario ual items similar to those of the mesa or altar tabl shamans and healers in Ancient Peru into the pres day. Tibet, Early 20th., century, A.D.

5.023 : Hindu puja utensils laid out in a traditional manner similar to the mesa known in Peru from before the Conquest. Uttattur, South India, Early or pre-20th., century, A.D.

It is known that the Moche were seafarers since they occupied the island all along the coast from Ecuador to the southern most Chincha Islands off the coast of Paracas in South Peru suggesting a shared ancestral heritage with the people of the Nazca Plains. The Chincha Islands would be a region where mariners, arriving on the most northerly section of the West Wind Drift Current flowing onto the Pacific Coast of South America, might expect to arrive off the shore of Southern Peru. This may well be one of the reasons why these islands were occupied in recognition of an entreport and perhaps to intercept such voyages arriving by the more southerly route across the Pacific Ocean. This would appear to be so since it would appear that both Moche and Nazca peoples were in contact with Ancient India reflected in the deities and iconography, and this forms an important element in the theme of this book. The northern-most reaches of the Moche Empire overlapped the sphere of Ecuadorian influence in the Huarmey Valley, settling in the Vicus region of the Piura drainage, and it is thought that the Moche colonists may have reached these zones by sea[18].

The Sacred Precincts of Pachacamac

Pachacamac is one of the most important sites in Peruvian history, not because it is so old, since it is recent by Peruvian standards, being founded in its final state at about 200 A.D., but because of its focus for the people of Peru and beyond by the time of the Inca Empire. This site was built around an oracle, perhaps from an older period, and the pilgrimage site was second only to that established by the Incas in Cuzco. It would appear that when the Incas conquered the coast where Pachacamac stands they dared not to despoil or demolish it because they feared a popular uprising both within and beyond the region so widespread was the devotional draw of this shrine. The monumental site is located about 30 km south of the modern capital of Peru, Lima, in the Rimac Valley. This site of Pachcamac is significant since it stands on a prominence overlooking the sea and clearly has important connections with oceanic travel since the myths relating to this centre, including some of those regaling the great Andean hero, Viracocha, suggest that this was a landing and departure point associated with mariners and culture-bearers from abroad over the centuries. These will be of note later, but it is sufficient to state that Pachacamac was considered the counterpart of the deity Con or Kon in Ecuador far to the north[19], and the coast there is also associated with mariners and sea travellers from the Pacific.

The original large platform constructed in the early period at Pachacamac is orientated north-south and this, along with the temples and enclosures in and around the sacred precinct including residential compounds, were constructed of hand-made bricks and adobe. The burials at Pachacamac were also oriented in the same direction and among them one was found laid out on a litter and accompanied by two human sacrificial burials, probably with the intent that their soul should carry the litter in the afterlife. The number of interments around the sacred site suggests that the status of this shrine was of such a high order that others, apart from those resident at the site, sought to be buried there so that they could be associated with its sanctity for eternity[20]. It may be that Pachacamac fulfilled the same role as Benares (Varansi) had anciently to the present day in India where to be buried or cremated there was an act of great sanctity and said to reduce the possibility of returning to this "world of woe" in a future life. The buildings at Pachacamac were often several stories high and there were compounds for many different purposes. High status goods such as carved shells and semi-precious stones, bronze implements and fine ceramics have been recovered along with sacrificial caches, and frequently, human skulls that were secreted under the floors[21]. The first settlement at Pachacamac is also noted for its irrigated agricultural development expanding away from the seashore into the valley eastwards.

This first stage of the ceremonial site was later built over and formed the core of the Huaca of the Sun and adjacent to it was the construction known as the "Pachacamac Temple". The status of Pachacamac remained high and was witness to the rise and fall of kingdoms and petty states throughout Peru over a long period. However, the pilgrimages continued and the oracle, and the officiating priests in residence, attended to the inquiries and needs of the multitude of devotees who frequented its hallowed portals from the disparate regions of Peruvian society for one and a half millennia.

The Nazca Plains of Southern Peru and the Nazca Lines or Geoglyphs

The region of the Nazca culture extended throughout the Ica and Nazca River drainages and from Chincha to the Acari Valley in Southern Peru. The Nazca ceramics were justly renown throughout the world for the colour, design and form and appear to have been initiated from the Paracas cultures of the Necropolis, or second phase succeeding the first of Paracas Cavernas. The most startling element of these ceramics, in terms of Ancient Peruvian pottery finds up until that time, was their realism and natural proportions of the birds and animals, including humans, that they produced. Symbolic references in the iconography included in the ceramic designs, representative of some aspects in other cultures, were also evident. In Nazca iconography, as at Tiahuanaco, the existence of the many inclusions of trophy heads in these symbolic and realistic depictions has lead to the speculation that such fearsome relics of warfare and their ritual meaning must have played an important part in their social and particularly religious life.

The landscape of the Nazca plain has provided one of the greatest puzzles for two generations of archaeologists and historians. Known only since the invention of the aeroplane these remarkable landscape patterns, now called geoglyphs[22], have been the centre of some of the wildest speculations of all archaeological remains in the surviving ancient landscapes of the world. They were first studied in modern times by Mejia Xesspe in 1927, his work was published in 1939[23] and he called these geoglyphs sege, known as ceque among the Inca in Cuzco. These lines have also been subject to astronomical research in an attempt to link them to the points on the horizon where stars or constellations would appear in their annual cycle, but this

has only had limited success. It is now realised that many of these lines are in fact focused on hills and mountains, many in radiating patterns[24]. These patterns appear to imitate water run-off from the mountaintops, and not calendrical directions as some have attested and appear therefore to relate to rainmaking ceremonies. There have been 62 converging or radiating centres located of this type[25] but other features on the plain include stone circles and junction nodes marked with cairns that may been intended as orientation markers[26].

These "rainmaking" lines, along which the lines are "walked", or ritually perambulated, focus in mythology and legend on the mountain named Cerro Blanco on the Nazca Plain and this in turn is identified with the snow covered peak of Illa-Kata in the high Andes to the east. These two mountains are in their turn associated with that of Carhuarazo further east than Illa-Kata, and one nearer the coast called Tunga - this latter being linked to the sea in surviving cosmology[27]. These mountains were believed to draw water cyclically from the sea the water from the Pacific Ocean, under the earth and this was believed then to flow upward to the top of the peak and then down the sides of the mountains as the rivers and streams of life-giving water to irrigate their fields. A large lake of water was believed to exist under Cerro Blanca and this corresponds to the general belief still extant among the Peruvian Indians of water cycles flowing under the Earth.

Offerings on each of the sacred mountains are believed to have been made frequently and human sacrifice and a trophy head cult culture appears to have been long established associated with the supply of water, crop increase and fertility of the soil[28]. These traditions closely mirror those in Indonesia and among the Nagas of Assam and some of the Aboriginal tribes of India such as the Gonds as well as among the Melanesians. Leading up to the time of the severe climate change in the 6th., century, A.D. there was a marked increase in the number of trophy heads found in graves. This phenomenon is recorded in the depictions on the surviving ceramics interred as grave goods as well as actual trophy heads, suggesting that these were offered as propitiations to a rain god believed to have turned against his people.

The long straight lines, tracks and "runways" along with those carefully marked out as geometric designs, some representing birds, fish and animals, cover an enormous area and extend into the mountain terrain to the east (*5.024/5*). These were ritual pathways along which ceremonially constituted groups of people would perambulate while chanting to the accompaniment of musical instruments[29]. A few of these ritual pathways are readily recognisable designs and one clearly defined example represents a needle and thread[30] or a form of spear using a cord instead of a spear-thrower more common in South America. Perhaps more realistically it probably represents a harpoon used in whale-fishing on the nearby Pacific coast. A basic measurement unit appears to have been used and that was a length of about 38 to 40 centimetres or the distance between the forefinger and the elbow, in other words the Ancient Egyptian cubit[31]. The cubit was not exclusive to the Ancient Egyptians and was found elsewhere in the Ancient Near and Middle

East and with the vast number of elements common to both this West Asian region and Ancient Peru it can hardly be coincidence that they should occur in regions exhibiting so many other aspects of Ancient Middle Eastern culture.

One important calendrical correspondence has been recognised in the lines at Nazca and that was those pointing to the important agricultural point on the horizon where the Pleiades a constellation associated with agriculture rose and this has been calculated to coincide with the period between 500-700 A.D. This tends to confirm that, more or less, the whole scheme of the lines was agriculturally related since the annual cycles of the Pleiades was utilised for the commencement of sowing in the whole of the Americas and also in Polynesia. The Pleiades was called Collca, a "storehouse"[32] and is associated with the constellation of Orion where the "Belt" and "Sword" of this constellation were referred to in Nazca as the "plough"[33].

Of some interest is that the Nazcans described to the constellation of Orion as the Pelikan and this seems to correspond with similar cosmological beliefs in Aboriginal Australia where Punjil or Bunjil was perceived as the Pelikan and has correspondences to Aboriginal myths and iconography in India noted in an earlier chapter. In Nazca, the Southern Cross was recognised and called the small "cross" while parts of the constellation of Scorpio were called the large "cross"[34]. Important in the cosmology of the Nazcans was the point at which the Milky Way, or great Sky Serpent, Amaru, rose and set in the early evening and before dawn and this corresponded with aspects of astronomical observation and the belief system in the Andean highlands at Cuzco[35].

Other geoglyphs are known along the coast of Peru and are found south of Nazca in Northern Chile and on the Central Coast of Peru in the Zana, Santa and Sechin Valleys and more immediately in the valleys to the north and south of Nazca[36]. It is also known that among the Aymara people living around Lake Titicaca, and beyond on the Bolivian Plateau, that they continued constructing and walking the ceremonial pathways into more recent centuries. These were associated with specific shrines and the walking ceremonies were undertaken on the festival days associated with that shrine[37].

Nazca Imagery, Textiles and the Problem of the Red Haired Mummies
The Paracas ceramic designs were transferred recognisably into the art of Nazca during the early period but the realistic elements began to become more prominently represented in later phases. By Phases 6 and 7 elements recognisable in Moche ceramic designs were becoming evident and tend to confirm that Moche influence, noted earlier on the Chincha Islands off Paracas, was transferred from the North by sea to these islands and then to Nazca. After these phases there were two later phases, the first ending about 755 A.D. and the second about 800 A.D.[38].

More fine textiles have been retrieved from the interments in the Nazca region of Southern Peru than any other part of Peruvian South America. These follow also the same tradition as the ceramics in receiving their initial impulse from Paracas but then developing their own high quality in technique and design incorporating new motifs and the wool of camelids - llamas and alpaca in textile production. Lama wool had long been utilised in weaving elsewhere but that of the alpaca was rarely used but in Nazca greater quantities of both llama and alpaca wool were utilised in textile manufacture. The textiles recovered from the Nazca interments indicates the importance of their use in the rites of burial and the preservation of vast quantities throughout the region was due to the extremely arid climate. These interments were also noted for their seated position, a custom also known locally in the uplands to the east of Nazca around modern Ayacucho and this also connects them to the highland traditions in Southern Peru and in Bolivia.

Much has been written on the subject of the Paracas and Nazca mummies found from the Paracas Peninsula, and in the Ica and Nazca Valleys. The bottle tombs of Paracas are the oldest in Peru and they are of special interest in the considerations of the physical type that formed these cultures and appear not to be unrelated to those contemporary on the North Central Coast. A subject of great interest among the historians, archaeologists and educated, interested parties in the first decades of the twentieth century was the origin of these peoples. In the extraction of the mummy bundles from their bottle tombs it was noted on unwrapping that the hair and physical type was clearly non-Amerindian, that is, decidedly not of the Mongoloid races forming the large mass of indigenous Indian peoples (*5.026; 6.124/5*). The earliest Paracas peoples were frequently blond, fair or brown-haired with a high proportion who were red-haired and there are many examples still retained in the museum collections of the world where they can be readily seen. The quality of the hair was also different being of a much finer type and begin clearly of the Caucasian type not the uniformly black, wiry type normally associated with the mongoloid races. In fact this evidence was recorded by other explorers in the late 19th., century, such as Werthmann in the Reiss and Stubal explorations, but is less well-known[39]. Overall, these Paracas mummies tend to confirm the iconography, myths and legends that the culture-bearers, deities and heroes so noted in the Peruvian myths as white, bearded and from abroad is correct and were responsible for the "abrupt" innovations and technical advances so noted in the archaeological record.

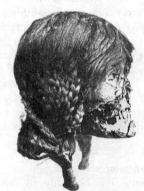

5.026 : Fair or red hair often braided as shown was common in early settlements along the Pacific Coast of South America (see *6.124/5*). Calama, North Chile, 500 B.C. - 600 A.D.

In the phase called Paracas Cavernas, immediately before that of Necropolis from about 500-200 B.C. the mummy bundle was wrapped in gauze-like fabrics in bundles and before being placed in the bottle tombs. These mummy bundles were further protected from the soil and climatic conditions because the cavern form of the tomb itself prevented salts in the soil penetrating into the bundles themselves. Another aspect of protection was that these tombs were often very large appearing to have been the preserve of specific families or clans since there were up to 55 mummy bundles found in them and in this Paracas Cavernas phase burials were accompanied by notable examples of ceramic art[40]. The accumulation of bundles further protected the mummies even if the bottle-tomb eventually collapsed since each bundle tended to protect the other except those around the outer perimeter. The red hair varying to even the most flaxen blond found among these mummies has been explained by more recent historians as due to exposure to the saltpetre in the soil. This, however, cannot be since, as above noted, so many of the mummy bundles were protected from direct contact with the soil in tombs that did not all collapse and the high degree of protection afforded anyway by the many wrappings of textiles. Those that were exposed through tomb collapse and by the looting by grave-robbers, the huaqueros, do exhibit the characteristic orange bleaching due to exposure but this is obviously natural even to the least qualified observers and has nothing to do with the clearly natural fair hair colouring found from Northern Chile and Argentina through to the far North coast of Peru in the same time frame. It is particularly noted in the Paracas Cavernas

5.027 : Seated priest with the large beard tending to suggest foreign influences and evidence of Asian people on this coast. Chimbote, Moche, North Central Peru, 200-600 A.D.

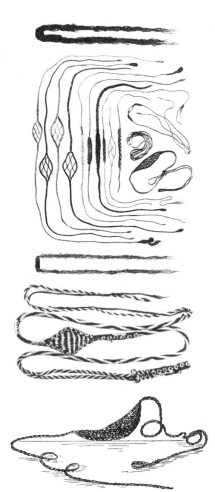

5.028 : Large selection of slings utilised traditionally along the Peruvian coast and the Andes through to Argentina and Chile identical to those of Polynesia, Melanesia, Indonesia and South Asia. Inca Dynasty, Peru, 1350-1500 A.D.

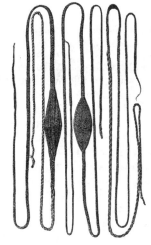

5.030 : Typical group of slings in Eastern Polynesia identical to those found in South America. Marquesas Islands, Eastern Polynesia, Late 19th., century, A.D.

5.029 : Sling and stone of the Melanesian type identical to South America and South East Asia. New Guinea, Melanesia, Late 19th., century, A.D.

5.031 : Decorated woven sling of the type found along the foothills of the Himalayas, but identical to those found in Arabia, the Pacific Islands and South America. Nepal, Early 20th., century, A.D.

5.033 : Slings of the type identical in South Asia and South America. Malay Peninsula, Late 19th., century, A.D.

5.032 : Basic form of woven sling of the type typically found among some Aboriginal tribes in India through the Pacific Islands to South America. Godavari Delta, East Central India.

5.034 : Slings from South East Asia of the South American and West Asian type. Karo Batak, Sumatra, Indonesia, Late 19th., century, A.D.

phase that many of the skulls exhibited trepanation, from surgery that had been frequently successful, and it is not known whether this was the result of frequent wars or internecine strife, brain disorders, or religious reasons (*4.002-4*).

Many examples of sectional sketches and diagrams through mummy bundles taken from archaeological sites in Paracas Necropolis show that the mummies themselves were seated with the knees drawn up to the chin. There were usually wrapped in lavish, brightly designed textiles, these being tied with cords (*4.107*; *4.108/9*) and embellished with symbolic ornaments before being placed in a reed basket. This basket and its contents were then also enclosed in a textile shroud before being enclosed in another tied at the top and in many cases an outer layer was added to seal the whole within[41]. Many of the outer textiles were about 4 metres long and this, along with the lavish use of textiles in the inner layers, has protected the natural attributes of the mummies from the saltpetre-rich soil in which their rectangular pits were located.

Characteristic of other Peruvian cultures was the ritual use of the obolos of small gold plates placed over the orifices, including the mouths, of the deceased before interment. This is an identical practice known anciently in Asia and the daubing of red ochre of the bodies is also known in the Old World and unlikely to be of independent origin[42]. Paracas Necropolis is a period dating from about 200 B.C. to about 200 A.D. and its end appears to correspond with that of end of the Cahuachi ceremonial centre in Nazca.

Textiles at this time appear to have been extremely important in death as they must have been in life since remarkable inclusions with inhumations have been recorded in terms of the weaver's art. Between the layers of the mummy bundles shroud textiles have been found richly ornamented and with folded cloths and in some bundles as many as 150 textile cloths such as tunics, scarves, breech clouts, bags, headbands, headdresses, fans, and slings[43].

Slings in Ancient Peru (*5.028*) are of particular interest since they are identical in technique and design found through Polynesia (*5.030*), New Guinea (*5.029*), Indonesia (*5.034*) and into South East Asia, India (*5.032*), the Himalayas (*5.031*) to Arabia. Various thread were used in these funerary textiles and include cotton, llama and alpaca wool, agave fibre and human hair. It is interesting to note that the last of these was also used frequently in ornamentation and symbolic ornaments in Aboriginal Australia. This lavish use of textiles associated with the dead, so richly preserved from the Paracas and Nazca region, was characteristic to a larger or lesser degree throughout Ancient Peru and Bolivia, and into Northern Chile and Argentina. It is also true of Ancient India and found by extension in the Philippines and Indonesia almost identically with Peru, where the name of the textiles used were called kumbi or kumbli in India, pa kumbu in the Philippines and Indonesia and cumbi or cumbli in Ancient Peru and will be considered in a later chapter.

In the second phase of Paracas, that of Necropolis, the trophy head motif becomes more apparent and this appears to have been subsumed into the Nazca region and became augmented in textile art, evident in the many surviving examples of ceramic iconography contemporary with it, and so widely admired in the present day. These motifs are associated with agricultural societies where human sacrifice and trophy heads were believed to impart fertility to the soil at the sowing of the seed in the agricultural cycle and rain-making[44]. These beliefs appear identical to those found anciently in headhunting societies in Indonesia, India and Assam and indicate a probable common origin.

The iconography at Nazca appears to have derived in large part from that of Chavin de Huantar through Paracas and then developed more realistic and individualistic iconographical references in creating its own recognisable tradition. In one textile design a throne or chief's seat is depicted supported by addorsed pumas[45] or native lions and this motif in turn appears to relate to that found at Palenque in Mayan Mexico dating to about the 8th., century, A.D. It has been shown that this originated in Ancient Buddhist India[46] over two thousand years ago suggesting contact between these far distant regions.

Another iconographical representation found in other cultures in Peru, as well as preserved on Nazca ceramics, is the spear-thrower. Some believe that this element is the "rod" represented being held by the Staff or Sun God on the Gateway of the Sun at Tiahuanaco, and entering the iconography of Nazca through Huari, or perhaps directly earlier. This spear-thrower motif is also found about the same time or a little later among the early Chimu or Sican phase. One of the few Amazonian Indian tribes to use the same type of spear-thrower has been identified in North-East Brazil[47] and this suggests that there were riverine traders travelling via the Amazon from the river delta in that region to the Andes and then across the cordillera to the Pacific Ocean. This appears to have been a fundamental principle of many of the major cultural influences from the earliest times in the Andes and Pacific Coast of Ecuador, Peru and Chile. The Nazcan Sun God of this period is noted by some to be closely similar to the Mexican Sun God culminating in that of the Aztecs[48].

One of the most interesting forms of weapon is the wooden sword used by the Tupinamba tribes of the Amazon Basin and Gran Chaco, called a tacape. This sword was found also represented in related types among Chiriguanos in Southern Bolivia, and the Guarani, and further in Northern South America in Guiana as well as among the Incas. The wooden sword, for peoples such as the Incas who had access to a long metallurgical tradition, seems anomalous. However, with so many aspects of South American culture appearing to derive from Asia via Indonesia in South America it is not surprising that among the Indonesian was known and traditional used a wooden parang or sword. In Nazca also the mace or club head is of interest since the local type appears to have spread from Pachacamac north to the Chimu[49]. The mace head types are found widely in Melanesia (*5.006/7*) in the islands that collect and filter any influences flowing from the East from Polynesia and South America, through the only bottleneck available. This is the Torres Straits leading to Indonesia and South East Asia and to India. These mace heads have their identical counterparts in India, and the star club head so characteristic of Peru and the symbol of state rulership of the Inca appears to derive from the earlier fluted clubs of India and Ancient Assyria.

Nazca Irrigation - Puquios and Qanats

Because of the extremely arid climate Nazca could only expand if irrigation was intensively applied and extended to ensure sufficient water supply to crops. Subsistence was therefore more acutely tied to water and to the deities believed to allow the water to flow from the mountaintops who were, therefore, more perspicaciously propitiated and appeased. The pressure to provide an adequate supply of precious water was undoubtedly the reason why innovations, such as the underground channel system, were undertaken on the Nazca Plains. Considered unique to Nazca in Peru a system of puquios that were as these underground stone-lined channels with nodal access junctions and ventilation shafts and their close similarity to the qanats of the Ancient Middle East is admitted[50] even by conventional Americanists who oppose the notion of any contacts between the Old World and the New. It is thought that these may have been introduced in the 5-6th., century A.D., a little before or perhaps after the massive eruption of the volcano Krakatoa between Sumatra and Java in Indonesia in 535 A.D. occurred. This was an event that dramatically changed the climate for decades after and the effects were particularly notable in South America but also in Asia. The puquios may have been introduced before that period but no date of introduction is yet available. The fact that this equivalent of the Middle Eastern irrigation system is found on this part of the coast influenced by Tiahuanaco is significant since the Iranian architecture and customs, and iconography such as decapitation of prisoners in Assyria, at this date and before around Persepolis and bears striking resemblances to those at Tiahuanaco. In the middle of the 1st millennium A.D. Nazca appeared to be experiencing a period of protracted aridity that may have preceded the extreme climate change experienced in the middle of the 6th., century A.D. Whether the massive eruption of Krakatoa in 535 A.D. set off adverse El Nino events and a period of extreme dryness after that date were El Ninos is unknown, these usually occurring in a 9-year cycle. It is clear, however, that the increase in trophy head rituals suggests a long period of decline and aridity on the Nazca Plain. The archaeological evidence from the Nazca region indicates that crops such as maize and beans were less frequently planted, while the cultivation of peppers ceased. These long-cultivated crops were replaced by others requiring less water and a shorter growth period such as the calabash[51]. In the Marquesas Islands, in Eastern Polynesia, the nearest of the Pacific Islands to the Americas, Pukeo is the name of a star that related to the months of December-January[52]. It is interesting to note that the rising Pleiades was observed to indicate the beginning of the agricultural season in the Pacific Islands as it was in the Americas. December-January was the month of the Makara, the Ganges River crocodile

5.035 : The temple shown in *5.038* with angled inner rooms deliberately designed to allow a sightline angled obliquely through the building from outside at point from where the photo was taken. Recauy, Huarez, Wilkawain, Peru, 300-1000 A.D.

5.036 : Sightlines to the mountain peaks were of primary importance in architectural orientation in Ancient Peru. This temple in Central Peru was orientated to the mountain peaks surrounding it. Recauy, Huarez, Wilkawain, Peru, 300-1000 A.D.

5.037 : Turbanned warrior with inverted trophy head in the Mexican manner hanging from the neck. The shield displays the identical saltire cross found in Western Mexico and India . Recuay, Callejon de Hauylas, Huarez, Central Peru, 300-1000 A.D.

5.040 : Two warriors with shields with saltire construction identical to that depicted in Central Highland Peru and Central America. Andra Dynasty, Central India, 100-300 A.D.

5.039 : Turbanned warrior with trophy head hanging from the neck. The shield displays the identical saltire cross found in Western Mexico and India. Recuay, Callejon de Hauylas, Huarez, Central Peru, 300-800 A.D.

5.041 : Bearded warriors with shield displaying saltire cross of the type found also in Central Peru and Mexico. West Mexico, First millennium, A.D.

5.038 : The angled sightline to the peak on the horizon from inside the temple shown in *5.035/6*. Recauy culture, Huarez, Wilkawain, Peru, 300-1000 A.D.

deity, so widely represented in the Americas (*11.024-9*; *11.031*) and the disgorger of the waters of the World in traditional iconography in India (*11.022*; *11.032/3*).

Nazca and the Congregational Ceremonial Centre of Cahuachi

Situated beside the River Nazca was what was considered originally to have been a "congregation" centre, Cahuachi dating from about 2200 years ago. This site was regaled with ceremonial enclosures that eventually grew into what is believed to have been the religious and possibly the political capital of the Nazca region. The city at its apogee of its development was a ritual centre for the region rather than a residential and administrative centre of the Moche types much further to the north. By Phase 3 this site had assumed pre-eminence in the South Coast Peru region and appears to have been a ceremonial centre boasting 40 mounds or more along with courts and plazas of various sizes and shapes. The largest mound, or "Great Temple" was a stepped platform 20 metres high and the associated court measured 75 x 47 metres. The mounds are of interest since they are formal structures built over remodelled hills and eminences with infill to form the mound's perimeter and supported and faced by adobes. Some of the finest textiles from South India were in fact recovered from elite burials within these mounds along with ceramics and other goods[53]. The early coastal building construction techniques using conical mud-bricks, called adobes, was utilised at Cahuachi[54] indicating that ancient techniques were retained over millennia when other, perhaps simpler constructional forms were adequate for the task.

Cahuachi, considered the capital of the early the Nazca plains efflorescence, appears to have been influenced by the Paracas culture and achievements in the Cavernas phase, but was abandoned by 200 A.D. This corresponds with a resurgence of the Paracas iconography dating from almost a millennia earlier and may indicate new influences from the land of origin that initiated Paracas, arrived to re-establish their original culture from abroad, that is by sea. Cahuachi was not abandoned through threat of war or other violence but was carefully covered over under a mantle of soil suggesting ritual cessation perhaps associated with the end of some calendrical cycle and, or a return of the elite ruling clans to the land of their ancestors.

Late Period Moche and Kuelap
On the North Coast of Peru the Moche were in full control and had reached the peak of their culture in the early centuries of the first millennium, A.D. At the headwaters of the Moche River a great hilltop construction at Marcahuamachuco was commenced at about 300 A.D. and this has been called one of the greatest monuments in the Peruvian highlands, but otherwise little known. This building is placed at the edge of a plateau giving panoramic views over the countryside but its purpose is unknown. Characteristic of this period, it featured extended galleries in long narrow buildings, and this building type is also found at the capital, Cerro Blanco, near the coast. Buildings reflecting a similar style were built until the 6th., century some featuring great halls that were constructed measuring 48 x 8 metres. The Marcahuamachuco-type buildings were also built as curvilinear galleries along the edge of steep plateaus where the lower floor was used as a residence and the upper level for storage. At this time also interment above ground in chullpa-like buildings, and mausoleums, of important people was usual and this form of burial was also known around the highland region of Lake Titicaca[55].

Recauy in the Callejon de Huaylas in Central Peru
This regional site area is one of the lesser known in Peruvian history but is located at the headwaters of the Santa Valley near modern-day Huarez. This site is considered a later extension of Chavin de Huantar not far distant and the partially preserved site of Willkawain indicates that the surviving building was aligned to the surrounding peaks where even the internal walls were located to allow direct site lines from the outside (*5.035/6*; *5.041*). The iconography clearly incised or carved into the many stone monoliths represent warriors and are thought to indicate connections to trophy head rituals. The cross banding in saltire form of the shields depicted on many of the monoliths (*5.037/8*) reflects identically those of the soldiers in India (*5.039*) in the same time band and in Mexico (*5.040*). The many examples of armorial animals also reflect those found in India and particularly the type found on the carved pediment rails surrounding the massive relief-carved stone railings around the Buddhist pilgrim centre at Bodh Gaya in India (*11.033*). Interestingly also at these centres is that the ceramics found in burials were ritually smashed, a tradition found throughout the Americas and in Asia, suggesting a major cultural transfer[56].

Ayacucho, the Ancient Guamanga in the Southern Highlands of Peru
The first reclamations of land in the highlands of Peru occur and are late attributed to the people known as the Huarpa who constructed terraces in the rugged terrain and utilised irrigation and dry farming methods. Some of these terraces extended up the hillside for as many as 100 steps extending from the valley floor to near the summit of the mountains. Waterproof clay-lined

canals, some 1.5 metres wide, springs and cisterns were constructed to ensure an adequate supply of water for these terraces over wide area[57]. Houses were usually stone built, two-roomed and of elliptical or circular plan. The main civic centres feature the H-form of construction where large monolithic stones were placed several metres apart and filled between with coursed or horizontally laid stones. This is a similar form of construction to that found at Tiahuanaco, and also in Polynesia. The capital of this region is thought to be the largest settlement known as Nawinpukyo, and there several platforms formed the civic centre along with courts, terraces and high status residences[58]. In the nearby region of Andahuaylas the first gold, along with gold-smithing tools, were found previously at Waywaka, dating to 1900-1450 B.C. [59].

Tiahuanaco - 1500 Years of Growth and Empire on the Altiplano

The ceremonial centre of Tiahuanaco is so exceptional in the development of South America that it has inspired many extreme beliefs as to its origins and the people believed to be responsible for its construction. These culture-bearers have been considered to have arrived from outer space as aliens, while others have more modestly considered them to have descended from a master race who were refugees from the mythical sunken Atlantis. More realistically others have considered the builders to have derived from one of the high culture in the Old World but many of these assertions suffer from the problem of dating since the need to identify these great initiators with primal avatar teachers or mythical heroes in the Old World corresponding to some fabulous date seems irresistible. Recent developments in dating techniques have consigned most of these theories to well-deserved oblivion, but a few of those who linked Tiahuanaco to Ancient Near and Middle East and India may have substance in them.

It is generally thought that the great city of Tiahuanaco was constructed and expanded by the same people for over a thousand years who shaped the social and cultural destinies of those far beyond the immediate environment of Lake Titicaca in the Bolivian highlands. Radiocarbon dating has indicated that the first settlement was founded about 400 B.C. and that this grew into the capital and ceremonial centre covering five phases. Phase 2 appears to indicate the growing dominance of Tiahuanaco the region with the decline of Pucara sited at the other end of Lake Titicaca. It was in Phase 3, however, that Tiahuanaco emerged into period of great construction projects and expansive irrigation works and this dated from about 100 A.D to 375 A.D. In Phase 4 at Tiahuanaco began to expand into the surrounding regions and realise its imperial ambitions either through desire, or necessity, and connected their centres with caravans expanding also trade as well as state control[60]. The city became an administrative centre that was a focal point for its far-flung colonies, aimed largely to the west to the Pacific Ocean shore, and south into Northern Argentina and Northern Chile, but also with influences in the north. The highland region where the city was located suffered severely in the dramatic climate change in the 6th., century A.D. that so ravaged the coastal regions and devastated the Moche in Northern Peru but survived somewhat diminished. This was followed in Phase 5 by another great building program but its power base had been eroded throughout the Empire and decline set in lasting for several centuries before the final collapse in the early 11th., century, A.D. This may have been the result of another climate change initiated by a severe El Nino event or the results of another volcanic eruption. It has been noted in recent research that climate change brought about collapse in the Late Classic Mayan period in Central America at this same time.

The Akapana as the Sacred Mountain

The Akapana, a stepped pyramid and the largest construction at Tiahuanaco, was first recorded in his eyewitness account by Cieza de Leon, and this structure appears to have risen to a summit with a sunken court reflecting the earlier Chiripa tradition. Chiripa appears to have been the fore-

5.043 : Massive monolithic size stone steps and uprights photographed over a century ago at Tiahuanaco before restoration (*5.058*). Tiahuanaco, Bolivia, 200-800 A.D.

5.042 : Massive stone upright 6 metres high with large stone blocks facing the massive platform of the Kalasasaya. High quality stonework and sophisticated drainage channels are typical of the great centre. Tiahuanaco, Bolivia, 200-600 A.D.

5.044 : Carved monolith as a model of a sunken court shown being measured by early Victorian researchers. Putuni, Tiahuanaco; Bolivia, 700-1000 A.D.

5.045 : Finely carved architraves around a window virtually identical to many examples of Chalukyan and Hindu Temple architecture in Central and Eastern India. Tiahuanaco, 700-900 A.D.

runner, or major contributor to the foundation of Tiahuanaco almost a thousand years earlier, located also around Lake Titicaca. Of particular interest are the recent excavations revealing sacrificial burials around the base of the pyramid. Dozens of male victims were interred and dismembered before final inhumation. A sunken court flanks the Akapana about 200 metres to the west (*5.058*) and this was constructed of stone lined walls into which carved tenoned heads, portraits and human skulls, were inserted. Centred in this sunken court was the best-known monument in Tiahuanaco called the Bennett monolith (*5.057*) after its excavator. The carved monolith appears to represent a priest holding a sceptre or baton and a keros or ritual vessel to his chest, but bears striking resemblances to other examples known in Eastern Asia (*5.054*; *5.056*).

To the east of the Akapana is a rise where numerous large carved stone slabs are found together with many sculpted as miniature portals called the Kanta Tayita. This site is only partially excavated and the purpose is yet to be determined but this is also true for the rest of the site. This site features gigantic stone blocks carved and sometimes broken, possibly as a result of grave robbing, and the whole represents a prodigious testament to the stonemason's art and engineering skills.

The miniature portal shapes, windows and niches still to be seen at the Kanta Tayita are characteristic of those found carved at other locations at the site and also miniature representations of a ceremonial sunken court (*5.045*). Not least of these is the most famous monument of all found at the site - the monolith known as the Gateway to the Sun. Although these carved portals, windows and niche forms are characteristic here at Tiahuanaco they were not usual in the rest of the Andean sites. The profiles appear to represent architraves carved around regular rectangular openings and these appear to be based upon an earlier reflection of the post and beam construction for a doorway, but adapted in a particularly individual manner. The sophistication and polished highly quality of the carving and the lack of precedents or anything that might parallel this development suggest that this tradition was probably introduced from elsewhere.

In fact, in the same time band, closely similar examples are found in India among the Chalukyan monuments of South India and in North East Central India in Orissa

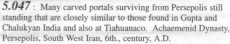

5.046 : The great portal into the Palace of Darius at Persepolis showing the king himself entering under a parasol. These portals are probably the prototypes of those at Tiahuanaco in Bolivia. Persepolis, S.W. Iran, 6th., century, B.C.

5.047 : Many carved portals surviving from Persepolis still standing that are closely similar to those found in Gupta and Chalukyan India and also at Tiahuanaco. Achaemenid Dynasty, Persepolis, South West Iran, 6th., century, A.D.

5.048 : Carved rock architraves to the cave shrine portal in a T-formed virtually identical to those of Tiahuanaco and carved in the same time frame. Gupta Dynasty, Udayagiri Caves, Central India, 320-606 A.D.

5.049 : Carved rock architraves to the cave shrine portalg in a T-formed virtually identical to those of Tiahuanaco and carved in the same time frame. Gupta Dynasty, Udayagiri Caves, Central India, 415-425 A.D.

5.050 : Carved architraves around a portal still standing a century ago similar to the T-portals found almost identically in the Gupta and Chalukyan Dynasties in India. Tiahuanaco, Bolivia, 700-900 A.D.

5.051 : Architraves surrounding portals are virtually identical to one of the greatest stone carving dynasties in India - the Chalukyas and in Iran. Putuni, Tiahuanaco, 700-900 A.D.

(*8.016*; *8.018/9*). The areas of influence preceding these local developments in India are regions that were influenced by earlier Buddhist ceremonial sites inspired from Iran, before and after the Greek invasion in 326 B.C. under Alexander. Alexander later laid waste to Persepolis in South Western Iran and the refugees in part sought haven in India and from this great centre it is clear that the later kingdoms of India drew their artisans along with architectural and iconographical inspiration. From India, these two regions of the Chalukyan Empire and those of Orissa clearly influence Sumatra and Java. It is from India that the artisans are known to have transferred their religious iconography to Indonesia and no doubt some continued further east to the Maya in Central America[61].

Although there are many who will insist that the traditions of fine stonework at Chavin de Huantar and other sites were the forerunners of that at Tiahuanaco a study of the exceptional monolithic stonework at Tiahuanaco suggests that is in a separate tradition albeit from the same origin. At all other sites stonework is utilised either used as

5.052 : Stone carved tenon heads in the walls of the Parthian capital of Hatra. Similar carved tenon heads were a characteristic in contemporary Andean sites. Hatra, Mesopotamia, 250 B.C. - 191 A.D.

5.053 : Stone carved tenon heads similar to those in contemporary Mesopotamia found widely in the Andean sites in the first millennium, B.C. and A.D. Tiahuanaco, Bolivia, 200 - 800 A.D.

5.054 : Carved stone statue showing an ancestor or deity with votive vessel similar to those found in Tiahuanaco. Mongolia, mid-first millennium, A.D.

5.055 : Insitu heads in the manner known for centuires before as tenons in the shrines carved from the living rock in Western India. Chaitya Temple, Nasik, 2-5th., century, A.D.

5.056 : Carved monolith representing a deity holding a sceptre and votive vessel in a similar manner to those in North East Asia and Tiahuanaco. Assyrian, 9-7th., century, B.C.

5.057 : The finest monolith found at Tiahuanaco depicting a priest or deity holding ritual implements to his chest, similar to those found in Mongolia and Manchuria (5.054). Tiahuanaco, Bolivia, 4th., - 8th., century, A.D.

5.058 : Large sunken court showing the many tenon heads, portals and freestanding statues closely similar to those known in contemporary Mesopotamia. Tiahuanaco, Bolivia, 200-800 A.D.

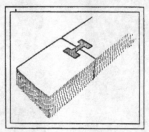

5.059 : Metal cramp identical to those found at Tiahuanaco found at Angkor Wat. 11-12th., century, A.D.

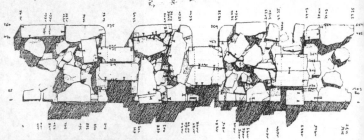

5.061 : Finely carved stone masonry with characteristic metal cramps inherited by architecture and construction in India and then found also in the Puma Punku at Tiahuanaco (5.063). Parsagadae, Southern Iran, mid-first century, B.C.

5.060 : Fine masonry showing the facing blocks, some irregular in shape connected I metal cramps similar to masonry in South America and the rarely found cramps found at Tiahuanaco. Dorozan, Iran, Mid-first m lennium, B.C.

5.062 : Finely carved stone masonry showing the metal clamps still insitu surviving from 1300 years ago. Udaigiri, Orissa, India, 7-8th., century, A.D.

5.064 : Finely carved stone masonry closely similar to that in the contemporary time band in India (5.062). Puma Punku, Tiahuanaco, Bolivia, 700-900 A.D.

5.063 : Metal cramp incision in the massive stone block in the bottom right of the illustration similar to those of the Puma Punku (5.064). Note also the crosses identical to those of the Chalukyan Dynasty (6-7th., cent., A.D.) carvings in South India (8.018). Putuni, Tiahuanaco, Bolivia, 700-900 A.D.

rough coursed stone or boulders as rubble walls, but at Chavin de Hauntar the stonework is shaped and coursed with stone panels that are fitted and carved in a careful manner along with ashlar facings to stone infill walls. The technique at Tiahuanaco is equally fine but very different in technique where large stone monoliths and slabs and shaped and fitted with almost machine precision and polish. Post and lintel examples occur but the Gateway of the Sun and other examples of exceptional stonework are carved from a single piece that is more reminiscent of rock-carved temple traditions in Iran and India.

The rock carved tombs of the Achaemenid and Sassanian dynasties at Persepolis, dating from the 4th., century, B.C. and 3rd., century, A.D. respectively, show a form and technique closely similar to that of Tiahuanaco but inherited in India and utilised by the Buddhists for a thousand years from about the 3rd., century B.C. or earlier. Rock carved tombs and temples were also adopted into the emerging Hindu religion, and contemporary dynasties, and are found still being assimilated into the Gupta and Chalukyan dynasty from about the 5th., century, A.D. in South India and through into the Pallava in South East India from about the 2-7th., century, A.D.

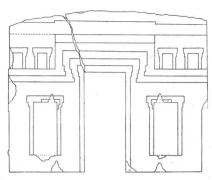

5.066 : Carved Staff Deity over the door opening identified with the Sun and/or the lightning god in Bolivia. Tiahuanaco, Bolivia, 300-600 A.D.

5.065 : Rear face of the Gateway of the Sun showing the recessed shapes of portals architrave and niche insets. These T-shapes are closely similar to those found throughout India in the same time-frame but particularly found on cave temples. Tiahuanaco, Bolivia, 200-600 A.D.

5.067 : Gateway of the Sun from the front as it was over a century ago showing seismic damage. Tiahuanaco, Bolivia, 400-800 A.D.

5.069 : Carved monolith similar in proportion to the carvings found at Tiahuanco some centuries earlier. Aztec, Central Mexico, 1300-1500 A.D.

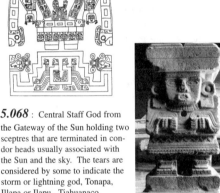

5.068 : Central Staff God from the Gateway of the Sun holding two sceptres that are terminated in condor heads usually associated with the Sun and the sky. The tears are considered by some to indicate the storm or lightning god, Tonapa, Illapa or Ilapu. Tiahuanaco, Bolivia, 400-800 A.D.

5.070 : A trumpeter from the Gateway of the Sun with a puma-headed serpent foot of a type found similarly among the Maya, and the early Buddhists. He holds a trophy head typical of some early deities in Buddhist iconography. Tiahuanaco, Bolivia, 400-800 A.D.

Perhaps one of the most convincing elements in this Iranian tradition and its origins and diffusion into to India and South East Asia but extending to Tiahuanaco is that the last named is the only place in the New World where copper cramps[62] are found utilised in the same way as Iran, India and Angkor Wat (*5.059-64*).

The copper cramps themselves were largely sought out by the Spanish Conquistadors after the gold had been largely dug out from Tiahuanaco, and melted down but the recesses to take these essential elements are still clearly evident in the surviving stonework at the Puma Puncu site (*5.064*). Metal cramps are not known at any other site in South America and indicates that these and the unique form of building construction at Tiahuanaco derives from the builders and artisans that must have been introduced from abroad, and from India in particular. Metal cramps are found at a number of sites in India and are found particularly in Buddhist structures and later Hindu works into the period before the British Colonial Period. Examples are also known from the Khmer sites of Angkor Wat in Cambodia (*5.059*).

The overall stepped pyramid form of the Akapana and the giant platform known as the Kalasasaya have their prototypes in principle from the earlier millennia in the Andes and coastal Peru. But this only means that whoever the Tiahuanacans were they adapted local traditions to their own or imported construction techniques. It is most likely that there were at least one major intrusion of immigrants - most or entirely male as was usual in cross-Pacific transfers, in the first half of the first millennium B.C. introducing the abrupt advances in metallurgical and weaving techniques among others and these intruders would have taken their marriage partners from the local ruling or elite clans as the Spaniards did two thousand years later. These newcomers would have formed new ruling clans and the merging of races to some degree would also be reflected their own belief systems with elements of the indigenous or naturalised peoples. This would have been true of social institutions and the customary means of social planning and temple building necessary when dealing with the ultra-conservative nature of the Amerindians. Certainly, as proposed in this work and in other earlier works, the incomers would have recognised many aspects of South American culture since there were many common traits introduced many centuries earlier through former contacts.

The metal cramps so unusual at Tiahuanaco were found securing the stonework at the Puma Punku, this being a later building, a half kilometre from the main site, dating to about the mid-first millennium A.D. possibly after the 6th., century, and is constructed of the "very finest andesite and sandstone masonry"[63]. This stepped platform measured 150 metres square and stood about 5 metres high with two or three separate stairways and these were graced with elaborate monolithic portals, or gateways similar to the Gateway of the Sun. The Gateway of the Sun now stands at the rear of the great platform Kalasa-saya but it is believed that this was not its original position.

Kalasa-saya - Ritual Platform on a Megalithic Scale

The sunken court in front of the Akapana is due west of the Kalasa-saya and aligned to its great entrance stair upward to its summit (*5.058*). The platform measures about 150 metres square and over 6 metres high and it is the supreme example of the so-called H-shaped structure where giant monoliths are set apart and filled with stone masonry in horizontal courses (*5.042*). On the sum-

5.071 : Vast ground design that may represent a tree and therefore fertility but that can only be seen from the sea. This suggests that it might have been a form of beacon for mariners. South Coast Peru, 3rd., - 6th., century, A.D.

5.072 : Hittite lightning staff as a trident identical to those found in India. Anatolia, 2nd., millennium, B.C.

5.073 : Staff God of the Huari type inherited from Tiahuanacan imagery. Pachacamac, South Central Peru, 700-1000 A.D.

5.074 : Trefoil "blossoms" depicted at the end of each branch characteristic of the Siva trefoil and the lotus flame illustrated extending from the Buddhist topknots. North Coast Peru, 1st., millennium, A.D.

mit there was a large court and this was flanked on its north and south side by religious or state buildings and the so-called "Ponce" monolith was centrally placed[64].

Putuni - Elite Residences and Palace Complexes
Due west of the Akapana is the mound known as the Putuni where it is considered to be the main residential complex or palace for the Tiahuanacan elite or rulers. Finely constructed conduits have been uncovered in this complex and this careful manipulation of water falling on this section of the site is noted also in the Akapana and the Puma Punku. It is believed that these conduits were constructed not only as drainage but also for imitating the descent of water from the sacred mountaintop thereby emulating the sympathetic magic origins of similar ducts and conduits associated in rainmaking traditions found also at the earlier Chavin de Huantar temple.

Gateway to the Sun - Fabled Monolith Depicting Tears of the Sun or Lightning God
The Gateway to the Sun has long fascinated researchers, historians and explorers and the imagination of those less inclined to scholarship than others. In the case of the latter Tiahuanaco has been seen as the landing place of aliens and by others as the location beside Lake Titicaca as the last remnants of Atlantis believed to have sunken beneath the Lake. In another more interesting treatise H.S. Bellamy, in attempting to decipher the bas-reliefs, believed them to be a record of the cycles of a moon, before the present lunar body, been drawn into the gravitational pull of the Earth that resulted in its disintegration about 10-12,000 years ago. This was an elaboration of the earlier Horbieger Theory. This is now thought impossible at any time in the last hundreds of thousands, or millions of years but certain aspects resulting from his interpretation and symbolic meaning from the iconography surviving may be of interest in due course.

The main staff god figure, so often identified with the Sun God placed over the head of the opening in the monolith, may represent the Sun or a lightning god. However, in the ancient world the symbolism associated with that representation, and the number of times it is shown, may give a clue as to the meaning intended behind its presentation. The "tears" carved on the cheeks are now seen as representing aspects of deity as the Ccoa or wildcat indicating hail and by extension rain so necessary for the growth of crops. But around the image of the Sun the "rays" number nineteen and this indicates that this number was a signification in the meaning of this representation. Further symbolic aspects in relation to surviving myths and legends will be reserved and considered in due course. It is sufficient at this point only to recognise its importance as an architectural unit as part of a broader, fundamental symbolic whole in the planning of Tiahuanaco.

Tiahuanacao - The Agricultural Support System and Extension Toward the Pacific Coast
To support the growing capital of Tiahuanaco and it's expanding imperialist ambitions the agricultural support system had, by necessity, to advance and extend in production and efficiency. Apparently adapted from the Chiripa traditions a ridged-field reclamation system was used for intensive high-yield cultivation of crops, more efficient that that utilised in the present day. Agricultural systems were associated on the Bolivian plateau around Lake Titicaca not only at Tiahuanaco but in the satellite centres of Pajchiri to the north, and Luqurmata to the south. Both of these centres featured stone-faced platforms, sunken courts and monumental gateways in the Tiahuanaco tradition along with carved monoliths and stelae[65].

Reclamation systems for agriculture were also found in the Azapa Valley - a section of the zone of the expanding influence of Tiahuanaco to the west. In the Moquegua River area, above 1500 metres, the Huaracani people began also to irrigate their land and manufacture fire-tempered ceramics styles apparently related to Chiripa. After the severe climate change commencing in 535 A.D. immigration is noticeable extending from the highlands around Tiahuanaco into the lower valleys and this is called the Omo phase[66].

The results of this climate change and migration were seen in the collapse of the Moche whose reliance on intensive irrigation, from already naturally poor environmental conditions for agriculture, bordered on the precarious. In Tiahuanaco, however, the capital as power-base of the Empire had always drawn people and trade to itself, but now migration away to the surrounding lower lands of the upland Andes appears to have saved it from collapse and allowed another great phase in its existence. The flow of the population into the western Azapa and Moquegua valleys provided the short route to the Pacific coast, but another great stream appears to have flowed to the north west into the already settled region around Guamanga now Ayacucho. This region formed the home ground for a new expression of the Tiahuanacan parent called Huari or Wari.

Huari or Wari - Expansion and Technical Advance after Tiahuanacan Decline

Although Tiahuanaco was much weakened by the climatic changes affecting the fragile eco-system of the altiplano that occurred in the 6th., century, A.D. it survived probably because of its assured position as a pilgrimage centre sanctified by almost a millennium of established tradition. Its location was probably perceived as mystical and symbolic and the reduced agricultural resources were probably supplemented from the established colonies in the lower highlands, including the Ayacucho region, brought by adoring devotees from these later settlements and a centralised government determined to maintain control or at least its influence.

However, as the extensive climatic changes lasted for decades the former colonies probably realised they had the whip hand and began to institute measures that would establish their independence from the parent state. The 600 miles of rugged terrain between the region around Huari, the capital of the Huari state, or modern Ayacucho, and Tiahuanco meant that communication and defence were clearly advantageous to the people of Huari. They controlled the route to the Rimac Valley, where the important pilgrimage site of Pachacamac had been established half a millennia before, and to the north that was clearly important since the Huari state influence is seen extensively in that direction.

The capital of the state of Huari was apparently also called the same name and this covered an area of about 3-4 square kilometres beside an extensive band of dwellings beyond the urban complex located on a hilly plateau about 25 kilometres north of modern Ayacucho. The central core featured multi-storey masonry buildings housing about 20-30,000 people. The strategic location of the city is emphasised not only by its links on the trade routes from North and Central Peru to Tiahuanaco in the Bolivian Highlands but also with long-standing access and contact with the Ica Valley and Nazca Plain to the West and therefore to Pacific shoreline of Coastal South Central Peru and Paracas.

It must be significant that the iconography that is distinctive to the Huari state, but clearly derived or influenced from Tiahuanaco, appears in its home region about the 7th., century A.D. This suggests that there was a migration from Tiahaunaco because of the severe weather at this time to an already established trading post or colony linking to Ica and Paracas. It is worth conjecturing that the climatic changes due to the eruption of Krakatoa in 535 A.D., taking several decades to affect the climate throughout the world, initiated some migration from the people of Java and the other Indonesian islands to South America. The Ica Valley and Huari region may have been a place of settlement for these refugees and joined later by Tiahuanacans when the dramatic climatic affects were being felt in later decades on the altiplano around Lake Titicaca.

The proposition that there was a migration from Indonesia or perhaps India may not be so farfetched since it is evident in the archaeological remains that the city was "heavily partitioned by towering sections and compound walls". These enclosures have been considered indicators of a system of segregation, defining rank, kin, class and occupationally related and where some of these enclosures were from 2-3 stories high and 40-100 metres on a rectilinear side. The buildings within these enclosures were usually grouped around rectilinear, and sometimes, oval courts and the galleried buildings forming the courtyard itself were usually reminiscent of those at Marcahuamachuco[67]. This suggests their origins in the caste system of India where caste status was preserved from those of lower standing by occupying their own compounds and village areas. It may be suggested that at Huari the Aryan caste so noted by some authors of the Incas was instituted first here in Huari and then inherited by the later Incas. Clans and castes that appear to have developed during the Inca dynasty will be an added interest in following chapters.

5.075 : Wizened portrait vessels were common along coastal Peru as they were in Central America. Sican or Chimu, North Coast Peru, 700-1400 A.D.

One of the enclosures made of carefully cut stone slabs called the Cheqo Wasi revealed the remains of looted subterranean megalithic chambers. There appeared scant respect shown for remains of the human burials within these chambers, disturbed by the quarrying and reuse of the burial chamber stonework, and these were accompanied by abundant luxury grave goods and many finely wrought artefacts including of gold. It is thought that these interments may have been former ancestral Huari lords whose earlier chambers had been built over, or of Huarpa people who had irrigated terraces in this region long before the Huari took over. The Huarpa appear to have abandoned many of their own settlements and moved into that of the Hauri and the capital and Conchapata[68]. It is clear that their society was in contact with distant lands since these elite grave goods were obtained from lands a great distance away and included Spondylus shell from Ecuador, as well as imported items made from lapis lazuli, greenstone and chrysacola, and metal artefacts of gold, silver and copper[69].

The Huarpa were well adapted to periods of drought and drew there water from higher elevations to their inclined hill terraces and by extending the feeder channels they were able to utilise the snow melt from the higher altitudes even in periods of drought to supplement their existing irrigation supply. This the Moche on the North Coast were unable to do since the snowline was at a much greater distance from their lowland irrigation areas and hence the latter fell when the long period of aridity in the 6th., century A.D. caused crop failure, starvation and chaos. The first foundation of the Huari, however, survived due to the adaption and extension of the principle of the earlier terraced irrigation systems of the Huarpa[70].

5.076 : Old gods were frequently depicted or found as stone carved heads or figures in Central America. Pantaleon, Pacific Coast Guatemala, 400-700 A.D.

This period, in the late 6th., and into the 7th., century, in Huari is called the Okros period and the iconography identified particularly with Huari is first seen in their homeland at the capital and Conchapata. Some have suggested that the first Huari were immigrants from Tiahuanaco and brought and adapted their existing beliefs and associated iconography to the new environment. Others have considered the Huari to have been pilgrims to Tiahuanaco and returned with influences enriching and deflecting their own local belief system into a new direction utilising modified imagery borrowed from the great city of the high altiplano[71]. Contact with Tiahuanaco colonies in the Moquegua Valley, where a Huari settlement was established, may also have influenced that in the Huari valleys. Whatever the truth is it is clear that the staff god, so common in Tiahuanaco, was adopted by the Huari and modified in a freer adaption to their own belief system. More common in the Huari staff god tradition is the trilobed or plumed staff and this appears to have close similarities with the Hindu trisula or trident staff of Siva in India. Seated burials, earlier adopted in Tiahuanaco, was adopted by the Huari and among the latter Moche in the Vicus Valley in North Coastal Peru, and become the norm and this also is a characteristic of Saivite Hindu burials in India rather than cremation more common among the Vaishnavites. Also characteristic of India was the ritual sweeping of the temples and sacred precincts around it and at Huari a particularly fine example of a rectangular sunken court has been excavated dated in the earliest phase to 580 A.D. +/- 60 years. The floors were repeatedly re-laid but notable for their having been constantly kept swept clean and later related dates are given as 720 A.D. +/- 60 years. The court and associated structure were then ceremonially buried after a century and a half of use suggesting a building of some importance[72].

The Staff God of Tiahuanaco has been seen as a solar deity in the Lake Titicaca region but its adaption among the Huari appears to have favoured associations with agriculture and fertility. Rites were reminiscent of Tiahuanaco where keros or ceremonial beakers were involved then smashed and buried after ritual usage. These vessels were particularly associated with the ritual consumption of chicha, the Andean equivalent of the Polynesian awa or kava, followed also by the ritual breakage and burial rites. In some ceremonials these vessels are found in association with the ritual sacrifice of young women at Conchapata[73].

Huari is seen as a military state and fortifications were common in the architectural constructions undertaken throughout their empire. At Moqegua, in this Okros phase, they fortified two hills behind their settlements and when the Incas attempted to impose their rule 600 years later the people retired to these impregnable fortresses and only succumbed after a long siege because of the lack of water. On top of one of these fortified hills, Cerro Baul, the Huari constructed large monumental buildings of halls enclosing expansive terraces[74]. The second largest of all of the known Huari compounds is found only 3 km away from Marcahuamachuco, appearing to have been a model for the Huari architectural style, and this was called Vira-cochapampa[75] - the prefix of this term will be of interest in due course in furthering the arguments for contacts between India and Ancient Peru and Bolivia.

Tiahuanaco Phase 5 Extending from 500-750 to 1000-1100 A.D.
The Moquequa drainage in Southern Peru was occupied by the Tiahuanaco Empire in the Phase 4, a period ending with the severe climate change dated to the 6th., century, A.D., a phase known as the Omo. This phase, contemporary with the Huari, features platforms with central monoliths reminiscent of Tiahuanaco and the cranial deformation so popular at Tiahuanaco is found extending into this southern region of Peru[76]. In about 800 A.D. a settlement known as Chen Chen was violently attacked and resulted in its overthrow including the destruction not only the civic buildings but also the canals and cemeteries[77]. It is not known whether this was caused by an internal revolt or by attacking, external forces but the site was never reoccupied suggesting that Tiahuanaco was not able to remain in control and possibly an indicator of central decline setting into its heartland around Lake Titicaca. The Omo phase was followed by the Chiribaya when polychrome painting was introduced and in this region they appeared to have preserved some of the elements of their Tiahuanacan heritage[78].

Tiahuanaco - The Development of Ridged Fields and Irrigation Channels
The most studied section of the ridged field system that supported the agricultural basis of the Tiahuanacan economy for almost a millennia and a half is found at Pampa Koani. The engineers who masterminded these remarkable irrigation feats controlled the run-off from surface rain rising ground water and annual fluctuations in the levels of Lake Titicaca. This was done through extensive and highly competent system of channels utilising springs and the beds of streams and rivers. Some channels were conducted across aqueducts to remove this excess water and redistribute it into those areas requiring extra supply. The ridged fields themselves were located between the water channels and were narrow but the very long strips of elevated soil above the

5.077 : Reed canoe illustrations from North Coast Peru but depicting solar and lunar references indicated by the "running feet" reflecting the identical motif found for millennia in Ancient Iran. Sican or Chimu, North Coast Peru, after 7th., century, A.D.

5.078 : Reed canoe illustrations from North Coast Peru but recording solar and lunar references indicated by the "running feet" reflecting the identical motif found for millennia in Ancient Iran. Chicama Valley, Late Moche or Chimu, North Coast Peru, after 7th, century, A.D.

5.079 : The sky canoe carrying the gods was considered to have its own spirit and this was anciently depicted as an anthropomorphic figure with legs and appears to be the prototype for the later Moche and succeeding Chimu period depictions in Peru. Akkad, Mesopotamia, late 3rd., millennium, B.C.

natural ground level were easily attended to and drained. The raised field system at Pama Koani covered an area of 75 square kilometres, a massive undertaking by any standards, but were certainly not the only one of its type. Research using reconstructed and reactivated ridge fields in this region in the second half of the 20th., century has shown that they are productive to, and some times more than double the yield than cultivating the earth directly without ridging, channel or furrows[79].

Irrigation in the Ancient Middle East was known almost from the first known settlements from the headwaters of the Tigris and Euphrates through the great plains of what is now Iraq to the joint delta in the marshes at their meeting with the Persian Gulf[80]. The use and reuse of these irrigated regions make it difficult to fully assess the earliest techniques but it is believed that "violation of fallow" methods led to an "engineered disaster" in Ancient Sumeria. The irrigation channels drained the water table and excessive use of such methods caused salting of the subsoil sterilising the land for productive usage. This excessive overuse of the land and its resources was reflected in the rapid deforestation of the region between 4-2nd., millennium, B.C.[81] and undoubtedly resulted in disasters that were both economic and political. Irrigation agriculture was more widely practised from 2600-1600 B.C. and this saw the development of progress in the arts and political influence in the Kaftari period at Susa and Tal-i-Malyan[82] extending from the Tigris-Euphrates lowlands into the Iranian Plateau. By the Sassanian Dynasty in the first half of the first millennium, A.D., so reflective in its iconography and imagery among the Moche on the North Coast of Peru, an extensive network of canals, dams, weirs supported agriculture and this appears to have had its origins in the earlier Parthian Dynasty in the region in the late 1st., millennium, B.C.[83].

The farming policy under Imperial Tiahuanaco was focused on the flatlands where ridging could be more easily applied, and part of this overall channel system for water supply was a large canal running from the ceremonial and residential centre to Lake Titicaca itself. In the later Inca period, a couple of centuries after the collapse of the Empire centred on Tiahuanaco, the emphasis in agricultural production was in terracing the hillsides[84] suggesting that the vast areas of ridged fields required a large degree of centralised control in construction and maintenance. It may also indicate influence from Huari indicating a possible origin, or intermediate residence for the Incas themselves.

It earlier noted that the irrigation systems maintained in Peru up until the first millennium, B.C. were basic and very low-tech to primitive in their application. Only at the period of the abrupt introduction of radically more advanced technologies in the early to mid-first millennium, B.C., when so many of the advances in irrigation techniques were adopted in the Andes and Coastal Peru, are most likely to have originated in the contemporary late Babylon, Assyria and the later dynasties of Ancient Iran.

Moche - From Dessication to Collapse

The severe climate change recorded and dated to the 6th., century, A.D., confirmed more recently since the development of dendrachronology, or the science of dating from tree-ring (annular) growth, was so destructive in its effects that it was clearly marked in the surviving archaeology and readily recognisable to those researching in the field. In more recent years, together with ice-core studies and modern dating techniques the massive eruption of Krakatoa has been fixed as occurring in 535 A.D., being declared the most singular event affecting climate change since the last Ice Age, and this triggered off catastrophic climate changes that lasted for many decades after.

5.080 : Leather sheath armour characteristic of the Nagas of Assam up until the early twentieth century, but virtually identical to that depicted among the West Mexicans in Jalisco. Rengma Naga, Assam, North East India, early 20th., century, A.D.

Assisting in climatic studies apart from dendrachronology is that of the examination of the annular stratifications from ice cores either from the Greenland ice cap, or for local information from nearby glaciers. In Peru, ice cores drilled from the Quelceaya glacier located between Cuzco and Tiahuanaco, reveals climate changes that have occurred in the last 1,500 years. These record El Nino episodes that struck on the following dates: 511/2; 546; 576; 600; 610; 612; 650; 681 A.D. One of the more interesting references was that gleaned from the later data indicating that a mini-Ice Age occurred in the highlands in 1500 A.D. a generation before Pizarro conquered Peru and that it lasted for three centuries.

These ice cores are now a generation old but one of the conclusions based on the data obtained was that there was period of "great drought" that began in 562 A.D. and continued until 594 A.D. The rainfall during that period dropped by about 30% and there was a marked increase in dust in the atmosphere[85]. The eruption in 535 A.D. would have had an immediate effect in the local environment in Indonesia, located as it is on an island between Sumatra and Java in Indonesia, on the other side of the globe. The long term effect would have become more apparent elsewhere later as the dust from this eruption entered the atmosphere and was carried around the world during the next decades and was undoubtedly the cause of the climate change in South America. It is now believed that this major drought so reduced the food supply that this lead to a period of strife and ultimately increased the need to develop military strategies to protect agricultural land and workers as well as the centres of religious and social administration in Peru.

Moche to Sican - An Epoch of Brilliance

The name for the Moche civilisation was given by the German archaeologist, Max Uhle, who named the culture exhibited in the burials from the pyramids first excavated after a small nearby village in the Moche Valley in Northern Peru[86]. In considering brief his-

5.081 : Leather armour identical to that found among the Nagas of Assam. Jalisco, West Mexico, 300 B.C. - 300 A.D.

5.082 : Typical armoured vest similar in design to those depicted in both Ancient India and Iran. Note the tumi sacrificial knife in the raised left hand identical to those in Moche and Tibetan headdresses. Moche, North Central Coast, Peru, 300 B.C.-300 A.D.

5.083 : Quilted armo with leather o metal plates, transferred fr traditions in Ancient Iran probably the model for the Moche in Per Gandhara, Northern Pakistan/Afg stan, 1-2nd., tury A.D.

5.084 : A rollout from a ceramic design illustrating mythical deities or warriors with Tumi knife head-dresses. Moche, North Coast Peru, 200-600 A.D.

5.085 : A front and side view of a fine portrait stirrup vessel showing a high-born man with a Tumi headdress. Moche, Chicama, North Coast Peru, 200-600 B.C.

5.086 : An Assyrian war-rior showing cross-braces similar to those adopted in India through to South America, and a feathered helmet comb probably the inspiration for the tumi of Peru in the Moche period. Assyria, 9-7th., century, B.C.

5.087 : A warrior dis-playing the Tumi headdress with a "apron" reflecting the simple geometric check pat-tern typical of the later Inca and the Maori of New Zealand. Moche, Trujillo, North Coast Peru, 200-600 A.D.

5.088 : Wrathful deity typical of the Bon Po that infused the Buddhism of the Himalayas after the 8th., century, A.D.. Note the Tumi-like, sacrificial knife, headdress virtually identical to those found in Peru. Mahakala, Tibet, 18th., century, A.D.

89 : Helmet with inte-tumi-like crest that is ably the prototype or ration for those of the he on coastal North ral Peru. Nimrud e, Kalhu, Assyria, Iraq, - 7th., century, B.C.

5.090 : A cross-legged carved stone figure dis-playing a Tumi headdress. Recuay, Huaraz, Central Highland Peru, 200-1000 A.D.

5.091 : A monster fish deity holding a Tumi sacrificial knife. Sican or Chimu, North Coast Peru, 700-1200 A.D.

5.092 : A fine ceramic platter depicting war-riors with Tumi headdresses. Captive warriors show their tor-ture postures and their being ush-ered to sacrifice. A three-moun-tain image plus one of two prob-ably relates to identification with the five sacred mountains and its deity. Moche, Chimbote, North Coast Peru, 200-600 B.C.

torical references it is interesting to note that when Cieza de Leon travelled through North Coastal Peru in the mid-16th., century, he noted "Mocha" buildings beside the Ambato River. This latter is a name that may have been introduced from Melanesia where the Megalithic cul-ture-bearers of Malekula through to the northern island of the New Hebrides (now Vanuatu) were called Ambat and the same term Ambattan occurs in South India and will be of interest later in this work[87].

It is more recently considered as a result of extensive studies in iconography, that there were many traces of the declined Chavin de Huantar culture in that of the emerging Moche tra-dition on the North Coast of Peru extending from the Lambeyeque to the Nepena Valleys over about 250 kilometres[88]. Chavin iconography appears to have been heavily influenced by Amazonian imagery and elements appear also in Moche imagery and that of other northern sites such as Cupisnique[89]. The corpus of Moche civilisation is preserved in the large majority of its ceramics[90], and these are of the highest value in projecting the people and culture of the Moche across the centuries reflecting their daily lives through religious and state rituals to the complexities of their religious and cultural symbolism recorded in their iconography. The realism achieved so sublimely in Moche art is considered by some to have derived from the Chorrera culture in Ecuador at least in part, first appearing there about 1000 B.C.[91].

After this period of severe climate change there appeared to be periods of excessive rain and this phase exhibits new types of maize being introduced from the upland regions into the lowlands. In the Moche region there are representations of the Staff God similar to that over the Gateway to the Sun at Tiahuanaco found in one of the courts of the Huaca de la Luna in the Moche capital, Cerro Blanco. The Moche still survived but were reduced in power to local control and this formed the period known as Phase 5. Sand dunes were, however, encroaching inland as a result of climate change and the capital had to be abandoned and by 700 A.D. this period also came to an end presaged by an increase in fortifications of towns and other centres[92].

It would appear that the Moche Empire spilt apart into two separate states, those from the Moche Valley moving north, and those in the Central Coastal region becoming independent. Interestingly a focus on storage of grains and other foodstuffs became a prominent feature of these later settlements, apparently reflecting the fear of another long period of starvation and warfare. Construction moved from adobe or mud brick, to masonry, and occupation and development from cave structures in the immediate phase followed before a new initiative could begin. The Moche occupied the Vicus Valley in their move north into the Pirua drainage and the settlements were located some distance from the sea indicating again a fear of climatic changes and El Nino events causing havoc in their coastal settlements. Here the later Moche built gigantic pyramids but overall there were fewer references to the old Moche periods to the south. In the new Late Moche ceremonial centres at Pampa Grande few indicators exist to link it and its architecture to the Huaca del Sol and the Huaca del Luna in the Moche Valley, although mud brick maker's marks are still to be found). In this new capital the largest construction in the North West of South America was constructed known as the Huaca Fortaleza. The construction is also notable since chambers were built and then filled in rather than building block upon block or brick on brick[93].

5.093 : Ritual vessel showing the mountain deities and the five sacred peaks, a religious motif found also in ancient India. Moche, Chimbote, North Central Peru, 200-600 A.D.

Sipan and the Iconography of Ancient Iran and Tibet
The great mud-brick pyramids built by the Moche appears to have been intended for ceremonial purposes since the burials found in them

5.094 : The mountain god of the Moche was known as Ai Apaec and is frequently depicted with human sacrifices and the five mountains - sacred also in Ancient India. Moche, North Coast Peru, 200-600 A.D.

5.095 : The mountain god Ai Apaec is often depicted in combat with demon shark deities, possibly representing hostile intrusive mariners, and his sacred five mountains are indicated to the bottom right. Moche, North Coast Peru, 200-600 A.D.

5.096 : Serpent-headed belt characteristic of Peruvian coastal iconography. Note also the tumi sacrificial knives. Moche, North Coast Peru, 200-600, A.D.

5.097 : Double-headed serpent belt characteristic of Peruvian coastal iconography. Note also the tumi sacrificial knife and the circle and dot ornamentation. Moche, North Coast Peru, 200-600, A.D.

5.098 : Chavin feline god are paired into male and female with serpent belts appearing to parallel the Moon's Node in India. Chavin de Huantar, Highland Peru, 800-400 B.C.

5.100 : Dual feather headdress typical through-out South America and the Pacific Islands into South East Asia. Note also the double-headed serpent belt that probably derives from the double-headed serpent of India identified with the ecliptic, and the Moon's North Node, Rahu. Moche Culture, North Coast Peru, 200-600 B.C.

5.099 : A stela with a depiction in low relief carving of the boar incarnation of the Hindu deity Vishnu. Note the two intertwined serpents the deity is treading on. Baragaon, North India, Mid-first millennium, A.D.

5.101 : A seated figure with a tumi blade surmounting his crown and two serpents descending from this ceremonial knife on the opposite sides and closely similar to representations of serpents forming a sky arch in India. Moche Culture, Chicama Valley, North Coast Peru, 200-600 B.C.

5.102 : Deity surrounded by descending serpentine forms of the two halves of the sky arch or torana similar to those found among the Moche on the north coast of Peru. Chalukyan Dynasty, Aihole, South Central India, 5-6th., century, A.D.

were not originally intended as an integral part of the structure but inserted afterwards[94]. Moche inhumations were always laid out full length, supine on a mat, and usually wrapped in a textile as a shroud. In some cases textiles were sewn to form a coffin and an obolos of copper was placed in the mouth of the deceased and sometimes pieces of copper or other metal were placed in the hands. At Sipan, in more recent decades, an interment of fabulous proportions of a young ruler was excavated and the whole sequence of Moche funerary ceremony and ritual was revealed. It was one of the few graves in a mud-brick pyramid to have been left unlooted and the original, remarkable contents have been removed for safe keeping but replicas have been made and placed at the site in their place and can be seen by visitors to the site. In the last Moche phase the pyramids were abandoned and the people moved to inland, defensible sites at Galindo lacking in major ceremonial constructions. It is thought that there may have been a threat from the southern state of Huari in its early stages of military expansion[95].

The main Sipan burial revealed an unusual wood plank coffin and the many objects immured with him suggest that he was a warrior. Of particular interest is that several of the figurines and the superb gold mask (6.120) show the Moche with blue eyes[96] and this is, in fact, a characteristic of many items found in realistic faces preserved among the Moche and other Peruvian cultures. Of note also is the plated armour (5.082) virtually identical to that depicted in Ancient Iran and in the early Buddhist depictions of soldiers in Gandhara (5.083) and North

303

5.104 : The Hindu deity Kankali also called Bhairava, both forms of Siva, displays the characteristic hairstyle of the mendicant standing on entwined serpents characteristically associated with this deity. South India, 10th., - 13th., century, A.D.

5.106 : Serpent design with circle and dot design inside a bowl characteristic of South East Asia. Huacho, Peru 200-1000 A.D.

5.105 : Interlocking serpents symbolising the balance of opposing forces later transferred into India. Elam, Western Iran, 2nd., millennium, B.C.

5.108 : Coiled rattlesnake in greenstone revered among the Ancient Mexicans. Aztec, Central Mexico, 1300-1520 A.D.

5.109 : Serpent image prominent in the Inca Dy and appears to reflect that India. Lerma, Argentina, 1521 A.D.

5.107 : Stone carved bowl with serpents integrally carved on the sides. Inca, Peru, c1450 A.D

5.103 : A larger than life size clay statue of a priest with a headdress depicting an addorsed jaguar head and a double-serpent headed belt. This form of belt is found widely in the Central America and South America. Addorsed felines are typical of iconography in the Ancient Middle East and India as well as South America. The figure is an ageing priest or eunuch indicated by the prominent sagging pectorals and the fold underneath. Remojadas Culture, Veracruz, East Coast Mexico, 600-900 A.D.

India. The coloured lower legs of the Moche warriors appear to indicate either greaves of the European type for protection, or painted for some ceremonial or imitative reason (*5.084*). It is of some interest to note that the first rank of warriors of Tahiti were called the Arae Parai, one of the nearest island groups to South America in Eastern Polynesia, also ritually painted the lower leg[97]. These Polynesian mariners appear to be related to the mystical sect in the Marquesas called the Areois and aspects related to them will be considered later in this work. There are many references that link the Marquesas to Peru and these will be of note in the following chapters. Of special interest, however, is the repeated depiction in Moche iconography of the stepped crown identical to that of the Sassanian kings in Iran. This occurs to such a degree that the crown associated with the reign of the particular dynastic king appears copied by the contemporary Moche (*6.051-6*). The Sassanids succeeded the Parthians in Ancient Iran and both were a conduit, and responsible for many Hellenistic influences transferred from Greece through Parthia to Bactria and then Gandhara and into India over the centuries from the 3rd., century, B.C. until about the 3rd., century A.D. The Moche warriors, rulers and priests depicted from objects retrieved from the Sipan tombs dated to about 300 A.D., show many examples of this stepped crown widely found as an element of iconography. It is unlikely therefore to be a coincidence that the Moche lunar deity was named Si and preserved for a thousand years into the Chimu period, the identical name for the ancient Moon god of the Ancient Middle East named Si or Sin and in found in Polynesia as Sina. The Moon-god was of paramount importance on the north coast of Peru noted in the earliest days of Spanish control by Antonio de la Calancha in the late 16th., century[98] who will be of interest later in this work.

Another element of iconography preserved with the Sipan burial, also ubiquitous in Moche imagery is the Tumi headdress (*5.084/5*; *5.087*). This remarkably unique headdress used

5.110 : Serpent deity sitting on his own coils with a star symbol and the fire altar before him. Akkad Dynasty, third millennium, B.C.

5.111 : Cylinder seal roll-out depicting interlocking serpents from a mythical scene. Akkad, Iraq, late third millennium, B.C.

5.112 : Serpent frieze carved around the whole building under the cornice indicating the importance of serpent worship influenced from India. Chandi Panataran, Java, Indonesia, 8-9th., century, A.D.

5.113 : Serpent deity sitting on his own coils with a star symbol and the fire altar before him. Akkad Dynasty, third millennium, B.C.

5.114 : Serpentine water channel, reflecting the descent of water from the rain on mountains, utilised in rainmaking ceremonies. Sacsahuaman, Cuzco, South Peru, 1350-1500 A.D.

5.115 : Dancing Siva, also called Nataraja, holds the serpent aloft as a representation of the Sky, imagery identical to that of Central and South America. Aihole, Central South India, 6-7th., century, A.D.

a sacrificial knife or time instead of feather plumes or other displays and is found identically from in the earliest Assyrian imagery (*5.086*; *5.089*) in the Ancient Near and Middle East and in the religious iconography of Tibet (*5.088*). Such iconography, incorporated into ritual display identically on the opposite of the world in similar time bands, cannot be a coincidence and indicates that cross-Pacific travel by mariners and traders occurred over centuries and millennia.

The imagery preserved on the gold and inlaid ornaments recovered from the site of Sipan are remarkable and of particular interest is the anthropoid eagle appearing to be the identical copy of the Tibetan and Himalayan form of the eagle deity otherwise known as Garuda (*5.132*). The Sipan examples show a fanged deity or eagle form with a human body and taloned hands and feet and often with a serpent headdress, and in Hindu myths the Garuda is the enemy of the serpent (*5.129*; *11.023*) - an iconographical duality frequent in the iconography of the Americas.

The iconography of Moche indicates that a major shift in emphasis took place in the Phase 5 period after the severe, disruptive climate change of the 6th, century. The phasing out of the older iconographical icons and deities to be replaced by those who had originally

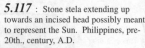

5.117 : Stone stela extending up towards an incised head possibly meant to represent the Sun. Philippines, pre-20th., century, A.D.

5.116 : Opposing serpents carved over a door in Cuzco similar to imagery in Melanesia (*5.118*). Inca Dynasty, Cuzco, 1300-1521 A.D.

5.118 : Two serpents carved on the first floor edge indicating the importance given to serpent symbolism in the Western Pacific. Bukaua, New Guinea, late 19th., century, A.D.

5.119 : Serpent symbolism illustrated in headdress imagery worn by so-called devil dancers of a type found in the Western Pacific. Parava Tribe, South India, early 20th., century, A.D.

5.120 : Serpent imagery transferred to the landscape where the representation of an egg or pearl emerging from its mouth is identical to iconography in Asia. Loudon, Ohio, 800-1350 A.D.

been minor sea deities is apparent and these are later adopted and adapted by the Chimu. This iconography appears to indicate a greater emphasis on maritime associations and the prominence of the so-called aged "wrinkle face" god also found in Guatemala (*5.075/6*) and an iguana deity suggest that these may be linked to the Maya and Central America where similar deities were prominent.

These deities are depicted together on reed boats and apparently are shown with Strombus shells from Ecuador, suggesting their direction of origin but this region is long noted for its contacts with Central America. These changes have been seen as "unprecedented" in the history of Peru, and that "many of the observed changes could not be anticipated from the preceding 500 years of Mochica cultural evolution"[99]. If there is little in the previous several hundred years that logically would be seen as leading up to these changes then here is another example where sudden changes and developments occur without an explainable developmental process and clearly indicates outside intrusions and innovations of major importance deflecting the direction of cultural evolution. This suggests that these cultural events, sufficiently powerful to deflect the whole of a long established culture, came from abroad and this may have been from Ecuador or, as the myths and legends state, from the West, across the Pacific Ocean from Polynesia, Melanesia, Indonesia or Asia. Others have suggested the Huari expansion from the South of Peru[100] but there appears to be insufficient remains to indicate that they were responsible although the traditional burial patterns changed to the seated form reflecting the customs in the south and at Tiahuanaco. As will be seen these regions themselves appear to have been the recipients of influences from the far west in the Pacific recorded in their culture-hero myths, their iconography and religious imagery.

In Moche ceramics frequent realistic depictions of reed boast with bound captives are found and there are many depictions of supernaturals riding in reed boats constructed from totora reeds represented as serpent boats[101]. So much of the imagery of Moche and the later Chimu ceram-

5.121 : Serpent mound as a sacred ceremonial focus for Aboriginal Australian peoples but these have close mythical connections with India. Warramunga Tribe, Central Australia, late 19th., century, A.D.

5.122 : Incense burner in the form serpents one in the form of a disgorging makara. Shan Tribe, Burma, 19th., century, A.D., or earlier.

23 : Serpent deities were prominent in both dhist and Hindu iconography. Ajanta, West tral India, 5-6th., century, A.D.

5.124 : Coiled serpent with emergent anthropomorphic winged deity - the probable prototype of that found in Peru (5.125) and Spiro, in Ohio, North America. Aihole, South Central India, 5-6th., century, A.D.

5.125 : Coiled serpent with a seated cross-legged deity identical in posture to illustrations in Indonesia. The coiled serpent appears to be based on the closely similar types at Aihole in South Central India. Tiahuanaco provenance, Chimbote, North Coast Peru, 300-1000 A.D.

ic imagery is orientated to the sea and its images that there must have been an overriding reason beyond just fishing and sea trading behind these depictions. Of special note are the supernatural reed canoe depicted with "running legs" (5.077) clearly derived from the imagery of celestial canoes in the very Ancient Middle East (5.078) and retained in their iconography until the end of the first millennium B.C. corresponding to the beginning of the Moche in Peru.

From Moche to Sipan - Double-headed Serpent Belt and the Five Mountain Peaks

In Moche iconography the double-headed serpent belt is ubiquitous in the Moche art of North Coast Peru. The snake-belted, fanged deity is considered to be the son of the Sun god or the mountain god, and it is of interest that many ritual vessels show the mountain god seated with the five peaks. These mountain peaks are also depicted on Moche ceramics as the site of human sacrifices[102] and it is of interest that in the Hindu mythology of India there are five sacred mountain peaks dedicated to Siva[103], the pre-Hindu deity absorbed into their pantheon, was said to be five-faced as Isana or Pancanana (Panca, or Panch = five)[104] and he is considered to be identified with the Himalayas. It is in the high mountains that Siva's abode, Kailasa, was believed to be located - an aspect of Hindu religious myths to be of great importance in later chapters of this work.

5.126 : Coiled serpent of a more elaborate type than that found elsewhere in the same ceremonial site shown in 5.125. Durga Temple, Aihole, South Central India, 5-6th., century, A.D.

After the fall of Moche at the end of Phase 5 there was a dramatic change in the orientation of the belief system and associated rituals supported by the people and this featured seat-

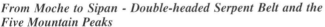

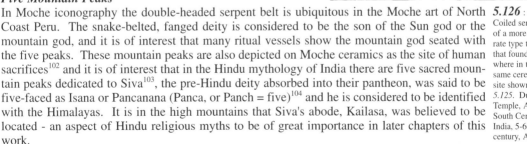

5.127 : Finely carved low relief stela reflecting the importance of serpent symbolism from the most ancient epochs in the Middle East the overall carvings being "guarded" by the serpent at the right side of this boundary stone. Babylonian period, Iraq, c1000 B.C.

5.129 : Eagle charm in the form of the Garuda (Hindu Eagle sky deity) yantra identical to iconography found at Sipan on North Coastal Peru. Tibet, late 19th., century, A.D.

5.128 : Jain thirthankara, or saint, in typical stance with a serpent arch descending either side representing the sky similar to that shown among the Moche. Jinanathapura, Central South India, 12-13th., century, A.D.

5.130 : Eagle impersonator with headdress similar to the Moche in North Central Peru. Jama Coaque, Ecuador, 13-14th., century, A.D.

5.131 : Kannaras or Garutman represenations as the Buddhist equiavlents of the Hindu Garuda bird. The Kinnaras are identical to contemporary eagle imagery in Iran. Sanchi, North Central India, 200-100 B.C.

5.132 : Serpent Sky arch headdress depicted worn by this eagle deity, probably intended to be a representation of the Garuda bird of India. Sipan, North Coast Peru, 3rd., century, A.D.

5.133 : Serpent Sky Arch headdress identical to those depicted on the Peruvian Coast centuries earlier that probably originated from India. Mysore School, South India, 19th., century, A.D.

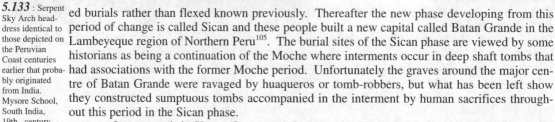

ed burials rather than flexed known previously. Thereafter the new phase developing from this period of change is called Sican and these people built a new capital called Batan Grande in the Lambeyeque region of Northern Peru[105]. The burial sites of the Sican phase are viewed by some historians as being a continuation of the Moche where interments occur in deep shaft tombs that had associations with the former Moche period. Unfortunately the graves around the major centre of Batan Grande were ravaged by huaqueros or tomb-robbers, but what has been left show they constructed sumptuous tombs accompanied in the interment by human sacrifices throughout this period in the Sican phase.

In one tomb in Huaca Oro, over 12 metres in depth, grave goods to the depth of 10 metres were excavated. These included human sacrifices, bundles of caste bronze metal, gold, tumbaga (gold/copper alloy the colour of gold or brass), silver jewellery, Spondylus and conus shells, beads and other artefacts. These many items were layered over a litter covering a seated burial of a man aged from 40-50 years whose body was sprinkled with cinnabar wrapped in a cloth with squares of precious metal foil sewn on to it. He wore a gold mask and had two tumbega gloves at his side along with thousands of beads shaped from various stones. Sican lords were accompanied by the wealth they had accrued in their lives into their graves, in the belief that they really could take it with them, and this follows the custom of the earlier Moche chiefs. Metalworking was of major importance to the Sican people and their graves show that the kurakas and rulers controlled this valuable resource. This is reflected in their tombs not only because there was an abundance of metal ornaments but also because metal scrap, and pieces waiting to be fashioned at the time of the persons' demise, were interred with him. Among these grave goods were included hundreds of pieces of copper axe-money, examples of gold masks and many other metal objects[106].

Late Intermediate Period from 1000 A.D. - The Aymara Kingdoms

It is thought that the Aymara were the earliest inhabitants of the altiplano in Bolivia and the Andean highlands generally whereas the uplands and lowlands were considered the preserve of the Quechua. Others have suggested that the people of Tiahuanaco were Pukina speakers and formed a separate, probably Aymara subdivision, or perhaps an elite who ruled over Aymara subjects. It has also been suggested that the Aymara seized the opportunity to invade the region of Lake Titicaca after the fall of Tiahuanaco and is a dilemma that has not yet been resolved. However there are contrary indicators since archaeological evidence indicates that the Aymara moved away from the Lake Titicaca basin into the foothills where they built terraces for irrigation and in the Moquegua Valley to the west toward the Pacific Coast. Pottery. after the fall of Tiahuanaco, does not reflect their style in the following Lupaqa kingdom suggesting a break from the people or elite of that great city. There are no ceremonial sites at this period and evidence of oval and circular huts and corrals for llama herding[107] indicates that these people took little part in the Tiahuanaco Empire. Inhumations in circular cysts (*5.137-9*) were continued from Tiahuanaco into the succeeding Aymara kingdoms and the tradition of seated burials was also continued. However the most distinctive mortuary practise was the erection of round or square burial towers[108], or chullpas (*5.134*), up to about 10 metres high, and these may be a reflection of those found further north at Marcahuamachuco, in the late Moche Phase 4 period. The term chullpa is of interest since these constructions resemble the relic towers as a form of stupa in the Tibetan plateau and Himalayan foothills called the chorten (*5.135*), possibly deriving from them in form and name. This may well be a merging of the two terms, stupa and chorten to form chullpa. Some of the chullpas concealed the burials of up to twenty adults and children. The Colla or Aymara moved their capital to Hatun-Colla (also Hatunqolla) near modern day Puno and the chullpas are the only monuments left standing to any degree to indicate its existence (*5.136*).

Chiribaya - a Culture in the North of Chile

The Chiribaya, located in the Victor Valley of Northern Chile around the modern city of Arica, extends toward the Moquegua Valley in Southern Peru. They maintained their independence from both the Tiahuanaco and the Huari empires and were a succession of petty states rather than a central polity of power and influence. Their ceramics and textiles reflected the more elaborate styles of the later Tiahuanco and Huari states but their town and cities were modest in comparison with the architectural achievements of these great states[109].

Inhumations were seated both in the dwellings and cemeteries and sometimes also enclosed in stone-lined tombs and accompanied by grave goods including textiles and pottery. In the graves in the uplands llamas were also included in these burials and in one region the burial was left on the litter, carrying the deceased to his last rest on top of the tomb. Of particular interest is that some of the interments located near springs away from the coastal excavations have

5.134 : Aymara burial tower, or chullpa, near La Paz. Acora, Bolivia, 1100-1350 A.D.

5.135 : Chorten or relic stupa, or chaitya, found widely in the Himalayan kingdoms and Tibet from the earliest Buddhist times in the late first millennium, B.C. The cross designs formed by the foliated central division may have been the inspiration of the cross found on the chullpas, a term that may have originated in that of the chorten, in *5.137* on the Peru/Bolivian border. Tibet, pre-20th., century, A.D.

5.137 : Rare depiction of a burial tower, or chullpa, showing a pennant-like giron (swastika) and saltire painted design on plaster finish. The design appears to have parallels in Ancient India and Tibet (*5.136*). Peru/Bolivia border, 1100-1350 A.D.

5.136 : Burial towers, called chullpas, in the late period before the beginning of the Inca dynasty. Hatun-Colla, Peru-Bolivian border, 1100-1350 A.D.

5.139 : Typical plan and section through a circular burial tower or chullpa characteristic of the region west of Lake Titicaca. Peru/Bolivia 1100-1350 B.C.

5.138 : Finely carved masonry typical of stone burial tower or chullpa. Sillustani, Puno, Southern Peru, 1100-1350 A.D.

revealed that miniature log rafts with sails accompanied the burials. This is likely to indicate mariner descent for at least some of these people near a coast directly connected to Melanesia and Australia and therefore Asia by direct ocean currents. Small canals extended from the naturally occurring springs in this Chiribaya period and this culture reached its maximum extent or apogee about 1000 A.D.[110]

Huari Decline to Inca Ascendancy

In the early Cuzco region the terracing of the valleys is of particular interest and a prominent feature of the landscape. It is in this area, however, that they are attributed to the Huari and then maintained and extended by the Incas suggesting that there may have been an ancestral link between the two Empires. The Huari terraces appear to have been centred on the region around Pikillaqta in the Lucre Valley and then extended into the Urubamba Valley. This tradition is termed the Killke and is directly ancestral to that of the Inca[111].

The valleys around Cuzco show that this was a period of fortification and retreat to hilltop villages and some of the Inca Origin myths note that there were several epochs where the encroachment of the Incas toward Cuzco was resisted and, having won territory in which to settle, were required to defend it in fierce battles. The Huanca (also Wanka), Chichaycocha and Tarma were known to have resisted the Incas in their incursions[112] and their later established settlements and they are particularly noted in the records for their resistance to Inca rule after the latter settled at Cuzco.

From about 1000 A.D. cultivation of maize of a large kernel variety was replacing the herding of llamas in the valleys around Cuzco and the Urubamba. It appears that the Huanca capital at Wari Wilka was influenced in style and construction by that of the Huari less than 200 kilometres to the west[113]. This tends to confirm that the agricultural terraces and agricultural patterns generally were propagated from there. The Huanca, along with their neighbours, the Chinchaycocha and Tarma, followed the more traditional agricultural practise of contiguous vertical swaths of agricultural cropping related to climatically distinct environmental altitudes. The land resource related to the various environmental zones from the warm valleys or coastal plains through to upland, highland and montane, was subject to rotation cropping and herding and this system was long developed from the earliest cultural epochs. The Huanca, Tarma and Chinchaycocha were inland kingdoms but applied these principles in agriculture to the eastern slopes of the Andes from montane heights down to the warm river valleys of the Amazon tributaries.

The Inca, the Ichama and Pachacamac

The Ichama were a people who occupied the coastal valleys of the Lurin and Rimac Valleys where the modern capital of Lima was founded and a little to the south the great oracular site of Pachacamac had been long established. This was such an important focus of religious attention that the Inca felt the need to form an alliance with the Ichama and later this was activated in military action resulting in the defeat of Chimor in the north exploiting an apparent reported long held rivalry between the Chimu and the guardians of Pachacamac[114]. It is said that, when the Inca Tupac reached Pachacamac, he had an interview with the huaca and it spoke to him alone stating that he must take riches to the Chimu and honour him more than Uiracochan Pachayachachi. This appears to have been taken as a confirmation that the Inca would succeed in a campaign against the Chimu, and in this undertaking from that interpretation he was proved to be successful[115]. In the interregnum after the collapse of the Empire of Tiahuanaco, and before the full control of the Incas was achieved Pachacamac saw a period of efflorescence when many elaborate and richly endowed shrines and buildings were constructed. It is likely that many of these were initiated from devotees from outside the zone of Ichama control since this sacred site had received donations and religious beneficiaries over many centuries before.

The Late Central Highland Florescence that was Chancay

During the Late Intermediate Period, before the Inca and Ichama formed an alliance against the state of Chimor, this northern state expanded south into the Chancay Valley and possibly into that of the Chillon. The result was a local style known as Chancay and was characterized by bright colours and a geometric style of realism in their iconography and simplified textile patterns. Mould-formed ceramics were common although not exclusive, characterised by red or black on a white background, and with human faces as a common subject moulded or painted onto the ceramic base surface.

The architecture of Chancay displays innovations such as tapia construction where walls were constructed in panels of adobe formed by pouring into a wooden frame and allowed to dry before erection. This was a form of mass production and provided the means to erect many substantial buildings in the Central Coast region of Peru. The tombs of the Chancay people provided evidence for elaborate interments and were found to be rich in textiles, brocades, complex gauzes and openwork fabrics. The burials were seated and elaborately supplied with grave goods and there was an apparent extension of a more affluent intermediate class who could afford to supply themselves with some of the trappings of wealth and status. It was clear, however, that the elite retained their monopoly on the symbols of status and the control of metalworking[116].

Cerro Azul, the Incas and the Huarco in the Lower Canete River

Further south on the coast of Southern Peru the distinct regional occupation in the lower Canete River appears to have been a settlement of the Incas on the coast of Peru. Here Cieza del Leon described the "… most adorned and handsome fort" in Peru and was found to be made of "great square slabs" of stone clearly in the style of Cuzco. This place is called Cerro Azul and became a prominent maritime centre where at least ten monumental complexes were constructed in the

5.141 : Contrasting geometric design similar to that of the Incas. Maori, New Zealand, Late 19th., century, A.D.

5.142 : More complex patterned feather-cape showing designs probably related to those of the Incas. Maori, New Zealand, 19th., century, A.D.

5.143 : Fibre cloaks with geometric borders designs but of particular interest if the centre feather cape with a typical Peruvian pattern. Maori, New Zealand, Late 19th., century, A.D.

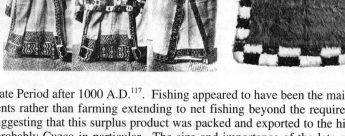

5.140 : Stirrup vessel showing a figure in a checked mantle similar to textile designs found among the Maoris. Peru, 1st., millennium, A.D.

5.144 : Fine feather cape showing geometric pattern border reminiscent of the Inca designs. Maori, New Zealand, Late 19th., century A.D.

Late Intermediate Period after 1000 A.D.[117]. Fishing appeared to have been the main occupation of the settlements rather than farming extending to net fishing beyond the requirements of the local people suggesting that this surplus product was packed and exported to the highland communities and probably Cuzco in particular. The size and importance of the late period monumental complexes, however, indicates that fishing was not the main reason for their apparent importance. It may be that the coastal connection was an important one, as it is in some of the Inca Origin myths, and contact with mariners, perhaps from the ancestral homeland alluded to in the myths was continued at these coastal centres.

In the Ica and Nazca Valleys during this Late Intermediate period there is evidence for seated burials, probably inherited from Huari influence. This newer tradition did not fully supplant the earlier traditions of flexed burials and both these forms of interment were accompanied by textiles and ceramics along with other grave goods.

Chincha and the Merchant Mariners

In the section of the coast further south than Cerro Azul the Chincha had long been associated with marine travel and it appears to have been a region supporting well over 100,000 people. It has been noted that the later Moche had, centuries before, appeared to extend their influence far to the south by sea. By the Late Intermediate Period they had succeeded in controlling the sea trade along the Peruvian Coast from the far south to the North and onto Ecuador. After the Incas had conquered Chimor in the early 15th., century the monopoly in this sea trade was assumed by, or turned over to the Chincha[118].

Many of the high status items found from the late fourth millennium B.C. through into Inca times in the first half of the second millennium A.D. came from the Amazon forests where feathers and other exotic items such as jaguar skins were imported over those four to five millennia. However, also during this time was the presence in high status inhumations of Strombus shells for trumpets and other religious items along with Spondylus shells obtained from Ecuador. Since these appeared to have been traded also through the eastern cordillera of the Andes and along land routes from the earliest times there was only limited dependence upon the sea trade for these, and fishing alone would not explain the necessity of each of the expansionist states to

5.145: Chief's feather cape displaying typical geometric Polynesian designs. Hawaii, North Polynesia, 20th., century, A.D. or earlier.

occupy coastal strips for part or the whole length of Pacific Peru. This suggests that there were other reasons why this accessibility was paramount and probably originates in the contact of traders from outside South America as the reports initiating the voyage of the Inca Tupac into the Pacific indicates. Ancient traditions repeatedly note the coast as the location where culture heroes arrived and later departed and some of these are preserved in the Inca Origin myths these will be of more interest in due course.

Chimor - The Second Largest Empire in Peruvian History

The Chimu were an expanding state extending its influence southward into the valleys of Peru toward Cuzco and it is not known whether they offered a real threat to the Incas or whether the Incas simply coveted their economic power and extensive trade infrastructure. It is believed that the Inca defeated the Chimu in about 1470 A.D. However, this may have been achieved a few years earlier since the Inca Tupac was sent by his father Pachacuti to undertake this mission and, after having defeated the Chimu, he is said to have met traders from other lands who informed him of the lands of gold far to the west across the Pacific Ocean. It was this meeting with these traders that initiated his legendary voyage and this will be of more interest in a following chapter.

It is recorded in the oral traditions that the first dynasty of the Chimu was the Taycanamu, and in the period of their rule the founder of the second dynasty, Naymlap, arrived on a flotilla of rafts on the North coast of Peru. Naymlap, his family and supporters, all of whom accompanied him on this flotilla, settled in the Lambeyeque region and when established they succeeded as the second dynasty of the Chimu. Some historians have seen these legendary rulerships, preserved in these traditions, as indicating complementary leaderships reflecting the dual social organisations or moieties believed endemic in Peruvian society[119] but characteristic also in India.

Naymlap and the 12 Sons of Zolzdoni

Alternate suggestions to the founding dynasties of Chimor indicate that the Naymlap period refers to the first half or phase now called the Sican whose capital, located in the Lambeyeque

5.146: Very old photo illustrating the ceremonial feathercapes, or kaitaka, worn as they were before the European entered the Pacific Ocean where one chief standing at the back holds a ceremonial spear, the Taiaha, identical to that of the Maya. Maori, New Zealand, Mid-19th., century, A.D.

5.147: A group of Maoris displaying the dramatic geometric patterns similar to those of the Incas in Ancient Peru. Maori, New Zealand, late 19th., century, A.D.

Valley, was called Pama Grande dating in this early phase from 700-900 A.D. The legend of Naymlap notes that he built a capital called Chot, thought to be the modern Chotuma, located about 4 kilometres from the Pacific shoreline. One of the extraordinary sections of the Naymlap legend is that he determined to have himself entombed to allow his son, Zolzdoni, to succeed. This remarkable act is highly reminiscent of the Sun kings

5.148 : Fine inlaid plaque with rampant armorial animals in the top register and central hero or deity, usually considered to be the mythical hero-king, Gilgamesh. Ur, Sumeria, 3rd., millennium, B.C.

5.150 : Addorsed animals were long found in the imagery of Mesopotamia, and identical to that of the Andes. Babylonian, Mesopotamia, c1000-900 B.C.

5.151 : Addorsed birds with ce hero or deity closely similar to th the Andes and Mesopotamia. Ne Guinea, Melanesia, pre-20th., cen A.D.

5.152 : Addorsed jaguars that appear to emulate iconography in Mesopotamia. Costa Rica, 800-1450 A.D.

5.149 : Armorial animals facing on each side of central deity - possibly intended to represent the legendary Chimu founder, Naymlap. Sican, North Central Peru, 800-1000 A.D.

5.153 : Armorial animals facing in mythical arrangement as a bronze orna-ment. Luristan, South East Iran, c1000 B.C.

5.154 : Tiahuanacan armorial ani-mals focused on central figure of tur-ban browband typical in Iranian designs. Tiahuanaco, Bolivia, 600-900 A.D.

of Asia and retained in later introduced form in North East Africa from the Ancient Near East. This first son had in his turn 12 sons who each founded settlements in legends closely similar, or from the same traditions found in Polynesia where these derive originally from the Ancient Near and Middle East. Even in South America the most conservative historians have linked these 12 sons to the signs of the zodi-ac unconsciously associating the legend with that of Ad and his twelve sons named Thamud, Tasm, Djadis, Amlik, Oumayim, Abil, Djourhoum, Wabar, Jasm, Autem and Hashen in South West Asia. Ad was the local version of the earlier legendary Cushite or possibly Ethiopian hero, It or Ait - the Greek Aetus, probably the origin of the Polynesian Atea[120]. Interestingly another related tradition notes that Ad was the son of Chan and it may not be a coincidence that the Chimu capital was Chan Chan[121]. Miles Poindexter, the former U.S. ambassador to Per, also notes that many aspects of South American terminology leads back to the term "chan" in Asia and his work is of interest read in conjunction with aspects indicated in this present work[122]. The Arabs have a tradition that they are descendants of Joktan through his twelve sons and the Ishmaelites claim descent through his twelve sons. The Babylonians also preserved a tradition of descent though the twelve sons of El or Il, a date of special note later in this work, and in Polynesia and the Marquesas in particular some of the tribes claimed descent through the two eldest of the twelve sons of Toho, Atea and Tani. The Hawaiians, with whom Fornander was most concerned since his daughter married one of their chiefs, descent was claimed through the youngest of the twelve sons of Kini-Lau-a-Mano[123].

The legendary descent from 12 sons is also found in India and there is little doubt that the evidence of the twelve-son myth cycle and the arrival of Naymlap from the west across the Pacific Ocean is one of the last in a long history of contact with Polynesia and Asia over the millennia in Peruvian history. The ending of the dynasty also terminates with an Asian twist where the last ruler in the dynasty, Fempellec, was said to have been so objectionable in his relations with a sorceress that he was seized by the kurakas, bound, and set adrift into the sea[124] - a mythical tradition found in myths around Lake Titicaca relating to Tonapa; in Polynesia and among the Hittites.

In Polynesia, Edward Mariner, who lived for 7 years among the Tongans, witnessed the binding of captive enemies in battle who were placed in, and set adrift in a canoe that had been tampered with only sufficiently to ensure that it would be carried away from the shore before sinking on its way to the open ocean[125]. This tradition probably originated from a more ancient custom recorded where the Hittite king, Urhi-Teshub, was driven from the throne for insulting behaviour and was "sent aside to the sea", thought to be a reference to his being exiled far away across the sea so that it would be difficult for him to return to cause more mischief[126]. This was probably a custom established in the Sican or Chimu traditions at that time, or perhaps it was used in the same was as the Polynesians retained until two centuries ago. Evidence for a foreign intrusion in the Lambeyeque Valley is not forthcoming from the present state of archaeology in that region but in fact the cultures of the Peruvian coast were advanced and it is more likely that any migration into the country, particularly if on a small scale, would largely adopt local traditions and introduce new ideas interpreted through them rather than dominate.

The version of Naymlap myth given by Miguel Cabello Balboa printed in 1586 A.D. notes that Naymlap arrived on balsa rafts with his wife, Ceterni, and his many concubines. This ruler was said to have been accompanied by forty officials among whom was Ninacola, the Master of the Litter and Throne; Occhocalo, the Royal Cook, and Llapchiululi, the Purveyor of Feather-cloth Garments. This version notes that the last of the dynasty attempted to remove the idol placed in the shrine at Chot by Naymlap[127] but it could not be moved until he fell in with sorcerers and from this action he was subverted and his rulership was ended by his being seized, tied up, and thrown into the sea. The Keeper of the Feather Garments illustrates the importance of certain mantles as designating status and the feather cape as an indicator of rulership was known also in Mexico, Polynesia and particularly similar to those of the Inca were the feather capes of the Maori (*5.146/7*). The textiles of the elite clans among the Chimu were known for the brilliant colours and magnificence although perhaps with less subtle designs and techniques than those of earlier epochs[128].

Other versions of the Naymlap myth states that he brought with him on his raft flotilla a green idol called Llampellec - possibly a confusion with the name of the last ruler of the dynasty[129]. There was certainly a tradition of green idols made out of emerald in Ecuador, noted later, and it may be that Naymlap originated from Ecuador or the greenstone idol was a confirmation of origin in or via the Pacific Islands where greenstone idols were greatly revered. It is also of note that greenstone Buddhist and Hindu carved deities were also important in Orissa where contacts with Central America are noted in an earlier[130]. Other myths state that the Chimu were considered to have descended from two sets of stars[131].

The Sican iconography is seen as a mutation of both the late Moche and Huari styles and this may indicate that these newcomers represented by Naymlap recognised something in both of these traditions possibly originating with their own ancestors and related mariners through which they could identify and project their own belief systems. In the later phase at

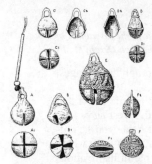

5.155 : Various pellet bells found in Celebes among the Koelawi and Kantewoe. Indonesia, Late 19th., century, A.D.

5.156 : Finely cast bronze finials to standard poles showing the traditional Siva trident based on cattle horns and the central spearhead. Such trident forms are the symbols of Siva, one of the supreme Hindu gods of India but found also in Ancient South America. Peru, 1st., millennium, A.D.

5.157 : Copper axe money found on North Coast Peru and Ecuador and similar to that of Pacific Coast Mexico. 700-1350 A.D.

5.159 : Finely cast copper/bronze ceremonial object with hung pellet bells. Chimu, North Coast Peru, 9-12 century, A.D.

5.160 : Wire-formed pellet bells closely similar in design and wire technique to those traditional in Orissa in North East India, but also to copper techniques found on the West Coast of Mexico. These are a selection of bells found in Peru, Colombia and Mexico. 1st., millennium, A.D.

5.158 : Traditional dancing dress including a fez-like hat similar to those in Indonesia and South America. Note the bunches of copper bells around the waist virtually identical to those found in Ancient Mexico and South America. The Sun disk can be seen high up on the dances' backs and identical to those found in Ancient Mexico. Gond, , Central India, Early 20th., century, A.D.

5.161 : Interesting bronze ornament with interlocking chain links similar to interlocking stone carved chain links known from at least the middle of the first millennium, A.D. in India. Chimu, North Central Coast Peru, 700-1200 A.D.

Sican monumental architecture is more notable and of particular interest is the imagery of the so-called "Sican Lord". This is an elite image of a contemporary lord with small wings projecting from each shoulder, a beak-like nose and sometimes talons for feet (*5.149*). The image is, in fact, almost identical to the Tibetan version of the Garuda bird or Sky Eagle of Hindu mythology (*11.023*). There is much in the symbolism and dress of Peru and Bolivia suggesting that there must have been connections between North India, Tibet and the access to both regions, the cojoined Ganges and Brahmaputra Deltas into Assam and the Himalayas to the north, and this will be of more interest in the following chapters. This bird image of the Sican Lord is depicted sometimes in flight surmounting a double-headed serpent[132] reminiscent of Vishnu as the boar deity surmounting double serpents, a symbol of triumph. In Hindu mythology the myths surrounding the Garuda bird are focused fundamentally on the perceived opposition between the sky and earth represented respectively by the Garuda bird or Eagle as the Sky and the Earth, represented by the Naga or snake. The double-headed serpent is a motif noted among the earlier Moche particularly as a serpent belt (*5.096/7*; *5.100*) and the waist was identified traditionally in Asia with the waist in the Anthropos, or Cosmic Man, in philosophic tradition. In Ancient India the double-headed serpent also represented the ecliptic and here also found confused with the eclipse demon named Rahu, a double-headed serpent[133]. In recent interpretations of North Coast Peruvian iconography this Sican Lord is identified with Naymlap himself[134].

At its height the vast irrigation system in the Lambeyeque supplied more large cities and monumental complexes than any other part of Peru. Some consider this as evidence that the twelve grandsons of Naymlap may indeed have been a reality each setting up their own clan territories within the overall state ruled by this immigrant family. It is also thought that the two-storey Huaca Gloria at Chotuna may have been the mausoleum of Naymlap sited in his family burial ground. One tomb of the period yielded 200 gold and silver necklaces, masks and repouse vases, tumi ceremonial knives, and other artefacts. Besides these grave goods shells, turquoise, lapis lazuli, emerald inlays, and other ornaments were included. In another tomb excavation was revealed 17 human sacrifices accompanying an elite burial beside Spondylus shells, lapis lazuli precious metal artefacts and 500 kilogram of copper items including a substantial number of copper axe-money called naipes[135]. These were stacked in piles of 500 and are the I-shaped hammered copper currency almost certainly the late forms of the "oxhide" copper ingots traded as currency known from very ancient times in the Near East and West Asia (*5.157*). These are also similar to contemporary forms of axe-shaped copper money found in Western Mexico and China. This form of copper currency was found in large amounts in graves at Batan Grande and measured 50 to 70 mm long and 30 to 50 mm wide and were found also in Ecuador already noted. The axe money in Ecuador must have been imported since copper is rarely found there naturally. It would appear that it was the Chincha merchants from the far south of coastal Peru who distributed the money and raw materials utilising this form of currency. There is readily available evidence that the copper was smelted in Peru and Bolivia from the first millennium, B.C., and at Batan Grande it might be assumed that these copper naipes might have been manufactured here using copper smelted from ore imported from elsewhere. It may also have been that this was a major centre of the production of copper axe money from about 850 A.D. and this date corresponds closely with the appearance of the first copper products in Western Mexico[136].

5.162 : Reed canoes with reed sail made from Totora reeds, traditional on the altiplano for thousands of years. Bolivia, Early 20th., century, A.D.

Because the same axe money is found in Western Mexico along with many other aspects of Ecuadorian culture it is likely that these were utilised as a common form of exchange on the Pacific coasts linking Mexico with Ecuador and the north of Peru. In the second half of the twentieth century it was bordering on anathema to suggest that there might be contacts between North and South America since this would contravene the dictates of the Americanist school that imposed the indigenous development theory. This theory in general insists that all cultural developments were local, and any contacts were secondary, limited and incidental. Miles Poindexter and others such as Reginald Enock a generation or two earlier noted however, that there must have been extensive contacts between North and South America concluded from the available evidence at the time. Professional archaeologists such as Joseph Needham and Robert Heine-Geldern, Gordon Ekholm and others clearly saw the parallels and did not hesitate to support cross-Pacific cultural transfer from Asia to Polynesia. It is only in the archaeologically based research in the last decades that modification to the Americanist view has had to be accepted, albeit grudgingly and noted where applicable in this work.

It would not be thought that objections could be made to contacts between North and South America but because the distance over which copper axe-money and other aspects are found is so great (between 3-4000 miles) it is illogical not to expect that such mariners and craft capable of completing this journey would also sail west into the Pacific. Such possibilities are considered abhorrent to Americanists but mariners who sailed the Pacific Coast of the Americas must have been forced on many occasions by the prevailing winds and the powerful flow of the ocean currents into Polynesia and Melanesia to the west from Central and South America. The interesting legend of the Inca Tupac's journey to the west from Manta in Ecuador will be of interest later in this work, but it is also worth mentioning that Naymlap is only one of several legends of cultural influences, incursions and expeditions from, or landing onto the Peruvian and Ecuadorian coast. Before Tupac and Naymlap there were the Manta "giants" and several heroes such as Viracocha who were said to have sailed to, or arrived from the west across the ocean and some of these will be considered in due course.

The capital of Sican, Batan Grande, came to an end about 1100 A.D. when, as the result what may have been a tidal wave or perhaps an exceptional El Nino event occurred. Perhaps because it was associated with the legendary founder, Naymlap, Chotuna was rebuilt but Batan Grande was abandoned. There is evidence that wood was piled against the pyramids and temples and the whole city was burnt by fire closely similar to the apparent end of Pampa Grande, the last Moche capital. It has been thought by some that this may have been a judgement against the ruling clans and kurakas by the people for allowing such catastrophes to befall them since it is generally believed that they were considered the intermediaries between the people and the gods[137]. A similar belief was held in Polynesia.

Glacial ice cores from the Andes show evidence for a catastrophic event initiating a period of torrential rains, severe flooding and droughts about 1100 A.D. and the flooding in particular wrecked the irrigation systems evident at Pacatnamu, Chan Chan and the rest of the Jequetepeque Valley extending into the Moche Valley. From these disasters it must have appeared to the people that the gods and their supposed intermediaries, the priests, ruling clans and kurakas must have deserted them and the latter failed in their interpretations or were considered no longer acceptable to the presiding deities. Although the events of c1100 A.D. appear similar to those of 562 A.D. the former was probably the result of the Krakatoa eruption of 535 A.D. while the latter is from and unknown cause. The period of famine and pestilence recorded in folklore that followed the 1100 A.D. event appears to have a foundation in truth but from the aftermath radical cultural changes emerged.

Following this great period of disaster and the abandonment of Batan Grande, the city of Purgatorio in the Leche Valley became the capital and here massive mounds were erected and later an enormous platform was constructed. Following this period of instability there are several versions of the events that lead to the establishment of the Chimu state originally the Chimu was considered to have covered the whole period to the Inca conquest from 700 A.D. but the first half is now separated off into the early Sican followed by Chimor. The earliest record by the Spanish describing this period is from their own sources and this states that a general from Chimor named Pacatnamu became the first provincial governor and after building the centre gave it his own name. This governor was expansionist and undertook the construction of another centre in this epoch called Farfan and this site in recent datings from excavations from this period indicate a foundation date at about 1200 A.D.[138]. This indicates that this legend was in a fact an encapsulation of several generations of expansion, and this is also true for the developments at Lambeyeque, since these sites were built some time before the reign of Minchancamon.

However, other versions, following the most important origin myths in the Andes, attribute the founding of the state of Chimor to a culture-hero called Taycanamu who was said to have arrived by boat on the coast of Peru having been sent from afar to govern the people. He settled in the Moche Valley, possibly at Chan Chan, and subjected the local peoples to his rule. His son, Nancenpinco, carried the conquest further inland in the Valley that were succeeded by campaigns beyond to the Santa River in the South and the Jequetepeque in the north. This conquest was followed either by five or seven rulers culminating in the reign of Minchancamon who initiated a second series of conquests along the Peruvian Pacific coast from the Chillon River to the Tumbes River in the far north. Tragically for this ruler he was faced with the Inca expansionist campaigns and was defeated by them. One of this ruler's heirs was installed as a puppet and he and his descendants remained as such until the Spanish Conquest only two or three generations later[139].

The oral histories preserved among the Northern Coastal Peruvians records that the lords lived in expansive compounds with courts for receiving their subjects including the kurakas - the clan leaders and visiting dignitaries. In the Chimu period the platform mound, once the preserve for the intercession of the priests with the gods, became a burial mound perhaps suggesting that the rulers had developed a cult of identification with the gods assumed by themselves. Over the course of a thousand years a total twelve mounds that were constructed in the Moche 5 - Chimor phases are still standing in the Moche Valley. The first of these is located at a constriction in the valley called Galindo dated from the period of Moche 5, but most of the subsequent platforms were built later at Chan Chan near the Pacific seashore. The last great, related platform was built at Chiquitoy Viejo under the Inca puppet dynasty in the south of the Chicama Valley[140].

An Inheritance from Moche 5 - Chimu Architecture and Artisans
With the end of Moche 5 period the Moche Valley had reverted to petty states and with the incursion of Taycanamu into the valley possibly consonant with the Huari influences in the region from the far South of Peru, a new iconographic tradition developed. This new period is generally called Chimu and maritime iconography and themes become much more prominent. The creation of friezes and murals becomes very much the architectural flavour of the time and this appears as a prototypical examples in the earlier Moche 5 times.

In the Chimu period the shrine of ceremonials focused on a form of binding that was a relic from the very ancient U-shaped ceremonial buildings of the Initial Period within the great compounds after Moche 5 and this is the so-called audiencia. The audiencia was a gabled building constructed on a raised floor set in a small courtyard about 4 metres square. It had external niches, reminiscent of the pre-ceramic period, and it is thought that these were the offices of the ruling king who was, it appears, identified with the gods[141].

When Chan Chan was at its height the conurbation covered 20 square kilometres although there were areas not built on within that perimeter but perhaps earmarked for future expansion - its founding appearing to date to about 850 A.D. The civic centre itself was densely occupied and included the great compounds of the ruler, associated clans and kurakas, along with the serving masses. The majority of the low class workers lived in irregularly shaped rooms constructed of cane set on small terraces and many of them were employed in wood-working or as carvers and as skilled craftsmen in metals and precious stones.

It would appear that the only people allowed to reside in the city centre were the elite along with their servants and the artisans since metal production and the manufacture of high status goods was of primary importance to the economy of Chan Chan[142]. The overall population of Chan Chan appears to have been between 40-50,000 at its height and probably less than 6,000 were the ruling elite and their families. Farmers and fishermen appear not to have been allowed to live in the city recalling the exclusion of certain castes in India from the main centres of religious and civic importance and to be of further interest in the following chapters.

There is early evidence for woven mats being extensively utilised in the practical sense for wall partitions or external cladding for houses. In the dry, warm, coastal climate this type of walling allowing inhabitants to roll up these mats for ventilation and this aspect of cladding recorded on ceramics is depicted on the huts of women weavers and as floor coverings. Mats were also used for wrapping the bodies of the dead in their burials but further afield woven mats were used as sails for rafts along the Peruvian coast to Guiana on the Caribbean. Woven reed matting sails were also found utilised by the Mojo and Paresse in lowland Bolivia and among the Aymara for their reed canoes on Lake Titicaca[143].

Chimu Clans and Castes

One of the most interesting social aspects known about these Chimu people related to their marriage arrangements since there appeared to be a caste system similar to that known in India operating among these craft guilds in Chan Chan and beyond. It is known that the metal-smiths took their marriage partners from the weavers in an identical marriage tradition between clans or moieties divisions between acceptable occupational castes known throughout India and still operating from over two and a half thousand years ago. These artisan people at Chan Chan, and probably generally elsewhere, had the right to wear ear tubes or cylinders, and similar traditions also occurred in India and South East Asia. Ear cylinders appeared originally to have derived from the practical, personal use of storing narcotics on sea voyagers since mariners at sea in hot climes rarely bothered with any form of clothing. Small containers hung as pendants around the neck, or in cylinders, and were usual and there are many examples recorded of these cylinders being worn through the ear. This practise was particularly notable among the Nagas of Assam and through into Indonesia in South East Asia, and who exemplify such close cultural parallels with South America traditions.

It is known that the dual organisation systems or dual moieties divided into 10 subgroups as a marriage arrangement existed among the Chimu and it was this system that was adopted and extended by the Incas. The dual system provided two groups of five clans and one set was permitted to arrange marriage partners with a corresponding section in the other five[144]. This reflects identically the dual organisation marriage moieties in India, Aboriginal Australia and elsewhere will be of more interest in due course.

Evidence for catastrophic flooding around 1100 A.D. destroyed most of the earlier constructions in this coastal region and possibly suggests a tidal wave struck the coast overwhelming the inland floodplain sites[145]. The Chimu period is also noted for its irrigation works and the initiation of hydrographic works including the construction and clearance of deep wells that were a feature of that system. Of particular interest was the 70 kilometre El Cumbre canal that was constructed from the city of Chan Chan to the Chicama River to ensure a permanent water supply to the capital[146] and connecting five valleys[147]. From this canal also water was drawn to supplement irrigation water supplies and this canal construction was no doubt a response, and highlights the vulnerability of these Northern Peruvian cities to the common natural calamities of drought and El Nino events.

This period of catastrophe suggest another volcanic event of great intensity in the Pacific Region since Peru is certainly prone to tidal waves emanating from the eruptions in the Pacific Rim on the other side of the Pacific Ocean. The North Western Pacific region, from the Philippines, Japan and through to the volcanic peaks in the Aleutian Island south of Alaska as well as those of the Hawaiian Islands have long been a source of tsunamis. These are initiated by volcanic eruptions and seismic disturbances that affect South America as the tsunamis sweep diagonally across the Pacific Ocean. Such a dramatic change in climate may also account for the fall of Tiahuanaco at about the same date and the decline of the Huari.

From the fall of the Chimú, engineered by the expansion of the Incas, this greatest empire of the Americas that followed extended their control over most of the Andean region from their capital at Cuzco south to central Chile, and north over much of what is now Ecuador, and virtually all of Peru between. The history of the Incas has been told and retold many times and it is unnecessary to repeat it here. However, in this work, a closer examination of the recorded myths, religious beliefs and social inheritance relating to their origins and later efflorescence is of greater importance since there are many aspects recorded that indicate that their origins are not indigenous. The Incas themselves allude to this in some of their myths and from other native sources and seems to be confirmed not only in archaeology but in many aspects of their life, religion and culture in eyewitness accounts recorded by the Spanish chroniclers and in a few cases by high born Incas themselves.

INCA ORIGINS MYTHS

Origins of the Inca - Myth and Propaganda
The historical outline of North West South America has shown that there must be special reasons why the "high" cultures developed first, and were concentrated for millennia along the northwest shoreline of the Pacific coast. This is one of the least hospitable shores in South America and yet high cultures did not develop anywhere else in the same way and for the whole of the Atlantic shore even though it is much longer and climatically more suitable. A glance at a map of the Pacific Ocean indicates clearly that this must be related to the ocean currents washing the shores from Mexico in Central America all the way down to Ecuador in South America. These coastal strips are entirely washed by the Equatorial Current flowing from Asia direct to the Americas and separating with a branch curving southwards extending to the Central American shores and the south branch washing the shoreline of Ecuador and the extreme limits of Northern Peru. The southern coast of Peru, and all of Chile, is washed by the Humboldt Current and is also called the Peruvian Current. This rapidly flowing current, separating from the north section of the West Wind Drift in the Antarctic Ocean, flows north along the Peruvian Coast to meet the southern branch of the Equatorial Counter Current. The Humboldt Current delivers directly from Southern Polynesia and further west from Australia, New Zealand and Melanesia.

There are many anomalies in the history of South America, not least the unique and abrupt developments of technological advances emphasised by an apparent lack of evolution in the technology and development of metals and textiles. Ancient metallurgy in South America has been the subject of some extraordinary explanations on the part of those who refuse to consider that they were not in any way the result of imported advances or technology but insist that they were the result of indigenous development. The South American people, they consider, were following a totally different evolutionary track to other metalworking peoples in the world. Elaboration of the principle espoused, therefore, of the finished product without apparent, or little development, is not forthcoming but such scholars would still refuse to consider that such developments were linked in any way to their evolution in Asia.

In the brief overview of the history of the Andean peoples and more general extension into the surrounding regions in the previous chapter it has been considered in a broad chronological sequence that these locations associated with "sudden" unexplained advances are almost always related to the coast and in legends to mariners from the sea. From the section of work, because there is much more recorded from the last of the Andean dynasties up until the Spanish Conquest, the Incas, the evidence in terms of archaeology and the written record in legend and myths, will be considered in reverse order from the Incas back to the earlier periods of Andean history. Because the evidence is so much greater for the Incas this area of consideration will extend for a larger proportion of the work in the related time band and diminish the further back in time.

The Incas - The Last Great Pre-Conquest Dynasty

The remarkable technological skills and constructional skills of the Incas has been marvelled at and commented upon by many historians and researchers since the Spanish Conquest. Even their conquerors, the Spanish Conquistadors, were fulsome in their praise even while destroying so much of it. The skills developed by the Incas have been considered to be the result of a long Andean history and explainable in terms of inheritance from the earlier traditions and particularly that developed by the Tiahuanacans. It is from the great progenitors of the Tiahuanacans that the Incas appear to claim descent, or at least attempt to identification with them, and thereby lay claim to be their rightful successors. Since actual archaeological and written records are not available to substantiate much that is recorded in these oral traditions the origin myths and legends propounded by the Incas are of some importance. It is also of note that the myths and legends gathered at the time of the Conquest are little changed when compared with those recorded from local peoples even into recent centuries and as late in the last decades of the 20th., century. There are many recent interesting and authorative books being written largely based on the fiercely conserved ceremonies and rituals practiced in the remoter Andean and coastal villages by the descendants of pre-Conquest Indians. From these studies it is notable that their renditions are clearly closely similar to those described by the Spanish soon after the Conquest. For the most part in this work the most ancient sources are preferred since they are less likely to be contaminated by later events and apologists but later work is used to fill in the gaps where they exist or where comparisons are required. Many of the earlier myths are associated with the culture-heroes Viracocha and Tonaca, or Thunapa, and these will be considered in a separate section.

Inca Origins Myth - Version 1

Yamqui-Pachacuti Salcamayhua was a christianised Quechua Indian living in the 16th., century, two generations after the Conquest but proud of his heritage and wrote down his memories of the Inca rule while still reasonably fresh in the minds of those subjected by the Spaniards. Salcamayhua recorded that the origins of the Inca were invested in the founder Manco Capac, as they were for almost the majority of the known versions of the Inca origins myths. His version records that the famous rod or staff that was later credited with being driven into the earth on Mount Huanacari, or at Cuzco, was delivered by Tonapa, the great proselytising hero identified with Lake Titicaca, to Apu-Tampu Pacha. At the birth of Apu-Tampu's son, Manco Capac Ynca (Inca), the staff was said to have turned to "fine gold". Manco Capac's parents then produced seven brothers and sisters and the names of three of the brothers are recorded as Ayar-Cachi; Ayar-Uchu; Aya(r?)-Raeca. After the death of his father and mother, Mama Achi, Manco Capac gathered his people to determine what should be done to expand their estates. However, apparently they would not follow him and he decided with his brothers to seek new lands elsewhere to settle or conquer. Manco took with him his arms, rich clothes, and the golden staff called the Tupac-Yauri, left to his father by Tonapa, and inherited by him along with two gold cups called Tupac-Usi. Manco set off with his brothers in the direction of the Sun and arrived at a hill - the highest point in the land. Arriving at the brow of this hill a very beautiful rainbow appeared and this was followed by many others so that he appeared to be enveloped by their many colours. This he took as a sacred sign of great promise and success and advanced with his brothers into the next valley to Collcapampa and at a place called Sanuc he saw an Indian far off and the youngest brother ran ahead to investigate. When the younger brother approached he discovered that this creature was a fierce and cruel huaca with bloodshot eyes and it said to him that he was now in its power. Because the younger brother had not returned after a long time Manco sent one of his sisters to fetch him. She too became ensnared by the huaca. After both younger brother and sister did not return Manco, angered, went himself to find out the cause and discovered their almost lifeless bodies each side of a stone and asking them why they had not returned they told him that they could not move because they had been captured by the huaca - the stone between them. Manco then struck the stone many times in great fury with the sacred staff, the Tupac-Yauri, and the voice from the stone retorted that if he did not have the staff Manco too would have succumbed to the huaca's power. The huaca told Manco that it was right for the brother and sister to remain at the stone since they had sinned. The huaca represented the infernal regions called Pitusiray Sanasiray that translated to mean "one person fixed on top of another". Manco was greatly perturbed and grief-stricken at his sibling's fate and went back to the place where he first saw the rainbow - the names being Cuchi, Tumumanya and Yayacarui. Manco bewailed the fate of his brother and sister, and of his loss and the fate that had befallen, them but the rainbow comforted him and removed his grief. From here Manco went with his sister named Ypa (Eva? or Ivi? in Polynesia, the Eurasian Eve?) Mama Huaco, and with another sister and brother led the way to Collcapampa with the Tupac-Yauri in his hand. Here they stayed for some days before travelling on to Huamantiana staying there for some time before relocating to Coricancha determining that this was a suitable place for a settlement. They found good water from two springs named Hurin-Chacan and Hanan-Chacan in this place. The local Indians were the Allcayrie, Cullinchinas and the Cayau-Cachis and Cuzco-Cara-Urumi who occupied these lands at the time of the arrival of Manco and his siblings and a rock named by these Indians, Cuzco-Cara-Urumi (Urumqi) gave the name for the locality, Cuzco-Pampa and Cuzco-Llacta. Because of this the Incas were called the Cuzco-Ccapac and Cuzco-Ynca. Ynca Manco Capac then married his sister Mama Ocllo, and this incestuous marriage was undertaken so that the family caste would be preserved. From here and from that time the Yncas set about extending their boundaries by inclusion of allied peoples and conquering those who opposed them. In the early stage of the Ynca expansion it is said that the Ttahuantin-Suyu came to do homage and brought gifts suggesting that this name, later adopted for the Inca Empire, was in fact one that preceded them and probably represented a dominant people in the region. Manco Capac is said to have ordered his smiths to make a large plate of fine gold representing the Sun as Creator of Heaven and Earth. This was formed in an elliptical shape rather than a circle and it was ordered to be placed in the great temple known as the Ccuricancha Pachaya-Chachipac Huasin. Of special interest is that it is recorded that Manco Capac was opposed to all huacas (shrines) and it is said that he destroyed the Curaca Pinao Ccapac "with all his idols" and conquered Tocay Ccapac, "a great idolator"[148].

This version from Salcamayhua must be of interest since is recorded from those who were in direct contact with the Inca traditions preserved not long after the Conquest and is likely therefore to be more genuine. There are references in this tradition not appearing in other versions and of particular interest are those to the huaca of the Underworld, to the two springs, and the gold disc. There are indicators here too that there were at least one, or two brothers and at least two sisters as there are in some other versions. More recent researchers have found that Pachacuti's record is more accurate in its references corresponding to many Andean Indian rituals and customs still retained from the Conquest into the present day and his work will be of further interest in this work.

Inca Origins Myth - Version 2

The record of Fernando Montesinos has been largely ignored because his writings appear somewhat garbled, many borrowed from secondary sources, but there are his first hand reports appearing to be authentic and clearly related. He arrived in the Americas in 1628, and is recorded to be in Arica, on the North Chilean Coast, in 1634, and in Lima between 1636 to 1639 A.D. One of these is his record of a meeting arranged by the Corregidor of Cuzco, Juan de Saavedra, with

Cayu Tupac, a surviving descendant of Huayna Capac. He also consulted other Inca descendants, whom he calls Orejones, because of their custom of enlarging their ears to accommodate large disks. Montesinos believed that the history that these Incas told him was exaggerated to magnify their own greatness but he otherwise records the history as he was informed of it and is as follows in an edited version: In ancient times, when all races who lived in the region were fighting among themselves and slaughtering each other and had sunk into vice, three men and three women appeared at Paccari-tambo, not far from Cuzco. The three men were named Ayar Ucho, Ayar Cachi Asauca and the third Ayar Manco. The women were named as Mama Huaco, Mama Coya and the third Mama Rahua. For some of these brothers or sisters other names were given instead of these but these are the ones given by the Orejones themselves. It was said that these people came forth dressed in long mantles and without collar and sleeves, called tapa-cu meaning "vestiture of kings". Each of the men ("lords") carried in his hand a golden sling with a stone in it. The women also wore rich clothing and had a great deal of gold. The brother named Ayar Ucho declared to his brothers that they should go forth and find more gold and make themselves the sole masters of the land. They built a settlement with the inhabitants of the region and called it Paccari-tambo and built up a great hoard of gold, silver and jewels and these were later looted by Hernando Pizarro and Almagro. Ayar Cachi was a great warrior and had such a power with the slings that it was said he hurled stones from his sling splitting mountains so that dust flew up to the clouds. His brothers resented him his power and were very much envious of him and finally they hatched a scheme to be rid of him. They requested that he fetch a golden vase which they had forgotten and required so that they pray to their father the Sun so that they might be lords of the land. Ayar Cachi, not believing that his own brothers would deceive him did so and as soon as he entered the cave they sealed it up with stones and it is said when they had done so the earth trembled to such a degree that the hills fell into the valleys. After this event the two brothers together with others who had joined them formed a settlement naming it Tambu which Quiro translated as "Teeth or (of) a residence or of a palace". They remained for several days at this place but began to regret the murder of their brother Ayar Cachi. Soon after the brothers beheld Ayar Cachi flying toward them in the sky with wings of coloured feathers and, seeing they were terrified, he told them not to be afraid. He informed them that he had come to advise them to move to a new site further down the valley where the Incas may found a great city with a great Sun temple and expand and become great lords. He further informed them that he would remain at the cave but that they should call it Huanacari and that they should offer gifts and sacrifices there. Ayar Cachi also told his brothers that they should have their ears bored in the manner in which his were now displayed with gold disks inserted and fixed with gems[149].

Version 2A

An extension to this myth seems to be that recorded by Augustin de Zarate, the royal Treasurer in Peru, on visiting the altiplano in 1543, one of the earliest of the Spanish chroniclers, noted in his book published in 1555: "These lords kept their Indians at peace and were their captains in the wars they had with their neighbours, and there was no general lord of the whole land, until from the region of Collao, from a great lagoon is (in it), called Titicaca, which has eighty leagues in circumference, there came a very warlike people which they called Ingas. These wore the hair short and ears perforated, with pieces of gold in the holes which enlarge the apertures. These called themselves (are called) ringrim, signifying ear. And the principal among them they called Zapalla inga, (the) only chief, although some mean to say that he was called Inga Viracocha, which is 'froth or grease of the sea', since, not knowing where the land lay whence he came, (they) believed him to have formed out of the lagune." ... "These ingas began to settle the city of Cuzco ..."[150]. This version from Zarate goes on to note the claimed Inca direct descent from

the great Andean hero-deity Viracocha, as
"grease or froth of the sea", and particularly that Alcauiza is named by Viracocha as the leader
of his people. Alcauiza appears in other versions as occupying Cuzco before Manco Capac suggesting that hc was the rightful appointee and that Manco was a usurper when he defeated him,
or his lineage, to seize control of the city and the surrounding valley.

This myth notes the special role played by Ayar Cachi and his being immured into a
cave bearing striking resemblances to Asian myths but not least to some found in Melanesia. The
winged "angelic" guardian is particularly noted among the Asian Near East myths from the earliest times and is a feature in the iconography of Akkad, through to Assyria and preserved to the
Sassanids in Ancient Iran in the first half of the first millennium A.D. Such references were
inherited and survived in India also and other elements will be considered in due course. After
Ayar Cachi was immured into the cave it was also said that and it was also said that his brother
Ayar Oco (Ocho/Uchu) turned himself into a sacred stone and his other brother Ayar Ayca
became the protector of the fields leaving Ayar Manco to capture, and then settle in Cuzco[151].

Version 2B
Another variation of this myth notes: "... Four brothers and sisters emerged from the caves of
Pacari-tambo. The eldest climbed up the mountain and threw a stone to each of the four cardinal points, saying that it was a token that he had assumed possession of the whole land. This
angered the other three, the youngest of whom was the cleverest. He made up his mind to get rid
of his brothers and reign alone. He persuaded the eldest to go into the cave, and shut him up with
a huge rock. Then he got his second brother to come up into the mountain with him under the
pretext of looking for the eldest brother. But when they reached the top he threw the second
brother into the void, and by magic changed him into a stone statue. The third brother fled in terror. So the youngest built Cuzco and had himself worshipped as son of the Sun under the name
of Pirrhua or Manco Capac"[152]. This version indicates that Pirrhua is a title of Manco Capac
rather than an ancestor as in other versions and this will be of more interest in a later chapter.

Inca Origins Myth - Version 3
When Adolf Bandelier visited Lake Titicaca and its environs a century ago, investigating the
ancient cultural remains in the region, he did not ignore the fact that the contemporary Indians
were the inheritors of the traditions from the time of the Inca and earlier. He recorded many
aspects of these surviving traditions found among them at that time and wrote down a version of
the Inca origins myths preserved by an Indian from Copacabana and related by him to the parish
priest of Tiqinia, Father Nicanor Vizcarra. The friar in turn retold this myth to Bandelier who
recorded it as follows: "The peninsular of Copacabana was inhabited prior to the time of the Inca
by a tribe of rude Indians who owned flocks of llamas. Every evening the herders returned the
flock to the care of the chiefs of the tribe, and among their number was a dumb girl. For several months this girl failed to put in an appearance. The fact of the matter was that she had given
birth to a male child in some cave on the peninsula, and that a female deer was nursing it. The
fatherless boy grew up in that cave and his mother visited daily toward evening. This went on
for a number of years until at last somebody followed her stealthily. He saw her approach the
cave. A boy rushed out of it to embrace her and she returned his caresses. When the boy reached
the age of manhood the boy begged his mother to give him a club and to make him three slings.
With the aid of these weapons he soon became powerful, and thus was the origin of the Incas"[153].

Inca Origins Myth - Version 4 [Migration by Sea from Colombia]
Some of the myths recorded for the Incas' origins are more interesting in terms of the theme of

this book and it is possible that some of these in fact reasonably preserved memories of more complete migrations, but doubted by others. Anello Oliva recorded the following migration myth: "After the Deluge, the first people came to South America from parts unknown, landing somewhere on the coast of Venezuela. From there they gradually scattered over the whole continent, one band reaching the coast of Ecuador near Santa Elena. Several generations passed, many made voyages along the coast and some were shipwrecked. At last one branch took up its abode on an island called Guayau, near the shores of Ecuador. On the island Manco Capac was born, and after the death of his father Atau he resolved to leave his native place for a more favoured clime. So he set out, in such craft as he had, with two hundred of his people, dividing them into three bands. Two of these he never heard of again, but he and his followers landed near Ica, on the Peruvian coast, thence struggled up the mountains, reaching at least the shore of Lake Titicaca. There Manco separated from the others, leaving them with orders to divide after a certain time and to go in search of him, while he took the direction of Cuzco. He told his people, before leaving, that when any of the natives should ask them their purpose and destination, to reply that they were in quest of the son of the Sun. After this he departed, reaching at least a cave near the Cuzco valley, where he rested."

"When the time elapsed, his companions started in several groups in search of him. One of these crossed over to the Island of Titicaca, where they were surprised to find a rock, and in this rock a cave lined with gold, silver, and precious stones. Thereupon they sunk the craft in which they had reached the island, and agreed among themselves, if anybody from the surrounding country should appear, to say that they had come out of a cave to look for the son of the Sun."

"A few days after, on the day of the full moon, they saw some canoes approaching, and they forthwith retreated to the cavern. Those who came in the canoes, when they approached the cliff and perceived the strangers viewing the cave apparently with the greatest unconcern, were surprised. The strangers gave them to understand that they had just come out of the rock and were in quest of the son of the Sun. This filled the others with profound respect for the newcomers; they worshipped them and made offerings to the rock, sacrificing children, llamas, and ducks. All together went back to the mainland, and shortly afterward learned that at Pacari Tampu the son of the Sun had come out of a cavern, called Capactocco, in great splendour, bedecked with gold, as brilliant in appearance as his father, and that with a sling he hurled a stone with such force that the noise was heard for more than a league off, and the stone made in the rock a hole as large as a doorway."

"At these news all the people of those regions went to see the miraculous being. Manco Capac received them as subjects. On this artifice he began to base his authority and he subsequent sway of the Inca tribe"[154].

An interesting indicator from this myth should be noted and that is Manco Capac's father name is given as Atau, a Polynesian name for god(s). In some Inca Origin versions is given as Apo Tambu - also reflecting Polynesian overtones in part.

Inca Origins Myth - Version 5

Many of the myths recorded by the early Spanish chroniclers have been thought too absurd to be considered and one of these is noted in a version by William Bollaert over a century ago. He records in his book and, probably difficult to accept by many present-day researchers, it has the dubious association of being associated with Montesinos. Bollaert noted: ".... Rivero and Tshudi, however, observe that the traditions of the Indians and the opinions of historians relative to the origin of the Incas differ much, some there are which by their simplicity and verisimilitude, cannot fail to satisfy, while there are others, which, by their silliness, arbitrary assertions and historical improbability, do not deserve the slightest credit. Such as, for instance, the one which makes an English sailor the legislator of Peru. A Peruvian prince, Cocapac, who chanced to be on the seacoast, met a white sailor. On asking him who he was, he replied, 'an Englishman', a word the prince repeated (as) Ingasman. Cocapac took the white man to his home, where he had a daughter, and she became the wife of the stranger. They had two children, a boy and a girl, and then the Englishman died. The boy was called Ingasman-Cocapac, the girl Ocllo. From accounts given by the stranger of the manner in which other people lived, and who they were governed, Cocapac determined on exalting his family. He took the boy and girl to Cuzco (some 4 degrees from the coast! Through sandy deserts and over the Cordillera!) where one of the largest tribes of Indians resided, and informed them that their god, the sun, had sent them two children to make them happy, and to govern them. He requested them to go to a certain moun-tain on the following morning at sunrise and search for the children. He moreover told them that the Huiracochas children of the sun (sometimes spelt Viracocha) Montesinos says, this means on account of extraordinary actions, but Vira or Huira is fat or scum, or such like matter that floats on water, also sacrificial oil, cocha is a lake or sea, or that these children came from the sea) had hair like the rays of the sun. In the morning the Indians went to the mountains Condor-urcu and found the young man and woman, but surprised at their colour and features, they declared the couple were a wizard and a witch. They sent them to Rimac-Malca, the plain on which Lima stands (only 6 degrees distance!) but the old man followed them, and next took them to the vicin-ity of Lake Titicaca, or among the Aymaras, (8 degrees back again!) where another powerful tribe resided; Cocapac told these Indians the same tale, and requested them to search for the Viracocha at the edge of the lake at sunrise; they did so, and found then there, and immediately declared them to be children of their god, and their supreme governors. Cocapac to be revenged on the Indians of Cuzco (probably Quichuas) privately instructed his grandchildren in what he intend-ed to do, and then informed the tribe that the Viracocha Ingasman Cocapac had determined to search for the place where he was to reside; he requested they would take up arms and follow him, saying, that wherever he stuck his golden rod or scepter into the ground, that was the spot he chose to remain at. The young man and woman directed their course to the plain of Cuzco, and the Indians surprised by the re-appearance of the Viracocha and overawed by the number of Indians that accompanied them acknowledged as their lords and the children of their God"[155].

In a rejoinder to this version Bollaert notes that Stevenson considered that this may have been related to the story he heard in Brazil in 1823 A.D. This Stevenson reported as being that before the Portuguese discovered the country an Englishman who had been shipwrecked was captured by the Coboculo Indians. This Englishman had retained a musket and ammunition from the shipwreck and with this he both delighted and kept the Indians in fear until the Portuguese arrived when he was taken to Portugal and King Emanuel granted him a valley near Bahia[156]. Such reports are difficult to research but there is more likelihood that the name of the white sailor in the Inca Origin myth sounded like "Englishman" in retrospect and since it sounded so similar to "Ingas" noted in other myths was subsumed to the more ancient legend. At the Conquest it is extremely unlikely that any Indian had ever heard or come across the name of another country let alone one named England until long after the Spanish, had arrived as the first contact with Europe. However this does not invalidate the whole myth since a number of its elements appear to be broadly confirmed in other recognized genuine myths.

Inca Origins Myth - Version 6

Montesinos also records a variation similar to that given by Garcilasso de la Vega (Version 9) but notes that the first Incas marched towards Cuzco led by four brothers whom he names as Ayar Manco Topa, Ayar Cachi Topa, Ayar Anca Topa, and Ayar Uchu Topa, who were accompanied by their four wives. The youngest brother rid himself of two of the brothers by sealing them up in a cave and the third fled. Ayar Uchu Topa reigned 60 years and left his throne to his son Manco Capac[157].

Inca Origins Myth - Version 7

The several versions already presented note the possibility of the Incas emerging from a cave or associated with it in one way or another. In several of the most accepted myths either they were associated with Viracocha, or other deity, while in some versions they were the founders of Cuzco but in others usurped the city already established. Betanzos records a myth of this type as follows: "And from there (speaking of the journey of Viracocha from the country around the Lake northward) the Viracocha departed and came on, he was made chief, to whom he gave the name of Alcauiza, and also named the place of that chief (he) made, Cuzco, and, leaving directions how, after he would be gone, the 'large ears' should come forth, he went on performing his task." Bandelier, commenting on the other elements of this myth notes: "He goes on to relate how, while Alcauiza was chief of the little hamlet of thirty houses that then constituted the settlement, four men came out of a cave at Pacaritambo, among them Ayar Mango who afterward became Manco Capac and the first Cuzco chieftain of the Inca"[158].

Inca Origins Myth - Version 8

The most celebrated version of the Inca Origins myths was recorded by Garcilasso de le Vega, himself of mixed blood parentage, with a Spanish Conquistador father and a mother who was a royal Inca princess. This gave him privileged access to highborn Inca relatives from whom he learnt the current Inca lore regarding their descent and state of the country before the Spanish Conquest. However, many commentators accuse him of attempting to sanitise his maternal history and the rule of the Incas over subjected peoples providing only a saccharin version of that history, the legends and associated mythology. However, the Montesinos version of the Inca origin myth appears to be the only one deliberately recorded from the Incas themselves apart from de la Vega's record of their own version of the Inca's origin and the latter also draws from those outside the royal court for two other versions.

The first of de la Vega's from outside the intimate Inca circle is from the provinces of Colla-suyu and Cunti-suyu to the south and west of Cuzco respectively. This is as follows from the Markham translation[159]: "Their account is that, after the flood subsided, a man appeared in Tiahuanacu (Tiahuanaco), to the southward of Cuzco, who was so powerful that he divided the world into four parts, and gave them to four men who were called kings. The first was called Manco Capac, the second Colla, the third Tocay, and the fourth Pinahua. They say that he gave the northern part to Manco Capac, the southern to Colla (from whose name they afterwards called the great province Colla), the eastern to Tocay, and the western to Pinahua. He ordered each to repair to his district, to conquer it, and govern the people he might find there. But they do not say whether the deluge had drowned people, or whether they had been brought back to life again, in order to be conquered and instructed, and so it is with respect to all they relate touching those times. They say that from this division of the world afterwards arose that which the Incas made their kingdom, called Ttahuantin-suyu. They declare that Manco Ccapac went towards the north, and arrived in the valley of Cuzco, where he founded a city, subdued the surrounding inhabitants, and instructed them." ... "But they do not know what became of the other three kings; and this is the way with all their accounts of ancient times, which is not to be wondered at, seeing that they had no letters wherewith to preserve the memory of their ancestors."

Inca Origins Myth - Version 9

De la Vega recorded another account as follows: "The Indians to the north and east of the city of Cuzco give another account of the origin of the Yncas, resembling the above (Version 8). They say that, in the beginning of the world, four men and four women, all brothers and sisters, came out of certain openings in the rock near the city, in a place called Paucar-tampu. There they came forth from the central openings, which are three in number, and they called them the royal window. Owing to this fable, they lined those openings with great plates of gold, covered with precious stones, while openings on the sides were only adorned with gold, and had no precious stones. They called the first brother Manco Capac, and his wife Mama Ocllo. They say that he founded the city called Cuzco (which, in the special language of the Yncas, means navel). That he conquered the nations round that city, teaching them to live like men, and that from him the Incas are descended. The second brother was called Ayar Cachi, the third Ayar Uchu, and the fourth Ayar Sauca. The word Ayar has no meaning in the general language of Peru, though it probably has in the special idiom of the Incas. The other words are in the general language. Cachi means the salt that we eat, and Uchu is the condiment they use for seasoning their dishes, which the Spanish call pepper (Chile pepper - Capsicum frutescens), the Indians of Peru had no other kind. The other word Sauca signifies pleasure, satisfaction or delight." Interestingly de la Vega noted that when pressed for further references in myths and legends regarding the Inca origins the Indians he noted that "...they repeat a thousand foolish tales..."[160] and sadly, because these were so considered in their time, they were never recorded and they are among many "tales" that would have preserved elements of legend and myth that may have been of great value to the researcher.

Inca Origins Myth - Version 10
The Licentiate, or viceroy appointed by the Spanish crown to Peru, who succeeded the line of the first, Francisco Pizarro, in the middle of the 16th., century, was Polo de Ondegardo. He record-ed another version from his privileged position as follows: "The first story that these Yncas put forward, though it was not the title which they finally asserted, was an idea that, after the deluge, seven men and women had come out of a cave which they call Paccari-tampu, five leagues (about 15 miles - 23 kilometres) from Cuzco, where a window was carved in masonry in most ancient times; that these persons multiplied and spread over the world. Hence every province had a like place of worship where people came forth after the universal destruction; and these places were pointed out by their old men and wizards, who taught them why and how the Yncas venerated the cave of Paccari-tampu ..."[161].

Inca Origins Myth - Version 11
Joseph de Acosta, a Jesuit, who resided in Peru from 1569 to 1585 A.D. provided some of the most valuable post-Conquest records about the myths and legends of the Inca and their forebears. He deliberately make the distinction between the oral records from the Incas themselves and that current among the people indicating that these were not necessarily the same. Among the myths of the peoples of Bolivia (the Aymara) he notes: "However it may be, the Indians say that with this their deluge people were all drowned, and they relate that from the great lagune of Titicaca there came out one Viracocha, who made his abode at Tiaguanaco, where to-day are seen ruins and parts of ancient and very strange edifices, and that from there they came to Cuzco, and so the human family began to multiply. They point out in that lagune (Lake Titicaca) an islet where they fable that the sun concealed and maintained itself, and for this reason they anciently made to it, there, many sacrifices, not only of sheep, but of men. Others say that out of a certain cave, through the window, there came six or I do not know how many men, and that these made the beginning of the propagation of mankind, and this was at what (the place which), for that reason, they call Pacari Tambo. So they are of the opinion that the Tambos are the oldest lineage of

mankind. From there, they say, proceeded Mangocapa, whom they recognise as the founder and head of the Ingas ..."[162].

The Incas' Origins and Their Lines of Descent Recorded in Myth

The many versions of the Inca origins myths reflect two or three apparent prototypes. One clearly attempts to identify with the great Andean hero Viracocha and, or Tonapa and the region of the altiplano near Tiahuanaco sited beside Lake Titicaca. This reflects a claim of hereditary and therefore right of descent from the previous rulers of the longest known empire in the Andes. The second appears to claim the right to rule by right of descent from the Sun, usually associated with the mountain above which the Sun rises in the east, and it is from a cave in this mountain that the Inca ancestors were said to have emerged. The third is much less often referred to and that is the Incas ascendancy as a result of a long migration from the north and the search for a place in which they can establish themselves, expand, and ultimately form an empire.

In the several versions of all of these myths there is evidence of influence by some part of another myth(s) through constant retelling but it is clear that there are elements relating exclusively to the Incas themselves. All of the myths appear to have been part of pre-Inca cycles adapted for themselves by the Inca propaganda machine and it is not always easy to establish which elements are from those earlier cycles and what might have been the rightful elements from the Incas themselves. The elements relating to Viracocha and Tonapa will be considered more fully in a later chapter and mentioned here only for continuity or as a starting point. In Version 2, however, the term Viracocha is used to associate the Incas not necessarily with the deified hero Viracocha but more with his physical appearance since traditionally among the Aymara of the Bolivian altiplano around Lake Titcaca he was said to have been white-skinned and bearded and even into more recent centuries white people were described or addressed as Viracocha as a term of respect. When Bandelier researched among the Aymara over a century ago he noted that he was informed by them that in very ancient times the island of Titicaca "...was inhabited by gentlemen (caballeros) similar to the viracochas (name given to whites by the Indian today)"[163]. It is in this more general use of the term and its association with the ancient hero Viracocha that the term is used in Version 2.

The relation in Version 5 referring to the white sailor Ingasman, who is later married to Cocapac's daughter and the children as a result of their union attempts to explain the Incas' light-skin colouring as the children of the Sun. This reference is highly reminiscent of Polynesian identification of Europeans as the Children of the Sun earlier noted, particularly among the Morioris. This is consistent with other myths indicating that the Inca and their previous incursive ruling groups and forebears married into local tribes to produce heirs and evident also in the earliest Aymara myths relating that the Viracochas who inhabited the island of Titicaca intermarried with local women[164]. This element is one that "rings true" since most of the sea migrations, and mariners who undertook them, were exclusively male and among some of the Oceanic people a woman was never allowed to approach or look at a canoe, ocean-going or otherwise, let alone travel in one. It is therefore one of the main tenets of historical research into ancient migrations and particularly in myths that incursive males of one race or tribal group acquired marriage partners from the lands into which they were penetrating. This lead to the many myths, legends and customs of bride capture or purchase sanctified by long tradition and becoming accepted as part of the marriage rites between one group and another.

The fact that the white sailor Ingasman noted in Version 5 was from overseas is not without precedent in Andean myth as Version 4 indicates but this in turn follows other myths predating the Inca and will be of more interest later. Version 5 indicates therefore that the main elements of the myth are no more fanciful than any other myths and deserves more consideration than it has received. That the bard who related the version identified the "Ingas" as Ingasman with "Englishman" is forgivable since it is not unlike white people today, and recent centuries, being identified with Viracocha in retrospect and should be understood in those terms.

Version 4 is of importance since it does indicate that many of the myths have some basis in truth in the present day long after this myth was recorded. This is so because it is known through archaeological research and dating techniques that many influences arrived from the north either through Colombia, or Venezuela, into Ecuador and Peru and this may be reflected in the fact that the first pottery in South America was made on the Caribbean coast and the introduction of maize from Mexico also took this route. However, the inclusion of the father name of Manco Capac must surely be significant - Atua, since this is the generic name of ancestral gods in Polynesia, suggesting that the line was from, or came via Polynesia or identified with other migrations from that direction while the clan was resident on the coast of Ecuador. It is likely that this myth is a redacted version of many migration myths assimilated into one myth retaining only the most prominent aspects necessary for the retelling and they are of particular importance to this work since they clearly indicate origins from the sea specifically noted also in Version 5.

The evidence from some of the myths, such as it is, or can be gleaned, suggests therefore that the Incas were of mixed race, the male originally from a foreign land and consorted with the indigenous women of South America out of necessity, at least for the most part. However, in the other myths there is a strong intimation that the Incas, particularly the ruling line of Manco Capac, were incestuous, retaining the tradition of marrying their sisters or blood kin "to preserve their caste". Certainly it is recorded that Manco Capac, the founder of the Inca dynasty, married his sister Mama Ocllo and one of the last Incas Huayna Capac, was known to have married his sister and his son Tupac married his aunt. This custom was long known of royal families in the Old World and here appears to be in direct contradistinction to the intermarriage with local women in some myths if the Incas were foreign. This appears to be confirm that the Incas were of a lighter colour skin intimated in Version 5 and identifying with Viracocha's appearance in Version 4.

In Version 2 there are references to a sacred mountain and a golden vase. It is probably not a coincidence that there are important references to sacred mountains with revered names, such as Kailasa, in the Himalayas that are also identified with ritual vessels known as Kalasa and this is possibly related to that in the Inca myth perhaps derived from earlier links with Tiahuanaco. These parallels and associations will be of more interest in a following chapter.

The most prominent aspect in Inca Origins myths and common to all the versions is the repeated use of the title Ayar and usually only applied to the men. This is a term frequently noted in the later known terminology applied to some place names but this title is so clearly of great importance to the Inca myths since it designates the most heroic founders of the dynasty. This has never been explained by any simple or extended references in local Andean terms or related to any other within, or outside the Americas except by Miles Poindexter. The fact that it applies to the male line tends to confirm that the first Incas were from elsewhere and since they are said to have arrived in the Andes with their sisters the whole of the incest episodes as preserved suggests that this relationship was based on the Asian model perhaps similar to that recorded in the epic called the Mahabharata in India.

Ayya; Aiyar and Aiyenar - Clans and Titles in India

If any man, women or child in India were to be asked who the Ayar brothers were they would be able to discourse, by chapter and verse, at length for hours and longer sufficient to satisfy any inquirer. This title and associated histories derive from the Pandava brothers, and sometimes including their sister Draupadi, who escaped from the defeat of the great civil war among the

Aryan tribes in the North West of India. After their defeat they travelled deep into the south of India thus creating myth and legends surrounding their exploits[165].

The Ayars as a whole were the Aryans tribes who invaded India from the Iranian Plateau across the Indus River, in what is now Pakistan, and settling around the Sarawati River in the early first millennium, B.C. This great legendary river has long since dried up and is now the focus of scientific efforts to relocate its bed from the Himalayas to its delta in the Great Rann of Kutch opening onto the Arabian Sea in the northern Indian Ocean. After the great legendary civil war recorded in the great Vedic/Hindu epic, the Mahabharata[166], between the rival Aryan clans of the Pandavas and Kauravas (Kurus), the defeated Pandavas escaped south and east and their heroic battle became embedded in the many myths and legends associated in the Deccan and South India. It is these Panadavas, and the five brothers, although sometimes of varying number, in particularly along with their sister Draupadi, who are more broadly identified with the Ayar brothers across tribal India[167]. Interestingly the Todas in the Nilgiri Hills, of some interest in this work, believed that they were descended from the Pandavas and from Ravan - the term for the wind god in the Ancient Middle East but also the name of Ravanna, the demon king of Sri Lanka[168]. The references to the five brothers, and Draupadi, are seen by some as a reference to former practices of polyandry and the Todas pointed to this aspect of this vestige of their ancient lifestyle as evidence of their descent from the Pandavas[169]. The myths and legends surrounding the Pandavas and particularly references to polyandry are highly reminiscent of those surviving as the Origin Myths of the Ayar Incas. Among the Gonds of Central India, of such note throughout this work, the father of the five Pandavas, Pando Raja, was said to have been born from the same egg laid by the mythical vulture (identified with the Condor?) Mohami. The great Gond hero, Linal, was said to have been born from this egg along with the Pandavas and his name derives from the fact that he had lings (phallic symbols) on his hands, feet, throat and head at his birth[170]. These are highly reminiscent of the phallic references and pendant identified with the phallus in Polynesia and in Coastal Ecuador. The myth of heroes born from mythical eggs is also paralleled in the Andes in the Pariacaca myths to be of some interest later in this work.

Ayar or Aya is the most desired title that can be claimed to in the history of India since this is associated with descent from the ancient Aryan culture-bearers who were the warriors in the Vedic legends who swept into India from Iran. They thrust aside the naturalized and indigenous people of the Sub-continent in wars for possession of Northern India and these were recorded in many surviving works of Indian literature. Most important of all are the deeds and battles recorded in the Mahabharata and Vedas. Because of the importance of the connections between the Inca as the last Andean dynasty and the traditions of India the intermediate geographic steps across the Pacific and South East Asia as connections between two continents will be considered briefly in later chapters although important in themselves. For this reason these connections with India will be established beyond doubt that cross-Pacific voyages did occur before the Spanish Conquest since more reliable recorded historical, legendary and mythical material is available than for earlier epochs. For this reason the historical sequence will be reversed and considered from the Incas back to the earlier civilizations preceding them. The interaction between South American and Central American cultures will briefly be reviewed only when reference to shared imagery since the connections between India, Mexico and the Maya and the cross-Pacific voyages that introduced cultural transfer has been considered in earlier works by the present author. The constant pressure of migrations from Central Asia forced many populations in the warmer climes to be displaced as periods of severe cold weather forced those from colder climates to seek warmer regions to the south in which to live. Since all the available territories were occupied violent clashes ensued and many of the existing peoples in the warmer climes were forced to flee or face violent deaths or enslavement. However, in all of these disturbances it was the women and children who tended to succumb to famine and cold in the northern climate of Eurasia and therefore the incursive peoples were largely male. To perpetuate their lines the women of the subdued population were taken as wives but the men who survived battle were either killed or retreated to displace other peoples ahead of the raiders. The male intruders in a region captured, traded or bought women from local tribes or arranged marriages through, and to secure alliances but in many cases they considered the hereditary of their own male line superior and that of the women of subjected peoples as only a function for securing heirs. In Iran, the main entreport from Central Asia to the Indian Sub-continent, the Aryan peoples supplanted, and in turn were themselves supplanted by later Central Asian peoples, mostly themselves of Aryan or mixed stock.

Since the British entered the Sub-continent in the 18th., century, and extended their control over the whole of the region a century or so later to create modern-day India, the subject of the Aryan incursions into the Sub-continent has been broached many times and a great deal written on the subject. Some are commentaries on the surviving works of the Hindus, Buddhist and Jains and many translate and provide commentaries on the myths, legends and oral traditions relating to the origins of the peoples of India both of Aryan descent and those considered Dravidian or Aboriginal. Of particular interest to this work are the references and researches into the caste system of India and its origins and its strict imposition by the peoples of Aryan descent through the majority Hindus. It will be shown that the caste system operated through the social organization that was very similar to that of the Incas and the model on which this latter was built probably derived from that found long established among the peoples of India.

In ancient India the term Ayya or Aiyar is the term for father, derived from the ancient Vedas, preserved among many tribes and castes in India[171]. This usually indicated a claim of Aryan descent, real or imagined, or as justification for an attempted rise of social status by some of the lower status castes in India - common up into the twentieth century. The term Ayara is the Ancient Iranian term Yairya meaning "Lords of the Year" or "Year-Lords" and the month lords were called Mahya"[172]. This term is probably the origin of the Vedic Indian term Maha, but interestingly, the Iranian term might be the origin of Central American name Maya. Another early term, Ayavas, also Yavas, referring to the "lord of creatures" but more appositely to the calendrical division of the lunar month into an increasing light half that followed the darkening half. In this the Yava is the first, light half and the Ayava is the decreasing or waning half of the month[173]. These terms are especially associated with the rites at the sacred fire altar since the main celebrations took place there fortnightly at the beginning of the rising half and at the full moon two weeks later. In the celebrations of the god of fire, Agni, at the altar these two deities were considered to have special references to the human figure in its symbolic arrangement and the breath control associated with these fire rites. These attributes associated with Ayava as the Lord of Creatures number thirty three, ten fingers, ten toes, ten vital airs, two feet (touching the sacred ground on which the human celebrant is supported), and the trunk[174]. This may have origin references to the beginnings of the fire altars found from the 3rd., millennium, B.C. through into the Inca Dynasty deriving from Ancient Iran. In considering the fire-god, Agni, as the supreme deity of the Aryans, it is worthy of note that Ayu ("life") was also a name of Agni[175] as well as relating as a term for the tribes themselves, Ayus. This and related aspects are noted elsewhere under the clan and caste system as the probable origin of the Incan term for clan - ayllu.

In South India the separate Dravidian people, the Tamil Brahmans, and a division of the Tamil Pallan Patnul-Karans - who will be of more interest later, also used the title of Aiyar even thought their claim of descent from the Aryan peoples of Iran, in the last wave dating to about the early first millennium B.C., cannot be supported. However, they identified with these later people through religion and perhaps a former contact from sea migrations direct from the Ancient

Middle East.

The only prominent male deity, except in very rare cases, in South India among the many village deities was Aiyanar[176], otherwise known as Sasta, and of interest in an earlier work in connection with cultural transfer to Mexico from India[177]. Aiyenar was considered to be able to guard the village at night and was believed to be the son of the native god Siva and the Aryan sky god Vishnu in a female incarnation. Many of the village deities required animal sacrifices and originally human sacrifices, but when any sacrifice was being performed a curtain was drawn across the opening to Aiyenar's shrine so that the god could not see rites considered abhorrent to him[178]. This probably derives from the fact that the Brahmans were not permitted to kill animals in their ceremonies even though the most ancient texts indicate that five sacred sacrifices included animals, the highest of these originally the human male, before entering India. The village deities were often represented by stones, usually small, laid around or at the foot of the sacred village tree[179], and these appear to be the counterparts, and origin, of the conopas of the Peruvians Indians.

Other very poor tribes and castes were forbidden to enter the temples of the Aryan Hindus and were usually not allowed to approach to the sacred precinct within stated distances measured in paces, while others were not allowed even to be seen near the outermost boundary. It was these latter people who usually retained their own primitive pre-Aryan deities represented often as very simple crude images or as stones associated with tribal trees or huts. One of the poorest of these was the Holeya and they worshipped the fierce Aboriginal female deity Kali, and in her most extreme skeletal form of Chamunda (*11.071*), was adopted into the Hindu pantheon and identified with Siva in his wrathful form as his wife. They also worshipped as their male deity Eiyappa[180] (Aiya-appa) who is clearly derived from an Aryan god.

The Holeyas were originally in the early first millennium A.D. the rulers of the far south of India and were later challenged by the venturers of the priestly Brahman caste, the Machis. By the second half of the first millennium the Machi Brahmans[181] had established control notwithstanding being evicted by the unwilling host a few centuries before, ultimately relegated the Holeyas and other tribes and castes, perceived as a threat, to the lowest rung of the social ladder where they remained into the twentieth century. It is of special note, considering the many cultural aspects associated with the Aryan Brahmans evident in Peru, that the term Machi appears frequently as the term for a priest in many parts of South America particularly among the Mapuche[182].

Among a few tribes the term aiya appears as a subdivision indicating a belief in the descent from an Aryan hero or part tribal descent from an Aryan group. Confusion occurs when one of the titles derives from an honour associated with warrior status and this occurs among the Kapus and Baligas where the title of Aiya was conferred on them by royal favour by a king, or Raja, for their loyal service[184]. A subdivision of this warrior caste is found among the Kapus called Aiya-Rakulu, and this is also the name of a separate caste divided into the classic sub-divisions probably, originally relating to the calendrical divisions of four or five clans, or gotras, including those originally with totemic animals, the tortoise and the cobra[185].

The Aiya-Rakulu were a caste of cultivators in South India and cross-cousin marriage was customary among them where menarikam, or the marriage of a young man's cousin to the daughter of his maternal uncle's daughter, was the norm. This caste also called themselves Razu, and this is a term deriving from Rao or Rayo meaning "king" and an identification in ancient days with the Sun's rays. In Ancient Peru the Inca and his ancestors identified with the Sun and it is unlikely to be a coincidence that snow-covered mountains where the ancestors were believed to dwell were called Razu, but also Rao or Ritri recorded by Arriaga, terms identical and coinciding in meaning with Razu in India[186]. This connection between South India and Peru is emphasised by the fact that the Incas entitled themselves Ayar, identical to titles of this and other tribes in India claiming Aryan descent.

Other variations on the title of Aiyar were Narayan and Nayanar and from these it may well be that the Chimus, said to have arrived on the coast of Northern Peru on rafts from the west, were associated and descended from the peoples of South India. The Chimu king was called Naymlap and it is interesting to note that their means of entry into Peru on rafts is the same for other legends of peoples from the west and will be of more interest in due course. The last ruler of the Chimu, Fempellec[187] was said to be so dissolute that the people bound him and caste him of into the ocean from whence the dynasty had come, a punishment known in Ancient Peru in the Tonapa myth, Polynesia[188] and in Asia[189].

Other titles identified with Ayar, Aiyar, and Ayya are Anna and Amma. Amma appears to have derived from an earlier identification from the Ancient Middle East most likely having arrived earlier by sea with traders and mariners since it is largely found in South India. Sea trade had long connected South India with the Ancient Middle East and Iran separately from land migrations before, and after the Aryan land migrations across the North West frontier from Iran into the Subcontinent. Ana and An were originally male titles millennia earlier in Ancient Sumeria during the period of high civilisations centred on the Tigris and Euphrates Rivers. Role and gender reversal was common in the cultural transfer of titles as well as in the nature of gods and goddesses. This occurred frequently not only in Asia but elsewhere and in South India the title Ama or Amma usually designated a village goddess. Anna was the retained male form as a title of the corrupted form of the female counterpart of An or Ana.

The Gavara were a people who originated from the Eastern Chalukyian capital of Vengi, near Ellore, but who fled from persecution of the king. They took to the sea and sailed down the coast and founded a village a little way inland on the South Coast of India called Wada-Palli meaning "the village of the people who came in boats"[190]. Wada means a boat, particularly a sailing boat, and is probably the early form of waka, the Polynesian term for a boat. The personal clan titles the Gavaras used were Ayya, Anna (Amma), Ayya, and sometimes Nayudu[191]. A Telugu fishing caste found on the Southern Coasts of India are the Neyyala and they reverenced the cobra, or Naga, as their caste deity. They claim the caste title of Ayya and their ceremonies are conducted, as with most who claim this title, by the Aryan priestly caste of Brahmans[192].

Another fishing caste located on the Malabar coast in South India were the Mukkavans who were also boatmen and palanquin-bearers and their hereditary chiefs were called Arayan[193]. In North Malabar these people are divided into four castes one of which is called Ponillam where pon = gold[194]. This corresponds to an early form of Son or Sun and probably indicates a tradition of adoration for the Sun found in other castes. The Arayans as the chiefs were entitled to all the porpoises or dolphins caught by the Mukkuvan fishermen and this identification with this special sea creature has references to the myths and legends of the Eastern Mediterranean and West Asia. The porpoise was often associated with oracles and among the Mukkuvans their seers were called Ayittans also called Attans[195]. Their goddess Bhadra-Kali was represented by a log of wood and this form or representation is found among the people of Orissa in Central India. Log gods are also found among the Nagas, far to the North East, in the Himalayan foothills north of the Bay of Bengal and also in the Marquesas Islands far to the east in Eastern Polynesia and these Mukkuvans will be of more interest in due coarse.

A Telugu people called the Golla claimed descent from the deified Hindu Aryan hero Krishna and were respected by others because of this association and as a result they retained the privilege of guarding the sacred cow. Their name is said to be a shortened, or corrupt form of the Sanskrit Gopala, a term for cowherd and their titles were Ayya, Anna, Konar, Kon-arlu and sometimes Nayudu[196]. One warrior division of this caste of local chiefs was said to have given their name to the famous Golconda fort in Hyderabad. The southern branch of this caste around Mysore was divided into Uru, village and Kadu or forest. The term Uru is of interest since so many of the terms in India are traceable to the Ancient Middle East and this clearly derives from the Uru from Ur. Miles Poindexter notes the many associations of this term with the Aryans, or Ayya in India and the Ayar Incas and the earlier peoples around Lake Titicaca called the Uru. He was not the only one to note such connections; the American archaeologist A. Hyatt Verrill also noted the many parallels in words he found among the Uru and Aymara of Lake Titicaca in comparison with those of the Ancient Sumerians of Ur[192].

The terms Konar and Kon-arlu are derived from Kon or Konan meaning "king"[198]. These are derived from the Ancient Aryan terms for Sun, where Kon, or Con, is recorded in Ancient Western European myths as a name for heroes identified with the Sun or as the Sun itself. A Tamil caste, called the Idaiyans, in South India was divided into shepherds and palanquin-bearers, or Puvandans. The term Puvandan was another form of Pon-dan[199] and the term is difficult to determine until it is realised that Pon is another confused form of two terms for the Sun - Pun and Pon or Kon (Sun and Son). In other words it was anciently perceived that the palanquin-bearers were carrying in their litter the incarnation of the Sun, or the Son of the Sun, the king - the Rao, Rayo, Raya, Rayadu or Razu[200]. This group of related terms includes Iraya, a closely similar, and related form of the Latin Rei, still used in the Southern Mediterranean countries to this day along with Ritri and Rao noted in 16th., century Peru by Arriaga and together form the name of the Peruvian hero, Con-i-Raya. The term Rao is still frequently to be encountered in India and was more specifically the title of the Desastha Brahmans, but found also among the Maratha classes, many of whom claim Kshatriya (Warrior) status. The title is also found, or has been adopted by other religions or castes, notably among the Jains, Servigaras and Perikes[201]. Related terms will be of more interest in later chapters in this work.

Living on the coasts and therefore associated with the coastal trade and mariners were the castes who manufactured palm-wine. One of these was the Idiga and they claimed descent from, or connection with the Aryans by retaining the titles, Aita and Appa[202]. Another coastal fishing caste was the Milas where the term Mila-vandhu meant "fishermen". Their caste titles were Ayya and Anna[203].

Dispossessed tribes and castes were many in the history of India and some of the dispossessed became mendicants or carried on a precarious existence in trades and professions necessitating a footloose existence. These lonely occupations were not always a guide to their origins but more to the vagaries of their unfortunate fate. The caste of Jogis earned a living as beggars and street entertainers, specialising as jugglers. Their claim to the deity Ayya-Varu[204] suggests that their origins may have belied their present state and been one identified with the illustrious and revered Aryans in North India.

A forest tribe in South India called the Kadirs gave worship to a deity called Iyappa-Swami, and the representation of this deity was a stone placed beneath a teak tree. It was believed that this deity protected them against illness and disease and was, as in so many tribes one of the few male deities among the primitive people in the forested regions[205]. It is unlikely that the Kadirs, and indeed many other of the South Indian tribes, were in fact descended from Aryans, either from the last, more celebrated incursions recorded in the Mahabharata, or earlier, or later incursions from the sea. It is likely that the origin of the male gods was in fact as a result of the idealisation of earlier contacts with Aryan peoples who had more advanced curative knowledge than they themselves. Similar parallels as examples of deification of this type occur as a result of the first Spanish contacts in North, Central and South America before the full scale Conquest itself and later of the British and others in Oceania, and Africa.

In a myth preserved of the Telugu weavers known as the Karna-Bhattu it was said that a king of the Godavari district in Central East Coastal India petitioned the deity Siva to assist him in ridding the country of pestilential demons troubling his domains. Siva produced nine warriors from his ear called Karna-Bhattus, or "ear-soldiers" and they cleared the kingdom of the demons and established themselves as both warriors and weavers in that district[206]. The story is reminiscent of the soldiers who were originally turned-to-stone who returned to human form when called upon by the Incas to assist in defeating their enemies in the time of Inca Viracocha and may not be unconnected. The titles used by the Karna-Bhattus are Ayya and Anna, and the term Bhattu in their name derives from the Brahman Bhatta or Patta and will be of further interest in due course.

Another caste in India claiming a special relationship of descent from Aryan hero Krishna are the Krishna-Vakakkar, meaning "belonging to Krishna". Their caste titles were Ayan and Acchi, and claim that their ancestors migrated south from Krishna's birthplace called Ambadi in North India[207]. The term Ayar entailed a special kinship with others from the same recognised tribal group and among the Kummara, Kumbara or Kumbaro, and another term, Ayam, indicated a relationship of equality among the tribal members and this extended to another related term for the hereditary village officers - Ayagar[208]. The Kunnavans in extending their territory in more ancient times were assisted by feudal chieftains named Ayya-Kudi, clearly claiming their cherished tribal descent from the Aryans[209]. This sense of brotherhood was also found among others of the barber caste named the Mangala, their titles being Anna and Gadu, where Anna meant "brother", and their other main title used was Ayya and meant "father"[210]

The Kurubas are one of the most important and extended tribes in Central and South India. They are particularly noted for their weaving skills, especially in earlier centuries, who claimed the titles of Ayya, Appa and Anna among others[211], and these people will be of more interest in later chapters. Among some of the suppressed tribes who were relegated from their original ruling positions, such as the Malas, tribal names often indicated an original separate identity indicating contact with Ancient Iran such as the Mala Arayan[212]. These people worshipped the deity Arayan and tigers were said to be his "dogs"[213].

Another caste of weavers was the Paidi, and they were also employed as agricultural workers. These clans are related to the hill peoples called the Panos and Dombos although they are considered of a lower status caste. Some Paidis claim descent from Valmiki, the author of the great Hindu epic the Ramayana, a distinction claimed also by the Boyas[214]. It is possible that these people may have had some contact, even intermarriage with the ancient Aryan insurgents but it is also likely that this contact has been exaggerated to extend to fill a void in the traditions of caste origins, a common problem in India.

Claims by association or intermarriage in Ancient India are difficult to prove except when recorded or noted in texts or copper plate grants. The Pallans were an agricultural class in South India and were treated only on a slightly higher level of status than the Paraiyans. However, at one time these tribes were in fact were, along with the Paraiyans and others, the rulers in their own land and were relegated by later Hindu Brahmans and their supporters[215]. The names applied to family members appear either to have originally been derived from Aryan descent or adopted by association from their suppressors. These were Aiya = Father; Amma = Mother; or Anja = Father and Atta = Mother[216]. One of their tribal divisions was called Konga Pallans in the far south of India and the term Kon-ga (Kon = Con = Son or Sun) appears to derive from an early form of Sun worship, a subject to be of interest in later chapters[217].

As a variation, where intermarriage has occurred between castes not necessarily of Aryan descent and those that retain some memory of Aryan ancestors, the commonly found dual divisions into clans, septs or gotras indicate some clan ancestor of Aryan descent or Hindu saint and utilised the suffix of Ayya, Appa, or Amma in the clan division name. This characteristic

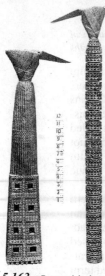

5.163 : Ceremonial adzes, following the exact design of similar staffs found in Tibet. Mangaia, Central Polynesia, pre-20th., century, A.D.

5.164 : The proctors of the monastery at Sera flanked with the symbols of their office including maces of a type similar in design to ceremonial adze maces in Melanesia (5.163) and Polynesia. Tibet, Early 20th., century, A.D.

5.165 : Foot-ploughs traditional among the Maori similar to those found in Ancient Peru. Note the traditional kilts - one exhibiting patterns similar to the India. Maori, New Zealand, Early 20th., century, A.D.

5.167 : Gond farmers with their traditional dray found in India from the early Indus Valley civilisation over 4000 years earlier. Sirpur, Central India, Early 20th., century, A.D.

5.166 : Four taclla, the traditional foot plough used anciently in Peru, and depicted also in 16th., century drawings by Huaman Poma de Ayala (5.168/9). Peru, early 20th., century, A.D.

occurs among the Wodeyars near the South India city of Mysore[218]. The Namdaris, were called Nambis and Desaris and the chiefs of the latter were called Annal-ayya; Godgul-ayya, Tuttul-ayya and Kurum-ayya[219].

Such claims of descent are exhibited by tribes and castes who are clearly merged Aryan and Aboriginal tribes or earlier peoples before the Aryan invasion nearly 3000 years ago. The Upparas or Uppiliyans were salt collectors and in the Tamil section, as Hindus, it was believed that the soul went to the abode of Indra, the storm god, called Swarga, and then to Kailasa, the paradise Himalayan mountain abode of Siva. Their caste god was a pot-god represented by a pot of water, margosa leaves and Avaram flowers[220]. Similar pot gods are found throughout India and in Indonesia and further east in Melanesia, clearly disseminated from India itself.

The Meda, Medara, Medarlu or Medara-Karan are a caste of bamboo workers in the Oriya, Telugu, Canarese and Tamil regions of Central and South India. Their origin legends state that they came from the mountain of Mahendrachala, the mountain of Indra, the storm god. Their caste myths state that the bamboo roots, so indispensable to their caste occupation, was a reflection of the serpent of Siva. This has references in flood myths where serpents are located at the roots of the World Tree or its substitute, bamboo. Indra was the quintessential Aryan deity

TRAVAXA HAILLI CHACRAIAPVIC

AGOSTO CHACRAIAPVI

5.168 : A sketch of agricultural work with the men using the foot-plough, or taclla, and the women sowing the seed. The high-born supervisor wears and apron similar to those retained by the Nagas of Assam into the 20th., century, and also significant is the brow disk worn by the middle man using a taclla identical to those found among the Maya and throughout the Pacific into Asia. Poma de Ayala, Peru, Early Post Conquest.

5.169 : A similar sketch in theme to *5.168* and both indicate the similarity to the foot-plough used among the Maoris (*5.165*). The highborn supervisor is indicated with his apron similar to pectoral designs among the Toradja in Indonesia and the apron traditional among the Nagas of Assam. Poma de Ayala, Peru, Early Post Conquest.

imported into India from Ancient Iran but where the first record of his existence is among the Hittites in Anatolia over three thousand years ago[221].

In every Medara-Karan family there were special spirits whom they worshipped only in that family called the Virullu. These may be boys who have not married before their deaths and an image of them is made of silver and kept in a basket and this is brought out and worshipped at the appropriate festival occasions[222]. Many of their myths and legends have Biblical or Middle Eastern references and one refers to a tribal hero named Medara Chen-ayya who was said to have fed thousands of people with one pot full of rice and is highly reminiscent of the "five loaves and twelve fishes" story in the Bible[223]. The name ending confirms the connections with Aryan descent and Ancient Iran. Even though some of the castes have forgotten the history and associations of the titles directly with the Aryans the titles, prefixes and suffices remain as a mute reminder to that connection and this is as true of ayya as it is with the often-met term karan.

The Telugu temple priests in the Godavari River district were the Tambalas, they regarded as the Brahmans in that region, and among them were Saivites and Lingayats and their titles were Aiya and Appa[224]. The lingayat was a small carving of a phallus representing Siva, wrapped into a pendant form and hung around the neck, resembling in principle the Tiki of the Polynesian Maoris. Sir Peter Buck, himself a Maori (Te Rangi Hiroa), noted the special relationship of the carved jade (usually) tiki with the male phallus and all its concomitant associations and iconography[225]. As such the tiki was a symbol of courage and virility and this appears to reflect the carved linga (phallus) worn around the neck of the Hindu Saivite Linga-yats.

One of the great anomalies of the Aryan Hindu religion was that it adopted to a large degree a vegetarian diet. As descendants of traditional cattle herders in Central Asia and the Iranian Plateau it would have been natural for the cattle to supply all the needs and benefits of a herding life for the cattle-herding Aryans. This included the keeping of cattle for their meat and their milk as modern cattle-herders do in other parts of Asia and Africa, as well as for their leather for clothing, weapon sheaths and many other necessities. Fundamentally there would be little other reason to tend and herd these animals except where they were used for dragging cart and drays and yoked to the oil and agricultural presses and grain grinders. Certainly the greatly revered Rishis, among the first of the mythical tribal progenitors, were meat-eaters and followed a typical cattle-herders life as recorded in the ancient texts and traditions and leatherworking would have been one occupation that produced elite goods for their horses, weapons and personal adornment. Tanning and leatherworking was reduced, over successive centuries of growing Hindu influence in India, to one of the lowest status occupations and the workers in leather were rigidly caste-bound by that occupation.

In South Canara, in the South West of India, the Samagara were leather-workers and the principal class or leather workers in that region. They were divided into two separate divisions, the Canarese Samagaras and the Arya Samagaras, the latter speaking Marathi, suggesting that they, in part at least, were northerners. Low status tribes in India were often those associated with the darker complexions of the Aboriginal races through intermarriage between them and some of the mixed race Aryans. The Arya Samagaras were noted for their pale complexions and "comely" features suggesting that they were in fact a separate Aryan people who may have descended from earlier Aryan migrants or an independent group of leather-workers and tanners from the Middle East who settled in South India. The dual organisation was therefore likely to have been established by the Aryan Samagaras formed of the purer Aryan males who took their brides where necessary from the surrounding Canarese while the Canarese Samagaras were formed of acceptable status local peoples and their part-Aryan descendants as secondary or illegitimate descendants of their union. The leather process of these Samagaras has been described elsewhere but it is interesting to note that the hides of the animals, after being soaked for a period of a month and the necessary procedures to preserve the hide, are sewn up and stuffed with bark of cashew, daddala and other trees and hung up[226]. This tanning process appears closely similar to the analysis of the filling for the eviscerated bodies of the dead in Northern Chile thousands of years ago, and the many examples of the stuffed human hides of enemies hung up and described by the first Spanish after the Conquest in South America.

The Aryan Samagaras were Marathi speaking suggesting their immediate earlier origin in India, but Marathi also were the Servegaras also found in Canara and South Central India. They are believed to have been a soldiering caste, as were many Marathis clans, and their titles were among others, Aiya, Rao and Nayak[227]. Nayak appears to have been a localised corruption in South India from Narayan, a title deriving from terms, Arayan or Aryan. The Nayars were a local high caste military people in South India and were the highest status caste of servants and supporters of the local Brahmin families and their castes. It is likely that these titles were also derived from early Aryan titles by association or perhaps arriving independently from the Middle East into Canara and Tamil Nadu (country) having a common origin with those of the Vedic Aryans in Ancient Iran.

The Tamils figure large in the possibilities of those who may have travelled by sea to Ancient Peru beside the mariners of Canara. The largest caste of palm-wine makers in the Tamil region of South East India was known as the Shanans. They claimed descent from the Indian Flood Survivor, Manu, or Sabyavrata, one of whose grandsons was called Atri, probably the Ait found in the myths of Western Asia and the Cushites. The Shanans claim the titles of Aiyar, Pillai, etc., and their caste name is recognised as a corruption from Saundigar to Shanan. The Tiyans appears to be connected to

5.170 : Shrine of Grama-Devata, or stone gods, raised on a circular platform not unlike those in parts of Pacific Coast Mexcico and Peru. India, Pre-20th., century, A.D.

them and these will be of more interest later, but their related titles are Aiyangars, and Raos[228], and the family title, usually Nadar, probably derives from Nayar. Of a much higher status, second to the Brahmans only were the Padma Velama (also Yelamas) who retained the titles of Ayya, Anna and Nayadu. Their caste divisions follow the classic sections originally related to the four cardinal directions plus the fifth as the World Axis (North and South combined) these being Naga (Cobra); Sankha (Conch Shell); Tulasi (Sacred Shrub) and Tabelu (Tortoise, local name)[229].

It will be shown that the fundamental dual organisation on which the Inca social system was based, and from which the caste system evolved, has its close parallels in Ancient India where it survives in the Sub-continent to the present day. These are so similar that they probably derive from almost identical origins, and for the same reasons - so much so that it is likely that the Inca system originated from that earlier developed in India. This appears to be confirmed by the consistent use of similar terms still in use at the time of the Spanish Conquest.

CHAPTER 6

CLANS and COSMOLOGY in PERU and INDIA
REFLECTED in TUANTINSUYU of the INCAS

The problem of clans and castes in the Inca Empire have received little attention in the last century and a half of growing and more intensive research into the largely artefactually based history and archaeology of South America. This is certainly not because there was anything hidden or obscured in terms of lack of reference since these clans divisions were known and reported from the first entrance of the Spanish under the Conquistadors. However recently, more occasional comparisons with other cultures both inside South America and abroad have thrown some doubts on the hereditary arrangement among the Incas and this research culminated in the work of R. Tom Zuidema in the second half of the twentieth century. Zuidema himself, along with some of his contemporaries and those since, draw comparisons with similar social structures on the other side of the Pacific Ocean far to the west in Melanesia[1]. Although these comparisons have all stopped short of actually attempting to indicate that there must have been a connection between them, inevitably by sea, they point to parallels that are unlikely to be coincidental. This is of particular importance since other aspects of research noted throughout this work undertaken by recognised authorities points in the same direction.

Clans and Castes of Ancient Peru

In the clan system proposed, structured on a dual social organisation of a superior and inferior, or a basic upper and lower polarity usually called moieties, each are further divided into a mirrored clan subdivisions similarly found throughout South America but more particularly in Ancient Peru. The dual organisation system was however not limited to the Inca Empire but appears to have been maintained earlier among the Aymara of Bolivia around Lake Titicaca where the greatness and might of Tiahuanaco survived for over a thousand years before the rise of the Incas.

Largely ignored by more recent historians and researchers is the fact that two generations ago Miles Poindexter, the American ambassador to Peru in the second decade of the twentieth century, wrote of the close similarities in caste, clan structure and titles assumed by the Inca to those of the Aryans in Ancient India. He provides an abundance of evidence in his work to support his view with arguments and sources ranging much broader than from the history of India alone[2]. It is interesting, therefore, that Zuidema and his supporters, in pointing to parallels in Melanesia and Australia in support of their own theories of the development, of Inca castes unintentionally reveal fundamental aspects and structures, that are so similar to those recorded in British Colonial India. It is also significant that both of these western regions of the Pacific were highly influenced from India directly as well as through South East Asia. Poindexter notes in particular the edicts and impositions by the Brahmans, or priests of the Aryan invaders, upon the tribes of India whom they relegated to the lowest status, and the resulting caste system that was so similar to that imposed by the Inca. He also noted that both used the title indicating their racial origin from these Vedic Aryans in India - Ayar, and this will be of more interest in due course.

The Ayar Incas and Ceques related to their Caste System

It was early noted by the Spanish that the Inca Empire was divided into four quarters corresponding roughly to the four cardinal points of the compass. The names of these quarters was Chincha-suyu = North; Colla-suyu = South; Anti-suyu = East and Cunti-suyu = west (6.002). These were related to the basic ceque structure, radial lines centred on Cuzco as the capital city of the Incas, where there were nine of these lines for each of the quarters, except for Cunti-suyu where there were fourteen, totalling forty one in all[3]. Each of these ceque lines distributed to the corresponding four quarters and many shrines and huacas were located along each of them. The

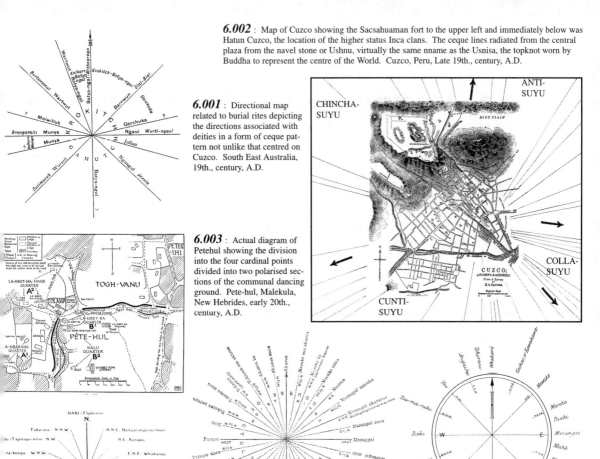

6.002 : Map of Cuzco showing the Sacsahuaman fort to the upper left and immediately below was Hatun Cuzco, the location of the higher status Inca clans. The ceque lines radiated from the central plaza from the navel stone or Ushnu, virtually the same nname as the Usnisa, the topknot worn by Buddha to represent the centre of the World. Cuzco, Peru, Late 19th., century, A.D.

6.001 : Directional map related to burial rites depicting the directions associated with deities in a form of ceque pattern not unlike that centred on Cuzco. South East Australia, 19th., century, A.D.

6.003 : Actual diagram of Petehul showing the division into the four cardinal points divided into two polarised sections of the communal dancing ground. Pete-hul, Malekula, New Hebrides, early 20th., century, A.D.

904 : Maori compass with the names of the relat-divisions and wind names. Ngati-Porou, Maori, w Zealand, Early 20th., century, A.D.

6.005 : Radial ceque lines radiating from the centre of Cuzco divided into the four quarters related to the cardinal points. Inca Dynasty, Cuzco, Peru.

6.006 : A diagram of a Moriori compass that also indicates deity names associated with those and intermediate directions. Chatham Islands, New Zealand, pre-20th., century, A.D.

renown 17th., century missionary priest, Bernabe Cobo, lists and describes most of these huacas and their locations as well as the associated deities, heroes or ancestors to whom they are dedicated and the sacrifices offered at the shrines correspondingly[4]. The maintenance and propitiatory rites associated with the nine ceque lines in each of the four quarters or the fourteen of Cunti-suyu were entailed upon the clans located within each of the four quarters[5]. The radiating lines of the ceques are known to have been determined from, or focused on a stone "navel" or omphallus sited in the main square of Ancient Cuzco (*6.002*) called the Ushnu and it is unlikely to be a coincidence that the topknot of Buddha representing the World Tree, Pillar or omphalus was known as the Usnisa.

The clan groups were the descendants from one of the previous rulers where each ruled over by its own clan chief called the Panaca, a name to be of interest later, and where each succeeding Inca formed his own clan subdivision or ayllu in addition to those already formed. The organisation of the Incas into a dual social organisation was instituted into two divisions called the Hanan or upper moiety, and Hurin or lower moiety. In the earliest reports it is noted that the first four Inca rulers including the founder, Manco Capac, all belonged to Hurin, or lower moiety, while the succeeding rulers belonged to Hanan, or upper moiety[6]. This has led some to believe that there was an alternating succession from upper to lower and back again after a certain number of rulers, while R. Tom Zuidema suggested that there may have been a corresponding dual ruler-ship where both Hanan and Hurin clan leaders ruled jointly. This contention was supported by evidence of joint ruler-ships occurring elsewhere in South America and particularly among the Aymara, from whom some researchers believed the Incas to have originated.

Zuidema contests the views recorded in the early Spanish records as to the structure of the clan system and its relation to the ceque system and records at some length, and in written and diagrammatic detail, his reconstruction of the Inca clan system as he saw it[7]. It is not necessary to go into that detail here but it is interesting to note that his views and fundamental clan concepts applied to the social structure of Cuzco, and outside of the capital in Peru generally, appears to be closely based on those developed by John Layard a generation before in Malekula, one of the islands of the New Hebrides (now re-named Vanuatu) in Melanesia, of which it is a part[8]. Zuidema even utilised the term for the nominated subject from whom the clan relationships are determined denoted, that is "ego", almost certainly derived by example from Layard's earlier work.

There can be no doubt that, even if the clan system as derived from outside of Peru, it would be adapted in part to suit the prevailing political and cultural influences in South America, and particularly so in the more extreme environment in the highlands of the Andes. In the east of Brazil in the Amazon Basin resemblances among the Bororo and Ge tribes in their social organisation to that of the Inca were noted by Zuidema. Other elements of similarity have been recorded by specialist researchers and it has been generally considered by them that the Inca system along with Andean culture generally originated among the Amazonian tribes.

However, Zuidema also notes that Claude Levi-Strauss considered in his extensive and celebrated researches that the social systems of South America were similar to those found in North America but even more so to those of Melanesia, and Indonesia[9]. More particularly he notes that Levi-Strauss indicates that these clan systems are reflected more prominently among certain of the tribes of major cultural significance in the Amazon - the Bororo, Canella, Apinaye and Cherente and their social strictures appear more related to the clan systems of Aboriginal Australia[10]. Further references to parallels between the Inca and moiety systems, or South American dual organisations of clan and marriage structures, are clearly determined on a fundamental, simple stratified system and therefore more easily administered. Zuidema suggests that the parallels between Melanesia and South America are superficial and that these conclusions were influenced by the similarity of basic structure[11] rather than as a product of imported cultural influences.

However, there are many more references beyond the system of the dual moieties linking these far-flung regions that are so directly connected by the sea currents of the Pacific Ocean. Zuidema does also note that Levi-Strauss recorded that the Indians of South America "exhibited contradictory elements which could not have originated in their present habit-hangovers or 'pauperized' from higher cultures'"[12]. In other words there were intrusive elements that could not have derived from the Incas and those of the higher cultures earlier in Ecuador, Peru and Bolivia or South America generally or apparently generated by contact with other Amazonian tribal groups. This view of Levi-Stauss's work therefore is in opposition to those who are determined to pursue the line of total indigenous development and also that of Zuidema who considered the dual organisation and clan structure among the Inca and Aymara to be only superficially similar to those of Melanesia, Indonesia and Aboriginal Australia.

6.007 : A form of panpipes called the Sumpotan identical to those found in the Ancient Middle East. Dyak, Borneo, Early 20th., century, A.D.

6.009 : Double rowed, ornamented panpipes. Chincha, Southern Peru.

6.008 : Simple tribal panpipes. Amazonia, South America, Early 20th., century, A.D.

6.010 : Clay and reed panpipes typical of South America but also in the Solomon Islands. Peru.

6.011 : Large Amazonian bark trumpet similar to those found in the Solomon Islands. South America.

6.012 : Trumpets of a closely similar type to those found in the Amazon Basin (*6.011*) along with panpipes and other cultural parallels. Solomon Islands, Early 20th., century, A.D.

6.013 : Variety of typical panpipes with a conch used for signalling at sea and religious rituals. Melanesia and Marquesas Islands, Eastern Marquesas, Late 19th., century, A.D.

6.014 : Panpipes characteristic of the Solomon Islands and South America. Buka, Solomon Islands, Early 20th., century, A.D.

One of the elements common between the Melanesians and the Incas, and the earlier high cultures along the Andean mountain chain and Pacific Coastal strip, is the quartering of the regions under their control reflected in their traditional ceremonial centre on Malekula, Pete-hul. The four quarters of the ground plan corresponding to the cardinal points is similar in principle to that of Cuzco and in the Andes this was extended with the Empire as a fundamental division in administration of their domains. In these Melanesian islands also there are to be found many aspects associated more famously with the Peruvians, such as trepanation, cranial deformation, panpipes and bark trumpets, as well as star clubs and other weapons, virtually identical in Melanesia to those found in Peru, not to mention the many parallel in the motifs of myths and legend.

In the first examples recorded earlier after the Spanish Conquest it appears that the first dual organisations in Inca Peru was based on a three part division called Collana, Payan and Cayao and from these groups there were formed four marriage classes. The group known as Collana was that of the rulers, Cayao the priests, with the Payan as the "Lords of the Land"[13] and

345

6.016 : Clay trumpet of a type called the Pututa, a similar name as that in the Marquesas Islands, the Putona. Moche, North Coast Peru, 200-600 A.D.

6.018 : Wind instruments developed from the first flutes are widely known in Asia and this example in early Iran is clearly the origin of the Sumpotan in Borneo (*6.007*) and other parts of South East Asia and a possible divergence from the panpipe. Sassanid Dynasty, Iran, 600 A.D.

6.015 : Ornamented panpipes made from bamboo from the Wai-Wai of Northern South America.

6.017 : Finely moulded clay conch trumpet. Moche, North Coast Peru, 200-600 A.D.

6.019 : Shell trumpet extended and bound securely to a wooden rod known as a Putona. Marquesas Islands, late 19th., century, A.D.

this system as a whole appears to have derived from that of the Aymara around Lake Titicaca[14]. In Tiahuanaco, dual organisations were known among the surviving tribes at the Spanish Conquest. Tripartite divisions were recorded and in city or town ground plans ceremonial centres were divided into four quarters and best known of Tiahuanaco itself. This suggests that the social structure imposed by the Inca may have been formed on the basis of the that applied in Tiahuanaco centuries earlier but survived in memory long enough to be adopted by the Inca.

The Inca introduced revisions to traditions adopted or developed initially into one that was structured as a dual organisation of five divisions, that appears to have been influenced by the model found among the coastal Chimu[15]. As in Peru and South America generally, along with the Ancient Mexican cultural region, the number five was of special significance and this was also true in India. It is likely that the division of five was related to this clan division because of its religious and traditionary connotations and this is likely to have initially been imported in principle from Asia. In Cuzco the city was divided into the dual social organisations of the higher status Hanan and lower status Hurin and these terms also have Asian connotations and will be considered in due course.

The origin of the wives of the Incas is of particular interest since it is noted by Zuidema that they were not all of Inca blood. It is suggested that there were certain regulations whereby an Inca was expected to take his principal wife as the Coya, or queen, from certain of the marriage groups and these had to be the clan divisions assigned exclusively to those of Inca descent reinforced by traditions of cross-cousin marriage[16].

The cross cousin-marriage system is one that is widely known throughout the world and existed for many millennia in Europe into very recent times. The reasons for its development were almost invariably ones of inheritance through race, tribe and economy to retain the wealth and tribal integrity under the control of the related clan members. In South America it is clear that the Incas imposed, or were traditionally used to the cross-cousin marriage alliances to maintain control among what appears from the records to have been extremely hostile tribes in Andean and North West Coastal South America. It is interesting to briefly consider, therefore, the first apparent origins of their clan system from the fundamental dual organisation they developed or inherited.

Clans and Clan Structures of the Andes

The earliest known records indicate that the clan system, rudimentary or otherwise, developed from the three-group system predating the Inca dynasty and appears to have had its parallel among the Quechua as among the Aymara. The parallel between the two systems can be summarily given as follows:

Quechua divisions				Aymara divisions
Collana	=	Alluaca	= Right	Cupi
Payan	=	Chaupi	= Centre	Chaupi or Taypi
Cayao	=	Ychoc	= Left	Checa

The division and their structures are developed by Zuidema at length and need not be considered here but it should be remembered that these appear to be closely influenced or based on the numerous examples given by John Layard. In his development diagrams Layard shows the close relationship existing in the clan structures of Malekula, and in the New Hebrides and generally, with similar clan structures in China. He also notes that the ground designs retained in the traditions by these same Melanesians also occur in South India and are further described in a separate book by him. As already noted the methodology utilised by Zuidema, so similar to Layard's, is reflected also in his use of his nominated subject term "ego"[17] but he appears to give no credence to actual contacts between Melanesia and Peru and certainly no credit to John Layard by whom he appears to be so obviously influenced.

Some of the terms used in the group arrangement above appear to derive, or have similarities, to terms in the Western Pacific and India. These will be of interest later, but it is interesting to consider why a three group system such as this is shown is developed from the principle of the dual organisation. It would appear that the history preserved by the Incas is far from clear or complete. Some of the Inca Origin myths indicate that the Ayar brothers emerged from a cave with their sisters or wives, but most do not, indicating that the single hero, Manco Capac, or the four or more brothers emerged or arrived alone. If the Ayar brothers were mariners or migrated from the far north, or south, as some of their myths indicate, it is likely that they would have entered Peru without related women. The Chimu myth of Naymlap is unusual since it is recorded that he arrived with his whole family on the coast of Peru and this is certainly uncommon for ancient mariners. The giant myths of Manta, north on the Ecuador Coast, are more usual in that the arrivals were specifically noted as male.

The fundamental principle therefore that developed from outsiders entering a foreign land and carving out a kingdom is no different to that applied in Asia, Europe and the North of Africa and Australia. The Ayar brothers would have selected the most suitable of the ruling tribes in seeking allies and from them, or if they had clan divisions already, from the ruling clan, and from them selected their wives to establish a dynasty. The physical characteristics of their descendants would have been mixed reflected that of the incursive males and the indigenous tribal clan. If able to establish superiority over these and the surrounding tribes, this mixed clan then is more likely to have become the ruling clan and the clan from which it chose, or abducted their brides is relegated to second-class status but above the clans over whom they previously ruled. Exactly this same principle operated when the Conquistadors entered Peru where they also selected their marriage partners from the relegated Inca clans having established political and military control over the Inca Empire. This appears to be at the root of the Inca system where the Inca had their own group, Collana, the higher status indigenous people were assigned to Cayao, and the mixed tribe, or mixed race children of the marriages that took place between them were assigned to the "centre" or Payan group. From this simple dual organisation of "us" - the superior ruling clan wishing to maintain its racial, tribal and, or economic identity; and "them", the relegated or indigenous people - the "ruled", who had to be kept as lower status divisions and represented the workers for the ruling clan. These several social combinations developed to accommodate the complexities of allowable intermarriage and their corresponding position in the social scale.

The Ayar Incas maintained the Collana as their own higher status clan division in a system based on patrilineality, or "us", while the indigenous tribes inhabiting the region controlled by the Inca was assigned Cayao, or "them", maintaining matrilineal descent and these in turn were subdivided into family sections with their own hierarchy. The intermediate division named Payan was that containing the subdivisions of those who were the mixed race descendants between Collana and Cayao and was that the endogamous group of Collana used as a natural buffer between it and the "outside world" represented by Cayao. As the simple divisions expanded over time and generations, the divisions themselves became occupied with many of the descendants of the former Incas and their principal wives, their lesser status secondary wives, children, and the brothers and sisters of their respective generations. In time, the distance of relationship through first and second cousins and beyond meant that the degree of blood relationship diminished and therefore these naturally formed a more peripheral association with the ruling Inca and his immediate family. The primary division of Collana therefore was in turn subdivided into a three part relationship reflecting the overall main division, of Collana, Payan and Cayao within the main division and this also applied to the main divisions of Payan and Cayao. In a few generations the Inca was able to draw his marriage partners from Collana exclusively and this might include his own sister or his aunts retaining the "Blood Royal" from his own clan subdivision while those of his lesser wives came from one of the three subdivisions within Collana. The concubines of the Inca were usually drawn from the Virgins of the Sun who were assigned Cayao in the main divisions, but their resultant children were assigned to Payan.

The earlier reference to the priests in Inca Peru being assigned Cayao is interesting since it is notable that in India the priesthood for the non-Aryans people in Hindu South India were correspondingly not from the Aryan Hindus but were local people. Although in India the Hinduised priests adopted the Aryan Vedic rites from the Brahmans as well many of the most strictly held aspects of the rites were lost in the translation from North to South and the earliest European writers in India noted: "The non-Brahmanic character of the worship is still further marked by the fact that no special direction from the homestead is prescribed in selecting the site for the shrine. No orthodox Hindu temple can be built south of the village site, as this quarter is regarded as the realm of Yama, the god of death; here vagrant evil spirits prowl and consume or defile the offerings made to the greater gods"[18]. Reflective aspects of this structure are found in Peru and the colour of Yama, derived from the Iranian Yima, was black, where in Peru the tern yana meant black[19]. It is likely therefore that many aspects associated with traditions imported from India or Iran were in fact modified but the priestly association outside and within the Inca clans appear to be paralleled, and will be of more interest in due course.

The final arrangement of the Inca clan divisions system devised as two dual organisation with five clan divisions each appears to have been imposed by Inca Pachacuti, the ninth Inca, but this still retained the basic dual organisation system recognisable elsewhere in the Andes and, of special note, in India. In Malekula there is an upper and lower clan division, reflecting that of the Hanan-Cuzco and Hurin-Cuzco in Peru and these are called the "high" and "low" Maki reflected in the naming of corresponding opposite ends of the ceremonial dancing ground marked by small monoliths. The term Machi is that found also in India of a particularly group of trading Brahmans and relates separately to rites in North East India, as well as the name of the shaman priest among the Mapuche in Chile already noted.

In a section quoted from Betanzos, Zuidema notes that that the region of Cuzco located between the fort of Sacsahuaman on the hill overlooking Cuzco and the confluence of the rivers, between which the main body of the ceremonial section of the city was sited, was assigned by the Inca Pachacuti to Hanan Cuzco when he rebuilt Manco Capac's first town centre. The main ceremonial centre surrounded, and was measured from the Temple of the Sun located there and in the district topographically lower than the Hanan ayllu was allocated by Pachacuti to Hurin ayllu. Pachacuti's dictates were recorded by Betanzos as follows: "…the chiefs (senores) who were his closest kin, and descendants of his lineage in a direct line, who were the sons of noble men and women (senores y senoras) of his own kin and lineage; for the three chiefs whom he permitted to dwell in the section stretching from the temple of the sun downwards, as you have already heard, were the subsidiary sons of the chiefs who, although they belonged to his lineage, had been born from alien women and were of low descent. Sons begotten in this manner they call Guaccha Cconcha, which means 'deriving from poor people and of low origin', although sons of the Inca, they are called thus and no honour is paid to them by any one from among the noble people, with the exception of the orejones (nobles) who also belong to the commoners[20].

This relation by Betanzos clearly indicates that the Inca town was arranged by Pachacuti in the same manner that the Brahmans constructed their own residential areas where they had control. They imposed living quarters or zones within the city exclusive to the recognised castes established under the Laws of Manu and excluded others to regulated distances beyond the town or city perimeter. This is still evident in some of the less industrialised towns and cites in India today where the Brahmans' quarters are located on a higher prominence if available nearby. They also reserved the colour blue for painting the external walls of their own dwellings and this, defining their enclaves, is readily seen in towns such as Jodhpur in Rajasthan in North West India (*6.110*).

Caste Divisions in Ancient Peru and India
In India the ruling dynasty was usually drawn from the warrior caste known as the Kshatriyas, since they fought the battles and established rule under their own chiefs. The highest social stratification was arrogated by the Brahmans to themselves since they were the priestly caste and "nearest to god". The other recognised caste was that of the agriculturists called the Vaisyas and these divisions were clearly based on the ancient Iranian model. Although there was a fourth caste eventually recognised, the Sudras, they were an outcaste group formed of the indigenous non-Aryan people and their mixed descendants from the three recognised Aryan castes. Zuidema notes that in the divisions at Cuzco the Incas established the three recognised lineage groups of Collana, Payan, and Cayao, but established also a fourth group assigned to those "who could be collectively be called outcasts, for they were regarded by the Inca as not belonging to organised society"[21]. The close similarity between the Aryan Hindu and the Ayar Inca social divisions can hardly be more pronounced and even Zuidema was moved to use the same term as that describing the Sudras in India by the British to the fourth division in Cuzco - "outcasts", more usually called "untouchables".

Interestingly, in the translation of Salcamayhua's important 16th., century work, the term the translator, Sir Clements Markham, found most appropriate - "caste", when describing the relationships established between the first Incas said to have been set up at Cuzco by Manco Capac, was that from the model applied in the social system in India[22]. It is clear that the earlier translators and researchers saw the parallels between the social system of Ancient Peru and that of India and found that of India the only one that adequately provided a model to explain the system imposed by the Incas or that they adopted from their predecessors in Tiahuanaco to be adjusted and imposed by themselves.

Zuidema also discovered from the Spanish records that a system of colour division was inherent in some of the older, perhaps original systems of social division in Ancient Peru just as it occurred in India, where in the latter the term varna, "colour", was used to determine fundamental divisions[23]. In the Peruvian region of the Collaguas a similar system and set of terms was found and reflected in other regions such as in Anta, where Capa, Hatun and Huchuy were synonyms for Collana, Payan and Cayao. Among the Chanca who inhabited the region around modern Ayamarca, ancient Guamanga, these terms corresponded to the two hierarchic extremes, probably originally applied racially, of Usco or Anco = white; Ticlla; and Yana = black[24]. It can hardly be a coincidence that the term yana was that for the colour black in Peru since the god of Death in India was Yama and his colour was also black. It is significant that one of the dual organisations preserved among the dark-skinned Tamils in the far south of India, a Dravidian, non-Aryan people or at least having little claim to that descent, is called Velattatu (white) and Karuttatu (black)[25] suggesting that they retained the ancient Brahmanic divisions from the first pre-Manu contact between Aryans and Dravidians.

One of the foundation words preserved in the Inca clan system is that of Cayao and this derives from the term khalla meaning "beginning, origin", and this where many of the mythical origins relate to heroes, ancestors, clans and tribes emerging from stones, or turning to stones[26]. These stones, huacas, or foundations were maintained with great devotion and it is interesting to note that similar myths associated with stones occur in India where the most anciently preserved term is kal, a sacred stone among many of the Aboriginal tribes and virtually identical to that indicated here in Peru[27]. It is particularly notable that this term, kal, is preserved by the Gonds into the present day since they have erected megaliths into the twentieth century and preserve the term kal for their sacred sites of standing memorial stones[28] (*1.062*). A large stone set on four boulders among them was called the Danya-Kal and the small stones at the foot of the menhirs were called Hanal-Kutul or ghost stools, perhaps the origin of the term Hanan in Cuzco in Peru. The Gonds are of exceptional interest in this work and will be more so in the following chapters. The term kal and other variations appears to derive from the Ancient Middle Eastern term for the priest, kallu, who officiated at the ancient stone altars, or a bat, batu, or baetyl[29] - another aspect of cultural transference. Khallu might also be the term of origin related to Titi-Kala (Wildcat Rock or Rock of the Sun - Titi = Wildcat; Kala = rock), the most sacred rock in the Inca Empire usurped from the Aymara and the former Tiahuanaco Empire (*6.020*) by the Inca, situated on the Island of the Sun in Lake Titicaca (actually Lake Titi-kala). Kallu was also the name retained by the Incas in praise of themselves meaning "smart ones"[30] and possibly derives from the same origin, or imported directly from India and the Ancient Middle East.

This fundamental tribal division in India on the basis of colour corresponds to the original principle of the white Aryans tribes entering the Subcontinent and encountering the indigenous dark-skinned people. This in turn instigated an intermediate group between them and including the racially mixed descendants of those in the Aryan tribes who could not find brides among their own people in the centuries before the Laws of Manu were instituted. This appears to be the identical basis upon which the Inca and pre-Inca peoples of Andean and coastal Bolivia and Peru established their own caste system so closely similar and probably descended from the ancient Laws of Manu model in India.

The probable connections of the Ayar Incas as immigrants into Peru from India was the subject of two volumes written by the former U.S. ambassador to Peru almost eighty years ago, Miles Poindexter. He saw not only that the titles used by the Incas were exactly the same as those of Ancient India but other aspects of their culture including their clan system. He notes; "The sublime thought of the enlightened Incas of the upper caste, like that of the transcendentalists of the Hindus, conceived the one true god as the 'infinite cause, the fundamental principle, the light of the world, the great teachers' (Markham quote). This conception of the Ayar caste of Peru is the same as that of the Aryan-Brahman caste of their god,

6.020 : One of the most revered huacas or shrines in the Inca Dynasty and before was the sacred rock called Titi-Kala, believed to be the place where the Sun rose at the beginning of the present Creation. Island of the Sun, Lake Titicaca, Bolivia.

Brahma, - 'the Supreme Soul, or impersonal all-embracing divine essence, the original source and ultimate goal of all that exists' (Eggeling quote). This is our own Aryan God, and eternal, omnipotent spirit, - our knowledge of whom we inherited from the same Aryan sources."

"The appeal of the Ayar-Amauta Tupac Cauri Pachacuti to the Peruvian people to abandon their idolatries seems, like a page from the history of Moses struggle with the apostate Israelites ..."[31]. Poindexter also notes; ..."As to the Chinese and the Hindus, the religion of most vital import to the Quichuas was the worship of the spirits of the ancestors of the ayllu, - the family or the clan"[32].

Poindexter perceives the Incas as an extension of the Aryan Brahmans and Hindus in India but also recognises the many similarities of both of their religious belief system and social organisation with that not only of South Asia but also with Western Europe and the West in general. He also clearly indicates in his work that he considers the Quichua in the Andean region of Peru the same as the Quiche of Central America relating the Maya with the Peruvians and the Mexican Colhua, Mayan Chol as the Colla of Bolivia.

The caste system of India, although ancient, derives its origins not to one system but two as a result of the influences and mutation or mergers where necessary due to local environmental and social conditions existing at the time the Vedic Aryans entered India. The first system is one derived from ancient traditions formulated in Iran that was less racially biased in the way later found in India. The second was the imposition by the Brahmans of the so-called Laws, or Institutes, of Manu, a great legendary sage who wrote down the laws and social mores that should be applied by the Aryans to themselves and the indigenous people that were confronted in India. These laws codified the relation of each person and clan in their daily lives within, and between the different Aryan groups, their own tribes, and the clans within those tribes, and the indigenous or naturalised peoples inhabiting the Subcontinent after their invasions into India centuries before.

The term "caste" applied to the Vedic Aryan system instituted over the two and a half millennia since the Laws of Manu were initiated is largely misunderstood and the bad press it has received from the observations of the first Europeans derives from the worst examples of its application after centuries of degeneration from the first principles. The word caste derives from the Portuguese term casta signifying "race", but can also be translated as "mould" or "quality", applied when they first set up trading colonies in South India and elsewhere in the fifteenth and sixteenth centuries A.D. The word used in India for caste was jat indicating the birth of a child and inherent in this term was the allusion to lineage and rank, reflected in the term jatha meaning "well-born"[33]. Developing later than the original application of the fundamental division based on varna, or colour, was that the references for caste reflected the common occupation preserved by a community. These clan members, who traditionally intermarried among themselves, reflected the very ancient traditions of cross-cousin marriages extant in India before the Vedic Aryans.

Even among the non-Hindu tribes of India a dual organisation system similar to that operating in Aboriginal Australia was found in India particularly among the Aboriginal tribes such as the Mundas and Kols but also those who reflected limited earlier Aryan intrusions. Clearly these various forms of organisation were also brought into India across the North West frontier from the Iranian Plateau and appear to derive from Anatolia in part from the second half of the second millennium B.C.[34]. More recent archaeological evidence in the Indus valley indicates that cultures from the Ancient Middle East and Iran entered India from at least as early as 5000 B.C. and probably earlier. It is likely, therefore, that the Indus Valley civilisation itself appears to have emerged from these many and very ancient intrusive influences, both racial and cultural, and these imported aspects were also reflected in trade items, and other cultural influences[35].

The Ancient Iranian Caste System; Tetrads and Cardinal Points

The caste system in Iran was critical to the development of that later in India and this ise evident in records preserved from the epoch of the fire-religions, of Zervanism and Mazdaean Zoroastrianism. In the earliest religious texts from Ancient Iran three castes are defined; the first that of the priest associated with the religious rites celebrating the deity of light, Ohrmazd; the second that of the warrior associated with the wind deity, Vay; and the third that of the "husbandman", or herder, associated with the deity Spihr[36]. A fourth "caste" emerged rather tentatively and that was the caste associated with the demon Varan in opposition to the other three, and each of these castes appears to have its roots in the Zervanite doctrines that in turn were probably derived from an earlier time. The ancient dichotomy of the relationship between the divine trinity and the quaternary has occupied philosophers for millennia and the inclusion of a fourth element in the basic trinity of the caste system may indicate something of this philosophic thought applied to the practical issues of social organisation.

The first three "castes" of the Zervanites and Mazdaeans applied to the race of people from whom they were engendered, the Iranians, but the emergence of the fourth element in opposition, associated with the evil Varan, may have been instigated in response to non-Iranian peoples and intruders who were outside their original territory. It is most likely that they were seen as hostile, including their religious and social practices, and were condemned socially to an "external" caste epitomised by the demon Varan. Tetrads were a developing trend in the late second and early first millennium B.C. and there are several examples of the deity Zurvan being arranged in tetrad order along with the Sun, Moon and the Signs of the Zodiac. In what was called the "Tetrad of Being" Zurvan epitomised Time and as such formed a tetrad with Space (Asoqar), Wisdom (Frasoqar), and Power (Zarogar) and this grouping is typical in the social and religious speculations of that time in Ancient Iran[37].

These Ancient Iranian speculations were all in the cause of explaining the nature of the god Zurvan and his ideal structure reflected in the perceived right actions and social order expressed through mankind. These same concerns were conveyed by the Ancient Iranians who transferred these belief systems into India and were in turn inherited by the Vedic Brahmans. This priestly caste of Aryans codified these beliefs to a more extensive degree to define social structure of the Aryans internally and their power reflected in their dealings with the Dasyus, dark or dark peoples, indigenous in the Subcontinent and this movement reached it highest degree under Manu dated to about the 8th., century, B.C. The castes as they now exist were formed either by occupation, or by marriage, and related to the three Aryan caste divisions, evident in principle in the much earlier Iranian Zervanite system. The Aryan castes intermarried between themselves, and when necessary with the women of Sudras[38], the lowest of the recognised castes, a non-Aryan caste, corresponding to the Iranian Varan, or fourth division.

Many of the castes in India developed and retained their own form of pre-Aryan organisation, while numerous of them were structured based on the dual organisation marriage system similar to those of Aboriginal Australia, Melanesia and Peru. Others instituted, because of their long history and tribal or caste numbers, divisions based on four clearly related to the tetrad of the cardinal directions or four quarters, while others such as the important high status traders, the Banias, were organised on the basis of ten or twenty subdivisions[39]. As with the term Van so frequently met with among the coastal tribes the term Ban probably derives originally from a Middle East connection where Ban = Van. This is the name of the country around Lake Van, once Armenia, or Ancient Urartu, the region where the original Vedic gods of Indra and Varuna are first recorded.

When the British entered India the caste system as they saw it had been instituted for many centuries and in a less than consistent manner. One report based on material collected a century ago noted of the caste system as it appeared in daily life in India that; "The highest consists of those castes who now claim to be directly descended from the Brahmans, Kshatriyas or Vaishyas, the three higher of the four castes. The second comprises what are generally known as pure or good castes. The principal mark of their caste status is that a Brahman will take water to drink from them, and perform ceremonies in their houses. They may be classified in three divisions, the higher agricultural castes, higher artisan castes; and serving castes from whom a Brahman will take water. The third group contains those castes from whose hands a Brahman will not take water; but their touch does not convey impurity and they are permitted to enter Hindu temples. They consist mainly of certain cultivating castes of low status, some of them recently derived from the indigenous tribes; other functional castes from the forest tribes, and a number of professional and menial castes, whose occupations are mainly pursued in villages, so that they formerly obtained their subsistence from grain payments or annual allowances of grain from the cultivators at seed time and harvest. The group includes also some castes of village priests and mendicant religious orders, who beg from the cultivators. In the fourth group are placed the non-Aryan or indigenous tribes ..... The lowest group consists of the impure castes whose touch is considered to defile the higher castes"[40]. Inevitably the caste rules, imposed more than two millennia before, were applied unevenly throughout the many and varying tribal and Hindu societies of India. As an example, although water could be taken by Brahmans without pollution from lower caste warrior (Kshatriya) and agricultural (Vaisya) Aryan castes, some such as the Marathi Brahmans refused to take water from any apart from Brahmans, while others interpreted the caste rules to suit themselves and these variations became fixed and ossified in custom and tradition.

Some writers have doubted whether the stigma attached to the lowest castes, such as the tanners, bamboo-workers, sweepers, hunters and fowlers, village musicians and weavers, along with meat-eating peoples, or that it was in fact part of the original dictates of the Hindu caste doctrine. It has been noted that in the period of Buddhist supremacy in India, in the time of Asoka in the 3rd., century B.C. meat-eating was acceptable[41] and it may have been that the establishment of the vegetarian strictures attached to the Hindu doctrines were imposed as an attempt to claim and elevate their own belief system to what they considered a higher moral order than that of the other religions in India at that time.

Caste Streets and Quarters in India and Peru

The fundamental division of society into four sections was applied in Ancient Iran long before it was transferred into India around 1000 B.C. This was adapted into India suit the new conditions firstly within the highest Aryan divisions of the dual organisation and later became more indistinct after the Laws of Manu were applied in the middle of the first millennium B.C. This was as a result of intermarriage between the dual organisations causing many sub-groups that required marriage classifications reflecting great complications as a result of the fundamental racial duality, and opposition between the Aryans and indigenous people and their resulting interrelationships in early Northern India. The northern quarter was associated in the early Vedas with the region of the ancestors and therefore this was reserved for the Brahman caste. The south was the direction of the despised indigenous dark-skinned peoples, including the Dravidians, and was associated with the black God of Death, Yama - a transferred god from the Iranian deity Yima. It was forbidden to build any sacred temples or other structures in the South of a sacred precinct or location, or open to the South because of this association, reflected in many of the holy cities of Hinduism located on the sacred rivers there are no buildings whatever on the South shore.

Attempts were varyingly successful in imposing this fundamentally simple principle to an increasingly complicated caste system and fundamental dual organisations between the Aryans and indigenous peoples.

This division of the towns and villages of early India into castes resulted in the exclusion of the outcast peoples from their precincts, and they were accommodated in hovels or little better at prescribed distances so as not to "pollute" the living zones of the accepted, recognised castes. Each of these caste groups lived in their own barrios or caste streets originally associated with the cardinal points. This tradition had been imposed over such a long period in India that even the smallest settlement was usually divided into caste streets known as teri and diminishing evidence for their existence still exists in the more established cities such as Jodhpur already noted. In the small villages in the country in South India the most ancient pattern appears to have been preserved into the twentieth century where the Kota tribes in the Nilgiri Hills, neighbours of a tribe to be of some note - the Todas, retained the strictly orthodox layout of the village that consisted of three streets. These were called in their own variation of the usual term keris one street being called the Ter-Karan or Devadi, and the other two Muntha-Kannans or Pujaris. At Kotagiri, a major settlement of the Kotas, the three streets were named Kil-keri, Nadu-keri, and Nil-keri, or lower, middle (central) and upper streets. These keris were strictly related to the marriage clans and were said to belong to the same family, each originating with the same ancestor. They could not intermarry with any from the same street, that is, not with any other who was closely related. Clearly this arrangement reflects the basic dual organisation with the later development of a third division for those who were the result of the two polarities established long before when outsiders, be they Aryan or other Middle Eastern peoples, settled among alien, indigenous peoples, notably the Dravidians, and others in South India. This follows this same pattern recorded as having been the basis for the first Incas in South America and among the Aymara. The fundamental separation of the ground plan into Upper and Lower Cuzco appears also in first settlement of Cuzco and was maintained in the rebuilding by Pachacuti. This corresponded in principle with the earliest of those in India where the trinity of three separate streets for the three divisions was a later inevitability of intermarriage between the two racial, tribal and clan polarities.

In South India the dual organisation is found reflected in the strict division of acceptable tribes and castes claiming Aryan descent where in the Tamil country land allotted for the village, (Ur), is separated into two portions. These clan territories are called either by the Sanskrit name graman, ("village") or by the Dravidian name of cheri ("gathering place"). This arrangement was reported two generations ago when it still was common as follows: "In the graman live the Brahmans, who sometimes dwell in a quarter by themselves known as the agrahara, and also other Hindus. In the paracheri live the Paraiyans. The paracheri and the graman are always separated at least by a road or lane, and often by several fields. And not only is it usual thus to find that, in every village, the Paraiyans as a community possess a house-site, but there are many cases in which more than one cheri is attached to a graman[42]. This containment into a specifically defined caste enclaves or villages outside the Hindu town for low castes was also applied to other low castes such as Pallans and Valaiyans[43]. The Malabar Chaliyans also retained the tradition of living in caste streets into the twentieth century, largely a dying tradition among other castes by then, and these streets were called Teru[44].

This same grouping of castes into streets is found also in South India among the Tamils as well as the non-Dravidians but these caste zones appear to have largely lost their associations with the cardinal points originally intended in ancient, Vedic times. The Vellalas resided in caste streets[45] and these people will be of more interest in later chapters in this work. The Nayars were a military caste associated with the former royal families in South India. They were originally split up into sections of 600 and each of these sections was given a nad or "country", or province, to protect. The province or nad was further divided into caste streets or taras, the Dravidian equivalent of the Tamil Teru; the Telugu, Teruvu; and the Canarese, Tulu teravu[46]. The Pallis, a caste found in South India, also lived in caste streets called known as Palli Teru or Kudi Teru[47] and these people will be of some importance in a later chapter. In light of these terms for caste street, teri, cheri, teru or tara, and the probable relation of kal or kala to khallu or kallu to a sacred stone or priest officiating at the stone altar it might be conjectured that the term for one of the sacred enclosures at Tiahuanaco, the Kheri Kala[48], was in fact related to the caste divisions into two separate dual organisations believed to be the basis of Aymara society in Ancient South America as well as in India.

In Inca Peru the city of Cuzco was founded on the dual divisions of Hanan-Cuzco and Hurin-Cuzco reflecting the basic separation of the Inca and his relations in the upper moiety, those without Inca rank and the submissive or subjected indigenous tribes, and those descendents of the Incas who appear to have intermarried with them. Not only does this Inca dual organisation, divided into marriage moieties, reflect in the built structure of Cuzco but it follows closely that already known in Ancient India and still evident in India into the twentieth century. The teru or caste streets found in South India in particular are also reflected in Ancient Peru into the present day. In Misminay, a Peruvian village at the centre of a study of the cosmology surviving from Ancient Peru, caste streets and social divisions are still preserved. Here distinct streets relating to upper, middle and lower philosophic cosmological constructs remain associated in relation to the sight lines of the summer and winter solstices are still the main axis of the village landscape. These points of reference relate to the horizon points of the rising and setting Sun and the "quartering", or suyus, of the village and land associated with the urban area[49]. These cosmological structures imposed on the landscape appear to have their earliest references around Lake Titicaca and the Aymara in their cosmological references to the environmental landscape of Uma-suyu and Urco-suyu and these correspondences with the perception of the sacred landscape will be of much more interest in a later chapter.

Dual Organisations in Ancient Peru and India

The association of the dual organisation social system with caste appears greatly diluted and complicated in more recent times in India and this is no doubt due to the repeated movement of the tribes and castes in India across the Subcontinent throughout many centuries since the Laws of Manu were instituted by the Brahmans. Originally, however, the dual system was one of clarity, "them" and "us", noted almost a century ago on one of the first reports on the tribes and castes in Central India. This is recorded as: "The institution of caste as it is understood at present did not exist among the Aryans of the Vedic period, on their first entry into India. The word varna, literally 'colour', which is afterwards used in speaking of the four castes, distinguishes in the Vedas the two classes only: there are the Arya Varna and the Dasa Varna - the Aryan race and the race of enemies. In other passages the Dasyus are spoken of as black, and Indra is praised for protecting the Aryan colour. In later literature the black race, Krishna Varna, are opposed to the Brahmans, and the same word is used of distinction between Aryas and Sudra. The word varna was thus used, in the first place, not of the four castes, but of two hostile races, one white the other black. It is said that Indra divided he fields among his white-coloured people after destroying the Dasyus, by whom may be understood the indigenous barbarian races"[50].

The same author recorded: "To the Aryans the word Dayu had the meaning of one who not only did not perform religious rites, but attempted to harass their performers"[51]. This author quotes another passage from the Rig Veda recording: "If some pious king belonging to the Kshatriya or some other caste should defeat the Mlechchhas and establish a settlement of the four castes in their territories, and accept the Mlechchhas thus defeated as Chandalas (the most impure caste in ancient Hindu society) as is the case in Aryavarrta, then that country also becomes fit for sacrifice"[52]. The Mlechchhas referred to are these "barbarians" whom they confronted in the Central North of Asia, or their homeland of Aryavarrta, and this termed was then applied to the Dasyus in India. The term Aryavarrta might be preserved in a diminished form in the Inca term of Arairaca referring to a division in the ayllu (clan) system of Ancient Cuzco[53]. This was one of the oldest sections appearing to be associated with the Inca founder Manco Capac and the four principal founders in one of the Inca Origin myths centred on Tiahuanaco[54]. The predecessors who were antecedent to Manco Capac, or who submitted to him when he occupied Cuzco were associated with the Arayraca section of the ayllu clan system[55] suggesting an earlier foundation from Aryan India.

In Ancient Peru the dual organisation system appears to have developed long before the Incas since it is endemic among the Aymaras around Lake Titicaca in Bolivia. It probably also occurred among the cultures of the coastal regions where duality in the construction of the pyramid culture millennia before witnesses to a probable similar social system. This does not, however, preclude the fundamentals of duality at the root of this system from being imported in the very first efflorescence of the Pre-ceramic period. On the coast of central and northern Peru there appears to have been dual "corporate" organisations recorded in the surviving cultures to provide the necessary organisation to develop and maintain the irrigation systems into the 16th., century. The conservative nature so frequently noted of these people suggests that this was true also centuries, and millennia, before when irrigation was first introduced and developed in that region. Interestingly, comparisons of labour divisions on the North Peruvian Coast is made with those for the Balinese water temples far to the west, connected directly by the ocean currents of the Pacific Ocean, but without committing to the possibility that they may have common origins[56].

The social system at Misminay in Peru was seen as a reflection of the cosmic order projected into the landscape and the human populations were not seen as separate from that order but an essential part placed in their correct order in correspondence. The footpath, the main artery through the village, called Chaupin Calle, the "middle" or "centre" path, divided the upper and lower moieties located in the settlement area[57]. This formed the actual and symbolic divisions of the basic community into the essential dual organisation so long imposed in Peru and Bolivia. Another path called Hatun Raki running from southwest to northeast further divided the village into quarters relating to the summer and winter solstices[58]. The "upper" moiety of the dual organisation above Chaupin Calle was topographically higher and this formed a corresponding polarity with the lower section nearer the valley floor called Mistirakai. This division into actual upper and lower sections reflects similar divisions in India where higher and lower, or mountain and plain were essential concepts in the location of superior and inferior castes.

In the first reports on the altiplano of Bolivia around Lake Titicaca there are reports of dual organisations, or implied in their dual leadership. In the 16th., century the Aymara-speaking Lupaqa kingdom was ruled by two chiefs named Qari and Qusi, and they apparently ruled their kingdom jointly which was divided into upper and lower moieties as well as the provincial subdivisions[59]. In 1612 the Jesuit priest named Ludovico Bertonio, who resided in the Lupaqa kingdom at that time, wrote that the terms Alasaa (Alasaya) and its complementary term Maassa (Masaya) were the names of the dual moieties found in every village. In the late nineteenth century the dual organisation system was still preserved by this most conservative of peoples and Adolph Bandelier noted that the moiety division passed through the central square at Tiahuanaco[60]. This was probably in response to some very ancient tradition that existed at the time of the fall of Tiahuanaco in the 11th., century, A.D. and was likely to have existed there long before that period of decline[61]. In examining the church records Bandelier noted that the groups

6.021 : Brahma showing three of his five, or four, faces depicted astride his vehicle the divine goose sometimes identified with the flamingo. Chidambaram, South India, 9-11th., century, A.D.

6.022 : Brahma as Universal Creator astride his vehicle the divine goose or hamsa. Aspects of myths associated with him appear in the Ancient Andes cultures. Aihole, Central South India, 6th., century, A.D.

6.023 : The Hindu creator took many forms and these were often assimilated by Siva, here shown when facing South. This image is a reference to the world creation as the ruler of the World - Jnana-Dakshinamurti. Note he sits on a representation of the sacred mountains similar to that of the Moche Ai Apaec (5.094/5). South India.

of ayllus were in fact a development of marriage phratries and corresponded to those in Cuzco where the two moieties were known as Hanan-Cuzco and Hurin-Cuzco[62].

The meaning of the two terms, Ara-saya (also Ala-saya) and Ma-saya, where it is known that -saya indicates the domain or location, is not known entirely understood. The resulting terms Ara (Ala) and Ma (Masa or Mara) must have some qualifying significance to indicate higher and lower in a topographical sense or to status in earlier times but now lost. The many parallels between Ancient Peru and Bolivia with Asia have been noted by Miles Poindexter and others and the terms Ara and Ma or Mara find correspondence in the traditions and terms of Ancient India.

Clans and Castes of India
In the ancient Vedic texts of the Aryan settlers in Northern India the term Ara was the name of the lake sacred to Brahman, the supreme Creator god of the Aryans. This lake, Ara, was one of two, the other was named Nya, both said to be located in the third heaven above the Earth. The text also records that in this heaven there was the lake Aira-mmandiya and where the Asvattha tree showered Soma - the nectar of the gods; the city of Brahman, Hiranyagarbha or Aparagita, and with these was located also at the golden hall called Prabhuvimita (Prabhu = Brahma)[63]. The term Ara and Aira-mmandiya may originally have been intended for the same lake and the term Ara, and Aira are both derived from Aiyar or Arya, that is the Aryans. Mmandiya probably derives from the term manda, related to the sacred temple of the Mandaeans, and the temples of the Assyrians in the early first millennium B.C.[64]. It is unlikely therefore that the Aymaran term Ara, preserved adjacent to Lake Titicaca in Bolivia, should have a name of such significance out of coincidence particularly in relation to the sacred landscape dual divisions of Uma-suyu and Urco-suyu to be considered in a later chapter.

The term Ara for the Aymara, related to the higher, more elevated castes of the Ara or Arya and probably also to Ayar, probably has a common origin therefore to the title claimed by the Incas along with their identification with Tiahuanaco and Lake Titicaca. For the comparison with the cosmology of the Vedas to be of significance the complementary term of Ara, representing the upper regions both topographically and socially, Ma or Mara would need to clearly indicate the representation of the lower geographical and social spheres. In the Vedas Ma or Mai appear to have the same origin and represents the ancient mother goddess in India and therefore the Earth as the womb, appropriate in philosophic terms. Mara, however, represented the "evil one" - the serpent king, and was a synonym for the Nagas among the Buddhists for those who were serpent worshippers. These people were said to have lived in lakes and holes in the ground and were perceived as an ever-present threat to mankind and by symbolic correspondence, to the righteous. The Buddhist texts refer to the worlds of Brahma, and that of the Maras, as the worlds of opposites corresponding to the world of the gods and the world of men[65], where duality is inherent in such a polarity. The idea of subdivision by a physical barrier between two zones so clearly imposed on the landscape at Misminay in Peru by the path called Chaupin Calle[66], is reflected in the Vedic texts as two upper and lower zones separated by the Ganges in India, the zone of the gods, the foothills and the Himalayas to the north, and the lowlands to the south[67]. It was Mara that Buddha defeated and it was this serpent king that was to be found at the foot of the sacred banyan tree and who grieved at Buddha's death. It is likely therefore that the many references to serpents emerging from the base of the sacred tree found in many myths in Oceania and also South America[68] are derived from this early Buddhist myth.

In India the dual organisation system survived in recognisable form among many of the tribes and castes across the Subcontinent. The Baligas were, and are a major trading caste divided into two main divisions called Desa (or Kota = a fort), and Peda (Street). The first of the divisions were said to be the descendants of the Nayak kings of Madura, Tanjore and Vijayanagar in South India. The second division was made up of those who were the Gazulu, bangle-sellers, and the Perike, or salt-sellers[69]. Not all admit that the Baligas were of such elevated stock but the dual organisation of their tribes and castes is the important element here.

The Izhavas were a group of South Indian people who migrated to Sri Lanka returning some generations later to settle on the mainland and who, tradition states, were invited back to India by the Syrian Christians. Interestingly the term Ambanat appears among them[70] suggesting a contact between them and the Ambats, Hambats and Kabat found among the Bhuiyas of Orissa in North East India, in Indonesia and Malekula, this latter island being of note throughout this work. The Izhavas were divided into three groups suggesting that originally they were a dual organisations and that the third group was the result of intermarriage between them as appears to have occurred in Ancient Bolivia and Peru. During the Onam festival the Izhava divided themselves into two sections and fought each other in what usually turned out to be more than a mock battle[71]. This tradition tended to confirm that they originated from the imposition of one superior tribe, who invaded and controlled the lands over the other, relegating the original people to become their serfs or slaves but from whom they originally also took their marriage partners to form the third intermediate division.

Many of the hill tribes in India retained their traditions long after the control of India had been established by the British, and this was because of their relative isolation. The Khonda Dora was such tribe and they retained the "well-defined" dual organisation of Pedda (=big) Kondalu, and Chinna (=small) Kondalu, fundamental divisions common throughout India. In these more basic divisions the exogamous clans, gotras or septs still retained a cosmological basis preserved in their subdivisions and for the Pedda Kondalu these were Naga (= Cobra), Bhag (= Tiger); and Kochchimo (= Tortoise)[72] originally relating to the cardinal directions.

The Gond of Kondh tribes are of special significance throughout this work, and their name may have derived from Kon the very ancient term for Sun, but nothing apart from very old myths relate their origin in tribe or name[73]. The dual organisation and division into marriage phratries is described in a long myth extending to agricultural practise and the Meriah Sacrifice, a human sacrificial form recorded to have been known also in the Andes in Ancient South America considered later in this work.

One of the poorest of the South Indian tribes is the Konga-Vellalas who retain a dual organisation. This is composed of the Konga-Vellalas and the Tondan, also known as the Ilakanban-Kuttam (servant or inferior) made up of their illegitimate descendants[74]. Perhaps the Koravas in Central South India illustrate the various forms that dual organisations can develop from the basic principles of more advanced tribes imposing upon lesser tribes but applied in other fundamental ways. A report describing the organisational traditions of the Koravas was recorded as follows: "The Koravas are said to be divided into two large families, which they call Pothu and Penti, meaning male and female. All the families included in the first division noted above are Pothu, and those in the second Penti. The families in the third division, being the product of mixed marriages, and the position of females being a lowly one, they are also considered to be Penti. The Pothu section is said to have arisen from men going in search of brides for themselves, and the Pentis from men going in search of husbands for their daughters. When a Korava, male or female, wishes to marry, a partner must be sought in a division other than their own. For example, a Korava of the first division is bound to marry a female belonging to the second or third division, who after marriage belongs to her husband's division. This may be a little hard on the women of the first division, because they are bound to descend in their social scale. However, their daughters can rise by marrying into the first division. For the purpose of religious ceremonies, each division has fixed duties. The members of the first division have the right of decorating the god, and dressing him in his festival attire. Those of the second division carry the god and the regalia in procession, and burn incense, and those of the third drag the temple car, and sing and shout during its progress. For this reason, it is said, they are sometimes called Bandi (cart)."

"The major divisions," ..... "are four in number, and according to their graduation they are Sathepati, Kavadi, Manapadi, Mendragutti. They are all corrupted Tamil words."

The same author continues: "Of these four divisions, the first two are, or rather were, considered superior to the other two, a Kavadi man being styled Pothuvadu (man), and a Sathepadi man Penti (female)"[75].

The localised adaption of the dual system follows not the religious or cosmological divisions but the racial or tribal incursions of males into the lands of indigenous peoples from whom they took their marriage partners. But this observation from South India illustrates a pattern that is strikingly consistent with that resulting from Zuidema's analysis of available material relating to those of the first Incas after entering the valley of Cuzco. The vast numbers of tribes and castes in India preserved every possible social variation imaginable but in essence they all appear to commence with the cosmological introduction of the Tetrad prototype and these are then modified and adapted to a lesser or greater degree by contact and control by the Vedic and later Hindu Aryans. The adaptions were aimed at the Aryan racial and tribal necessity of preserving their own identity together with the practicality of selecting marriage partners from indigenous peoples all of whom they considered of a lesser status than themselves. In this the Inca myths and legends of caste and social organisation are consistent with the fundamental model in India as Miles Poindexter noted over two generations ago.

The Kota tribe, located in the Nilgiris south of Mysore in South India, already noted above for their caste streets, is also noted in one region for their four caste street village planning, or Keri, apart from the three street model. These are called Amreri, Kikeri, Korakeri, and Akkeri, otherwise "near street", "lower street", "other street" and "that street". These resolved themselves into two exogamous sections where Anreri and Kikeri form one group and Korakeri and Akkeri form the other[76]. Among the Kota there were two classes of priests, one of higher rank than the other. The Munthakannan or Pujari was the higher ranked and he was involved in the most sacred ceremonies related to the tribe's cattle herding, seed sowing and reaping rites along with the fire rituals and is the spiritual leader in the various regions of the tribes[77]. The Ter-Karan or Devadi is the lesser ranked and there may be more than two of them in a village, but they should belong to different keris or caste streets. The Munthakannan corresponds to the formal caste priest while the Per-Karan corresponded to the shaman or paye in South America. This arrangement of two priests, one of higher status and the other of lesser status, is found throughout India and across the Pacific into South America. This seems also to have correspondences reflected in the idea of dual clan leaders sharing power in Ancient Peru, and possibly among the Incan in particular postulated by Zuidema.

A Sudra (fourth division) caste of higher status potters in South India were the Kummaras or Kumbaras, who derived their named from the Sanskrit for "pot-maker", Kumbhakara. The word derives from ku = earth. They were divided into a dual organisation composed of two mutually exclusive endogamous (marrying within the clan) divisions and in these they were further divided into two exogamous (marrying outside their clan or bali, another name for sept or gotra). Characteristically one of the two divisions claimed superiority over the other[78].

The Kunnans were a tribe in South India whose caste is divided into three divisions, a development from the dual organisation where intermarriage between the two was allowed but their descendants were not admitted to the other two. These were the original dual organisation of Periya (Big) Kunnuvar, and Chinna (Little) Kunnuvar, and their intermediate division was called Kunnuvar, and these three divisions were called Vaguppas and cross-cousin marriage was strictly maintained among them[79]. The Kunnans maintained a ceremony common in Hindu India where an unmarried young man, but more likely an unmarried female, was married to a tree or other sacred object if a partner could not be found. The Kunnans, however, maintained their own variation to this custom in that if a girl was not claimed by the maternal uncle's son as was usual she was married to the door-posts of the house and a silver bangle was put on her right wrist instead of the tali (marriage badge) around her neck. The girl is then allowed to "consort" with any man of her caste and her earnings go to her parents. In this form of arrangement the girl becomes their heir and the son born from these liaisons inherits any property through her[80]. Marriages to trees, common in India are also found among some of the peoples of South America.

The Kurni are a caste of weavers and the name derives from kuri = sheep and vanni = wool, and it may have been that they were originally specialist weavers in wool. They are subdivided into a dual caste organisation named Hire = Big and Chikka = Small. They also retain the tradition of a dual priesthood, where the Hire employed Jangam priests and the Chikka accepted priests who were men from their own castes. The Hire maintain the higher status and do not eat meat, smoke or drink alcohol, in other words maintain the traditions of the Aryans Hindus while the Chikkas do all three indicating that this again is another example of a higher status group entering the territory of an alien people and setting up a dual organisation to separate their own traditions from that of the indigenous people. Each of the dual organisations were divided into gotras or clans, theoretically into sixty-six, claimed to have been established from the model of the Kuruhina Settis[81].

Left and Right-hand Divisions in Social Organisations

The fundamental duality of the organisations was imposed in the historic period as a result of the Aryans entering India and establishing such divisions to maintain their own integrity and mutuality from the indigenous peoples. This is reflected in this structure of "higher" and "lower", "big" and "small" - for the most part references to status, and there were also dualities in the same way but described as "left" and "right". The most extreme ends of the social scale tended to retain their caste and social systems in the purest form since the highest status, the Brahman had the most to loose while the lowest, such as the Chandalas, Paraiyans and Malas, had these systems in their most undiluted form imposed upon them from which they had no escape. But because these lowest status people were largely outcast they tended to retain the earliest pre-

Aryan social structures.

When the Vedic Aryans first entered India and encountered the Dasyus, many of whom, toward the south, were dark-skinned Dravidians, they vilified them as devilish people addicted to the most primitive and brutal practises. In Ancient India the philosophic belief in the right and left paths relating fundamentally to good and evil, light and dark, male and female, had been endemic for millennia and aspects of this belief appear also in the ancient Iranian beliefs. To the Aryans the natural principle that they should correspond, because of their light-coloured skin, with the light, day, the Sky, and therefore the Sun and their identification therefore to the male therefore to the right-hand side, was inevitable. Where such a belief system was so ancient it was seen as a natural correspondence therefore that the Dravidians and Negrito Aboriginal tribes of the Subcontinent would also correspond to the night, dark, demons known as Asuras, and the Earth, the female and the left hand side followed without difficulty. The Moon was not seen as part of this dark, left-handed system since it was bright and white and was particularly associated with the right, male side, since the lunar sphere was that associated with the white seminal fluid of the male, the Soma also known as the ambrosia of the gods. It is probably from this identification and cultural transfer that the Sperma cults of New Guinea derive.

The Mukha Dora hill tribe in South India claimed Aryan descent, even if only in part, reflected in their titles of Ayya and Anna. They were divided into a dual organisation where one section, the Kora-vamsam, worshipped the Sun (Kor or Kon = Sun) and therefore the Sky, and Nagas-vamsam who revered the Cobra (Naga) representing the Earth[82].

The Malas, as a low caste weaving tribe, preserved many of the most ancient traditions from earlier epochs in India, retained because they had for many centuries no access to the slow changes or advances introduced only in the higher echelons of Hindu society. They maintained a dual social organisation of two divisions - left and right. The right was divided into two further sub-sections and these divisions were separated into exogamous septs[83]. Other South Indian tribes are divided also into large and small such as the Malayalis where there are Peria (Big) Malayalis and Chinna (Little) Malaialis and these appear to derive from traditions relating to an

6.024 : A spatula reflecting a pillar with a hero or deity atop characteristic of imagery known in Peru in carvings and Inca myths. New Guinea, Melanesia, pre-20th., century, A.D.

6.025 : A pillar as the Axis Mundae or World Tree assimilated into the Jain religion from Brahmanic origins. This Jain pillar is called the Brahmadeva and is probably in principle the origin of references in Inca myth to one of the Ayar brothers becoming petrified atop a pillar. Panchakuta Basti, Kambadahalli, South India, 10th., century, A.D.

6.026 : Maori warriors performing the "haka", or war dance. The kilts reflect the bold geometric designs favoured by the Maori but also highly reminiscent of those traditional in Peru. Note the seated deity atop the gable pillar identical to those found in Melanesia and in a lesser scale in Ancient Peru. Maori, New Zealand, early 20th., century, A.D.

6.027 : Seated figures elevated on pillars are identical to those found on the Pacific Coast of South America. Melanesia, late 19th., century, A.D.

older and younger brother and therefore status and inheritance. In another tribal myth the Malayalis state that three brothers left the holy city of Kanchi (Conjeevam) near Madras, and set out for the hill regions to the west to carve out a territory for themselves. They took three different routes and set up three different territories. This legend undoubtedly attempts to explain the origin of their tribe but also the implied status of the three groups when interacting one with another. The elder brother retained the highest status and therefore corresponded with Peri or Big in the Aryan derived systems. The middle brother corresponded with the central mediating division where three organisations were established and second brothers were always considered the stand-by should anything fatal occur in the life of the elder brother. The youngest brother was always of the lowest status and in many situations was the "give-away" in any problematical negotiations, particularly where the highest status clans of the second group were seeking to increase status in marriage by association with the first division or some other necessity. The youngest brother was often seen as a threat by his siblings because of his lowest status among them and lack of inheritance, and in some traditional societies, these youngest brothers were sometimes outcasted or even killed by their siblings to avoid rivalry. There are many examples of the youngest brother seeking to usurp the older brothers inheritance and status in Melanesia and these customs probably derived from India. In Burma (Myanmar) a retained tradition into the 19th., century was that when an heir to the throne succeeded his father was to round up his siblings and kill them all, often by burying them alive in a large pit.

Among the Malayalis also there was a variation on the tradition of the three brothers that a priest, who was the brother of the king, left Kanchi for the west of South India together with his three sons and daughters. They entered the country ruled by the Vedans and Vellalans who resisted their entry, but the "conch-shell blew and the quoit cut" and the priest and his family defeated the people of that land. After the battle there was no food and the brothers sold one of the sisters to obtain supplies. This curious legend has elements reminiscent of the Inca's entering the new lands of the Cuzco valley from Huarochiri. where one of the brothers, Ayar Cachi (or sometimes Ayar Uchu) was walled up in a cave, and another turned to stone on a pillar (*6.025*). This reflects other losses among the origin four brothers, some say more other say less and where Manco Capac is ultimately the only one left with his sister, Mama Ocllo, to establish the city of Cuzco[84].

The Mangala are a barber caste in South India who retained the Aryan titles of Anna and Ayya. They were divided into a dual endogamous, mutually exclusive organisation called Telapa and Kapu. The ancestors of these dual divisions were said to have been half-brothers with the same father but different mothers[85], illustrating the recognition to remove too closely related peoples from allowable marriage structures.

Another form of dual organisation occurs among the Omanaito, an Oriya cultivating tribe, centred originally in Orissa whose dual divisions were called Bodo (Big) and Sanno (Little). The Bodo are the legitimate tribal members but the Sanno are the section formed from the illegitimate children of the Bodo and other women from outside their tribe or caste. The legitimate division represented the original descendants of the tribal or caste ancestors while the larger number of other peoples with whom they came into contact were too many or too scattered to be separated into an attached menial, or inferior class and the descendants from the Bodo. These other peoples became what was the second of the dual division but would, in other more stable regions, have been the intermediate division of three[86]. The Odde or Voddas were a prominent working caste associated with major earth and stone works in the Central India. They were divided into two divisions forming a dual organisation, one branch known as the Kallu Vaddas who considered themselves of higher status, while the other was the Manu Vaddas[87]. The former formed a more stable caste while the Manu Vaddas were largely nomadic suggesting a similar

6.030 : Squared form of studded headdress similar to those at La Tolita in Ecuador. Assyrian, first half of the first millennium, B.C.

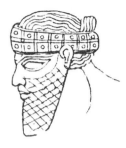

6.031 : Plated form of studded headdress similar to those at La Tolita in Ecuador. Assyrian, first half of the first millennium, B.C.

6.028 + 6.029 : Finely modelled portrait head wearing a headdress reminiscent of the plated form and design from Assyria. La Tolita, Esmeraldas, Ecuador, 400 B.C. - 500 A.D.

6.034 : Bird Headdress similar to that found among the Maya and those in China. La Tolita, Esmeraldas, Ecuador, 400 B.C. - 500 A.D.

6.033 : Bird headdress worn by a ballplayer, a figurine headdress closely similar to those depicted in China)in the T'ang Dynasty and from the Ecuadorian Coast . Mayan, Jaina, Campeche, Yucatan, 700-900 A.D.

6.032 : Bird headdress on female figure in the T'ang Dynasty, China, 8th., century, A.D.

6.035 : Studded regal helmet made from glazed pottery with bronze nails probably related in principle to the studded Assyrian browbands noted in *6.030/1* and those from Tumaco in *6.028/9*. Elam, Mesopotamia, 2nd., millennium, B.C.

arrangement developing in a slightly different way to the Omanaito in Orissa.

In Orissa also are the Patra caste who are silk-weavers, a higher caste occupation because of the finer, more expensive product. They are an Oriya caste and both of the divisions of their dual organisation are engaged in silk production but they did not eat together indicating that one was of a higher status than the other reflecting separate ancestral traditions[88]. The overall caste head was called Maha-Nayako, a title associated with, and almost certainly derived from the Aryan traditions where maha meaning "great". A Canarese caste of silk weavers, the Patvegara, were also divided into a dual social organisation called Bodo (Big or Genuine) and Sanno (Little) and the latter were considered to be the illegitimate descendants of the former. The Bodo were divided into the classic subdivisions more related to the ancient Aryan-Hindu cosmology where septs or clans were called Kurum (=Tortoise); Bhag (=Tiger); Nag (=Cobra) and Surya (=Sun)[89].

Canara and Orissa were at opposite ends of India, Canara being on the South West Coast and Orissa in the North East Coast, a little south west of the Ganges and Brahmaputra Deltas. Their dual organisations and clan arrangements are so closely similar it is almost certain that they have a common origin in transfer by mariners and traders travelling over long distances around the coast of India before the advent of European influence in the Subcontinent. Another high status caste of weavers was the Sale, from the Sanskrit, Salika - a weaver. Their dual organisation was divided into the two endogamous divisions called the Padma, or Lotus, and the Pattu, or silk, where the former were of a higher degree and status than the latter[90].

One of the most prototypical of the dual organisations occurs among the Semman who were low caste Tamil leatherworkers. These people were considered a section of the Paraiyan peoples but their dual divisions, named Tondaman and Tolmestri, were arranged so that the men from the Tondaman took their wives from the Tolmestri, but the men of the Tolmestri could not marry women from the Tondaman[91]. This undoubtedly derived from a time when the incursive invaders of the region, usually all or mostly male required to purchase, seize or capture their brides from local tribes, either by arrangement or force. There would have been so few females of their own tribe or race forming the Tondaman for some generations that women were not allowed to marry outside their higher status division in an attempt to preserve the tribal identity, a characteristic long known of the Aryans, and probably borrowed from contact with them or as an earlier offshoot from them. Similar traditions formed the basis of a number of tribes in South America and were also fundamental to that of the highest caste of the Incas, in the Collana division.

Where intermarriage has occurred among the two fundamental dual organisations and a third, or more, is formed this can be treated as a repository of lower status or resulting undesirables unacceptable to the other two divisions. It may also be that where the original dual organisations remain separate and endogamous or mutually exclusive, the illegitimate members of both of these divisions are assigned to the third. This section can be treated as an exile or excommunication from the legitimate dual divisions or as a division from which are drawn marriage partners only by necessity. This form of organisation occurs among the Sondi, an Oriya palm-wine merchant caste[92] and is likely that the original dual divisions had been developed in a similar way among the Incas in the earliest generations.

6.036 : Bejewelled helmet with elaborate makara-serpents descending from the top each side. Such headdresses are probably the prototype for those of the Muisca, Chibcha and Inca of South America. Sembadavan Mayana Kollai Tribe, South India, early 20th., century, A.D.

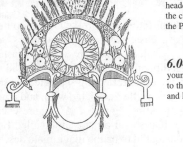

6.038 : Headdress of the high priest of the Inca Empire. Note the cranial form similar to the earlier headdresses in Colombia among the Muiscas but with the circle and dot patterns common in South India and the Pacific. Cuzco, Peru, early 16th., century, A.D.

6.040 : A Velan dancer and musician group. The young lady wears a crown that appears closely related to those found in Colombia (*6.039*) in South America and Peru. South India, early 20th., century, A.D.

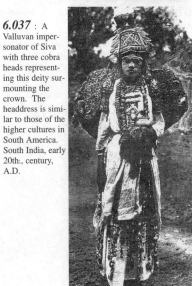

6.037 : A Valluvan impersonator of Siva with three cobra heads representing this deity surmounting the crown. The headdress is similar to those of the higher cultures in South America. South India, early 20th., century, A.D.

6.039 : The crown of a Chibcha or Muisca style but apparently related also to the Inca. Note the shells surrounding the crown rim similar to that of the hornbill headdresses of New Guinea (*4.024*). Colombia, 1000-1500 A.D.

6.041 : Pill-box style cap so similar to those depicted in Ancient Peru and Bolivia. Dyak, Borneo, early 20th., century, A.D.

6.042 : Typical traditional Indonesian pill-box hat some being plain while others are elaborate. Dyak, Borneo, early 20th., century, A.D.

6.043 : Tapestry velvet pile cap typical of Tiahuanaco and Ancient Peru but closely similar to those in shape and design to those traditional in Indonesia. Tiahuanaco, Huari period, 700-1000 A.D.

44 : Fine carving of two rulers or high status men with that resemble those found traditionally in Indonesia and ng the Gond of Central India (*5.158*). Embroidered caps in uanaco and the Huari also resemble those of the Dyaks of eo (*6.041; 6.043*). Tiahuanaco, Bolivia, 400-800 A.D.

6.045 : Traditional pill-box style hat worn by a Andean highland dignitary similar to the characteristic woven cap long traditional in Indonesia. Tiahuanaco, Bolivia, 1st., millennium, A.D.

6.046: Traditional Semai Senoi pill-box woven cane hats typical in Indonesia and the Malay Peninsula. Ancient forms of these hats appear to have been the model for those found from the Moche period through to the Inca Dynasty. Padang, Perak District, Malaysia, mid 20th., century, A.D.

In one of the most interesting variations of dual organisations, so obviously having common origins with those so widespread throughout India, is that of the Vannan (also Bannan) in South India. It has been suggested earlier that the term Van or Ban drives from Lake Van in what was Armenia, although the origins have long been modified and forgotten, but there are now known contacts between the Caucasus and Anatolia in India as far back as the Hittites. Another practise that links these people with the Ancient Middle East and the Todas of South India is that one of their main divisions practised "fraternal polyandry", or brothers marrying the same bride. Interesting also was the term for the higher status endogamous division, this being Peru-Manna, where Peru meant "big" or "great", and Tinda-Mannan where Tinda = "pollution"[93]. The probable transfer of the many elements from India to Peru in more ancient times must beg the question of whether the Vannan term for "greatness", peru was also the name adopted in some reference through links to South America. Similar references including the term Peru are found in clan names. Before an answer can be posited more research requires to be done, but the Vannans were professionally employed with cleansing and ritual cloths from the washermen caste indicating that their lives were associated with the weavers and cloth producers and ritual use of textiles after their production. The Vannan women were usually employed in the actual washing even with the higher status castes and the men were exorcists, "devil-dancers" and physicians and claimed the right to carry the ceremonial parasol at the Puram festivals[94].

The principle of left-handed and right-handed applied in India appears to derive from Iran where right- and left-handedness was an essential element in their philosophy. The right hand was that used by the priests in benediction, greeting, and purifying and was used for eating and these tenets were assimilated into Hindu India. The right side of the body was where the liver was located, used in diagnostics in both medicine and divination in the Ancient Middle East as in India, parts of Indonesia and Ancient Peru[95]. The right side also was symbolically that associated with the Moon and the constellations, and these were considered masculine in the earliest recorded period of Mesopotamian history. The Moon (and the Sun) was considered masculine also in India and reflections of this gender association and the name for the Moon, Sin, or Sina are found across a wide distance that could only have been transferred by mariners at that, or a later time. The left side was considered reflective of evil, and demons and the early kings were depicted protected with the left-leg uncovered and advanced possibly as an indication of protecting attack from that side[96].

6.047 : Fine textile design with unusual crown designs in South America displayed by the two winged figures more typical of those in West Asia. This example was found beneath the temple at Pachacamac where other aspects of Asian culture are prominent. Pachacamac, South Peru, 1st., millennium, A.D.

The division of clans into greater and lesser dual divisions in India, where the descendants of the Aryan invaders, who imposed the rules, considered themselves the right-hand, and the lower status castes from whom, where necessary, they selected their brides, were deemed the left-handed. This also corresponded to their religious beliefs where they observed the laws of sacrifices to the gods and the Dasyus who formed the indigenous and Dravidians tribes were considered demon-worshippers and were therefore designated left-handed. Although many of the Aryan tribes became degraded as centuries passed with increasing intermarriage with lower status the Dravidian castes or Aboriginal tribes of India, the division into dual sections, and frequently also the identification of one with the right and the other with the left, remained firm within the Hindu society of India into the twentieth century.

Because the lower castes, and left-handed sections, were considered to pollute the higher status castes or right-handed divisions, strict regulations in their association and customs were applied. References to such caste disputes between the left and right-handed section of the Komatis were recorded during the governorship of Aaron Baker in 1652 A.D. in Madras and in that of William Pitt in 1707 A.D. In the latter dispute Pitt was able to finalise an agreement where one section settled on the opposite, east section of the town, the other on the west[97]. The Ganigas

6.049 : Stepped crown of the Sassanid king, Shapur 1, identical to those found on the Peruvian Coast in the Moche epoch. Sassanid, 3rd., century, A.D.

6.050 : Finely carved blue stor crowned head found in the Hall o the Thirty-two Columns. The stepped crown is identical to thos depicted on contemporary carvin and silver platter designs and in India. Achaemenid Dynasty, Persepolis, 4th., century, A.D.

6.048 : Stepped crown motif with an abstracted tumi elevated from the centre probably originating in Iran but also found in Tibet. Central Peru, Peru, 1st., millennium, A.D.

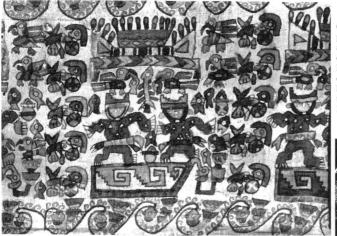

051 : A fine [pain]ted textile [dep]icting two [figur]ies with serpent [head]s and Stepped [Cro]wns in the style [fou]nd among the [Mo]che but also [iden]tical to those of [the] contemporary [Sas]sanids in [Anc]ient Iran. The [figures] stand on a plat[for]m of two South [Am]erican spiral [motif]s. Pachacamac, [Sout]h Coast Peru, [first] millennium,

6.052 : A section of the centre of a fine silver platter showing the Sassanian king, with the characteristic stepped crown, and surmounting crescent found also among the Moche on the Peruvian coast. The queen wears the dual horn crown probably one of the origins of similar headdresses and feather substitutes in India throughout the Pacific to South America. Iran, First half of the first millennium, A.D.

6.054 : Finely carved head, probably by Iranian craftsmen, showing the king with a stepped crown of the Iranian type. After the fall of Persepolis there was a large movement of craftsmen into India and their presence is clear in the fine stone sculptures in the last centuries B.C. Mauryan dynasty, Sarnath, 3rd., century, A.D.

6.055 : The stepped crowns clearly derived in inspiration from Ancient Iran that could only be imported by cultural diffusion by mariners across the Pacific Ocean to the Moche of Peru. Sassanian, Iran, 309-79 A.D.

[6.0]53 : Fine silver platter dating from the Sassanian [dyn]asty in Ancient Iran showing the king, Shapur 1, with a [crow]n identical to those found so frequently on the North [Cent]ral Coast of Peru in the contemporary time zone. This [stepp]ed crown is not only the same but also with a lunar [cresc]ent as found among the Moche. The mouth binding is [typic]al of the fire-religions in Iran and the layered couch on [whic]h the king sits is also found among the Maya. Sassanid [dyn]asty, Iran, 6-7th., century, A.D.

6.056 : Bronze Moche warrior with stepped crown identical to those in the contemporary Parthian and Sassanid Dynasties in Ancient Iran and Mesopotamia. The tumi surmounting the crown is also found there. Loma Negra, Vicus, 300 B.C. - 300 A.D.

were also divided into left and right-handed divisions[98], and one of their tribal divisions is called Kallu meaning a stone, a term almost certainly derived from the Ancient Middle East and apparently found in Ancient Peru. Other left-handed castes were the Gollas and Mutrachas and difficulties were often a common problem in their relationships[99].

The weaving castes, who will be of more interest in the last chapter, were in some cases recognised as left or right-hand castes. The Padma Sales, dealers in fine cloths, were designated right-handed befitting their higher status while the Devangas were considered left-handed and of a lesser status[100]. In some regions such as at Conjeeverum (Kanchi) the Devangas were identified with right-handed section. Many anomalies occur in caste customs, but this is understandable when it is known that the left and right-handed sections relate also to status and alleged pollution. Such problems that arise cause friction therefore between the two divisions often one, the higher right-handed section, refusing even to dine with the other and such problems as these

6.057 : Unusual headdresses traditional in Celebes in the land of the Toradjas similar to that found among the Indians of North America. South West Celebes, late 19th., century, A.D.

6.058 : Unusual headdress worn by a North American Plains Indian a century, ago apparently derived from the people of Celebes in Indonesia. Omaha, North Plains USA, late 19th., century, A.D.

occur with the Kammalas[101].

The duality of left and right occurred occasionally between two castes, probably with common origins, who have spilt apart into separate tribes or castes. A Madiga sword dance, banned by the British in 1859 A.D. and 1874 A.D., was accompanied by a song including one verse as follows: "I shall cut with my saw the Malas of the four houses (caste divisions) at Nandgal, and, having caused them to be cut up, shall remove their skins, and fix them to drums"[102]. The Madigas and Malas were low status castes in Southern India but who were anciently the probable ruling tribes who had been relegated by the later Hindu Aryans. It would appear that they were two sides of a left- and right-handed tribe or allies where the Madigas were considered to be "left-handed" and the Malas "right-handed". The ancient threat preserved in the sword dance to use the skins of the Malas to cover their drums reflects the identical customs so widely known in Indonesia and in South America[103].

Other anomalies occurred in the long development and the inevitable corruption of the dual organisation system applied in India and among the Pallis, in South India, a people to be of some interest in the last chapters of this work, the caste was considered as left-handed but the men were employed in fighting for the right-hand castes indicating the modification and compromises instituted over millennia. The Chakkiliyans also were classified as left-handed and their women took the stance opposite to that their husbands supported. This suggests that there were traditions of marriage capture in their ancestral history where brides from incursive males, either migrating or displaced, seized women from whichever tribes occupied the lands they usurped, and to whom they remained hostile. Among this caste the women were known to resort to connubial denial when their husbands were being employed to support the right-handed castes[104]. This has reflections among the Kurnai women opposing and fighting their men in Aboriginal South Eastern Australia[105].

Left-Right and Child Sacrifice in India Madagascar and Peru

The Mala tribe in South India, already noted, were themselves divided into a dual organisation system and one was considered left-handed the other right-handed[106]. One of the most interesting customs banned by the British was that of child sacrifice among them known also among other tribes in South India. This was the sacrifice of a child that must have had very ancient origins among the cattle-herders of Central Asia where the child was placed in a hole in the ground at the entrance to the village and back-filled with the excess earth allowing only the head to protrude above the ground level. A herd of cattle was then driven across the spot and anointed with herbal ointment called Poli as they did so[107]. This form of sacrifice was also known among other tribes such as the Korava[108], Lambadis[109] and the Todas[110]. It is believed that this form of sacrifice was exported to Madagascar where it has been recorded and it seems that this sacrifice was intended to originally provide the child's spirit as a guardian to the entrance gate of the cattle pen or the road along which they were driven. Although there is no written evidence that the South Americans sacrificed children in this way, since they had no equivalent of cattle, the Incas were known to have placed their children in pits wrapping them in "dirty napkins" while their mothers were occupied during working hours or otherwise employed[111]. This may have been a vague memory of the tradition associated with cattle-driven sacrifice that lapsed as a result of the lack of suitable replacement animals in South America. Placing children in pits to secure them without reference to child sacrifice was also known in India, above referred to, and thc Malas in the 20th., century eventually substituted a pig for a child in their rituals.

Right-Hand and Left-Hand Reflected in Australia Aboriginal Traditions
Aboriginal Australia preserved many cultural aspects transferred from India, particularly South India, and other references that are clearly derived from the Mundas and Bhuiyas of Orissa. One of the unusual aspects noted of the Wakelbura tribe in South East Australia, a region noted for its Polynesian cultural contacts, was that they believed that right-handed men went up to sky after death while the left-handed men went down into the ground[112]. The Wakelbura believed that the white-people were the left-handed ancestors returning to them and in this their belief is opposite to that held in India and Polynesia where the European explorers and settlers were identified with ancient mariner ancestors or "papalangi". The Wakelbura belief that the right-handed were identified with the sky is identical with those in India where Vishnu was the supreme Aryan deity of Hinduism associated with the right-handed tribes and castes. This Sky deity formed a polarity with Siva, the deity associated with the serpent who emerge from the Earth, and as the river Ganga, and patronised particularly by the left-handed tribes and castes along with the pre-Aryan "demonic" village religions and their gods.

The clan systems in India were greatly complicated with the long period of cultural and tribal interactions among the peoples of India and they appear to be reflected in the adaptions in the transference of Aryan ideals by the Ayar Incas into Peru. Only a few references to the left hand are recorded in Peru by the Spanish but Father Pablo Joseph de Arriaga noted that; "When they have made their offerings brought by the priest they invoke the huaca, as we have said, by raising their left hand and opening it toward the huaca with a motion as if they were kissing it. On such occasions they must wear no Spanish clothing, not any hat or shoes ..."[113]. The references may not appear to have great significance but such ritual "kissing" was particularly associated by the Spanish priests with demonism in the Old Testament of the Bible and this will be of more interest later in this work. However, the priest here uses his left hand suggesting a recognition of the officiant's inferiority to the god or huaca being addressed indicating that the huaca spirit or god itself was superior to himself and the congregated worshippers in these ceremonials and corresponds with the general symbolic presentations in the Ancient Vedic ceremonies and Hindu rites

Beliefs in Pollution Rituals in India and Peru
Close similarities between the traditions of India and Peru have been noted many times throughout this work and another of some interest is that surrounding the rituals considered essential to cleanse where pollution was considered to have contaminated, either spiritually or physically the person or clan. These were particularly associated with funerary rites where to touch the deceased human body was considered to contaminate the persons preparing the body for burial and extended even to those attending the funeral and subsequent interment.

The observant Spanish priest, Father Pablo Joseph de Arriaga, although sent to eradicate the rites and "superstitions" of the native Peruvians, did in fact leave to posterity one of the best eye-witness accounts of the existing belief system still surviving into the 16th., century. It was Arriaga who related that a Peruvian Indian girl was married to a tree to preserve her virginity[114], and such a marriage rite was also widely known in India anciently into the last century. The touching of the body at death was believed by many of the Peruvian Indians to incur pollution and both in the cleansing ceremonies and the funerary rites the procedures are highly reminiscent of those in India and the Near and Ancient Middle East.

6.059 :
One of a series of the Incan rulers painted by an Incan descendant, Dr. Justo Sahuaraura. Peru, Late 16/7th., century, A.D.

Arriaga recorded; "At death" .... "Under the winding shroud they frequently dress the dead in new clothing, whereas at other times they merely folded clothing on top of them, without putting it on. They perform the Pacaricuc, or all-night vigil, with sad songs, etc.," .... "Then, when the dead man is carried out, they close up the door that he passes through and never use it again."

"In some localities they scatter corn meal or quinua meal about the house in order to find out, so they say, by the tracks in the meal whether the person has come back."

"In some towns in the lowlands, the clan come together with the relatives ten days after a death occurs to accompany the nearest relative to a spring or flowing stream that has been agreed upon. There they duck him three times and wash all the dead person's clothes. After this they have a picnic at which they spit out the first mouthful they chew. When the drunkedness is over, they return to the house and block off the dead person's room. They throw out the rubbish while the sorcerers sing, and they keep on singing and drinking all the next night for the soul of the dead. They say he returns to eat and drink, and when they are well into their wine they say the soul is coming, and they pour out a lot of wine (that Arriaga alludes is chichi, acca or azua) and offer it to him. The next morning they say the soul is now in Zamayhuaci, or the house of rest, and will never return again. The Pacaricuc (Pacaric = reborn, what returns, the dawn) usually lasts for five days, during which they fast, eating only white corn and meat and abstaining from salt and pepper. And they play a game called Pisca (variant is Pishcia or Pichca = 5) which uses the names of five days. It is played with little sticks with stripes. I do not believe there is any mysterious reason for this but that it is used to beguile their sleepiness. When the five days are up, they wash the dead man's

TUPAC INCA IUPANQUI

6.063 : Dual feather springing from a flat cap similar to depictions of the Inca crown. Campa, Eastern Peru, Early 20th., century, A.D.

6.060 : Gold pectoral showing the dual feathers indicating status. Also depicted if the dual spiral found anciently in Assyria, India and through to Indonesia to South America. The cord bindings around the figure are similar to bindings found in Indian mystical postures. Colombia, 700-1000 A.D.

6.061 : Textile figure with turban and dual feathers projecting upward. Chimu/Chancay, North Central Peru, 100-1450 A.D.

6.062 : Gond youth with traditional turban surmounted by twin feathers in the identical manner known of the Incas (6.059) and other South American cultures (6.062) and found throughout the Pacific region. Tinmar, Central India, Early 20th., century, A.D.

6.065 : Dual headdress found on this incised obsidian flake and this is identical to that found on the Moche ceramic in *6.064*. Maya, Belize, Late Classic, 600-900 A.D.

6.066 : Mosaic crown with upward extending dual imitation feathers in a step form reminiscent of South American designs. Aztec (Mixtec?), Central America, 1300-1521 A.D.

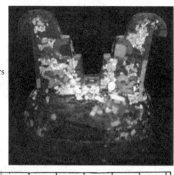

6.064 : Dual feathers or split headdress are characteristic in Ancient South America but also common throughout Polynesia through to Indonesia and South East Asia. This example is from a Moche ceramic design. Moche, Chimbote, North Central Coast of Peru, 200-600 A.D.

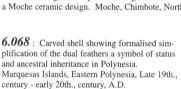

6.068 : Carved shell showing formalised simplification of the dual feathers a symbol of status and ancestral inheritance in Polynesia. Marquesas Islands, Eastern Polynesia, Late 19th., century - early 20th., century, A.D.

6.069 : Gold figurine with dual headdress as serpents. Diguis Delta, Costa Rica, 800-1525 A.D.

6.067 : Dual horns presented in a manner that was emulated by rulers in rams' horn crowns in Ancient Iran (*6.052*) and probably the model with feather substitutes throughout the Pacific region and South America. Winged Griffon, Persepolis, S.W. Iran, 6th., century, B.C.

6.070 : Wall drawing showing a tribal goddess with the characteristic dual headdress and hairstyle typical in many depictions in Ancient India through to South America. Golla Ganga Muggu, South India, Early 20th., century, A.D.

clothes in the river."[115]. Arriaga notes similar rites occurred at Huanacari, a place of great importance in the Inca Origin myths associated with Manco Capac.

The laying out, washing and dressing the body in new clothes is a characteristic known not only in the Near and Ancient Middle East and India but also throughout the Mediterranean and these are rites still adhered to from before Biblical times into the present day. These ancient rites are virtually identical to those in Peru witnessed by Arriaga and other Spanish eyewitness accounts. After the burial the second Peruvian rite of scattering corn meal on the floor to elicit whether the soul of the deceased has returned is of particular interest since this occurs identically in India and Polynesia into the last century.

In India there are many similar rites to those taken as a whole or as individual sectors of the funerary traditions in Peru and among the Bhondari, as among the Peruvians the burial ceremony focuses on, or is conducted by the nearest male relative, either the eldest son or a brother. After the funeral; pyre the ashes of the deceased are heaped up on the ground and an image is carved with a stick representing him and food is offered. Agnates partake of a meal and after ten days, being shaved, the son and agnates go to the bund, or water tank, and there in a hut anoth-

er feast is undertaken in the memory of the deceased. After this all bathe to cleanse the pollution and after this two bone fragments of the deceased are placed in a pot and buried under the root of a sacred pipal tree (banyan family) and this is lustrated with water. Other aspects of the interment tradition are carried out before the eliciting of the soul's return is undertaken. Edgar Thurston records this custom among the Bhondari; "If an important elder of the community dies, a ceremony called jola-jola handi (pot drilled with holes) is performed on the night of the tenth day. Fine sand is spread over the floor of a room having two doors, and the surface is smoothed with a tray or plank. On the sand a lighted lamp is placed, with an areca nut by its side. The lamp is covered with an earthen cooking-pot. Two men carry on their shoulders a pot riddled with holes, suspended from a pole made of Diospyros Embryopteris wood, from inside the room into the street, as soon as the lamp is covered by the cooking-pot. Both the doors of the room are then closed, and not opened till the return of the men. The pot which they carry is believed to increase in weight as they bear it to a tank, into which it is thrown. On their return to the house,

6.073 : Dyak warriors many displaying the long single plume depicted frequently in early Dongson imagery of North Vietnam and the dual feathers are characteristic also among the people from the Nagas of Assam, some of the Aboriginal tribes in India through to the Maoris and into South America. Murats, Sarawak, Borneo, Early 20th., century, A.D.

6.071 : Carved pillar with turban and dual "feathers" similar to the traditional depictions of Naga memorial effigies. Paracas, South Central Peru, Early first Millennium, A.D.

6.072 : A plaque with dual feathers headdress projecting from the crown of the turbans. Traditional clubs and the "megalithic S" survive from at least before the Moche period two thousand years earlier. Inca Dynasty, Peru, 1350-1500 A.D.

6.075 : Maori high status woman, named Goldie, displaying the dual feathers common among the arikis and high status clans and rulers through the Pacific, India and South America. She also wears the tiki as a pendant around her neck. New Zealand, Late 19th., century, A.D.

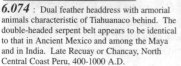

6.074 : Dual feather headdress with armorial animals characteristic of Tiahuanaco behind. The double-headed serpent belt appears to be identical to that in Ancient Mexico and among the Maya and in India. Late Recuay or Chancay, North Central Coast Peru, 400-1000 A.D.

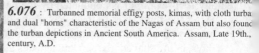

6.076 : Turbanned memorial effigy posts, kimas, with cloth turba and dual "horns" characteristic of the Nagas of Assam but also found the turban depictions in Ancient South America. Assam, Late 19th., century, A.D.

they tap three times on the door, which then opens. All present then crowd into the room, and examine the sand for the marks of the footprints, of a bull, cat or man, the trail of a centipede, cart-track, ladder, etc., which are believed to be left by the dead person when he goes to the other world."[116].

The funerary rites of the Bhondaris are closely similar to the Peruvian rituals reported by Arriaga and another similar variant of the rite in India is also noted by Thurston and given here in part only; "Like other Oriya castes, the Haddis observe pollution" ... "Some Haddis proceed, on the tenth day, to the spot where the corpse was cremated or buried, and, after making an effigy on the ground, offer food. Towards night, they proceed to some distance from the house, and place food and fruits on a cloth, spread on the ground. They then call the dead man by his name, and eagerly wait till some insect settles on the cloth. A soon as this happens the cloth is folded up, carried home, and shaken over the floor close to the spot where the household gods are kept, so that the insect falls on the sanded floor, and is covered with a pot. After some time, the pot is removed, and the sand examined for any marks which may be left by it. This ceremony seems to correspond to the Jola Jola Handi (pierced pot) ceremony of other castes."[117].

In these closely similar rites in India to those of Peru sand is used instead of flour to detect the returning spirit. It should not be surprising therefore that the Bhuiyas, so important in this work and earlier expositions should also have similar traditions. Sarat Chandra Roy recorded from his researches among the Hill Bhuiyas of Orissa that as part of the funerary rites a pot containing some cooked goat's flesh is set up on a tripod at the village boundary. Another man carries a new pot containing rice-flour; a third man carries two sickles or a brass cup in his left hand and a stick in his right. At sunset the pot on the tripod is smashed and the men call the spirit of the deceased who is thought to be attracted by the smell of the cooked meat and it is thought that he enters the pot containing the rice-flour. This is carried back home and the rice flour is then examined for footprints believed to be left by the soul of the dead man. When the footprints or tracks have been detected the rice-flour is then cooked and eaten and this may be the origin of grinding and eating the bones of the deceased known in India[118] and in South America[119].

In a Hindu rite called the Sraddha or among the Bhuiyas, Suddha (Purification), an annual celebration directed toward the ancestors, the relatives of the deceased among the Hill Bhuiyas go to the crossing of two roads and after cleansing of the spot, offer arua rice and turmeric powder. The offering is made to the high god, Dharam the Sky god, and Basuki, the Earth mother, as well as the ancestor spirits. Roy notes following this offering; "If a red ant or a white ant or some other worm is found on the cleaned crossing, it is taken up and carried hone in a leaf; and if no worm or other thing is found on the spot a leaf or a grain of rice is picked up and carried home. After reaching their home the ant or worm is let loose on the floor and it is thought to bring them happiness[120].

Other examples of the soul being detected as a worm or insect are found among the Nagas of Assam. The Sema Nagas believed that the soul entered a butterfly, or other insect after death[121] and similar beliefs occur among the Lhota Nagas and the other tribes[122]. Laying out a cloth after the death of a friend and waiting for an insect to crawl across it, this being recognised as the soul, was known in Samoa[123] and this is confirmed by earlier reports by the Reverend John Stair[124]. The pollution and other aspects of the burial rites in India are too extensive and well reported to include any further here but it is sufficient to point out the close similarities in all aspects of the corresponding rites in Peru with those of Asia to be considered coincidental.

The Inca Ayllu

In Ancient Peru the tradition of the dual organisation expressed through the ayllu or clan system has been the subject of an intensive study already referred to in part by R. Tom Zuidema and to

6.077 : The heroic statue of Ashurnatsirpal 111 holding a club and to the left in his right hand an implement believed to be for the ritual opening of the mouth after death, a ritual known among the Moche at Sipan in Coastal North Peru. The same implement is seen in *7.005*. Nimrud, Babylonian Period, Mesopotamia, c9th., century, A.D.

6.078 : Hydra or the seven-headed dragon probably related to the mushussu deity associated with the solar deity Marduk. Akkad Dynasty, Iraq, Late third millennium, B.C.

6.079 : The World Tree was perceived in Buddhist myth to be a great spirit and was depicted as a serpent or dragon. The inheritance from the Mesopotamian Mushussu is clear in this Chinese stela. Eastern Wei Dynasty, China, 546 A.D.

a lesser degree by other scholars and need not be considered in as great a depth here. The ayllu is recognised as a kinship organisation[125] parallel to similar clan divisions found in the Old World. These form the governmental basis of Inca society and in Cuzco, at the centre of their Empire, there were two shrines representing the dual organisations of Hanan-Cuzco and Hurin-Cuzco[126]. Interestingly one of the rituals recorded of the Incas was a ritual mock battle between the two main ayllu groups representing the dual organisations at Tambo near Pacariqtambo in the Andes[127]. This suggests that these were originally associated with left and right-handed identifications between the ayllus and the imposition of the higher status over the lower status divisions that is virtually identical to that found so widely in India where mock battles of a similar type and for similar reasons were common earlier noted.

More recent scholarship indicates that the regional model or bipartition of the Inca state into Hanan and Hurin originated in Tiahuanaco[128], but as will be shown both the Inca and Tiahuanaco almost certainly derived their traditions through transfer from Ancient India. The archaeology and investigation into the surviving Spanish chronicles and texts as well as surviving traditions among the Peruvian Indians suggests that their ancient society was divided into these dual organisations and that they cooperated in earthworks and engineering undertakings for civil works, irrigation and construction of agricultural terracing. It is likely that the higher status ayllu provided the directors and architects, corresponding to present day European "white-collar" workers, while the lower status ayllu provided the labourers and artisans corresponding to "blue-collar" workers in present-day society, much as the dual organisations were so divided in India.

More recent research into the ayllu and their structure defined by the early Incas has been recorded from Salcamayhua and other Peruvian and Spanish writers. The Bolivian mountain community of Kaata was researched and explored by Joseph Bastien in the third quarter of last (twentieth) century. His study is held to be a model of the form the ayllu system evolved into or the principles on which it was established at the time of the Inca Empire. Kaata was a settlement at the centre of a region divided into high, middle - or centre, and low zones related to environmental regions and here a social structure was conceived on cosmological principles that was reflected in the daily life of the inhabitants in economic and ritual exchange through social intercourse. Aymara-speaking peoples inhabited the upper regions while the lowlands were occupied by Quechua-speakers. The conceptual view of the community was that the highland within the zone was the "head", the centre the "heart and bowel", and the lowlands the "legs". The head was uma meaning "head" in Quechua but "water" in Aymara and was considered the place where the souls of the newborn descended to commence their life cycle and at its end the departed soul returned to complete that cycle[129]. This followed, in principle, the ritual decent of water from the mountaintops down through streams and rivers to the "great ocean" where it was believed to return underground and emerge again at the top of the mountain. The cycles associated with water and that of the human soul is found almost identically in India as it is in Ancient Bolivia and Peru. This apparently prototype ayllu concept from which the Inca concept evolved appears somewhat more sublime than that imposed by the Inca at Cuzco suggesting that its origins were earlier than simply derived from that during the Inca control in the Empire period. The centre of the three zones was therefore seen as a median point between the two environmental extremes of mountain peak and valley floor and these were seen to correspond to the two caste divisions in the dual organisation system. This social structure appears identical in Bolivia and Peru where the centre of this duality was the third division resulting as the interaction or breeding between two different tribes and races. This seems to reflect exactly that of the Aryans and Dravidians in India, whereas this principle is reflected in South America by the Aymaras and Quechua at Kaata, but probably also early by the Ayar Incas and the Aymaras and later the Quechua when they migrated to Cuzco in Peru.

The original dual organisation into three divisions appears in the written records of the early Spanish and was retained in their more original form in the clans of the Aymara. The Incas, however, developed the clan system to correspond with a decimal system of 10, but where each section was further divided into two. The fundamental divisions of ten provided organisational units of 5, 10, 50, 100, 500, 1,000, 5,000 and 10,000. This system was used in association with the Inca clan system that was based at Cuzco, and evident only there but where the division of 5 derived in principle from the Chimu, where ten clans were divided into two groups of five[130].

When adopted by the Incas the ten clans divided into two groups of five were then assigned to the four quarters or suyu and these were characterized by the four major roads that radiated from Cuzco into the respective quarters roughly corresponding to the cardinal points. Two of these quarters, Anti-suyu and Chincha-suyu, had a special identity with upper or Hanan Cuzco while Cunti-suyu and Colla-suyu were considered special to lower, or Hurin-Cuzco. In each of these moieties of two groups of five, two of the five clans stood in a special relationship to one of the suyu and three to the other. One clan noted as an anomaly in these clan system assignments is the first and possibly the second of the Hanan-Cuzco where these were the highest allocated to the ruling Incas themselves and were associated with Chincha-suyu, not Anti-suyu as might be expected in the symmetry of the assignments to the four quarters[131]. Chincha-suyu was the direction of the north, but more accurately the northwest, and this suggests that in a few of the Inca Origin myths, indicating that the male line of Incas migrated from the North West by sea either from Ecuador of Colombia, may have some foundation in fact. Anti-suyu was the eastern quarter where some of the myths indicate that the Incas first entered and settled Peru from Tiahuanaco or the Lake Titicaca region before entering the valley of Cuzco.

The many correspondences between the ceque lines along which the huacas or shrines were located and the clans at Cuzco and the Ayllus have been reported on at length by Bernabe Cobo[132] in the 16th., century, and Paul Kirchhoff[133] and R.Tom Zuidema in the mid and latter half of the twentieth century. It is necessary here only to indicate that the ceques lines may have been derived from the people called the Aymaras in the Collaguas Province and these people retained the fundamental three divisions characteristic of Kaata and the Aymaran divisions generally at

6.080 : Rear view of ceremonial cross braces. Marin-anim, Highland Papau-New Guinea,Late 19th., century, A.D.

6.081 : Ritual cross braces were frequently found in the body paint designs among the Australian Aborigines and clearly derives along with many mythical references from India. Arunta tribe, Central Australia, Late 19th., century, A.D.

6.082 : Cross braces shown as ritual dress. Antioquia, Cauca Valley, Colombia, 1000-1500 A.D.

6.084 : Ceremonial cross braces. Marin-anim, Highland Papua-New Guinea, Early 20th., century, A.D.

6.085: Priest with ceremonial cross braces. Babylon, Iraq, 2nd., millennium, B.C.

6.083 : The stela of Samas-vul 11 showing the ceremonial cross braces frequently depicted in surviving Mesopotamian reliefs and carvings and found similarly expressed in India through Oceania into South America. Note also the Maltese cross depicted in Daguita pectorals (*4.065-7*). Assyria, 7th., century, B.C.

the root of their social organisation and it is this that appears adapted by the Inca for their own ceremonial and social structure at Cuzco. The people in Collaguas consistently applied their division of three and their three clans were composed of 300 Indians each and where other divisions were based on the division of three[134]. This fundamental association between the ayllu, Uma-sysu and Urco-suyu - the upper and lower dualities or polarities evident in the Aymara highlands is of major interest in the theme of this work and will be of more interest in a later chapter. The ayllu retained a chief, the Curaca, whose family formed the only apparent aspect of hierarchy in the clan and his position was usually hereditary. These clans were each responsible for a collective land ownership, management, seeding and cropping, and providing labour and expertise for communal works beneficial and undertaken within the region of more than one clan. In more recent research it has been shown that some traditional villages, where the clan system has survived in some of the ayllus, had been identified in earlier colonial times with traditional constellations or stars[135].

TAHUATIN-SUYU and the FOUR QUARTERS

Pawa; Paua; Paowa - Wind Deities and Myths from the Caucasus to Tahua of Peru

The term Tahua is significant not only in the Andes where it was used to signify the number four but appears to have been derived from the Pacific Islands, or Mesoamerica where the term is found among the Maya. The term is widely found in Polynesia and Melanesia but there it was in fact imported from India and West Asia and derived from Pahua, Pawa or Pavan. These terms are related in the same way in Asia to the number four, particularly relating to the cardinal points or four quarters, and the deities associated with the wind as they are in Central and South America. It will be shown that the term Tahua in the Andes and the Pacific was in fact preserved in the same context as Pahua among the Maya and transferred intact with the same intent.

Among the Mandaeans of the Middle East the name Pawan was applied to their sacred "white mountain" and is said in their religious texts to have been the birthplace of John the Baptist, a shared saint with the Christian religion. This Mountain of the Madai was said to hold a secret chamber called by the priests the "Inner Haran". This interior world was considered special to the Nasurai, the esoteric sect of the Mandaeans, since the access road to the "Inner Harran" was believed only to permit them entry but to exclude the Yahutaiia, or Chaldeans[136]. Baptism was considered central to the Mandaean belief system and the use of pure, running water was critical to the success or failure of their rituals, reaching its highest aspiration in the "Waters of Life", or Life Giving Water so widely found in a similar concept throughout Polynesia and parts of Central America.

The Mandaeans receive their name from their ritual hut, the Manda, located always beside the flowing waters of a river or stream, since still or stagnant water would be abhorrent in the context of their beliefs[137]. The Mandaeans called themselves the Subba or Sabba[138], "Baptisers", and it is thought that they may be related to the better-known Sabaeans located at the mouth of the Red Sea in Southern Arabia in the first millennium B.C. The term Hiia among the Mandaeans related to flowing water, preferably in streams from the Caucasus and meant "life-giving" and this term is virtually identical to that used throughout Polynesia and traces are also found of it among the Maya[139].

It has also been proposed that the Umman-Manda may have had common origins with

6.088 : Ceremonial cross braces depicted here and undoubtedly inherited from symbolism transferred from the Ancient Middle East. Siddharta, Nanda Shrine, Pagan, Burma, 11-12th., century, A.D.

6.086 : Ceremonial cross braces as part of traditional military uniform. Oraon tribe, Orissa, North East India, late 19th., century, A.D.

6.087 : Cross Braces used as ritual dress are found throughout the Pacific Ocean islands and the Americas particularly related to mariners and occurs early in the Ancient Middle East. Rio Verde Style, Costa Rica, 800-1525 A.D.

the Mandaeans of about the 6th., century B.C. and is recorded when king Nabonidus stated that he had had a dream in which the god Marduk had appeared to him and directed him to restore the Moon temple at Harran. It was said that the idol for this temple was still in the hands of the Umman-Manda[140], and it was necessary for him to retrieve it from them. Some historians have suggested have suggested that this Umman-Manda was in fact related to the Madai or Medes of Biblical fame. In Iranian the word mandi means a covered market, and in India mandapa means a temple but more particularly the ceremonial porch as an antechamber entrance to the temple proper, and is a term and architectural structure found widely throughout India. Among the Toda of the Nilgiri Hills in Southern India the term mand refers to their sacred milking shed and these people have been of note in earlier chapters and are believed to have migrated from the Ancient Middle East or Caspian region[141]. This term, and its derivatives, has already been noted among various clans, and in context among other cultural aspects, as being derived from the Mandaeans. It should be noted that there are references to the Ancient Babylonian languages still traceable in the Mandaean texts, as well as the Jewish Talmud and these references extend into the ancient Nabataean language of the Petra region, a rock-cut temple site now in modern Jordan, and their descendants in Western Iraq.

The term Pawan is particularly related to the Mandaean zodiac that was composed of 12 months each of 30 days. This totals to 360 days per year and leaves five intercalary days at the end of the year called the Parwanaia or Panja[142]. The twelve months were divided into four seasons, but because of the precession of the equinoxes they have lost their association with the original equinoctial and solsticial points. Each year is named after the day on which it commences and the corresponding five intercalary days are closely similar to that of the Mayan[143] system in Central America[143]. It was believed that during the five days of the Parwanaia the 360 days of the year the deities of Mandaean religion were created and after this was done "it was daybreak"[144]. Reflecting similar beliefs among the Mayans these last five days of the Mandaean calendar were considered unlucky and a disaster for the soul of anyone dying in that period[145]. The Parwanaia was celebrated, or propitiated, by feasting and ritual cleansing. It is also of special note that the spring feast of Pthatha (Opening) was associated with a festival linked to this name of Parwanaia. In these rites the souls of the deceased were said to be received by the deity Pthahil who is almost certainly the Tohil of the Mayans of Central America Mayan[146]. It is thought that there are close connections between the Mandaean rituals and those of ancient Babylonian and the "opening" was seen as probably deriving from the "opening of the mouth", or "pit pi" (*6.077; 7.005*), of the Babylonians period[147]. It is probably no coincidence that closely similar regalia associated with the "opening of the mouth" rituals for the dead have been found at the end of the twentieth century at Sipan, near Chiclayo, in Northern Peru.

Panch or Panj was the number particularly related to, in this case, the "five powers of darkness"[148], and is the direct antecedent of the panch meaning five in India - in Peru five was pishga, pichca or pisca, clearly deriving from panch. These days were considered polluting and required both personal and social rituals to cleanse away effects of these dark days - similar cleansing rites after pollution being almost obsessive among the higher castes of India, but also noted in ancient Peru. It was necessary during this time to "eat for the dead", a tradition that was also found throughout the Pacific and the Americas[149].

It was noted by earlier researchers that the Mandaeans claimed that their sacred mountain was located either in the Caucasus, North East Iran, Turkestan or in the Himalayas[150]. It is therefore of particular interest that the sentinel peak to one side of the main focus of Hindu belief Kailasa or Kailas, shaped remarkably similar to a stepped pyramid, was named Parwan (*7.091*). This suggests that Kailas may in fact originally have been Parwan and this latter became displaced in time to a side peak. In the Hindu belief the four rivers of creation flowed from Kailas, or Siva's hair, as they were poetically referred to, and in the Mandaean creation it is noted that Parwan is related to the great rivers of the world. These were probably numbered four original-ly, corresponding to the cardinal points, and were said to flow from the Frat-Ziwa (the "Light Euphrates" probably intended to refer to the headwaters) - the primal mountain of Karimla. The Karimla is an unknown mountain but was probably located near some early location in a territo-ry the Mandaeans once occupied. Here it is believed they formulated their fundamentals of their religion and probably has the same origin to an ancestral region corresponding to that of the Hindus[151].

Hittites and the Gods Ill, El, Bel and Ba'al - Rivers, Serpents and the Mountain Gods

It has been noted in this work earlier and in other publications by the same author that the first references to the deities usually associated with Vedic India in the first millennium B.C. origi-nated from the Ancient Caucasus. Among the first gods recorded in the Vedas of India dating to the first millennium B.C. are Indra, Mitra and Varuna but these were recorded also in ancient Hittite inscriptions dating to the second half of the first millennium B.C.[152]. This indicates that they were clearly derived from the Caucasus region and it is also known that they were also the deities of the contemporary Aryan Mitanni kingdom at the headwaters of the Tigris and Euphrates rivers. The great volcanic eruption of Heckla in 1159 B.C. appears to have been the reason for the civil unrest in that century as a result of dramatic climate change and many sub-sequent years of famine. The fall of most of the ancient kingdoms, from the Hittites in Anatolia to the Shang in China, appear to have been casualties as a result of this catastrophe. This date also appears prominent in the archaeology of the Americas where major cultural changes occurred among the Olmecs in North America and in the Peruvian cultures. It is likely therefore that the exit of the Aryan peoples from Anatolia and the Iranian plateau toward India was a result of these enforced migrations due to the severe climatic changes. India was the unwilling recipi-ent of these settlers over the next few generations since they devastated the pre-existent Indus civilisation and those on the margins further afield on the Sub-continent. It is clear therefore that the major gods of these people were imported at that time along with the adherents of several independent fire-religions of Iran feeing the advancing Aryan surges from North West and South of the Caucasus. Among them must have been the Mandaeans and related peoples and it is like-ly that the references to the Parwaniia and to the sacred winds relating to the four cardinal points of the compass, and other aspects of their religion were swept into India ahead of this Aryan advance. It is also likely that there were migrations before that time where traders and mariners were making contact in India long before the first millennium B.C. now recorded in recent archaeology dating back to the 6-5th., millennium, B.C.[153].

Apart from the records of the Ancient Aryan gods there were other aspects of cultural transfer that the immigrant peoples took with them into India. Serpent worship was particularly endemic in the Ancient Near and Middle East among the broad mass of the people and this appears most prominent in the records surviving from Elam in what is now Eastern Iraq and Western Iran. Serpent worship was also known in the Caucasus region and among the Hittites the storm god known as Teshup, or Teshub was the slayer of the dragon or great serpent called Illuyankas[154]. In Hittite tradition each spring the festival to revitalise the Earth was celebrated in a performance known as the purulli - the re-enactment of the combat between the weather god and the dragon. There are many curious unaccounted twists in these Hittite myths, such as the weather god, Teshup, slaying the dragon but also having to slay his own son. This curious episode results from Teshup despatching the serpent and, in response, his son demanded that his father slay him also[155]. Other myths suggest that the dragon or great serpent was in fact the dom-inant deity in earlier times. These curious twists and turns in the narratives of existing texts and surviving descriptions suggests that Illu-yanchus was in fact an earlier storm god who had been overthrown and demonised by the people who had supplanted the old order and who had replaced the original state myths with their own[156]. It is likely then that the term Il or El was that related to the early storm gods of Babylonia and found among the adjacent peoples probably through cultural imposition, or from an earlier common origin. Vestiges of mother-right or hereditary through the female line are found in the Hittite myths being contrary to the male lineal right known to have been that adhered to during the Hittite dynasty[157]. This would confirm the supplanting or relegation of an older indigenous population by insurgent people imposing their own beliefs and system of hereditary. It is also of interest that the term for a sacred stone among the Hittites was huwasi and this bears a remarkable resemblance to that of a sacred stone or wayside shrine in Peru huaca[158].

The increasing belief in the ending of many polities and dynastic states as a result of exceptional volcanic activity is now gaining ground and the end of some of the greatest of all ancient civilisations occurs too widely at the same time not to have some validity. However just as many older civilisations were terminated by the social unrest caused by climatic changes and the resultant famines so others were born after such catastrophes. In Anatolia the Hittites themselves appear to have been the strongest survivors from the earlier eruption of Thera on the island of Santorini in 1628 B.C. since the first king, Tudhaliyas from Kizzuwatna, assumed power in Anatolia in the middle of the 15th., century B.C. The Hittite empire is generally thought to have extended across the whole of Anatolia, the modern Turkey, during the time of its existence but in fact there were several smaller kingdoms flanking the more dominant state centred on Hattusas. The kings of the Hittites then initiated control of their kingdom to adjacent neighbouring states and it is interesting to note that they included the Mitanni who were generally known as the Hurrians, while the Hittites ruling at Hattusas were called Hatti. Both of these more major states that formed the Hittite Empire were Aryan and here there is the subjection of one by the other, that is, the relegation of social status of the Hurrians by the Hatti[159]. However, both the Hatti and Mitanni royal families had been considered for suitable marriage partners in their time by the Egyptian kings[160]. The suitability of marriage partners to those of equal status, or at least as near as possibly so, after the Hatti had conquered the Hurrians was still essential and liaisons occurred between the two royal families. This meant that in the social strata one was superior and the other, for the time of the Hittite supremacy, relegated to a lesser status recognisably reflecting a long established dual social organisation structure.

The term Hatti or Katti are found widely in India among the "Aboriginal" tribes and confirmed archaeological evidence indicates cultural transfer of Anatolian influences in North West India dates to 1450-1200 B.C.[161] and Mesopotamia generally from the 3rd., millennium, B.C.[162]. It is also of note that the term Haran, that of the very ancient region of Canaan - in what is now Syria, was a place within the sphere of influence of the Hittites. There appears to be the probability that those of the Hatti who settled here formed an elite section of that society and may have assumed the name of Harrians as opposed to Hurrians. This is also the city most identified with the Nasurai, the esoteric sect of the Mandaeans. When the great schism occurred between the sects of the Mandaii the followers of Ruha, those most dedicated to the study of the stars and associated secret doctrines, left or were forced to migrate. The Mandaean texts do not divulge their destination but it has been proposed by the author that they did in fact migrate to India, perhaps concentrating in Sri Lanka and the region around the Ganges Delta where aspects of their culture were still preserved in local tribes into the twentieth century. However, many of their expressions linked to temple and social buildings are too widespread, such as mandi, mandar and mandapa to be considered as only being safe havens. It must be considered that many other aspects were also imported and this might be reflected in the naming of the typical dual organisation social system. These are traceable before that time and are also extended into the four-caste system found in ancient Iran noted elsewhere in this book.

The terms Haran and Hatti, appear to have been applied to those who were the former esoteric sects and who would therefore be more inclined to insist on endogamy since they were the educated elite. The term Hurrians was used for the broader mass of the country people and artisan classes in the city. Correspondingly it is probable therefore that the same or similar terms would have been found among the Mandaeans at the times of the Babylonian and Assyrian empires and they are likely to have formed a section of the Umman-Mandaii referred to by King Narbonidus earlier. The followers of the Nasurai, these elite being concentrated in Haran, who were the less educated would form the "others" or being identified with the Hurrians. From these national, racial or tribal terms it is possible to perceive that the term in Peru for the dual organisations Hanan and Hurin may have been derived. It has also been shown by the author in an earlier work that many of the aspects of Mandaean culture survived in India and appear to have been transferred both from India and directly from the Ancient Middle East into the Pacific and Central America.

The term Ruha, describing the esoteric "sky-gazers" of the Mandaeans, was almost certainly the origin of the sea god Ru and associated mythology found among the Polynesians[163]. Inevitably these cultural expressions became modified in their transfer both directly to South America via the Pacific Islands and in other cases through India and then on to the Pacific Rim independently.

Among the ancient texts of India one called the Harivamsa records two different catalogues of divine serpents, when attributed to mountains deities, identified with the rivers flowing from them because of their respective river courses, reminiscent of the Peruvian myths in the Americas. In this manuscript one catalogue records in one section twenty-six divine serpents and in another gives eighteen names. In less extensive texts there are nineteen and twenty names recording the description of the court of Varuna, a deity associated with mariners and oceans, and who lived in the high mountains of the Himalayas. These serpent names appear to be associated, typically, with numbers that have a calendrical base. Eighteen appears to be the number associated with the years in the cycle of the Moon's Node and twenty-six is two quarters of the lunar cycle. This latter might also be a reference to half of the fifty-two year cycle found anciently among the references in the Jain texts of India and those in the oral traditions of the Aboriginal tribes of India[164].

The Bhuiyas and the Assurs in Central India

The Bhuiyas were thought by some to be the remnants of one of the great ancient military heroes of India, Jorasandhu[165], also called Jarasanda but whom others identify with Alexander the Great. Several historians consider the Bhuiyas to be largely intermixed with the Aboriginal tribes and forming a section of the larger mass of the Munda peoples. They are into more recent times, at the beginning of the anthropological studies initiated by the colonial authorities in India, considered to be related to the southern tribes of India and therefore more Dravidian or Kolarian. The Mundas were particularly noted to be represented in a wide range of modern Indian people and classes from traditional Hindu to remote and isolated animists who were spirit worshippers. Of special interest is that they are represented on the coasts of Bengal around the Ganges Delta and near Madras where they are called Buis[166]. Their traditional oral histories and legends note that they came from the north-west of India and there are elements in these tending to confirm that they share themes and motifs as well as hero and place names with many of the important works in the Ancient Near East myths and legends.

It is clear that many of these myths, legends and particularly place names have been pre-

6.089 : A finely carved low relief reflecting a mythical scene from the sea of milk from which the world was said to be churned depicting the turtle which was said to have drawn up the first earth, a motif found also in the Americas. Angkor Wat, Cambodia, 12th., century, A.D.

6.090 : A stylised turtle supported on a representation of the head legs and tail in the four quarters or cardinal points identifying with identical mythical beliefs among the Maya to those of India. Copan, Honduras. 500-700 A.D.

6.092 : An abbreviated symbol of the turtle with the legs indicating the cardinal points and the head displays the common symbol for a flame, or fire emanating from the head, to that found also in India. Codex Dresden, Mexico, Pre- or post-Conquest, 16th., century, A.D.

6.091 : A turtle reflecting the same creation symbolism as found in Ancient India. Codex Dresden, Mexico, Pre- or post Conquest, 16th., century, A.D.

6.093 : Large finely carved turtles revered as a symbol as the supporter of the world, represented as pillars supported on their carapaces, preserved in the Imperial Tablet House. Seoul, Korea.

served in spite of encroachments of the Hindu faith in its many reflections throughout India. The Hindu culture as a whole is in many aspects assimilated from that of the Aryans who overwhelmed North India in the first millennium B.C. but those Near and Middle Eastern aspects reflected in that of the Aboriginal Mundas and Kols or Kolars and Dravidians appears to date from an earlier period. These earlier assimilated aspects among the Aboriginal peoples, or those such preserved by the Bhuiyas reflect earlier Aryan peoples from Iran with assimilated aspects more clearly from the Caucasus, that of the Anatolian Hittites or Hurrians, or the Mandaeans. Although modified by intermarriage with local tribes these migrant peoples still retained recognisable aspects of their ancient paternal cultures into the last century. This is particularly illustrated in the adoration of certain deities having clear derivation from Ancient Iran. In Bhuiya legends there are references to Lutkem Haram that appears to preserve references to an ancient descent from the Middle East reflected in the name Haram among others[167] and where this name is also associated with the ancestors[168].

Not least of the ancestral gods is the popular monkey scribal god Hanuman (ILLUST), who is considered the son of the wind Pawan and is called by the Bhuiyas, Pawan-ka-put, or "Son-of-the-Wind". Pawan here as the wind is clearly the same as Pawan among the Mandaeans and the Bhuiyas applied to the title Pawabans, "Sons-of-the-Wind", to themselves[169]. In Mandaean literature the island of Sri Lanka (Ceylon) was considered in some of their texts as their land of origin, unusual for a supposedly land-based people. Before the Hindu ascendancy in the early centuries of the first millennium A.D. this island was said to be ruled by the great king named Ravan, or Ravana. This name is a clear reference to the ancient wind deity of the Middle East, Pawan, from whence the traders and mariners arrived on this island as a windfall over millennia in their ventures to the Ganges Delta and South East Asia. No doubt the name refers to Ancient Middle Eastern control over the island and this king no doubt was a personification of many generations or dynasties who ruled as descendants or tributaries to these ancient mariner lords.

In the myths of India Hanuman was the ally of the early Vedic Aryans in their battle against the king of Sri Lanka and he is considered the personification of the Aboriginal tribes of India who supported them. Hanuman as Son-of-the-Wind, Pawan-ka-put, provides another link between the Bhuiyas, Sri Lanka and the Ancient Middle East. It is possible that the Bhuiyas were a section of the Aboriginal army or were the result of intermarriage between the Aryan soldiers and the Aboriginal women from the tribes who supported them[170].

The importance of the wind to the ancient mariners was critical and the support of the deity presiding over this element of nature was greatly sought by those who traded by, or ventured onto the sea. Undoubtedly the references to being "Sons-of-the-Wind", or Pawabans refers to the contacts that the Bhuiyas must have had related to the sea as fishermen or more probably as mariners. The term is found widely around the Bay of Bengal suggesting that they were descendants not only of the land armies or migrations from the North West of India but also from those who sailed from Sri Lanka along the coast of Eastern India to the Ganges and Brahmaputra Deltas. The settlements of the Bhuiyas as the Buis near Madras certainly suggest this and these people will be of more interest in a later section.

The Wind God Vay, Vayu - Parwaniia of the Five Evil Days and the Mayans

It has already been noted that the Parwaniia of the Mandeans appears to have been the prototype of the festival of the five "bad" or unlucky days of the Mayans. This transfer appears along with the close similarities of the adoption of the other term for the wind god from Iran Vay and its variation. The term Vay for the wind deity has been preserved more widely in India than Pawan and he is identified with Pawan and is therefore also the father, as was Vay of Pawan-ka-Put, or Hanuman[171]. Parwan was the sacred mountain of the Mandaeans called by them the "Great White Mountain" and in their texts the winds were considered to have special relationships with the four quarters of the cardinal points[172]. In other references the rivers were also associated with sacred mountains and such references reflect no only the philosophical speculations recorded of the Maya but also the Peruvians in the Ancient Americas. Certain rituals among the Bhuiyas are similar to the Mandaeans and take place by a running stream. Terms derived from them are reflected in sacred objects and buildings including their sacred drums called mandar and the bachelors' house in which they were kept was called traditionally the Mandar-ghar[173]. In some of the bathing rituals the binding and tying of the belt knot appears to be modified versions of that of the Mandaeans[174]. In Keonjhur the government of the hill villages was the council called the Pawri, and among these villages an oligarchy composed of sixty chiefs was called the Pawri Desh[175]. This use of the sexagesimal is of import since it appears to be another vestige of the Ancient Middle Eastern numbering system. It is also interesting to note that when a joint clan council was to be summoned a knotted string was passed from village to village to inform the elders of the event. This appears to be a relic of a more extensive numbering system before the introduction of writing. This method of notification also appears to be highly reminiscent of the quipu system and its use in the Inca Empire.

There are many other aspects of Bhuiya culture appearing to have derived from the Ancient Middle East indicating that they were the descendants from there from both land migrations and sea mariners. Not least among them is the fact that one of the deities of the Bhuiyas was named Boram, and this deity is also called Bir, or Vira, or Mahavira, "Great Ape", that is Hanuman[176], but is also the Sun[177]. This deity is found among the Australian Aborigines and could only have been transferred there by mariners from India. Another deity is Karo Byro and this undoubtedly derives from the widely appended term Karan or Karun in South India and is found as a deity also among the South East Asians as Karo, Karei and in Aboriginal Australia as Kari[178]. The term Karun appears to derive from the Middle East where it refers to the people who dwelt by a river of some importance in Mandaean texts called the Karun[179].

It is, for this work, the connection between Hanuman, as Pawan-ka-Put and the Bhuiyas as the People of the Wind, that is the Pawanban, that is of special importance in this section. This is the link to the ancient cultures of the Americas since the ancient deities of the four cardinal points and who were considered wind deities among the Mayan were the Pauahtuns - clearly the Pawabans, the "People-of-the-Wind" - the sea-going Bhuiyas of India[180]. It is clearly shown that Pawa and Pawan are wind deities and relate to Bir and Viri or Vira and have long been known as such from the Ancient Middle East to India.

The sacred mountain of the Mandaeans originally appears to have been the great mountain now known as Kailas in the Himalayas and the original name of Pawan appears to have been displaced to a sentinel mountain now called Pawan, and the range itself named the Kailas Parvat by Hindus[181] (*7.091/2*). Not only therefore were the Bhuiyas likely to have been partially descended from the Mandaeans but they were, and are still located not far distant from their probable sacred mountain originally called Pawan, or "Great White Mountain" and nearer to it than their parent race. Now called Kailas, the mountain resembles closely a stepped pyramid and although not the highest in the Himalayas it was this reflection of the traditional pyramid that was considered to be of special importance. It is very likely that in pilgrimages in the ancient past the Mandaeans and others who worshipped that sacred mountain to the east extended their journey along the Tsang Po to the Ganges Delta and from there into India and South East Asia or used the more western passes for the south. There is nothing especially problematical about this since the Buddhists are known to have penetrated from India far beyond the Himalayas into Central Asia late in the first millennium B.C. and from such places as Khotan travelled through eastern Tibet to the Ganges Delta back into Bengal and South East Asia. It is likely that these routes had been used for millennia before them, particularly from the Middle East and Iran from the earliest times.

The Iron-Working Assurs or Agaria

The Agaria are a people similar to the Bhuiyas who reflect vestiges of important Middle Eastern culture and developments. The Agaria are considered both by earlier Victorian researchers and those in the middle of the twentieth century as possibly being the ancient Assurs or Asuras noted in the Vedic and Hindu texts. The Asuras were said in the ancient texts to be the anti-gods who opposed the encroachment and overthrow by the Aryans from Iran of the naturalised, indigenous and Aboriginal peoples in the Indian Subcontinent. The Assurs, or Agaria were still ironworkers into the twentieth century and there is much to convince the serious researcher that they are the remnants of once powerful iron-working guilds that existed before the arrival of the Aryans. As the great researcher into the myths and legends of India, Verrier Elwin noted of them: "The Agaria as a group are a people absorbed in their craft and their material; they seem to have little life apart from the roar of the bellows and the clang of hammer upon iron"[182]. After so many centuries in contact with other Hindu and Aboriginal cultures that of the Asur is permeated with references derived from deities and histories not strictly their own. However, other elements are found only among them and are of considerable interest. Their name is derived from Nag possible an abbreviation of Agni the Vedic god of fire who is clearly related to the Agaria, Agyasur, the fire demon that is said to leap from the flames of the forge. Another derivation is that the name comes from the iron mines in nearby Udaipur[183].

The name tends to confirm the association of these people with the opponents of the Hindu gods, and who are probably related to with the Asuras in legend such as Lohasur, Koelasur and Agyasur[184]. Elwin also notes that: "It is thus possible to trace an Agaria belt across the centre of India within which the primitive iron-smelters are quite distinct from the Hindu-workers on every side of them"[185]. It is particularly interesting that they are found firstly in the western state of India called Mandla and from here gradually migrated eastwards to the east coast of India[186]. In one of their myths there is a reference to the twelve sons of Sabai Sai, who were called the Asur brothers and tends to confirm a connection between the Ancient Near East and India before the Aryan invasions. It must be remembered that iron is first known in Anatolia and production there is first dated during the Hittite Dynasties - another connection confirmed by recent archaeology in North West India[187]. Saba and Subba are the names the Mandaeans gave themselves - "Baptisers". The link to the Bhuiyas appears also to occur not only in their references to the sacred manda of the Mandaeans in several elements but linked to them as a related people are the Savaras who also have founding tribal deities called Suba. The Savaras have an iron-working subdivision called the Laura or Muli and these are linked to the Agarias, and there is some uncertainty as to whether they are a Gond subdivision intermarried with Agarias or an otherwise related tribe in India[188]. The Gonds also appear to have a very old association with iron-working and the only metal they have a name for is iron - "Kachi". Their traditions state that their first settlements were founded in the Red Hills in Kachikopa Lahugarh, or Iron Valley in India[189]. This term for iron is an interesting one since it is the prefix for the ancient name for a turtle - Kach-appa, and this is possibly an ancient reference to the ingot, bun- or loaf-shaped, in the ancient Indus civilisation resembling the turtle or tortoise, greatly revered in India from the earliest times. The Sanskrit name for iron seems to denote its origins - Ayas, a possible reference to the Hittites of Anatolia in Aryan India[190].

The Vedic and Hindu epics relate that the Asuras fought the Aryan gods and that they included the Nagas who had their homes in the caves of mountains, in the depths of Patala, or at the bottom of the sea[191]. All the pre-Aryan peoples are demonised and almost all fought against them in their onslaught into the Subcontinent. They are variously described by the Aryans but in some of the relations they are called the Daitya, Danava, Dasyus, and Dasa. The Dasyus are further described as "noseless", "black", "without rites", indifferent to the gods", "without devotion" and "lawless", and recorded as worshippers of the phallus[192]. It is clear that these jibes are meant to refer to the pygmoid and small statured aboriginal peoples located for the most part in the forests then widely covering India. In the great epic, the Mahabharata the Asuras and their allies are described as cannibals, living on flesh and blood, and of great strength and courage. Their appearance is further described as dark as a thundercloud, with red eyes, frightful appearance, great teeth, red hair and beard, spear-shaped ears and neck and shoulders as thick as tree-trunks[193]. They wander by night, transforming themselves into alluring shapes to draw men to their destruction, and they prevent those devotees from penance and offerings. In other texts it is said that they built three great forts of gold, silver and iron and that the Aryans destroyed their great cities[194]. Some scholars have placed the origin of the Naga peoples in Khotan in Western Tibet and as the allies and, as the "backbone" of the Asuras, they were in fact considered to be the peoples also of the Indus Valley who were swept into the Indian Subcontinent by the Aryan hoards. In their flight they were immured into the dark forests and hills of Eastern India and Bengal and there became so mixed with the local Aboriginal peoples that they were clearly no longer the people they had once been[195].

This latter description of the Asuras is clearly not that of the Aboriginal peoples but of a tall strongly built, red-haired people who certainly did not fitting the description of the textual rendition of the native peoples who were generally described as the small to pygmoid stature of the forest peoples. The red-hair of the Indus people described here appears to be related to the reddish-eyes also recorded of some of the early people, a characteristic of red-haired people but almost invariably associated with fair-skinned people. The physical characteristics of the Indus peoples are known and they are not Aboriginal negritoes but Caucasian and were no doubt the result of thousands of years of immigration from the Iranian plateau. The Indus people therefore are more likely to have been an admixture of earlier Caucasian and Central Asian peoples accounting for the red-hair noted in the text. It is notable also that the Mandaeans record that there was, in earlier millennia, a high incidence of red-hair among them as it is frequently noted to be so in their texts relating to the calendar and zodiac[196].

The Indian scholar Sarat Chandra Roy noted a century ago that the Asurs, or Agaria were far from primitive in their historic existence. The fear in which they were held among many tribes was as a result of their superiority in development of metalworking skills unmatched by other people[197]. He attributed many of the older pre-Aryan constructions to them with the detection of the migration routes said to have been undertaken and preserved in their oral histories. Of some interest are the records in the Hindu texts stating that the Asurs were cheated out of their share in the rich products of the sea at the mythical "churning of the ocean". There are also traditions clearly reflecting something of the same idea in the Agaria oral histories where Bhagavan (god) tricks the first Agaria raja, Logundi, and destroys his city. Elwin notes further similarities in the records: "As Arjuna and the Padava fight against the Asura and capture their forts, so do the Pandava, led by Bhimsen, attack and destroy Lohripur, the Agaria citadel. As the Asura Rahu for ever seeks to devour the Sun, so does the Agaria Jwala Mukhi, and in Mandla at least there is a strong tradition of enmity between the Sun and the tribe and a strict taboo on working iron in the Sun's rays"[198].

Sarat Chandra Roy recorded traditions a century ago in Munda myths and from them describing the old Asur giants as "'... a pundi or white people of enormous stature, strength and agility, who could in the course of one night walk a hundred miles with giant strides to attend dances at distant villages and walk back to their own homes before dawn. They are said to have lived in huge brick palaces, to have engaged most of their time in smelting copper and iron, and the tradition goes that they even ate iron and blew fire from their mouths'"[199]. The description of these people is probably one that derived originally from the small dark Aboriginal forest people of India who in many cases can be classed as pygmoids. The appearance of Caucasians as these "Pundi" people clearly is more apt in describing peoples who appeared among them and therefore appeared to be giants. The Pundi appeared to have inhabited the Indus region from Iran and then relocated to the east of India proper. This record also suggests a reasonably accurate preservation in memory of these ancient people indicated by the fact that it was more likely that they were not exclusively ironworkers and in this legend being noted more realistically as producing both copper and iron. The division into minute sectors of occupational castes was much more reflective of the later splitting into vocational exclusivity as a result of the imposed Hindu system.

Pawan - The Asur Wind Deity

The story of the Agarian equivalent of Rahu the Hindu eclipse demon, Jwala Mukhi, notes that unlike other boys who had fathers the Agaria hero had a mother only. When he asked his mother why this was he was told that his twelve fathers had been killed by the Sun. Jwala inquired as to where the Sun lived and was told that he lived beyond the seven seas and the sixteen rivers, and there also dwelt the Moon. He was further informed that the Sun and Moon played with the sand on the shore of the great ocean every morning at dawn. Jwala went off to seek the Sun and as he rose in the east he caught him in a net, and it was the wind Pawan Daseri, related to the Bhuiya Pawan, and they as Pawan-bans, "Children of the Wind", related to the Pauahtuns of the Maya, that released the Sun[200]. A more complete version will be included later in this work.

This myth encapsulates many of the characteristics of the elements of the mythology of Aboriginal India. The solar divisions of the yearly, or solar calendar, are reflected in the twelve

6.094 : Pot god raised on a pillar almost identical to those found in India (6.097). Minembi, Melanesia, Pre-20th., century, A.D.

6.095 : A clay incensario or pot shrine of the type closly similar to those found in Aboriginal India. Tlatilco, Early Teotihuacan Period, Central Mexico, 300 B.C.-100 A.D.

6.096 : Pot shrines common in village India from the earliest times and found in some of the islands of Indonesia. South India, Early 20th., century, A.D.

6.097 : Pots raised on forked posts usually represent a god or deified ancestor, here the god Torosam Persa Pen, among the aboriginal tribes of India but also found identically in Indonesia and Melanesia but also in parts of South America. Gond tribe, Sati shrine, Rompalli, Central India, Early 20th., century, A.D.

brothers. In other myths the twelve brothers are often assisted by thirteen brothers of an allied race, tribe or people representing the thirteen lunar months in the year. Here there are twelve fathers probably representing the twelve previous yearly cycles or the 12-year cycle of Jupiter. It is interesting to note that this myth is preserved by a people who are supposed to be land-locked but this tradition included many references to the sea and what is beyond in the middle of the ocean. This is also the case in the Gond myths suggesting that the Agaria were at one time associated with the sea or employed in connection with sea travel. The great ocean referred to here is possibly the Indian Ocean but may actually represent the Pacific since other references in Polynesian myths are remarkably similar and will be of interest later. Seven seas are noted in most readings of the myth and this would be taken to represent the seven spiritual spheres so noted in the texts and cosmology of India. But here it may indicate that this is a reference to reports by ancient mariners that were adapted to religious speculation contained in traditional philosophic structures. The sixteen rivers reflects another philosophic speculation relating to the division of the four cardinal directions into four and commonly illustrated in the iconography of India. The hero, the boy Jwala Mukhi, catches the Sun in a net having hidden himself until the Sun has risen in the east and this is virtually identical to that in the Gilbertese myth of Bue, to be considered in due course. The Sun was released when the world fell into darkness, by the wind Pawan Dasari, and here is another reference to travel, the wind necessary for travel across the sea by sail boat and probably by the Bhuiyas but ultimately probably derived from the Mandaeans. It is noted in some of the Asur myths that they claimed to have come from Lohripur, "beyond the sea" and hid in the jungles of Suriya (the Sun) when first in India. As with the Gonds, they spread claimed to have spread all around the world once they reached the sea[201]. The wind was of particular importance to the Agaria since it was perceived as so necessary for the bellows to work their fire-pits of their forges. It is also of interest to note that the Gilbertese have a similar myth to that of the first Agaria where he is made from the sweat of the Creator similar to one from another tribe, the Sondi[202] and others in India[203]. Similar to the Maria Gonds and the Bhuiyas, the Agaria had boys', and sometimes girls' houses where the teenagers slept apart, and their clans intermarried with the Gonds and Baigas[204]. Marriage was cross cousin and tattooing of women in particular was common and "indeed the tattooing seems to have been a substitute for clothes" customs both preserved in the Pacific Islands and the Gran Chaco of South America[205].

6.098 : Stepped stone pyramid and other stone structures that form the sacred site of Tongatapu, probably constructed by immigrants from Tiahuanaco in South America. Tonga, 10-12th., century, A.D.

6.099 : Traditional Muria Gond burial mound in the form of a stepped pyramid. A stone monolith has been placed in front before the lowest step for ancestral sacrifices and worship. Gudripara, Central India, Early 20th., century, A.D.

6.100 : Traditional stepped pyramidal shrine with the sacre Tulsi bush growing from the to symbol of the World Axis and World Order exactly imitating those depicted on Buddhist shr over two thousand years before Bhubanesvar, Orissa, Eastern I 20th., century, A.D.

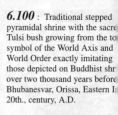

6.102 : Three-tiered stepped pyramid made from wat rounded stones sim lar to those found a Izapa on the Pacifi Coast of Mexico an many other later si in Central and Sou America. Samoa, Central Polynesia, 500-1000 A.D.

6.101 : Three-tiered stepped pyramid with a stone built temple on top with cerer nial central access stairway. El Meco, Eastern Yucatan, Mexico, Late-first millenni B.C.

6.103 : Stepped and battered platform constructed of river stones and similar in design to those found in Polynesia and Indonesia. Izapa, South West Coast Mexico, 200 B.C.-200 A.D.

Pawan, Pavan and Pavana as the Wind God in India from Iran

In the texts of India Pavan, or Pavana meaning "Purifier", is also the name of the deity Vayu the ancient god of the wind in the Vedic texts and in Iran but is also the symbolic name for the sacred number five[206]. The name is found attached to some of the castes in India where the sea trade is important and who may be descended from mariners or merchant stock such as the Chit-Pavans of Bombay who are a subdivision of the Mahratta Brahmans[207]. In Tanjore in the South of India the sea god is named Pavad-airayan linking both the name of the wind and Airayan relating to the Aryan people[208]. The clan divisions among the Hill Bhuiyas are adopted from their Hindu neighbours and they call themselves Pawan-Bans or "descendants-of-the-wind"[209]. The Bhuiyas also claim descent from the Riks[210] or Rishis the seven sacred sages usually identified with the Great Bear constellation and Rik is also found as a title among the Mandaeans. In a flood myth Pawan Dungar was one of two hills where this one was the male, and is probably a memory of the Mandaean "White Mountain"[211].

An interesting Burmese legend records that a ruler named Thag-gya-min wished to marry a Burmese girl but returned to Tawa-Deintha, his homeland, before doing so but promised to return in seven days. In his homeland he had four principal queens but did not return so a letter was sent by a rishi or sage on the prospective bride's behalf by a parrot to Thag-gya-min and

6.104 : Stone monoliths and a dolman known as kuraskal characteristic of several Aboriginal tribes in India and the Nagas of Assam from ancient times into the 20th., century, A.D. Gond, Central India, Pre-20th., century, A.D.

6.105 : Ho monoliths as memorial stones to their ancestors. Chota Nagpore, Central India, Pre-20th., century, A.D.

6.107 : Large stone monoliths erected over many layers of ancient Munda graves. Central India, Late 19th., century, A.D.

6.106 : Miniature monolithic groups sacred to the Toda similar to those found widely in the Middle East including the Arabian Peninsular. Nilgiri Hills, South India, Pre-19th., century, A.D.

by return he sent back some celestial water in an emerald cup courtesy of the same parrot[212]. It is remarkable that the name Tawa-Dein-tha could be Tahua-ntin, the name of the Incan Empire.

Pawabans - Sons of the Wind as the Old Gods or Pauahtuns of the Maya

The deity Pawaban, the Sons of the Wind, or Bhuiyas in the Ganges Delta opening onto the Bay of Begal, are clearly the Pauahtuns, or Wind deities of the Maya. This has been more fully explored in an earlier work[213], but there are other aspects of this term relating it to South America. In India the scribal monkey god Hanuman was more widely known than just among the Bhuiyas under his title of Pawan-ka-Put, "Son-of-the-Wind", but was also known under his more usual Vedic title of Marutputra - also meaning "Son-of-the-Wind God"[214]. Maruts were said to be the sons of the wind god Vay or Vayu and this has been derived from Ancient Iran.

In North Borneo the dowry of a bride among the Dusun people was called Bawahan. Most of these people had contacts with the sea and many of their myths and legends refer to incursive mariners as heroes, plunderers or traders. The term Bawahan probably derives from a connection with the Bhuiya or Gond mariners in centuries past when they were of a more elevated status[215]. The term Murut appears among the Borneo people as a Dyak division, probably deriving from the mariners who referred to themselves as Maruts, the followers of Hanuman as the son of the Wind god and therefore a deity favourable to mariners. The Dusun are linked to these people and their creator god, Kinaringan is said to have had a son called Tawar-dakan, clearly a derivative from the Bhuiya's Pawan-Ban, "Sons-of-the Wind"[216].

On Easter Island a special group of warriors called paoa kai tangata, also called the tai tangata, who practised cannibalism[217]. It is probable that the prefix paoa was originally a reference to their ancestors as long distance mariners, having therefore a special association with wind deities, who were forced to resort to cannibalism to survive the long weeks and months at sea without seeing landfall. Paoa is the Maori version of the name for the wind deity and corresponds closely to the original wind god name of Pawan in India and the Ancient Middle East - the Maori form as elsewhere in Polynesia being pronounced pa-owa.

Pawa and Paoa In The Myths Of The Maoris and Polynesians

In New Zealand, the Maoris called ariki or ocean-going canoe captain and the legendary waka, or canoe, Horouta by the name of Pawa or Paoa[218]. Although not specifically related to the wind deity it is clear that mariners and sea-going craft are associated with the wind and navigation across the Pacific Ocean. The hero is particularly of interest since it was he who is said to have brought the kumara, or sweet potato, a Peruvian tuber, to New Zealand and it was he who is also revered in the rituals associated with the kumara. In the myth associated with this importation of the sweet potato it is said that Paoa visited the demon woman, Te Ruahine-mata-maori, who knew the rituals for growing the kumara, and she gave him a meal of this tuber. He tricks her into seeking something away from her home and Paoa stole her sweet potatoes, burnt her home before he left and fled in his canoe, the waka. She pursued him in the form of a shag but he killed her and made off with her precious red feather cloaks[219]. When he landed in New Zealand with his men on the waka, Horouta, he took his men into the forest to fell a tree, and then urinated bringing the four main rivers into existence. This act undoubtedly related to the cardinal points so similar to the four sacred rivers in other Asian myths, and those of India in particular. After creating other important landmarks in New Zealand Paoas's descendants became one of the important tribes of Maoris in the Turanga region of New Zealand[220]. In other myths Paoa, or Pawa is marooned on the islands of New Zealand after importing the kumara[221] but there can be little doubt that the name for this hero derives from the wind god of India and the Ancient Middle East, Pawan.

In the Marquesas Islands an interesting variation occurred where the wind was harnessed to display particular ornamental symbolic designs. Those worn by both sexes were called ouoho, literally "head-hair", made from the hair from the head of adults and therefore black or brown. Hair ornaments called Pava-hina were made from the beards of old men and worn for the most part by men at festivals and in war because they were silvery grey or "Moon-like". When at war the Pava-hina ornaments were displayed by allowing the wind to blow them and give the effect of swiftness or speed[222]. Pava-hina were sometimes worn on the backs of the hands of women dancers to display the speed and flow of the movements[223]. Pava clearly refers to the wind, and Hina, or Sina is the name for the Moon or brightness throughout Polynesia and undoubtedly derives from the Ancient Middle Eastern term for the Moon Sin - the same term, Si, is found for Moon on the Peruvian coast.

Pawa as the Origin of the Pauahtun in Mayan Culture

The first references in the Americas to the term Pauahtun were those recorded by the Friar Diego de Landa in his attempts to justify acts of cruelty and vandalism under his direction in Mexico immediately after the Conquest. He refers to the Bacabs who were said by the Maya to be placed at the four cardinal points to hold up the sky and the terms applied to these included for the South - Hobnil, also named Kan-Pauahtun. The Bacab of the North was known as Sac-sini, also called Sac-pauahtun; the Bacab of the East was called Muluc or Chac-pauahtun, while the Bacab of the West was known as Cauac or Ek-pauahtun[224]. Since these were all considered wind deities it can hardly be coincidental that they reflect the name of the "Sons-of-the-Wind" - Pawan-Bans in the Ganges delta both having the root Pawa or Paua.

The attributes of the Pauahtuns are more extensively described in the "Ritual of the Bacabs" and they also appear to be wind gods and there are references that they guard also the access to Metnal, or the Underworld of the Maya[225]. This book is largely a book of incantations and remedies for curative purposes and the cardinal points and their presiding deities, the resident Pauahtun of each compass point, receives the sick person for healing and the effect the disposal of the various demons supposed to be afflicting the patient[226]. Where an illness is cast to the wind deity of the West the presiding deity is called in these incantations Ek-Pauahtun, and in India this compound term including Pauahtun is clearly identical to those of the Bhuiyas and others near the Ganges Delta. Ek means black among the Maya and is one of the terms associated with Siva the Hindu god of time, but also "the One"[227], and he is also identified with the cardinal points. This deity Ek-Pauahtun, as the Mayan wind god of the west, refers to the direction of the setting Sun but it is probably no coincidence that this is the direction of the Pacific Ocean west to India[228]. A deity assimilated to Siva, Rudra, has aspects associated also with the colour black[229] and this deity will be of some interest in later chapters. Each of the Pauahtuns were not only associated with the four cardinal points but each of these regions was designated a colour in almost the identical fashion to the colour attributions of India, Tibet and China[230]. For the Maya these colours related to the cardinal points were Chac - red; Sac - white; Ek - black; and Kan - yellow[231].

Closely related deities are those associated with the "Uayeb" - the five unlucky days of the Mayan calendar[232]. This is shown elsewhere in this work to be a version of the wind god of India, Vayu, and hence the close similarities between the Mayan Pauahtun or Pawans and the uayeb or uoh with the Vay or Vayu of India and Iran. The gods of the Mayan uayeb have been designated Gods, G2; G2a; and G2b since their names have not yet been deciphered and probably will never be known. Another deity, apparently derived from the Pauahtuns, is God N who appears to be closely associated with the turtle, an animal of mythical significance, and he is described as one of the "old gods" and associated with the number five[233], a sacred number also in India.

The many aspects of culture and iconography transferred from India, and the Ganges Delta in particular, is clearly detectable or visible among the Maya but of particular interest there can be no doubt that this same term reached South America. It is most likely that the Ayar-Incas were originally from India but it is also clear that they were closely related to the early Aryan invaders of India or from Iran. They would, in migrating across the vastness of the Pacific Ocean, have relied heavily on their own wind gods, Vayu or more particularly Pawan. This deity's name they immortalised in the name for their empire - Tahuatin-suyu, that is Pahuatin-suyu or Pawatin-suyu, the empire of the four parts or four winds. This could of course be written Pauahtan-suyu thereby emphasising the three-way connection developed over many centuries between India, Mexico and South America.

In his book, "Wizard of the Four Wind", Douglas Sharon investigates the shamanistic rituals and belief system of the Peruvian Indians into the present day away from the major cities. Their ancient belief system and its associated rituals are being patronised and performed recognisably in the same way as they were before the Spanish Conquest. It is clear that the deities and mystical associations identified with the cardinal points of the compass and with the winds in particular are the fundamental base for the essentially curative system, although not always so, and appear to be derived from, or similar to the Inca rituals 600 years ago in the Andes[234]. This is true also for the term Vira related to the deity named Viracocha shown to be associated with the wind in another chapter of this work. One of the deities or heroes associated or identified with Viracocha is Tagua-paca, as the deified eagle, emphasising wind-borne aspects, probably originally Tahua-paca relating to the four cardinal points or quarters[235]. The name given by the Incas to their kingdom, Tahua-ntin-Suyu, literally meant Tahua = four, ntin = ("multitude")[236] and Suyu = parts or divisions. It was in the term Tahua therefore that the four cardinal points and the four winds, believed to originate from those aspects, is implied.

The Peruvian Malca; Malquis; and Malku as the Middle Eastern Malke; Melke, Malek and Malik

In the many apparent connections between the Ancient Near and Middle East, India and South America is the term variously recorded as malca or malquis in South America is of some interest. In the Inca Origins myths recorded in Chapter 5 the term malca occurs once only but it is notable in that it is within a version recording migrations to the coast of Peru and appears to indicate that the term was in use before the first Inca arrived on the coast of Peru (Version 5). It is a term recorded several times by Father Joseph de Arriaga in his inquisition into Andean beliefs and in recording the burning of the ancestral mummies of the Peruvians he refers to them munaos and malquis[238]. He later writes: "…it was a mistake not to have burned the munaos of the lowlands, which are called malquis in the sierra, for the Indians esteem them more than their huacas; a mistake not to have destroyed their machays, or burial places of their grandfathers and progenitors to which they carry the bodies stolen from the church …"[239]. Arriaga does not always define the difference between the Huaca, a sacred stone or shrine often associated with a natural object, and the malquis and refers to them in the "same breath". He associates the practices of sorcery with both the huacas and malquis and records that illness is often perceived as "an affliction imposed as a punishment by them"[240]. The prayers and demands are made of the malquis similarly also to the huacas[241].

Interestingly it was the first haircut given to a child, Arriaga records, "that they called this pacto or huarca, was dedicated to the malquis and huacas also"[242] and this ceremony appears closely similar to that performed on Brahman boys in India and copied by other castes. In reference to the justification for the methods of destruction imposed upon the Indians of Peru by the Spanish friars Arriaga again records: "… the Devil and his ministers have persuaded and blinded the Indians. The first is the belief and conviction that what the fathers preach is the truth, that the God of the Spaniards is a good God, but that this teaching is meaningful for the Viracochas and Spaniards only whereas the huacas and malquis are intended for the Indians together with the festivals and everything else that their ancestors, old men, and sorcerers taught them"[243].

In Huanacari, prominent in Inca Origins myths, Arriaga noted that. "… they washed the bodies of the dead, dressed them up, and stayed up all night in drunkedness" …"The principal worship of this town is of malquis, or the mummies of their ancestors, of which they say there is a great abundance…"[244]. Arriaga also described some of the mummies and statues he found before burning or destroying them. "In the ancient town of Huahalla," … "…we dug up an armless stone giant. The whole body was buried with only the head protruding, and the latter was well covered with flagstones. The old men of the clan say of this huaca, which is called Huari, and also Chani, that they used to give it chewed coca by placing it in its mouth. From another place we removed two whole mummies called Caxaparas and his son Huaratama, which were famous and highly respected by everyone. They rested in their burial places, decked out as if for war, with plumage of various colours and dressed in garments that had become worn with time. A little way away was another mummy in storage, dressed like the others, and called Vinchos"[245]. The "sorcerer" who attended the mummies was called the Malqui Villac[246].

It is clear from Arriaga's account that the term malquis in fact applied to the ancestral mummies retained in the temples and houses of the Peruvians from the Inca to many of the broad mass of the people. In Montesinos's account of the Inca Origins myths he notes in Version 5 that it was to the plain of Rimac-Malca, where modern-day Lima is located, that the young man and woman were sent by the Indians after they were found on the mountain of Condor-urcu. The name appears to have special reference to the ancestors and is possibly a location of a landing for those from overseas who were believed to resemble the fair-skinned couple and may have been a repository of ancestral mummies[247]. In present-day Chile the term of mallku was attached to sacred mountains since it was believed that the earlier peoples, after their earthly life lived inside the mountains and the term had the additional meaning of "great"[248]. As well as referring to the mountain deities to emphasise the elevation of the status of something the term was multiplied either two or three times, Mallku Mallku Mallku - "great great great"[249].

In the Nazca region, in coastal South Peru, a town following the religion associated with Viracocha was called originally Kasha-Malka. At the Conquest it was known as Nanasca, this later believed to be a term derived from Nanay the name of a form of supplication to Viracocha[250]. Caxa-Malca (Kasha-Malka) is located on the Nazca plain near Cerro Blanco, the sacred mountain that was noted by Jose de Acosta in 1590 A.D. as the focus of worship in that region to Viracocha[251]. Among the ancient Chipaya, on the altiplano south of Lake Titicaca, small covered conical shrines were constructed to house "effigies of spirits" and these were noted as similar to those of the Manda Indians of North America (see possible link between Mandans and Mandaeans in and earlier work[252] and the Armenians. Miniature shrines were well known among the peoples of India from Ancient time into the present.

Among the highland peoples of the altiplano at the time of the Conquest were the Aymara and one of their tribes, the kingdom of the Lupaqas, was divided into a dual organisation system and each moiety was represented by a headman called a Mallku. This indicated that the Mallkus or Malquis were in fact derived from headmen or chiefs and that the title was originally intended to define status. It is likely therefore that Malquis was the title of prerogative of the ruling people or clans and then probably only the chiefs among them, but had become a privilege granted as a favour to allies and other clan supporters, a characteristic of Inca rule. In Inca times the name for the Inca royal mummies was in fact also mallqui and this meant in their language, Quechua, "seed". It has been noted by some researchers that the mummies were often interred in urns with seed symbols painted on the surface. This has led to the speculation that they were perceived as seed that was reborn from the afterlife back into this world - the concept of reincarnation[253]. The meaning of the term mallqui is seen to extend also to the term covering both "seed" and the Underworld or Inner World. The soul seed dwelt, or was confined for a period of time, in the same way as in the agricultural sense and the whole of the concept appears to have been referred to as mallqui[254].

Of particular interest is the use of the term mallqui to refer to Uchu Pacha, the Underworld, where a special tree grew and in the Upper World, or Hananpacha, where children who died young cultivated flowers in a garden for God[255]. This bears striking resemblances to the "child suckling" tree found of special note among the Mandaeans in the Ancient Middle East and the Aztecs where, among the latter this same tree was called "Chichiuaguauhco" or the "wet-nurse tree"[256]. In the diagram sketched by Pachacuti-Yamqui Salcamayhua (*9.159*) the mallqui tree, symbolising the ancestors, is shown in the lower right of the drawing[257].

It is not surprising therefore that the term Malke, Melke, Malka and Malik or Malek is found in a similar sense in the Ancient Middle East up until the present day. The revered hero-deity of the Yazidis in Northern Iraq is called Taw-us Melke or "Peacock Angel", and is the equivalent of the Spirit of Light known among the Mandaeans, Malka Tausa. This has been linked to the deity who appears to have been transported by mariners across the Indian and Pacific Oceans called variously, Tewa among the Bhuiyas in India; Tawuna in the Indonesian Islands; Teweia in the Gilbert Islands; Taiau the father of Tangaroa in Eastern Polynesia, and Taiowa among the Hopi of Western North America[258].

In Mandaean texts it is noted that their people came form the north, perhaps the Caucasus or beyond in Central Asia and some have identified them with the Parthians. The term they record for their supreme leader was Malka equating to "king"[259]. The Supreme God was called variously Malka d Nhura - King of Light; Mara d Rabutha - Lord of Greatness; Mana Rba - "The Great Soul"[260] and Melka as eHshukha - King of Darkness"[261]. Of major interest is that Melek or Malka is used in the term Melek Ziwa[262] and Ziwa has been shown to almost certainly relate to the same term found among the Maya[263]. The melki in Mandaean thought relates to spiritual beings[264] and this is clearly evident in their many manifestations of the word. In the context of the cross-cultural affinities in which the terms are so clearly exhibited in a related manner in the cultures of South America it is surely they who were among the foremost culture-bearing mariners sailing from Asia to Peru and then overland to Bolivia.

Among the Kois of India the term Malka is found as a term related to a specific clan, and these were a people who erected stones or megaliths as memorials[265]. The Pandarams in South India are a caste of non-Brahmanical priests and their employment in the rites of the temple is known as Melkaval (body-guard of the god)[266]. Malku is also a name used among the Gonds in India[267]. The term malku appears among the Australian Aborigines referring to one of a particular clan member after death when being buried with certain colours that were applied according to their rank in the clan - this rank is a "Tippa-malku"[268]. The term malka in Aboriginal Australia also referred to the mulga tree[269] in its mythological associations and therefore appears again to be a mid-point in the transferral from that of the Mandaean child-suckling tree found also in North and South America.

The Hatti, Hattu, Katti and Huttu, Hurrians, Haram, Haran with Links to Peru

It has been noted that the name Hatti generally referred to the people whose capital was Carchemish and occupied the region now known as Syria. They are referred to as the Kheta in Egyptian texts and as the Hatti by the Assyrians to the east[270] in the second half of the second millennium B.C. However the Hattians, who gave their name to the land were not actually Hittites but have since become confused with them[271]. The Hittites were an Aryan people who imposed their rule over the Hattians relegating them to lesser status and whose empire stretched across into central Anatolia. The Mitanni were usually known as the Hurrians and occupied the region in North Mesopotamia and south of the Caucasus[272]. The fall of the Hittite Empire occurred in the late second millennium B.C. but the state of Hatti is still recorded in the ninth century B.C. when the Assyrians had overrun the region and incorporated the smaller states into their empire. By the end of the eighth century these small states were no more[273].

In India the term Hatti and its variations are widely found, as are many Ancient Middle Eastern terms and expressions, related to those particularly with religious or social status connotations. In South India villages are usually called ur and hamlets are called hattis and the funeral "car" or cortege is called gudi-kattu[274]. Among the Katti or clan subdivision of the Idaiyans the Pancha-ram-katti derive their name from a gold ornament called panja-ram or pancha-ram shaped like a rayed Sun with a trefoil in the centre, worn by widows[275]. Panj is the term for five among the Mandaeans as Panch is among the Indians themselves and derives from it while the trefoil is a sacred symbol spread from the Ancient Middle East into India and across to the Americas at an early date. Characteristically many of the castes and tribes in India were divided into dual organisations and the Kappiliyan Canarese farmers were divided into two endogamous divisions named Dharma-Kattu and Munnu-Kattu[276]. Among the Kondhs (Gonds) they revered an ancestor called Mandia Patro who was brought to their present lands by four deities[277]. One of their revered deities was the elephant called Hatt-Mundo[278]. The Kolas of South India reflect many aspects of culture from the Ancient Middle East and among them Ariya (Polynesian

Ariki) meant "noble". Ara-shina referred to sacred spice or turmeric and Sinnata meant Gold similar in fact to a related hero title of Siki-ana in the Solomons. The term hatti meant hut and their special religious temple was called Katta-illu[279]. Among the Okkiliya (Vakkaliga), a Canarese caste, one of their clans was called the Hatti sept[280].

In Borneo, among the Dusun the pot god was called Hantu Gusi[281], an apparent derivation from the Bhuiyas deity Kutkam Buria and Lutkam Haram[282]. Other associated tribes in India are also known for their pot gods such as the Gonds[283]. These pot gods are found from India to Indonesia and through into Melanesia[284].

On the artificial island of Sika-iana in the Solomon Islands the people were almost of pure Polynesian blood having "drifted in a canoe to the lagoon" and the island itself was named after them. This island was thought to have been built in the 16th., century, A.D. and featured, apart from the artificial construction of the island, a coral block wall running across the whole of the island from South to North. It was constructed so the inhabitants, said to separate the original inhabitants and those who subsequently arrived from a place called Lua-Hatu, thought to have been located in Tonga or Samoa. The Polynesian term kaupa for the wall was used to describe it and tends to confirm Riesenfeld's researchers that many stone-using peoples came to Melanesia from the East - that is Polynesia, and this probably also was an intermediate stop for those from South America.

Among the Hill Bhuiyas in Central Eastern India the bachelors' hut was called the Manda Ghar, a clear reference among others to connections with the Mandaeans of the Ancient Middle East[286]. Each village had its own patron deity generally termed the Pat[287], and represented by one or more stones, and this is also a term derived from West Asia where the usual ancient term for a stone was bat or baetyl. Their hero-gods were termed "Birs", such as, Tulsi Bir, Hanuman Bir and Basar Bir[288] and Bir has already been shown to be an alternative of Vir or Vira = "hero". A related people, the Mundas, usually considered one of the indigenous races of India and in many cases displaying physical evidence of Aryan infusions, called their villages Hatu, or in Santal, Atu[289]. The gods among the Mundas were termed the Hatu Bongako[290]. This term does not have Sanskrit origins; the ancient language of the Vedic Aryans in India, but along with the many other references to Anatolia and Northern Mesopotamia and would certainly indicate that the term derives from Hatti or the land occupied by the Hatti and Hittites. This place of origin is also true for the later Vedic deities, Indra and Varuna, who are first found inscribed in Hittite in Anatolia in the second half of the second millennium B.C.[291]. In the earliest times the village clearing made by a family in the virgin forest in the Ranchi district of North Central India was called by the Mundas the Hatu and later called the Khunt-katti-hatu, or clan village as these family groups expanded[292]. Hattu may derive from the capital of the Hittites Hattusas[293]. In fact there is so much to suggest that these names and customs of the Munda are so closely linked to those of the Ancient Near East that their name is probably in fact a modest corruption of the name Manda, the Mandaeans or related people who came to India before the Aryan invasions in the early first millennium B.C. An interesting marriage custom among them takes place before a rectangular mud pulpit called a Mandoa[294] and this is likely to derive from the ancient religious ceremonies associated with the religious mud- or clay-rendered reed temple of the Mandaeans, the Manda, after which they were named.

Other elements of Munda culture also suggest contacts with the Hatti of the West Asian regions of Anatolia, Syrian and Iraq such as the term for the headman of a village Patti[295], and their term for the ancestors, haram-horoko, seems to be a memory of the ancient ancestral city in Syria named Haran, a city of importance in Mandaean texts. Other references to this ancient city may be preserved in the first people of the Santal residing in the same region as the Mundas and Bhuiyas in Chota Nagpur. The Santals relate that one of the two first beings was Pilchu Haram, and in another myth it is said that two children sprang from the eggs of a divine bird, a boy and a girl, and the Supreme Being created Marang Buru as their guardian[296]. It is probably not a coincidence therefore that the homelands of the Polynesians in the Gilbert Islands were Matang and Buru, the latter often being identified with Buru in Indonesia as an intermediate staging post from India.

Among the Mundas again there is a myth of an old couple named Lutkum Haram and Lutkum Buria, who protected and assisted the deity Sing Bonga - Sing probably deriving from the Mesopotamian Moon deity Sin, and in fact this relation appears to have derived in some part from the Assurs, already noted under their more recent name of the Agarias[297]. Haram here means old man and probably indicates an ancestral link[298]. Among the Mundas the Panch was, and still is the village council[299], and the number for five referred to the five elders who represented the village in its council. In Mandaean, Panj is the number five and no doubt is another reference confirming the Munda origins, at least in part. One of the villages associated with Munda burials was called Choka-Hatu (literally - "place of mourning") and these sacred grounds were filled with menhirs as stone memorials to their ancestors[300] (*6.107*), a custom widely known in the Ancient Near and Middle East. Interestingly the agricultural fields of the Mundas are called Hatu-Japa-Piri[301] and the rice was called tewa whereas in Nias off the coast of Sumatra the rice soul was also called Tewa, and may have been derived from the term for the deity of light in Mandaeans, Tawsa earlier noted. There are many aspects linking the Bhuiyas and Mundas to Australian Aboriginal culture and onwards eastwards to Polynesia and Peru. Of interest also is the term Kacha for the tortoise or turtle in myth the foundation of the World since this is also found among many other tribes in India as Kawachi[303] - a term also found as the capital on the Nazca Plain in Southern Peru.

These references in the foregoing are a few of the many found among the tribes and castes in India indicating their cultural inheritance from the Ancient Near and Middle East. Of particular importance to this work are the Gonds of India, probably once rulers of large stretches of territory in Central India. Among the Gonds the sacred staff is of special importance and this was called Kati, and will be considered in another section[304]. One of the most interesting myth cycles of the Gonds is that of Kati Kolasur Jeitur - a collective term for the semi-divine mother and son worshipped by the four ancestral Gond brothers[305]. These will be of more interest in a later chapter but the term Kati is here again linked to ancestral beginnings.

Among the Bants of India, an important merchant class, the rules of inheritance are called Makkala Kattu[306]. Although in historical terms they came from North India the name of these people suggests that they may have originated in the Caucusus region where Bant appears to be the people of Van, or Dan from around Lake Van in what was greater Armenia.

Herodotus notes that the Phoenicians originated from what is believed to by intended by him the coast of India. Recent Israeli researches indicate that the people known as Dan, probably the Van from Ancient Central Armenia, suddenly disappeared from history after 1000 B.C. and that they were noted as sea traders[307]. These Dan were also noted for their belief in their claimed descent from the fiery, redheaded hero named Mopsos. Red hair is a characteristic of many hero mariners from the Ancient Eastern Mediterranean, Middle East, India, and through into the Pacific Islands, and onto the Peruvian coast[308].

Already mentioned is the panja-ram, the gold ornament worn in marriage by widows, and it is associated with the subdivision called Pancha-ram-Katti in the caste of Idaiyans. The subdivision name combines three Ancient Middle Eastern terms, Panch or Panj ("five"), Raman and Katti. Typically this caste was divided into a political dual organisation system and that of higher status called themselves Yadavas[309]. Yadava was the term applied in India to peoples deriving from Greek or Roman stock, and a catch-all for other foreigners, and in India these were usually the descendants of traders. Among the Kavilgars in South India the marriage tali, or marriage ornament, is called the "Katu"[310].

Among the Kallan of South India the bull is a daily object of reverence and the centre of their lines and social interaction. The Kallans excelled at the rituals and games centred on the bull and their rites involving these animals were called Jetti-Kattu[311]. Bull races were an aspect transferred from South India to Indonesia where they still occur to the present day but that almost certainly derived from the Ancient Middle East. Among the Kallan also a grinding stone was called the kallu-katti where Kallu meant a stone[312], but in a cross-over in meaning Kallu was actually the name of the Ancient Middle Eastern priests who presided over the sacred stone altars or memorial menhirs stones representing ancestors or deities. Kal in other parts of India likewise meant a stone, while the Middle Eastern derived term of baetyl or bat was retained in its original form in Indonesia and Melanesia, while in other parts it meant the presiding priest. The Maravans, also resident in South India, participated in similar games but these were generally termed "bull-baiting" and called by them Jelli-Kattu, and must have had a similar origin to that of the Kallans[313]. Among the Todas located in the Nilgiri Hills in Southern India the stone walls surrounding the sacred dairy were called Katu and clearly derive or assimilate the term bat for stone[314]. In Polynesia, and particularly among the Maori the term "Pat-u" refers to the stone, sometimes a wooden substitute, ceremonial club and this clearly derives from the Ancient Middle Eastern term bat, or Indonesian batoe.

Among the Karna-Battu caste the term katta meant the construction of an embankment or dam and the term Battu in their name suggests that they were originally associated with stone working or erecting sacred stones in their former existence[315]. The Paniyans worshipped various deities and among them one called Kattu Bhagavati was a deity more associated with the forests but probably originally included stones[316]. On the coasts of South India the conch shell (turbinella rapa), or chank, highly prized in India for its religious associations, and those associated with its preparation for the sacred ceremonies were called Lanku-Katti[317].

The Tottiyans, also called the Kambalattans, located in the Tanjore district of South India have a sub-division called Kattu Tottiyan. Their headman among the Tinnevelley Tottiyans was called the Mandai Periadanak-Karan, suggesting clear connections with the Mandaeans in the Ancient Near East[318]. The Valluvans are referred to several times in other sections of this book and both male and female of this tribe in South India wear the linga in the form of a small, carved stone pendant. Also mentioned elsewhere in this work this symbol of Siva is probably the origin of the Tiki of the Polynesians also associated with virility and the phallus[319]. There can be little doubt, therefore, that the mystical and legendary associations of the stones with the recent ancestors, and the male aspects of procreation and virility were transferred from the Ancient Middle East either directly, or through India into the Pacific Islands and thence to the Pacific Coast of South America.

6.108 : Panorama of the ceremonial site of Machu Picchu showing its spectacular but isolated location that preserved its existence from the world until rediscovered in 1910. Machu Picchu, Peru, 15th., century, A.D.

6.109 : A ritual vessel from the Classic Maya showing what apears to be an elephant deity depicting reasonably faithfully, probably from a mariner's description from Buddhist or Hindu India, this special deity as Ganesa - the god of protection and luck in ventures. Of particular interest is that fact that these figures are both shown from the rear - a characteristic particularly noted in Buddhist reliefs and imagery in early India (*12.075-6*). The long nose and tail and the exact copy of the crook-shaped elephant goad shown under the figures arms to the left indicate that this is meant to emulate the elephant deity of India. The legs of the far left figure are faithfully drawn as those of the elephant while those on the right appear to reflect the anthropomorphic aspect of the Hindu elephant god Ganesa (*12.077*) . Yalloch, Guatemala, Late Classic, 600-900 A.D.

6.110 : Upper northern caste enclave of Brahmans with character-istic blue-painted houses seen from Meherangarh, the Maharajah's fortress palace. Jodhpur, Rajasthan, India, 20th., century, A.D.

6.111 : Ancient terraces still in use. The paths to the right lead to the ceremonial Inca site of Pisac with its Intihuatana. Pisac, Peru, late 20th., century, A.D.

6.112 : Ancient terraces on the Island of the Sun. Lake Titicaca, Bolivia.

6.113 : Panorama of modern La Paz overlooked by the sacred mountain of Mount Illimani on the horizon. Bolivia.

4 : Massive "cyclopean" stonework with what some believe to be the mythical windows through which the first Ayar Inca brothers emerged. u Picchu, Peru, 15th., century, A.D.

6.115 : Intihuatana, or Hitching Place of the Sun - carved living rock. Machu Picchu, Peru; 15th., century, A.D.

6.116 : A Mayan lord grasps the hand of a Pauathun, or Old God, whose shell earring and shell carapace suggest that he is a mariner. This is em... sised by his Middle Eastern appearance. The red lips and face applications suggest that this is part of greeting rituals such as was known in the Ku... Western Pacific until a century ago. The ruler hides a flint knife behind his back suggesting that treachery was his intention and is a subject found... Chama vases (*1.025/6; 1.033*). Guatemala, 600-900 A.D.

6.117 : Ground designs were common in parts of Indonesia, Melanesia, and Central America. They were, and are still used for sacred rituals in South India to this day. Kanchipuram, 2001 A.D.

6.119 : Fine portrait head crown headdress similar to... found in South East Asia. Tiahuanaco, Bolivia, 300-7... A.D.

6.118 : Face paint and tattoos were common in Polynesia and known also in Tiahuaanco and Coastal Peru. Tiahuanaco, 400-700 A.D.

6.120 : Fine goldmask image of an ancestor or deity showing blue eyes almost invariably depicted where eye colour is indicated in most images retained from Ancient coastal Peru probably referring to legendary descent from Aryan Asia. Moche, Sipan, North Coastal Peru, 200-400 A.D.

6.121 : Finely woven "poncho" with design of the Inca type. Lake Titicaca, Bolivia, 1250-1500 A.D.

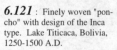

6.122 : Surviving original "cyclopean" stone masonry built upon by Spanish Colonial structures. Cuzco, Peru, 15th., century, A.D.

6.123 : Red ochred hair has been common in South America for many centuries and is a tradition found also in Tasmania, the Western Pacific, and South and South East Asia. Warau Tribe, Amazon Basin, Mid-20th., century, A.D.

6.124 : Peruvian mummy with shell pectorals, representing attachment to probable sea origins of the ancestors and a characteristic cap showing the lighter red-brown hair typical of the peoples from the first millennium B.C. to 15th., century A.D. Ica, South Peru, 800-1000 A.D.

6.125 : Peruvian Inca mummy with natural blonde hair, characteristic of the fair red and light brown hair found among many South American cultures from Ecuador, Peru, Bolivia into Northern Chile. The hair quality is that of the fine Caucasian and not the coarse black Mongoloid type and the parchment skin colour of the mummy and the tall skeletal type is typical of the Caucasian type. Inca period, Peru, 14-15th., century, A.D.

6.128 : Sacred banyan with Siva trisulas or tridents ceremonially smeared with red ochre. Chandigarh Fort, Rajasthan, India, Late 20th., century, A.D.

26 : Brahman priest performing the evening ... to the fire god Agni, as the fundamental ...ciple of the Sun, on the banks of the Ganges ...er after sunset. Varanasi (Benares), India, ...I A.D.

6.127 : Jade mace heads, one inlaid with emeralds. Jade and greenstone was much sought after in Central America and throughout the Pacific Islands, and into Asia. The form of these mace heads is closely similar to those known anciently in Asia. Pasto, Colombia, 1st., millennium, A.D.

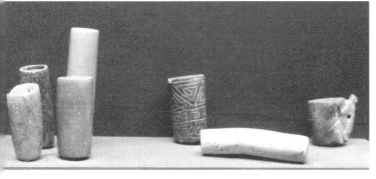

6.129 : Finely carved jade and greenstone vessels and objects. Pasto, Colombia, 1st, millennium, A.D.

CHAPTER 7

VIRACOCHA AND
THE TESTIMONY OF TONACA

Viracocha in Myth and Tradition

The great Andean creator hero Viracocha is found throughout the myths and rites of the Incas and the many generations before the founding of the Inca Dynasty. It has been argued by some that this deity or hero was a fiction of the Inca's imagination but research outside the Inca strongholds suggest otherwise. Those who have suggested that Viracocha was a late fabrication include Guardia Mayorga who claimed that this deity was a "creation of the Jesuit chroniclers" and suggests that he was only a hero in the immediate Pre-Columbian period[1]. However, the evidence for Viracocha being a separate deity, particularly outside or on the extremities of the Inca Empire appears to militate in favour of his being both an ancestral hero and a god. Others claim that the term Viracocha has no meaning even though its separate parts are identifiable, that is, he was "a god with no name"[2], a belief derived from Garcilasso de la Vega's dictate that the name had no meaning. However, this is against all the earliest records indicating that the Indians themselves provided the meaning through translation, "Foam of the Sea", "Sea of Grease" or similar meanings, and it will be shown that these earlier records are more likely to be correct.

The word Vira-cocha appears to be a merging of two Quechua components and suggests that they derived from their pre-Inca past[3]. This is true also for the term Pacha-camac[4] where Pachacamac is identified with Viracocha[5]. Earlier researchers have suggested that the Quechua were naturalised descendants of the Quiche from Central America[6]. It is further attested from the same sources that the Quiche were themselves probably the Toltec immigrants from Central Mexico into the highlands of Guatemala and who then migrated further south into South America. It is interesting to note that one of the celebrated Peruvian researchers, Julio Tello, earlier last century, considered that the Lanzon at Chavin de Huantar, dating to the middle of the first millennium B.C. (*4.014/5*), represented Viracocha[7].

Other researchers have identified Viracocha with the deity Pachacamac whose shrine at the coastal site of the same name south of Lima was one of the oldest and most famous in South America. In some versions of the Viracocha myths, retained along the Central and Northern Coasts of Peru, this hero is said to have disappeared over the sea westward from Pachacamac and not much further north at Manta in Ecuador as other versions record. This region of Peru appears also to identify the deity Coniraya, as a an early form of Viracocha and possibly also the Pachacamac deity, with the same stretch of coast[8].

In a myth recorded by Antonio de la Calancha recorded in the second half of the sixteenth century, A.D. the destruction and recreation of the World is attributed to the Creator, Viracocha Pachayachachic, translated as "Viracocha the Invisible Lord". There were in fact two periods of destruction preserved in the oral traditions, one by fire and the later one by flood, not dissimilar to World destructions recorded in Central American myths. It was said by the Indian informants that Viracocha did this because they allowed their attention to drift from concentration upon him to the worship of the forces of nature, focusing on those relating to water and springs, rocks and mountains. These traditions note that at the time of the flood there were a few survivors and from these people the World was said to have been re-populated"[9]. A modified version of this myth is recorded by Molina and in a similar myth Sarmiento notes that it is a male and female pair that survive the Flood[10].

In myths recorded by Betanzos, Molina and Sarmiento all identify the place of creation and genesis of the next generations after these catastrophes with Tiahuanaco[11]. In the myths recorded it has been noted that the period of the year that Viracocha seems to be associated with is that of the winter Sun, at the solstice, and the beard that he is said to have worn has been considered to reflect the rays of this solar aspects[12]. The justification for believing that Viracocha predated the Incas by a few centuries at least, if not much longer, is that his worship was still retained in the Nazca plain region of South Peru. The town of Kasha-Malka on the southern edge of the Nazca desert was the place where droughts were common in the present day as well as the ancient past. Ancient pleas for their god Viracocha to have mercy upon them and send rain for their crops to avert starvation are recorded that are considered to long pre-date the Conquest. It is said that the later term nanay was that cried out by the priests and people in supplication so that he would shower them with his "tears". The name given to this town noted at the Conquest was Nanasca apparently derived from this same term[13]. Nanay is thought to have developed from the Quechua term for "pain" and from this the name Nazca is also thought to have originated. In response to the peoples' prayers and plaintiff cries it was believed that Viracocha shed "tears" that were then believed to stream down from the top of Mount Cerro and accumulated as rivulets flowing out to the irrigated fields to be gratefully utilised by the populace[14].

It is interesting to note in the traditions, still retained to the present day in Nazca, that it was believed that the hero called Tunga was attempting to reach the ocean shore but was turned into a mountain that still bears his name. It is also said that Illa-Kata's wife, identified as Cerro Blanco, was buried under a blanket of white maize, probably an allusion to snow, representing the fertilising power of water, as it melts and by which power the maize grows and fruits[15]. In the attempt to attract the attention of their deity by sympathetic magic the people of Nazca delegated a man to collect a pitcher of "foamy" sea water where the waves crashed against the cliffs and this is ceremonially "splashed" on the peaks near Nazca to encourage Viracocha to "shed his tears". The translation of the name Viracocha as "Foam-of-the-Sea" is also considered here as a proper rendition of the name and will be of further interest as well as the term for the local priest, the Pongo.

Some of the simpler versions relating to Viracocha as the Creator derive from Andean peoples and are recorded by researchers in the mountains in the middle of the 20th., century. One record states that, "First there was a flood, Uno Pachacuti, which symbolised the centrifugal dispersal of water. After the waters receded, earth was uncovered with lagoons, rivers and lakes formed. Mamacocha (Mother Earth) emerged to rule the aquatic elements, and Viracocha ("Lake of Fat") performed his creator acts and disappeared into the ocean"[16]. This is a very simplistic version but illustrates that the foam or "fat" lying at the edges of lakes was identified with the name of Viracocha. Montesinos also recorded the fact that Vira or Huira is to be translated as "fat" or "scum" and this clearly has been received from the Indians themselves when asked the meaning of these words. These terms were apparently used when any oily substance floated on the top of water such as sacrificial oil, and the term cocha actually meant a lake or the sea or large body of water[17]. Garcilasso del la Vega, however, disputes that the name of Viracocha is anything more than a name without any meanings attached to the whole or its constituent parts[18], but as will be shown the traditional attribution of foam, wind and sea are in fact correct.

In the Andean regions visited by the Spanish missionary Father Pablo Joseph de Arriaga he noted in the last decades of the 16th., century, that llama fat known as "Bira" was used as an offering to the huacas (shrines) and conopos (sacred stones). Arriaga records that in the town of Parquin the local people, in a ritual very similar to the Voodoo rites known in Brazil, formed a figurine out of a small lump of llama fat representing the Spaniard Hernando de Avendano. This they burnt in attempt to destroy his soul and this method was considered an effective means long honoured in their traditions[19]. "Bira" is clearly related to the rite of destroying the soul or spirit and it is interesting to note that this may be related directly to Vira both in Peru and India. Arriaga further noted the difficulties in the conversion of the Indians from their own long-held and conservative beliefs to that of Christianity writing: "...the Devil and his ministers have persuaded and blinded the Indians. The first is the belief and conviction that what the fathers preach is the truth, that the God of the Spaniards is a good God, but that this teaching is meaningful for the Viracochas and Spaniards only, whereas the huacas, and malquis are intended for the Indians, together with the festivals and everything else that their ancestors, old men, and sorcerers have taught them"[20]. It is probably fair to say that the true indigenous Indian was never actually fully converted and small offerings and propitiations are still to be found at many of the ancient sites on both the coast and in the Andes in both Peru and Bolivia.

In more recent times, a century ago, Adolf Bandelier visited Bolivia to research the ancient cultures among the descendants of the peoples who were resident at the time of the Conquest. The myths of origin he collected from Indian sources confirm the conservative nature of the mind of these Indians and that they had preserved, with little appreciable change, their ancient traditions compared to those collected immediately after the Conquest. He also noted the long-held requirements for offerings and rituals among these Indians and noted that the "articles for conjuration were: Coca, uira-koa, llama-tallow, the two llama foetuses, a piece of the skin of the 'titi', or wild-cat, grape-brandy, wine, and especially 'mullu' noted by Bandelier as being a "fetish of white alabaster representing a bull or cow similar to New Mexico"[21].

From one of the local old men Bandelier collected a myth of origin relating to Viracochas as noted: "In very ancient times," he said, "the Island was inhabited by gentlemen (caballeros) similar to the viracochas (name given to whites by the Indian today). Whence these 'gentlemen' came he knew not ..."[22]. This among other references indicates that the long tradition noted from the time of the Conquest onwards was accurately preserved that the first creators and progenitors were considered similar to the Spanish and Europeans generally.

The Spanish chronicler Betanzos, a companion of the Conquistador Francisco Pizarro, who had married an Inca princess, recorded from the traditions preserved by his wife and her family the known traditions relating to Viracocha after 1532 A.D. Of Betanzos Bandelier notes: "... the early traditions of the Indians of Cuzco and especially of the Collas or Aymara, gathered by Betanzos within ten, or at most fifteen years after 1532 (the Conquest). At such an early date Indian folk-tales and myths could not have much been contaminated through contact with the whites, and, while there are some of the traditions recorded by Betanzos, inklings of extra-American influence, the substance of which appears to be authentic and primitive."[23]. The point that the early Inca traditions preserved elements that were evidently from outside the Americas is here clearly indicated.

The tradition Betanzos wrote down about this Andean hero and the creation of the World is as follows: "In ancient times, they say the country and province of Peru was in darkness, having neither light nor day. There were, at that time, certain people in it, which people had a certain chief who commanded them and to whom they were subjected. Of the name of the people and of the chief who commanded them they have no recollection. And in those times, when all was night in this land, they say that from a lagune in this country of Peru, in the province of Collasuyo, there came a chief called Con Tici Viracocha who, they say, had with him a certain number of people, which number also they do not recollect. And after he had sallied forth from his lagune, he went from there to a site that is close to the lagune where to-day is a village called Tiaguanaco, in the aforesaid province of the Collao. And as he went thither, he and his own, forthwith there, unprovisedly, they say, that he made the sun and the day, and ordered the sun to move in the course it now moves and afterwards, they say, he made the stars and the moon. Of this Con Tici Viracocha they say he had appeared once before, on which occasion he made the sky and the earth, leaving everything in obscurity, and then he made the people who lived in darkness as aforetold, which people did some sort of wrong to this Viracocha, and being angered by it, he turned to come out again this last time and came forth as on the first occasion, and those first people and his chief he converted into stones, in punishment for the anger they caused him"[24]. Bandelier notes of this version that the actual term used in Viracocha's title was Titi not Tici and that Titi referred to the sacred rock on the Island of the Sun in Lake Titicaca, and that this was the usual name for the wildcat and that Titicaca was actually Titi-Kala in the Aymaran tongue[25].

Pedro de Cieza de Leon recorded of his South American sojourn from 1532 to 1550 that in the region of the Collao (Aymara) they "… say the same as all the other people of the Sierra, that the Creator of the world was called Huira-ccocha, and they know that his principle abode is in heaven; … they take account of time, and know some of the movements both of the sun and moon. They count their years from ten months to ten months, and I learnt from them that they called the year Mari, the moon or month Alespaquexe, and the day auro"[26].

In Ayacucho, now known to have been the region in which the Huari, or Wari capital was situated, Cieza de Leon noted of a location near what was Guamanga (Ayacucho): "The largest river near the city is called Vinaque, near which there are some great and very ancient edifices, which are now in ruins, but appear to have stood for many ages. When the Indians are asked who built these ancient monuments, they reply that a bearded and white people like ourselves were the builders, who came to these parts many ages before the Yncas began to reign, and formed a settlement. These, and some other ancient edifices in this kingdom do not appear to me to be like those which were erected by order of the Yncas, - for their buildings were square, and those of the Yncas are long and narrow. It is also reported that certain letters were found on a tile in these buildings …"[27].

In what seems to be a blatant piece of Inca propaganda a tradition was preserved among the Incas, apparently firmly believed by them, claiming direct intervention by Viracocha on their behalf in the war against the Chancas who occupied the region around Ayacucho (Guamanga). It appears sometimes to have been the custom among the Incas to select the most suitable successor to a ruling Inca rather than by primogeniture, that is the eldest son. The heir of the Inca Viracocha was considered unsuitable, stripped of his right of succession, and banished to become a shepherd but, while tending the sheep he had a dream or vision where the god Viracocha appeared before him warning him that the Chancas were plotting to overthrow the Inca dynasty. The myth of Viracocha's intervention against the Chancas and the hapless heir recorded by Garcilasso de la Vega was translated as follows after the reports of the vision reach the ruling Inca: "The prince, as soon as he had been brought before his father, said. 'You must know, O sole Lord, that, when I was lying down at noon today (…..) under one of the great rocks that are scattered over the pastures of Chita, where I am employed by your order in watching the flocks of our Father the Sun, a strange man stood before me, different in dress and appearance from our people. He had a beard on his face more than a hand's breadth long; he wore a long loose robe down to his feet, and held an animal, unknown to me, fastened by its neck. He said to me: 'Nephew, I am a child of the Sun, and brother of the Ynca Manco Ccapac and of the Coya Mama Ocllo Huaco his wife and sister, the first of the ancestors; wherefore I am a brother of your father and of you all. I am called Uira-ccocha Ynca, I come on the part of the Sun our father to make an announcement to you that you may deliver it to the Ynca my brother. The whole of that part of the provinces of Chincha-suyu, which is subject to his empire, as well as other parts still unconquered, are in rebellion, and a great multitude has assembled to drive him from his throne, and destroy our imperial city of Cuzco …"[28]. It is said that the Chancas rebelled three months later but since the Incas were forewarned they were ready to contain the uprising in the most ruthless manner after which many of the Chancas fled to the eastern forests to avoid annihilation. One of the extraordinary reports preserved from Inca Viracocha's reign relating to the Chancas' defeat is that he is said to have announced to his soldiers that "… they had not conquered their enemies but that the victory had been gained by certain bearded men sent by Uiraccocha who were visible to none but himself, and that they had afterwards been turned to stones, etc."[29]. The Inca Viracocha was so named, it is claimed by the Incas at the Conquest, because his skin was very white as was also his hair. De La Vega wrote from his mother's relations accounts that: "The prince is said to have hair on his face, while the Indians are usually beardless, and he wore his clothes down to his feet, which is different from the usual custom of the Indians, whose clothes only come down to their knees,…"[30]. This description suggests that there appears to have been a religious fixation, or identification by this Inca on the mystical character of the ancient deity of Viracocha and assumed the believed characteristics of the hero-god, in the manner Christian mystics, and imitate the dress code reported of him. An alternative explanation might be that he was in fact an albino since the white hair and more abundant body hair is a characteristic of albinoism. Covering the body from head to toe is in fact another characteristic of albinoism since their skin is extremely sensitive to the Sun's rays and may explain the Inca's dressing in the manner, reported to cover as much of the body, from harmful exposure.

In the temple dedicated to the Inca Viracocha a statue stood described by de la Vega: "The image represented a man of good stature, with a long beard measuring more than a palmo, in a wide loose robe like a cassock, reaching the fee. It is held a strange animal of an unknown shape, with the claws of a lion, with a chain around its neck, and the end of it the hand of the statue, carved out of stone …". De la Vega commented on this report that: "The statue resembled the images of our most blessed apostles, and especially that of St. Bartholomew, who is painted with a demon chained at his feet, like the figure of the Ynca Uira-Ccocha with the unknown animal"[31]. References to either St Bartholomew or St. Thomas by the Indians or the Spanish chroniclers were recorded several times in various parts of South America and it will be shown that this was probably not a coincidence.

In the more recent researches into the Inca calendar and associated calendrical or geomantic lines Valcarel (1959) noted that the quarter designated Anti-suyu was the direction in which the Sun rose in the east. The Sun that set in the west and there the calendrically orientated empire divisions that was the allocation of Conti-suyu. The Sun set in the region of Chinchaysuyu at the Winter solstice and was given this name since it was believed that the Sun was "swallowed" by a feline called Chinchay, the name of a constellation, in that North West direction. The Southern quarter was called Colla-suyu after the Collas who occupied that region around Lake Titicaca. It has been noted that the axis that runs from Lake Titicaca through Cuzco to the North West - the extreme point where the Sun sets at the winter solstice is the path taken in the ancient myths relating Viracochas route from Lake Titicaca or Tiahuanaco to the point on the North Peruvian coast or Ecuador where he is said to have departed across the sea to the West[32].

In some myths and iconography the Creator as Viracocha is seen as bisexual and ovoid, or depicted as the primal egg, and from this both male and female emerged along with creation - in type a very Asian rendition. Interestingly Pachacuti Salcamayhua, whose works are now extensively scanned by recent researchers, records some aspects of interest relating to Viracocha and significantly in this version, relating to the primal egg, to Viracocha he ascribes a cosmological diagram of the Southern Cross, considered to be a hearth formed by crossed poles. This imagery is closely similar to that of the Huichol in North West Mexico[33]. The Huichols retained a ritual where crossed arrows placed over the Hikuli or peyote are believed to induce moisture onto the cactus and is possibly a distant reference to crossed arrows relating to lightning heralding rainfall.

Father Bernabo Cobo is considered one of the most reliable of the first Spanish chroniclers, but being a missionary priest his views were prejudiced against many of the beliefs of the Indians and what he, and other friars considered their fables. Cobo travelled the road from Lima to Cuzco in 1609 A.D., examining the surviving monuments, and took the opportunity to interview the surviving Incas while at his destination. In 1610 A.D. and 1615 A.D. he travelled to the Lake Titicaca region of Bolivia, and possibly went there on other occasions, learning Quichua and Aymara so that he could elicit their traditions and culture as well as proselytise on behalf of the Church[34]. He notes in at least one section of his writings that the Indians preserve "a thousand absurd stories"[35] about their Creator deity Viracocha, but, regrettably, does not record more than a few of these. The myths, legends and rituals, and the belief system generally, he record-ed have proven as accurate, or more so, than some and he does preserve elements that are of par-ticular interest. In one of the "fables" relating to the creation he noted that the people in the provinces around Quito, the capital of modern Ecuador, preserved the tradition that the Creator came across the "North Sea" and travelled through the land "creating men", "assigning provinces" and "distributing languages"[36]. In one of these places he brought forth "all things" and some believed that the Creator managed this from nothing, others said it was from clay while some said he formed creation from stones, birds and the animals. Cobo preserves an interesting element believed of Viracocha and that is he was said by some not have any joints in his body and was very "swift" and these elements appear to be similar in some ways to myths in Aboriginal Australia but originating in India[37].

In a remarkable section of the Ancient Vedic texts in India the oldest preserved notes that the "body" of the early Creator Prajapati could not rise since his joints were "relaxed", that is they either were unable to operate or did not exist and in exoteric meanings this would be accepted as such by the faithful and illiterate majority. The gods were said to have healed Parajapati's joints so that he could arise, however, the text clearly indicates that there was an underlying esoteric meaning that alludes to calendrical aspects. The reason that Parajapati's joints were relaxed is also given and this relates to the dawn, sunset and the Moon as follows:
"35) After Prajapati had created living beings, his joints (parvan) were relaxed. Now Prajapati, doubtless, is the year, and his joints are the two junctions of day and night (i.e. the twilights), the full moon and new moon, and the beginnings of the seasons."
"36) He was unable to rise with his relaxed joints; and the gods healed him by means of these havis-offerings: by means of the Agnihotra they healed that joint (which consists of) the two junctions of day and night, joined together; by means of the full-moon and the new-moon sacri-fice they healed that joint (which consists of) the full and new moon, joined together; and by means of the (three) Katurmasyas (seasonal offerings) they healed that joint (which consists of) the beginnings of the seasons, joined that together."[38].

Beside referring in this text to the joints as the nodes of the sunrise and sunset the cor-respondence with the joints to the rising, or brightening half of the lunar month and the second darkening half, so ubiquitous in the calendrical and religious formulations in the Vedic and Hindu religion is referred to here also. The text suggests that Prajapati created the world and did not actually have joints before that period and this bears remarkable similarities to the Andean con-ception noted of Viracocha who was also associated with the Moon, dawn and the sunset noted elsewhere in this book and appears to derive from the Vedic prototype along with other aspects. Interestingly also is that Prajapati's joints, as the "twilight" of dawn and sunset, is termed parvan and is the name for the Vedic wind god derived from the Ancient Middle East. This term is prob-ably the original for the Pahua or Tahua forming the fundamental Inca term for their Empire - Tahua-ntin-Suyu and considered in another section of this work.

In the Viracocha myth it is further said that he used the end of his staff to break-up the soil and plant seed for cultivation, including maize, and vegetables grew from the seed. In a few myths Viracocha was said to have turned to stone after creating Tiahuanaco[39], a stone built cere-monial city, but others indicate that he travelled northwards performing further acts of creation before heading west across the Pacific Ocean after reaching the coast in Peru or near Manta in Ecuador. This calendrical form of the myth tends to be confirmed by the considerations associ-ated with the solar path that is said to have originated in, and risen over Lake Titicaca in the myths of creation and setting at the Winter Solstice in the North West and therefore a heavenly reflection of the route that Viracocha took while on Earth[40].

Viracocha's name is particularly identified with the great Flood recorded in many myths throughout North West South America centred particularly on the altiplano or Bolivian plateau.

The Great Flood was believed in Cobo's records to have been caused by Viracocha, and this concurs with the versions preserved by other chroniclers. Cobo stated from his Indian sources that there was darkness during the great Flood and the Sun hid in Lake Titicaca for its duration but at its end it arose before "anything else". He notes that there are others versions relating events after the Flood and records one indicating that while the Flood lasted all the mountain peaks were covered and only one man and one woman survived by climbing into a drum that floated down with the subsiding waters and came to land at Tiaguanaco[41]. This version Cobo claims was the most prevalent that he heard about the aftermath of the Flood, but many others record that those who survived the waters did so by climbing to the top of the highest mountain not covered by the Flood, this Cobo also notes but his primary version is not unique.

Viracocha - Creator of the World

Cobo notes that in some versions of the Great Flood all the people died from drowning and after it subsided the Creator used clay to form the people of "all nations". He painted on the clay figurines the style and colour of clothing they were to dress in and designated the languages each should use. He gave them songs to sing and seeds, foods and vegetables and then ordered them to go down into the earth, each nation by itself, and emerge at their predestined spot that he had ordained for them. Some of these peoples emerged from caves, hills, springs, lakes and tree trunks, and each began to worship as huacas that place of their own particular origin. These first people after the Flood as the progenitors of their race having had offspring to perpetuate themselves and their people, then changed into falcons, condors, and other birds and animals and these were then associated with their huacas, or shrines to be worshipped similarly by that people[42]. The Flood myths will be considered further in another section of this work.

Among the Incas it was believed that the souls of the Inca themselves, after their earthly sojourn, would reside in a heaven where there would be eternal bliss. This was described as a place where they would be associated with the Sun forever and enjoy "perpetual bliss". This heaven was said to have been provided for them by Viracocha and in this divine place there would be no need for food or drink, sleeping or women. This version sounds very similar to that of the Brahmans of India and the more traditional heaven of the Polynesians. Cobo noted also, however, that this was not the view of the majority who believed that in heaven they would enjoy splendid repasts of the best food and drink and that this was ensured by the many food and drink sacrifices they performed throughout their life, and which they were therefore careful to perform for the whole of their earthly existence. These were directed towards Viracocha who created and enabled them to reach this heaven and the store they built up was provision in part for their ancestors supplying food and drink for their mummies during their lives so that they would guard for them that store built up in the afterlife[43].

In the pronunciation of the name of god it is remarkable that the general term used in China, parts of India and South America was Ti. Cobo noted that in pronouncing the Christian version Dios was pronounced by the Indians Tios as the "d" was difficult for them to utter since it did not occur in their language[44]. "Dios" therefore became Tios and it is perhaps no coincidence that Deo and its variations, such as Io in Polynesia, occur as Tia in pre-Conquest Peru South America. Cobo noted the importance of titles among them. Honorific titles were granted by the Inca including Ticci Viracocha or Viracocha Yachachic, and the former of these was considered to reflect an aura of mystery and meant "divine origin", while the title Pachayachachic and Viracocha Yachachic mean "Creator of the World". At the time of the Incas, however, Viracocha, although greatly revered, was not considered superior to the Incas sacred deity, the Sun. Only during the reign of the Inca Viracocha, Pachacuti's father, did the ancient deity Viracocha attain supremacy in their dynasty. This may have been because that Inca ruler may have been an albino and therefore resulted in a personal reaction against the Sun as deity. In reforming Inca society and rebuilding Cuzco Pachacuti assigned lands to support the temple of the Sun but not for Viracocha. This suggests that the Sun had regained favour in its role as the Inca dynasty's own symbol, but Viracocha was still provided with his own temple called the Quishuarcancha - Quishar being a sacred tree[45]. The temple of Viracocha and his other shrines drew tribute and support from all the other gods since he was universal lord over everything and the Inca himself made offerings from his own property to him[46]. For the people in the Empire, however, Viracocha retained his supremacy and was considered the Creator as such of all things including the Sun and therefore superior to it. Even when directing a prayer or propitiation to another deity, or ancestor, Viracocha was always first addressed[47]. The Sun was called "Apu Inti" and was prominent for its importance in cultivation, being visualised as a man, and where the Moon was considered his wife and the stars were said to be their daughters[48].

Animal Sacrifices - the Coloured Sheep of Indra
In the Vedic texts of India animal sacrifice is noted many times and of interest is that the colour and blemish free qualities of the finest available were of great importance. A brown cow with red-brown eyes was considered suitable for the Soma sacrifice and a ruddy one was reserved as the appropriate to sacrifice to Indra. Red cows were appropriate because they resembled the "…red clouds, which appear after the thunderstorm", Indra being the storm god[49]. In another section of the same texts it is noted that animal sacrifice was considered appropriate to assist in dispelling the great darkness said to have fallen over the earth when the demon Svarbhanu struck the Sun causing darkness to fall. It is noted that; "The gods sought the expiation for that (darkness): the first darkness of his which they dispelled became the black ewe, the second a red one, the third a white one; and what they cut off from the surface of the bone (?) that became a barren sheep, etc."[50].

The Andean myths are noted for that distant epoch when a great darkness fell upon the Earth and here in the Vedic texts is a similar relation. Of interest is that the sacrificed sheep where in fact offered in the very ancient tradition of the "scapegoat" where the purpose was that the evil that caused the darkness, believed to be tangible, would enter the sacrifice as indicated in the Vedic text. The various coloured ewes, the females, were related in ancient beliefs to wrathful and demonic forms, appears similarly in, and to be the origin of the Andean traditions. In Vedic myths these, and goat myths associated also with Pushan[51], are found in the myths and belief system associated with the storm god, Indra, who will be of more interest in the last chapter of this work.

In animal sacrifices, common in the rituals of Peru and Bolivia, llamas were selected with regard to their colour since white-fleeced llamas were due to the Sun and brown were allocated for Viracocha. This follows a similar practise in India where specifically coloured, blemish free goats, sheep and bulls[52] for sacrifice were selected for their colour above noted in the Vedic texts of India but derived from Ancient Iran. Interestingly, in the buffalo sacrifice of the Todas of Southern India, after the bull was sacrificed all the men would weep as part of the ritual suggesting that this was again linked originally to the storm god Indra and the rain believed to be sent by him[53]. Compare this to the references to weeping for Viracocha noted on the Nazca Plains in South Peru noted earlier in this chapter. Every day a white-fleeced llama was sacrificed in Cuzco and coca leaves were thrown on it when it was burning. Every morning at dawn the Sun was saluted with a prayer and sacrifice of food burnt in a special fire as the Sun appeared above the horizon - almost an exact copy of the Vedic Brahman rites in Ancient India[54]. Also remarkably similar to the ancient Brahmans' rituals was that the Incas bathed to cleanse themselves of sin and "pollution". The Inca in these cleansing rituals had to bath in a running river[55]. This is virtually identical to the bathing rituals of the Mandaeans where running water was considered the only true "baptismal" water, or the "water of life", and the only type of water that was endowed with divine power of cleansing as well as life-giving power[56]. The confession of sins was also required from the broad mass of people in the Inca Empire, as well as from the Incas individually, and they too were required to cleanse themselves in the running water of rivers[57].

In the sacrifices during the second month called the Camay festival, having kept the ashes from the festivals for the whole of the previous year, they collected this and the ashes from the present festival and assembled in Pumachupa where two streams met. The Inca and two hundred men with staffs also assembled. The two hundred men then walked, following the stream, until they reached Tambo and there these men took their positions on each side of the stream. The Inca then directed them to take the ashes of the sacrifice down to the town of Tambo and there they opened the first dam so that the water rushed downstream in such a volume, and gathering such force, that it broke the dams further down its route. The two hundred men with their staffs then followed the river and thrust away into the stream any of the offerings or ashes that had become stuck on the banks or edges of the stream. When they reached Tambo the water was unleashed with a declaration uttered: "Water, it is in your power to carry these ashes as far as the sea, to Viracocha, to whom our republic sends them, and thus we beg the wind to help you because we cannot go any further than here"[58]. Respects were also paid to the Inca Pachacuti since it is said that he initiated this part of the festival ceremony.

This ceremony indicates that there is an intimate connection between Viracocha and the sea and suggests further that there is a close link and a belief that that the legends of his leaving South America to travel west over the Pacific Ocean had some truth, and are at least consistent with the other myths relating to him. There is here also recognition that Viracocha is associated with the wind since there would be little purpose in invoking this element unless there was some mythical or legendary association between the wind and Viracocha.

Animal Sacrifice and the Principle of Foetal Sacrifices

When considering animal sacrifices in the Andes it has been noted that the llama foetus appeared to have a special place in these rites and this is confirmed by anthropologists and archaeologists in recent decades[59]. Foetal sacrifice appears to relate particularly as the corresponding motif of fertility for grain sown into the earth paralleling the gestation process[60] - a foetus probably indicating that germination was successful and therefore perceived as inducing the same in the grain by sacrifice, giving the grain "life" so to speak. In the territorial expansion from Tiahuanaco, the more restricted areas of influence in the Tiahuanaco 5 period in Southern Peru known as the Omo, foetal sacrifice is found under the southern corner of the temple structure. This offering was found together with a starfish indicating references to the sea and probably mariner influences. This region was an important route from the highlands of Bolivia, where Tiahuanaco is located, to the Pacific Coast and Alan Kolata notes the probable symbolic association of mountain plateau and the deep sea referring to similar offerings in the Templo Mayor at Tenochtitlan (Mexico City)[61].

The close similarities of the animal sacrifices in Ancient Iran and India with Peru have been noted and it is of some interest that foetuses were also of symbolic importance in Ancient North India being recorded in the Vedas. When the Aryans entered India, as cattle-herders, they brought with them their cattle and probably also sheep and goats. In time the goat became more widely kept in the rugged terrain and anciently this was considered an acceptable sacrifice when sheep and cattle were not available. Advantages occurred in this substitute where the goat, after sacrifice, was easier to cook[62] and even from very ancient times the he-goat was considered sacred to Agni, the fire-god[63].

In the Vedas the principle of Aga is given as meaning that of undeveloped principles in the womb of nature where the term literally means "unborn"[64]. In these texts the aga is identified with the goat, and resultant from this principle is that it is identified as being coloured red, white and black and that this aga is the he-goat and the offspring he produces are in his image[65]. In this aspect of Vedic philosophy the aga is identified with the true Self of an individual that proceeds to birth, the soul and is independent of Brahman and therefore appears to identify closely with the foetus. In this "birth" the self is identified with the rising and setting Sun and believed to be caused by the aga, or he-goat lying in the womb with Prakriti, deduced to be the she-goat[66]. Although this is a point of contention among Western scholars it is more or less accepted among the Hindu philosophers who do not rationalise their texts in the same way.

The Aga is seen as the causal light[67] from which all creation proceeds and this is paralleled with the emergence of the human as the microcosm and the Sun as the fundamental principle of light from either the womb or the dark womb of the night. As an identification with the Sun the divine goat is called Aga Ekapada, one footed or one legged and particularly identifies with its rising from the darkness of the night in the east[68] and this expressly emphasises his attribute as the "unborn"[69] or foetus.

The foetus therefore appears to have a special identification with the soul or life-force and in the winnowing of the grain harvest an offering of pure grain is made by sprinkling it with water and a piece of gold is dropped into it together with a Gayatri - metrical prayer, and then held up before a goat[70]. This has parallels with the grain offering associated with the llama foetus in Southern Peru suggesting closely similar beliefs, probably imported from India, and in one Vedic reference one claim is that the sacred goat "upholds the sky and the earth with his "efficacious spells"[71].

Animal Tallows in Sacrificial Offering

Important in the sacrifices of both Ancient Andes and India was the acquisition of tallow or animal fat. In Bolivia this foetal tallow from the llama was called uira-koua and appears to have been widely used in sacrifices and offerings throughout the Andes[72]. Father Pablo Joseph de Arriaga wrote that in the 16th., century A.D., when Hernando de Avendano visited Parquin, a tallow image was made of him in a form of voodoo, a rite called Caruay-Quispina, in an attempt to destroy his soul[73]. In South India the Paraiyans (Paraiahs) were well known for practising forms of black magic akin to West Indian voodoo. When attempting to despatch an enemy that cannot be approached a wax image is made of that person and the rites followed included burning the image and it was said to see the person's demise in two weeks[74]. The Odi or Oti cult ("breaking the human body") is, or was a black magic cult that practised the killing of people by ritual means and it was said that, similar to shaman cults in the Americas, the practitioners could render themselves invisible in an animal form. One of their specialities was the use of human fat in their potions and foetal fat was especially prized. One of their rituals to acquire the desired human foetus was describes by Edgar Thurston two generations ago that required the pregnant victim to yield her unborn foetus[75]. The practise of using human fat in rituals was more widely spread both inside India[76] and outside and was particularly described by interested researches among the Australian Aboriginals[77].

In another reference the renown 19th., century, architect scholar James Fergusson recorded in his "Tree and Serpent Worship" a myth that closely follows the myth of Pundariki considered elsewhere in this work. He recorded that the Brahmans, who preserved the Vedas as their own texts in direct descent from the Vedic Aryans, stated that the first king of the Naga dynasty of Magadha, at the time of the Buddha in the 6th., century, A.D. and the legendary founder of this dynasty was Sisunaga who origins were as follows: "On a certain occasion one of the chiefs of the courtesans bore a child to one of the Lichchhawi Rajas, but the child proving an abortion was put into a basket, and at night thrown on a dungheap. A certain nagaraja, the titular of the city, observing it, encircled it with its folds, and sheltered it with its hood. The people who congregated there mad a noise, 'Su, Su', to frighten the snake, and on examining the basket found the abortion matured into a male child with every mark of greatness on it. In consequence of this incident he received the name of Sisunaga, and in time ascended the throne of Magadha. ..."[78].

This myth appears to indicate that the foetus was as sacred as the healthy new born child and his elevated status underlines the point, but may also have been a gloss to references to the earlier noted Vedic texts. There can be little doubt that the foetus was of importance either in the strictly held and observed Vedic texts as in the broader base of the tribal myths and customs in India reflected in this Naga myth and the use of the foetus in ritual magic and voodoo applications in the lowest status tribes. These are clearly reflected in the Andean and Coastal Peru traditions and are too similar to be coincidental. In other sections of this work the Maoris are noted as considering the foetus as a soul to be respected and these formed the lowest strata of the gods, the Atua[79], in their pantheon and related to Maui in his foetal form when depicted. It is likely that these aspects were received perhaps partly from India, but probably also from Peru.

Viracocha as Healer

In treating illness Viracocha was invoked by the medicine man or "sorcerer", and preparations of ground maize and seashells were placed on the sick man's hand from which he had to blow it off as an offering. Coca was also placed on his hand and he blew that as an offering to the Sun. Small pieces of gold and silver were then given to the sick man to scatter about as a further offering to Viracocha, and food as an offering to the ancestors was placed on their graves, or given to their mummies since it was believed that the sickness was a curse placed on him by them because he had not sufficiently fed them or revered them. If he was able to walk the sick man was taken to the confluence of two rivers or streams and there bathed with the running water and white flour, otherwise this was performed at home. Remedies were applied to the man's stomach and sucking of the part of the body where the pain or illness lay was also applied by the sorcerer in the belief that the disease in the form of worms or small stones could be drawn out through the skin[80]. In the case of serious illness the patient was placed in a "secret" room and the walls and floors were swept clean. Black maize was used to be "scrubbed" on the walls and floors, and it was also used for blowing it everywhere and burning it in the "sick" room. They repeated the same actions with white maize. They then sprinkled the floor with a mixture of water and maize flour and when this was done the room was then considered to be purified. The patient was placed in a trance and the sorcerer "pretended" to operate on the patient with a crystal knife, and they "extracted it is said, snakes, toads and other filthy things" and burnt them in a fire[81]. These ancient Peruvian curative procedures are virtually identical in part or whole to those known among the Australian Aboriginals and in parts of India.

In considering Cobo's records more recent researchers have recognised him to have been accurate in his perceptions and descriptions of the Indians' belief system as far as he was allowed to penetrate and understand the Indian conservative hold on their traditions. It is evident in many of the writings of the Spanish friars at the time that they believed that the Devil, Satan, had deliberately attempted to subvert their attempts at proselytisation by developing a religious belief system imitating that of Europe among the Indians. Thus was due to the rites and beliefs of the Indians apparently so closely resembling that of the Christian Church along with a white, bearded Creator Saviour deity, Viracocha, whose resemblance to Christian saints was undeniable. These ancient deified missionaries were reputed in myth and legend to dress in an almost identical fashion to the Christian friars and led to some of the Spanish priests questioning whether St. Thomas had indeed preceded them and had attempted to convert the Indians many centuries before[82]. They were, it seems, closer to the truth than they could have realised at that time and possible contacts by the missionaries of St Thomas will be proposed later in this section of this work.

Viracocha - Name Origins

The earliest translations of the name Viracocha give it as made of two words each with their own meaning. vira means "foam" and cocha means "sea", or "lake", hence these translations give the name meaning "foam of the sea". Much more rarely is the meaning given as uira or vira being a corruption of pirua meaning the "storehouse" of creation - an explanation supported by Miles Poindexter. Montesinos, in quoting others, relates that the name Illa Tici Uira Cocha is made up of words with independent meanings, where Illa = "light", Tici = "foundation of things", uira = "storehouse", and cocha = "lake". However, most of the more recent researchers tend to revert to the first and more usual interpretations of Viracocha meaning "Foam of the Sea"[83] noted earlier in this chapter. On the coast it will also be shown that there is a significant connection between Viracocha and his named son, Paria-caca, a relationship rarely noted in myths and legends[84].

The most expansive account of the creation of the World by Viracocha is provided by Betanzos who married an Inca princess and derived most of his accounts from a position privilege. An edited version notes: In ancient times there was no light or day in Peru and the land was dark. The people of that time were ruled by an overlord whose name they no longer remembered. In those days there came from the lake in the region of Coallasuyu, a Lord named Con Ticci Viracocha who brought with him a certain number of people. After emerging from the lake he went to the place nearby now called Tiahuanaco in Collao. While he was there with his followers it is said that he made the Sun and caused it to follow in its course in the sky. He also made the stars and the Moon. They said that Con Ticci Viracocha had emerged on an earlier occasion and that during this appearance he had made heaven and the Earth and left everything dark. It was at this time that he created the men that lived at the time of the darkness. Viracocha was angered with the actions of this people and turned that people and their overlord to stone in punishment.

When he emerged (the second time) and had made the Sun and Moon he made at Tiahuanaco stone models or patterns of the races he was afterwards to produce and did it as follows: He made from stone a certain number of people and a lord who governed them and many women who were pregnant and others who had young children in cradles as was the custom. After this had been done he set the stone figures apart and made there another province in Tiahuanaco and figures also of stone in the same manner. When this had been done he kept only two of the people with him (Sarmiento says three, in a separate version re Taguapaca)[85] and commanded all the other people to journey forth, but to the two who remained with him he said: "These are called so and so and will issue forth from such and such a fountain in such and such a province and shall increase and populate it; these others shall issue from such and such a cave and will be named such and such and shall populate such and such a region. As I have them here painted and fashioned of stone, so shall they issue from fountains, rivers, caves and rocks in the provinces that I have indicated to you." Pointing to the east, the place of sunrise, he said, "And all you my people shall go in that direction dividing them up and indicating the title which each shall bear".

"After this the viracochas went off to the various districts which the god Viracocha had directed them to take and as soon as each had arrived in his assigned district he took up his position close by the designated site and called the stone figures which Viracocha had commanded in Tiahuanaco were to issue forth in that district. After this had been done at Tiahuanaco Viracocha spoke in a loud voice: 'So and so, come forth and people this land which is deserted, for thus has commanded Con Ticci Viracocha who made the world."[86]. At this the peoples came forth from the places and regions preconceived by Viracocha and as he had instructed. Thus they went on calling forth the races of men from caves, rivers and fountains and the high sierras and peopling the earth towards the east.

When Con Ticci Viracocha had accomplished this creation he sent the two men who had remained with him at Tiahuanaco to call forth the races of people in the manner as noted. He sent one through to the province of Cuntisuyu, that is to the left if one stands in Tiahuanaco with one's back to the sunrise (facing West), to bring forth the Indians native to that province. The other man he sent to the province of Antisuyu, which is on the right if one stands with the back to the sunrise in Tiahuanaco.

After Viracocha had despatched these two men to their respective destinations he went to Cuzco, this place lying between these two provinces, travelling by the royal road toward Cajamarca. As he went he called forth the races of men in the manners described above. When he came to the district called Cacha, the district of the Canas, eighteen leagues (about 55 miles) from the city of Cuzco, he called forth these Canas and they came forth armed. When they saw Viracocha, not recognising him, they rushed towards him weapons in hand with the intent to kill him. Reading their minds Viracocha commanded a fireball to fall from heaven scorching the mountain peak in the direction the Canas were attacking from. This so terrified the Indians that they threw their weapons down and knelt on the ground before him and when he saw their submission he used his staff to beat out the flames caused by the fireball.

When the fire had been put out Viracocha told the Canas that he was the creator and they built for him a sumptuous huaca (an idol or shrine) in the place where this event took place. They and their descendants were said to have provided many offerings of gold and silver to this huaca. In memory of their confrontation with Viracocha and the fireball they sculpted a huge stone figure on a large stone base about five yards long and one yard wide.

Betanzos records that he himself had seen the place where this fireball event had happened and confirms that the landscape appeared to have been devastated by a fire and that the scorched region extended for about a quarter of a league (about ¾ mile). He notes that, having seen this sight and the huaca or shrine to the event adjacent a stream that ran in front of it, he enquired from the local people the legend behind the huaca and they related the story above to him personally. He further asked then about the god Viracocha and his appearance when the first people of their race had seen him and they told Betanzos that he was a man of tall stature, clothed in a white robe extending down to his feet, this being belted around the waist. His hair was tonsured similar to that of the Spanish priests and he went barefoot and carried in his hands a "thing" recognised by the Indians as being similar to the breviaries carried by them after the Conquest. Betanzos asked the Indians the name of this man-god and they said it was "Con Ticci Viracocha Pachayachachic, which means in their language 'God, Creator of the World'".

The creation story noted by Betanzos continued further and the Indians told him that after this fireball event Viracocha went on his way, intent on his work. He travelled on until he came to a place that is now called the Tambo of Urcos, six leagues (about 18 miles) from Cuzco, and there he climbed a mountain and sat down. At this place he created more Indians commanding them to emerge from the mountain and their descendants were said to be those who lived in the region at the time of the Conquest. In honour of this event the Indians made a "very rich and sumptuous huaca" including a throne of "fine gold" and a statue sitting on it, set up in Viracocha's honour, "also of fine gold".

Viracocha continued on his way from this mountain at Tambo and proceeded to Cuzco where he created a lord named Alcaviza, and it is said he also gave the name of Cuzco to the place now bearing this name. He instructed Alcaviza that after his departure Orejones, or "long-ears", should be created and travelling on he met up with his followers, whom he had sent forth earlier at Tiahuanaco. This occurred in the district of Puerto Viejo, near Manta in modern Ecuador, and they then "put to sea" and they travelled as "easily across the water as they had done so on land". Interestingly Betanzos noted at the end of this relation that he could have written down many other stories about Viracocha but preferred not to do so as to avoid "prolixity and great idolatory and bestiality"[87].

It was said among the Aymaras that the great sacred mountain of Illimani looming over the valley that modern La Paz occupies was the favourite peak of Viracocha. This roused the envy of the adjacent peak which complained to Viracocha about his favouritism and the god in turn out of anger, broke off the top of its peak with a sling and as a result it now appears to be truncated. The upper section broken off was hurled through the air and became the present mountain of Sajama. The Omasuyus and the Pacajes, local Aymara clans, both claim Illimani as their ancestor[88]. In a closely similar myth, perhaps the prototype for the Andean myth, the wind god Vayu in India was incited by the sage Narada to shatter the top of the sacred mountain Mount Meru. Vayu blew at great force for a year but this mountain, sacred to Vishnu, was shielded from this attack by Garuda spreading his wings, and thereby thwarted Narada's scheme. Narada then decided to wait until Garuda had been called elsewhere and then incited Vayu to blow again and this time his designs were successful since the top of Mount Meru was blown off and it was thrown into the sea to become the island of Sri Lanka[89].

It has been noted not only by earlier researchers a century ago, but more recent historians, that there are close similarities between the Andean high gods and those of Mexico. Not only are the deities and their iconography similar but it has been shown that in both cases the imperial dynasties altered and adjusted the myths and imagery to suit their own political ambitions and to extend and identify themselves with national religious symbolism[90]. The earliest records of the original myths relating to Viracocha indicate that he was indeed an Andean and coastal Peruvian deity before the rise of the Inca dynasty, and that he was also known in the north as far as Ecuador.

Vira-Cocha and the Wira-Pora Wind Deities of the Pacific

A main element of disagreement regarding the name Viracocha is whether the term vira meant "foam" or "grease", as indicated in the earliest records already noted, and whether Viracocha as a deity had a special relationship with the sea over which he was said to have travelled to the west when last seen on earth. It has also been shown that the ashes of the sacrifices from all the previous festivals was floated down the river into the Pacific Ocean in the Camay festivities, and that he is specifically related to the wind in these rites. Others have argued that there is no meaning to the name Viracocha and this finds its authority in the dictate of Garcilasso de la Vega against all stated translations in the records of other early chroniclers.

It has been noted in an earlier chapter that at least two 16th., century myths relate that the Incas immigrated from the north and more recent researchers have suggested that the Quechuas, whose language they spoke, were the Quiche of Central America. Others have indicated, that the secret language spoken by the Incas, reported by Garcilasso de le Vega[91] and others, was in fact Pukina, a form of Aymara. Whatever the case may be one of the myths states that the first Inca progenitors came from the sea coast of North Colombia and it is interesting to note that it is here that evidence that the term vira originally related to the wind is preserved in that region.

The Tukano are an Indian people who inhabit the Amazonian rainforest in the northwest of South America in the eastern shadow of the Andes in Colombia. There are many aspects of their culture that has close similarities and parallels to many aspects of Polynesian culture and beliefs and these will be considered in due course. In the ensuing pages the continuity in the search for the origin of the term vira and relating it to the wind is of importance and it is to one of the Tukano divisions, the Desana, where that connection with the Incas, and India, is preserved. The name that the Desana give themselves is Wira-pora - "Sons of the Wind"[92], the identical term found among the Bhuiyas located in East Central India and around the Bay of Bengal who arrogated it to themselves. Here the Tukano wira is clearly the same as vira and therefore likely to have been related to that of the Quechua Vira in Viracocha. The Desana less often call themselves Mimi-pora or "Sons of the Hummingbird" - this being their tribal animal. In cosmic myths the Milky Way was conceived as an extended skein of fibres that had been blown by the wirunye boga or "wind skein" in a current from a lower zone from east to west[93]. In a remarkable parallel with India the wind forms the complement of the soul and is called ka'i, and was thought to reside in the brain and there called the "head wind", dihpu ka'i[94]. This parallels exactly the idea that the soul was the especial responsibility of the former Vedic wind deity in Iran and India, Vay, probably the prototype for the name and meaning of the Tukano, Ka'i.

Among the Desana, the priest, the Kumu, has a very high status and is said to represent the Sun[95]. The priest among the Incas was called the umu and is clearly derived from a common origin as that of the Desana. It has to be noted that kumu is also the name for one of the Polynesian ancestors as the first god Tu or Tumu. In an extraordinary rite, after the death of a kumu, he is buried in the centre of his malocca or tribal house. After five years or so he is exhumed and the bones of the toes and hands are removed, ground up into powder, and mixed into chichi and then drunk by the men to incorporate into themselves the wisdom of the deceased kumu[96]. It is interesting to note that the hands, and or feet in the human sacrifices of captives at Sipan were removed in interments dating to about 300 A.D.[97]. Sometimes part of ritual cannibalistic rites were considered the finest part and were retained for the chief and priests in Polynesia and parts of Melanesia in Melanesia[98]. In the Kula circuit, of interest earlier, the hero Tokosikuna was said in one version to have no hands or feet possibly a reference to human sacrifice or to elevated status indicating Polynesian descent[99].

The Desana indicate in their mythology the importance of the rainbow as a symbol of their tribe and this reflects the same symbol as the emblem of the Incas. Desana myths record that the rainbow was said to represent the Sun and in mythical times it was believed to be a fish, or type of eel, named Buime. This eel was said to have emerged from the great waters to find out what had happened after the great fire had destroyed the world in an earlier time[100]. Biume, the eel, established itself as an intermediary between earth and heaven in the time after this great conflagration. This deity name appears to be the same as that of Bue in Polynesia and Baiame in Aboriginal Australia and these will be shown to have derived from India also. The great mythical, sky-supporting eel called Riiki[101], is found in Polynesia, and no doubt is reflected here among the Desana.

An element of Desana myths of central importance is the Pamuri-gahsiru - the Snake-Canoe that carried the first ancestors from their sacred Tukano heaven Ahpikondia to their forest home. This element will prove of considerable importance later in this section of the present work since they bear close resemblances to the beliefs and ceremonials associated with serpent canoes in India and South East Asia. Having made the connection between the Incas, Vira-cocha and the Desana of Colombia, with the term for the wind apparently having a common origin, it is necessary to consider the origins of Vira, and Ka'i, or Paye as Vay in India and the Ancient Middle East.

Andean Wind Gods Origins from Vay, and Vayu, the Wind God of India and Iran
The term Desana name for themselves, Wira-pora - "People-of-the-Wind", has been noted and that it corresponds exactly to the same expression used by the Bhuiyas in East Central India and around the more northern reaches of the Bay of Bengal, Pawanbans - "Sons-of-the-Wind". At first glance there seems to be a glaring dissimilarity in half of the terms comparing the two expressions in their respective languages but when it is considered in the last chapter that Pawan also equates to Vir or Bir in India it becomes clear that they have an identical origin. In parallel the term Pawa in India has been shown to correspond to the Pauah or Paua among the Maya of Central America equating to the Tahua of Ancient Peru - all deriving from the wind deity of Iran

and India earlier noted. Among the Hindus the spirits of the heroes were called the viras and was an expression widely preserved into the present day from ancient times. This is also the case among the mixed Aryan and Aboriginal peoples such as the Bhuiyas. These "Sons of the Wind" also took to the sea and there is a section of their tribes settled near Madras in South East India called the Buis who may in fact have been the origin for the myths or legends relating to the Desana and the Bue of Polynesia[102].

The Bhuiyas greatly favoured the worship of the monkey god Hanuman, widely popular in India, and it is of particular interest that he was considered to be the son of the wind god Pawan. He was therefore called Pawan-ka-put - the "Son-of-the-Wind", and as a result the Bhuiyas called themselves Pawanbans in honour of their special deity[103]. The Bhuiyas of the Keonjhur Hills worship the Sun as Bharam, also Boram, who was called Bir or Vira, otherwise known as Mahabir Hanuman. These people were more privately devoted to the bloodthirsty goddess Thakurani, an even fiercer version of the Hindu Kali, who required to be propitiated with blood sacrifices, and these were almost invariably human victims in earlier centuries. In the cosmology of the Bhuiyas, Bhima, the great Achilles hero of India, a Pandu, was the brother of Hanuman and both were said to have been the sons of the wind god Pawan also known as Vay or Vayu[104]. It is also significant that the most valorous fighters among the Hill Bhuiyas were the Pawris or Poris a contraction of Paharis. These Hill Bhuiyas retained an oligarchy called the Pawri Desh composed of 60 chiefs and it is of special interest that in summoning a council meeting they notified other sections as follows: "A knotted string passed from village to village in the name of the sixty chiefs throws the entire country into commotion, and the order which is verbally communicated in connection with it, is as implicitly obeyed as if it emanated from the potent despot"[105]. This form of communication also was found in other parts of India but it should be noted that this is virtually identical to the quipus messages conveyed along the highways for the Incas in Peru. The term Pawri or Pori is found also among the Desana as Pora and the council construct based on sixty is a sexagesimal system probably derived originally from the Ancient near East consistent with other elements of Bhuiya culture.

In other parts of India, in the south, the term vira is usually associated with hero or an honorific title. The great first cosmic man was Vira-purusha and the four castes of India were said to derive from his substance. From his mouth it is said the Brahmans issued (from his breath), from his arms came the Kshatriyas, from his thighs came the Vaisyas, and from his feet came the Sudras[106].

The various village deities imaged in clay were collectively termed Virans and these were said to keep watch over their master. Offerings to the temples were collected by the Virans, permanent attendants, and if the offering was an animal it was they who despatched it with a knife[107]. In an interesting myth preserved by the Kaikolan caste of weavers, who will be of further interest in later chapters, a myth relates aspects of their favoured deity Vira-bahu. Edgar Thurston recorded this myth as follows: "The demon Suran was troubling the Devas (angels) and men, and was advised by Karthikeya (Subramanya) and Virabahu to desist from so doing. He paid no heed, and a fight ensued. The demon sent his son Vajrabahu to meet the enemy, and he was slain by Virabahu, who displayed the different parts of the body in the following manner. The vertebral column was made to represent a pole, round which the other bones were placed, and the guts tightly wound round them. The connective tissues were used as ropes to support the pole. The skull was used as a Jaya-Mani (conquest bell), and the skin hoisted as a flag. The trident of Virabahu was fixed to the top of the pole, and standing over it, he announced his victory over the world. The caste section called the Nattu-Kattada Nayanmars claim direct descent from Virabahu who in caste disputes set up a pole having 72 internodes and measure the same number of feet. The number of internodes is supposed to correspond to the number of nadus (countries) into which the Kaikolans are subdivided. The Nattu-Kattada Nayanmars climb this pole

7.001 : The serpent identified with the sky serpent and the arch of the sky is closely similar in concept and reflected combination to the iconography associated with the sky in India called the Torana. Chimu Dynasty, La Huaca del Dragon or Arco Iris, Trujillo, North Central Coast Peru, 1200 - 1450 A.D.

and perform various feats or acrobatics under the patronage of the deity Kamatchiamma. The final act is performed by their principal acrobat who "balances a young child in a tray on a bamboo and, letting go of the bamboo, catches the falling child." These acts are said to be inspired and to commemorate Virabahu defeat of the demon's son, and the pole represents his spinal column above noted[108]. The headman of the Kaikolans is the Patta-Karan and this term will also be of more interest later.

Many ceremonies revolve around paying homage to the ancestral spirits particularly those associated with the warriors or the caste. At many marriages across the castes a part of the ceremony is set aside to pay respects to their ancestors called Vira-Gudi-Mokkadam or "worship of the heroes". This is also known as Vira Puja[109], often called collectively when several or many are referred to as "heroes" - vira-lu[110]. Sometimes the caste gods are deified ancestors, occasionally joint male and female, and it is usual to apply, or separate the male by attaching the title of Vira, or ancestral hero, to him[111]. The Kurubas of South East India are an important tribe and former rulers, and their "patron saint" is Bir-appa, or Bira Varu. Both of these appear to have the same origin but, as in Peru and among the many other tribes and castes of India, Bir is interchangeable with Vir or Vira and relates to the wind and therefore to monkey scribal god, Hanuman as son of the wind[112]. As with so many examples in South America, and among the Incas, sacred objects wrapped in sacred bundles or boxes were also prevalent in India and the southern branch of the Kurubas near Mysore revered and worshipped a box, which they believed to contain the garments worn by the god Krishna[113].

The Kurubas are known for their extensive monoliths temples that were constructed of megaliths resembling the dolmens so well known in Europe. The main structure is usually constructed from four stone pillars and covered with a large stone slab and centred under it is the large stone monument with the image of the chief to whom it was dedicated carved on one of its faces (*7.002*). The Kurubas were also known for building miniature dolmens about 500 mm or 18 inches high. In the interiors of these dolmens were placed two stones painted red representing "the deceased resting on his mother earth below"[114]. Edgar Thurston reported that, "In the open country near Kadur in Mysore, is a shrine of Bira-devaru, which consists of four stone pillars several feet in height surmounted by flat slabs as a cap-stone, within which the deity is represented by round stones, and stones with snakes carved on them are deposited"[115]. Such stone structures are highly reminiscent of those found at San Agustin (*12.003*) in Southern Colombia, Peru and Bolivia as well as in New Caledonia (*12.005*).

One of the most interesting of the tribes and castes of South India are the Pallis also called Vanniyans. Some of its members claim descent from the Agni-Kulas, or "fire-races", a section of the warrior caste called the Kshatriyas. An early writer on the cultures of India H.A. Stuart wrote three generations ago that the name Vanniyan was derived from the Sanskrit vanhi (fire) resulting from the following legend: "In olden times, two giants named Vatapi and Nahi, worshipped Brahma with such devotion that they obtained from him immunity from death from every cause save fire, which element they had carelessly omitted to include in their enumeration. Protected thus, they harried the country, and Vatapi went the length of swallowing Vayu, the god of the winds, while Mahi devoured the sun. The earth was therefore enveloped in perpetual darkness and stillness, a condition of affairs that struck terror into the minds of the devatas, and led them to appeal to Brahma. He, recollecting the omission made by the giants, directed his suppliants to desire the rishi Jambava Mahamuni to perform a yagam, or sacrifice by fire. The order having been obeyed, armed horse men sprang from the flames, who undertook twelve expeditions against Vatapi and Mahi, who they first destroyed, and afterwards released Vayu and the sun from their bodies. Their leader then assumed the government of the country under the name Rudra Vanniya Maharaja, who had five sons, the ancestors of the Vanniya caste. These facts are said to be recorded in the Vaidiswara temple in the Tanjore District." The same author adds that "this tradition alludes to the destruction of the city of Vapi by Narasimbha Varma, king of the Pallis or Pallavas"[116]. Vatapi was the capital of the Chalukyas and it has been noted that the Chalukyas, particularly their iconography, appear to have a special relationship with the Maya of Central America notable especially at Palenque and at Tiahuanaco.

Historically the Vanniyan myth appears to have been founded on historical fact and the defeat of the Chalukyas and their king Pulikesin II, by the Pallava king Narasimbha Varman is dated to 642 A.D.[117]. The Chalukyas and Pallavas of South Central and South East India respectively were great combatants in the seventh century A.D. and the names and origins of the founders of these dynasties has been conjectured by some to be indigenous while others have considered them to be immigrants from the Ancient Middle East.

In another myth the Pallis or Vanniyans relate that they are "...descendants of one Vira Vanniyan, who was created by a sage named Sambuha when he was destroying the two demons named Vatapi and Enatapi. This Vira Vanniyan married a daughter of the god Indra, and had five sons, named Rudra, Brahma, Krishna, Sanbuha, and Kai, whose descendants now live respectively in the country north of the Palar in the Cauvery delta, between the Palar and Pennar. They have written a Puranam and a drama bearing on this tale. They declare that they are superior to Brahmans, since, while the latter must be invested with the sacred thread after birth, they bring their sacred thread with them at birth itself"[118].

Although in more recent times the Vannis are a less well-known agricultural class they were, it seems in earlier epochs, of higher status and, as surviving manuscripts record they were, as the Agnikula, victorious warriors and were famed for their skill as archers. In one manuscript they are recorded to have refused to pay tribute to the Rayar, or local king, who was unable to reduce them to submission. Rayar, or Raya is the term for king or ruler is the earlier equivalent of Rao[119], and appended to the caste names of those whose clans have supplied kings, usually the warrior castes. Apparent in the name is its derivation from the term Arya, and is believed directly linked to European term ray relating to the Sun. Extraordinarily this coincides with Miles Poindexter's theory of the Peruvian contact with the Aryans from India since the term Raya is founding the elevated term for one of the first pre-Inca gods Con-I-Raya, or Kon Raya[120] and noted later in this chapter.

The Patta-Navans in South India have a special sea god named Kutti-yadavan but animal sacrifices are not offered to him but to the other deities named Semu Virappan and Minnodum Pillai[121]. Yadavan appears to exalt an external deity since Yadavas was the collective name given to Middle Eastern peoples, Greeks and Romans who settled as traders in India but Vir-appan is more widely known and is characteristically the cult hero. They represent the deity Ayyanar (Aiyanar or Sasta) among others as sand mounds on the seashore emphasising their foreign associations.

The term Vira is clearly recorded as relating to heroes both state and religious. The Lingayats are a caste who are usually worshippers of Siva, the god of the linga or phallus. Originally it was the custom for the Vira-mushti to only wear the ling, a small phallic carving enclosed in a wrapping or case to be hung as a pendant at death as a symbol of regeneration in the afterlife. However, it had become the custom for the initiation to take place earlier in life and these Vira-mushtis are usually associated with the Lingayats or Komatis. Thurston records; "Whenever a Devanga, Lingayat Komati, or other Lingayat wants to make a hero (vira) of a deceased member of his family, he sends for a Vira-mushti (or hero-maker), and has a slab planted, with a recognised ceremonial, at the spot where he is planted." ... "I am informed that they

7.002 : Sophisticated dolmen covering massive central monolith traditional since about 500 B.C. in Central and South India. Kuruba Tribe, Biradevaru Temple, Pre-19th., century, A.D.

correspond to the Virabhadra Kayakams of the Canarese Lingayats, like whom they dress up, and adorn themselves with small lingams, the figure of Virabhadra, a sword, a plate bearing a star, and heads of Asuras (demons). Every important temple has one or two Viramustis attached to it, and they are supposed to be the servants of Siva. One of their chief duties is to guard the idol during procession, and on other occasions. If during a car procession the car will not move, the Viramushtis cut themselves with their swords until it is set in motion ..."[122].

The carved lingas worn about the neck are considered of great importance in the worship of Siva, as for the majority of Hindus resembling the larger lingas found in the Saivite temples (*12.007*). It has been shown that the linga is probably the Tiki so well known in Maori carved stone art and myth, and probably was the prototype for similar aspects of belief and artefacts found in the America. There are many of aspects of deities specifically associated with heroes qualities and therefore prefixed with the term vira, such as Vira-Bhadra, a fierce god demanding animal, and originally, human sacrifices. This same prefix was used by the Chola Kings in the 10-12 centuries A.D. in South India where they and the Pallava dynasty influenced the South East Asian countries and the islands of Java and Sumatra in Indonesia[123].

The Tottiyans are a South India caste who repeatedly crop up in the researches of possible cross-Pacific contacts between India and South America. At the marriage ceremonies of a Tottiyan couple a special traditional pandal (hut) is constructed in the village, and a smaller hut constructed each side, one for the bride the other for the groom. An unusual rite then took place where the slaughtering of an unblemished red ram takes place and the blood used to mark the brows of the bridal pair. Before sacrifice the ram is first sprinkled with water and if it shivers it is thought to be a good omen. The rite also includes the pursuit by the bridegroom with a bow and arrow of a man who pretends to flee but who is captured and bound. Clearly the pursuit is a memory of the rites still in force among the Nagas of Assam and peoples in some of the more remote islands or parts of Indonesia where a bridegroom was eligible only if he had collected at least one human head before marriage. These later, modified forms of pursuit seem to have their counterparts among the Incas and where large numbers of unblemished llamas (or sheep as the Spanish called them) were sacrificed in their frequent festivals[124].

Another section of the Tottiyans, called the Vekkiliyans, for their marriage festivals, erected two huts outside the village and the main pandal was constructed in front of them. This was built up of twelve posts and roofed with the branches of the Pongu tree. The bridal couple are conducted to their huts and the bride herself is carried by her maternal uncle. They worship their ancestral heroes (viras) who are represented by new cloths folded and placed on a tray. A mock ploughing ceremony is undertaken in the bridegroom's hut and upon leaving the hut they took up a child and carried it three times around the huts. This was a substitute for the former practise of the couple having to remain in the marriage huts until a child was born to them[125].

The Tottiyans appear similar to other lesser status tribes who were believed to have once been rulers in the land and Thurston quotes Hemmingway on their caste deities: "The Tottiyans," Mr. Hemmingway writes, "do not recognise the superiority of the Brahmans, or employ them as priests at marriages or festivals. They are deeply devoted to their own caste deities. Some of these are Bommaka and Mallamma (the spirits of women who committed sati long ago), Vira-Karanor Vira-Mati (a bridegroom who was killed in a fight with a tiger), Patta-l-amma (who helped them in their flight from the north), and Malai Tambiran, the god of ancestors." .... "The

Tottiyans are known for their uncanny devotion to sorcery and witchcraft." ... "All of them are supposed to possess unholy powers, especially the Nalla Gollas, and they are much dreaded by their neighbours. They do not allow any stranger to enter their village with shoes on, or on horseback, or holding an umbrella, lest their god should be offended"[126]. It is worth noting that in the Americas also, particularly among the high cultures, it was forbidden to wear shoes in a sacred place in the same manner and this custom is also found to the present day in India and known from the Ancient Middle East.

Among the Badagas, a people who lived closely associated with the Todas of South India, when, at the time when death for one of their tribe was drawing near, an obolos in the form of a gold coin called the vira-raya hana was smeared with clarified butter (ghi), and given to the dying person to swallow. A century ago an eyewitness account was recorded by a Mr. Glover as follows: "If the tiny coin slips down, well. He will need both gold and ghi, the one to sustain his strength in the dark journey to the river of death, the other to fee the guardian of the fairy-like bridge that spans the dreaded tide. If sense remains to the wretched man, he knows that now his death is nigh. Despair and the gold make recovery impossible, and there are none who have swallowed the Birianhana, and yet have lived. If sensibility or deathly weakness make it impossible for the coin to pass the thorax, it is carefully bound in cloth, and tied to the right arm, so that there may be nought to hinder the passage of a worthy soul into the regions of the blessed"[127]. In this relation Vira clearly equals Bira of the Birianhana as it does among the Bhuiyas far to the north and among others. The term Vira-raya refers to the soul where Vira refers not only to "heroic" qualities but reveals its probable origin as being another derivative of Vayu - Vayu as wind deity being the god of the soul in Ancient Iranian and Hindu mythology. Raya refers to "royal" in the European sense since Raya or Rao is title the king much as Rey (Rei) is in Spanish - but also has the associated meaning of shining like the rayed Sun. In this sense it is used in this myth and appears to indicate that the soul is a "spark" from the cosmic fire - the beginnings of life, "the spark of life" so to speak, and this would correspond with the derivation of the name from the old fire religions of the Ancient Near and Middle East. The Badagas and Todas are believed to have been vestiges of Ancient migrations from West Asia and the name of their villages, hatti[128], suggests that they may have had Hittite origins.

In India the sky god of Hinduism is Vishnu, and his popularity as supreme deity of the pantheon meant that he accrued, or was endowed with many titles. One of particular interest is that of Vira Tarupa and this meant that he assumed the great stature of a hero - vira = hero, and where the literal meaning of the whole title is "having the figure of a Vira-ta"[129]. In transferring such titles and in an attempt to preserve or proselytise abroad it is unlikely that the intellectual meaning would be conveyed, only an impression of the name indistinctly remembered and a few of the qualities it was supposed to convey. It may be significant that the term Vira is clearly sim-

7.004 : A Birhor sacrifices at small mounds representing gods and deified ancestors, or manita, similar to those constructed in Burma as miniature stupas or pagodas. Behind the man is a hut dedicated to the ancestral spirits. Central India, Early 20th., century, A.D.

7.003 : Earth mounds constructed as miniatures representations of the Buddhist stupa, originally a relic shrine. Burma (Myanmar), Early 20th., century, A.D.

ilar to that of Vira-cocha and that Tarupa may have been remembered as Tarapaca or Taupaca, other early names recorded variations of Tonaca or Tonapa, identified with Viracocha in Bolivia. Many references relating to the transfer of culture from India, and Southern China to Western Mexico have been recorded among the Huichols, and it is worth noting that among them the name Huichol was in fact given to them by the Mexicans, while the name they gave themselves was Visha-lika or Vira-rika. The Huichol terms means doctors and healers[130] but in a direct translation in India would be Wind God or Heroic Lord. In Polynesia the term A-rika meant a sea-going canoe-captain. The first of these terms appears to reflect the name of Vishnu while the second that of the wind god of India Vay as Vira, while rika is the term in India for the rishis or the seven sacred Aryan sages identified with the Great Bear constellation.

The Tamils of South India, a Dravidian people, used the term Vanni and Vanniyan to denote king, or kingship. In South India it is recorded that there were small local kingdoms ruled over by Vannis, or Vanni-raya[131]. It is interesting to note that the Vannis, also known as Pallis, lived in separate caste streets or quarters known as Palli teru or Kudi teru (ryot's quarters - a term derived from raiyat in Hindi, and rayah in Arabic), a practise known in Ancient Peru and still retained in some of the more isolated villages earlier noted.

Fire walking is practised in Southern India as it has been for many centuries where it was considered an essential rite associated with the Agni-kula peoples. "Treading the fire" was a privilege claimed by the Vanniyans and the myth associated with this rite was recorded by a British observer in South India as follows: "Draupadi's temples are very numerous, and the priest at them is generally a Palli by caste, and Pallis take the leading part in the ceremonies at them. Why this should be so is not clear. The Pallis say it is because both the Pandava brothers and themselves were born of fire, and are therefore related. Festivals to Draupadi always involve two points of ritual - the recital or acting of a part of the Mahabharata and a fire-walking ceremony. The first is usually done by the Pallis, who are very fond of the great epic, and many of whom know it uncommonly well. In the city of Madras there are several Draupadi Amman temples belonging to Pallis. The fire-walking ceremony cannot be observed thereat without the help of a member of this caste, who is the first to walk over the hot ashes."[132].

The fire-walking rituals were recorded not only widely in South India but also in Fiji, among the Maoris, and the Pacific North West Coast of North America when first contact by Europeans was made and it is clear that this ritual was dispersed from India along the ocean currents running through the North and Central Pacific. Draupadi was the sister of the five Pandava brothers who lost their kingdom the North West of India in the great wars between rival Aryan tribes, and they fled south and became very popular cult heroes in South India. Interestingly it is also said that they lost their kingdom through losing at the game of Pachisi, identical to the game known as Patolli in ancient Mexico, where the outline of the gaming pattern is inscribed on ancient floors exactly repeating those of India. One of the great heroes of the Mahabharata, Krishna, was a cousin of the Pandavas[133], as was the greatest, Arjuna and the giant Bhima beloved of the Bhuiyas[134]. Interestingly also is that the architect Maya built a great hall for worship for the Pandavas[135]. The connection between this architect and Central America have been recorded in an earlier publication[136] but is should not be missed that the term Palli, formerly so prominent in South India and associated with other elements transferred to the Americas is probably the origin for the name for the Inca women of high birth - Palla. It was said in the Pandava myths that Draupadi was married to her brothers and was therefore an example of polyandry, known in parts of India into the twentieth century but also known in the Ancient Middle East. In the Inca origin myths several of them state that the first Incas, usually numbered at four married their sisters.

Another myth associated with the Pallis, or Vannis, is a very unusual one but that appears to have references to Andean myths. One of the deities of the Vannis was named usually Aravan, more correctly, originally Iravan, but also Kuttandar. The name Iravan clearly indicates its origin - Iran or Aryan. This deity was the son of Arjuna, the hero of the great Aryan epic the Mahabharata and the cousin of the Pandavas. Edgar Thurston recorded that; "Local tradition says that, when the great war which is described in the Mahabharata was about to begin, the Kauravas, the opponents of the Pandavas, sacrificed, to bring them success, a white elephant. The Pandavas were in despair of being able to find any such uncommon object with which to propitiate the gods, until Arjuna suggested that they should offer up his son Aravan. Aravan agreed to yield his life for the good of the cause, and, when eventually the Pandavas were victorious, he was deified for the self-abnegation that had thus brought his side success. Since he died in his youth, before he had been married, it is held to please him if men, even though grown up and already wedded, come now and offer to espouse him, and men who are afflicted with various diseases take a vow to marry him at his annual festival in the hope thereby being cured ..."[137].

This Vanni myth betrays its Ancient Middle Eastern name in the racial origins of the heroes, the Pandavas, but also in the presumption that only male sacrifices were acceptable to the gods - a element to be of note later in this work since it is found in Melanesia. The rites of this festival associated with Aravan were recorded in eyewitness accounts as follows; "The festival occurs in May, and for eighteen nights the Mahabharata is recited by a Palli, large numbers of people especially of that caste, assembling to hear it read. On the eighteenth night, a wooden image of Kuttandar is taken to a tope (grove) or mound, and seated there. This is the signal for the sacrifice of an enormous number of fowls, etc." ... "While this is going on, all the men who have taken vows to be married to the deity appear before his image dressed like women, make obeisance, offer to the priest (who is a Palli by caste) a few annas, and give into his hands the talis (marriage badges) which they have brought with them. These priests as representing the God, ties round their necks. The God is brought back to his shrine that night, and when in front of the building he is hidden by a cloth being held before him. This symbolises the sacrifice of Aravan, and the men who have just been married to him set up loud lamentations at the death of their husband ..."[138].

The sacrifice of the youth appears as a motif widely in the myths of India and Oceania and is probably one of the elements that had become merged with the deity Tonapa in the altiplano of Bolivia, and in Andean and coastal Peru identified with Viracocha, who was also called there Arnauan[139]. Among the Paraiyans, believed by early British researchers to have been rulers but now reduced to outcastes in their own land, the ancient traditions regale them as once having been superior even to the Brahmans. During a festival to their village goddess they repeat a refrain of "extravagant praise of their caste" as follows: "The Paraiyans were the first creation, the first who wore the sacred thread, the uppermost in the social scale, the differentiators of castes, the winners of laurels. They have been seated on the white elephant Vira, Sambavans who beat the victorious drum." Thurston noted of this, "It is a curious fact that, at the feast of the village goddess, a Paraiyan is honoured by being invested with the sacred thread for the occasion by the pujari (priest) of the temple, by having occasionally having a turmeric thread tied to his wrists, and being allowed to head the procession. This, the Paraiyans say, is owing to their exalted origin."[140]. There are many festivals that require the involvement of one of the lower castes in recent centuries to occupy an apparent far higher social position than they hold in the everyday social scale in India and this is just one important example illustrating the former exalted position of this tribe. This tribe will be of more interest later in this work.

Extending the Origins of the Terms of Vira, Vay; Vayu - The Wind as a Soul Deity
The term Vira in Vira-cocha is identical in Indian mythology to Vira, Vir or Bir in India, and this has been shown to be closely related to Maha-Bir, the monkey god Hanuman who was, along with Bhima, the son of Pawan or Vay or Vay the wind god[141]. It has also been shown elsewhere

that Pawan is the prototype for the examples of the wind deities, the Pauahtuns among the Maya, but that the alternative name of vay or vayu was also known among them as uo; uay, uayeb, and u-vayey-ab[142]. The wind deity as Vay or Vayu was particularly associated with the wind as an element of the soul in the mythology of Ancient Iran and India and among the Maya. The elements derived from Pawan, as wind deity, have been shown to derive from the Ancient Middle East in India and reflected in the Andean civilisations in South America in the previous chapter. This deity, Pawan, is clearly recognised as that much earlier associated with Western Iran and the Mesopotamian region, but the primary god Vay or Vayu was originally a separate wind god at the head of a cosmology in a separate cultural region in Eastern Iran dating from the second millennium B.C. and earlier.

It appears that the pressure of migrations from the Caucasus region into the southern regions of West Asia occurred regularly with peaks around the massive volcanic eruptions of 4370 B.C., 3195 A.D., 1628 B.C. and 1159 B.C. These catastrophic events caused dramatic climate changes and forced the northern peoples south into South Asia driving all in their path to flee by the only escape route available for most of them into, and from Iran to India. Such events appear to have forced the merger of the Eastern and Western Iranian civilisations producing an incomplete hybrid preserving two lines or pantheons of various deities. This resulted in duplication to a large extent but in time relegation or elevation of one or the other occurred without either being totally lost. This occurred also in India where the supreme Vedic Aryan deities such as Indra and Varuna were eventually relegated to the second rank while other such as Vishnu and Siva emerged as the new supreme deities of the Hindu religion.

From Eastern Iran both wind gods, Vay or Vayu and Pawan, were imported into Indian mythology and were largely interchangeable, although Vayu appears to be more favoured than Pawan. Among the fire religions of Ancient Iran and the Near East in the second millennium B.C. the deity named Zurvan was prominent but in later Mazdaean religion he was relegated and then virtually excluded from this religion under the Zoroastrian revisionism. In this earlier time the deity Vay, the wind god, was largely identified with Zurvan ("He who conquers deceit")[143]. Vay in later texts, such as the better known Avesta, Vayu as he is called in the text known as the Yast, appears frequently and, as noted above Vay appears unconnected with early Zoroastrianism[144]. He appears, when ultimately assimilated to Zoroastrianism, divided into two powerful deities or one with intense dual natures of darkness and light. The dual natures of Vayu are from this time, at the beginning of the first millennium B.C., identified either with the god of light Ohrmazd (Ahura Mazda) or darkness, Ahriman, and these deities are recorded in ancient texts as being revered by a number of mythical heroes[145]. Because of the all-pervasive nature and strength of the wind he is thought to be the pursuer (vayemi) of both the creations attributed to Ohrmazd and Ahriman. In this context he is also considered the "catcher" - apayate. Vayu was considered to be the deity above the qualities of good and evil and was patron of the warrior caste and invoked in battle. Vayu was depicted wearing a golden helmet and a golden crown riding in a golden chariot with golden wheels. His weapons of war were also golden and he wore golden garments, shoes and girdle[146].

Vayu was associated with the soul particularly immediately after death when the soul was thought to undertake the "journey of the soul" to a place in the afterlife. This deity was the judge at the entrance to the Cinvat Bridge, or the bridge across the river of death. Vayu guarded this bridge and the only option available to the soul was to attempt to pass over it where, if the soul had lived a worthy, blameless life the bridge would provide it access to the hallowed land of the ancestors and a happy afterlife. If the soul had led a life of wickedness it would fall into the chasm below and be tormented for eternity by the demons who dwelt there. The duality of the nature of Vayu appears to be associated with the perils of this Bridge, and his "good" nature was exhibited if the soul was good and passed over it unharmed, but "evil" if the soul itself was found wanting. The "good" Vayu was termed Vay i veh and the "evil" Vayu was called Vay i vattar and reflects his original principle of the wind that connects Heaven and Earth and extended to mean the intercessor between Darkness and Light[147]. These terms are very reminiscent of those recorded among the Maya noted above, but more so in the expressions developed in the mythology of India where he is called "pervader" - vyapya[148].

As wind god Vay is considered the element that gives life to the soul since this is considered to be a spark from the "atmospheric fire" (vayik atachs) and fire burns in air of the atmosphere (Vay). This fiery nature of the "breath-soul" corresponds to the "fiery-wind" of the soul of man unifying both the elements of fire and wind[149]. Vay is also identified with Spihr, or the great "arc" of space" and had the "wheel" as its symbol, suggesting zodiacal connections. The assistant of Spihr was named Sok and he was believed to be the helper who delivered the pre-designed advances by the heavenly spirits to Spihr who then devolved them as benefits upon the Earth's people[150]. This may be the origin of the Suk or Suque, a ceremonial related to initiation cycles among the Melanesia in the Pacific Islands. In some texts Vay is identified with Ram who is considered to be the chief of the spiritual warriors[151], and it is interesting to note that Ram or Rama was also the great, deified hero in India who defeated his namesake, Ravan or Ravana the king of Sri Lanka in the texts of India. Ravan is identified with Pavan or Pawan the wind in Western Iran and the Ancient Near East. As in India Vayu as Pavan, or Pavana, was also associated with the sacred number five[152].

Vayu in India was also the god of the Sub-continental month Vaisakha (April-May)[153]. As the wind, Vayu was believed in Ancient Iran to have "ruled" over the rain and the Satapatha Brahmana, the oldest recorded Vedic text dating from the mid-first millennium B.C., states of the blowing one (Vayu, the wind); "...and he, it is true, blows as one only; but, on entering into man, he becomes a forward and backward moving one; and they are these two; the out-breathing and the in-breathing"[154]. In later Hindu cosmology Vay became the dikpala or guardian of the North West quarter, undoubtedly because this was the direction of several deities' origin in Iran to the North West. He is also considered the god of the mouth, no doubt because the breath is associated with the wind and the soul. It is also considered that he was the charioteer of Agni, the Vedic god of fire, confirming the association of wind and spark of fire in the Zoroastrian cosmology from which it was drawn[155].

In a Brahmanic myth the man-god called Purusha, was sacrificed in a similar manner to Merodach recorded in Ancient Iraq. From him animals were created that were subject to Vayu - the wind god, since they required air to live and breathe. This life-power was called vayavya - a term remarkably similar to a related meaning of the Mayan term u-vayey-ab, and parallels have been considered in an earlier work[156].

The term Vay, in Iran, appears to have derived from earlier deities in the Sumerian or even Uruk period of Mesopotamia since it is preserved in Mandaean texts that Ayar-Ziwa - "radiant ether" or "radiant brilliance" represented the pure ether. From this ether it was believed that all things emerged and life in particular - not dissimilar to the Zoroastrian beliefs, with whom the Mandaeans have been compared. The Ancient Iranian term for the ether was Vayah[157], clearly Vayu, but possibly originating much earlier deriving from a principle representing the emergence of the Aryans or Ayars as preserved in the Mandaean myths personified as Ayar-Ziwa. The term Ziwa is also found among the Mayans and Mandaean myths appearing to have been transferred with little loss of context or significant deity name changes[158].

As wind deity Vayu was seen as the provider of the path to the gods since from the magical ether it was said the great rivers that provided life flowed into material creation and he is also associated with the four quarters of the cosmic construct. The "paths of the gods" also figure in his remit as provider and this is associated with the aspirant or soul after death finding the right route to the gods. In the Upanishads, perhaps the most famous of the ancient texts of India after the Rig Veda, reference to the soul attempting to reach the most central abode of the gods is recorded: "He (at the time of death) having reached the path of the gods, comes to the world of Agni (fire), to the world of Vayu (air), to the world of Varuna, to the world of Indra, to the world of Pargapati (Virag), to the world of Brahman (Hiranyagarbha - Golden Embryo). In that world there is a lake Ara, the moments called Yeshtiha, the river Vigara (age-less), the tree Ilya, the Salagya, the palace Aparagita (unconquerable), the door-keepers Indra and Paragapati, the hall of Brahman, called Vibhu (built by vibhu, egoism), the throne Vikakshana (buddhi, perception), the couch Amitaugas (endless splendour), and the beloved Manasi (mind) and her image Kakshushi, eye), who, as if taking flowers, are weaving, the worlds, and the Apsaras, the Ambas (sruti, sacred scriptures), and Ambayavis (buddhi, understanding), and the rivers Ambayas (leading to the knowledge of Brahman). To this world he who knows this (who knows the Paryanka-vidya) approaches. Brahman says to him: 'Run towards him (servants) with such worship as is due to myself. He has reached the river Vigara (age-less), he will never age.'" (Kaushitaki-Upanishad, 1 Adhyaya, 3)[159].

References to the wind providing the paths to the sacred centre of the universe suggest that these are also related to the broad cosmic constructs of the four quarters based on the cardinal points of the compass. It is Vayu who is seen as the god of these forms since the wind is said to blow from the four quarters as is replicated in Mayan cosmology where the wind deities, the Pauahtuns, or Paua, derived from the Iranian Pawan, are also located there at the cardinal points. Vayu as Pawan is also associated with the winds, and among the Mandaeans, the sacred mountain, and from the sacred mountain the four sacred rivers fertilise and maintain life on earth. This suggests that the prototype for the Inca's ceque system may have derived from this principle of cosmology found throughout the Ancient Near East and in India. To this day there are recognised pilgrim paths extending from the plains of India to the shrines at the headwaters of the Ganges and other sacred rivers and these are still pursued to this day reflecting the pilgrimage routes, or ceque, so noted by the first Spanish such as Bernabe Cobo and more recent researchers.

Tonaca or Tonapa - Viracocha; the Andean Saints and the Syrian Christians

None can read the myths and legends and research papers on the Andean hero-deity Viracocha without realising that there existed a confused identification between him and the hero-saint named Tonaca; Tonapa or Thunapa. To confuse the matter further Tonaca is also identified with Tarapaca, Taguapaca as well as with the thunder deity named Illapa. It was believed by some of the early chroniclers that the Andean plateau around Cuzco south through to Lake Titicaca was peopled from immigrations forcing their way from the south (Northern Chile and North West Argentina) onto the Bolivian plateau. After these people had settled in the altiplano, and known as the Collao (Aymara), it is said that a bearded man named Tonapa, and identified with Viracocha Pachayachchican, travelled the land "performing miracles" and whom Salcamayhua identifies with St. Thomas the Apostle[160]. This native Indian from Peru writing in the late 16th., and early 17th., century, A.D., described his wanderings and tribulations at the hands of the Indian peoples in those ancient times. He concluded by writing; "...they say that the said Tonapa, after having liberated himself from the hands of those barbarians, remained some time on a rock called Titicaca, and afterward he passed through Tiguina toward Chacamarca, and on his way came to the village of Tiahuanaco, where the people ridiculed his teachings. In punishment he changed them into stones. From Chacamarca he followed the Desaguadero to the south, finally reaching the ocean where he disappeared. While in the Collao, Tonapa met a chief called Apotambo, who was the only one who lent an ear to his teachings, in consideration of which Tonapa gave him 'a piece of wood from his walking-stick.' This Apotambo was father to Manco Capac, to whom Salcamayhua attributes the foundation of Cuzco, which place was then already occupied by Indians, so that by 'foundation' the establishment of a formal village must be understood. In regard to the teachings of Tonapa, the author states: 'The modern old men from the time of my father, don Diago Felipe, are wont to state that, it was almost the commandments of God, especially the seven precepts, only the name of God our Lord was lacking and that of our Lord Jesus Christ, as it is public and notorious among the old men and the penalties were severe for those who broke them'"[161].

In the history written by Fra. Alonzo Ramos Gavilan, entitled "History of Copacabana", published in 1621, a popular belief is recorded mentioning the origins of Manco Capac on the Island of the Sun in Lake Titicaca. Ramos was a contemporary in that region with Cobo around the first decade of the 17th., century, A.D. and he records the legends "of a mysterious white man called Tunupa and Taapac, murdered by the Indians on the Island. Mention is also made of the belief that, after several days of obscurity, the sun came out of the Sacred Rock"[162]. These legends referred to by Ramos Gavilan are also accompanied by another remarkable reference to a very similar cross resembling a Christian Cross destroyed by the first priests since it was so greatly revered by the Aymara Indians and called the Cross of Carabuco[163].

This extraordinary report is confirmed by Salamayhua who recorded that Tonapa was said to have erected a large cross at Caravaya and carried a cross to the mountain of Carapucu where he "preached in a loud voice, and shed tears. And they say that a daughter of a chief of the province was sprinkled on the head with water, and the Indians seeing this, understood that he was washing his head. So afterwards Tonapa was taken prisoner and shorn near the great lake of Carapucu"[164]. The ritual performed by Tonapa appears to suggest a form of baptism and there can be little surprise at Salcamayhua's questioning as to whether this might have been St. Thomas, centuries in advance of the Spanish representatives of Christianity, along with many other Indians and Spaniards at the Conquest[165].

The most comprehensive reports on Tonaca and his progress through the land are recorded by Salcamayhua himself and an edited version of these reports are as follows: In the kingdom of Tahuantin-suyu, after the Hapi-Nunus Achacallas (demons) had been driven out of the land, there came a bearded man of medium height, long hair and dressed in a "rather long shirt". He was a man of middle age because he had grey hair and was "lean". He travelled with a staff and taught the peoples of the land, expressing love, and calling them his sons and daughters. As he went through the land it was remembered that he was able to speak the native tongues of the people and that he performed miracles and the sick were cured with his touch. He was known as Tonapa or Tarapaca where the latter means an "eagle"; Uiracocha-rapacha Yachipachan or Pachaccan meaning "steward" or "head servant" (later the term for a Chamberlain to the Incas); Uicchay-camayoc meaning a "preacher"; and Vicchay-camayoc where Vicchay or Huichay means "ascend" and camayoc an official in charge; Cunacuy-camayoc meaning an "adviser or preacher", and also Tonapa Uiracocha Nipacachan. Although he preached tirelessly to the people he had little effect and he eventually entered a town where a chief named Apo-tampu lived. This was the father of Manco Capac noted in a few of the Inca origin myths and it was said that Tonaca entered the village, very tired from his exertions, at the time when a wedding feast was being celebrated. The chief listened to Tonapa expound his doctrine but that his servants were hostile, but because of the sympathy aroused in Apo-tampu he was allowed to stay as his guest. Because of this hospitality Tonapa gave Apo-tampu a "stick" from his own staff and on this marks and scoring, related to the precepts of the doctrine, was preserved.

Thonapa (as Salcamayhua also spells it) was said to have visited all the provinces of the Colla, or the land of the Aymara, but one day entered the town of Yamquesupa. In this place he was harassed and "treated with great insolence and contempt, and driven away." The legend recorded stated that Tonapa slept in the fields with no other covering except the "long shirt", a mantle and a book. Having been driven away in such a manner from Yamquesupa he cursed the village and that as a result it was then submerged under water in the middle of a lake. It became known as Yamquisupaloiga but its location could not be identified by Salcamayhua.

One of the miracles attributed to Tonapa was the destruction on a high hill named Cacha-Pucara, of a shrine housing the idol of a female deity to whom were offered human sacrifices. This he destroyed and burnt and reputedly the whole of the hill where it stood[166]. Cacha is the famous temple referred to in de la Vega's reports regarding Viracocha's progress northward from Tiahuanaco to Ecuador earlier noted.

In a continuation of the Tonapa myth, after the Indians had shaved his head and incarcerated him, it is said that a bird that sang four times to herald the dawn, named Pucu-Pucu and perhaps related to the name of the place, Carapucu. Then a beautiful youth came to him saying, "Do not fear; for I come to call you in the name of the matron, who alone watches over you, and who is about to go to the place of rest" and Salcamayhua continues, "So saying, he touched the cords by which Tonapa was tied hand and foot, with his fingers. There were many guards for Tonapa since he had been condemned to a cruel death. But at dawn, being five in the morning, he entered the lake with the youth, his mantle bearing him up on the water and serving in the place of a boat. On his arrival in the town and province of Carapuco, the chiefs and principal men were disturbed at having seen their idol thrown down and destroyed. They say that this idol flew like the wind to a desert place, which was never visited by men. Here the idol or huaca was mourning and lamenting with his head down; and in this plight it was found by an Indian, whose report caused the chiefs to be exited at the arrival of Tonapa, who had been imprisoned. They say that Tonapa, after he had been freed from the hands of those savages, remained for a long time on a rock called Titicaca, and afterwards he passed by Tiquina to Chacamarca; where he came to a town called Tiyahuanacu (Tiahuanaco). They say that the people of the town were engaged in drinking and dancing when Tonapa came to preach to them, and did not listen to him. Then, out of pure anger, he denounced them in the language of the land, and when he departed from that place, all the people who were dancing were turned to stones, and they may be seen to this day. Tonapa then followed the course of the river Chacamarca until he came to the sea. This is reported by those most ancient Yncas"[167].

These reports are strikingly similar to the myths and legends of Viracocha and there is clearly a confusion between Christian teaching and the ancient folklore regarding Viracocha, Tiahuanaco and the Incas. However, the elements of Christian myths incorporated such as the appearance of the youth in the jail, so reminiscent of Daniel in the lion's den, need not have been as a result of Christian contacts after the Spanish Conquest. The "beautiful youth", along with people being tuned to stone, is a motif found widely among the Pacific Islands and in India and is also reflective of elements in the Coniraya myths in South America itself and these will be considered in due course. The section of twig from Tonapa's staff given to Manco Capac's father Apo-tampu was, in his hands in the Inca myth, turned into fine gold and then called the Tupac-Yauri. Apo or Apu is the term for a chieftain in the Andes and also in Polynesia.

Salcamayhua notes that when Manco Capac was very old he prayed for the prosperity of his son the heir. He is reminded of words spoken by Tonapa and his purported words were recorded. After this invocation Salcamayhua records; "Having said this he watched to see if he might have a sign from the Creator. He offered a very white lamb upon the altar, which sacrifice is called 'Arpay'. When no answer was given, he ordered the most beautiful of his sons, aged about eight years, to be offered up, cutting off his head, and sprinkling the blood over the fire, that the smoke might reach the Maker or heaven and Earth. To all these offerings no answer was even given in the Coricancha" (Sun Temple in Cuzco)[168].

This remarkable reference could not be considered to be recorded to sanitise and elevate the memory of the Incas as de la Vega is accused of attempting. Here there is failure to communicate, or rejection of the gods, by the so-called "Son of the Sun", and hardly to be considered an auspicious legacy for the Incas from their founding father. It also records the sacrifice of his own son and many researchers over the last half century denied such acts occurred and references to capacocha, as it is called, and were considered to be an ethnocentric bias promulgated by the early Spanish friars. With the recovery of capacocha burials over the last two decades it is now realised that the reports by the Spanish chroniclers were more nearly accurate than presumed. This extended not only on this aspect of human sacrifice but in reports of the many other rituals and ceremonies of daily life and belief in the Inca Empire. Urgent re-evaluation is being undertaken by more recent researchers into the historic texts left by the Spanish friars and chroniclers in the last couple of decades as a result. Here also, in this report, is the motif of the "most beautiful" child considered the highest and most acceptable sacrifice and this was also the case in Ancient West Asia.

In the dynasty of the Incas the ruler Inca Pachacuti, not to be confused with the chronicler Pachacuti-Yamqui Salcamayhua sometimes referred to by historians as Pachacuti, was considered the Great Reformer. He rebuilt Cuzco and was said to be responsible for the construction of the Sun Temple, Coricancha, as recorded by the Spanish Conquistadors. The worship of haucas, such as stones, springs and other natural objects, considered to be the dwelling places of spirits and in some cases were the places believed to be where the ancestors emerged, was prevalent from the earliest times. Inca Pachacuti, however, was said to be opposed to the worship of anything other than a supreme god and confronted the keepers, and supposedly the spirits inhabiting these places, to banish them. Salcamayhua notes these events and records that a magical spell called the Yacarcay was used to dispel the spirits and sorcerers; "With these words the Yncas made all the huacas tremble; although they had not left off performing Capacochacocuy (capacocha). If these Yncas had heard the gospel, with what love and joy would they have believed in God! They say that this Ynca Ccapac Yupanqui had a son, by his wife, Mama Corillpaycama, named Ynca Ruca, at whose birth there was much festivity. But this Ynca did not entirely separate himself from idolators, as he allowed the Huacas of each village to be worshipped. It is said that the Ynca sent men to search for the place called Titicaca, where the great Tonapa had arrived, and that they brought water thence to pour over the infant Ynca Ruca, while they celebrated the praises of Tonapa. In the spring on the top of the rocks the water was in a basin called Ccapac-chama-quispisutec unu (footnote: Cacpac = rich; chama = joy; quispisutu = crystal drops; unu = water). Future Yncas caused this water to be brought in a bowl called Curi-ccacca (footnote: "golden rock"), and placed before them in the middle of the square in Cuzco called Huacay-pata: Cusi-pata: where they did honour to the water that had been touched by Tonapa"[169].

The association of Tonapa with baptism was noted above where he had his head shaved for "washing" - that of an apparent convert. It is clear that the Yncas appeared to have adopted an elaborated version of that instituted by Tonapa among the Aymaras of Collao around Lake Titicaca (Bolivia). They resemble closely Christian baptism rites and the possible apparent connection to earlier Christian missionaries cannot be ruled out.

In another version of the Tonapa legend Salcamayhua records the following: "In those days the Curacas of Asillu and Hucuru told the Ynca how, in ancient times, a poor thin old man, with a beard and long hair, had come to them in a long shirt, and that his name was Tonapa Vihinquira. They said that he had banished all the idols and Hapi-Nunu demons to the snowy mountains. All the Curacas and chroniclers also said that this Tonapa has banished all huacas and idols to the mountains of Asancata, Quiyancatay, Sallcatay, and Api Tosiray. When all the Curacas of the provinces of Ttahuantinsusyu were assembled in the Huacay-pata, each in his place, those of the Huancas said that this Tonapa Varivillca had also been in their land, and that he had made a house to live in, and had banished all the huacas and hapi-nunus in the province of Hatun Sauas Huanac to the snowy mountains of Pariacaca and Vallolo. Before their banishment these idols had done much harm to the people, menacing the Curacas to make them offer human sacrifices. The Ynca ordered that the house of Tonapa should be preserved[170].

It is particularly interesting to note that Tonapa, and then Pachacuti were opposed to the worship of the long endemic worship of huacas, or natural objects and forces in the landscape, and that Tonapa is associated with a cross and identified so readily with a Christian apostle, St. Thomas. The opposition and destruction of the huacas, idols and religious buildings in South America is notoriously attached to the Spanish friars after they entered South America and is also more widely reflected in all the missions from European countries in the more recent colonial past where they had sufficient power to do so. The identification of Tonapa with St. Thomas was not only thought, but actually considered possible by the Spanish as well as the Indians themselves and there is in fact some merit in this possibility. Salcamayhua considered Tonapa to be the personification of St. Thomas while another Indian, Huaman Poma de Ayala, whose sketches of Inca life are illustrated throughout this work, considered him to be St. Bartholomew[171]. Not only does the name of St. Thomas actually sound similar to Tonapa but in fact was seriously thought as possibly explaining other parallel missionary heroes in other parts of the Americas.

The Andean Deities Thunapa and Ekkekko (Ecaco)

Thunapa has understandably been identified and associated with the Tonapa myths, also called Tarapaca and Taguapaca. Tonapa as Thunapa was a deified hero preserved in myths by an Augustinian friar, Antonio de la Calancha, published in 1638, and therefore preserved earlier less than the three generations after the Spanish Conquest. These myths record that this revered culture hero is found in the oral histories of the Bolivian Indians and believed to have arrived on the altiplano in ancient times and who carried a cross on his back to Carapucu. He was described as a man of great presence, bearded and blue-eyed, wearing the native mantle called the cusma, and a long shirt extending to the knees. Accompanying him were five followers identified as disciples, and he preached against drunkenness, polygamy and war. Carapucu was the capital of a chief named Makuri, and Thunapa scolded him for his cruelty and warlike manner, but was rebuffed and scorned by the chief, the Indian priests and sorcerers also opposed him. Thunapa then departed for Sicasica where his preaching so incensed the people that they set fire to the hut where he was sleeping but, escaping, he returned to Carapucu. While he had been away one of his followers had fallen in love with the chief's daughter and converted her, and when Thunapa returned he baptised her. The girl's father, Makuri, was furious and he had all the disciples killed and Thunapa himself was left for dead.

The Indians placed the body of Thunapa in a totora reed boat and set it adrift on Lake Titicaca. The boat suddenly sped away with the winds piloting the boat and the waves acting as paddles to the astonishment of the Indians since this lake was known to have no current. The translation of Calancha's version continues: "The boat came to the shore at Cochamarca, where today is the river Desaguadero. Indian tradition asserts that the boat struck the land with such force it created the river Desaguadero, which before then did not exist. And on the water so released the holy body was carried many leagues away to the seacoast at Arica"[172]. It is significant that Tonapa is said to have reached the Pacific Coast, in at least one legend, at Arica since Miles Poindexter considered this town name a localised form of the Polynesian for the name of a sea-going canoe-master - Arika. This section of the South American coast is the most obvious location for those arriving from across the Pacific Ocean from the west utilising the southern route from Southern Polynesia, New Zealand, Melanesia, Australia and South and South East Asia (*1.007*).

Other Indian traditions assert that the Indian people attempted to destroy Thunapa's cross by burning and by cutting it to pieces but were unsuccessful. They attempted to sink it in the lake but could not do so and finally they buried it in the ground where it was said to have been discovered by the Augustine fathers in 1569 A.D.[173]. The references to the Inca ruler

Pachacuti being inspired to bring baptismal water, considered to have been blessed by Tonapa, also applies to Thunapa and it is clear that they are the same hero deity.

The myths and legends associated with Tonapa or Thunapa appear similar to those associated with Viracocha and the more recent researchers have identified the former as the Viracocha in his aspect as the "thunder god". This has also been extended to identify the named thunder god, Illapa with Tonapa and Thunapa, and consequently with Viracocha also[174]. Because of these identifications among other references Viracocha has been seen as a pre-Incan deity of the Aymara and not a later fiction of the Incas or the Jesuits as some have attested[175]. In Aymara myth the Thunder god is the brother of the Sun and this is a similar belief to those reported on the Peruvian Coast[176]. Among the Incas Curi-Inti was the "Son of the Sun" and this deity is equivalent to Punchao. The affix chao is a title indicating status, and corresponds to Chau in the Caroline Islands, Au, Hau and Sau in Polynesia generally, Ahau also among the Maya, as well as Chao in Burma. Viracocha also, in some of the versions of ancient myths, appears as a solar deity and this has been linked to the migratory route he was said to have taken corresponding to the solar path from Lake Titicaca or Tiahuanaco through Cuzco to Manta on the coast of Ecuador. He is identified in this form with various aspects of his being, or with other heroes, namely Conticci Viracocha, Ticci Viracocha, Pacha Yachachi, Pachacamac and Tonapa, Thonapa, Thunapa[177], and elements also of Kon Raya or Coniraya, and possibly Paria-caca. Some of these hero-deities are compared to the Sun that is said to have risen in great splendour over Lake Titicaca, after an extended period of "great darkness", hence their identification with the Sun and its transit with their migration route across the Peruvian landscape towards the constellation of the wildcat or Chinchay.

The thunder deity, Illapa, has been identified with Thunapa by several eminent scholars and this is considered to be most evident in the creation myth. The oldest creation myths are from the Bolivian plateau around Lake Titicaca and is the region traditionally inhabited by the Aymara. In their myths it is Thunapa who is identified as the creator and this is the name in Aymara for the Quechua term Illapa, the brother of the Sun, and the god of thunder and lightning[178]. The Aymara have a similar alternative name for the thunder - Ilapu, and probably the origin of the Inca thunder god Illapa. In the Aymara version of the creation myths it is the thunder who travels the countryside performing miracles not Ticci Viracocha. In other myths Viracocha and Thunapa/Illapa are unified in a single godhead as aspects of the whole, forming a tri-unity with the Sun[179]. It has been suggested that the Inca version of the state religion was a more specific and defined version of the generality of the Aymara creation myths in the Bolivian Highlands around Lake Titicaca[180] and not the other way round.

The influence of the pre-Inca Andean thunder god extended far beyond the Bolivian Plateau or Altiplano and is found in coastal region where the thunder and lightning god is identified with Catiquilla and Pariaraca whose attributes of the thunder and lightning was the Ccoa, or wildcat with the same symbols that are anciently found identified with Thunapa or Illapa on the Altiplano[181]. This aspect of the thunder and lightning, symbolised as wildcat, reflected the spirit of the storm as lightning, hail, etc., was identified by Arriaga after the conquest with the Christian saint St. James[182]. The Aymara, into recent centuries, raised metal plates inscribed with crossed serpents to propitiate Thunapa as the lightning deity (*7.008*) that reflects similar iconography known at Cerro Sechin (*7.010*) and in the Ancient Middle East (*7.006*).

The Aymaran fertility god was called Ekkakko, or Ecaco, and this was considered another aspect of Thunapa and therefore also the wildcat, Ccoa. An animal associated with Thunapa is the puma and this corresponds with the identification of this creature with Viracocha[183]. Associated also with Thunapa was the snake and this appears to be a result of the apparent serpentine form of lightning when it strikes from the sky[184] just as the rivers descending from the mountain tops are also similarly identified with the serpent. It is now considered

7.005 : Winged deities of the type found also in South America (7.012) in later millennia. The storm god holds a modified arrow symbol in each hand. Note the sickle-like implement hanging from the upraised arm thought to be for the opening-of-the-mouth rituals also in 6.077.. Marduk (Bel), Babylonn,First half of the first millennium, B.C.

7.006 : Lightning god, Teshup, holding his axe, alway associated with lightning in Ancient Middle East, India and South America. He also holds a group of arrow shafts almost identical to those found at Cerro Sechin on the Central Peruvian Coast. Nimrud, Assyria, c900, B.C.

7.007 : Lightning symbols with a stream with nodes characteristic of constellations in North America and Asia emerging from the back of the neck probably depicting here the constellation of the llama. Wankcani (Wankarani), Lake Titicaca, Bolivia, Mid-first millennium, B.C.

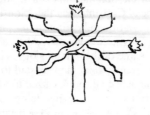

7.008 : Thunder and lightning symbol similar to that of Cerro Sechin three thousand years earlier but also similar to depictions in the Ancient Middle East. Aymara, Copacabana, Lake Titicaca, Bolivia, Late 19th., century, A.D.

7.009 : Head of a deity probably representing the lightning god Illapa indicated by the lightning streams emerging from the eyes. Wankcani (Wankarani), Lake Titicaca, Bolivia, Mid-first millennium, B.C.

7.010 : Priest or deity holding a group of three rods or arrows identical to those of the early Ancient Middle Eastern cultures and adopted by the Assyrians in the first millennium B.C. The "pill-box" crown the deity wears is similar to that known anciently in Indonesia and the Ancient Middle East (6.041-6). Cerro Sechin, Central Coast Peru, Late second millennium, B.C

that Thunapa was probably the original of the recorded Andean deities and that others such as Catequilla, Chincha Cama, Pachacamac, and Viracocha were regional variations. Even though they exhibit certain differences they are sufficiently similar to indicate that they have derived or identified with Thunapa who appears the oldest known deity and recorded by Samcamayhua as the oldest creator[185]. This is not agreed to by all historians or researchers. However, it must be remembered that Viracocha, who is most similar to Thunapa originating in the identical place, departed in one version of his myth not from Ecuador or northern Peru but from Pachacamac suggesting more than a coincidental association[186].

The supreme deity, often called the Staff God, carved above the central opening in the Gateway to the Sun is shown with "tears" falling from the eyes down his cheeks. This is a characteristic of the depictions of the wildcat deity Ccoa, and parallels drawn conclude that this figure is in fact Thunapa or Tonaca. Others have identified the Staff God with Tuapaca or Ticci Viracocha who are also identified with Thunapa or Illapa[187]. Although there appears to have been a theological tri-unity between these deities, the Sun, and Punchao as Son of the Sun, this is rarely expressed outside of the intellectualised deliberation by western scholars on Inca cosmology. The less complicated adoration of the Indians probably worshipped each one as separate deities although broadly understanding that some were more closely associated through inclusion or exclusion in festivals or propitiation rites established over many centuries.

7.012 : Griffon style winged puma-headed llama with "cross-of-Lorraine" staff. The depiction is similar to a type of "griffon" found in the Spiro Mound in Ohio (*7.017*) and both appear to derive from Ancient Middle Eastern types. Wankarani, Bolivia, Mid-first millennium, B.C.

7.011 : Lion impersonator at the local Muharram festival similar to those known in Mexico and South America. Central India, Early 20th., century, A.D.

7.013 : Fine low relief carving of the Hindu monkey god Hanuman who defeated the armies of Ravana of Sri Lanka. The armorial lion-headed, demon-masked "horses", derives from Ancient India and the Middle East but also found in Tiahuanaco in Bolivia. Angkor Wat, Cambodia, 12th., century, A.D.

7.014 : Armorial lions suspended upside-down being ridden in an unconventional manner. The lion heads are in fact a mutation of the Makara, the Ganges crocodile and the Garuda sky eagle reflecting Tibetan traditions and found also in Ancient South America. Angkor Wat, Cambodia, 12th. century, A.D.

     The Staff God is earliest recorded in the works of the Spanish chroniclers and these note that the Incas considered that this image exhibited the "stance" or ceremonial posture associated with Illapa. One of the three golden images housed in the Coricancha was said to be similar and possibly to include an image of Illapa[188]. The two staffs this deity holds are thought by some to be serpents but in the surviving similar images from Tiahuanco the tears from some of the cheeks of the carved faces still retain the gold disk inserts representing the tears and the staffs on the gateway are clearly terminated with heads of the condor and not the snake[189]. If the tears were representative of hail and therefore the thunder god Illapa it might be expected that they would have been inset with silver disks not gold. Interestingly hail was seen as white flint[190] - reflecting the association of crystalline nuances associated with lightning in the Western Pacific, Indonesia and India elsewhere noted. It is likely that the three golden images in the Coricancha at Cuzco of the original deities of Tiahuanaco, or of the Aymara, were in fact exact copies but adapted to emphasise the Inca's own predilection and elevation of the Sun as Punchao. In this Temple of the Sun, Punchao was given higher status than Thunapa or Viracocha and therefore all "gilded" to impose and project that preference and superiority. In the same period as that most associated with the greatest period at Tiahuanaco from about the 7-8th., century A.D., the region around Ayacucho, formerly Guamanga, long an ancient seat of innovation and culture, saw the rise of a people called the Huari or Wari, who shared the Staff God of Tiahuanaco[191]. This suggests a common origin, or as the result of an extension of empire, or major influence, or even colonisation from Tiahuanaco. The shared iconography extends to many aspects and includes the double-headed serpent staffs, belts, headdresses, pectorals and other regalia[192].

7.015 :
A rollout of a cylinder seal depicting the column representing Marduk supported on the back of the dragon named Mushussu at the left with the Moon god Sin standing in the crescent Moon at the left.
Babylonia, 1200-900 B.C.

7.018 : Tenoned fanged serpent head similar to puma heads found in South America. Maya, Guatemala, Late Classic Period.

7.016 : A column with a capital resting on the back of a puma identical in principle to many depictions found in the Ancient Near and Middle East and India. Mantero Culture, Manta, Ecuador, 500-900 A.D.

7.019 : Carved stone tenon head of a puma closely similar to examples in India and Guatemala. Huar Huaraz, Central Highland Peru, 800-1000 A.D.

7.017 : A fine shell carving from Eastern United States depicting a "griffon" that is clearly derived from the long traditional composite lion figures found for millennia in the Ancient Near and Middle East and closely similar to that found on the Bolivian Plateau (7.012). Sprio Mound Culture, Ohio, 800-1350 A.D.

The legend recording Viracocha's departure from the coast of Peru from Pacahacamac suggests that there was a well-trodden path between Tiahuanaco to Pachacamac with Huari located between the two regions. These apparently separate political entities would have shared the iconography and material culture conveyed by those who travelled between one regional extremity to another. This same route would convey the myths and legends along with religious ideas and rituals these would have been assimilated to a lesser or greater degree eventually diverging by the degree of predilection that each political region would have for these new innovations and ideas.

The regional variations to the name of Tonaca or Tonapa or Thunapa such as Taguapaca, Tarapaca are the result of just such divergences and identification with local, or other imported deities from the names and belief associated with the original Andean gods. It is therefore far from certain in fact that these were not actually representative of several or many missions from outside the region, who became identified with, and assimilated in a few cases with the existing deities. In pre-Inca times these gods may have included Illapa and it is this deity that can be shown to have originated from outside South America and itself possibly displaced the original thunder gods of the Andes no longer remembered even in the Inca Dynasty. This would certainly appear true also of Tonaca, Viracocha, Taguapaca and Gagua[193] who have already been shown to have derived from Asia via Oceania.

Tonapa as Tonaca of Mexico
In Mexico a deity called Tonaca is identified with the Quetzalcoatl myth cycle. Brinton recorded a tradition about this deity: "Another myth represents him as the intermediate son of the All-Father Tonaca-tecutli, under his title Citlallatonac (Citlalla-tonaca), the Morning, by an earth-born maiden in Tollan. In that city dwelt three sisters, one of whom, an unspotted virgin, was

named Chimalman. Chimalman's two sisters were struck to death by fright at his awful presence, but upon her he breathed the breath of life, and straightway she conceived. The son she bore cost her life, but it was the divine Quetzalcoatl, surnamed Topiltein (Topilzin), Our Son, and, from the year of his birth, Ce Acatl, One Reed. As soon as he was born he possessed speech and reason and wisdom. As for his mother, having perished on earth, she was transferred to the heavens, where she was given the honoured name Chalchihuitzli, the Precious Stone of Sacrifice."

"This, also, is evidently an ancient and simple figure of speech to express that the breath of Morning announces the dawn which brings forth the sun and disappears in the act."

"The virgin mother Chimalman, in another legend, is said to have been brought with child by swallowing a jade or precious green stone (chalchiuitl)."[194].

In these myths there is a clear connection between Viracocha and, or Tonapa commanding the Sun to rise from Lake Titicaca and the dawn, particularly of a New Age, and this Mexican version one time must have been the same myth or from a common origin. This associates him with the emergence of the Sun from the Cosmic morning as he is in the Mexican myth and his miracle birth also is reflected in the South America myths of Con-i-Raya and Paria-caca. Brinton records other aspects of Tonaca also related to Quetzalcoatl noting: "In ancient and purely mythical narrative Quetzalcoatl is one of four divine brothers, gods like himself, born in the uttermost or thirteenth heaven to the infinite and uncreated deity, which, in its male manifestations, was known as Tonaca Tecutli, Lord of our Existence, and Tzin Teotl, God of the Beginning, and in its female expressions as Tonaca Cihuatl, Queen of our Existence, Xochiquetzal, Beautiful Rose, Citlallicue, the Star-skirted or the Milky Way, Citlalatonac (Citlala-tonaca), the Star warms, or The Morning, and Chicome Coatl, the Seven Serpents."

"Of these four brothers, two were black and the red Tezcatlipoca, and the fourth was Huitzilopochtli; the Left handed, the deity adored beyond all others in the city of Mexico." Brinton footnotes the title Tonaca: "The usual translation of Tonaca tecutli is 'God of our Subsistence' - to 'our', 'naca flesh', 'tecatli' chief applied to edible flesh - that expressed by the word 'nonoac' - but is the flesh of our own bodies, our life, existence."

Codex Telleriano-Remensis is quoted by Brinton in another record relating to Tonaca, and he writes: "This document tells how Quetzalcoatl, Tezcatlipoca and their brethren were at first gods, and dwelt as stars in the heavens. They passed their time in Paradise, in a Rose Garden, Xochitlycacan ('where the roses are lifted up'); but on a time they began plucking the roses from the great Rose tree in the centre of the garden and Tonaca-tecutli; in his anger at their action, hurled them to the earth, where they lived as mortals!"[195].

Tonaca appears to have been a supreme deity in some of the Mexican codices or myths and the suggestion that he was able to expel these major deities has Biblical overtones and certainly parallels with Tonaca, Thunapa and Viracocha in South America. It is very likely therefore that the names of these deities in North and South America are not coincidentally linked but are in fact one and the same deity. The explanation that Tonaca-tecutli is related to the term nonoac, above referred to, may be coincidence or an example of an "otiose" god. Brinton explains the term "Otosis": "This is the substitution of a familiar word for an archaic or foreign one of similar sound but wholly diverse meaning. This is a very common occurrence and easily leads to myth making. For example," ... "In an Algonkin dialect missi wabu means "a great light of the dawn"; and a common large rabbit was called missabo; at some period the precise meaning of the former words was lost, and a variety of interesting myths of the daybreak were transferred to a supposed huge rabbit!"[196]. The god Viracocha has also been described in the present generation of researchers as an otiose deity[197].

7.020 : Carved representation of a priest or deity from Tiahuanaco showing gold foil insertions in recesses carved in the surface representing tears. Tiahuanaco, Bolivia, 700-900 A.D.

It is likely therefore that the name Tonaca was in fact a reference to a deity, hero or missionary who was known both in North and South America and adopted into both retaining the memorable name or a closely similar one and something of a religious reformer throwing down idols and expelling other deities from Paradise. Other reports so similar to those of Tonapa and Viracocha are found elsewhere in South America and associated with pre-Colombian apostolic missions. Brinton again records the known writings describing "Our Ancestor" - Tamu, Tume or Zume: "The early Jesuit missionaries to the Guaranis and affiliated tribes of Paraguay and Southern Brazil, have much to say of this personage, and some of them were convinced that he could have been no other than the Apostle St Thomas on his proselytising journey around the world."

"The legend was the Pay Zume, as he was called in Paraguay (Pay = magician, diviner, priest), came from the East, from Sun-rising, in years long gone by. He instructed the people in the arts of hunting and agriculture, especially in the culture and preparation of the manioc plant, their chief source of vegetable food. Near the city of Assumption (Asuncion) is situated a lofty rock, around which, says the myth, he was accustomed to gather the people, while he stood above them on its summit, and delivered his instructions and his laws, just as did Quetzalcoatl from the top of the mountain Tzatzitepec, the Hill of Shouting. The spot where he stood is still marked by the impress of his feet, which the pious natives of a later day took pride in pointing out as a convincing proof that their ancestors received and remembered the preachings of St. Thomas."

"The story was that wherever this hero-god walked, he left behind him a well-marked path, which was permanent, and as the Muyscas of New Granada pointed out the path of Bochica, so did the Guaranys that of Zume, which the missionaries regarded 'not without astonishment.' He lived a certain length of time with his people and then left them, going back over the ocean toward the East, according to some accounts. But according to others, he was driven away by his stiff-necked auditors, who had become tired of his advice. They pursued him to the bank of a river, and there, thinking that the quickest riddance of him was to kill him, they discharged their arrows at him. But he caught the arrows in his hand and hurled them back, and dividing the waters of the river by his divine power he walked between them to the other bank, dry-shod, and disappeared from their view in the distance"[198]. Characteristically, Tumu or Zume promised to return and it was this firm belief that the ancient missionary would return that ultimately brought the downfall of both of the great civilisations contemporary with the Spanish Conquests - the Aztecs and the Incas. There is, therefore, the possibility that Tonaca, identifying with Thunapa and Tonapa on the Bolivian Altiplano, was in fact a memory of St. Thomas. This raised the question of how he, or missions in his name, may have reached the Americas and the Andean Altiplano in particular.

It has been shown that there are intimate but ultimately clear parallels between the Andean gods of the Incas, the Inca name for their empire - Tahuantin-suyu, the wind deities of the Maya in Central America - the Pauahtuns, the wind god Vay, and Pawa and Pawan in India and the Ancient Near East. The earlier deities in the Andes, Viracocha, Thunapa or Tonapa are clearly the same as those found also anciently in Mexico and the wind gods under another name, Vir, Bir, or Vayu in India and the Ancient Near and Middle East. There is another consideration linking the gods of the Andes, India and the Ancient Near East already mentioned in part and that is the thunder deity of the Aymara and Incas Ilapu or Illapa and Il or El in West Asia and these will be considered and extended in the next chapter. This will also include the possibility of connections between St. Thomas, also centred in the Ancient Near East but also known in South India and the Americas.

The Syrian Christians and the Missions of St. Thomas in India and Beyond

The first reports known in modern times that there were Christians in India were recorded in the reports of the Portuguese who were the first of the European powers to reach and colonise the west coast of India at the beginning of the 17th., century, A.D. The Portuguese had set up mission stations on the Central and South West coasts of India and there, rumours that there were Syrian Christians of St. Thomas in the southern inlands of Malabar reached the "Lord Bishop" Dom Frco Ros. He sent out a mission and on reaching a place called Todramala they came face to face with the people who proved the rumour to be correct. The reports noted: "They are a somewhat white-skinned race and tall of stature; they grow long beards and wear their hair after the ancient Portuguese fashion, bushy on the head and falling on the shoulders behind ..."[199].

The Syrian Christians of Malabar relate that St. Thomas himself landed on the south west coast of India at Malankara, an island in a lagoon near Cranganore, and preached to the native people there and baptised them. In time he was able to establish seven churches along the coast and he then ordained two priests to take charge of the new church before he departed.   It is said that he went from the Malabar coast to the Coromandel coast of South East India near Madras, and at Mailapore, a suburb now of Madras, he converted the local king and the people and from there sailed to China before returning to Mailapore. After his return it is said that he "excited the jealousy" of the local Brahmans and they incited the people to stone him after which the Brahmans "thrust him through with a lance"[200].

Near Madras there is a hill revered by the local Christians as the place that St. Thomas reputedly took refuge before his death, and there his footprints are shown still etched in the rock along with a cleft that, it is said, he created to allow a spring to form. Located here also is the church and a cave revered also by the local people who consider the oral history of St. Thomas proselytising in South India as literal truth. There can be no doubt from known history and archaeology that the Romans traded with South India by sea and these routes taken through West Asia were those known for at least two thousand years before via Arabia, Mesopotamia and the Persian Gulf. An abundance of Roman coins and trade items have been recovered since the beginning of the British Archaeological Survey a century and a half ago in South India[201] and it is also probable that earlier than the Romans the ancient Greeks also had contact from their colonies in Egypt and Arabia.

These contacts between Rome and South India contemporary with the first Christians in West Asia are considered evidence by some that St. Thomas could easily made his way from the Western Mediterranean to South India by sea or overland. There have been more recent scholars who have argued for the mission by St. Thomas to India to have been an actual event. Others have, however, argued cogently against this "history" but the story of St. Thomas as an Apostle is first related in an apocryphal text - "The Acts of the Apostles"[202]. One of the historians of the latter persuasion was George Milne Rae who came to the conclusion that "...the several passages in Church history which have been often applied to the history of the Church in Southern India, can be proved to have no connection with it whatever. They apply, as we shall show at a later stage, to other localities known likewise in those days by the writings and monuments of the first five centuries for any attestation of the existence of a South India Church"..."Not, St. Thomas, but only the tradition, migrated to Southern India"[203]. Milne Rae, through his researches as a Professor of Theology based in South India a century ago, seems to prove his case beyond reasonable doubt, and indicates that the term "India" was a catch-all name referring to "... the whole area between the Indus and the eastern frontier of Persia, and between the Indian Ocean and the northern boundary of Afghanistan, was formerly denominated India"[204]. He concludes that St. Thomas probably never travelled beyond what was then Parthia in Eastern Iran or West Afghanistan[205].

It is recorded that Constantius in 356 A.D. sent an embassy to "Arabia Magna", or "Arabia Felix", the capital being Saba, and it is interesting to note that this was the land of the Homeritae and Philostorgus who formerly called these people Sabaeans or Indians, and that one of their countries of influence was India[206]. This is an early record that the people known as the Sabaeans were connected with other regions and it is probably that they were, or were related to the Saba, the Subba or Mandaeans in Mesopotamia, and the Subba or Savaras of India. The Savaras are related to the Bhuiyas already referred to in earlier chapters and in later sections of this work. In other texts it is stated that Apostles were sent to other regions and St. Matthew was assigned to India Ulterior - the name usually given to Ethiopia[207] this being another cautionary indicator in accepting ancient texts too literally.

The Christian Church in South India is considered to be a direct offshoot from the Church of Persia, and this was itself a section under the Patriarchate of Babylon. At the Council of Ephesus in 431 A.D. the Bishop of Constantinople was condemned on doctrinal issues and the Nestorian supporters fled to Persia to form their own branch of the Christian Church in opposition to Rome[208]. In 498 A.D. the Persian Church, then totally separated from the Church at Rome, adopted the name of Chaldean Church and their religious head assumed the title of Patriarch of Babylon. The Nestorians, as the Chaldean Christians, became noted for their learning and preserved many references and texts from Ancient Greece and Mesopotamia covering both religious and cultural studies including music, poetry, and the sciences including astronomy music and medicine. The local ruling dynasties in turn employed the Chaldean Christians to translate and apply the treasures of learning from other earlier and contemporary peoples and thereby the Christians retained a privileged position in their kingdoms[209].

The first known report of Christians in India is recorded by an Alexandrian sea-merchant named Cosmas who had undertaken trading voyages to India between the years 535 and 550 A.D. He retired as a monk and wrote a book about his travels including references to Christians on the island of Ceylon (Sri Lanka) and on the Malabar Coast of South India. He is known to have had friendly contacts with the Nestorians in Persia and it is possible that he was a Nestorian. It is known that there had been sea connections between Persia and the south coast of India in the early 6th., century A.D. and it is possible therefore that the Chaldaean Church or Syrian Christians may have first sent missions at that time[210]. Earlier than this there is no record of Christian missions to South India, only speculation and oblique references. On St. Thomas's Mount in Mailapore, near Madras (now renamed Chennai), there is an inscription on a cross found there in 1547 A.D. in Persian and this has been determined to date it at 7-8th., century A.D. and provides the earliest datable material.

The term Mailapor is derived from Mayil - the peacock, and from this name come the name of the place Mayil-a-pur, Peacock Town[211]. There appears to be some consensus that the term used in the original text of the Bible for peacock - Tukki-im is the Tamil word spelt from Hebrew. This is noted by Milne Rae as reflecting the Hebrew plural inflexion dating from the period of Solomon at the beginning of the first millennium B.C. and this is considered to be evidence that there was contact between the Hebrews and South India from that date[212]. Milne Rae continues: "The ordinary name at present for the peacock on the Malabar coast and in Tamil is Mayil (Sanskrit, Mayura); it is sometimes called Siki (Sanskrit, Sikhi), a name given to it on account of its crest; but the ancient, purely Tamil-Malayalam name of the peacock is Tokei, the bird with the (splendid) tail, Sikhi = Avis Cristata; Tokei = Avis Caudata. It seems reasonable therefore, to infer that Solomon's historiographer became acquainted with the bird and its name in consequence of visits made by that great king's sailors to the west coast of Southern India. Nor is it improbable that similar visits may have followed in the course of the centuries subsequent to Solomon's time ..."[213]. It is not known whether the King sent immigrants or set up trading posts in South India or Ceylon at that time but Jewish settlers did in fact arrive some time early in the first millennium A.D. and there was still a community in Cochin into more recent decades of last century.

The available evidence suggests that St. Thomas could have reached South India since the terminology found among the Dravidian Tamils suggests that there was contact from about the 10th., century B.C. between the East Coast of the Mediterranean and Ceylon now called Sri Lanka by sea. Other evidence indicates that several centuries before this time there were contacts between the Caucasus and the Hittites and India, probably for the most overland, since there are many cultural elements in India suggesting such contacts. However, actual archaeological evidence would indicate that those who reached South India at Malabar (Mylapore) and then Coromandel were in fact missionaries acting under the aegis of St. Thomas for the Syrian Christian church. This hypothesis tends to be confirmed by the Mailapur legends stating that "St. Thomas", soon after arriving, went on to China and later returned to die at the hands of the Brahmans or the "fowler" recorded in the legends.

The earliest linguistic evidence is preserved on a cross as earlier noted for the Persian characteristic of the 7-8th., century A.D., and there is in China inscriptions recording a Nestorian colony dating to the 636-781 A.D.[214]. It is unknown whether this is actually the result of the Syrian Christian missions personified by St. Thomas arriving from South India, but it seems perhaps too great a coincidence that these should both date to the 7th., century A.D. and therefore six centuries too late to have been undertaken by St. Thomas himself. Records indicate that the Bishop of Tyre, Dorotheus (254-313 A.D.), stated that the Apostle St. Thomas preached to the Parthians, Medes, Persians, Germanians, Bactrians, and Magi (Iran) before suffering martyrdom at Calamina a place said to have been in India. This is also a town mentioned by St. Jerome a century later, and St. Gregory of Torus states that he died in India and his body was transferred to a monastery and temple of great size in Edessa in Syria[215]. These reports does not however, define where Calamina was in Sub-continental India or whether India is here related to India Maxima including Afghanistan and Eastern Iran.

Other traditions have associated the Apostles, Thomas with Parthia, Philip with Phrygia, Andrew with Syria, and Bartholomew with India. However, there are also some references to the Apostles drawing lots in the division of the countries to which each was to be sent[216]. Some historians record that Demetrius of Alexandria received a message from a section of the population of India begging for teachers to be sent to instruct them in the doctrines of Christianity. Pantaeus, an Athenian stoic and Principal of the Alexandrian Christian College, sailed from Berenice for Malabar between 180 and 190 A.D. He found "some who were acquainted with the Gospel of Mathew, to who Bartholomew, one of the apostles, had preached, and had left them the same gospel in Hebrew, which was also preserved until this time"[217]. It seems that it may have been possible for St. Bartholomew to have founded a Christian Church in South India, but it is surprising that no mention is preserved in the records of later centuries, unless they became assimilated back into Hinduism before the advent of missions of those under the patronage of St. Thomas centuries later. It may also be that he stayed too short a time to accomplish a permanent Church before going onwards, perhaps to the Americas.

The 7th., century is an important watershed in the history of Asia since it saw the beginning of the expansion of the Muslim religion toward India. By sea the pre-Muslim Arabs had long had contact from Arabia and the Middle East with South India in particular and where it is known that the last Perumal converted to Islam in 827 A.D.[218]. Perumal is the name of the pre-Brahman rulers of the indigenous Dravidian people in Malabar and meant "big men"[219]. The primary warrior caste was that of the Nayas or Nayars, and the elders, in whose hands the power of the villages and towns was invested under, the ruler were the Karanavar, and these Nayars appear to have retained a social structure based on divisions of six hundred[220]. These divisions of Nayars into six hundred are mentioned twice in a Syrian Christian document dated to 925 A.D.[221]. Evidence of the Syrian Christian colony in Malabar occurs apart from the dated first cross, to the copper plate charters, or Sasanams, on which were inscribed the rights, and land allocations, ascribed to any foreigners who were allowed to settle granted by the rulers of the region[222]. The earliest surviving charter appears to be dated at 774 A.D. but a generation before this, another Thomas, known as Knaye Thomas or Thomas of Cana, arrived in South India with a company of Christians from Baghdad, Nineveh and Jerusalem in 745 A.D.[223]. Some authorities have considered that this is the Thomas with whom tradition has confused with St. Thomas and, for the historians, his recorded arrival matches too closely to the available archaeological and textual evidence such as it is to not be so. However, this Thomas appears to have been sent on the orders of the Catholic bishop of Edessa and does not explain how or why the Church in Malabar became Syrian Christian rather than Roman Catholic unless there was a surviving Syrian Church strong and large enough to absorb over generations the Catholic immigrants. Whatever the outcome and identifications it is known that the Syrian Christians were evangelists in their early days and evidence occurs not only in South India and China but in Mongolia where wall sketches clearly indicating their religious activities are known[224] (*7.026; 7.029*).

By the 6th., century A.D. Nestorian Christianity had spread their interpretation of Christianity into East Central Asia and ultimately to the North East of Asia. In China, translations of Christian documents have been recovered from Dunghuang and there is a stela with a Nestorian inscription dating to the 7th., century A.D. (*7.021*) in the former capital at Chang'an[225]. A cross discovered at Singanfu records the appearance of Nestorian missionaries in Shensi in the early seventh century coinciding also with the first records in Southern India[226]. Because they had for such a long time resided in China it is said that in 551 A.D. the Nestorians monks travelling to Constantinople brought with them the eggs of the silkworm[227]. This implies that the Syrian Christians, the Nestorians, had in fact been in China before the 6th., century A.D. A record notes that Cosmos, called Indicopleustes, an Indian, in his travels visited Male "where the pepper grows" in 522 A.D. and referred to the "fully organised" church in Malabar where the Bishops were consecrated in Persia[228]. The depiction of the Nestorian Christian, on his horse in the Central Asia (*7.029*), and wearing a cap with a simple equal arm cross is characteristic of that found also in South India but also in Codices and figurines in the Americas (*7.025; 7.027/8; 7.030*). The many references to St. Thomas in South India, China and probably Mexico and South America appear too similar to those of Tonapa or Tonaca, in both iconography and myth, to be coincidental. Through all the vicissitudes faced by the Syrian Christian Church in among the local peoples of Malabar and Coromandel, the hostile Brahmans, the rise of the Hindu faith and the gradual incursions of the Muslims in South India, none were more perilous than when they suffered through the Portuguese importing the Western faith of the Church of Rome. From the beginning of their arrival the Catholics demanded the subjection of the Syrian Church, considering it heretical, and in 1599 A.D. the inquisitor Alexes de Menezes, Archbishop of Goa, had all the books written in Syriac and Chaldaean burnt so that all the records of a millennium were consumed in the flames. With them went any records that might have established that the Syrian Christians reached not only China but the Americas in the first millennium A.D.[229].

There have been discovered three crosses among the ancient Christian remains in South India. The most recent has been dated to the 10th., century and exhibits the inevitable integration of extraneous cultural influences from the surrounding Hindus. Peacock armorials were included in the panel and these birds were a symbol of the Mailapore (Mayil = peacock) district where the first Christians were converted in Coromandel. In the reports attributed to Marco Polo who passed through this part of India it is related that he was told that while St Thomas was praying one day in a grove a "fowler", who was employed there in shooting birds, having shot his arrow at a peacock missed it and the arrow struck St. Thomas. As he lay dying St. Thomas was said to have been "sweetly addressing himself to his Creator"[230]. Another legend recorded by John de Marignolli, when he visited South India in the mid-14th., century, A.D. notes from local tradition that St. Thomas was shot by an arrow in a similar way but that he was riding on an ass and was wearing at that time a shirt, a stole and a "mantle of peacock feathers". The Portuguese

Duarte Barbosa was told in the 16th., century that St. Thomas was badly treated by the people and he retired to solitude, when a "Gentile hunter", out with a bow and arrow to shoot peacocks, saw many of them together on the slope of a hill, and, aiming at the one in the middle because it was a "peculiarly handsome creature" sent the arrow into its body. The peacocks then "rose up flying" and in the air the wounded peacock "turned into the body of a man". The hunter watched as the body fell as that of the Apostle. He hastened to tell what he had seen to the "governors" who came to see the body and who saw that it was indeed that of St. Thomas. They saw at the place where he was struck with the arrow that there were left the impressions of footprints where he flew up as the peacock[231].

In the tenth century, A.D., Persian influence in South India was by then long established and this connection was a conduit from the Ancient Middle East continuing in a refreshed flow as it had in former millennia. The ruling Pallavas, dating from the first centuries A.D. in South East India, have been considered by some to have been related to those sharing the similar Persian name and who originally came from there along with so many other influences over the millennia. In the tenth century the Perumals, the rulers of South West India, were contemporary with the reviving Pallavas after the demise of the Chola kings.

The Syrian or Nestorian Church after breaking from Rome in the early fifth century A.D. did not remain without its own divisions. In the Council of Chalcedon there was a great debate about the true nature of Christ as to whether He was in fact a tri-unity of Father, Son and Holy Ghost or whether he existed in his sole nature. Those who supported the latter were condemned as heretics and were regaled with the term Monophysites. The adherents of the West Syrian Church became attached to the Monophysite heresy and the reason is given in the following remarkable relation recorded by Milne Rae: "Now it came to pass in the days of the Emperor Justinian that the Monophysite party in Syria was threatened with becoming gradually extinct; when a man arose among them whose indefatigable zeal did much to revive and extend the Monophysite communion. This was Jacobus Zanzalus, commonly surnamed Baradaeus, or the man in rags; from the circumstance that he went about in the guise of a beggar. Ordained by certain imprisoned bishops to be the metropolitan of their Church, he visited the Syrian and neighbouring provinces, ordained clergy for his party, and gave them a Patriarch of Antioch

021 : A Nestorian - Syrian .ristian, stela with a long inscrip-.n indicating the missionary zeal this religion in China from the ddle of the first millennium, A.D. ..n-Fu, Shensi, N.W. China, 635-.1 A.D.

7.022 : Persian cross similar to that on St. Thomas's Mount in Madras indicating contacts from the Ancient Middle East. Cottayam, Malabar, South West Coastal India, 7-10th., century, A.D.

7.023 : Syrian Christian cross of the Persian type with armorial peacocks surmounting over the main panel. Cottayam, Malabar Coast, South West India, c10th., century, A.D.

7.024 : Cross of the Persian type indicating probable Christian migration from there in the middle of the first millennium, A.D. St. Thomas's Mount, Madras, 7th.,- 8th., century, A.D.

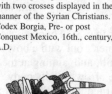

7.025 : A form of the deity, Xolotl, depicting a headdress with two crosses displayed in the manner of the Syrian Christians. Codex Borgia, Pre- or post Conquest Mexico, 16th., century, A.D.

7.026 : Nestorian or Syrian Christian inscription in South West China. Hsi-an-Fu, China 636-781 A.D.

7.028 : The god Xolotl, the brother is some myths of Quetzalcoatl, depicted with a cross on a turban closely similar to the type found among the Syrian Christians in Southern India). Codex Borgia, Pre- or post Conquest Mexico, 16th., century, A.D.

7.027 :The lower supine deity is depicted as a form of Tlaloc the rain god sometimes identified with Quetzalcoatl, with crosses displaced on his headdress in the manner of the Syrian Christians. Codex Borgia, pre- or post Conquest Mexico, 16th., century, A.D.

7.029 : Syrian Christian missionaries depicted riding horseback are found in Central Asia. The cross on the brow is identical to those found in Mexico and Ecuador. 6-9th., century, A.D.

7.031 : The culture-hero deity associated with the sea, Quetzalcoatl, showing a cape that probably was intended to identify with the Mexican Tonaca, probably intended to represent St. Thomas. Codex Vaticanus, pre- or post Conquest Mexico, 16th., century, A.D.

7.032 : Two seated priest or rulers seated on their traditiona[l] stools indicating status. Their fez-like caps are similar to thos[e] found early in India, such as worn by the Gonds and the Indonesians with crosses identi[-]cal to those worn by the Syrian Christians. Manteno, Manabi, Ecuador, 850-1500 A.D.

7.030 : The wind deity particularly noted among the Zapotecs in Southern Mexico, identified with Quetzalcoatl. He is depicted with a cross on a turban identical to that of the Syrian Christians and lower on the headdress similar to those shown on the traditional cowls of Coptic and Syrian Christian headdresses. Codex Borgia, Pre- or post Conquest Mexico, 16th., century, A.D.

for their superior. For more than thirty years he continued his labours with great success till his death in 578. It was from him that the Syrian Monophysites were called Jacobites, and it was by his ordination of Sergius as a successor to his master that the heretical succession was kept up"[232]. This remarkable record will be of interest when considering in the following section the Cora and Pariacaca myths - the latter hero identified with Viracocha and Tonaca.

In Syrian Christian tradition the Izhavans from Sri Lanka were invited back to Malabar at their suggestion and it is also recorded that they had brought with then the palm trees with which they were usually identified. They are also said to have imported into Kerala a variety of areca nut palm, champak and lime trees, to whose vernacular names the term Izham was prefixed into the present times. The name Izhavan is the southern counterpart of the Ilavans and Tiyans and is said to be a corruption of the Sri Lankan name Simhalam and ancient name of Sri Lanka. One of their traditions states that a Pandyan princess named Alli married a Rajah from Karnataka named Narasimbha, and they eventually migrated with their followers to Sri Lanka. When their line died out in later generations it is said that their descendants returned to South India but were accorded a very low status in society. They are mentioned in a grant of 824 A.D. recording that their headman leading a guild planting up the "waste lands"[233].

7.034 : Syrian Christian pontiff wearing a traditional cowl headdress with crosses more similar to stars. Malabar Coast, South India,

7.033 :A group of the priests and church elders in the Syrian Church of South India at the beginning of the 20th., century, A.D. showing the headdresses long traditional from their beginnings in India from the mid-first millennium, A.D. Malabar Coast, South India, Early 20th., century, A.D.

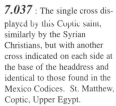

7.036 : A Bolivian Indian wearing a traditional hat of the Tibetan type with star designs applied reminiscent of the Syrian Christians. Potosi, Bolivia, Early 20th., century, A.D.

7.037 : The single cross displayed by this Coptic saint, similarly by the Syrian Christians, but with another cross indicated on each side at the base of the headdress and identical to those found in the Mexico Codices. St. Matthew, Coptic, Upper Egypt.

7.035 : The fundamental single cross was typical of Asian Syrian Christian missionaries throughout Asia. Coptic, Egypt.

In the copper grant held by the Syrian Christians dated to 824 A.D. there is also recorded that there were four families of Vellala carpenters existing on the sea coast and these were the Karalars or trustees of growing plants. These Vellalas are the same as those in the original Pandyan domains, but who adopted local customs, but it is important here to note that they are associated with other notable players among those with whom the Syrian Christians were bound up in the second half of the first millennium A.D.[234].

In Peru, Garcilasso de la Vega, apart from the Cross of Carabuco already mentioned, refers to another cross inherited by the Incas from an earlier time as he notes: "The King Yncas kept in Cuzco a cross of fine marble, of the white and red colour called crystalline jasper, and they know not from what time they have had it. I left it, in the year 1560, in the sacristy of the cathedral church of that city, where it was hung to a nail by a cord passing through a hole made at the top of the upper end. I remember that the cord was a selvedge of black velvet, but in the time of the Indians it must have had a chain of silver or gold, which may have been exchanged for this selvedge by the man who first found it. The cross was square, that is, as long as broad, being three-quarters of a vara long, rather less than more, and three fingers deep; and almost the same breadth. It was all of the same piece, very well carved, with corners carefully squared, and the stone brightly polished. The Yncas kept it in one of the royal houses, in a huaca or sacred place. They did not worship it, beyond holding it in veneration on account of the beauty of its form, or for some other reason which they could scarcely give expression to. Thus it was kept until the Marquis Don Francisco Pizarro entered the valley of Tumpez; and, owing to what there happened to Pedro de Candia, they began to worship it and hold it in greater veneration, as we shall mention."[235].

The equal-armed cross was particularly associated with the orthodox Christians and would correspond well with Tonapa and identifying with St. Thomas. The same type of cross was adopted by the early Christians from crucifix forms long known in the Ancient Near and Middle East (*8.035*). It is likely, however, that the same cross was imported much earlier into South America before the arrival of the Syrian Christians.

Thunder and Lightning Gods from Il, El and Baal and Illapa and Ilapu

Illapa as the Inca thunder deity and Ilapu that of the Aymara, clearly relate to thunder and lightning both in myth and ritual propitiation by the pre-Conquest Indians of the Andes that continues into the present day. This has been considered in terms of local relationships of deities in South America in South America where those of the Inca probably derived, in part at least, from the Aymara (Colla). Other references clearly indicated in the Andean names are paralleled in those of the same deities in West and South Asia.

Of particular note is that the lightning diagram inscribed by the Indians themselves on metal plates are of crossed serpents in the shape of the serpentine forms of the thunderbolt or lightning strike. Adolph Bandelier a century ago sketched a typical representation of the "Cross and Snake" commonly found on the gables of the people living on the Bolivian puna (*7.008*). The arms of the saltire cross, that is oblique cross, represented the serpent while the cross proper were the vertical and horizontal arms with manos or hands terminating the ends. Both the traditional cross, with hands, and the saltire represented the lightning as serpents. This diagram corresponds with the age-old Aymara belief in the thunder and lightning deity Thunapa otherwise called Ilapu by them but Illapa by the Quechua and the Incas. Among the reports not yet considered is that of Arriaga who calls the lightning god Hillapa but also Libial[236]. Hillapa is clearly the Quechua Indian form of the lightning god, Illapa, and completes the triune form with Inti,

7.038 : An example of a multiple crosses depicted on the brow of the cowl worn by this Coptic saint some exhibiting dots or stars between the arms compare to those traditional on the headdresses in Bolivia and crosses on each lower end side on the shoulder. St. Sarapamon, Egypt.

7.040 : A group of three women wearing traditional Bolivian hats with star designs reminiscent of designs of Syrian Christian designs depicted on a hat similar to a traditional Tibetan style hat. Potosi, Bolivia, Early 20th., century, A.D.

7.039 : Multiple crosses depicted on the brow of the cowl worn by this Coptic saint some exhibiting dots or stars on the shoulders, compare to those traditional on the headdresses in Bolivia (*7.040*) and crosses on each side of the shoulder ends of the headdress. St. Anthony, Egypt.

7.041 : The Syrian Christian pontiff in South India from 1865 A.D., Mar Dionysius V, with the characteristic equal arm cross so typical of the orthodox Christian churches. Malabar Coast, South India, Late19th., century, A.D.

7.042 : The traditional cross that may have shared a common origin from the Syrian Christian missions on the South West Coast of India and on to Peru and Bolivia in the late first millennium, A.D. Cherakon, Malabar, S.W. Coastal India, Pre-20th., century, A.D.

the Sun, Viracocha the Creator[237]. Illapa may have been a manufactured form by the Inca themselves, and Pachacuti in particular, although each deity in original type appears to pre-date the Incas themselves among the Aymara. Among the Inca, de la Vega asserts that Yllapa (Illapa) represented thunder, lightning and lightning bolts[238] and this deity was visualised as a bright, shining god. As his personal huauque or "familiar spirit", Pachacuti had Inti-Illapa, the Thunder[239].

In other parts of Peru Illapa is combined in a triad as Inti-Illapa with Chuquilla, and Catuilla at Huamachuco on the Peruvian North Coast[240] where sky serpents are often associated with this deity[241]. There does, however appear to be ancient connections before the Incas between Viracocha and Illapa since he is referred to in some traditions as Illa Tecce Viracocha, the "great white bearded man" and where his beard is conceived as the brilliant white rays of the Sun[242]. This reflects the ceremonial use of the beards cut from old men in the Marquesas Islands, called Pava-hina, being especially revered and identical with the brilliant white of the tropical Moon noted elsewhere in this work. The Quechua Illapa or Aymara Ilapu is also identified with Pariacaca who was the deity worshipped on the south coast of Peru[243]. On the South coast also, in the Nazca Valley, the most ancient creator was Inkarri and Illapa was more commonly conceived as the Ccoa or wildcat. The Ccoa was believed to spit hail, and urinate rain, hurling lightning or hail from its phosphorescent eyes[244].

The Wamanis in Nazca were the ancient mountain gods, the counterparts of the Achachilas of Andean Peru and Bolivia, and considered largely beneficent. They were believed to assist the flow of the rivers and streams from the mountains to the irrigation channels constructed by the people. The bounty provided by these mountain deities was presided over by the earthly priest or Pongo who dealt out punishment to any who contravened the Wamanis' will[245]. Valcarels' report of the cosmology of the Incas preserves the myth of the two serpents who emerged from the Underworld, Yacu Mama and Sacha Mama, into this world before continuing on to the Upper World where Yacu Mama turned into the lightning god of thunder, storm and rain, Illapa[246]. The Jesuit Father Blas Valera referred to the Sun God as Illa Tecce suggesting that the term Il, extended to Illa and then Illapa, was in fact the root for all the deities of this name both solar and those of thunder and lightning[247]. It is interesting to note that in all the references to Illapa there are no significant connections reported between the sacred mountain towering above the modern city of La Paz named Illimani. Even the Aymara term for the lightning god, Ilapu, is not recorded as having special connection with the sacred mountain. To even the most casual observer a mountain with such a prefix as Ill or Illi-mani should be connected in some way with the deity so closely identified with mountain tops in actuality as well as in myths and named Il-apu or Ill-apa. Apu or Apo is a term used a prefix to denote sacredness, e.g., Apu Saqro = "the sacred mountain of the cat (or devil)"[248], or to denote high rank as a chief, e.g. used in the Inca myth to name Manco Capac's father Apu-Tampu. This term is found among the Maya as Apho but is a term, among many others, leading across the Pacific to Asia.

Exactly the same association and symbolism of the serpent with the lightning strike or thunderbolt illustrated in myth and iconography among the Aymara of Bolivia was used anciently in the Near and Middle East. It has already been noted that the Hittite deity Illu-yankus was depicted as a dragon or giant serpent was the opponent of Il or El the creator deity. It is likely that there is some mirroring of the name and prefix Il, in the name of this dragon and was probably originally conceived as the dark reflection of the mountain god El and probably a supreme god subjected by his successor[249]. This Hittite myth is similar to the Peruvian myth of Yacu Mama and Sacha Mama, the serpents or dragons who emerged from the earth. Hittite iconography depicts the weather god Telipinu holding aloft thunderbolts and other serpentine forms clearly as a reference to the dragon and the serpentine form of lightning others illustrate a trident (*7.005*).

The deity El was considered the first of the Canaanite gods, "old", "master of time", benevolent and merciful", and he was said to dwell on Mount Saphon[250]. El dwelt not only on the mountain but significantly also in a pavilion on the seashore where rivers flowed into the sea. It was he who ensured that the rivers flowed into the divine abyss of the ocean where this was perceived as a reflection of the divine cosmic structure reflective of the time. This is a closely similar mythical construct to that of the Mandaeans where the primal rivers flowed from the divine ether to give life on earth[251]. The deity Il or El was usually depicted seated and wearing a crown of bulls' horns, a symbol of strength[252]. One myth cycle associated with El or Il is that of his son Keret whom Il assisted in finding a suitable second wife who later presented her husband with "seven sons, yea eight"[253]. Another myth cycle features the second son of El whose name was Aghat and who possessed a wonderful bow. This son is identified with the "dying and reviving" heroes and therefore to the agricultural myths associated with the seasons referring to the sowing and reaping of the grain. In a fragmentary surviving text the association of El with the rivers from the mountain and the fields as the intermediate plane before they drained into the ocean is recorded as follows: "... Anat ... (she planted) (her) feet and the earth did quake; then (verily she set) (her) face towards El (at) the source(s) of the rivers, (amid the channels) of the two oceans, she penetrated the fields of El."[254].

The reason that there was an identification of the mountain deity Il or El with the seashore was because he it was who ensured that the sea would yield water as clouds to fall as rain on the mountains - this being exactly the concept that the Ancient Peruvians and Bolivians had preserved. It is said that El advanced along the shore on the edge of the ocean as the Abyss. He plunged into the waves and grasped the wave of the ocean and placed it in the sky and it fell as rain upon the earth identically to the concept preserved in Peru. The myths associated with El and the ocean are therefore related to the fertility of the earth. Other references also occur to the god making his wives fertile and he is said to have exclaimed that their lips were as sweet as a bunch of grapes - doubtless another reference to rain and the cultivation of the vine[255].

In more ancient times there are references to a warrior deity in the Akkadian Dynasty and there are records of a "weapon of Ilaba", possibly a club. This mariner deity as Ilaba may have been a weather god where the striking of the club produced a spark such as Thor's hammer[256]. It seems too great a coincidence that this reference to a lightning god, Ilaba, should so closely resemble Illapa or Ilapu in Ancient Bolivia and Peru.

The mace is very early depicted in Near Eastern art and many ancient examples have been found which are ritual forms of the actual clubs used in war and celebrated in the myths of the gods as follows: "The mace whirled in Ba'al's hands(s) like an eagle, (grasped) his fingers it crushed the shoulder of prince Yam, the chest of judge Nahar; Yam did gather strength, he sank not down, his face quivered not and his features crumpled not up. Kathur fetched down a mace and proclaimed its name, (saying): Thy name, thine is Aymurr, expel Yam, expel Yam from his throne, Nahar from his dominion ..."[257]. The club was also a mythical and no doubt real symbol of war and regal authority among the Moche of Northern Peru and is depicted many times among them. Star clubs were also depicted as a symbol of authority among them and the later Incas, found also on the coast of Ecuador, and was probably a reduced version of the fluted clubs depicted so widely in India. Ba'al was in usually considered to be in the Canaanite myths the son of Il or El but he is sometimes considered to be El himself. Because the deity, Ilaba, is so similar to that of the Bolivian Ilapu it may be that the associated hero named Aymurr from Ancient West Asia, or Near East, is the prototype for the name Aymara. These connections will be of more interest in a projected future publication.

The epics in the Canaanite myth cycles revolve around the need for rain in a hot and dry land and in some myths Baal is the son of El. He is noted to have defeated Yam in several myths similar to that above and this Yam is almost certainly the origin of the deity of the Underworld in India, Yama, the Iranian Yima, and a related term preserved as the Underworld god Yomi in Japan. It is probably no coincidence therefore that yana is identified in the Inca world with the underworld and particularly the colour black noted earlier. It is clear that many of the Hittite references in myths to deities were transferred through Iran to India and along with them other aspects of ancient myths, from contemporary and earlier peoples were also swept along with them, and were integrated to a lesser or greater degree in the Vedic texts and into later Hinduism. El or Il is identified with the divine Bull[258] in West Asian mythology and undoubtedly the progenitor of many of the bull cults extending from the East Mediterranean across into Iran and India where in South India in particular rites associated with similar aspects of the divine bull, the transfer appears to have been transferred reasonably faithfully and practised into the twentieth century.

There are many aspects of West Asian cultures preserved among the peoples of India and South India in particular and it has been shown abundantly that these Aryan peoples from Anatolia, the Caucasus, and Mesopotamia were driven through Iran into India over millennia. Their origins in India are traceable, as has been shown, and the terms used for deities or racial or tribal origin are in some cases preserved exactly or with elements still identifiable from their origins in West Asia. It is notable in many cultures that World Trees are closely identified with the Axis Mundae or World Axis, usually conceived as pointing at the Pole Star in corresponding myths. In the subjection of one religion by another the symbol of that religion is often recorded as being defeated, if an animal or person, or destroyed or dispersed if a building, or other object such as the Biblical Tower of Babel, where it is overthrown. The converted Naga or serpent-worshipper in Buddhist literature was said to have destroyed the tree called Ila in the days of the Buddha's successor Kasyapa[259]. He was said to be a gigantic serpent or dragon in form and this suggests that the myth was a transfer of the Canaanite myth of Illuyankus into India.

The problem of gender reversal among the deities was noted in early texts from the Ancient Near East and is found also more widely including in the Americas. In the Near East Albert Clay noted a century ago: "... the generic designations or titles as El 'god', Ba'al 'lord, owner', with the corresponding feminine form Ba'alat, were used in connection with deities of different localities. It seems Malik, or Melek, probably the same as Molech in the Old Testament, was another such appellation. In only a few instances can names of the deities who are represented by such designations be surmised; to cite a single example, the Ba'al of Harran was the moon god Sin." ..." 'Am written in cuneiform Amma, Hammu, etc., which some regard as a designation of the 'the father-uncle', borne by the husbands of a wife when polyandry was practised, is also used instead of a deity in personal names, cf., 'Am-ram', 'Ammi-el', 'Ammi-hud', etc., ..."[260].

It is clear from this textual reference that not only gender reversal, similarly found in the Americas, has early examples in the Ancient Middle East, but that there are associated gods of near identical names appearing in these same disparate regions. The El, Il, and Ilaba of the Ancient Middle East occurs with Malik, Melik, Malca and Sin, corresponding to the Il-apa, Il-apu or Ilaba as well as Libial together with Si, Malca and Malquis in Ancient Coast and Andean Peru and Bolivia.

Lightning and the God Baal, Il or El outside Iraq and Iran

In Borneo a chest of a manang, a medicine man, contained various stones, usually connected to lightning or the conductors or healing energies from the spirit world. Stone is invariably denoted from the West Asian derivative from bat or baetyl and the term found throughout Indonesia

7.043 : The World Axis as the World Tree is shown extending from the throne of the Buddha. The parasol is also a symbol of the Axis Mundae. Amaravati, South East India, 2nd., century, A.D.

was bat, batu or batoe. The medicine chest had stones, among others known as Batu Bintang a stone representing his authority, a transparent stone; Batu Lintar (or Nitar) - a dark-coloured stone called a "thunderbolt"; Batu Kran Uiranan - the petrified ginger root; and Batu Ilau - the "sparkling stone"[261]. The term Ilau corresponding to sparkling appears to reflect the resplendent Il or El of West Asia and the luminous image of Illapa devised by the Incas. The term Uiranan may have some connection with that of the wind in India, always associated with the soul whether in sickness or in health, and Uira (Vira) in Peru.

In Fiji early British researchers considered the cult of the Nanga to reflect that of Baal and Ashtoreth in Canaan[262]. This may well be but in fact the Nanga rites and megalithic ceremonial areas more closely resemble those of the villages of the Gonds and related peoples in Central East India who are frequently mentioned in this work. On Erromanga, an island in Melanesia, another writer recorded that, "Some of the Erromangan navilah stones are quite circular and like a ring or wheel. Such also were some of the symbols of Baal and Ashtoreth, the deities of productiveness, the Sun and Moon, in the ancient Syrian world ..."[263]. In Polynesia Abraham Fornander researched the association of sacred stones and the name derivatives applied and recorded that his conclusion was that the stone, the name, and the practices associated with it were derived from West Asia. He traces their names of the term batu, found so widely in South India and Indonesia to the god name Il, Illu or El[264] noting parallels in Hawaiian myths and monuments, and similar associations are found in the New Hebrides with the term bat. Some Mexican deities seem to preserve aspects of Ancient Middle Eastern contacts in the terms used for them. Il-ama-Tecuhtli was a goddess of earth, death, the Milky Way and midwifery[265]. The name Tlal-tecuhtli means "Earth Lord"[266] and Tlal may be simply El or Il inflected in the Mexican tongue. This appears also likely for the serpent goddess Coatlique (Co-at-li-kay) probably an extended inflection of the fierce goddess of India - Kali, while Cihua-coatl (Cihua-serpent) or Cihua-teteo (Cihua-god)[267] may be gender reversals, a characteristic as noted also found in Asia, and referring to Siva. Siva was said to be the origin of the great serpent, the Ganges River, and this is noted more fully elsewhere in this work. In Southern South America, among the Teheulche Indians, is should not be a surprise to find a hero named Elal who was born of a "cloud-woman"[268]. In another myth the Evening Star is called Karro (see Karo and Karei in India and South East Asia), and Elal falls in love with her. They fly up into the sky where the souls of the people go to him after death and are taken there by a spirit called Vendeuk, clearly the localised form of the Iranian myths where the soul is taken to the Cinvat Bridge by Vayu[269]. There are many references in the myths of this people paralleling those of India and the Ancient Middle East but cannot be considered here but reserved for a projected later publication.

The Origins of Thunder and Lightning Gods in Andean Myths

Lightning on the Bolivian highlands was represented by figures of two "crossed serpents"[270]. Those who had been struck by lightning and lived to tell the tale were called Yatiri and considered supernatural[271]. Some of the earliest chroniclers among the first Spanish such as Bernabe Cobo and Pedro Pizarro noted that the "fetishes" of the Sun, Thunder and Lightning as deities were always worshipped together, at least in Public[272]. It is also notable that the "tears" of the Staff God were identified with the Ccoa and these were considered to represent the hail that fell in a storm, but in some of the Tiahuanco carvings the gold disks are still in place suggesting that these represented rays or "tears" of the Sun (*7.020*). In Peru the hail, falling from a storm was considered to represent Supay, the spirit of evil, while on the Bolivian Puna (Altiplano) his counterpart was Anchancho[273].

In the agricultural cycles in the Inca Empire certain stones in the fields and the aqueducts were regaled with offerings at the time the seed was sown. Twins who had died young were preserved in urns in a hut near the fields since one of the twins was considered to be the child of the lightning[274]. Arriaga noted: "... when twins are born they call them Chuchus or Curi, and in Cuzco Taqui Huahua, and they believe that twins are a sacrilegious and abominable thing, although they say that one of them is the son of lightning. They do penance on this account as if they had committed a terrible sin. Usually the father and mother both fast for many days, as Dr. Avila has shown, eating neither salt nor pepper nor having intercourse at that time. In some places they carry this on for six months. In others, both father and mother lie down on one side and remain without moving for five days. One foot is folded under them, and a lima bean or kidney bean is placed under the knee, until with the effect of perspiration it begins to grow. For the next five days they do the same thing on the other side, all the while fasting as described. When this penance is over, the relatives go hunting for a deer, and after cutting it up they make a kind of canopy of the skin. The penitents pass beneath this with ropes around their necks, which they must wear for many days"[275].

This interesting belief associating twins with evil of the lightning appears to be evidence of another direct connection with the Ancient Middle East. The evil twin in religious myths of the fire-worshipping Ahura Mazdaeans, who became the revisionist Zoroastrians, was Ahriman (Aharman) the spirit of darkness while his twin was the god of light Ohrmazd or Ahura Mazda. This dark spirit took many forms and in the Pahlavi Texts he appears as a young man of fifteen years although his actual body in this reports was that of "a log-like lizard's (vazak - varanus in India) body", suggesting a large monitor lizard or crocodile. It is said in the text that he stood up inside the sky "and he sprang, like a snake, out of the sky down to earth". In the following verse of the text it is said that he rushed into the world at noon and the sky was shattered and that, "He came on to the water which was arranged below the earth, and then the middle of this earth was pierced and entered by him"[276]. The text does not mention Ahriman as the lightning serpent but there can be little doubt that he is represented here as a catastrophic storm and is reminiscent of the Yacu Mama and Sacha Mama in the Peruvian myths already noted. The mention of the water below the earth is identical to the beliefs held by the Ancient Peruvians.

In Vedic myths of India, inherited for the most part from the Aryan invaders originating in Iran in the first millennium B.C., Indra was the god of the thunderbolt, or lightning. In an ancient myth, Indra, having committed a desecration of sacrifice, was required to undertake penance and it is recorded in the texts of the Satapatha Brahmana that he was consecrated after this "on a black antelope skin" as part of the sacrifice[277]. In the same text a verse records a section of the ritual: "He then throws down a gold and a silver plate (beneath his feet, the silver one beneath the left foot) with, 'Protect (me) from death"', 'Protect (me) from lightning! The Virag doubtless is the rain, and of this there are these two terrible forms, lightning and hail; of these the gold plate is of the form of lightning, and the silver one that of hail: against these two deities he affords protection to him, whence who has performed the Sautramani has no fear of these two deities, ..."[278]. Here gold and silver are also associated with hail in this oldest of the ancient Vedic texts of India as it is in Peru and Arriaga noted that silver in particular is revered as part of their rituals.

Among the Araucanians, in what is now North and Central Chile, the deity associated with thunder and lightning was Pillan, said to dwelt in the Andes mountains and who manifested as the fire and smoke of the volcanoes[279]. In the Bolivian and Peruvian Andes this deity became Hillapa or Libial[280] - the Ilapu of Bolivia or Illapa of the Incas. Julio Tello identified the Lanzon, the famed carved monolith at Chavin de Huantar (*4.014/5*), with Viracocha[281] and he in turn with Thunapa of Bolivia and consequently Ilapu or Illapa as deities of the thunder and lightning but this identification with the Lanzon is not clear and not explained.

Guardians of huacas or sacred stone shrines in Ancient Peru were occupied as hereditary posts but also assigned to those who had been struck by lightning and survived[282]. This is reported by Arriaga in an earlier chapter in this work and he further notes: "When they have made their offerings brought by the priest they invoke the huaca, ... by raising their left hand and opening it toward the huaca with a motion as if they were kissing it. On such occasions they must wear no Spanish clothing, nor any hat or shoes ..."

"They worship the sun and lightning in this same fashion, and when they come down from the sierra to the lowlands, they look upon the sea and worship it also. They pull out their eyelashes and offer them, and they beg to stay well and return in health and with much silver to their own country"[283]. The custom of pulling out the facial hair, including the eyelashes is a custom well known among the Dyaks of Borneo, a people who share many customs with the peoples of South America.

This interesting passage confirms the importance of lightning with its association with stones, and reflects also the Asian tradition of walking within sacred precincts barefoot (*7.089*). This relationship between lightning and stones is also illustrated further by Arriaga when he wrote: "Above the town of Yamor we removed the huaca Libiac, or lightning, which was a huge stone cleft in two by a bolt of lightning, and around it was as abundance of sacrifices of llamas and other things"[284]. Stones associated with lightning in other villages are sometimes called Ll'uviac and are clearly from the same origin[285].

In ancient Peru the term Amaru referred to the mythical serpent and was usually applied to the great rivers flowing into the Amazon[286], but these were also associated with the lightning since they were conceived as flowing from the clouds down the mountain sides in their serpentine form as rivulets and becoming the great rivers of the Amazonian drainage east of the Andes[287]. In the Amazon Basin forests the mythical rainbow serpent was called turu amaru[288], and appears to be known from east of Cuzco from its tributaries[289]. On a Kassite (Aryan Dynasty) seal from Mesopotamia, the god Amurru (Amaru) is depicted as a sea god in the characteristic fish garb and holding a crook-shaped sceptre[290].

All three manifestations of the thunder, lightning and the thunderbolt were called Yllapa, Illapa or related derivations in Peru[291]. The religious men, dealing with the agricultural sections of the Nazca plains, were said to be guided by the Ccao or lightning wildcat deity. The earth during August, or mid-winter was believed to be alive and during that time stones called incaychus thrown up in the fields were used as amulets. The Illas are the counterpart of the incaychus and these appear to have connection between the lightning and the sacred stones similar in traditions long known in Asia. The initiation rituals of the shamans in Peru are closely paralleled by those in Siberia. Near Cuzco the lightning was believed to be sent by the apus or mountain spirits who were the shamans' protectors in that region as the Ccao was in the coastal lowlands[292]. The power to practise magic by these shamans with their stones or amulets is believed endowed by the lightning and it is unlikely to be a coincidence that the term for white magician among them is defined by the term white pago where that of white among the Tibetans is Pai, and this connection will be of more interest in due course.

In the mountains of Peru where the thunder was Illapa, "the Flashing One", all male children born during a storm were considered his children as were the stones dedicated to him. As storms were so enveloping in the mountain themselves the thunder and lightning deity was considered an omnipresent, "heroic" male deity and when he flashed his golden sling the lightning was emitted from the all pervasive cloud cover[293].

Lightning in Myths of Central and North America

Among the Maya the lightning deity was Chac and he was usually depicted holding a stone axe or a serpent[294], both symbols associated with the lightning and thunder deities in South America, India and West Asia. The Maya appear to have extended this symbolism to represent the serpent aflame to indicate the flaming or inflammatory aspects of the lightning bolt. The manikin sceptre of the Mayan rulers is now believed to represent the lightning rod depicted as a serpent, fire and axe and is known as God K and also kauil[295], and these aspects are paralleled by those of the Mexican deity Tezcatlipoca[296]. The Zapotec counterpart to the Mayan deity for the thunder and lightning was Cocijo[297] and this name has been defined more accurately as Pitao Cocijo or "Great Spirit within Lightning"[298]. A flying deity with a turtles carapace on its back is believed to be a lightning deity of the Mixtecs called by them Yahui and found also among the Aztecs at the beginning of the first millennium A.D.[299]. The Post Classic counterpart was the Xiuhcoatl characteristically wearing a serpent headdress and tail with a turtle's carapace on its back, carries a conch trumpet and also flint blades[300]. The best known representation of the lightning god in Central America is Tlaloc and he is often depicted holding a serpentine lightning bolt and is found depicted on ceramic vases from at least as early as the 1st., century B.C. at Tlapacoya in Central Mexico[301].

7.044 : Fine ceramic portrait head showing the sling bound around the forehead. Nazca, South Coastal Peru, 200-600 A.D.

Among the Nicarao, of Mexican descent, in Nicaragua arrows were a symbol of lightning hurled to earth during a thunderstorm[302]. Among these people are deities such as the first creator pair named Tamagastat and Cipattonal. Tamagastat has been identified with the Muysca deity Tamagata in Colombia[303] and this deity is also most certainly derived from Tangaroa in Polynesia. Cipattonal is certainly the same as Cipactonal in Mexico, the Aztec Earth Monster, probably originally the caiman or crocodile, and identified also with Oxomogo[304], where this same creature is the crocodile of Hawaii[305]. The prefix Cipa from Cipactonal is probably derived from Siva of India where Coatlique is almost certainly the Kali of India.

Among the Quiche of Guatemala the full title of lightning is Caculha Huracan, and Raxa Caculha is a "green flash" but others assert that this latter is the general name of lightning[306]. The neighbouring Cakchiquel call the lightning Raxhana-hih, but generally racan means a long thin rope or cord[307]. This rope or cord appears to have some parallels therefore with the cord tied around the necks as penance for parents who have had twins in Peru, one of whom was considered the undesirable child of the lightning earlier noted.

Lightning Deities in Indonesia/Melanesia/Polynesia

Characteristic of many lightning myths is that it was believed that it represented the dragon's teeth, a belief widely held in the Mediterranean region. Among the Galela and Tobelo of Minahassa in the north of Celebes in Indonesia the people believed that ancient implements such as axes and celts were the teeth of the lightning dragon who lived in the sky and the clouds. These were called therefore "thunder teeth" or "lightning stones"[308]. Similar beliefs were held widely and are only likely to occur by transfer of cultural myths by mariners. The peoples who find the stone celts or axes almost invariably consider them not to be from their own ancestors but were gods or peoples who walked the earth in ancient times. Beliefs associating celts and stone axes with lightning of this type in Indonesia are virtually identical to those held among the Cuna of Central America[309].

7.045 : The fish god with censer indicates the importance of the sea and sea travel to the Ancient Mesopotamian peoples from the earliest dynasties. Nimrud, Babylonian Period, 1200-900 B.C.

In Pasemah on the island of Sumatra the many celts, or ancient stone axes and tools, found in the soil were associated with the lightning and called by them gigi njaroe meaning "tooth of the lightning"[310]. Also in Sumatra, in Palumbang, it was believed that the lightning was caused by the elephant sharpening its teeth, while others say it dispenses the lightning from its trunk, or from the hairs raised by the anticipation of a storm at the sound of thunder[311]. In Sumatra the lightning was traditionally associated with the four cardinal points of the compass (North, South, East and West) plus the intermediates - 8 in all, and in the rituals associated with it a secret language was used together with the magic wand or sceptre[312]. This is represented by a ground drawing identical with one found in Mexico[313] (*7.047/8*; *7.051*) where the cardinal points are depicted as a square with loops at each corner and an the same is used superimposed at 45 degrees on it representing the intermediates. The ground design is said to represent the lightning serpent itself. Ph. L. Tobing records in text and illustrations the ritual that the Toba-Bataks preserved where the performing priest identifies with the naga (serpent) of the underworld in their celebration associated with the High Gods[314] that resemble the myths of the creator serpents emerging from the underworld, Yacu Mama and Sacha Mama, on the Nazca Plain in South Peru. Lightning in Ancient Peru and Bolivia also appears connected to the four corners, but less emphatically than those of Sumatra, and Garcilasso de la Vega also records that the Incas used a secret language[315].

In the islands off New Guinea the Yokala preserved a myth relating that the inhabitants of the village had, at one time in the past, attempted to erect a "high pillar" reaching to heaven. It fell down and one of the men was marooned in the sky above and now sends the thunder and lightning[316]. In the myths from Yetar a woman struck by lightning eventually gave birth in the grave to a boy named Taimi, who took arrows to revenge himself on the lightning. The lightning was named wiri[317] suggesting that this derives from Vira, and South America where Vira-cocha was identified with Thunapa, the thunder and lightning. Also in the islands north of New Guinea Malinowski wrote: "The oarsman swing their leaf-shaped paddles with long, energetic and swift strokes, letting the water spray off them and the glistening blades flash in the sunlight - a ceremonial stroke which they call 'kavikavila' (lightening)"[318].

In Polynesia the eel became the substitute for the "lightning" serpent and this deity was called Rongo-mai-tauira - the last part of this name perhaps too closely similar to Uira or Vira of Peru to be coincidental[319]. In the Gilbert Island this deity - known as Riiki the Eel has been noted earlier in this work. In the Gilbert Islands also, a myth relating to Bue, a mythical hero to be of more interest later, the term iti is the name for lightning[320] and this probably relates to Ticci or Tikki in the name of Tecce, Ticce or Tiki Viracocha often noted as such by the first Spanish chroniclers. In South East Australia the Aboriginal deity, Kohin, was said to dwell in the Milky Way, and roamed the earth in the night as a gigantic warrior killing those he met. He sent the thunder and lightning and appeared to the ancestors of the race as a carpet snake. He is said to have presented two tikovias to the ancestral elders (*1.053*) and these have a pattern that is clearly derived from the sacred textile patterns of India and found across the Pacific Islands to the Americas.

The term Kohin or Koin was early seen to represent the same deities as Mungan-ngaua, Daramulen and Baiame[321], the first found in India, and the last considered to be a corruption of the name of Buddha, but more likely actually Brahma, found in India, and found also among the Tukano Desana in South America. In the far north of Australia also, in the North West corner of Arnhem Land, the lightning man is called Narmargun (the Thunder and Lightning Man) and a mythical place associated with him was called Ungandun ("where the lightning was")[322]. These names appear to have a common origin from the term for the Tamil god found in South India, Murugan, noted also widely in South East Australia. Among the Tiwi, on the opposite side of Australia, Pakadringa was considered to be the lightning god among the Tiwi and he also was described similarly with a "pendant abdomen caused by continuous overeating[323].

7.047 : Sacred designs as graffiti were anciently known among the Maya in Central America. Copan, Honduras, Classic Period.

7.049 : Ground design identical to those found in Indonesia. Codex Borbonnicus, Early-post Conquest Mexico.

7.050 + 7.051 : Ground design as a sand tracing from the New Hebrides similar to those from Southern India. Oba, New Hebrides, Early 20th., century, A.D.

7.048 : Ground designs were of great importance in Toba-Batak ritual in Western Sumatra. They were particularly linked with the lightning god and in design identical to those found in Ancient Mexico (*7.047*). Batak, Sumatra, Indonesia, Early 20th., century, A.D.

7.046 : Sacred designs are also applied to the walls as well as floors in India and are similar to those drawn in the New Hebrides (Vanuatu). Pariah Tribe, South India, Early 20th., century, A.D.

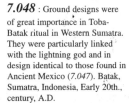

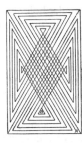

7.052 : Sacred ground design used for divination closely similar to those traditional in Malekula in the New Hebrides (Vanuatu). Pulluvan Tribe, South India, Early 20th., century, A.D.

Lightning Gods of India and West Asia

In India a Puranic tradition notes that forty-nine Vayu (winds) were born together as one in the womb of Indra's mother Aditi. Indra, fearing that he would loose his kingdom by being taken away by these Vayu, he divided them into forty-nine inside his mother's womb. When the forty-nine winds of Vayu were born Indra ensured that they remained in "pieces" by hurling his thunderbolt at them[324]. This is reminiscent of the division of the deer in Peruvian myth from Nazca, but the Hindu myth as a whole confirms the many myths locating Indra's home in the high Himalayas and the intimate relationship between the winds, thunder, lightning and storms.

The Maria Gonds of Central East India referred to the thunderbolt as "the seed" and relate it to the male seminal fluid. Among the Gonds in the Karanji district it is said that rice, vegetable and trees could only bear fruit after hearing thunder - if there is no thunder then it was believed the crops would always be poor[325]. This seems to reflect also the Peruvian association with fertility in agriculture conveyed by the Pongos earlier noted. Among the Andaman Islanders a large iron spike fixed to a large pole about 6 feet long to which toys, dolls and "fancy weapons" are tied in festivals, is kept in the rainy season to "prevent" thunder and lightning and called a Merahta[326]. This term probably derives originally from the name of the sacred Buddhist mountain of Mt. Meru. Spears were also considered to be the cause of lightning and this potency was engendered in those being thrown against the enemy in Burma and no doubt all these references originate from a common source in India.

In China also the association of arrows is recorded associated with lightning[328] and in other myths it is identified with the eyes of the cosmic anthropos, Pan Kua, a dwarf, a being from which all things were born[329]. The myth follows that of the Vedic Creator, Brahma but this version also has its parallels in Ancient West Asia. In China the Pi, or circular disk, always had a

453

circular hole in the centre called the lie-chhui and through this the lightning was said to flash[330]. Among the Ainu of Northern Japan the thunder god was called Kanna Kamui and he was believed to fertilise the soil and was identified with a serpent[331]. An early missionary, John Batchelor, noted that among the Ainu the first serpent had his genesis in the heavens, and suggests that the origin of this myth may have had the same origin as that in ancient Iran as Ahriman[332]. The first serpent was said to come down to earth with the goddess of fire as the Creator's deputy. Batchelor noted; "This serpent, descending as he did in the lightning, came down with such mighty force that his fall made a large hole in the ground. Even at this present day some of his offspring who were left behind in heaven, and have a longing to visit their father, likewise descend in lightning, and the force of their fall also makes holes in the ground. These holes, when known to exist, should by no means be approached, for they lead down to Hades, which is now believed to be the true home of the serpent kind ..."[333]. There are reflections here of the Yacu Mama and Sacha Mama myths from the Nazcan Plains of South Peru.

The Pauri Bhuiyas of North East Central India call the Moon (Jana) as their maternal uncle (mamu - see Mamas of Tukano). The lightning is called Bijli and is the son of the Sun, Bero, and the Moon, Jana, and is also the son of the Sun and the brother of the lightning[334]. The god Indra as the most ancient Vedic deity was believed to bring rain-clouds from the ocean as rain[325]. This suggests the belief that there is a cycle recognising that evaporation from the sea formed the clouds around the mountains resulting in storms, the region of Indra, the god of the storm and thunderbolt, and that is then descended as rain or in the rivers. The peoples of the Himalayas have long identified the wreathing, coiling, serpentine flash of lightning with sky serpents and by these "serpents" the contents of the rain-clouds are spirited to the lakes and rivers to nourish the earth[336]. Interestingly the lightning is also associated with the coils of rope and it has already been noted that parents of twins in South America had to do penance with ropes around their neck. There the lightning was also considered by the Peruvians to have condemned the parents through the birth of the "unnatural" pair. Among the Maya the lightning was associated with coils of rope.

Among the Mandaeans the lightning is called Guha[337]. In the earliest depictions of the lightning god in the Ancient Near East the deity associated held a bunch of arrows and later was depicted standing on the back of a bull holding a "sheaf"[338] (*7.006*). The lightning deity is also anciently depicted holding a trident and this also appears to parallel that of the deity holding a sheaf of arrows known to the Sumerians as Iskur and to the Akkadians as Adad[339].

Among the Sema Nagas of Assam the flashing of sheet lightning is called the "Flashing of Iki's dao". The dao was a type of battle-axe and Iki was considered an excessively cunning fellow and seems to have much about him that derives from the Tiki of Polynesia and possibly Ticce or Tikki of Peru. Forked lightning was called amusuh and was thought of as a celt thrown from heaven onto a pre-chosen object[340].

The Lord of Tears - Hail and Rain Gods in India

The lightning has been irrevocably linked in the Bolivian highlands with the lightning deity, Thunapa, Tonaca; Ilapu or Illapa, and these with the wildcat called the Ccoa. It is believed by some historians that the Staff God carved over the centre of the Gateway of the Sun is a representation of the Thunapa while others retain the earlier belief that it represents the Sun as Inti or Punchao. It has long fascinated researchers that there are many representation of gods with what are considered "tears" on their cheeks depicted on South American ceramics and carvings - the most famous being the central figure itself on the Gateway of the Sun and have lead to many poetic descriptions such as "tears of the Sun". However, just as the references to the other deities closely resembles that of India or the Ancient Near and Middle East, so too do references to tears and, or hail in Bolivia and Peru.

In Southern Highland Peru it was believed that hail actually originated from a cave located on the road to Chichasuyu from Cuzco. This was the fourth huaca or shrine on that journey and was named Cirocaya. As the cropping season approached the people frequented the shrine to make offerings and pray that the hail would not be sent to destroy their crops[341]. On the road to Antisuyu, the eighth shrine or huaca from Cuzco, named Picas, was also dedicated to hail, and this was composed of a small stone located on the hill named Larapa. Small pieces of round gold were offered at this shrine[342]. When hail appeared the people were reported to shout and make sacrifices[343]. Hail was identified by the Bolivian highlanders as the spirit of the devil Supay sweeping across the landscape[344].

In a regional myth preserved in the Yungas, a valley on the sub-tropical region of the eastern Andes, at a lower altitude than the altiplano, it was said that their ancestors descended from the highlands, entered the valley, and prepared the land for cultivation. In so doing the smoke from the burning of the trees and scrub from the land clearance polluted the sacred mountains of Illimani and Illampu. These peaks were considered to be the "ice mansions" of the god Khuno (Kon or Con?), the god of rain and hail and in revenge he sent a torrent of rain and hail into the Yungas. This swept everything away and resulted in landslides closing off the valley from the rest of the Andean Cordillera. In their hunger and despair the survivors ate a brilliant green leaf which stayed their hunger and gave then strength. Renewed in their energies they returned to Tiahuanaco to reveal their discovery to the auquis, or elders, and the seers known as amautas and this leaf was named the coca[345].

The rites associated with the beliefs in the traditional deities were not eradicated by the Spanish friars outside the main cities of Peru and Bolivia and these were still reverenced into the present day. A curious ritual witnessed in the middle of last century, reported of the Aymara of Bolivia, was that it was believed to imitate that undertaken in one year when the essential rains were very late and fell in January instead of November instigating the traditional divination ceremony. In the witnessed rite it was ascertained through divination that the mountain deity, the achachila, had gone off to attend his daughter's wedding, and was remiss in not ensuring the normal rains for the people at that time. "When the achachila finally returned Segundino (the "medium") 'whipped' and scolded him and forced him to 'drink' pure alcohol during a séance until the achachila excused himself for his absence and promised to produce rain again ..."[346]. Rituals are also undertaken to avoid hail as one of several serious threats to the crops. In some villages there is an area reserved for "whipping" to cleanse a ritual item of evil spirits[347]. This practise of whipping the images of the deities was carried out also in Polynesia to discipline or keep the deity up to scratch. The belief that drought was the result of the absence of the rain god has close similarities to that of the god, Telipinu's absence and the resulting drought in Hittite myth earlier noted.

Characteristically, along with the Eurasian deities, the storm and lightning god into the present day is conceived by the Andean peoples as an armed warrior and was immediately identified by them with the Christian St. James, whose sacred site is at Santiago in Galicia, and whose name was yelled by the Spaniards when charging into battle. In Cuzco, Illapa was depicted covered in gold with a golden sling as another reference to the warrior and hunter[348]. Deities wielding staffs are found in the Andean regions dating back to before 1000 B.C. and some consider these staffs to be thunderbolts or serpents. On the Nazca plains the famous lines crossing the landscape are considered to be ritual paths connected to rainmaking. Accompanying them are many landscape delineations of objects and animals. One of these is what are considered "needles and thread" but in fact these probably represent javelins or spears, or spear-throwers with lengths of cord attached to them to assist in retrieval and may represent the weapon wielded by the thunder and lightning god[349].

Tears of the Sun or Hail of the Lightning God in the Andes

Small gold disks are noted as being identified with hail in the Andes and on the coast and among the Nagas of Assam the Sun is conceived as a large metal plate on which one basket of seed rice is sown[350]. The references to hail being defined in symbolism as gold and silver plates in Vedic texts has already been noted corresponding to similar references relating to gold and grain on the Nazca Plains into the present day.

It has been shown that the hail, but also rain and snow was considered to be the "tears" of the Ccoa, or wildcat, on coastal Peru and in the Andean highlands[351] and identified further with the Staff God on the Gateway of the Sun. It has also been recorded that rain on the Nazca plains was considered to be the tears of Viracocha in myths recorded at the Conquest[352]. On the pleadings and propitiations by the Nazca peoples Viracocha's tears were said to run down the sides of the Cerro Blanco to form rivulets and then rivers into the irrigation ditches of the Nazca people[353]. In Colombia masks of gold also included tears worked into the iconography[354]. In the myths of the Tehuelche Indians of Patagonia the tears of the deity Kooch, "sky", formed the primordial sea and his breath went forth as powerful storms[355]. This may be the same deity as the lightning god of Illimani and Illampu in Bolivia and the rain and hail god of the Yungas is Khuno (= Kooch, Kon or Con).

References to Tear Symbolism in Polynesia and Melanesia

On Easter Island there are numerous sculptures with "tears" displayed on the cheeks[356]. In Melanesia, on the great island of New Guinea, there are many references in myths that are highly reminiscent of India and Peru and this island was an essential mid-point landfall on the direct sea routes between these two distant cultures regions. In a myth recorded on Manam Island, in the North Papuan region, there is a culture called the Wogeo and it appears to have been the location of an earlier megalithic or "stone-using" people. This region reflects many myths regarding these remarkable prehistoric people and it is said that the Wogeo state that an early stone-using race called the nanarangs lived long ago but no longer existed. It was said that these nanarangs alone inhabited the island and that eventually these people took to canoes and sailed away and changed themselves into new islands. The oral tradition further notes that the great spine of the high and almost impenetrable mountains of the main island of New Guinea was the spine of one of the Wogeo nanarangs; the island of Koil was the hand of another nanarang; the head of another nanarang was the volcano of Manam. It was believed by the Wogeo that all the customs, magical rites, the objects and arts the natives used into the present were left to them by the nanarangs. It was said that the institution of marriage was commenced by the marriage of the first male and female nanarang, a second early nanarang built the first men's house, a third the fishhooks while another carved the first flutes. The first nanarangs constructed houses that were said to have turned-to-stone and were identified with the boulders found on the island, and depressions in the rocks are pointed out as the footprints they left behind, while the streams were said to be their tears flowing from the mountain tops.

These nanarangs were identified by researchers with the Ambats of Malekula[357] in the New Hebrides and these have been considered in an earlier work to be culturally transferred from the Gonds and Bhuiyas of Central East India[358]. The term nanarang appears almost certainly, to derive from Nanga found imported into Fiji but probably from India where the Gonds also refer to their priests as Anga. In Fiji this term refers to their sacred priests and rites called the Nanga[359]. Of special interest is that among these people there are references to mythical tattoos being applied to the woman's genital region and there are a number of ceramics found in ancient Peru with this practice clearly indicated (*1.043*) and found also in Ponape (*1.044*). It must be questioned therefore whether the name Nanorca of the Nazca Plain, a name for Nanay or Nazca, was also related to Nanga and Nanarang. This term, and the Gonds, will be of more interest in due

7.054 : Bronze halberd head with armorial animals reflecting closely traditions in Ancient Peru and Bolivia. Khinaman, Iran, 2nd., millennium, A.D.

7.055 : Puma cast onto a bronze axe as a lion substitute closely similar to those long known in Iran, and from Luristan in particular (*7.054*). Similar traditions are also found in the Southern Andes and Tiahuanaco in particular. Ecuador, c1st., millennium, A.D.

053 : Old types of dao or battle axes ed for a wide range of activities apart om war. Lhota Nagas, Assam, North East dia, 19th., century, A.D.

7.056 : Moari chief holding a traditional club identical to the Naga dao in Assam. He also wears a dog skin cape. New Zealand, Mid-19th., century, A.D.

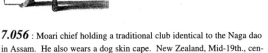

7.058 : A battle axe typical in Ancient Iran but similar to those in Peru. North West Iran, Early first millennium, B.C.

7.060 : A Bhil tribesman displaying his battle-axe or dao tucked into his belt of the identical type found among the Nagas of Assam and the Maoris in New Zealand. Central North India, Late 19th., century, A.D.

7.057 : Maori weapons, both ceremonial and practical, called "tewhatewha", are almost identical to those of the Nagas of Assam illustrated here in these dao-like weapons. Maori, New Zealand, 19th., century, A.D.

7.061 : Halberd bronze axe-head identical to those found of a similar type and also the probably model for the Tumi found in Ancient Peru. Luristan, South East Iran, Early second millennium, B.C.

7.059: A fine textile depicting a clenched-teethed deity with the upturned snout more typical of the makara in Ancient India. The staff he holds with the right hand reflect the trisula or trident typical of Siva in India. Note the axe-head pectoral probably indicating a warrior deity. Note also the "flames" typical of those emerging from the crown or topknots of representations of the Buddha and bodhisattvas in India. Tiahuanaco, Bolivia, 700-1000 A.D.

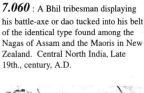

7.062 : Gond Dancers with representations of Sun disks on their backs and rays or streamers of peacock feathers extending from it sacred to the Son of the Sun, Skanda. Muria Gond, Central India, Early 20th.,century, A.D.

7.063 : Guardian deity with Sun disk worn on the back, shown here separated each side at the waist, and leaning on his halberd of the Luirstan-Iranian type but also similar to examples found in Peru and Bolivia (*7.057*). Udayagiri Caves, Vidisha, Central India, 5th., century, A.D.

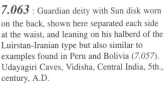

course.

In a Garhwali myth from India, a tribe located in the Central Region of India along with the Gonds and other pre-Vedic Aryan tribes, a myth indicates that the creation of the world was as a result of the tears linked to fertility. This myth states that at the beginning of time there was no earth, not sky or water - only Nirankar, the Guru who existed alone. Nirankar rubbed his right side to scrape off the sweat and from this a female vulture was born named Soni Garuri (Garuda). From the sweat he scraped from his left side he created the male vulture Brahma Garuri (Garuda). The male eagle came to Soni Garuri to marry her but she rebuffed him because they were brother and sister and therefore could not marry and she followed this rejection by a stream of caustic comments about his ugly shape. Brahma Garuri wept at these taunts and Soni Garur relented and collected the tears that fell from his eyes, but as she did so these tears penetrated her womb and she became pregnant. Realising her condition she flew to Braham Garur and begged him to build her a nest for the eggs she was expecting but he in his turn taunted her for her apparent lack of chastity, declaring her as ugly and unacceptable to be considered as his wife. She in her turn wept so much that Brahma Garur also relented and offered that, since there was no earth, nor water, she could lay her egg on his wings. Soni Garur declared that since he was the vehicle (vahana) of the sky god Vishnu, she would pollute him by laying the egg on any part of him. The egg fell from Soni Garur and divided into two halves. The lower half became the Earth while the upper half became the sky, and egg "white" or fluid became the oceans[360].

The myth illustrates that tears were frequently associated with fertility not only in Bolivia and Peru but also originally, in India and beyond in Asia. It is probably not a coincidence that here in this myth from India that the eagle is also associated with mythical creation and depicted half a world away also in the iconography of the Gateway of the Sun at Tiahuanaco by Lake Titicaca. The ultimate result of the eagle's fertile tears is the egg and this association of creation myths with cosmic eggs is found in India and the Andes and will be considered in a following chapter.

Among the Gonds, and the later Aryan Hindus, the peacock was considered to have special association with the Sun. The Gonds used a large disk on their back symbolising the Sun and the tail of the peacock extended below them on the dancers back and this same imagery is identical to that found in Mexico[361]. In Hinduism the son of the Sun (Surya) was named Skanda and his special animal, or vehicle, was the peacock and almost invariably depicted with him in traditional iconography. The peacock was mythically considered to be condemned to reproduce by seed from its mouth or beak. It is said that as part of that judgment, when the dark clouds of the monsoon arrived, "joyfulness will come", meaning a rise in libido to reproduce. When the male peacock with his "beautiful tail" is dancing "beautifully on the mountain", and when he tires from his exertions and "with sweat covering your face", the seed will come from his mouth "with a cough". The female peacock must then eat the seed and she, "from that day", will "without fail become pregnant"[362].

Another myth associating the peacock with the Sun states that he was in love with the peacock and the "spots" or eyes on the tail are "the tears of the Sun". In a further myth the peacock, dissatisfied with his legs for dancing wept tears, and the female peacock was said to "catch his tear-drops and generate eggs"[363]. The Gonds were notorious for their ceremonies associated with agricultural fertility practices requiring human sacrifice in the earlier centuries of European contact. This was called Meriah Sacrifice where the victim was tied to a symbolic plough or sacrificial post and set upon by the local peoples at the rite

7.064 : Sun disks worn on the back were often depicted in front orientated carvings or drawings spilt either side in the same manner as those in India *(7.062)*. Ritual Vessel, Guatemala, Late-Post Classic.

with knives to strip the live male of his flesh. The pieces of flesh were buried and considered to be endowed with the spirit of sacrifice that were believed to assist in the fertility of the soil for the coming seed cycle. An alternative method was recorded and that was a method of "slow burning" using red hot brands and the "amount of tears extracted relates to the proportion of rain to be received. The victim is then cut to pieces"[364]. A poem recited at the Meriah Sacrifice by the Gonds in the North East of India reflected a form of sympathetic magic in Chapter 4 in this work recorded by Herbert H. Risley a century ago in "People of India" published in 1908[365].

It is noted by recent researchers that there were seashells included as part of the worship of the gods associated with tears in Peru including Viracocha and others. In a myth from India a legend is recorded in the text called the Harachacharita relates that a present consisted of "...a wonderful pearl necklace which was presented to the king by a holy man. The pearls of this jewel were born from the tears of the Moon-god, which had fallen down in pearl oysters and become the antidote against all poisons, ' in consequence of its having been produced from the Moon, which is the ever-cooling fountain of ambrosia'. This precious necklace came into the possession of Vasuki, the King of the Serpents, who presented it to Nagarjuna during his stay in the Nether World (Patala Rasatala)"[366]. These references in India appear too closely parallel those of Peru even in the least aspect of imagery and ritual.

Tears in Mandaean Ritual and Tradition
In the myths of India it is recorded that the tears coalescing from the clouds of Rudra on the mountains of the Himalayas in Northern India were said to be the origins for the great rivers, particularly the four corresponding to the four quarters. This aspect of cosmology, along with so many others, appears to have its earliest origins in the Ancient Near East where such elevated identification was often counterbalanced by their opposite in myth and with their mythical associations appears to reveal an onerous side. It was believed by the Mandaeans that to weep at a funeral was forbidden since it was said that it would cause a river to form that hindered the progress into the afterlife[367]. It is notable that when children, sometimes the only child of an Inca couple, were required for capacocha the parents were forbidden to weep or show any emotion.

Rudra - Lord of Tears in the Myths of India
In India, tears, reflecting specific or general attributes of with the gods is far from unknown and one deity in particular is titled "Lord of Tears", and that is the pre-Vedic god Rudra[368], the equivalent of the Dravidian deity Siva, Lord of Time, who was absorbed into the Aryan Hindu religion. He is said to have sprung from the forehead of Brahma, the Immense-Being - the Creator, and then to have divided into male and female where the male half went on to further subdivide into eleven beings, some white and gentle and others black and furious[369]. Rudra was considered to be a principle of dissociation and the destroyer of the Universe and in these aspects identified with Siva in particular[370]. Siva was more associated with the violent aspects of disintegration while Rudra represented the long-term effects of relentless action or reaction such as erosion by water over long periods of time[371]. The Earth was seen as the complement of the Sky and believed in the philosophic speculation in India to form two halves of the divine cosmic egg (see Chapter 8) and these as a dual principle were said to be the two "laments", rodasi, or the "abodes of the Lord-of-Tears" - Rudra[372]. He is therefore considered in some texts as the ruler of the Universe[373].

In India, a myth recorded that the first Creator, Prajapati, attempted to commit incest with his daughter, a myth with a virtual identical parallel among the Huichol of North West Mexico[374], and it was Rudra who attacked him to prevent such an act[375]. Rudra had a less militant aspect and he was particularly asso-

7.065 : The Hindu deity Karttikeya, a form of the Son of the Sun Skanda, seated on his vehicle - a peacock. Post-Gupta, Harikatora, Bihar, North India, 7th., century, A.D.

7.067 : Fine textile depicting four deities, two holding ceremonial sceptres and two holding bows and arrows. The bow in India was particularly associated with the vault of heaven and the arrow with lightning as it was in Ancient Peru and Bolivia. Tiahuanaco, Bolivia, 700-1000 A.D.

7.066 : The ruler as the Moon god Sin enclosed in a lunar cartouche and a deity with bow at the left probably indicating the Sky god (Indra in India) where the curve of the bow represented the Arch of Heaven . Note the phrygian cap worn by this armed deity. Achaemenid dynasty, 6-4th., century, B.C.

ciated with the flute[376]. This god though is usually portrayed as a dangerous and fierce deity although it is he who is responsible for the dispersal of darkness in the cosmic sense and the dynamic increase in the power of illumination. Rudra was also considered to be the father of the wind deities and the "howling god of the storms"[377]. He is described as three-eyed (Tryambaka) but is also described as having a hundred heads and a thousand eyes, and the bearer of a thousand quivers. In battle he was the bringer of death to the warrior on the battlefield, the causer of tears, and was usually invoked, or propitiated, when fear of death was immanent or threatened[378].

The root of the name Rudra is rud, "to weep", but the name also appears to mean "the howler", where his howling in the sky is considered to be the thunder and lightning regaling their violent natures upon the Earth. The name Rudra is also thought to mean "red one", and it may have been this that identifies him more closely with Siva since it is believed that this name came from the Tamil, or was imported into that language since sev-, or sivappu is "red"[379]. In other derivations the name is thought to relate to the root for sleep, sin where Siva was considered also Lord of Sleep. In the Vedic texts and the Puranas Rudra means, however, "Lord of Tears", because he makes men cry or grieve, and in this sense by extension to all parallels in nature and cosmic philosophy, to most things alluding to tears in the formation a water droplet, such as rain. Interestingly Rudra is identified also with Agni, the Lord of Fire, and in this form he was identified with the heat of the Sun - this being called the "breath of Rudra" (rudra-prana). In alchemy, mercury was anciently considered the result of solar heat stored within the Earth, and quicksilver was called rudra-virya, or the "semen of Rudra"[380], thereby extending the metals normally attributed to Rudra, the gold of the Sun and the silver of the Moon to Mercury.

Rudra was also pictured with serpents wound round his head and was associated in this form with cemeteries and skull necklaces, common in Tantric mythology of North India, Nepal and Tibet. In the cosmic sense "time" is said to be kala, and Transcendent or Absolute Time was Maha-Kala, and it is Siva who is normally identified with Time and its cycles[381]. In the religions of India the principal deity was also considered to be the sum of his parts and these were aspects of his being that were worshiped under their separate names. This was long the practise even though it was recognised by all that ultimately they were in fact worshipping only a part of the greater deity. Rudra-Siva as Bhava was the element of water and is equated with another aspect as rain personified by the god Parjanya. It is probably significant that the deities called Vira-Bhadra and the other lesser Bhairavas (*1.050*; *7.069*) were considered Rudra's attendants or aspects of him[382]. The consort of Bhava was called Uma, or "Peace-of-the-Night, and their son was said to be the planet Venus[383].

7.068 :Offerings placed before a group of bows representing the Sky during the Wijja-Weta ceremony - possibly the origin of the Watawuts ceremony at Buka in the Solomons. Indra's bow, the Vedic storm god, was anciently identified with the Sky and is found in various interpretations through into the Pacific Islands influenced through Indonesia from India. Bison Horn Maria Gonds, Central India, Early 20th., century, A.D.

7.070 : Sky Arch formed by serpentine extensions from the peacock's tail, an influence from South India. Ponteay-Prea-Khan, near Angkor Thom, Cambodia, 10th., century, A.D.

7.069 : The wrathful aspect of the Hindu deity Siva, known as Bhairava, with his dog at the bottom right. South India, c9-12th., century, A.D.

Uma was said to be the daughter of Himavat, the divine spirit of the Himalayas, and was considered also to be the consort of Siva, and her more usual name is Parvati. Uma originally was not the daughter of the mountains but of the cloud and in the same way Rudra was not the "Lord of the Mountains", the Himalayas, girisa, but "Lord of the Clouds". Uma meant flax, from va, "to weave" and it has been suggested that this term, more usually reflective of the female or wife, derives from a later Semitic introduction from the Ancient Middle East[384]. In the Upanishads Rudra is particularly described as a mountain deity and his association with the arrow also illustrates his fierce nature and as the harbinger of death[385]. In a Vedic hymn a few lines of one to Rudra is recorded as:

"4. We implore Rudra, the lord of songs, the lord of animal sacrifices, for health, wealth, and his favour.

5. He who shines like the bright sun, and like gold, who is the best Vasu among the gods,"[386].

In another hymn Rudra is associated with the thunderbolt:

"3. In beauty thou art the most beautiful of all that exists, O Rudra, the strongest of the strong, thou wielder of the thunderbolt! Carry us happily to the other shore of our anguish, and ward off all assaults of mischief."

In a further verse his appearance is recorded:

"9. He, the fierce god, with strong limbs, assuming many forms, the tawny Rudra, decked himself with brilliant gold ornaments. From Rudra, who is lord if this wide world, divine power will never depart"[387].

A further hymn to Rudra appears to extend the associations of his thunderbolt with comets rather than lightning alone:

"3. May that thunderbolt of thine, which, sent from heaven, traverses the earth, pass us by! A thousand medicines are thine, O thou who art freely accessible; do not hurt us in our kith and kin!"[388].

In the early commentaries of the scholars, saints and sages over the centuries it is noted that the god "Trishamdi, was one of those who was said to assist in the defeat of armies and that he used a club with three joints. And this object appears to have been the basis for Rudra's light-

461

7.071 : Sky arch represented by a serpent common in the mythology of Central and South America but also linked to the deity Siva in India. Costa Rica, 1000-1500 A.D.

7.072 : Buddhist cosmic diagram of the Western Paradise of Amitabha with characteristic concentirc arches representing the progressive higher levels of existence away from Earth existence similar to beliefs in Polynesia (*11.048*). Tibet, pre-20th., century, A.D.

7.074 : Aboriginal Australian with a curved nurtunja or sacred pole curved to represent the Sky Arch. Arunta, Central Auatralia, Late 19th., century, A.D.

7.075 : A formal standing goddess framed with a flowing drapery formed as a Sky Arch. Paharpur, Bengal, North East India, 8th., century, A.D.

7.073 : Curved Sky Arch or torana that is in the Hindu and Buddhist tradition depicted above the Sky deity, Vishnu, that was probably the model for those on the North Peruvian Coast. South India, 7-9th., century, A.D.

ning"[389]. United with Siva, Rudra was associated something of a near reflection of this deity in warfare and this extends to the symbolic weapons in the iconography depicted with him and his aspects. The battle-axe (parasu) was one of Siva's better-known symbols and this he gave it to the hero Parasu-Rama, so well known in the myths of South India. Of special interest is that Siva held a bow resembling the rainbow and this is depicted as a sky serpent with seven heads and poisonous teeth. This bow was called Panaka, or Rudra, and the image of Siva as "Giver-of-Peace" he is called Pinakin (the bowman). This bow was also called Ajagava or the southern Sun-path and will be of more interest in the last chapter[390]. These curious references may not be coincidental since the path of the southern Sun probably indicates the summer season in the Southern Hemisphere when the journey across from Australia to South America would have been more favourable along the West Wind Drift. The name Panaka is the same as that of the headman of the Inca clans and the ancient name of the capital of Bhutan in the Himalayan foothills and this Pinakin may be the origin of the ancestral term Pinahua in Inca Origin Myths.

The lion, tiger in Asia and the puma or jaguar in Central and South America has been a symbol of both religious and secular rulership and appears to be indicated in the iconography at Kotosh (*3.056/7*) in the Peruvian Highlands in the 3rd.-2nd., millennium B.C. The myths surrounding the hero-deity, Coniraya, note that the puma pelt cape was sacred to him and when the Spanish arrived in Peru this pelt was brought out on festival occasions at the time of the digni-

7.077 : Sky deities in the typical posture of flying gods with the goddess holding aloft the arched cloth in the form of a torana or Sky Arch indicating wind deity associations. Gwalior, Central India, 4-7th., century, A.D.

076 : Standing aboriginal deity with a double-headed serpent forming the Sky Arch. Bengal, second half of the first millennium, D.

7.078 : A "flying"deity in characteristic pose holding a cloth arch above his head typical of the wind god, Vayu, but enclosed by the traditional portal arched representing the Sky known as the torana. Nalanda, Temple 2, 6th., century, A.D.

7.080 : Serpentine sky arch or torana characteristic of Late Chalukyan architectural design reflecting the sky arch as serpents disgorged by the Makara or Ganges crocodile at their base. Late Chalukyan Dynasty, 11-13th., century, A.D.

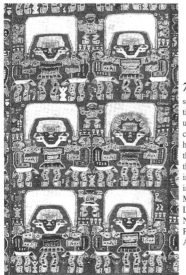

7.079 : A section of a textile showing figures holding a cloth above their heads in exactly the manner of those representing the wind god in India. Moche, Lambeyeque, North Coast Peru, 250-550 A.D.

7.081 : Gold figurine with a serpent extending from the body rising from the left side above and over the head to represent the sky serpent or arch. This appears to reflect similar iconography in India. Costa Rica, 1000-1500 A.D.

fied man who sacrificed a llama as part of the rite[391]. In the myth of another hero, probably originally related in the distant past, a hero-deity named Huathiacuri, the son of Pariacaca, is recorded as wearing the jaguar pelt in a dancing contest as one of several ordeals to achieve success[392].

    In India the tiger skin was particularly identified with Rudra who became absorbed to the aspects of Siva, the Lord of Time, and referred repeatedly throughout this work in relation to South American myth, legend and iconography. Textual references from the Skanda-Purana describes Siva in his seated form, known as Maha-Kailasa, where it is said he was regaled with a garland of skulls and wore a tiger skin, as did the Ekadasa-Rudras[393]. In some temples dedicated to Siva the priest or attendant wears the tiger skin at devotional ceremonials[394]. The tiger's skin is also worn by some of the wrathful goddesses such as Chamunda[395] and Kali[396].
Siva was said to have slain the tiger who was the mount of the Sakti, the power of nature, and wore its skin as a garment. This tradition is anciently known in the north, east and west of Asia long before being adopted in India and appears to be a tradition imported in the second or first millennium B.C. The Sukla Yajur Veda notes that Rudra also wore the tiger skin[397]. Interestingly

7.082 : Carved stone stela from the Ecuador coast showing a stepped torana or sky arch over the deities' head similar to those among the Maya, Java and India. Note the 6 panels with sky supporting godlings similar to the Pauahtuns among the Maya and Ganas (*7.092*) in India. Cerro Jaboncillo, Ecuador, 850-1400 A.D.

7.083 : Stepped Sky Arches are common among the Mayan carvings that are closley similar to those of Indonesia and India but also to stela in Ecuador. Stela K, Quirigua, Guatemala, 8th., century, A.D.

7.084 : Headdresses throughout many cultures reflect aspects of sky orientated deities and cosmology. This headdress reflects the sky arch and the drums have their counterparts in India. The headdress also includes a brow disk identical to those found in India, Melanesia, Polynesia and the Americas. Wagawaga tribe, New Guinea, Late 19th., century, A.D.

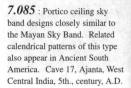

7.085 : Portico ceiling sky band designs closely similar to the Mayan Sky Band. Related calendrical patterns of this type also appear in Ancient South America. Cave 17, Ajanta, West Central India, 5th., century, A.D.

the Dragon's Tail, the Moon's South Node, Ketu, was said to be the son of Rudra. The Dragon's Tail was the half of the eclipse serpent that was cut into two by Vishnu's disk, where the head became the Moon's North Node, Rahu, and the South, Ketu[398]. The month in India covering part of November and December was called Marghsirsa and its god was Rudra[399] the darkest part of the year in the Northern Hemisphere

At the death of a Gammalla caste-man an effigy was shaped of the person heaped the ashes from the cremation when it was over and three conical shapes were constructed from mud and ashes near the head of the effigy. These represented Yama, the god of death, Rudra, and the spirit of the deceased, and cooked food was offered to them on leaves[400]. These small mounds created from the ashes after cremation appears to represent the earliest form of burial - that is the corpse being covered by a mound - cremation being a later Aryan introduction. These mounds were called tilas or tolas and is the same term used on the anciently on the Ecuadorian coast where mounding both for burials and ceremonial platforms was usual.

Rudra was the fierce face of Siva, one of the most popular deities in the Hindu pantheon and it was said that that from the crown of his head the purifying "primal" waters of the Ganges River flowed. The term for this image of the primal waters flowing from the Himalayas, where Siva was said to have his pleasure palace, Kailas, was termed Ap[401], and this clearly derives from the Ancient Sumerian term Ap-su. In his mendicant role, Siva's matted hair represented Vayu,

464

the wind deity, and esoterically the topknot or jata represented the soma, or divine ambrosia of the Gods. This was the equivalent of the earlier form in Iran - the Hoama, and in the Rig Veda, Rudra is also noted to have had similarly matted hair[402]. In Hindu tradition Siva's hair topknot, the Jata, represented the Lord of the Wind, Vayu, and is said to reflect the flow of the Ganges in the ringlets extending from it[403]. There are many depictions of Siva with matted hair and the topknot, or Jata, is said to represent the lord of the wind, Vayu. The ringlets extending from the topknot are said to represent the river that are the Ganges and its tributaries [404]. Rudra is considered the Vedic counterpart of Siva who later became identified with this non-Aryan Lord of Time. In this identification Rudra is depicted with an animal-hide garment and matted hair called Kapardi - the "wearer of matted hair", and common in depictions of Siva and his mendicant aspects (*5.104*; *7.086*). This hairstyle features in this case a "crown of snail-shell like jatas on his head", and these appear to reflect similar depictions of "rayed" shells forming a crown in the Pacific Islands (*4.026*) and Colombia (*6.039*). Siva is also identified as an aspect of Isana and in some texts he is identified as Rudra as "Lord of the Paths" to protect travellers and pilgrims from bandits and vagrants in forested or remote regions, suggesting another possible origin for ceques in Peru[405]

7.086 : A mendicant idealisation of the Hindu god Siva named Bhikshatana showing his association with serpents. This deity is occasionally identified as a eunuch. This deity may be the model for the mendicants known as Guacucae in Ancient Peru. Pandananallur, South India, 10-13th., century A.D.

Mendicant Mystics as the Areois; Arya and Araha

In the cultures of Mexico and South America hallucinogenic substances appear to be of special importance with allusions to sea origins and long distance trade. Traces of these substances and the ritual artefacts utilised to inhale them are found in coastal graves and appear associated with peoples who are probably from mariner occupations. Alcoholic beverages are also included in these references and this would appear to parallel aspects of Oceanic cultures recorded from the observations resulting from the first contacts that European made in the Pacific Islands. There are similar known traditions in Central or South America and these were often noted or compared with parallels or origins in India, particularly those of the Tantric sects.

Aspects indicating the cultural transfer probable introductions from India by mariners, but adopted and applied in a debased or misinterpreted manner, are found widely and in Aboriginal Australia where certain aspects of the medicine man reflect those of India, Melanesia, Polynesia and South America. A.W. Howitt recorded the practises of one tribe: "Among the Wiimbaio one man, being a Mekigar, could initiate another and make him a Mekigar in the following manner. They procured the body of a man, usually by digging one up. The bones were pounded up and chewed. One of my correspondents (Dr. McKinley) saw one of these men being initiated in the office of Mekigar. He was plastered with human excrement, and carried about with him the humerus of a disinterred body wrapped round with twigs, and he kept gnawing at it. These men are, at such times, brought to a state of frenzy, their eyes are bloodshot, and they behave like maniacs"[406].

This description closely parallels the practices of both Hindu and Buddhist Tantric sects that developed in the middle of the first millennium, A.D. and were clearly influenced from the Tibetan Bon Po. Into the present day Tantric initiation includes isolation in a cemetery and where similar practices reflected in those of the distant Australian Aboriginals clearly are maintained except ashes from the cremation pyres are used in covering the body of the initiate. They also reflect the mendicant "sorcerers" known as Guacacue in Peru and the Areois in Polynesia.

It has been shown in this work and earlier publications that there are many parallels between India and the Nagas of Assam in the culture of the Marquesas Islands, the nearest islands to the Americas in Eastern Polynesia. The Tohua has been shown to closely reflect the Tehuba of the Nagas and used also for similar rituals. There were mystic sects who pursued a lifestyle outside that of seers and ceremonial priests and these sects extended to other islands in Polynesia including Tahiti. Here the reports of the Reverend William Ellis still provides some of the few accurate eyewitness accounts of these people before the adoption of the Christian religion among the native peoples. These mystic sects were called Areois and Ellis provides a description as he saw them and of their practices: "On public occasions, their appearance was, in some respects, such as it is not proper to describe. Their bodies were painted with charcoal and their faces, especially, stained with the 'mati', or scarlet dye. Sometimes they wore a girdle of the yellow 'ti' leaves; which, in appearance, resembled the feathered girdles of the Peruvians, or other South American tribes…"[407].

In his reports Ellis unfortunately considered the practices of these Areois too "terrible" to record[408], but does note that they were avid participants in wrestling[409], an activity well-known throughout South American tribes (*2.099*), and in India and Assam (*2.096/7*). Ellis also notes that they represented their gods by stones[410] and goes on to describe the various sects that made up their number. Of particular interest were the highest ranked among them called the Arae parai - "painted leg" and writes that their signature was "the leg being completely blackened from the foot to the knee"[411]. This is identical to the leg-blackening so noted of the Moche on the Peruvian coast (*5.084*; *5.096/7*), and he notes the special position that these men had in the society of the Tahitians. This includes a myth stating that the Areoi were imitators of the demi-gods Orotetefa and Urutetefa who were created by the Supreme God, Taaroa, or Tangaroa[412]. The terms Oro and Uru since they occur frequently in Polynesian myths and legends and also among the Cuna of Panama, and may have their origin in the legendary Uru of Sumeria and from here Miles Poindexter, and A. Hyatt Verrill relate them to the Uru, the "first people" of Bolivia.

The Areois are clearly the proto-types of the Pulque Gods of Mexico. These Pulque gods are called the Ahuia-teteo, and of note is that these gods were associated with the number 5 since this number in this relation meant a loss of control after this number of cups of pulque imbibed[413]. Teteo means gods generally, and is clearly a derivative of Io in Polynesia and the name for god in India - Deo. The term Ahuia clearly refers to the Polynesian term Ahua, or tribe or clan leader, identically among the Maya and found also similarly in South America. It cannot be a surprise therefore that the Ahuia-teteo was related to the demon goddess of the west, Cihua-teteo, and here the west refers to the direction of the Pacific Ocean and ultimately further west to Polynesia, Asia and India. It is likely therefore that this is another reference where Cihua is a characteristic role reversal of the Hindu deity, Siva, pronounced in the same way earlier noted.

Pulque is a maize beer and is the counterpart of Chicha in South America, known as awa in Colombia and the counterpart of the Polynesian kava. There can be little doubt that these pulque gods originated from mariners who used beverages, and probably the maize beer itself, to sustain themselves over long periods at sea. This would have been used in conjunction with the narcotics drugs derived from the coca leaf and the St. Pedro cactus in South America and the Hikuli cactus, the Peyote, in Mexico. These over many centuries of use would have become deified through the use and identification with these mariner gods as they did among the Huichol in Western Mexico. The representation of many "old" and gaunt, skeletal gods among both Central and South American ceramic portraits probably derives, at least in part, from premature aging caused by very long periods at sea through malnutrition (*5.075/6*).

In South America in Peru, in the dynasty of the Ayars, Arriaga recorded the rites and customs associated with some of the religious sects and in one he notes that initiation was approached as follows: "A person about to assume one of the offices has to fast for a month, or, in some places, six, in others a year, eating neither salt nor pepper, nor sleeping with his wife, nor washing, nor combing his hair. In some localities they are forbidden to touch the body with their hands, and it is told of a man in San Juan de Cochas that during his time of fasting he neither washed nor combed his hair, and as a result his hair became infested with lice; in order to keep his oath and refrain from touching himself, he used a little stick to scratch himself"[414]. He further notes that people affected by a "sudden frenzy" are considered to have been chosen by a huaca (spirit of a shrine) as its guardian[415].

Douglas Sharon reported from the writings of Father Martin de Murua in 1590 A.D., only two generations after the Conquest, that there were in Inca Peru diviners called the Guacacue and latterly referred to using the Greek term "gymnosophists"[416]. These people went about naked and were noted as philosophers and "doctors" and resided in the desert regions. They were reported to stare at the Sun and from these lengthy privations and disciplines received great knowledge and were able to avoid illness and disease and died in very old age. The description given could be from any one of hundreds of reports into the present day of sadhus, or holy men, in India and who have been known from several thousand years ago and still are found in great numbers into the present day. These reports are virtually identical to those recorded in Aboriginal Australia, the Pacific Islands and Mexico but more particularly are identical to the many reports of the Siva mendicants in India who anciently, into the present day, adopted such privations and physical austerities. The quintessence of the Saivite mendicant holy man was Bhikshatana and he is particularly associated with remote isolated regions, absolute nudity as a rejection of false appearance and wealth, and serpent worship so noted of Siva[417] (*7.086*).

In Melanesia there are references to "light-skinned" immigrants chiefs generally entitled Arai, and these are usually identified with the Araha or Alaha in the Solomon Islands[418]. These are regions where identical cultural artefacts such as star-clubs, panpipes and bark trumpets among other cultural references are noted in common with South America (*6.007-19*). In connection with other references to the Ari people, who occupied Cape Vogel in New Guinea, the sea-hawk was the totemic bird of the stone-using sea-going immigrant peoples known in myth and legend and this bird was called "the father of the Ari tribe"[419]. The Islands of Melanesia cluster around the only return route from South America to Asia as well as providing an alternative route from north of the Equator from Asia to South America as a crossover to the southern route. It is clear that Ari and Araha in Melanesia, Areoi in Polynesia and Ahuia-teteo in Mexico are all derivatives, or have the same origin as the Ayars of Peru and the Ayas or Aryas in India.

7.089 : A priest dressed typically to perform puja or prayer rituals, essentially bare-foot, similarly also in Ancient Peru and Mexico, and frequently bare-chested. South India, Early 20th., century, A.D.

7.087 : Indra, the Vedic storm god, holding his thunderbolt sceptre or vajra aloft. He rides his vehicle, the elephant called Airavata, named after the home of the Aryans. Baital Deul Temple, Bhubanesvar, 6th., century, A.D.

7.088 : A mendicant sahdu or holy man whose forebears were probably the prototype for the Areois and Guacacue in Polynesia, Mexico and Peru. India, Early 20th., century, A.D.

The Mountain Paradise of Kailasa as Kalasaya and Akapana in the Andes

The pleasure mountain named Kailas, the location of Siva's palace in the Himalayas, is also called Meru and in this form it is the World Axis pointing towards the North Pole. From this high point in the Himalayas the Ganges was believed to emanate and for many centuries into the present day pilgrimages took place, and still takes place to the headwaters by people from all over India and abroad. In the Bhagavad Gita this great mountain is called Meru, probably a name derived much earlier from the Ancient Middle East, and one of the texts notes: "Of all mountains, the great Meru is stated to be the first born. And among all the quarters and sub-quarters, likewise, the eastern quarter is the first. Likewise the Ganga going in three paths is stated to be the first-born among rivers. And likewise of all the wells and reservoirs of water, the ocean is the first-born. And of all gods, Danavas, Bhutas, Pisakas, snakes, and Rakshasas, and of all men, Kinnaras, and Yakshas, Isvara (Rudra), is the lord. The great Vishnu, who is full of the Brahman, and than whom there is no higher being in the three worlds, is the source of all the universe." ....
"The unperceived is the source of the worlds; and the same is also the end of everything. Days end with (the sun's) setting; the night ends with (the sun's) rising; the end of pleasure is ever grief; the end of grief ever pleasure. ..."[420]. These extracts are paralleled in the text called the Santi Parvan, Parvan being a name for the wind deity in the Ancient Middle East.

Among the Jain Sutras the sacred mountain of Meru was also adored as it was among the Buddhists. In a text devoted to the praise of the last Tirthankara, or Jain saint, Maha-vira, literally "Great Hero", but also "Great Ape", it is stated in comparison that: "By his vigour he is the most vigorous; as Sudarsana (Meru), the best of mountains, or as heaven, a very mine of delight, he shines forth endowed with many virtues.
"(Meru) a hundred thousand yoganas high, with three tiers (Kandaka, one of stone, one of gold and one of turquoise), with the Pandaga (-wood) as its flag, rising ninety-nine thousand yoganas above the ground, and reaching one thousand below it;"
"It touches the sky and is immersed in the earth; round it revolve the suns; it has the colour of gold, and contains many Nanana (parks); on it the Mahendras enjoy themselves."
"This mountain is distinguished by (many) names; it has the colour of burnished gold; it is the greatest of all mountains, difficult to ascend on account of its rocks; this excellent mountain is like part of the earth on fire."
"The king of mountains, standing in the centre of the earth, is seen in a pure light like that of the sun. With such beauty shines forth this many coloured, lovely (mountain), which is crowned with radiance."[421].

The mountain is repeatedly associated with cardinal points; four quarters and other calendrical aspects and essentially with the Sun and Moon. It was believed that the mystical city of the gods, Amaravati, was said to be located on top of Mt. Meru and the city of the Asuras, or anti-gods, Iravati was said to lie beneath it[422]. In a reference not dissimilar to the many myths associated with the end of world cycles in the Americas including the Andes, a battle, where demonic forces are fended off by a sage is likened to that predicted to end this present age in the Buddhist texts repeated here in small part as follows:
"38. Some, having lifted up stones and trees, found themselves unable to throw them against the sage; down they fell, with their trees and their stones, like the roots of the Vindhya shattered by the thunderbolt."
"39. Others, leaping up into the sky, flung rocks, trees, and axes; these remained in the sky and did not fall down, like the many-coloured rays of the evening clouds."
"40. Another hurled upon him a mass of blazing straw as big as a mountain-peak, which, as soon as it was thrown, while it hung poised in the sky, was shattered into a hundred fragments by the sage's power."
"41. One. Rising up like the sun in full splendour, rained down from the sky a great shower of

live embers, as at the end of an aeon blazing Meru showers down the pulverised scoriae of the golden valleys."

"42. But that shower of embers full of sparks, when scattered at the foot of the Bodhi tree, became a shower of red lotus-petals through the operation of the great saint's boundless charity."[423].

It has been noted that the wind deity Pawan, or Parvan, is closely related to with the better-known alternative, Vayu, both having derived from the Ancient Middle East, and from there were transferred by immigration into India. The name of the ancient sacred mountain in the Himalayas was Meru, and in this name and form it is found in Buddhist and Jain texts as well as in those of the Hindus. It is more usually referred to as by them as the Axis Mundae, or World Axis believed to be pointed towards the Pole Star. However, other names and titles have been applied, and the more usual in India is to identify it with the mountain of Siva, or his pleasure palace situated on the summit of Mt. Kailas, or Kailasa, and also identified with Airavata, the home of the Aryan ancestors. Airavata or Airavana was also the sacred mount of Indra and this was said to be the four-tusked white elephant who stands at the entrance to heaven, Kailasa, and believed also to have been a ancient serpent king reborn[424]. This sacred mountain is located in Tibet, and since the beginning of the Chinese occupation in the second half of the twentieth century it is a place very difficult for pilgrims and researchers to reach.

The deity Siva has been thought to have originated from the Dravidian, pre-Aryan deities, but he is depicted on an Indus clay seal dating to the middle of the second millennium B.C. in the far North West in what is now Pakistan next to modern Iran. It is more likely that his name was actually a corruption, or derivative, from the ancient Sumerian and Akkadian Moon deity, Sin, since Siva was also a Moon deity and was often depicted with a crescent moon in his hair. Similar depictions are found in Ancient Peru and the name of the Moon god of the Moche was Si, linked to the fanged Ai Apaec a radiant armoured war god who was his prototype[425]. Between the two continents of Asia and South America in Polynesia the term Sin-a for the Moon is often found[426], clearly a direct transfer from West to South Asia and then across the Pacific to Peru.

Many of the tribes and castes of India claim that they were specially created by the deities on Kailasa to raise the culture of humanity in Ancient India. A typical myth of this type is preserved by the Linga Balijas and is recorded by Thurston as follows: "On a time when the god Pralayakala Rudra and Mochari Rudra and his five sons with other celestial attendants, were assembled on the Kailasa parvata or mountain of Paradise. The god directed the latter to descend into the Bhuloka, or earthly world, and increase and multiply the species. They humbly prayed to know how they were again to reach the divine presence. He answered 'I shall manifest myself in the Bhuloka under the form of the lingam or Priapus; do you worship me under that form, and you will again be permitted to approach me.' They accordingly descended into the earthly regions, and from them the present casts of Baljwaris deduce their origins"[427]. The association of tribal origins or caste birth is extended to the general belief that human beginnings were intimately associated, if not derived from the gods. It was believed that the power of the goddess Mata Januvi, or Janami, rested in a sacred bead, a belief closely similar to that of Juno Lucinda among the Romans, and in Northern India midwives carried around beads blessed with this power known as Kailas Maura, or "the crown of the sacred mountain Kailas"[428] (*7.091/2*).

In many Hindu funerals the faithful are believed to go to the region of the gods "when they say that their relatives have died and have gone to heaven, that is Kailasa"[429]. Indra, the great storm god of the Hurrians or Mitanni and later of the Vedic Aryans in India was also believed to live in the high Himalayas. The Uppara people in South India at the final ceremony sixteen days after the funeral of a man, among the Tamil division of the caste, poured milk over the enulka shrub (Calotropis gigantean) "just before the jackals howl", with the words, "Go to

Swarga (the abode of Indra), and make your way to Kailasam (heaven)"[430]. It is significant that Kailas also appears in the myths of the Gonds, a people in India of considerable importance to the theme of this work and they refer to this mythical heaven as "Kailasdip"[431].

The iconography related to the myths of Kailasa are famously expressed in the great rock-cut temples at Elora in West Central India, and considered by some the finest rock-cut building anywhere in the world, where the mythical beings associated with Siva's mountain heaven are depicted in full display. This great carving appears to have been influenced by the 7-8th., century A.D. Pallava temple at Kanchi near Madras in South East India, and by the nearly contemporary Virupaksha temple at Pattadakal, a Chalukyan temple dating to the mid-7th., century A.D.[432]. Another fine representation is found at Lakkundi (*4.090*).

The most complete reports available of the mountain identified as Mount Kailas were published in the mid-twentieth century before the Chinese closed the borders of Tibet to visitors and pilgrims. From the earliest days of Hinduism there were probably monasteries located around the great mountain, although those that exist are now Buddhist. Associated with the holy mountain are the two associated lakes - the larger, the very sacred Manasa-sarovara, with its two islands, and the smaller, Rakshas Tal. From this smaller lake were said to issue the four sacred rivers of Indian philosophy, the Brahmaputra, the Indus, the Sutlej and the Karnali[433]. Although the Hindu pilgrims traced the headwaters of the Ganges into the high Himalayas they were well aware that the river did not actually reach to the sacred mountain or lakes. The Ganges was believed to flow under the Himalayas, from its headwaters in underground conduits![434]. Benares as the sacred city of Siva on the Ganges, or Ganga, was originally called Kasi, and today has been renamed Varanasi, another ancient name for this same place. Kasi was also related to philosophic aspects of the three planes of an individual's being and the point or node at which they united or made contact was called by this name. The city of Kasi was also perceived as the union of three aspects of the Ganges, these being the Celestial Ganges - the Milky Way, the earthly river Ganges, and the Underworld Ganges (Patala Ganga) said to travel underground from the Himalayas and run southwards through Kasi, and not predominantly east west as the earthly Ganges does.

There were five sacred temples associated with Siva and in each of these were one of the five lingas, or carved stone phallus, representing the five elements. These were to be found in Kasi (Varanasi), representing the element water; Kanchi, representing the element earth; Chidambaram, representing ether; Kalahasti, representing the element air, and Tiruvannamalai, representing the element fire[435]. These clearly form, along with many other pilgrimage paths with their intermediate shrines and lodges the type of routes known as ceques, or pilgrimage paths along which shrines to deities are located in Ancient Peru.

Although the sacred mountain and lakes of Kailasa have been known and frequented from the rise of Hinduism in the early first millennium A.D. they were in fact the centre of much more ancient attention confirmed by occasional references in the early texts. There can be little doubt that this same mountain was known to the earlier Near Eastern and Middle Eastern peoples since it probably bore the name Pawan before being replaced by the Hindus own appellation. In fact confirmation of this is not difficult to find since to this day the adjacent smaller peak flanking Mt. Kailas is named Pawan (*7.091*). This was probably the original name of Kailas and then downgraded to an adjacent peak in recognition of those who still retained it as their sacred mountain. Pawan was still retained in Hindu myths as the wind god along with Vayu, both from ancient Iran, and it was likely that the former inhabitants of the now deserted rock-cut cave city of Pangtha not far distant were devotees and provided a centre for pilgrims to stay on their visits to the holy mountain.

Perhaps the question that must come to mind is why this mountain in particular should be chosen as especially sacred, particularly when the Himalayan range and plateau to the north

7.091 : Near view of the sacred mountain of the Himalayas called Kailasa showing its shape similar to a stepped pyramid. Tibet, Mid-20th., century, A.D.

090 : Ravanna the mythical demon ruler of Sri Lanka depicted in this finest relief ving of him holding up the sacred mountain paradise of Siva, Mount Kailasa. isually Ravanna is depicted from the front and note the sky supporters, Ganas, to right. Lakkundi, Central South India, 13th., century, A.D.

092 : The holy mountain of Kailasa seen from across the sacred lake called the nasarovar and highly reminiscent of the sacred mountain flanking Lake Titicaca in ivia. Tibet, Mid-20th., century, A.D.

provide so many, and more accessible possibilities, and many nearer to the peoples of the ancient Near and Middle East. One glance at a photo from almost any angle, however, would soon reveal the reason. In the most ancient texts of the Mandaeans, and probably those earlier than the second millennia, there are references to sacred mountains, and it must also be remembered that the local, artificial, constructed sacred mountains, the ziggurats, were invariably stepped pyramids. Mount Kailas reflects, startlingly, the form of a stepped pyramid from any angled it is viewed, and this must have struck travellers from a very early time when stepped pyramids were a focus within the sacred ceremonial precincts in the Ancient Middle East and reported this fact on their return. This suggests that such an identification must have taken place by the latest in the second millennium B.C. but more likely earlier in the fourth or third millennium B.C. More recent research on the Iranian plateau indicates that there were many advanced, for their time, sites in Elam to the east of Sumeria. There can be little doubt that long distance trade routes were operating from at least the period of Uruk in Ancient Iraq to Anatolia in the North West and to Iran and beyond in the East by the fourth millennium B.C.

It is probable that these traders and religious travellers would have named the sacred pyramidal Himalayan mountain in their own language regaling it, correspondingly, with their own myths and iconography just as the European colonial powers did throughout the world in more recent centuries. This is reflected in the term Pawan and is likely to have been one of perhaps several as a vestige from that earlier time before the Hindus renamed the peak Kailas for themselves and dedicated it to Siva probably early in the first millennium A.D.

Twenty miles (32 km) from the peak is the lake of Manasa-sarovar, usually shortened to Manasarovar and is described by Swami Pranavananda who visited it in the 1930s and 1940s as "… the holiest, the most fascinating,

7.093 : The goddess Ganga, identifying with the river Ganges. She holds the water pot named Kalasa as the source in myth of the River Ganges said to flow from the sacred mountain of Siva, Kailasa in the Himalayas. North India, 6-8th., century, A.D.

the most inspiring, the most famous of all the lakes in the world and the most ancient that civilisation knows" … "Before the dawn of history Manasarovar had become the sacred lake and such it has remained for four millennium. She is majestically calm and dignified like a huge bluish-green emerald or a pure turquoise set between two mighty and equally majestic silvery mountains, the Kailas on the north and the Garla Mandhata on the south and between the sister-lake Rakshas Tal or Ravana Hrada (Langak Tso of the Tibetans) on the west and some hills on the east"[436].

It is immediately apparent that in "traditional" Hindu terms related to their temple architecture are those associated with the Mandaeans and their contemporary Ancient Middle Eastern equivalents. These were probably transferred before the rise of Hinduism, one being mand-hata and mandapa from Manda, and Ravana or Ravan another term associated with them. This latter term was the name for the "demon" king of Sri Lanka and the Mandaeans have a tradition that they originated from that island at the south of India. Rawan is another form of Pawan or related to the wind in the Ancient Middle East and calendrically to the last five "unfortunate" days in the solar year - the Parwaniia. This tends to confirm that these names were applied long before their imposition or being inherited by the Hindus. Another reference to such terms is that the mountain range in which Kailasa is sited is called Kailas Parvat[437] and this along with Parwan and Rawan derive from the attributes of the wind deity in the Ancient Middle East. Both mountains of Kailas and Mandhata were especially sacred to pilgrims who made the extremely difficult journey to this sacred Tibetan region and especially so since these two peaks reputedly "glow in the light of the sunrise"[438].

Among the ancient texts the Kailas Purana states that their mountain is the "… centre of the whole universe towering right up to the sky like the handle of the millstone, that half-way up its sides is Kalpa-Vriksha (wish-fulfilling tree), that it has square sides of gold and jewels, that the eastern face is crystal, the southern sapphire, the western ruby, and the northern gold. It also says that the peak is clothed in fragrant flowers and herbs, and there are four footprints of the Buddha on the four sides, so that the Peak might not be taken away into the sky by the deities of that region and four chains so that the denizens of the lower regions might not take it down"[439].

The resident deity of Kailas guarding the mountain was named Pavo or in Tibetan Demchhok (Buddhist Dharmpala). He is depicted wearing the tiger skin and holds a "vibrant" drum in one hand and a trident (Khatham) in the other, and wears a garland of human skulls. Apart from the Hindu belief that this mountain is the abode of Siva this sacred mount is also claimed by the Buddhists who consider that it was the home of Buddha and his 500 attendants a

7.094 : The sacred mountians of the Marquesas include Tai Pi that clearly relates to the Taypi-Kala, or "Centre of the World", at Tiahuanaco. Nuku Hiva Island, Marquesas Islands, Eastern Polynesia, Early 20th., century, A.D. map.

7.095 : A sketch of the mystical associations with the sacred Hindu mountain of Kailasa showing the two sacred lakes of Manasarovar and Rakshas Tal and the four cardinal points symbolised by animal heads. Photo - Late 20th., century, A.D.

7.096 : Koati or the Island of the Moon South West of the Island of the Sun in Lake Titicaca looking toward the sacred mountaind of the Bolivian Plateau, Ilimani, in the distance.

more ancient claim than that of the Hindus. It is believed by the Hindus that the monkey scribal god Hanuman also resides at the foot of this mountain. Swami Pranavananda records from the Hindu texts that there is believed to be…" "…seven rows of trees round the Holy Manasarovar, and there is a big mansions on it, in which resides the king of Nags (serpent-gods) and the surface of the Lake is like an arc with a huge tree in the middle. The fruits of the tree fall into the Lake with the sound JAM; so the surrounding region of the earth is named Jambu-ling, the Jambu-dvipa of Hindu Puranas. Some of the fruit that fall into the Lake are eaten by the Nags and the rest become gold and sink down to the bottom".

"At one place it is written that in the centre of Jambu is the glorious mountain of Meru of various colours; on the east it is white like a Brahmin; on the south it is yellow like a Vaisya; on the north it is red like a Kshatriya; and on the west it is black like a Sudra. Four mountains form buttresses to Meru and on each of these stand severally a Kadamaba tree, a jambu tree, a pipal tree, and a fig tree"[440].

The ancient Hindu texts relate that the Lake Manasa-sarovar was created by the thought from the mind (Manas) of the supreme creator Brahma. And later it was said that the lake was discovered by the Maharaja Mandhata (a mythical figure) and he gave his name to the hills were he did penance. It is also suggested that this lake is the same as another mythical lake called Manasa-Saras, but nobody is certain of this but judging from the name it would appear to be identical with that adjacent to Kailas, and the Buddhist texts also refer to the lake as Anotatta or Anavatapa and in the Jain texts it is sometimes called Ashtapada[441]. In the great Vedic Aryan legends of their entry into India there is a reference to Kailasa as Bindu-sara, where bindu means "seed" in the cosmic sense.

In the Tibetan version of the Kailas Purana it states that the Ganges River originated from the peak of Kailasa and then descends to the spring known as Chhumik-thumgtol and that the four main rivers associated with the cardinal points emerge from this spring in copper pipes through Laka Manas. The Ganga was spouted out the mouth of the mythical elephant (Langchen Khambas, or the Sutlej River) near the Dulchu Gompa on the west and went to Chhembo Ganga in Gyagar in India where it officially emerges as the Ganges. The Sindhu went northwards in the beginning and then emerged through the Peacock's Mouth (Mapcha Khambab, or the Karnali River) and proceeded westwards then to Sindu-yul. The Pakshu or Vakshu went west from Lake Manas and arrived at the Horse's Mouth (Tamchok Khambab or the Brahmaputra River) and emerged from a mountain in Cheme-yungdung in the east. It then flowed to Chang (Tashi-Lhongpo) and then onwards to Kamarupa in India where it was called Lohita before flowing southward to the joint Brahmaputra and Ganges Delta in North East Bengal. The last of the four was the Sita said to flow southwards from Lake Manas and then emerged through the lion's mouth (Senge Khambab, or the Indus) located in the mountain called Senge north of Kailas and then flowed on to Baltichen and Changhor before rising as the Indus[442].

Swami Pranavananda relates that the traditions regarding these four sacred rivers, in the religion and calendar of the Hindus were as follows: " …the water of the Sutlej (Ganges headwater) is cool, the water in the Karnali warm; the water of the Brahmaputra, cold, and the water of the Indus hot; that there are sands of gold in the Sutlej; sands of silver in the Karnali; sands of cat's-eyes in the Brahmaputra; sands of diamonds in the Indus; and that those who drink water from the Sutlej would become strong like elephants, those who drink water of the Karnali would become beautiful like a peacock, those who drink the water of the Brahmaputra would become sturdy like a horse, and those who drink water from the Indus would become heroic like a lion. It is also said that these four rivers circle seven times round Kailas and Manasarovar and then take their course towards west, south, east and north respectively"[443].

The River Saraju combines with the Gogra to form the Ganges and some believe that it is the former river that rises from Lake Manasarovar. This is believed so because the first part of the name Sara-ju refers to its abbreviated form of the name Manasa-sarovar as Saras[444], and this also is considered to be part of the name of Saras-vati, a river (long dried up) as well as the goddess.

The smaller lake of Rakshas Tal also known as Ravana Hrada, Rakshas Sarovar or Ravana Sarovar, is located at about 4 miles (6.5 km) west of Manasa-sarovar. It is said that the demon king of Sri Lanka Ravana did penance here and the name Rakshas, also Rakshasa, refers in Hindu myth to the former demon people said to have inhabited India called Rakshasas of whom Ravana was one. However, it is more likely that this was evidence of an earlier people represented by Ravana who were defeated by the Vedic Aryans in the first millennium B.C. These people knew of, and frequented the mountain region as traders and pilgrims long before the Hindus and his defeat and penance is a reference to Hindu deities replacing or displacing those of the former peoples. This former (mythical) king of Sri Lanka has references to the Gond peoples and to the Bhuiyas of Central and South India and these in turn have close cultural ties to the Nagas of Assam near the confluences of the Ganges and Brahmaputra Deltas above noted. Since the smaller lake is believed to be the origin of the four sacred rivers it too is greatly revered. There are also two islands in the lake of Rakshas Tal, or Ravana Sarovar, one called Lachato and the other Topserma.

On the island of Lachato there was a heap of white stones - a cairn, and mani-slabs, these being stela or carved rocks with early Tibetan inscriptions. Topserma is larger than Lachato (about 1 mile square), and the southern section was called Tonak. On the eastern projection of the hill there was, two generations ago, still standing a ruined, walled building called a Pucca[445]. In disposing of the dead the monks are cremated, no doubt an ancient tradition, and this custom, along with their religion was influenced from India. The broad mass of the Tibetan populous, however, are hacked to pieces after death and thrown into a river or exposed on the distant high rocks for birds of prey to consume - a custom probably with a common origin to those of the Parsees and the Early Zoroastrians. When cremated the monks' ashes are collected and mixed with clay and modelled into small pyramids and then placed into a small stupa known in Tibet as a Chhorten[446] (*5.135*).

The remarkable association of ancient myths, legends and names with the great stepped pyramid mountain of Kailasa and its two sacred lakes leaves anybody who may have had some acquaintance with South America myths, but who has not fully made the connection, thinking "where have I heard this before?" or "there is something very familiar about some of these records!" It has been noted that the term Kailas was only applied after the rise of Hinduism in India and overlaid on the probable former ancient name of Parwan, relating to the wind deity of India. This deity derives from the Ancient Mandaeans and of the Ancient Middle East to the West, where there it is conventionally identified with Media in the Ancient Near East adjacent to the Eastern Mediterranean. In the Mandaean texts it is identified as the Tura d Madai, the sacred mountain. The name of Parwan probably dates from the second millennium B.C. and this was believed by some of the Mandaeans to be located in the Caucasus while others thought it was in Iran, or east in the Himalayas as noted by Lady Drower[447]. But before that, no doubt, the mountain was well known by the people of the Ancient Near East and probably given the name of their supreme mountain deity Il or El earlier noted. This mountain and its physical resemblance to a stepped pyramid tends to date its sacredness to the period in which stepped pyramids were being built in the Ancient Middle East and this tends to confirm a probable third millennium date for its first elevation to the mystical level of sacred mountain. It is noted also that there were two mountains revered because they captured and reflected the dawn sunrise and this appears to correspond with the sacred mountains of the Bolivian Altiplano, Illi-mani and Il-ampu, and the first of these, towering over modern La Paz, reflects also the form of a stepped pyramid and the sunrise at dawn (*6.113*).

7.098: Variations of Vaishnavite tikas, tilaks or brow marks, with two from Saivite sources. India, Early 20th., century, A.D.

7.099 : The term for the ithyphallic god of the Himalayas is Urdhva, here as an aspect named Nilakantha and this is probably the origin of Urco in Aymara cosmology. North India, 5-6th., century, A.D.

7.097 : Brahman youth with Vaishnavite brow mark, and shaved forehead found also among the Amazonian Indians. South India, Early 20th., century, A.D.

7.101 : Enchique Disk showing the Sun's face with "tears" as faces on the cheeks. This exact symbol is found in Ancient Mexico and as a trefoil in earlier depictions. The brow symbol is similar to those found in India among the Vainavite Hindu sects. Tiahuanaco design, Cuzco, Peru, 1000-1450 A.D.

7.100 : The god is Siva - here as the aspect named Hara. The top-knot represents the sacred mountain Kailasa and the braids or flowing locks the rivers of sacred life-giving water descending from the Himalayas onto the plains of India via the Ganges. Hara and Parvati, North India, 200-500 A.D.

The fact that there is a large main lake, Manas-sarovar, associated with the sacred Mount Kailas also reflects a similar relationship between the Tibetan Plateau and the Bolivian Altiplano where Lake Titicaca is located near Illimani and Ilampu. The second sacred lake of Rakshas Tal or Ravana Sarovar in Tibet is reflected by that adjacent to Lake Titicaca where a second lake is named Lago Huinaymarca beside which Tiahuanaco stands. On the banks of an inlet off Lake Titicaca called the Golfo de Puno, is Hatun-colla, considered possibly the oldest of the Aymara settlements, and this may have some other sacred association with the two main lakes. The two sacred islands in Tibet are intimately related to Kailas are located in the smaller lake of the two lakes whereas on the Bolivian plateau they are found in the larger, Lake Titicaca, as the islands of the Sun and the Moon, otherwise called respectively Titicaca (Titi-Kala) and Koati. On one of these islands in Tibet it is noted that one portion of the island named Topserma was called Tonak, and it seems far too great a coincidence that the name for the deity, associated with thunder, who emerged from Lake Titicaca, was named Tonaca or Tonapa. The name for the walled building on this Tibetan island, called Pucca, seems too close to the Peruvian term for fortress - Pucara, for any doubt that there must be a connection between these two mountainous regions on the opposite sides of the world. It will be remembered that the rival city to Tiahuanaco located at the other end of Lake Titicaca was named Pucara and dated from about 600-200 B.C. This suggests that very early, probably in the second half of the first millennium B.C., mariners and venturers from the Ancient Near and Middle East discovered the Bolivian plateau and saw the close parallels between the sacred stepped pyramid mountain in Tibet with its two lakes and those

475

on the South American Altiplano and deliberately settled the region inevitably imposing their own terminology and philosophical constructs.

It has been noted that the term Sarovar, in Manasa-sarovar, refers to the lake and is found also abbreviated as Saras while the term Manas refers to its creation as an act of the mind of Brahma. Since the Lake is closely identified with the four cardinal points in being considered the origin of the four sacred rivers and the mountain of Kailasa as having four sides, aspects and colours also relating to the cardinal directions the term Sara is itself therefore identified in the same way whether originally intended or not. In many of the main endings related to castes tribes, legendary of mythical, the affix sometimes suffix, is often applied to indicate its origins or associations. In deities and tribes or individuals this is demonstrated by the affix of ayya to record the racial derivation or inheritance from the Aryans. This has also been earlier noted in the adoption, rigorously adhered to with great pride, by the tribes and castes in India and reflected in the titles such as Ayya, Ayar, and Anna. In other affixes, apart from tribal or caste names, the term Saras seems to have been adjusted in time to, or derived from a common origin as saya and to have been identified in the same way with terms clearly derived originally from the Ancient Middle East such as Am or Amma and reflected in the term for the New Moon - Ammavasaya (Ammava-saya)[448]. This term for the New Moon implies that it relates to the first quarter of the Moon's cycle and this quartering is indicated by the term saya.

A caste of particular note, the Bants, traders along the West and South Coast of India were divided into a number of balis or septs (clans). In one tribal example all the divisions recorded by Edgar Thurston (13 + 1 variation) the clan name was suffixed ayya. Some of these are the Bellathan-naya (jaggery clan); Chalian-naya (weaver clan); Kochattaban-naya (jack-tree clan) and the Puliattan-naya (tiger clan)[449]. Among the Shivalli Brahmans of Southern India the clan names reflect their pride in their Aryan descent and the term for "belonging to" probably derives from the term for Aryan since this was emphasised from the earliest days in their occupation of India: Kudret-taya - belonging to the horse clan; Tali-taya - belonging to the Palmyra palm clan, etc.[450]. However some suggest that these affixes, even when retained by tribes and castes, having lost much of their original meaning, are sufficiently related in occupation to suggest a link to cardinal directions. The basic principle of the four castes was indicated to be related one to each of the four sides of the sacred mountain Kailasa earlier noted.

Among the Dasaris the "chief people" were the Guru who was titled Annal-ayya, the Umbrella Men, the parasol always being symbolic of the World Axis pointing to the Pole Star in India - the Godugul-ayya, and Horn-blowers - the Tuttul-ayya, always associated with the deity of wind and in India associated with the North East[451]. In Peru also the term saya is used to define the clan regions of Hanan Saya and Hurin Saya - Upper and Lower Cuzco respectively[452].

The division of the Inca Empire was into four quarters or Suyu[453] and this may also have developed from the term Saras in India also since there is little more than an linguistic inflection in the way both words are pronounced considering they developed originally on the other side of the world. This Peruvian term may also have developed from Surya, the name for the Hindu Sun god, and it is probable that this god's name and saras became confused and interchangeable in Peru. This is likely since Surya as the Sun related to its path and consequently to the cardinal points and these related aspects will be considered in the next chapter. This is all the more likely to be so considering the association of the terms saya for the New Moon quarters above noted in India and there being only the most moderate linguistic divergence from saya to suyu it is likely that the transfer from an Aryan language to the alien Quechua of Peru would have exacerbated its exact assimilation in Ancient Peru. The four suyu were Chincha-suyu, north; Anti-suyu, east; Colla-suyu, south; and Cunti-suyu, west[454], and this term was incorporated into the title of their empire, the "Land of the Four Quarters" - Tahuantin-suyu. As among the Hindus the quarter divisions of Saras are related to the cosmic dimension of Mount Kailas and in Peru it was also considered a division applicable to the Milky Way by the "two alternating, intercardinal axes"[455].

The Sacred Landscape of Uma-Suyu and Urco-Suyu and Taypi - the Centre of the World

The fact that these parallels are found among the people who claim descent from Tiahuanaco and the Islands of the Sun and Moon, located in Lake Titicaca, suggests that none of this can be coincidental. There is too much surviving evidence showing such close parallels between the Himalayan traditions and those of the Andes to be consigned to coincidence, and indeed, there is more to reveal. Tahuatin-suyu has been recorded as the Inca concept of the world, one divided into four quarters, but among the Aymara their vision, recorded in the 16th., century, was of a dual division into an eastern and western world more of less corresponding to the split of the Andes mountains to the north and south into two flanking the Bolivian Altiplano. The eastern zone was called Uma-suyu and the western Urco-suyu and in the middle, focused on Lake Titicaca and Tiahuanaco in particular, was Taypi - the Aymara "centre of the world". The flanking zones of Uma-suyu and Urco-suyu were perceived as a duality each being rooted in the ecological environment found predominantly in their respective region, and where these physical attributes of the altiplano were a focus reflected in the cosmic speculation preserved by the Aymara[456].

Uma-suyu was a zone where hunting, fishing and agricultural pursuits were the norm and reflected the fecundity of the earth since it encompassed the lower zones of the Andean Cordillera, being a warmer, wetter region. It was associated with abundance and less severe hardship in winning a living from the earth than the higher elevations of Urco-suyu and recognisably corresponded and formed a parallel with the Yin, or feminine principle in Chinese philosophy. Urco-suyu on the other hand encompassed the cold, dry, "aggressive", celestial qualities of the Andes reflecting the power, strength and "solidity" of the high Cordillera that would correspond, therefore, to the male, or Yang principles in Chinese Taoist philosophical concepts. These dual zones of extremity, or polarities, were perceived as united in the vastness of Lake Titicaca and appears to be at the root of Aymaran concepts in the location of Tiahuanaco as a ceremonial centre, itself based on a quartered designs reflecting the cardinal points. The name given by the Aymara to Tiahuanaco appears to have been Taypikala[457] and this would break down into the terms of Taypi and Kala. The two culture heroes, Tocapa Viracocha and Ymay Mama Viracocha are identified by some as the primal, male-female, Creation couple and associated with the West and East respectively[458].

In Aymaran philosophy concepts Uma means head and when wearing a headdress the expression is Uma-chucu[459], but is also the term for water in Aymara[460]. The primal waters in Polynesia was Unu - almost certainly derived from Umu a term related to storm[461] and the primordial sky god An or Anu in the Ancient Middle East. The correct name for the high Inca priest appears to be Villca Uma where villca means priest and uma head or mountaintop. In rank below the Villca Uma was the Hatun Villca and below him stood the Yana Villca who were the ordinary priests[462]. In climbing the mountain Tom Zuidema relates that Ayar Uchu, Manco Capac's brother, was the Inca brother who was associated with the mountain height and the guardian who resided there. The priests were considered to be guardians of high mountains since was there that the gods were believed to reside[463]. The deceased souls were believed to travel along the underground waterways and channels to the mountain's head, the uma pacha, and from the highland lakes on the mountains they arose to the earthly plane of the living[464]. In South India, Occhan priests were called Umai Archaka[465] and the term Occhan probably has the same origin to Uchu in Peru to be of note later in this work.

It is clear that the term uma derives from the association of the revered mountaintop, where the gods reside, and the intercession of the priests with those deities, and the head priest in particular. Needless to say this concept appears to have derived from India where Uma is

7.103 + 7.104 : Two views of the puma or jaguar deity surmounting his human victim that appears to derive from earlier examples in India and the Ancient Middle East. San Agustin, South Colombia, 50 B.C. - 800 A.D.

7.102 : The so-called Lion of Babylon excavated at Kasr Mound depicting the lion surmounting its human victim, a symbol of the Babylonian king defeating his enemies. Babylonia, c900 B.C.

7.105 : The Hindu deity Siva as Sarabha trampling the Sky God Vishnu both in the man-lion form representing pride. The symbolism is clearly inherited from Babylon and Assyria. Dharasuram, South India, Chola, 9-11th., century, A.D.

especially related to the mountain god Rudra, since it is his "wife" Uma who was particularly identified with the mountains. Rudra, when identified with the mountains' top, as an extension of his being the cloud deity, was reflected in his shared, dual role with Siva, the god of the male phallus or linga, and was known as, in this role, Udhva[466].

In Hindu texts the first mention of this goddess, Uma, appears in the Kena Upanishad and she is noted as a mediator between the gods and the Supreme Creator Brahma but she is also identified with the power of speech, Vac, deriving from Vayu or the wind deity. Of particular interest is that she is the principle of fecundity, and it is she who provides the power of germination for her husband's seed, Rudra's essence in the cosmic sense. Along with her spouse Rudra she was identified with the mountain tops where the couple resided and where he was particularly identified with the clouds that send the fertilising rain into the river torrents from the high mountains[467]. It is quite clear, therefore that there is a direct transfer of the name and principle from the Himalayas to the high Andes with a minimum of change, even the gender of Uma remaining the same in the cosmology of the Aymara extended to the environment.

Uma, as the female aspect of the mountain deity Rudra, has been seen to be the descendant of the Ancient Sumerian goddess Umu[468]. However, Rudra in his identity as the forerunner to Siva was also known, as earlier noted, Urdhva-linga[469], the ithyphallic Siva, linga being the name of the phallus itself, and Urdhva meaning erect. Erect also means to stand erect and therefore was also applied to the mountains of the Himalayas towering above the plains of the Ganges to the south. In this sense also the name for the brow-mark applied to the forehead of the devotees of Vishnu was called the Urdhva-pundra since it was drawn as upright marks from the bridge of the nose to the hairline[470] (7.097). The ithyphallic depictions of Siva are very common in India, but they are also found abroad including in a very specific pose as Eka-pada found in Peru - the one-legged pose popular in Orissa (3.041). This pose therefore is the very epitome of the male principle as Urdhva in India and as the term Urco among the Aymara of Bolivia. Therefore this ancient term of Urco from Tiahuanaco must surely be a corruption of the term Urdhva in India. It is unlikely to be a coincidence, therefore, that the term for the male fluid, virya, associated with Rudra as the clouds providing the rain and considered the basis of the male essence[471], is associated with Ymay Vira-cocha above noted in Aymaran myths in this aspect. This concept of the phallic associations of rain, and depicted in corresponding iconography, is reflected in a very similar concept that appears to have been portrayed in the iconography of the Olmecs in Ancient Mexico.

In considering the foregoing at the revered mountain of Kailasa, and its lesser companion, Parvan, its two associated lakes - one with two islands, formed a sacred region identified with the gods and it cannot therefore be a coincidence that there are two sacred mountains in Bolivia, associated with two sacred lakes one of which has two sacred islands. The names of both of the Bolivian mountains with their prefix of Il, or El, corresponds to the almost certain similar name derivations given to the peaks of the Himalayas at the earliest epochs and where vestiges of the following, but pre-Hindu epoch are still retained in the names Parwan and Mandhata. The term Kailasa is the Hindu name that probably dates from the late fist millennium, B.C. to the beginning of the first millennium A.D. This superimposition may also be evident on, and corresponding to the Bolivian altiplano in the construction of Tiahuanaco and the names of the adjacent peaks.

Sacred Mountains as the Dwelling Place of the Ancestors from the Andes to Asia

In the very far south of the Andes, at land's end in Tierra del Fuego, resided the Ona who lived according to their earliest memories in this cold and bitter land. In their oral traditions they record that the mountains separated from the main range of the Southern Andes as human beings who lived in ancient times and were greatly revered. To point at them was considered a lack of respect that could bring retribution from the ancient spirits said to inhabit them[472]. Far to the north this same belief was found and still survives among the Andean people in Chile, Bolivia and Peru through to Ecuador. So revered were mountains in the Peruvian cultures that the Moche depicted in their ceramic imagery human sacrifices to the five sacred mountains[473], the same number revered by the Ancient Hindus in the Himalayas. Models of the human fist have also been retrieved from the Moche period and these are believed to have represented the five sacred mountains[474] (*5.093-5*).

In Melanesia it was noted in early researches that the headdresses in some of the tribes in New Guinea were meant to represent the mountains (*7.084*) and this was true of tribes noted for their Polynesian traits such as the Mekeo in the South East of the island[475]. The headdress form appears not only to represent the mountains but also take the form of the torana or sky arch known and identified with the sacred mountains in India (*5.128; 6.023*). These same tribes manufactured drums of a similar type to those from Aboriginal India and the brow-disks similar to those in India through Indonesia into the Pacific Islands to the America (*7.084*) indicating cultural transfers and influences from both South and South East Asia through the Pacific Islands to the Pacific Coasts of South America and back again.

Sacred Mountains in the West, South and South East of Asia

In the oldest Ancient Sumerian texts the great god of the air, Enlil was said to have carried off his mother Ki, the Earth, and his father An carried of heaven. Ki is identified with Ninhursag who was the "queen of the Cosmic Mountain"[476] and this union between earth and the sky as the air god indicates the probable origin of many of the rites and ceremonies performed to the great gods on the tops of mountains. These sacred mountains in the Ancient Middle East were believed to be the personification of deities or ancestors as they were in India and South America. It has long been recognised that Ancient Sumeria and the following civilisations that existed in that region of Mesopotamia and Ancient Iran flowed into India over many millennia to eventually be assimilated into the Vedic, Jain, Buddhist, and Hindus traditions. The earlier migrations focused upon the Indus River civilisations into the first millennium B.C., when these indigenous religions took their root, and later extended along the Ganges to the east to the Bay of Bengal, and south into the Deccan.

CHAPTER 8

The FOUR QUARTERS and
the SUN in RITUAL AND MYTH

Taypi-Kala - The Navel of the World

The third element of the Aymara conception linking the sacred landscape in their environment to cosmological precepts was Taypikala, the "stone in the centre", which was focused Tiahuanaco[1], linking both of these polar extremes. The other two noted are Uma-suyu, relating to warm dark and wet of the Amazonian forests and the Yungas, and Urcosuyu, relating to the high, cold, hard and dry Montana. This concept of a "centre" has the same connotations as the Greek omphalus, a carved stone set up to mark what they believed to be the centre of the world and in Easter Island, Rapa Nui, in mythology the island itself was believed to be the "Navel of the World". In Aymara thought the concept of Taypikala was considered central to maintaining the equilibrium between the two polar extremities represented by Uma-suyu and Urco-suyu, and each of these was focused through the divinities associated with the culture hero deities Ymay Mama Viracocha and Tocapa Viracocha respectively. As the place of balance or mediation between these two environmental and cosmic zones Tiahuanaco was seen as the place of emergence, but also a place of integration and communication within the breadth of the environments covered by these three zones. The ceremonial city was therefore the hub of both earthly activities in terms of agricultural and craft related production and political and social balance within the zones of influence. This was enmeshed in its focal role as the ceremonial centre where worship of the ancestors, who were believed to dwell in the surrounding mountains, was directed. The great Lake of Titicaca was a natural focus for the agricultural industry in the fertile valley, between the mountains ranges, covering a broad area around it and the dominance in the landscape undoubtedly created a feeling of entirety or that of a holistic world existing apart from, and above all other Andean zones.

In terms of the Aymara clans it was noted in an earlier chapter that the equivalent of the three-clan division, corresponding to those found in Peru, was Cupi, Chaupi or Taypi, and Che-Ca[2], and here the central position is an element consistent with the cosmic thought of the Aymara centred on Tiahuanaco as Taypi. In the province of what is now Ayacucho the Ayamares were divided at the time of the Conquest into four subdivisions - Collana Ayamares; Taypi Ayamares; Yanaca Ayamaraes and Cayao Ayamaraes, suggesting that these were an Aymara people who had migrated west from Lake Titicaca to the region and brought their triple sub-divisions with them and added a fourth, lowest division into which to categorise the people among whom they found themselves[3]. This bears close similarities to the early caste organisation of the Brahmans in India adding a fourth division, Sudra, division to include for the local populations whom they subjected, and later a fifth for those whom they outcasted or were considered too primitive to rate within their system - the Untouchables.

The term Taypikala is recorded in the 16th., century, by Bernabe Cobo as Taypicala when he visited and described the great ruins of Tiahuanaco crediting the term to the local Aymara language and defining its meaning as "the stone in the middle"[4]. In Quechua, the term Taypi in Aymara, is paralleled by Tinkuy - the principle of balance and represented in cosmology as a beam in equilibrium[5].

The most interesting intermediate contacts, reflecting that there must have been contacts between Polynesia and consequently also therefore with Asia, are those found in the Marquesas Islands. On the island of Nuka Hiva there is a high sacred mountain called Tai-pi Vai and in the valley adjacent to it there were remains which Craighill Handy, almost a century ago, considered to be the ancient sacred centre of the island. He determined from oral traditions that the original population responsible for this site were the Na Khi[6]. There are many remarkable comparisons between the culture of the Marquesas Islands and Tiahuanaco and it is surely not a coincidence that the sacred centre of the regions of both should share an almost identical name of Tai-Pi or Taypi. Craighill Handy noted that were noticeable variations in the people and cultures in the Marquesas Islands and that this must have been a result of migrations and pressures of populations in and through the islands. From the earliest days of European missions in Polynesia it was noted that there appeared to have been Chinese influences, among others, and the term for the earlier vanquished race was called, as Handy notes, the Na Khi. The Na Khi have been noted elsewhere as a people otherwise known as the Lolos in Southern China[7], and who appeared to have been a Caucasian race who retained their independence until more recent centuries and who extended their influence from Eastern Tibet into South East China. Their iconography and contacts from a very early date with Buddhist India and the Nagas of Assam appear closely similar to that of the Maya in Central America[8] and these references in the Marquesas suggests that these are the same people with the same name.

The sacred precincts among the Marquesans were used for ceremonials including the essential sacred chants relating to the genealogy and deeds of the gods and chiefs called the Vavanas, and it is noteworthy that is paralleled in India by the Ramayana, the great Hindu epic also performed in drama chants and verse from India to Indonesia. There is little doubt the vavana is simply an adaption of the Indian saga - the Ramayana. The sacred trumpet among the Peruvians was called the Pututu[9] and among the Marquesas it was the Putona[10], and other references will be considered in due course with parallels in iconography in the illustrations where appropriate included in this work.

Aspects of Taypi as Thai Ki or Tao at Tiahuanaco

The term Taypi-kala, however, is pure Asian and appears to derive directly from the Chinese term Tai-Ki or Thai-Pi. In Ancient Taoist philosophy, attributed largely to Lao-Tze in the middle of the first millennium B.C., (born it is said 604 B.C.), a sage living more or less contemporarily with the Buddha in India, Thai Ki was identified with the Tao as the union of Heaven and Earth. Practices aimed at attaining union of these opposites are the subject of the Tao, and aimed at disciplines and rituals reuniting both as a social ideal and individually in the person, and as these polar extremes[11]. In oracular rituals the throwing of the yarrow sticks, interpreted according to the trigrams of the I Ching, reflects the opposites of Yang - male, spirit; firm, unyielding through the single undivided line; and Yin - female; matter; yielding; reflected in the divided line[12].

In an interesting myth from the writings of Kwang-sze, Ta Ki or Thai-kwei was identified with a youth who was a horse-riding herder on the side of the sacred mountain of Ku-shze[13]. It is interesting to note that such divine youths, or beautiful boys as they appear in Polynesia myth and legend, are also found in Andean myths, later noted. In another section of the same writings it is stated that:

"Now, the Tao (shows itself in two forms); the Pure and the Turbid, and has (the two conditions of) Motion and Rest. Heaven is pure and earth is turbid; heaven moves and earth is at rest. The masculine is pure and the feminine is turbid; the masculine moves and the feminine is still. The radical (Purity) descended, and the (turbid) issue flowed abroad; and thus all things were produced."

"The pure is the source of the turbid, and motion is the foundation of rest."

"If a man could always be pure and still, heaven and earth would both revert (to non-existence)."[14].

This interrelationship of dualities is identical to that expressed in the Aymaran cosmology around, and focused on, Lake Titicaca and Tiahuanaco. The lyrical aspects noted in the text above reflects that of the Chinese perception of dualities mirrored also in that of the Himalayan focus in both Buddhist and Hindu philosophy.

8.001 : A Buddhist stupa as the centre of devotion but also representative of the omphalus or "Centre of the World". South East India, 3-5th., century, A.D.

In Ancient China the term for god was "Ti" and Supreme god "Shang Ti" where and Tao meant the Way of Heaven[15]. Thien was the term for Heaven[16] and in Kwang-tse's writings there are references to the five Ti's. Thai-ki in Chinese philosophy was considered to be the primal ether[17] from which all things emerged but which unified and held all things together in an invisible web and it is this, with other elements of the Chinese Taoist thought, that bears such a close resemblance, in philosophical construct as well as in the terms, to that applied in the thought of the Aymara. The name for the deity - Ti or Tia is also found widely in India as well as in the Americas and clearly derives from a very early Eurasian original relating Ti or Tia to Deo and Deus.

From an inscription on the stone tablet said to have been preserved at the Temple of Lao-Tze recorded by Hsieh Tao-Hang in the Sui Dynasty (6th., century A.D.) the commentary on it is translated as follows:
"After the Thai Ki (or Primal Ether) commenced its action, the earliest period of time began to be unfolded. The curtain of the sky was displayed, and the sun and moon were suspended in it; the four-cornered earth was established, and the mountains and streams found their places in it. Then the subtle influences (of the Ether) operated like the heaving of the breath, now subsiding and again expanding; the work of production went on in its seasons above and below; all things matured and maintained. There were the (multitudes of the) people; there were their rulers and superiors"[18].

The substance of such a text appears so similar to that of the Aymaran beliefs and with virtually identical corresponding terms that coincidence is extremely unlikely and points to transference by mariners and missionaries from China but also in similar principles from India. In the consideration of the two polarities of Uma and Urco it is clear that these have developed from the equivalents in India of Uma and Urdhva and it is in the Himalayan region that Chinese and Indian influences combined to lesser and greater degrees. This is clearly evident in Tibetan Buddhism where it is heavily permeated by the indigenous Bon Po rituals and regalia and this later extended to early Chinese influences. It is clear that the Buddhists in Western Tibet and the Na Khi in Eastern Tibet received influences periodically from the Chinese and these were from there transferred to India itself just as India was exporting its culture by missions dating from at least the Mauryan dynasty under Asoka in the 3rd., century, B.C. This was also true of much earlier epochs in the greatness that was the Indus civilisation that ended a millennium earlier.

In considering Tibetan influences transferred from the Himalayas to South America another region that is of consequence, and as a preliminary mention, is the country of Burma more recently known as Myanmar, that appears to have been an important stop-over on that journey. Mention is frequently made in the religious myths of the Karen people of Southern Burma to the sacred Mountain, Thaw Thi (T-haw-T-i) - clearly Tay-Pi. This mountain is a high peak situated between the valleys of Sittang and Salween and is called by the Burmese Nattung or "mountain of the Nats" - nats being the nature gods or mountain spirits. There is another peak in this range a thousand feet higher and is considered the male and Thaw Thi is considered his wife, named "Ta La", but Thaw Thi is the most conspicuous. One of the myths associated with this mountain is that a Great Flood submerged the world and only the ridge on the highest point of this mountain was left above the water. When the waters subsided a peacock or pheasant alighted on the summit. Another myth stated that this was the highest mountain in the world. It is said to the abode of the god Y'wa[19]. The fact that the gods were to be met with on the top of the mountain emphasises the common belief that mountaintops were special zones where intercession between heaven and earth could occur. That is the place of equilibrium between the two polarities of heaven and earth, and this was as true of the Karen in Burma as it was for the Aymara in Bolivia.

The Origins and Myths of Kala; Kalasa and Kaleya

A component part of the Aymaran term Taypicala, or Tapi-Kala, in Bolivia - their apparent, esoteric name for Tiahuanaco, was the term Kala as the affix and this clearly has its own meaning and was not appended accidentally. In India the term means "black", "age" or "time" and is therefore closely linked to the God of Time, Siva, and has references to the Kali Yuga, the "Black Age" or "Age of Conflict"[20]. The Kali Yuga is said to be the present World Cycle in Hindu philosophical constructs and is believed to commenced in 3102 B.C.[21] as one of the four cosmic cycles as almost identical date found among the Maya. Kala is also visualised as the "serpent of Time" - Kala tattva[22]. The serpentine motion of time, perhaps inspired by the rhythmical "flow" of the meander motion of the forward movement, and perhaps also the coils of the snake, is reflected in the god Kaliya who was said to inhabit the sacred Yamuna River (Yama's River)[23].

Kala is also the epithet of the God of Death, Yama, whose colour is black and has been noted of the term Yana where it was used in Ancient Peru to denote black[24]. Yama is also called the "binder" and one of his names means "twin", and as he was said to be the first-man or ancestor of mankind he rules over the sphere where the departed ancestors dwell[25]. The fact that he is described as a twin is a probable, obscure reference to the derivation from the equivalent deity Yima in Ancient Iran where the dark Ahriman was the twin of the god of light, Ohrmadz. Because of his association with death he is usually depicted as an ugly misshapen person with dark green complexion and glowing red eyes. He holds a noose to seize the souls of the departed, but when associated with Time he is depicted as an old man with a sword, very like the Western, Grim Reaper, but in a few cases he is shown as a handsome man[26]. The identification with Time Cycles and as "binder"[27] would suggest that Yama as Kala at Tiahuanaco was associated with Taypi as signifying holding the two polar opposites together. This binding principle is represented by Uma-suyu and Urco-suyu together focusing them upon the "stone" or focal centre in the ceremonial form of the artificial mountain or pyramid known as the Akapana.

Kalasa is the Indian term for a water pot, urn or jar, or a pot filled with sacred water[28] and is frequently depicted in the early carvings in India but particularly atop the Sikharas or towers attached to temples in Orissa. The tower is in the stylised shape of the sacred mountain and the Kalasa represents the flow of the sacred waters from the Himalayas in the form of the Ganges. It is probable, therefore, that the term originally derived from Kailasa, and represented the mountain and Lake Manasa-Sarovar, earlier considered. It should also be noted that kal is in fact a term for a priest officiating at the sacred stone altar and for an ancestral stone generally in the Ancient Middle East and in India. This term therefore, may also have been included in the merging of several imported terms to form the localised belief system inherent in the name Kala among the Aymara.

The Four Quarters of Tiahuanaco -
Cosmic Aspects of the Akapana, Kalasaya and Puma Punku

The term Il or El corresponds to a date in West Asia surviving until about the middle of the first millennium B.C. It may have survived longer in India were the influences were transferred by migration and preserved for a longer period. The term Parwan was probably imported into India in about the beginning of the first millennium B.C. to the Himalayas and subsequently was replaced, or overlaid in part by those of the Hindus some centuries later. On the Bolivian altiplano it is now known that there were pre-Tiahuanaco settlements around Lake Titicaca and this

8.002 : A high status Mayan woman holding the mask of the old god, probably representing the Pauahtun, associated with the wind and mariners. Maya, Late Classic.

8.004 : A circular disk representing the cardianl points and a half lotus design clearly derived from India and related to that of the Maya. Huacho, Peru, 1st., millennium, A.D.

8.005 : Low relief carved wooden box showing the identical half lotus design found widely over many centuries in India (*8.010*). Pachacamac, Peru, c500 A.D. or later.

8.003 : Lotuses appearing similar to those found in Mexico at Cacaxtla and among the Maya. Note also the headdress beads strings hanging either side of the masked faces of performers of the topeng or lyric dance drama representing the traditional ringlets worn from the most ancient times by mariners in the Ancient Middle East and India. Java, Early 20th., century, A.D.

had been called Chiripa. These villages are believed to have been constructed about 1000 B.C. around the Lake and reflect elements of iconography found in later Tiahuanaco. The first settlements at Tiahuanaco proper date from about 600 B.C. and these coincide with major developments in India and significantly the end of the Assyrian Empire in West Asia. The proselytising Buddhists were founded in the 6th., century B.C. and the Jains also become notable at the same time. These movements reflect much that can be traced to the Aryan migrations from Iran centuries earlier and it is likely that the population movements did not cease with just the one major invasion. The very earliest South America settlements reflect the developments in Ancient Near East and Middle East closely, and the "sudden" advances in weaving ceramics and metallurgy date from the Chiripa phase, throughout the Central Andes, and are then followed by another leap forward in the middle of the first millennium B.C. Although Tiahuanaco was developing from about 600 B.C. there was another sudden "surge" that occurred about 200 B.C. when the cultural influences from Tiahuanaco began to be noted more widely in the region and this is considered the beginning of the Empire period. The city and Empire of Tiahuanaco suffered, along with the Peruvian cultural zones in the middle of the first millennium A.D. from collapse, probably brought on be severe climate change, but revived in the late 7th., century A.D. to rebuild and survive until the 10-11th., century A.D. at its final collapse.

If the earlier impulses and advances were due to migrations or an increase in traders from Asia from the beginning of the first millennium B.C. then this would probably account for the names of the sacred mountains in Bolivia reflecting the name of the mountain god in West Asia, El or Il. It is notable that it is the Aymara who preserved these names and it is they also who retained the concept of duality in a closely similar form to that of the Chinese Yin-Yang, in Uma-suyu and Urco-suyu. Both these terms and the origin concepts in China that probably derived from an earlier epoch in Iran and applied to the heights of the Himalayas before the rise of Hinduism filtering thereafter in China. In Mexico it has been shown in an earlier work[29] that there was a considerable influence from the Buddhists and this is particularly evident on the coast of Guatemala. It is likely also that the foundations of Tiahuanaco were laid by Ancient Middle Eastern people in that precise location because of their long-held beliefs that reflected principles of cosmology associated with the proximity of lakes and mountains sacred in their own traditions

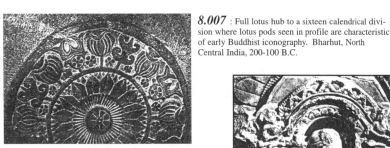

8.007 : Full lotus hub to a sixteen calendrical division where lotus pods seen in profile are characteristic of early Buddhist iconography. Bharhut, North Central India, 200-100 B.C.

8.008 : Elaborate torana, or sky arch, supported on characteristic pilaster columns showing the outer arch decorated in high relief half lotuses. The widely favoured elephant deity Ganesa stands in his anthropomorphic form under the arch. Harsatmata Temple, Abaneri, North India, Early 9th., century, A.D.

8.006 : Half lotus carved into the eloborate hairstyle found as a symbol throughout Ancient India. Cave Temples, Aurangabad, West Central India, 5-7th., century, A.D.

8.009 : Lotus hub with extended petal forms similar in form to collars found in the Sipan civilisation on the North Coast of Peru. Bharhut, North Central India, 200-100 B.C.

8.010 : Ceiling design based on the half lotus in the lower centre register and with a full lotus showed at the lower left. Kont-Gudi, Aihole, Central South India, 6th., century, A.D.

8.011 : The lotus was the most famous ot symbols of all the religions of India and the half lotus was commonly used as a border in many relief carvings as shown in this example. Paharpur, Bangladesh, 8th., century, A.D.

8.012 : Ceremonial collar or pectoral in the form of an octopus, but closely similar in principle to those of lotuses in India (*8.009*). Sipan, North Coast Peru, 200-300 A.D.

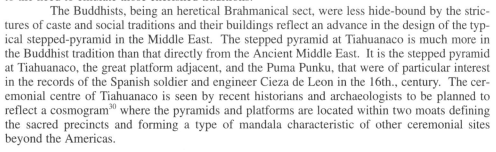

perceived similarly reflected in Bolivia. The settlement of this site was undoubtedly in response to the need to emulate those cherished traditions.

The Buddhists, being an heretical Brahmanical sect, were less hide-bound by the strictures of caste and social traditions and their buildings reflect an advance in the design of the typical stepped-pyramid in the Middle East. The stepped pyramid at Tiahuanaco is much more in the Buddhist tradition than that directly from the Ancient Middle East. It is the stepped pyramid at Tiahuanaco, the great platform adjacent, and the Puma Punku, that were of particular interest in the records of the Spanish soldier and engineer Cieza de Leon in the 16th., century. The ceremonial centre of Tiahuanaco is seen by recent historians and archaeologists to be planned to reflect a cosmogram[30] where the pyramids and platforms are located within two moats defining the sacred precincts and forming a type of mandala characteristic of other ceremonial sites beyond the Americas.

8.013 : A row of smaller stupas flanking the main stupa showing the cruciform plan typical of the period similar to cruciform patterns in the Andes. Tapar Sardar, Swat Valley, Afghanistan, 400-800 A.D.

8.014 : Soma platform in the symbolic shape of a cruciform. Hirapur, Orissa, pre-20th., century, A.D.

8.015 : Small shrine in Java showing a characteristic lower register of typical crosses displayed on the architecture of India for many centuries. Chandi Sawentar, Blitar, Java, 13th., century, A.D.

The Akapana at the Centre of the Cosmic Construct

Cobo is one of the first to report on the buildings at Tiahuanaco and he notes that the local Indians refer to the stepped pyramid as "Acapana"[31]. Cieza de Leon describes it more accurately in terms of its construction indicating that it was about 200 m on the sides and 15m high and was particularly interested in the enormous stone blocks used in its construction[32]. The ceremonial city of Tiahuanaco was built on a characteristic plan bisected into north and south and reflecting the "solar axial partition" into quadrants of four quarters corresponding to the cardinal directions of the compass[33]. It has been discovered that these are common to the planning of many such ceremonial sites throughout the world evident in the theme of Paul Wheatley's book "The Pivot of the Four Quarters" (1971). Far from the claim that it is an indigenous response to common environmental criteria they are all more likely influenced or diffused from the Ancient Near and Middle East as far as can be determined at this time.

It is now thought that the bi-partition of Tiahuanaco in plan and social reality was the model for the Incas at Cuzco reflected in the division of Hanan-Cuzco and Hurin-Cuzco, the former being higher status than the latter[34]. An extensive description of the Akapana and the archaeology undertaken to date is available in Alan Kolata's work and need not be repeated here, but this structure is considered the oldest surviving major structure at Tiahuanaco and dates from the 3-4th., century A.D. having been renovated several times until the final decline in 11th., century A.D. One particular aspect of its final appearance is the sunken courtyard on its apex, reflecting an early Chiripa style a millennium before it was constructed in Tiahuanaco, and this is associated with an even more interesting feature. The upper surface of the pyramid and the upper terraces features a construction of deep "chunky clay" layers between which were laid thin layers of bluish-green gravel. These clay layers were considered by Poznansky, in the first half of the twentieth century, to be symbolic of the Great Flood believed to have covered old Tiahuanaco in legendary traditions. More extraordinarily is that this gravel is known to have been brought from the Quimsachata Range south of Tiahuanaco and is noted for its "arresting" colour[35]. It is postulated that because this gravel is found naturally at the bottom of the mountain slopes, washed out

16 : Carved monoliths, one showing the characteristic
s found in the Andes from ancient times in South America
lar to those of India. Putuni, Tiahuanaco, Bolivia, 400-
A.D.

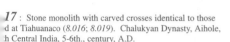

17 : Stone monolith with carved crosses identical to those
d at Tiahuanaco (*8.016*; *8.019*). Chalukyan Dynasty, Aihole,
h Central India, 5-6th., century, A.D.

8.018 : Walls covered in
a regular relief of carved
crosses clearly indicating
the importance the symbol
held for the Incan people
but identical to that found
in Java (*8.015*) and at the
Spiro Mounds. Temple of
Viracocha, Sicuani
(Raachi), Southern Peru,
1350-1500 A.D.

8.019 : Crosses carved and ornamenting ceramics and reliefs throughout the Americas appear
to derive directly from India. Three crosses can be seen at the lower, nearer end of this finely
carved monolith are identical to those found at the Chalukyan capital of Aihole (*8.018*). This
monolith also shows recessed architraves identical to the outlines in those found around portals
in India. Putuni , Tiahuanaco, Bolivia, 400-800 A.D.

by water running from the mountain peaks above, that it had
been seen to have a special association with rich lowlands
fertility. This green gravel was also, therefore, symbolic of
the rain cycle from the mountaintops fertilising the plains
for agriculture, and sustaining life itself, and travelling
onwards to the great blue-green ocean. On reaching the
ocean of water was believed to be transferred through underground canals or rivers to the mountaintops where it would
rise to form clouds to complete the cycle and initiate the
next one.

    This principle of covering a surface with symbolic
material is also found later in Cuzco where one of the principal plazas, the Haukaypata (Aycaypata), was covered with

8.020 :
Cruciform niches
were commonly
used in the archi-
tecture of India
traditional in the
earliest dynasties.
Those in the low-
est register are
identical to those
in Tiahuanaco.
Vishnu Temple,
Osian, Rajasthan,
North West India,
A.D. 850-75.

a layer of sand transported from the Pacific Coast to Cuzco over a distance of 500 km. The
Indians considered the sand sacred and buried small gold figurines and vessels in it, and was
therefore removed by the Spanish in 1559 A.D.[36]. The Akapana is considered to have represented in the microcosm of the sacred cosmological construct of the Aymara. The pyramid itself is
believed to represent the sacred mountain reflected in the ceremonial ascents by the priests and
rulers on days set aside for ritual propitiation and display[37]. The internal drainage system constructed in finely cut and coursed stone is believed to conduct rainfall through channels to the
base in a symbolic manner imitating that of the rain falling on a mountain and emerging at the
base, or part of the way down, and then flowing as streams or rivers to the fields[38]. The conduits

8.022 : Cross design developed from traditional designs long utilised in India. Gwalior Fort, North Central India, Mid-second millennium, A.D.

8.021 : Sacred cross carved on the lower centre of this owl-like monolith or masked figure. Nicaragua, 800-1500, A.D.

8.023 : Seated saint known as Agastya, the son of the sea god Varuna, with a meditation strap around his legs displaying cruciform ornamentation typical of the symbolic forms found from the earliest Vedic times into the present day in India and in Ancient South America. South India, 8-9th., century, A.D.

8.024 : Kilts of priests show crosses of the type found in Java and Peru on this engraved shell. The Sun disk on the right is identical to those found in India (*7.101*) and in Ancient Mexico and Maya. Note the pot shrine found similar also to the pot gods of the Gonds of India and Indonesia. Spiro Mound, Ohio , U.S.A., 800-1350 A.D.

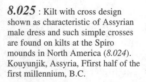

8.025 : Kilt with cross design shown as characteristic of Assyrian male dress and such simple crosses are found on kilts at the Spiro mounds in North America (*8.024*). Kouyunjik, Assyria, Ffirst half of the first millennium, B.C.

so constructed in fact bear remarkable parallels in principle to the four sacred rivers believed to flow from the smaller sacred Tibetan lake of Rakshas Tal in "copper pipes" to Manasa-Sarovar and then through to the point of emergence as spouts from the animal's mouths associated with the cardinal points.

It is particularly of interest that the rising Sun can only be seen to rise over Illimani from the top of the Akapana, and in its setting over a part of Titicaca to the west[39]. This emphasises the East-West Axis fundamental to the layout of the Akapana and the other ceremonial buildings on the site reflecting solar principles and orientation. The form of the Akapana as a step pyramid was less usual in that it was based on a cruciform, the fundamental shape that occurs in the Moche Pyramid of the Sun at Trujillo[40]. This is the iconic shape found throughout Tiahuanaco (*8.016*; *8.019*) and Ancient Peru (*8.018*) and also in the Jama-Coaque phase (*8.026*) on the Ecuador Coast, and appears to have its origins in the cruciform shape of the early Buddhist and later stepped platforms in India (*8.013/4*; *8.017*; *8.020*). The shape of the cruciform appears to relate to that of the lotus and half lotus, fundamental to Buddhist and Hindu symbolism, found in both India and Ancient Bolivia and Peru.

8.026 : House or shrine in the form of typical Batak houses found through Indonesia and Melanesia through into Micronesia. The cruciforms and crosses are identical to those in Tiahauanco and contemporary India. Jama-Coaque, Central Coast Ecuador, 200-400 A.D.

8.028 : Simple and elaborate crosses of the type found in India and the Ancient Middle East depicted on these plaster relief columns. Hatuncolla, South Highlands Peru, 700-1400 A.D.

8.027 : Cruciforms and crosses similar to those found at Tiahuanaco and in India. Chavin de Huantar, Cental Highlands Peru, 600-400 A.D.

8.029 : Earrings with crosses occur frequently in Ancient South America as well as across the Pacific and in India. Recuay, Central Peru, 300-1000 A.D.

8.030 : Cross of exactly the type found in Java (*8.015*) and throughout Ancient Peru and Bolivia. Ica, South Coast Peru, 200-600 A.D.

Origins of the Akapana from the Asian Apadana and Apana

The platform on which the palace of the Archaemenid Persian kings was built was famously known as the Apadana[41]. The illustrations in this work show clearly that architectural elements and particularly those of the stone carved portals appear to have been the prototypes for those at Tiahuanaco and epitomised by that carved in the monolith of the Gateway to the Sun (*5.066/7*). Significantly, after the fall of the Achaemenids in the 4th., millennium, B.C., their architectural, symbolic and iconographical heritage began to appear in India in the Maurya dynasty and finds it surviving apogee at great Buddhist temple site of Sanchi and subsequent Buddhist Dynasties (*8.013*). Architecturally both the Hindu Gupta and Chalukyan Dynasties show architectural elements and closely similar fine stonework similar to the Achaemenids and later Iranian Dynasties and display cruciform plans[42]. Elements of these Dynasties are traceable in the imagery in Central and South America (*5.063*; *8.016*; *8.019*) contemporary with the early and first apogee in Tiahuanaco from 200 B.C. to 600 A.D.

Because of its appropriateness the term apadana is used for ancient mounds or acropolii in Elam that have been transformed into platforms for habitation and particularly for those supporting civic architecture[43]. The term probably has its origin in much more ancient times two or three thousands years earlier and possibly links to the term, or has a common origin with apkallu, the term for sage[44], where stepped platforms were used by such men in their intercessions with the gods. In the transfer of culture, either with the Vedic Aryans in the early first millennium,

8.033 : Priest wearing a cape with sacred cross pattern found earlier also at the Spiro Mounds in Eastern U.S.A. British Colombia, Canada, Late 19th., century, A.D.

8.032 : Saltire cross painted on forearms with four dots in each quarter identical to those found in the Americas. Siva, India, Early 19th., century, A.D.

8.034 : Traditional cross found widely in the Ancient Middle East and utilised in architecture and in ceramic designs. Susa, Elam, Second millennium, B.C.

8.035 : The cross was a characteristi symbol in the most Ancient Mesopotar and this appears to have been transferre India and South America. Akkad Dyn Late 3rd., millennium, B.C.

8.031 : Pierced wall of simple crosses typical for the period and influenced from India behind the image of the Buddha being protected by the Naga (cobra) king named Mukalinda. Mandalay, Burma, c13th., century, A.D.

B.C. or from the later Archaemenids, the term apadana, as aparna, appears in the Vedic works relating to the ancient fire-altar and in Buddhist rites as Arapacana.

In Vedic texts the term Aparna is utilised as a general term for the special breathings forms called "vital airs" used in the construction of the sacred fire-altar by the presiding priest and is particularly defines extensively in the oldest of the Vedic texts named the Satapatha Bahmana. This may indicate that this term was preserved from before the Achaemenid period, perhaps and even before even that of the Babylonian a millennium before, at about the time of the Aryan invasions of India. Here, the Vedic texts, the pure essence of the fundamental act of the priest constructing and performing the appropriate rituals before the stone fire altar is preserved regardless whether or not it was elevated in the more lavish state and royal ceremonies for the elite on civic platforms. It is likely therefore that, since in Vedic ceremonies derived from Ancient Iran the fire altar was usually private to the family or clan, the term for the Archaemenid platform, the Apadana at Persepolis, probably derived from the fire-altar being within the palace on this platform giving its name at least from their time for the generally accepted named for this monumental construction that was transferred Tiahuanaco.

In Vedic texts there are considered five vital airs generally terms Aparnas, or Pranas, when constructing the fire-altar, and the term for the downward vital air was specifically aparna[45]. The dictates in constructing the fire-altar are extremely complex and specifically defined for every action, posture and the breath and also in the rituals to be performed after completion. These Aparnas are particularly identified with the top surface of the fire-altar and there can be little doubt that this is identified with the larger ceremonial platforms built for Public display. Of special interest is that in the first layer of construction of the fire-altar the bricks are set out in the form of a circle with a central squared block extending beyond the rim to its externalised "spine". Over this the altar is built and extraordinarily this form closely resembles the fire-pits and sunken

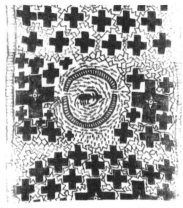

8.036 : Crosses incised into both animal figurines reflecting an important symbolic meaning. Guanacaste, Costa Rica, 800-1200 A.D.

8.037 : A sacred cloth or geringing printed in Bali in Ikat work with cruciform patterns of two types similar to those in Peru and Bolivia. Early 20th., century, A.D.

8.038 : A mawa that is a sacred textile with crosses typical of South East Asia and Coastal South America and the Andes. Toradja, Celebes, Indonesia, Early 20th., century, A.D

circular court so well known in Ancient Peru. The construction of the circle is achieved by using a knotted cord extended from a fixed point in the centre to the east end of the altar, that is the direction of the rising Sun, as Agni, the fire god[46].

In finishing the construction of the fire-altar after drawing in the aparna, the vital inward breath, is held while the presiding priest places the surface bricks, often marked, and this he does also when placing the small image of the golden man on the altar representing Agni himself[47]. Of some interest is that when the altar constructed, laid out corresponding to the cardinal points, has been sanctified and identified with Agni, the fire god, he is described as the "animal". Undoubtedly this is because animal sacrifices, and human sacrifices, were performed for millennia on these altars. In other sections of the text the altar was specifically laid out in the form of the male warrior, considered the highest of the five sacred sacrificial victims in Vedic texts, but here the text appears to indicate modified strictures to accommodate the period after human sacrifice ceased generally - initiated probably in the first millennium, B.C. The text notes of this sacrifice:

"3) Now that Agni (the altar) is an animal, and (as such) he is even now made up whole and entire, - those (bricks) which he lays down in front are his fore-feet, and those behind are his thighs; and those which he places in the middle are that body of his. He places these in the region of the two retahsik (bricks), for the retahsik are the ribs, and the ribs are the middle, and that body is the middle (of the limbs). He places them all round, for that body extends all round."[48].

This section of the texts is an interesting one when considering the sacred precincts in South America since it is known that several, including Cuzco were laid out in the form of the highest deified animal, the puma[49]. Sangay ceremonial site on the Amazon Basin side (east) of the Andes in Ecuador[50] was also planned reflecting the form of a puma and this is believed to derive from the Olmecs of Central America. The Incas were the last of the Andean cultures to focus their worship of deities on the fire altar and their "burnt sacrifices" closely resemble those in Biblical narrative, but also in Vedic India. In Ancient Babylonian sculptures the lions surmounting a human victims (*7.102*) is a powerful and evocative image but the identical carving is found at San Agustin in Southern Colombia (*7.103/4*). This imagery may originally have represented the fire-god, Agni, as the "animal" consuming the finest of all sacrifices, the human male warrior and therefore intimately identified with fire worship reflecting a transfer from the Old World to the New. Old World deities are often identified with the lion as king of the animals (*7.105*), others with the elephant in India, and both of these icons are represented in imagery found in Central and South America.

It is significant that the Aparnas, or Parnas, are five in number[51], the sacred number in the Ancient Middle East and India, but also in Ancient Peru. Associated with the origins of the fire-altar in the texts are the five priests[52] and the five-fold distribution through the body[53]. The Aparnas are perceived as the rays of the Sun that extend downwards to convey vitality and life-force through these breathing rituals[54] and this appears to have more baleful influence when directed from planets (grahas)[55]. Of particular interest in relation to this aspect of Agni worship are the Karakas, mendicant fire-worshippers[56] who may have given their name to Kuraka, the term for a clan chief in Ancient Peru.

The aparna, sacred breaths, are each identified with the cardinal points, and as breath they are related to the wind-god, Vayu, and the soul noted elsewhere in this work. In an extraordinary part of the text it is noted at some length that the first or earliest Creator, Pajapati, lay down on the fire-altar and Vayu imbued him with, and activated his vital Aparnas, or sacred breaths. When the ritual is at its end it is noted that Prajapati "relaxed", interpreted from "disjointed", and the gods took him away. Vayu, the Wind god, is specifically noted as taking the upper part "above the waist" and below the head that became the "deities and the forms of the years"[57]. This reference may have been fundamental in the original purpose of the rituals at Tiahuanaco and adopted by the later Incas since Vayu, the wind deity of the soul, here is the Pawan (Pahuan or Tahuan) of Ancient Iran, and identical to the name that the Incas gave, or preserved for their Empire - Tahua-tin-suyu. Decapitation was a common ritual in both the Old World and the New but here that part above the waist is seen as separate and the text appears to indicate that the lower half was that temporarily associated with Worldly existence. Clearly the upper half is identified with the world of the gods and this may be the origin of the "severed-at-the waist" imagery found both in Central America (*4.116*) and in Ancient Peru (*4.117*) deriving from the Ancient Middle East and later reflected in the Brahman penalty recorded elsewhere in this work.

In other early textual references in India the term aparna referred to a "leafless tree" supporting a "leafless creeper" and was equated symbolically with the vulva of Parvati, the consort of Siva[58]. It was perceived that the creeper itself was the female element and the "leafless tree" as the phallus and represented the Changeless Being. The Intihuatanas erected in Inca Peru (*8.078*), Bolivia and through into Northern Argentina (*8.079*) may have embodied this iconography particularly as they are set up on platforms resembling akapanas or apadanas. It is likely therefore that the Akapana of Tiahuanaco derived from the Apadana of Achaemenid Iran and later assimilated the various related meanings derived from India.

Other derivations from the associations of the Apadana, or Aparna, from Ancient Iran appear to be preserved in Buddhist symbolism and myths. The term Arapacana refers to the "mystical collective", called of Manjurisi - the five names of the Buddha[59]. These deities originate from the five syllables, A, R, P, C and N and the principle deity, therefore, incorporates all of these where his name is made up by these sounds - A-ra-pa-ca-na. However, the association probable derives from Brahmanism and devised by, or derived from the Brahmanic five priests associated with the fire-altar noted above. It is likely that the Buddhist reference derives from earlier Middle Eastern associations where names and letters were related to sounds and numbers in esoteric meanings related to the fire-altar and tending to confirm this is the fact that this deity, Arapacana, is associated with the Sun, Surya-prabha - "light of the Sun"[60].

In the cultural transfer from one land to another

8.039 : The sacred fire altar of the Vedic Indians is based on a series of circular, superimposed courses closely similar in design to the sunken circular courts known in the fire religions of the Andes in Ancient Peru. This diagram is taken from analyses of the Vedas a century and a half ago. The Vedic fire altar appears similar to those of Early Peru (*3.017*).

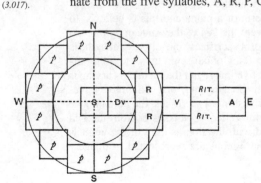

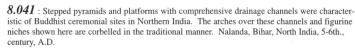

8.041 : Stepped pyramids and platforms with comprehensive drainage channels were characteristic of Buddhist ceremonial sites in Northern India. The arches over these channels and figurine niches shown here are corbelled in the traditional manner. Nalanda, Bihar, North India, 5-6th., century, A.D.

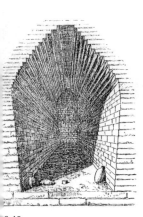

8.042 : The ruins of the Inca or pre-Inca monastery or convent on the island of Koati, dedicated to the Moon in Lake Titicaca. The corbelled door heads and window niches are virtually identical to those found at Paharpur, the Buddhist University at Nalanda, and other sites in North India dating from the 5th.,-8th., century, A.D. Inca or pre-Inca., Lake Titicaca, Bolivia, 1350-1500 A.D.

040 : Corbelled arched brickwork the finest type found from the earliest times in Mesopotamia typified by s example from a tomb-chamber. ghier, Assyria, 900-700 A.D.

8.043 : Corbelled arches are found traditionally in brick and stone throughout the Ancient Near and Middle East and also in India. Here at Petra in the inverted form carved in stone is purely decoration. Jordan, West Asia, Early first millennium, B.C.

8.044 : Close-up of a single door at Koati showing the probability of influences from Buddhist India in the first millennium A.D. Inca or pre-Inca., Lake Titicaca, Bolivia, 1350-1500 A.D.

should include in the equation both time and distance. It is clear that if all the references applied to the finished built platform in Iran and, or India are transferred in their pristine state along with all of the contemporary and later adaptions associated with subsequent, but related cultural intrusions from the same regions and their developing or declining religions, then in time divergence and mutation would naturally occur. Clearly this occurs in India with cultural influences from Iran where these alter and adjust as a result of incoming influences from the source country particularly at the change from one dynasty to another and the intrusive changes caused by North Eurasian invasions in their territory. As these influences, changing over the generations and centuries, entered India they in turn would cause further change to the local cultures, and be assimilated to a lesser or greater degree to reflect the developing or declining cultures religions and political developments in the Sub-continent. When cultural influences were transferred from either Iran and the Ancient Middle East direct to South America or from India the same process would occur and it is likely that identification, mutation or rejection would occur in the same way for similar influences confronting those that had already developed in the Andean regions. This would certainly by true for Tiahuanaco where so many aspects related to Ancient India and Iran are clearly visible in the architecture and related terms and myths preserved from the mid-first millennium, B.C.

8.045 : Ceremonial corbelled arched portals to the ceremonial staircases up the stepped pyramid typical of those in North India and at Koati in Bolivia. Borobodur, Java, Indonesia, 8th., century, A.D.

    In Bolivian scholarship there are now several books on the belief system and deities of

8.046 : Mud brick pierced court walls characteristic of the sacred lozenge textile design in India and throughout South East Asia. Chan Chan, Northern Coastal Peru, 9-15th., century, A.D.

8.047 : Stepped motifs probably descended from Moche and Tiahuanacan traditions in earlier centuries. Chan Chan, North Central Coast Peru, 8-1200 A.D.

8.048 : Stepped motifs similar to stepped motifs sho[wn] on the crowns of Moche rulers, ancestors or deities. Chan Chan, North Central Coast Peru, 9th.,-15th., cen[tu]ry, A.D.

8.049 : Ceremonial staircase at the Apadana indicating the stepped gable features characteristic in the crowns in Ancient Iran and the architecture and headdresses of the Moche and Chimu. Persepolis, Iran, 5-3rd., century, B.C.

8.050 : Conical house type found on the banks of Lake Poopo in Bolivia virtually identical to those constructed 2-3 thousand years ago. Uru, South Central Bolivia, Early 20th., century, A.D.

Tiahuanaco and its symbolic layout and some aspects from them are referred to in this work. In the foregoing, in this section of this work, references to the term Akapana being ultimately derived from Apandana and Aparna are made. Extending from the Buddhist terms last noted above, two other elements might be considered in the association of the sacred platform as a physical touch-point with the Earth for mystical rites that might apply to Buddhist transfers to Tiahuanaco.

The purpose of building platform or pyramid was almost entirely in imitating the sacred mountains as a focus of aspiration and ritual in the contact with their deities since high regions were believed to be closer to the gods or ancestors who dwelt, usually, in the Sky. The platform or pyramid was therefore an elevated sacred precinct usually reserved for officiating priests whose vocation was to transfer sacrifices and propitiations to these gods and to receive, and transmit omens, signs and guidance through trance, visions or dreams. In Buddhist rites the term Akarsana meant "attraction"[61] and this would appear to have been a reference to rites in an attempt to attract the god and ancestors. As well as this mystical application there was a more mundane ritual associated with physical contact and attraction between the supplicant and an absent person or party using set intonations and formulae.

In what appears to be a related term, to aparna or apadana, in Buddhism Akasagarbha meaning "sky womb" where its essence was ether in the mystical sense. The term itself implies having "space in the womb" tending to indicate that this was a void or "world" where another form of existence, perhaps non-material was possible. It is said in Buddhist myth that the Boddhisatva, the angelic and saintly beings of Buddhism, lived in this "sky womb" in the sky and that its colour was red[62]. Both of the terms, Akarsana and Akasagarbha would appear to have some relevance to the name of Akapana in Tiahuanaco as well as in the rituals of "attraction" essential in mystical rites and ceremonies between man and his gods focused on the sacred platform or pyramid.

Kalasasaya as the Counterpart of the Himalayan Kailasa

The Kalasa-saya is the second of the most important ceremonial buildings on the site of Tiahuanaco and concurs in axis to the main East-West lines of orientation relating to that of the adjacent Akapana. The great stone-faced platform measures 130m x 120m and opened onto by a ceremonial staircase to the subterranean courtyard located in front of the main entrance (*5.058*). The Kalasa-saya varied from the Akapana, to the south of it, in that it appeared to have been the focus of the priests' accommodation and, or shrines around a central court on top of the main plat-form and there were at least a number of large scale sculptures associated with it[63] (*5.057*). It would appear from more recent research that the Kalasa-saya was reserved in ceremonial rites for the worship of the city's elite ancestors as well as the centre for agricultural rituals[64]. This would tend to reflect closely the sacred water pot of India and the identification with Kailasa, the sacred mountain from whence the life-giving waters of the sacred rivers flowed into the plains of India relating essentially to life essence, and nourishment through agriculture. The breakdown of the term Kalas-saya into its two basic elements reveals how closely it follows that of India were saya is probably derived from Saras, the early abbreviation for lake Manasa-Sarovar and identified with the four cardinal points, and Kalasa referring identically with the term for the Sacred mountain of the Hindus, Kailas, or Kalasa the symbolic container of sacred, fertilising water. It seems, even when not considering any other aspect or parallel between India and Tiahuanaco, to be too much of a coincidence not to have some validity in the proposition of a direct cultural transfer. This is particularly so for the Kalasa-saya as it was known to be a centre for fertility and rituals associated with water, as the whole complex appeared to be in various ways. The importance of the name Kalasa-saya has wider implications and the relationship between this important ceremonial platform and the sacred mountain of the Hindus, Kailasa, and other extensive parallels in iconography and myth has been indicated in an earlier chapter.

The Puma Punku - A Latter-Day Akapana or Sacred Mountain

The Puma Punku, along with the Kalasa-saya, appears to have been constructed from the begin-ning of the last phase of Tiahuanaco commencing in the 7th., century A.D. and lasting until the 11th. At both the Akapana and the Puma Punku there were twin staircases ascending the East and West side of the pyramids[65], and the finest stone masonry at the site is found at the Puma Punku itself and perhaps more reasonably called a terraced platform. This ceremonial building exhibits no residential content and appears entirely reserved for rituals. The Puma Punku never-theless appears to have been constructed as a sacred mountain as the Akapana had been, and includes in the same way stone-lined water channels clearly with symbolic or for ceremonial intent. It has been suggested that the Akapana was perceived as no longer suitable for its pur-pose and was replaced by this new edifice away from the old dedicated to the ancestral gods. This new building was constructed after the very major climate change in the 6th., century A.D., when this and other sites in South America preserved evidence of cultural collapse. It is also believed that the climatic change resulted in major drought lasting perhaps decades and then was followed by a prolonged major period of rains and floods probably due to the El Nino phenom-enon. This later phase is noted for its remarkable stone masonry and it is significant that this and the earlier phase also saw irrigation systems, with symbolic overtones, being constructed and these included the puquios on the Nazca plain, and both of these regions feature elements unde-niably found also in the Ancient Middle East. The puquios built on the Nazca plain of Peru were virtually identical to closely similar systems constructed in South East Arabia called qanats[66] and these are found also in South West Iran. Also of interest is that fact that the masonry is so close-ly similar in design and finish to that in the Chalukyan Dynasty in South India but more so in that surviving at Persepolis and Pasargadae where metal cramps, similar to the one used in the Puma Punku, are found tying the finest of masonry dressed blocks together (*5.064*).

The Sun in Ritual and Myth in Peru and Ancient India

When the name Inca or any reference is made to the Andean civilisations, gold inevitably comes to mind. Gold, as the golden man of Lake Guanavita and the associated legend of Manoa - the fabled land of gold; the golden "tears" of the Tiahuanacan Sun Gateway; the gold ransom paid in part to Pizarro for the Inca Atahualpa - the largest part still missing, or the more recently discovered gold treasures interred with the rulers found at Sipan in northern Peru. Gold above all is associated with the Sun kingdoms of both the Old and New World and in this there are many shared traditions and principles of some interest. However, it would appear that adoration of the Sun as the chief deity was more a special preoccupation of the Incas, but not all of the Andean or coastal peoples, since elsewhere the Moon deity appears to have been accorded greater prominence.

On the Island of the Sun in Lake Titicaca, it was the sacred rock rather than the Sun that was worshipped although the Sun and Moon had certain prominence[67]. It was out of this rock that the Sun was believed to have emerged at the end of a period of great darkness. This period of darkness is recorded in many myths throughout the world and in the Andes this was said to have been relieved by the Sun rising from here in "great splendour" over Lake Titicaca that initiated a new world order[68]. On this island the Sun was represented, according to one of the earlier Spanish chroniclers, Gavilan Ramos, by three statues called Apu-ynti, Chusip-ynti and Yntipquanqui, and this appears to reflect the imagery of the Sun god in Colombia[69].

The Andean Sun and the Origins of Punchao

Among the Incas the name for the Sun was Inti although Punchao appears to have been in more general use throughout Peru. Among the first Spanish chroniclers it was noted that the Sun was among the highest deities to be revered and it was the Bolivian and Peruvian Indians custom in that worship not to wear any Spanish clothing and to approach the representations of these deities barefoot[70]. On coastal Peru, Coniraya Viracocha was identified with the Sun and he is noted in one section to have been a handsome young man dressed in radiant golden clothing befitting the Sun[71]. Belief in the immortality of the soul appears among the Peruvians who considered the deities Con, Pachacamac and the Sun the judges of the deceased soul as it entered the afterlife[72].

For the Incas in confession the Sun was considered the intercessor, and the Inca perceived the Sun as the brother of the Thunder Illapa already considered, and worshipped as a triad with the Viracocha, and his son was considered as Churi-Inti or Punchao[73]. Punchao was considered as the Sun at the Summer Solstice (December) and Viracocha the Sun at the Winter Solstice (June)[74]. Viracocha is identified with the Sun rising over Lake Titicaca and setting in the north west consonant with his migration across the landscape to Ecuador, a reflection of the Sun's orbit, where he "sets" as the dying Sun "walking over the water" as recorded in the myth[75]. Viracocha's beard is seen as the rays of the Sun as they appear over the horizon. Churi-Inti, or Punchao is reflected in the Sun's life-giving force as Inti-Guauqui[76], this latter term appearing to relate to that of the Chibcha of Colombia whose name for the Sun was Guagua.

In Cuzco solar pillars were erected to determine the Sun's progression through the seasons corresponding to the monthly divisions and as markers to observe the daily orbit from sunrise to sunset[77], and the eyewitness reports state these numbered between 4 and 16. One chronicler noted that there were four pillars placed on the high ridge of the mountains to the west of Cuzco at about 2-3 leagues away and two hundred paces separated the first pillar from the last. When the Sun passed the first pillar towards the second it indicated that it was time for planting in the higher regions and when it had reached the space between the second and third pillar it was time for general planting on the plains[78]. Festivals throughout Peru were regulated toward the adoration of the Sun and each day the Sun was worshipped at sunset as its strength faded. As the

Sun approached the horizon all work stopped and the people knelt to face the orb and prayed[79]. These central pillars were called Sucanas and were destroyed during the period of the "extirpation" of the traditional images and iconography from the pre-Colombian period.

In Inca myth the royal clan itself was claimed to have descended from the Son of the Sun, Manco Capac, and they therefore considered that in worshipping the Sun they were adoring their ancestral father, or grandfather - Inti as the Inca Sun where "Villca" was the equivalent of the Aymara. The fourfold division was seen as a model relating to the cosmological four quarters since this was defined by the path, or orbit, of the Sun daily and throughout the solar year[80]. The Inca influences, or that from a common origin among the Araucano in Northern Chile, is perceived in the Sun being called Anti (Supreme Being)[81] and clearly is a name related to Inti.

The Successive Sun Gods in India

In India, among the Brahmans, the Sun was represented among one of five sacred gemstones, placed in miniature shrines, so favoured by them in their private rituals, as a piece of crystal. The other four were Salagramma (sacred stones) representing Vishnu; Bana Linga representing the essence (male fluid) of Siva; jasper - a red stone representing Ganesha (the elephant-headed god); a lingam representing the male phallus of Siva, or a piece of metallic ore representing his wife, the goddess Parvati[82].

Among the Pulayas of South India the chief deity is the rising Sun, and they named him Utaya Tampuran and they are a people who use the kokkara, or rattle to drive away evil spirits from their ceremonies[83] similar to the Peruvians. The Thanda Pulayans when swearing an oath raise their hands to the Sun declaring - "By the Sun, I did, or did not do ..." etc.[84].

In many of the tribes or castes the social organisation is divided into dual moieties, as earlier noted, and among the Mukha-Dora these moieties are named after the Sun - Kora-vam-sam, and the other is named after the cobra - Naga-vamsam[85]. In South India generally, the image of the serpent, whose imagery is widely revered in the Travancore region, is usually placed on the northwest side of gardens and plantations. In the Aboriginal, or less Hinduised people in India, the serpent is worshipped as widely as the Sun itself[86]. In other castes there is a distinct fourfold division resembling those of Peru such as the Rona, an Oriya hill people. Among these people the septs or clans of these divisions are related to clan status where the highest is Kora, the Sun; and the others are typically Bhag, tiger; Nag, cobra; Khinbudi, bear, and Matsya, fish[87].

Among the Nayars, the great military caste of South India, during the marriage ceremonies the women worship the Sun[88]. A sub-caste of the higher status Amabalavarsis are the Pisharati who make flower garlands for the temple. When a child has reached the age of between four and six months it is first brought out from its house to see the Sun by its maternal uncle[89]. On the Malabar coast of South India the Tandan caste have a custom where on the first Sunday in January, after the Winter Solstice, they offer cooked food to the Rising Sun[90].

Among the Paraiyans the Sun god is their principal deity. They claim that their first caste ancestor was a Brahman who had been cursed by Brahma, the Supreme Vedic and later Hindu deity. To remove this curse the Sun gave to them, as the descendants of the Brahman, objects to worship representing forty-eight thousand deities and eight special gods[91]. Other of the tribes such as the Bhuiyas, who identify the Sun as the Supreme Being, consider the Moon as his younger brother, instead of his wife as some others do[92].

In many myths in India the Sun is looked upon as a godling, or hero, that once lived on Earth and was rewarded with a mansion in the Sun or as its ruler. As a godling the "man-in-the-Sun" was known as Suraj, Surya or Suraj Narayan or as an incarnation of Vishnu and in these terms the Sun god is considered to emulate that of Helios among the Ancient Greeks[93]. The worship of the Sun is also fragmentised and some worship him in the morning at sunrise, some at

8.051 : A priest with a traditional circular gold pectoral representing the Sun similar to those found in South America. Lhasa, Tibet, Early 20th., century, A.D.

8.052 : Finely modelled ritual urn showing a ruler or priest with a pectoral of the type found among the Toradja, in Indonesia traditionally. Moche, North Coast Peru, 200-600 A.D.

8.053 : An apron form of pectoral reflecting that of the Toradja in Celebes and dual headdress similar to those found in South America. Lhota Naga, Assam, North East India, Early 20th., century, A.D.

8.056 : Pectorals appearing to be based upon those found among the Toradja and other Celebes peoples and the Nagas of Assam. Aboriginal tribes, Taiwan, Early 20th., century, A.D.

ALGVAZILMAIOR
CHACNAICAMAIOC
LVRIN CVZCO

8.054 : Inca noble with an apron pectoral similar to those traditional among the Toradjas of Celebes and the Nagas of Assam. Note the coca bag at the top of the staff. Inca Dynasty, Poma de Ayala drawing, Post Conquest.

8.055 : Pectorals of a type found in the Philippines but also among the Nagas of Assam and the Inca of South America. Note the embroidered caps similar to those found in Ancient Bolivia and Peru. Toradja, Celebes, Indonesia, Early 20th., century, A.D.

mid-day, and others still in the morning while some worship all three aspects, with certain sects only eating when the Sun shines[94].

Myths preserved by some of the South Indian castes are highly reminiscent of those in Australia and South America. One of these preserved in the oral traditions from the Jalia caste, where the Sun, Moon and Venus figure predominantly in their pantheon, noting that stars and planets are the Moon's children and were always in danger of being eaten by the Sun[95]. These resemble the eclipse myths found in the rest of India[96], Mexico and Central and South America. The image of the Sun in India is of a golden being with a golden beard and hair who lives within the Sun. In a few references he is portrayed as a dwarfish man with a body colour of "burnished copper and reddish eyes". In other descriptions he is said to have a neck like a tortoise and this allows him to extend to all quarters of heaven to illumine it[97]. According to the Kurma Purana, Surya had four wives, Samjna (Knowledge), Rajni (Queen), Prabha (Light), and Chaya (Shadow), and these were probably, originally related to the four quarters of the sky. In other myths he is considered to be the husband of the dawn, Usas, and he is also spoken off as the

498

"child of the dawn"[98]. The name of Surya comes from the root sur or svar and from the same root come the name for heaven - svarga.

The Sun and the Four Quarters and the Calendar

In references to the Sun related to the four quarters the Satapatha Brahmana notes that the concept is a very ancient one since it is stated in this reputedly oldest of the recorded Vedas that the Sun is, " 'The four-cornered', - four-cornered, indeed, is he who shines yonder, for the quarters are his corners: therefore he says, 'Four-cornered'"[99]. This clearly indicates the Sun in Vedic myth and texts as being essentially related to the four cardinal points, or "four quarters", as apparently so in Inca myth and cosmology reflected in their adoration of the Sun and naming their Empire the Land of the four Quarters. This special emphasis on this relationship between Sun and cardinal points is reflected also in their arrogation as the Sons of the Sun.

The Gold Disk - the Sun - Gods and Priests

In many solar orientated civilisations the ritual ornaments worn have often reflected the adoration of the Sun as chief deity and in the Americas this orb is often represented by a gold pectoral disk. This was also so anciently among the Brahmans and this fact is recorded in the oldest known Vedic text, the Satapatha Brahmana dating to about the middle of the first millennium B.C. An extract from this book reflects the associations of the golden pectoral disk in India: "1) He hangs a gold plate (around his neck), and wears it; for that gold plate is truth, and the truth is able to sustain that (fire): by means of the truth the gods carried it, and by means of the truth does he now carry it."

"2) Now that truth is the same as that yonder sun. It is a gold (plate), for gold is light, and he (the sun) is the light; gold is immortality, and he is immortality. It (the plate) is round, for he (the sun) is round. It has twenty-one knobs, for he is twenty-first. He wears it with the knobs outside, for the knobs are his (the sun's) rays, and his rays are outside."

"3) And as to why he puts on and wears the gold plate; - that plate is yonder sun, and man, in his human form, is unable to sustain that fire: it is only in this (solar or divine) form that he bears that (divine) form."

"4) And, again, why he puts on and wears the gold plate; - this fire is seed poured out here; and the gold plate means vital energy (or brilliance) and vigour: he thus lays vital energy and vigour into that seed."

"5) And, again, why he puts on and wears the gold plate; - the gods now were afraid lest the Rakshas, the fiends, should destroy here that (Agni) of theirs. They made that (plate), yonder sun, to be his (Agni's) protector (standing) by his side, for the gold plate is yonder sun: and in like manner does this (Sacrificer) now make that (plate) to be his Agni's) protector by his side."

"6) It is sown up in a black antelope's skin; for the black antelope skin is the sacrifice, and the sacrifice is able to sustain that (Agni): by means of the sacrifice the gods carried him, and by means of the sacrifice he now carries him; - with the hair (inside), for the hair are the metres, and the metres are indeed able to sustain him: by the gods carried him, and by the metres he now carries him."

"7) It is sown into the black and white hair, for these two are forms of the rik (hymn-verse) and the sama (hymn-tune), and the rik and the saman are indeed able to sustain him (Agni): by the rik and saman the gods carried him, and by the rik and saman he now carries him. The hempen sling of the gold plate is a triple (cord): ... ."

"8) He wears it over his navel; for that gold plate is yonder sun, and he (stands) over the navel (of the earth and sky)."

"9) And, again, why over the navel, - below the navel is the seed, the power of procreation, and

8.057 : Sun with legs similar to those found in North America and in the myths of India. Bronze, Peru, 1st., millennium, B.C.

8.058 : Ceramic decoration depicting the Sun with legs probably indicating its track along an orbit. Moche, North Coast Peru, 200-600 B.C.

8.060 : Sun with legs found widely as an image in South Peru, and the Spiro Mounds in Ohio. Milagro Culture, South Ecuador, 800-1200 A.D.

8.059 : A "turtle" clearly reflecting the Sun disk with its two legs similar to the iconography found in South America. Spiro Mound, Ohio, Eastern USA, 800-1350 A.D.

the gold plate represents vital energy and vigour: (he does so, thinking) 'Lest the gold plate burn up my seed, my power of procreation, my vital energy and vigour."

"10) And, again, why over the navel; - sacrificially purer is that part of the animal (victim) which is above the navel, and more in contact with ordure is that part below the navel: he thus carries it (the plate) by means of that part of the animal which is sacrificially purer."[100]

The twenty one knobs (rays) of the Sun are given as the sum of the twelve months of the year, the five seasons, and three worlds plus the Sun itself adding to twenty-one[101]. The rituals dedicated to Agni as the sacred fire in the Sun continue and include a few other verses that are of interest:

"27) Now then the (mystic) correspondence (of the number of objects to the nature of Agni), - the seat, the fire-pan, the sling of the gold plate, the fire, and the gold plate, - these amount to six; - six seasons are the year, and the year is Agni: as great as Agni is, as great as is his measure, so great does this become. Two pads, that makes eight, - the Gayatri has eight syllables, and Agni is Gayatra: as great as Agni is, as great as is his measure, so great does this become."

"28) Now the total correspondence, - four feet and four boards (of the seat), the netting, and the sling of the gold plate, or any other corded netting; after that the pan and fire, and the gold plate, - that makes thirteen; - thirteen months are year, and the year is Agni: as great as Agni is, as great as is his measure, so great this become."

In the performance of the ritual these required items are considered necessary and it is noted in the Second Brahmana: "1) Standing he puts on that (gold plate), - for that gold plate is yonder sun, and yonder sun stands, as it were; and moreover, while standing one is stronger. (He does so) standing with his face towards the north-east: ... ."[102]

It is remarkable that this Sun disk represents the exact form and intent of identical disks in South America but even of more interest is the reference in paragraph 8 where it is stipulated that the gold disk is the Sun that stands on the "navel" that clearly is intended to link the Earth with the Sky. Clearly this is imagery that finds its exact parallel at Tiahuanaco and later at Cuzco where each of these centres was considered the Navel of the World in exactly the terms intended to unify or focus symbolically the polarities of Earth and Sky in the Andean world. It hardly seems credible that these Ancient Andean peoples developed the same philosophic concepts including terms so exactly similar without inheriting much of it from India and, or the Ancient Middle East.

The Sun, the Sacred Mountain and Solar Orbits

The earliest philosophic constructs in the Ancient Middle East reflect several views of the cosmic beliefs associated with the Sun. That of the earliest Zoroastrian sources preserved in the

Pahlavi texts notes:

"3) Of Mount Albruz it is declared, that around the world and Mount Terak, which is the middle of the world, the revolution of the sun is like a moat around the world; it turns back in a circuit owing to the enclosure (var) of Mount Alburz around Terak.

"4) As it is said that it is the Terak of Alburz from behind which my sun and moon and stars return again.

"5) For there a hundred and eighty apertures (rogin) in the east, and a hundred and eighty in the west, through Alburz; and the sun, every day, comes in through an aperture, and goes out through an aperture; and the whole connection and motion of the moon and constellations and planets is with it: every day it always illumines (or warms) three regions (keshvar) and a half, as is evident to the eyesight.

6) And twice in every year the day and night are equal, for on the original attack, when it (the sun) went forth from its first degree (khurdak), the day and night were equal, it was the season of spring; when it arrives at the first degree of Kalakang (cancer) the time of day is greatest, it is the beginning of summer; when it arrives at the sign (khurdak) Taraduk (Libra) the day and night is equal, it is the beginning of autumn; when it arrives at the sign Vahik (Capricorn) the night is a maximum, it is the beginning of winter; and when it arrives at Varak (Aries) the night and day have again become equal, as when it went forth from Varak.

"7) So that when it comes back to Varak, in three hundred and sixty days and the five Gatha days, it goes in and comes out through one and the same aperture; the aperture is not mentioned, for if it had been mentioned the demons would have known the secret, and been able to introduce disaster."

"8) From there where the sun comes on on the longest day to where it comes on on the shortest day is the east region Savah; from there which it comes on on the shortest day to where it goes off on the shortest day is the direction of the south regions Fradadafsh and Vidasafish; from where it goes in on the shortest day to where it goes in on the longest day is the west region Arzah; from there where it comes in on the longest day to there where it goes in on the longest day are the north regions Vorubarst and Vorugarst.

"9) When the sun comes on, it illumines (or warms) the regions of Savah, Fradadafsh, Vidasafsh, and half of Khvantras; when it goes in on the dark side, it illumines the regions of Khvantras; when it is day it is night there."

Professor Max Müller notes of these texts in his commentary: "The five supplementary days added to the last twelve months, of thirty days each, to complete the year. For these days no additional apertures are provided in Alburz, and the sun appears to have the choice of either of the two centre apertures out of the 180 on each side of the world. This arrangement seems to indicate that the idea of the apertures is older than the rectification of the calendar that added the five Gatha days to an original year of 360 days"[103].

These textual references indicates the Sun moving in and out and across apertures and appears to be derived from the ancient Sun circles in megalithic structures that would reflect this apprehension of the Sun through the day. From this it is likely that the Inca, and pre-Inca solar pillars derive from closely similar practises in Eurasia developed from, and in conjunction with these megalithic monuments. Such cultural transfers are emphasised by Professor Muller's references to the five Gatha days, identical to the Mandaean Parwaniia of five days, and the five unlucky days of the Mayans in Central America.

In a curious reference to the disappearance of the Sun after sunset it is stated in one part of the Satapatha Brahmana that the fiery globe "enters the wind" and is recorded as follows: "Now, when that fire goes out, it is wafted up in the wind (air), whence people say of it, 'It has expired,' for it is wafted up in the wind. And when the sun sets it enters the wind, and so does

8.061 : The Sun disk being suspended by a deity by a rope depicting the fundamental four cardinal points and the intermediate directions from the "Sun-God Tablet" record-ing the restoration of the Sun temple at Sippar. This is probably the origin of "noosing" the Sun in Polynesia and Peru. Babylon, Iraq, c9th., century, B.C.

the moon; and the quarters are established in the wind, and from out of the wind they issue again. And when he who knows this passes away from this world, he passes into the fire by his speech, into the sun by his eye, into the moon by his mind, and into the quarters by his ear, and into the wind by his breath; and being composed thereof, he becomes whichever of these deities he chooses, and is at rest."[104].

The text appears to indicate that the sun was not considered philosophically to become the wind but be "waft-ed" by it after sun set. Correspondingly, since the wind was associated with the soul of mankind, it was the medium through which the Sun transited through the night after sun-set. This night phase section of the orbit corresponded to the Underworld where, carried by the wind noted elsewhere, the soul of the deceased was destined to remain.

The idea that there was an actual deity dwelling within the Sun is emphasised in the Brihaddaranyaka Upanishad, from the Aryan Vedas, and this record note these references as follows: "Now of the person in that (solar) orb Bhuh is the head, for the head is one, and that syllable is one; Bhuvah the two arms, for the arms are two. And these syl-lables are two; Svar the foot, for the feet are two, and these syllables are two. Its secret name is Ahar (day), and he who knows this, destroys (hanti) evil and leaves (gahati) it."[105].

This deity or spirit within the Sun is a very ancient concept and the name Ahar appears to point to the Ancient Near East, however, it is remarkable in this Vedic text that in describing this deity he is considered to have two arms and two feet, but there is no reference to an anthropomorphic body. For most Western people reading this it would be assumed in imagery of this type that the deity was meant to be a man, "with two arms and feet", and sitting or standing within the orb of the Sun. Others peoples, however, do not necessarily take the same line but attempt to interpret what they hear, rather than read, where literal and iconographic interpretations are more likely to be evidence of cultural transfer than logical adaptions. The text actually describes a body-less figure consisting of a head with two arms and legs, and the visualisation of Ahar therefore is more likely, as the orb, Bhuh, to be a disk with two arms and legs. In fact there are representations interpreting this or similar iconographic references of this figure within the Sun and these are par-ticularly noted as evident in North and South America (*8.057/8*). There is no absolute proof that this visualisation was transferred from India but the South American images match so exactly the description in the texts that transfer seems likely. This appears to be the case even accounting for variation through the retelling to reach the opposite side of the world and that this, along with so many other similar or identical cultural references, is probably one of a myriad elements absorbed from Ancient India.

Identification with the Sun as a being was important in early Vedic India by the Brahmans since the Sun was considered a giver-of-life and because there was considered to be a deity within the Sun, identification with this being was the focus during the sacred rituals. In the same Vedic book a verse identifies the "Self" with that deity within the Sun and here, the high-est caste in India - the Brahmans, relate that it is the highest part of one's being that is so identi-fied. In Vedic society in India the highest castes were identified with the head of the anthropo-morphic Brahma, and the lowest with the feet and in social subdivisions the priests are consid-

8.062 : A deity in his sky canoe typical of a reed boat of the type found also among the Maoris, on the coast of Peru and Lake Titicaca. Babylonia, 2nd., millennium, B.C.

8.063 : The gods in their canoe depicted in the reed marshes of South Mesopotamia (Iraq). Akad Dynasty, Late 3rd., millennium, B.C.

ered higher even than the ruler. Priests were of lower status except in more established surviving non-Hinduised societies or among non-Aryans. In the strict Vedic interpretation it is the priestly caste who are the highest, but in reality this only applied where they held absolute sway. It follows naturally, therefore, that the ruler himself was identified with the Sun and this became emphasised where the Sun was considered the Supreme Being or Creator. In relating aspects and attributes of the highest Self of one's own being the same texts relates: "8) …. He is also he who wars, the Sun, hidden by the thousand-eyed golden egg, as one fire by another. He is to be thought after, he is to be sought after. … (See him) who assumes all forms, the golden, who knows all things, who ascends highest, alone in his splendour, and warms us; the thousand-rayed, who abides in a hundred places, the spirit of all creatures, the Sun rises."

"9) "Therefore he who by knowing this has become the Self of both Breath and Sun, mediates (while meditating on them) on his Self - this meditation, the mind thus absorbed in these acts, is praised by the wise."[106].

The identification of the highest Self, or the ruler, and the Sun with the "World Egg" is repeated in Vedic texts and noted in another as follows: "As a lamp burns so long as the vessel that holds the wick is filled with oil, these two, the Self and the bright Sun, remain so long as the egg (of the world) and he who dwells within it hold together."[107]. The association of gold, animal sacrifices, and the number five are inextricably linked in the Vedic rituals where the Brahman priest presiding at the sacred fire is emphasised in the record of the Satapatha Brahmana where it relates: "4) "He makes an underlayer of ghee (clarified butter)(in the offering-ladle): this he makes a type of earth; he then puts a chip of gold thereon: this he makes a type of fire; he then puts the omentum thereon: this he makes a type of air; and he then puts a chip of gold thereon: this he makes a type of sun; and what (ghee) he pours upon it, that he makes a type of the heavens. This, then, is that five-portioned omentum, - fivefold is the sacrifice, fivefold the sacrificial animal, and five seasons there are in the year: this is why the omentum consists of five portions."[108].

An interesting reference found repeatedly in the Americas is that the sky was considered to have been constructed as a "web", frequently associated with a divine spider. In India it is the Sun who wove the "web" by its many orbits through the sky and this is recorded in a text as follows: "22) 'To the web-weaver,' - the web-weaver, doubtless, is he that shines yonder, for he moves along these worlds as if along a web; and the Pravarga also is that (sun): thus it is him he thereby pleases, and therefore he says, 'To the web-weaver'"[109].

The Sun is, therefore, indicated as the divine spider in the philosophies of the Ancient West Asia and later, as here, recorded Vedic India. However, it is clear that references to the divine spider have become dissociated from their original contexts in the transfer across the Pacific to the Americas and are considered as separate myth cycles that are more usually opposed in principle to the light and the Sun in particular. This in fact tends to have original references in Ancient Iranian myths where the planets were considered malevolent and aspects of these are noted earlier in this work.

Surya as the Sun and Sky Serpents - Rahu as the Eclipse Serpent
In the earliest rituals of the Vedic Aryans the three supreme deities were Agni the god of fire, Vayu, the god of wind, and Surya, the Sun. In a rite associated with the full-moon day of the

Sravana month sacrificial foods were offered and salutations rendered to the serpents associated with each of these sky deities and a section in illustration notes:

9) "To the lord of the serpents belonging to Agni, of the yellow terrestrial ones, svaha!"

"To the lord of the white serpents belonging to Vayu, of the arial ones, svaha!"

"To the lord of the overpowering serpents belonging to Surya, of the celestial ones, svaha!"[110].

The importance of the sky serpents is underlined by the worship of the Nagas, or serpent deities in all aspects of Hindu myths, but is less evident in the earlier Vedic myths above noted. One of the most important in Vedic and later Hindu myths is the serpent associated with the ecliptic, and the eclipse, Rahu, considered extensively elsewhere[111]. In the earliest myths Rahu is known only as a head, perhaps disembodied in myths no longer remembered or recorded and perhaps a myth woven around a trophy head from its origins in the Ancient Middle East. The demon Rahu was particularly damned for attempting to swallow the Sun and Moon and thereby associated in ancient thought with the greatly feared eclipse and therefore believed to evil. In the Upanishads, one of the earliest sections of the Vedas captures the association of Rahu and the Moon is recorded: "From the dark (the Brahman of the heart) I come to the nebulous (the world of the Brahman), from the nebulous to the dark, shaking off all evil, as a horse shakes his hairs, and as the moon frees herself from the mouth of Rahu (at the eclipse). ..."[112].

It can be seen here that another aspect, so clearly evident in many surviving elements of Peruvian iconography, relate to the serpent belt noted elsewhere in this work, but clearly reflecting the Solar and Lunar eclipses. This is a further example where the broad extent of the Sun worship recorded of the Incas is so closely exemplified in the texts and imagery of Ancient India.

The Sun - Our Father

Many references in the Inca liturgy, rituals and expressions are highly reminiscent of those of Vedic India. The Inca is frequently recorded as referring to the solar disk as "Our Father, the Sun" and in the Aryan Vedic rites of the early Brahmans the presiding Brahmin priest implores: "'Thou art our father!' - for he who shines yonder is indeed the father, and the pravarga is that (sun): it is him he thus gratifies, and therefore he says, 'Thou art our father: be thou our father!' - 'Reverence be unto thee: injure me not!' - it is a blessing he thereby invokes."[113]. The Brahmans were considered the most religious of men where every aspect of their life was governed by strict rules and rites relating to every action in life as well as religious ritual. This extended to prescribed strictures where every breath taken and the food and water eaten and drunk as well as the relationships between the Brahmans themselves and extended to all other classes of people. It was also noted among the Ayar Incas that they were the most religious of people and the fact that their rituals were so similar to the Brahmans seems to further indicate that this was due to their forebears having migrated from India and in so doing transferred their cultural inheritance from the Aryan Brahmans in India noted elsewhere in this work.

In Vedic India the Sun is considered the counterpart of Agni, the God of Fire, who is one of the three chief deities in the Vedas worshipped by the Aryan Indians, and where Agni is represented as the fire within the Earth and the Sun was seen as the celestial fire[114]. The Sun was considered as the gateway to the gods[115], and this reflects the zodiac as the celestial vortice through which celestial influences were focused into the world. It was through this vortice that the soul returned on its journey to reach the abode of the gods or ancestors after death. In some creation myths it was said that at the beginning of time the cosmic egg came into being and split into two parts, one gold and the other silver. The earth was created from silver half and the sky from the golden half, and the golden half, the sky, and was ruled over by the Sun, while the silver part, the earth, was governed by the Moon[116]. It is noted in the ancient texts, the Upanishads, that the Sun rises entering the eastern quarter and sustains all the beings of the east. It then illumines the south, west and north and all that lies between them, and sustains all beings with its rays[117]. These aspects of the Sun are noted more fully in the later part of this chapter so that it is only necessary here to record that this element of Solar worship appears to be closely similar to beliefs found anciently in Peru.

Sun-Zodiac

In the Inca zodiac there were considered to be twenty-four compartments and this appears to reflect the characteristic dual aspect philosophic constructs of India where all cosmology was composed of all aspects were based on a light rising half, and a dark descending half, undoubtedly derived from the earlier lunar zodiac. Each month was considered to consist of two weeks when the Sun was rising and the second half when it was descending, resulting in 12 solar months but consisting of 12 light halves and 12 dark halves, 24 in all.

Sun as the Fire God Agni - and the Inca Inti-huatana

In an finely carved stone tablet from Sippar, dating to about 870 B.C., the golden disk of Samas, or Shamash, is shown suspended by a thick rope from the sky arch held by two deities before the king of Babylon[118]. The depiction reflects the fundamental belief that the Sun's disk was controlled by deities in the sky and its clearly depicted divisions into two sets of four indicate the relationship with the cardinal points related to its orbit designated as the four corners or quarters of the Sun or the Earth as a result of its cycle. It is probably from examples such as this iconography that transferred ideas relating that the Sun could be tied to a "hitching post" or could be caught by a noose, characteristic in Polynesian and South America myths derives.

Among the Polynesians, early recorded by William Ellis, it was said that Maui caught the rays of the sinking Sun and tied them to a tree until he had finished building the sacred marae (ceremonial platform) since it had to be completed before sunset. This allowed him the extra time he needed to complete his task[119]. This same tradition appears to be the basis for the "Inti-huatana", the "Hitching Place of the Sun" in Peru.

The term for the Sun as Shamash is Semitic, (Akkadian), but in the myths of their predecessors, the Sumerians, he was called Utu. In the later Aryan Kassites Dynasty he was called Surias or Sah[120] the former of these two names being transferred to India to become the Vedic and Hindu Surya. In early records of the fire religions of Iran, in Mazdaeanism that underwent revisionism to become Zoroastrianism, the Sun was identified with Mithra[121]. It is said when Ohrmazd (Ahura Mazda) made the world of light he created the "firmament", the universal sky with its myriad stars. He appointed four major stars, or clusters, to rule over each of its quarters, Tistar (Sirius) over the East; Satves (Scorpio) over the South; Vanand (Vega) over the West, and Haptoring (the Great Bear) over the North. Over all he ensured control by placing the Pole Star, as the "Nail in the middle of the Sky". Within this universal space he created the zodiac in the form of a wheel, and then the Sun, Moon and planets[122]. These were considered "maleficent beings" associated as they were with the zodiac and were tied to chariot, or the brilliance of the Sun, to prevent them from doing "excessive harm". The planets were also considered to be maleficent and these were "bound by two ropes" to the Sun and Moon and "clothed in the light of Ohrmazd"[123]. In other texts the Sun and Moon, are typically depicted and described as boats or canoes usually carrying the "man-in-the-Sun", or solar deity[124].

In Mazdaean philosophy the deity Orhmazd was considered the "Original Man" and that he created mankind as imitations of himself or in his own image. He was said to have created man from five principles; body, spirit (breath), soul, prototype and Fravahr. The body is here considered the corporeal reality as a person appears to another, while spirit was the life-breath and related to the wind, Vayu, earlier noted. The prototype was associated with the Sun and situated in the heart and no doubt gave rise to a number of myths regarding the miniature "familiar spirit" said to be associated with the individual human being called in Nias[125] Tanoana, and among the Kwakiutl the Tamanoas[126]. The Fravahr was the part of being associated with each person that derives from Orhmazd and protects man against the attack of demons[127].

The ropes, cords, binding or capturing of the Sun in a noose, so clearly indicated in these myths will be of more interest in a later chapter. These mythical associations with the Sun are reflected in Polynesia and South America and will be considered with the epic voyages of the Polynesian in some of their oral histories.

The Problem of the Incan Punchao and the Sun God Inti

The Inca retained two names for the Sun god, Inti and Punchao. It has been shown that Punchao was thought to be an aspect of the Sun at the summer solstice and yet there appears to be little etymological connection between them. The same can also be said of the Sun at the Winter Solstice were he is identified with Viracocha. This suggests that at least one, or both of these deities was adopted into the pantheon when the Incas were in their ascendancy from the tribes they had conquered or had assimilated one or either before that time. The term Viracocha has been shown to have close links with the Colla (Aymara) people located around Lake Titicaca in Bolivia. Punchao, however, has been considered as an Andean term referring to the Sun[128] and requires some investigation.

Miles Poindexter, Reginald Enock, and other earlier researchers noted the close similarity of Punchao to the Polynesian term for chief Ahau, Au, Hau, Sau and most telling of all to the same term Chau of the Caroline Islands in Micronesia. This term Ahau for chief or ruler is also found among the Maya[129], however, perhaps more significant is that the term Chau as Chao is the term for chief among the Shans in Burma (Myanmar). The Shan, many centuries ago, migrated from Yunnan and Szechuan in Southern China from the region associated with the Na Khi or Lolos people in that region.

Bernabe Cobo mentions the term Punchao several times, and first notes it when referring to their most revered image in the Coricancha, the Temple of the Sun at Cuzco, and he records that it "was entirely made of the finest gold". He describes it in the form of a human face with rays extending around it and notes that it is exactly the way that the Spanish themselves depict the Sun. This golden disk faced the east and was so positioned that it caught and reflected the Sun's rays when it rose in the morning and Cobo particularly notes that there was a golden chair provided for this Punchau[130]. He describes the meaning of the term "Punchau" as "the day" but Arriaga notes it, probably more correctly, as meaning the name of the Sun during the day and that the name of Inti also applied to the Sun[131].

On the "high hill" known as Chuquipalta there were three images carved of stone representing Pachayachachic (Creator - Viracocha), Inti Illapa (the Thunder) and Punchau as the Sun[132]. This was considered a very sacred shrine and children were sacrificed and figurines offered, and high quality clothing made and burnt as sacrifices to these deities[133]. Here Punchao is more specifically noted as the Sun while Inti is seen to be associated with the Thunder. This raises the question of whether Inti was originally the Sun god and only later became separated from the Thunder deity and adopted as an aspect of the Sun in evolution becoming more prominent in later Inca dynasties. Another term for Punchao as Son of the Sun was Churi-Inti[134] and this term appears to equate with Apu-Inti. In other records he is seen as an aspect of Viracocha[135].

More recent researchers have noted that in less well-known records Punchao formed a triad with Inti-Guauqui and Apu-Inti[136] and this reflects Cobo noting that there was a triad of images associated with the Sun in the Temple of the Sun at Cuzco[137]. The group, however, has not previously been noted perhaps for an obvious reason and that is that each of these terms include a known deity, heroic, or chiefly name in Polynesia, the nearest landfall to the West and North West of the Peruvian coast. The affix Chao, or Chau, already noted appearing in several forms in Polynesia and Micronesia and in South East Asia in Burma; Apu is also a term found meaning chiefly in both Peru and Polynesia. The term Guauqui, appears to be the same as Gagua, the Sun, in Colombia to the north of Peru, and this surely has the same origin as Tagua-paca[138], a name for the Creator, Sun or Thunder god around Lake Titicaca. But the phrase Inti-Guauqui appears to be associated with Venus and the Aymara Thunder god Thunapa[139], although the term is thought to be specifically Incan[140] and a special "mocha" or offering was made to him[141]. Another term appears to represent the same deity as Tagu-pac[142], referring to the eagle, and these variations seem to lead to an identification with Taga, Taghar, Tagaro and to Tangaroa, perhaps the best known god of Polynesia. The terms Taupota and Taupaca also appear in Melanesia even more distinctly than Polynesia[143]. The fact that there was a sacred chair or stool associated with Punchao suggests that there was an intimate association in iconography between the Inca ruler as personification of the Sun and the sacred stool on which he alone was allowed to sit. In fact there were a number of cultures who maintained this form of status symbol, not least the Polynesians, and this is reflected earlier in the sacred platforms or elaborate raised platforms or thrones found in India and South East Asia denoting status. Apu is another term for chief in Polynesia and found also among the Maya.

Tagua-paca as a deity name, appears therefore to have shared aspects with Punchao, and it has been shown that Tahua was the fundamental term used for the four quarters of the name Tahuantin-suyu. These names are related to the four winds, where Tahua or Pahua was the name of the wind deity in Mesopotamia, India and known as Paowa (Pao-wa or Pa-ahua) in Polynesia. Taguapaca is also identified, as earlier noted with the eagle, usually emphasising the connection with a Sky god, and this again links to Tahua or Paowa, the wind, and Tangaroa the Polynesian Sky god.

It was noted be early researchers that the term for the Naga clan elders' platform, these being considered sacred, the Tahuba, corresponded to the Tahuba, the sacred dancing ground in Polynesia, also called Tahoa. The stool appears among the Nagas of Assam to denote chiefly status and it is therefore unlikely that the term for the Inca stool, Duho[144], was a coincidence, being virtually the same as that of the Nagas, Daho[145] and Tehuba as a burial platform[146]. These elements are considered elsewhere in this work.

By extension Punchao may have broader references since in Australia the revered deity, Pundjal was considered a deity of great power. In several Peruvian references Punchao as Apu-Inti is associated with Venus, but among the Australian Aborigines Pundjel was a great creator figure[147] and this deity is known by this name in South East Australia. Punchao is also associated with Viracocha who, in the creation myths, destroyed the First World because the people began to behave evilly and he decided to cause a great flood to be rid of them. In a myth from the South East of Australia the Pund-Jel became angry when the people began to behave wickedly so he caused great winds and storms to rage across the land. When all was confusion he descended to Earth and with his great knife began to attack the people and cut then to pieces, but, although dismembered the pieces themselves continued to live. Each of the pieces moved as a worm does and they resembled snow. They were drawn up into the clouds and were then carried randomly across the landscape and dropped to earth as the clouds being then blown about. Pundjel caused the pieces to drop where he pleased but the good men and women he transformed into stars[148].

This Aboriginal myth bears striking resemblances to the elements of the Viracocha myth earlier noted even paralleling the references after destroying the original population with the flood where he then to travel across the country and calls the new inhabitants from certain places across the landscape. There are numerous parallels in the myths of Aboriginal Australia and the Andes but also between Aboriginal Australia and India and these will be considered further in later chapters.

In Indonesia, a large "stump-shaped" rock in North Borneo was called Batu Punggul and was said in Dusun and Murut folklore to have been a great rock that had extended into the sky when the world was only inhabited by seven brothers and their sister. Rocks such as these tend to mark the centre of the world in mythology and the fact that there are seven brothers tends to reflect largely forgotten elements of the seven sacred spheres in the cosmology of Asia where the Sun is the corresponding centre of the solar system[149]. The term batu means stone and derives from the term bat and baetyl in the Ancient Near East.

Pushan and the Stone Circles called Pun

In Southern India the first European researchers became fascinated by the Todas and their unique culture located in the Nilgiri Hills on the plateau of the same name near Ootacamund south of Mysore. Many believe that they were lineal descendants of a very ancient migration from Sumeria long before the more famous migrations of the Aryans from the Iranian plateau in the early first millennium B.C. They were, and largely still are cattle herders, and their social life revolved around the sacred milking shed and the many rituals centred on their cattle stocks. The relationship of the Todas with their environment and the deities that inhabited it was especially interesting and recorded by their earliest researchers, as the celebrated Victorian historian and anthropologist W.H.R. Rivers noted: "The Toda gods are definitely anthropomorphic beings, who are believed to have lived in this world before man existed. Both man and buffalo were created by the gods, and the Todas seem to picture a time when gods, men, and buffalos lived together on the Nilgiri Hills, and the gods ruled men." He further notes, "The earliest of the gods was Pithi, who was born in a cave, and the Todas and many of their buffaloes were created by his son On and his wife. Later death came to the gods inn the person of Puv, the son of On, and On followed Puv to the world of the dead, called Amnodr." Once these gods had departed from the world it was left to a goddess, Teikirzi, to govern the Todas and she too is considered to have a special hill designated as her dwelling.

Rivers notes the broad hierarchy of gods and the environment that they inhabited as: "There seems to have been many other gods contemporaneous with On and Teikirzi, and certain of these are believed to have been related to these deities and especially to Tiekirzi. The gods are believed to be very numerous: the Todas speak of the 1,600 gods, the 1,800 gods, but it would seem that these expressions are used in the sense of 'an infinite number'. The gods are believed to have held their councils, meeting on some special hill, to which each god came from his own hill-top. The hill of Polkab, near Kanodrs, and the village of Miuni are both renowned as meeting places of the gods."

"There is a very definite association between the Toda gods and the hills of the Nilgiri plateau. Nearly every one of the gods has his hill where he dwells, and often when speaking of the gods the Todas identify the god with the hill. There are two river gods, Teipakh and Pakhwar, associated with the two chief streams of the district, but there is some reason to believe that even these gods have their hills where they sometimes live, while at other times they inhabit or are identified with their streams."[150]

The deities appear similarly associated with hills as the Andean peoples, Uru, Aymara and Quechua, did so with their ancestral gods and they too were considered as ancestors, or "Grandfathers". In the Americas stone circles, usually considered to be related to the zodiac or the Sun's annual cycle are found long before the Incas in both North and South America and appear to have been revered from the earliest high cultures in the Andes (*10.042-5*). Among the

064 : ...glets extend-...in front of...ears charac-...stic of early ...ddhist depic-...1 but inherit-...from the ...ient Middle ...st. Domoko, ...nese ...kestan, Early ...t millennium,

8.065 : Fine ceramic portrait head showing braided hair at each side of the face. Nazca, South Coastal Peru, 200-600 A.D.

8.066 : Double braids long traditional in the Ancient Near and Middle East through into recent times around the marine states of the Arabian peninsular. Rwala Bedouin, Arabia, Early 20th., century, A.D.

8.067 : A braided wig typical of those known in Orissa in North India in the 7-8th., century, A.D. Coastal Peru, 1st., millenium, A.D.

068 : Braided hair char-...eristic in New Guinea dis-...yed by this Baramura man ...possibly introduced by ...ddle Eastern mariners sail-...from South Asia via ...lanesia to South America. ...w Guinea, Melanesia, ...ly 20th., century, A.D.

8.070 : Braided hair traditional from long before the Inca Dynasty in the Andes and Coastal Peru. Aymama, Bolivia, Early 20th., century, A.D.

8.071 : Braided hairstyle typical of the Amnanga similar in appearance to that of the Peruvian Incas. Marind-anim, Papua New Guinea Highlands, Early 20th., century, A.D.

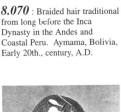

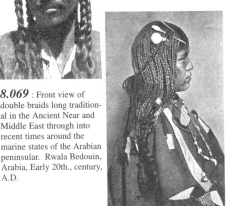

8.069 : Front view of double braids long traditional in the Ancient Near and Middle East through into recent times around the marine states of the Arabian peninsular. Rwala Bedouin, Arabia, Early 20th., century, A.D.

8.072 : Braided hair extending to the knees traditional among the women in the Baramura tribe a century ago. Fly River region, New Guinea, Early 20th., century, A.D.

Todas stone circles are similarly associated as Rivers notes: "There is one important feature which is said to be common to all the hills inhabited by deities. They all have on their summits the stone circles which the Todas call pun."[151].

Rivers noted that the Todas, although revering the circles, appeared indifferent to anyone grave robbing or digging within their boundaries. This has led to the speculation that these megalithic circles in fact pre-dated the Todas, and their lack of interest was because they were not considered by them as their ancestral heritage, and yet, as Rivers noted, the Todas did appear to link the monumental circles with their gods in the hill on which they were erected. Rivers concluded that: "There seem to be three chief possibilities. One, that the cairns are Toda remains and that the association of the stone circles above them with the presence of the god is the last surviving relic of the fact. The second is that when the Todas came to the Nilgiri hills they found mysterious stone circles on certain hills, which marked out these hills as possessing features out of the common, and that this gave them a sanctity which led to the idea that they were inhabited

8.073 : Akimbo pose characteristic of many deities in Ancient India, here the Hindu Sun god Surya. Anandmata Temple, Nosal, North India, 8th., century, A.D.

by gods. A third possibility is that the same peculiarities which led the original builders of the circles to choose certain hills also led the Todas to choose them as the abodes of their deities, and that it was only later that they came to recognise the association between the circle and the presence of the god."[152].

Whatever the true situation between the Todas, their hill gods and the stone circles crowning them, the name pun must surely be of some significance, since it is likely to have some relation to the so-called Sun circles. This appears to indicate that a very old name associated with the Sun is pun (Sun = Pun), the prefix of Pun-Chao. Chao has been shown to be a common term for leader or ruler in the country with which India shares a North Eastern border, Burma. This suggests that the term Pun-Chao may have been originally been an ancient title for the ritual leader or high priest who performed ceremonies in the Sun-circles or megalithic sites in Southern India and perhaps Burma.

Megalithic sites, as elsewhere in the world are associated with giants and there is a legend among the Mundas, an aboriginal people of India, that there was at one time ancestral to the Assurs, two white giants, called generally, pundi[153], and this may have been a distant memory of a megalithic people associated with Sun circles. The Assurs, as has been shown earlier, were iron-workers and were probably the descendants of the Anatolian peoples from West Asia probably migrating into India after the 12th., century B.C. In India the surviving megalithic sites are dated to 500-300 B.C. and these in the Toda heartland probably date from that time. It is likely therefore that if the Todas had come from Sumeria in the early third millennium B.C. then it is most likely that they must have taken the slow route to South India and travelled overland. After entering India it is likely that they were gradually driven south from the natural migration entry point in the North West by later immigrants, such as the Vedic Aryans,who displaced them and drove them deeper into Central and South India. Equally, it is possible that after migrating by sea from the Middle East, the Todas may have survived on the west coast for several thousand years, and then retreated inland after the beginning of the first millennium A.D. This would accord with the scenario recorded of the Aryan Brahmans in their gradual settlement further south in India from this latter time.

Whatever the history and fate of the Todas it is clear from the researches carried out in the last century that they have had a wide influence since there are elements of their culture appearing into the Pacific, and these will be referred to later. The Kal referred to as the sacred stone, usually as an altar or representing a deity, is found among them and this undoubtedly was derived from the Ancient Near East where in Assyrian religion the Kal-lu was the priest who officiated at the sacred stone altar and was associated with animal sacrifices. This same term is also found among some of the tribes intermixed with Aboriginal blood in India such as the Mundas and Bhuiyas already noted.

Pushan or Pun-shan - An Ancient Sun Deity of India

In all ancient civilisations there are many layers of culture and influences as a result of immigration and, or invasion, trade, and religious missions depending upon the strength and forcefulness of the impact received. This has resulted in many terms for the same deity since, where those propounding a new religion or way of life are not able to dominate sufficiently to eliminate the old deities and social order and replace it with their own, the old survives and becomes subsumed to the new order and gradually assimilated to the new gods as one of their attributes. No other country exhibits this tendency so clearly in the many cultural overlays that have been imposed over many millennia on India. Since the Sun god by necessity must be a prominent, if not the supreme deity in almost all ancient countries, it is he, usually a male god in India, who preserves these attributes and titles under various names. Included in these are the more ancient forms of this Hindu god's name (and Ancient Iranian name) usually known as Surya in Hindu India, who were older gods who have faded from memory as this name became more used as the Hindus gained power in the early first millennium A.D.

A prominent Sun deity in the Vedic texts originating in Iran was Pushan. In the earlier Vedic texts Pushan is more prominent and he is noted in the Upanishads as follows:
"15) The door of the True is covered with a golden disk. Open that, O Pushan, that we may see the nature of the True."
"16) O Pushan, only seer, Yama (judge), Surya (sun), son of Prajapati, spread thy rays and gather them! The light which is thy fairest form, I see it. I am what he is (viz. the person in the sun)."[154].

This identifies Pushan with, and as the Sun, the God of Death as Judge, and Prajapati, the very early Supreme Creator, but above all with the "man in the Sun", that is the Spirit of the Sun and the "gold disk". In a similar text it is said that the face of the Brahman, representing the Truth, is covered with a golden disk, and this is considered to emulate the man (purusha) in the Sun, hence his face is concealed behind the golden disk of the Sun[155]. However, it is more than likely that Pushan was in fact a very early corruption of Pun-shan, where Pun = Sun (see Todas) and Shan is the Ancient Aryan term for a settlement and in these terms perhaps as a sacred precinct related to a stone circle. Shan is another form of An, and Chan found widely in Asia and indicated as such in the work of Miles Poindexter[156]. This is especially so since in South India, among the Mukhavans, Pon = gold (Pon=Pun=Sun) the colour and sacred metal of the Sun[157].

In an interesting section it is Pushan who is considered to distribute the portions of the "fivefold" sacred sacrifices to the gods. There were only five types of sacrifices considered acceptable to the gods, and these in order of precedence were man, bullocks, rams, and he-goat[158], and where the highest was not available the next lowest was considered appropriate. These are enumerated in the most ancient texts and are vestiges left over from very ancient days in Iran and Central Asia, but were still carried out among some of the Aboriginal tribes of India on the periphery of Hinduism until the early part of last century. Whenever the Brahmans sacrificed, and that was regularly, in their rituals around the sacred fire hearth and altar, they were always careful to move in the same direction as the Sun's orbit[159]. The Sun was said to be the gate to the Gods, in the North East and the Moon was the gate to the ancestral Fathers in the South East[160]. The rituals also reflected the four cardinal points where each of the Sun's rays were said to relate to these - one for each of the four quarterscorresponding to the cardinal points, one each for North and South (opposite ends of the World Axis, the Axis Mundae), and one for the Sun itself[161].

Pushan was also identified with the thunderbolt, and this is reminiscent of Punchao considered to be associated with the Thunder god Illapa, and this reference in the Vedic text notes of Pushan: "Pushan is the distributor of the portions (to the gods): with his hands he therefore takes it, not with his own; for it is the thunderbolt, and no man can hold that: he thus takes it with (the assistance of) the gods."[162]. Pushan's thunderbolt is noted again in other texts where it is used to cut off the heads of Rakshas or demons[163]. In another portion of text it states that: "13) He (the Brahman) receives it (offering), with the text, 'At the impulse (prasava) of the divine Savitri (another name for the Sun) I receive thee with the arms of the Asvins, with the hands of Pushan."[164].

The Asvins are here closely identified with Pushan as the Sun and these are the horse deities and will be of note later. Needless to say, because of the associations of Pushan with the thunderbolt, the storm god more favourably known for his thunderbolt is associated with him and Pushan was considered to accompany Indra just as Punchao is associated with the Thunder god Illapa in Peru[165].

In an extraordinary Vedic myth recorded in the Satapatha Brahmana it was said that the ancient Creator deity, Prajapati, attempted to "unite" with his own daughter, the Sky or Dawn. This was considered a sin by the gods and Rudra shot an arrow at him in an attempt to separate him from his daughter. This part of the myth is closely similar to a Huichol myth related to Orion and has been noted in an earlier work[166]. In relenting and curing Prajapati the gods sent Rudra's arrow, broken during extraction from the Creator, since it contained some of the offerings to the gods, distributed to the gods. When the arrow reached Pushan it was said that it broke his teeth and from that time only special offerings made of rice were considered appropriate. This may be the origin, at least in part, of so many peoples along the sea routes in the Pacific Ocean practising teeth evulsion, the removal of some or all of the front teeth, in emulation of this Sun god.

The name Pushan is said to derive from pus, meaning "nourisher"[167], and therefore relates in some aspects to the earth and the products developed from the earth to nourish mankind. This is more likely a latter attribution identified with Pun-shan since his name is more clearly derived from Pun - the Sun.

Since the Sudras were designated the labouring castes the Sun as Pushan was said to have a special association with Sudras. The text states: "13) ... He created the Sudra colour (caste), as Pushan (as nourisher). This earth verily is Pushan (the nourisher); for the earth nourishes all this whatsoever."[168]. The mouth is of special importance in the rituals of the Brahmans since apart from the obvious means of consuming nourishment the priest during the rituals actually consumes portions of the sacrificial food on behalf of the deities, not a practice exclusive to the Aryans of India, and requires special attention in the rituals itself in the ceremonial implements and regalia. A text notes:
"The mouth of the true (Brahman) is covered with a golden lid; open that, O Pushan (sun), that we may go to the true one, who pervades all (Vishnu)."
"He who is the person in the sun, I am he."[169].

In both Central America and South America gold masks appear in many examples of the iconography of the deities depicted (*6.120*). Even the ritual of opening the mouth, known as the Peruvian site of Sipan, near Chiclayo[170], and these appear to have their prototype in the Brahman "gold mouth lid" and probably applied for the same or similar reasons. Alva and Donnan note that this ritual of "opening the mouth" at Sipan is another example of a very sophisticated ritual of appearing suddenly without antecedent in South America. Clearly this must have been derived from Asia where such rites were well known and reflected a long period of incremental development.

Pushan was considered also the guardian of the path, perhaps because journeys were usually made in daylight relating to the Sun[171]. In some texts he is implored to make the paths difficult for the enemies who are adversaries[172] and is declared the "overlord of roads" and petitioned by those who wish safe journeys, particularly when riding horses[173]. He is especially considered the protector of travellers and declared as such in the oldest of the Vedic texts of India, the Satapatha Brahmana[174]. This suggests that this deity is related to pilgrim shrines along known trading routes that became sanctified by age and may by the origin of the "ceques" - radial routes extending from the centre of Cuzco.

Pushan was also associated with the shaving rituals of the hair and beard and was said to have shaved the deity Brihaspati's (teacher of the gods) head or beard in a ritual requiring stepping towards the east three times, while repeating a metric text[175]. In the shaving or tonsuring of a Brahman child's head the male relative or priest who performs the ritual invokes the mythical shaving of Brihaspati's head by Pushan. In this ceremony the boy is seated to the west of the sacred fire facing east and his mother stands at the north of it to receive the locks when they are removed[176]. As an epithet of Rudra, the Vedic clan, and Pushan "Kapardin" or "Kaparda" means a shell where the name denotes the hairstyle where the hair is twisted in the form reminiscent of the shell and is reflected in ringlets or braiding[177]. Braided hair, associated with Rudra and Pushan tends to indicate the early origin of these deities since such braiding is more associated with the Early Near and Middle East (*8.064*; *8.066*; *8.069*), and is found similarly in Melanesia (*8.068*; *8.071/2*) and traditionally also in the Andes (*8.065*; *8.070*).

The Brahman male child was the centre of ritual and adulation and in their birth they were considered to have been assisted by Pushan and Aryaman. In chants and prayers offered to assist in parturition these deities are implored as follows:

"1) Aryaman as active hotar-priest shall utter for thee the vashat-call at this (soma-) pressing, O Pushan! May (this) woman, (herself) begotten in the proper way, be delivered, may her joints relax, that she shall bring forth!"

"2) Four directions has the heaven, and also four the earth: (from these) the gods created the embryo. May they open her, that she shall bring forth!"[178].

Aryaman - The Noble and True Gentleman

Aryaman is a deity specifically identified with the Vedic Aryans in India since he is, along with the deities such as Indra, Varuna and Mitra, found in the older texts of the Ancient Near and Middle East and was brought with them in their migrations into India. Aryaman is particularly associated with "chivalry" and the virtues of being a man and correct actions in the aristocratic society of the Aryans - a true gentleman was therefore called an Arya. This deity was considered to preside over contracts including those in marriage alliance, law, tradition and religion, as well as family wealth and the possessions both in the family and tribal sense[179]. Interestingly Aryaman's royal path was considered to be the Milky Way and he was considered by the true Aryans as the Great Ancestor and the source of the aristocratic blood that ran in their veins. This appears to follow closely the attitude and beliefs in the deification of the first ancestors among the Incas.

The cult of Pushan is rarely found in India today and his name has almost disappeared from the daily pantheon of the Hindu faithful[180]. The associations of Pushan as the Sun, however, appear to be too closely similar to those of Punchao to be accidental. The variations in pronunciation and spelling within the related languages of India, especially those of its many deities, is wide and some deviate and so much so that they separate and become deities in their own right. If the Sun deity Pushan was transferred by Aryans Indians to South America then it would be expected that some inflexion would evolve and that it may mutate with other terms associated with ruler-ship such as "Chao" in Burma and Ahau in the Americas. This would allow a hybrid to evolve such as Punchao and this would follow in the tracks of many other deities being transferred from Asia into the Pacific and beyond noted in this and earlier works.

The proper vehicle, or vahana, for the Sun was the horse Tarksya (also Tarksa), and the Sun in iconography is frequently carved and painted as a radiant human hero riding on one or several horses (*8.073*; *9.158*). In later times the Tarksya is shown as a bird and identified with Garuda. Tarksya was the proper name for Asva the vehicle of Surya, Asvin being the mythical pair of heroes said to be the fathers of Pushan[181]. In Buddhist mythology Vairocana meaning "coming from or pertaining to the Sun", and a representation of this deity was seated in the inner shrine of the stupa[182]. In another work it has been shown that Buddhism had greatly influenced the iconography of the Maya and the cultures of Mexico[183] and this might lead to the possibility that they also had influence in South America and that Viracocha was in fact a reflection of

Vairocana adapted to the later influences of the Vedic and Hindu Indians.

The Sun in Pre-Aryan India

Among the Mundas, an Aboriginal people in India the Sun was called Sing-Bonga[184], where Sing is almost certainly derived from the Moon god, Sin, millennia before in the Ancient Middle East. Myths clearly derived from the Ancient Near East were still preserved by the Mundas into last century and noted elsewhere[185]. "Sin" or "sina" is found frequently in Polynesia in particular where it meant also "bright" or "shining" and this clearly derived from the intensity of the lights of the Sun and Moon. Si was known to be Moon god of the Moche[186] and preserved among the later Chimu people, and appears to be related to the fanged mountain god, Ai Apaec (*5.093-5*). This deity, Si, clearly derives from the same origin as the Polynesian Sina, and the Sin of Mesopotamia.

Among the Todas the Sun was highly venerated and virtually all the sacred dairies located their entrance doors facing east so that when the dairyman emerged from inside at dawn he would see the rising Sun. The priests salute the rising Sun each morning and interestingly the Sun salutation anytime after the morning, that is afternoon or sunset, was still performed facing the point on the horizon over which the Sun rose. After a woman had given birth in the seclusion hut, on leaving, she faced the Sun in salutation[187]. Unlike the Aryan Hindu traditions the deities and gods of the Todas appear to have nothing to do with the Sun nor considered to be related or derived from him even though these salutations were rigorously observed[188]. This suggests that they originally had a religion that has largely become shorn of its cosmological elements, retaining only the Sun, and Moon in the simplest terms, while ancestral deities appear to have gradually replaced these and other aspects. This has resulted in two apparently unrelated systems consisting of the Sun Moon and the remnants of a cosmology composing of stars and constellations, along with the deified heroes.

8.074 : Trench surrounding the stepped pyramid at Cuicuilco showing remnants of the three rings along the floor of the trough. Cuicuilco, Mexcio City, Valley of Mexico, 600-200 B.C.

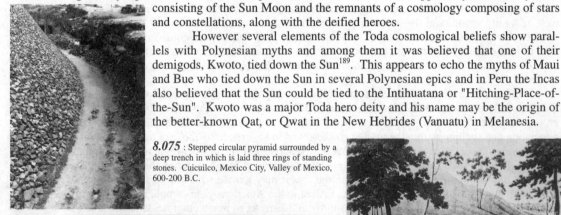

However several elements of the Toda cosmological beliefs show parallels with Polynesian myths and among them it was believed that one of their demigods, Kwoto, tied down the Sun[189]. This appears to echo the myths of Maui and Bue who tied down the Sun in several Polynesian epics and in Peru the Incas also believed that the Sun could be tied to the Intihuatana or "Hitching-Place-of-the-Sun". Kwoto was a major Toda hero deity and his name may be the origin of the better-known Qat, or Qwat in the New Hebrides (Vanuatu) in Melanesia.

8.075 : Stepped circular pyramid surrounded by a deep trench in which is laid three rings of standing stones. Cuicuilco, Mexico City, Valley of Mexico, 600-200 B.C.

8.076 : Earth mound with three raised earth arcs discovered by the first British in Sydney. These resemble the stepped pyramid at Cuicuilco, near Mexico City, surrounded by three outer rings o stones laid in a wide trench around its perimeter. Sydney, East Coast Australia, 18th., century, A.D. or before.

The term "Pun" among the Todas has been shown to relate to the Sun as an expression of the Sun circles and among the Bhuiyas of North East Central India there is a myth told of their ancestor's origins that is shared also with the Rajas of Chutia (or Chota) Nagpur. This myth relates that a Naga (serpent) ancestor named Pundariki secretly assumed the form of a Brahmin. In learning the sacred scriptures as a Brahmin the Guru who taught him was so pleased with his abilities that he gave him his daughter as a wife. However, Pundariki could not rid himself of his forked tongue and his foul breath, and he insisted that his wife never asked of him the reasons why. However, on a pilgrimage to Puri she became so insistent to know that he eventually told her of his origins and then reassumed his real form and plunged into a pool and disappeared from sight. His wife was grief stricken and gave birth immediately to a son, but while she was contemplating sati (immolation by fire) a Brahman bearing an image of the Sun God appeared and he found the child being protected by a "huge hooded snake", actually Pundariki in his natural form. Pundariki addressed the Brahmin and told him that the son would become the Raja of the country and admonished him to bring the child up and that the Sun image was to be his tutelary deity[190]. A similar legend existed among the Bhuiyas of Central and East India and there are many similar myths through into the Pacific region regarding child heroes being protected by great Nagas or serpents that have clearly derived from India. The term Pundariki appears to indicate that, as with the Toda, the term pun or pund relates to the Sun, while Riki is another form of the term Rishi. This is the name for the seven sacred sages on India, but who were originally ancestral heroes in the Aryan epics deriving from Ancient Iran, and were identified with the Great Bear constellation. The term Riki, or here Ariki, may in fact be the original form of the term for a Polynesian sea captain - Ariki. The coils of the serpent, Pundariki, may have references to the earlier noted rope coils associated with lightning among the Quiche-Maya and that placed around penitents' necks in Peru as an expiation.

The Spaniards when they first entered Peru heard of the fabled garden in the Temple of the Sun courtyard composed of trees and plants made of gold and silver[191]. The Peruvians considered the garden was dedicated to the Sun and that the trees also were an essential part of that adoration. The Vedic texts of India record that the tree called the Asvattha was known as the "tree of the golden leaves" and those who arrived at the tree left "possessed of wings"[192]. The subtleties of the meaning of this tree would have been lost on most of the adherents and they would have accepted that the description in the text was meant literally, although the scholarly commentators indicate that it was to be read symbolically as beneficial and pleasant in aspect. It might be remembered that the Ayar Inca hero, one of the first four legendary Inca brothers was called Ayar Uchu and he, after being enclosed in the cave by his brother was "possessed of wings" when he appeared before Manco Capac to assist him later (Version 2).

Sun Myths Among the Naga

In the researches of a number of first anthropologists and interested British officers in the colonial administration of India it was repeatedly noted by them that the Nagas exhibited many cultural aspects appearing to be reflected closely among the peoples of South East Asia, the Pacific islands and the Americas. Among the Ao Nagas in Assam, in North East India, it is said in the origins myths of the Anichar, meaning "Sun clan", that they are descended from a woman who, while drying rice in the Sun, fainted from the heat and fell over onto her back. When she recovered she found that she had been impregnated by the Sun and the child born from this event was the first man of the clan. In some versions there were said to have been two women impregnated in this manner, one by the rising Sun over the hills and the other by the setting Sun over the plains[193].

J.P. Mills who recorded these myths noted that a closely similar myth occurred among the Guacheta Indians in Colombia in South America and were very similar to myths found in the Gran Chaco. These reflect attribution to the powers of impregnation by the Sun closely similar to those of the Hindu Sun god Surya. The myth recorded of the Guacheta Indians notes that the ancestress was in fact one of two sisters and that one had conceived. It is related that the two sisters were exposed to the Sun's rays with the intent that they should conceive from the Sun's rays, but that that neither was impregnated by the rising Sun, one only being impregnated by the setting Sun[194]. Similar myths are also noted among the people of the island of North New Guinea, Samoa and Tahiti as a link between Asia and South America[195].

Apart from "accidental" or divine impregnation a closely related traditional practise in Northern India for a barren woman who desired a child, up until the early colonial period in India, was recorded and this was that she was required to stand naked before the Sun imploring him in her prayers to relieve her of the bareness[196]. Fertility of the soil was encouraged through ceremonies of the imitation of the Sun's disk and a ritual was performed where round flat cakes were laid on the earth to be cultivated along with sweetmeats. Having been exposed for a period of time these flat cakes were then eaten by the family cultivating the plot. Interestingly this was believed to fertilise the goddess of the soil known as Bhumiya Rani, or "Soil Queen" in the North West of India, but in other regions she is a male deity and known as the godling Bhumiya, or Bhumi. This deity was also referred to as Khetpal or Kshetrapala - "the protector of the fields", Khera or the "homestead mound", and in the hills, Sayam (Sanskrit, Sayama) - "the black one"[197]. This emphasises the care in attributing and researching mythical and legendary heroes and heroines, since gender reversal is common within the one tradition let alone in non-related cultures that have assimilated them from imported traditions. This tendency has been found to be deliberately applied by some peoples and among the Huichol in North West Mexico a century ago the explorer Carl Lumholtz noted that these people consciously reversed the gender of aspects of culture assimilated from the Spanish to depotentiate them so that they did not feel quite so subjected or overwhelmed in the face of a technologically superior tradition[198].

Among the Sema Naga there is a myth that the Sun (Tsukinhye - Eye of Heaven's House), shone during the night and the Moon during the day. The Moon's name was Akhi, but it shone so intolerably bright and hot that the Sun threw a cowpat at it to reduce its light. It is said that the darker patches on the Moon are caused by this cow dung and still seen today[199]. This motif of the Moon being scarred or obscured by dung, mud or ashes being thrown at it is found widely beyond India and preserved in many myths among the peoples of the Pacific Coast of North West North America but also in South America[200].

The Sun in Myth in Australia, Melanesia and Polynesia

In Aboriginal South Australia the men of the Wotjo-Baluk tribe called the Sun, Ngaui, and they described themselves as Ngau-na-guli or "men of the Sun"[201]. It has already been noted that Punjal may actually have been a form of Punchao or Pushan, and the Wotjo-Baluk equivalent was Bunjil (Pun-djel), considered elsewhere in this work. A tribe with similar traditions, the Wurunjerri, thought the Sun was a woman and that it travelled by the sea every night from the West and returned to the East to rise in the morning[202]. Other tribes, isolated and landlocked far from the seaboard considered that the Sun descended through a hole in the ground in the West and travelled by a tunnel-like underground route to reach the East to rise again - a concept very similar to many found in India and the Americas. This place was called by the Dieri tribe, Killa-wilpa-nina[203]. The term nina means "vagina" in their language and there are many myths among the Pacific peoples that fire was obtained originally from the vagina of a mythical woman204, and the term for the fire-god in India was Agni, probably corrupted here to nina. However, it should also be remembered that nina was the term for fire among the Quechua in Peru and there-

8.077 : Intihuatana, a stone phallic stone seen at the centre above the surviving wall of this sacred building said to be where the ritual of tying the Sun to this stone was performed. Pisac, South Highland Peru, 1350-1500 A.D.

8.079 : The Intihuatana in the cave mouth at Cerro de Intihuasi Mostrando. San Luis, N.W. Argentina, 1300-1521 A.D.

8.078 : Large stone monolith as the Intihuatana as the "Hitching Post of the Sun". Qenko, Cuzco, South Highlands Peru, 1300-1521 A.D.

8.080 : A broader view of the monumental ruins of Pisac near Cuzco with the stumped form of the Intihuatana visible in the centre left of the Portal into the Sun chamber. Inca Dynasty, Pisac, 1300-1521 A.D.

fore both may have derived from India. The Urubunna tribe, located in South Central Australia, called the Sun Ditji and the hole where he was said to disappear each night was called Minka and this place was located about 25 miles from Lake Eyre.

Of particular note is that the Sun is called by the Arunta tribe located in the very centre of Australia, Alinga and this name seems to correspond to the name of Alluna, whereas when the Sun is referred to a mythical being it is female and called Ochirka[205]. The Moon was called Atninja, and the term for Sun and Moon appears to have close associations with similar names among other tribes but this might also be a corruption of "Agni". The Kaitish tribe believed that the Sun sank at a place called Allumba[206], and in Arnhem Land, one of the most northerly points in Australia, the Milky Way was named Ataluna[207]. In Yirkalla tribe myths the Moon man was named Alinda[208] and among them also there was the belief that there were two suns[209]. Belief in the two Suns was a principle of Jain myths in India[210] and among the Nagas of Assam[211]. The term Alinda, Alluna and similar titles for Moon-related associations appears to have a direct connection to similar Moon-related terms among the Kogi, also called the Kaggaba, in Northern Colombia in South America. Among them the term for the sphere of spirit was called Aluna and associated with the night[212]. The two distant geographical regions are connected directly by the Equatorial ocean currents and where sea craft are assisted by the prevailing winds blowing from the Americas towards Asia and Northern Australia.

The early researchers were frequently reminded in studying Australian Aboriginal myths of parallels in India, Asia generally, Europe and Egypt. James Bonwick wrote in his book published in 1870, regarding the Tasmanian Aboriginals with reference to those of the mainland, as follows: "In Australia the name Baal repeatedly occurs, and has been considered by some writers related to solar worship. Some of the traditions have quite a Maori type, and remind one of the story of a New Zealand god waylaying, catching, and severely beating the sun to make it go less quickly. The Australian spirit Koen is the sun. It is she that kills her husband Taorong (Tangaroa?), the moon, every month. Such is the story of her in Western Australia, Eastern Australia, and Queensland. The name has been thought connected with the Egyptian Kron or

Khun (Kon or Con?). According to the Lake Macquarie people, Koen carries a firestick about with her. One tale is that Koen is a male spirit, seizing Blacks at night, carrying them a great distance, but restoring them to the camp fireside. His wife Tippakalleun cruelly spears children, and takes them below in her bag. Koyorowen skewers and roasts women, and his wife Kurriwilban impales men on horns growing out of her shoulders. In another part they said the sun was an emu's egg, thrown by a spirit in the darkness."

The Victorian writers were usually writing out of interest and were highly educated men with a broad classical education so that when confronting the myths of peoples so very far from Europe, Asia and Egypt, with which they were most familiar they were immediately able to compare them and discover the many parallels. Bonwick wrote further: "The Sun in all ages has been regarded as the conquering foe of darkness, or the Evil One. A singular dance was once seen by myself in South Australia. A man came into the circle limping as if lame, and groaning as if in pain. He was supported by two companions, who pretended great sympathy with his sufferings. All at once he sprang into the air with a loud laugh, in which all the tribe heartily joined. Vulcan, otherwise the sun, was the halting god. Baal Thalatth means he that halteth. The priests of Baal, says Kitto, limped at the altar. The Druids in some rites did the same."

"The sun was variously known by the Blacks - being in Van Dieman's Land (Tasmania) petreanna, loina, nabageena, pugganoobra, etc.; in Port Phillip (Melbourne), noweenth or ngerwein; at Grafton, tharoo; on the Darling Downs, boroka; in Eastern Queensland, mungarra; at Wilde Bay, ngananth; at the Macquarie River, jeeralang."

"Mounds, to be found in Tasmania and all over Australia, were once supposed to be only native ovens, as the loose soil was suitable for cooking purposes. But as a small hole was sufficient for cooking, and some of these mounds are eighty feet in circumference, consisting of earth, stones, ashes, bones, and charcoal, they have been associated with sacrifice of bodies to the sun. A Victorian surveyor writes: 'I believe these mounds have been altars used by the Aborigines at a remote period in their worship of the sun.' The name given to some of them - noweenth weenth, sun fires - is very significant."[213].

These examples are some of the many indicating the sometimes vast divergence in names for the same objects and deities occurring between tribes who have shared the same, smallest continental mass in the world. Any similarities in names between disparately located tribes highlights probable special connections in origin but the possibility of mounds built to the Sun is certainly not fantasy since sketches by the earliest British explorers shows similar mounds with three sequential platforms, possibly seats but similar to those in a trench at the mound at Cuicuilco in Southern Mexico City (*8.074-6*). Bonwick's references to the god Baal of West Asia is not so far fetched as it might seem since connections to this deity are illustrated in references elsewhere in this work. The writings of Abraham Fornander, a judge residing in Hawaii over a century ago, recorded many parallels in the cultures of the West Asians and the Pacific and provides indicators of a very early sea migration route between these vastly distant regions[214].

In Melanesia there is a tradition among the Bae Guu people of Northern Mala that the bow originally fell from the sky and that this bow belonged to the stone-using people who anciently inhabited their islands[215]. These legendary people were always likened to Europeans, since they were said to be fair-skinned and this appears as a common factor among many traditions relating to these early people in the Pacific. In the mythology of India the bow was in fact the Thunder God of India, Indra's bow, and it was also considered to be the rainbow - Indradhanus[216]. On the island of Malaita this tradition is linked to the hero Vulanangela who was said to have been swallowed by a large fish while tying to catch it. He was carried inside the fish until it was grounded and he then cut his way out through the belly of the fish using a flint stone. He travelled on with the Sun until he reached the house of the Sun, and here he remained some time, until he was lowered from the sky with the gift of fire[217]. The association of the hero with the Sun and reaching his house is reminiscent of the legend of Bue - to be considered in due course, and being swallowed by a giant fish and cutting himself out of the belly is frequently found in myths in the Amazon and Gran Chaco regions of South America noted in a later chapter.

Sina was the name for the Sun in some of the Solomon Islands, highly influenced from Polynesia, and depicted as a rayed disk[218]. The Bae Guu people, also noted earlier, believed that it was possible to conceive by the Sun's rays. In some cases an unmarried girl, who wished to conceive a child by the Sun, remained in the village and did not accompany the other women to work in the fields. She sat out in the village's open spaces and as she weeded she sweated as a result of the heat of the Sun, and it was believed that she conceived in this way. It was said that the great culture hero of the region Sina Kwao was conceived by his mother, Bira'ana hato ("Cleave to the Sun") this way[219] and his name means "Shiny Bright" and is clearly derived from the origins of the name of the Moon, Sin, in the Ancient Near East and related to the Polynesian Sina.

In the Torres Straits Islands, on Mabuig Island, it was necessary for the men to process around the sacred platform on which were laid their catch of turtles, in the direction of the Sun's orbit while whirring bullroarers. If they inadvertently marched opposite to the Sun's orbit it was believed that it would drive the turtles away from the island[220]. In Polynesia the Sun's path was closely observed as might be expected of a mariner people, and the two extremities of the orbit, the Tropic of Cancer, and the Tropic of Capricorn was called respectively "the black shining path of Kane" and "the black shining path of Tangaroa"[221]. The Sun is linked to lightning in the Gilbert Islands[222] and this connection reflects that of the Andean peoples anciently and will be considered further in due course.

Sun Gods and Myths in Colombia

In Colombia, in South America, the chief Sun deity among the Chibcha was Gagua and he was identified with Zue, Xue, Sua and Zupa, and the day, Chia[223]. The practices among the Colombians was similar to those of Central America in adoration of the Sun where young male warrior prisoners were sacrificed and their blood sprinkled on the sacred stones that the Sun's rays first struck on rising[224].

At harvest time, a child who had been chosen from a particular town on the plains and who had had his ears pierced, was brought up in the Temple of the Sun until he was ten years of age. At the appropriate time he was led out on a "walk" said to commemorate the "peregrinations" of the Sun deity Bochica, and then beheaded in the belief that his soul would go and live in the Sun. The youth represented the culture hero Bochica, who was said to live in the Sun, and he was instructed, before decapitation, to intercess on the behalf of the people to ensure a good harvest[225]. In another ritual a youth who had been bought for a high price was secluded in the Temple of the Sun where he was raised until the age of fifteen. The youth was then entitled Guesa, meaning "without a home" and also "mouth" since he it was who was being trained to be the mouthpiece on behalf of the people with the ancestral gods. The most important of gods was Bochica and the sacrifice was also called Quihica, or "door", since he passed from one level of existence to another as if through a door between the earth and the abode of the Sun and Moon. In a ritual similar to the Tezcatlipoca rites in Mexico, where this deity was called "Soul of the World", the youth, Guesa, at the age of fifteen, was sacrificed and his heart and entrails torn out and offered to Bochica[226].

Bochica as Sun was considered married to the Moon, Chia, and Bochica was considered to have three heads and one heart - the identical reflection of Siva in India where he was depicted as three-headed[227]. Siva was an all-consuming deity and was identified with the roles and attributes of the other former prominent deities as he assimilated their special qualities but as three-headed he was more associated with the Moon than the Sun and the three heads represented where the three phases of the Moon.

A Sun Myth from the Amazon

Among the Bororo the Sun was called Meri and the Moon named Ari[228]. Among the Ge Indians the Sun was considered to tirelessly pursue the Moon and an eclipse occurred when one caught up with the other. It was said that in anger the Sun became so frustrated that he turned against humanity and burned then turning their hair red[229]. One of their tribal groups, the Apinaye, laid their villages out as a Sun-wheel suggesting a very ancient form of Sun worship[230]. In another Apinaye myth the Sun creates the winged serpents[231].

Myths of the Noosing the Sun and Hitching at the Inti-Huatana

Among the most interesting sets of myths are those suggesting that the Sun could be controlled in its orbit across the sky. Usually this was said to have been possible after a period when the Sun shone too warmly or too coldly, or that a hero or deity required more time to ensure a particular task could be completed. Most famously there are ancient monuments, accompanied by only a minimum amount of mythological material describing the use or associations with the Sun, erected or carved specifically for this purpose and this is the Inti-huatana - the so-called "hitching place of the Sun" found at certain sites in the Andes and usually attributed to the Incas. The best-known examples are found at Macchu Picchu, Pisac, Hatun Colla near Lake Titicaca and Vitcos near the Nusta Issapana. The term Inti-huatana is interpreted in the sense that it is the pillar where the Sun is " held fast", and the Intip-huatana as it is also referred to is translated as "the measure of the sun or measure of the year"[232] (its course or orbit). It has been speculated that ropes may have been used in relation to the short stone pillar for measuring the height of the Sun, or some other measurement or ritual since huatana meant "rope"[233]. This interpretation appears to relate directly to the most famous of the "noosed Sun" myths in Polynesia where a cord or rope was said to be used and illustrations deriving from the Ancient Middle East 3,000 years ago.

In the Marquesas Islands, it has been noted that the sacred mountain was named Tai Pi and this appears to relate directly to Taypi-Kala at Tiahuanaco. The god Tai was considered the deity of the sacred house reserved for tapu (taboo) chants and at the rear of this building was a decorated altar or Ahu. Associated with the altar was a sacred rope (Tou'a Kaha), and usually kept in, or near it. Under the altar were one or two sacred stone blocks, called Fatu, and from this, on the appropriate occasion, a piece was removed to make an adze for the rites associated with the coming-of-age of a boy. The legend associated with the sacred blocks is one relating to the demi-god Motuhiki, the legendary canoe builder and patron of the craft, and it was said that the sacred rope, the Tona Pou, was the rope with which this hero "noosed the Sun". It was reported that the Marquesans did not associate this legend with Maui as recorded in most of the other Polynesian myths and legends. The post that stood in front of the sacred rope, or Tona pou, was 3 or 4 inches thick (75-100mm) and about 10 feet (3 m) high. On the morning of the ceremony a rope made of seven strands of plaited sennit, woven so that it lay flat, was hung on the post. On top of the post a horizontal stick with coconut leaves attached was secured. On the afternoon of the ceremony the boy approaching puberty who was to receive his adze along with fish, perhaps octopus, or taro root and the stone piece, covered with shells collected by the boy's father, was tied to the post. The post was then called the Fata Tau Enata - "the post landing-place of men". It was thought that the cross piece was in fact the perching place for the ancestral spirits who came to watch the ceremony, and the male elders of the clan chanted during this rite in their honour. The post was left standing for two weeks after which all the elements of the sacred pole were dismantled and secreted in the sacred tribal house. It is not known whether the rope wrapped around the pole was believed to be the actual Tona Pou[234].

The ceremony appears to have some memory of ancient rites connected to their nearest continental neighbours in South America and particularly so as they share also religious and mystical elements such as Ta Pi or Taypi, and where the sacred conch trumpet was called Putona in the Marquesas and Pututu in Peru. The Reverend William Ellis was one of the first missionaries to write of the Polynesian beliefs, when based first in Tahiti, after the earliest European contacts in the latter part of the 18th., century. He wrote in relation to Maui and the myths of the Sun: "One of the most singular of their traditions, respecting the sun, deserves attention, from the slight analogy it bears to a fact recorded in Jewish history. It is related that Maui, an ancient priest or chief, was building a marae, or temple, which it was necessary to finish before the close of the day; but, perceiving the sun was declining, and that it was likely to sink before the work was finished, he seized the sun by his rays, bound them with a cord to the marae, or an adjacent tree, and then prosecuted his work till the marae was completed, the sun remaining stationary during the whole period. I refrain from all comment on this singular tradition, which is almost universally received in the islands"[235].

In the Solomon Islands a myth preserved by the Mwara clan notes a flood legend where it is said that an ancestor caught the Sun with a noose to lengthen the day and all the Mwara people who had died during this catastrophe were turned into stone pillars[236]. This clearly has its origins in the Maui myth and the name Mwara may well have a common origin with the name Maui. Another group who might also have a name derived from a common origin with Maui are the Maori. Sir Peter Buck, himself a Maori, recorded the following myth from Maori traditions: "When Maui laid rope snares around the opening through which the sun emerged for the daily round, he instructed his brothers not to pull on the ropes until the sun's head and shoulders were above the noose. Thus, when he gave the signal, the sun was rendered helpless because his arms were pinioned to his sides. Maui beat the sun with a club formed of the lower jawbone of his grandmother Murirangawhenau, (Great son of the sun?). Thus, the personal name of the sun became known for the first time. As a result of his heating, the sun moved more slowly across the sky and man had more ample time to procure food ..."[237].

Needless to say there is a corresponding myth in India regarding the slowing of the Sun's progress through the sky and a Buna tribe myth notes that in the most ancient times the days were much shorter that they now are. This myth relates that people were unable to complete all their tasks since the daylight lasted for insufficient time so their ancestors called a council meeting to decide on how the daylight hours may be lengthened. There was one man who could bear the heat of the Sun and he said that if they could manage to bind the Sun to slow it down in its course the days would be longer. All agreed to this proposal and next morning several of the young men climbed a tree with a rope to capture the Sun. However, there was a mistake in tying the noose so that the Sun instead of remaining in the sky longer for each day and the same amount of time for every day of the year, it caused the Sun to orbit faster during one half of the year and slower for the other half and this was the origin of Summer with longer days and Winter with shorter days[238]. The myth is so similar to the Maori myth, and those of Polynesia generally, in its main principle that it is unlikely to have a independent origin.

In another myth the Todas, from the Nilgiri Hills in Southern India, preserved a myth where a young god was considered to be an upstart by the other gods and they attempted to do away with him. They tried several methods and these ended in failure so decided to impose ordeals to control him and these were an attempt to determine his strength by trials as tasks set for him to complete or that would destroy him. In one of these trials his ability to tie the Sun was challenged and this he did by binding it with a stone chain to a tree that grew beside a pool surrounded by trees. This caused great darkness in the world and the people begged the hero, Kwoto, to restore the Sun to its proper place and this he did but only after the gods acknowledged his superiority[239]. In a similar myth the reason given in this undertaking was that in a rite requiring the sacrifice of a calf, Kwoto, the tribal hero, had sacrificed the calf and dismembered it as required but had thrown the pieces among the gods and demanded that they should eat the flesh since he declared them to be sacred flesh. The gods refused but would do so only if Kwoto tied down the Sun. After he had done so the gods acknowledged his superiority and consumed the flesh[240].

It has already been noted that in the ancient texts of the Mazdaeans in Iran it was said that the Creator bound the planets by a rope to the Sun and Moon so as not to cause "excessive harm". The irregular motion of the planets was said to be caused by the planets reaching the end of the rope when they are pulled back again[241]. The "noose" so frequently found in the iconography of India is probably, originally, as in this Iranian example a refection of the rope as their orbits or as the ecliptic - the path along which all the planets travel around the Sun (*8.061*). Similar myths appear to derive from the Ancient Middle East and then were transferred along with many other cultural aspects into India. From there, or independently and directly from the Middle East, they were transferred in modified form into the Pacific and ultimately into South America. Other references to the Sun being caught in a noose will be of more interest in the myths of Bue in due course. In one myth from Melanesia the noose used to catch the Sun was in fact a sling exemplified by one from the York Islands. This is an unusual version clearly borrowed, but distorted, from Polynesia, since the hero not only catches the Sun, but kills him, and in turn is killed by his son[242].

Sun-Too-Hot Myths

An aspect of the Sun found in Asia and distributed throughout the Pacific Islands and into the Americas is related to stories telling of a time in the world's history when the Sun was considered "too hot" for the inhabitants of the earth. These are often bound up with the belief that the cause was that there was more than one Sun in the Sky and that there were in some mythologies up to ten suns, perhaps more. It is possible that these "Suns" were in fact meant to relate to various zodiacal periods or ages when the Sun was perceived to rise at the Spring Equinox on one of these zodiacal signs. In the last two thousand years the Sun has entered the zodiacal sign of Pisces and is immanently entering Aquarius for the next two thousand. The apparent progression of the Sun, backwards through the zodiac is a result of the Precession if the Equinoxes and is due to the "wobble" of the earth's axis pointing northward to various "pole" stars as the millennia progress. This precession has long been recognised by the more advanced civilisations but is rarely found among the less developed except where they have clearly been influenced by those more advanced. The Earth's axis at this present moment in time points towards the Pole Star and it was noted that this in principle was the case several millennia ago by the Mazdaeans who declared the Pole Star as the ruler of the zodiac[243].

Each "new Sun" occurred as a result of precession when the next and subsequent zodiacal signs rose at the Equinox until the 12 signs (or Suns) had risen over a period of about 26,000 years when Aries would again return as the "rising sign" for the Age resulting in 12 Ages. Other alternatives might promote one complete revolution of the Precession of the Equinoxes as an Age lasting the whole of the 26,000 years.

Contemporary with the Mazdaean ascendancy in Iran, or perhaps antecedent to it deriving from the early Babylonian or Akkadian traditions, the Mandaeans record a version stating that when the Sun God Shamash first set sail in his sky boat his light was so intense that it consumed and burnt up all things. Because of this the souls of Mleka d Anhura seized Shamash and imprisoned him for 360,000 years. The mother of Shamash was Ruha and she begged that her son should be released and, as a result, the deity Melka d Nhura placed him back in his orbit but provided 12 natri (Nats), or guardian spirits, to ensure that he did no further harm. It is said that the light of Shamash came from his banner or drafsha and in those days it is also said that there was no solid earth but only black water before Pthahil entered the World and created Adam and Hawwa[244].

The account is an interesting one since there are several elements found more widely than West Asia where the Mandaean traditions are preserved. The number of years placed at 360,000 clearly refers to a cosmic reflection of the solar year accounted in their tradition as 360 plus the 5 "evil" days of Parwaniia - a tradition found also among the Maya in Central America. The 12 natri clearly relate to the zodiacal signs or 12 houses or stations of the Sun and the term natri is almost certainly the origin for the term Nats or nature spirits among the Burmese but also found among the Gonds and other tribes in India[245]. Among the Gilbert Islands (Kiribati) the deities and heroes were represented by banners, as Shamash is said to be in the Mandaean myth, and in Micronesia to the North West of the Gilbert Islands the deity name of Tohil is found, identical to that of the Mayan and clearly the local form of Pthahil[246].

One of the most unusual references, that the Sun was at one time was too hot, is recorded in the Mahabharata, the great epic of the Vedic Aryans portraying their struggle to gain territory during the first entrance into India in the early first millennium B.C. The text record that the spirit of Knowledge - Sanja (the wife of the Sun[247], left Shadow - Chaya, to retire to the forest to devote herself to religion. Chaya, attempting to hide from the heat, took the form of a mare but the Sun saw her and mounted her and she gave birth to the horse-headed gods of agriculture. Because of the intensity of the Sun's heat Chaya's father, Visvakarman, the cosmic architect, placed the Sun on his lathe and cut away one-eighth of his rays, trimming every part except his feet[248]. The pieces cut off fell to earth and were used to fashion his weapons. Such a myth is understandable, since the Aryans had arrived from a cooler climate, and in India they must have felt the enervating heat of the tropical Sun. A myth among the Aboriginal tribes of Queensland noted that at the place where the Sun descended at sunset through a hole in the ground was the place they could "knock a piece" off it and obtain from it fire[249]. This seems to reflect the Hindu myth that the pieces shaved off the Sun were used for his weapons.

In a myth resembling those of the Cuna of Panama, the Lhota Nagas of Assam in North East India state that the Sun is a flaming plate of hard metal "as big as a piece of ground on which one basket of seed rice is sown". During the day its travels its path in the sky above the earth and at night it follows a route to light the Land of the Dead as it returns from west to east under the Earth. It was believed that the Moon did the same but in ancient times it was said that the Moon was much hotter than the Sun, and the latter, seeing that the earth was being scorched, smeared the face of the Moon with cow-dung to greatly reduce its light[250]. This myth is found among other Naga tribes and also in India[251], but more importantly it is found in the Pacific Islands and the Americas earlier noted. J.H. Hutton noted that a closely similar myth is found among the Nicobarese, the Malays and in Japan[252]. He also notes that there is a similar myth in Mexico where the Moon's brightness is diminished by throwing a rabbit at it[253]. Another Nagas myth, from the Ao tribe, notes that dung was also thrown at the Moon's face to reduce the intensity of the brightness, and that there is another myth where there were believed to have been 7 Suns and six of these were shot down with arrows by ancient heroes[254].

A Kond (Gond) myth records that in ancient times a boy was guarding his pulse field when a pregnant barking-deer attempted to steal some of the crop. But as the boy prepared to kill the deer a voice came from inside of it and said if he did not shoot he will tell him something very important. The voice was that of the Sun god in the deer's belly and he told the boy that in eight days the world would turn upside-down and everything will be covered by water. He instructed the boy to make a cottonwood boat and fill it with food for him and his sister. The boy went home and faced the wrath of his mother for not returning with food for the table and, after telling her about his encounter, she refused to believe the prediction. The boy and his sister prepared the boat as instructed and placed food and seed in it and when they stepped into it the world turned-upside down. The boy and his sister were the only two to be saved and the boat drifted along until it brushed against a great fig tree growing out of the water. The Sun eventually dried up the water since in those days there were seven Suns and they were "very hot", and the boat settled on the land, but soon the land became parched and began to split. The Moon, seeing the fierceness of the Suns was causing such desolation, pretended to eat her children and went to the Sun with her mouth red telling him to look at what she had done and the Sun decided to do the same and ate his six brothers. But when the night came the Moon revealed her children as the stars and the Sun was very angry because he could not do the same and bring his brothers back to life[255].

This myth records several myths motifs in one. The flood; the world turning upside-down; the cotton and banyan trees as sacred trees, and the multiple Suns scorching the Earth. The deceit practiced by the Moon on the Sun in tricking him into eating his own brothers or children is found widely from India into the Pacific Ocean islands, as are the other motifs. The world turning upside-down is best known in the Hopi myth from the South West United States, but is found widely in India besides among the Gonds. Here similar versions and variations are found among the Uraons, Santals and Bunas[256].

In Australia the Aborigines also preserved a myth noting that the Sun woman was accompanied by her two daughters but the intensity of the heat was so great that the Sun woman had to send them away. Among the Yirkalla it was said that there were two Suns and this appears, as earlier noted, to have derived from a Jain concept[257].

The Solomon Islanders preserved a myth regarding the Sun and the problem of the Moon's intensity recorded as follows: "Once the world was a very hot place with few streams, and vegetation only along the course of the streams, and everywhere else bare rocks and sand. This was because the Moon was as powerful as the Sun, and was the enemy of mankind, burning things up every night he shone. So the Sun, who was man's friend, got some trees and bit them in half through with his teeth and made a bridge where the Moon was to cross the sea. Thus he fell into the sea when the bridge broke and became cold. Since then mankind has had cool nights, plenty of water, trees and plants growing plentifully, and good seasons"[258]. The myth is clearly identical to those found in India and there can be little doubt that it has been transferred by traders and venturers from Asia into the Pacific region.

In Polynesia the hero Bue in the Gilbert Islands was said to have pelted the Sun with coconuts to reduce the Sun's heat[259] and Bue will figure in other aspects of cultural transfer in a succeeding chapter. The throwing of objects or shooting arrows at the Sun, as recorded among the Nagas of Assam, is repeated in a myth featuring Chuvalete, a personification of Venus, among the Nayarit, or Cora, in Western Mexico. It was said that "when the Sun first appeared, the Morning Star, who is cool and disliked heat, shot him in the middle of the breast, just as he journeyed nearly across the sky. The Sun fell down to earth, but an old man brought him to life again, so that he could back and make a fresh start"[260]. Chuvalete will be of further interest in due course but it is clear that there is a close parallel to the myths of India in this version probably due to cultural transfer.

In Peru Bernabe Cobo noted that the three golden images found in the Temple of the Sun were represented together because it was believed that three Suns at one time appeared in the sky[261]. However, Cieza de Leon records that the Andean peoples believed that in ancient times, when a "great multitude if devils assembled in these parts" that five Suns appeared in the heavens and these demons and their leader Huarivilca disappeared with "groans and screams" because of these Suns and were never seen again[262]. A similar myths recording the appearance of five Suns was recorded among the Aztecs[263]. More recent researchers have noted the parallels between the five manifestations of the Sun, the five World Ages, and the five Sacred Eggs from which Pariaraca were born[264].

The Sun-Too-Hot myths have been dealt with in the context of cross-Pacific cultural transfer context in an earlier work[265] and need not be considered further here. It remains only to mention another element briefly and that is the believed Underworld path of the Sun after sunset to illustrate that this also likely to have been another element transferred by mariners or traders from Asia to South America.

The Sun - Illuminated Underworld and Underworld Path

Among the Indian peoples of Peru the earth was called Kaipacha, and was the plain on which humanity dwelt. Below this there was considered another world and the original name appears to have been forgotten but is known in present times by a Spanish term Otra Nacion - "Other Nation" or "Other People". It was considered that everything in this world was the opposite or the reverse of things in the Earth world, and that when the Sun set on Earth it entered this world and become the sunrise of that world. Correspondingly, therefore, the day here was the night there and the converse[266]. This "Otra Nacion" was said not to be the so-called Underworld of the Quechua, the Ukhu Pacha, or "internal world". This suggests that there were two different traditions, one perhaps an indigenous form, the latter in this case, and the other an imported form, although both ultimately may have been imported.

Among the Todas of South India it was believed that when Kwoto tied down the sun it caused darkness in both the Earth world and that below it implying that the same Sun actually was thought to light this world and an Underworld[267] in a similar manner to that of the Peruvians. It has been shown that many of the researchers into Toda culture believed that they migrated from the Ancient Near or Middle East and in Mesopotamia it was also believed that the Sun illuminated the Underworld during the night hours on Earth after sunset[268].

Among the Ainu of Japan the idea of a reversed world seems to have something in common also with the Peruvian belief. Their concept was that the people in that world beneath the Earth actually walked upside down so that their "feet meet ours"[269]. Such concepts of an invert-

8.083 : Finely carved stonework forming the portal at the late Inca capital of Vitcos near the Nusta Issipana. Late Inca Dynasty, Vitcos, 16th., century, A.D.

81 : Carved stone outcrop with altar terraces and priestly or ruler seats platforms similar to carved stepped outcrops in the Eastern iterranean. Inca period, Nusta Issipana, Vitcos, East Central Peru, 1350- A.D.

8.082 : Detail of stone carving on the surface of the rock known as Yurak Rumi associated with Intihuatanas in the Eastern Andes. Inca Dynasty, Nusta Issipana, Vitcos, East Central Peru, 1350-1500 A.D.

ed Underworld are found among the Tukano of Colombia and they perceived this relationship as a "mirror-image" of the Earth world[270] suggesting a common origin with others of this type. These elements of the Underworld and particularly relating to the Sun suggest that the fundamental beliefs and terms used for the Sun and the mythical cycles surrounding them are derived from the Ancient Middle East and India. These interrelationships and cosmological concepts are still sufficiently obvious for there to be little doubt that they were transferred long before the Spanish Conquest from Asia to South America.

The Itihuatana of Vitcos and Mocha, Mochar or Mucha - Kissing the Sun and Moon
One of the least known chapters in the history of the Incas is the period of exiled Inca rule after the fall of the Dynastic capital at Cuzco that occurred with Atahualpa's death in 1532 A.D. There were, however, successors and these were four or five succeeding emperors depending on whether all claimants are recognised or not. These heirs were descendants of Huascar's line since he was in the recognised direct line of hereditary rather than Atahualpa's. Four are usually recognised and these are Manco Inca, Sayri Ttupac, Titi Cusi and Tupac Amaru. These Inca rulers, except for the appeasing "puppet" Inca Sayri Ttupac who returned to Cuzco, ruled from their last stronghold in the rugged mountains around Vitcos. This was located in what had been the lands of refuge for the Chancas in East Central Peru in the mountain fastness opening onto the foothills of the Andes giving access to the Amazon Forests.

After the betrayal and cruel death of Tupac Amaru and the end of the last of the Inca Dynasty by 1572 A.D. the region of Vitcos was claimed back by the forest and was rediscovered by Hiram Bingham in his expeditions in search of the last capital of the Incas in the early part of the 20th., century. In rediscovering Vitcos, Bingham also discovered the large natural outcrop called the Nusta Issipana, carved into the characteristic altars and ceremonial seats found, and better known at Machu Picchu and Pisac[271]. The Nusta Issapana was also the location for another Intihuatana, or "Hitching place of the Sun", a projecting phalliform section of the white stone outcrop located over a natural spring. The twenty years of the last Incas saw their retention of the pre-Spanish rites and beliefs in parallel with the Christianisation of the rest of Peru. This meant that some of the beliefs and rites were therefore either witnessed or recorded as they were practised and not subject to previous interpretations handed down to descendants without actual experience of the associated ceremonies. Some of these records were preserved from reports of Spanish missionaries or envoys from Cuzco who attempted to negotiate with the court at Vitcos. Others appear to have been derived from those who lived under the last Incas' rule in their jungle fastness and one rite in particular was associated with the Intihuatana, no doubt the same as that that was celebrated originally at the others, at Pisac, Qenko and Machu Picchu. These ceremonials including devotions called "Mucha" or "Mocha" where word mucha means "to kiss" and the term muchani means to "kiss the hand"[272].

Bingham, in his search for understanding of the rituals held at the great Intihuatana of Nusta Issipana, refers at length to Antonio de la Calancha's report collected from the available records surviving two generations after the death of the last Inca and the fall of Vitcos. The Intihuatana is actually located outside Vitcos near a small village called Chuquipalpa and the Spanish eyewitness reports noted that the term used for sacred places of worship of this type was mochadero. The Nusta Issipana was the principal of those places in the forested regions of Eastern Peru away from the more populous and accessible regions at, or near Cuzco. This term, mochadero, actually derives from the term for kissing among them, mocha or mucha, and therefore these locations are where the ceremony of "kissing" was performed. Of particular note is the fact that Calancha records that this "kissing" was the principle act of worship at these shrines and at the Intihuatana in particular. The most telling of all of his references is that he notes that the whole ritual was in fact virtually identical to that described in the Book of Job in the Bible.

The object of this "kissing" as preserved in the Bible was the adoration of the Sun and Moon and it is this rite that Job "abominates" in the rites of the Gentiles. These Gentiles were described as raising their outstretched arms with hands raised toward the great orbs in the sky and to "throw kisses to them". This was considered the highest and "finest" act of worship that could be shown towards the Inca deities. Calancha reports these acts as a "grave iniquity" and in so doing was an act by the Peruvians of "denying the true god" as proselytised by the Christian Fathers. The Spanish friars were incensed that the "idolators" at Vitcos should perpetrate such acts in rejection of their own advances in attempting to enlighten them into acceptance of their god[273].

This remarkable report has three points of interest, the first being the virtual identical ritual of kissing being found on the other side of the world to its apparent first place of origin - the Ancient Middle East. The second is the term mucha itself and the third is the identification by the Spanish friars of the ritual, and other aspects of Ancient American culture unequivocally with the pre-Christian religions of the Ancient Middle East. The reference to the prophet Job and the Biblical record of this type of worship is to be found in the Book of Job, Chapter 31:26-8, and is generally ascribed to the rituals to the Moon called "Esbat" but similar references to "kissing the hand" also occur in Kings 19:18 and Hosea 13:2. The second point refers to, and extraordinarily, illustrates not only that this is the same rite found in the Ancient Near and Middle East but the term mucha or mocha is found in the Vedic Indian term mukti meaning "liberation". Mukti is the worship of the linga or Saivite phallus when identified with the Sun, the exact form of worship the Intihuatana, as a phallic stone reflected in its shape, appears to emulate[274].

The third point to be considered is the fact that not only in Peru but in Ancient Mexico and Central America the first Spanish recorded the evidence of so many aspects of Ancient Middle Eastern culture, particularly Biblically related, were to be found that were virtually duplicated in the Americas. Consequently they believed and recorded that Satan had anticipated the Christians arrival in the Americas and had deliberately set about deceiving the people by masking his own "devilish deceits" with the clothing of Christian symbolism to deceive the Indian peoples. The notorious Bishop Diego de Landa cites just such "deceits" in his famous work "Yucatan Before and After the Conquest"[275] and among many others, and not least the report by Calancha, that record the same Satanic conspiracy theory thought to be behind the beliefs and rites of the Incas themselves.

There can be little doubt that the first Europeans believed that there had been some contact between the Old World and the New and this was also true of many researchers and historians up until the middle of the 20th., century. However those who have been most voluble against contacts in the second half of the twentieth century have been swayed by Americanist theories of indigenous development and have repeatedly derided contacts between the Old World and the New as anything from "preposterous" to "racist".

Even though there are abundant reports referring to probable intrusions from the Old World, historians and archaeologists still attempt to deceive the Public and one of these specifically refers to these early Spanish reports. It is in this Isolationist environment that Norman Hammond, one of the most prominent Mayanists toward the end of the twentieth century, felt able to record that, "Throughout this period, Mayan civilisation progressed without any contact with the Old World"[276]. This is true of many other of those prominently placed, who are able to project their own similar, or less modest views, having sufficient Establishment support without fear of opposing views or need to justify their own.

Viracocha and His Son Paria-Caca

Of the first Spanish chroniclers to record the myths and religious practices of the Andean peoples few have noted the lesser-known deities before or after the more famous Viracocha. Dr Francisco de Avila arrived in Peru only a generation after the Conquest and later recorded his impressions from his missionary forays among these peoples only two generations after the fall of the Inca. He notes, as few do, that the great, revered culture hero and deity Viracocha was said to have had a son called Pariacaca.

It was Dr. Francisco de Avila who recorded, beside this one, another remarkable myth about Coniraya, or Kon Raya. Pariacaca was of some interest since it is attested that he is, similarly to Coniraya, thought to be a variation on the myth of Viracocha. The first oral tradition is that of Huathiacuri, whose father was Pariacaca the divine falcon and followed by that of Coniraya. Avila's account of the these long myths are worth considering since it is rarely presented outside the first translation in English a century ago, and given as he wrote it: "It must by understood that in the time after the deluge in every district, the Indians chose the richest and most valiant man among them for their leader, and this period they call Purun-Pacha, which means the time when there was no king. They say that in those days there appeared five large eggs on a mountain between Huarochiri and Chorillo, towards the south, (and this is the origin of Pariacaca) called Condorcoto. At that time there lived a poor and ill-clad Indian named Huathiacuri, who, they say, was the son of Pariacaca, and who learnt many arts from his father. They say that he was called Huathiacuri because his food was all huatyasca, which means parboiled, not properly cooked, or, as we say here roasted "en barbacoa". Being poor, he could afford nothing better. At the same time they say that a very rich and great lord had his house on Anchicocha, about a league and a half from the place where the five eggs appeared. His house was very richly and curiously adorned, for the roof was made of the yellow and red feathers of certain birds, and the walls were covered with similar and even more curious materials. This lord had a great number of llamas, - some red, others blue and yellow and of other bright colours, so that, to make mantles, it was unnecessary to dye the wool, and he had many other kinds of riches. For these reasons people came to him from all directions to pay their respects, and he made himself to be very wise, even saying that he was the God and Creator. But at last a great misfortune befell him, which was that he fell sick of a tedious and disgusting disease, and everybody wondered that a man who was so wise, and rich, and he was a God and Creator, should be so ill and be unable to cure himself. So they began to murmur against him. During all this time the pretended God did not fail to seek for remedies, trying various cures, procuring extraordinary medicines, and sending for all who had any knowledge of the healing art. But all was of no avail, and there was no man who understood either the disease or the cure. At this time they say that Huathiacuri journeyed towards the sea, and slept on that height called Latallaco, where the ascent commences in going from Lima to Cienehuilla. While he was there he saw a fox going towards the sea, and another coming from the coast towards Anchicocha. The one coming from the sea asked the other whether there was any news, and the other answered that 'all was well except that the rich man was very sick, and was taking extraordinary pains to get cured, and to assemble learned men who could tell him the cause of his illness, and that no one understood it. But,' added the fox, ' the real cause is that, when his wife was toasting a little maize, one grain fell on her skirt, as happens every day. She gave it to a man who ate it, and afterwards she committed adultery with him. This is the reason that the rich man is sick, and a serpent is now hovering over his beautiful house to eat it, while a toad with two heads is waiting under his grinding-stone with the same object. But no one knows this,' concluded the fox; and it then asked the other fox whether it had any news. The other fox replied that a beautiful daughter of a great chief was dying for having had connection with a man. But this is a very long story which I shall; tell presently; and now we will return to the proceedings of Huathiacuri.'"

"Having heard what the foxes said he went to the place where the rich man was lying sick, and with much dissimulation, he asked a young and beautiful girl (who, with another elder sister already married, was daughter to the sick God) if any one was ill. She said, 'Yes, my father is sick.' He replied: 'If you will consent to show me favour and to love me, I will cure your father.' The name of the girl is not known, although some say that she is the same who was called Chaudinaca. But she did not wish to consent, so she went to her father and told him that a dirty ragged man said he could cure him. Then all the wise men who were assembled laughed heartily saying that none of them could effect a cure, and how much less could this poor wretch succeed. But the sick man, by reason of his earnest desire to be cured, did not refuse to place himself in the hands of the stranger, and ordered that he should be called in, whoever he might be. He entered, and said that he could certainly effect a cure if the sick man would give his young daughter to him for a wife. The sick man replied that he would willingly do so; which the husband of his elder daughter took very ill, holding it to be a shame that his sister-in-law should be the wife of a poor man, who would thus appear to be the equal of himself, being rich and powerful. The contention between these two will be related presently."

"The wise Huathiacuri commenced the cure by saying - 'Do you know that your wife has committed adultery, and this is the reason of your sickness? Do you know that there are two great serpents above your house waiting to eat you? And that there is a toad with two heads underneath that grind-stone? Before everything else we must kill those animals, and then you will begin to recover your health. But, when you are well you must worship and reverence my father, who will appear before many days, for it is quite clear that you are neither God nor Creator. If you were God you would not be ill, nor would you be in need of a cure.' The sick man and those who stood round were astonished. The wife said that the accusation against her was a wicked lie, and she began to shout with rage and fury. But the sick man was so desirous to be cured that he ordered search to be made, and they found the two serpents on the top of the house and killed them. Then the sage reminded the wife that when she was toasting maize one grain had fallen on her skirt; and she had given it to a man; and that afterwards she had committed adultery with him. So she confessed. Then the sage then caused the grindstone to be raised, and there hopped from underneath a toad with two heads, which went to a spring that now flows by Anchicocha, where they say that it still lives, making those who go to it lose their way and become mad, and die. Having done all this, the sick man became well, and the wise Huathiacuri enjoyed the girl. They say that he generally went once a day to the mountain of Condor-coto where were the five eggs, round which a wind blew, and they say that before this there was no wind. When the sage wanted to go to Condor-coto, the sick man, now recovered, gave him his daughter to take with him, and there the pair enjoyed themselves much to their own satisfaction."

"To return to the brother-in-law of the girl, that rich man who, as we have said, was displaced that she should be given Huathiacuri, - he was very angry when he was told that Huathiacuri had enjoyed her, and declared that he was a poor wretch and not a sage. So one day he said to Huathiacuri, 'Brother, I am concerned that you, as my brother-in-law, should be ragged and poor, when I am so rich and powerful and so honoured by the people. Let us choose some thing at which we may complete, that one may overcome the other.' Huathiacuri accepted the challenge. Then he took the road to Condorcoto, and went to the place where his father Paria-caca was in one of the eggs, and told him what had taken place. Paria-caca said that it was well to accept any challenge, and that he should come back and tell him what it was. So with advice Huathiacuri returned to the village."

"One day his brother-in-law said - 'Now let us see which can vanquish the other in drinking and dancing on such a day.' So Huathiacuri accepted the challenge and posted off to his father Pariacaca, who told him to go to a neighbouring mountain, where he would turn into a dead huanacu. Next morning a fox with its vixen would come to the place, bringing a fare of chichi on her back, while the fox would have to approach Paria-caca, because the object of their coming was to give him drink, and to play and dance a little; but when they should see the dead huanacu on the road, they would not wish to lose the opportunity of filling their stomachs; and that they would put down the chichi, the drum, and the flute, and would begin to eat; that then he would come to himself and return to his own shape, and begin to cry aloud, at which the foxes would take flight, and that he would then take the things they had left behind, and might be sure of victory in the challenge with his brother-in-law."

"All this happened as Paria-caca had said, and Huathiacuri went to the place where his brother-in-law was drinking to those who stood round with great quantities of chichi, and was dancing with many of his friends. His drums were beaten by more than two hundred women. While this was going on Huathiacuri entered with his wife, dancing with her, and she charging his cup and playing on a drum. At the first sound of her drum the whole earth began to shake as if it was keeping time to the music, so that, they had the advantage of the rich man, for not only the people but the earth itself danced. Presently they went to the place where they kept the drinking bouts, and the brother-in-law and all his friends came to beat Huathiacuri in drinking, thinking that it was impossible for him to drink alone as much as the rich man and his friends. But they were deceived, for he drank all they gave him without showing a sign of having had enough. Then he rose and began to drink to those who were seated, his wife filling the cups with chichi from the fox's jug. They laughed because they thought that before he had given cups to two of them the jug would be empty; but the chichi never failed, and each man that drank fell down in a state of intoxication. So in this also he came out as conqueror."

"Then the brother-in-law challenged him once more, saying that people should now see who could enter the public square, with the best lion-skin on his shoulder, for dancing. Huathiacuri went again to his father Pariacaca, who sent him to a fountain, where he said he would find a red lion-skin with which to meet the challenge; and when he entered the square, men saw that there was a rainbow round the lion's head; so Huathiacuri again obtained his victory."

"Still the conquered brother-in-law was determined to have a final trial. This was a challenge for each to build a house in the shortest time and in the best manner. Huathiacuri accepted it; and the rich man at once began to collect his numerous vassals, and in one day he had nearly finished the walls, while Huathiacuri, with only his wife to help him, had scarcely begun the foundations. During the night the work of the rich man was stopped but not that of Huathiacuri. For in perfect silence, an infinite number of birds, snakes and lizards, completed the work, so that in the morning the house was finished, and the rich man was vanquished to the great wonder of all beholders. The a great multitude of huanacus and vicunas came next day laden with straw for the roof; while llamas came with similar loads for the rich man's roof. But Huathiacuri ordered an animal that shrieks loudly, called oscollo (wildcat) to station itself at a certain point; and it suddenly began to scream in such a way as to terrify the llamas, which shook off their loads, and all the straw was lost."

"At the end of this competition Huathiacuri, by advice of his father Pariacaca, determined to put an end to the affair; so he said to the rich man, 'Brother, now you have seen that I have agreed to everything that you have proposed. It is reasonable, therefore, that you should now do the same; and I propose that we should both see who dances best, in a blue shirt with a white cotton huara round the loins. The rich man accepted the challenge, and, as usual, was the first to appear in the public square, in the proposed dress. Presently Huathiacuri also appeared, and with a sudden shout, he ran into the place where the other was dancing; and he, alarmed at the cry and the sudden rush, began to run, insomuch as to give him more speed, he turned, or was turned by

Huathiacuri, into a deer. In this form he came to Anchicocha, where, when his wife saw it, she also rose up saying, 'Why do I remain here? I must go after my husband and die with him.' So she began to run after him and Huathiacuri after both. At last Huathiacuri overtook the wife in Anchicocha, and said to her, 'Traitress! It is by your advice that your husband has challenged me to so many proofs, and has tried my patience in so many ways. Now I will pay you for this by turning you to stone, with your head on the ground and your feet in the air.' This happened as he said, and the stone is there to this day; and the Indians go there to worship and to offer coca, and practice other diabolical superstitions. Thus the woman stopped; but the deer ran on and disappeared, and it maintained itself by eating people; but after some time the deer began to be eaten by men, and not men by the deer."

"They say that those five eggs in Condorcoto, one of which contained Pariacaca, opened, and five falcons issued from them, who were presently turned into five men, who went about performing wonderful miracles; and one was that the rich Indian, who we have mentioned in this chapter as pretending to be God, perished, because Pariacaca and the others raised a great storm and a flood which carried him and his house and wife and family away into the sea. The site of this man's house is between two very lofty mountains, the one called Vicocha, near the parish of Chorrillo, and the other Llantapa, in the parish of San Damian, and between them flows the river of Pachacamac. There was a sort of bridge, consisting of a great tree called Pullao, forming a most beautiful arch from one hill to the other, where a great variety of parrots and other birds passed to and fro. All this was swept away by the flood."

"Having come forth from the five eggs with his four brothers, and having caused the above tempest, Pariacaca aspired to perform great and mighty deeds throughout the world, though the region he traversed did not exceed twenty leagues in circuit. Especially he conceived the idea of encountering the valiant Caruyuchu Huayallo, to whom they sacrificed children as we have related in the first chapter. So Pariacaca went in search of Caruyuchu, of whose end and defeat I shall speak presently; but first I must relate what happened to Pariacaca on the road."

"On his way from Condocoto to the residence of Caruyuchu, he came to the place where now stands the village of Santa Maria de Jesus Huarochiri, at the bottom of the ravine in which the river flows, and by which one goes to the parish of Quinti. Here there was a village called Huagaihusa, where they were celebrating a great festival. It is to be noted that all this country was then Yunca, with a hot climate, according to the false opinion of the Indians. Pariacaca entered the place, where all the people were drinking, in the dress of a poor man, and he sat down with the others, but at the end of all, as is the custom with those who are not invited. But no man drank to him nor gave him a drink during the whole day. Seeing this, a girl was moved with pity and compassion, and she said, 'How is it that no one gives a drink to this poor man or takes any notice of him?' And she put a good draught of chichi into one of those large white calabashes called by the Indians Putu, and took it to Pariacaca, who received it with thanks, and told her she had done a very good deed, and had gained his friendship. 'This,' he added, 'is worth to you the same as your life, for at the end of five days wonderful things will happen in this place, and none of the inhabitants shall remain alive, for their neglect has enraged me. You must put yourself in safety on that day, with your children, that you may not share their fate; but you reveal this secret to any other inhabitant of the village, your death is also inevitable."

"The woman was thankful at receiving this warning, and on the fifth day she took good care to go far away from the village with her children, brothers, and relations; leaving the rest of the inhabitants off their guard, and still engaged in drinking and feasting. But the enraged Paraicaca has ascended a high mountain called Matrocoto, which overhangs the village of Huarochiri, and below which there is another mountain peak called Puipu-huana, which is on the road from San Damian to Huarochiri. Then an enormous quantity of rain began to fall, with hail and yellow and white stones, which carried the village away into the sea, so that no man escaped. This flood is still a tradition, among the people of Huarochiri, and some high banks were left, which may be seen before arriving at the village. Having completed this work, Pariacaca, without speaking to anyone in the other villages, or communicating with them, crossed over to the other side of the river, where he did what I shall describe in the following chapter."

"Having crossed the river, Pariacaca travelled over the fields which now belong to the Ayllu Copara, and which then in great want of water for irrigation. They did not then procure it from the river, but from a spring on the mountain called Sienacaca, which overhangs the village now called San Lorenzo. A large dam was built across this spring, and other smaller dams were thrown across it lower down, by which means the fields were irrigated. In those days, there was a very beautiful girl belonging to the Ayllu Copara, who, seeing one day that the maize crop was drying up for want of water, began to weep at the small supply that came from one of the smaller dams she had opened. Pariacaca happened to be passing by, and, seeing her, he was captivated by her charms. He went to the dam, and taking off his yacolla or cloak, he used it to stop up the drain that the girl had made. He then went down to where she was trying to irrigate the fields, and she found that there was no water flowing at all. Pariaraca asked her, in very loving and tender words, why she was weeping, and she, without knowing who he was, thus answered: - 'My father, I weep because this crop of maize will be lost, and is drying up for lack of water.' He replied that she might console herself and take no further thought, for that she had gained what he had lost, namely his love, and that he would make the dam yield more than enough water to irrigate her crop. Choque-suso told him first to produce the water in abundance, and that afterwards she promised willingly to yield to his wishes. Then he went up to the dam, and, on opening the channel, such a quantity of water flowed out, that it sufficed to irrigate the thirsty fields, and to satisfy the damsel. But when Pariacaca asked her to comply with her promise, she said that there was plenty of time to think about that. He was eager and ardent in his love, and he promised her many things, among others to conduct a channel from the river which should suffice to irrigate the farms. She accepted this promise, saying that she must first see the water flowing, and that afterwards she would let him do what he liked."

"He then examined the country, to see whence he could draw water, and he observed that above the site of the present village of San Lorenzo (in which the Ayllu Copara now resides) a very small rill came from the ravine of Cocachalla, the waters of which did not flow beyond a dam which had been thrown across it. By opening this dam and leading the water onwards, it appeared to Pariacaca that it would reach the farms of the Ayllu Copara, where were the fields of his ladylove. So he ordered all the birds in those hills and trees to assemble, together with all the snakes, lizards, bears, lions and other animals; and to remove the obstruction. This they did; and he then caused them to widen the channel and to make new channels until the water reached the farms. There was a discussion as to who should make the line for the channel and there were many pretenders to this duty, who wished to show their skill as well as to gain the favour of their employer. But the fox managed, by his cunning to get the post of engineer; and he carried the line of the canal to the spot just above the present site of the church of San Lorenzo. Then a partridge came flying and making a noise like Pich-pich, and the unconscious fox let the water flow off down the hill. So the other labourers were enraged, and ordered the snake to take the fox's place, and to proceed with what he had begun. But he did not perform the work so well as the fox; and the people to this day deplore that the fox should have been superseded, saying that the channel would have been higher up and better, if this had not taken place: and because the course of the channel is broken, just above the church, they say that is the place where the fox let the water flow off, and, which has never since been repaired."

"Having brought the water to irrigate the farms in the way that is still working, Pariacaca besought the damsel to keep the promise, and she consented with a good grace, but proposed that they should go to the summit of some rocks called Yanacaca (yana = black, caca = a rock). This they did, and she was well repaid for her love when she knew who he was. She would never let him go anywhere alone, but always desired to accompany him; and he betook her to the head-waters of the irrigating channel which had constructed for her love. There she felt a strong wish to remain, and he again consented, so she was converted into a stone, while Pariaraca went up the mountains. Thus Choque-suso was turned into a stone at the head channel which is called Cocochalla."

"Above this channel there is another called Vim-lompa, where there is another stone, into which they say Coniraya was turned"[277].

This long epic, rarely repeated, about Pariacaca suggests that this myth is in fact an aggregation of several myths, and that his association with Viracocha may be purely a manufacture of a later period to identify with him. There can be little doubt that Viracocha was a missionary, or culture-bearing hero from outside South America and Pariacaca may have actually been the son, racial or lineal descendant, or the cultural inheritor of this earlier hero, having the same origins and being perceived so by the local peoples. This would follow in the same tradition where the Spanish were identified with Viracocha when they first entered Peru and this tradition was retained as Bandelier noted into the late 19th., century, A.D.

There are several elements to consider relating to this myth, the first being the "divine eggs" myths and the number five in the traditions of Peru; the poverty of the hero; the trials, or ordeals set for Pariacaca by his brother-in-law, his association with irrigation, and his name. It is the "egg myths" as the element of divine creation that are to be considered first.

The Divine Egg in Creation Myths
The reference to Pariacaca being born from one of five falcon's eggs is remarkably similar to the myths in India recorded elsewhere in this work regarding the primal "egg" coming into existence in the first act of Creation and divining into two halves, one of silver - the Earth and other gold - the Sky. Before considering the Hindu myths it is worth consider investigating whether or not the name of Pariacaca had also been derived from India or that only the mythical.

In an extraordinary myth relating to rain-making the Paraiyans in South India preserved a ritual which clearly indicates their origin, at least in part, from the Ancient Near East. This suggests that they were earlier Aryan peoples from there who settled in India before the Vedic Aryans and who were later relegated by them. The rain god in Hindu India is Varuna, who is himself mentioned in the Hittite inscriptions carved in the second half of the second millennium B.C. in Anatolia, indicating migrations from soon after that period that associates him with the Vedic Aryans. The Paraiyan myth translated a century ago states: "In times of drought some of the lowers orders, instead of addressing their prayers to the rain god Varuna, try to induce a spirit or devata named Kodumpavi (wicked one) to send her paramour Sukra to the affected area. The belief seems to be that Sukra goes away to his concubine for about six months, and, if he does not then return, drought ensues. The ceremony consists in making a huge figure of Kodumpavi in clay, which is placed on a cart, and dragged through the streets, for seven to ten days. On the last day, the final death ceremonies are celebrated. It is disfigured, especially those parts which are usually concealed. Vettiyans (Paraiyan grave-diggers), who have been shaved, accompany the figure, and perform the funeral ceremonies. This procedure is believed to put Kodumpavi to shame, and to get her to induce Sukra to return, and stay the drought. Paraiyans are said to wail as though they were at a funeral, and to beat drums in the funeral time"[278].

The Paraiyan myth appears to be a reflection of the Hittite myth of the so-called Missing God that illustrates in mythological form the desolation of the earth when the rains fail, a repeating problem in all hot dry countries. The rain is depicted usually as a young male deity and in the Hittite myths he is named as Telipinu. An edited version of the myth is as follows: The Sun god gave a great feast and all the guests ate but could not drink enough to quench their thirst. The Sun god then belatedly complained that his son Telipinu had gone away because he was angry and had taken all the good things with him. The gods set out to find him and the Sun god sent out an eagle to search for his son with the instructions to seek his whereabouts in the "hollow valleys" and the "dark-blue waters", but the eagle could not find him. The Weather-god spoke to Hannahannas complaining that they would die of starvation, and this goddess urged him to go himself and look for Telipinu. The Weather-god rapped at the gate of the town with his hammer but broke the handle and could not pass through and sat down dejectedly. The goddess Hannahannas then sent out a bee to sting Telipinu when it found him and after a very long search it found him asleep in a meadow near his cult centre of Lihzina. The bee stung Telipinuas as directed, on the hands and feet, and he awoke in a rage and then, instead of returning as planned, went on the rampage and proceeded with destroying mankind, sheep and oxen. Eventually he was calmed enough to return on the back of an eagle. The text of this section of the myth states that Telipinu hastened and there was thunder and lightning in the sky and below the earth was dark and in turmoil. The "eagle's wing brought him from afar". The goddess Kamrusepas saw him coming from afar and she stilled his anger, wrath and his rage and fury. In returning he restored the earth to its fruitfulness and the endangered social institutions were again stabilised[279]. The myth continues on for some length but is less important to this study.

The references in the Paraiyan myth to a ritual cart also seems to have been derived from the Ancient Near East. The gods of renewal and rebirth were also important in the far north of Europe where the Scandinavian myths record the myth cycle of Balder. Associated with him, but perhaps from a separate lineage are the Vanir who may have derived from the Lake Van region in the Southern Caucasus - the same region likely to have been the ancient homeland of the Bants and Vannis of West and South India. The connection between the Ancient Near Eastern deities and those of Northern Europe has long been established and the cart or wagon used in the rites of the dead Freyr or Frodi appear to have the same origin as similar rituals associated with those of Cybele in Western Asia[280]. It is probably from the early forms derived from the fertility worship of the gods and goddesses both the Hittite, Canaanite and Syrian goddess patronised throughout millennia in the same region that the Paraiyans (or Pariayans) derived their somewhat garbled myths and associated rites.

As already noted the Pariayans claimed to be superior to the Brahmans even though the Brahmans had successfully relegated them to the lowest strata of society and inevitably therefore, to abject poverty. - a process inveigled upon them from about a millennium ago. There are some references as noted in myths and vestiges in some of the ceremonials and rituals still performed into the twentieth century that suggests that they were as they claim at one time the rulers of the land, and reflected their name, and this caused their severe subjection by the Brahmans resulting in their abject poverty. The name of the Pariayans derives from Paria and their original linkage anciently may have been Paria-Raya to denote their ruling status as a former kingly caste. It may be that raya = raca = caca where the suffix raca appears to also be identical to raya, a term for king in India earlier noted but where caca referred to a stone in Peru, and priestly kings of the Ancient Middle East officiated at stones. Overall this probability is also reflected in the other related deity, Con-I-raya where raya clearly identifies with ruler as raya, a king, in Ancient India, and found also in South America as I-raya. It seems probable therefore that the South Indian tribal name Paria (Pariah) may have been the origin of the deity Paria-raya, named Paria-raca or Paria-caca in Peru. This would mean that this culture-hero would have arrived in Peru some centuries after Viracocha probably after the 10th., century, A.D., but it is also likely that there were regular contacts over the centuries long before the advent of both Viracocha and Pariacaca, or Paria-raca from Asia. This means that any one from abroad from India would be generally identified with Viracocha just as the Spanish and later Europeans were in more recent times. If this is so, then origins of the Peruvian deity, and Chuvalete in Mexico, reflect a time when the Pariayans were being relegated socially to the ragged, lowest strata in South India society, and account for the references to that relegation and the subsequent extreme poverty occur in the Mexican and Peruvian myths. And it is probably significant therefore that this region of South India is the same where the Syrian Christians settled.

The myths of ancient pre-Vedic India were incorporated into Hindu mythology when the Brahmans were not powerful enough among the more remote regions of India from the North West were they entered from Iran. Many of the Aboriginal or pre-Vedic naturalised immigrants, before the later Vedic Aryans, retained myths and deities already familiar to the Aryans and these were readily adapted centuries later to the new religion growing out of Vedic Brahmanism - Hinduism. Creation myths, elaborating the principle of world evolution from an egg is widely known in Eurasia and this was also true of India, and there is, inevitably, at least one myth cycle attributing creation to development from the egg to Brahma. However, these myths are also found among the earlier people and it is likely therefore that the Paraiyans also retained a more complete mythology including this cycle before them in the centuries when they were rulers before the tenth century A.D. Equally there may be connections with their decline and degradation at the hands of the Brahmans is some myths.

In the earliest complete myths recorded in the Vedic texts it is said that Prajapati created or "hatched" the worlds. In other texts it is said that at the beginning of time only non-Being existed. This developed into existence and then "turned over" to form a cosmic egg. It remained in this form for a "cosmic year" and then split into two, one became silver while the other was gold. The half of the cosmic egg that was golden became the sky while the other, silver half, became the Earth. The outer membrane became the clouds and mist while the veins became the rivers and the white of the egg became the ocean. The elemental deity Virat-rupa Agni, the Fire God as the Cosmic Cause, who was the spiritual essence of the egg or the seed principle of existence within, thought, and from this he wished a second half of himself be produced and he was therefore able to unite with himself to produce all things[281]. Sexual symbolism is a natural part of the cosmology in Hinduism where the phallus is the central focus of its most popular sect, Saivism or the worship of Siva, whose symbol is that of the linga. In terms of the Cosmic Egg, "space" was considered to be the linga and the earth the altar, and in the Tantras the egg shape is equated to the linga. Brahman as Cosmic Principle is likened to the curve of the universe that reflects the shape of an egg, and in this imagery it is described as the "golden egg resplendent like a sun" of Manu[282].

In the Bramanda there are two primal eggs, the smaller is man as the microcosm of the Universe called Ksudra Brahmanda - "Small Egg of Immensity", and the other is the Cosmic Being called Samasti or "Egg of Immensity" and these are compared to two birds in the Vedas[283]. In the Great Void, or "Egg of Immensity", there are said to be fifty forms of void. Five of these belong to the Tara, the "power-of-hunger", while the others belong to Kali, the "power-of-time"[284]. Here Tara is identified as "The Star" and was the life-force of the "Golden-Embryo - Hiranya-garbha. Tara is identified with the "power-of-hunger" since when an embryo is born it requires constant feeding and "wants only food". The Golden Embryo is usually considered male, and here the derivation of the term Tara has been considered by some to originate with Ishtar in the Ancient Near East from a time when Venus was considered a male star. However, others have derived it from the Tantras where the Tara as the Star leads souls to "the other shore"[285] and suggests a link to Vayu as wind deity. Consequently both of these deities are linked to sea mariners who require the assistance of wind to fill the sails to reach that other, distant shore. This is indicated in a term associated with Vayu and that is Vata and this appears to have given the terms for the names for canoes with sails from India and throughout Oceania where vata, vaka, and other related terms denote this type of canoe[286]. Interesting in the Golden Embryo or Egg myth Tara is associated with the sacred number five and this number frequently occurs similarly in South America.

In the Vedic myths and rituals of Ancient India the divine egg, as above noted, and the human embryo, perceived as a spark of the Sun, are seen as a consistent correspondence from the Divine Cosmic Egg, through the divine Solar Orb, to the fundamental embryo of the human or animal being. The individual human being was perceived as being a "spark" from the God of Fire, Agni, and Agni was seen as being representative of the Sun in the microcosm at the sacred fire in the altar hearth at the centre of the Brahman rituals. These rites appear to have their echo in the Inca rites and ceremonies and particularly so since they were required to be performed at the time of the sunrise or sunset, and a portion from those of the oldest Vedic texts are included as follows:

"1) The Agnihotra, doubtless is the Sun. It is because he rose in front (agre) of that offering, that the Agnihotra is the Sun."

"2) When he offers in the evening after sunset, he does so thinking, 'I will offer, while he is here, who is this (offering);' and when he offers in the morning before sunrise, he does so thinking, 'I will offer, while he is here, who is this (offering):' and for this reason, they say, the Agnihotra is the Sun."

"3) And when he sets, then he, as an embryo, enters that womb, the fire; and along with him thus becoming an embryo, all these creatures become embryos; for, being coaxed, they lie down contented. The reason, then, why the night envelops that (sun), is that embryos also are, as it were, enveloped."

"4) Now when he offers in the evening after sunset, he offers for the good of that (sun) in the embryo state, he benefits that embryo; and since he offers for the good of that (sun) in the embryo state, therefore embryos here live without taking food."

"5) And when he offers in the morning before sunrise, then he produces that (sun-child) and, having become a light, it rises shining. But, assuredly, it would not rise, were he not to make that offering: this is why he performs that offering."

"6) Even as a snake frees itself from its skin, so does it (the sun-child) free itself from the night, from evil: and verily, whosoever, knowing this, offers the Agnihotra, he frees himself from its skin; and after his birth all these creatures are born; for they are set free according to their inclination."[287].

The Brahman rites and the commentaries upon them are here already ancient and there are many aspects that had become garbled and lost their meaning with time even before they had been written down. They do, however, reveal a very sophisticated philosophical mind-set in the fundamental understanding of the development of the human or animal from the embryo dating from at least as early as the first half of the first millennium B.C. Compared to that recorded in South America at the time of the Spanish the Brahmans appear to have a far superior form of understanding and coherent cosmic philosophy than that of the Incas. This therefore tends to confirm along with all the other shared aspects of cultural heritage that the flow was largely, but not entirely, from West Asia and India to the Americas rather than the other way round. This probably explains why there are only elements without the developed all-embracing references either in myth or ritual in the recorded myths such as those of Viracocha or Pariacaca where only certain elements such as the eggs and their number and little else is remembered of the related cosmology. Other elements such as the Sun compared to a snake shedding its skin are not integral in the South American myths but exist where they occur as clearly separate elements and were probably received as such via Indonesia, Melanesia and Polynesia.

The appearance of Pariacaca as a poorly dressed Indian is reminiscent of the Coniraya myths and those of the Nayarit (Cora) Chuvalette. The lack of the Amerindians exhibiting what might be considered a parallel of European morality was noted not only in the Americas but also in Africa and throughout Melanesia and Polynesia to a large extent by early explorers and missionaries. The appearance therefore of myths such as those relating to these three culture-heroes and their apparent "moral" tales admonishing the listener not to judge a person by the clothes he wears, or a "book by its cover", appears to be very much out of character among the generality of their myths and heroic type. These few examples, therefore, stand out in contradistinction among the many other myths exhibiting not the slightest interest or development of a morality of the European type. This is more characteristically reflected in the early part of the Pariacaca myth indicating that a chief may be chosen by his display of wealth and power including fine clothes and the broader eulogy and overt admiration for wealth and power in these cultures. These so-called moral elements in these few myths could be explained by the fact that they were indeed foreign elements imported into otherwise locally engendered myths. Similar references were imported in earlier Christian contacts but of particular note is the possibility that they may have been introduced by the missionaries of St. Thomas from Southern India and similarly distributed with related iconography onto the Pacific Coast of North and South America reflected in the Tonaca-Tonapa myths. The idea that a manifestation of a hero as the Sun should go about dressed in rags is completely alien to the Amerindian mind and they considered that a strong man or leader should look and act the part and that if he dressed otherwise he could only be a fake or impostor. This is particularly illustrated in the Coniraya myth following where it would be totally unbelievable that the hero, dressed in rags for the first part of the myth should then suddenly revert in a later section to dressing in the finery of the Sun simply to impress the person with whom he is infatuated. Such motifs are likely only to have been foreign introductions.

Kon Raya or Con-i-Raya as Hero-Deity

Avila was the main source of the Pariacaca myths and also records more fully that of Coniraya or Kon Raya. He recorded the myth as follows that is an apparent extension, or parallel that of Pariacaca: "It is also said that there was another idol called Coniraya, of which it is not known certainly whether it existed before or after the rise of Pariacaca. It is, however, certain that it was invoked and reverenced almost down to the time when the Spaniards arrived in this land. For when the Indians worshipped it they said, 'Coniraya Viracocha (this name is that which they gave and still give, to the Spaniards), thou art lord of all: thine are the crops, and thine are all the people.' In commencing any arduous or difficult undertaking, they threw a piece of coca (a well-known leaf) on the ground, as an oblation, and said, 'Tell me, O Lord Coniraya Uiracocha, how I am to do this?' The same custom prevailed among the weavers of cloths, when their work was toilsome and difficult. This invocation and custom of calling the idol by the name of Uiracocha certainly prevailed long before there were any tidings of Spaniards in the country. It is not certain whether Coniraya or Pariacaca was the more ancient, we will first relate his origin and history, and afterwards that of Pariacaca."

"They say that in most ancient times the Coniraya Uirococha appeared in the form and dress of a very poor Indian clothed in rags, insomuch that those who knew not who he was reviled by him and called him a lousy wretch. They say that this was the Creator of all things, - and that by his word of command, he caused the terraces and fields to be formed on the steep sides of ravines, and the sustaining walls to rise up and support them. He also made the irrigating channels to flow by merely hurling a hollow cane, such as we call a cane of Spain; and he went in various directions, arranging many things. His great knowledge enabled him to invent tricks and deceits touching the huacas and idols in the villages which he visited. At that time they also say that there was a woman who was a huaca. Her name was Cavillaca, and she was a most beautiful version, who was much sought after by the huacas, or principal idols, but she would never show favour to any one of them. Once she sat down to weave a mantle at the foot of a lucma tree, when the wise Coniraya succeeded in approaching her in the following manner. He turned himself into a very beautiful bird, and went up into the lucma tree, where he took some of his generative seed and made it into the likeness of a ripe and luxurious lucma, which he allowed to fall near the beautiful Cavillaca. She took it and ate it with much delight, and by it she was made pregnant without other contact with man. When the nine months were completed she conceived and bore a son, herself remaining a virgin; and she suckled the child at her own breast for a whole year without knowing whose it was nor how it had been engendered. At the end of the year, when the child began to crawl, Cavillaca demanded that the huacas and principal idols of the land should assemble, and that it should be declared whose son was the child. This news gave them all much satisfaction, and each one adorned himself in the best manner possible, combing, washing, and dressing in the richest clothes, each desiring to appear brighter and better than the rest in the eyes of the beautiful Cavillaca, that so she might select him for her spouse and husband. Thus there was an assembly of false gods at Anchicocha, a very cold inhospitable spot between the villages of Chorrillo and Huarochiri, about half way. When there were all seated in their order, Cavillaca addressed them as follows: 'I have invited you to assemble here, O worthies and principal persons, that you may know my great sorrow and trouble at having brought forth this child that I hold in my eyes. It is now aged one year: but I know not, nor can I learn, who was its father. It is notorious that I have never known man nor lost my virginity. Now that you are all assembled, it must be revealed who made me pregnant, that I may know who did this harm to me, and whose son is this child.' They were all silent, looking at each other, and waiting to see who would claim the child, but no one came forward. They say that in this assembly, in the lowest place of all, sat the god, Coniraya Uiracocha in his beggar's rags; and the beautiful Cavillaca scarcely looked at him, when she addressed the gods; for it never entered her head that he was the father. When she found that all were silent, she said: - 'As none of you will speak, I shall let the child go, and doubtless his father will be the one to whom he crawls, and at whose feet he rests.' So saying, she loosed the child, who crawled away, and, passing by all the others, he went to where his father Coniraya in his rags and dirt, and when the child reached him, it rejoiced and laughed, and rested at his feet."

"This conduct caused Cavillaca great shame and annoyance, and she snatched up the child exclaiming:- 'What disgrace is this that has come upon me, that a lady such as I am should be made pregnant by a poor and filthy creature.' Then she turned her back and fled away towards the seashore. But Coniraya Uiracocha desired the friendship and favour of the goddess, so, when he saw her take her flight, he put on magnificent golden robes, and, leaving the astonished assembly of gods, he ran after her, crying out:- 'O my lady Cavillaca, turn your eyes and see how handsome and gallant am I,' with other loving and courteous words; and they saw that his splendour illuminated the whole country. Yet the disdainful Cavillaca would not turn her head, but rather increased her speed, saying:- 'I have no wish to see anyone, seeing that I have been made pregnant by a creature so vile and filthy.' She disappeared, and came to the sea coast of Pachacamac, where she entered the sea with her child, and was turned into a rock. They say that the two rocks may still be seen, which are mother and child, Coniraya continued the pursuit, crying out, and saying, 'Stop! I cannot see you?' As he ran he met a condor ... ", etc. The myth includes lengthy references that appear to be imported from other myths relating that after this confrontation he met a Fox, a Jaguar, falcon, Humming Bird, Parrots and wears an animal headdress (*4.058-64*).

The myth continues after this section: "Thus he rewarded and granted privileges to all the animals that gave him news that accorded with his wishes, and cursed all those whose tidings were not agreeable to him."

"When he reached the sea-shore he found that Cavillaca and her child were turned to stone; and as he walked along the beach he met two beautiful young daughters of Pachacamac, who guarded a great serpent, because their mother was absent, visiting the recently arrived Cavillaca in the sea. The name of this wife of Pachacamac was Urxayhuachac (Urpi-Hua-Chac). When Coniraya found these girls alone without their mother, he did not care for the serpent, which he could keep quiet by his wisdom, so he had intercourse with the eldest sister, and desired to do the same with the younger, but she flew away in the shape of a wild pigeon (called by the Indians Urpi); hence the mother of these girls was called Urpi-Huachac, or mother of the doves."

"In those days it was said that there were no fishes in the sea, but this Urpi-Huachac reared a few in a small pond. Coniraya was enraged that Urpi-Huachac should be absent in the sea, visiting Cavillaca; so he emptied the fishes out of her pond into the sea, and thence all the fishes now in the sea have been propagated. Having done this, Coniraya continued his flight along the coast. When the mother of the girls returned they told her what had happened, and she pursued Coniraya in a great fury, calling out, until at last he determined to stop and wait for her. The she addressed him with loving and tender words, saying, - 'Coniraya, do you wish that I comb you head and pick out the lice?' So he consented, and reclined his head on her lap; but while she was pretending to do this, she was forming a rock over which she might hit him when he was off his guard. He knew this through his great wisdom, and told her he must retire for a few minutes. She agreed to this; and he went back to the land of Huarochiri, where he wandered about for a long time, placing tricks both to, whole villages and to single men and women"[288]. In the Pariacaca myth Coniraya turned to a stone on the top of a mountain.

The myth has several remarkable elements and these are the association of this hero named Coniraya with the Nayarit hero, Chuvalette, a ragged deity already noted but more importantly, along with the name Tonapa or Tonaca, is that this myth illustrates that the coastal regions of Mexico and Peru were anciently connected before the advent of the Spanish. In the last decade it has been finally admitted by some in the broad stream of archaeology in North America that there were contacts between North and South America, although fiercely denied by others in the second half of the twentieth century. The Latin American researchers have usually been more positive about the possibility of cross-Pacific contacts between Asia and the Americas and of particular note were Miguel Covarrubias in Mexico and Emilio Estrada in Ecuador. For those who support isolationist attitudes any contact between North and South America meant pre-Colombian peoples had the marine technology to construct and steer ocean-going rafts in opposition to the natural flow of the oceanic currents for over 1000 miles (1600km) to the north to Central America from Ecuador or a further distance from Northern Peru. Thor Heyerdahl long supported such a proposition, but the problem for the Isolationists, propounding the Indigenous Development Theory, was that if the Amerindians could achieve such marine feats then they could also reach the Polynesian Islands to the West. This is certain to have occurred since storms or freak weather conditions, such as the regular El Ninos, must have driven them to the West assisted by the normal prevailing winds and Equatorial Currents that flow for the most part from east to west.

The Cora (Nayarit) Myth of Chavalete - Venus as the Morning Star

A myth recorded by the Nayarit people preserved a myth recorded by Carl Lumholtz a century ago in Western Mexico and is given here verbatim as follows: "Chuvalete was poor, and the rich people did not like him. But afterward they took to him, because they found that he was a nice man, and they asked him to come and eat with them. He went to their houses dressed like the 'neighbours'. But one day when they invited him he came like an Indian boy, almost naked. He stopped outside of the house, and the host came out with a torch of pinewood to see who it was. He did not recognise Chuvalete, and called out to him. 'Get away, you Indian pig! What are you doing here?' And with his torch he burned stripes down the arms and legs of the shrinking Chuvalete. Next day Chuvalete received another invitation to eat with the 'neighbours'. This time he made himself into a big bearded fellow, with the complexion of a man half white, and he put on the clothes in which they knew him. He came on a good horse, had a nice blanket over his shoulder, wore a sombrero and a good sabre. They met him at the door and led him into the house."

"'Here I am at your service, to see what I can do for you,' he said to them."

"'Oh, no'" they said. 'We invited you because we like you, not because we want anything of you. Sit down and eat.'"

"He sat down to the table, which was loaded with all the good things rich people eat. He put a roll of bread on his plate, and then began to make stripes with it on his arms and legs.'"

"'Why do you do that?' they asked him. 'We invited you to eat what we eat.'"

"Chuvalete replied: 'You do not wish that my heart may eat, but my dress. Look here! Last night it was I who was outside of you door. The man who came to see me burned me with his pine torch, and said to me, 'You Indian pig, what do you want here?'"

"'Was that you'" they asked.'"

"Yes, gentlemen, it was I who came then. As you did not give me anything yesterday, I see that you do not want to give the food to me, but to my clothes. Therefore, I had better give it to them.' He took the chocolate and the coffee and poured it over himself as if it were water, and he broke the bread into pieces and rubbed it all over his dress. The sweetened rice, and boiled hen with rice, sweet atole, minced meat with chile, rice pudding, and beef soup, all he poured over himself. The rich people were frightened and said that they had recognised him.'"

"'You burned me yesterday because I was an Indian,' he said. 'God put me in the world as an Indian. But you do not care for the Indians, because they are naked and ugly.' He took the rest of the food, and smeared it over his saddle and his horse, and went away.'"[289].

Along with the Coniraya and Huathiacuri myths this of Chuvalete reflects this uncharacteristic "moral" element not at all usual in Mesoamerican tradition. It is more likely that these are another aspect of evidence that supports the probability of the Syrian Christians proselytising along the Pacific Coasts of both North and South America utilising morality tales in their sermons more characteristic of the Christian tradition of Eurasia.

Not only do shared aspects of iconography in these Amerindian myths between the far north west of South America correspond to that of Mexico but is found in the same contexts along with myths clearly naming the same heroes and their superhuman feats and tasks. For this to be so these vastly disparate people must have all been in contact and the most logical means was by sea where sea mariners or traders were in at least occasional contact to convey their myths and corresponding iconography and rituals abroad. In the middle of last century researchers in the Amazon recorded to perceive parallels with Central American cultures and these included well-known names such as Donald Lathrap, and Meggers and Evans. Betty Meggers also wrote on the archaeology of Ecuador and recorded parallels and probable derivation of iconography and cultural transfer from Polynesia and South East Asia. More recently others such as Anna C. Roosevelt have opposed connections between the forested tributaries of the Amazon and have supported Indigenous Development of the Amazonian tribes. However, the myths and legends from that region point to so many parallels between their own myths and Central America and beyond that contact must have been more than sporadic. Some of these will be considered but firstly there are a few comments required on the Coniraya myths indicating ordeals as a major myth motif and their parallels beyond Peru.

Ordeals and Trials in Myth and Tradition

In a series of myths similar to the one described in the Pariacaca myth those recorded of the Amazon Indians also preserves similar motifs to the examples in Peru and beyond suggesting that they are all connected. In a myth relating to the trials of the tribal hero of the Bororo - Toribugu, it was said that his father wanted to kill him because he believed that his son was having relations with his wife and the young man's stepmother, so he devised a series of trials. The first test was to acquire a jaguar from the forest, the second was to obtain rattles from the Land of Spirits, the third was to acquire nuts from the babassu palm that grew in the middle of a swamp guarded by a fierce demon, and the fourth and last was to climb a cliff to obtain the chicks of a macaw. In all these tests, just as Huathiacuri had elicited assistance from his father, Pariacaca, so Toribugu is aided by his grandmother to succeed in each of these trials[290].

These trials or ordeals appear to be similar to those already noted among the Todas in Southern India. These were the tests imposed on the culture-hero Kwoto by the gods in their demand that he should tie the Sun down to a tree and he used various types of chains before he succeeded with the stone chain[291]. Between India and South America the Islands of Indonesia provide a convenient stopover and also reveal closely similar myths to that of the Bororo and are illustrated in the myths focused on the hero named Seroenting known throughout the Central and Eastern Islands of Indonesia. In another myth from Borneo there are not only the trials that the culture-hero must succeed in completing but there are references to closely similar aspects of flood myths found widely in South America but rarely elsewhere[292], and this myth will be considered in a later section.

After leaving India, and departing or passing Borneo, a mariner would reach the great Melanesian island of New Guinea or the islands off the mainland to the north. It is here that there are some remarkable customs and myths associated with the Kula, or ceremony, a trading circuit between the island and the mainland and some of these are of great interest. This region would be an essential stop-over in the journey from India to Peru since the Equatorial Current to the Americas only flows from Asia to the Americas to the north of New Guinea. The Southern branch of the Equatorial current is ideal for travelling from New Guinea south through Melanesia, Polynesia and using the north section of the West Wind Drift to sail directly to Chile and Peru in South America.

The Kula has already been considered earlier but preserved in the Trobriand Islands, forming a central region in the ceremonial Kula circuit, is a myth that bears considerable resemblances to the Bororo and Pariacaca/Huathiacari myth in South America. This was recorded in two versions, the more coherent is as follows as recorded by Bronislaw Malinowski: "Tokosikuna, …, is also slightly, lame, very ugly, and with a pitted skin; so ugly indeed that he could not marry. Far North, in the mythical land of Kokopawa, they play a flute so beautifully that the chief of Digumenu, the village of Tokosikuna, hears it. He wishes to obtain the flute. Many men set out, but all fail, and they have to return half way because it is so far. Tokosikuna goes, and, through a mixture of cunning and daring, he succeeds in getting possession of the flute, and in returning safely to Digumenu. There, through magic which one is led to infer he has acquired on his journey, he changes his appearance, becomes young, smooth-skinned and beautiful. The guya'u (chief) who is away in his garden, hears the flute played in his village, and returning there, he sees Tokosikuna sitting on a high platform, playing the flute and looking beautiful. 'Well,' he says, 'all my daughters, all my granddaughters, my nieces and my sisters, you all marry Tokosikuna! Your husbands, you leave behind! You marry Tokosikuna, for he has brought the flute from the distant land!" So Tokosikuna married all the women."

"The other men did not take it very well, of course. They decided to get rid of Tokosikuna by stratagem. They said: "The chief would like to eat giant clam-shell, let us go and fish it." "And how shall I catch it?" asks Tokosikuna. "You put your head, where the clam-shell gapes open." (This of course would mean death, as the clam-shell would close, and, if a really big one, would easily cut off his head). Tokosikuna, however, dived and with his two hands, broke a clam-shell open, a deed of super-human strength. The other were angry, and planned another form of revenge. They arranged a shark-fishing, advising Tokosikuna to catch the fish with his hands. But he simply strangled the big shark, and put it into the canoe. Then, he tears asunder a boar's mouth, bringing them thus to despair. Finally they decide to get rid of him at sea. They try to kill him first by letting the heavy tree, felled for the waga, fall on him. But he supports it with his outstretched arms, and does no harm to himself. At the time of lashing, his companions wrap some wayaugo (lashing creeper) into a soft pandanus leaf; then they persuade him to use pandanus only for the lashing of his canoe, which he does indeed, deceived by seeing them use what apparently is the same. Then they sail, the other men in good, sea-worthy canoes, he is in an entirely unseaworthy one, lashed only with the soft, brittle pandanus leaf." The myth continues with the canoes reaching their first destination and while the other men trade their goods in the Kula they obtain only inferior shells and goods for theirs in return while Tokosikuna returns always with the finest quality trades and inflames the anger and jealousy of the other men. They notice, however, that Tokosikuna's lashings for his boat are rotten and will not last and they declare among themselves that he next day he will drown in Pilolu. Next day they all paddle for Vakuta and as they adjust their canoes for the wind the lashings on Tokosikuna's canoe break and the canoe sinks. The other men refuse to attempt to save Tokosikuna and he is forced to swim to the rock of Selawaya on the eastern slope of Gumasila where he stays and turning to the other canoes on their journey he utters a curse against them[293].

The ordeals here are clearly not identical but the fundamental principle is the same as in the myths from Peru and the Amazon through to New Guinea and Indonesia where the influences from India are undeniable and is the likely origin from where it was derived. This myth is certain, therefore, to have been a result of diffusion along the oceanic currents and trade routes from India to Indonesia, Northern New Guinea to Melanesia and through to South America. The term Pilolu is clearly the Pulotu of the Polynesians, the Land of Departed Souls and indicates the direction, the East, from which at least a part of the influences included in these myths must have been imported by mariners and, or traders. It is also interesting to note that the Melanesian name here for chief, guya'u is almost certainly derived from the corresponding Hindu term, guha[294].

Nakawe Myths - From Huichol to Amazonia into Oceania

In a previous work by the present author there were described an important myth, and related myth cycles, reflecting certain motifs of unusual type found preserved within the oral traditions of the Huichols in North West Mexico and through into Polynesia, Melanesia, Indonesia and to India itself. One of these included a motif categorised under the title of the Woodchip Myths where heroes, in attempting to cut a giant tree down return later, usually next morning, to find all the chips that had been hacked from the trunk had reformed in their original place and the tree restored and standing normally[295]. These were shown also to occur in the Quiche-Mayan sacred book, the Popol Vuh, but this myth is also known in the Amazon Basin.

In the Mexican myth the mythical Great-grandmother was named Nakawe and for the Huichols she was mother of the gods as well as the goddess of vegetation. She is always depicted leaning on a staff since she is believed to be the serpent goddess herself, and the bamboo staff was her symbol[296]. The flood myth in which she plays an important part records that a Huichol was felling trees growing on his field ready to plant maize but when he reappeared each morning after cutting them down the previous day they were all standing in their original position as if never touched. This re-occurred for four days and on the fifth day he determined to find the reason for this phenomenon. As he lay in wait an old woman arose from the ground with a staff in her hand and it was no other than the Great-grandmother, Nakawe, the goddess who caused the vegetation to rise from the ground. The Huichol man did not recognise her but she pointed to the South, North, West and East, as well as above and below. All the trees the man had cut down the day before then stood up in their former position. Angered he confronted her and demanded to know why she was undoing all his hard work. She said it was because she wanted to talk to him to warn him that he was working in vain and that there was going to be a great flood in five days. A very cold wind would arise and that would be the warning, and she further admonished him to construct a box in which to secure himself which would float, and take with him five grains of each of the colours of maize, and fire along with five stems of the squash plant to keep it burning and finally a black bitch[297].

The number five occurs repeatedly in the Americas as a sacred number and is also found similarly in India and the Ancient Middle East. The flood myth itself will be of more interest in a later chapter, but it is interesting to note that a similar myth, including a localise version of the Woodchip Myth, occurs 4000 miles (6400 km) South East of the Huichol among the Cayapo Indians of the Ge tribe. In a myth regarding the discovery of corn a woman, while bathing with her son, was annoyed by a mouse jumping onto her shoulder so she knocked it off but it immediately returned to her shoulder again. She again tried to rid herself of this apparent pest but unsuccessfully, and he then spoke to her. He also gave her corn seed unknown to the Indians until then who had always existed on a diet of "rotten wood". The woman ate the corn and then the mouse guided her to the place in the forest where it could be gathered although there was no sign of the plant from which it grew. One day an Indian noticed that in a huge tree there were macaws and monkeys eating cobs up in the branches and from these the seed was falling. The Indians decided to cut down the tree but were unable to complete their task before nightfall so they returned next day to find the woodchips had returned to the tree and it was standing fully restored. The Indians sent two small boys back to the village to collect another axe, and when returning, the boys killed a lizard and ate it but then suddenly they aged so much that they found the axe was too heavy to carry. The Indians succeeded in chopping down the tree that day and since then corn has been grown and distributed throughout the world[298].

It is clear that this myth in principle has much to do with, and probably from the same origins as the Huichol myth and the interlude of the boys aging suggests that this was a substitute, through long, garbled retelling, of Nakawe the aged goddess of corn and the earth. The restoration of the woodchips is unmistakable and much further south in the Gran Chaco of Central South America among the Toba Indians there is a goddess named Nasore who may well have developed from Nakawe[299]. The Ge Indians also preserve versions featuring this goddess in their myths[300]. Interestingly the researchers into Erromangan culture from have recorded oral traditions that have parallels originating from the megalithic-based culture found on this island to that of the rites associated with Baal and Astoreth in Ancient West Asia. The megalithic artefacts include ring stones and stone disks used until the late 19th., century in the islands ceremonials[301]. On the same island in Melanesia there are myths that record mythical old men named Nate, probably the Tate or Tata of South and South East Asia and the Americas. Tata also occurs among the Huichol, and their goddess Nakawe is probably the Erromangan "old woman" recorded as being called Name (Namay)[302].

543

CHAPTER 9

MARINERS, SUN MYTHS - TUPAC AND THE PACIFIC

The myths of Pariacaca, his son Huathiacuri, and Coniraya are reflected in the previous chapter among the Huichols of West Mexico, and with their common aspects west into Melanesia. It is worth considering also the other myth motifs contained in these myths where they indicate contact from further afield indicating a broader, more distant transfer of cultural influence from, and in return, with Asia through to North and South America.

The Hero Myths of Si'wit and Kixwet

The vast distances covered by these myths suggests that sea travel must have been entirely normal in centuries, and millennia, before the Europeans arrived in the Americas although not necessarily reflective of contact on a weekly or monthly basis. Another example of a people whose myths and culture were orientated towards the sea are the Kwakiutl in British Colombia. A major culture hero among them was Si'wit and he was, inevitably, noted as being a great sea traveller. The close similarities of the Kwakiutl myths and those recorded in Asia have been noted elsewhere[1]. One of the places he visited in his travels was a legendary place called K'wit[2]. A feature of many of the tales of the coast of North West America is that the heroes were said to be away for so long that they returned as old men, and many were said in those travels to have been secreted in the dark of a whale's stomach. These myths bear striking resemblances to the story of the Biblical Job where he too was swallowed by a whale and returned after a long period of time. The whales are probably references to ships, where the rowers were accommodated, or stowed as slaves, in the lower decks and the long voyages referred to, relates to their being willingly or press-ganged into service aboard ships that did not return for many years perhaps decades.

Si'wit is associated in myths with Q!o'mogwa, a frequently featured hero associated with copper among the Kwakiutl referred to earlier, and in many aspects appears similar to Coniraya in the Peruvian myths both as a trickster and hero figure at the same time with little reference or aspects to what might be called in the West as morality. The hero changes form to suit the occasion and disappears "into" (across) the sea and reappears as a dolphin[3], invincible, larger than life, or as a pauper and performer of the sacred rituals. He is often portrayed in conflict with his family and his brother in particular, and repeated cycles of death of or different types, coming back to life in one form or another are a feature of the myths of the Indians in this region. In one section his special symbol of power is a quartz object placed in his brow[4]. This is clearly a reference to the brow jewel worn by the Hindu and Buddhist deities[5], and these were undoubtedly aspects of hero myths assimilated by Kwakiutl men returning from Asia or contact with early Buddhist missions and traders from India. This element is also found in other myths in the region and undoubtedly originates from either Buddhist China and Japan or India itself[6] as well as being found among the Nagas of Assam[7] and around Lake Titicaca in Bolivia[8]. Other references to Si'wit building a house with four platforms and with five birds on their respective poles suggests symbolical aspects to ancient rites among the Kwakiutl referring to the cardinal points and common to other cultures of the Americas and Asia[9]. Found among the cultures of Asia, particularly India, South East Asia, Mexico and South America are the double-headed serpents said to have flanked the entrance door to his house and these were noted as having their tongues protruding[10].

Among the South American tribe of the Chorote in the centre of the continent Si'wit has almost his exact counterpart as another hero, or trickster figure, even down to his name as locally known, Kixwet. Si'wit is a name undeniably similar to Kixwet, and this is similar to the place where said to have visited by Si'wit named K'wit. In one myth Kixwet is considered a giant along

9.001 : Carved one bird deity probably intended [to] sit atop a pillar. [M]anta, Ecuador, [2]00-1000 A.D.

9.002 : Birds atop poles are found all around the Pacific Rim along with carved posts. Manchuria, Pre-20th., century, A.D.

9.003 : Throughout all the islands of Indonesia, Melanesia and Polynesia the careful observation of bird flight paths and migration routes was of such importance that they were elevated to deities or identified with them. These birds deities were raised on poles and were associated with omen ceremonies but identical beliefs and pillars are found all along the Pacific coast of North and South America. Borneo, Late 19th., century, A.D.

9.004 : Carved stone pillar with eagle carved atop from the early Mayan highlands. Kaminaljuyu, 4-7th., century, A.D.

9.005 : Carved stone bird [pi]llar. Bilbao, Santa Lucia [C]otzumalguapa, Guatemala, [4-]7th., century, A.D.

9.006 : Sceptres in the form of birds atop pillars were common in Ancient Peru and probably referred to bird navigation utilised by Pacific mariners. Pachacamac, South Coast Peru, c1st., millennium, A.D.

9.007 : Carved bird pillars virtually identical to those found in Indonesia and Melanesia and found also in Central America and on the Pacific coat of South America. British Colombia, Canada, Late 19th., century, A.D.

9.008 : Stone carved bird atop stem of ceremonial pounder or sceptre. New Guinea, late 19th., century A.D. or earlier.

9.009 : Stone carved bird atop a ceremonial sceptre closely similar to examples found in the Pacific Rim and Ocean area. Antilles, West Indies, 500-1500 A.D.

with his brother and in several confrontations with women makes a nuisance of himself in the trickster manner typical of Si'wit. In one of these conquests a Chorote woman complained to Kixwet's brother and after searching for him, then kills and incinerates him in a fire. He tells the girl to go and look for an armadillo in the ashes and sfter she finds it, the animal is restored to Kixwet in his human form and the brothers join up and continue on their way[11]. This element of the myth has parallels in the Popol Vuh where, after the brothers Hunaphu and Xbalanqúe had been challenged by the Underworld Lords, Hunaphu deliberately allowed himself to be incinerated and his ashes thrown into the river where he was restored to life again[12].

There are numerous aspects related to Kixwet recorded in the Chorote myths and many have their parallels in the myths of Melanesia far to the west on the other side of the Pacific Ocean. Deities or heroes who create from their own substance are a feature widely found in Melanesia and some closely follow those of Ancient Egypt. Kixwet among the Chorote is said to have closed his hand and from the act of self-fertilisation, almost identical to that of Tum in Ancient Egypt, a son was born[13].

In several other myths there are close parallels with myths in Melanesia or Polynesia that cannot be considered to be accidental. In one of these myths, where Kixwet is identified with the armadillo, it is said that a beautiful girl was admired by all the armadillo "shell people" and three of their men wanted to have relations with her but she rejected all approaches. One armadillo named Ithlio decided the only way he could succeed was to deceive her and he dig a hole near her and attempted to possess her by stealth from under the ground but failed in his intentions.

Kixwet-Aseta was bigger and stronger than Ithlio and decided to try the same technique, and dug his hole next to her and entered her from underneath without her being aware. From this illicit action a boy was born and when he grew up he recognised his father immediately. This is reminiscent of the son of Coniraya recognising him at the assembly called by Cavillaca after eating the fruit given also in an illicit manner to her. The myth continues to inform that Kixwet-Aseta's son was called the father of fish since he recognised his father when he stood guard over the bottle tree in which were many fish. These lived inside the tree where a "lagoon" had formed and where the fish were secreted and the boy shot a fish with an arrow and took it home for his grandmother to eat. The boy became the inventor of the weaving of fishing nets that were used by the tribe to catch the fish in the tree. In another related myth the wily fox wanted to know where the fish that Kixwet owned came from and he followed him to the tree. When Kixwet had left the fox lifted the "lid" of the tree and took out some of the fish but forgot to replace the lid and the water gushed out from the tree to form a flood. Kixwet used his magic rod to return the waters to the tree and replaced the lid, but decided to provide the fish with an environment outside the tree and placed his rod into the earth as he walked and the water flowed from the tree as a rivers in which the fish now live[14].

The attempt to penetrate the beautiful Chorote woman by Kixwet-Aseta is found in other Amazonian tribes and one from the Rio Campa states that the Moon was imaged as a boa in the sub-aqueous waters of the Amazonian rivers who extended his penis into the ground when his niece attended the fish trap and it entered her and caused a pregnancy[15]. In Polynesia, in a myth recorded from the Gilbert Islands (Kiribati), Ne Areau, the trickster creator deity, impregnated a woman by exactly the same means, by extending his penis under the ground[16]. A closely similar myth is found in Central Australia where it was said that the leader of Arunta and he extended his penis in a furrow in the ground to penetrate women from underneath[17]. These myths appear to be part of a large body of Vagina Dentata myths, so common in India, that had been diffused throughout the Pacific and the Americas by mariners and traders.

A myth from New Guinea, on the direct route by the ocean currents from South America to Melanesia, notes similar motifs of fish origins from a tree. The myth has been given in full elsewhere[18], and requires only a shortened version here for comparison. A man named Duagau and his dog found a flying fish on the ground and he took it home where he ate it and Duagau found that it tasted better than any of the other river fish. Next day he went to the same place and waited to see if another fish would be found there. After several hours he heard a splashing sound coming from inside a tree trunk and eventually fish fell from the branches. Climbing the tree Daugau found that there were many fish inside, and taking another fish home, he gave it to his mother to eat. After sleeping for a while she was awoken and demanded that all the men chop down the tree for more of the fish so the men from the two clans of Lavarata and Aurana set about chopping it down. However the tree was so large that the men had to leave at sunset before the work was completed and when they returned next morning the chips had all returned to the tree and it was standing fully restored. This folktale follows those of the Woodchip myths found in the Americas and Polynesia and in attempting to chop down the tree to find the following morning that it is standing fully restored again except for a single chip[19]. This relation follows similar examples recorded in an earlier work[20] and numerous others in Melanesia such as the Qat myth cycle[21]. The outcome of this myth, in attempting to fell the tree, was that the answer was to burn all of the chips, as they were cut from the trunk, and this prevented the tree from being restored. When the tree fell the water inside gushed out across the ground, and in other myths it is this that causes the oceans and provides fish for the sea[22]. There are here some aspects of the fish kept in the pond by Urpi-Huachac at Pachacamac, and their being emptied into the sea by Coniraya. These myths are clearly related to the myths of the Amazon, the Gran Chaco through into the Western Pacific Islands and to India and are too closely similar to be coincidence especially when considered along with the broader mass of mythical, legendary and artefactual evidence.

Miracle Conception Myths by Fruit in Melanesia

In the Coniraya myth it is recorded Cavillaca is impregnated by a fruit placed in her way as a temptation by Coniraya, and conception by such magical means occurs widely in the Americas but also in Melanesia. In a myth from Malekula, an island in the former New Hebrides, now Vanuatu, the exploits of Ta-ghar, the Melanesian version of the Polynesian Tangaroa are preserved in a local form illustrating the conception by fruit motif. In the native town of Pete-hul, noted elsewhere in this work as a possible intermediate point between the fourfold village caste planning of India and Peru, Ta-ghar is said to have founded the site by causing a fruit to fall and, splitting on hitting the buttress root of the tree, gave rise to the first man and woman. Their first son is said to have cleared away the bush around the tree to construct the first dancing ground. Behind the town was a cliff cave in a range named mbarang, where the creation is said to have taken place, and the nearest quarter into which the town was divided to it was named La-mbarang meaning "At the Cave"[23]. As with all myths there are variants but the main thrust of the myth includes an extension where the first man and woman, after being born from the fruit, lived separately in the compartments formed by the root buttresses but eventually united and produced four sons who were the founders of the four quarters of Pete-hul. The myth has much that suggests a common origin with the Incan myths and it is not surprising therefore that this island group was also known for the practices of cranial deformation and trepanation. This among other cultural achievements noted in Peru, are found on this island group forming a mid point between India and South America. The island has many cultural aspects shared with India suggesting a common origin from there and with the Munda and Bhuiyas peoples in particular noted elsewhere[24].

A myth from North West New Guinea states that an old man named Mangundi (also known as Manseren; Manamakrie; Mansariji, etc.), who had lived on Biak a long time ago, was engaged in the preparation of his palm wine when he noticed that some of it and his utensils were repeatedly taken. He lay in wait to catch the thief and caught the Morning Star in the act, and let him go only after he had been given a magic fruit which had the power to make women pregnant. Mangundi used this fruit on a young woman and she bore a son called Kon-ori. However, because her relatives did not approve of this association he drew a canoe on the sand that immediately became a real canoe and the small family climbed into the canoe and it moved of its own accord to another island. This island was a small, uninhabited sand spit and Mangundi stamped his foot and the island magically increased to a much larger size. He placed four sticks in the ground and these became four villages and he gave fire to the people who inhabited them. Mangundi suffered from a skin disease so he built a fire and, standing in it, he became a "beautiful young man". The skin that fell off became rings and bangles of gold and silver with pearls used in trade with other island peoples. Nothing else was known about Mangundi but certain myths and legends about Konori state that he finally returned to the sky to join his father there, and that this grieved his mother so greatly that she turned into a stone[25].

The myth has much in principle common with the Malekula myths, besides the magic inseminating fruit in all these myths, but the name Kon-ori is certainly reminiscent of Coniraya or Kon Raya. The elements of poverty (skin disease associated with poverty and low status in some places) and the mother turning to stone certainly indicates that this myth generally may have derived circuitously from Coastal Peru. As at Malekula the four sticks forming the villages seems to reflect the fourfold division of Pete-hul and the fourfold division of Cuzco and the Incan empire.

In India, needless to say, there are myths relating that fruit could inseminate a woman. A Gond myth from Central India notes that Ghokhchand Raja and his wife had no heirs and were desperate for children. They went to a holy man, a sadhu, and he gave them a stick and told them to throw it up into a particular fruiting mango tree, a tree sacred in India, and to pick up the first mango that fell and to eat it. They did so and the Raja's wife conceived after having to fight off witches who took the form of bees that attempted to sting them[26]. A Baiga myth, a people closely connected with the Gonds and Bhuiyas, preserved a myth that stated that a Gond and his wife were living in Koeli-Kachhar childless - considered a shame in India. The wife eventually went to Mahadeo and focused her devotions on the carved phallic monolith of the god for 12 years. At the beginning of the thirteenth year the god Mahadeo was pleased with her and asked what it was she wished for and she told him of her plight. The deity informed her that she must come to him in the peak of her next menstrual cycle and when she appeared as instructed he gave her two mangoes to eat and he lay with her and she conceived and bore a son and a daughter[27].

In the Amazon Basin a similar myth illustrates the diffusion of similar motifs along the sea routes from Asia to South America. A myth states that a young man lived at home with his aged mother and each night she arranged the mosquito net around her son's hammock. One day she noticed a shopan - a type of watermelon fruit. Since her son was unmarried he had been using it as a substitute for a wife in the frank unabashed way of the Amazonian Indians. One day the old woman decided to throw it away and as it hit the ground the fruit broke open and two male babies stepped out. Their aunt decided to adopt them since they were large and already growing quickly and fed them on chichi, a maize beer, used in sacred rituals. On enquiring as to why they had no mother the aunt replied, instead of telling the truth, that she had been killed by the lightning man. The two boys made an arrow and went off n search of him and finding him they killed him. The myth is a very long one and in the rest of the myth their canoe become a caiman and with their elder brother, who shot arrows into the sky so that stuck one into the other so that there they could climb the arrow ladder into the Sky World. They took with them the caiman' mandible and this became the Hyades (Huishmavo)[28].

The myth reflects many elements found in Melanesia, the birth of miracle children that grew quickly; the killing of the ogre in the form of the lightning;, arrows shot into the sky to form a ladder and the serpent or caiman/crocodile that turned into a canoe. The elements of the old woman or couple unable to have children who, late in life, give birth to a miracle child and the heroes or deities born from fruit are found in Melanesia and in the myths from India. This one from the Amazon Basin is just one of many that is recorded above that are too closely similar not to be connected. The miracle child motif is also found in Peru but is more similar to those of India than Melanesia while other motifs found in the Peruvian myths are reflected in the following myths.

Myths of Gods and Heroes Turned-To-Stone

In several myths, including the Inca Origin myths there are references to a main mythical figure or hero turning to stone. Ayar Ucho[29] was said to have turned to stone, at the mountain of Huanacauri or on a pillar, the first sacred site of the Incas in Peru itself, as was Ayar Cachi (Version 2 and 2A) in another myth. The use of megaliths and stone to represent deities and heroes appears to have been widespread in Andean and Pacific Coastal South America. This is also the case across the Pacific through Polynesia, Melanesia, Indonesia where so many of the deity names are prefixed by the term for stone, batu, a Middle Eastern derivative, and in India.

The earliest Spanish chroniclers note the focus on worship of stone as idols and as the believed dwelling places of ancestral spirits and deities. One of the most interesting of the origin myths throughout the highlands of Peru and Bolivia believed that Viracocha had turned the first people, who existed in that creation, to stone and that the statues found or still standing at Tiahuanco were considered the material evidence for this act[30]. In another version it was Tonapa, having reached Tiahuanaco, angered when the people refused to give up their drinking and dancing to listen to him preach, turned them all to stones. In a parallel legend, Tonapa, rejected by the people of the Bolivian plateau around Lake Titicaca, is said to have turned the people to stones while they were celebrating a wedding[31].

In Peru, Tonapa was said to have turned a female huaca and a man from Huancas to stone because he caught them fornicating at the foot of a small hill near the river at the entry of the Xauxa Valley. These two stones were called Atapymapuranu-tapya. The term taypi, found at Tiahuanaco can be found in this expression referring to "navel" stones, or omphalli, and these stones are said to utter that they had become Huacanquis[32] and these were apparently common before the time of Pachacamac influence from the coast.

Another group called the Pururaucas were believed to have been soldiers who had been turned to stone and these could, and were in legend called back to life fully armed to assist the Inca when required, and this was believed to have occurred whenever a ruling Inca required their services. Bernabe Cobo opined that this was a "fiction" created by Ynca Viracocha, the father of Pachacuti, to terrorise and retain subjection of his people and a deterrent aimed at opposing tribes[33]. One of the stones on the ceque, or road to Cuntisuyu was called Pururauca and this stone, placed on a stone bench next to the Temple of the Sun, was said to be representative of the Pururaucas as a whole[34]. One of the shrines on the road to Chinchasuyu was the eighth house called Mamararoy, and in this place there were stones said to be the wives of Ticci Viracocha the god who, when out walking one night, turned to stone[35].

In the Coniraya myth Cavillaca fled before the pursuit of the disguised Sun God and on reaching the coast near Pachacamac turned into stones with her child as she plunged into the sea[36]. In the Pariacaca myth his son Huathacuri turned his sister-in-law into stone because she had incited her husband to impose trials on him unfairly[37]. At the end of this same myth the woman whom Pariacaca loved and who had given herself to him wished to remain on a mountain and she too was turned to stone at the head of a water channel called Cocochalla[38]. In myths recorded by Cristobal de Molina there were stones believed to have been giants or very large people who were petrified by the Creator. This Creator had two sons named Imaymana Viracocha and Tocapo Viracocha to who he delegated creative and destructive powers, at Jauja, Huarivilca, Pachacamac and Cajamarca[39].

It was not only heroes, or heroines, gods and demons who were turned to stone but many of the clans at the time of the Incas claimed that their founding fathers, or prominent ancestors had been turned to stone[40]. Usually they were able to determine the exact stone alleged to be that person and this invariably became the family shrine still frequented into the times after the Spanish Conquest. The Incas themselves had stone carved images as their "doubles" or "brothers" located in geographically significant locations reinforcing the land claimed by themselves, and these were allocated houses, fields for planting, and servants[41]. On the Amazon slopes of the Eastern Andes certain of the tribes thought the bones of the deceased turned to stone[42], while far to the south in Patagonia among the Teheulches, when the father of the hero Ellal reached the ocean he too turned to stone[43].

In a myth from the Yucatan in Mexico it was said that the world was first inhabited by dwarves and the great cities there were believed by the Maya at the Conquest to have been built in that time of darkness before the Sun was created. When the Sun first rose in the sky the Mayans say that these dwarfs turned to stone[44]. The Huichols, in searching for the sacred Hikuli - the peyote cactus, consider that many of the stones along the prescribed route were in fact the gods, who were also to be found in springs and mountains reflecting a similar belief system to that attached to stones and other natural phenomena in the Andes[45].

There are an abundance of myths in Melanesia indicating that natural rocks, menhirs or megaliths were believed to be heroes or ancestors turned to stone. One of the more extensive myths cycles in Melanesia is that of the hero Sido known in the islands around New Guinea. He is probably the same hero from the islands some distance further east in the New Hebrides known as Sina Kwao, "Shining Bright". Sina in Melanesia is clearly related to the term for the Moon in Polynesia and also originally derived from the Ancient Near and Middle East. The term Si is known to be the name of the Moon in the Moche culture of Northern Peru and there are many other aspects clearly related to this term and diffused commonly throughout the Pacific Islands and continental Rim. It is said in the Sido myths that his shrines were associated with the megalithic culture of the islands and his wives were said to have turned to stone[46].

In New Guinea a people called the Yee anim, located on the headwaters of the Upper Maro river, consider many of the prominent stones represent their Yavar or Yawar, ancestors turned to stone, and who address them by their individual names. They were of all different shapes and sizes, some as rounded stones while others were small and obtained from the rivers. Another stone was considered to be the petrified, legendary canoe that their ancestors were said to have travelled up the river to the highland. Interestingly these people also possessed the star-shaped club made from crystalline rock and identical to those known from the Inca and earlier epochs of Andean South America[47].

In New Guinea also a myth among the Wagawaga people records that a red eel-man, named Tuisuheaia was able to take a human form. He stole away a village child from its mother by deceit in exchange for a basket of coconuts. The child was dashed against the rocks and eaten by the eel-man and, in searching for the child, the parents found that the eel-man had killed it and sought to destroy the eels and their living place. In thrusting a pole into the eel's lair there came a great storm and the father and mother of the child were turned to stone[48].

The Kula trade district extends into the islands and to part of the mainland of Northern New Guinea. Within this region on Fergusson Island near Dobu, there are two dark rocks on the shore at the end of a sand spit and these are said to be the legendary notables Atu'a'line and Aturamo'a. The locale with its rocks is associated with large-scale inter-island canoeing expeditions[49]. On the nearby island of Sanaroa is the area where the Trobriand Islanders look for the Spondylus shell for ceremonial trading expeditions[50]. On this small island it is said that the sister of these two heroes was petrified and is represented as a stone here where it is regaled with offerings. In another myth three sisters were said to be angry with the canoe building mariner, Toweyre'i, and they flew off in the air but one of them, named Na'ukuwakula, deviated to the west and arrived at Simsim and turned to stone[51]. These sacred rocks were all the focus of offerings and they were also considered to have healing qualities and to assist in sea voyages[52]. The lunar term sina is found among the sacred places in the Kula region such as Sina-keta, and the name for legendary rain, Sina-matanoginogi[53].

In Indonesia the sacred or revered stones were considered to be the result of the wrath of the gods in many cases and they were propitiated to prevent the indwelling spirit to harm those who lived in the vicinity. A report on the Dyak people of Borneo is typical of the myths associated with these stones: "In the bed of the Sesang River there is a rock which is only visible at the lowest of the ebb-tide. It is called Batu Kudi Sabar. The story goes that in olden days the inmates of a Dyak house tied to a dog's tail a piece of wood, which was set alight. They all laughed at the sight as the dog ran off in fright, dragging after him the burning torch. Suddenly there was darkness, and a great storm came on. There were thunder and lightning, and torrents of rain, and the house and its inmates were turned into this large rock..."[54]. Other oral histories and folklore preserve similar myths and are recorded in North Borneo where a similar relation attaches to Batu Uko, or Dog Rocks along with others of this type[55].

Some myths in Sumatra are associated with spittle from a demons mouth causing petrifaction[56] and these are closely similar to myths found in India and no doubt derived from there. The most prevalent myths of people-turning-to-stone appear to be associated with the Indonesian island of Celebes (Sulewasi) where megaliths and other stones are so prolific in the central region of Poso[57]. In one myth there are apparent Biblical reference to a woman fleeing a flood, caused by a great storm, who stopped to look back and was turned to stone that is reminiscent of Lot's wife turning a pillar of salt.

Aboriginal Australia has a great number of myths relating that heroes and mythical people had been turned to stone. The Bunya-Bunya people from North Queensland had a fear of the rainbow, called by them Thugine - "large serpent". A tribal group went fishing and left two boys at camp with strict orders not to go to the beach. The boys, eventually tired of being at the camp with nothing to do, decided to opt for disobedience and went to the beach. As soon as they arrived the Thugine emerged, caught the two boys, and turned them into two rocks between Double Island and Inskip Point[58].

In a more remarkable myth from South East Australia from the Yaurorka people myth preserved over a century ago was recorded as follows: "A Mura-mura belonging to Kilyalpa, named Ngura-tulu-tulu-ru, started on his wanderings. He came to Paia-tira, where he saw women beating out Paua and cleaning it. As he came nearer to them, they saw him, and surrounded the stranger. They looked at him inquisitively, and could not help laughing at his crooked legs and arms. Nor could they help being surprised at the light-coloured flies which accompanied him, because those with them were black. Then they began to discuss where he came from, and who he was, for not one of them know him. But they thought of one old woman who was a little distance away, and called her, thinking that she might know who he was. Hastening to them, she recognised him as being her Ngatamura, and took him upon her lap, and sobbed unceasingly, crying, 'Palingi! Palingi!' (my brother's son). When she had wept over him, she sent him to her husband, his Yenku (father's father), who was in the camp with other men eating Paua. Before he reached the camp he could hear the men grinding the seed which the women had collected and cleaned. He thought to himself, 'That is a good grinding stone; I wish I had it.' The he went to his Yenku's camp, and after he had spoken to him, made his own camp close at hand, and lay down as if to sleep. As he lay there, the whole camp collected there and made themselves merry over his crooked legs and arms. He, however, secretly watched where they had put the wonderful Tayi-stone, which with so little rubbing had ground so much Paua. When all the people had gone to sleep, Ngura-tulu-tulu-ru rose up, and taking some glowing coals and a piece of fungus, he powdered both and scattered them over the whole camp, to make every one unconscious. To make sure that every one was fast asleep, he shouted 'Bai! Bai! Bai!' loudly, after he had spoken his spell, but no one moved. Then he touched each one with a burning coal, to try to wake him, but without effect, and he then took the grinding-stone out of the damp earth where it had been hidden, washed the mud off it, and walked away quietly, about midday, with it on his head. When he had gone a long way from the camp, the people woke up, and to their sorrow found that the stranger Ngura-tulu-tulu-ru and their Tayi had both disappeared."

"The they formed a Pinya (blood-revenge party), and having found the track of the thief, they followed him hastily."

"At Ngapa-kangu they met with a man whom they killed, thinking him to be Tayi-tampana, and it was only after he was dead that they found out their mistake. Then they again followed Tayi-tampana's tracks to Malka-malkara, where they overtook him, and came upon him from two directions. When he saw himself suddenly surrounded by a Pinya, he took the Tayi from his head, and using it as a shield, stopped all the boomerangs thrown at him. These he collected, and when attacking the Pinya, he pursued them as far as Pinya-maru, where he killed them, and turned them into stones, which are black because the men of the Pinya were painted of that colour. Going back for the Tayi, which he had left behind, he was attacked by the remainder of the Pinya, whose weapons he stopped with the stone for a shield; and having gathered them up, he followed his enemies, and killed them. So deeply did he strike them into the ground that a deep pit was formed, from which that place has been called Yidni-minka."

"Having done this, he went back, and on his way he again slew a number of those sent against him at Madra-yurkuma. Then taking his Tayi under his arm he went to Meriwora. The Pinya had by this time collected against him. When they began to throw boomerangs against him, he threw himself on the ground face downwards, and placed the stone in such a manner on his back that no weapon could injure him. But he was buried under the Tayi and was turned to stone."[59].

The myth is an interesting one since it contains elements that appear to have references to South America. The magical grinding stone is called Tayi and this may have derived from Taypi, the "navel" stone central to the founding of Tiahuanaco. The term also occurs in the sacred mountain of the Marquesas Islands as Tai Pi. Sacred rituals involving grinding maize and hallucinogens were also central to Andean and Coastal Peruvian rituals and it seems too great a coincidence that similar references are found in the Australian myth. Also found in this myth is the term Malka-malkara where the prefix appears to relate to malquis - the term for sacred stones and other objects including ancestral mummies in Ancient Peru and Bolivia.

In the far north of Australia in Arnhem Land in mythical times when the ancestor called Inigia appeared his camps they were said to have been transformed into trees, but when he transformed himself into a goose he became a group of boulders[60]. The Onkaparinka ancestors are now thought to be a group of rocks on the seashore[61]. In a myth known as the Myth of Jarapiri, a mythical serpent, his physical representation was considered to be a stone on top of a hill, and it was considered too dangerous for the Aborigines to ceremonially rub it as part of an increase ritual[62]. The Ngalia men were those associated with this sacred spot and the name itself suggests that it originated from Naga, the term in India for serpent. The myth of Jarapiri has many parallels in the myths of India and among the Bhuiyas themselves[63], and these will be of more interest in a projected future publication.

In India the Pardhans are a caste of musicians usually associated with the Gonds of Central India. In a myth from Balaghat District the Raja from Hardinagar, named Karsanbira, had a son named Ram Darwai, and in Bandadaur lived the Raja of Singhbahani who had three daughters. It had been arranged that Ram Darwai was to marry one of the daughters named Nakti Deva. When the time came the marriage party of the bride went to Hardinagar but when they saw the great number of people forming the marriage party of the groom they felt embarrassed and wanted to hide. In a series of moves only available to mythical people they changed their form and shrank into a liquor pot and there performed dances, etc. Eventually, next morning, they emerged from the liquor pot and made their escape but as they did so the people of Hardinagar turned to stone. The bridegroom attempted to pursue them but they escaped and they too turned to stone[64].

The Todas of South India have been mentioned several times in this work and again one of the shorter myths notes: "When Teikirzi (the main goddess of the Todas) was living at Nodrs the people of Mysore came to fight her, but as they approached, the woods made a great noise. When the Mysore people heard the noise they stopped, and then Teikirzi cursed them and said, 'Let them become stones,' and they were turned to stones, which are still to be seen below Nodrs"[65]. In another myth the body of a man struck by a sacred wand flew through the air and fell dead and could not be moved so the burial hut was constructed around him. Instead of two doorposts two women with pounders were placed either side and they turned to stone[66].

These few myths show the transfer of the basic belief that people could be turned to stone from India to South America and probably derives from the megalithic cultures of South India dating from about 500 B.C. Ultimately, however, it is probably rooted in the ancient association of ancestors with megalithic stones in the Ancient Near and Middle East. These stones were often placed in circles where they were the receptors for the invocations of priests and the temporary touchstones and habitations for the spirits during rites and ceremonies where contact between the people of the Earth and the ancestors was considered necessary. Frequently it has been found that there were stone seats or blocks at the foot of these monoliths and this was the place where the priest sat during the rites and this point that is of more interest in this work.

The Conopos and Stone Worship from Peru to India

Long before the coming of the Incas worship of sacred stones and carved images and idols was endemic in Peru. Dr. Francisco de Avila wrote two generations after the fall of the Incas to the Spanish Conquistadors: "It is the most ancient tradition that, before any other event of which there is any memory, there were certain huacas or idols, which together with the others of which I treat, must be supposed to have walked in the form of men. These huacas were called Yananamca Intanamca; and in a certain encounter they had with another huaca Huallallo Carunincho, they were conquered and destroyed by the said Huallallo, who remained as Lord and God of the land. He ordered that no woman should bring forth more than two children, of which one was to be sacrificed for him to eat, and the other, - whichever of the two the parents might choose, might be brought up. It was a tradition that, in those days, all who died were brought to life again on the fifth day, and that what was known in that land also sprouted, grew, and ripened on the fifth day; and that all these provinces were then a very hot country, which the Indians called Yunca or Ande; and they say that these crops were made visible in the deserts and uninhabited places, such as that of Pariacaca and others; and that in these Andes there was a great variety of most beautiful and brilliant birds, such as macaws, parrots and others. All this, with the people who then inhabited the land (and who, according to their account, led very evil lives), and the said idol, came to be driven away to other Andes by the idol Pariacaca, ..."[67].

The proliferation of haucas, or natural objects, left un-worked, or carved, as shrines was one of the greatest problems faced by the zealous Spanish friars when they confronted the newly discovered polytheistic world of North West South America. Stone worship in particular is singled out as a major problem since these were worshiped as the dwelling places of ancestral, tribal and national heroes and deities and extended from the public shrines at the centre of villages and around the landscape to any prominence or unusual place natural or otherwise. Even worse for the Spanish Fathers was that virtually every house and hut also had these huacas or stones believed related to the ancestors of the family itself and personal gods also known as huacas. This form of personalised clan focus upon sacred stones and associated ancestral deities was so ubiquitous so that some Spanish friars described conceded that they were among the most religious of men[68]. Similar stones were also used as guardians, or the dwellings of spirits as guardians, of towns and temples called Marca Aparac or Marca Charac[69]. Many of these marked the sacred places where emergence of the first tribal people was believed to have occurred and these were called Pacarinas[70].

Dr. Francisco de Avila noted that conopa was the name used by the Indians for the small stone idols found in abundance by him and others. He also notes that the small ritual vessel with a face of the "Devil" moulded below its lip was called "Uncu-raya"[71]. At Huarochiri, de Avila discovered about 600 idols of this type mostly wrapped in a sacred blanket called "Cumbi"[72], a fact that will be of special importance in a later chapter in this work. These conopas were kept in the houses of the people as well as in the temples and other sacred buildings. These stones were kept together with other revered objects such as children who had died at childbirth (more especially those born feet first called Chuchus[73] and given due worship daily.

The Peruvian Indians not only reverenced the stones themselves but also the places from which they were taken and named these as zamana. The places where they propitiated or carried out rituals or invoked the sacred stones were known as cayan[74]. Conopas were not always stones but anything that had assumed or grown into an unusual form such as potatoes and maize. Corn conopas or "totems" were known as Micui conopa or Zara conopa[75]. The conopas were usually kept high in the rafters of the house and this loftier part of the dwelling was known under the names of Chichic, Huanca or Chacrayoc. Larger stones were used in the fields ostensibly to protect the irrigation ditches and to ensure a good water supply and these were known as compa or larca villana[76]. One of the signs that the Spanish Friars noticed when seeking out the conopas to destroy them was that these were always associated with the fruit the Indians called Espingo, a small fruit from the Chachapoyas region in North East Peru, and ground for medicinal purposes[77]. Lowland Quechua peasantry searched the hills for these stones and they were considered by them to be mementos from the mountain deities called Apus[78].

When the time had arrived for a woman to be delivered at childbirth the conopas she considered to house her own special guardian was clutched by her to her breast during the birth itself. Arriaga noted: "On such occasions, in some places, they invoke the moon, as the Romans did under the name of Lucina"[79]. Arriaga rued the decision not have confiscated and destroyed the many haucas, idols and conopas immediately on detection as he recorded, "...it was a mistake not to have burned the 'munaos' of the lowlands, which are called 'malquis' in the sierra, for the Indians esteem them more than their huacas; a mistake not to have destroyed their 'machays', or burial places of their grandfathers and progenitors to which they carry the bodies stolen from the church; a mistake not to have deprived them of their 'morphis', as they call them in the lowlands, or 'Chancas', as they say in Cuzco, or 'conopas', as they are called in this archbishopric; which are their household gods, passed on from father to son as the richest and most precious of their few jewels. Rare are those who do not have them, for they are the principle inheritance of the family, and sometimes they have two, three, or four of them"[80]. There are several names as indicated for these sacred stones and one of these has already been compared to malka, the term also associated with elevated status in the highlands of Peru and kingship in the Ancient Near East and among the Mandaeans. Other modern researchers have noted that the passing of these sacred family stones patrilineally through the family resembled the lares and penates in Roman times. Another lowland Peruvian name for the stones was Alecpong, and considered the sons of the Sun[81].

The efforts of the Spanish friars was sometimes frustrated since they were often itinerant in the early years, and even if they had succeeded in eliminating the primary cult idols in a town or village the more extensive worship of personal stones remained almost unchecked until the more determined efforts of those such as Father Pablo Joseph de Arriaga. When the priests preached and sought out the idols for destruction they often planted a cross on the central sacred site, or huaca, and then moved on to the next town. Only in the later follow-up by Arriaga and others who remained longer in the towns was the problem perceived and attempts to deal with the conopas undertaken. Arriving at one town named Choquechuco Arriaga noted that huacas had been buried by the local people under the cross planted by the earlier friars and the cross itself had been adopted as the centre of the village cult. The assemblage around the cross included a large "...liver-coloured stone with a face and eyes stood upon a stone base with twenty-five conopus, or lesser idols around it". He also notes that at Humivilca a stone idol had been placed under a cross, and another beside it called its brother and records that; "...Both were seated on a flat stone with thirty-two conopas and many sacrifices around them." Other crosses subsumed to the belief systems and rites of the local Indians were found at Quichumarca and Chochas[82].

Arriaga's accounts are some of the few recording any information about the worship of stones and huacas and their value lies in their being eyewitness accounts and not just hearsay. In some coastal villages the name for the conopas associated with the lightning was ll'uviac[83]. Above the town of Yamor Arriaga had the lightning stone called huaca li'biac, or "lightning destroyed", this being "... a huge stone cleft in two by a bolt of lightning, and around it was an abundance of sacrifices of llamas and other things"[84]. In the town itself Arriaga noted: "... In the midst of these buildings and fortresses of the ancient town they brought to the visitor a huaca which was on the surface of the ground, called Huair Yurac, son of Apu Yurac. They told the visitor that this idol had been burned by Friar Francisco, but they assured me that he had turned into a falcon, that he had sons, and that this falcon was to be found in this place. I ordered them to start digging, and at a depth of about two yards we came upon a storage place in a kind of a cave where there was a stone falcon sitting on a little sheet of silver surrounded by many conopas, representing his servants. There were also many sacrifices and a trumpet. Nearby were four whole mummies, with plumes, and rich garments, though worn with time. They call these the sons of the huaca and the progenitors of the clan, and so worshipped them and consulted them whenever they deemed it necessary. These mummies are more harmful than the huacas, because the worship of the latter takes place once a year, whereas the dead are worshipped every day[85].

Arriaga records the typical approach that the Indians made to the huacas noting that they usually called the name of the particular huaca and said this with a characteristic "sucking noise" made with the lips called mochar (also mochi and mocha). Arriaga further noted: "Saying this and similar things -, he pours out the chichi (fermented corn liquor) in front of the huaca, or over it, or sprinkles the huaca with it as if he were giving it a rap on the nose. He anoints the huaca with the blood of guinea pigs or llamas and then burned, or blows towards it, the rest of the offerings, according to the nature of each one."[86].

If the offerings do not affect the required blessing from the huaca and bad luck follows it, or they had omitted to make sacrifices, it was always assumed by the Indians that they had acted incorrectly or had not sacrificed sufficiently to the spirit of the huaca and the ceremony of forgiveness is undertaken. Arriaga noted: "The blame themselves for not having appealed to the huacas, and the sorcerer tells them to mend their ways, etc. The Indian then places the powders for the offering on a flat stone and blows them. The confessor holds a little stone called pasca, meaning pardon, which is brought to him by the Indian. The confessor rubs the Indian's head with the stone and washes him with corn meal and water in a stream where two rivers meet. And this is called Ticuna ..."[87]. This remarkable ritual is of more interest in another section of this work earlier noted.

Sacred Stone Worship in India

In India, among the Todas, the buffalo are the centre of social and religious life and they have been taken on seasonal migrations to and from traditional pastures for many centuries. Because of the sacredness of this migration there are ceremonial objects that are also taken on this march and these are collected near the sacred stone for sanctification called the Pepkusthkars, and this is located in or near the sacred dairy called the Tu[88]. At the stopping-places along the route to the new pasturage the sacred milking vessels were laid by sacred stones called Perskars. Other stones along the way were at one time rubbed with clarified butter after the cattle had passed by[89]. In the funeral ceremonies cremation was the usual means of disposal for both men and women, and the ashes of a woman were swept into a hole within the stone circles of these people and covered with a stone, while that of the man is also placed in a hole and covered with a stone. As part of the ritual for a male a new pot of water was broken over the stone and the officiator knelt and touched the stone with his forehead before the end of the rites[90]. The Todas otherwise had many ceremonies relating to the sacred stones and these appear to be too similar to those of the Ancient Near and Middle East not to have been connected.

Among the other tribes and castes of India sacred stones were, and still are central to the religious rites of both Aboriginal and Aryan descended people in the Sub-continent (*5.170; 9.010*). The Brahman practises have been retained in recognisable form for over two thousand years and adopted in many modified and often misunderstood versions throughout India. The Vaishnavite sects of Hindu Brahmans centre their daily domestic worship around salagrama stones. Before eating it was traditional to retain the water that had been used to bath the sala-grama stone to wash the hands and also to drink the water at the same time. An investigation as to the origin of these stones was reported a century ago in India and noted: "Salagams are fossil cephalopods (ammonites), and are found chiefly in the bed of the Gandak river, a mountain tor-rent which, rising in the lofty mountains of Nepal, flows into the Ganges at Salagrami, a village from which they take their name, and which is not far from the sacred city of Benares. In appear-ance they are small black shiny pebbles of various shapes, usually round or oval, with a peculiar natural hole in them. They have certain marks ..... and are often flecked and inlaid with gold (or pyrites). The name Salagram is of Sanskrit derivation, from sara chakra, the weapon of Vishnu, and grava, a stone; the chakra or chakram being believed to be engraved thereon at the request of Vishnu by the creator Brahma, who, in the form of a worm, bores the holes known as vadanas, and traces the spiral coil that gives the stone its name"[91].

The salagrama stone is reminiscent of the stones sought out by the Peruvians searching the mountains for their unusual shapes for their personal use noted by Arriaga five hundred years ago. Similar also is their seeking pardon at the junction of two rivers or streams reflecting the Brahmans searching for their stones washed down from the Himalayas at the junction of two rivers. Among the lowest castes in society were the Pulayan, and among their Cheruman sec-tions they represented their gods and ancestors in the characteristic South Indian manner with sacred stones[92] placed in a sacred hut or at the foot of a sacred tree, often the banyan. This is cer-tainly true of the characteristically peripheral Hindu castes made up of the Aboriginal or part Aboriginal tribes such as the Irulas, one of the Nilgriri tribes near the Todas, who were one of the darker-skinned peoples in the region. They worshipped Vishnu under the name of Ranga-swami, suggesting that there might be a connection between Vishnu as the Hindu sky god and Ranga the Polynesian sky deity, and this might account for their being-darker skinned. The Irulas fre-quented a sacred thatched hut as the temple of the smallpox goddess, greatly feared throughout India, and this goddess was represented by the Irukas as a stone. Both the sky god and his wife

9.010 : Grama-Devata shrine or sacred stones rep-resenting the vil-lage deities. South India, Early 20th., cen-tury, A.D.

9.011 : A typical village shrine consist-ing of a raised platform sur-rounding a sacred tree and a carving of the local deity, often found stones of spe-cial quality. South India, Early 20th., century, A.D.

were also represented by a stone for each deity. Victorian writers from the nineteenth into the twentieth century recorded many aspects of Nilgiri hill culture and it was recorded of the Irulas (and Kurubas) that, "... after every death among them, they bring a long water-worn stone (Devva Kotta Kallu), and put it into one of the old cromlechs sprinkled over the Nilgiri plateau. Some of these have been found piled up to the capstone with such pebbles, which must have been the work of generations. Occasionally, too, the tribes mentioned make small cromlechs for burial purposes, and place the long water-worn pebbles in them"[93].

The association of special qualities projected onto stones is here derived from many centuries, and millennia, of stone worship from before the Vedic Aryans through to the Hindus of the modern day. In the many other poorer sections of the peoples of India a stone of a special shape or quality, if it can be found, otherwise any stone or plank of wood placed on the ground or attached to a wall, were considered and sanctified as a Bhuta, that is a demon, or a deity[94]. The type of stone was, however, more important to some caste than others. For the Paliyans, located near Madura (Madurai), their god Mayandi was usually represented by a stone, preferably reminiscent of some special shape, where one reflective of a serpent was most highly prized. The stone itself was not considered the god who was said to dwell elsewhere although it was not known exactly where, but the stone itself was kept in a simple thatched shrine at the foot of a tree. A chicken was the offering proffered and a fire hole in front of the stone reflected the origins of the beliefs associated with these deities in the old fire religions of Iran. In the famous temple to Subramanya the Stanikas, the temple servants, placed the cooked food and rice on the stone altar for sanctification called the Bali Pitam typical of many of the temples in India[95]. The Thanda Pulayans however, being forbidden to approach the temples as they were considered a caste of too low a status to be allowed near it, had a stone on which they placed their offerings about a quarter of a mile away from the temple. From the offerings placed on the stone a temple servant took the submissions to the temple and the priest sent sandal paste, holy water and flowers[96].

One of the most important tribes in India is the Kurumbas and they too are associated with the Nilgiri Hills. They also follow the burial pattern of the Irulas but they cremate their dead and place a small bone and a small, round stone or pebble in a selected ancient cromlech called by them the Savu-Mane or "death-house"[97]. Cairns and miniature cromlechs were constructed by the Arayans in memory of their dead and they often maintained small oil lamps burning in or on them along with "sweetmeats" to feed the dead[98]. Among some of the castes a sacred stone associated either with the bridal couple or the caste deity was placed under the pandal (marriage booth) and the bridal couple seated themselves before it during the ceremony. The Malayali form of marriage of South India was typical of this form of ceremony and part of the celebrations was, for the bridal couple, to walk three times around the stone before prostrating themselves before it to receive the blessing of the tribal elders[99].

The various tribes of India have developed or lost many elements according to their economic circumstances extending or degrading the many aspects related to megalithic or stone culture among them. The Kanakkans were the Tamil accounting caste in South India and in their domestic compounds there was often a raised platform, usually constructed beneath a sacred tree, on which were placed the stones representing their caste and personal deities[100]. In considering the healing powers attributed to stones in Peru this belief held so firmly in the Ancient Americas is found also among the many tribes and castes in India. Among the Kota, neighbours also of the Todas, the Kotas set up carved sacred stones considered to be capable of healing injuries and disease, and cures were claimed to be the result of rubbing the affected part against the stone[101].

In the Canara region of South West India the low cast Holeyas maintained that in the days of their forefathers, when a village was first being established, a stone called the "Karu

9.012 : An Amazon boy using elementary stilts that were probably introduced by Polynesians from the Marquesas Islands. Amazon Basin, Late 19th., century, A.D.

9.013 : A boy walking on bamboo stilts probably derived from contact with India. Toradja, N.E. Celebes, Indonesia, Late 19th., century, A.D.

9.014 : Traditional stilts celebrating the Pola festival found among some of the Aboriginal tribes in India. Gond, Central India, Early 20th., century, A.D.

9.015 : Hindu boys resting their stilts during the Pola festival. Central India, Early 20th., century, A.D.

9.016 : Finely carved stilt stirrups typical of those found in the Marquesas Islands. Eastern Polynesia, Late 19th., century, A.D. or earlier.

Kallu" was set up[102]. Offerings annually were made to this stone and this appears to be a closely similar ceremony to the marking the possession of the land with a boundary stone in the manner recorded from as far back as the fourth and third millennia B.C. in the Ancient Near and Middle East. The term kallu appears to confirm the connection since this is the term for a priest who officiated at the sacred stone or carved altar in those distant times and into the first millennium A.D. It may be that the term Karu was actually the origin of the name Cara or Kari in South India giving it the name Canara for that region. Some researchers have considered the name Canara to originate from Kannada or Karnata and these to derive from a mutation of the Dravidian words kar = black and nadu = country alluding to the black soil of that South India region where cotton was anciently grown. However, this appears to have little base in the ancient textual references although there was a Kannada region and is largely the intellectualisation of later British researchers[103]. It is much more likely, as with other Ancient Middle Eastern terms such as Pallava, and Yaksa derived from the Jaxartes River region, that they are a naturalised adaptation by immigrant peoples and traders and they appear without their previous recorded history. It is more likely therefore that Karan, Caran, Canara and Kannada are all adaptions resulting from the incursions of peoples and influences from the Karun River region in Ancient Iraq among whom were the Mandaeans whose influence in India is so marked. This connection with the West Asia appears also to be further confirmed by the term used to describe Holeya servants - Huttu-alu.

Among the Raj Gonds of South Central India the village was usually considered to be guarded by a village deity whose dwelling was a stone located on the outskirts of the settlement and placed under a tree. The largest of their villages in the Madura region preserved the stone of the village guardian, Aki Pen, placed under a tamarind tree, and nearby a small group of stones was dedicated to the Village Mother - Auwal[104]. The flowers of the Mahua tree are very important to the Aboriginal and part Aboriginal peoples of India and the Gond revered it as greatly as any other using their flowers, as other do, to make a liquor. Against this tree they lean stones representing the god Iruk Pen and fresh mahua flowers are offered at this shrine in the season[105]. Often this god was called Persa Bhimana and he was associated with stones representing Chenchu Bhimana[106].

Other sacred sites are dedicated to ancestor and deities represented by stones and these are sometimes placed adjacent or between prominent natural features such as between two hillocks having special significance for the local people[107]. As with the Todas earlier noted the Gonds were associated in the earliest times with cattle-herding suggesting, along with other aspects of culture, that they may have been migrants from the Iran plateau in an earlier migration than that of the Vedic Aryans also from the Iranian plateau. A stone, sacred to the god of the salt-lick, Chopun Pen, was also revered by them and adorned with offerings when the cattle were driven to the salt-lick itself. Among the Gonds, stilt-walking was long known and ritualised and in myth it was said that these were in honour of the deity Bhimul, attributed to having been made by his mother Gorondi for him. At the end of their use in the Pola Festival by the Gond boys, they are piled up over the stone representing the goddess Gorondi and to them and the stone are made offerings, while the Muria Gonds throw the stilts onto a stone sacred to Bhimul Pen[108]. Stilts are known also in the Marquesas Islands far to the East in the Pacific Ocean much nearer to the coast of America than to India and found among Amazon tribes.

Similar to other tribes in India the Gonds anointed their sacred stones with red ochre, the symbol of life and rebirth. Small stones and oil lamps were often so thickly coated in red ochre, applied as a vermilion paste, that they were almost unrecognisable[109]. There can be little doubt that there was a close link between human and animal sacrifice where blood smeared upon the sacred objects and where red ochre was a substitute for it or as a symbol of blood and there-fore life itself. The Gonds in their animal sacrifices smeared the freshly collected animal blood over the sacred sacrificial post and then those present embraced the post. Clasping the post in this way occurred only at this sacrifice except for the munda-posts set up as memorials to the departed ancestors[110]. In Ancient Peru Bernabe Cobo noted that the Indians threw offerings into the sea made of white maize flour and red ochre, among other things[111]. In attempting to cure ill-ness they would smear maize powder on themselves and used llimpi or mercury oxide, red ochre, widely, including rubbing it over their bodies, and utilising it also in other rituals[112]. In South East Brazil the dead were buried in rock shelters and covered with red ochre from about 7000 B.C.[113], and this was a practise widely known from then until the first millennium A.D., - a prac-tise also known widely in Asia from the earliest times. Red face paint was used in the Moche burials at Sipan[114] and in others associated in the same site the floor was covered in red pig-ment[115].

The rituals recorded by Arriaga in post-Conquest Peru records that conopas more usu-ally were small stones but he also notes that corn or other objects were included within this term[116]. An interesting ritual performed by the katora, or Gond priest included a ritual performed by the Atram clan in the middle of their maize field in the presence of the clan men and boys. In the standing stalks of the maize field the katora cleared an area where two "longish" mounds of cow dung were constructed. One of the clansmen broke a few maize cobs, and together with beans, small cucumbers, and ears of the sama, a grain, from another field, these were burnt with some incense. These were then dropped onto a pile of newly threshed sama grains while other of the sama grains were distributed to the men and boys present. Holding the sama grains between their hands they all prayed, and then bowed down to the ground. The katora then made on each of the dung mounds six plus one small heaps of cooked sama that had been brought from the village and dipping his finger into a small cup of ghee (clarified butter), he allowed the ghee to drip onto each of the sama heaps. This ceremony was repeated by all the men and boys pres-

9.017 : Large stone dolmen as a sacred clan altar or tehuba. Naga, North East India, Late 19th., century, A.D.

9.018 : Male and female monoliths standing on a stone faced circular platform. Note the sleds used for dragging suitable stones over long distances. Rengma Nagas, Assam, North East India, Late 19th.,-early 20th., century, A.D.

9.019 : Massive carved stone being towed on a sled similar in principle to those found among the Nagas and on some Indonesian islands. Assyria, First half of the first millennium B.C.

9.022 : Massive monolith being dragged to its final location using traditional rollers. Sumba, Central Indonesia, Early 20th., century, A.D.

9.020 : Sacred stone being transported in an alternate to the sled. Here a frame is constructed to allow a shared load around the carriers surrounding the perimeter. Lhota Naga, North East India, Early 20th., century, A.D.

9.021 : Typical sledge for dragging selected monoliths to their predetermined sites. Chazubama, Manipur, North East India, Early 20th., century, A.D.

ent[117]. These rituals appear similar to those of the Peruvians noted by the Spanish and that still survive in the more remote areas, and since there are so many other aspects of apparent cultural transfer it is likely that they have a common origin.

In South India the Pariahs or Paraiyans shrines to local deities often had carved images of the deity, sometimes quite large, and sometimes very crude, and in front of them a number of small stones. When offerings were being made at the time of festivals, associated with the deities the people anoint the stones and wash, the deities, with oil, milk, coconut milk, limejuice, and water and regale them with new cloth and garlands of flowers. Animals are also offered and then sacrificed to these deities in ceremonies not dissimilar to those in Ancient Peru witnessed by the first Spanish and still preformed into the present century. Blood is collected from the animal sacrifice and when the people have departed the priests mix it with boiled rice and then perform a ritual about 100 yards (or metres) outside the shrine throwing it to the "north-west, south-east, south-east and south-west" at the end of the festival[118]. It is interesting to note that the intermediate cardinal points of the compass are here recognised as they are in the earliest Vedic texts. It is these intermediates to the cardinal points that are more prominent in the calendrical constructs of Ancient Peru.

Stones - Increase Rituals

It must not be forgotten, however, that in the fundamental symbol of Hinduism, the linga is itself a formalisation of the megalith or menhir as the male phallus of the supreme male deity, where the yoni is the corresponding female organ of the female deity. As fertility symbols they were, and still is peripheral cultures, carved stones - one male the other female, and these remained in their crude state in many less affluent sections of Hindu society in India. These stones were perceived as essential elements as reflecting abundance and increase in the human population, and by extension into the agricultural symbolism throughout Asia and retained as such in India to this day. It has been noted elsewhere in this work that many cultural aspects of Aboriginal and Hindu India were transferred by mariners and traders to Australia and those aspects are still clearly visible in the reports of the first anthropologists who recorded their cultures as they found them over a century ago.

The bathing and anointing of sacred stones, so widespread among all the religions and castes of India, appears to be the origin of the "increase" rituals among the Australian Aboriginals. The sacred stones of the Aborigines are considered to relate to the mythical times known as the Alcheringa. The personal stones in which the soul of the individual is sometimes said to reside is known as the Churinga, and this is rubbed to produce manna[119] - similar to the Melanesian and Polynesian mana or spiritual energy on which the individual and tribe can draw. The Todas in South India sacrificed buffalo only on special occasions and this took place near the funeral hut at a place that was usually marked by a stone called Teiks. If there was no stone the place it was marked by a wooden post with the same name. It is thought that this is the name of the timber required for the post of teak suggesting that the stone was a substitute for a sacrificial post known as the Yupa[120] in Hinduism and deriving from the sacrificial posts of Ancient Iran. This is probably the origin of similar posts in the Pacific and Americas, and known as Yopee among the Zapotecs in Southern Mexico. The original purpose of the sacrificial post was to despatch suitable male warriors, or other of the finest specimens of manhood, to the gods in Central Asia in the most ancient times and traces of the associated rituals are still preserved in the Vedas of Ancient India[121]. In some less advanced and peripheral societies the original sacrificial stone is preserved and the victim was laid out on it before being despatched. In others the post, or megalith was retained and both these traditions were preserved in the cultures of the islands and Aboriginal Australia in the Western Pacific.

Stones in the Cultures of the Nagas of Assam

It has been noted that in Peru stones represented the personal gods of the families and clans of the Indians. In Assam the Nagas also revered stones kept within, and outside of the home. These stones were called oha and when a new house was built these were sanctified and placed in their houses[122]. The central feature of a village was often the sacred tree or mingetung, a member of the ficus family usually planted on an earth mound near the centre of the settlement. In this tree the trophy heads of the enemy were tied and at its base were placed the sacred oha stones[123]. These stones are usually smooth worn from a river and vary in size from a pebble to the size of a man's hand. They are usually kept apart from the foot, or under the sacred tree, or at the foot of the carved posts each side of the morung (or clan house), or in their houses or granaries. The ratsen, or clan healer also had the tradition of retaining small oha somewhere in their head[124], reminiscent of the Australian Aborigines who pierced their tongues into which they secured crystals. Such traditions among the Nagas probably derive from the brow jewel myths of India earlier noted.

Stone sacrificial slabs were essential to the ceremonial life of the Naga village and these usually took the form of a flat slab raised off the ground with other stones. These are associated with grain rituals and resemble in principle those of the Central American site at Izapa. At both the Naga sites and those at Izapa there are stones clearly believed or known to represent male and female associated with the their respective cultures, and found also in India. The artisan was taught that stones were considered either male or female detected by their "ring", or sound given off when struck, and selected appropriately as to whether the carver was going to represent a male or female deity[125]. Among the Sema Nagas, they typically reflect the Naga predilection for sacred stones. And some of the villages, such as Lazemi, had at one time a pair of stones considered male and female and who were believed able to breed and produce offspring[126]. The several methods of transporting, or dragging stones among the Nagas are found related to megaliths being conveyed on rollers in less mountainous terrain of the Indonesian Islands such as Sumba. These various methods probably duplicate those used in Peru, and Bolivia in particular, where ruts in stone level outcrops suggest that sledding was common and was probably imported as a technique among others from the ancient Middle East as indicated in the illustrations found in Assyria.

In some of the villages when hauling the stone monoliths to their sites in the villages, the main stone, dragged by the men using ropes was secured on a large sled-like construction together with a smaller stone that was also taken along as the "wife" for the main stone[127]. The Lhota Nagas also revered oha stones and dual male and female menhirs, or monoliths, and these were more usually associated by them with the Y-posts where one arm was considered male and the other female[128]. In the Melanesian island of Tikopia, influenced from Polynesia, male and female stones were associated with the deities to which offerings were made[129]. In the Upper Waghi district of New Guinea male stones were upright, clearly derived from the linga of India, while the female stones were placed at the base of it[130].

GOLDEN STAVES; PORTALS and the SEARCH for AVA-CHUMBI and NINA-CHUMBI

Golden Staves of the Incas

In the Inca's own account recorded in their Origins myths, including that of Pachacuti-Yamqui Salcamayhua, the first Inca, Manco Capac, used the golden rod, staff, or wedge to determine the place where the Incas were ordained by the gods and ancestors to settle. The staff used in such a way is certainly not unique to Inca mythology and is found in principle widely in Asia. The ceremony in memory of the act of the first sacred rod entering the earth from Manco Capac's hand was imitated in rituals commemorated annually by the reigning Inca[131]. In Bolivia, the most ancient representations of lightning are highly reminiscent of the early Asian representations where two "rods" of lightning are depicted in the cross form[132]. The ceremonial rods shown held by the Sun or lightning god carved centrally on the Gateway of the Sun appear to be serpent- or condor-headed rods. These may have been clad in gold foil since the application of gold to other carvings have been retrieved from this or related sites and may have been the prototype for immediate predecessors of the Incas and given rise to the Inca myths themselves. There are several references to the fact that the carved figures of the Sun or Inti, Punchao - the son of the Sun, and Illapa - the lightning god, were all covered in gold and Cobo himself describes the three images located in the Temple of the Sun at Cuzco, the Coricancha[133]. The images of the Sun and the sacred rock, Titi-Kala on the Island of the Sun in Lake Titicaca were covered with gold noted by the early Spanish chroniclers[134] as were the many statues to Viracocha[135]. Viracocha and Tonapa along with the other Andean heroes were noted for the staff they carried and these appear to resemble those of the Asian and Christian records in form and function along with those so frequently depicted in Mayan iconography (*9.029; 9.033*). It is likely, therefore that the golden rods and staffs of South American myths are in fact probably modelled on those used and reported in original myths imported from Asia, India and the Ancient Near and Middle East in particular. These staffs from both the Americas and South Asia incorporate the trilobe or trefoil that is so closely identified with the god Siva in India.

Golden Rod in Myth in Colombia
The Chibcha in the highlands of Colombia were said to have been punished by the deity named Chibchacum "for their excesses" by causing the waters of the Sapo and Tihito rivers to rise and flood their lands. The people fled to the mountains and they implored the deity Bochica to save them. He appeared at sunset on a rainbow and promised to open a breach at Tequendama, and he threw his golden rod at the dammed water causing it to pour down to the plains below to bring greater fertility than before. Bochica further decided to chastise Chibchacum for his act against the people and forced him to carry the Earth on two pillars made of guayacan wood - a very hard wood resistant to the copper axes of the Indians[136]. Although not specifically recorded as gold the staff in the traditions associated with a female deity named Chia, Yubecayguaya, or Huitaca, note that she was transformed into the Moon by the use of this rod of her husband Botschica and he was also called Zuhe and Nemquetaba. Botschica appears to be another version of Bochica, and Zuhe has been identified with Zue, Sua, Zume - names identified with Tonaca of Bolivia and Peru, and Tumu of Polynesia. Botschia was also reputed to have created the waterfall of Tequendama that subsequently drained the waterlogged plains in the high plateaus and valleys, and then retired to Sogomoso for 2000 years[137] Interestingly Chicha, the fermented beverage made from maize, was known as aba or ava in parts of Colombia[138] and this appears to have a common origin with the Polynesian form of the drink - ava or kava. Aba was also the name in Colombia for the maize itself[139].

The Golden Spindle and the Sacred Turtle of the Maya
The Maya revered the turtle as a fundamental creative element in the primal world of the first creation and this was virtually the identical belief to that held in India[140]. In texts referring to the Bacabs, the rulers of the four quarters - a later reflection of the Pauahtuns, it is said that the "golden spindle" was the tail of the cosmic turtle, that is, the Axis Mundae, or World Axis[141]. This corresponds to some aspects of Asian imagery particularly related to the vajra or magic sceptre, or dorje in the Tibetan form, and it is probable that the golden rod of the Incas derived from similar cosmological speculations since the rod sank into the earth at the centre of the four quarters at Cuzco. The Earth in the Hindu myths of India was said to support the world Axis or Tree is recorded as such and depicted also in the myths of "Churning the Cosmic Ocean" in Aboriginal India, and in South East Asia.

In India, sacred sceptres and staffs are commonly identified with many sages, heroes, and deities. The throwing of the golden rod by Bochica to open up the dammed water is highly reminiscent of the high Hindu deities of Vedic origin, particularly Indra, who frequently is recorded as throwing his rod or thunderbolt to alleviate some threatening situation. For reasons that will become apparent in a later chapter the Gonds myths are worthy of note in respect to golden rods.

Golden Staffs in Myths and Traditions in India
In a few of the texts preserved from the Gupta Dynasty traditions in North India, dating to between 300-500 A.D., some of the more famous commentators or sages of the time recorded their own view of the earlier and current philosophic traditions prevalent at that time in the first major Hindu dynasty in India. It is recorded that in this early time it was believed that the great god of the large mass of the Hindu population, Siva, lived in the great paradise he ruled from his

"pleasure mountain" located in the high Himalayas named Kailasa. It was stated that the symbol of his authority was his golden staff and this was depicted resting on his left forearm while he remained in Kailasa, and described as such in the Kumarasambhava; III, 41[142]. Siva's usual symbol of authority was the trisula, a form of trident and this appears in earliest iconography as a spear, originally used by Iranian herdsmen, with horns attached and probably linked to the lightning symbol of the Ancient Near East shown in Hittite carvings (*5.072*). This form of the trident or trisula is still constructed in this way today. Lightning and storms must have been a feared event for the plains herdsman and a great danger to them much as it is for present-day golfers exposed on the open fairways and greens. In fact there are many reflections of the Siva trident in South American (*5.074*) and Mayan iconography and other trilobed imagery appears to have been directly transferred from India[143]. The celebrated ground drawing on a dune at Paracas, known either as the "trident" or "candelabra", is about 600 feet high and 200 feet across and is drawn so as to be visible only from the sea. This trident is in a recognisable form of Siva's trisula and the fact that it can only been seen from the Pacific Ocean tends to suggest that it was a guiding marker for mariners approaching the coast of Peru using a symbol they would understand as a form of beacon[144] (*5.071*).

Golden Staves of the Raj Gonds Gods

In their tribal origin myths the Gonds note that their founding fathers were in fact deities who had been liberated from a "primeval cave" by the semi-divine hero Pahandi Kupar Lingal. In the myth preserved by the four-brother clan of the Pardhans it is noted that when Sri Shembu (Siva) sealed the twelve threshing floors and their associated gods in the in the cave he placed a female demon to guard the cave who was to devour anyone who dared to approach. After twelve years the Gond hero Pahandi Kupar Lingal found the cave, and, placing his foot on the head of the demon pushed her down into the ground and then proceeded to release the Gond gods from the caves. These "gods" had "become men" and required to find the deities that they must worship who were designated the Persa Pen. Pahandi Kupar Lingal was detailed to find the gods and found the house where they existed.

9.023 : A finely carved section from a Buddhist complex showing a group of devotees in front of the centrally placed stupa in the characteristc form of an omphalus. Amaravati, East Coast India, 2nd., century, A.D.

The myth continues that the golden staves were located inside that house were the gods of the Gonds resided and when the hero entered he found that they were guarded by one of the two earth goddesses. While she was asleep Pahandi Kupar Lingal stole the four golden staves and made away with them but she awoke and threw a firebrand at him this hitting him with a glancing blow on his shoulder and as a result the four staves caught fire and turned black and became iron. The bamboo shafts of the staffs to hold the metal spearheads were also considered a symbol of the Gond along with four fly whisks and sets of bells for each of the Gond clans, together with cloth[145]. Other myths note the magical healing qualities of the rod possessed by another group of Gond heroes, the seven Panoir brothers[146].

A Canarese caste of betel-leaf sellers called the Pentiya instituted a highly organised caste system governed through the local heads of the castes. These headmen were connected by a caste messenger carrying a silver rod as a symbol of his authority to summon the caste members to meetings[147]. The Canarese appear to be prime movers in the extension of trade and ventures to South East Asia and the Pacific Islands and among the Polynesians the Sun god was said to have given the hero Bue a divine rod to prevent him

9.024 : Carved Staff Deity over the door opening identified with the Sun and or the lightning god in Bolivia. Tiahuanaco, Bolivia, 300-600 A.D.

9.025 : A brass guardian deity standing holding a magic staff with a mace head to command and defeat demons and unwelcome demonic energies. Central India, Early-mid 2nd., millennium, A.D.

9.026 : A section of a fine textile showing a deity holding a sceptre or staff in each hand possibly branches relating to fertility. Moche, North Coast Peru, 200-600 A.D.

9.028 : Ceremonial sceptres similar to those found among the Batak in Sumatra considered temporary shrines for ancestral spirits. The sceptre at the left is said to represent the deity Rongo; the middle Maru, and both at the right, Tangaroa. Maori, New Zealand, Late 19th., century, A.D.

9.027 : ...remonial staff ...mounted with ...arved head vir-...lly identical to ...se of the ...ori 5,500 ...es away in ...w Zealand. ...tak, Sumatra, ...e 19th., centu-...A.D.

drowning at sea[148].

In Sumatra, in Indonesia, the Toba-Bataks still preserved in the present day the rituals and myths surrounding their "magic wand"[149]. These wooden staves were originally carved with seven figures, called "pusaka-magic wands" (the tunggal panaluan), and these are recognised as closely resembling those found in the totem-pole carvings on the North West Pacific Coast of North America. In a remarkably similar motif to that of Tonapa in Bolivia where he gave a piece of his staff to Manco Capa's father, the Toba-Batak wand is said to have been broken off the World Tree by the High God and given to the high priest (the datu) of these people so that they could communicate with him[150]. The datu uses this wand when dancing around the square drawn on the ground representing symbolically the interaction of lightning with the cardinal points[151] noted elsewhere in this work, and it should not be forgotten that Tonapa in Bolivia is also the Andean lightning god.

Golden Rods or Staves in Mandaean Myth

In a myth recorded in the Mandaean texts in the Ancient Middle East it is stated that a Mandaean hero travelled far from his homeland with the aid of Shamash, the Sun God. He travelled each day the distance of forty day's journey making a distance travelled in 30 days that would be normally covered in about 1200 days. It appears, from the myth, that he travelled to the icy north and to have reached a region that corresponds to the far north of North America where he emerges from a long dark tunnel through a hole in the ground with a staff in his hand. The staff was "all of gold and bore an inscription", this being a talisman to protect him on his journey[152].

9.029 : Staff God with ceremonial cross braces reflecting similar imagery to that from Asia through Oceania to the Americas. Chimeltenango, Guatemala, Late-Post Classic.

9.030 : Trefoil on a typical fez-like cap found anciently into the present day in Indonesia and South Asia. The staff also displays a trefoil and stepped motif probably derived from the Ancient Middle East. Note also the globe at the lower end displaying four border markers and central circle usually indicative of the Sun at the centre of the four cardinal pints found in Ancient Burma but also in Mexico. Cerro Sechin, Casma, Central Coast Peru, Late second millennium, B.C.

9.032 : Bat or Eagle deity holding staffs, in gold, with dual plumes extending from his head, and demon mask pectoral on the chest. Chavin Style, Chongoyape, North Coast Peru, Mid-first millenium, B.C.

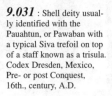

9.031 : Shell deity usually identified with the Pauahtun, or Pawaban with a typical Siva trefoil on top of a staff known as a trisula. Codex Dresden, Mexico, Pre- or post Conquest, 16th., century, A.D.

9.033 : Finely carved Mayan stone stela showing spear staffs identical to the ceremonial Taiaha found among the Moaris of New Zealand and the Nagas of Assam. Guatemala, 8th., century, A.D.

The staff was the special symbol of the Mandaean priest and was called the margna, associated symbolically with water, and was often called the "staff of living water"[153]. In the fire-religion of the Mazdaeans the barsom, or bundle of twigs was considered the emblem of the priesthood[154] and this was also noted in the early Vedic religion of India.

The golden stave appears to be a merging of the magic wands such as that used by Moses in the Biblical accounts and symbol of the Axis Mundae or World Axis upon which the world revolves that and pointed northward to the Pole Star. In ancient accounts the two are clearly the same since the magic wand was a symbol of authority, right, and command over the whole world and the power it wielded was considered derived from the gods who lived in the sky or were in fact personified by the stars.

Magic Wands; Rods and Staves in General in India and Burma

In South India the Todas used a wand or sceptre when praying called a Pohvet[155]. In one of their myths it was said that their primary female deity, Teikirzi went into a cave beside a river and their gave birth to a son called Azo-mazo. The afterbirth fell into the river and floated downstream and became tangled with riverine plants and gradually it was transformed into a boy. This boy was named Korateu and he lived in the river until he was eight years old and was said to be the brother of the river named Teipakh. Large sections of the original myth are missing but it is said that Korateu played with the horns of a buffalo, made a male and female buffalo out of earth mounds, and built a dairy and buffalo pen. He is associated with buffalo horns in other parts of

566

9.035 : A trilobe design with circle reflecting a trefoil and both characteristic of a sacred design found in the Ancient Middle East and India. Tiahuanaco, Bolivia, 700-1000 A.D.

9.034 : Trefoil symbol typical of the Siva trisula in India held by a Tocharian merchant, a red-headed people in Central Asia probably of Celtic descent. Central Asia, 2-5th., century, A.D.

9.036 : A carved stone pediment showing a makara or stylised fish-crocodile depicting a trilobe on the gills identical to the same symbol found in South America, among the Maya and in North America. Mathura, North Central India, 100 B.C.-200 A.D.

9.037 : A finely shaped ceramic of apparently a horned serpent, a type of iconography identical to West Asia. The body design is of trilobes found widely on the Peruvian coast and similar to those found in India and the Ancient Middle East. Peru, 200-600 A.D.

the myth and he is particularly noted as having cut off the horns that grew downwards and gave them to one of the temples. The myth is too long to repeat here but he is also said to have carried a "stick of iron" and one day when he came upon a Kurumba woman Korateu "knocked her on the head" with the iron stick and she became pregnant[156] . Clearly the myth is so old that there are a series of creation myths apparent and preserved here linked together although garbled and the horns reflect the early reverence the Todas and other Middle Eastern peoples had for their cattle herds. Bringing forth the first cattle from earth mounds reflects the early Middle Eastern creation myths, and it is likely that the horns themselves were related to lightning in the homelands from which these people had come but had become dissociated in time and lost in their traditions. The magic rod tends to indicate that they had links to early blacksmith or iron-making traditions, possibly with Anatolia and the Hittites. The horns and the iron "rod" appear to be the earliest forms of Siva's trident or trisula in India.

In Burma (Myanmar) a legend current into modern times was that a Nat, or nature spirit, buried Buddha's staff under a kanyin tree on Theingottara Hill[157]. This appears to have some connection with the Toba-Batak magic wand earlier noted where the wand was carved from the World Tree. The Buddha's staff became converted and identified as the lightning rod, the dorje in Tibetan Buddhism, but is better known in this form as the vajra of the storm god Indra (7.087) where the rod represents lightning preserved from the original clutch of three arrows so widely illustrated in Ancient Middle Eastern iconography (7.006). Indra was relegated in importance in the development from Vedic Brahmanism to Hinduism but his less elevated status appears to have survived transfer to South America, although only alluded to, and will be of further interest later in this work.

9.040 : A finely cut gold foil plate showing armorial animals and a central figure with "ear muffs" of a type found among the Nagas of Assam, and also in the Marquesas Islands. Note also the cruciform located in the centre of the figure of the type found in Tiahuanaco and also the Chalukyans among others in India. Moche, North Coast Peru, 200-600 A.D.

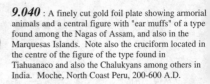

9.039 : A trefoil design within the trilobe found at Tiahuanaco but also in South and West Asia. Bolivia, 400-900 A.D.

9.038 : The great ruler Sargon standing before a stylised tree clearly indicating the importance of the trefoil applied to the leaf or blossom structure and to the symbolic branch in his left hand. This depiction reflects the trefoil associated in Hindu India but more reminiscent also of similar depictions in Ancient Peru. Akkadian, Late third century, A.D.

9.042 : Trilobes depicted on these shell fragments identical to a type also found in Ancient Buddhist India. Spiro Mound, Ohio, Eastern USA, 800-1350 A.D.

9.041 : Three eyed demon mask showing the trefoil so important in the symbolism of Ancient Middle East, India and Tibet, Pre-20th., century, A.D.

9.043 : A ceramic in the form of a puma or wildcat, possibly the hail deity the Ccoa, displaying trilobes of the type found in Ancient India, the Ancient Middle East and in Central America and North America. Recauy, Huacho, Central Peru, 200-600 A.D.

Magic Rod or Wand in Aboriginal Australia

The spear was considered to be the most sacred weapon in Australia and one or more spears was wound with string made from human hair, then decorated with down, and known as the nurtunja[158]. The fact that several could be used seems to indicate that this is a reflection of the barsom traditions of stick, or twig bundles used by the Parsees and Mandaeans. Other examples recorded by the early British researchers in Central Australia note that this magical sacred staff, or nurtunja, was made from the central spine of the spear wrapped with grass stalks and these tied by human hair until the pole was about 8 feet (2.5 m) high and 6 inches (150 mm) diameter[159]. In the kangaroo totem their nurtunja was made from twenty spears tied together[160]. Interestingly, among the traditions of Central Australian Aborigines regarding the Evening Star, it was believed that when it set it descended into a "big white stone at Ulkni-wukulla, where Auadaua sat in the Alcheringa" (dreamtime or distant time of the ancestors)[161]. The many connections in mythical traditions between the Australian Aborigines and India have been noted in other chapters in this work and here the mythical deity is probably the Pole Star and in India this star is called Arundati[162] not dissimilar to the Aboriginal Auadaua. The myths in Australia are much less integrated than the traditions of India but sufficient links are detectable, when searched for parallels and transfers, to be certain when read with other evidence.

568

9.044 : A figurine of Mahakala displaying trefoils on all the armbands, wrist-bands, and ankle straps typical in early Buddhist symbolism inherited from the Ancient Middle East. He is shown trampling on an elephant-headed demon named Vinataku. Tibet, Mid-second millennium, A.D.

9.045 : The ruler or priest shown in this low relief carving wears a trefoil cap of the type found anciently in Tibet and India. The staff he holds has a calendrical division at the upper end and a Sun symbol of the type found among the Maya and in Buddhist India. Cerro Sechin, Casma, Second half of the second millennium, B.C.

The Magic Rod or Staff in Myth and Ritual in Melanesia and Polynesia

The magic rod is a prominent item in of the many myths recorded in Melanesia and Polynesia, and local myths on the Solomon Islands note that the hero Ao-marau in his haste dropped his magic rod on the island of Arosi in the Solomon Islands. The evidence for this belief was pointed out by local people as being the large luxuriant clumps of bamboo that grew at the point it fell to earth[163]. The prefix Ao is the Melanesian equivalent of the chiefly Polynesian designation Au, Sau, Hau, Chau and Ahau and their correspondences are found also in South America. In Polynesia the insignia of a chief included the leaf fan, virtually identical to examples found in Western Mexico and in Peru. This was called Tahi'i (Taiaha) while in other Polynesian societies such as the Maori it was the spear that was called the same name, while in the Marquesas the spear associated with kingship was called the To'o-to'o-pio'o, or Toko-toko-pio'o. This latter was a staff about 6 feet (1.8 m) long and at the top a band of sennit was wound around it surmounted by a small tuft of curly black hair[164]. These spears are identical to those found depicted as insignia of rulers among the Maya and in South America. This form of staff was known among the first Polynesian settlers in New Zealand, the Morioris, and known as the Tokotoko. Both the Maoris and Morioris possessed the Patu as a ceremonial hand-club and was a symbol of king-ship[165] and this appears to have been the same as that used by the Kwakiutl and others Indians on the North West Coast of North America. The sacred sceptre of the priest was composed of three fau sticks wrapped in cloth and resembles the barsom of the Mandaeans and Parsees. The inspirational priest also carried a sacred staff, or rod, and was composed of three fau sticks wrapped in cloth. The staff was made from ironwood, and called a hoto[166].

Magic Staff or Rod Among Amazonian Tribes

Among the Bororo in the Central Amazon the creation myths suggest in part contact with West Africa. For the present purpose it is necessary only to record that the first creator, Jocoramodogueddu, a monkey god of the Paiwoe clan, tired of being alone, used his magic rod to create all the different colours of human beings, animals, plants and the forests[167]. Aspects of the myth resemble also the Hopi myths of the South West United States and these will be of more interest in a projected later publication. In a further myth from the Chorote, noted earlier, Kixwet

used his magic wand to return the waters, that flooded out from the great tree of the myth, back to the trunk[168]. This myth clearly relates to the Si'wet myths from the far North American West Coast, originating with the Kwakiutl Indians, and is indicative of the long distance routes travelled by sea and the culture that they dispersed along the way.

The magic rod is most famously the symbol of the special magical powers of the great sages and semi-divine heroes of history but more particularly better known in the Biblical legend of Moses using it to separate the River Nile to allow the Israelites to pass. Even with the myths from the North West Coast of North America it is possible to trace these myths back to the Ancient Near and Middle East and India, along with many other aspects illustrates the dispersion of myths, legends, material culture and contemporary technology from there throughout Eurasia and Africa.

9.046 : A Buddhist saint wearing a traditional fez-like crown with a symbolic five circlesmotif similar to those found at Cerro Sechin where three circles on a similar cap are found. Tibet, Pre-20th., century, A.D.

Three Golden Windows or Jewelled Portals and Cave Origins in Inca Myths

The golden staff or wedge associated with the origins of the Inca occurs only with versions deriving from the Incas themselves. This is also true for the references to jewelled treasures stored up by Manco Capac and his descendants, but more interestingly there are references to gold and jewelled architraves or surrounds to these openings in the fabled Cave of Origin. This sounds rather like grandiose propaganda, but was there in fact some truth in these reports? It is known that there was a vast gold treasure delivered as a ransom for Atahualpa's release from the Spanish confinement at Cajamarca. An even greater treasure was on its way when it the news that the Inca ruler had been assassinated by the Spanish Conquistadors reached those conveying it and the ransom was then spirited away and secreted in a place that has never been detected. Certainly it is recorded from first hand accounts that a golden garden was associated with the Sun temple, where all the elements were made or covered with gold and silver and possibly bejewelled.

The golden garden and other historically confirmed references may have their origin in the much earlier traditions interpreted in these later architectural wonders at Cuzco. Of special interest were the references in the Inca origin myths recorded by Version 9 to the apertures forming the three entrances to the cave of origin being jewel faced. This certainly sounds like gilding the myths to associate the line of descent with the reflections of wealth and power. However, there may in fact be some truth in this report, and although it occurs only in one written report, but as hearsay in others, this in fact may be part of its validation that might be found in the reports of Inca Tupac voyage to the west across the Pacific Ocean.

In the records by Sarmiento, one of the most important and reliable of the Spanish chroniclers, there is a report that the son and successor of the Inca Pachacuti Yupanqui, Tupac, after defeating the Chimu in the 15th., century A.D., led an expedition west across the Pacific Ocean. In the first reports Sarmiento records that, "Marching and conquering on the coast of Manta (Ecuador), and Tumbez, there arrived at Tumbez some merchants who had come by sea from the west, navigating in balsas with sails. They gave information of the land whence they came, which consisted of some islands called Avachumbi and Ninachumbi, where there were many people and much gold." Not fully trusting the reports from the merchants Tupa, (Tupac Inca), consulted a "necromancer" who accompanied him on his campaigns, who had a great reputation and "could even fly through the air" named Antarqui. Antarqui "thought the matter out" and he replied that the merchants reports were true and that he would go there first and that, "They say that he accomplished this by his arts, traversed the route, saw the islands, their people and riches, and, returning, gave certain information of all to Tupac Inca. Tupac having received these confirmations then determined to go there and caused a great number of balsas (log rafts) to be built"[169].

The logistics of constructing sufficiently large numbers of ocean-going log rafts is not challenged by Sarmiento or later scholars to accommodate the reported 20,000 soldiers who accompanied Tupa and the seven generals. Interestingly the Inca was accompanied also by his captains, named as Huaman Achachi, Cunti Yupanqui, Quihual Tupac and also Yancan Mayta, Quisu Mauta, Chachimapaca Macus Yupanqui and Llimipita Usca Mayta, the first three being noted as from Hanan-cuzcos, and the last four being from Hurin-cuzcos. Tupa was also accompanied by his brother Tilca Yupanqui and the commander of the fleet was named as Apu Yupanqui.

Having sailed off into the Pacific Ocean to the west it is reported by the Incas that Tupa returned, "… bringing back with him black people, much gold, a chair of brass, and a skin and jawbone of a horse." Sarmiento then reported that: "These trophies were preserved in the fortress of Cuzco until the Spaniards came. An Inca now living had charge of this skin and jaw-bone of a horse. He gave this account, and the rest who were present corroborated it. His name is Urco Huaranca. I am particular about this because to those who know anything of the Indies it will appear a strange thing and difficult to believe. The duration of this expedition undertaken by Tupac Inca was nine months, others say a year."[170]. Sarmiento was so interested in this story that he examined the legends and the Incas who preserved it and decided that he could fix the point of the two islands noted in them, Hahua-chumbi ("Outer Island") and Nina chumbi ("Fire island"), and encouraged and undertook expeditions into the Pacific resulting in the discovery of the Galapagos Islands off the coast of Ecuador and the Marquesas Islands in Eastern Polynesia as well as the Solomon Islands in Melanesia.

This report recorded by Sarmiento has long intrigued researchers and historians since, if Tupa did sail west and returned, the Inca reports that they returned after so long and with a great deal of gold and a jawbone of a horse certainly does not fit the Galapagos Islands. This is compounded by the surviving relic preserved by the contemporary Inca, and more particularly the preserved jawbone appearing to be identified by both the later Incas and Spaniards who saw it as definitely that of a horse. These records have long baffled historians and some have rejected them as fantasy while others suggest that Tupa must have sailed to Central America where gold was plentiful, as the Spaniards could attest, and from there returned with his trophies. However, such propositions are not logical since the Incas and their ancestors were master builders and planned the orientation of their buildings accurately to the cardinal points or other prominent features of the landscape. An army commander such as Tupa would have had to be entirely aware of the compass directions in the campaigns he undertook over the length of Peru and into what is now Ecuador. That he, or others, could not detect or report on whether they went west into the Pacific or North to Central America or Mexico is inconceivable.

Other researchers, such as the greatly respected historian a century ago, Sir Clements Markham, the translator of Sarmiento's report, have suggested that the landfall Tupa reached was the Galapagos Islands, since these were situated to the west of Ecuador, consonant with the record, and now form part of their territory. Markham does not attempt to explain the gold treasure claimed by the Incas to have been brought back by Tupa, nor the brass chair or the "black people", and these are essential in the confirmation of the record of the journey. There was no culture contemporary then, or before, exhibiting any sort of culture let alone technical development and metallurgy skills or production in the Galapagos since these were an uninhabited island group until the Europeans entered the Pacific. All that has been found on the Galapagos in the mid-20th., century is some pottery from the Incan period, perhaps left by Tupa's expedition, but unlikely to be the final destination that would attract an heir to the Incan throne to risk his life and future on such a spurious venture. These is nothing in the Galapagos that would have attracted merchants to visit, let alone to report on, and certainly nil of interest for the Inca prince, Tupac.

It is likely from the available evidence to detect that the destination for his voyage and his determination to undertake it was in fact much further west.

The Galapagos Islands are located about 400 miles (720 Km) due west of Ecuador, while the nearest of the most easterly of the Polynesian Islands, the Marquesas Islands, are about 3500 miles (6300 km). When Thor Heyerdahl attempted to prove his theory that the Peruvian Indians had sailed into the Pacific Islands he had a balsa raft constructed and with limited training sailed with his companions and made landfall in the Marquesas 101 days later. This would average out at about 35 miles per day, and in considering a Peruvian royal expedition it must be assumed that this Inca prince would have had at his command the very best mariners and raft builders who were superior in their craft and navigational skill than Thor Heyerdahl centuries later. Even if Tupa's raft fleet had sailed at the same rate as Heyerdahl's solitary craft he would had taken two weeks maximum to reach the Galapagos.

Sarmiento's report notes: "After Tupac Inca disembarked from the discovery of the islands, he proceeded to Tumipampa, to visit his wife and son and to hurry preparations for the return to Cuzco to see his father, who was reported to be ill. On the way back he sent troops along the coast to Truxillo, then called Chimu, where they found immense wealth of gold and silver worked into wands, and into beams of the house of Chimu Ccapac, with all which they joined the main army at Caxamarca. Thence Tupac Inca took the route to Cuzco, where he arrived after an absence of six years since he set out on his campaign."[171]. More recent researchers have determined that Tupa, Topa Inca or Tupac Inca's campaign in Ecuador began in 1463 and lasted until 1471 A.D.[172]. However, the Inca reports recorded 6 years[173] absence and this period appears to include a period searching for opponents in the eastern forests. Even if the war had begun at the beginning of the first year and lasted until the end of the last of these it would have taken a maximum of four years. This leaves two years unaccounted for and possibly nearer three allowing for up to three years in which the voyage undertaken by Tupa would have occurred lasting for the "nine months or a year" recorded by Sarmiento. It is interesting to note that in the last section of Sarmiento's report he relates that he was told by his Inca informant that when Tupac Inca Yupanqui returned Cuzco in great triumph, his father Pachacuti Inca Yupanqui was consumed with "avarice" and "jealousy that his son should have gained such honour and fame in those conquests". It was said that he had his other two sons, Tilca Yupanqui and Auqui Yupanqui, who accompanied Tupa, or Tupac, killed because they had disobeyed his orders by delaying longer than the time he had fixed and that they had taken his son to such a distance that he thought he would never return to Cuzco[174].

If Tupa's destination was further west than the Galapagos then, as the original reports noted that he was absent for 12 months or more then it can be assumed the furthest he may have reached before having to return within that time is a six month voyage there and six months back. For a six-month period using a minimum of Heyerdahl's progress of 35 miles per days means that Tupa would have managed to sail 6400 miles (9500 km) approximately. This would have meant that he could have reached the Samoan Islands or Tonga or Fiji as a minimum. However, it is said in some reports that Tupa was absent from Peru for longer and with the most skilled mariners would have travelled much further. The reports recorded of this venture undertaken by Tupa state that he was given to understand that the island group he was headed for consisted of two main islands where gold was in abundance and there were other attractions deserving his attention. A prince from the Inca court would be unlikely to be allowed or want to go on such a mission unless it was certain there was something of great value to be gained. The only lands to the west where gold, and the metallurgical expertise to exploit it was available was in Indonesia where the two great islands of Java and Sumatra were located. These had long been centres of Brahmanic Hindu and Buddhist learning and an architectural tradition exhibiting a unique style focused on these religions transferred from India. It is not only possible but almost certain, therefore, that Tupa's destination was in fact Java and possible further west to Burma and India.

Thor Heyerdahl suggested that Tupa had reached the Tuamotu Archipelago to the south of the Marquesas Islands and he noted that there were certain legends referring to him in their oral traditions. However, these Pacific Islands were unlikely to be the destination for Tupa since they had none of the attractions said to have initiated his desire to undertake the voyage. The Spanish records again preserve the references indicating that Java was at least one of the destinations if not the main voyage. Sarmiento notes that the lands Tupa visited were named Ava-chumbi and Nina-chumbi. Ava-chumbi, however, in the original text is referred to as Hahau-chumpi, and Markham suggests that Nina-chumpi refers to the volcanic island of Narborough Island (Fernandina) in the Galapagos since the term nina refers to "fire" in Quechua, and chumpi means "island"[175].

Although there are many islands in the Galapagos there are not two major islands, but one large with many lesser ones, and as noted, there were none of the attractions to incite the desire to visit them by an Inca prince. The term nina means fire but is probably related and derived from "Agni" ([ag]-ni[na]), the god of fire in Vedic India. This term will be of more interest, as it has been earlier in this work, since it relates to the Sun and was perceived by the ancient Brahmans as representing the Sun on Earth, as a microcosm and therefore also the Sun within as the "divine spark".

The terms Ava and Hahua, prefixing the names of the islands, are of great interest, however, since in the earliest texts in the first millennium A.D. the island of Java was always referred to by its original name Hawa (Hahua), and this island derived its name from Hawa in the ancient Middle East. Not only do the names correspond to the two main cultural islands of what is now Indonesia but both are highly volcanic and correspond therefore to the Incan myth as "fire-islands". Indonesia was the perfect entry point from South and West Asia into the Pacific and from the Pacific, and the Americas, to South East Asia, South Asia and West Asia.

Another region that was influenced from India and Java was Burma, where one of the most famous of its several states was that of the Kingdom of Ava - the famous "Kingdom of Gold". This fabled land was noted for its portals and window architraves of gold foil and many were also bejewelled (*9.058/9*). It is likely that this land was of special importance for the Tupac expedition.

The Three Windows of Origin of the Incas - The Divine Doors
Among the most famous elements of Inca mythology is the fact that they were said to have emerged through three windows. In fact this element occurs only a few times in all of the major myths that were recorded and given some accreditation. The emergence from the sacred cave, not through windows, was in fact the main motif and occurs in the myths also preserved around Lake Titicaca by the Aymara. Needless to say the version (9) where the cave is elaborated to its golden and jewelled state is from a direct Incan source, and is likely therefore not to have ever been related into the Public domain. In the light of Tupa's voyage to the west his motives for undertaking the voyage have been questioned above and whether these were initiated by information received from the Chimu he had recently defeated. The Chimu are known to have controlled the sea routes before their defeat, and if there was a land of gold to the far west, or whether there may have been other traditions already known, it is possible that this was confirmed by the Chimus after their defeat. It is likely that there may have been family traditions among the Incas, closely guarded and withheld from the Public, that did preserve some reference to their origins apart from attempting to ensure the Public propaganda did link them as the natural heirs and successors to the rulers at Tiahuanaco, particularly if those origins were outside and distant from

Peru. This would be very likely if the preservation of their clan title of Ayar was so important that they retained it up until and beyond the Conquest itself, just as the descendants of the Brahmans and other Aryan castes have done in India for the last 3,000 years.

The sacred windows are likely to have actually been intended as portals or some other symbolic reference but that became garbled in the retelling as windows. Polo de Ondegardo noted from the Incas that there was a single window only. It is notable that in the only other importance myth cycle recorded from the Incas or by an Inca, in this case Pachacuti Salcamayhua, the "windows" he describes and sketches he made indicate that they were in fact symbolic plaques or wall designs and not apertures in the true sense[176]. These were said to have been ordered to be made by Manco Capac and to represent the lineages, first window that was called Tampu-toco, the second - Maras-toco and the third Sutic-toco, and these were references to his uncles and paternal and maternal grandfathers. Between the three "windows" were placed two trees, one between each of the windows, separating each of them, making five elements in all. This suggests that these windows were a reference to apertures linking the present to the ancestors of the past and had become divested from their original intent. These may have been intended to link the "holes in the sky" or "dark clouds" in their calendrical cosmology where deified ancestor heroes descended to imitate clan beginnings. This is a common principle to those mythical beginnings claimed in Australia, Melanesia, Polynesia, Indonesia through to India.

In virtually all temples and Public buildings throughout the world the main entrance doors were considered to have special ritual and ceremonial significance, and it is clear that these windows or portals referred to in this private Inca Origin myth were of a special importance to the Incas. The Incas repeatedly claimed mystical descent from the Sun itself and therefore it is probable that they originally associated divine portals or apertures with Sun myths. It is likely therefore that the gold plated and jewelled window architraves or reveals were in fact a reference derived from real contacts in the past rather than confused with other aspects of ancestral mythology and belief systems.

Divine Doors - The Gateways to and from Heaven

In a hymn to Agni, the fire god, he is imaged as driving through divine gates to descend to the sacrificial altar of the Brahmans in the Vedic texts[177]. During the fire altar rituals further invocations are made to assist the divine doors to open without sticking so that "the gods may come forth"[178]. In another reference to Agni it is stated that the divine doors are many and that they "have sent forth streams of ghee"[179]. Ghee is clarified butter and the primary facilitating offering to the gods, and probably the original model for the Peruvian mollo, a treated form of shell powder forming a fetish essential in the shaman's, or medicine man's rituals in Peru up until the present day. The special association between the gods, ancestors and the Vedic Aryans is delineated in the following verse from the ancient Vedic texts after the invocations to assist them had been performed:

"5. May the divine doors which are easily passable, open themselves wide when invoked with adoration. May they, the far-embracing, undecaying ones, open wide, purifying our glorious race which is rich in valiant men."[180]. Such an invocation certainly has its parallels in the epics recorded in the myths and legends of the Incas, but the whole point of the fire rituals, always performed before dawn, was to ensure that the Sun rose àt dawn a right arrogated by the priests and rulers who considered themselves Sons of the Sun[181].

Three Portals - Openings and Triadic Symbolism

The importance of the openings of the portals to heaven was that they were directed toward the Sun and to facilitate it's rising at dawn through the day. The Brahmans were thought the holiest

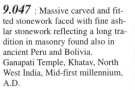

9.047 : Massive carved and fitted stonework faced with fine ashlar stonework reflecting a long tradition in masonry found also in ancient Peru and Bolivia. Ganapati Temple, Khatav, North West India, Mid-first millennium, A.D.

9.048 : Cyclopean stonework characteristic of some masonry at Angkor Wat in Cambodia in South East Asia. Angkor Wat, Cambodia, 11-12th., century, A.D.

9.049 : Remarkable finely fitted cyclopean stonework fort. Inca period, Ollantaytambo, Southern Highland Peru, 15-16th., century, A.D.

9.050 : Cyclopean masonry surviving after partial demolition by the Spanish and used as the foundation of Colonial buildings. Inca Culture, Cuzco, 1350-1500 A.D.

9.051 : Finely carved stonework similar to that of Ancient Peru from Tiahuanaco through to the Incas. This stonework is ashlar rough stone constructed platform facing as found also in South America. Easter Island, South Eastern Polynesia, 8-12th., century, A.D.

of men, and in their original rituals they considered every section of the day and night to be subdivided into structured sections philosophically based, with their own corresponding dedications and deities. Fundamental to these divisions was that of the triad as the Vedic texts note: "… The light in the sun is goodness; the heat is the quality of passion; and the eclipse on the Parvan days must be understood to be of the quality of darkness. So in all shining bodies, there exist three qualities. And they act by turns in the several places in several ways. …. The day should be understood to be threefold, the night is stated to be threefold, and likewise months, half-months, years, seasons, and the conjunctions. Threefold are the gifts given, threefold the sacrifices performed, threefold are the worlds, threefold the gods, threefold the (departments of) knowledge, and threefold the path. …"[182].

The Parwan days are mentioned here and in this case refer to the conjunctions and oppositions of the Moon. Whether it refers to ancestors, gods or other aspects of the Sun it is clear that three is a fundamental number in the rituals of the Vedic Aryan Brahmans and this is likely to have inspired the "windows" or portals to the ancestors and deities as a fundamental principle and inherited by the Ayar Incas. In references also in the Vedic texts the number of horses associated with the deities is three since "what is three-fold belongs to the gods"[183]. The divine horse was Indra's mount, the deity imported with the Aryan migrations from the Caucasus into India, but his mount in India was Airavati[184], the elephant a name also linked to the Aryans (7.087).

Interestingly it was recorded in Vedic rituals and texts that the south-east was the domain of the ancestral fathers[185] and that it was in that direction that access could be obtained to them by invocation and rituals. The former capital of the Andean highlands, Tiahuanaco, the claimed ancestor of the Incas, and from whom they claimed descent, was south-east of the Inca

9.052 : Natural crevice as a shrine in the living rock sacred to the Ancient Peruvians. Inca Dynasty, Machu Picchu, Central Southern Peru, 1350-1500 A.D.

9.053 : Finely carved altars in the caves and tunnels of a rock outcrop. Inca, Qenko, near Cuzco, Southern Highland Peru, 1350-1500 A.D.

9.054 : Sacred rock outcrops particularly with natural phallic shapes were revered in India and South East Asia and often enshrined in a temple as in this illustration. Angkor Wat Period, Ta Muen Thom, Thailand, 11-12th., century, A.D.

9.055 : Selected rock outcrops were considered sacred in Peru and particularly so among the Incas and frequently enshrined as illustrated here. Inca Dynasty, Machu Picchu, Central South Peru, 1350-1500 A.D.

capital of Cuzco suggesting that the latter location was deliberately chosen by Manco Capac in exactly the way the early Vedic Indians were known to do. In claiming to be Ayars they appear to have been well aware of their Aryan descent as Miles Piondexter asserts. This possibility appears to be confirmed by the name of the great town of their ancestors buried on the field of battle named Aya-viri meaning literally in the Aryan tongue "(place of) Aryans heroes". It is likely therefore that the golden rod or staff of Manco Capac was indeed a calendrical reference to the symbolic World Axis and compass bearings to determine the correct bearing to locate Cuzco from Tiahuanaco in the South East. Along with the admonition in addressing the correct direction to approach the "fathers" of the race, there are also stipulations in the text to locate a tomb so that the soul of the interred man may face the right direction for untrammelled access to this "land of their fathers" - the South East[186].

In Vedic texts also the "fathers" as the ancestral spirits or manes are considered to roam about as birds[187], and this appears to refer in Inca myths to the five cosmic eggs in the Pariacaca myth recorded in the last chapter (*5.131*). In what may be a reference to the ceque lines leading to the mountain, and similarly in the city of the ancestors, Cuzco, it is said in the Vedic Aryan texts that the ceremonial rituals performed at the fire altars established the road that lead to the fathers in the heavens[188]. The "fathers" were believed to follow the Sun in their ancestral home[189]. Perhaps more telling than anything else is the fact that one of the Vedic texts states that there were three ancestral fathers. This undoubtedly refers to ancestral progenitors of the race and in the Brahmanic Sraddha ritual these are defined as "father", grandfather and great-grandfather[190] seemingly to relate to the three windows myths of the Incas as defined by Pachacuti Salcamayhua.

Burma - Jewelled Temples with Gold Plated Portals

Burma (now renamed Myanmar) was a land of unusual development in the history of cross-cultural contacts with its powerful neighbour India and those countries to the east and north. The evolution of a recognisably different culture, while being heavily influenced from India, can only be a result of those influences being assimilated and reinterpreted by a people who thought and responded to such stimuli in a different way that reflected their origins. The several states that

9.056 : The great Shweze-Dagon pagoda in Rangoon traditionally covered with gold foil. Rangoon, Burma, 13-15th , century, A.D.

9.057 : The Shwesandaw pagoda showing a stepped pyramid with great ceremonial access staircase along the centre of each side similar to those of Mexico rather than India supporting a traditional pagoda built on the top level. Thaton, Burma, 11-12th., century, A.D.

made up what was called Burma, amalgamated by the British, until a decade ago were later developers in terms of apparent material culture but are clearly recognisable as being more related in their final expression of that material culture in terms of the other South East Asian countries to Tibet and China than to that of India.

One of the problems in determining the evolution of Burmese history and art is that many of the influences imported from India were derived from Bengal and the architecture and arts were modelled and constructed on the widely available biodegradable materials in these largely forest-covered monsoon countries. Being highly perishable in such a hot damp climate little remains of the early periods in Burma's history to be able to construct a clear understanding of its earliest development and chronology. The several peoples, who consider themselves separate races, that make up Burma are largely immigrants from Southern and Central China - the Shans in particular, Tibet, Thailand, Ceylon (Sri Lanka), and India itself. There are many references in the myths and legends of Burma suggesting that there were substantial influences from the Near and Middle East also. Broader

9.058 : Fine architrave covered in gold foil and studded with jewels traditional in the architecture in South East Asia but noted also in Inca myth. Mandalay, Burma, 13-15th., century, A.D.

9.059 : Gold sheet covered architraves, here surrounding the Lily Throne, long traditional in South East Asia and noted also in Inca myth. Mandalay, Burma, 13-15th., century, A.D.

influences appear in the form of the ceremonial centres surviving from the middle of the first millennium A.D. clearly reflecting planning, constructional forms and iconography derived from many near and distant regions.

The earliest known people to settle in Burma were the Mons between 2500 and 1500 B.C. who were to be an important element in the later development of the temple city of Pagan. Of particular interest is that the later Pyu who migrated from Central China were a megalith-building people and who also penetrated into Davaravati, that is modern Thailand after it had received its independence from Fu-nan in 150 A.D., and then these people migrated onward to the island of Sumatra[191]. Together with the Pyu and Shans they provided the dissemination of major elements of Chinese cultures into the very southern coasts settlements of South East Asia and these were then transmitted by mariners and traders into India to the west and Indonesia and the Pacific to the east.

On the Arakan coast, facing East India across the vast expanse of the Bay of Bengal, temples are known to have existed since they are recorded in Western writings by the Romans from the 4th., century A.D.[192]. The Ancient Pyu capital, established by these people who had immigrated through the region of the Himalayan foothills, dates from about the 5th., century A.D.[193]. The ancient capital of Pagan, the celebrated temple city with its myriad temple and shrines in Southern Burma reflects Brahmanic influences in its original name of Arima-Ddanapura[194].

Although there were revivals of early Brahmanic influences from Northern India into Burma from time to time throughout the first millennium A.D. it was Buddhism that influences and took root in the mainstream of Burmese culture and from the first centuries A.D. into the present day was, and is the major religious influence upon the Burmese as a whole. One of the great mysteries of Burmese history is that their next-door neighbour, Dvaravati (Thailand), appears to have developed sooner and at a greater rate through the influence of cultural stimulus from India, although further away, than Burma itself. It is clear that this development in Thailand was closely influenced by the early kingdom of Fu-nan in what is now Cambodia. It is also known that both Sumatra and Java were early developers with direct stimulus from India, but also receiving influences from the Dongson in the Red River valley and delta now in North Vietnam and considered elsewhere[195]. In the ninth century A.D. influences from Sumatra, from the state known as Srijaya in Sumatra, were prominent in Thailand and then reached Burma[196]. In this same period, and commencing from at least about 5-6th., century A.D., Pala influences from North Eastern India, that is Bengal, were prominent in India. In the arts and through dynastic relationships the connection with Pala India reflected through considerable trade and communication between the Ganges and Brahmaputra Delta through Burma and beyond to Sumatra and Java in a counterflow of cultural exchange. There are textual references also confirming that sea travel was undertaken from Orissa, adjacent to Bengal on the East Coast of India, indicating that commerce and travel were common in that period from India to South East and Eastern Asia[197]. Certain aspects of temple design and construction reflect those of India from the earliest time, and these are largely derived from Northern Indian models. However, some periods and aspects of Burmese architecture relate specifically to Kanchi near Madras, in the far south of India at its apogee in the middle to late first millennium A.D.[198]. The overall appearance of the Burmese stupa reflects the traditions related to Tibet and the Himalayan foothill kingdoms such as Sikkim and Bhutan extending in the later Buddhist traditions into Northern Tibet, Sinkiang (Western China) and Mongolia.

For those with a general interest in the cultures of South East Asia this fascination must be arrested for some time by the fact that many of the temple buildings as stupas are of a unique form to the region. Particularly eye-catching is the fact that they were, and some still are covered in gold foil, and many of the portals, statues and other carvings were, and are numerous still studded with jewels or semi-precious stones (*9.058/9*). The religion surrounding the teachings of Buddha originally imposed religious and material austerity and despised ostentation, but by the end of the first millennium B.C. Buddhism had become saturated with conspicuous display, along with the language and iconography of the profane. The Buddhist texts, or sutras, became permeated with the ostentatious display of religious and profane objects incorporating diamonds, gold, precious metals, and stones in their descriptions of the Buddha and the possible higher philosophic based states to be attained, not to mention the religious regalia associated with the worship and rituals surrounding the later developments of that religion.

Buddhism was a proselytising religion, and this was famously emphasised when the great Mauryan emperor Asoka (Ashok) sent his son Mahinda and daughter to Sri Lanka to preach at the request of the local king. Another of Asoka's sons is known to have ministered in Khotan, now Western Tibet[199], so that Buddhism was being exported in missions abroad by at least as early as the 3rd., century, A.D. and probably earlier. Certainly it is known that Buddhism was a

9.060 : A fine Tibetan statue in a similar combative stance of a warrior guardian deity traditionally typical of Mahakala and that found in Ecuador. Tibet, Mid-2nd;, millennium, A.D.

9.061 : A fine traditional brass figurine in a stance typical of Mahakala and wearing a long sacred thread identical to that found in Ecuador. Tibet, Mid-2nd., millennium, A.D.

063 : A mendicant Buddhist monk with a human femur bone trumpet similar to those found in tantric India and Central and South America. Tibet, Early 20th., century, A.D.

མཚོ་རྒྱལ   ཐུགས་རྗེ་ར།

9.062 : A traditional wrathful Buddhist guardian deity in a pose typical of many figurines found throughout the Himalayas and in Ecuador. Tibet, Late 19th., century, A.D.

9.064 : A finely constructed clay figure identical in stance to those traditional in Tibet and the Himalayan regions. This figurine also wears a yajno-pavita, or sacred pearl thread almost exclusive to the Buddhist Hindu and Jain cultures in India and evidence of ancient contact between Asia and South America. Jama-Coaque culture, Ecuador, 100-600 A.D.

major force in Srijaya, or Sumatra, known as Suvarna-dvipa, in the Orissan texts[200] in the early centuries A.D. On the mainland west of the mouth of the Mekong Delta a "city of gold", Oc Eo, must have been of great influence from the 2nd., to the 8th., centuries in the first millennium A.D.201, reflecting Brahmanic influences and probably also Buddhist, since the Brahmi script has been found here[202]. Indian writing is found at this site until the 5th., century suggesting that there were influences from India possibly initiating the building of this trade centre from perhaps the Buddhist period and lasting into the succeeding Hindu Gupta Dynasty in Northern India. It is proposed that the name usually identified with Sumatra, Suvarna-dipa, actually referred to Oc Eo or at least jointly with this golden city[203]. Coins and medallions from Rome and jewellery either from, or inspired by Mediterranean people, along with Chinese mirrors from the same period have been recovered dating to the first and second centuries A.D. Most of the raw materials for the wide range of luxury trades and crafts found at this city came from long distances since most were not available locally and confirms that long distance sea travel by that time was frequent and over very long distances.

It is now known that the island of Bahrein, considered by some to be the fabled Dilmun in Sumerian myths, had trade relations with India and that at least some of those goods reached the coast of Burma by the middle of the first millennium B.C. or earlier[204]. Other indicators suggest that tin, required in the making of bronzes in the Indus civilisation more than a millennium earlier in the third millennium B.C. came from Tavoy in Burma[205]. This suggests that the architecture at this time in Burma was mostly constructed from perishables such as timber and perhaps more temporary accounting for the lack of surviving monuments from before the 6-7th., century A.D.

The great majority of the great stupa constructions in Burma were erected from the 8th., century A.D. and have from that time reflected the traditions of the South and South East Asian people. Apparent in the associated iconography is the revisionism of later Buddhism, relating religion with the finest attributes of known material objects applied to the most valued icons known in human experience. Gold, therefore, became a symbol of kingship and earthly power, diamonds to the eternal and unyielding precepts of truth and light of the Buddha's teaching as set out in the sutras or teachings current at the time. All these aspects are recognisable adaptions of the earlier doctrines inherited from Brahmanism and preserved in the ancient Aryan fire religions of Iran. In the extension of these precepts, the associated iconography and temples forms and construction throughout South East Asia many become pilgrimage sites that resulted in the inevitable counterflow of devotees and students, but also of artisans, craftsmen and religious teachers would return to or visit also the motherland over long periods after the first contacts abroad. The Chinese records in particular note that the often long, arduous sea journeys were not infrequently suffered by these people throughout the first millennium, A.D.

The counter-flow of pilgrims brought local influences and interpretations from Java, Sumatra and from China to India and such voyages had been long established before the major influences of India in Burma by the 5th., century A.D.[206]. The surviving evidence indicates that influences from Sumatra are reflected in Burma before the 10th., century A.D. From the Ancient Middle East through to the present day there were sea routes long established between these vastly distant regions frequented by mariners and whose expertise and skill were utilised by missionaries and venturers from India and West Asia. It is clear therefore that, long before the known settlements in Burma, the Melanesian and Polynesian Islands of Oceania were being intruded upon by these same mariners and traders. These islands still reflect the early energies and initiatives of these early peoples since they have long been populated from before the Lapita at about 1500 B.C. and that the shores of North, Central and South America were only a small step in comparison beyond these myriad stepping-stones across the vast ocean of the Pacific.

In the scheme of history the Incas were very late indeed, and Tupa's voyage across the Pacific would have been routine for the Asians mariners who are likely to have made up at least a part of his crew on the return journey to their homelands. Having reached Java probably four or five months, perhaps less, after the commencement of his voyage westward, it is unlikely that he would have decided to return immediately. This would be especially unlikely when he would have been informed of greater, golden glories to be found further westward - especially as such reports were indicated to have been the reason he undertook the voyage in the first place.

In journeying further west, actually northwest, he would have arrived at Angkor Wat where the stonework of the temples exhibits close parallels to that of Tiahuanaco. Here is the finely carved stone, also the polygonal "cyclopean" stonework identical to that of the later Inca work (9.048). Most importantly, at Angkor, identical metal cramps are found to those only known in South America in the Akapana and Puma Punku at Tiahuanaco (5.064), and dating from about the 400-800 A.D. and therefore in the same time frame as the greatest of the monuments at Angkor Wat. Such metal cramps are known in the development of fine stonework from Ancient Iran and are notable in Iran at Parsagadae (5.061) where cramps of a similar shape to those at Angkor, and at Tiahuanaco are found dating to 6th., century A.D. Later more contemporary examples are found linking the fine stonework of the Ratnagiri temple complex in Orissa in North India (5.062) through to the later periods a little before the British colonisation beginning in the 18th., century.

9.066 : Soul net of the type found also in Western Mexico, the Peruvian Coast, and in South East and South East Asia. Tahiti, Early 20th., century, A.D.

9.067 : A clay Nayarit figurine holding a soul web of the Huichol and Peruvian type identical to those in the Pacific Islands and Asia. The textile designs are identical to those found in Ancient Peru. Ixtlan del Rio, Nayarit, 400 B.C.-400 A.D.

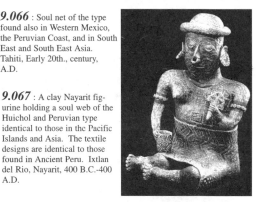

9.065 : A soul net or spirit tablet of the exact type found on the Coast of Peru (*9.073*) in a scene depicting the Greek defeat of the Persians. Greek, Mid-first millennium, B.C.

9.069 : Soul "net" of a type identical to those found in South America, South China, India, Tibet and the Nagas of Assam. Huichol, Western Mexico, 19th., century, A.D.

9.071 : Elaborate soul net typical of those in the Himalayas but probably the model for those in the Americas along with near identical types in Assam and Southern China. Tibet, Late 19th., century, A.D.

9.068 : Soul webs of the type typical of the Nagas of Assam, South China, West Mexico and Coastal Peru. Bali/Lombok, Indonesia, Late 19th., century A.D.

9.070 : Soul net, called locally a titu-ititui, identical to those found in Western Mexico and the Peruvian Coast as well as South China, Tibet and Assam. Torres Straits, Melanesia, Late 19th., century, A.D.

9.072 : Traditional woven soul webs adorning a grave similar to those long known throughout the Himalayan regions and South China but found on the Pacific Coast of the Americas. Angami Nagas, North East India, Early 20th., century, A.D.

One of the features found in some of the surviving temples at Angkor Wat from that period is that some of the natural rocks were outcrops enclosed within their own shrines or alcoves associated with the temples highly reminiscent to those found in Macchu Picchu (*9.052; 9.055*). These appear to have developed from the Hindu shrine known as the jyotir-linga that is an enclosed natural outcrop of rock resembling Siva's linga or phallus. In some cases the projecting phallic shape of the rock has been destroyed by rampaging non-Hindus but in this case a carved one replaces them where necessary. It is likely therefore that the Inti-huatanas of the Incas were in fact a replica of the same idea.

Comparisons have been drawn by several historians between the close similarities in basic planning and structure at Angkor to the Mayan temple site in Central America, but in the next likely stopover for Tupa would have been Pegu and, or Ava in Southern Burma. Here he would have been amazed, as all are, at the remarkable collective structures of the many stupas and not least the brilliantly reflective glow of the sunlight on the gold claddings of the temples. This site includes an infinite number of carvings, statues and plaques for which these once separate countries were, and are still famous. Covering the walls and stupa surfaces with gold therefore is likely to have made a great impression upon any such as Tupa who saw such magnificence and wealth so conspicuously displayed and it is probably, therefore not a coincidence that the walls of the Coricancha, the Temple of the Sun in Cuzco were likewise covered with gold.

9.073 : Woven grave tablets showing various types of soul webs identical to those of West Mexico, the Pacific Islands, and Asia. Compare the example at the left to that in the Greek scene at left also (*9.065*). Ancon, Central Coast Peru, 1st., millennium, A.D.

9.074 : Woven "grave tablets" or soul webs closely similar in type and intention to those found throughout the Pacific Islands, West Mexico and South Asia. Chimu, Peru, 1350-1500 A.D.

The intimate relationship between the Buddhist religion of Tibet and that in Burma was mediated through the great Buddhist establishments in Bengal of Paharpur (8th., century, A.D.) and Mainamati (7-13th., century, A.D.) and others not yet excavated. This is illustrated by the unglazed terracotta jataka plaques (scenes from the life of the Buddha) still surviving around the Shwe-hsan-daw pagoda and the finer examples in the East and West Hpetleik pagodas built in the 8th., century, A.D.[207]. Paharpur itself has been singled out in previous works[208] as a centre exhibiting wall panels depicting the Mayan Cauac or Earth Monster in the exact form known among the Maya at Palenque. This major Buddhist centre was clearly a focal point of distribution of cultural influences as well as providing access to Tibet to the north and from the Himalayan plateau into India, South East Asia and throughout the Pacific across to the Americas.

From the 10th., to the 13th., centuries the great temples now associated with Burma were built and during the reign of Kyanzittha it is recorded in the Burmese chronicles that eight Brahmans arrived at his court offering their services to build something rivalling the temples of India. It is believed that the great temple of Nanda (Ananda) dating to about 1105 A.D. was the result[209]. This was based on the Pala temples of North East India and reflects also the Buddhist constructions at Paharpur built two centuries earlier - considered by more recent historians as a "holdover" in style and construction[210]. This example of perhaps several styles indicates the long period of influence from Bengal and the importance of the region in distribution of long traditional aspects of temple construction and design. Paharpur, however, is of greatest importance as the gateway to Tibet from the Bay of Bengal and from this centre the easiest route to Lhasa. This shortest of available routes into Tibet was known and used for millennia up until the present day, and that route was through the valley of Chumbi. In more recent times the valley became the focus or World attention when the present Dalai Lama of Tibet, fled Chinese occupation through this valley to India in 1950[211].

Tibet and the Route to Kailasa

Virtually every book relating to the British colonial period in India, when referring to missions to Tibet or by explorers venturing into the plateau extending northward from the sentinels of the high Himalayas forming the southern boundary of Tibet, mention Chumbi as providing the most accessible route by land. Today this valley is located in the small state of Sikkim, and this nestles between Nepal to the west and Bhutan to the east, both with their own more difficult routes into Tibet through which trade, migrants and refugees have flowed for centuries and even millennia. It has been proposed in previous works that early Tibet, possibly before the Buddhist conversion in a large part of the plateau in the 8th., century, A.D.212, had connections with the

Pacific islands - but certainly with China and India for long before that time. Earlier, debased forms of Buddhism had been introduced from Northern India about 640 A.D.[213] but the later mission, invited by the king of Tibet included the revered teacher Padmasambhava from the university at Nalanda, instructed the court in Buddhist doctrine in its more conventional form for that time. It has been proposed earlier in this work that there were connections from a very early period between the high Himalayas and Ancient Iran and that the sacred mountain of Parwan was the original name for Mt. Kailas in South West Tibet. This latter name is noted as the abode of Siva in Hindu myths from about the beginning of the first millennium A.D. and must have been known to have existed, and been accessible, long before this to become identified with Siva.

The influence of pre-Buddhist Tibet has long been recognised in the foothills of the Himalayas and into the Bengali and Orissan region of North East India manifesting itself in the Tantric forms of Hinduism and Buddhism. The "wrathful" forms of deities derived from the native Bon Po religion of Tibet permeating Buddhism in that country after missionaries attempted to convert the Tibetans in the mid-first millennium A.D. Buddhism had been established much earlier in Western Tibet in Khotan[214] and Asoka's son was known to have visited there in the third century B.C.[215]. The wrathful forms of the deities assimilated from the Bon Po into Buddhism such as the deity Mahakala are shown wearing a form of magic regalia and apron made from carved human bone and this was adopted into Himalayan Buddhism by the monks and worn into the last century in their rituals. The bones of a Brahmin, the priestly caste of India, were preferred in the manufacture of this item of regalia[216]. This exact form of magic apron is found among the Maya of Central America along with other aspects of imagery and iconography from India and Tibet[217] (*3.005-10*). Skulls found in Western Mexico[218] reflect the Tibetan and Indian Tantric custom of cutting the skull through the eyebrows and ears into two parts . In these Asian traditions the cranium was then used as a ritual cup (kapala) or two of them were used as an "hour-glass" drum known as a damaru[219]. The earliest known examples of this form of cutting of the skull is recorded from Zhengzhou in China[220] dating to about the 2nd., millennium B.C. in South China it is thought that the Na Khi, already noted as possibly being linked to the Marquesas and other Polynesian islands, were a literate people and possessed their own script. They were Buddhists and there are references that they may have had contacts with Asoka's court in the 3rd., century B.C. in India[221]. Their iconography has also been connected to the Maya[222] and their origins appear to have also been in Tibet. However, there is a direct ancient route from the Middle East through Khotan, to Lhasa and then eastwards to the headwaters of the Red River and its delta in the China Sea and thence into the Pacific Ocean proper. The myths and ancient terms used by the Na Khi may indicate that they may have been originally migrants from Ancient Iran who used this route finally settling at the headwaters of a region that not only gives rise to the Red River but also the Yangtse (China), Mekong (Laos, Cambodia and Vietnam) and Irrawaddy (Burma) Rivers.

In Tibet the term for monk, llama, means "the Superior or Exalted One". Of particular interest in this work is that it is the literal translation into Tibetan of Arya or Aryan and this term itself derives from the Early Aryan or possibly Sumerian term Ar - "exalted" or "noble"[223], is the same as it is in the early Vedic texts. The Tibetans adapted the term in the religious sense rather than the racial sense used by the Vedic Aryans in India. It must be remembered that the focus of what was the new Tibetan religion in the 8th., century was the Buddha, named Gautama, who was the former Aryan prince of the Sakya (Scythian) tribe[224]. It is interesting to note that the term for "Lord" in India was Nath and from this derived the term Nat in the Hindu dramas or plays[225] and the probable origin of the term for nature spirits as an indigenised term in Burma. In India the meaning of the term degenerated into nat for a dancer" and eventually translated in English as nautch for a temple-dancer or prostitute[226]. The initial dispersion of terms such as these

9.075 : The Indonesian islands are populated by mariner peoples and many traditionally preserved the Phrygian cap typical of mariners in Eurasia. The young man on the right exhibits the constricted waist also found widely into recent times in the islands through to Melanesia undoubtedly traditionally to attempt to offset the pangs of hunger on long distance sea voyages. Indonesia, Late 19th., century, A.D.

9.078 : Phrygian cap depicted on this fine ceramic head from Southern Colombia. Tumaco-La Tolita culture, Southern Colombia, 400 B.C.-500 A.D.

9.077 : A headdress derived from the Phrygian cap typical of Tibet and of long distance traders and mariners. South India, Early 20th., century, A.D.

9.076 : Phrygian cap with ear flaps worn by the standing monks characteristic of those worn in South India and also traditionally in Ancient Peru into the present day. The seated magician wears traditional cross braces found in Ancient Middle East through to South America. Tibet, Early 20th., century, A.D.

9.081 : Phrygian caps were traditionally worn by Sinhalese, a mariner race as an island people, shown here massacring the Dutch colonial commander. Baldaeus Drawing, Sri Lanka, 17th, century, A.D.

9.079 : Typical depiction of the Central Asian Phrygian cap associated with long distance traders and mariners. Himalayan, 18th., century, A.D.

9.080 : Headdress in the form of a Phrygian cap fitted over the head. Note also the "serpent" forms emerging from both side of the mouth characteristic also in Ancient South America and also probably derived from the serpent myths of India (*12.090*). Tuxla Gutierrez, Mexico, Late Classic.

9.082 : Typical depiction of the Phrygian cap long known in Ancient Iran and India. Gandhara, Jammu, 1-200 A.D.

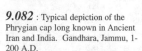

9.083 : Peruvian caps undoubtedly derived from Pacific mariners from Asia showing also the earflaps consistent with those of Tibet. Cuzco, Southern Peru, early 20th., century, A.D.

appears to derive from Asoka, who first appears to have instituted these didactic plays about the life of Buddha after his conversion and who is known to have sent missions to Nepal, Ceylon, Burma, Kashmir, Afghanistan, Bactria, Persia, Mesopotamia and Syrio-Palestine[227].

The swastika as fly-flot relates to the Sun in its orbit through its "four-quarters" and is often drawn in ancient iconography as an equal-armed cross with its angular plumes extending from the extremities of the cross forming section of the perimeter of a circle. The ancient term for the Sun has been noted as Pushan or Punshan, which may have been the origin of the Inca term Punchao. The name of the fly-flot, or swastika, the particular emblem of the Buddhist Aryans, was known in Tibet as the Punya. This again seems to have derived from the term for the Sun, Pun, and relate to the Burmese term Pongyi for priest, whereas Ponya means "holy

9.084 : Fine textile depicting warriors wearing Phrygian caps. This is one of a series and many appear naked as here and this is a characteristic of Pacific mariners such as the Polynesians into recent centuries. Note also the "Megalithic S" border so common in Eurasia. Early-Middle Chimu, 900-1150 A.D.

9.085 : Quechua Indians shown wearing the full breadth of traditional headdresses corresponding identically with those of Tibet. Ollantaytambo, Southern Peru, Early 20th., century, A.D.

9.086 : Coya or Inca queen wearing a mantle with a typical Phrygian cap hood more typical of Tibet. Poma de Ayala; Inca Peru, 16th., century, A.D.

9.087 : Phrygian caps shown in a sculptured group representing aspects of Siva in the Himalayas. Panchavaktra Temple, Mandi, Northern India, 14th., century, A.D.

9.088 + 9.089 : Two examples of the Phrygian mariner's cap found among the Maya that clearly relate to those found at Tumaco in Colombia (9.078). Palenque, South Mexico, 8th., century, A.D.

man"[228]. It has been recorded by eminent modern day historians that there are close similarities between the architecture along the coast of South West India, Nepal and the foothills of the Himalayas. It appears that this term, Ponya, also travelled by this same route to those who migrated from the North to the southern coasts since the term for priest among some castes was Pongo[229] and it cannot be a coincidence that this exact term for a shaman priest found in Peru[230]. Bon Po rites and rituals

Mt. Kailas, and its sacred two lakes of Manasarovar and Rakshas Tal, was worshipped by both the Buddhists and the indigenous Bon Po, and is also the sacred mountain of the Hindus where Siva was said to dwell. Myths associated with the mountain state that there were fierce battles by Buddhist and Bon Po magicians in attempts to gain supremacy over the sacred sites and that in succeeding the Buddhist saint Milarepa left his foot imprints on the mountain slopes where his Bon Po opponent was turned-to-stone in defeat[231].

The Bon Po and its religious iconography and myths are still a viable force in Eastern Tibet, and in more isolated regions throughout the Himalayas. In Bhutan the local protective deity was the dam can sGo Bdud chen po and he is depicted as a form of a black giant with fire issuing from his eyes and human fat dripping from his mouth. In his right hand he brandishes a bow and arrow, and in his left a serpent snare[232]. The name for a mountain god or deity in Tibet and regions of influence is Iha and this may have originally derived from an imported term derived from Il or El in the Ancient Near East.

9.090 : Monk wearing a ceremonial crown derived from the Phrygian cap with extended earflaps. Lhasa, Tibet, Early 20th., century, A.D.

9.091 : Dyak warrior with Iranian type helmet similar to the Tibet Phrygian cap with ear flaps and identically found in Burma and clearly related to the headdress in Peru. Dyak, Borneo, Early 20th., century, A.D.

9.092 : Tibetan headdress all of which appear in one form or another in the Pacific Islands. Tibet, Late 19th., century, A.D.

9.093 : Carved circular stone showing a priest or ruler on the right with a characteristic Tibetan hat. Mayan, Guatemala, 600-900 A.D.

9.094 : Traditional hats similar to the metal types found in gold images among the Tairona in Northern Colombia and the Tibetan ceremonial hats. Maudslay Expedition, Guatemala, Late 19th., century, A.D.

9.097 : Bark hat with walrus whiske adornments similar the hats depicted among the Himalay peoples (*9.092*). Tlingit, Alaska, late 19th., century, A.D. Early 20th., century A.D.

9.095 : Ceremonial hat perched on the elevated hairstyle of this Mayan portrait head. This hat type almost certainly derives from that of Tibet where the characteristic types are found singularly and in combinations through the Pacific Rim countries. Maya, Uaxactun, Yucatan, Classic Period, 300-600 A.D.

9.098 : A Mayan figure holding a parasol-type hat of probable Tibetan influence in the same tradition as that shown in *9.093*. Yucatan, South Mexico, Late-Post Classic.

9.099 : A man with a traditional felt hat that appears emulated throughout the Pacific Rim and by the Maya (*9.095*). Go-lok, Tibet, Early 20th., century, A.D.

9.100 : Woven hat close similar to those found in tl Pacific Rim and among th Mayans in Central Americ Lepcha Tribe, Sikkim, Ear 20th., century, A.D.

9.096 : The metal hat or crown worn by Himalayan monks finds an almost exact parallel to the metal hat of the Tairona figurines in North East Colombia (*9.160*). Phodong, Sikkim, Early 20th., century, A.D.

In the North East of Tibet, a region influenced by Mongolian plainsmen, the local deity is called yul lha of Ordos sometimes identified with Jenghiz Khan. He dwells on the red clay mountain surrounded by a sea of "billowing" blood. He is imaged as being of red colour, and three eyes on his face, flaming eyebrows, and teeth bared and clenched. He usually is shown holding a lance in his right hand and a snare in his left. One leg is bent while the other is extended, and his whole figure is surrounded with a halo of fire. Another deity called Dung skyong dkar po is a brilliant white colour and holds a lance with a red pennant in his right hand and holds a snare in his left. He wears hair bound together into a hairstyle wrapped above the brow around a small conch-shell projecting[233].

These wrathful deities in their sculptured forms and associated imagery are virtually

9.101 : Wide-brimmed hat of a type typical and traditional in Tibet and closely similar to those found among the Ancient Peruvian Indians and retained into the twentieth century. Lhasa, Tibet, Early 20th., century, A.D.

9.102 : Bronze tupus or mantle pins. Peruvian and Bolivian type, 700-1500 A.D.

9.103 : A group of Quechua Indians displaying the long traditional hats and headgear identical in range and form to those of Tibet. Ollantaytambo, Peru, Early 20th., century, A.D.

9.104 : Feathered headdress with ear flaps in the tradition of the Phrygian cap. Coastal Peru, c1st., millennium, A.D.

identical to those known on the coast of Ecuador in the period from 9-10th., century A.D. This South American culture is the Jama-Coaque and many aspects appear to derive from India and, or Tibet. The general name given to the demon protectors was Gon-Po, and Mahakala is the most important and best known, and it is probably this wrathful form that was the prototype of the demon or deity preserved in a clay figurine of a warrior with a Brahmanic sacred pearl thread to Ecuador[234] (*9.060/1*; *9.064*). It may be that this term, garbled in India among the Gonds[235], have been the origin of their term Pongo and related to the pongu tree in South India[236].

In the Northern region of Tibet there is evidence of human sacrifice, and of children in particular and the blood of an eight-year child but also from a child who was the result of an incestuous region was considered appropriate for certain rituals in the Khalkha region[237]. Of special interest is that human sacrifice could be traditionally replaced by felt or textile dolls and have been compared to those found so widely in the early culture of Peru (*4.109*). The wrathful forms of deities, or dvarapalas, absorbed into Buddhism from the Bon Po, appear not to have been entirely freed from their demand for propitiation with human sacrifices. In Tibet, human sacrificial flesh was called sha chen, or "great meat" of Tantra rites, and the equivalent of mahamamsa in Sanskrit. The flesh of a child, in similar rites and requirements in the Khalkha region, were known elsewhere and sometimes it is stipulated that human intestines, liver, bowels and the heart were to be included in the prescription for appropriate offerings. In the black, or destructive forms of rites the earlobes, tip of the nose, eyebrows, lips and heart of a man killed in a fight were utilised in the magical rituals. Sometimes the vagina of a prostitute of notorious reputation was prescribed. The human bones, particularly the skull and femurs were utilised for kapalas, or ritual cups and the thighbones for trumpets. In some rituals the ground human bones, teeth, nails, skin among other elements were necessary in the performance of the black magician's art. Interestingly the feathers of birds and animals was used and the excrement of an Indian rhino was also highly prized and requirements of this type are reflective of similar prescriptions in the shamans' magic or altar in Peru[238].

The tribal peoples each have their own view of the journey of the soul after death and the Giljaks, Golds, Orochons and Olches imagined that after death the soul traversed a string stretched from a hut across a river to the other bank, to reach the afterlife. This belief clearly has a common origin with the Cinvat Bridge preserved in Mazdaean myths in Ancient Iran and a similar concept occurs throughout Indonesia, Melanesia through to, and into North and South America. The Buriats of North East Asia believed that the soul travelled across the rainbow to reach their particular heaven[239].

587

Thread-Cross Ceremonies and Soul Nets in the Himalayas

Soul-Nets or crosses are among the most interesting elements of cultural development evident in the transfer by mariners and missions across the Pacific Ocean. In Tibet they are called thread-crosses and appear to have been representative of the four cardinal point of the compass, or the four divisions representing the four quarters of the Earth. In Tibetan tradition the World Tree or Mountain stood on three or four steps. In some cases the World Tree is deflected standing on a mountain and represented the Axis of the World. Similar to many Asian concepts, the Yakuts of North East Siberia believed that the World Tree had no branches but was covered with "whorls" out of which the shamans were said to originate from eggs[240]. This is reflected also in the Na Khi myths, a branch of the No Su in South Western China. There are clear parallels between the divine eggs myths of North and Central Asia and those of the Vedic Brahmans and these in turn appear to be the origins of the Pariacaca myths in Peru. The thread crosses were used by shamans, Buddhist llamas and Bon Po priests in weather-making ceremonies and utilised as such in the rites associated with the divine figure called "old mother Khon ma", where the earth god-dess is implored to close the hole from whence illness was believed to issue in the earth[241]. Among the Nagas of Assam and the Na Khi the soul-net or thread cross was a symbol of the soul of the departed. In some traditions the soul on departure from its body was required to be caught by the presiding deity to be conveyed to the land of souls or land of purgatory depending on the quality of life the soul had led on Earth. In considering the name of the deity Khon ma it is inter-esting to note that Khon or Con is the name given to the male deity in Peru earlier noted and clearly derives from Kon as one of the most ancient Sun related deities in India.

In determining exported influences from Tibet one of the main problems is that it was never fully recognised as being one homogenous cultural region. Tibet, depending on the region being described, had been called Bod-Yul, Both, To-Both, Tuboth, Ti-Both, Tebet, and the east-ern, more independent region retaining a larger proportion of the old Bon Po religion was called Kham and the chiefs these were known as Gyalpos. Tibetans called their country generally, Po, Both, Bod, or Chan-Thang (Northern Plateau). In Sanskrit, viewed from the Indian Subcontinent - Tibet was called Kinnara Khanda, Kim Purusha Khanda; Trivishtapa; Svarga Bhoomi; Svarna Bhoomi, and Tibet. In India also, North Burma was called Shree Kshetra, Siam was called con-fusingly Kamboja Rashtra; Indo-China or Vietnam was known as Malava or Amaravati; Sumatra as Svarna Dvipa[242] but also Hawa. This means that some terms were exported with missions and mariners or other travellers and one region became known by several names and these diverged from their original pronunciation in time. The same can be said for the great mountain chain known as the Himalayas also known in India as Himavat, Himachala, Himadri and Giri Raja[243] so it is understandable that original names for the various notable cities, temples and mountains should be confused, mispronounced and much later miss-spelt.

It was noted by Edward Mariner during his enforced residence in the Tonga Islands in the first decade of 19th., century., 200 years ago, that the widespread custom of teeth evulsion made the language "exceedingly indistinct". Unfortunately this caused the local pronunciation of the names of heroes, deities and other references very problematic for those who wished to imitate or record, apart from the natural difficulty of transferring, an alien language and pronun-ciation. The great variation between the terms and names of Tibet for the identical Buddhist deities in India is just such a case in point and the Sanskrit derived names are usually applied because they are more easily remembered. The same problem must have existed when mariners and traders from India entered Chile, Peru and Ecuador. The sacred mountain of Kailas was revered by all religions in Tibet, from animist, Bon Po, Buddhist and from outside the Bon Po region in Northern India. The Tibetan name for Kailas was Te se or Ti se and reflects the East

9.105 : The winged deity Ahura Mazda, as the Sun in orbit, with winged armorial supporters. Achaemenid Dynasty seal, Iran, 6-4th., century, B.C.

9.106 : A winged Sun god, Ahura Mazda typical of the Babylonian period in Iran. The bow held represents the arch of the sky reflected in the imagery associated with Indra in Vedic India. Babylonia, Iran, Late second millennium, B.C.

9.107 : Large scale carving at the tomb of the Acheamenid king, Artaxes III, depicting the Sun deity Ahura Mazda. Persepolis, 4th., century, B.C.

9.108 : The winged Sun is found in the Ancient Mesopotamian form little changed in India and Ancient Peru and is clearly seen in the alternating decoration band on this stone carved trough. Machu Picchu, 1300-1521, A.D.

9.109 : The winged Sun is found on many symbolic decorative reliefs in Ancient Peru and here on this trough a variation to that shown in 9.108 is depicted. Machu Picchu, Highland Peru, 1300-1521 A.D.

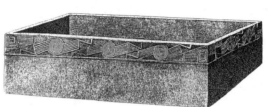

Asia name for supreme deities Ti or Tia and known also in India itself[244].

The mystical land of Tibet was no less exciting to the imagination of ancient peoples, particularly in North India, than it was to the British colonialists and more recent explorers. If the Inca prince Tupa had reached Burma and the kingdoms of Ava, Pegu and Arakan, then in this country, more influenced by Tibet than any other in South East Asia beyond those in the foothills of the Himalayas, then he too would have been magnetically attracted to that distant land high in the clouds so reminiscent to that around Lake Titicaca. It would have been necessary for him to sail to the Brahmaputra Delta forming part of the great confluence of the river outlets of this sacred river and the other even more sacred river, the Ganges at the head of the Bay of Bengal, but providing the nearest sea ports to Tibet itself.

As already noted the most convenient and accessible of the valleys linking Bengal to the heights of Tibet was the Chumbi. Adjacent to the Sikkim territory in which it lay was Bhutan and little has been recorded of this closed Buddhist kingdom in the Himalayan foothills anciently or through into the present day. Its people, architecture and history and culture generally are more intimately connected to Tibet rather than India.

Bhutan - The Capital Punagha and the Origins of Panaga, Panaka and Pakeha

There can be little doubt that the plateau environment and the revered mountains of Bolivia and Tibet appear to be too closely related in terms of architecture and religious focus that developed so closely in parallel not to have been connected anciently. In both distant regions these high plateaus supported similar terms such as Mountain Kailas, also known as Kailasa reflected in the great sacred raised platform called Kalasa-saya near Lake Titicaca in view of sacred mountains. It cannot be a coincidence that there is also a pyramid constructed adjacent representing the sacred mountain and probably derived from another aspect of early Vedic culture related to the Apadana in South East Iran and in Tiahuanaco called the Akapana. The parallels continue where forts in Peru, pucara, have their counterpart in the walled structure known as pucca in Tibet. In the kingdom of Bhutan, adjacent to the valley of Chumbi, the ancient capital was called Punagkha, and this may have been the origin of the term Panaka among the Inca - where in Peru this was the name of the Inca clan leaders. There has been no archaeological excavations of any significance to determine the age of the earlier occupation layers of Punagkha, but the name itself seems to be derived from Pun, perhaps related to a priestly or ritual Sun centre, or circles earlier noted, but possibly also relating to the Sun from the Vedic Pushan, etc. The suffix appears to derive from Naga; e.g. Pun-naga, and it is known that before Buddhism the Himalayan foothills were strongholds of the Nagas or serpent worshippers so noted in the early texts of India.

The name Panaka refers to the Inca clan leaders themselves and suggests that possibly Bhutan may have been the homeland or an intermediate safe haven before immigration by at least some of the Ayar Inca clan to South America. It might also have been a more general name divorced from the capital itself but there is here a closely similar name for heroes or semi-divine deities known in India and throughout the Pacific. This term is Panaga and is a synonym for snake in Amarakosa[245] and is itself an extension of the term for snake or serpent - naga and this aspect will be considered in a following chapter.

Serpents and Sacred Jewels

The importance of the symbolism of jewels dates back into the first millennium B.C. when the Buddhist sutras use the language of exaltation in comparing the Buddha and his works to the finest riches or most desirable commodities of the time such as gold, silver and precious stones. The outward display of wealth adorning the later temples was perceived as a rightful manifestation of Buddhist teaching, or doctrine and its munificence and influence in society. Where precious stones, gold and silver were not available then lavish wall murals or silk banners and wall hangings were commissioned reflecting the riches of the earth and the best of contemporary civilisation for the same didactic purposes. Burma, where such mundane riches were readily exploited from the earth, did not hesitate to use such wealth to enrich the temple to focus the attention of the population on the teachings of Buddha as they perceived them and these gold-covered temples must have made a profound impression on all who saw them both those of the faithful and the profane.

Hindu and Buddhist texts note that the motifs illustrated by jewels overflowed into the general myths adopted into the faith at an early date when the Naga peoples, distained by the Buddha himself, infused the religion with their own serpent-based symbolism. References occur to Nagas, or serpent deities with jewels in their brow or sometimes throat, and these appear in Buddhist literature very early, but importantly, this same symbolism was transferred to the Far East, found in Japan[246], and conveyed to the North Coast of North America[247]. In South America it is probably not surprising to find that this element of iconography is also found at Tiahuanaco. It is recorded that among the mythical attributes of the wildcat deity, the Kowa of Ccoa, there was featured a "carbuncle", or protuberance on his brow and that this was a blood red jewel fixed in his forehead[248]. This reflects exactly the beliefs recorded from Buddhist iconography and myths preserved into the present day in India. Such references also occur in the Amazon region and they appear also to have been diffused from India rather than a development from indigenous element of imagery and myth[249].

The Phrygian Cap from the Ancient Middle East to South America

Virtually unmentioned over the centuries since the Spanish Conquest is an element of imagery that is quite distinctive and representative particularly of mariners in the Mediterranean cultural sphere of influence - the Phrygian cap. This very distinctive form of soft cap is found earliest, (or depicted earliest) in Western Asia, and not always in a marine context. Sometimes it is illustrated as a crown in ancient carvings, particularly in the Hittite Empire, but also in the Near East of West Asia. These socially elevated forms often include earflaps indicating that the design evolved in the cold north of Eurasia and recognisable variations are found in Tibet. The mariner versions may have developed from the same origin and are widely depicted in the coastal nations of the Mediterranean but also in South Asia including India where it was worn traditionally by the mariner castes along the coasts of the Sub-continent and also by the Indonesian island peoples.

In Tibet, the Phrygian cap was adapted as an element of regalia for the various religious orders and their earflaps were also included in the overall design. The ordinary Phrygian cap, however, was made in several modified form suitable for common use as the standard cap in the very severe climate of the high Himalayas as well as for religious headdress of a more elaborate type. For mariners, more usually operating at sea level in much more moderate climates, the earflaps were eventually dispensed with and the cap took its adapted form fitting tight around the brow but with a soft capacious, extended crown. This large soft cap was not accidental or an affectation since mariners in ancient times wore a minimum of clothing partially because of the climate and particularly so around South and South East Asia and into the Pacific where it was largely tropical or equatorial, and in the Mediterranean. Because of the lack of clothing weapons and necessary implements, such as knives and daggers, were kept in a belt or girdle and personal effects were kept in the extended crown of the cap. This form of mariner's cap is found widely depicted in ancient and more recent depictions on sculptures, ceramics, murals and paintings in Ancient Greece and beyond but into more recent centuries worn by the mariners themselves well into the photographic era in Asia (*9.075*).

Early British reports note the prevalence of this cap among the fishing and mariner castes of India. In the 19th., century, Lord Dufferin[250], arriving by boat at Madras, wrote an account of his arrival and noted that the rower for the log catamarans wore a "fool's cap" as it was colloquially known in England, probably because it was associated with Punch in the Punch and Judy puppet shows. Early British researchers noted the similarities in the North Indian myths and those of Phrygia particularly relating to serpent worship. William Crooke was one who noted the similarities in the practises and iconography of the Ophiogeneis or serpent worshipers in Anatolia and those in India. He suggested that there was a close connection between these and the Cheros of the eastern districts of India and the Bais Rajputs in the North Western Provinces[251]. It has already been noted that there has been found more recently archaeological evidence that there were connections between Anatolia, or the Caucasus, and India dating back to the 2nd., millennium, B.C.[252]. Many such references occur in the myths of the pre-Vedic Aryan peoples in India and similar references have been noted by more recent historians writing on India[253].

In Indonesia the mariner's cap was worn by men almost universally and was made out cloth or in less advanced areas from rattan or pandanus leaves[254]. Among the Mayan the so-called Jester God were a crown depicted with a tri-pointed mariner's cap with a bobble shown at the end of each one and depicted (*9.078; 9.088/9*). These Mayan examples clearly resemble closely those from Tumaco in Southern Colombia and indicate a connection between the two regions. These Phrygian type caps, "fool's caps", or mariner's caps are sometimes called "stocking caps" and as such they have been found in Peruvian coastal graves on the heads of bodies which were otherwise naked and wrapped during interment in a barkcloth shroud[255]. This suggests that the caps themselves were of some symbolic importance and probably associates the early culture-bearers in Peru with a mariner paternal line. This would tend to confirm sea links with the coast in a number of the Moche, Chimu, and Inca themselves as well as those preserving similar myths and legends outside the Empire itself. Yet there is nothing new in the perception that this form of cap depicted in Central and South American was not an independent development but connected to those in the Old World, as the American archaeologist A. Hyatt Verrill noted in his book written with his wife Ruth half a century ago recording that, "... Even the tight-fitting woollen caps with extended crown and ear-tabs worn by the Incan men, and still universally worn by their descendants of today, are duplicates of the 'Phrygian caps' worn by the Phoenician sailors in south western Asia from time immemorial"[256].

An early sculpture from Tumaco in Southern Colombia clearly depicts a tasselled form of mariner's cap (*9.078*), as do textiles of a later period from the Chimu period dated to 900-1150 A.D. (*9.084*). More connected to the voyage of Tupa into the Western Pacific is that the Coya, the Inca queen, and their children are depicted by Poma de Ayala as wearing capes extended with integral hoods clearly intended to depict a derivation with the Phrygian cap (*9.086*). This would suggest that there were connections between the Incas and sea mariners, or a people whose elite wore a modified type of Phrygian cap in the style the Tibetans or perhaps Bhutanese. This may otherwise sound far fetched except that the identical form of common Phrygian cap worn in Tibet is found anciently into the present day as the traditional Peruvian cap (*9.082/3*). This is unlikely to be a coincidence since another form of flat disc shaped hat is worn as commonly in both Peru and Tibet (*9.085*; *9.102*) and a further type of metal brimmed helmet or crown associated with the monks in Tibet is identical to those depicted also in the North and Central Andes. Link to this the fact that the poncho is known in Tibet, but more widely found in Burma, and the connections become far more than can be attributed to coincidence (*12.033-9*). The tupu, or copper pin to secure a mantle, also depicted on the Coya's cape, are virtually identical to those known in bronze from Luristan in South East Iran and the addorsed heraldic motifs depicted in the latter's bronze ornaments are virtually identical to those found at Tiahuanaco (*9.103*).

The Inca Prince Tupa - Black People, Horse's Skin and Skull and the Asvins

In returning from the sea voyage into the Pacific Ocean it is stated by the Inca informants that Tupa brought back, besides an abundance of gold, "black people", a brass chair; the pelt of a horse, and a horse's jawbone noted earlier. The reference to black people is an interesting one since people of a darker skin than those found in South or Central America, who are almost never exhibit very dark skin apart from that due to exposure in the sunlight, are rare in the indigenous population. The Polynesian peoples due west are more honey-skinned in colouring and lighter, not unlike the Peruvians themselves, and truly dark skin colouring is found only in Melanesia and Australia in the Western Pacific or in Central and South India among the Dravidians and Aboriginal tribes of India. This would tend to confirm that Tupa and his maritime expedition did in fact reach the Western Pacific islands, and possibly Australia - at least on the return voyage, and probably at reached as far as the great cultural magnets, the two great volcanic islands in Indonesia - Java and Sumatra.

9.110 : Very ancient means of utilising the sacred Brahman bull for grinding grain from a centrally fixed radial arm. North India, Early 20th., century, A.D.

Another aspect relating to Tupa's voyage is also of interest and that is he was said to have been brought back to Peru, on his return, a "brass chair". Copper production has long been known in India and such thrones or chairs are depicted frequently in the carvings and paintings surviving from India, Burma and Java in Indonesia. Brass, manufactured from copper and tin, tended to succeed the use of copper for prestige items, being more similar in appearance to gold, and requiring more processes and greater skill and therefore was more expensive to manufacture anyway. Such copper or brass thrones, solid or veneer clad, are unlikely to have existed among the Maya, or in Mexico, the only other likely location for thrones resembling those of India, Burma and Java.

The last elements, reported to have been brought back to Peru by Tupa, were the pelt and jawbone of a horse. It was reached that Sarmiento de Gamboa, who married an Inca princess, saw the horse's skull, and a skin still in the possession of the Inca who reported Tupa's voyage to him first hand, and he confirmed that they were indeed those of a horse[257]. Other reports of finds of the bones of "giants" confirming the existence of pre-Colombian giants in myths have had doubts cast upon them but the Spanish report in this case has more veracity since Sarmiento de Gamboa has been proven to be one of the most accurate chroniclers, and he had direct access to the highest surviving Inca inner circle denied to most others. Of particular import is the fact also that the Spanish Conquest was achieved on the back of the horse, and in Spain for these Conquistadors as for most people, travelling by horse was an essential of daily life and they would generally have been more intimately knowledgeable about this horse than any other domestic animal. The horse was not only their means of travel but along with the mule was their pack animal as well as in many

11 : Bark-belt
a pattern
rently derived
the calendri-
alf-cycles and
ions character-
of Indian
nomical specu-
ns defined by
earliest
dhist relics.
ulu Tribe, New
nea, Melanesia,
y 20th., centu-
.D.

9.112 : Gold cast figure clearly based on traditions shared by the minimalist string wedges ??? of the Polynesians preserved from Tahiti. This figure shows clearly the wound cord girdle characteristic of parts of Melanesia, New Guinea in particular. Colombia, 800-1500 A.D.

9.115 : Aboriginal ceremonial bark-belt characteristic in many islands in Melanesia. Kakadu Tribe, North Australia, Early 20th., century, A.D.

9.113 : Brahman with traditional wound girdle closely similar to those found among some of the people in the Pacific Islands. Nepal, Early 20th., century, A.D.

9.114 : Girdle constructed of many windings of cord indicating ancestral descent and clan status but probably originating in early incursions from India through Indonesia into Melanesia. West Iran, Early 20th., century, A.D.

9.118 : Carved stone captive figure displaying a girdle almost certainly a bark-cloth type similar to those in Melanesia. Linea Vieja, Costa Rica, 800-1525, A.D.

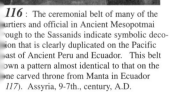

116 : The ceremonial belt of many of the
urtiers and official in Ancient Mesopotmai
ough to the Sassanids indicate symbolic deco-
ion that is clearly duplicated on the Pacific
ast of Ancient Peru and Ecuador. This belt
own a pattern almost identical to that on the
ne carved throne from Manta in Ecuador
117). Assyria, 9-7th., century, A.D.

9.117 : Rear view of carved stone seat with cal-endrical edge design identical to those in Assyria and India. Manta, Ecuador, 700-1000 A.D.

9.119 : Silver dish with the representation of the king seated on a lion. Note the enclosing circlet design with saltire crosses identical to those used in early Buddhist cosmology (*9.122*) and in South America. Choresmian, Iran, 672 A.D.

9.120 : Bronze mirror back with central square design related to calendrical iconography. The squared structure and the four-fold divisions are a development of those of the Buddhist (*9.125*) and closely similar to similar representations found in South America particularly at each corner. Japan, 5-6th., century, A.D.

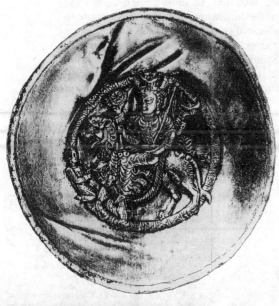

9.121 : Gold plate pectoral with a band around the perimeter composed of squares showing designs found in Mayan sky band iconography and found also in India. The central image is probably representative of the Sun. Calima, Colombia, 700-1000 A.D.

9.122 : A ringstone of the type found in Gandhara, and across North India from Gandhara to Patna. The two outer bands show crossed links probably derived from the contemporary circlets common of contemporary Iranian silverware. North India, 3rd.-2nd., centuries B.C.

9.123 : Buddhist high stone relief depicting an altar with two saltire crosses, normally included on all four sides of the altar pedestal, indicating calendrically related fundamental aspects of Buddhist cosmology. This same motif is found across the Pacific Ocean into Central and South America. Gandhara, Northern Pakistan, 100-200 A.D.

9.124 : Large clay urn with traditional cross design alternating with vertical stripe divisions identical to many surviving from Ancient Central and South America (*9.125*), particularly relating to apparent calendrical designs. Susa, Elam and Anwan, 3rd., millennium, B.C.

9.125 : Ceramic ritual cup with decorative band identical to that long known in the Ancient Middle East and India depicted in *9.124*, probably originally having calendrical significace. Lapaya, Diaguta, N.W. Argentina, 800-1400 A.D.

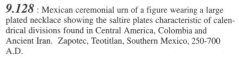

9.128 : Mexican ceremonial urn of a figure wearing a large plated necklace showing the saltire plates characteristic of calendrical divisions found in Central America, Colombia and Ancient Iran. Zapotec, Teotitlan, Southern Mexico, 250-700 A.D.

9.126 : Fine bronze pin with rayed image probably representing the Sun. The sixteen rays are usually considered a fourfold division of each of the cardinal points and are found as such in over two millennia of philosophical speculation and iconography in India. Luristan, South East Iran. c1000 B.C

9.127 : Browband probably of the calendrical type found further south in Ancient Peru. Cerro Jaboncillo, Guangala, Valdivia, Ecuador, 400 B.C. - 500 A.D.

9.129 : Ceremonial bowl with a pattern probably related to cosmological or calendrical traditions. The stepped imagery are also characteristic of Central American iconography. Nazca, South Coast Peru, 200-600 A.D.

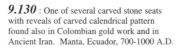

9.131 : A pectoral or tabard that appears to reflect those worn by the Toradja of Celebes and the Nagas of Assam and probably relating to calendrical symbolism. Moche, North Coast Peru, 200-600 A.D.

9.130 : One of several carved stone seats with reveals of carved calendrical pattern found also in Colombian gold work and in Ancient Iran. Manta, Ecuador, 700-1000 A.D.

9.132 : Akimbo goddess that is probably the local version of the Earth goddess of India, Adya-Sakti. She is shown under a stepped Sky Arch made up of nine halved squares that probably relates to the half cycle of the 18 year eclipse cycle of the Moon's nodes. Manteno, Cerro Jaboncillo, Ecuador, 850-1400 A.D.

cases their source of meat as well as providing pelts in common usage. Of all the animals this was the one, and so much more than any other, that they might be relied upon in terms of eyewitness accounts to correctly identify in terms of the reputed preserved skin or pelt and a jawbone.

The horse was an unknown animal in the Americas before the Spaniards and was therefore not obtainable earlier from Central or North America. For any other native animal, such as the deer or llama for which it might have been mistaken, these were common in South America that it is unlikely to have been confused with that of a horse by the Incas or the later Spanish and would have soon been ruled out as being of special significance. Horses were, however, not only a feature in the landscape of India but probably had a special symbolic reason for Tupa to have brought the pelt and a jawbone back with him from a visit there rather than any other exotic animal not found in South America. It was earlier noted that the vehicle of the Sun was the Asvins - the sacred horse deities of the Aryans. As a worshipper, and indeed as an Inca, a claimed representative and son of the Sun itself, this close association between the horse and Solar disk in

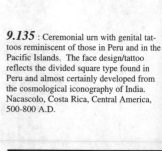

9.133 : Gold mask with radiating halo probably as divisions of the Sun and the calendar. The divisions shown have the vertical divisions evident in calendrical bands in India. Colombia, 700-1500 A.D.

9.135 : Ceremonial urn with genital tattoos reminiscent of those in Peru and in the Pacific Islands. The face design/tattoo reflects the divided square type found in Peru and almost certainly developed from the cosmological iconography of India. Nacascolo, Costa Rica, Central America, 500-800 A.D.

9.134 : A standing priest or ruler with a pectoral of the type found in Inca drawings but also among the Toradja in Celebes. The outer perimeter shows a "portal" of 16 panels with the characteristic squares representing light and dark, and day and night. The tabard or extended pectoral design appears similar to those of the Inca and the Toradja of Celebes as well as the Nagas of Assam (8.051-6). The whole design appears to derive from similar more realistic carvings in Buddhist and Hindu iconography. Cerro Jaboncillo, Manta, Ecuador, 9-14th., century, A.D.

9.136 : Finely finished spouted stirrup vessel with the characteristic divided square design usually called "stepped". This version however shows its intention to link or "teeth" both halves of the square together suggesting the "light" and "dark halves" characteristic of the cosmology of India. Moche, Trujillo, North Central Coast Peru, 200-600 A.D.

9.138 : Chinstrap turban portrait stirrup spout vessel of the characteristic North Central Coast of Peru. The browband reflects the typical divided squares probably of calendrical significance. Moche, North Central Coast Peru, 200-600 A.D.

9.137 : A keros or ritual vessel reflecting designs clsoely similar to those found on the Manta Coast of Ecuador (9.134). Tiahuanaco or Huari influence is reflected in the overall appearance of this vessel. Lapaya, Diaguta, N.W. Argentina, 800-1000 A.D.

9.139 : Peruvian stirrup vessel depicting a seated turbanned male. The turban has the characteristic dual division motifs almost certainly indicative of the dual half-monthly divisions so frequently noted in India and derived from early Buddhist iconography. Moche, North Central Peru, 200-600, A.D.

9.140 : Remarkable model of an early Buddhist stupa. The first, highest register under the carved lotus petals reveals the saltired square panels indicating almost certainly a formalised pattern representing the ecliptic. The step pattern evident throughout Coastal Peru is almost certainly derived from this early form in North India. Loriyan Tangai, Swat Valley, Gandhara, 1st.,-2nd., century, A.D.

9.141: Two exampless from a cache of dishes displaying identical designs illustrating constellations in Ancient Mexico and China. San Jose de Moro, Cajamarca, North Highland Peru, 1st., millennium, A.D.

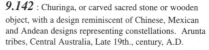

9.142 : Churinga, or carved sacred stone or wooden object, with a design reminiscent of Chinese, Mexican and Andean designs representing constellations. Arunta tribes, Central Australia, Late 19th., century, A.D.

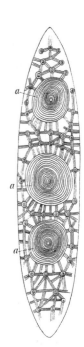

9.143 : An astrological diagram constructed as if held by a tortoise in the rectangular, or repeated squares, representing each zodiacal "house" that was adopted from Mesopotamia into Ancient India surviving into the present day. This is also probably the basis of the calendrical square patterns found widely in Ancient South America. The structure is based on cosmological data that is clearly emulated in the early dynsties of Japan (*9.120*). Tibet, Pre-20th., century, A.D.

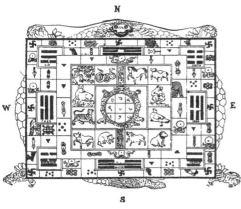

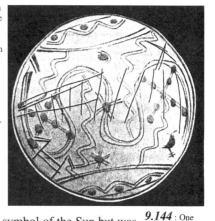

9.144 : One example of a cache of dishes illustrating more similar designsreflecting constellations typical in Ancient Mexico and China. San Jose de Moro, Cajamarca, North Highland Peru, 1st., millennium, A.D.

India would have been of major interest. Not only was the horse the symbol of the Sun but was the specific symbol of Aryan nobility so vaunted in India while other animals were considered related to the peasantry or common peoples except perhaps the bull, an important distinction in a land ruled by caste regulations and strictures[258].

The Aryan horse deities, the Asvins, the vehicles or mounts of the Sun, were considered the Adhvaryus, or priests, of the gods[259]. The embryo of the highest castes of Brahmans in India was believed to be created by the two Asvins with their golden kindling sticks and placed by them in the mother's womb[260]. In a text, as a comparison, the priest intonates the following: "'As the earth is pregnant with Agni (fire god), as the heaven is with Indra (storm or lightning god) pregnant, as Vayu (wind deity) dwells in the womb of the regions (of the earth), thus I place an embryo into they womb'"[261]. The connection between birth and lightning, and the wind and the soul, are evident here as is the "spark" from the fire associated with the internal fire of the earth as a reflection of the fire of the Sun. In the Vedic hymns the Sun supported by the two Asvins at

9.148 : Masterly carving of the Buddha seated on a throne in the entrance of the Indrasaila cave w adoring attendants. The throne is banded under the cushion in the characteristic calendrical divisions a saltired square. Note also the half lotus band base found identically in Mexico, among the Maya in Central America and in South America. Gandhara, Loriyan Tangai, Swat Valley, North Pakistan, 100 200 A.D.

9.145 : Incense urn with decoration probably intended to signify calendrical or cosmological references. The divided panels appear to indicate the light and dark halves of the day, the month and the year characteristic in India. The vertical separations are similar to those found in sky bands in India and among the Mexicans and Maya. Siquiros, Linea Vieja, Costa Rica, 800-1512 A.D.

9.146 + 9.147 : Band from a clay votive vessel that clearly relates to the sky bands of Ancient Mexico and the Maya. The panels appear to be abstracted versions of those of the Maya but also similar to those of the sky bands found in Orissa and among the Chalukyans in India. Chircot, Costa Rica, 800-1400 A.D.

9.149 : Maori design possibly based on calen- drical divisions. New Zealand, 19th., century, A.D.

9.150 : A deity wearing several elaborate neck- laces, one a sacred thread, the other much larger one is divided into rectangular sections each with mythical images that almost cer- tainly has calen- drical signifi- cance. Sacred threads are occaisonally found identically in the Americas among the Maya and in the Jama- Coaque culture of Ecuador (9.063). Trailokya-vijaya, Pala Dynasty, Bihar, 8-10th., century, A.D.

dawn is likened to red birds while Agni itself is per- sonified as the "red man"[262]. The winged Sun was a symbol of Ahura Mazda in Ancient Iran (9.105/6) so closely related in texts to the Vedic texts and beliefs and this same symbol are found widely throughout the Americas.

Because the Sun was essential to agriculture and its orbit through the solar year issued in cycles of seasonal weather, the mounts of the Sun, the Asvins were, by extension also associated with the benefits and dangers imposed by the solar orb. Among the Vedic peoples, as well as the Ancient Mexicans and the Inca, the initiating principle inherent in the basic ceremonial structure of the fire rituals was to secure the cyclic structure of favourable weather and condi- tions on Earth. It was perceived by the priests that it was necessary to ensure that the cycle of the Sun was maintained and for this purpose sacrifices were regu- larly undertaken to stabilise its orbit in the sky and guarantee that it would shine daily upon the Earth and thereby mankind may continue to prosper.

In an interesting text relating to the Asvins there are references to these horse deities, as mounts of the

9.151 : Polynesian chiefs and priests preparing the sacred kava, probably from the South American cassava, virtually identical in its ceremonial preparation and consumption to that of chicha in the Andes. Samoa, Central Polynesia, Early 20th., century, A.D.

9.152 : A ritual vessel similar to those found in parts of N. W. India. The prominent testicles of the figure suggests that this is a Soma vessel related to the Sperma cults in New Guinea but ultimately to Ancient India where such rites were associated with the Moon. Tazumal, Chalchuapa, San Salvador, 1st, millennium, A.D.

Sun, being sent to fetch the king to assume his rightful throne. In the Artharva-Veda, Agni is invoked to seek over the "far-reaching hemispheres of the world" to seek out the wandering "king" and the red steeds are prepared to undertake the mission. Verse four in Chapter 3 notes " An eagle shall bring hither from a distance him that is fit or be called, (yet) wanders exiled in a strange land! The Asvins shall prepare for thee a path, easy to travel. Do ye, his kinfolk, gather close about him!" References are also made to crossing the sea, and in the following chapter the king is then called to the throne. There is, of course no written record that Tupa reached India let alone read or heard any of the verses of the Vedas but if he had then the text seems appropriate particularly since it refers to the Sun deity, with whom he would have identified and believed to be his ancestor, and the Asvins, as the horse deities, whose pelt and skull he was said to have brought back with him. The text

refers to the king in waiting being sent for and the Spanish recorded that Tupa's father believed that he had perished with his expedition because he had been away so long. Perhaps, as in the text, his father had actually sent representations to Tupa while abroad to remind him of his duty back in Peru and, as Son of the Sun, the heir to the ruling Inca. Tupa may had seen something of the dutifulness required of an Inca prince and heir if he had been informed or read this text.

9.153 : Two priests preparing chicha or similar preparations for ceremonials. The obliquely divided squares around the base of the platform on which they stand number twelve indicating that they relate to similar zodiacal iconographic diagrams found in Ancient India. In Japan the mirror back (9.9.120) indicates squares in each corner of the calendrically related central decoration exactly of the Moche design. Moche, North Coast Peru, 200-600 A.D.

In the other reports of the Inca and their dynastic history it is noticeable that there is an uncompromising control imposed on the royal princes and the Inca clan through the absolute authority of the Inca ruler and to oppose this usually meant death. In retrospect it is remarkable therefore, that Tupa is said to have simply decided to initiate a voyage with 20,000 of his men across the Pacific Ocean to the west without the permission or knowledge of his father, the absolute ruler. It would have taken weeks, and probably months to simply prepare for such an undertaking and it is likely, and indeed necessary, that his father would have been informed and in support of the initiative. This was so since all the resources of the Inca empire were entirely at the disposal of the ruling Inca and not of his sons or any other high-born person and only he retained the authority to authorise such an incredibly expensive and risky operation. It is certain therefore that Tupa's father was not only informed but that he knew where the expedition was headed, and if he had doubts as to whether his son and heir and all those who set out with him were in danger or had perished it is likely that he would have sent a mission to determine their fate.

The records state that Tupa was absent for "more than a year", and as has been written so many times by recent historians, the Indian concept of time was, and still is, a very vague one and this could have meant a little more than a year or several, the term actually been given as

9.154 : The water god Enki ascends the sacred platform where he will commune with the Sun god Samas. The platform corresponds to the sacred mountain and the fire god is seen in the pit representing the volcanic fire below. Akkad, Mesopotamia, Late 3rd., millennium, B.C.

9.155 : Fire urn characteristic or those dedicated to the Mexican fire-god Huehueteotl. Note the characteristic eye motifs on the urn rim separated by vertical bands characteristic of Mayan calendrical bands but also found among both Buddhist and Hindu sky ba in India. Aztec, Valley of Mexico, 130-1521 A.D.

9.156 : Iconography depicting eyes were often associated with the fire gods in Mexico and Central America. In this example the shell design probably relates with its eyes to a mariners' star cosmology or navigational reference. Aztec, Central Mexico, 1350-1500 B.C.

9.157 : Eye motifs surround what is a closely similar representation of the torana or sky arch of India. Eyes related to sky deities are characteristic of India. Teotihuacan, Central Mexico, 6-7th., century, A.D.

meaning " a very long time". The knowledge and techniques to determine more accurate calendrical observations and constructs were limited to a small elite band of priests and did not extend into the general populace or even necessarily among the elite populace. An illustration of the vagueness is in Mexico where it is stated that when the number 400 is mentioned in myth or in general conversation among the Indians it does not necessarily mean that actual number but "much more than" that number[263] and references to Tupa's voyage must be considered in this light. The various objects and people reported to have been brought back with him tend to prove the point. As noted earlier the overall 6-7 years of Tupac's campaign in Ecuador cannot be fully accounted for in much more than three or less than four years. This suggests that his voyage across the Pacific took two to three years.

It is likely that the black slaves and the objects brought by Tupa would naturally have been trophies to prove the success of his mission. The horse pelt and skull, however, and the myths attached to them in their Vedic Aryan homeland, were likely to have been an important indicator related to his role as Son of the Sun. These clearly correspond to the Sun personified in Peru as the ruling Inca, and this symbolism extended to include the logic of returning with the Asian status symbol of the copper or brass throne. It was likely to be perceived that the horse relics were an important symbol of continuity related to the claim of inheritance where the Aryan peoples first settled Tiahuanaco through to the Inca. These objects were possibly also to assuage the temper of his father; to mollify him with symbols that reflect his dutiful response to his father's summons to reassume his duties as the heir to the Inca Empire - Tahuatin-suyu.

The Asvin Horse Deities and Agni
The two horse deities, the Asvins, as the mount of the Sun itself, were intimately associated with the Sun in all of his manifestations. As the Sun was a sky object, birds were frequently associ-

ated in the long history of symbolic references as the definitive representatives of Sky beings - the Sun was often depicted in the Ancient and Near and Middle Eastern art as winged. In the oldest Vedic text, the Satapatha Brahmana, Agni, the solar spark, is regaled as "A well-winged bird thou art! - the well-winged bird means vigour; ..."[264]. The texts were written in the time when the lunar calendar was that used in India in the Vedic period, and another text refers to the brick construction of the fire altars dedicated to the fire-god Agni, as reflecting the bird shape of the god himself in his bird-like characteristics. The same text above is recorded in the same section that notes the placement of the bricks in constructing the altar:

"9) One of them he places in the middle, with the front side towards the east: this is the body (trunk); - three in front, fitted to (the position of) the head: that is the head; - three on the right: that is the right wing (side); - three on the left: that is the left wing; - three behind: that is the tail. Thus this his body, furnished with wings and tail, is just like that of Agni (the fire-altar)."[265]. It is undoubtedly significant that throughout the Americas there are bird, often eagles, related to altars and fire rituals and this text appears related to those of the fire religions known to have been celebrated for two to three millennia before the Incas. The special bird fetish of the ruling Inca clan - the India bird, was said to be a falcon and will be of interest in due course.

As the red birds of dawn, the Asvins were closely related to Agni the red man of the dawn and the sacrificial altar. The intimate relation of Agni, as the fire god and the Sun is obvious and early recognised by the Vedic Aryans since they imported this worship in the virtually identical form to that of the early fire religions of Iran. The altar necessary for these rituals was prescribed and referred to in detail in an earlier publication[266] and this related specifically to the shape of the human male form. Among the most suitable of the five recognised sacrifices was anciently a male warrior of the finest type but before or soon after the entry of the Vedic Aryans into India this was discontinued and the lesser sacrifices of animals was extended to cover the need for a human. To ensure the maintenance of the Sun in its orbit the fire altar was built according to the Aryan concept of the cosmos, and the World as seen as energised by the Sun, reflected in the solar orbit of the year and where each element was associated with a specific supporting deity. The Satapatha Brahmana records that the Asvins are associated with the laying of the bricks for this sacred hearth[267]. The verses also indicate that the thirteen months of the lunar calendar were associated in the earliest texts with the hearth and this confirms the origin of these Vedic fire rituals from Ancient Iran.

The sacrifices at the Vedic fire altar, both animal and grain, were usually burnt after the invocations and prayers and resemble closely those described by Bernabe Cobo and others soon after the Spanish Conquest. In a text relating to the birth of Agni as the fire god he is said among other things to be born of the daughter of Manu, named Ila, the great lawgiver of the Vedic Aryans. The Laws of Manu have been noted in the chapter dealing with the caste system, but this reference to Ila is more symbolic. As a deity she was considered to be more related to the spirit of the cattle herds of the Vedic Aryans before they entered India and while still residing on the Iranian plateau in the second millennium B.C. In the oldest text, the Satapatha Brahmana, Ila is said to dwell at the "navel of the earth", and it is there that Agni is born, clearly indicating the sacred fire-hearth where all rituals devoted to him were carried out. The text then states: "Having conceived and quickly given birth to the manly one. He whose summit is red - bright is his splendour - the son of Ila has been born in the (due) way"[268]. This text seems to reflect the fire rituals believed to have been carried out at Tiahuanaco long before the Inca epoch and this Andean ceremonial centre was located only a short distance from the sacred mountain Illa-mani, suggesting that this may well have been another element of the contacts between West and South Asia and the high Andean altiplano. In Vedic cosmic concept the divine cow was believed to represent the Sky and all that was contained in it, a similar concept to that of Ancient Egypt, and the

9.158 : The Sun God, Surya, here missing his head, depicted riding cross-legged on a lotus atop his chariot drawn by the two Asvins, the horse deities representing the Rising and Setting Sun. The imagery is inherited in Hindu tradition from the Aryans and similar mythical beliefs are found among the Andean peoples. Kusan Dynasty, Gandhara, Mathura, N.W. India, 1-2nd., centuries, A.D.

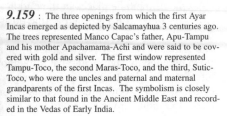

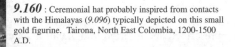

9.159 : The three openings from which the first Ayar Incas emerged as depicted by Salcamayhua 3 centuries ago. The trees represented Manco Capac's father, Apu-Tampu and his mother Apachamama-Achi and were said to be covered with gold and silver. The first window represented Tampu-Toco, the second Maras-Toco, and the third, Sutic-Toco, who were the uncles and paternal and maternal grandparents of the first Incas. The symbolism is closely similar to that found in the Ancient Middle East and recorded in the Vedas of Early India.

9.160 : Ceremonial hat probably inspired from contacts with the Himalayas (*9.096*) typically depicted on this small gold figurine. Tairona, North East Colombia, 1200-1500 A.D.

6.190 : A ceremonial hat reflecting a mask similar to the Tibetan religious hats often made from metal (*9.096*). This headdress type reflects similar traditional hats worn into the 20th., century in Guatemala (*9.094*) and among other ancient representations including the Tairona in Northern Colombia (*9.160*). Tikal, Guatemala, 600-900 A.D.

ancient Sky god in the near East was Il or El earlier noted and it would seems that Ila was a later gender reversal of that deity.

Agni as the red man, earlier noted, and the counterpart of the red bird at dawn, is also associated with the red sky at sunset. He was in these aspects the son of the two mothers, dawn and sunset[269], and in association with references to him being the spirit of lightning seems to closely reflect the mythical references of surviving traditions in the Andean kingdoms[270]. Agni is considered the son of Dyu, the highest god and this deity is in fact none other than Deo of India, or Zeus of Greece. This is the same term found among the Polynesian and some Melanesians of Io[271].

The link between the lightning strikes and resulting fire outbreaks links the fire god Agni at the fire hearth and the Sky world. Agni was sometimes called the golden-haired god as an aspect of the Sun and the serpentine form of lightning links its imagery with that of the earthly snake. A verse from a Vedic text links these iconographic elements appropriately as follows:

"1) The golden-haired in the expanse of the atmosphere, the roaring snake, is hastening (through the air) like the wind; the brightly resplendent watcher of the dawn, he who is like the glorious, ever active and truthful (goddesses)."[272]. The "roaring snake" is the lightning and Agni was the red man of the Dawn whereas the Asvins were the red birds of the Dawn. The terrestrial serpents were divided up between the deities depending on their attributes. The yellowish coloured snakes were considered to be under the aegis of Agni. The "overpowering serpents" belonged to Surya, the Sun, and the white serpents belonged to Vayu, the wind deity[273].

Other Vedic textual references to the fire-god Agni, or [Ag]-ni(na), undoubtedly the origin of the Inca term for fire - nina, and lightning illustrate the similarity to the connections recorded between lightning and the two aspects of the Sun as sky deity and Punchao as the son of the Sun and corresponding to the fire god - in India as Agni. A verse from the Vedic Hymns states, "2) The whirls fly quickly. Fiercely flaming touch (them). O Agni, (send forth) with the ladle they heat, the winged (flames): send forth unfettered thy fire-brands all around."[274]. The text notes the sacrificial ladle, an essential element of the ritual in the rites at the fire altar hearth, but in the language of the Vedas the ladle can also mean the flame of the sacred fire itself[275]. The ladle used for the ghee (clarified butter) is virtually identical to those found among the Moche and also particularly those in the shape of an extended arm with the hand as the ladle reflecting those from Ancient Egypt.

Agni and Asvin - Bridle as Noose
One of the most important aspects of Agni in terms of this work, when related to the Asvins or divine horses, is preserved in the Vedic Hymns and eulogises the Aryan heritage and their primary and probably oldest deity - the fire god himself. A Vedic hymn records:
"7) Three are those highest, true, and lovely births of this god Agni. Being enveloped in the infinite he has come thither, the bright, brilliant, shining Aryan."
"8) He, the messenger, longs for all seats, the Hotri (priest) with the golden chariot, with the lovely tongue, with the red horses, of marvellous appearance, brilliant, always lovely like an assembly abundant in food."
"9) He, the kinsman of sacrifice, has enlightened men. They lead him forward by a great rope. He dwells in his (the mortal's) dwelling, accomplishing (his task). The god has obtained the companionship of the mortal."[276].

This verse notes the drawing of the horses and chariot, the vehicle and mount of Agni identifying with the Sun. The rope is often identified with the orbit of the Sun and the shape of the orbit is that of a noose, a symbolic element of regalia common in the iconography of India. The commentary on these verses states the rope is the "shape of praises", that is a rhythmic looping or spiral associated with the "musical" repetitions, or "metre" of poetry known as gyatri[277]. This undoubtedly corresponds to the many myths related to heroes and deities who are said to have "noosed" the Sun from India through to South America via Polynesia.

The Myths and Traditions of the Agni-kayana
As supreme Sky deity of the Hindus of India, Vishnu, is intimately involved with the Sun cycles within his universal domain and consequently, since the sacred fire was seen as the microcosm of the Sun, he was a reflection of with its orbit through the sky and the yearly cycle it formed. Vishnu was considered to mark out his territory or domain by his "strides", and was said thereby maintained it in its place, and the cycles described by these strides were reflected in the Vatsapra rite preformed at the sacred fire hearth. The whole of the yearly cycle, and that of the Sun through its orbit creating that cycle, as well as the cycle of the Moon's monthly cycle were considered to be formed of two halves characteristic of all Vedic philosophy - the light in the arising half-cycle and the dark in the following descending half-cycle. So in philosophic reflection, light was followed by dark and activity was followed by rest. In performing this rite the Brahman priest consciously "constructs" the universe symbolically at the hearth and thereby believes that he assists the deity to maintain the cosmic structure to ensure stability extends to all aspects. This ritual is directed in intent so that the Sun may follow its course unimpeded and without a problem in its proper place.

The imagery the priest invokes in his ceremonial performance at the fire altar is that of the sacred oxen yoked to a long timber beam, fixed at the fulcrum of a central grinding wheel where the animals plod around in a circular course for many hours to separate the grain from chaff. Periods of activity required in this process during the day are symbolically enacted in the pre-dawn hours followed by those of the night representing a long period of rest. The Vedic text notes:

"12) He proceeds with these two alternatively, even as one would accomplish a long way by (repeatedly) unyolking. Both before and after (the Diksha - priest), he combines both, the Vishnu-strides and the Vatsapra; for the Vishnu -strides are the day, and the Vatsapra the night (when the fire ceremony at the hearth is performed); and Pragapati, both he was about to gener- ate and when he generated this universe, enclosed it on both sides by day and night: in like man- ner the Sacrificer now, both when he is about to generate and when he has generated this uni- verse, encloses it on both sides by day and night"[278].

The circular orbits described by the track of the oxen are the symbolically enclosed describing the universe so generated, and reflects the famous wheel of the zodiac. This has long corresponded to the spokes of the cartwheel in Central Asia and among the Ancient Chinese, and known as the cakra in India. The symbolic loop, circle or "wheel" described by the oxen is reflected by the noose, so common in the attributed "weapons" of many of the deities of India indicating that they are associated with the sky or the ecliptic in the religions of India. Just as a noose formed by a cord has a beginning and end so the universe and the orbits linked to the sym- bology of the oxen tracing a circle around the central grinding stone was considered to have a beginning and end. As the priest commences the generation of the universe at the hearth, the beginning of the cord at one end of the noose, so he must finish it at the hearth as the text notes: "15) .....Let him (the priest) not conclude by performing the Vishnu-strides, for that would be as if after going for a drive he were not to unyoke; but when he concluded by performing the Vatsapra - the Vatsapra being the halting-place - (it is) as if he made a halt and unloosed (the team): let him therefore conclude by performing the Vatsapra"[279].

In time the practical use of the oxen during its life of service to the Aryan peoples were appropriated in all its daily activities to be related in symbolic terms reflecting an applied cos- mology. The first act of the gods on Earth was seen as the first insertion of the plough into the virgin earth to create the first furrows extending in their mythology to these furrows reflecting their migrations across the Iranian Plateau into India. Essentially, however, the Vedic texts appear to link the origins of the myths and rituals of this circular motion at the grinding stone to peram- bulations of the circular track reflecting the perception of the universe and the orbits of the Sun, planets and stars.

The association with the fire rituals at the sacred hearth and the structure of the universe is emphasised where the fire god, as the personalised microcosm of the Sun, is addressed in the following section of the text: "5) Now on any day which he (the priest) may intend to drive, he gets the chariot placed north of the fire (with the pole) to the east; and he puts a kindling stick on it (the fire) ..."[280]. Here the priest is imitating the movements around the fire altar of the Sun where Agni the fire god is at the centre just as the Sun as the centre of the universe and when the Pole Star is toward the East. The priest imitates the actions of commencing his mimicry by using a miniature "toy" oxen and cart in urban districts, actual in country districts, and starts by moving from the fire altar to the east with Agni the fire god placed in a small ritual vessel. The priest therefore describes the orbit of the Sun and in so doing is believed to be able to influence and control the movements, in the microcosm of the fire altar, on which the Sun as the centre of the solar system and the Earth depend. The imagery of the Sun in the cart follows closely similar imagery of the deities in their orbits and particularly of Rahu in China where the cart symbolised the ecliptic along which it was believed to travel[281]. In China also the axle of the wheel, was perceived as the symbolic univer- sal axis around which the zodiac, the wheel and its spokes revolved. This has its counterpart in the Vedic rites as described in the following verse: "15 Now, then, the (symbolic) correspondence, - with the first (formula) he puts on a kindling-stick, with one he lifts him up, with one he starts, with one he addresses the axle, with the fifth he puts on a kindling-stick, that makes five, - of five layers consists the fire-altar, five seasons are a year, and the year is Agni: as great as Agni is, as great as is his measure, so great does this become"[282].

That Agni as the fire god was seen as the microcosm of the Sun is readily illustrated by a paragraph describing the launching of the fire in the ritual performance of the perambulations around the altar by the priest with his real or "toy" oxen and cart to revitalise and energise the Sun recorded as follows: "9) 'Go forth, O Agni, brilliant thou with propitious flames!' - that is, 'Brilliant O Agni, go thou forth with propitious, shining flames'" - 'Beaming with great beams injure not my people with thy body!' - that is, 'With great shining flames do not injure my people by thyself!'"[283].

The term Ag-ni derives from very ancient Iran where this term for the ancient Vedic homeland Ir-an is the same as Ary-an, where the fire god is considered possibly the most ancient of their gods before entering India. The term Ag-ni probably originally was I-ni or Ig-ni relating to the Indo-European word Ig-nite deriving from ignis from the related original ancient root for fire. Ag-ni therefore as Igni is clearly the origin of the term for Inti, the Ayar Inca term for the Sun. A century ago the former US ambassador to Peru, Miles Poindexter, noted the many Aryan words among the Quechua language and also those of other peoples in the Americas, and in his conclusions he may well have been correct.

The Aryan Agni-Kayana, Fire Altar and the Peruvian Inti-Huatana

In a section clearly related to Agni as the molten centre of the earth it was recorded in the texts in the rituals of the Agnikayana the ancient Vedic Aryan fire altar that he was to be found in the sky, the sea and the sky[284]. In preparing the sacred fire altar for rituals the priest seeks out a suitable lump of clay and, from this, the fire-pan to contain the sacred flame itself is made and placed in the east of the altar. The altar itself is perceived in some rituals as an ant-hill representing the Earth itself[285]. The clay-pan is considered to be lodged in the east part of the ant-hill since this is the region where Agni as the fire god first manifests as the rising Sun. As the Sun rises it is considered to throw down the anthill and expose the fire-pan or "lump of clay", so it is said that the Sun, riding on his winged horse, mounts the fire-pan to ensure that the horses' hoof "steps" are imprinted on the "lump of clay", since the horses' hoof was identified with the thunderbolt. The horses' hoof was also considered to be able to dig into the earth and reveal Agni in his dwelling in the centre of the Earth, and this textual reference therefore appears to links the Sun to; the fire on the earth in the fire-pan on the altar; symbolically under the earth; as revealed in volcanic eruptions, and from lava earth fissures. This is illustrated in the text: "10) And again, why he makes it step thereon; - the gods then were afraid, thinking, 'We hope the Rakshas, the fiends, will not slay here this our (Agni)!' They placed that thunderbolt upon him as a protector, to wit, yonder sun; for that horse is indeed yonder sun; and in like manner does this (Sacrificer, or priest) now place upon him that thunderbolt as protector"[286]. The horse then is identified with Agni, the Sun and the Thunderbolt and this appears to be the exact model for these three elements found among the Incas and described by the first Spaniards in Cuzco and described by Bernabe Cobo and others earlier noted. The trophy of the horse; skin and jawbone then becomes significant as one of the main trophies acquired and brought back to Peru by Tupa but it is likely that these were reminiscent of the practices already initiated by the first Ayar Incas in the earliest years of the dynasty and therefore seen as elements specifically related to their descent and religion from the Vedic Aryans of India.

Of special interest in the texts, therefore, is that the term for these rituals was called Agnikayana and that these textual references relate that the fire-god Agni, the Sun, and the Sun's mount as the horse are so completely reflected in the Incan Inti, Punchao, and Illapa. The other texts have been shown to consider the zodiac and the rituals prescribed at the fire-altar as a noose describing the ecliptic or Sun's orbit. These rituals are not separate but are sections of the one rite including very long ceremonies performed for hours up until a little before the time that Agni rose as the Sun at dawn. The clay-pan in the fire altar, the linkage of the horses' hoof as the lightning rod, identifying with the "axle" of the wheel in the rituals, and the noose of the ecliptic indicates that the anthill, as the fire altar, was clearly the omphalus to which the Sun was "tied" and relates directly to the Inti-huatana of the Incas at the centre of the religious beliefs in Peru. It has also been noted that Ag-ni was in fact Ig-ni and undoubtedly the Inti of the Incas. The parallels and symbolic associations that existed in the mind of the Brahmans when celebrating the rites were commented on by the great Victorian scholars. They saw that the linga, or phallus, was an equivalent in many ways to the fire-altar of the Vedic Aryans since the Soma, or male seminal fluid, was intimately linked to both and in one rite the sacred cup was called avivakya and in the other manasa[287]. The stone-carved phallus, or linga, is the ultimate representation of the god Siva (*12.007*) and the term manasa links to Siva since the term is already noted under the mystic, mythical palatial residence of this deity on Mt. Kailasa in the Himalayas of such note in this work. Needless to say the stone-carved phallus or linga is found identical to those of India at San Agustin in Southern Colombia (*12.006*; *12.009*). The Agnikayana in the Vedas, therefore, must be the Ig-ni-kayana[288] and the origin of the term Inti-huatana, the rock phallic pillar found at those sacred places in the Inca Empire - Macchu Picchu, Pisac, Hatun-colla and the Nusta Issapana at Vitcos.

One of the interesting elements included in the text referring to the Agnikayana is that it is noted that Brahma's son Atharvan is considered the divine breath that first gave Agni life and therefore of major importance to the rituals involving the lump-of-clay - the fire-pan[289]. In many of the myths of Aboriginals of India they and Hindus record that Brahma or his equivalent was born from the lotus that floated upon the primal waters when the universe did not exist. In some of these relations it is said that his son churned Agni, the fire god from the lotus and supplied the air essential for the fire to burn. It is unlikely that this deity named Atharvan, here so intimately associated with Agni as the fire, the Sun and the lightning, bears the almost identical name to Arnavan identified with Tonapa, the lightning deity among the Aymara of Lake Titicaca on the high altiplano in Bolivia[290].

It must also be recalled that the Vedic Aryans brought their very ancient culture from the steppes and mountain regions of Iran into North West India, and most aspects of their recorded religions, and deity names derive from there. The deity Agni, the Vedic fire god, corresponds to and originates from the fire deities known much earlier in Iran and the Ancient Near and Middle East, and the texts clearly indicate that he was considered the supreme deity of the Aryans before and after their entry into India.

It has been noted that the Vedic Aryans considered the clan system an essential to the preservation of their ancient race, history and the ancestral deities who accompanied them and guarded on their long trek into the Subcontinent from Iran. This clan system was formalised in the statutes of Manu who prescribed every aspect of the clan life and the regulation of those within the clan in their dealing with those outside of it. This was considered essential where the tribes encountered by them in India were so very different in term of culture (or lack of it in their eyes) and their darker skin colouring.

In a verse in the Vedic Hymns, Agni is eulogised as the deity that the Aryans clans had long adopted as their own god and these clans are called the Ayus[291]. Another verse in the gods praise is given:

"3) May our new, beautiful praise, born from out heart, reach him the honey-tongued (Agni), whom the human priests in our settlement, the Ayus, offering enjoyment have engendered"[292]. In many of the texts it is stated that all gods existed in Agni and therefore he was the first, and greatest among the gods in terms of "gods own people" a text highlights this deity as special to the Aryans themselves:

"2) By the ancient Nivid, by Ayu's wisdom he has procreated these children of men. With his irradiating look (he has procreated) the Sky and the Waters. The gods have held Agni as the giver of wealth." This is followed by the third verse of this particular hymn:

"3) The Aryan clans magnified him as the first performer of sacrifices, the son of strength, the Bharata (the ancient Aryan people), the bestower of mighty rain. The gods have held Agni as the giver of wealth."[293].

The first Aryan clans before entering India were therefore known as Ayus and the first ancestor of mankind was known as Ayu[294]. The Vedic hymns notes their belief that they and their ancestral progenitor were descendants from the gods themselves and therefore higher status than any other and this is reflected in a verse from the Vedic Hymns:

"8) Being kindled after dawns and nights may he shine with his red light like the sun, Agni, being a good sacrificer with the help of offerings of man (or, of Manus), the king of clans, and the welcome guest of Ayu"[295]. In another verse from one of the many mandalas in these hymns appears not only to indicate Agni as their supreme deity but the implications perceived by the translator in his notes indicates that the Aryans identify themselves with the deity itself, much as the Incas did with the Sun in Peru. This is translated as:

"1) How, O Agni, have the resplendent ones worshipped thee, aspiring through the powers of the Ayu, when the gods, obtaining kith and kin of both races (human and divine?), rejoiced in the song of Rita (or Right)?"[296]. Professor Max Muller noted of this verse that "The Ayu seems to be Agni himself...." and that this might also refer to the ancient line of the "... mythical sacerdotal tribe of Ayus, the ancient worshippers of Agni"[297] who are reflected as the Earthly representatives of their deity Agni.

In one verse from the Vedic Hymns Agni is likened to a demon evoking the imagery reflected in many of the face carvings and ceramic paintings found not only in India but in the Pacific Islands and the America: "7) He indeed, the beast, mows of the deserts and habitable lands like a mower, the golden-bearded with brilliant teeth, the Ribhu of undecaying strength"[298]. Here Agni is described when he reflects his attribute of relentlessness but this also records the many images invoked of him as a fair golden-haired and bearded god in many of the texts and this image of him appears to have been conveyed far into the Pacific Ocean islands and beyond.

It is clear from the foregoing, therefore, that the Aryan clans, the Ayus, must have been the Ayllus of the Ayar Incas and is reflected in the fact that there is no more than an inflection in the pronunciation of the name that separates them. Compounded with this is the Inca term Ayar and this is also the same as that in clan usage to reflect Aryan decent in India from those ancient times into the present day. The term Ag-ni in its original form is the same as In-ni or I-g-ni and Ni-na is the name of the fire god in India, and this clearly is the solar deity of the Incas In-ti. The reason the name for fire in Inca Peru, nina, does not follow more closely that of the Vedas, Agni, appears to derive from an abbreviation of the name of the fire-altar itself, Ahavan-niya, the last section of this term being emphasised and it is clearly this vestige that remained when it was transferred to South America. When all is considered it is clear, therefore, that the Inti-huatana, the Peruvian "hitching-place-of-the-Sun" is derived from the Ag-ni-kayana or Ig-ni-kayana of the Vedic Aryans or Ayus, where the attendant fire rituals were undertaken similarly to assist and ensure that the Sun remained in the sky and continued in its course to confer its beneficent glow upon mankind.

Ushas - the Red Dawn and Ucchu the Priests

In Versions 2 and 2B of the Inca origin myths there is reference to one of the brothers, Ayar Uchu ascending the sacred mountain of Huarochiri and there turning to stone. This aspect of the myth suggests that he is associated with the dawn since this mountain reflects the rising Sun seen from Cuzco. Depending on the which version of this myth Ayar Ucho, on the summit of this mountain, turned-to-stone seated on top of a stone pillar (*6.025*), although some commentators have considered this to be confused with his brother Ayar Cachi or Ayar Auca turning to stone sitting on a pillar marking the sacred centre of Cuzco[299]. Other references state that he simply climbed the mountain and turned to stone but also that this place became the most sacred place of the Incas[300]. One of the myths relates that when the Inca brothers climbed the mountain they saw a rainbow and this was retained as their special emblem of the Incas and that Ayar Uchu later turned to stone on the summit[301]. Since this stone became the foundation of the Inca religion it was associated with the priests and special religious rites[302]. In these Inca Origin myths Ayar Ucho was sealed into the cave on this mountain and later emerged as a winged demi-god to assist his treacherous brothers in their first settlement. In a curious reference it is recorded that the Allcabiza, the name of the king of the district that became Cuzco under the Incas, was the name also of the ayllu, or clan, of Ayar Uchu and they were linked with the district called Pauca-marca. Puca-marca was also the name of the palace built by Tupac Inca Yupanqui, who sailed off to the west, and this was situated in Hanan-Cuzco, the higher status moiety district of Cuzco[303]. Linked to this report was the fact that Allcabiza were identified with Ara-iraca ayllu[304]. The term Ara here appears to indicate Ayar, and therefore Arya in India and Iran, while Iraca is clearly the ancient name for Ira, or Iran and the Maori term for the original homeland - Irihia. The term raca probably has the common origin from raya meaning a king or noble as it does in India.

It is clear that the name of Ayar Uchu is relevant in these myths, related to the Sun rising and therefore the dawn since Uchu, or Ucchu, since the mountain on which he remained as a stone was that over which the Sun rose. Miles Poindexter noted the close similarity between many of the Quiche-Maya terms and place names and those of the Quechua in Peru the later he considered descendants of the former. In the Popol Vuh, the sacred book of the Quiche-Maya one of the main "branches " of the "trunk" of the Quiche family is stated to be the Uchabaha[305]. Among the Cuna the term uchu designates a shaman or seer and their images were carved from ancient wood believed to have survived the great flood[306]. In Peruvian cosmology Uchu Pacha meant the Underworld or the Inner World, where Pacha meant space or time[307]. This term is the same as Uku Pacha[308] or Ukhu Pacha[309], where ukhu means "going in", and presumably, if not specifically implying also "going out". In other references, seed is related to the east and the rising Sun and this is also reflected in the texts of Ancient India, no doubt because the Sun was an essential ingredient for germination and growth.

The association with first growth seems to have translated among the Aymara to their name for "chicks", that is chhi-uchhi[310]. Among the early Buddhist in Northern India the name for a child or infant was ucchu-sma[311]. Just as the mother gives birth and she is therefore considered related to the night (the dark of the womb) and the child as it enters the world corresponds to the emerging of the light or Sun into day so among the Ao Nagas of Assam the term Ucha is the Chonghi term for mother. This seems to reflect the Peruvian belief that the term relates to "going out" or Ukhu from the Inner World of the womb to the outer world of the Earth. Interestingly the Naga mother's brother, the mentor and guardian of the male children, was called Akhu[312], the Polynesian term for Ancestral spirit and protector where Apu was a similarly used term in Peru. The deity named as Ucchi-pillaiyar, a South Indian (Tamil) name for the elephant god Ganesa and a translation of its Hindu name Uchchishta-Ganapati, is recorded in an inscription relating that he is the lord of ganas or spirits. Ganapati is said to be the guardian of the village, and accordingly a statue of him was "installed in one of the four corners of the village"[313]. This clearly relates the deity to the cardinal points and where Agni was considered the ancient ruler of the East.

In South India around Madura (Madurai) hill deities were called Uccha-veli and these demons were believed to have survived on human sacrifice in times past[314]. In Peru the hill deities were called Acha-chilas and these probably originated in the hills of India since Acha is clearly a variation on Ucha or Uchu and among the Central Australian Aborigines their corresponding term was Alcheringa. The Pulayas, a section of the pariahs or Paraiyans in India worshipped deceased ancestors called Anchu Tamprakkal[315], and these were believed to be the five Pandavas who escaped after their defeat in the Maharbaharata, the great civil war among the Aryan tribes after they entered India in the first millennium B.C.

Among the Malayans of Southern India a ceremony named the uccha-veli appears to have been an ancient ritual involving "devil dancers" but where the theme of the rite was one of human sacrifice[316]. In an ancient inscription dating back to the ninth century A.D. the temple priest is called Uvac-chan[317] and this appears to relate to the rites associated in all Hindu temples, in essence with the cardinal points and the inner life of the faithful, and this appears to relate to an ancient title associated with Achu or Uchu and probably therefore related to the identical Peruvian titles.

The Dawn - From Agni as Arusha and Aruna to Ushas

Arusha was Agni as the bright red of the morning Sun, and it has been shown that this term actually is related to the Greek, Eros[318] and the name itself translates as "the Red". In Professor Max Muller's commentary he notes its relationship with Ushas, the Dawn: "The night retires from her sister, the Dawn; the Dark one yields the path to the Red one, i.e. the red morning" and further notes that here "the name Arusha share the half-mythological character as Ushas." The importance of the Sun and the morning in Aryan myth is reflected in a line from a hymn of praise: "O mortal, i.e. O Sun (dying daily), thou hast been born with the dawn."[319]. This refers to the dawn as an independent entity, as Ushas, rather than the Red light of the Sun as it rises over the horizon, and the Incas appeared to have revered the breaking of the dawn with the same reverence as the Vedic Aryans. The rituals commenced to the Sun by the hotri or priest must start after midnight but must conclude before daylight appears. His recitation and oblations are directed to the "early-coming" deities, and these are Agni, the fire-god as the essence of the Sun, Ushas, the dawn, and the two Asvins, the mounts of the Sun who are the precursors of the Sun before it is first seen above the horizon[320].

It is clear therefore that the Sun rising in the east represented by Ayar Uchu in Inca myths is in fact the same as the name of the dawn in ancient Vedic and Hindu myth in India. Even the name, Uchu, is virtually identical no doubt indicating its transference in Peru from India or ancient Iran. The more localised forms of the term Ushas in India indicate that they also derive from the same name and the associated religious functions are modified versions of temple worship or identified with hill deities as they are in Peru.

Agni-Eyes in Myth and Ritual

One of the more interesting aspects of iconography associated with Agni are the son called "eyes", no doubt associated with him because he is considered particularly potent in the night where he acts "watcher" as the guarantor of continuance as the essence of the Sun in the dark hours. These eyes are the personification of the stars and when referring to them in the text he is called the "thousand-eyed" and thought particularly effective in this aspect as defender against a myriad "demons"[321]. In this thousand-eyed form also Agni was believed to dwell wherever his tribe of Aryas existed and to defend them against those most feared demons of the Vedas, the "Rakshas "[322].

In another text relating to fertility where Agni is paralleled with the vigour of a bull he is termed "one-hundred eyed"[323]. In one of the Vedic Hymns, Agni, where he is associated with the sky, and the redness of the Dawn and Sunset are considered his mothers, he is described as four-eyed. This reference no doubt associates him with the cardinal points and more generally that he has the capability of seeing all around himself and the earthly world[324]. It is therefore particularly significant that the crouching, figured altars with the large fire-pan surmounted the image of the fire-god has in some cases a frieze around its rim, or aura depicting eyes in Mexico (*9.155*).

Another aspects of Agni is that he is depicted in some sculptures as twins, sometimes co-joined (*3.034*). The close relationship of Agni as the Sun with the two horses, the Asvins, appears to have some probable influence upon the texts relating to Agni and being depicted as a twin. There may also be another explanation and that is, since he is considered the son of both the Dawn and the Sunset, that the twins reflect the dual nature of the Sun rising, as masculine, and the Sun setting into the night which is feminine. This may have been the underlying origin of a text stating that:

"8) He who is born is one twin; he who will be born is the other twin - the lover of maidens, the husband of wives"[325]. It is significant that the image of co-joined, or Siamese twins, are found not only in traditional images of Agni in India but also in Polynesia (*3.035*), and on the West Coast of Mexico (*3.032*) and Peru (*3.036*).

The Inca Tupa - a Summary

The jewelled windows, featured in the myths of the Incas relating to the three windows (probably portals), would suggest that Burma, possibly Thailand or Java, was the land from which such influences were derived. Here also are found, from ancient times into the present day, ponchos and patterns resembling so closely those of the Andes and these are also found in Tibet along with the several forms of headdress so noted in Peru. It is the mariner's enticing descriptions of these distant lands to the west that were related in Ecuador that attracted Tupac attention and determined his undertaking to visit these distant, probably ancestral lands.

CHAPTER 10

The TUKANO DESANA; the POLYNESIANS
and MARINERS from ASIA to SOUTH AMERICA

The Tukano and the Amazonian Heritage from India

The Amazonian and forest peoples are much lesser-known peoples of South America than those associated with the great wealth and glamour of the Pacific coast and Andean high cultures. Among these forest people are the Tukano and among them are one of the Maku tribe, a sub-division of the Tukano, whose constituent tribe is that of the Desana[1]. In an earlier section of this work is noted that the Desana called themselves Wira- or Vira-pora - the "Sons of the Wind". This has been shown to be directly derived from the Bhuiya and related tribes near or on the north-east coast of the Bay of Bengal near the Ganges and Brahmaputra Deltas. The wind deity of these Bhuiyas and related tribes is named Pawan and the Bhuiyas entitled themselves Pawabans - also "Sons of the Wind". Pawaban is clearly the same as the wind deities related to the four cardinal points among the Maya, the Pauahtuns, and is derived from the Vedic deity originally from Iran, Pawan.

One of the most interesting validations that many references in the myths and legends of the Desana actually derived from India via Polynesia is that not only do the myths actually state that they came from the West, the most logical and appropriate direction for mariners to reach South America directly from South East Asia, but that the interface between the indigenised Indians and the ancestral males were women. The first male heroes who arrived in the "snake-canoe", the Pamuri-Gahsiru, are obscure in the surviving myths and legends and there are no great outstanding heroes as there are among the Incas[2]. From this canoe came the Sun and Moon, both male and the ancestral men aboard were said to wear copper cylinder tubes in their ears[3] and to have brought with them the sacred drum[4].

The myths relating to the Desana ancestral men suggest that they settled with women from the indigenous tribes, the Maku, and formed separate clans. Clearly all children would have been half Maku and if, as so often occurred and noted in the myths of sea travellers, they did not all remain tied to village life it is likely that their descendants in time would have resembled the Indians themselves as each generation took their brides from the full-blooded Indian Makus. The imagery of the Desana is dominated by the great serpent that was the giant anaconda of the Amazon region. The original, related mythical serpent mother ("mother-of-all-serpents") dominated the mythology of the Desana and she is said to have devoured the first son of the Desana[5]. It is recorded of this subdivision of the Tukano Indians that, "... There is no male personification in Desana mythology that represents a model or example"[6]. This suggests that the descendants from first male intruders from the serpent canoe were absorbed back into the tribe in a few generations and that there appeared to been no other intruders from the same racial origin for many generations that reinforced the male descent in the tribe, or sub-tribe if the original descendants had remained separate.

The belief that monsters, usually from the river, were liable to carry off women was a firm belief among the Desana[7] and suggests that these "monsters" were in fact raiders in canoes seeking women for wives, or temporary comfort, or perhaps as objects for barter or trade. This was a characteristic in the Indonesian, Melanesian and Polynesian islands and is likely also to have been a custom transferred by them to the rain forests of the Amazon Basin.

The Mythical Snake Canoe - the Pamuri-Gahsiru

The Desana retain no specific myth recording the contact that the first Desana or Tukano had with the revered mythical Snake Canoe. Considering its importance in the beginnings of the tribe this is surprising but may indicate that the contact was in fact many centuries ago and, without the aid of writing, the details and impact of the entrance of this mythical boat into their lives has been lost. The memory of the mythical canoe is preserved to a certain degree, however, as an element in other myths and from this some idea of its power in initiating the beginnings of this tribe can be gleaned. In certain elements of the myths the name of the canoe, Pamuri-Gahsiru, is also the name of a mythical person believed to have guided it, and the verb pamuri, means to ferment in the manner of yeast[8]. The respected Colombian anthropologist Gerado Reichel-Dolmatoff considers this reference to ferment material was meant to identify in the Desana myths with the male fluid, and that the hero himself was in fact a reference to the male phallus and the Creator as the new Sun. In this context, where the guiding Canoe-man was the phallus of the Sun, the snake canoe was considered the female element and related to other female elements such as the great serpent known as the "mother-of-all-snakes".

Of interest to the theme of this book is the fact that this canoe was thought to be connected by an umbilicus to the mythical land of Ahpikondia. It was believed even into the present day by the Desana that all human beings were connected in a similar way by an umbilicus to the same mythical land. This umbilicus was believed to extend back from the snake canoe along the rivers systems to the headwaters of the river itself where the mythical birthplace for Pamuri-Gahsiru was to be found. In a myth relating to the snake canoe it is said to have collided with a "perforated" rock and the men left the canoe through a hole in the front and "gushed forth like white bubbles"[9]. The myth states that the captain of the canoe, Pamuri-Mahse, did not want the people to leave and blocked the opening with his foot but all the canoe-men had already "rushed" through the hole. Since he was unable to contain them he gave them all the "objects" they had brought in the canoe from Aphikondia and they travelled throughout the rivers and streams of the Amazon creating the various tribes. These men who "escaped" from the snake canoe were clearly incursive in the Amazon, as implied in the myth, not only in the fact that they came for the far west but that after this event Pamuri-Mahse himself is stated to have returned to Aphikondia[10].

Associated with the Snake Canoe are the serpents, turtles and fish believed to have come with the canoe along with the "first human beings". The serpents associated with introducing the first fish are not considered to be the boa but another unspecified type[11]. The snake Canoe was therefore seen as part of the creation of the Desana world and one that brought civilisation and expansion of culture to their lives[12]. This has resonance with other tribal myths in the Amazon where fair or red-haired people are associated with creation and the emergence of the first culture-heroes from the river or canoes.

The Desana lived in an Amazonian maloca, or communal house, and the walls were clad with bark painted with yellow clay, charcoal and colours made from vegetable dye. The designs represented the ancestral land of Ahpikondia described from the visions of the shamans in an hallucinogenically induced trance. Above this were representations of the Pamuri-Gahsiru, the snake canoe, and on other sections of the wall the skin of the great serpent or anaconda (makha piru) was hung and decorating it were designs representing the male seminal fluid[13]. It is interesting to note that the term used for the anaconda, makha is the identical name for the Ganges crocodile in its most ancient references, makha, or makara. The maloca was said to be constructed in the image of this serpent and because of this it attracted the protection of the Blood-people, the Diroa-mahse[14].

The sacred drum of the Desana was believed to have been brought in the Snake Canoe and was made from the same wood. The drum was constructed from a log and hollowed out with a straight slit between to circular holes at each end and resembled Western Pacific drums and slit gongs. The Desana drum was hung on ropes outside the maloca entrance and was considered to be a replica of the Snake Canoe and reflected its sexual symbolism. The drumstick was seen as the "penis of the Sun" and the slit in the drum itself the female vagina of the serpent as the Snake Canoe[15].

Ahpikondia - The Land of the Ancestors in the West

The term given to the ancestral land, that all good Desana were said to seek after their earthly life has concluded, was Ahpikondia. This was said to derive from the root ah and ahpi found in sexual symbolism referring to the breast, the womb, and is extended in their meaning where ahpi also means coca and aphikon the maternal milk. The term aphikon-dia is a female element underneath the aphikon-yeba the male element of the conception of the Desana cosmic world and aphikon-ni'i is the enveloping shroud around and imitating these two. Interestingly this cosmic structure is reminiscent of the Polynesian deities Rangi, the male sky and Papa, the female earth considered to be wrapped in an embrace before the evolution of man. There are good reasons for there being similarities since the term for the Desana priest was Kumi, a high office in Desana society, and in Polynesia the first god was called Tumu, and the first ancestor was a derivative called Kane. Tumu must also be related to Tume, Zume, Xume[16] and other divine heroes among the higher cultures of the Chibcha in the highlands of Colombia and may have been related to the Wira-pora or "Sons of the Wind" as the Desana hero. While Tumu is better known as a Polynesian deity, he also a deity known, and is probably the link with the Tumu of the Na Khi located in Yunnan in Southern China of note in several chapters of this work[17].

The Desana believed that the present Sun was not in fact the Sun as the Creator where this latter deity was said to have remained in the far west in Ahpikondia together with the Moon. The present Sun was considered to be only a representative of the main Creator Sun and when he sank in the far west his splendour was as nothing when he faced the great Creator in Ahpikondia where he was believed to exist[18]. The same was believed to obtain for the Moon, as it is now seen, since it also was a substitute for the Moon who remained with the Creator in the far west suggesting that these concepts were recognised as copies of another more prominent culture. Interestingly the Sun and Moon were both considered male, this paralleling beliefs in India, while the concept of an ancestral land located where the earth and sky meet on the far western horizon closely parallels the beliefs of the Polynesians. There are recorded references where the Polynesians described the first Europeans as Papa-langi, or "sky-bursters", because they thought they had emerged from the ancestral lands found at the point where the sky met the horizon. In Polynesian myth Papa is the earth goddess; Langi is the sky god, and Pulotu or Bulotu was the name of their ancestral home in the far west. The Europeans were believed to be their own, much-eulogised fair-skinned ancestors returning to them who managed this by lifting the edge of the sky and, sailing under it, to reach them[19].

The ancestral land of the Tukano Desana ancestors was believed to be situated on the western horizon and was otherwise known as the "Dark Region" and was under the rule of Nyamiri-Mahsa - the "Night People". This was a region that was considered an interface between this world and the lower world where the Earth was said that it was connected to the Milky Way, and where "residues" of illnesses was to be found, although not generally considered in opposition to the earth as a place of evil. On the other side of the Pacific Ocean the Australian Aborigines almost universally believed that the Earth was a flat surface surmounted by a solid sky. A legend among the Yuri-ulu relates that in mythical times, after performing the Wilyaru ceremony, they went on their nomadic way and finally passed beyond the mountains and through a region where there was "hard darkness" into another country and realised that they had passed through at the edge of the sky[20]. There are many aspects of similarity noted over the past two centuries that appear to relate aspects of cosmology of South America with those of Aboriginal Australia, Melanesia and Polynesia and these will be of more interest in due course.

Aphikondia is imaged by the Desana as a great heap, perhaps deriving from the idea of a midden mound, where the "Night People" lived in a giant maloca, or communal house[21]. The souls of the Desana who had lived virtuous lives when on Earth went to the land of the ancestors and when they arrived in Aphikondia were transformed into hummingbirds. The majority of the Desana, however, recognised that they did not fall into that category, and apparently reflection on their future existence caused them "profound anxiety". The lesser souls were destined for the great "uterine" maloca in the underworld beneath the Earth or under the aqueous world and they shared this environment with the spirits of the rivers and forests. From this great "storehouse" of soul-stuff new creatures were fashioned and some into fish where they are said to be the replacement for the fish that are caught by the Desana in the rivers and other creatures. It is believed that the paye[22] or shaman was able to determine whether the individual soul was destined for Ahpikondia or the Underworld[23]. It was also believed that the lower part of the human body was associated with the yellow of the Sun and that Ahpikondia was bathed in this colour of light[24].

The paye or shaman after death was buried in the centre of the maloca and the communal house then abandoned. His soul, if exhibiting an exemplary character in life, was believed to go to Ahpikondia. If the shaman was of dubious or evil character his soul was believed to flow down the rivers to the east where it entered the hills or rapids and existed in a spectral form accompanying the "Master of Animals" - Vai-Mahse[25]. However, there are many aspects of Desana culture that suggest the land of the "Night People" was a real place and that it was indeed in the far west but much further west than most historians and researchers have considered.

In Assam, among the Sema Nagas anyone who died from lightning strikes, fire, water or wild animals was considered categorised under Apo-dia deaths. This was considered an "accursed" way to die and the body buried behind the house where nobody is likely to go near it[26]. Api means woven cloth[27] and many of the cloths woven had special significance in the festival rituals and prohibitions. Among the Dyaks of Borneo, api meant fire and clearly derives from Agni of India[28]. The term khondia almost certainly has other derivations from India and will be of further interest in due course.

Tumu, Kumu and Zume in Tukano Desana and Polynesian Tradition

In the myths of Hawaii the first man or deity was Kumu-Honua and his first son was recorded as Laka while his second son was named Ahi. Fornander recorded the many cultural links between Polynesia and South and West Asia, and notes that Laka killed Ahu[29] in a way that reflected Biblical similar myths in the Ancient Middle East. Similar versions are found among the other Polynesian islands but of interest is that he links these oral traditions to the myth cycles of a Biblical or other Middle Eastern hero, or deity and his 12 sons found so frequently in Near Eastern and Middle Eastern records and who gave rise to 12 tribes[30]. It has also been noted that there are similar myths in South America already noted of the Chimu and these are so similar that they are likely to derive from the same origins. Fornander notes that the earliest versions of this myth of a patriarch with 12 sons are found earlier in Ancient Egypt and even among the Etruscans of Central Italy. From Kumu-Honua's twelve sons the Hawaiians claimed descent from the youngest son named Kini-lau-a-mano, while the Marquesans claimed descent from the two eldest sons, named Atea and Tanu, or Toho, the Eastern Polynesian equivalent of Kumu-Honua[31]. In the Kane legends relating to Kumu-Honua there are associated flood myths bearing close similarities to those of the Ancient Middle East and where Kane or Kumu-Honua survives as the first man[32].

In Tahiti, it is said that Ta'aroa (Tangaroa) made the first man and woman, Tumu-nui, and Papa-raharaha[33]. In the genealogical records of the Polynesians of the Cook Islands (Raratonga, also known as Tumu-te-varo-varo)[34], the oral histories show that Tumu was the most ancient name utilised as a personification for describing the "cause" or "foundation" in the lineages of clan descent[35]. In their oral histories it is said that Te Tumu, as the first man, married Papa and they were the parents of five children who were the gods Rongo, Tane, Tu and

10.001 : Sgaw clan herbal or betel bag. Karen, Southern Burma, Late 19th., century, A.D.

10.002 : Bwe clan herbal or betel bag and below a Sgaw clan herbal or betel bag. Karen, Southern Burma, Late 19th., century, A.D.

10.003 : Herbal or betel bag. Toradja, Celebes, Indonesia, Late 19th., century, A.D.

10.004 : Naga type of herbal or betel bag. Kachin, Assam, North East India, Late 19th., century, A.D.

10.005 + 10.006 : Two men's carrying bags. Mindanao, Philippines, Late 19th., century, A.D.

10.007 : A group of 15 coca bags and pouches known as chuspas clearly related to the betel bags in South and South East Asia. Inca, Peru, 1350-1532 A.D.

Tangaroa[36]. In Easter Island the patterns of exchange among the clans was called tumu possibly after the deity or ancestor considered to have instituted the exchange[37]. In the South East Solomon Islands the term for a clan was Komu or Kumu[38] and this reinforces the breadth of cultural distribution of heroes and deity names through the Pacific islands.

In an earlier publication the case was made for substantial contacts between the No-Su otherwise known as the Na Khi in Southern China and the Pacific Islands through to the Maya of Central America[39]. The term assimilated from the Chinese, for a landowner of rank, was Tumu, and princes were called Nzemos[39], these appearing to relate directly to the terms found among the Chibcha in Colombia - Tumu and Zume. Of note also is that the term for an early Ainu deity in Japan was Kamui to which the personal, or descriptive name was attached[40]. The name of the fire goddess was Kamui Fuchi and known also as Abe Fuchi, and Fuchi is related to the root for fire uhui - "to burn"; and ui or uhui is the root for Ma-ui, the Polynesian fire god[41].

Phallic Symbolism Among the Tukano Desana

Sexual symbolism is at the root of Tukano Desana thought in religious and mythic motifs. This is highly reminiscent of the religious and myth motifs and iconography at the heart of the symbolism of India. It is unlikely to be a coincidence that one of the most importance megalithic sites in South America is located in the Andean highlands not far form the forests of Colombian Amazonia where the Desana live and that this site at San Agustin reflects so closely the megalithic motifs of India. One of the fundamentals admonished through the ancient texts of India relating to caste divisions and status of physical types reflecting their castes was that, for the male, a small penis was a symbol of high status. This is recorded in the texts known as the Kama

10.009 : Nose labrets identical to those found among the Maya. Apa Tanis Nagas, Assam, North East India, Early 20 th., century, A.D.

10.010 : Maya nose labrets of a type identically found in the Western Pacific and Assam. Guatemala, Late-Post Classic.

10.008 : Nose labrets on the top of the nose and a bone through the septum both forms of ornament found also among the Maya. Marind Anim, New Guinea Highlands, Melanesia, Late 19th., - early 20th., century, A.D.

10.011 : Nose labrets similar to those found among the Maya and in Melanesia. Mayoruna tribe, Amazonia, South America, Mid-19th., century, A.D.

10.012 : Characteristic bored septum ready to take the nose bone or ornament. Kiwai tribe, New Guinea, Melanesia, Late 19th., century, A.D.

10.013 : Nose ornaments that seem to imitate the mucus from hallucinogenic inhalation in Ancient Peru. Amnanga, Marind-anim, New Guinea highlands, Melanesia, Early 20th., century, A.D.

Sutra, but were also known from Ancient Greece. Totemism was fundamental in the origins of the Desana beliefs and it was said that the Coati had a very small penis and that those who were considered the Mihpi-pora, or "Children of the Coati", reflected the highest status according that this was believed to confer[42]. Conversely those who were distinguished by a large penis were called Bugu-pora, "Sons of the Anteater", since this animal was said to have a very large phallus, and this was a sign of low status[43] exactly paralleling the Hindu beliefs in Ancient India. It was believed by the Desana that hallucinogenic drugs were stolen in the form of a finger or a phallus suggesting that the whole identification of rituals, megalithic pillars as phalluses, and hallucinogens were in fact probably derived from ancient ritual centres such as San Agustin.

The Desana retain a myth recording the origin of gold and silver relating that a "strange" man named Nyapa Mahse, who was "not from any tribe", appeared with moulds of yellow clay. He taught the Desana to make copper cylinder earrings and their name for him was derived from nyahpa = gold. The stranger collected the small grains of gold, probably washed from the rivers, and taught the Desana to form moulds to make small figurines such as those of butterflies and other small creatures. The description preserved of Nyahpa Mahse was that he was tall and red faced and his eyes were like fire. He was said to have worn long earrings that "shine a lot", but their contact with him ended when the Spaniards arrived although others claim to have seen him since[44].

The reports of a culture-bearer teaching the Desana metal-working and of a clearly different race to themselves suggests that this person was from the Chibcha or other peoples who

10.015.: Nose ring and solar pectoral closely similar to those found in Colombia and Ecuador. Melanesia, Early 20th., century, A.D.

10.014 : Nose ornament with a nose ring behind similar to those known traditionally in India and in Assam. La Tolita, Tumaco, South Colombia, 400 B.C. - 400 A.D.

10.016 : Nose ring identical to those found in Melanesia and India. Bahia, Ecuador, 500 B.C. - 300 A.D.

10.017 : Nose ornaments were common in Ecuadorean cultures as they were in South India and Melanesia. Bahia, Ecuador, 500- B.C. - 300 A.D.

10.018 : Finely crafted gold nose ornament of the type found in Colombia among the Calima, Chibcha and Muisca. Nitendi, Melanesia, Early 20th., century, A.D.

10.019 : Gold nose ornaments typical of Melanesia and South America. Limbu woman, Kirati Tribe, Himalayan Foothills, Early 20th., century, A.D.

10.020 : Late Olmec head with a nose ring of the type long known in India, Assam, and the Coast of South America, and the Western Pacific. Miraflores Culture, Guatemala, Early first millennium, A.D.

occupied the highlands adjacent to the Amazonian Basin stretching into the South East of Colombia. There are many references in the local cultures of the Indians in Colombia and elsewhere suggesting that Polynesian influence at one time must have been substantial throughout Western South America but also that they were in contact with traders from India. Even a cursory glance at the oceanic currents in the Pacific Ocean indicate that there are not one but two major currents delivering onto that coast from all parts of Polynesia. The term for "red" in Colombia and parts of the Amazon region, kuru, was the same as that of the Polynesians. This name was usually associated with the highly prized red feathers for crowns, as well as the feather-capes throughout the Oceanic region and South America.

Virtually all of the contact between Polynesia and South America would have been by male mariners and cultural transfer depended on the strength of representation. In terms of sexual symbolism the Desana term for the male penis, a major element in their symbolism and mythology, was called yeru. Quartz, much revered as the transmitting of divine energies was called abe yeru, or "penis of the Sun". Here Abe is equated with the Sun and appears too similar to the term found in the Ancient Near and Middle East where Abe or Abba was God, identified with the Sun, and also to be coincidental. There are many aspects of Polynesian terms and

10.021 : Nose ornament identical to those depicted on Spiro mound shells in Ohio, U.S.A. shown here incised on obsidian. The notches and dots around the perimeter number twelve suggesting that this has calendrical references. Tepeau, Tikal, Guatemala, 400-600 A.D.

10.023 : Nose rings and ornamented tusks resembling those nose marks from the septum to the ears (*2.093*). Papua New Guinea, Melanesia, Late 19th., - early 20th., century, A.D.

10.024 : Nose ring worn by a youth of the type found in Melanesia and South America. Nepal, Early 20th., century, A.D.

10.022 : Nose ring of the type found in the Western Pacific and Pacific Coast Americas. Pahari Woman, North India, Early 20th., century, A.D.

references to the same region in Asia and the Polynesian term for penis is ure, clearly the origin of the Desana yeru. The whole imagery of the hero Pamuri Mahse standing in his serpent canoe is so completely that from the Ancient Near and Middle East via India that it must have been imported from there via Polynesia. Further evidence of contact between South America and Polynesia will be of more interest in due course.

Some aspects developing from the assimilation of external motifs and myths appear, however, to be all the Desana's own and it was said that the horsefly, immediately after the period of primal Chaos, flew about stinging and causing a great nuisance although there are here certain parallels with the stinging of the Hittite god Telipinu noted earlier. This appears to have been some kind of fiendish initiating force since it was said that the name of the horsefly was nua-mee. This combination appears to have developed from muriri, meaning to "bite" or "insert" the penis. This expression has overtones of the Vagina Dentata myths, so common in India, and with almost exact equivalents among the Huichols in North West Mexico and found widely also in the Amazon Basin.

Hallucinogens - the Sun's Navel and Tobacco

Hallucinogens were a universally used stimulant to assist in the shaman's trance states in making contact with the ancestors in rituals and in the healing and oracular consultations required for the ordinary tribesperson. The Desana were no exception and their myths and legends associated with them are also of some interest. The Sun was believed to have retained the hallucinogenic powder in his navel, called by the Desana, Viho, and it was said to be obtained from this deity by his daughter scratching that part of his body[45]. Coca was known to the Desana and in their myths it is noted that the ancient birds associated with the Sun, the eagles, chewed these leaves[46]. The first people associated with the snake canoe, and the deities commanded by the Sun, all appear from outside the Desana themselves.

Preserved in the tribal memory is that heroes and teachers imported and taught them their skills rather than indicating that they were developed from within the evolution of the tribe itself. It is implied, and hardly disguised, that these first men from the serpent canoe spread to other parts of the Amazon Basin to form clans and tribes by the capture of marriage partners. It is likely that each man had more than one wife and their descendants were therefore mixed race, where all the women were Amazonian. Their offspring, however, were neither one nor the other and formed a separate racial descent and this aspect is reflected in the myths of the Desana who clearly reflected such a tradition in considering themselves separate from the other Maku. Researchers during the twentieth century noted that the Desana were different from their other Maku tribal relations and they were divided into patrilineal clans each with a claimed descent from the boreka - a fish ancestor. The Desana despised the other Maku divisions and considered them "not quite human"[47] and this is reflected in the myths particularly related to the Sun, the first ancestors and deities, and their descendants in the first generations. Long held traditions appear to be reflected in the references to the daughter of the Sun, named Abe Mango, where she was said to have been sent to earth, along with the other deities, to teach the Maku and particularly those of them who became the Desana. She lived with the people and taught them pottery and basket making and which fish and fruits to eat. Abe Mango lived with her father "as if she were his wife" but in time she became thin, ugly and lifeless, because of her sexual cravings. As her life ebbed away he father, the Sun, decided to save her and smoked tobacco and wafted it over her, she revived, and these tobacco biased rites formed the foundation for menstrual rites among girls reaching puberty[48] into recent times.

The fact that the daughter of the Sun could appear to be able to die suggests that she was in fact one of the first generations descended from the mariners who followed the Sun - as they did in Polynesia. The narcotic leaves were of particular importance in assuaging hunger and thirst in the long, island-hopping voyages across the Pacific Ocean, and seeking out supplies of this narcotic when reaching the shores of South America would have been of primary importance. The myths of the Viho, the Desana ground narcotic being retrieved from the navel of the Sun god, appears to have close similarities with the Hindu myths of Vishnu when he was said to have emerged from the navel of Brahma while others say it was Brahma the god of fine essence that emerged from a lotus. The blue lotus of Ancient India appears to have been utilised for hallucinogenic purposes as it was in Ancient Egypt.

An aspect associated with hallucinogens through its believed introduction by the Sun's daughter, was that of the ear-cylinder, usually utilised in South and South East Asia for holding narcotic leaves during long distance voyages, and here made from copper[49]. It is said in Desana myth that the daughter of the Sun had two sons and both were apprenticed to become payes or shamans. One was successful but the other was "withering away" because he "was always thinking of sex"[50]. This same affliction was suffered by his mother, but her father, the Sun as noted, revived her with tobacco smoke but she was unable to save her son and he became the first Desana to die. This tends to confirm that the first ancestors who arrived in the snake boat were

10.025 : Ear disks of a medium size found widely in the Amazon Basin and Gran Chaco. Early 20th., century, A.D.

10.026 : Traditional ear cylinder, inserted after the ear lobe opening is extended over months or years with expanded rolled leaves. South India, Early 20th., century, A.D.

10.027 : Ear cylinders were a characteristic of mariner peoples who used them to carry supplies of narcotic leaves or other substances. This same type of cylinder is found from the most ancient time in Central and South America and the ear lobes are extended from the early years as children. South India, Early 20th., century, A.D.

10.028 : Ear "muff" ornaments identical to those of the Nagas of Assam. Taiohae, Marquesas Islands, Eastern Polynesia, 1804 A.D.

10.029 : One largely ignored element of transferred iconography is that of the "ear muff". The purpose is unsure but the importance clearly has been transferred from India to South America. Those drawn in the first drawings from Polynesia are identical to the Nagas of Assam. Taiohae, Marquesas Islands, Eastern Polynesia, 1814 A.D.

10.030 : Extended ear decorations less elaborate than those in *10.032*. Nanda Temple, Pagan, Burma, 7-8th., century, A.D.

10.032 : Extended, elaborate ornamental ear flares displayed on a gold covered Buddha. Cross braces are found from the Ancient Middle East through India to South America. Burma, 8-9th., century, A.D.

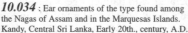

10.033 : Fanged mask typical of many tribal imagery in Indonesia but here the extended elaborate foliated ear "muffs" undoubtedly influenced from the earlier South East Asia Buddhist examples. Indonesia, 19th., century, A.D.

10.034 : Ear ornaments of the type found among the Nagas of Assam and in the Marquesas Islands. Kandy, Central Sri Lanka, Early 20th., century, A.D.

10.031 : Extended ear ornaments clearly based on those of the Nagas of Assam and the Marquesas Islands. Temes Malau Mask, Nalawan Society, Malekula, New Hebrides, Melanesia, late 19th., century, A.D.

considered true gods and did not die, perhaps leaving them after commencing their clans and returning to their own countries in the West. This would have been perceived by them Desana that they had not died since the death rites were never carried out, and they were therefore considered to still live on Earth in the West. The descendants who remained would have reflected more of the Amazonian culture and physical appearance in successive generations and, remaining in the Amazonian forests, lost contact with their paternal progenitors and their traditions. Certainly the myths reflect this principle in the origins of many of the Amazonian tribes not only the Desana or Tukano.

The "Ancient Eagles" were associated with coca and believed to have fed on carrion and were therefore seen to be associated with sickness and disease. As sky creatures they were associated with tobacco smoke that was seen to rise into the sky and therefore considered as a link between the Earth and the region of the gods, the Milky Way. These eagles were therefore invoked at rituals designed for the removal of health threats to the people and they were believed to carry afflictions of this nature to the Milky Way - this region being considered a type of "dung heap"[51]. Tobacco was used also to kill the embryo of the horsefly that could threaten mankind and lay its egg under the skin. The tobacco leaf was chewed and placed on the swelling and this caused the embryo to wriggle out, but the horsefly was earlier identified with the first people on earth. The whirring of the horsefly was identified with the bullroarer and is a ritual item found also in Australia and parts of Melanesia, and was considered to be the "voice and power of the Sun"[52]. It is the tobacco leaf that was believed by the Desana, when rolled into a cylinder and extended as a "forked cigar" from Ahpikondia to the Desana homeland that allowed child spirits or souls to emerge in their land, and the forked cigar holder is perceived as a symbol of man himself[53]. When a child is born in the maloca, or tribal communal dwelling, the father lights his cigar of tobacco leaves and proceeds to exhale the smoke inside. While smoking and expelling the smoke he forms a ring of it around the maloca as he runs to perform a circuit around the outside reciting prayers and invoking the protective powers of the ancestors to look benignly on the child and the house in which it will dwell[54]. The forked cigar holder is the symbol of men and of a man as its owner during life. After death it is placed in the ground beside the grave after a few months during a ritual of remembrance to celebrate the life that has passed[55]. This ritual element appears frequently in the preserved symbolism of the Maya and appears to have had similar oral traditions attached (*4.024*).

Blue is the colour particularly associated by the Desana with the Milky Way and this was perceived by them to also be the colour of the tobacco smoke itself as the subtle form of communication between the Earth and the great star highway in the sky. There appears to be some confusion as to the location of Ahpikondia since the Desana sometimes considered that there was also that this land was bathed in a pale green light, the colour of the "land of coca"[56], and this could only refer to the Andean slopes of the highlands of what is now Colombia, Ecuador or Peru. However, in other myths it is described as being bathed in a golden light of the Sun and this dichotomy no doubt derives from the fact that the paternal line lost contact with the Pacific Ocean probably many centuries ago. This would allow prominence in time for traditions from the female line, who probably never knew of the Pacific Ocean, from the Amazonian peoples to dominate or infuse. These maternal tribes are certainly those who have occupied the rain forests separated from the Pacific Ocean by the broad band of the Northern Andes.

Associated with the Milky Way is the wind, named by the Desana as miru-nye, and purire means "to blow", and where it has also been earlier noted that Wira-pora - "Sons of the Wind" is the name they give themselves. It is said that the ancestor named Mirupu received the hallucinogenic powder named Viho from the ancestor called Viho-mahse[57], and it appears very likely that this Miru-pu is probably the Polynesian Milu or Miru or Miluk, and known in the Easter Island legends among others. This is a direct reference of transfer between the wind deity among the Desana, noted particularly as wira or miru, or puri, and the wind deity of the Hindus of India, and the Bhuiyas in particular. These Desana terms appear to a general term deriving from Vir or Bir, and the alternate term pawan earlier noted and the Polynesians located between these disparate geographical regions.

Many of the Amazonian tribes have been noted by anthropologists, even to the present day, to have very fair-skinned children, a trait recorded also of the Polynesians on many of their islands, and particularly noted of the Parakana in the Amazon Basin[58]. Contact between the Amazon and the Polynesians has been more recently confirmed with blood analysis suggesting that they "may not be genetically independent"[59]. When the Europeans entered the Pacific they were believed by the Polynesians and many Melanesians to be the fair-skinned ancestors returning to claim their lands, and this was also famously true of both the Aztecs and the Incas. There are references in Desana myths alluding to lighter-skinned deities and among the people pale-skinned children were not unusual. A term used for a child of this type was pumbora where pu referred to the pu leaf that turned pale when it dried, and where bore was descriptive of a light colour. Another derivation if from puri, to "cohabit", and bora, the "house-post" since the revered ancestor was said to have "a penis like a house-post". The latter references are interesting since, if Puri relates to the wind above noted among the Desana, then it corresponds directly with the belief in India that the wind deity had special responsibilities and associations with the soul. This Desana term bora referring to a house-post reflect rites in the Pacific Islands associated with the sacred dancing grounds along with the pillars and ridgepole of the adjacent temple that were widely spread in Polynesia through Melanesia to the East Australian coast. These dancing ground and, or the sites celebrated with them were also called the bora and noted in and earlier chapter. Among the many Amazonian tribes light-skinned people or heroes formed a major element in the myths and legends of their formative cultures, and usually were designated by the term yuri - "white". The Desana note also that they are descended from the mythical progenitors who are identified with the snake canoe otherwise calling themselves the Sons of the Aracu Fish or in their language Boreka-pora, where Boreka derives from Bore, or boreri - to turn white. This is an allusion to the white gelatinous matter secreted in the head of that fish and is by extension, because of its appearance, an allusion to the male seminal fluid[60]. This might be seen as a reference to ancestral males being white-skinned, as noted in Polynesia, where the phallus was called ure, so similar to yeru of the Desana. Among the Desana also are references to the Umu-si-pora or Sons of Oropendola, and this derives from the yellow-tailed bird called the umu, umusi, or pendola and is identified with the seminal powers of the Sun[61]. The term Oro for deities and, or as a prefix is widely found particularly among the Cuna in Panama to the north and these people have close apparent connections with the Nagas of Assam in their terminology, myths and ritual associations[62]. They also appear closely connected to the Caroline Islands of Ponape and Pelew and other aspects of Polynesian culture[63]. Significantly, in terms of South American connections, the Desana retained references to the rites associated with the mythical or legendary Yuri-pari and among them this relates to initiation ceremonies exclusive for, and only attended by, the males and during these ceremonies the large flutes are played[64].

Yuru-pari - The Legendary White Peoples in Amazonia

Among the tribes inhabiting the slopes from the Gran Chaco leading up to the Bolivian plateau the Yurucares, literally the "white men", were said to reside at the time of the Conquest and later between what is now Santa Cruz de la Sierra and Cochabamba in Bolivia[65]. These people were located in 1768 A.D. and the name appears to have an Quechua origin where yurak means "white" and kari means "man" and refers to their natural, very pale skin colouring although, as with many of the tribes of the Amazon and Gran Chaco, they suffered from large patches of cutaneous pigment loss usually called Piebaldism or Vitiligo. The Yurucares were considered by the early writers who saw them to be the tallest and best made of all the South America peoples[66].

Juru-pari as a god appears to be another form of Yuru-pari and who, among the tribes along the Uaupes River was identified with the thunder and it was said that natural death among them occurs when this deity has "killed them"[67]. The Yurupari ceremony was created around the myth of the boy who was perceived as the bringer of fruits to the people of the Uaupaes River region. The myth relates that in earlier times a small boy came from the Great Water-House, the name for the house of the Sun, and his name was Milomaki. He was said to sing so wonderfully that the people came from long distances to hear him, but when the people had returned home and ate fish they fell down dead. It was stated that Milomaki grew very much more quickly than a normal child and when the relations of these dead people seized Milomaki, believing that he was responsible for their deaths, he was already a youth. The relations tied Milomaki to a pole placed on a pyre and set it alight but he kept on singing even more wondrously than before. He did not cease singing even as his body swelled from the heat and as he disintegrated into ash his soul rose to heaven. Even on the day when he had been reduced to ash a large green leaf arose from them and it kept growing ever larger and by the following day it had become a large tree. The men made flutes from its wood and from these it was said that the most wonderful "melodies" arose and were those Milomaki had sung while among them. The tree became the origin of the first fruiting trees and when that time comes each year for the trees to again fruit the men sit below them and perform dances and blow their flutes in honour of the singing boy deity. Women and children are not allowed to be present and suffer severe penalties should they contravene that prohibition[68]. It is likely that Milomaki is also related to the hero-deities named Moshikishiki, Matahiki, Matik-tiki and Maui in Polynesia and Melanesia[69].

The fact that this festival, not exclusive to the Desana, is called the Yurucari suggests that this is identified with fair-skinned intruders from outside and the myths and legends of the origins of peoples emerging from trees and fruit, or from the skull or body of a hero or deity are too closely similar to those in Oceania not to be as a result of cultural transfer[70]. This tends to confirm that this Desana myth derives from those found widely in the Pacific Islands and that are also found through into Indonesia to India. There are clear references also in the myths and legends of Central America among the Mexicans and Mayans to similar beliefs and the famous funerary slab over Pacal's tomb at Palenque is an example of iconography developed from these same myths and legends[71]. Yuri-ulu were a people in Australia who had a closely similar concept of the sky to that of the Desana, and it is unlikely to be a coincidence that there are other aspects clearly related[72]. In Western Mexico there is an origin myth among the Tarahuames who stated that the sacred dances and singing were called Yumari and were given to them by deities of the same name who lived with the Sun[73].

Boraro and other Demons - Transfer of the Na Areau Myth from Polynesia

Some of the most interesting aspects of the heroes, gods or demons in Desana mythology are those about the demons who were believed to plague them in certain circumstances or at certain times of the year. The boraro is the most feared of these and this terms derives from borei, meaning "white", and commonly called kuru-pira and is a name occurring more widely for this demon in Amazonia[74]. The term kuru means red among the Colombian Indians as well as in Polynesia, and clearly indicates another probable connection. This boraro is described as a tall naked man with a hairy chest with eyes glowing red and large curved fangs along with a huge penis. It was said that his name derives also from the name sound of his cry when attacking a victim and is likened to an "enraged jaguar". The ears of the boraro are said to be very large and erect and point forward to hear better, and his feet are also very large - the length of a "human forearm". He has four toes on each foot but they point back so that they appear reversed with the heels forward, but has no joints in his legs so that when he falls he has great difficulty in regaining his balance. There are many different versions of the boraro and he is believed to live at the headwaters of rivers and also with Vai-Mahse in the hills. It is said that he is always found with a large swarm of mosquitoes and insects around him because of his fetid smell and is sometimes discovered sunning himself in a clearing of the jungle and is seen with a stone hoe hanging over his shoulder. It is said that one of the way he kills his victims is by urinating on them, since this is a very strong poison, and then the boraro punctures the skull with his fangs and drains the brain and internal organs from the body. After this he repairs the body so that it appears to come back to life and return home. The advice given to those who are attacked by this creature is to runs backwards facing the boraro and there is a chance of escape. The animals associated with him are the tapir and the toucan.

Vai-mahse - the Dwarf Deity of the Tukano Desana

Dwarf deities are notable in the Desana mythology and the boraro is said to live in the cliffs and hills with the Dia-Mahse, dwarf beings, and the evil Black Jaguar people. Lord of these beings is Vai-Mahse and is a red dwarf[75] living in a cave at the entrance to the underworld[76] and is the Master of Animals. He is sometimes imaged as a small lizard.

The Urubu tribe had a supernatural mediator between the Master of Animals, Vai-Mahse, and the boraro, a dog-monkey named Ae reminiscent of the Hindu monkey god, Hanuman. He is portrayed as red haired and red-eyed, but has blue bones and a blue penis and came out only at the full Moon. The Urubu hero is named Mair identified with the Sun and its animal representation the Yellow Jaguar[77]. In the Witoto myths it was believed that monkeys first emerged from a hole in the ground and then turned into men, but if they misbehaved they reverted to animals again[78] - the same belief existed in Indonesia, Malaya and India into the last century. With so many connections to Polynesia the name of the Urubu hero, Mair, may be a corruption of the Polynesian hero Maui sometimes described as a dwarf deity.

The Glowing Red Eyes of Amazonian Mythical Beings

The description of the boraro given here from Desana sources conflicts with the believed derivation from the jaguar by some researchers, the natural top predator in the Amazon rain forest. The various elements for this figure suggest otherwise and that this may be an imported deity. Although the eyes of the jaguar are prominent and see very well in the dark and could be termed glowing they cannot be described as red. Another form of the boraro is the Anyang, known among the Urubu tribe, and is considered the most unpleasant of the demons that wander the forest. It too is considered as a naked male but there are references to females accompanying him or as part of a group. The Anyang's hair is allowed to grow to their waists and it tends to be matted and tangled, and their skin greenish and is compared to the colour of "decaying corpses" and their bodies are thought to lack bones[79].

The term boraro and the attributes of these wrathful demons appear to have derived from the name and characteristics of Bhairava - "the Terrible", a fierce for of the god Hindu god Siva. As Lord of Time, Siva, in his aspects as Bhairava is said to relish death and destruction, it is he who wields the weapons for the defeat of enemies and termination of World Cycles[80]. This aspect of Siva is associated with another of his aspects, Rudra, "Lord of Tears", of such interest in other sections of this work[81]. Bhairava is associated with a dog that almost always is depicted accompanying him (*7.069*), and it is this companion that "sniffs-out" the way to his goal where destruction or retribution is destined. Bhairava's appearance is described as red skin colouring, always naked in the form of the mendicant sadhu, or holy man, usually holding a trident, a kapala or skull cup, and the only clothing occasionally associated with him is an elephant's hide and he is usually considered to reside on the mount of Mandara, a reference to be considered in a projected future work[82]. These aspects of Siva closely relate him to the wrathful Bhairava (*1.050*) as an aspect of his being and the naked mendicant form of wandering saint, Bhikshatana (*7.086*). Both aspects appear to relate to the Gaucacue in Ancient Peru[83], considered elsewhere in this work. This may be the origin of the Anyang noted in the myths of the Desana.

Among the Kaingang tribe, the Yoin is considered the most horrific of devils, and his head is described as large with extensive hair said to be red or in some cases "woolly like a Negroes". His eyes are white with red rims and his mouth has large jaws, his body thickset, and with a very long penis. His food is human beings and his mouth is always red with their blood. In most cases all the ogres of the forest are considered to have "excessive" sexual appetites extending not only to the males but also to the females and when attacking the forest people, when not eaten, they often died from this excessive sexual appetite being perpetrated upon them.

This aspect of people dying attacked by giants imposing their sexual wants upon the small to pygmoid sized people of South America and elsewhere is of great interest and will be more so in due course.

Among the Lengua of the Gran Chaco their most notorious demon was called the kilyikhama and was thought to thieve from the Indians and was particularly a danger at night. This was because it, or they, was at one time believed to have walked as men upon the Earth and was looking for a body into which it could co-opt for themselves while the Lengua was sleeping since the soul was believe to separate from the body during sleep[84]. This demon was also said to have red eyes and missionaries who first contacted the Lengua and lived with them over some years were undecided as to their origin and one noted: "That these kilyikhama are not the deified souls of the men seems clear from the fact that there is no veneration shown them, but whether the Indian idea was originally that they were a distinct spiritual creation, or simply the souls of a prehistoric race, is not clear"[85]. In this observation the fact that they might have been demonised earlier race seems to be nearer the mark than many other opinions.

The same imagery of the forest demon is found among other peoples in South East Asia and Australia. The beliefs of the Engami people of Western Indonesia were similar to those of Mentawei, and derive much of their influence from Hindu India. They retained the idea of the giant world serpent who supported the World and this aspect of cosmology among others is virtually identical to that of the Bataks on the highlands of Western Sumatra and the Dyaks of Borneo. The Enganes also believed that earthquakes were caused by a giant sea fish with fiery red eyes. The Mentawei considered that in ancient times a powerful magician was buried under the centre post of their temple, or uma, and that he was responsible for earthquakes when they occurred, and he was considered to be their prime ancestor, or Teteu[86]. This term, Teteu, is undoubtedly related to, and having a common origin with the Central and South American term Tata. The temple name uma clearly relates to that of the Polynesian ruma, the name for house.

Serpents with red eyes are also found in Japanese mythology and these are usually associated with the cardinal directions[87]. Other deities are reminiscent of demons and one in Japan is a God who was said to have dwelt at the eight crossroads of heaven and to have been seven fathoms high and that his enormous eyes emitted a "ruddy glow"[88].

The Jakun Besisi, who live in the forests of the Malay Peninsula, preserved the belief that there were demons that infested the forests and fed upon human beings. It was believed that the Jin Sa-ribu, or "Legion of Demons", dwelt in the earth and fed upon these humans as required: The description of them was recorded a century ago: "They are as tall as the loftiest trees, and very long black hair, which in the case of males is grown to the waist, but in the case of females falls below their feet. They have conical heads and walk with the greatest swiftness ....As they go, they make a shrill whistling voice, ... At the full of the moon their bodies are perfectly white, in fact, as a sheet"[89].

Another demon was called Huntaman, in Besisi, Hantu si Buru, and, "... is full ten feet high, and his face is very hairy (with beard and whiskers). From nightfall onwards at the full of the moon he goes hunting deer and pig. He has two hunting dogs, both of them small and with reddish fur ..."[90]. It is clear that the demon Huntaman is the deified monkey deity Hanuman of Hindu India and the Besisi term associates him with the Buru - a similar name perhaps indicating a shared a common origin with the Boraro in the Amazon Basin. He is also associated with the pig where the Amazonian counterpart is associated with the tapir, a large pig-like animal but with a small trunk relating to the elephant.

The origins of such demons appear most likely to have been transferred not only into South East Asia but across the Pacific Ocean into South America. Red-eyed deities are associated almost exclusively with wrathful or demonic deities such as Chamunda (*11.071*) who was often depicted as dark or black-skinned with red hair and black eyes and who wore a tiger's skin[91]. Red hair is commonly associated with these deities and appears to derive from the Tantric depictions of demons from Tibet.

Particularly interesting among the demons of India are the Airi, or Hill Bhutas, and these were all said to have their feet reversed and this is a characteristic also of the Churel, from which the Anglicised term churl derives[92]. It is likely however that there are other aspects suggesting that these elements were not only confused with Hanuman, the Hindu monkey god, but with the elephant since the very large ears and the fact that they were moved forward as if to hear better, seems to relate to the Desana myth demons that were derived from garbled accounts from South India and their elephant myths. This is also reflected in other myths in Southern South America noted in due course. There are other references clearly related to intruders who wore animal skin capes with the head of the animal still attached and worn as a headdress, but these myths tend to refer to four ears and four eyes when it is clear that these are being described. There are many illustrations of such heroes or deities in Central and South America (*4.058*; *4.062*) and similar headdresses are still worn by the tribes of North America. Such headdresses were also known in India and north into Central Asia.

Large Ears Motifs in Amazonia, Oceania and Asian Myth

In the Pacific Islands there are no large animals and even the crocodile does not extend beyond the large western islands of New Guinea. But among the islands there are references to large-eared creatures that may have been the model, or at least supplied certain elements, for the Amazonian boraro. The birth of children in the Northern New Hebrides was associated with the deity named Yetar, but in some districts this deity is named Tautai or Soo[93]. This name reflects associations with the boraro equivalent among the Engai and Mentawei in Western Indonesia, and featuring a myth recorded from Malekula in the New Hebrides referring to a coconut that was a black woman with large ears[94]. In the islands to the north of New Guinea it is said that the souls of the dead, called barom, went to the small island of Tuma to the northwest of the Trobriand Islands. The spirits of the dead travel to the upper world but after a time they descend to the world below the earth. On arriving in the Underworld they find a track leading to the land of "shades" presided over by the Underworld lord, Topileta. It was said that this deity was in every way similar to a man except "... that he has huge ears which flap continually" - and it must be remembered that the elephant-headed god in India is, in the many images still in existence, portrayed mostly as an elephant human or anthropomorphically represented (*4.087*). This deity was also said to be covered with tattoos and caused earthquakes[95]. It was said that the first people to inhabit the world emerged from Topileta's world, through a hole in the ground on Tuma, bringing with them their bird totem and a pig[96]. The island of Tuma was important in the Kula trade among these islands and here, when a man died, his trade items of high ceremonial value, the vaygu'a, were left on his grave out of respect for the Underworld Lord, Topileta[97]. The term vaygu'a is interesting since the Kula trade was dependant on sail craft moving around the islands in an accepted sequence, and this may have in centuries, or millennia past have derived from Vayu the Wind god of India, just as the term found for canoe in Polynesia and parts of Melanesia, waka derived from vaka in India.

In another report from the Malay peninsula it was recorded a century ago that the Gergasi were giants who molested the people and were characteristic in some ways of the boraro in the Amazon and one record notes: "The giants (Gergasi) are believed to be represented by two huge black men with projecting tusks in both jaws. They are said to devour those who lose their way in the mountain chains of the north of the Peninsula." Another section expands on this recording, "... that southern Siam was once invaded by man-eating giants with dark skins and two projecting teeth resembling the canine teeth of tigers. The Raja fought with them, and in a single battle killed all but seven, who fled to Southern Kedah, where each of them sought for a hill for himself to dwell in. Here they henceforth dwelt in caves. According to some they had many heads, or elephants ears, or large wings. By the poorer Malays they were believed to bury treasure, and in many parts of Kedah a Malay who has dreamt of such a treasure will go and dig for it. At length, however, they died out, and if they were killed and their blood fell on the earth leeches arose, but if it fell upon the grass it turned to mosquitoes"[98].

These references to cannibals with large ears appears to have connections with others known in the myths preserved by the Nagas of Assam. Among the Ao Nagas there was a tradition stating that there was a land where these cannibals had such large ears that they used one as a mattress at night and the other as a covering[99]. In Malayan forests it was recorded that small ears and woolly hair were identified with the pygmoid negrito peoples who were much despised and it was thought that, conversely, by extending the ears it was a signature of higher civilisation. This identification and contempt for the negrito for apparently similar reasons was known among all the straight-haired Nagas tribes[100]. Similar associations regarding woolly hair were known among the Polynesians. The trickster dwarf Na Areau in the Gilbert Islands (Kiribati), was said to be a "stinking black dwarf with frizzy hair and flapping ears" and this appears to be an intermediate version of the Malay-Naga beliefs and those of the Amazonian people. The figure of Na Areau appears in many guises both in the Gilbert Islands and in South America, noted in other sections of this work.

In the Cloncurry region of Queensland in Australia the Mitakoodi people retained a belief in a giant supernatural being "with immense eyes and very big ears" called Ten-gul-a-goo-lun. He was said to be a familiar of the shamans or medicine men and taught them how to "point-the-bone", a ritual used to kill an enemy[101]. Many aspects relating to the cultures of India are found among the Australian Aborigines, and in India, the wrathful smallpox deity Sitala, exhibited in her most fierce form as the "terrible elephant form" or Matangi. She manifested in eight aspects as William Crooke noted over a century ago, and in naming them he states that they are "… a collection of names which indicates the extraordinary mixture of beliefs, some of them importations from the regular mythology, but others, obscure and local manifestations of the deity, out of which this worship developed. She is described as having ears as large as a winnowing fan, projecting teeth, a hideous face with a wide open mouth"[102]. The term Matang is known among some of the Polynesians, such as the Gilbert Islanders, as their place of ancestral origin and to which they expect to return after this life ends.

Among the Gonds (Konds or Khonds) of Central India, a tribe of some importance in this study, an oral history regarding their settling the land was recorded by Edgar Thurston as follows: "There is a tradition that, in olden days, four Konds, named Kasi, Mendora, Bolti, and Bolo, with eyes the size of brass pots, teeth like axe-heads, and ears like elephant's ears, brought their ancestor Mandia Patro from Jora-Singha in Boad, and gave him and his children authority over the whole country now comprised in Mahasinga, and in Kurtilli Barakhumma, Bodogodo, Balliguda, and Pussanga, on condition of settling their disputes, and aiding them in their rights …"[103]. The four deities clearly indicate some original derivation from a calendrically orientated myth where they represented the four cardinal points but the description of these deities appears to indicate that they belonged to the Demons, or Rakshas so noted in the myths of India. Interesting also is the reference to one of them with the name Mandia Patro (Patro being father as in the ancestral sense) and Mandia probably relating to the Mandaeans noted in other sections of this work and with the Mundas, Bhuiyas and Assurs in particular.

In another part of South India the Velans, characteristically fearful of smallpox, in previous centuries propitiated the deity known as Karin-Kali, an aspect of the great Hindu goddess

Kali. This goddess was invoked by the priest in the following intonation: "Oh! Thou, round-eyed short Karinkali with big ears, born from the third incessantly burning eye of Siva, come, come and be in possession." This was intonated sixteen times and then regaled with the following prayer: "Oh! Thou, Karinkutti (black dwarf) of Vedapuram in Vellanad, that pluckest the fruits of the right hand branch of the strychnine tree (Strychnos Nux-vomica), and keepest toddy in its shell, drinking the blood of the black domestic fowl, drumming and keeping time on the rind of the fruit, filling and blowing thy pipe or horn through the nose. Oh! Thou primeval black dwarf, so long as I utter the proper mantrams, I beg thee to cause such demons as would not dance to dance, and others to jump and drive them out. Oh! Thou Karinkutti, come, come, and enable me to succeed in my attempts"[104]. The association of large ears, black demons and red eyes are all found in India and these appear to have been transferred across the Pacific Ocean and been assimilated in all or a few of their elements among the various Amazonian peoples.

In the Desana myths one of the forest demons, the boraro, was imaged as having a hoe hanging over his shoulder. Among the Gonds of India a female demon formed always from a mother who dies in childbirth called the Ondar Muttai was said to have only one breast and this was hung over her shoulder. She was considered with the "greatest horror" and was said to have teeth as "long as your hand", a bulbous nose, ears like winnowing fans, and her feet, as red as fire, were said to be "turned back-to-front"[105] a reference noted of the boraros.

Tukano Desana Concepts of the Soul

The Desana concept of the soul is that of the wind blowing against a "little cloth" that begins to flutter as the soul comes to life. This reflection of the soul in terms of the wind appears directly parallel to that in India where the wind god, Vayu, was responsible for the soul and conducted it on its journey to the afterlife. The wind is literally seen as breathing life into the soul after its creation. The cloth seems to be a vague memory of wind associated with the sails of mariners as it was in India and Oceania. The soul is seen as a direct manifestation of the Sun's will and is given the name simpora and its "soul-stuff" appears to have been derived from Ahpikondia, the land of the ancestors, and the "milk" of the soul appears to be coca. When the soul leaves the body, either in the sleeping hours, or during trances, or after death it is perceived as a humming-bird[106].

Separate from the soul, perhaps best visualised as the Sun's spark, is the mind soul - the ka-i thought to reside in the brain. This is the accumulation of experience during the life and is believed by the Desana to survive after death with the soul itself[107]. Ka-i appears to be related to the Chinese term Ki - life energy, and it has been noted by others that the astrological concepts and constructs among the more advanced people of the Colombian highlands at the time of the Spanish Conquest appear to be remarkably similar to those of China[108]. Further, it has been pointed out in this work that the term for the Desana priest, Kumu appears to have derived from the Polynesian Tumu and the Na Khi (Southern China) Tu Mu. It would seem, therefore, that the Desana concepts of the soul have been acquired from incoming influences from the Pacific Ocean after they had been assimilated in the Colombian Highlands cultures.

When the soul has departed this life, and if it has been virtuous, it travels to Ahpikondia in the far west situated at the place where the sky meets the earth, and there becomes the hummingbird. These souls no longer are attached to this world and are called nyamiri-pora, or people of the night[109]. The term nyam is also of interest since apparently related terms are found widely throughout Melanesia and the Western Pacific[110] but particularly in India[111]. Among other references in Vedic texts the souls of the righteous went to the Aryan heaven and there a lake called Nya existed that may be the ultimate origin of these terms[112]. It was believed that the paye, the shaman and healer, or kume, the priest[113], could influence the destiny of the individual soul and direct it to either the land of the Ancestors or the feared Underworld beneath the Earth.

Kumi, the Priest and Paye the Shaman - Crystals in Myth and Tradition

The kumi had a high status in Desana society and was believed to be the direct representative of the Sun[114]. In colour symbolism the kumi, also called kumu, and his sacred rituals were assigned to white while black represented the west[115] and also found so designated among the Maya. It was believed that the kumu was created by the Sun so that his representative could be trained to "perpetuate" the "highest moral teachings" and he was not concerned with the healing and curative aspects in tribal life[116]. The paye as shaman and healer embodied various aspects of mystical beliefs and rites. Contact with his personal spirit familiars along with the ancestors of the people during consultations as well as attracting beneficial influences into the tribal life of the Desana were some of his functions. Physical, mental and spiritual strength were also an essential basis on which these seem to function as shamans and it is interesting to note that this was termed tulari[117], whereas physical training which also embodied less prominent aspects relating to the spiritual aspects of the shaman was known as kalari[118] among the warriors of South India. The term also had phallic associations and included the act of procreation by penetration in the symbolic sense, and by extension the shaman's ability to penetrate the more subtle spheres during his ritual performances and induced trances[119]. It is clear therefore the priestly function of the kumu, as the name suggests, is probably imposed from outside by earlier paternal related peoples arriving from the Pacific Ocean and who first had some contact with the highland peoples of Colombia. The paye, as shaman, on the other hand represented the long indigenous tradition recognisably descended from that introduced by migration from North East Siberia and transferred over many millennia from there through North and Central America into South America evident in the characteristic rituals of the maternal lineage of the tribes.

Although shamanistic healing was part of the maternal heritage of the Amazonian tribes it was strictly passed down among the Desana through the male line. Prized and revered crystals were considered to focus the power of the shaman and it was thought that the shaman focused his healing energies into the patient's body that entered the patient as a form of "semen" or male essence imparted from the shaman. Interestingly toothache was thought to be the result of a small worm gnawing at the root of the tooth[120], and this exact concept was found among the Maya[121], in New Guinea among the Mafulu[122], and in the Ancient Near East[123].

Sun, Moon and Eclipse among the Tukano Desana

In formal salutations in rituals of the Desana the Sun is addressed as Sun Father but in general references he is called go'a-niee meaning "god", or "supreme force", etc.,[124]. The word go'a derives from "bone" and the rest of the name indicates "power" or "force"[125]. It is noted that the Sun is particularly related to the kumu and his teaching of the Indians and that he is also thought to have special connections with the land of the ancestors in the far west since it was in Ahpikondia that the Sun set[126]. It must be significant also that the Sun is the deity from whom the hallucinogen, Viho was obtained[127], since narcotic substances were used by long distance mariners to assist in suppressing the effects of hunger and thirst in the long weeks and months at sea. The Desana usually referred to the Sun by its appearance as a rayed being rather than to its attributes of heat and light, and to its colour of yellow - this having references to the male seminal fluid[128]. In an interesting section of beliefs to edible worms or larvae the white meat is considered another aspect of the Sun's seminal powers[129] and to procreation, and it is unlikely to be a coincidence that worms have similar mythic parallels in Polynesia. In reference to the Sun's seminal powers it was thought by the Desana that lightning was the ejaculation of the seminal power to fertilise the Earth. The crystal was thought to be residue in material form of such strikes

10.035 :
Ladders were considered symbolic of ascent to the sky necessary to reach the land of the ancestors and that shown of a log with angled wedges cut out for steps is one of the oldest type known. Mairava, Milne Bay, New Guinea, Late 19th., century, A.D.

and subsequently were sought out and greatly valued by the shamans[130].

In Desana thought there were two concepts of the Sun, one in terms of Creation and the other mundane. The Sun as Creator was not considered to be the Sun seen daily in its orbit through the sky as earlier noted. The Sun and Moon appearing in their orbits were considered to be two halves of the same principle, where the Sun represented "sublime fertility" and the Moon his twin brother representing "carnal sexuality"[131]. The Sun and Moon are both considered male and this relates much more to concepts found widely in India and originally in the Ancient Middle and Near East.

The theme of duality relating to the Sun and Moon is exemplified by the name of the Sun, nyami abe, meaning nocturnal Sun reflecting dark and light aspects of the Sun's nature this appears to have some parallel with the half cycle constructs known in India. There are aspects in Desana myths relating to incest between the Sun and the Moon where the latter abducts the daughter of the Sun. Other aspects of the Moon are considered sinister since he is thought to descend to Earth at night to cohabit with unsuspecting women and to partake in necrophilia acts at cemeteries. The Moon is also characterised by his copper ear cylinders and this suggest also contacts with the Western Pacific peoples[132].

When an eclipse occurs the Desana believed that the Moon was falling asleep and they shot arrows at it in an attempt to awaken him. For some activities the eclipse, unusually, was considered auspicious and the men went fishing and the woman grated manioc and performed activities during this short period that were believed to be of great benefit for the children and later descendants of the tribe[133]. This parallels some beliefs in India and Indonesia where certain fishing targets, or turtles, were reserved for this time[134].

It was said by the Desana that, when death first entered the world, it was the daughter of the Sun who caused it through neglect of her son, who was the first to die, and whom she buried in the earth. This is perceived by them as a primal act of the male representing the phallus being driven into the earth, representing the female, and the place he was buried was called abe-goro. The first prefix of this means the Sun is identical to the Ancient Near and Middle East term from god the father and goro means a flower[135]. "Abe" is the male term and the flower is the female and therefore the concept is identical to the sexual symbolism of the linga, or phallus, and yoni, or vagina, in Hindu myth where the yoni is equated with the lotus.

The Desana Sun and Buime as the Rainbow

In the mythical past the rainbow was believed by the Desana to be a fish and was in those times called Buime. At the time of one of the great cataclysms that destroyed most of the people on the Earth, that of the great fire, this great fish was recorded in myth as appearing in the form of an eel, emerging from the waters to see what had happened. The myths relate that when Buime found no people he went to buime goro, a place corresponding with abe goro, the first cemetery, and established himself as a "new intermediary" between the sky and Earth, so that the Creation of the Sun may continue[136]. This myth is unusual in South America and it follows closely that of a tradition found in the Gilbert Islands (Kiribati) in the Central Pacific.

It has been noted that the Desana traditions follow those known in Polynesia regarding the eel deity supporting Creation and allowing mankind to be re-established. Even more extraordinarily is that the Desana believed that the rainbow should never be pointed at since it would cause an infection in the fingernail[137]. In India it was also stated in the Vedic texts that it was unwise to point at the rainbow and that there were penalties imposed on those caught[138]. In one listed penalty for pointing at the rainbow, among several prohibitions, the sentence was to loose 12 years from one's life[139].

In a myth related to Creation of the World it is said in the Gilbert Islands myth cycles referred to above that at the beginning, when heaven and earth were clasped together, there was Na Areau te Moa-ni-bai - "Sir Spider-the-first-of-all-things". In a long myth describing the creation process resulting in heaven and earth being forced apart the first creatures kept hitting their head on the sky because it was too low. Na Areau called on the eel god, Riiki to force them further apart[140]. In another myth Na Areau the Younger was ordered by his Father, Ne Atibu, to enter the swamp that lay on the ocean and between the sea and the swamp was a "great rottenness", and there a large number maggots grew. Na Areau the Younger asked the Butterfly, Tiku-Tiku-Toungang, their names and he settled on the foreheads of the maggots as he named them, one of whom was Riiki-the-Eel[141].

Other references note that Riiki-the-Eel had many legs originally and these were struck off by Na Areau, son of Na Atibu, and fell into the sea to become eels. Na Areau then ordered the Eel to take up its place and Riiki lay across the heavens as Naiabu, the Milky Way[142]. It is interesting to note that here the Eel, as the rainbow, is related to the Milky Way and in the Desana myth the Eel god[143] earlier identified, is associated with Ahpikondia. The electric eel, born from the great serpent, is in turn also associated with the Milky Way and the serpent Canoe of the ancestors - Pamuri-Gahsiru[144]. The references to worms or maggots associated with rottenness is found widely in Amazon myths and represented life emerging from death. The connections between South America and India with the Gilbert Islands as an intermediate stop-over will be of more interest later.

The name of the Gilbert Islander Eel God, Riiki, appears to derive from the serpent deity in India named Punda-Riki. It has already been noted that Pun or Pund appears to relate to ancient solar megalithic circles in India and Rik or Riki is the older term for Riki or Rishi and among the Bhuiyas known as Rikmun[145]. In Hindu myth the Rishis are the seven sages identified with the seven stars of the Great Bear, its form in the night sky being serpentine. Among the Bhuiyas the Rikis are identified with the ancestral deities named Birs, and as has been earlier noted, these are the Virs or Viras apparently sharing a common origin with that of Vira-cocha in the Ancient Andes. This is consonant with the term Tahuantin-suyu apparently deriving from the Bhuiya wind deity Pawan[146] and related to the Mayan wind god Pauah-tun. Some myths associated the Bhuiya Rikhmun with the sea[147] along with those of the Kols or Munda tribes who are related to the Bhuiyas and Gond peoples in Central and Eastern India who retain the myth of Pundariki, or Pundariki Nag (Nag = Serpent)[148]. This relates the story of a great serpent god who found an abandoned child in the forest and protected it by taking it to Madra Munda[149]. This long myth a reduced simplified version noted earlier from another tradition records the believed origins of the former ruling Chotanagpur Raj family. This myth states that in ancient times, when Raja Janmejaya was attempting to destroy the entire race of serpents, one of these nagas, Pundariki Nag, changed himself into a human form and travelled to the holy city of Benares. There he succeeded in wooing the daughter of a Brahman of Benares but his true identity remained unknown to the Brahman and his daughter since such a marriage or liaison was strictly against their caste laws. Although his human form was convincing he was unable to change his serpent's tongue so he had to be very careful not to reveal himself. The couple had a son but soon after the Brahman's daughter found out the truth and Pundariki jumped into a pool and disappeared. The Brahman's daughter was stricken with grief and abandoned her child, and threw herself on a funeral pyre in an act of Sati. Soon after this act a Sakaldwipi Brahman appeared carrying an image of the Sun, and, being thirsty, he placed this on the ground while he drank from the pool, but when he had finished he found that he could not lift it again. As he looked about for an explanation he noticed to his amazement a great cobra with its hood raised and its coils surrounding a child to protect it. Pundariki, who had emerged from the pool earlier to protect his son, spoke to the Brahman, and told him of his story and that the child was destined to become the Raja of the country. He then committed his son to the Brahman's care and that he was to care for him and act as his guru and the Sun-god image was to become the tutelary deity[150].

This myth finds its exact counterpart in the many similar myths of children being protected by a serpent ancestor or by accidental discovery as in the Pundariki myth in Melanesia. In the Solomon Islands on the island of San Cristobal serpent deities were often identified with stones. Cairns formed of stones thrown by a person each time they pass it is characteristic of peoples in India through to South America, and known also in Eurasia and Africa. The sacred serpent spirits were usually called figona in the Solomon's Islands and the myth cycle of a serpent called Agunua is of special interest. The figona or serpent is also called Hatuibwari, the winged serpent, and this name is found as Hatui in the Huichol myths in Western Mexico and appears to derive from Hatu, a term found widely in Munda and Bhuiya culture in Eastern India from where the myths surrounding this serpent probably derives. In one of a number of similar myths from the islands to the south of the Solomons, Banks Island, it was said that a woman who was descended from a large snake married a man and they had a child. During the day the man went fishing and the woman went to the cultivated land to work and the child was left in charge of her grandmother, the great serpent identified with Hatuiwari or Agunua. The husband, however, did not known of his wife's serpent descent nor that her grandmother was the serpent, and when he returned home unexpectedly one day and found her he challenged his wife to tell him who the serpent was and why it was there and she had to confess. The husband awaited his chance and taking the child burnt down the house, and when the wife returned the serpent head spoke to her and told her to plant her body in a particular spot and fence it round and later from the grave a coconut palm sprang[151]. This version is one of many but illustrates the far distances that myths have been diffused by mariners and others in a recognisable form. It is clear that Riiki in the Gilbert Islands has similar origins to that of Hatuibwari and there are other cultural references linking the Gilbert Islanders closely to India relating to the construction of their sacred temples.

In considering the serpent deities and their dissemination it can be noted here that among the Desanas' far northern compatriots, the Kogi, or Kagaba, a goddess, sometimes identified as the eagle, was said to have laid the Egg of Creation, but where all the many images are generally called the "Mother", Gaulcovang[152]. This serpent was also conceived as a great serpent in the well-known Urobos forms, that is circular and holding its own tail, an image particularly associated with Ancient Greece and India. From the Creation Egg came the nine tiers in the three dimensions of Creation. This appears to fit the image of Hatuibwari who was both male and female, and as a winged deity was both eagle and serpent residing on a high mountain and who taught mankind all the arts and crafts necessary for survival and development[153].

Connections in myth and tradition between the Desana, South America and the Gilbert Islands is of more immediate interest in the Desana name for the eel god, Buime. This name clearly indicates, that not only the eel myth, but other myths are incorporated in this term and prominent also of note in the myths that connect Gilbert Islands and Aboriginal Australia. This name is reflected in the great Polynesian epics connected with these islands indicating that they sailed from their Central and Eastern Polynesian islands to Central and South America and will also be considered further in due course.

The Tribal House as the Maloca and the Ridgepole Myths

The construction of the malocas, or tribal communal dwellings among the Amazonian tribes, follows a structure where the overall plan often follows a traditional orientation to the cardinal points. The construction itself, after the basic orientation, is defined following certain prescribed traditions indicating that the maloca was built to correspond to certain cosmic strictures. Consistent with the phallic symbolism of most of the mythical, religious and philosophic structures it appears that the Desana perceived the maloca itself as the tribal or clan "uterus" and consequently as a model of the universe itself. At the centre of its construction are the "three red jaguars" - the three pairs of large forked posts, making six in total. Connecting these "jaguar" posts are three large lateral beams centrally placed as well as at the two edges and where the longitudinal beams were an integral part of the philosophic structure. The centre of the roof construction was the ridge known as the gumu and this part of the structure is thought to relate to the priest, the kumu - representative of the Sun. Interestingly the ridge beam is considered a divine "ladder" by which the priest is able to ascend in trance to reach his "father" the Sun and it is this beam that represents a World Axis emphasising the cosmic and symbolic associations that the maloca's construction reflects. The inclined rafters forming the sloping members of the roof's construction are identified with the male clan members in the maloca and are called vahsuni having phallic associations reflected by the sloping rafters themselves. When the clan or maloca is threatened wood is cut to reflect these vahsuni and are used against their enemy to defend the integrity of the clan and its sacred home. The roof cladding is formed of woven palm leaves and is considered to be the reflection of the "Owner-of-the-Roof", Milu-mahse[154].

After the completion of the maloca, and following the purification and protection rituals, trees are planted as perches and "look-out posts" for the Ancient Eagles. It is believed that these mythical eagles fly down from their perches when the paye undertakes rituals to rid the maloca of illness and they are thought to throw a net around the illness so that it can be ejected and then throw the net into the Milky Way[155]. The cosmically based construction of the Tukano Desana maloca resembles temple structures or communal houses in Polynesia and Melanesia and the phallic references to the rafters reflects much that even contemporary researchers admit is reminiscent of the far west on the other side of the Pacific Ocean. In the construction of the maloca, the vahsuni, the sloping rafters were duplicated in smaller replicas and were made and painted red when used for war. Similar ideas are noted to occur among the Abelam and Iatmul tribes in New Guinea by accredited researchers and historians[156]. However, characteristically among more recent historians, although the parallels are recognised with the Western Pacific Island cultures, no attempt to validate probable connections is advised or undertaken.

The Gilbert Island Manabea and the Sacred Ridgepole

In an earlier work[157] it has been noted that there are myths relating to the ridgepole of the sacred temple in the Gilbert Islands that have their parallel with those in the Popol Vuh, the sacred book of the pre-Conquest Quiche-Maya in Guatemala[158]. In a myth, Bue, where this Gilbert Islands' hero is almost certainly the origin of Baime among the Desana, is the local version of the great fire deity of the Polynesians Maui and the myths surrounding him will be of some interest later in this section.

The construction of the sacred temple in the Gilbert Islands was the responsibility and privilege of two clans in its building according to ancient tradition - the Ababou and the Maerua, and the kings they served were those of Karongoa[159]. It is the clans forming these three groups who held the secrets associated with the rituals relating to the Sun and Moon and these were performed in the temple to ensure a good pandanus harvest[160]. Bue, the mariner hero, is particularly associated with the clans of Ababou and Maerua and is said that he sailed under their canoe-crests, or pennants so resembling those known in Asia. It is further said that it was the Sun who gave him the knowledge to layout and construct the Maneaba according to cosmic principles. The sitting places, boti, specified in this tradition, were rigorously prescribed according to these traditions and that of the Ababou was under the middle rafter, kiaro-matua, on the western side, facing that of the Karongoa[161]. In Gilbertese myth the divine ancestor was named Teweia and it was he who is said to have held the secret of the first fruits ceremonies and was the father of the great Karongoan hero and high Chief of the ancestral land of Beru, considered by some to be the island of Beru in Central Indonesia. This deity probably related to Ta'arua, or Tangaroa in the rest of Polynesia and appears to be Taiowa, the hero of Hopi myth in the South West United States. Taiowa of the Hopi and their myths of origin appears to record migration from India across the Pacific to Mexico and then northwards across the Rio Grande[162]. This provides another link between the Gilbert Islanders with the Americas besides the Tukano, and the Desana in particular, but it is the temple itself, the Maneaba, that is of most interest here.

The Maneaba, or temple, is called by the Karongoa clan "the enclosure of the Sun and Moon" and it was believed that any who violated its sacred precincts was dealt with severely by the Sun himself. In the structure of the temple pillar supporting the roof beam in the middle of the eastern side of the eastern side was called the "Sun". Against this pillar the Karonoa-n-nea retained their hereditary sitting place and on the opposite, western wall was the pillar of the Moon where the clans of the Ababou and Maerua were seated[163]. Among the Gilbertese, therefore, the term Ababou may also be separated into Aba and bou where the first is the term also found among the Desana as the prefix for the Moon's name, or Ao-bau: bou being either a corruption of Ao or related to the sacred Gilbertese stone monolith called Boua[164.] This sacred stone was about the height and breadth of a man and stood in the centre of a circle of flat stones. The circle was about twelve feet or about 3.65 metres diameter and the skulls of successive generations of clan elders were buried under the white shingled surface, except that section due west of the Boua since this was reserved for offerings. The Boua represented the deity Teweia who initiated the first fruits ceremony[165], who has elsewhere been noted.

The Gilbertese Maneaba is recorded as being of three types, and given three names, 1) Tabiang, where the breadth and width are about the same; 2) Tabentebike, or Te Tabanin where the building is of equal dimension on all four sides; and 3) Maunga-Tabu whose breath is about two units compared to about three on its length and considered sacred to the Sun[166]. The Maneaba is set up according to a set "Sun" formula and the first timber to be dressed is that for the tatanga or roof plates. The construction begins before noon on a day when the Sun and Moon are seen together in the sky and after the building master has mounted the platform on which it is to be built to intone the sacred chant prescribed for this occasion[167].

When construction is near completion the Ababou and Maerua workers place the ridge-capping and the master again mounts to the ridge and takes with him four coconuts filled with liquor representing human blood. As in India, when trophy heads, Ata, were not available coconuts were used in sacred ceremonies and he anointed the ridge intoning the sacred formulae and chants appropriate for the occasion, and each of the heads is used consecutively as he faces the cardinal points in turn facing first from the north looking south and so on[168]. Standing on the north side facing south is highly reminiscent of Hindu rites where north was the direction of the revered ancestors and where and where priests stood in relation to the fir altar. Interestingly one of the salutes in reverence to the Sun was crossing the hands, called Te Kaanangaroi , and this also is associated with a salutation in cultivating friends[169]. This form of address is also noted of that a similar image found anciently in the fire temples of the early Andean culture at Kotosh in Central Peru (*3.057*). The lion skin ape of the priests of Ancient South Arabia crossed the paws across the chest of the priest in the identical fashion to that of Peru (*3.056*).

The temples of many of the Polynesian islands have now been recognised to be of related planning origin even though local variations and external influences have been assimilated the common elements and these expressed in different ways. Archaeologists in the last two generations have recorded that the altars in particular of Hawaii, Tahiti, Easter Island, Manareva, Tubuai, Pitcairn, Tongareva and the Maoris of New Zealand exhibit a rectangular altar with vertical upright monoliths in wood or stone often carved to represent figure of the heroes and deities[170]. Such low altars, of stone as mounds or dolmens, and surrounded by vertical menhirs, megaliths or carved posts are common in Asia and particularly noted in certain of the aboriginal tribes of India such as the Muria Gonds and the Nagas of Assam and other hill tribes in the Himalayan foothills (*6.104-7*).

The Muria Gonds and their Temple

The Muria and Maria tribes in Central India are sections of the Gond tribes so noted throughout this and an earlier work[171]. They are a tribe among whom the megalithic traditions still survived into the twentieth century and in parallel with many tribes in Melanesia and the Amazon Basin the custom of men's communal houses was still retained. The Halba form a caste of priests among the Muria and ministered to their ancient clan gods[172] called the Anga. It is thought by researchers in the myths of the Gonds that the Anga cult may have originated in divination rites associated with the ritual slaughter of a human male sacrifice[173] much as reflected in the rituals of hepatoscopy, or liver divination in the Ancient Middle East, Indonesia and South America. The most famous of their hero-deities is Lingo and the close connections with the ancient megalithic tradition is obvious since the name is actually that for the male phallus in its symbolic state carved in stone or represented by a natural outcrop or as a found stone reflecting the appropriate shape.

In a main Muria ritual centre called Kabonga the shrines looked like a small village. In the open framed temples the images or representations of the gods were slung high in the roof framework. Verrier Elwin, whose collection of myths and writings on the Aboriginal tribes of India is unsurpassed, and are often the only source for any research material upon the tribes included here, described the temples of the Murias half a century ago. He noted: "At the foot of the central pillar there is generally a flat stone which serves as a seat of the god, and there are several big stones placed together to form a hearth for the cooking of grains and pulses and sacrificed animals" ..... "Outside the temple, there may be a swing with a spiked seat on which mediums can prophesy; there is often a row of wooden pillars, each with a stone before it, to which certain visiting gods can be tied, and their may be a stone for special offerings for the dead." Elwin then utilises a witnessed example from another credible author of a temple in construction, that at Markahera to the deity Bhumiriya, recorded as follows: "The temple is built with nine wooden pillars, fixed in place by the clan-priest who puts iron slag at the bottom of each hole. Bundles of grass called 'gubba' were prepared by the Karanga, a clan akomana (a member of a different clan with whom a marriage can be contracted) to the Wadder clan; mahua flowers and water were offered them and they were tied to the top of the pillars before thatching. The roof was then thatched, but no walls were made. Every ten years the pen-rawar building was renewed"[174].

The special ghotul or sacred men's house associated in myth with the Gond hero, Lingo was said to have had as its central pillar a symbolic "python", and the roof poles were known as "Maha-Mandal snakes", the beam was thought of as a "daman snake", and the cross poles were considered "cobras". The usual bamboo roof framework, was instead of "kraits" (snakes), tied together with vipers and covered with the fantail feathers of the peacock (a symbol of the Sun). The roof of the veranda was made of bulbul feathers, and the walls of bod-fish bones. The door

10.037 : Massive stone megalith sacred to the Nagas. Maram, Manipur, North East India, Pre-20th., century, A.D.

10.036 :
Massive dolmen called the Maikel Stone said to mark the spot where the Naga tribes emerged from the Earth - a tradition of origin similar to those in the Andes. Manipur, North East India, Pre-19th., century, A.D.

was made from crimson silyari flowers, and the doorframes of the bones of ogres and the fastening of ular-malom snakes. The kutul-seats were "crocodiles" and the floor plastered with the flour of urad pulse. The Anga, or temple deity, was represented by the swing suspended from the roof beams by pirpitti snakes[175].

As in the Desana villages where an imaginary fence was considered to surround the village so in the Muria Gond village nails of iron slag were placed in a circle as a protection against an "incursion of magic"[176]. The Desana fence was thought of in terms of a close woven "grating" made of thin sticks called the imiki yaru[177]. This was believed to be in the image of the Sun's rays as a sort of corona.

There is a tradition among the Muria Gonds of India that a man may metamorphose into a were-jaguar and similar beliefs are found among the Malay tribes and in the Amazon Basin tribes[178]. This utility was attained by the man going to an ant-hill and circling around it seven times in a clockwise direction muttering the particular mantra associated with this rite. This is done each time he wishes to attack a victim and when done he repeats the circling to regain his human shape. In the Desana myths ants are also noted as containing male fertilising component, along with honey, although it was forbidden to eat both of these at the same time[179].

Among the Murias also is found the tradition of stilt-walking during the rainy season and although it is conjectured to be associated with growing crops it may have been a throwback to days when the tribes were located in swampy lands and required to elevate themselves above the dangers that lurked under the water surface. It is known that stilt-walking was found traditionally among the Marquesas Islanders in Polynesia and the Angami, Ao, Kuki and Kachari Nagas of Assam, all of whom have other cultural links with the Gonds, Kols and Mundas of India suggesting closer contacts in more ancient times[180].

The special construction of the temples of the Muria Gonds reflects that of the Gilbert Islanders where important aspects, particularly the placement of the deities or their ancestral descendants are similarly centrally located in at each. The term Anga, for the Muria cult, suggest the culture-bearing heroes well-known in Fijian myth as the Nanga, and these latter have long been associated with India by earliest historians[181]. Some authorities have connected the rites of this cult in Fiji with the Kurnai of South East Australia[182]. It is likely that the temple clans associated with the Gilbertese temple derived directly from those associations in the region of the Muria Gonds. The term for the ritually acceptable member who prepared the sacred grass for the temple was Karanga reflected in the Karongoa clan in the Gilberts. The Gilbertese Maerwa are surely the clans of the Muria themselves and the Ababou are probably the Ao Nagas who exhibit so many closely similar aspects of culture both with the Gonds, Bhuiyas and Mundas of India and those of Indonesia and Polynesia. These Ababou appear to be associated with the term Ao-Ba of Melanesia[183].

On the island of Aoba in New Hebrides (Vanuatu) there were castes operating among the tribes resembling that of the Hindu system in India, and where each had its own hearth, and loss of caste status was incurred if one had to cook on the fire of a lower caste[184]. Earlier researchers noted that the people on this island were "different from these of other islands" being of a lighter colour and with straighter hair reflecting physically some "Mongolian features".

10.038 : A Konyak Naga youth with an artificial trophy head pendant probably intended anciently to represent the Sun. Note the eye outline that is probably related to the Tlaloc imagery in Ancient Mexico. Assam, Early 20th., century, A.D.

10.040 : Inverted V chest mark is the traditional sign of a successful Chang Naga headhunter. Chingmei, Assam, North East India, Early 20th., century, A.D.

10.039 : A warrior from New Britain in the Bismark Archipelago with the inverted V marked on his chest in the manner of successful Naga headhunters in Assam. Papua-New Guinea, Melanesia, Early 20th., century, A.D.

10.041 : Trophy heads of slain enemies believed to be necessary in ensuring a good harvest. The same beliefs were held in Ancient South America. Dyak, Borneo, Indonesia, Early 20th., century, A.D.

They were also noted for their customs resembling those of the Polynesians as well as their cleanliness and intelligence and were also considered "good-looking"[185]. The Polynesian connections were far from superficial since the islands were known as the "Land of Ta-har", this being a local term for the great Polynesian god Tangaroa[186]. Because of the associations the island of Ao-ba with the Polynesian deity Tangaroa it is likely that Ao refers to the chiefly term Au or Ahau, also Hau, Sau and Chau, known throughout Polynesia but also occurring in Central America among the Maya and in South America.

On another island, called Ao-re, tumuli were recorded to exist and the light colour of the skin of the people suggested that they had been part of a megalithic tradition found throughout the islands of Melanesia[187]. In the Solomon Islands the great serpent deity, already noted called Hatuibwari, had its residence on top of the sacred mountain of Hoto was Ao-fa[188]. This indicates again connections with the elevated status of the non-Melanesian tribes who at one time occupied these islands.

In the New Hebrides the islands are known for celebrating the sacred rites of the Maki[189], as well as among the Mapuche of Chile, and it is interesting to note that maki or machis is the name of a shaman in some Amazonian tribes as well as the name of tribal group. Among the Borora Indians in the central Amazon Basin a culture hero noted in one of the myths is named Pari Ao, and it must be remembered that blood analysis has shown probable connections between at least some of the Amazonian tribes and the Polynesians. This tribe will be of further interest in another future publication.

Nagas of Assam and their Sacred Houses

Among the Nagas of Assam there were no temples as such and the sacred religious rites, such as they were, were celebrated within the individual houses where for the Lhota Nagas the sacred house is of considerable of interest because of its ridge construction. Most Naga villages were planned and similarly lining both sides of a road and were extended to form one long street. The house was called the Morung in which an extended family dwelt and was based on a common design where the construction was narrow but very long. In the public space between the houses burials were interred and genna stones were placed for clan rites. The ridge itself was called the "roof tree" and this composed of two very long bamboo trunks and where two of the roots extending from the base were retained. These were laid side by side with the roots of one laid exposed at the front, and the other, adjacent trunk were reversed so that it had its roots exposed at the other end. These roots were arranged so that they form a horn shape rising from the base of the bamboo trunk upward to resemble the horns of the sacred mithan or forest buffalo. A veranda is built from the extended downward turn of the eaves at the front of the house and centrally the carved post supported the front of the "roof-trees" and was called the humtse tachungo. At the base of this post were placed the sacred oha stones dedicated to the ancestral spirits and gods[190]. This construction of the Lhota Naga house appears to have much in common with the Maneaba of the Gilbertese in Central Polynesia and the Desana of Colombia and the bamboo "trees" appear to have been a reflection of the roof ladder symbolised by the ridge of the Desana maloca. The ringed sectional appearance of the bamboo trunk is reminiscent of a ladder and in many parts of South and South East of Asia trunks are "v"-notched to lean at an angle to act as a ladder into platform dwellings (*10.035*).

The connections between the Nagas of Assam and the Pacific Ocean peoples has long been noted in several many books written on their culture and the ornamental barbed spear has been considered identical to that found among them Igorots of the Philippines). This type was found among the Anagami Nagas and it is believed that the Ao Nagas used a miniature form as a type of currency, a rare type of Tanglshul dao (*7.053*) that resembles closely that of the Igorot dao also. A stone hammer used by all the Nagas was considered "scarcely distinguishable from a similar one found in the Philippines[191].

The Rites and Beliefs Associated with the Genna, Gehenna or Gahanna

The term genna is a remarkable one since it retained its original expression in terms of meaning and almost exact pronunciation from before Biblical times, being noted in the Bible, through to South America along with other terms and expressions. The Maikael stone (*10.036*) and that at Maram (*10.037*) are believed to mark the spot by the local Naga tribes in the foothills of Assam where the ancestors emerged from a hole in the ground from inside the Earth. It was said that the father of all the tribes was Asu and that he had three sons, Mamo, Alapa, and Tuto[192]. Another tradition from Maram, from the Marring Nagas, however, notes that at least some of the ancestors migrated from the west. Along with this legend there are references to a Biblical-type Great Flood and the prohibition of eating pig's meat suggesting that these tribes were in part descended from migrants from the Ancient Middle East. The couple who survived the Great Flood had two sons, Kela Sangmuk and Maram Pungsa, the elder went to Kachar and the younger founded the village of Maram with its impressive megalithic stone. From Maran Pungsa sprang the four sons who gave their names to the four clans at Maram[193]. In creating distinctions in clothing and means of dressing to separate the various tribes the men tied their hair in a brow knot and the women tied theirs behind the head[194]. This section of the Naga myths bears close similarities to those of the Incas and the Aymara where hairstyles clothes and even the colour the people wore were predetermined by the Creator and reflects their descent from the four brothers. The name for the place of origin was Haubum Maruk where "Hao" means Naga, and "bum" is an old form of "adjectival suffix" and Maruk is another form of Maru, meaning "source" or "origin"[195].

Similar to the Inca also are the references to cave origins reflected in a Naga myth with variations among the Thado Nagas. These references are to a horned deity emerging from a cave to defeat a beast as they themselves emerged from their own cave of origin. In one myth, recording the birth of a young man who became chief from one of two eggs lying in a paddy (rice) field, the relation is reminiscent of the oral tradition among Aboriginal tribes in India and the Pariacaca myth in Peru[196].

The term for a headman was Khullakpa or Genna-bura and he was associated with the magical and religious rites of the village. All who are mentally less able, or physically blemished or deformed, are precluded from the position[197] and this tends to suggest that this position has descended from Ancient Middle and Near East traditions where such strictures were applied rigorously and are still applied by those such as the Mandaeans. The Marrings worshipped the deity

Taiaru, and it is interesting to note that this deity may also have its origins in the early form of the Mandaean Tuasa; and the Yazidi Tawus; the Gilbertese Teweia; Tahitian Taiau, and the Hopi Taiowa[198]. The Taiaha is the Maori sacred ceremonial spear and these are identical in form to those of the Nagas, and of the Maya, and probably relate to this Naga deity named Taiaru.

The term genna means "forbidden" or "prohibited"[199] and parallels, at least in several practices and observances, the Polynesian term tabu or "taboo", hence applied to sacred stones and ceremonials presided over by the headman or gennaburi among the Nagas. The gennas were frequently associated with warrior rituals and headhunting and special cloths were worn by the warriors when they had completed all the gennas that the highest status man could achieve. A cloth associated with men was called the Aghao-pucho suggesting that this is connected with the poncho of South America and the name for cloth itself was api[200]. The gennas appear essential to village life and the builder of a house observed a genna, or prohibition on feeding, or even speaking to anyone for three days who enters from outside the village[201]. The posts supporting the ridge beam of the house of the Sema Nagas is called the genna post, and this is usually carved with many symbolic designs often of horned mithan heads[202]. The mithan is the sacred forest buffalo and any birth among the herds or domestic cows incurs a 3-day genna also[203].

The principal gennas are associated with headhunting and these are termed aghucho when hostilities are initiated and aghupfu when a successful outcome is celebrated. These gennas are focused upon stones usually found lying around near the chief's house which are identified by their being black, round, water-worn, and divided across the middle by a vein of white quartz or similar. Failing this exact type stones of unusual shape or colour may be substituted. The stones associated with the aghucho genna were less specific and appear to be any water-worn black stones of unusual shape and particularly those resembling a human head[204]. It was believed that these stones could breed resulting in smaller stones and that these could also, in turn, grow up and breed into further generations. Characteristically, warriors who had been on a successful headhunting trip returned ritually "unclean", being contaminated with the blood of their enemies, but they were also considered holy and therefore genna. Such aspects of ceremonial beliefs have their close parallels among the Indonesian, Melanesian, Polynesian and Amazonian tribes although some historians do not entirely agree. In some cases the genna used against a person in what might be termed black magic rites resembles the applications used by Gonds and other Aboriginal Indians as well as the voodoo of the West Indies[205]. The men who were considered to be able to deflect spears and missiles from their enemies among the Angami Nagas by magical practises were called Zhumma[206], and this name sounds perhaps a little too similar to Zume, Xume and Tume in Colombia to be coincidental.

Just as the South American trophy heads were suspended by cords so among the Nagas the most pre-eminent warrior in the village bored the hole through the top of the skull and this was called the akutsu-kegheheo or "head-hanger"[207]. The warriors had to undergo prescribed rites to cleanse themselves after a headhunting foray so that did not attract vengeful spirits into the village. They were required also to perform other ceremonies to feed the spirit of the decapitated soul to mollify the indignity he had suffered. There can be little doubt that these same traditions were as a result of diffusion from a common source, but, as South American history is pushed back further onto the past, it is uncertain whether the custom originated in South America or was transferred from the Old World into the new, since it is a tradition that goes back several millennia in Asia and South America. It is unlikely to be coincidence that trophy heads were an important item in the ritual display of victory and these were worn hanging as large pendants around the neck in the exact manner of those depicted of the Maya and Ancient Peru (*11.054-6*). Gennas were also performed in association with stone-draggling, chisu, and was performed by those who have celebrated the rituals associated with pounding paddy. These stones were set up in memory of having performed the many gennas. Stone-dragging was usually done by the young men, or, in some cases by the whole village of the man who is performing the genna. There are a couple of methods used traditionally to move the stones one being to lash the stone to a sledge made from the fork of a tree, and drag it by placing rollers under the frame (*9.018*; *9.021/2*). Another method is to construct a large framework lashing the stone into the middle of it and the stone is then lifted by a large number of young men around its perimeter (*9.020*)[208].

Among the Lhota Nagas stone pulling or dragging is a social genna of great importance and relates to a progressively larger stone being pulled ranking with status and importance of the event up to the most prestigious. The entitlement to drag stones at all is achieved by other gennas such as performing the mithan (ox) sacrifice and it is significant that acquiring smaller stones are associated with these sacrifices[209]. A variant of these rituals is the dragging of two stones and those who are chosen to drag them are entitled to wear a distinctive cloth where in this case the men chosen are from those who have performed the complete series of stone-pulling ceremonies. The full, recognised series of gennas is rarely attained by any man and since status is all in the ceremonials of Naga life to undertake most or all is of great importance celebrated by the wearing of the special cloth informing all of the high status reached. Such is the importance associated with stone-pulling that the person undertaking these tasks never announces it to any except to the elder, officials arranging it and to his best friend[210].

As among the Sema Nagas, the Lhotas use both the sledge and framed structure to move the stones. The reason the full sequence of gennas is not achieved is that the sponsor who is considered the performer must pay the costs. This includes all the labour and feasting associated with the acquisition of the stone for dragging, the pulling of the stone from its original location to its designated and erection of the stone. This has reflections in similar practices noted by Claude Levi-Strauss in South American social traditions. Inevitably there were pigs or bulls sacrificed for the event and the person who presided over this was the Wokchung, the pig-killer priest. When the stone has been acquired and the carriers and frame have assembled two Wokchungs and the performer and all hold the ceremonial axe and make eight cuts to the right and then eight cuts to the left imitating cleaving away the front face of the stone. The stone is then carried, if supported by a bamboo type frame, or dragged, if by a sledge to the front of the sponsor's house and left there temporarily while feasting commences. The following day the Wokchungs direct the carrier to the exact place where the stone is to be erected and the hole dug. Prayers are sung and plantain leaf cups full of the liquor named madhu, similar to those of the Ao Nagas in their pig sacrifices, are passed around. The sponsor's wife and three old women then emerge from the sponsor's house and the four proceed to the hole and walk around it waving one of their feet in turn over the hole each passes and then they proceed back to the house. The women wear cloth that is special to the occasion and before entering the house they wash their faces. The stone is then tipped into the hole and covered with mats and the rest of the day is spent in celebration. The following day the mats are removed and the rite is at its end but during the period of the stone-dragging and the final erection of the stone the sponsor is under genna and must not speak to strangers or eat "unclean" meat[211].

The recognised close similarities in aspects of culture between the Nagas of Assam and the Gonds of Central India have been referred to several times and the latter were well known for their megalithic culture and the erection of monoliths in memory of their ancestors. Eye-witness accounts dating from the middle of last (twentieth) century state: "They drag out the selected stone from its resting-place, and place under it several cross-pieces of wood, and on each side of it a long thick pole, to which the cross-pieces are lashed. The stone is then lashed to the cross-pieces, and the poles are lifted on to the shoulders of the bearers from twenty to thirty in number, and so the journey to the Kotokal begins"[212]. Reserve bearers were always on hand and there

10.043 : A gahanna or stone circle identical to those found in India and Assam and the Andes. Fergusson Island, Melanesia, Late 19th., century, A.D.

10.042 : Stone circle similar to those long known in Eurasia but closely similar to those found also in Indonesia. Naga, North East India, Pre-20th., century, A.D.

10.045 : Stone "Sun circle" found in South Peru created from stone monoliths similar to Melanesia and through to Asia. Sillustani, Southern Peru, pre Inca Dynasty.

10.044 : Group of ancient megaliths forming stone circles in the Naga Hills. Uilong, Manipur, North East India, Pre-19th., century, A.D.

were stops for imbibing mahua liquor made from the flowers of the mahua tree. The mahua liquor is widely favoured among the Aboriginal tribes of India and appears the origin of its use to anoint the stone originally before being transferred in established ritual to the Nagas.

The early Victorian and British Colonial historians noted the close similarities between the material culture and ceremonial practices of the Naga tribes in Assam and those of Indonesia, the Philippines and parts of the Americas. The methods of transporting large megaliths retained by the Nagas into the twentieth century in their stone-dragging ceremonies may well have a common origin with those in the Andean highlands and Peruvian coast. In the surrounding hills at Tiahuanaco, what have been described as "wheel-marks", are preserved in rock surfaces leading some to believe that the Aymara knew the wheel. In fact they are much more likely to have used a sledge of the type the Nagas utilised since driving wheels into, or along wheel ruts is difficult and damaging for wheel-rims but ideal for the sliding movement of the sledge.

In the later half of the twentieth century Karl Luckert perceived that the tradition of the "Y-post", or "horned-posts", and the customs associated with them appear to indicate that those found in the Americas were connected with those known around the Pacific Rim from North Asia to Australia and extending to India and Africa. It is not surprising therefore that the Naga tribes of Assam also exhibit this same tradition and large forked posts were traditionally utilised by them in both a practical, symbolic and religious sense in their social lives. Luckert notes that they are considered to be interchangeable with menhirs[213] by the various cultures in which they are found and this is also the case among the Nagas. This is also exactly the tradition found among the Aboriginal tribes such as the Gonds in India and the Hindu texts still retain the Vedic tradition of the sacrificial post known as the "Yupa". The victim was tied to the post and it is likely that the fork in the tree forming the "Y" was actually, originally intended to be utilised to lash the arms of the victim to prevent his protecting his torso from the strike of the sacrificial knife. The Y-trunk of a tree was of course used in the construction of the house, and particularly the sacred temple, but as has been noted of the Gilbertese Maneaba, human sacrifice was originally associated with its erection and sanctification.

It is not surprising therefore to discover that the Y-post was utilised in more than a constructional sense in South America and the mysterious, and still unexplained, "field" of Y-posts found at Paracas on the South Coast of Peru is unlikely to have been associated with a conventional building[214]. What is known and certain is that this region was known for its headhunting practices and not only have they been found in recent excavations on the Nazca plain but more widely and from earlier times in the Andes and North Coast of Peru. However, representations of this practise are found depicted on their many ceramic examples dating from the late centuries B.C. through to the middle centuries of the first millennium A.D. and at Tiahuanaco into the later part of that millennium. Interestingly the Nazca plain is best known for the so-called Nazca-lines - large geometric designs in the landscape associated with ritual perambulations and probably related to the rainmaking ceremonies on the plains-people. Luckert also notes the similarities to the ground designs of the peoples of the South West United States and compares them to the remarkable ground designs on the island of Malekula. The designs of Malekula and their associated mythology and practise were first reported by John Layard and he also showed that they are virtually identical to those found in South India and these latter he noted in a small, separate publication. It is from Layard's work on the clan systems, related to those of China in Malekula, that Zuidema has clearly derived his inspiration for the clan system theory he developed for the Inca social caste system earlier noted. It is clear that there are close cultural affinities between South America and Malekula extending not only to the four-divisions of the ceremonial village in Malekula of Pete-hul and Cuzco in Peru, but also to the clan system structure along with shared practices such as cranial deformation, trepanation, and associated cultural and mythical references.

The Lhota Nagas erected large forked posts called Tsongzu, and these were up to about twelve feet high (1.650 metres), and often composed of two trunks strapped together rather than a trunk with a fork. These were erected when a suitable stone was not available and illustrates the direct relationship as a substitution for a menhir in megalithic cultures. Other traditions associated with the Y-posts indicate that it was a symbol of the female organ, as the yoni was in Hindu India, while the generality of Naga tribes also associated the Y-posts with prosperity[215].

Among the Ao Nagas the genna represents more a sacred day, than the Polynesian tabu, and was more similar to that of the Lhotas, and others Nagas. It is believed by the Ao that they were in danger of importing illnesses, unwanted spirits who followed them home, and other undesirable influences after they had been away visiting, trading or other reasons for leaving the village. To combat this perceived danger among them a ceremony called the Ao-bi was performed once a year to rid the villages of any baleful influences so engendered. The priest, during this rite, visited each house with a basket into which were thrown the "contaminated" clothing believed to import those influences and he prayed in attempt to exorcise the house and its inhabitants, and these collected items were later thrown into the river. The importance of cloth repeatedly appears in the rituals of the Nagas, particularly those who have traditional long distance trading contacts and have apparent connections with Ancient and Aboriginal India. This appears to have resonance's not with only with the traditional weavings arts of India but through to Indonesia and further eastward to the coastal and Andean peoples of Ancient South America. Similar to some of the Indonesian peoples, and particularly noted among the Moche of North Coast Peru, the Naga ceremonial dress is highly reminiscent of that of the Toradja of Celebes. More particularly the pectorals worn on ceremonial occasions by the Nagas and Toradjas are clearly related also to those of the Moche (*8.052-6*).

The Ao Nagas retained a tradition that there were two Suns[216] and this is so clearly related to that of the Jains of India that there has to be a connection, but it may be that in fact they both have their origins in the Ancient Middle East. Probable contacts with the Ancient Middle East appear to be corroborated in the genna associated with the funeral rites. The sexigesimal (times 60; 1/60) system was a noted development in the Ancient Near and Middle East and at the Naga funeral rites 60 plates of meat and rice and 60 cups of madhu liquor[217] was traditionally dedicated to their associated deity Lichaba.

An ancient custom among the Ao Nagas was that after the funeral rites, the body of the deceased was wrapped in cloth and laid in the outer room of the house on a platform. A fire was lit under it and the body dried over this slow burning hearth until the time of the first fruits ceremony at the beginning of the next harvest. The shrouded body was then laid out on a platform near the village path. In more recent times, however, the bodies were only partly dried and the time for keeping it in the house was limited to seven days for the man and five for the woman and during that time the house was genna[218]. These platforms resemble those found widely in Madagascar, Indonesia, New Guinea and through to North America[219]. With the diffusion of material culture and specific myths such traditional platforms indicate that such practises were diffused by mariners along the oceanic currents that connect these regions.

Similar to the Anagami Nagas practices in particular the people of Mentawei in Western Indonesia, a people connected with sea trade and travel along with the Bontok Igorot in the Philippines, have their "rest" days called pena or punen derived from the Naga genna when all work in the fields was forbidden[220]. The punen is a period of religious festivals and among the Mentawei the temple was called the uma[221] and the name clearly indicates the origin of the name of the Peruvian priest, umu[222]. The priest of the Desana in Colombia was called the kumu, and he was always chosen from the Umu-sipora clan[223] clearly connected to the Peruvian umu. The Dyaks of Borneo did not usually build temples but the house of the headman was known as the Tua-Rumah, where Tuan was the chief and rumah the term of respect for his dwelling[224]. Among some of the Dyaks the supply of miniature grave goods including canoes or boats and miniature woven goods[225], was an ancient tradition and similar customs, were noted among the Chinchorros in early Northern Chile and in the later Andean cultures. The connections between the Indonesian, Malays and the Polynesians has attracted considerable attention and it need not be expanded here except to note that the uma, the house temple of the Mentawei, is the ruma of Polynesia and rumah of the Mapuche in Chile. It is considered acceptable for historians to utilise such linguistic connections to show that Malaysian and Polynesian related languages are connected but it is not considered acceptable to relate by extension such elements to the South American coast. Regardless, these are clearly other elements that has been transferred by ancient mariners following the marine highways along the sea currents of Oceania.

The connections between the Nagas of Assam and the Gonds of India has been repeatedly noted in this work, as they were in earlier studies on these tribes. The Gonds were a megalithic people and particularly notorious for their Meriah sacrifices carried out from the most ancient times and their influence appears similar to some of the Melanesian islanders in the Western Pacific. On Rossel Island stone circles were frequently associated with ancient settlements and these were used as ceremonial seating stone with upright backs in the exact manner known in the Ancient Middle East. These were called as jagega and appears to relate to the similar term found among the Gonds or deriving from the term for Jagga found in the Purari[226] Delta. At the death of a chief a victim was dismembered on the stones and eaten as part of the funeral rituals. The stones in the circle were also associated with trade transactions and as sitting places for the men, and it is probably significant that the stone circle was located a little below high tide level on the coast[227]. This suggests that traders or ancestors were associated with the circle and that it was here that trade with mariners identified with the circle was undertaken. These were probably also ritual exchanges similar to the Kula in the islands off Northern New Guinea and these may have been undertaken and linked to tidal changes of the Moon or yearly seasons observed by mariners. Significantly also was that the stone circles in the D'Entrecasteaux Islands and Milne Bay were called gahana, preserving the link between the Gonds and Nagas in South Asia into the Melanesian Islands.

In New Guinea, and the islands off the coast these gahana were of two types, one for cannibalistic rituals and the other for meeting and debating of tribal issues. Usually a coconut tree stood at the centre of the circle and in the cannibalistic circle the victim was tied to it[228]. At Milne Bay the stone circle composed of a number of stones with one much larger than the other. As so often was the case these circles were usually associated with distant ancestors, mariners or "unknown" people. James Chambers provided an eyewitness account of one circle being used in the second half of the nineteenth century[229] and some tribes or clans claiming to have continued the tradition into the twentieth century. However most of these circles appear not to have been used in living memory when the first researchers entered the islands at the beginning of the twentieth century.

Mummification in Tradition from the Nagas of Assam to South America

In has been noted that the Ao Nagas, among others who dried their dead and kept them in a mummified form, after drying the corpse over a fire, wrapped it in a cloth and placed the mummified body in the house with the living. It has been noted that the Andean peoples also kept the dried bodies of their ancestors and secreted them in specially constructed shrines or in their own houses. The Incas and clan leaders paraded their dead on litters or platforms on festival days . The Spaniards were appalled at such "heathen" practices and such customs are likely to have been only marginally unacceptable to Western tastes generally to this day.

The practise of drying the body of the deceased, almost invariably the men only, was known from Asia through the Pacific Islands to South America. The Ao Nagas wrapped the corpse after death in clothes and in one of the outer rooms of the house laid it upon a platform and lit a slow-burning fire under it to dry it. The dried corpse was then kept in the house until the next first fruits ceremony and then it was placed on a platform expressly constructed outside the house for the purpose[230]. In Melanesia, in the Solomon Islands, mummifications rituals occurred where incisions were made in the body and then a fire to dry it was placed nearby. The body was sometimes packed in wood shavings suggesting another form of preservation and placed in a canoe and stowed in a cave[231]. One island was often more sophisticated in its practices relating to the preservation of the body while on others only memories are recorded in myths and legends. On the island of Malapa there was noted in a myth that immigrants from other islands brought mummification practices with them[232]. Perhaps more similar to the Peruvian practices were those in the Gilbert Islands where the dried mummy of the deceased was kept in the north gable of the house[233]. Even more similar to Peruvian practises was that of the Samoans who called their process of mummification, Ole fa'a-Atua-lala-ina, meaning "made into a sun dried god"[234].

Further east in Tahiti Captain Cook recorded at length many of the customs as he witnessed them when visiting the islands in 1789 A.D. and among the descriptions given are those of corpses hanging from the rafters of the funeral hut[235]. In Nicaragua, the culture denoted the Rama is noted for their tribal leaders and other men of rank, at death, being dried over a fire, embalmed and then kept in the palace or chief's compound - the same practice found in Polynesia and South America[236]. This is clearly the identical, and well-known custom of the Inca and it is known that this dynasty preserved at Cuzco the mummies of the Incas (*6.125*) and their wives as well[237]. In Peru a curious symbolic relationship in more recent times it is attested that the term for a potato that is alternately frozen and thawed for long term storage is ch'uno, the same term as that for the dried ancestral mummies. The ancestors are related in Ancient Peru to the north and this appears to confirm the direction of origin for the first Incas into South America either from Ecuador, indicated in the Inca Origin myths, or from Central America. The same direction was associated with the ancestors of the Ancient Vedic Aryans and Buddhists in India but was identified as such with the North Pole paralleling similar beliefs in Ancient Central America and Mexico.

It is clear that special terms for sacred events, festivals and periods of cleansing and contamination have been introduced into the Pacific Region directly related to the ocean currents as the marine highway washing the shores of the surrounding Pacific Rim continents facilitating dispersion of many aspects of Asian culture. From there, although much less applied in their original terms, this dispersal can be traced into South America and preserved more nearly in their original form in the Amazon forests, and to a more modified degree in the Andean regions. On the South American coast they appear to undergo their greatest changes and adaptions since there all cultural developments are affected by the import of succeeding influences and these in turn were assimilated and adjusted to suit the long history of cultural development on the coast of Ecuador, Peru and Chile.

The Tehuba, Dahu, and Status Stool as the Dahu in Transfer from Assam to Peru

Among the Ao Nagas in Assam the term used for a man's spirit double was tiya and in Polynesia it was tii[238]. Among other Nagas wooden statues were erected as effigies to accommodate the souls of the deceased and among the Konyak Nagas the skull was placed on top of the effigy so that his soul could pass from his body to the effigy as a more complete copy of himself. When an Angami Naga died too far from his home for his body to be brought back home some of his hair was returned and attached to a wooden image of himself and his vital essence was believed to infuse the statue during the funeral rites in his memory[239]. The Polynesian tii is also accommodated in a wood or stone image for the soul to reside in, is given due worship, and "fed" in the same manner as were the carved figures among the Nagas.

It has been noted that the Angami genna, also penna and Sema Naga pini, was similar to the Polynesian tabu, or anglicised taboo, and that it occurred in Indonesia and similarly among the Mentaweai and Philippino Igorot Bontoc as pena or punen. The Malay equivalent was buni; the Maori, punipuni, the Tahitian, puni and the Tongan, tapbuni[240]. It should not be surprising therefore to discover that the term for the Naga dahu and tehuba, their ceremonial platforms or sitting places, are reflected in the Polynesian ahu and tahua.

The Naga tehuba was an open air structure either framed or constructed in masonry serving as a ceremonial platform and meeting place for the clan elders and the men of the tribes

10.047 : Massive sacred banyan growing from a platform adjacent to a finely carved stone temple. Gupta Dynasty, Chikka-gudi, Badami, South Central India, 3-5th., century, A.D.

10.046 : Large spreading sacred banyan growing from a stone platform of the type found widely in Polynesia. Chikka-gudi, Badami, South Central India, First millennium, A.D.

or clan. They were often located so that they could be used as a lookout but their main function, since there was no other communal place for congregation such as a temple, was for the clan rituals associated with their ancestors and gods (*10.049*; *10.051*; *10.054*). These were frequently placed in front of, or adjacent to the chief's house since he was the primary functionary for the clan. However, the tehuba most usually was placed opposite the chief's house as a banked-up earth construction, since so many Naga villages were located on the side of hills or on ridges for protection from their neighbours, and this banked structure was faced with stones or delineated by small monoliths[241] (*10.048*). Where the tehuba could not be used as a vantage point a timber structure was erected in place of the earth or stone construction and this was called the daho[242] and this appears to be the prototype for the characteristic dobu, or dubu, found on the shores of New Guinea. Unlike the stone encircled dancing grounds or ceremonial places in Melanesia the head-hunting and sacrificial rites associated with them were reserved in the Angami villages for a special monolith standing a little inside the village gate called kipuche. This stone was held in great veneration and the focus of gennas related to these sacrificial rites[243].

Among the Angamis the tehuba is the site where the deceased kemovos (chiefs) are interred and considered therefore a very sacred place. In all villages there was a tehuba outside the Kemovo's house but clan villages were socially ranked and in dancing festivals the tehuba outside the chief of the highest ranked village was the one chosen when all clans were dancing together and they would progress from that to the lower ranked tehubas in turn. It was considered very unlucky to be performing a dance sequence on the tehuba when it rained and it was thought to presage death[244].

The Dyak Tanju as the Naga Tehuba

In Borneo among the Dyaks the open-air platform used for religious or ceremonial purpose was called the tanju[245] and this appears to derive from the Naga tehuba or Polynesian tahua. Here also

10.048 : Masonry clan seating place and lookout among the Naga tribes called a daho where the Inca's throne in Peru is called dohu. Angami Naga, Jotsuma, Assam, North East India, Early 20th., century, A.D.

10.049 : Clan elders sitting or meeting platform called a daho the same name as the Inca seat or Dohu. Sema Naga, Assam, North East India, Early 20th., century, A.D.

10.050 : Clan or tribal meeting platform called a dubu, clearly derived from the Naga daho or Incan dohu. Motu tribe, Gaile, New Guinea, Melanesia, Late 19th., century, A.D.

10.051 : A traditional tehuba in the form of a stone circle of the type found widely in Melanesia but also anciently in the Andes. This is built over the grave of the legendary first Kemova or ancestor of Khonoma. Naga, Assam, North East India, Early 20th., century, A.D.

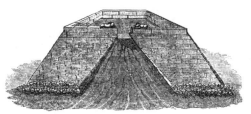

10.052 : Framed and roofed clan meeting platform, also known as a dubu. Kalo, Hood Peninsula, New Guinea, Melanesia, Late 19th., century, A.D.

10.053 : Mounded masonry faced lookout similar to the Angami Nagas stone constructed lookouts. Inca, Huanuco, Central Highland Peru, 1350-1500 A.D.

10.054 : Framed sitting and clan meeting platform doubling as a lookout. Angami Nagas, Kohima, Assam, North East India,Early 20th., century, A.D.

pigs liver were examined in the same way[246] (*11.083*), known as hepatoscopy, as they were among the Peruvians using that of the llama and their entrails[247] anciently and into the present day. In more recent decades in Peru, following the ancient tradition, one form of liver divination was that of a guinea pig (coyu) this being first rubbed on the patient and then examined for a prognosis and portents[248]. Needless to say this form of divination was long known in the Ancient Middle East[249] and clay models have been found illustrating this practise (*11.084*).

Polynesian ceremonial sites were known by several names one of which was marae, meaning "meeting place", and these usually referred to the raised constructions in stone or were elevated mounds of compacted earth that were stone faced. There are usually located near the shores along the coasts of the Polynesian Islands. Similar platforms are known as tahua or tohua[250] in the Marquesas Islands and heiau in Hawaii. In the Southern Marquesas, Tuamotu, the Society Islands and Austral Islands the term ahu referred to the ceremonial raised platform at the end of a ceremonial court, whereas in the Northern Marquesas and Easter Island it meant the whole ceremonial precinct[251].

The tohua as the ceremonial platform as it was called in the Marquesas, was considered the property of the chief, similar in context to the placement of the tehuba next to the chief's house among the Nagas. In these islands it was considered the place for sacred feasts and dances which was usually associated with a temple. Near these temple platforms, banyans were grown[252] and these too were considered sacred and suggests that this practise is so closely similar to that found in the villages of India that the tree and the custom were imported from there (*11.046/7*). In more specific cases the Marquesan dance floor is called the tohua and the surrounding platform was called the paepae[253]. The tohua was often paved and more or less a rectangular shape, sometimes of great size, and was adjacent to one or more platforms, or in larger centres was surrounded by them[254]. In the early part of the twentieth century Craighill Handy recorded in his researches into Marquesan history and culture a description of the tohua: "...On the dance area there was frequently, if not always, a special place marked off by stone slabs set on edge for the choirs of old men who chanted. Hii Tohua is given by Dordillon as meaning seated on stones around the public place, Tuu, as being the name of the square place surrounded by red tufa (lava) stone where rites over sacrifices were performed. There were stone backrests (kepo) against which chanters leaned. On the paved area itself were sometimes special small platforms on which a chief or chiefess sat. On the platforms at the times of festivals temporary houses were erected, different platforms and different parts of platforms being reserved for special purposes. At one end of, or on one side of the area was a place of sacrifice (me'ae = marae) on which stood the house of the high priest (tau'a) and where the priests and their assistants performed their rites. Opening on the feast place (tohua) or near to it was always the chief's house; and on or near it was the warriors' tapu house. Theses dance areas were regarded as the property of the tribal chief, and as such constituted community centers for the tribe"[255].

One of the most important rites to be held at the tohua was the ceremony called the Hakahe'e or honouring for the first born male and female child[256]. This rite bears strong resemblances to the rites in the Ancient Near and Middle East where the first-born son was regaled with special celebrations. During the frequent wars in the Marquesas Islands it was required that the women slept on the tohua or dance floor for the period of the battle until the outcome was known[257]. The warriors' tapu or tabu house appears to have served the same purpose to isolate the warriors after they had become stained with the blood of battle for a period to ensure cleansing rites to prevent the angry souls of the defeated to enter and wreak havoc in the settlement. This so closely resembles the Naga tradition, noted earlier, that it is likely to have a common origin - the same custom existing among Amazon tribes[258]. Even the drinking from the skull of the decapitated enemy[259] resembles that of the Nagas and Tantric practices in India (and West Mexico) where the sawn upper cranium so used was known as the kapala. For a single individual who was in tapu a raised stone platform at the back of the house was called the Ahu Tapu and here the individual was closeted until the necessary time period and associated rites had passed[260].

In New Zealand the colonising migrations had left Central Polynesia before the development of the stepped pyramid and before the succeeding transition that saw the ceremonial platform type change from ahu to marae[261]. The platforms of the Maori therefore were more in the tradition of the earlier Polynesians and retained the name of ahu or tuaha. In Central Polynesia the great marae of Raiatea overbuilt on an older platform was 141 feet by 24 feet wide and 12 feet high and was called the Tapitapuatea marae. This was erected in the early part of the second millennium A.D. and constructed of very large blocks of coral limestone set on their ends reminiscent of the construction techniques at Tiahuanaco. An even more exceptional structure was that of the great step pyramid of Mahaiatea of Tahiti, this being located in a court 377 feet on the longest side and 267 feet wide, where the ahu platform measured 267 feet long and 87 feet wide. The final structure was a building composed of 10 steps and said to have been completed a little before Captain Cook's visit in 1769 A.D. but tragically was completely demolished after 1798. Fortunately this occurred after the visit of Captain Wilson who sketched the pyramid in its final glory[262]. Other less well-known stepped pyramids existed in Tonga (*6.098*) and these would suggest that they are related to the fall of Tiahuanaco in the 11th., century A.D. and diffusion from that time into the Polynesian islands.

It is likely that the Maoris themselves were in the vanguard of those who left Peru, and Bolivia and Ecuador, perhaps before the final collapse, and travelled to Tahiti and then onwards through Polynesia to New Zealand rapidly enough to retain many aspects of their original designs and crafts so clearly related in these islands to those of the Incas and Peru. The Maoris were one of the few peoples to have cultivated the sweet potato, a native of South America and this tuber was clearly developed and acclimatised early to allow local varieties to develop. It has been suggested that the Maori peoples left Central Polynesia, or Tahiti, about 1350A.D. and this date corresponds to the conventional inception of the Inca dynasty in Peru[263]. New Zealand was earlier occupied by another Polynesian people, the Morioris, referred to elsewhere in this and other publications[264].

On Easter Island itself there are striking similarities in the construction of the oldest of the stone platforms, Vinapu in particular, and the masonry of Tiahuanaco especially at the time period in which they were built coincides with that of Tiahuanaco and its empire (*9.051*; *9.049/50*). The subject is highly controversial but there are many more comparisons to be made than just the platforms since stone carvings in some cases are virtually identical, the totora reeds found on Easter Island and in Lake Titicaca are identical, and reed boats of the Andean type are identical to those of the Maori (*2.025-30*), along with related terms that are also similar.

In Melanesia, on the large island of New Guinea, there are many references to Asian cultures and among the Abelam, inland from the coast, unusually shaped stones were believed to the incarnations of the Wale, or spirits of the streams and springs[265], similar to beliefs in Peru and the Nagas of Assam. Among these same people the dancing ground was the centre of ceremonial life, as it was in Polynesia, and this was named the amei. These Wale (warlay) appear to correspond to the Wagan among the tribes living in the upper reaches of the Sepik River. The Wagan were the spiritual beings claimed as their ancestors or pre-existent beings by the Iatmul tribe and their myths and culture indicate that they had migrated from the coast. Among them also "floating islands" in the lakes of the highlands were said to be the work of Agwi[266] and this appears to be a variation of the Vedic Indian deity of fire, Agni, who ruled volcanic uprisings from the sea. Other highland tribes claim heroes clearly derived from abroad and the Kai claim a hero named Mau around whom myths clearly similar to those of the Ambat and Kabat in the New Hebrides are wound. It has been shown that these Ambat are the megalithic peoples clearly originating, or having a common origin among the Mundas and Bhuiyas of Central India[267]. In the New Hebrides also Mau is clearly recognised as Maui, the Polynesian fire-god, and Taghar is the local version of the Polynesian Tangaroa. Among the Iatmul there is a culture-hero named Mwaimnanggur[268] who is almost certainly the culture-bearing Nanga of the Fiji Islands and probably derived from the village deity - Anga, of the Gonds or Naga of Assam.

The designs produced by these people have long fascinated anthropologists and it is now accepted that the Sepik River region was an intermediate staging-post connecting Southern China and the Maori of New Zealand. The non-Melanesian speaking Arapesh tribe were similar in many respects to the Iatmul and with whose language their appeared to be common origins. The Iatmul and Abelum also shared common cultural references and the name of their dancing ground, amei appears to be derived in common from the Polynesian marae, while that of the Arapesh was named agehu[269], clearly derived from the alternate, and earlier names, ahu and tahuba or tohua, derived from the Nagas of Assam. Defining the agehu were stone monoliths associated with the ancestors and outside the perimeter medicinal shrubs and trees were grown, and some for dyes, associated with the magical rites to be performed within the dancing ground itself. The men's house and coconut palms were also located on the grounds, and around the foot of the palms there were raised small mounds[270]. The ancient cultivations throughout highland New Guinea have raised speculation as to their age and organisation. It is now known that there were raised fields in the highlands dating from about 7000 B.C.[271] and among the later residues at these sites the sweet potato has been found, following the so-called "Kumara Line" from its native South America[272], the date uncertain, but in any case, long before European contacts in recent centuries. It is interesting to note that this was a similar system of cultivation so successfully used around Lake Titicaca during the Tiahuanaco epochs and that is being reintroduced in test beds nearby at the present day.

The Roro-speaking tribes of New Guinea exhibited many Polynesian influences. The sacred clubhouse, a substitute for a temple, was called the marea, clearly a reference to the Polynesian marae[273]. The dobu or dubu was claimed to have been first introduced by the Sinaugolo people and spread from them to other tribes. The myth associated with the dubu states that, "... when the Sinaugolo came forth from their ancestral cave on the slopes of Mount Taborogoro, they had with them one carved post and taking this as their model made three others like it, and these posts became the corner posts of the first Sina-ugolo dubu in their village on Taborogoro"[274]. The front right post was considered the most important of the four and this probably derives from the origin myth of the ancestral Sina-ugolo[275], each was named, and this front one was named vamaga varo. The next most important was the left front post named vaga varo; then the back right post named dura vainaga and finally the left back post called dura vaga[276].

10.055 : Spirit seat reminiscent of similar spirit chairs among the Huichol and other Amerindian peoples. Guriu, Papua-New Guinea, Melanesia, Early 20th., century, A.D.

10.056 : A traditional Huichol spirit chair found into the 20th., century in Western Mexico and similar in principle to those in the Western Pacific Islands. North West Mexico, Early 20th., century, A.D.

As in Naga myths there are alternative myths stating that these Roro-speaking people emerged from a hole in the Earth on the other side of Mount Taborogoro. A group of these tribes possess not an open dubu (*10.050*) but a closed one resembling a house called a koge and is otherwise known by Europeans as a steeple temple[277] (*10.052*).

Turtles were sacred to the dubu and when eaten in sacred rituals the skulls were painted red and attached to the front end of the ridgepole, but the turtles were not eaten by the chief suggesting that this was the chiefly line's totem at one time[278]. Carved heads higher on the posts probably indicate that trophy heads and ritual sacrifice were previously essential to the rites of the dobu, at least in its sanctification[279]. Among the Elema people and Motu-Motu it was said that the supreme deity Semese lived in the sky with his wife, Kauue, and a younger brother. His sons were Hiovaki and Semese, although some versions give them as two brothers. Hiovaki descended from the sky to make the land, the sea, and to plant the tree. He cut down a coconut tree and made from it men and women. He then built separate houses for the men and women and the dubus were then designated as men's sleeping areas and small houses were allocated for the women. The deity's son then returned to heaven and it is believed that fighting men who died in battle went to live with him in the sky[280].

This myth indicates clear influences from Polynesia where Hiovaki is clearly a misinterpretation of the sacred land of the ancestors Havaiki, and Kauue is clearly Kaua, another Polynesian deity. The dubu was considered sacred and to it on certain occasions the spirits (sua) came and where the men of the village resorted to sit and discuss clan issues[281]. There were few examples that remained at the beginning of the twentieth century and those that had survived were disappearing quickly through lack of ceremonial usage at that time[282].

The Dahu and the Incan Tiana in Ancient Peru

In Ancient Peru it has been noted that the term tahua meant four and that in its application in the Inca term Tahuatin-suyu, the name for their Empire, it mean the four parts[283] but is a term that appears to have a direct common origin with the tuaha of the Maoris and the tahua or tohuba of the Marquesas. Soon after the Spanish Conquest of Peru Bernabe Cobo noted that the houses of the people were not furnished with tables and chairs and that the people sat on the ground on mats, a Polynesian custom. Stools and seats were reserved as an indicator of status for the chiefs and priests and these were called duho[284], a term almost the exact name used by the Sema Naga for their communal ceremonial platform and sitting place, the dahu, and identical to the Angami Naga, tehuba. When a person died in the Inca Empire most tribes buried their dead in a seated posture and this closely resembles the custom of seated burials among the Saivite Hindus but where in India also the Vaishnavite Hindus usually cremate their dead. It the deceased was a chief, or cacique in Peru, he was placed on his stool, or duho, and entombed seated along with wives and retainers[285].

Status, Stools and Benches

Many of the South American tribes considered the stool the prerogative of the chiefs and priests, although some such as the Tukano also extended its use to men and boys more generally. The

Tukano called the stool sea-peno and it was carved from a single block of wood. It was believed to aid concentration and was a symbol of stability and wisdom. The four legs were painted yellow and symbolised the seminal power of Ahpikondia, the ancestral world, the flat seat the Earth. The seated chief or priest therefore formed a cosmic representation and it was he who was the means of communication with the ancestors and deities in Ahpikondia[286]. The stool therefore formed a microcosm of a fairly conventional mythical perception of the earth being supported by four pillars. The seated priest, the kumu, under the ridge beam of the maloca was considered a potent line of communication between the Sky being, including the Sun, and those on the Earth and in a continuous line of communication with the ancestors in which he was placed as the central and pivotal lynch-pin[287]. In other Amazonian tribes the stool was referred to as the "Divining Stool" and strictly forbidden to all except the chief or the priest[288]. The Zurinas located on the Amazon itself were renown as expert stool craftsmen and for their carvings[289]. The revered stool and its use is connected with the ancestors and deities closely resembled the long traditional seats for priests at the foot of pillars and menhirs when they were required to communicate with their ancestors or gods thought to inhabit these stones.

The stool in Inca society was exclusively the prerogative of the Inca and symbol of his authority and power throughout the Empire[290]. This traditional right appears to have been allowed for the approved local chiefs, noted by Cobo, and called the dohu - the same name found among the Nagas of Assam. The Inca stool for the ruler, called more specifically the ti-ana, was made from solid gold, had a curved seat, and was placed on a large square gold "board" or plate for official occasions[291]. This name and the prefix ti referring to the deities and gods appearing to be derived directly from the Aryan heritage of Ancient India.

In Central America early Spaniards noted the special significance of the stool in the rituals of the Indians and there it was noted that "certain cloths" were associated with these stools and their "devil" was represented carved on the stools[292]. Stone carved stools were also widely found in the cemeteries of the Talamanca district in Costa Rica at Guetar, and in Panama[293].

Carved stools, as elements of social status virtually duplicated those found in South America and in Tahiti these were called iri or nohorea[294]. Those in Tahiti and among the Tongans were often four-legged, as the Desana were, and also carved from a single block of wood[295]. One of the stools, said to have been used in the legendary canoes that transported the ancestors to Samoa, was seen by early British missionaries who noted that it was sprinkled with holy water on ceremonial occasions. Included in the canoe was one of the skulls of those ancient people[296]. The wooden stools of the Melanesians tended to follow closely those of the Polynesians and these were shown to have been as much for the purpose of providing the ancestral spirits a place to sit as the living chiefs and priests (*4.092-9*). The Iatmul tribal myths and legends indicate that their stools were once made of stone and associated with the cult of the dead as they were in the islands of Indonesia[297]. This is also believed to be the case for the stone thrones found on the coast of Ecuador and known as the Manteno culture on the Manta coast and suggests direct contact.

In Nias, an island south of Sumatra in Indonesia, every village has stone seats erected for the spirits of their ancestors to sit on and they are also located in the forests and beside streams and springs. In the south of the island the bench is called daro daro and in the north

10.057 : Stone seat, the udamgarya, defining chief's status and priority in clan meetings characteristic in Ancient India and also in the Pacific Islands to South America. This group of elders forms the traditional Panchayat or clan council. Hill Maria Gond, Itulnar, Central India, Early 20th., century, A.D.

behu and harefa[298]. It is likely that behu and daro daro were simply modified pronunciations of dahu or dohu derived from their closely allied cultural relations the Nagas of Assam. On an island where the burial of chiefs consists traditionally of placing them in canoes, to assist in their return across the sea to the land of the ancestors, it is fair to assume that such traditions were introduced from abroad[299]. Many of the traditions of Nias were reflected among the tribes on the mainland of Sumatra and there a wooden ceremonial seat was called a pepadon, with the head of a bird, dragon or elephant carved on it where a tradition associated it with high status. This status was acquired as follows: "Formerly a pepadon might only be erected after a man had cut off four heads. These heads were struck against the bench and later kept in a chest under the seat. The jaws of the wooden animal's head were smeared with blood. In Kroe the seat was called krosi boelampok; it was placed on a great stone, around which was hung a drapery with the picture of a ship. The tribal chief and his wife were brought to the festal grounds in a wooden ship on wheels (a similar custom was known in China). The prow had an animal head, usually that of a rhinoceros bird, an elephant or buffalo. In the middle of the ship was a baldakin, on which was paced a rhinoceros bird or a serpent made of cloth. To the right and left were poles decorated like trees, - on the branches hung heads, shells, little pots, pieces of cloth, coins delicacies, etc."[300].

From this description seats or stools were as central to the conspicuous display of status as they were in the Pacific islands through to South America. It is also obvious that the stool was here associated with the four cardinal points reflected in the four trophy heads and the World Tree imitation as an essential element in this ceremonial boat. As in Nias the fact that the whole symbolic display was conveyed in a boat suggests that the ritual was the importation of mariners peoples from outside Sumatra.

It is clear from even a cursory study of the maritime culture of Nias that it was greatly influenced from India and the Nagas of Assam but also shows clear references to the broad culture of the Polynesians and consequently to that of Amazonia and Andean South America. In Assam it has been shown that the Nagas erected male and female stones and in Celebes the same practise was found as well as further East into Melanesia. The stone seats in Celebes consisted of the seat proper, being considered female, and the back or vertical member associated with it was the male. The menhir, or the vertical male stone, was considered to conduct fertility from the ancestors who possessed or visited the stone to the earth and were therefore due offerings and tokens of gratitude by their descendants[301]. In Minahassa in the north of Celebes, at the foot of a hill named Tonderukan, a stone was called watu rerumeran ne empung, or the "seat of the empung". This expression empung is translated as "the great or mighty spirits" and the whole expression has been translated as "the stone upon which the gods are accustomed to sit"[302]. The term watu for stone is a variation for the more usual batu in Indonesia and is the local adaption from the Middle Eastern bat, baetyl or bethel and is found in all these variations in Aboriginal Australia. The variation watu is related to the early Middle Eastern term Wad, Wadder and Odde and anciently share a common origin with bat along with other derivatives in India.

Among the Nayar, a high status warrior caste Tamil people in South India, the bridal couple were arrayed on stools during their marriage ceremonies, but these were of a three-legged type[303]. However, it was strictly forbidden, when the astrologer was examining the horoscopes of suitable marriage candidates, to sit on a stool[304]. The Todas were also known for their ceremonial seats and these were called kwottun[305]. The keeper of the sacred Toda dairy hut was called the Palol, and he was only allowed to eat his food while seated on his special stool just outside the dairy entrance indicating the high degree of ritual function and special focus that the stool accrued over many centuries[306].

Inevitably, stools reserved for the men were found among the Gonds and during the ceremonies and festal occasions they usually sat on designated stones. During these ceremonial occasions the headman, or Gaita, sat on the Uddamgarya, constructed of a flat stone raised on stone legs[307] (*10.057*). At the burial ceremonies among the Hill and Bison-Horn Marias, tribal sections of the Gonds, a menhir was erected in memoriam of the departed in the kotokal or uraskal, or memorial area. Other divisions erected a wooden post and a hana-garya seat for the departed along with the appropriate offerings[308]. Among the Sema Nagas in Assam, when a man died his stool, the alaku, it was wrapped in cloth and buried with him. It was believed that during life his essence naturally permeated the stool and it was necessary to ensure that it was available for him in the next life since it was so completely a reflection of himself and his status[309]. As noted it is among the Nagas that the sacred sitting place was called the dahu or dohu the exact name for the stool in Ancient Peru. However, this term dohu or dahu may have been introduced from Peru in a counterflow at the fall of Tiahuanaco or more generally in several influxes of mariners, who were themselves of ancient mariner descent. It is possible therefore that the original in South Asia, was tehuba, related to tahua in the Marquesas because the dohu of Peru before returning as the dobu of New Guinea and dahu among the Nagas.

The Bue Myth in Polynesian Epic Voyages to the Americas
In an earlier publication it was noted that in myths found widely from Asia to South America it was stated that the Sun at one time was too hot[310]. Other variations state that this excessive heat was caused by there being more than one Sun, numbering up to ten in the myths of China. This same myth is found among the Gilbert Islanders (now Kitibati) and this notes that it was the semi-divine hero Bue who pelted the Sun with coconuts to reduce its heat[311]. In another myth Bue is recognised as the local counterpart of the Polynesian fire-god, Maui, and he is said to be a child of the Sun "engendered" by a sunbeam that penetrated his mother Matamona, as she was bathing in a rock pool. Bue, when he grew up, wanted to know his paternity and in response to his demands he was advised to seek his sire beyond the horizon in the far east where his father, the Sun, was to be found. There he was to obtain the power of creating and undoing the power of eclipses and this he was said to have transmitted to his descendants, the clans of Ababou and Maerua. From this myth the right, and that of their hereditary, claimed by the two clans to represent the Sun and Moon in the construction of the sacred temple, the Maneaba. This right is represented and embodied particularly in the central monolith of the five in the temple construction supporting the ridge beam beside which they always sit during ceremonial occasions[312].

Of special interest in this work is the saga relating Bue's great voyage to find his father the Sun, beyond the eastern horizon, where he was informed by his mother he dwelt. His mother had six children by the Sun and Bue was the fifth but the first four were said to have died and only he and his younger sister, the sixth child survived. This sister, named Nei Te-raa-iti, her father the Sun took with him to the east, and there he built a rock enclosure to house her. When Bue had grown up he decided to visit his father so his mother gave him the instructions for the route necessary to be undertaken to find him. Bue built his canoe out of the shell of a coconut, named it Te Kuo-n-aine, and before setting out his mother gave him six items to take with him. These items were two smooth stones of red coral, one fruit of the non-tree, an old fallen coconut, the first leaf of a seed coconut and finally the strong green leaf of the coconut tree and, at the same time, gave him instructions on their use.

Bue was then said to have sped in his canoe to the far east in search of his father, but first visited his sister, Nei Te-raa-iti. He explained to her the purpose of his voyage and she requested that when he had seen his father to return to her on her rock in the sea. Setting out again for the east he finally arrived before dawn at the "side of Heaven where the Sun rises". Bue waited until the Sun began to rise and then sprang into action to "smite" the Sun as he began to rise at "his six mounting-platforms" (kai-ni-katoka), these being "three rocks upon which he began to move up from the depths and three rocks upon which he climbed up over the sea."

As the Sun reached the first rock in the depths below the horizon the first of his rays sprang up into the sky and Bue hurled his first stone of red coral at it and it fell dead into the sea. As the Sun reached its second rock his second ray sprang into the sky and again Bue hurled his second piece of red coral at it and it also fell dead into the sea. As the third ray leapt upward Bue smote it with the fruit of the non-tree and the fourth ray he hit with the old coconut both with the same result. When the Sun reached his fifth rock, a rock above the sea, the Sun burned so fiercely that it scorched Bue's face but Bue was not afraid and he ran forward to fan his father's face with the coconut frond given to him among the other gifts by his mother. As the wind from the fanning blew upon the Sun his heat abated and the Sun "winced" and he spoke to Bue asking who he was and where he came from. Bue declared that he was his son, the Son of the Sun, and told him his name.

The Sun dragged himself up onto his sixth rock - ati-ni-kanenea, the rock of his blazing, but as he was tiring Bue, seeing this ran forward and caught him in the strong green coconut frond. The Sun floated on the sea and Bue bound him and the Sun asked who his mother was, and Bue answered that it was Nei Matamona, and then the Sun asked why he had come to see him and Bue answered that it was to be given cleverness and knowledge.

The Sun gave Bue knowledge and imparted the secrets of the construction of building sea craft (katei-bai). He also taught him the methods and principles of constructing the maneabas of Kings called Te Nama-kaina and of the maneaba called Te Tabanin, and the long maneaba called Maunga-tabu, and finally the maneaba where the breadth is greater than the length called Te Ketoa. The Sun also imparted to him the magic for "raising and stilling the wind" and to make rain. Along with this knowledge was the magic associated with the Moon, called Te Kabueari, giving the ability to protect children, the health of the people and rituals to protect the maneaba and the chants for ceremonials. The Sun also taught Bue the three forms of burial, the first being that for the kings, the second for the people generally and the third being that for those who practised the fructification rituals, this latter being called the "grave of Bue." This was a form of seated burial and resembles that of the probable origin of this rite, that of the seated burial of Siva worshippers in India.

Before Bue left his father the Sun, he was given by him the white staff with three black rings called Te Kai-ni-kamata as a memento of his visit to his father and in memory of him, and told him to attach it to the sail and it would protect him while at sea. This staff and pennant became the crest for Bue's descendants retained by both the Ababou and Maerua clans. His father, the Sun's final gift was to impart the magic to defend himself against "fierce fish" and waterspouts while at sea.

When Bue commenced his return journey he called first at the rock where his sister resided and she left with him when he resumed his journey westward. However, instead of being carried by the canoe they swam beside it and they committed incest as they went. The Sun saw this and was angry and sent the porpoise to overturn their canoe and the brother and sister sank to the land of Mone in the depths of the sea. There they discovered their ancestors and Bue's sister was led away by them to the north while Bue himself travelled west to the enclosure of the old woman known as Nei Bairara.

Bue hid himself in the enclosure since he wished to steal the magic of the old woman and he waited concealed until his father, the Sun had appeared in the west. Bue, being in the Underworld was considered to be in a region that was the reverse of the Middle or Earth World. The Sun, therefore, was considered after setting in the west in the Middle or Earth World, to travel from the west across in the Underworld to the east to rise again there in the Earth world. When the Sun was above the old woman's enclosure, after rising in the west in this Underworld, his father asked her to repeat the spell for the first wind, which she did. She also complied with his requests for her to repeat the spell in turn for the other three winds. In this way Bue learnt by eavesdropping all the spells for the four winds and then was able to reveal himself before departing since he feared his father's reactions should he stay.

Bue travelled on westwards until he arrived at the country of Roro, where he met the old woman named Nei Temaing ("the left-handed"). She was keeper of the rain and winds that distributed the rain-clouds and he remained until he had learnt her magic tricking her into relating it by the same method he had used on the other old woman, Nei Bairara. As Bue was preparing to leave Nei Temaing he asked her if she would go with him but she refused and he then requested that she give him her uri tree so that he might use it as his canoe. This she also refused but pieces of coral had washed up under the roots of the uri tree and Bue then dislodged the tree and ran off with it. Nei Temaing gave chase and because she could run faster than Bue he raised the winds he had stolen from the first old woman but they did not hinder Nei Temaing. Bue then raised the winds he had stolen from Nei Temaing herself and the winds howled and the rain poured down and so she was prevented from reaching him. Bue escaped carrying with him the uri tree and from them he made fire-sticks.

Bue continued to sail east until he arrived at Tarawa and there was hospitably received by Riirongo of Tawara, who fed him "in the midst of the sea." Bue had reached Tawara after a long voyage but his sister reached there directly since the ancestors had led her to the place after leaving Mone. Riirongo was the son of Kirataa who had become the husband of Bue's sister, and they gave Bue a house called Ababou and he remained there for some time. As Bue walked around Tarawa it is noted that the pandanus and coconut trees were all withered and Kiritaa asked his wife, Bue's sister, if Bue himself could assist since it was a result of Bue that the landscape was so parched as a result of his being (as fire-god) setting alight the trees. She begged her brother to send the rain and he acceded to her request and the rains quenched the fires, but as it continued to descend in torrents, Bue again had to be requested to stop this. After this Bue asked Kirataa to build him a maneaba and two were built, that of the Maunga-tabu and the Te Namakaina.

Bue requested his sister to make him some string and when she had done so Bue made a dip-net usually used for catching flying fish. On a rainy day he went to the reef to the west of Tarawa where he first met Riirongo. When Riirongo appeared Bue caught him in the net and taking him ashore took him back to Tarawa where they lived as brothers. Bue and Riirongo moved to other places to live on Tarawa before embarking on another voyage with Riirongo's mother, in the canoes named Te Bakakai and Te Kai-ni-kamat, sailing to the islands of Beru and Nikunau. On these islands the descendants of Bue and Riirongo live who are the clans of Ababou and Maerua and they construct the sacred maneabas for the "Kings of Karongoa"[313].

In considering this myth it must be realised that the overall relation displays a certain lack of consistency and unity for an original myth and therefore appears to have lost many clarifying aspects through constant retelling. This tends to be confirmed by the inclusion of another element of note and that is incorporated in the section recording that the Sun was too hot, this is illustrated to a limited degree in another reference to Bue throwing coconuts at the Sun to reduce his heat[314]. This appears to be derived from other myths common from Asia through the Pacific to the Americas and noted elsewhere as the "Sun-too-Hot Myths"[315]. In the Bue relation, the Sun-too-Hot Myth is adapted to the first part of the theme and along with the cursory manner in which Bue reaches the Far East where the Sun rises appears to be a much shorter version than an original. Where many prominent aspects and adventures recorded in reaching such an important place would be expected as in other epic voyages noted in Polynesian myths, there is lack of explanatory narrative. This is evident where loss of narrative has been glossed over by using such terms as "sped" in reaching the eastern horizon as well as connectors in other sections. It must be remembered that these epics among the Polynesians some times took hours to relate and such an important hero as Bue would have originally consisted long sagas describing every detail along the way and the whole of the surviving saga suggests that this is a very old myth with only the main elements remembered merged with other myth motifs.

The identification of Bue with the fire-god of Polynesia, Maui, has long been acknowledged, and in the Maui myths this hero prevents the movement of the Sun by noosing it and lashing him to a post - undoubtedly an element of influence reflected in the Inca Intihuatana - the "Hitching-place of the Sun". Each of the elements of the myth, except the section where he confronts his father, the Sun, is dealt with in the same cursory way. It is interesting to note in the Bue myth that, when he reaches beyond the eastern horizon, there are references to the "six mounting platforms and this appears to be distinctly a garbled reference to the stepped pyramids, almost certainly a reference to the Americas along with the observation of the Sun at certain angles made in its ascension after dawn to mid-day. Such divisions of the day, and night, appear in the philosophical constructs of the Vedic Aryans and later Hindus as well as among the Jains. In the Vedic rites, ceremonials directed at the rising of the Sun it was essential that they should be commenced after mid-night but completed before the dawn and this is implied also in the Bue myth where he had to prepare himself before the Sun's rays were apparent.

The white clan staff with its black rings and pennants guiding and protecting Bue, given to him be his father, is remarkably similar to those preserved in the texts of the Mandaeans in the Ancient Middle East. In returning from the eastern horizon Bue collected his sister and they sailed further west until their canoe was capsized by the porpoise sent by the Sun. They descended to the land of their ancestors and Bue then sailed on further to the west until he reached the "enclosure" of Nei Nairara and here his father appears from the West. This element in the myth appears to his father transiting to the east in the Underworld after the western Sunset but this might also be a reference that Bue was sailing westward during the night using the stars to navigate after the Sun had set in the West. This section might also be a reference to magical rites carried out at night since Bue was associated with both the Sun and Moon as well as eclipses.

From this "enclosure" Bue sailed further west to the land of Roro and here also night was of importance since at this place he met the woman named "left-handed", another reference to the magical rites of the Moon - in India the Sun was considered to refer to the right and the male and left to the Moon and the female. After escaping from the woman named "left-handed" he then sailed east and eventually reached Tewara and from there to Buru and Nikanau. The references in this myth suggest that the episodes of the myth are condensed epics from ancient sea voyages from one side of the Pacific Ocean to the other. The stealing of the winds and other means of controlling the winds and weather suggest the learning process in achieving mastery over the sea and the fine art of sea navigation and oceanic travel.

The episode where Bue and his sister reach Mone, the underworld land of the ancestors, suggests that it was not the land of the Gilbert Islands where the hero is considered to have started his journey since the usual ancestral lands were believed to be somewhere distantly located in the west or north west of Polynesia. This might, however, be a reference to Samoa since the myths state that the Gilbertese were descendants from the "Tree of Samoa" and "Au-the-Skull"[316]. Before Samoa the ancestral lands specifically mentioned in the Gilbertese myths are Buru, noted in this myth, and Gilolo, and here Buru is associated with Nikanau. There has been considerable discussion as to where these islands may have been located and most accept that they refer to the islands of Gilolo, now called Halmahera in the Eastern Indonesia, and the island of Buru next to Ceram in East Central Indonesia..

The islands of Buru and Ceram along with Sumba are renown for their former mega-lithic cultures and almost certainly related to those of Celebes to the North East. Gilolo has been shown to be closely connected to the cultures of the Ancient Middle East, India and particularly to those of the No Su, or Na Khi, in Southern China. It has been shown that there are references to the Na Khi in the Marquesas and the Maori appear to be connected to this same region of Southern China[317]. The land of Buru is also associated in Gilbertese myths with the golden-haired, fair-skinned ancestors of Matang and both of these terms, sometimes as Matang and also Marang, are found as deities, or associated together in the pantheon of the Santals[318] and other Aboriginal peoples in India[319] suggesting that at least one strand of Polynesian descent came from these tribes in India. These same tribes form a section of the Munda and Kol tribes of India and are therefore closely associated with the Bhuiyas and Gonds, of such note in this work and to be of further interest. The record of Bue sailing continuously westward after leaving his father, the Sun, from what appears to most likely to be the South America coast suggests that Bue sailed, so far west, using the prevailing winds to reach India, and that this was his final destination before turning east, correctly, to the named islands of Indonesia. Tarawa noted in the Bue myth may be a reference to Java, often called Hawa or Jawa, and finally from where he sailed on to the island of Buru. Bue's mother was from Tibongiroro and this has been thought to derive from Gilolo.

Sir Arthur Grimble, who was the resident governor of these islands for some years in the early twentieth century, noted the many environmental and marine related signs that the mariners observed at sea essential in assisting the successful navigation over long distances between islands and known locally as betia. These he listed and included such observations as noting the flight of birds, the swarming of fish, the distance and number of peaks in ocean waves, swarming of jelly-fish, the direction of sea currents and their strength, debris trails and types, mist and clouds - their forms and shapes, and the geographical locations where these might be expected to be found or signified among many others[320]. These are essential in realising that the Polynesian and the Gilbertese in particular were expert mariners and were fully capable of reaching the west coast of the Americas by using this accumulated knowledge, probably gleaned over millennia. Interestingly, incestuous relationships between brother and sister were forbidden among the Gilbertese except among the chiefs and this reflects the same regulation among the Incas[321].

One of the most interesting aspects in the myths of the Gilbert Islands is the fact that there are recorded ocean journeys to a land to the Far East[322] that appears to indicate clearly that they had reached the Americas and returned to tell the tale. It is said in these myths that the first person to reach this distant land in the east was Raaka but little else is known of him except to suggest that this is the hero Rata noted in Central Polynesian myths. In one myth it is Ne Areau who, as the trickster figure described as a dark-skinned pygmoid, visits a land described as "Heaven" and learns that its name is Maiawa, and that there appeared to be some special associ-ation with the star Antares[323]. This land has been considered to be a reference to the Maya of Central America and expanded upon more fully elsewhere[324]. Also interesting and as convinc-ing is the legend of the voyage undertaken by the hero Na Utonga.

This myth states that Na Atia and Nei Ikiiku lived in Te-bongi-roro and they had three girls and the youngest, named Nei Ikiiku the Youngest, one day, quarrelled with her parents and she left them in anger. She took with her the seed of a tree called Te Kimatore and went to a dis-tant place. She dug a hole and threw in the seed and sang over the spot. After a short time the tree grew rapidly and eventually reached Heaven and Nei Ikiiku climbed it and, arriving in Heaven stood before the Woman-of-Heaven, Nei Ni-Karawa who adopted her as her own. When Nei Ikiiku the Younger had been in Heaven for some time she married Kirata-n-Karawa and they had one child named Nei Ni-Karawa. This child saw a pandanus tree full of fruit but her father forbade her to climb it but she disobeyed and as she did so the branch she held to broke and she fell to earth. The place where she fell to was called Aba-tiku and she then changed her name to Komake since she had fallen to earth on the east side of the garfish (make - pronounced makay) in a pond on Aba-tiku. The only inhabitant of Aba-tiku was Na Utonga and he took Komake for his wife and they had two children. One day Komake wished to go out for a time and she left the youngest child, Nei Mata-noko who was five seasons old, in her husbands care requesting that he should not allow her to go out into the Sun.

When the mother had gone, however, the child cried and Na Utonga picked up the child to still her cries. Nothing stopped the crying so Na Utonga took the child out into the Sun and she stopped crying immediately. But the child refused after that to ever enter the house and it was not long before she again cried ceaselessly. Nei Komake then said to Na Utonga that there was only one solution and that was for her to be taken by him to the Sun and Moon and only then would her crying cease. In the night Na Utonga was visited by his ancestral spirit, Nei Tituaabine, who told him that he could not carry the child to Heaven himself but to seek the assistance of a man named Nabenabe who dwelt in the "midst of the sea." Na Utonga sought out the man with the child Nei Mata-moko, and was received hospitably and Nabenabe agreed to speak to the navigator whose name meant literally "half-spirit-half-man", Te-anti-ma-aomata. This man agreed to the proposal and instructed Na Utonga to construct his canoe. He required that the canoe be built with seventeen sails, a ro or plaited anchor, one tanai or shell-bladed adze, and six other items or implements including a maneka, a climbing step cut tree trunk. Na Utonga returned to Aba-tibu to construct his canoe and provide all the items required by the navigator and then set out with his seventeen sail canoe to where Te-anti-ma-aomata awaited him using just one of the sails.

With the navigator and the child on board they all set off sailing at speed toward the East. The first major hindrance was that a giant deep-sea octopus grasped the canoe with its tentacles and Na Utonga had to cut it away to free the canoe with the adze and they continued on their journey to the East. The first landfall was the land of the long-eared people known as Taban-noto, Waituru and Katatake-i-eta. They stayed a long period here before setting out again for the East. They voyaged for a very long time, in this time they used each of the seventeen sails in turn as they worn out, until they arrived finally at the land "… at the side of Heaven to eastward that were beyond all lands, which is called Maiawa. There was no end to that land north and no end to south; it spread over the north and the south and the middle, as it were the wall containing the sea." This is a remarkably apt description for the two continents of the Americas and the spread from the centre south of the "great wall" that is the Andes and to the north the Mexican plateau and Rockies to the Artic Circle. The myth further notes that here there was a rock in the sea where the Sun rested and they anchored their canoe at the rock to await the Sun when it arose. When the Sun appeared at (over) the rock on the "eastern horizon" Na Utonga offered his child, Nei Mastanoko, to him but the Sun responded that she should be given to the Moon since she would be burnt if he took her. They sailed to another rock in the sea where the Moon rested and anchored their canoe. When the Moon arrived Na Utonga addressed the Moon saying, "Moon, thy granddaughter loves thee" and the Moon took the child and carried her away and it is believed that, from that time to this, Nei Mata-noko sits in the Moon and plaits all night[325].

This myth is truly remarkable in that is not only describes a very long voyage to the east but gives a recognisable description of the Americas as viewed on approach from the Pacific Ocean and a name that is also appropriate in terms of the Central America civilisation of the Maya. This description has been referred to by other authors and some have seen the obvious implications that the Polynesians reached the Americas and clearly knew of its existence long before the historical period. Some have seen the description of the long-eared people as references to the Marquesas Islanders and, or the Easter Islanders while the former are the most likely in any crossing of the open ocean from the Gilbert Islands or Samoa to the West Coast of the Americas. Certainly, as has been shown in this work as well as a previous publication by the same author, there are many cultural parallels between the Maya and the Marquesas and the Marquesas and the cultures of Colombia, Ecuador and Peru.

In the Na Utonga myth the last section refers to his canoe anchoring at the rock of the Sun as well as after this at the rock of the Moon. The myth states that these were in the sea, but in fact it is possible that these are distant memories to the inland sea of Lake Titicaca where the Island of the Sun also called the Island of Titicaca and Koati, the Island of the Moon appear to emerge from the Lake as large rocks. On the Island of the Sun there is the famed sacred rock where the Sun was believed to have risen for the first time in "great splendour" and where the Sun was believed tied to the rock, Titi-Kala, and it is likely that it is from these sacred places and their associated myths that the references in the Na Utonga myth have been derived and co-opted. These gaps in the narrative and associated references noting that they stayed for long periods, and it may be more that one of these long periods covered the landing on the Peruvian coast and the overland trek to Lake Titicaca to the islands of the Sun and the Moon - Titicaca and Koati.

Jwala Mukti - Eclipses and the Voyage to Bind the Sun

The similarities of the myths of neighbouring tribes in India has been referred to in this work a number of times and results from social and cultural interaction over centuries or millennia. The wind god of the many tribes of India and the Bhuiyas in particular from whom the Polynesian hero Bue may have originated, Pawan, is shared by the Assurs and called Pawan Dasari. Jwala Muhki is a hero of special note among the many mythical sagas of the Assurs who are also known as the Agaria. The name means "Mouth of Fire" referring to the long tradition of these people as a caste of smithies who are conjectured in this and earlier publications to have probably derive from Anatolia. A myth that may be the origin of the Bue myth in the Gilbert Islands (Kiribati) is preserved by the Assurs and is of great interest in the overall theme of this work and given as an edited version as follows: As Jwala Mukhi grew up with the other boys they shot birds with arrows. When any of the boys had shot a bird he exclaimed "Good for father" but when Jwala Mukhi succeeded he cried "Good for Mother". Eventually the boys began to shun Jwala Mukhi since they began to believe that he had no father, a great disgrace in traditional India. Jwala Mukhi was sorely hurt by these jibes and demanded of his mother to know about his father. She told him that "his twelve fathers" were killed by the Sun so, in his anger, he insisted on knowing where the Sun lived. His mother replied, "... beyond the seven seas and the sixteen rivers, my son, live the Sun and Moon; every day at dawn they play with the sand on the shore of the great ocean."

That night Jwala Mukhi built a great furnace and fashioned a great lump of iron called kuari loha (Virgin Iron) and from this he constructed an iron net and an iron cage - this was said to be the size of a seven storied house. Next morning he told his mother to give him food for twelve years and that he would return in the thirteenth. He departed for the east, crossing the seven seas, the sixteen rivers, and finally arrived on the shore of the great ocean and there he hid in the sand.

At dawn the Sun came to play with the Moon on the shore and Jwala Muki caught him "as fishermen catch fish, in his net", and shut him up in the iron cage. The whole world then plunged into darkness and everyone searched for the Sun but he could not be found. The people then approached the "blind" Pawan Daseri, the Wind, for assistance and he found a tiny crack in the cage and emerged with the Sun. On seeing each other the Sun and Jwala Mukhi cursed each other where the Sun relegated the Agaria to poverty and Jwala Mukhi restricted the Sun to see his wife, the Moon, only "during her period", that is at the eclipse.

The myth is closely similar to that of Bue, also associated with the eclipse, in principle but the Polynesian version it is possibly one transferred by the Bhuiyas rather than the iron-working Agaria and therefore was identified by their name thereby loosing its connections with the forge. It might also be that Mukhi sounded to the foreign ear too similar to Bhuiya or Bue to be differentiated. The reference to Jwala Mukhi burying himself in the sand to wait the rising Sun may well be a distant memory of the long sandy coast of Peru and Chile over which the Sun would rise when approached from the west - Asia and Polynesia.

In another section of the Agaria myths it is noted that lightning was believed to fall from the Sun, or in more graphic terms was described as the "excreta or slag" of the Sun. This belief seems to reflect a closely similar association of lightning with the Sun as it was in the Andean beliefs. These myths from the Assurs or Agaria were collected over some years by Verrier Elwin (pages 98-101) in his work on these people and their culture and there are many others suggesting that they were in some way connected with ancient sea travel in to the Pacific and possibly to South America.

Tahaki and the Myths of his Epic voyage to the Land of Maiawa

There are many myths regarding the exploits of Bue's counterpart Maui and another demi-god Tahaki. All are clearly localised versions of the great epic myths from the earliest epochs of Polynesian (or Asian) exploration into the Pacific. Another possible contact with the land that may include South America is reflected in the myth of Tahaki relating his great and perilous voyage to the lands of the ancestors but possibly incorporating some memory of Tupa's voyage from South America to the lands of the far west. Only edited excerpts can be given here from this very long myth cycle.

The section of the myth relating the voyage of Tahaki opens with a boast by the ancestress Arimata that her sons would be great voyagers on the seas and shall "go to the remote oceans". In response Huauri declares in a chant that her son Tahaki would do the same and the two women quarrelled and it was finally agreed that, since Arimata was the older of the two mothers her sons would be the first to venture across the seas. Arimata then sent her sons Niukura, Niu-mea, Niu-takave-a-puga and Tau-mai-puga to venture forth across the oceans. Huauri immediately on their departure called on her gods to descend and the sons of Arimata were swallowed up by the sea and turned to porpoises.

After a time Huauri sent her son Tahaki and her adopted son Karihi to venture across the ocean and chanted in their support for the success of "long pre-destined voyage" that had just begun. The myth then records a sequence of responses from Tahaki and Karihi and recognises the invocation of Tahaki's mother in raising the south wind to assist them in the venture and this passage reveals also that Karihi was Tahaki's elder cousin. In a particularly interesting section of the chant Tahaki declares that his "rod-of-life" rises above the land, and that on that land the rod "rises erect" and this is referred to as "Tupa-of-the-princely-lineage"! This appears also to be declared the "staff of love" and that it is borne upon the wind. In a reference to the rods' identification with the wind the refrain chant notes "As sinks the breeze - so sinks my wind-supported rod-of-life." Another section of the refrain notes:

> "My rod-of-life, floating on the wind, follows the foaming track
> The ocean trail of Tane,
> Tane - shadowy-shelter-of-the-land."

Long after Tahaki had left land his mother remembered that she had forgotten that she had not taught the correct greeting that her son should use in salutation of the "very great Prince" named Titimanu, and she pursued her son until she had overtaken him, and she then related the correct form of the greeting. She told Tahaki that when he approached Titimanu he should greet Tahaki with these words:

> "Tahaki the young growth,
> Tahaki the swelling sap,
> Tahaki the phallus,
> Tahaki the rigid,
> Tahaki the denuded -
> There is no such ardent fellow faring forth upon the seaways as Tahaki!"

The response from Tahaki must be:

> "Greetings! O Titimanu!
> I am the stormy-petral coursing hither over the bitterly cold expanse of the sea!
> Pleasantly warm are the inland valleys of Havaiki!"

A long series of chanted responses in the myth's chanting records the final departure of Huauri and Tahaki before he recommences his voyage with Karihi, and his mother declares that she will return to the sacred land. Tahaki then asserts his determination to set his course for Vaerota - the sacred land of Ru - "there where the Sun rises. Borne far away on tireless wings ...". In a final declaration Huauri states that her son Tahaki will go to the "night-realm of Kiho, the last bourne of repose." Huauari returns to the land of her ancestors, but then Tahaki sailed on to the land ruled by Titimanu.

The greeting ceremonies were performed as Huauri as predicted and provided for and Titimanu, who is revealed as the grandfather of Tahaki and Karihi then enquired as to the purpose of their journey and Tahaki exclaimed that it was to avenge his father, Hema. Tahaki then asked his grandfather, Titimanu, where the land of Horahora was to be found and he was told that it lay in the direction of "the flaming rays of the dawn!" Tahaki was eager to go on but his grandfather admonished him to stay a while and learn the "formalities" that must be rigorously observed when he arrived at that land. These formalities were directed in order that Tahaki may "rupture" the "hymen of the radiantly beautiful and noble-born Princess, Horahora" and their destiny, predicted by Titimanu in a chant, was to dwell together on the sacred temple platform - Mata-aru-ahau. The translation for this "sacred temple" is "First-tender-wooing" and other references to Horahora such as "freely shall gush forth the ichor of her maidenhood" sets the tone of the chant for numerous verses and this "nobly born" lady was said to be found in the land of Kiho.

Tahaki and Karihi departed and arrived at the land of Horahora and went to her house named "Marua-of-the-regions-of-the-gods." The result of Tahaki's time spent with Horhora is that a daughter was born, named Mehau, and all of Titimani's predictions were fulfilled during his time in this land. Eventually, from the land of Horhora, Tahaki and Karihi sailed to the land of Kuhi. Here the myth recounts the story restoring the sight of an old blind woman by throwing coconuts at each in turn and from here the two heroes sailed on to the land of the Matua-uru, the land of the "devil-possessed goblin band." The two young men then went across the land for a long distance and saw nobody, not a soul, and Tahaki called out to his father by name and Hema heard him and called back warning him of the "goblin creatures" who had plucked out his own eyes and left him in filth. Tahaki rescued his father and climbed the sacred coconut tree of the goblin hoards stealing the fruit from among its fronds and then set fire to the goblin's house catching all of them in a net and slaying them by a ruse. When the dawn glimmered on the eastern horizon Tahaki set out to retrieve the eyes of his father that were fastened to the belt of the woman Roi-matagotago. Tahaki slew her and removed the eyes of his father and took them back and in placing the eyes in Hema's eye sockets his sight was immediately restored.

From this distant land Tahaki, his father Hema and Karihi travelled on and finally arrived at the place where a tree called "The High-coconut-of-Hiti" grew. Tahaki left Hema and Karihi and climbed the coconut tree but as he reached the centre a violent wind suddenly blew but although he clung to the tree he was blown off and his girdle became detached and was blown far away. Tahaki fell into a fresh pool of water belong to Hina and she came by and found him in her pool. She enquired as to his name and he told her he was Tahaki and because his girdle was blown away she told him she would fetch the royal girdle, called "The Long-girdle of Hina", and she went to her husband Ituragi who ruled the land. Hina related the finding of a man claiming to be Tahaki in her pool to Ituragi who stated that she should take the girdle to him and if the girdle wound round his waist more than once then he was an impostor, but if it wound only once it must be Tahaki himself. Ituragi accompanied Hina and when Tahaki took the girdle and put it on it did not meet even once so great and powerful was Tahaki. He was declared by Hina and Ituragi to be Tahaki, their grandson, and they embraced him and exclaimed him to be "A youth of crimson skin - of blood red skin" and Ituragi further averred that he was "A young noble of superb beauty - a radiant youth has come to Tuaraki, oh! Joyful event!"

Ituragi advised Tahaki to take Hapai for his mistress and an extended section follows relating the wooing and relationship of the young couple. After finally succeeding in taking her to his bed Hapai declared to Tahaki that she must go to "Tane-of-ancient-waters" to inform him that Tahaki had arrived in their land and was intending to visit Kiho the land of the ancestors. "Tane-of-ancient-waters" said that, when Tahaki arrived to see him, if he could "pass before his face, then he must be Tahaki; if he could sit upon his high four-legged stool he must be Tahaki; but if he could pull up his sacred tree by the roots, then he surely is Tahaki."

Hapai returned to Tahiki to introduce him to "Tane-of-ancient-waters" and he passed also the tests required of him, sitting upon the high stool and breaking it into pieces under him, and when he tore up the sacred tree he saw Havaiki, the sacred land of the ancestors below him. Tahaki declares: "My face turns landward - 'i Havaiki', to thee, to Havaiki dwelling in the realm of night - for I am as the drifting Moon descending to the underworld..." and he further muses: "It was Pug-ariki-tai who came at last to Fare-kura - templed abode of the veneered learning gods - there in the spirit-world where thou dwellest - for I am as the floating Moon sinking to the world below."

Tahiki and Hapai remained together for "many moons" until Tahaki angered Tane by sleeping with Hapai's younger sister Teharue. Tahaki is then said to have travelled "far away to a distant land hoping that he would be killed there." In the land known as the "Harbour-of-refreshing-rain" Tahaki was attacked and fatally wounded at the hands of the Manono clan who inhabited that country[326].

This myth is considered in the same milieu as those of Bue and Tahaki and the three demi-gods are identical in many respects. The overall theme is Tahaki's descent into the Underworld, a theme much favoured among the Polynesians and has, inevitably parallels to the better known descent of Nana, or Ishtar into Underworld in ancient Sumerian literature. There is no indication in what direction the hero is said to have begun his journey, but the Underworld of the Polynesians is usually considered to be in the far northwest or west of the Central Pacific islands.

Other oral traditions from the Gilbertese clearly indicate that Maiawa was in fact several months due east corresponding to the Americas. However, the mention of "Tupa-of-princely-lineage" suggests that this reference may have been an intrusion into a more ancient original and that this might correspond to Tupa's or Tupac's voyage into the Pacific west from Ecuador. Tupa's voyage, in the likely event that it did take place, would probably date from about 1465 A.D.[327]. Tupac's father, Pachacuti, initiated the invasion of Ecuador in 1463 A.D. and this campaign is believed to have lasted until 1471 A.D. - overall about 7, possibly 8 years!!! This adventure would be late enough for it to still be remembered, but not necessarily as a foreign incursions four generations later when the Europeans began to record the Polynesian myths. If this was a reference to the Inca Tupa linking with the direction toward the ancestral land west of Peru, traditionally west or north west of Central Polynesia, indicate the general direction to be correct. To travel to Indonesia, to Java and Sumatra from Ecuador, the probable two major islands noted in the Tupa legend, would require him to travel with his fleet along the wind-assisted southern route via the South Equatorial Current, south of the Equator, taking him through Central Polynesia, Melanesia and then through the Torres Straits north of Cape York in Australia and south of New Guinea. In returning the North Equatorial Current flowing, north of the Equator, from North of Indonesia across the north of New Guinea through Micronesia to the Northern Islands of Central Polynesia would deliver Tupa's fleet directly onto the coast of Ecuador where he started.

Tupa's journey outward, and from due west of Ecuador would be more difficult to plot in more detail since the South Equatorial Current broadens and separates as it reaches Eastern Polynesia. The islands most likely to be the first landfall would be the Marquesas Island, Samoa, the New Hebrides or the Solomon Islands (now Vanuatu) and then through the Torres Straits to Indonesia on the northern flank of the current. If the wind was blowing to send the expedition toward the southern flank of the Current then the Tuamotu Archipelago followed by Tahiti would be the first landfall. After this Tupa would sail to the Cook Islands, Tonga, Fiji, New Hebrides and then on through the Torres Straits. On the return journey the stopovers probably included the Bismark Archipelago, Gilbert Islands (now Kiribati), Phoenix and then Line Islands before the long hop to the Ecuadorian coast. In the references to Tahaki's initiative to undertake this epic journey it is his male energy that is praised and this is noted in the legend as his "rod-of-life". This in fact, as it is stated in one section, his erect phallus, and this symbolism is closely similar to, and probably derives from that attributed to Siva, the god of the linga (phallus) in India (*12.007*) but also reflected unambiguously in the phallic structure of the Peruvian Intihuatana. Interestingly it is when eulogising these male attributes that this phallus, as his "rod-of-life", the royal sceptre so to speak, that he is identified with the "princely-line" of Tupa. As has been noted earlier the golden sceptre was a cherished traditional symbol of the Incas and this is no other than the formalised manifestation of the male Sun and the creative symbol of the phallus.

Thor Heyerdahl, in his researches into the probability of South American incursions into the Pacific also recorded legends associated with Tupa and an expedition of rafts on the Polynesian islands of Magareva[328]. But it is likely that there were many other voyages from South America by traders, and it was these who were said to have informed Tupa that these western islands existed, and so convincingly that he risked his life and that of the whole expedition in such an undertaking. It is more probable that Tupa's voyage was an encapsulation of already known and sailed routes to the west and the Inca propaganda and myth making simply adapted it to aggrandise the name of Tupa in his undertaking.

The Tahaki myth indicates that the land of Havaiki was in fact the destination since this is revealed as one of the final and culminating acts of the legend. Havaiki is the most celebrated on the ancestral lands in the broad sweep of Polynesian myths. The location of Havaiki has long been the subject of speculation and controversy and some have identified it with Hawaii while others identify it with Savaiki in Samoa. Havaiki is essentially the land considered to be the island(s) from which the ancestral Polynesians spread into the Pacific. The central location of Samoa, and the fact that so many myths appear to name these islands as the land from which they originated, suggest that Savaiki might be the main contender. However, the Gilbertese myths also assert that their first ancestors came to Samoa from Buru, before dispersing on the fall of the Tree-of-Samoa, and that they were descended from the great fair-skinned heroes of Matang. These have been identified with the island of Buru in Eastern Indonesia and significantly not far distant from Java. Some have seen in the name of Havaiki the root of the name Java or its ancient name Hawa, that is Hava-iki, and this would appear to correspond not only with the Tahiki myth and that of Bue but the Tupa myth where one of the main two islands was Ava-chumbi or Hahua-chumbi (Hawa-chumbi).

In both the Bue myth and that of Tahiki there is the underlying theme of travelling from the lands beyond the eastern horizon to those laying on the western horizon, from Sunrise to Sunset. This is more specifically stated in the Bue myth where he seems not only to sail or travel westward from South America but right across the Pacific Ocean, and probably also the Indian Ocean, before sailing East again to reach Tarawa (Hawa or Java?) and then onward to Buru. The direction in the Bue myth is confirmed if this assumption of sailing from eastern to the western horizon in these terms is correct. There are known references that tend to support this possibility. Not only are there many cultural references in South America common to those in Polynesia but it is known, and not conjecture, that the Polynesians reached the island of Madagascar on the far west of the Indian Ocean, probably seen as a continuation of the Pacific Ocean by the Polynesian themselves. Even the name for a woman, vahine in Madagascar is the same as that in Eastern Polynesia[329]. There are universally known and accepted ancient connections between the Ancient Middle East, India and Indonesia and Madagascar, and the myth of Bue, although lacking in great detail, encapsulates in principle those ancient voyages undertaken by the Polynesians to the lands of their ancestors.

The Tahaki myths, only one of many, records in more detail mythical, and probably actual elements of those lands on the way to the ancestral lands and the section recording Tahaki's rescue of his father notes what appears to be the pygmy peoples of Melanesia, perhaps in New Guinea, where long distances through dense forests without seeing any person are noted. The myth is unlikely to be a linear travel documentary since there are references appearing which are purely mythical and others indicating places that are not easily identified. In one section of the myth Vaerota is named as the land sacred to Ru. Ru was the Polynesian sea god who lived at the bottom of the ocean but it has been shown elsewhere that this deity almost certainly derives from the Ancient Middle via India[330]. However, in the Tahaki myth, the land of Vaerota is identified with regions where the Sun rises and suggests that the diffusion of Asian influences was conveyed to the Americas and associated with transfer by sea, that is, under the aegis of the sea god, Ru. The land of Tahaki's grandparents is alluded to as being in Havaiki, but associated with the land of his grandfather, Titimanu, is the land of "swirling flame", suggesting a volcanic country or island, called Taka-mura. This would be an apt description for the most volcanically active areas in the world, Java, Krakatoa and Sumatra or the Hawaiian Islands. The land of Matua-uru, the land of the "goblin myriads" suggests New Guinea (*11.045*) or other larger islands, or mainland Asia where the pygmoid negritoes survive. This is unlikely to be the Hawaiian islands, or nearby, but might be Southern India or other forested less inhabited regions of South East Asia or possibly the Amazonian forests.

In reaching "Tane-of-ancient-waters" there are possible references to the Ancient Middle or Near East where rituals associated with life-giving and sustaining water were associated with the flow from the mountain height of pure water, being elevated to the mystical, and were long established and resembled closely those of Polynesia. Abraham Fornander, a century ago, traced the Polynesian myths through to the peoples in Western Asia and presented an abundance of evidence to support his theory. The fact that, in the myth, when Tahaki pulled up the sacred tree, he is said to have seen Havaiki below, suggests that this might be a reference to the other side of the world and if this was the case then the reference to Kiho being the land of the

10.058 : Serpent canoe depicted in the localised form of the reed boat, note the bird deities pulling the canoe by a rope indicating that this was intended as a sky canoe of the gods. Moche, North Coast Peru, 200-600 A.D.

10.059 : Superb low relief carving in stone of a royal serpent canoe and parasols almost certainly the models for those recorded in the myths and legends in South America. Angkor Wat, Cambodia, 12th., century, A.D.

10.060 : Large state serpent canoe a century ago that is almost certainly the prototype for those preserved among the Amazon tribes in South America. Cambodia, Early 20th., century, A.D.

ancestors, or Underworld, and being a night-land suggests that this is what is intended. When Polynesia was in daylight the opposite side of the world would be in darkness and this appears to have been known by the ancient Polynesian mariners.

The references to the sacred stool of "Tane-of-ancient-waters" appears to refer to the stool as the cosmic symbol, and the four legs to the cardinal points, necessary in navigating for long sea journeys. The breaking of the stool when Tahaki sat on it referred to his mastery of navigational techniques in sailing across the world to reach the ancestral lands, and the original ancestor was embodied in the person of Tane himself. The girdle had special symbolic references in India and the Ancient Near and Middle East and this was also true in Polynesia and Melanesia where it was considered the sacred belt or malo. The waist of the human figure was symbolically identified with the union of the two halves, the upper representing the spiritual world identified with the sky while the lower half was identified with the animal part of the person and corresponded to the earth. The girdle when undone represented the separation of the spirit from the body after death but when tied it represented material and the term of the Earthly lifespan - in some cultures there is the indication that it was the opposite. In the myth the implication of the girdle that could not be completely wound even once suggests that Tahaki was master of his existence and could not be bound by earthly stricture. This reflects ancient traditions from earlier centuries, and still in some parts of India, where the Sadhu or holy man abandons clothing, such as it is, and considered the naked state as the most pure form of spirituality. This appears to be another aspect derived from ancient transfer of cultural ideas from India into the Pacific.

Bue as the Bhir, Bir or Bhuiyas and the Gonds of India

Bue is clearly associated with major sea migrations and explorations by the early Polynesians but inherent in many of these epics is the fact that the heroes considered in many cases that their paternal line originated from the lands on the eastern horizon just as the Tukano Desana considered their land of the ancestors was on the western horizon. In some of the Polynesian myths the distant eastern lands are associated with the female line but this is always less notable than that of the paternal line, that is related to the rising Sun. Other myths indicate that the west was the ancestral land, Bulotu or Pulotu, or that this land of the dead was in the north west or under the sea (Mone). In other references, mostly Maoris, the land associated with ancestors is actually stipulated as Irihia[331] and this is unlikely to be anywhere other than Ancient India or Iran, Irihia being another name in India and Iran for Arya.

In Central Celebes (Sulawesi), in North Central Indonesia, there are villages associated with megaliths, or carved monoliths located in the centre of village. In this region one of the traditions retained by the Toradja, so noted in this island, is that they called the Sun was "the eye of Pue" who dwells "in the place where it rises and sets"[332]. This appears to correspond with the Gilbert Islanders Bue and also tends to confirm that Bue's voyages indicate that he sailed from the eastern horizon to that in the west since he is associated with both extremities of the Pacific and probably Indian Oceans in his own myths centred in the Gilberts.

In the Murray Islands a cluster of stars is named Bu, because it resembled a conch shell named by them bu, and called in the West Delphin, the Dolphin[333]. A myth retained by these people states that this constellation follows the star, Dorgai, known in the West as Altair. In these myths it is said that Bu slew Dorgai - an all-consuming female monster that lived in a bird's egg-laying mound[334].

From Tupa's probable navigational strategy of utilising the oceanic currents to reach his destination, and along with the myths and legends of the Polynesians, the most likely route to reach South America on his return directly was utilising the North Equatorial Current from the North Islands of Indonesia through the Caroline Islands, the Marshal and Northern Gilbert Islands, the North Line Islands (North Polynesia) and then to South America. The references to Asian culture along this current would therefore, by necessity, be more pronounced than influences from the Americas. In the South Equatorial current it would be expected that there is stronger influence from South America into Polynesia than north of the Equator, since the current flows from South America through Central and South Polynesia and Melanesia to Australia, and this is certainly the case in actuality. Along the North Equatorial Currents the reality of the Current being used as a marine highway distributing Asian influences is confirmed where the betel leaf, so well-known on the coast of India, is used into the Caroline Islands having diffused from India through into South East Asia on the way to the North Central Pacific Islands. A little further on the name of Bue appears, and in some islands in Melanesia, but this is not so for the rest of Polynesia. It is clear therefore that this name originated in India but did not proceed beyond the Gilbert Islands although other references associated with this hero did particularly when linked with other Polynesian heroes.

It has been noted that the Bhuiyas in Central East India are almost certainly the origin, among the Munda peoples of India as the racial group for the name of the Mayan wind deities, the Pauahtuns. This name is certainly derived from the name the Bhuiyas give themselves, Pawanbans, "People of the Wind"[335] and their wind god, and relates to their coastal settlements in Eastern India where they were both fishermen and employed as boat-hands or mariners. In South India, near Madras a people called the Buis, considered to be probably a branch of the Bhuiyas[336] are almost certainly an offshoot established locally when the sea trade to the sacred city of Kanchipuram (Conjeeveram) was at its height. This period was one of ocean-going trade and overseas pilgrims that demanded an extensive industry related to the sea and long-distance travel. The critical location of the Gilbert Islands in mid-Pacific for both the out-going sea travel to Central America and the Maya and the return journey back to Indonesia and India tends to suggest that Bue is the personification of the Buis as mariners. Ultimately such a connection reflects back to the Bhuiyas further north on the east cast of India in Orissa and Bengal near the Ganges and Brahmaputra Deltas. These deltas are the gateway to Assam and onward to the Chumbi Valley and Tibet. This route is most likely to be that the Bolivians and Peruvians and others from South America followed to reach the corresponding antipodean Himalayan plateau to the altiplano of Bolivia. Although it may not be possible to ultimately prove this assertion it is unlikely to be coincidence that so many aspects of the Andean and Nazcan cultures resemble those of the Naga tribes of Assam, the Tibetans, as well as those of the Polynesian, Melanesians and Indonesians in the intermediate island zones.

The Mundas and Santals are considered by recent historians to have originated from the same tribe and separated when they reached Eastern India from North West India probably in the first millennium B.C. It is also believed that their kinsmen preceded them, having migrated to the same place, and then continued along the Cossai River into the districts around modern Ranchi[337]. On reaching Eastern India and Bengal the Bhuiyars appears to have evolved into high and lower status castes and subdividing into clan subdivisions. Some of the higher status castes became Rajas, others were landholders called Bhuinhars and Baran Bhuiyas, and other sections socially much inferior to them[338].

The homeland of the Bhuiyas is considered to be the region around the Chota Nagpor plateau, but, where there have been Hindu incursions of later Aryan descent the Bhuiyas have been relegated in status over time. However, where they have retained control of their lands they have maintained higher status and a certain independence. It is believed that the Bhuiyas, along with earlier tribes now considered part or largely Aboriginal, were in fact earlier Aryan migrations from North West India and Iran who became immured into the Aboriginal peoples through intermarriage. Others such as Colonel Edward Tutte Dalton considered the Bhuiyas a Tamil people[339] who migrated north and it cannot be derived that there are many connections notable between the Bhuiyas and the myths and legends of Sri Lanka and the so-called demon king Ravanna. In this connection Dalton believed that they were one of the so-called "monkey races" under their leader hero, Hanuman, who defeated Ravanna in the fight on the side of the deified Hindu hero Rama so noted in the Hindu epic called the Ramayana[340]. Dalton states: "Hanuman, the general of the ape army, was Pawan-ka-put, 'the son of the wind;' and the Bhuiyas to the south of Singbhum call themselves Pawanbans, the children of the wind, to this day. That they are the apes of the Ramayana, there can be no doubt." Although Dalton describes the Bhuiyas as the "apes" of the Ramayana, their physical appearance reflects much less that prejudicial description than other Aboriginal tribes and even he describes them as "perhaps the most interesting and widely-diffused of the class."

Sarat Chandra Roy, a Hindu historian of some note, considered the Bhuiyas descendants of the Aryans from the North West of India who became part of the Aboriginal races in varying degrees as they progressed over the centuries across India through intermarriage with them on the way. Either way their name, their associations with the wind god, and the alternate names for the favourite deity Hanuman, called Vir or Bir, and the fact that the most powerful of the Bhuiyas, the Pawri, or Paharia, the Hill Bhuiyas, appear to be the element that influenced the Pacific peoples through sea travel in very early times is clearly important and reflected in the Desana among the Tukano of Colombia. It has also been shown that their Sun deity Boram[341] is found in Aboriginal Australia tending to confirm their connections with long distance sea travel. Among the Desana their name for themselves was Wira-pora - "Sons of the Wind"[342] and this clearly relates to the Bhuiya's deity Vir or Bir and the most prominent of the clans among them, the Pauris or Poris.

The Tukano Desana Serpent Canoe named the Pamiri-Gahsiru is of special note since the imagery of the canoe captain of the same name clearly reflects that of Polynesia, Melanesia, India and the Ancient Middle East. This highlights their links with the Bhuiyas of India, not to mention that with the Incas to the south in the Andes of Peru reflected in their symbolism, ancestral origins and mythology. The Desana term for the mythical deity identified with the rainbow, Buime, and also believed originally a fish, suggests that this is the Gilbertese hero Bue, but may also be confused with the name for the hero found in Melanesia and Australia named Baiame noted in an earlier chapter. Baiame is identified by some researchers with the Indonesia term for Buddha, or with Brahma, known there as Baima[343], but in any case they all refer to the dispersion of aspects of the cultures of India through into the Pacific Islands and then to South America.

The Serpent Canoes of the Desana - Origins in India and South East Asia

The Desana does not refer to ocean-going canoes but only to that of their great mythical canoe, the Pamuri-Gahsiru, that was said to have followed the rivers until it struck the mythical rock. At this point the mythical ancestors spilled out into the forest until the canoe captain blocked the hole. Clearly this is a mythical account but it is more likely that this is an encapsulated version of many such canoes carrying foreigners, some of whom remained among the ancestors of the Tukano, from whom they are descended. It is probable that large sea-going canoes arrived on the long Pacific coast of Colombia and that they either carried their canoes overland into the navigable river system of the Amazonian Basin or that, more probably, they landed on the Ecuadorian coast and crossed to the most extreme tributaries of the Amazon. This is the region of the Andes that provides a possible access to the Amazon Basin within striking distance of the Pacific coast and the Andean mountain range is more broken and very much lower. These canoes were in fact probably Polynesian, Hindu or Chinese or possibly Javan or Sumatran, and certainly, as earlier noted, there are detectable traces of related blood types to Polynesia among the Amazonian peoples. This only tends to further confirm that many cultural imports, such as bark-beaters and barkcloth traditions known from India, Indonesia into Polynesia entered South America from Polynesia, and that the sweet potato cultivated for at least a millennia in the Polynesian Islands and New Zealand were transferred by mariners undertaking sea voyages noted so widely in the Polynesian traditions from the South American Coast back to Polynesia and beyond.

In Samoa, the marine voyages were early recorded by the Reverend John Stair and he noted that these traditions record that these vast open oceans were transited by suppressing hunger and thirst for long periods of time by chewing the leaf of a particular tree, allowing them to drink sea water if necessary. His enquires never elicited the name of the tree of the leaf but he suspected that this was the South America coca leaf[344]. He links this to the fact that the Samoans, by the time the Europeans arrived in the 18th., century, had ceased their traditional construction of their long-distance canoes, and from this it might be inferred that when the Spanish arrived in South America the trade into the Pacific Islands ceased. The cessation of the essential trade items to sustain that sea trade included the importation into Polynesia of the coca leaf itself since no bushes of a suitable narcotic type were ever discovered in Polynesia.

Serpent symbolism and the power believed inherent within its symbolic display was certainly not exclusive to the Desana Tukano people of Colombia. The Serpent Canoe of the Desana, the Pamiru-Gahsiru, as a reflection of the canoe captain of the same name and associat-

10.061 :
Serpent legs reflecting a symbolic aspect of this representation of a deity from Ancient Elam. Elam, Western Iran, 2nd., millennium, B.C.

ed with the Sun, finds its close parallel in the numerous myths of the Ancient Middle and Near East. The Mandaean manuscripts dating from near the end of the first millennium B.C. depict the Sun and Moon in their sky canoes and similar, probably associated, beliefs and myths are found at least two-three millennia before in ancient Sumeria. The identification on the ecliptic, the band of the Sun's orbit across the sky as perceived geocentrically, with the sky serpent originates long before the Vedic period in India. The ecliptic and the orbit of the Moon's node have long been confused in early Hindu myths, and consequently the serpent, ecliptic and eclipse demon as the Serpent, Rahu, are inextricably linked and dealt with in an earlier publication[345].

The serpent canoe, relating to the ecliptic and as the "conveyor" of the Sun developed as a state symbol in the form of a canoe constructed and ornamented in the form of a serpent in regions influenced from the Ancient Middle East and India. Some of these canoes still exist in the impressive serpent canoes of the former royal houses and state canoes of Burma (Myanmar) (*10.060*) and Thailand, and other official canoes in India and South East Asia (*10.059*). Of particular interest, in a region repeatedly noted in this work as the major contributor to South American cultures, because of it natural location as a prime stopover and international maritime trading region on the way to South East Asia Oceania and the Americas from the Ancient Middle East, is South India and Sri Lanka. In Cochin, in the South East Coastal strip of South India, the Raja, as part of the ceremony of his coronation, was rowed in a special ceremonial canoe. Associated with the Valan caste as rowers were those of a slightly lesser status caste, the Katal Arayans, the name indicating that they were sea-going Aryans who possibly settled on the South India coast direct from the Ancient Middle East or North India.

In a "snake-boat", before that of the Raja, the headman of the Valan caste lead the way as an escort, a tradition retained as an ancient right jealously, and as part of this special ceremonial duties the caste supplied all the rowers for the water-borne procession including the other dignitaries. Of considerable note is the fact that the special privilege as the ceremonial guard who stood in the prow of the Raja's ceremonial boat in front of him was accorded to one of them and called Arnavan, who held a sword in hand[346]. The term Arnavan appears to have the same origin as unmarried hero of the same name earlier noted probably another name for Tonapa or Thunapa among the Aymara around Lake Titicaca in Bolivia. Tonapa or Tonaca appears to be another name for St. Thomas whose Syrian Christian Church has existed from at least as early as the 7th., century, A.D. in South East India and may have had representations there a few centuries earlier.

Aravan and Arnavan as names may have derived from the religious myths associated the son of Brahma - Atharvan. Brahma, the Supreme Vedic deity is said to have related all knowledge to his son Atharvan and the Arnavan in the Raja's boat holding the sword may be a reference to the sword guarding right actions and delegation through the rule of the Raja, who represented the Sun, and who was thereby admonished symbolically to proceed rightfully in his course or reign. It should also be noted that the term for the Parsi fire priest[347], immigrants into India from Iran in the first millennium A.D., was called the Athravan and this would appear to have a common origin with the name of Brahma's eldest son. The Athravan was identified with Ahura Mazda, in essence the Winged Sun of light, and the priests were often itinerant serving each community for a time as required[348]. Whether this was based on a predetermined circuit possibly related to the Sun's orbit as occurred in Peru, relating Viracocha's journey from Tiahuanaco on Lake Titicaca to the coast at Manta, is not known. Since Ahuara Mazda is the winged Sun it is very probable that such a reflection of the Sun's orbit among the Parsis, or other fire religions of the Ancient Middle East, was ritually followed and may have been the early prototype for South America.

The serpent is a characteristic myth motif associated with all cultural stages in the history of Ancient Near and Middle Eastern as well as in India. The serpent canoe in South and South East Asia, and in China, was the last reflection of these long traditions of association and none of the later Aryan based intrusions in India could eliminate it, even though the early Buddhists despised their adherents and attempted to do so. In the ancient Vedic texts, many dating originally from the middle of the first millennium B.C., and in later additions and commentaries in subsequent copies, the serpent reflects both the symbols for the elevated as well as the contemptible part of human, as well as its divine nature. In the Buddhist jatakas, or didactic panels illustrating aspects of Buddha's life, the naga-form of the serpent assumes all forms including that of the sea-faring ship[349].

The association of ecliptic of the Sun's orbit and appearing as an ouroboros (urobos), a serpent forming a circle holding the tip of its tail in its mouth is a common symbol used for the annual solar cycle. Inevitably the serpent is utilised for other calendrical aspects and it was recorded in the oldest Vedic text that the serpent belonged generally to the west. This is noted in a section defining the construction of a "house" (for worship - a rudimentary temple) in relation to the cardinal points and is recorded as follows:

"6) On this (ground) they erect either a hall or shed, with the top-beams running either from west to east; for the east is the quarter of the gods, and from the east westwards the gods approach men: that is why one offers to them while standing with his face towards the east."

"7) For this reason one must not sleep with his head towards the west, lest he should sleep stretching (his legs) towards the gods. The southern quarter belongs to the Fathers; and the western one to the snakes; and that faultless one is the one where the gods ascended (to heaven); and the northern quarter belongs to men. Hence in human (practice) a hall or shed is constructed with the top-beams running from south to north, because the north is the quarter of men. It is only for a consecrated, or for an unconsecrated person that it is (constructed) with the top-beams running from west to east"[350].

Julius Eggeling, who translated this section, provides an alternate commentary on the construction prescription of the sacred Vedic fire shrine from the text known as the Prakina-vamsa as follows: "The 'vamsa' are the horizontal beams supported by the four corner posts. In the first place the two crossbeams are fastened on the corner-posts, to serve as the lintels of the eastern and western doors. Across them tie-beams are then laid, running west to east, on which mats are spread by way of a roof or ceiling. The term 'parkina-vamsa refers to these upper beams (upari-vamsa), and especially to the central beam (prishtha-vamsa or madhyavala) the ends of which rest on the middle of the lintels of the eastern and western doors; .... Inside the Prakina-vamsa there is the Ahavaniya fire immediately facing the door; the Garhapatya fire facing the west door; between the two the altar; and south of the latter the Dakshinagni. The shed (vimita) is to be erected on the back (west) part of the sacrificial ground, after the roots have been dug up. It is described a square structure of ten (or twelve) cubits, somewhat higher in front than at the back; with doors on each side (except, optionally, on the north). The sala, or hall, is to measure twenty cubits be ten"[351].

10.062 : The divine Buddha depicted as a male child or beautiful youth, a state eulogised in Buddhist and Hindu myths. Gandhara, Pakistan, 1-2nd., century, A.D.

The importance of these quotes is twofold. The first is to note that the Vedic texts record the rituals and dictates of a religion brought by the Vedic Aryans into India and therefore records the cosmology then current in Iran in the early first millennium B.C. This reflects the worship of the fire-god Agni as the fundamental element of the rising Sun in the East. In the later Hindu texts and rituals developed from the Vedic the orientation changes and the south becomes the direction of the dead and a memory of the Vedic ancestry is more or less retained by moving their land to the South East. The North West became the land of the tribal ancestors in recognition from their decent from the Aryans of Iran from that direction. The overall development reflects a foreign tradition introduced from outside and assimilated and adjusted to accommodate the new topographical and environmental conditions of the Sub-continent but still retaining vestiges of the original cosmic constructs.

The second point to note of the strictures laid down to be observed when constructing the sacred Vedic "shed" was that these resemble the cosmology assigned to the framed temple building of Melanesia but particularly to those in Polynesia and to the Gilbertese Maneaba already noted. These find their reflection also in the temple buildings of the Tukano

Desana and other Amazonian tribes[352] together with other recognisable cultural imports - men's houses, so reminiscent of those in Aboriginal India[353]. The men's house, named ·Gamal in the New Hebrides[354] and Ghotul among the Gonds of India[355], clearly from the same origin, are all constructed to cosmic principles to a lesser or greater degree. Those of the Polyncsians follow much more coherent principles as illustrated in the Maneaba of the Gilbertese but Kjell Akerblom records[356] from recent contemporary reconstruction in a study that these beliefs projected were through their temple structures reflected the relationship between the cosmic associations of the night sky as perceived by the Polynesians and their use in navigation over long distances at sea.

It has been noted that the early serpent worship of India was probably derived, or at least augmented by that of Elam in the Ancient Middle East situated east of Sumeria in what is now eastern Iraq and western Iran. This must have been one of many aspects of Ancient Middle Eastern culture that was thrust before the Northern Eurasian invaders who had only one place to go and that was south east into India. Here there are many recognisable elements still recorded in the serpent mythology of India that are clearly derived from the serpent symbolism and associated mythology, from Elam and the Ancient Middle East. The religious tenets of Western and Central Asia were anciently based upon the cardinal points and the early fire religions perceived the basic principle as embodied in the rising Sun. This principle was imported along with many other aspects into India and is retained in the surviving Brahmanic and Hindu forms in the fire ceremonies to this day. Since serpent worship formed an integral part of the early Elamite cosmology it inevitably became reflected in the early Vedic forms in India after transferral, although strongly resisted initially, by that breakaway from Vedic Brahmanism in the mid-6th., century, B.C. - Buddhism. Buddhism, after a century or two became as "infected" with Naga symbolism as that of the Hindus, although Buddha and his follows recorded their contempt of the Nagas and their religious affiliations.

The importance of orientation to the cardinal directions in religious worship and the construction of their temples was important to both Buddhist and Hindus where serpent symbolism was clearly associated with these cosmological aspects. In some references the four cardinal directions of North, South, East and West are the only directions noted but in the most comprehensive two others are added and that is up and down - referring to the North and South Poles of the World Axis. This is reflected also in some of the cosmologies of the Americas such as that of the Huichols and in ancient Vedic references in India the are also six directions that are associated with six serpents. In describing the attributes and protectors of these sacred directions a prayer to Brahman notes that the "sovereign lord" of the East is Agni, the fire god, and the "black serpent" was the guardian for that direction. The lord of the South was Yama, the god of death, and his guardian was the "striped serpent". The lord of the West was Varuna and the guardian for that direction was the "pridaku-serpent", and for the North was Soma, the ambrosia of life, and the "svaga-serpent" is designated as the guardian. The nadir, or South Pole was said to be ruled over by the sky deity Vishnu, and the guardian serpent was the black-spotted serpent, and the North Pole or zenith was assigned to Brihaspati (the bowman) with the "light-coloured-serpent" as the guardian[357]. In other versions the attributions are given to the "four quarters" and not to the cardinal points and North and South Poles[358].

In one of the early texts it is said that there are "four royal breeds" of serpents and these are noted as the Virupakkhas, the Erapathas, the Khabyaputtas and the Kanhagotamakas[359]. It is likely that these have been adopted from identification with the cardinal directions but the references diminished and became vague as these were apparently adopted into Buddhism at a later date. These "royal breeds of serpents" were identified with ruling clan and sects and there appear to be some correspondence between the early Elamite and Vedic references to the revered dragon of the Ancient Chinese. In the Far East the dragon was identified as a symbol of the "superior man" and where the six lines of the "hexigram", used in the oracles of the I-Ching, appear possibly to have been derived from the six serpents of the four cardinal points plus the poles[360]. The great serpent as the Chinese dragon is identified with the sky, and spirituality, but more usually in a functional sense in the Chinese texts and commentaries. This has much in common in principle with the sky serpents in the cosmology of the Ancient Middle and Near East, India and through South East Asia to Oceania and the Americas[361].

The Chinese perception of the sky serpent is plundered in superficially applied practices adopted abroad in that more fashionable geomantic practice in the West derived from it - Feng Shui. In its original form it is a complex, philosophically sophisticated development and probably arrived in China from Ancient Elam by the ancient route north of the Himalayas. Implied or stated in many references to this sky dragon is the belief that the dragon flowed along lines of geomantic force. In the early Vedic texts, where the first concepts in the creation of the world creation are being expounded, the very first "concept" is that of the sky and that this appears to be associated with the concept of "paths" - these being described as notionally similar to those along which certain animals are perceived as moving - most notably serpents[362]. This would appear to have something in common with the Chinese geomantic concepts and in fact that of the early Buddhist iconography. This Buddhist imagery depicts serpents forming a geomantic pattern over the stupa (*8.001*) that clearly indicate influence derived from the Greek omphalus as the centre of the world shown in an earlier work[363]. This returns to the idea linking serpents with the apparent "serpentine" flow in their descent from mountaintops and the probably link to the formalised ceque-line system in Andean South America.

The mountaintop has long been considered the nearest and most desirable place to worship the gods and the symbolic portal represented the transition between the earthly sphere, and heaven as the inner sanctum into which only the priest could step. The life-giving water is symbolised by the goddess Ganga, deity of the River Ganges flowing from these sacred mountaintops reflected the interlocking serpent motifs extending from above her on each side of the portal architrave across and linking centred above on the lintel. In other myths Ganga is more associated with the flow of the Ganges across the North Indian Plain to its delta in the Bay of Bengal. However, it is Siva overall, whose abode is traditionally located in the Himalayas whose ringletted hair (as the Jata or topknot) was seen as the flow of rivulets and rivers down the mountain sides from the peaks themselves[364]. This is a motif particularly associated with post Gupta India from about the 5th., century A.D.[365]. The portal serpents therefore represent the transition between Heaven and Earth. Since the upper human (male), and particularly the priest, above the waist reflected the spiritual state and therefore identified with heaven, and the lower part below the waist identified with Earth, the waist was considered identified with the ecliptic through which the gods approached Earth and through which humanity ascended to reach Heaven.

Inherent also, and already noted, is the serpentine form of lightning associated with the cloud base at the top of mountain and this is both feared and adored as the giver but also taker of life. The lightning in some ancient texts in Iran as well as India perceived the clouds as well as the lightning to have serpentine connections where the winged serpent demon Dahak[366] was associated with the clouds and was probably a prototype for the lightning serpent. Dahak was depicted as an anthropomorphic demon with serpents growing from his shoulders reflecting the shape of wings. In another section of the early Iranian texts the equivalent of the Hindu god of death Yama, Yima from the Iranian, was said to have been overthrown by "the fiendish snake" of the storm cloud - Azi Dahaka[367]. Yima appears to be the prototype for the later Yama in India and this relation indicates that this god, originally a solar deity, was overthrown by intrusive non-Aryan peoples and replaced by their own gods, and he became demonised into the god of death. The identification of the cloud serpent to a specific deity is less clear in the texts of India where

Indra the storm god is said to have slain this demon[368]. This is probably due to the fact that Indra was an imported deity, first reported in the Hittite inscriptions in Anatolia, before being transferred via Iran where the associations with the cloud-serpent was expanded to include the Iranian Azi Dahaka, who became the equivalent in the Subcontinent as Vritra[369] before being gradually eclipsed by the rise of Hinduism in India.

Other references to sky serpents appear to have developed from sky-watching at night where certain groupings of stars or constellations suggest certain snake-like forms and are then confirmed in tradition through common usage. In Iranian myths, Gocihr, a "malevolent being", was said to be bound to the Sun, along with another, to prevent him from causing disruption[370]. He is described a being located in the middle of the sky, "like a serpent", with its head in Gemini and its tail in Centaurus. Between its head and tail there were six constellations "in all directions" probably meaning from one end to the other, that is, six on both sides making the full complement of 12 zodiacal signs in all[371].

Serpent Girdle and Double-Headed Serpent Belts - Eclipse Demon in Iconography
Iconographically the serpent belts so widely found in the imagery of Central and South America, but also further north, finds its exact equivalent in Asia from where it clearly derives. This was extensively noted in part in an earlier work[372] and this depiction was shown to relate to the eclipse serpent demon Rahu in the myths of India. It was further shown that the ecliptic was related to the waist of the deity or his representative on earth, the priest, and that the origin of the sacred belt or girdle was in turn associated with the ecliptic, the eclipse demon and the double-headed serpent belt. This symbolism was derived from the Ancient Near and Middle East and transferred to India to be identified with the world serpent representing the ecliptic but identified with the eclipse, or Moon's North Node, Rahu as the head and where its tail was also usually depicted as a head, the Moon's South Node, Ketu.

In the Buddhist texts the mendicant monks, or Bhikkus, are admonished to wear only girdles that are made of cloth. In the texts it is particularly forbidden to wear certain belts particularly those "made like the head of a water-snake"[373]. This appears to be a direct reference to the serpent worshipping people whose belts reflected their beliefs and iconography, and possibly also a reference to lunar worship. In a reference in a Buddhist text to the "venerable Bhaddiya", an early Buddhist saint, it is noted that he visited Rahagaha where he was allowed an audience with the prince Agatasattu. It is said in the text that he assumed the form of "a child clad in a girdle of snakes"[374]. The imagery from both the Ancient Middle East through into India appears to be duplicated in that of Ancient Coastal Peru, particularly from the time of the Moche.

Serpent Deities from Iran to India into Oceania
In the early Babylonian Assyrian texts the sea serpent Musrussu (Mushussu) is the constant companion of Marduk as Gibil[375], the most prominent of their deities. The name of Marduk meant "bull-calf of the Sun", was later known as Bel (El or Il) - "Lord"[376]. This horned sea serpent is probably symbolic of the importance of sea trade and power to the empire at that time and other iconographical references indicate that there must have been contact with India, Oceania and probably South America from that time. There are even references in the myths surrounding Marduk suggesting that this deity himself may have originated abroad, reflecting the earlier Sumerian deities recording that the sea god Ea came from the "middle of the sea"[377] and related to the people of the "south winds" or southern oceans.

Marduk is equated with the term Amaru-Utag and appears to be the form from which the name marduk itself derives and this in turn is apparently derived from Amar and the deity named Amurru[378]. The association of Marduk in his original form as Amaru-Utag and the sea serpent Mushurru suggests that this is the origin of the name for the Amazon among the Incas, Amaru. The Incas were late in Andean history and it is probable that this name was adopted by them from those who occupied the Andes long before them, going back to Tiahuanaco and beyond to Chavin and Chiripa. The oldest known people, possibly the descendants of the Chiripa around Lake Titicaca, are the Uru, remnants of whom still survive in Bolivia to this day. It has been shown a century ago that the term for the early storm god in early Assyria, Amurru or Amaru, was also written Ur or Uru[379]. This tends to confirm the American historian A. Hyatt Verrill's researches that there were several hundred words in the early languages of the Aymara and associated peoples in Bolivia that equate directly with those of Ancient Sumeria in the Ancient Near East[380]. His conclusion was that the Uru people south of Lake Titicaca were their descendants as the first surviving West Asian immigrants into South America.

The storm god and the association of the Assyrian deities to the Caucasus mountain and the river system that flowed from it - the Tigris and Euphrates, paralleled in name and symbolism that of the storm gods of the Andes and the descent of the Amaru or Amazon from their heights around Lake Titicaca. This also reflects similar symbolism and associations between the storm gods of the Himalayas and the four sacred rivers including the Ganges in Ancient India known that were based on the Aryan and pre-Aryan prototypes from Iran. All three regions portrayed the major river(s) flowing from their respective mountain systems and the associated storm gods as a giant mythical serpent.

Interestingly the term uru is also used for "West" reflected in the Babylonian word was amurru and this is best illustrated in the ancient phrase for the Eastern Mediterranean - the Sea of Amarru. The term ur or uru is also used to denote servant and the sign uru meant "brother"[381]. It is interesting to note therefore in this context, the term "brother" is used similarly in the Uru traditions in Bolivia, and in the language of the Kogi in the North West Colombia, and among the Hopi in describing other races where some races are considered to be the elder brother and others the younger brother. The association of the term uru or amurru with the West (of Western Asia) is far from spent in this reference and the conjecture that has raged over the century as to whether the people of the Ancient Near and Middle East, as well as from Europe, sailed to the Atlantic and the Americas will be of more interest in a later publication. The close parallels in the word and terms in language still surviving in South America having West Asian parallels and the evidence of the iconography clearly derived from the Ancient Near and Middle East apart from India suggest that the claims of the Assyrian kings to be the "Ruler of the Four Corners of the World" may not be entirely unfounded.

CHAPTER 11

SERPENTS and CAESAREANS; THE LOOM
- from FLOOD HERO KAWASI to NAZCAN CAHUACHI

Panaga and Panaka in Himalayan Myth

In the foothills of the Himalayas is the kingdom of Bhutan, and this region, along with neighbouring Sikkim is the access route and gateway into Tibet as well as the escape or trading route in the opposite direction from there to the Ganges Delta and the Bay of Bengal. The most accessible of the valleys leading to Tibet is the Chumbi Valley and it had been suggested in this work that it might be no coincidence that this name is reflected in the Inca Tupac legend. The ancient capital of Bhutan was called Panagka or Punagka but little has been recorded, even in myth, of its origins or the meaning of the name. This name being the same as the term of the Inca clan chief suggests that this may have been the place of origin of the Incas, or at least one of their ancestral lines. The name itself appears to have been derived from Pai-naga or Pun-nakga or, where Pai, earlier noted was associated is a term for "white" in Tibet and Peru. The term Pun-nakga has already been considered at length relating to Sun circles and the probable prefix of the ancient Vedic name for the Sun, Pun-shan. In a myth related more fully elsewhere in this work, Pund-ariki - who assumed the form of a Brahmin - his child by a Brahmin woman was committed to a Brahmin bearing an idol of the Sun god[1]. This relation clearly associates the serpent, its half-human child, as well as his name with the Sun-god confirming Pun being that term of identification.

The foothills of the Himalayas, in early Buddhist times in the second half of the first millennium B.C. were the strongholds of the Naga worshippers and the affix of the term Pan-nagka (naga = snake) may be a reference to a major settlement of these people. Equally it may derive from the Sanskrit term for mountain, nag, although its location so far from the main centres of Sanskrit usage and scholarship on the plains of India suggests otherwise. The widespread myth of the Pundariki serpent in the tribes residing to the south in Bengal and Orissa suggest that name Punagka derives from the association with serpent worship. This appears emphasised where the whole term Panaga is that used for the snake in certain regions such as Amarakosa[2], this term perhaps deriving from the Ancient Middle Eastern term identified with serpent Amuru becoming Amara. Pai-naga would mean "white snake" in the Tibetan languages of the Himalayas where pai = "white" and of particular interest is that the term paqo or pai-gho is a term used for white magician on coastal Peru[3].

In Melanesia there are several myths that have been derived from the term Pa-naga and these are remarkable in their content. Among the Motuna in the Solomon Islands it was said that the ancestor named Pa-naga were "discovered" or, that cultural advances were introduced by him included culture-bearing influences such as building houses. Of particular note is that mythical references state that before his time, when a an expectant mother was almost at full term, the child would be cut out in a crude form of caesarean operation with a knife resulting almost inevitably in the death of the mother[4]. Panaga is notable in this tradition because he did not wish to loose his wife so he initiated the custom of allowing natural birth, curiously, he is also said to have been the first person to commit adultery. The myths and legends about him report that he introduced the gong, a South East Asian instrument, into the islands suggesting that he was in fact from the continental mainland or perhaps from Bengal or the Ganges Delta region.

Rainbow Snakes and Sky Serpents in Myth and Tradition

Rainbow snakes are major mythical beings prevalent throughout the myths of Aboriginal Australia. In Arnhem Land the local Rainbow snake was a horned serpent and is also noted for his whiskers denoting his masculinity[5]. These appear as a fortuitous element apart from the whiskers being a male characteristic in the Aboriginal myths and do not have special signifi-

cance. However, these are recognisable characteristics of the serpent deities of the Ancient Near and Middle East as noted of the sea serpent, Mushussu, and are probably derived from there by the ancient mariners using the adjacent sea currents between New Guinea and the North of Australia where Arnhem Land lies. In the adjacent region of Kimberley, in North West Australia, there are caves with rock drawings clearly depicting the mariners of Central Indonesia, Sumba, or Celebes. To the North West of these islands in Halmahera, otherwise called Gilolo, the ancient deities reflect those of India but more particularly the Ancient Middle East as noted by the 17th., century English mariner, Thomas Hyde[6] and it is likely that these cave drawings are significant in their cultural dispersion to Kimberley. These rock drawings, discovered by Sir George Grey in an expedition there in 1837-9 A.D., clearly depict the turban types wore into recent times in these regions but found also on the coast of Peru a millennium earlier noted.

This Melanesian myth of Panaga is paralleled by myths preserved in the oral traditions of the Tsiruan people of Nissan in the Solomon Islands and Panaga is substituted for their own hero Uskawu or Manatchire who were said to have arrived from a far distance on a raft. They too abolished the crude form of caesarean childbirth and allowed natural birth to run its course[7]. It has been recorded that there are many elements among the Pacific Islands that appear to be close-ly connected not only with Asia but with Ancient South America. It had been noted, among others by Hyatt Verrill, that the Inca term for clan chief, Panaka, or probably originally Pa-naga, was similar to the name Pakeha of the Maoris. The Maoris are the only people in the Pacific to not only successively cultivate the South American sweet potato long before European arrived into the Pacific Ocean but to have been doing so long enough to have developed many varieties suitable for the cooler New Zealand climate. The sweet potato can only be propagated by tuber and therefore by human agency although some have recently suggested that seed may be obtained from the plant for replanting. It has been noted that Pai-naga would mean white snake in the Himalayas and the Maori used the term Pakeha to describe the white man when he arrived in

11.004 : Two men with simulations of turbans probably imitating those of ancient mariners. Taburi, Kolari,
New Guinea, Melanesia, Early 20th., century, A.D.

11.005 : A turbaned figure with chinstrap of the type
discovered in caves in North West Australia but probably depictions of Indonesian mariners. Kimberley,
North West Australia, Pre-19th., century, A.D.

11.006 : A group of men with traditional turbans with chinstraps. Sumba, Early 20th., century, A.D.

11.007 : A carved wooden
image displaying a turban with a
chinstrap of the type identical to
those anciently in Indonesia
through to India. Chimu, North
Coast Peru, 900-1450, A.D.

11.008 : Two men performing the
gumela dance showing turbans with
chinstraps of the type found throughout
Indonesia to South America. Gond
Tribe, Central India, Early 20th., century, A.D.

New Zealand. The apparently closely related Peruvian term Panaka is notable and the Maori
connections to Ancient Peru are of more interest in other sections of this work.

Panaka or Panaga reflects the name of its original components and relates to the serpent
associated with the creation myths in India, South East Asia and into the Pacific Islands. In the
mythological constructions of the Ancient Middle East the deities were largely based on
humanoid features and incorporated elements in their recognisable construction. This is reflected in these deities in human form and with attributes and items reflecting their status including
the thrones and conveyances utilising descriptive objects from human life in illustration. This
was particularly so in depicting sky deities where the canoe became the symbolic reflecting of
the orbit of the Sun, Moon and stars across the sky. After transfer to India these elements of
mythology became adapted to local myths and concepts and the serpent became the conveyor of
the deities often retained in the form of the canoe. In the subsequent transfer these elements often
became dissociated and the serpents became the deities and the residual elements of the myths of
India and the Middle East became separated and assimilated into other myths or retained some
sort of independent existence.

In myths from the Admiralty Islands north of New Guinea the serpent (malai) caused
the reefs to rise creating the land for settlement as well as the trees and food along with the first
people named Nimei and Niwong. In another myth it was these two first people who created the
earth and the food plants and trees along with the Sun and the Moon. It is said that Nimei and
his wife Niwong arrived in a canoe from far away. In another myth the first couple increased the
height of Mount Pounda on the main island so that it reached the sky to be able to communicate
with the Sky People. To achieve this they took large blocks of rock to the mountaintop until it
was high enough for them to ascend to the sky. In another myth associated with these islands it
is said the serpent called Muat, Mat or Moat arrived and invited the people to enter its mouth, go
into its belly to and take out the food plants and trees to enhance their existence. Only the "red
taro" was forbidden them but aside from this the snake also gave them fire, pottery and all elements associated with civilisation as they understood it[8]. It is said that the serpent left because
the people broke the prohibition by taking the red taro as well. The Melanesian myths rarely

attain the coherence and cyclical structure of the Polynesian myths and as with these example from the Admiralty Islands are composed of recognisable elements originating in various myths and traditions of India and the Middle East.

Caesarean Myths and Cultural Transfer into the Pacific and Amazonia

Among the most exceptional myths are those preserving extraordinary customs and traditions appearing to record early methods associated with human birth and a few excerpts have been given in the above. Important in this work is not whether they were entirely actual practises, if they existed as such at all, but it is their diffusion of related myth motifs along the ocean currents from Asia to South America that is important. These customs and associated myths are very ancient and again can be found to have almost certainly diffused by mariners from the Ancient Middle East on their way to South America via India, Indonesia, Melanesia and Polynesia. These routes are continuously confirmed by whichever myth cycle, or even an occasional motif, is examined in the surviving oral traditions along those marine highways.

In a remarkable cycle it is recorded in the Mazdaean myths of Ancient Iran that the wife of the supreme earlier deity, Zurvan, was expecting twins and that this god had decided to give his kingdom to the first-born. Unfortunately the god of darkness, the evil twin Ahriman, divined his father's thought and although his elder twin, Orhmazd the god of light, was nearer and blocking the passage of egress from the womb, Ahriman burst through his mother's side to claim the right of the first born[9]. It is clear from the widely dispersed versions of this myth and the attitude toward twin births that this has been the diffused model that has influenced the ambivalent traditions prevailing among many peoples in Asia, Africa and into the Pacific Ocean to South America. Frequently some local traditions have considered one twin evil and the other good, while if a few cases both were considered an ill omen and both killed. Interestingly also is that Abraham Fornander considered that many of the Polynesian cultures were influenced by migrations from this same region of West Asia. It is notable in this pre-Zoroastrian myth that the deity Zurvan is said to have declared that the first-born male child would receive the crown and the second born would be appointed the chief priest[10], and appears to have been the model for some of the Polynesian islands through to the Maya and the Inca.

The bursting of Ahriman from the side of his mother appears also to have been the model for the traditions noted among many other people all linked by the fact that they are located beside trade routes by land or sea. In a curious reference Lady Drower, half a century ago, noted a contemporary belief among the Yazidis in Northern Iraq where they considered the English to have been born by caesarean birth[11]. The Todas, still located in the Nilgiri Hills to this day in South India, have a tradition stating that the sacred buffalo were at one time attended by the women and when a calf was expected they would cut open the buffalo thereby sacrificing the mother[12]. The sacred buffalo were identified with their clan deities and since many of their traditions are clearly derived from the Ancient Middle East it is likely that this is a vague remembrance of the Ahriman myth, or has a common origin with it, among the cattle herders of Iran and Central Asia.

In a Gond myth it is stated that Indra Raja was born to the goddess Kamlapati but that he did not arrive through natural childbirth but burst thought the ribs. The child asked her for his bow and she gave him two handfuls of entrails and told him to stretch them across the sky to indicate to the people that he was their ruler and from the entrails they would be able to predict whether it will be wet or dry[13]. The myth is an interesting one since Indra was the god of storms in India and here Indra's bow, although not specifically mentioned as such was considered to be the rainbow in ancient Vedic and Hindu myth. Indra was derived from Anatolia via the Ancient Near East and his bursting through his mother's side reflects that of Ahriman, although his is likely to have derived from an older version. It should also be noted that Buddha was said to have emerged through his mother's side and this probably has a common origin with this Indra myth. The entrails given by the goddess and being used for divination is reminiscent of the liver divination of the Dyaks in Borneo and the Incas in the Andes of South America.

Other myths among the peoples of India record similar caesarean type births in their oral traditions[14] and one indicates a more recent Gond adaption that states that from the left side of Parvati the semi-divine hero, Shriyal Jhango, was born and from the right Angarmoti and each had twelve sons and twelve daughters. Those descended from Shriyal Jhango were the Gond and those from Angarmoti were the Muslims and English[15]. Verrier Elwin, who collected apparently related myths in India, noted the close similarities of these myths and those of the New Guinea and Maori peoples[16]. Other myths written down in South India recorded that the practice for many castes, when a mother died before childbirth was for the child to be cut out of the womb and placed on the funeral pyre beside its mother[17]. Among the Kappilan caste a similar rule applied to the removal of the child from a dead pregnant mother but, where otherwise the normal cremation rules would apply, the mother is buried as well as those suffering from cholera[18]. A similar custom was found among the Kems in Burma and probably influenced from India[19]. This practise appears to have reflections in the term used on San Cristoval in the Solomons where an Adaro means the ghost of a child born by a pregnant woman who has been buried, or the ghost of the woman herself[20].

In Melanesia it has already been noted in the islands near New Guinea that unusual myths associated with childbirth and the practice originally for a caesarean delivery were believed to be enforced in ancient times. In the Solomon Islands at Buka the culture-hero named Uskawu took some real lime from his lime pot, chewed it, and then spat it out. The men of Tsiraun thought he was spitting up blood, but through this habit introduced by this hero it became generally accepted in the islands[21]. Lime chewing appears to be the substitute for the coca leaf where in Colombia it was also associated with the use of this leaf that was not available in the Pacific Islands. This myth, in an extended form at Buka, has also been associated by the local people with the cessation of caesarean birth and the introduction of the natural method above noted.

In Australia, a myth associated with Ayers Rock in the centre of Australia notes that a large split boulder was the body of a Kunia woman who, in Tjukurapa times - the mythical ages, gave birth at this place. The myth states that the cavity between the two rocks was the womb of Bulari and that she had died while pregnant and having contracted so quickly after death that she split apart and the child emerged[22]. Where certain motifs are included in myth cycles they appear often appear to be elements that have little point within the whole. Undoubtedly this is because they have been adopted from foreign myths into their own mythologies as elements vaguely remembered by those who related them incompletely. Many such elements appear in the myths in Aboriginal Australia and these appear to have derived from India or the Ancient Middle East and this is true also for Melanesia.

In the Solomon Islands, Tolo myths preserve the belief that the panpipes, so widely found in the islands, so closely similar to those of South America, were made by the Gosite. These were children of women who died "enciente" - while still pregnant, and they were thought to live in the hills. They were described as of short stature with long hair and nails, and lived in holes deep in the forested regions, but did not know how to make fire therefore eating their food raw and were also cannibals. It was said that one of the Tolo caught a Gosile and stole his panpipes, copied them, and that was how they originated among the peoples of the Solomon Islands. Similar legends were preserved from the Tau people of Guadacanal[23].

In a myth, probably developed from the myth cycle surrounding the megalithic, stone-using hero called Qat, the pregnant sister of Qatu was killed while she was working near a thicket by a cannibal ogre named Taso. He did not eat her because she was near the time of delivery and it is said that twins were delivered as her flesh disintegrated - this having overtones of a caesarean myth. The twin boys were discovered by their uncle, Qatu, and the myth describes that the boys were "light in complexion, wonderfully fair" and he adopted them and in time they became heroes when they killed the ogre[24]. This relation reflects the myths and legends of numerous of the Polynesia and Melanesian peoples who identified these mythical and legendary heroes with the first Europeans when they entered the Pacific many believing them to be their own ancestors, heroes or deities returning to them. This myth also preserves beliefs recorded of the Mexican and South American peoples.

In the Western Pacific in the Reef Islands a myth relates that there was a woman who was pregnant by a husband who had married one hundred wives. When the child grew up he was very handsome and he lived entirely in the clubhouse. He only left the clubhouse at night but went no further than the gardens of his father's wives but his father had never seen him. When the father finally glimpsed him he enquired of his wives who he was and was told only that he was his kinsman. The father became very jealous and the son had to flee, sailing far away, and remained so long at sea that he grew thin and weak. Having landed he was rescued by a tree who, to save the handsome young man, stole the fish of the stars who came down each night to extract them from their nets. When their fish were found to be missing several nights in a row the stars demanded to know of the tree what had happened to them. He told them that he was feeding his "son", the handsome young man, but they scoffed at him since they were aware that the young man was a human. The stars took the young man up into the sky to dwell with them. When the wives of his kinsmen were nearing their term in pregnancy he descended and cut open their wombs and took the infants back with him. The stars eventually asked the young man whether he wished to return permanently to his kinsmen and he replied that he did, so they made him a raft. When he saw his "kinsman" who had driven him away - his father, he shot him dead[25] .

This myth is a very interesting one since the descent of stars to assist or harass humanity is a characteristic of the South American myths among the peoples of the Amazonian Forests. It has already been noted that the typical panpipes of South America are also found among the people of the Solomon Islands. Here the hero appears to be partly identified with mariner peoples who travel overseas and possibly those who are unable to recognise their own offspring probably because they were absent for many years on these long sea voyages by necessity. Another aspect is that many of these myths do indeed confirm that their culture heroes are mariners and have come from far away and these are usually identified with European or Caucasian people.

One of the less unusually noted aspects in the make-up of the Melanesians is the presence of the pygmoid called the negrito (*11.045*). These people are now largely confined to remote havens deep in the forests. Always in more recent centuries precariously few in number they had died out in some of the islands before or soon after first contact with European explorers or missionaries. This disparity between the confrontation and physical problems of the merging of two quite different racial types may have been behind the myths originating in ancient times and later identified, or integrated with the imported Asian myths. Bride capture or barter was common in these islands and it is likely that mariners who settled for long were few and relations with the very small local pygmoid women must have caused problems in the resultant development of the foetus inside the mother's womb. There are frequent surgical interventions in the present day in the birth of a child from the parents of the same race but for pygmoid women who bore children fathered by what appeared to be giant intruders must have been a very great problem. It is likely that this confrontation and fatal result was the origin of many of the ogre myths in Melanesia who seized women, whether for procreation or not, ended apparently with the problems resulting from crude caesareans. This must have resulted in many deaths of women beside the high mortality rates from normal birth complications. A child much above the normal size of a pygmoid child would have been very difficult indeed, but this problem must also have been known in South America where closely similar myths abound.

South America variations on the caesarean birth myth theme, that perhaps derived in part from the Melanesian traditions, were noted by Cieza de Leon in his travels from Colombia to Bolivia in the 16th., century. He reported that in Colombia, in Arma province, the Indians were so fond of eating human flesh that "... they have been seen to take women on the point of bringing forth, quickly open their bellies with knives of stone or cane, and take out the child; then, having made a great fire, they toast and eat it, together with the mother, and all is done with such rapidity that it is a thing to marvel at"[26]. Cieza de Leon reported the horror that the Spaniards felt for many of the practices they saw on their journeys, particularly among the Indians of Colombia, and they did not hesitate to wreak their own form of justice upon the natives for these vices.

This local form of caesarean practise may have derived from Oceanic travellers who, having endured many months of hunger and thirst at sea were not overly cautious in utilising practices apparently known in their own islands to satisfy their acquired cravings when reaching South America. Since some of the myths and legends of Polynesia and Melanesia suggest that cannibalism did occur, and probably, ultimately, as a result of extreme hunger, the lack of any other readily available food on these sea voyages would necessitate the extension of such practices anywhere they landed after many months on the oceans of the Pacific. Difficulty in acquiring sufficient food supplies was an ever present problem in the reports of many Amazonian forest explorers and this was true also for those with extensive experience including the native tribes in those regions. This has been the subject of many studies in recent decades and may have been one of the reasons why so many of the tribes in the forests resorted to cannibalism. Whatever the origins, whether the practise originated in the Amazonian forests and spread to the Pacific Islands or the other way round, it is almost impossible at this time to discover.

The connection between the Amazonian myths and those of Melanesia appear closely connected in the version preserved by the Shipibo people. In the Amazon tribes there are usually many longer and shorter versions of the same myth and one of these notes that the first women in earlier times went to defecate in the forest and came upon the tracks of a tapir. A malevolent trickster named Dika brushed over the tracks and changed the tapir into a huge, black man. This black man said to the woman that her husband was dead and that he wanted her but she refused his advances at first but finally gave in. She became pregnant with a "huge baby" and they returned to her former home where her husband's younger brother killed the tapir-man. When the time neared for the birth of the tapir's child he burst through his mother's side and she died[27]. This myth resembles not only the Melanesian myths but also the birth of Ahriman in the Mazdaean version from Iran, where he is often considered to be coloured black, or as the "dark half", and is always described as bursting through his mother's side rather than being cut out or through natural egress.

At the mouth of the Amazon there are sites of some importance designated as part of the Marajoara culture dating from about two millennia ago. Myths believed to have descended from them through the local Indians indicate that the Sun was a major cultural icon and that the ceremonial structures appear to have been laid east-west reflecting solar beliefs. The Moon is also of importance and the turtle was a mythical creature associated with both Sun and Moon. The turtle, recorded in these myths, is sometimes said to have torn the culture-heroes from the womb of the first woman and appear therefore to closely follow those of Melanesia[28].

Giants and Polynesians on the Ecuador Coast at Manta

Some of the most interesting myths recorded by the first Spanish in the Americas are those recording the incursion of the giants who terrorized the local people on the Pacific coast of Ecuador. The Indian peoples on the Manta section of this coast of Ecuador retained traditions that a giant race of naked mariners landed on their coast and the first Spanish note that this tradition or similar ones were "universal" among them and extended south as far as Peru[29]. Cieza del Leon, considered one of the most reliable of the early Spanish chroniclers, noted some of the legends surrounding the arrival of giants on the Ecuadorian coast. His version is as follows among other myths ands legends: "There are, however, reports concerning giants in Peru, who landed on the coast at the point of Santa Elena, within the jurisdiction of this city of Puerto Viejo, which require notice. I will relate what I have been told, without paying attention to the various versions of the story current among the vulgar, who always exaggerate everything. The natives relate the following tradition, which had been received from their ancestors from very remote times. There arrived on the coast, in boats made of reeds, as big as large ships, a party of men of such size that, from the knee downwards, their height was as great as the entire height of an ordinary man, though he might be of good stature. Their limbs were in proportion to the deformed size of their bodies, and it was a monstrous thing to see their heads, with hair reaching to the shoulders. Their eyes were as large as small plates. They had no beards, and were dressed in the skins of animals, others only in the dress which nature gave them, and they had no women with them. When they arrived at this point, they made a sort of village, and even now the sites of their houses are pointed out. But as they found no water, in order to remedy the want, they made some very deep wells, works that are truly worthy of remembrance; for such are their magnitude, that they certainly must have been executed by very strong men. They dug these wells in the living rock until they met with water, and then they lined them with masonry from top to bottom in such sort that they will endure for many ages. The water in these wells is very good and wholesome, and always so cold that it is very pleasant to drink it. Having built their village, and made their wells or cisterns where they could drink, these great men, or giants, consumed all the provisions they could lay their hands upon the surrounding country; insomuch that one of them ate more meat than fifty of the natives of the country could. As all the food they could find was not sufficient to sustain them, they killed many fish in the sea with nets and other gear. They were detested by the natives, because in using their women they killed them, and the men also in another way. But the Indians were not sufficiently numerous to destroy this new people who had come to occupy their lands. They made great leagues against them, but met with no success." ... "All the natives declare that God our Lord brought upon them a punishment in proportion to the enormity of their offence. While they were all together, engaged in their accursed ..."(acts of sodomy). "A fearful and terrible fire came down from heaven with a great noise, out of the midst of which there issued a shining angel with a glittering sword, with which, at one blow, they were all killed, and the fire consumed them. There only remained a few bones and skulls, which God allowed to remain without being consumed by fire, as a memorial of this punishment. This is what they say concerning the giants, and we believe the account, because in this neighbourhood they have found, and still find, enormous bones. I have heard from Spaniards who have seen part of a double tooth, that they judged the whole tooth would have weighed more than half a butcher's pound. They also have seen another piece of a shinbone, and it was marvellous to relate how large it was. These men are witnesses to the story, and the site of the village may be seen, as well as the wells and cisterns made by the giants. I am unable to say from what direction they came, because I do not know"[30].

Cieza de Leon notes further: "At the point of Santa Elena (which, as I have said before, is on the coast of Peru within the jurisdiction of the city of Puerto Viejo) there is a thing well worthy of note; and this is that there are certain wells, or mines, of such excellent tar, that as many ships as require caulking might be caulked with it. This tar must be some mineral that flows out at this place, and it comes forth very hot. I have not seen any other mines of tar in any other parts of the Indies which I have visited; but I believe that Gonzalo Hernandez de Oviedo, in the first part of the general history of the Indies, gives an account both of this and others"[31].

In present-day rational terms the remarkable myths surrounding these giants suggests that they were nothing but mythical. However, when considering the stature of the Amazonian people that was probably much more widely spread than today throughout South America, then any of the Pacific peoples apart from Negritoes would have seemed gigantic as the modern Caucasian (*11.041*) does to a lesser extent to the native peoples of South America today. Name of the Polynesian peoples are not only taller but their bones structures are more massive, a subject that greatly interested Victorian researchers, and in this they were compared to the Ona of Tierra del Fuego in South America earlier noted. The appearance on the shore of such comparatively gigantic people for any native South American must have been frightening and if the mariner intruders did force their attentions upon the men as well as the women the outcome was most likely going to be tragic. As mariners it was natural and convenient that in those tropical zones the giants, as recorded, did not wear clothes and the whole account suggests that these were Pacific Islanders arriving on the Ecuadorian coast. They may have been boatmen for Asian mariners and traders and probably not for the first time. Early Europeans noted several times that there were Semitic men among the Polynesians and Melanesians, who were greatly revered, and these may have been the last before European powers took over the apparently long established trading contacts between Asia and South America.

There are many references to the connections between the North West Coastal Indians, Oceania and South America in this work and it is therefore not unexpected that there are myths appearing to retain the same motifs as those of the caesarean myths. Among the Tsimshian myths, neighbours of the Kwakiutl, a people who appear to have common links with the Polynesians, a hero named O'mat, whose mother was the daughter of a sky chief, is said to have had a father who was a youth who had been cut out of the body of his dead mother and flew up to the sky[32] and then dropped into the sea. In a myth from the Coast Salish there are references to mythical women being thrown against rocks so that they burst open and that many children fell out[33]. Many motifs, apart from those relating to caesarean births, from the Kwakiutl, Coast Salish and the other tribes of the North West Coast of North America indicate that these are shared myth motifs with the Central and Western Pacific islands.

Ingested or Swallowed Heroes Bursting from Inside Serpent/Whales

Myth motifs similar to the culture-hero recorded from the descendants of the ancient Marajoara culture at the mouth of the Amazon are found also in Melanesia. From the island of Isabel in the Solomon Islands among the Bogatu people the hero Kamakajaku was said to have dwelt on the hill at Gaji. From there he could see far out to sea and saw that it was exceedingly dark in the distance and wanted to know why. He sent his grandchildren out to where the sea and the sky met, where it was "so dark", and when they returned they brought back white sea-salt but Kamakajaku still could not understand why it was so dark out there. He decided to swim out himself and when he reached the "darkness" he was swallowed by a giant "king-fish" and it swam off with him ingested, eastwards to the rising Sun until it became stranded on the beach. Kamakajaku cut his way out of the fish's stomach with an obsidian blade and then saw the Sun. He stayed with the Sun and his children but, once, when he was alone, in express defiance of the Sun's orders, he lifted a stone covering a hole in the Sky. Looking down he saw his home and he wept longingly for his people there so the Sun had a house made for Kamakajaku and, giving him a banana and the seed of the Pau to use for dyeing, lowered him down by a cane to his island[34]. This myth is almost duplicated by that of the Bae Guu people on Northern Mala in the Solomon Islands except that they associate this with another myth relating that the bow original-ly fell from the sky and this was associated by them with the stone-using culture heroes. These megalithic people are known throughout Melanesia and various guises and later identified with the first Europeans. This myth motif suggests that it is an element from the mythology of India where Indra's bow is the rainbow but is an element in myths closely related to those preserved by this people and those of Malaita that reflect the Bae Guu myth above noted. This notes that the hero Vulanan Gela was swallowed by a fish while trying to catch it and was carried for a long distance until the fish was beached. He cut his way out with a flint knife and travelled with the Sun until he reached his house where he remained some time. Later he was lowered to Earth car-rying with him the gift of fire[35].

Myths of the same type are found among the Kiwai of New Guinea and one states that a man was swallowed by a monster and while in its stomach he was taught to use the beheading knife and this appears to have much in common with these other myths[36]. Similar myths are found in New Caledonia where the motifs of the hero being swallowed by a giant fish, and trav-elling with the Sun and returning to Earth, are separate myths[37]. These were early recognised as being similar to those of the Biblical Jonah who was famously said to have been swallowed by the whale.

Myths of the Melanesian Biblical Jonah type are found widely among the Amazonian tribes where one recorded among them states that there was a giant serpent that always devoured those people who sat upon a particular rock on the riverbank. A man decided to do something about this and made a wicker figure out of cane and covered it with tree bark to give it a close resemblance to a human being and placed it on the rock. He sat inside this cane figure with a drum and a sharp knife and, after having been swallowed by the serpent, he began to drum con-tinuously in the serpent's belly. This noise greatly irritated the serpent and it swam desperately from one end of the river to the other in an attempt to alleviate this internal irritation. When the serpent finally settled in a shallow part of the river out of sheer exhaustion the man cut himself out of the serpent's belly killing it but, in so doing the worms that lived in the belly of the snake attached themselves to the man's ears, nose and eyes and he died shortly afterwards[38].

This version is interesting because it so closely follows versions so far distant on the other side of the world in the Ganges region of Northern India. It is to the Bhuiyas again that the preservation of an ancient myth so similar to those found in the Amazon so far distant from India is found. It was said that a crocodile lived in the Batarani River and that it used to ferry men across but when it took two men across then one would be taken for the payment and eaten by the monster. One day the great hero Bhimsen arrived alone with a load of grain to be ferried across the river. Because of the grain the crocodile insisted that the Bhimsen pay with his life so that his grain may be transported to the other side. It was agreed between them that the croco-dile would take the grain across and then return to eat Bhimsen and this he did and swallowed Bhimsen on returning. Bhimsen, however, had his knife with him and he began to slash at the crocodile's liver and entrails so that the crocodile roared with pain. In a frantic effort to expel Bhimsen he brought him up with a mighty "vomit" and, as Bhimsen came from the mouth, he cut out the crocodile's tongue and from that time no crocodile has been born with a tongue[39].

The myth ostensibly is meant to explain why the crocodile has no tongue but the myth motif of swallowing a hero and his attempt to cut himself out of the monster's belly is clearly that found so widely noted in the Pacific Islands and the Amazon Basin. The various adaptions of such motifs suggests that they are not original myths but may be traced from their original motifs in Asia which have become detached and re-assimilated to other myths abroad. Nowhere is this process so clear that in the Amazon Basin and this will be of more interest in a future publication.

In a Japanese myth the hero Issunboshi confronted a demon known as an Oni and, as he left a temple, he was mocked by it saying he could swallow the hero whole. The Oni proceeded to make good his boast and Issaboshi slipped down the Oni's throat and found himself in the monster's massive stomach. The hero had with him a "needle-sword" and he took it out of its scabbard and proceeded to bore into the creature's stomach walls[40]. This caused the Oni great pain and he belched out the hero. There are many aspects of Japanese and Chinese culture that are conventionally recognised to have originated in India and this appears to be a lesser myth motif that has been derived from the Ganges crocodile myth above noted and diffused not only far away to Japan but also to Melanesia and South America.

In another version from Southern South America, preserved by the Tehuelche Indians, the myths records that a great whale living in the sea pursued people and consumed them when it caught then and it is said that this whale could walk in open country. The hero, Elal, decided to remedy the situation and allowed himself to be swallowed with the intention of saving and releasing the people who had already been swallowed. He cut open the whale and all the people previously consumed fell out and Elal banished the whale to the seas as its only habitat[41]. There appears in these myth motifs a confusion between an Amazon caiman from one source emerging with a whale tradition in one much further south. Other myths involving this hero, stating that the world was said to have been created in a canyon north towards the Gran Chaco, also include the references to cutting open the great whale in the same way[42].

The myths recorded in this work illustrating both the caesarean myths and those of the swallowed hero cutting his way out of serpents are recognisably the same as those correspondingly found from India to South America. These myth motifs appear to have found fertile ground in Melanesia in particular as a geographic mid-point between Asia and South America and could only have been transferred by mariners.

Dismembered Serpent Myths

Serpents disgorging or being dismembered or in other ways cut up are found in abundance in the myths found along the same route from South Asia, into the Pacific, and extending into South America. In the early Vedic texts those who have been "torn by love" are compared to an ichneumon (a weasel-like animal of the mongoose family) who tore the serpent apart and joined it together again[43]. This is compared to the catlike play it has with its prey and this comparison exists over long periods in the literature of India[44]. There may also be here a reference to the origin for many serpent myths where the serpent having been cut to pieces, gives rise to many benefits for the good of mankind, but there are other references that are more specific.

An interesting tradition from the Gonds of India who preserve extensive myths relating to cultivation of the first grain featuring the Corn Queen and a hero who was a Raja - Bikram. In one of these, in a very long story, it was said he was seeking her on his horse and rode for more than six months without finding her. Soon after this he came to world that was yellow, where all the men, soil, stones, grass and trees were of yellow colour. Riding on for another two months he came to a world where everything in the same way was red. After this he passed on through a correspondingly black world, a white world, a world of brass, a world of copper, a world of silver and at last reached the world where everything, including the men, soil, plants and stones were all the colour of gold. In this world he came to a giant banyan tree and under its branches he rode for twelve years before reaching its trunk. Here he dismounted and tied his horse to the trunk, cut grass for his horse, and lay down and went to sleep.

When Bikram, the Raja, awoke after a long time he looked up into the tree and saw two nestlings in a bird's nest. He then heard the male nestling say to his sister that their parents had given birth every year but none had survived because a giant serpent came and ate their siblings before they were fledged. The nestling then said that the serpent would also eat the man and his horse who slept under the tree because that night coming was the night that the serpent was due to ascend the tree to perform his evil deed. The nestling continued to relate that if the Raja was wise he could save them all since, when the serpent emerges from the ground it is very small and, by the action of a wind, it will "spring up" as he grows larger and larger. It was necessary there-fore for the Raja to attack the serpent with his sword and cut it into two, then cut each part again into two until he had thirty-two pieces, and then cover them with a cloth. On the head of the ser-pent he would find two pieces of gold and these the Raja must cut off and at this time a frog, the friend of the snake, will hop out of the nearby well and he must also be killed and on his head will be two more pieces of gold. These four pieces of gold the Raja was to place near the well and then he would be able see the seven sacks of gold at the bottom of the well which he must retrieve.

The birds then spoke to the Raja and asked where he was from and why he had come to the tree. The Raja told them of his mission to seek the Corn Queen, and to find the grain to grow for his people, and the birds said that they would help him if he would slay the serpent and he agreed to do so. That night was the Full Moon and the snake emerged just as the birds had said and the Raja proceeded to cut up the serpent as they had instructed and all came to pass as they said, and after he had retrieved the sacks of gold the Raja laid down and slept from exhaustion. In the morning the parents of the birds arrived and the nestlings insisted that they help the Raja to find the Corn Queen because he had saved their lives. The parent birds then tied a cloth around the chest of the Raja and each took an end and flew high in the sky with him and over the sea. The myth goes on at length to describe the jawari, a type of millet, growing in the "middle of the ocean" and the means that the Raja collected it with his sword cutting of the grain heads for the seed as the birds passed over suspending him above it. The birds returned him to the land and he left them for his home only to find that inside the bundle the grain stalks had become the Corn Queen herself[45]. This is far from the end of the myth but importantly much more abbreviated versions lacking whole sections must have also been broadcast and only the essential elements of the association of a cut-up serpent and the gift of grain are likely to have survived among such versions.

The relation is also interesting in that, along with numerous other Aboriginal myths in India, the acquisition of grain and other essential food plants are obtained by heroes from over, or in the "middle of the sea". This could mean that it came from the Ancient Middle East by sea to the west and South Coast of India or from the East and that would point to the China or even to the Americas. There has been a great deal of conjecture as to where and how the development of food plants occurred and were derived but it is not conjecture to note that South America was the home of the majority of all known cultivars in production. In more recent years investiga-tion into cocaine residues found in the cloth bindings of the Egyptian mummies has shown that this could only have originated in South America. This is likely to have been the result of trade contacts from at least as early as the first millennium B.C. - the period when there was a major cultural revolution and the recorded, inexplicable sudden advances in technology and metallur-gy in the Andes and coastal Peru occurred. The myths cannot be treated as factual history but they do preserve general trends, cultural changes and developments without reference to a strict chronological context.

Among the Iban of Borneo, a Dyak people, a myth states that their ancestors were look-ing for food in the jungle and came to a giant serpent looking just like a log so that they cut it up. However, it began to rain and did not stop for many days until all the land was covered except the high mountain called the Liang Lajii. All the people were drowned except a woman, a dog, a rat and a few other small animals. On top of the mountain the dog rubbed itself against a creeper that was hanging there and the woman took the hint and attempted to create fire by friction with a piece of wood to warm herself. Because there were no men who survived the flood she took the creeper as her husband and gave birth to a child who was half-human. One day they found the rat in whose hole grain was stored and this became the first grain cultivated by the survivors of the flood.

This myth as given is an edited version of an extensive oral tradition and there is no need to include the complete myth here but it is notable that the serpent is associated with the great flood, the high mountain and where a serpentine-like creeper is clearly the later substitute for the serpent itself. These myths clearly originate in the flood myths of the Middle East but has parallels also with those of Melanesia, Polynesia and South America. The myth of Hatuibwari in the Solomon Islands, earlier referred to, is clearly related to this as well as other myths from India and at least some must derive from those of Pundariki known among the Mundas and Bhuiyas and already of note in this work.

A myth from Rossel Island in the Louisades, south east of New Guinea, from the oral tradition of the Temene people records that the people of the hero Wonaji was a race of serpents that lived at the bottom of the lake on the island. They moved to a new home called Ngwo on Mount Rossel and Wonaji created from there the Morning Star, stars generally and the clouds. He made shell money and when a sago palm appeared on the island he ordered two serpent gods to cut it down. The snake god, Mbasi, was dark coloured and he married a fair woman named Kon-jini who Wonaji had wooed but was rejected by her. The myth relates that after this Wonaji travelled with two snake friends on a "wooden dish" (a raft?) because they did not known the art of canoe construction. In another myth, however, he is associated with the outrigger canoe. A variant of these myths notes that the dark god, Mbasi, brought the Sun, Moon, a dog and taro in his canoe.

In another variant an egg developed from the union of Mbasi and Konjini and from this came the first two humans. Descended from them were the ancestors of the peoples of that part of Melanesia. It was said that Mbasi and Konjini eventually became stones on a beach at a sacred site - such places are termed yaba. In the myth it is stated that the Sun and Moon went into the sky but the Moon found the Sun "too hot" and the Sun complained that the Moon was "too cold". Because of this Wonaji arranged that the Sun should occupy the sky by day and the Moon by night and also raised the sky to its present height.

Found among the people of Rossel Island and among the Gilbertese are myths recording the struggles of "fish" people against others and this suggests that these are tribes or clans whose totems were the fish, the snake, or birds such as the eagle or hawk. It was said that Wonaji and Mbasi led the snake-men into battle against the fish-men. The snakes were five in number, these being Wonaji, Mbasi, Gadiu, Mbyung and Nongwa and each of these leaders had his own "host of snakes". The myths of Wonaji are recorded in unusual details for Melanesia and suggest that these traditions have been imported whole from other lands, not unlike the myths of the Qat cycle in the New Hebrides. It is said that in this war between the snakes and the fish Wonaji arrived with his "man-catcher" (probably a noose associated with Sina Kwao in the adjacent Solomon Islands). Mbasi and his snakes came armed with greenstone axes; Gadiu and his snakes with bows and arrows; Mgyung and his forces with stones (slings?), while Nongwa used his "fingers". In this battle the snake-men exterminated the fish-men[46].

The names of the main hero, Won-aji (Kon-aji?), and the female Kon-aji suggest that these myths may share a common origin with the Kon-ori myths earlier noted from the West New Guinea (Chapter 9) that appears to link directly to the Con-i-raya myths recorded in Southern

Peru. The Coniraya myths have been paralleled to those of Pariacaca also in Peru and in this myth the sacred number five and birth from divine eggs are also featured as they are in the Rossel Island myths. The term "Con" is less usual in Peru and its origin generally is a mystery unless Miles Poindexter's suggestion that it derives from Aryan myths in Asia is accepted. However, it may also be that Con is a simplification of Gond or Kondh, but either from this origin, or a similar deity name, is then consistent with the diffusion of myths from India, often confused with serpent myths, to South America and their return from there via the natural ocean currents through Polynesia Melanesia back to India. The Coniraya myths in particular are associated with Pachacamac and the surviving myths indicate that serpent worship in the shrine located there was itself of major importance[47].

Myths of Dismembered Serpents as Child Protectors
The serpent cut up for food is reflected in the Iban Dyak myth in the foregoing and this association of essential gifts for humanity is found in many myths in the Solomon Islands. This includes oral traditions recorded of the great serpent deity of the Solomons, Hatuibwari, told in several myths and versions. These are essentially those that note the belief that certain stones emitted lightning and this serpent arrived from the west by swimming and accompanied by a great flock of birds. The myth appears to link to megalithic people who came from the west and this element linked to lightning appears to concur with many other myths of stone-using, and megalithic culture-bearers in Melanesia. This serpent was also associated with the first fruits ceremonies of the native people underlining its origins with the serpent-worshipping immigrants who arrived from the west[48]. It is very likely therefore that these immigrants, as serpent people, were confused in time having arrived in a serpent-like canoe. The form of construction was common and the decoration of canoes in India and South East Asia, to the west of Melanesia often reflected serpents or the makara - the Ganges crocodile, and such mariners utilising bird migration routes in navigation and were culturally far in advance of Melanesia.

In another myth from the Solomon Islands, similar to those from the islands of San Cristoval, Malaita, Florida and Guadacanar, the serpent cult called pirupiru was associated with a sacred grove, much as similar cults in India are to this day. The story is a very long one but it states that a serpent named "eight fathoms" was killed and was cut into eight pieces but she returned to life after eight days of rain and that she made her house with eight leaves. When she was killed a second time her bones reunited after eight showers of rain. In revenge against the people who killed her she inundated their village under eight waves from the sea. This last section suggests that the serpent is regaled with elements borrowed from another myth relating the adventures of the hero Rapuanate reflecting heroic feats such as those recording that the land had been fished up from the sea by Mauua - a local version of the Polynesian Maui myth[49]. The number eight is usually related to the four cardinal plus the four intermediary points of the compass, particularly in India, and suggests that this myth derived from a calendrically orientated traditions originally.

In an edited version a Solomon Island myth relates that a woman named Huapiaoru, whose father's name was Porokalihidani, conceived but the child when born was a snake. This "daughter" hid out of shame and told her husband that the child had died and that she had buried it. Later the mother gave birth to another daughter and while she and her husband were out working in the gardens the snake came out and coiled herself around the child to protect it. The mother knew of this and when asked by the father how the child was being cared for while she was away from the house she told him her grandmother was caring for her. The husband later became suspicious and returned to the house to discover the serpent coiled around his daughter and cut the snake into eight pieces. The snake's mother was extremely distressed to discover the dismembered pieces but the snake's head said to her that she should fetch eight leaves of the sacred giant caladium plant and cover her. When this was done the snake then called upon the sky to rain heavily for eight days and the eight severed pieces reunited to become whole again. The myth records the many adventures of the snake in its enforced migrations in and around the islands until it is caught and dismembered again into eight pieces. The pieces of the snake are then cooked over a fire but only a woman and her child do not eat their share and to then the head spoke saying that she would reward them instructing them to gather all the bones and take them far out to sea and throw them in the water so that they sank far down in the depths. This they did and after eight showers of rain the bones reunited to become the snake who then caused eight great waves to cover the island. Although the people heard the noise of the waves as they came toward the island they were unable to escape and were drowned. This section of the myth is highly reminiscent of the reconstitution of the twin heroes of the Quiche-Mayan Popol Vuh where their ashes reform into their human selves after being thrown into the river in the Underworld. This is similar also to the myths of Quetzalcoatl in Ancient Mexico where the sacred bones of the ancestors are reconstituted. In the Solomon's myth all died except the woman and child who were found by the snake in the top of a banyan and she provided for them all the food plants including coconuts, yams and taro and created a stream for their water[50].

The myth contains most of the elements of the serpent myths so common in Melanesia. This example incorporates not only the myths of the serpent being the introducer of new crops and the benefactor of certain of the island people but incorporates calendrical references from a long forgotten, and probably foreign tradition. The myth also preserves traditions of what appears to be tsunamis, or tidal wave events having devastated the islands since they also record the characteristic "roar" heard ahead of a strike associated with such catastrophes. These serpent deities were often associated with caves and offerings were left at the mouth of the openings in the same manner as in India. In recent times reports into local traditions around Lake Titicaca near Mount Incahuasi, noted for its popularity in times past for human sacrifices, show that that Mount Kapia was perceived by the indigenous peoples as a giant serpent dismembered in the mythical past and that its head was said to be an extension into Lake Titicaca itself[51]. This extension of the base of the mountain to the Lake itself seems to be highly reminiscent of the serpent that lived on the high mountain of San Cristoval in the Solomons named Hatuibwari. The name of the sacred mountain, Kapia, is reminiscent of an important tribe in East Central India, the Kapus associated with the other Gond peoples both of whom appear to have been earlier intruders into South America before the Incas.

Lakes and water holes were often conceived as the entrance to the Underworld and into which, and from which heroes and whole clans could pass. Many myths note that heroes returned from the underworld to visit their ancestors and often there were said to be guardians who had to be defeated or negotiated in some way to survive the journey. In a myth from the New Guinea highlands around Lake Kitubu it is said that a man named Tauruabu was mourning the loss of his wife and, after the three death feast had, been held her bones were gathered from her coffin and hung up in a string bag over the door. Next to his wife's coffin he saw a large hole and he entered it and found a passage where he saw fresh footprints he thought were those of his wife. He decided to follow to see if he could bring her back but passed through a forest to a place where there was a field of stinging nettles - these opening to allowed him to pass and then closed behind him. He soon came to a giant gateibu lizard, a known lizard type but here probably a forgotten identification with the crocodile indicated in its size being compared to a large tree trunk. This giant lizard asked him the question as to whether he ate the flesh of the gateibu and he gave the answer in the affirmative. If he had answered no he would have been eaten, but having given the correct answer the jaws of the lizard closed and the man walked over its back to proceed on his jour-

11.009 :
Ceremonial
greenstone axes
and a club virtu-
ally identical to
those in the
Pacific Islands
through to India.
Paracas
Peninsula, South
Coast Peru, Mid-
late first millenni-
um, B.C.

ney[52].

The hero journeyed further on in this Underworld and faced other obstructions until he came to the Land of the Dead where he arrived at the house of this Lord of the Dead, Gaburiniki. This is described as a very large U-shaped building and here the Lord of the Dead is described as a man in his "prime, very handsome, and of gigantic size". In the end the man is allowed to take his wife back to the land of the living with the gift of sug-arcane and a special type of banana as a present from Gaburiniki. Interestingly the Land of the Dead was said to be in the East, called Takore, and the Land of the Living in the West, called Korere and this is the reverse of that usual in much of Melanesia and Polynesia. This might indi-cate that this myth refers to a journey made to the East and the U-shaped building and the gift of food-plants suggests that this may have been Polynesia or even South America. The description of the man's journey to the Underworld bears striking resemblances to the "Guardian Ghost" myths of Central America[53], the Cuna in particular, and those of the almost identical myths in the New Hebrides[54]. The crocodile appears to indicate the derivation from earlier myths of serpen-tine rivers such as the Ganges and its crocodile the makara, or the ocean. The traditional refer-ences in India and the Ancient Middle East to the Cinvat Bridge where the guardian asks a ques-tion and the correct answer must be given to pass over it appears here where the hero passes along the lizard's back in a local variant.

Humankind were considered to be particularly at risk from the predations of serpent demons at night, the night being a reflection of the day in the water of a pool, and some of the ancient texts in Asia preserve the necessary rituals to prevent their afflictions upon a household. A priest and householder were instructed to walk three times round the house pouring water upon the earth to provide a circle of protection from night demons in the form of serpents. Having per-formed the fire ritual at the end a bali, or offerings, is made to the serpents to pacify them[55]. In other texts the rightful place of the "great snake" is the lake in which it prefers to dwell and is so notable in the references preserved in the myths of India[56].

In the myths of the Tukano Desana and those of Melanesia, Indonesia and India all note the close association of the serpent, or crocodile/caiman with the underworld, and the serpentine form of the Milky Way. In the Ancient Near and Middle East the mythical dragon was Tiamat and serpents have long been associated with the Underworld as this demon was said to have been. So many of these references appear reflected in the myths of the mythical creation serpents Yacu Mama and Sacu Mama recorded from the Nazca Plains in Peru noted elsewhere in this work.

The Serpent Sky Arch

From the earliest times in the Ancient Near and Middle East the serpent has been associated with the Sky and the rainbow. The description of the Mazdaean serpent named Gocihr resembles the Mesopotamian Tiamat, and it is clear that this motif has been transferred from there to India. Gocihr was a reference to the name of the Moon[57] and the great serpent called Rahu was the name of the serpent's head and another name for the Moon's North Node. At Cerros in what is now Belize, south East of Mexico, the king was believed to have been the "pivot of the sky" and iden-tified with gods who emerged from the sky serpent represented heaven[58]. These similar beliefs in the Americas paralleling so closely those of Ancient Mesopotamia are not lost on historians and researchers a century ago.

Okinemutu—Rotorua Lake.

11.012 : Traditional carved memorial posts, called "kamk", closely similar to those found in North Australia. Gond tribe, Nanur, Central India, Early twentieth century, A.D.

11.010 : A vast field of traditional Maori memorial posts surrounding sacred site beside Lake Rotarua similar to those of the Gond in Central India. New Zealand, Mid-19th., century, A.D.

11.0011 : Gond carved burial posts of a type found on the North Coast of Aboriginal Australia. Nugur, Kutru Mar, Central India, Early 20th., century, A.D.

11.013 : Carved grave posts of the type typical of traditional memorial posts. Melville Island, North Australia, Early 20th., century, A.D.

In Ancient South America the serpent appears to have been associated with the sky and important rivers and in more recent archaeological finds the apparent supreme deity as a feline-faced eagle found at Sipan that was regaled with a double-headed serpent headdress[59] (*5.132*). This eagle deity appears to be as near an identical copy of the Tibetan form of the Garuda, or sky eagle, of Ancient India (*5.129*). In Aboriginal Australian myths the Rainbow Serpent crossed the landscape carving out the mythical features that became the focus of the vast body of their recorded myths. The Rainbow serpent is also identified with the sky and in South America this same or similar deity was called the Amaru, known also as the sky serpent. This was depicted as a double-headed monster was thought to have one head at one end buried in the landscape while the body arched up into the sky before descending into the far horizon where its other head is located[60]. No doubt many of the associated myths derive from the Amazon but there is much to suggest that the Peruvian Rainbow Serpent and that in Australia have some common origin and will be of more interest in due course.

Serpents as the Rainbow and Lightning

The best-known Rainbow Serpents are those mentioned in the mythology of the Aboriginal Australians. Serpents associated with the rainbow and Rainbow Serpents, not necessarily the same, are widely found in Australia and noted from the first British observers in Australia over a century ago. The Bunya Bunya tribes of Queensland called the rainbow Thugine meaning large serpent, but maintained that it was supposed to actually live in the sea. A curious belief among the Wotjo-baluk tribe was that to point at the rainbow was very dangerous and that as a result a

11.016 : Running-kneeling pose found anciently in Mesopotamia. This seal may show influences from Luristan. Iran, c2nd., millennium, B.C.

11.015 : Finely moulded bronze vessel showing the characteristic running kneeling pose found later in India but also characteristic in the Moche culture on North Central Coast Peru. Luristan, East Iran, 2nd., millennium, B.C.

11.017 : Running-kneeling pose as a corner Sky-supporter or Gana. Devarajaswami Temple, Kanchipuram, 14th., century, A.D.

11.014 : Running-kneeling pose found also in Central and South America particularly identified with the Hindu deity Nrittamurti, a form of Vishnu shown here holding up the Sky. Kanchipuram, South India, 7-9th., century, A.D.

person's fingers might become permanently crooked or contracted. Pointing at the rainbow could only be safely done if the fingers were turned over each other - the second over the first, the third over the second and the little finger over the third[61]. The Victorian explorers and early anthropologists, Spencer and Gillan, produced several volumes from their sojourns among the Central Australian tribes including a great number of photos remaining to this day as the finest collection as authentic records of the Australian Aborigines celebrating their original archaic state. Among these the serpent is a prime focus of the myths and rituals and the more recent records of Ronald M. and Catherine H. Brandt illustrated the Rainbow Serpent as fundamental to the myths still preserved among the surviving Aboriginal peoples.

Not quite as recent are the researches in the mid-twentieth century including the several studies of the tribes of Aborigines including some monographs of the Tiwi in the far north where the record of a series of Rainbow Serpent myths called the "Maratji" have been preserved[62] along with carved burial posts closely similar to those of the Gond in India[63] (*11.011-3*). In Arnhem Land prehistoric stone celts were associated with lightning coinciding with similar beliefs in the Melville Islands, and it was said that the lightning woman, Bumarali, caused lightning by striking the ground with a stone axe[64]. This association between stone celts or axes and lightning is found in Indonesia through into Asia and Europe and in parts of Africa. In this same region the Rainbow Serpent was said to be a woman named Narama and she had four sons, suggesting an origin from a calendrical myth where the four sons represented the cardinal points[65].

The Australian Aboriginal Pitjandjara tribe believed that a wanabi, a mythical snake, was believed to live in a deep waterhole named Uluru. This was situated above the Tjukiki Gorge on the summit of the great Ayers Rock in Central Australia. This snake was considered the most dangerous in the country and was said to have its home in the caverns under the waterhole itself. The description given by the Pitjandjara was that it was in length the equivalent of many hundreds of yards, with an enormous head, long projecting teeth and a beard. The skin was said to be the colours of the rainbow and this was the form it sometimes assumed. It was said if an Aborigine drank at the waterhole or lit a fire near by the snake would rise into the air as the rain-

11.018 : Running-kneeling pose of a warrior among the Maya but also of the Moche of Peru but originating in India and Ancient Iran. Mayan, Belize, Late-Post Classic.

11.019 : Running-kneeling pose characteristic of many Moche warrior poses but also found among the Maya, and in India and Iran. North Coast peru, 200-600 A.D.

11.020 : Running -kneeling posture characteristic of door guardians in India, S.E. Asia and Java. Chandi Sewu, Java, 7-9th,., cnetury, A.D.

11.021 : Garuda as the anthropomorphic guardian eagle deity in the characteristic running-kneeling pose found among the Maya, and the Moche in North Peru. North India, 8-10th., century, A.D.

bow and kill the offender by biting his spirit (kuran) with its long teeth[66]. These references to the relationship of the Rainbow Serpent with the waterhole and having special functions are closely similar to myths found in the Amazon Basin.

In South America earlier researchers such as Koch-Grunberg reported that the Indians of Guiana considered the rainbow as "theriomorphic"; it is identical to the many-coloured water serpent which inhabits the high cataracts"[67]. In some studies in the Amazon it has been noted that these animals were utilised in a basic system of colour coding. The rainbow was considered a metaphor for the rainbow since it reflected its shape and colour but this colour is not so much linked to the actual colour of the serpent's skin but to its blood when it had been captured or injured and the colours forms by it when spewing out upon the dark waters of the rivers or pools in the dim forest light[68]. The great serpent of the Amazon is of course the anaconda, and this is associated with the Thunder Jaguars. The Rainbow, together with the Milky Way, the anaconda and the Thunder Jaguars were all considered bringers of illness and disease when they are killed. The Thunder Jaguar was believed to be positioned at the entrance, through a cave, to the underworld[69] and bears close similarities to the references in Melanesia where this mythical being is called the Guardian Ghost. The imagery preserved from the archaeological sites of pre-Colombian South America records examples that appear to be related beliefs at the site of Moxeke where a bas-relief depicts a figure with upraised hands holding bicephalic snakes suggesting a symbolic link with the sky dating from about 1500 B.C. Unfortunately, although there are many wall relief's depicting sky serpents surviving from the pre-Conquest period, the associated mythology is largely lost and has to be conjectured and reconstructed through present day references descended from the post-Spanish Conquest periods or from conjecture.

Serpents - Double-Headed
The serpent symbolism of South America is perhaps more extensively expressed in the depiction of the double-headed serpent belts worn by so many of the imaged deities. This is also true of the iconography of Mexico and Central America and it has been shown in an earlier work that this is the conventional depiction of the ecliptic serpent known as Rahu in India and identified specifically with the Moon's North Node[70]. Moche pottery in particular depicts on its surface designs many illustrations of this serpent belt and its universal usage in this Peruvian epoch indicates the highly significant symbolic references it must have had for the priesthood and rulership along the coastal strip of Peru at that time (*5.082*; *5.100*).

In representations, where the double-headed serpent is actually used to divide the upper from the lower, it is perceived as a demarcation between earth and sky and some of the Moche

11.022 : Makara disgorging a deity characteristic of the iconography from the earliest Buddhist times in the late first millennium B.C. on for many centuries. Similar depictions are notable among the Maya and other parts of the Americas. North India, 5-7th., century, A.D.

11.023 : An eagle deity, probably originally the Garuda bird, disgorging a serpent. A motif found also in the Americas. Shunga Dynasty, Mathura, North Central India, 2nd., century, B.C.

11.024 : A depiction of a doubled headed dragon probably relating to the Moon and its North and South Node. Moche Culture, Trujillo, North Coast Peru, 200-600 A.D.

11.026 : A carved basalt monster head with a human, ancestor or dei head in its mouth typical of identic depictions in Ancient India. San Salvador, El Salvador, Central America, 550-950 A.D.

11.025 : Gaping serpent head decorative design emulating makaras or symbolic crocodile imagery in Ancient India. Maya, Santa Helena, Central America, Late-Post Classic.

11.027 : Deity or hero disgorged from a caiman or serpent head idetical to those found in the iconography of Ancient India. Pantaleon, Guatemala, 4-7th., century, A.D.

11.028 : Anthropomorphic basalt carved monolith with the head of a makara characteristic of the crocodile in Northern India. Linea Vieja, Costa Rica, 800-1525 A.D.

illustrations suggest that it is the equivalent of the Mayan sky band and is considered and extension of the rainbow serpent and equating with the Moon[71] (*9.153*). However, equating the sky serpent with the Moon returns the focus to the ecliptic and the Hindu version of the serpent equating to the ecliptic and the serpent head as Rahu himself in their mythology. It is much more likely that the more advanced cultures along the coast of Peru and Ecuador and on the Andean altiplano retained a more sophisticated view where the ecliptic was one specific type of Sky Serpent identified with the Sun's orbit. This is likely since the rainbow is only seen during the day and this is likely have extended to its use as the Sky Band in a form clearly similar to that of the Maya. Another type would be the double-headed serpent found so frequently depicted as a belt and that this related to the ecliptic and the cycle of the Moon's nodes, North and South and this would correspond to that of India. The sky serpent is depicted and described as such in India and corresponds to that of Ancient South America and identified also with the rainbow earlier noted, a favoured symbol of the Inca. The single or double-headed serpent belts so frequently depicted worn by the deities associated with the lunar deity, Siva, and his fierce altar-ego, Bhairava, as well as his son Ganesa the elephant god in India, has clearly been transferred from India to the Americas. Among the average person in India there was a universal belief in the dom-

694

11.029 : Elephant heads occur at Copan and early sketches show that plaster heads were also found at Palenque as this example by Waldeck demonstrates. Many were disappearing before modern archaeology was able to save them. Palenque, South Mexico, 8th., century, A.D.

11.031 : Remarkable stone carved examples of the makara or disgorging Ganges crocodile among the Maya. Copan, Honduras, 8th., century, A.D.

11.030 : Superb full relief of the Hindu sky deity, Vishnu, protected by the hooded cobra serpent attendants. Note that the deity wears two sacred threads, a small one of pearls and the longer one of human bones. Nalanda, Bihar, Central North India, 8-10th., century, A.D.

11.032 : Two serpents held by the Eagle deity, Garuda. Similar iconography of a deity holding two serpents together in this way is found also in India and in the Americas. Thamma-Nan, Cambodia, 10th., century, A.D.

nuba, a snake with a mouth (and head) at both ends and was feared because it was very "virulent" - a belief seemingly to have derived from the malefic eclipse serpent[72]. In one parallel the serpent in South American iconography is reduced to two formulae as follows: Dragon = Rainbow = Moon and from it by association - Drugs (Hallucinogens) = Rainbow = Moon[73]. The lunar deity Siva in India was associated with the ritual use of ganga, or marihuana, and these were associated with the night when the effects of hallucinations were more vivid. Since he is frequently depicted with the serpent as his belt and in some sculptures he is shown holding the sky serpent aloft[74]. These images and iconography identified so anciently with Siva appear to relate too closely to those of Ancient South America to be coincidental.

In the iconography of Sican on the North Coast of Peru it has been conjectured that the double-headed serpent depicted with the "Sican Lord" was none other than Naymlap, the legendary founder of the Chimu dynasty, although it is now believed that the Chimus were a later branch from this legendary figure[75]. The images of this Sican Lord are also associated with an eagle deity where he is identified with this bird and shown with a beak and wings much in the manner of the anthropomorphised Garuda eagle in India through to Indonesia (*5.129; 5.131/2*). The legend of Naymlap relates that he arrived with his family and retainers on the coast of Peru aboard a raft and this appears to be in principle a similar tradition claimed by the Incas in two of their origin myths, and reminiscent of the legends of giants arriving on a raft on the coast of Ecuador already mentioned.

11.033 : Two makaras or mythical crocodile-fish as armorial animals flanking a central figure. These face the same direction similar to examples found in Central Peru highlands. Bodh Gaya, Bihar, North Central India, 5-6th., millennium, A.D.

11.034 : Carved monolith showing two pumas or jaguars facing in the same direction with a central figure in an akimbo pose. Recauy, Haurez, Callejon de Hualayas, Central Highland Peru, 300-800 A.D.

The meaning of the serpent belts in South America is conjectural due to the lack of associated myths elucidating the symbolism in the depictions on the North West Pacific Coast of South America but the extent of the surviving illustrations indicate that serpent belts are of considerable significance in other parts of the Americas. On North Pacific Coast of North America there are references to the double-headed serpent with a human head centrally placed being carried aloft by the thunderbird undoubtedly identifying it with the sky serpent. In this form it is reminiscent of the ceremonial belts of the Maya where a central trophy head was centrally located on the belt was a serpent and this was often carved out of greenstone or jade. The serpent iconography above noted of the Maya is found among the Kwakiutl and another myth notes from the Comox clan that a double-headed serpent appears as one of the "people of the sea chief" indicating its probable origin from across the Pacific Ocean. In another myth it was said that the deified hero Q'a'nege'lak kills a double-headed serpent and uses its eyes as sling stones to kill whales by instructing the eyes to come to life. This hero paddled a double-headed serpent canoe named Xatetsem and from the skin of the serpent he killed he made a belt. When he gives the belt to a child who is going to "meet" a sea monster, after the child is swallowed by it, he shouts "child in the belly" and the belt kills the monster. This myth and the apparent derivation from "sea people" suggests that they originated from Polynesian epics where it relates to the swallowing of a hero by a crocodile in India, oni's or serpent's in Japan and Melanesia. It is also stated in the Kwakiutl myths that the scales and intestines of the double-headed serpent, when pulled along the ground, create the rivers paralleling the myths of India, Melanesia and the Amazon Basin - too closely to be coincidental.

The Sun was said to wear a double-headed serpent mask in Kwakiutl myth and this motif appears to be almost identical to the iconographical representations found in Peru and identifies the serpent belt with the sky serpent as the Sun's orbit[76]. The many other parallels between the myths of India and those of the North West Pacific Coast Indians of North America have been noted elsewhere[77]. The Sun's mask appearing as a double-headed serpent among the Kwakiutl, and resembling so many aspects of iconography among the Peruvians so far to the south, is reminiscent of the close similarities of the Si'wit myths of the Kwakiutl being so similar to those of the Chorote in the Gran Chaco and their hero Kixwet, earlier noted.

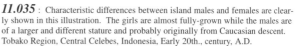

11.035 : Characteristic differences between island males and females are clearly shown in this illustration. The girls are almost fully-grown while the males are of a larger and different stature and probably originally from Caucasian descent. Tobako Region, Central Celebes, Indonesia, Early 20th., century, A.D.

11.036 : Group of Nattu Malayans displaying the result of Aryan tribal incursions among the Negrito or Veddah pygmoid aboriginal tribes in India. South India, Early 20th., century, A.D.

11.037 : A group of Gonds of stature and Caucasian features similar to the Ghasi and Ancient Middle East. Central India, Early 20th., century, A.D.

11.038 : Three Toda men displaying traditional hairstyles and dress that is remarkable reminiscent of Sumerian depiction surviving from 3,000 years before. Nilgiri Hills, Mysore, South India, Late 19th., century, A.D.

11.039 : A Ghasi man with a traditional gourd stringed instrument. He is typical of many of the part Aboriginal tribes who have assimilated Aryan immigrants from Iran and reflects that physical heritage. Manebhum, Chota Nagpore district East Central India, Early 20th., century, A.D.

Figures with serpents emerging from their mouth or nose are found among the Mayans and the Ancient Peruvians and the Moche in particular[78]. In India one of the most important mythical figures was the great serpent Sesha and it was believed that he incarnated as the hero Bala-Rama and was particularly attributed with instructing Aryan heroes in the use of the mace. When he died the serpent Sesha issued from Bala-Rama's mouth[79]. In a Buddhist text, an epic recording the battle between the forces of the Nagas and the Buddha, it is said that these demons, in attempting to vanquish Buddha seated under the Bhodi Tree, spat out serpents from their mouths[80]. This exact reflection of this imagery is found in a monkey image flanking both sides of a ceremonial stairway at Copan, in the identical form of the monkey god of India, Hanuman, and finds its reflection in South America iconography[81]. These serpents appear also to be identified with the mouth fangs and emergent spirals illustrated in carving in India.

Not only is such shared imagery common between India, Central America and South America but even the smallest item appears to have sometimes been transferred. In Melanesia there are many myths and legends associated with twins, or two boys, who slay ogres who oppressed or cannibalised the people. In one myth it is noted that the relation as a whole is identical with those associated with the megalithic stone-using people of pre-history in Melanesia but who appear to originate from the megalithic Mundas, Bhuiyas and Gonds in India. The Melanesian myth relates that the grandfather of the boys was in fact a giant serpent living in a cave and was fed through fear by the local people. Once a month the single large tooth the serpent possessed was extracted by the people and they were rewarded by him for this act although the tooth grew back quickly[82]. Clearly the giant serpent in fact represented the megalithic ancestors, probably originally serpent worshippers from India, from the distant past and who were encapsulated in the myth of this great serpent. Interestingly a post carving from Arequipa in Southern Peru depicts a single-toothed figure with a turban reminiscent of those worn by the Nagas of Assam and the Gonds into recent times (*6.071*; *6.076*; *11.040*).

Serpents - Vagina Dentata Myths

11.040 : A single tooth in the upper and lower jaws seems to relate to similar iconography and associated myths in Melanesia and South America. The carved post with a serpent rising to the head is characteristic of the Nagas of Assam in North East India. Paracas Peninsula, Central Coast Peru, First half of the first millennium, A.D.

In many of the traditions in the forested regions of South America it was considered that a woman was especially vulnerable during the period of menstruation. At this time it was believed that she was exposed to attack by evil spirits who attempted to enter her through all the openings in her body. These spirits were usually described as taking the form of snakes and that if they succeeded in entering her she would give birth to a monster, deformed babies, or herself become ill and die[83]. In some tribes it was believed that women could actively have relations with serpents and demons and the result would be a deformed child or half-human creature. In many of the tribes of South America the women were tattooed more frequently than among the men and it was believed that this form of body marking was imposed as a protection since women had "small power of resistance" to the attacks of evil spirits[84]. This identically replicates the beliefs in Melanesia and parts of Indonesia as well as India, and it is to be noted also that among these same Amazonian Indians cutting off a section of the finger as a sign of mourning is the same as that found in Polynesia[85].

These myths are far from exclusive to the Amazonian and Gran Chaco regions of South America and many form the basis of the so-called "Vagina Dentata" myths. These are myths that thematically consider the dangers of a male attempting intercourse with women, and usually result in dire consequences for the male. In India there are a very great number of this myth type recorded and some of these are almost identical to those in Central and South America. Many of these involve serpents that have been said to have entered the female and then prevented the male from having relations successfully with the woman.

It has been noted elsewhere that there are several of these myth types that occurred in India and are closely similar to those among the Indians of the North Pacific Coast of North America and the Huichol in the North West of Mexico. These are shown to have been distributed along the marines highways that are the ocean currents in the Pacific Ocean connecting directly those places where they occur most profusely in Central and North America with South East Asia and India. These have been recorded as particularly occurring among twenty-six tribes along the Pacific coast of North America Coast and in twenty-two of these the versions parallel closely those of India[86].

As in India there were many tribes where the female after puberty was deflowered by the priest since he alone was believed able to resist the malevolence of the evil spirits attached to the female that threatened to damage the bridegroom or other males of the tribe[87]. This exactly duplicates many of the myths and practices found in India and are probably introduced through transfer by mariners between the continents of Asia and the Americas[88]. These myths have occupied the minds of many learned people and Havelock Ellis believed that they might relate to the male spider being in danger of being eaten by the female after mating - that is the damage in intercourse that is usually done to the male reflected in human relationships[89]. However, it was attested in these myths that the male and his organ of generation was at risk due to teeth believed to have originally been located in the female vagina. Clearly there is no anatomical evidence for such a belief and is therefore symbolic of what has been called primitive psycho-pathology. It is unlikely that any acute observations of the fate of some of the male spiders, usually that of being eaten by the female, after mating, by tribal peoples gave rise to such beliefs. However, it may be that the many myths relating to incursive giants "killing the women" of indigenous tribes in their relations may hold something of a clue as to the origin of vagina dentata myths that were recorded of the Manta giants in Ecuador. These myths or legends occur where there are oral traditions preserved of giant men who have possessed the women of pygmoid tribes such as in the Manta records, in the tribes of the Amazon Basin, and in Melanesia. These pygmoid tribes were at one time more extensive and known as negritoes in the Western Pacific, and where there are still descendants of this small people in New Guinea (*11.045*). In fact the indigenous peoples throughout Central and South America are noted for their exceptionally short stature and this is still evident in many of the less mixed peoples with the mestizos, that is with some Spanish blood, and many qualify as pygmoid. So widespread were these very small indigenous people that it is possible that the vagina dentata myths originated with the considerable difficulty of the much larger males attempting to enter the female either voluntarily or by force. The result recorded of the imposition of the giants having relations with these very small women, and sometimes men, was usually death. Although such relations must have been dire for the indigenous people the inequity of corresponding male and female organs must also have been more than a little discomforting for the male giants if these reports were based on fact. Even among the partners of the same racial heritage and physical size the difficulties of entering the virgin are somewhat celebrated for the frequent difficulty encountered so that the confrontation between partners reflecting physical extremes must have been potentially and proportionally much more difficult. The variation in racial backgrounds between some of the male and females in the castes of India indicate that the male lines were from the considerably taller Aryan peoples. By necessity they took the only available women, either by force or barter, from the indigenous and negrito Aboriginal peoples and formed separate tribal groups whose descendants tended to retain their respective inequity of the male and female physical inheritances (*11.035/6*; *11.043*). This is also true in New Guinea and there is a body of myths recording that giant men crossed the Australian continent in mythical times[90] in an east to west direction[91]. They were said to be following the sea current flowing across the north coast of Australia but while doing so they preyed upon women suggesting that the original race of people were the pygmoid negritoes in Australia[92] probably related to those of nearby Melanesia. The vagina dentata myths are clearly as a result of dispersal along the ocean currents from India, South East Asia to the Pacific Coast of North West America - where they occur more frequently than anywhere else. They were also imported into Central America and South America indicating that it was the mariners who dispersed or were responsible for their origins. These were probably the fair-skinned giants, recorded in Gilbertese myths and in other parts of Polynesia, who experienced these sexual problems with the negritoes and pygmoid Amerindians of the Americas. They preserved the memory in their many myths along the destinations of their sea journeys and these became assimilated in time into the local folklore in those many distant destinations.

One particular example of the vagina dentata myth is worth extending from its inclusion in a previous work. This is because it occurs not only among the Huichols and is so closely similar to one preserved in India but is also found among the Amazon tribes far to the South East. The version in India derives from an Assur myth, a people already noted as possibly being descended from the Anatolian peoples, possibly the Hittites, and having references to the cultures of the Americas. This myth records that a Rakshasa (a demon) loved a human girl and from their union a daughter was born and when she grew up she declared that anyone who could survive intercourse with her would be raja of the district. Many young princes came to see her but after sleeping with her, the two teeth in her vagina cut of their penises. One day a young prince and

11.041 : Dwarf tribes are prominently mentioned in South American myth. The white explorer indicates the extremely small stature of some of the Amazonian Indians. Amazon Basin, Early 20th., century, A.D.

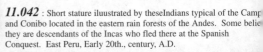

11.042 : Short stature iluustrated by theseIndians typical of the Camp and Conibo located in the eastern rain forests of the Andes. Some belie they are descendants of the Incas who fled there at the Spanish Conquest. East Peru, Early 20th., century, A.D.

11.043 : A Navarute family - a man and his three wives and their children. The noticeably taller male is a characteristic descendant of an ancient intrusive, taller races into the pygmoid tribes inhabiting the Amazon region. Amazon Basin, South America, Early 20th., century, A.D.

11.045 : Dwarf peoples are featured in many myths in Indonesia, Melanesia and Polynesia through to the Amazon Basin. New Guinea, Early 20th., century, A.D.

11.044 : A Naga couple showing the characteristic difference in height common among many peoples in Bengal and Assam as well as in South India probably due to male intruders from the Bay of Bengal. West Rengma Nagas, Assam, North East India, Early 20th., century A.D.

his friend, an Assur (a caste of smithies), came to visit her. The young prince slept with her and suffered the same fate as the others and he related to his friend the tragedy that befallen him. The young Assur man went to the smithy and had an iron hollow penis sheath made so that it fitted over his own closely. When he went for his turn with the Rakshasas's daughter, having fitted the penis sheath, he thrust it forcefully into her and the two teeth were broken off. The young Assur man then threatened to kill the girl unless he restored his friend's penis, to which she concurred, and then she married the Assur[93].

From North West Mexico the Huichol myth relates that the heroic Flood survivor, Kauymali, in a long myth that need not be expounded here relates to obtaining and planting the first corn. At the end of the myth, he wished to marry to produce heirs but it is said that it was necessary for him to remove the teeth from a woman's vagina before this could be achieved. Nakawe, the supreme goddess of the Huichols assisted in his efforts to produce children by advising him to place his magic horn over his penis before penetration and by this method the "teeth" were ground away. The goddess caught the horn as it was withdrawn so that it retained it magic power. It was believed that this act was done on behalf of all Huichols and that they can only reproduce because of this heroic act[94]. The myth is clearly so similar to that of the Assurs in India that this must have been effected by transfer, particularly so since, as noted in an earlier work, there are so many other aspects of Huichol myth and ritual that also corresponds. The Assurs themselves were closely connected to the Gonds and Bhuiyas on the Sub-continent of India and

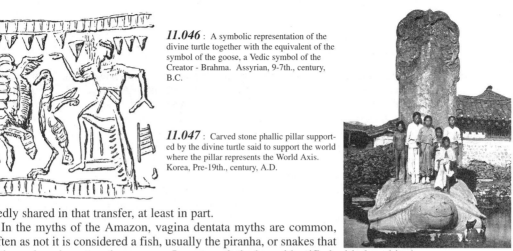

11.046 : A symbolic representation of the divine turtle together with the equivalent of the symbol of the goose, a Vedic symbol of the Creator - Brahma. Assyrian, 9-7th., century, B.C.

11.047 : Carved stone phallic pillar supported by the divine turtle said to support the world where the pillar represents the World Axis. Korea, Pre-19th., century, A.D.

undoubtedly shared in that transfer, at least in part.

In the myths of the Amazon, vagina dentata myths are common, and as often as not it is considered a fish, usually the piranha, or snakes that threaten the male as he enters the woman. In one myth the hero, identified with the white heron, was afraid to have intercourse with his bride as the First Woman because of the piranha fish[95] believed to inhabit the vagina, so he obtained an iron pin and made an phallus from it, some versions say it was inserted into his penis, and as he deflowered the girl the teeth were ground away[96]. This myth closely follows that of the Huichol of West Mexico and the Assur of India as the generality of the same type of myths do with others in those same lands. In the Toba and Mataco version from the Gran Chaco the fox and a falcon wish to have relations with a girl but the fox is mutilated while the falcon after him uses his magic staff to break the teeth of the vagina[97]. In a Makiritare myth the "masculine long-beaked bird" assists the fox by using an armoured artificial phallus similar to that of the Huichol and Assur mythical heroes. The First Woman was believed to have been created from a piece of the World Tree and the shape of the female was cut out be the beak of the creator in the form of the woodpecker[98]. Cutting out the figure and providing its with human features is a motif found widely in Australian myth and derives no doubt from similar examples in India.

Associated with the vagina dentata myths are those where the male penis was said to be originally very long and was often described as being coiled around the waist, or even around the head, and in some myths carried in a basket. In these myths this oversized penis was reduced to normal size or in stages by often very drastic means. An abundance of these myths are found in India[99], among the Huichol[100] and in the Amazon Basin and Gran Chaco regions of South America[101].

Kachchapa to Kawasi -
The Nagas of Assam and their origins in the Gonds of India to the Nazca Plains in South Peru
The connection between the Assurs, the Bhuiyas, Mundas, Kols and Gonds has been emphasised throughout this work since they share so many aspects of an ancient pre-Vedic-Aryan culture more characteristic before the migrations of the Aryans from Iran dating from the early first millennium B.C. The unifying elements of this pre-Vedic-Aryan culture appear also to have originated from the Caucasus region, and Anatolia in particular, and progressed through Iran into India before this last great migration across the North West border. These aspects appear to have been preserved in the cultures of these semi-Aboriginal tribes of India and also appear to have influenced the Pacific Islands into Central and South America before the rise of the later Vedic Indians and their successors, the Hindus. In Peru the Incas appear to have been a later migration who emerged after the collapse of the Altiplano empire of Tiahuanaco. They may have been either the legitimate descendants from their rulers in part or later migrations from the north of South America, possibly from Central America into Colombia, after migrating across the Pacific

from India. Certainly many of the myths are closely similar, such as the vagina dentata type, and this seems to indicate that the direct connection with Central America and Colombia from India was equally likely. From there the common influences appear to separate, some proceeding into the Amazon Basin while others went south into Ecuador and Peru. The Inca's own origin myths tend to indicate both this possibility and part descent from Tiahuanaco. The retention of so much of the original Brahmanic form of Vedic-Aryan culture from India suggests that the male lineage was centralised in South America for too little time for the essential caste divisions, still operating, to have been more eroded from the original model in India. The date usually given for the beginning of the Inca dynasty is the mid-fourteenth century A.D. - say 1350 A.D., and this would appear reasonably correct in the terms of lack of substantial modification of their Vedic-Aryan heritage. On the other hand the name they gave to their own empire, Tahuantin-suyu, associated with the Bhuiyas and part Aboriginal peoples in India suggests that this may have been adopted from Tiahuanaco, an empire exhibiting many aspects of iconography and constructional techniques known to the early Iranians at Persepolis and elsewhere and also later among the Chalukyas and Orissan peoples in India. This adoption from Tiahuanaco appears to have extended also to assimilation of mythical and religious rites derived from Tiahuanaco long preserved by the pre-Inca and contemporaries of the Aymaran people around Lake Titicaca.

It has also been earlier noted that the descendants of the Vedic-Brahmans in India paid, in some way, respect to the Gonds not accorded to other part or wholly Aboriginal peoples in India. These Brahmans were not a sentimental people and it may be that they early recognised that the Gonds (at least the paternal line) were an earlier migration from the Iranian plateau. Certainly the long myth cycles they have preserved are more coherent and sophisticated that among many other tribes in India and they preserved the assertion that they had once been masters in the land.

The Maria Gonds are largely located North of the Central East Coast delta of the Godavari River and this is the location of the Habla clan division and their chief "log-god" was named Kachchua Deo. This belief in a log representing the supreme god (Deo in India = Deus in the West) is shared to the North East in India and among the Nagas of Assam. This probably derives from the identification of the World Tree, or World Axis, with the cosmological systems in the earliest Hindu iconography and that of the Buddhist. The almost exact form of the log god to that of Orissa[102] is also found in the Marquesas Islands[103] among many other aspects indicating origins in India[104]. The log god of the Gonds is called Kachchua Deo and identifies with this Turtle deity noted elsewhere in this work. The Gond log god is usually represented at the Pen-Rawar by a framework of logs "criss-crossed with bamboos and bedecked with peacock feathers, spirals of quills, brass balls and other simple finery"[105]. Considering the many cross-cultural aspects shared by the Gonds with the Assamese Nagas and the coast people. This suggests that the log god may have represented a raft originally. Peacock feathers and quills are associated with the Sun god and the Sun disk worn by the Gond dancers (*5.158*; *7.062*) is identical with those of Mexico and Guatemala[106] (*7.064*). Brass bells utilised by these dancers in India are identical to those found in the Ancient Americas (*5.160*).

The name Kachchua, however, refers to the turtle or tortoise and among the Aboriginal tribes of India the turtle was believed to have drawn the earth up from the bottom of the primal ocean "before the world began"[107]. The identical cosmology, developed around the primal turtle, appears among the Maya and their associated beliefs are paralleled with that in India in a previous work[108]. In Hindu cosmology Siva is identified with Lord Kacchapesvara - "Lord of the Tortoise" and in aspects of his iconography the phallus is identified with the World Tree. This symbolism of the phallus or world tree being supported on the back of a giant turtle is widespread in the Far East and is found in surviving sculptures, particularly in China and Korea (*6.089-93*).

The clan system among the Gonds appears to preserve early clan divisions and has been recognised as being similar to those systems operating in Aboriginal Australia[109]. This reflects an ancient system whereby the tribe is organised into a dual organisation and then each subdivided into two or four, and a man takes his partners from one of the opposite subdivisions to his own. Among the Gonds, and some of the other Aboriginal tribes, the four main subdivisions appear to reflect the primal quaternary derived from a largely lost cosmology. The traditional terms used indicate that these clan names were usually totemic and probably related to the four quarters or cardinal points, but often there are five since this is the sacred number and the fifth, incorporating the other four as a reflection of the four cardinal points, is the World Axis. The names of the five divisions of one group of Maria Gonds are Baktahans (Goat), Nagams (Cobra), Kuhram or Kadiaribans (Cuckoo), Baghhans (Tiger) and Kachhimvans (Tortoise)[110].

Each of these clans is considered to be a "race" and appeared originally to have stood one to the other in an order of recognised status. Unfortunately the myths of origin, and indeed any folklore associated with most of the clan divisions, has not been preserved, except that only the Kacchimvans, or the Tortoise "race" retain any myths related to their origins. The legend told by this clan is repeated here as it was recorded: "… there is said long ago to have been a great flood, which the brothers Markham and Kawasi were unable to cross until a tortoise came and took them on his back"[111]. Other versions exist relating how the Gonds were stopped on their way to worship a god by a flood and, in attempting to cross it, each section held onto a particular support. These are noted as the trunks of various trees, or an iguana or a tiger, and from these the personal totems of the clans were derived. The Muria branch of the Gonds record that Kawachi was the "brother" of the Maria Gonds suggesting that there was an important link through this name and their hero in Gond mythology so apparent in the flood myth noted[112], and this relationship is also reflected in the naming of one of their clans, Kawachi (tortoise Totem Clan)[113]. Among the important Valluvan tribe of Southern India the term Katchi also referred to a clan subdivision probably derived from contact with the early Gonds in Central India[114]. In North West India, in Rajasthan, the totem of one of the thirty-six "royal races" of the Rajputs held the Kachhwaha, the tortoise, sacred[115].

The term Kawasi as one of the Flood heroes should be noted since this relates to the subsection themes in some sections of this work. The "Sons of the Wind" in India, the Pawabans,

11.048 :
Diagram of the cosmology of Mangaia in Central Polynesia showing the believed levels extending from the earth closely similar to Buddhist and Tibetan cosmic diagrams. Mangaia, Central Polynesia, Early 19th., century, A.D.

of the Bhuiyas, adopted the names of the similar deities to the Gonds and probably for the same reasons in association with the cosmology of the four quarters or cardinal points. Their clan names were the Nagas (snakes or cobras), Gadjas (Elephants), Kachhap or Kasyap (Tortoise) and the Kabutar (Pigeon)[116]. It can be seen that these not only represent the cardinal points but also the four "elements" of air, fire, water and earth corresponding respectively to the Pigeon, Snakes, Tortoise and Elephant. Other tribes of Orissa in North East Central India have similar divisions and among the Oriya their term for the Tortoise is "Kochipo"[117]. Other terms in the same region appear to have been extended from the original four or five clans but retained names of signifi-

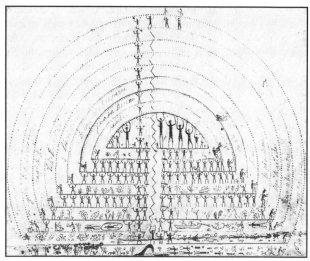

cant meaning such as the Sva (Parrot), Bhag (Tiger), Kochchimo (Tortoise), Naga (Cobra), Sila (Stone), Dhudho (Milk) and Kukra (dog)[118].

Among the Assurs the name for iron is kachi, and loha among the Gonds, while in Sanskrit, the ancient Language of the Vedas it was either lauha or ayas[119] suggesting that it was a particular metal introduced by the Aryan Hittites of Anatolia where it is first known. It is probable therefore that the earlier terms from the Gonds and related tribes reflecting clan names, status, and totems was also transferred to South America and only partly submerged by the assimilation among the indigenous Peruvians.

The name of the capital, or primary ceremonial site influenced from Tiahuanaco on the plains of Southern Peru was called Kawachi, and appears to derive from the Naga traditions in Assam and, or the ancient turtle/tortoise god in India. The fact that among the Raj Gonds it was the hero, Kawasi, that was one of the two Flood survivors and also the name of the most important clan retaining its traditions, Kawachi, suggests that it was they who transferred their name to Southern Peru. In Japan also there are surviving references to the same name where a river important in their myths, Kawachi, is notable. A river sprit named Kappa was said to live in the river Kawachi flowing beside the temple of Kawako-no-miya, in the small village called Kawahimura. This sprite was said to be polite, but fierce and quarrelsome if roused and travellers were supposed to pay homage to him[120]. Interestingly the Gonds in India are associated with the important tribe of Kappa or Kapia and in South America where Kawachi or Cahuachi was the foremost sacred ceremonial centre south of Nazca the sacred mountain was Mount Kapia.

In Ancient China the shell of the tortoise was used in divination and appears in the kingdom of Shu to have been used to select "worthy men" for the ruling council of ministers and was a method used to confirm other important state decisions[121]. In texts, as an apparent explanation of the importance of the number nine in government based on the cosmic constructs of Heaven, there appears to have been the belief that a great turtle appeared in the river Lo and on its back there were "well-defined marks" on its carapace from one to nine[122]. The texts go on to explain the importance of these numbers and their relationship to the seasons and elements. The means of divination in ascribing these relationships is said to have been themselves divined from the tortoise shell and the "reeds" of the Khi plant[123] yarrow stalks so well-known in the present day associated with the oracle of the I-Ching. One of the oldest textual references in the use of the tortoise shell was that of the proposed consultation regarding the illness of the king utilising the tortoise shell, two years after the fall of the Shang kings (c1200 B.C.). However, instead of utilising the turtle shell the Duke of Chao had constructed three altars plus one to the south, calendrically aligned, placing a roundel of jade on each altar[124] for divination rituals.

The association of the number nine and the turtle is also found in the Ancient Vedic texts and recorded in the section describing the Supreme god Brahma creating the world from the divine egg. It is said that he reached into the primal waters and drew up the egg and from it the Brahman (priestly caste) was brought from it first of all and the divinity declared that "they shall be his mouth" (that they would speak for Him). First born from the yolk was the god of fire, Agni, and this deity is identified with the Brahman (priest) as Agni's "mouth". From the eggshell Brahman, squeezing it to form the Earth, created the tortoise and the oceans as well as the sky and universe. The divine mythical tortoise in Vedic mythology is intimately associated with the oceans and believed to live deep underneath them and to support the World Axis in very much the same way as recorded in the myths of the Chinese and Koreans. In the Vedic texts the tortoise is identified along with Agni in this cosmology with the "nine creations" and the fire altar[125.] In an interesting section of the oldest recorded Vedic texts, the Satapatha Brahmana, the tortoise is identified with the fire-altar and the course of the Sun in the rituals performed on it. In performing the rituals at the fire altar it has earlier been noted that the whole of the ritual is performed before dawn in the belief that it was essential to be undertaken at that time to ensure that the Sun rose on the Eastern horizon. This corresponds largely to the principles of the Mexican rituals when large numbers of warriors were sacrificed to ensure that the Sun had the necessary energy to rise in the East and continue its course. The Brahmana records the ritual required of the Brahman priest at the fire-altar:

"1) He then puts down a (living) tortoise; - the tortoise means the life-sap: it is life-sap (blood) he thus bestows on (Agni). This tortoise is that life-sap of these worlds that flowed from them when plunged into the waters: that (life-sap) he now bestows on (Agni). As far as the life-sap extends, so far the body extends: that (tortoise) thus is these worlds."

It is clear from this first part of this fire-ritual that the tortoise is identified with the blood sacrifices of the five sacred animals, the finest of which was considered to be the male warrior. It is clear that the tortoise here, as a primal representative of the cosmic structure, was also considered a suitable sacrifice and as an appropriate substitute for the human and provider of the essential blood as the life force of the universe to enable the Sun to rise.

The second verse gives an interesting description of the tortoise, or turtle, as the cosmic model - from the text as follows:

"2) That lower shell of it is this (terrestrial) world; it is, as it were; fixed; for fixed, as it were, is the (earth-) world. And that upper shell of it is yonder sky; it has its ends, as it were, bent down. And what is between (the shells) is the air; - that (tortoise) thus is these worlds: it is these worlds he thus lays down (to form part of the altar)."

There are many aspects of Melanesian and Polynesian culture that clearly derive from India and the elevated deification of the turtle was notable among many of these islands and also in Indonesia that parallel such reverence in India. It is notable that the Polynesians in their cosmic constructs and in daily life considered the sky to be a hemisphere resting on the horizon much in the same way as the Brahmana text above describes the sky or universe represented by the tortoise shell. The Polynesians also considered that the first Europeans were "Papalangi" or "sky-bursters" since they were considered to have come from the ancestral world and entered their myriad island lands by lifting the sky at the horizon and sailing[126]. This would suggest again that the turtle formed an original model imported by mariners into the Pacific from India but which had become detached from the original Vedic model and ultimately from the turtle imagery itself.

The Satapatha Brahmana Vedic text records the anointing rites associated with the sacrificial turtle and the importance of honey in that ritual and then continues:

"5) And as to its being called 'kurma' (tortoise); - Pragapati (the early Creator, possibly pre-Vedic), having assumed that form, created living beings. Now what he created, he made; and inasmuch as he made (kar), he is (called) 'kurma;' and 'kurma' being (the same as) 'kasyapa' (a tortoise), therefore all creatures are said to be descended from Kasyapa."

Not only is the divine tortoise considered the supporter of the structure of the Universe but its identification with the phallus, although not specifically mentioned, is implied in being the generative principle inherent in its symbolism. This includes its depiction in many representations with a phallus, pillar or linga on the turtle's back in South and East Asia (*6.093*; *11.046*) and in some Chinese depiction of the extended neck and head in the form of a phallus.

In the following verse of the Vedic text the turtle is identified with the Sun and this is as follows:

"6) Now this tortoise is the same as yonder sun: it is yonder sun he thus lays down (on the altar). He lays it down in front with the head towards the back (west): he thus places yonder sun in the east looking thitherwards (or moving westward): and hence yonder sun is placed in the east looking thitherwards. On the right (south) of the Ashadha (he places it), for the tortoise (kurma - is

11.049 : Assyrians with trophy head hung by a cord in a similar way to those illustrated in Central and South America. Kouyunjik, Assyria, Iraq, First half of the first millennium, B.C.

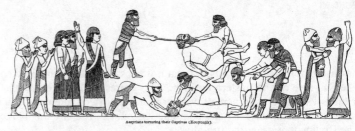

11.050 : Assyrians torturing their prisoners of war. Note the captive on the extreme right bond at the ankles and about to be struck by his captor. The trophy head hung as pendant upside down is identical to many shown among the Zapotecs in Southern Mexico, Central America and South America. Kouyunjik, Assyria, Iraq, First half of the first millennium, B.C.

11.053 : Elamite trophy head displayed after defeat by Ashurbanipal in a sacred tree characteristic also of the Nagas of Assam, Borneo, Central and South America. Babylon, Mesopotamia 7th., century, B.C.

11.052 : Assyrian scribes recording the number of trophy heads taken after the defeat of enemy warriors and other captives. Note the head hung up on the large rock at the left. Kouyunjik, Assyria, Iraq, First half of the first millennium, B.C.

11.051 : Battle scene showing a battering ram and captives impaled on sacrificial posts. This was the model for the Yupe in Ancient India and probably also the Ancient Americas. Nimrud, Babylonia, c900 B.C.

masculine) is a male, and the Ashadha (an altar brick a pada or foot square) a female, and the male lies on the right side of the female; - at a cubit's distance, for at a cubit's distance the male lies by the female. That Ashadha is the consecrated queen (mahishi) of all the bricks, hence being on the right (south) side of her, it (the tortoise) is on the right side of all the bricks."[127] .

The important identification with the Sun and its course is here confirmed and should be read with the other references that parallel the symbolic aspects of the fire-god Agni and those of the Andean deities in earlier chapters in this work. It is clear that the fire-god of the Andes derives from the Vedic fire-worship of India but also in the epochs before the Incas not only from India but from Ancient Iran. As in Melanesia and Polynesia the names of the deities, so clearly derived from India in many cases, were localised while others retained at least some reference to their original terminology in Asia and this was certainly the case exhibited by the Tukano Desana in Colombia and is likely also to be the case in the Andes. The name of Cahuachi or Kawachi as the main ceremonial site on the Nazcan Plains of Southern Peru appears to have been initiated as an extension from the later period of the Empire of Tiahuanaco. It is, therefore, largely influenced by a highland culture around Lake Titicaca, in existence for half a millennia, before lowland Kawachi was established. It is probably because of this that the name Kawachi was important since many aspects of Tiahuanaco culture are paralleled in Central and North East India, relating to the Mundas, Bhuiyas and Gonds, and reflects also Ancient Iranian connections in their architecture. The connection with the turtle appears to have diminished or been lost due to lack of contact with suitable alternative tortoise types in the highland, but retained important ritual connections in the ceremonial rites on the Nazca Plains reflected in the name Kawachi. Here they may have retained myths and legends associated with the turtle from India or because of the critical lack of water on the plains, identifying with the Flood hero, Kawasi or Kawachi, as a form of sympathetic magic or rain hero-god.

11.054 : Carved basalt warrior with a trophy head hung as a pendant on his back. Rio Verde, Limon Province, Central America, 800-1525 A.D.

11.055 : Shrunken heads were the famous trophies of the Jivaros in the Eastern Andes of Ecuador but also known in Indonesia. Jivaro tribe, Ecuador, Late 19th., century, A.D.

11.056 : Carved stone wall of trophy heads representing a tzompalli or skull rack. Chichen Itza, Yucatan, South Mexico, 10th., century, A.D.

11.057 : Stacked trophy heads carved in relief on the revetment at Cerro Sechin. Casma Valley, Central Coast Peru, Late 2nd., millennium, B.C.

11.058 : Trophy heads hung from the necks of warriors or rulers. Quen Santo, Guatemala, Post Classic.

11.059 : Large group of trophy heads as recorded on a cylinder seal similar to the Tzompalis or skull racks and other collected piles of prisoners heads recorded in Mexico and among the Maya. Assyrian, First half of the first millennium, B.C.

The parallels between the Tiahuanaco cosmology, although much less complete due to the lack of written evidence from the time, provides consistent evidence in comparison with the myths of India to be able to determine that their mythology derived in large part from India. Not only is Kawasi, Kachhapa, or Kasyapa the turtle as both flood hero and clan name of the Gonds but as the last, Kasyapa, he is associated with Brahma's son Arthavan. This hero-deity is identified with Aravan in Southern India and it has already been noted that this is an alternative name given for Tonapa, the god of lightning, among the Aymara around Lake Titicaca - Arnauan. Kasyapa is the name given to the turtle in the Arthavan writings and the amulets and charms said to have been handled by him were considered particularly effective. In these texts also Kasyapa as the tortoise was considered to be the Sun "that creeps its slow course across the sky"[128] relating again to the Sun symbolism of the Andes.

Kawachi; Headhunting and the Vedas

One of the most remarkable aspects of the Andean and coastal Peruvian civilisations is the universal depiction of human trophy heads as an apparent essential requirement for military ands religious ceremonies. Leading up to, and during the severe climate change that occurred in Peru about the middle of the first millennium A.D. a sudden increase is notable in the depiction of human heads on textiles, ceramics and carvings. This increase suggests that the climate change was considered by the people, or priests, that the gods who had stopped listening or were punishing their people for misdemeanours. This resulted in many more human sacrifices were being offered to the gods and their heads were then secreted in sanctified niches and pits around the temples, many of which have subsequently been recovered in the excavations at Kawachi on the

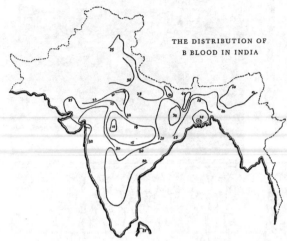

THE DISTRIBUTION OF
B BLOOD IN INDIA

11.060 : Blood group map of India showing the extension of blood groups away from the Bay of Bengal and the deltas of the Ganges and Brahmaputra Rivers giving access into the whole of India and into Tibet. This is probably a result of mariner intrusions and intermixing. India, Mid-20th., century, A.D.

South Nazca Plain in South Peru. Kawachi was considered an outpost of the Highland Tiahuanacan civilisation and here also trophy heads were common in contemporary ceramics, textiles and reliefs from centuries before. This begs the question as to whether headhunting was a mystically elevated and ritualised form of the Amazonian Indian customs or was instigated by, or at least augmented, by teachings derived from imported traditions from their mariners ancestors originating in the authority of the Vedic texts.

The construction of the sacred fire-altar in Ancient India, dating from the first half of the first millennium B.C., is set out in regulations and commentaries by the early Vedic writers. This was done since any fault in the construction and performance of the fire rites was believed to invalidate the ceremonies. In the earliest instructions the altar had to be in the outline of a supine human male and took the form that was initially imported by the Aryans in preserved traditions from their homelands in Iran. There are very specific references indicating that this was so because the finest sacrifice to the gods, and the rites associated with Agni as the life-force of the Sun, was the human warrior male and is described at length in an earlier work[129]. In later texts the altar is said to be also in the form of a bird but this "body" or "atman" was said to be four man's lengths square but usually measuring about forty feet where the first five layers are built of special bricks. The text notes that the ground of the "body" is then ploughed, watered and sown with seeds of all kinds including herbs. On this a square mound, the uttaravedi, measuring a yuga about 7 feet, on each side is constructed in the middle and the top levelled. Connecting the centre of each side are two "spines" forming a cross on top of the altar. At the centre of the raised cross the priest places a lotus-leaf and the gold pectoral plate he has worn during the rite up to that point as the symbol of the Sun. On this plate he places a small gold figure of a man representing Agni-Pragapati, and this figure is placed with its head to the East. The description given in the Satapatha Brahmana also notes among other aspects in the construction of the altar that a live tortoise is placed facing the small gold figurine of a man representing Agni and a wooden mortar and pestle. On the mortar the priest placed the firepan (ukha) filled with sand and milk and on this are placed the "... heads of five victims, after chips of gold have been thrust into their mouths, nostrils, eyes and ears"[130]. Such ceremonial items appear reminiscent of the trophy head rituals known at this time through Peru (*11.057*) and Bolivia and it is of particular interest that small gold figures were, and are frequently found in Ancient Peruvian and Bolivian graves - largely Inca.

The number of bricks in construction of the Vedic fire-altar is important and prescribed including one for the three hundred and sixty for the days of the year and twenty-four for the half-moons during the year (two per lunar month) as well as one for each solar month[131]. The number of three hundred and sixty for the days in the year, rather than 365 days, appears to be an old symbolic reference and corresponds also to the sacred year of the same number of days found in Mexico.

The construction of the fire-altar is of particular interest in considering the custom of head-hunting since, as has already been noted, the altar itself was considered to be the shape of the ideal sacrifice the finest human male, but in later constructions, that of a bird. However, all the elements still retained the connotations of human sacrifice and the five trophy heads, originally human but later certain animals, were placed on the altar as part of the fire rituals. The platform as the base for the altar was still referred to as the "body" (Atman) and this no doubt refers to a time when human sacrifices were interred as guardians under the platform. Similar rites were still retained as a tradition in many parts of the world including India, South East Asia and into the Pacific Islands through into the Americas up until a century or two ago. This "atman" meant "the self" and the "breath" and corresponds to the breath associated with the wind god, Pawan. It is this wind god who conducted the soul after death to the ancestral world and therefore the addition and identification of the sacrificed soul was seen as mediating on behalf of the priest at the fire-altar. The ritual prescribes five sacrificial heads but does not define whether all were human trophy heads or whether they were one of each of the five acceptable sacrificial animals - "man, horse, ox, sheep, and goat"[132]. It is most likely that they were all originally human since gold oboloi are not known originally for animal sacrifices, and similar oboloi are found in Ecuadorian, Peruvian and Bolivian interments. In either case since the Vedic fire-ceremony was ideally performed twice a month indicating that a considerable number of sacrifices were required and was also a purification rite to embark upon forays into enemy tribes to acquire these captives for sacrifice. Such forays were known to have occurred, and were still operating and described in some detail among the Nagas of Assam into the twentieth century, and in parallel to have formed an essential social requirement among the peoples of Ancient Peru and Bolivia.

Although the historic Vedic Aryans in India are not known to have sought trophy heads the remnants of such rituals are clearly retained in their texts and probably formed part of the fire ceremonies in the religion of Ancient Iran in earlier millennia. From this distant age such traditions may have been transferred into the Andean communities from the third millennium B.C. to first centuries B.C. and culminating at Nazca and in the Tiahuanacan Empire through until about the 11th., century A.D. The copies of the ancient Vedic texts in their original form in earlier millennia B.C. would have seen the rituals operating as defined in the originals and therefore human heads were certainly placed on the altars in those epochs. This tradition appears to be confirmed by the acquisition of trophy heads from local wars and skirmishes depicted in the reliefs of Assyria (*11.049/50*; *11.052/3*; *11.059*) which are remarkably reminiscent of the skull-racks of Aboriginal Formosa (Taiwan) and the Tzompalli of Mexico[133] (*11.056*).

The term Kawasi of the Gonds and Kawachi or Cahuachi in Nazca appears therefore to be intimately connected and this transfer is likely to have occurred before the supremacy of the Aryan Brahmans in India. It is likely also that the Gonds in India were an earlier branch of Aryan (males) who migrated from Iran bringing memories of some of their original fire-ceremonies and associated rituals with them, or, they were subject to incursions or contacts with early Iranian Aryans from whom they derived some fire-related cults. They also appear to have been the recipients of Mandaean influences from the Tigris and Euphrates regions. There are traceable contacts with Sri Lanka in their myths and from there diffusions of their cultural references are detectable towards the North East coast into India into the Ganges Delta region and these include references to some of the Gond people. From this it appears that earlier than the post-Vedic Brahmans and Hindus, the Gonds and related tribes were among those who transferred such rituals and associated headhunting requirements from India to South America.

It has been shown in a previous work that the Mandaeans appear to have been of major influence in North and Central America and this influence appears to be in concert with other peoples considered in part Aboriginal to India such as the Mundas, Bhuiyas, Kols and Gonds[134]. This influence is probable to have been long established by the time the Brahmans, and the Hindu religion had become more influential in India evident in the Gupta dynasty. This is particularly so in South India when their ascendancy and that of the Hindus becomes more apparent in the transfer of culture to Indonesia, Melanesia Polynesia and then into Central And South America in the second half of the first millennium A.D. The peoples who became the Incas appear to have transferred in the latter part of the first millennium A.D. and reflect much more of the old fire-religion of India overlaying that already assimilated in Peru and Bolivia essential in their Aryan heritage and the deity terms preserved by them in the Andean region of Peru in their Empire.

Although the Gond and other part-Aboriginal tribes exhibit close connections with the Nagas of Assam, located only a few hundred miles away in the foothills of the Himalayas, it is likely that the Nagas incorporated a large proportion of the mariners peoples who had plied the trading vessels from the Ganges Delta to South America and back again. Apart from them others, as relief crew, would also constitute inflow from the Peruvian Coast in subsequent generations since the earliest contact with South America and whose destination was in fact the Ganges Delta and probably also Tibet in the later period. It is likely that some would have remained in South America and intermarried and it was their descendants returned over generations as relief crews and settled back in the same region of their ancestral homeland. This is likely to have formed a pattern of flow and counterflow over many centuries. The demographic blood grouping illustrated in maps drawn up half a century ago show the expansion inland from the eastern Bay of Bengal coasts of Eastern India and into Assam and it was noted by the first officials in Assam, two generations before, that the tribes appeared to have gradually moved northward a way from the coast towards the Himalayas and Tibet[135] over the centuries (*11.060*). Early research by British officials indicate that at least some of these Nagas were in fact mariners and their culture was early noted to be closely similar to those of the islands of Indonesia in particular and the Philippines as well as parts of Melanesia. The close similarities in the former head-hunting and megalithic culture of Assam suggests that these may have originated in India and then transferred to South America before returning from the Nazca plain to the Ganges Delta. All along this route, on their way to their ancestral lands or to Tibet, where closely similar cultural references occur and human sacrifices were part of the ancient pre-Buddhist Bon Po rituals, there are aspects of South American culture that is evident in its return back to India and particularly evident in the New Hebrides and Celebes.

Cahuachi or Kawachi in South Coast Peru

Cahuachi in South Coast Peru was the centre of the Ica Valley to the north and the Rio Grande de Nazca in the south and reflecting Chavinoid elements of influence at its inception in about 350 B.C. and appears first to have been strongly influenced by Paracas Cavernas and Cavernas Necropolis styles. Cahuachi itself in its final and greatest stage is now thought to have been occupied and extended as an outpost of the Tiahuanacan Empire from the Bolivian Highlands in the early centuries A.D. and ceased to function by about 200 A.D.. Apart from its ceramics Cahuachi is most noted for its fine textiles, where one retrieved example from a tomb measuring 50m. long and 1.7m. wide[136] and is situated about 10 miles from the present town of Nazca[137]. Cahuachi appears also to have been a centre for the resurgence of influences, particularly imagery from a millennium earlier[138]. This may have been either a locally inspired expansion of conservative influences still surviving in the region or stimulus from the same external influences that had given rise to the first period of imagery in Southern Peru.

Cahuachi (Kawachi) began, it is believed, as a congregational centre and became an important settlement with the construction of forty mounds of various sizes along with forecourts and plazas. The mounds or stepped platforms were usually built around and over natural rises in the landscapes, or eminences, and faced with mud brick facades[139]. Importantly its is here in the surrounding Nazca plain that the puquios (pukios), the underground irrigation system incorporating wells or chambers, are found so closely resembling the qanats in South East Arabia and

Ancient South West Iran, although a slightly later date than Cahuachi at its height has been conjectured[140]. This is the area of Asia from where the portals and fine stonework, including metal cramps, appear to have originated in the construction of Tiahuanaco in its last expansive period from the first half of the first millennium A.D. Once again the iconography, architecture and irrigation systems of Ancient Iran appear connected to the areas of influence in East and South India and then to Peru and Bolivia in South America.

It should be remembered that the ancient connection of the imagery and mythology of the tortoise or turtle noted in the Vedas, probably derived also in Iran where the Vedic texts largely have their origin. In Iran to this day is the ancient and holy city of Kurma, the name given for the Tortoise in Vedic texts. Although this city has long been dedicated to Islam its origin may have been on the site of ancient pre-Muslim fire-worship dedicated in some way, or pre-eminently, to the tortoise as the foundation for the spirit of the universe. What is known is that the tortoise figures prominently in their iconography and therefore certainly in the religious myths of Ancient Assyria (*11.046*) and this may have been the origin from the name Kurma for Kawasi in India, or Kawachi in South Peru. Among the Mandaeans there is a hero named Kawila and this may have been the origin of the Gond hero Kawasi, but Kawila, the name for the Ark in the Great Flood[141], also appears among the Mayans in Central America as Kauil. This Mayan deity is identified with the wind deities, the Pauahtuns[142], and this leads back to the Bhuiya wind deity in India, Pawan, and themselves as the Pawabans, the "Sons of the Wind"[143] reflected among the Tukano Desana.

It should also be remembered that the Sacred Tortoise - the Kurma, Kachchapa, or Kachchua Deo (the name of the Gond log god earlier noted), was "squeezed out" from the shell of the World Egg along with the waters of the oceans hence he is associated with all great masses of water including the Flood and probably links in this way to the Gond Flood Survivor, Kawasi. Among the Mundas of India the Horo, or Kachua Kili (kili = clan), their ancestral origin is given in a myth as follows: "The ancestor of the Kili, while on a journey had to cross the swollen river. His 'Hagas' or kinsmen crossed the river safely. But he himself did not venture to do so unaided, and exclaimed, 'Whosoever will take me safely across the river, will be my kith and kin forever.' In those days all animals and vegetable creation could understand human speech and could themselves by understood by man. A tortoise, who heard the Munda's appeal for help, offered to carry him across the river. The tortoise succeeded in carrying on his back not the Munda alone but all his family and baggage safe to the other side of the river. True to his promise, the Munda henceforth assumed the name Horo or 'Kachua' (turtle), and his descendants came to form the Horo or Kachua Kili. No Munda of the kili will kill a tortoise or eat its flesh."[144]. The myth is a naïve one but it indicates the very ancient traditions associated with the tortoise or turtle related to floods and the oceans generally and the identification with animal totems, that many tribes in India and abroad retained for many centuries and millennia. The myth has probable similar origins to that of the Gond and their hero Kawasi and this would appear to be derived from the Ancient Middle East.

Turtles Deities and Turtle Ancestors

Among the Mundas of India and other tribes there are many references in myth to the turtles fetching up land to form the Earth in Creation myths[145]. These almost identical myths are broadcast throughout the Pacific Islands and have clearly been derived through diffusion from India and are noted in an earlier work[146]. In many myths preserved in the Pacific Islands it is clear that they have lost many aspects of their association with the Ancient cultures and myths of Iran and India but are still recognisable. In a myth from the Solomon Islands it is said that a woman was saved in the ocean by building up earth and stones until she had solid material to stand on[147] and in many islands of Indonesia[148], Melanesia[149] and Polynesia similar actions commonly resulted in totemic identification with the original myth attributed to the divine turtle. Turtles were, reflecting the same traditions as among the Mundas, sacred animals and in some cases special pools were created or reserved for their use.

On the Ecuadorian Coast in South America turtle bones were found in excavations undertaken a century ago suggesting that the turtle was considered sacred[150]. The name of this place was, and still is Manta and it must be conjectured whether this was in fact a localisation of the term Manda, for Mandaean. This is certainly not far fetched since the main deity of the Mandaeans, Pthahil is found among the Quiche-Mayan traditions as the deity named Tohil, and the term Kauil, identified with the Pauahtuns, is also a Mandaean name noted in their own texts and found also in Eastern India where Mandaean influences is ubiquitous. Marshall Saville, reporting on the excavations in Ecuador, noted that the local term for the wells was coconcha and he considered that this term actually derived from the Mayan chaltun in the Yucatan in Mexico. He also noted that the name of the Ecuadorian goddess Umina appears in Maya as Uminhah meaning the "true grandmother of them"[151].

The Mayan belief relating to the cosmic turtle notes that the human world floated, or rested on the back of a great caiman or turtle. These reptilian aspects of their cosmology were related to the cardinal points and the World Tree, Waca Chan, was believed to be supported on its back[152]. This imagery is identical to that of Ancient India, and Miles Poindexter, the former ambassador to Peru noted in his researches that the term chan appears frequently in the place names and myths in the Ancient Americas. He plots the transfer of chan to the original of the term from an in the Aryan heartland of Central Asia, and corresponding to l-an-d in the West and such terms as -ham in the place names of England, such as Birming-ham[153]. His researches are far more extensive than can be included further here, but it is clear that the fundamentals of many aspects in both North and South America can be traced back to West, Central and South Asia, and this includes the concept of the World Tree and its being carried on the back of the mythical turtle.

In the Amazon the turtle was associated with the Sun and Moon and it was said to have been the animal who tore the culture heroes out from the womb of the First Woman[154]. This appears to parallel the tortoise as the first animal in the myths of India as the Kurma or Kachhapa since the myths associated with it indicate that the first people came from it. The Vedic myths also identify the tortoise with the Sun, and as a water animal it is also associated with the Moon. Among the Ge Indians of the Amazon Basin there are what appears to be remarkable parallels with the myths of India. Here the mythical turtle is named Kapranapetti, and it was believed that he could send a deluge of water if annoyed. The name of the divine turtle in Hindu myth is identified with Siva in his phallic aspect as "Lord of the Tortoise" - Kacchapesvara, clearly the model for the Ge Amazonian deity. In the Ge myth the Sun is called Pud and the Moon his female counterpart is named as Pud-lera and this follows the feminised duplication of the male name in the most ancient of Near and Middle Eastern traditions as well as those of Ancient Egypt. Pud as the Sun is clearly derived from the ancient Aryan Asian term for the Sun, Pun and indicates that this myth appears to derive directly through being imported by mariners from India before the name Surya became more commonly used in the succeeding Hindu traditions to those of the Vedas.

In Ancient Sumeria the turtle was associated with Ea the water deity and is found depicted on the back of the goat-fish and sometimes used as a substitute for it[155]. Interestingly the name for the goat in Sanskrit was Kapra and the inclusion of this in the name of the Ge turtle may simply be an inflectual mishearing for the name of the turtle or actually preserved this more subtle derivation from the goatfish again suggesting an early contact with Ancient India or Middle East.

In Ancient West Asian thought the goatfish was a symbol of the zodiacal sign of Capricorn, the "old man" of the signs and it is notable that among the Mayans in Central America the symbol of the "Old Gods" or Pauahtuns included a deity with a turtle shell on his back[156]. This name again leads back to the Ganges Delta and the Mundas, Buhiyas, Kols and Gonds and their contacts with the Ancient Middle East.

The turtle, as a sacred or cosmic symbol, was transferred by mariners from India into the Pacific, including Melanesia, and it is identified particularly in the Solomon Islands with the hero Sina Kwao[157]. The myths and legends surrounding this demi-god have been referred to in an earlier work[158] but it is notable that he is said to have brought a turtle with him as his special symbol. The myth states that in certain places in the islands pools were set aside where the turtle was to be revered. This hero was said to be particularly notable for his red hair and this corresponds with the Maori saying "Red Hair - Chief's Hair[159]. The conspicuous reddish colour of many Pacific Islanders, particularly in parts of Melanesia, identifies this hair colour with that of the higher status clans and their clan heroes in particular and is a hair colouring particularly notable among the many surviving mummies excavated in Central and Southern Peru (*6.124/5*).

Sina Kwao is a hero found in the Solomon Islands and there too is to be found myths of the turtle fishing up the land from the bottom of the sea in a similar way to the myths found in India[160]. The fishing up of the land in creation myths is more famously associated with Maui, the Polynesian fire-god already noted earlier, but myths of a similar nature are found in the Americas. These have clearly been imported from India via Melanesia, Polynesia and more notable in the Americas as a motif among the Indians of the North Pacific Coast of North America.

There has been noted in this work a number of important parallels between the Peruvian myths, customs as well as iconography and that of the Marquesas Islands and this is unlikely to be coincidence. It has also been noted that there are many aspects of belief and ritual as well as the layout of the sacred dancing and ceremonial grounds with associated sacred banyan trees relating to India and the Nagas of Assam. The deity in the Marquesas Islands was noted as being a very ancient god and called Mata Fenua and he was associated with the capture of turtles. The ancient fish god of Ancient India was named Matsya and this appears to be the origin of the Marquesas name particularly as the main place for the capture of turtles was called Ke'eomana, undoubtedly derived from the name Kurma, Kachhapa, or one the other variants of the sacred name of the turtle in India. In fishing with the nets for the turtles the ancient chant was always intoned called the Mauta'a and this is recorded as being similar for other sacred events as Craighill Handy noted almost a century ago: "The same mauta'a with slight changes in the words was used also in connection with the operation of incision of the foreskin of the male child, and at the funerary festivals. It refers to certain gods, the heavens and lightning, the genitals of the chief, and ends with the words, expressed with great force, 'It is the turtle, ugh!'"[161]. It has also been noted that there are identifications of the turtle with the Sun and lightning in India apparently extended in the transfer to the Bolivian Highlands, and of particular interest is that the name of this sacred chant is mauta'a and this is similar to the name of the dynasty before the Inca and also the name of the special class of tradition-bearers and historians among the Incas who were the A-mautas. The Marquesas Islands, as the most easterly part of Polynesia nearest the Americas, appears to have been the lynchpin in the contacts between Asia and the Americas as well as vice versa.

The relation is an interesting one since the phallic association of Siva in India with the turtle appears here to be expressed as the generative power thought to be imparted in the rite of circumcision associated with the divine turtle. But it is clear in the Marquesan chant that the turtle was an iconographical element fundamental to all important aspects of their culture and in this sense it parallels the same basic cosmic associations as found in India and the Ancient Middle

East as well as in the Amazon Basin.

Cahuachi or Kawachi and the Kachcharis of Assam

The origin of Cahuachi appears to have originally been in the term for the sacred turtle, Kachapa, and variants of the term found among the Gonds relating to an ancient clan. It is also likely therefore that the Nazcan Cahuachi or Kawachi was also the name derived from Gond mariners who once formed a kingdom in Central East India as did the Chalukyans in South Central India and whose influence is seen at Tiahuanaco. It has also been noted that the capital or main ceremonial centre of the Nazca region was closely connected to Tiahuanaco in the Bolivian Highlands and a major outlet to the Pacific shore for the great city on the Altiplano. This was also true of the Moquegua Valley further south of Nazca and clearly indicates that these connections with the Pacific Coast were of great importance.

It has been shown that the artefacts similar to those of Ecuador, Peru and Bolivia are found so concentrated in Melanesian islands that guard the only natural flow of the ocean currents from South America and the Central Pacific to Asia as it tapers between Cape York in the North of Australia and New Guinea to Indonesia, Asia, and India in particular. It has also been shown in this and earlier works that many expeditions set out from the Ganges Delta at the head of the Bay of Bengal from North India; from the East Coast of India from Orissa; the Godavari-Kistna Delta, and from the Pallava and Chola kingdoms in the far South East of India. Forming the eastern section of the Ganges Delta is the delta of the Brahmaputra River that flows north to Manipur and the Naga lands in the foothills of the Himalayas and flows then eastward before turning in a broad arc westward into the highlands of Tibet. Here it flows more or less due west as the Tsang Po towards the great sacred mountain in southwest Tibet called Kailas with its two sacred lakes. This river delta, in its lower navigable part from the Bay of Bengal and its shared delta with the Ganges, forms almost the whole width of the modern day country of Bangladesh. Critically this allows entrance to the Himalayan foothills to the north and is the most direct route to the capital of Tibet and its sacred sites. This is achieved when leaving the river just south of Sikkim, then overland through the foothills into the valley passes through the Chumbi Valley in particular. These passes have been used for millennia as the main route from the Tibetan Plateau and Central Asia to the North and West and attracted strategic interest in the control of trade and possible enemy forces through the foothills themselves.

The Naga peoples who occupied these hills were called the Kachcharis, and this was a

11.061 : The deity Jambhala and his wife Hariti. He is a Buddhist form of Kubera, the Hindu god of wealth and good luck. Kusana, Mathura, North India, 2-3rd., century, A.D.

11.062 : The Hindu deity Kubera, the good of good fortune, trade and wealth and probably patronised by mariners. Kusana, Mathura North India, 2-3rd., century, A.D.

name given to them from the ancient name of the territory they occupied since the term actually applied to the hills that formed a defensible barrier between the plains of Manipur and the valleys to the passes into Tibet. These hills were called the Kachari dwars or "doors" and acted as sentinels and a defensive barrier where required. The "doors" formed access routes to the sacred highland sites of Tibet, and in the reverse flow from the Tibetan Plateau to the lowlands of Manipur, and the lower Brahmaputra River to its outlet in the Bay of Bengal. This appears to duplicate almost exactly in topographical principle the route to the Altiplano on the Andean plateau in Bolivia where Tiahuanaco stood and critically there was more than one route to the highlands from the Pacific Coast of Peru as there was in the Bay of Bengal to Tibet. In Peru, the Ica and Nazca Valleys formed one of the main routes to Tiahuanaco, where this route ran through the rugged terrain of the Huari who occupied the intermediate highlands, and it is on the southern Nazca Plains that Kawachi stands. This culture with its headhunting practices, so central to their social and religious rituals, is evidence of a civilisation that exhibited many common references to that of the Nagas in Assam guarding the routes from the Brahmaputra to the Valleys into Tibet. The Kachchari called themselves the Bodo, a name derived from the native name for Tibet, appearing to be indicate that they were a mixed race of Tibetans and the Manipuri plains people. It is probable that the Kacharis who were the guardians of the pass approaches hired in by the ancient Koch kings who were centred in their nearby capital of Koch-Behar[162]. Other traditions of related tribes, the Garos, preserved a legendary origin of descent from a Hindu fakir, or holy man, and a Tibetan woman[163].

Myths of origin and tribal legends suggest that there are connections with the East Coast of India and the Gond people and references to Roana, a local term for the mythical Sri Lanka king, Ranana, and the creation of thunder and lightning. Sri Lanka is an island far to the south and this legend suggests links to these people and connections with the sea trade between the Ancient Middle East and India into the Ganges-Brahmaputra Delta. In this region of the Himalayan foothills the term for tall flagpoles draped in fluttering pennants was parwa[164], a name associated with the wind deity among the coastal deities found among Bhuiyas near or along the Bengal Coast of India and preserved also in the name of the Mayan wind deities, Pauah-tuns, and the name of the "land of the four corners" of the Inca, Tahua-tin-suyu noted elsewhere in this work.

It may never be proved but it has been proposed several times throughout this work that the Nagas of Assam were in fact the earlier mariners from the Ganges Delta and East Coast India who travelled into the Pacific and to South America. It was they who were an essential part of the coastal cultures that flourished along the coast of Peru and in Nazca at Kawachi and who were referred to in numerous legends associated with culture bearers who arrived on the coast of Peru. In the many centuries following their voyages their mixed race descendants inevitably returned back to the land of their origin and took with them many of the less pleasant customs practised in the Andes. Undoubtedly this inflamed those practises that were already endemic in the more remote regions of Northern India and the Himalayas and were evident in the rites of the Tibetan Bon Po and the Tantric religions. The practise of headhunting can be traced from South America via the natural flow of the ocean currents through Polynesia, Melanesia, Indonesia and directly to the Ganges-Brahmaputra Delta in Bengal to the Nagas of Assam and this route corresponds also to a myriad of other shared cultural traditions. These later practises infected the long established Hindu and Buddhist, centred in Bengal and Orissa, on the coast that would most likely receive the returning mariners from South America. It is probable, therefore, that the Nazcan name Kawachi, the same as the Gond Flood hero or associated turtle deities derives as much from Kachar or Kachchari related to their settlements around the Kachari-dwars.

Aspects of Gond; Munda; and Bhuiya Culture from India Transferred into South America

It has been repeatedly noted that the Melanesian thought the first Europeans in the Pacific in the recent colonial period were their ancestors and that these stated to be the cultural heroes to whom they are attributed the many megalithic structures found throughout these islands. In some cases these ancestors were called the Pangku, Panka, Pura, or Puru[165]. Pura and Puru were terms also for white men[166] and the whole of the myth cycles associated with them appear to have derived in part or more completely from India. It is probable that the deity Pangku was no other than the Chinese Pan Kua[167], the giant from whom the universe was created[168] and who is paralleled in the myths noted of Brahma in India. These myths involve the identification of parts of the great body of the creator with elements of creation and peoples and animals much as those of the great serpent being severed into pieces and from whose parts all creation flowed. The Pankus were said to be four times the size of human beings and this may be a dim memory of the original Chinese and Indian myths associating Pan Ku or Brahman with the four cardinal points[169]. Reflections of the Chinese myth are found in the Dyak version of the giant named Usai from whom useful plants and benefits were derived[170].

11.063 :

Blowpipes identical to those found among the Amazonian basin forest tribes. These peoples reflect many other cultural transfers identical between the two distant regions that could only be transferred by mariners. Kenyah Tribe, Borneo, Early 20th., century, A.D.

Interestingly, there are references to elements in the ancient beliefs possibly relating to Pan Kua among the Mundas of India - the widely spread aboriginal peoples related to the Bhuiyas already noted. Alluvial soil, so important for crop growth, and therefore to the useful plants was believed to be derived from Pan Kua in Chinese myth and among the Mundas was called Pankua[171]. Of equal importance is that the fields divided traditionally over many centuries were called Hatu-japa Piri[172]. It has been noted that the term "Hatu" along with many others has almost certainly derived from Anatolia, and the Anatolian connection is particularly notable among the Bhuiyas and the Assurs. The term Hatu also appears in Peru, and since this is not alone with many other parallels in terms and customs it has to be probably that the term arrived in the Andes from India.

In India, serpents, such as the cobra are intimately associated with the cultivated fields and grain stores in reality and in myth. The term hatu-japa-piri, although not directly related to the serpent as such in India, but the soil in which it has its abode, appears to have been linked in garbled versions of Indian cosmology and myth in transfer to Aboriginal Australia. Many aspects from the cultures of India have long been noted by earlier historians in Australian Aboriginal traditions, myths and legends, and these appear to link more closely with the Aboriginal tribes of India that suggest early contacts. In considering serpents and their dismemberment, disintegration or immolation to provide humanity with sustenance it is worth considering the Aboriginal Australian myth local to Ayers Rock relating to the increase serpent Jarapiri. Jarapiri was the mythical serpent and the oral tradition relates its travels across the landscape creating places of "increase" or fertility and the events occurring as it passed other significant landmarks and mythical being[173]. Of significance is that Jarapiri's wife was called Jambeli, the name of a particular deity influenced by the Aboriginal myths in the Buddhist and Hindu pantheon in India - Jambhala, a gender reversal of Kali. This fierce mother deity is often painted black and said to represent the "supreme night"[174] and is associated with serpent symbolism and garlands of human skulls reflecting her aspects as the consort of Siva.

In India the term derives from having "large teeth" in a mythical sense of "devouring" and is usually associated in the Hindu pantheon with the deity Kubera, a god associated with trade, wealth and mariners[175]. An ichneumon or mongoose aspect of Jambhala is said to cause the disgorging or "vomiting" aspect and this is probably the origin of many acts related to this in the myths and particularly those featuring snakes[176]. The rainbow serpents of Australia are constantly referred to as vomiting up, among many other aspects, mythical peoples and this appears directly related to the myth of Jarapiri. Interestingly the name Jambeli is a term associated with a culture found on the Ecuadorian coast[177].

In the Australian myth, when Jarapiri shed his skin, it formed the dancing ground on the claypan of Bouala and the scales flaked off and became many small snakes whose bodies later became the serpentine and twisted forms of the tea tree on the western side of the dancing ground. The term for the dancing ground rites of Polynesia was the Bora found widely spread among the Aboriginal tribes on the East Coast of Australia and on this coast the sea current direct from Polynesia and Melanesia washes directly onto that very long shore. It is likely that Boula, therefore, is a name developed from Bora or perhaps also confused with the term Boua, the name for the ancestor-hero represented as a monolith that stood in the burial circle known from the Gilbert Islands[178].

In a myth from the Raj Gonds of Central India there is a description of the first settlements of the first Gond clans that relates the steps taken to construct their farming implements. The Earth Mother, at the court of the Supreme God, Shembu Pen - a Gond name for Siva, instructed the first Gonds to use the bullocks, train them and to construct the plough to be tied to it using, instead of ropes, subdued cobras to serve as substitutes. The whole is a mythical tradition and cannot be used as history but it illustrates the essential association of the land, the cobra that infested it, and construction of the plough, a symbol of advance from the state of the hunter-gatherer. The clearly retained aspects and terms of Gond, Munda and Bhuiya cultural traditions appear to link closely with the Assurs who appear to have been early iron-working peoples from Anatolia who became immured into the Aboriginal life of India. The Gond also have iron-working traditions and in the myth associated with constructing the plough and becoming agriculturists a section notes that in building the forge for iron-working the first Gonds were told to go to the blacksmith Visa Bama to make the sickle and agricultural implements from iron. However, it is said that he had no materials but his wife intervened and told him to take their son and cut the head of for the anvil, the arms to make the pincers and the legs to fashion the hammers, etc., and this relation appears to be an adaption of the Pan Kua type myth to the iron-working traditions[179]. It appears that many peoples interpreted such myths literally and it is little wonder that head-hunting, ritual human sacrifice, and the agricultural cycle became inextricably linked with them.

The term panku appears to be an imported term into India and this is probably also the case for China and was assimilated into the local languages more or less as heard. However, it may be that the term panku derived, as for so many aspects of Munda, Bhuiya and Assur culture, from Anatolia since this term appears among the Hittites. Surviving references from the second half of the second millennium B.C. note the term apparently used in referring to the "whole community" - the pankus[180], although other references suggest that it might mean a council such as the Panchyat of five elders later found in India (panch = five). It has been noted in this work that the first known references to the Vedic deities of India, Indra, Varuna and Mitra are found at this period in Hittite inscriptions in Anatolia suggesting that migrations, voluntary or enforced, transferred these aspects of Indo-Aryan culture through Iran then to India itself. The term panku probably arrived with these population shifts along with the deity names and iron-working practices first known in Anatolia. It is also likely, therefore, that similar references found in South East Asia were transferred either directly from West Asia or through later India.

Puri, Puru and the Pamuri

The term pamuri used as a descriptive term for the serpent boat and the captain in the Tukano Desana myths in Colombia appears to provide another link to the Himalayan region of South Asia. Over a century ago researchers among the Amazonian tribes described a tribe, located among others along the Purus River who called themselves the Pamouiris, but by others Purupurus. These people were noted for their flat bottom boats unlike the dugout canoes from tree trunks among other tribes[181]. The blood group analyses made a few decades ago suggesting that the Amazonian Indians and the Polynesians may have been in contact suggests by extension that the name Pa-mouris was in fact originally Pa-Maoris or Pa-Morioris since the latter were known for their flat bottom boats noted elsewhere as being similar to the wash-through construction of the traditional catamarans along the coast of South India constructed into the present day. The traditional Maori bark and reed canoes in New Zealand were identical to those of Lake Titicaca on the Bolivian altiplano and the feather capes and designs of the traditional Maori ceremonial dress are almost identical to those of the Inca. A form of greeting, the crying greeting noted elsewhere in this work (*2.089*), known among the Pamouris was also identical to that of the Maori and of the Andaman Islanders, the latter located in the Bay of Bengal near South India.

The great British naturalist, Alfred F. Wallace, the less well-known researcher into the history of the human species and who rightfully shares the theory of evolution with Charles Darwin wrote of the Amazonian tribes: "One of the singular facts connected with these Indians of the Amazon valley is the resemblance which exists between some of their customs, and those of nations most remote from them. The gravatana, or blowpipe, reappears in the Sumpitan of Borneo; the great houses of the Uaupes closely resembles those of the Dyaks of the same country; while many small baskets and bamboo-boxes, from Borneo and New Guinea, are so similar in their form and construction to those of the Amazon, that they would be supposed to belong to adjoining tribes. Then again, the Mundarucus, like the Dyaks, take the heads of their enemies, smoke-dry them with equal care, presenting their skin and hair entire, and hang them up around their houses. In Australia the throwing stick is used, and on a remote branch of the Amazon, we see a tribe of Indians (Pamouiris) differing from all around them, in substituting for a bow a weapon only found in such a remote portion of the earth, among a people differing from them in almost every physical character"[182].

The spear-thrower has now been found to be more widely used in Ancient South America but the fundamental principle of Wallace's perception that there are remarkable connections between the far east and the far west of the Pacific Ocean is still valid and require explanation. Arthur Poznansky, two generations ago, noted the raft dwelling made from the totora reed growing around the Lake edges was similar in principle to the raft dwellings constructed by the Paumaris on the Purus River[183], clearly the same people referred to by Wallace. The totora reed is found on Easter Island and has been used as an element in the argument for diffusion from South America into the Pacific and the term is also found among the Maoris in New Zealand along with the sweet potato and this is a tuber that could only have been transported by human agency from South America into the Pacific Islands. Some have suggested that puru meant painted, referring to the white patches caused by a skin disease suffered by these people but the references elsewhere associating the white blotches to a white-skinned person appears to have been the origin of this reference[184]. The term muri appears frequently as a term and in the name of tribes and will be of more interest in a projected future publication.

Among the Ao Nagas in Assam the clan priests were called Pachar Patir and, interestingly Pacha, meaning heaven or the sky among the Inca, and Patir may be the derivation from Pamir[185]. In Ancient India the Purus, Porus or Paurava, were one of the independent kingdoms in the North West of India encountered by Alexander the Great when he invaded India in the 4th., century B.C.[186]. The Purus was the common name for the Panchalas and this group has been identified by some ancient historians with the Phoenicians. One of the scripts of Ancient India, Brahmi was traced by philologists back to the Phoenicians[187] suggesting that Herodotus may have been correct in declaring the Phoenicians origins were from the Erythraean Sea, usually identified with the Persian Gulf or Indian Ocean and that part of the Indian Ocean lapping the shores of India in particular[188]. The actual region called Pamir was that in the northwest of India identified with the foothills of Northern Afghanistan[189]. The Pamirs was an elevated mountain region that separated the Bactrian kingdom in what is now Afghanistan and Chinese Turkestan and is a region that might have been identified with the Mandaean sacred mountain, the Tura d Maddai. The history of this region has been intensively studied from an early time in the British colonial period through to later works that are still of interest today[190].

Puru Ancestors in Peru

In the dynasty of the Ganga kings in Orissa a deity associated with overseas trade and sea-faring was named Puru-sottama and his wife, the goddess Lakshmi, was considered the daughter of the Ocean[191]. Pura is the number four in Southern India and is the proper number used in the planning of a house[192]. In parts of Southern India the wealthier Tiyans lived in houses called Nala-pura and this name derives from having been built around a quadrangle[193]. In terms of the castes employed by the temples extending its work outside of the perimeter were called the Pura-potu-vals - potuval meaning more or less an "elder"[194]. Among the Southern Indians the term Pura is identified with Tampu-rans, the high caste rulers[195], and this will be of more interest in the last chapter. Pura, or puram, in the general Aryan family of languages in India means a fort or stronghold[196] and appears to derive from the Sanskrit Pa - the same term also found among the Maoris for their forts.

Among the Hill Buiyas a pura was a small hung basket for holding the sacred grain[197] and among these people the Pauri or Pori was most prominent of these tribes[198]. These people appear originally to have been fire-worshippers and their skin colouring was noticeably lighter than other surrounding people[199] indicating Aryan origins. Their deity Boram is found also among the Mundas, Santals, Hos and Kharias[200], identified with the Sun god and is found also in Aboriginal Australia earlier noted. Among the Pauris there are two special deities who receive offerings of stones named Andya and Sandya and were said to belong to the Pundi tribe - a subdivision of the Assurs who were believed to have had superhuman strength. These names probably derived from the term for the Moon, Candra or Chandra, and the Candravansa were known as the "lunar race of kings" in India. They were a section of the Paurava clan in the great civil war between the Aryan tribes described in the Mahabharata[201] and it is likely that this is the origin of the Bhuiya clan name of Pauri. The myth goes to record that these were giants who travelled eighty miles in one night and back to attend special dance festivals but one last time they were waylaid by their enemies (some say devas, that is angels or spirits) and killed. Stones were heaped over them to form a cairn and since that time all that pass by the cairns throw a stone on as an offering[202]. Any one interested in archaeology will know that such cairns are found not only in Eurasia and Africa but also in the Americas and in this specific myth they are associated with white people. Pun-di is of course associated not only with white people, either as giants or of normal size, but the root of the word is Pun and this again relates to the stone Sun circle of the Toda on South India and Pun equates to the Anglicised term for the Sun.

The association of Bhuiya ancestral origins with white people is reflected also in a myth retained by a subdivision known as the Puran. Their origin myth states that "… the semen of Bhagwan (God) fell on the earth and produced an egg resembling a pea-hen's egg. From the white of this egg sprang the first ancestor of the Purans, from its membranous coating the progenitors of the Savaras, from its shell the first ancestor of the Kharias, and from its yolk the ancestor of the Bhanja (Bhuiya) Rajas of Mayurbhanj"[203]. There needs to be no proving that the egg with its central golden yolk is always perceived as a symbol of the Sun and this mythical model further confirms the association of the name Pauri, Pora or Puran with early Aryan ancestry indicated in the researches of Sarat Chandra Roy to derive from the Panchalas of North East India[204]. The ancient texts note that the Purus were worshippers of Agni, the fire-god, of such note in this work, and to this deity the defeat of the Dasyu, the primitive pre-Aryan peoples of India is attributed[205]. Puran, however, among the Bhuiyas is believed to be derived from Pawan, the wind deity, and this links again to their name for themselves - Pawanbans, "the Sons of the Wind". This is the identical phrase that the Desana of the Tukano tribe gave themselves, called Wira-pora, Wira or Vira also being another name in India for the wind deity. The Bhuiya Pawanban is also the same name for the wind deities of the Maya - the Pauahtuns, so that all the terms considered found in South America tie up in one way or another too closely with those in India to be coincidental.

As noted above among the Bhuiyas the name of the wind god was Pawan and that they identify themselves ancestrally with their most favoured deity Bir or Vir or Vira, Hanuman, the monkey god as the Son of the Wind, and themselves as the Sons of the Wind - Pawanbans. Pawa is also identified as being the origin of the Mayan Pauahtuns, the wind gods at the four cardinal points and the likely origin of the Inca term Tahua-ntan- suyu, the name of the Inca empire meaning the land of the four parts or corners. It is likely therefore that Pawa has been identified with the term Pauri and thence Pora and in this related context has been diffused to the Pacific Islands and to South America with less distinct references to the wind or Sun as it had in India.

In the transference from India into the Pacific the term Puru appears frequently as pura, puru or poro. In Melanesia, Puru is identified with the deified heroes Panku and Pangu, these being four times higher in stature than normal people reminiscent of the Manta giants in Ecuador[206]. On Rook Island, Puru was the hero who introduced from his canoe food plants and taught the people their language, and was said to have had a white skin[207]. In New Guinea the name of one of the main rivers where tribes with many aspects of Polynesian culture are noted is the Pura-ri. Here one of the tribes of the Ipi peoples revered a divine hero named Ivo[208], this god name clearly derived from the Polynesian Io and in turn undoubtedly derived from the god Deo in Aboriginal India. This same term in India appears in the god of Ipi warriors who died in battle named Hio-vaki[209]. The term Puru early associated with the Puravas in the Mahabharata in India, who were Caucasian Aryans and probably the same as the Purus in the Pacific, and Puro appears to have a common origin with the term for the officiant at the Brahman fire-altar was known as the puro-hita[210]. This provides the link in both cases with the dispersion of these terms but also the consistent identification with "white-skinned ancestors" in the Pacific Ocean islands.

In the Solomon Islands the name of the hero on the island of Mala was Mauwa (Polynesian Maui) whereas on the island of Ulawa his equivalent is expressed in a phrase - "Poro wa'I henua", meaning he who pulled up the land[211]. It is likely that he was initially the name of the hero as it is in New Guinea, Poro or Puru. A pre-European phrase was "Poro ni Haka" - "Man of Ship" and was a term used for the white explorers and traders when they arrived in the Solomon's[212]. It was soon discovered that the terms "Poro" and "Hu'e" were used in these islands as honorific terms in the manner the English use "Lord" and "Lady"[213]. Other terms are reminiscent of the Ancient Middle East where the term Ama was the term for father[214], and is the alternative found in West Asia as Aba, and this latter term is found also among the Desana in Colombia and among other Amazonian tribes as Abe. An alternate name for father in Melanesia was Mama'a and this term is found among some of the South American tribes to denote the shaman priest, the "Mama" - particularly notable among the Kogi in North East Colombia.

Interestingly, the term Tata or Teitei denotes "mother" in parts of the Solomon Islands whereas in the Ancient Middle East, India, Indonesia through the Pacific Islands and into the Americas it denote the father. In religious terms it is applied as "god the father", being used in this sense among the Huichols of North West Mexico among others[215]. The term among the Desana for priest, kumu, is found in the Solomon's to denote a clan, kumu or komu[216].

Because the Solomon Islands were on the direct route established by the prevailing sea currents from the Central Pacific towards South East Asia there are many aspects of the Solomon Islands cultures corresponding to, and influenced from Polynesia - and therefore also from South America. The islands in the Solomon's and New Hebrides occupy a unique position in the Southern Pacific Ocean since they spread across the only viable access route by sea from Polynesia and South America to South East Asia. The South Equatorial Current, assisted by the prevailing westerly winds drives any craft from any place on the South American Coast through South and Central Polynesia to these islands; 1) onto the coast of Australia to the South; 2) to the only direct sea route between North Australia and the large island of New Guinea through the Torres Straits, through Central Indonesia to South East Asia and onto India and the Middle East (*1.007*). This sea route through the Torres Straits is a "funnel" through which all at sea must pass from East to West. The evidence that the Polynesians utilised this route, on many occasions, is reflected in the cultures of the native peoples occupying the flanking coasts. It is clear from the cluster of many aspects of their cultures reflected in an unparalleled array of material objects notable in South America that peoples from Colombia, Ecuador and Peruvians also used this route.

In the Solomon Islands, the New Hebrides, and New Guinea, cranial deformation and trepanation have been frequently observed in the surviving skulls from previous centuries, and cranial deformation was still practised in all these islands into the twentieth century and reflects the traditions of South Central and North America. Star clubs of the identical type found among the Incas as a symbol of ruler-ship are found in the identical form in these Melanesian islands along with panpipes and trumpets also identical to those found in the Amazon and into the Andean peoples are found on the Solomon's in particular. Earth mounds, pyramids, shaft burials, megaliths and dolmens were also noted in the Solomon's a century ago, and terraced hills similar to those among the Inca, in the Philippines, South China, the Nagas of Assam, South Arabia and Ancient Ethiopia were noted in the New Hebrides. Megaliths, dolmens and stone-carved rituals implements were common throughout Melanesia but particularly so on the islands of the Solomon and New Hebrides and their distribution is best recorded in the work of Alphonse Riesenfeld. The ceremonial settlement of Pete-hul on the island of Malekula in the New Hebrides (Vanuatu) is closely similar in principle to the quartering of Cuzco and the clan system has been utilised as the model for that of the Incas of Peru.

Considered along with the many aspects of mythology and the apparent close links to Ancient India it is clear that these islands were host to many mariner landings of traders and explorers and other venturers. They travelled, like Bue and the other recorded heroes, from East to West and back again over many centuries and indeed millennia, between South America and South East and Southern Asia.

Evident from 3-2000 years ago as the path of the Lapita culture through the islands north of New Guinea into the Solomon's and Central Polynesia the progress from Asia illustrates that the sea currents are so disposed as to allow mariners from South East Asia travelling from West to East to enter the South Pacific through these islands. This provides, therefore, a crossover with the mariners using the natural sea currents and prevailing winds as marine highways sailing East to West from South America to meet in the Solomon's and New Hebrides and this route allows access further south to New Zealand, the home of the Maoris. Along with the many South

American cultural aspects readily identifiable in Melanesia it is not surprising therefore that the South American tuber, the sweet potato, was cultivated also along these routes known and dated in the Cook Islands from about 940 A.D.[217] and in the New Guinea Highlands possibly much earlier, but most notable of all in New Zealand earlier noted.

In the Solomon Islands in Melanesia, on the island of Sa'a, the chiefly clan were also known as Pawloto, undoubtedly derived from the name of the Polynesian Underworld Pulotu or Bulotu. The hereditary family of the priests was called Puu, undoubtedly derived from Puru and characteristic of their original Polynesian descent, the chiefly families also preserved the genealogies of their family descent[218]. The legends of the founding of the chiefly families on Little Mala are an example of the use of the title Poro as meaning "Lord" and the traditional splitting of the clans into sub-clans. These peripheral relations set off to found new settlements and their developed traditions focused on the importance of gardens and musical instruments, the gong in particular can be traced from Sa'a[219]. On the island of Ulawa a prominent ghost was called Siho i Salo, or "Descended from the Sky". He was the guardian of the gardens of Poro taki. It was recorded that: "The mark of his presence was the track left on the ground, like that of the crocodile. In himself the appearance of Siho i Salo was awesome, his bulk was huge, his ears were big enough to wrap around him as a covering at night and to serve as a mat to be on. His speech was that of (the islands of) Tolo, Mala, etc." Among the various guardians was one named Rahu-Maca[220]. This record of the Siho i Salo in local myths seems to preserve the memory of a crocodile where the path is clearly equated to one, but also of an elephant, and since the latter did not occur anywhere in Melanesia, the nearest being thousands of miles away to the west in Indonesia, its association has been introduced by diffusion. That this guardian ghost originally derived from India is emphasised by the term used in the second ghost, Rahu-Maca, since Rahu was the eclipse serpent in Hindu myths and maca (maka) is another name for makara, the crocodile in India. In the many islands of the Solomons the term Poro occurs frequently in the prefixes of these ghosts and on Sa'a and Ulawa the name for the holy man was, respectively, Poro-waa'i and Poro ni Mwane[221]. The adaption of such terms and expressions is observed in the usage of the betel leaf chewed with the areca nut, so widely found in India and South East Asia and used by mariners to assuage hunger and thirst while on long sea voyages. Its distribution is from India through into the islands of Indonesia through to Micronesia, north of the Equator, and into the Solomon Islands to the south of it. The expression pua tangaloa means "Areca nuts in abundance", the term pue derives from Indonesia, where the term pua is also used in Ulawa but not in Sa'a[222]. Tangaloa is the name of the great Polynesian god and clearly has been adopted in Melanesia because of its mariners association and their use of the areca nut in their sea journeys.

On the island of Raratonga in the Cook Islands, the human spirit medium was called pura-pura and he was considered the intermediary between the gods and humankind[223]. The association of the term "Puru" with white-skinned people in Melanesia is also noted in Colombia where the people known as the Purunas among others were of "whiter" skin colouring than others[224]. On the Puru River in the Amazon Basin the tribe called the Puru-Purus were so noted because of the whiteness of their skin enhanced, or disfigured by an hereditary pigmentation irregularity known as piebaldism. The Puru-purus were also known as Pa-maouris[225] and this is the term that the Desana Tukano sometimes applied to their serpent canoe hero Pamouri-Gahsiru.

The Incas referred prejudicially to the pre-Incaic empire as the Purun-Pacha or "Heathen Times" and this may refer to the time when there was greater influence directly from the Pacific Islands and India vaguely remembered in an encapsulation of an earlier expression. The term Purun Aucca meant unconquered and purum meant "savage" in terms of reference to peoples outside the Inca Empire, and Purum-puram referred to the uninhabited wilds. Purum-Pacha, or Heathen Times, was a reference to the ancient days when demons were worshipped and consid-

11.064 : Dyak warrior with a traditional tusk breastplate that appears to derive from influences from the Gonds of India but similar to those worn among the North American Indians and reflected in the Mayan codices. Borneo, Early 20th., century, A.D.

11.065 : Amazon tribesmen with breastplate representations appearing to imitate the exposed rib cage similar to those of the Maya and particularly similar to the Gonds of India. Rio Aiary, Amazon Basin, Late 19th., century, A.D.

11.066 + 11.067 : Apparent breastplates probably s an imitation representing the keletal structure of the rib age. Kaua Mask, Rio Aiary, Amazon Basin, Late 19th., century, A.D.

11.068 : A breastplate that signifies chieftainship known as the Eaii rove. This is made from boar tusks and probably originally related to the skeletal appearance of their mariners ancestors after long sea voyages. Roro Tribes, New Guinea, Late 20th., century, A.D.

ered to have enslaved humankind to their will, and these were called the Hapi-nunus and Achacallas[226]. The term Achachillas was the name applied to the ancestors who dwelt in the mountains, also known as Tias, and were much revered, and the Achacallas were probably originally the Aymara term for the same and the two had become confused or interchangeable. Pusa in the Inca Empire was the name for the water channels for irrigation[227] and this would appear to have some relationship with the Gond name in India for the Moon, ruler of water, Pusa[228].

The term Puru-raucas was noted by Bernabe Cobo and he stated that it translated as "hidden traitors". This was a term applied by the Inca Viracocha to gods who dwelt in stones but that he claimed he could raise to assist him, and his descendants, in times of war[229]. It appears that these were ancient warriors who had been turned to stone because they were on the losing side but could be enlisted when needed by the Inca before again being returned to the stones after victory had been achieved. It would appear that their term from these earlier times may be the same as that known as the true name for the Tarascans in Western Mexico who are believed to have arrived from South America via Central America - this being the Puru-pichas[230]. These people have been shown in an earlier work to almost certainly to have originally come from Polynesia and probably India possibly via South

11.069 : A skeletal guardian deity of the wrathful type with a pearl sacred thread similar to that illustrated on the coast of Ecuador (9.063). Hirapur, Orissa, North East India, 6-9th., century, A.D.

11.070 :
Seated fire god with brow disk and large ring earrings similar to those found in South America, in Melanesia, Indonesia and Southern India. Note the protruding ribs possibly indicating mariner origins. Remojadas, Veracruz, East Coast Mexico. 400-800 A.D.

11.072 : Exposed skeletal detail depicted on this deity, Lahun Chan, is traditional believed to express symbolic related to death. Codex Dresden, Mexico, Pre-post Conquest, 16th., century, A.D.

11.073 : A group of Gond dancers showing the ceremonial "waistcoat" apparently representing the skeletal rib cage probably the prototype of those depicted in the Mexican codices and in Borneo and the Amazon Basin. Hill Maria Gond tribe, Central India, Early 20th., century, A.D.

11.071 : A wrathful deity known as a Datura or guardian in the form of Chamuda with characteristics associated with death expressed through the exposed or delineated skeletal rib cage. Jaipur, Orissa, East Central India, 7-9th., century, A.D.

11.074 : Tibetan deities representing death as skeleton painted onto ceremonial clothing. The trefoil symbol of flames from the skull is found in some depictions in Ancient Peru and commonly so in Mexico and probably an influence upon the Gond traditions. Tibet, Early 20th., century A.D.

11.075 : Fierce deity as a carved ritual vessel with an extended skeletal frame hanging from under his chin but sharing the same skull as the body forming the vessel behind. Bilbao, Santa Lucia Cotzumalguapa, Guatemala, 4-8th., century, A.D.

America[231].

Eclipse Serpent Rahu and the Demon Tammui

In an extension of a myth motif noted in an earlier work[232], the serpent was considered to be the symbol of the eclipse and therefore represented by the double-headed serpent belt. It is worth noting the term Tammui among the Nagas of Assam appears to be that in the corresponding term, Tamoi, among the Amazonian Indians that was transferred across the ocean path between them. In the myths of the Ao Nagas in Assam the name of the eclipse demon is called Tammui[233] and appears sometimes to be perceived as a serpent but other times as an indistinct, but fierce mutation of animal characteristics. It clearly derives from the Hindu double-headed eclipse serpent Rahu this being identified with the Moon's North Node. Common also among the Nagas tribes are myths indicating that the Moon was said originally to have shone much hotter than it now does and that dung was thrown at its face to cool it down[234]. The frequently recorded counterpart of this myth, that there were at one time many Suns and all but one was shot down by a hero with a bow and arrows, is found throughout the Pacific and in the Americas including Peru and earlier noted.

On the Nicobar Islands, due south of Assam in the Bay of Bengal the Tamiluanas or medicine man was employed to subdue the ocean tides when these low-lying islands were being threatened with inundation[235]. The name suggests that it is associated with the Moon and its orbital effects on the tides of the sea and by extension with the eclipse where he would lead the fight against the eclipse demon to prevent it from "swallowing" the Sun or Moon. Characteristically, the people of the Nicobars revered their canoes and, along with other rituals sacrifices, offerings were made three times a month, at the New Moon, the Full Moon, and the Waning Moon[236]. The name of the shaman on these islands being Tamiluanas, particularly as he is associated with communicating with the ancestors and lunar aspects of the social life, suggests that the term is derived from that of the Nagas, Tammui.

The term for ocean in Southern India, samudra, samudran or samudrala, is recorded in the clan names of many of the tribes and castes. The corresponding term, tamudri, appears in the clan names of the sea kings of Calicut, on the coast of South West India, the Zamorin. The Naga term for the eclipse demon, Tammui, and that of the Nicobarese, Tamiluanas, and their variations, appears to derive from, or have a common origin with the term for sea tamudri or samudra. Of special note is the fact that the myth motifs associated with the Moon, both in terms of its heat being reduced by dung, earth or ash thrown onto its face, or the mythical serpent demon as the eclipse demon, are found in the Pacific Islands but also in South America. Here the fundamental term tamudri or Tammui, is associated with the "sea-kings"[237], and other aspects from these "sea kings" will be of more interest in due course.

In Melanesia, the "lightning stone" on the island of Netar was said to be a crystal and this was said to be the head of the Lightning deity, Wiri. In a related myth the motif of a caesarean birth is again apparent where a child is said to have emerged from his mother after she had been struck dead by the lightning. This child climbed a tree that grew up to the sky and killed Wiri while he was asleep and brought his head back from the sky and it turned to crystal. The boy's name was Taimi[238], and crystals were intimately associated with the shaman's healing role among the people. This myth suggests that originally Wiri was in fact identified with the serpent demon of the eclipse since lightning was usually symbolised by serpents. The name Wiri may be a vague reference to the deity Vir or Vira, or Vayi, in India - the counterpart of Pawa(n). The myths surrounding Taimi are usually identified with the first white men in the Pacific Islands before the Europeans by the Melanesians and it is said that Taimi turned into a snake[239] confirming the probable origin in the South Indian traditions of those found among the Nagas of Assam.

The South Indian name of samudra or tumedri for the sea appears to be reflected in Melanesia in the name for a prominent ruler of the ancestral world name Tumu-durere, and this may be in itself a mutation of kumu for priest found in South China, Polynesia and Colombia among the Tukano Desana, and as umu in Peru, all references to the name of a priest. The deity is associated with the megalithic cultures in Melanesia, and in New Guinea and it was believed that he ruled the netherworld under the sea called Hiyoyoa[240], identified with the Polynesian Pulotu. The hero, named either Tamudurere or Tamudulele, was known particularly for two elements in the myths preserved about his existence and they were his canoe and his axe. These have parallels among other heroes identified with the early megalithic cultures of Melanesia suggesting another variant, or another migration from India into the Pacific from the stone-using megalithic tribes known there. These myths correspond to the Sido myth cycle, along with those of the Mbasi serpent noted earlier in this chapter, and axe motif myths are typical of the Massim Highland District in New Guinea[241].

In South America, the Tamoyos were a large "robust" people in the Amazon Basin who considered themselves to be related to the Tupinambas. They also believed themselves to be the first people in the forests and from whom all other tribes sprang. The name Tamoi among them was that used to describe the grandfather, an important figure both in reality and in terms of being a general identification with the ancestors[242]. As the term for "Great Father" or ancestor, Tamoi was said to have originally lived among them and to have taught them the arts and crafts of civilisation, agriculture and all that they know[243]. This term for the Grand Father of the people appears to correspond to that of the Nicobarese medicine man and the Ao Nagas eclipse demon, in all cases the associations are with the Moon, the sea and the ancestors linked with it.

In a previous work the associations of the great god of Mexico, Quetzalcoatl, was linked to the Huastecs of North Eastern Mexico and it was concluded that he was a sea deity with many references to the ocean and to the Nagas of Assam. It was further noted that the capital of the Huastecs, named Tamuin[244], and that this name may also have referred to Moon worship and Quetzalcoatl as a sea hero-divinity as a founding ancestor from Polynesia or Asia[245].

Rahu - Eclipse Demon and Double-Headed Serpent Belts

The concept of the serpent as the Moon's North Node has a very long history and closely similar imagery and motifs included in associated myths in both Asia and the Americas indicates that the traditions and customs portrayed in these beliefs can only be by diffusion from Central Asia. The myths of the eclipse serpent transferred from India to Central America has been examined or referred to in earlier works[246]. However, the transfer of these myths to South America is also important and is further evidence of cultural transfer from India to Ancient Ecuador, Peru and into the Amazon Basin.

The Vedic texts first refer to the monster that was said to swallow the Sun or the Moon at every solar and lunar eclipse, and the mouth or the head of the demon is all that is recorded in the oldest surviving references. This may only be as a result of the loss of many of the original myths and texts after their transfer from Iran in the early first millennium A.D. but later references to the serpent body appear to have some imported indicators[247]. The later Hindu myths note that Vishnu was the sky god who destroyed the serpent and prevented it, as Rahu, from consuming a full cup of the ambrosia of the gods that would have imparted immortality to those who had partaken of it. Because of this he was able to destroy the body of the serpent but the head and tail survived, since Rahu had already consumed a little of the liquid from the cup, to become the dragon's head, Rahu, and the dragon's tail, also depicted as a head and called Ketu. There are a number of references in the various texts to the eclipse demon and his attempt to "swallow" the Sun or the Moon, but also their re-emergence from his belly, and it is clear that such fables were a means by the use of their mythical images to convey fundamental astronomical truths[248].

Many of the surviving ancient images of the lesser deities in India, and elsewhere, lack identifiable mythology to indicate their meaning and intent and only scholarly conjecture or comparative analysis can be applied. It is useful therefore to have comparisons to give something of the quality and intensity behind the imagery that is known and may be paralleled in similar iconography. In the transfer of mythology and iconography abroad the various images utilised, often based on local peoples or animals in India, need to be identified with indigenous peoples and corresponding animals when far distant from Asia. A passage from a Buddhist text, attempting to convey the impression of fear that overwhelmed King Milinda when he approached the great serpent saint Nagasena notes: "Then at the sight there came over king Milinda a feeling of fear and anxiety, and the hairs of his body stood on end. But nevertheless, though he felt like an elephant hemmed in by rhinoceroses, like a serpent surrounded by the Garuda (the snake-eating mythical birds), like the jackal surrounded by boa-constrictors, or a bear by buffaloes, like a frog pursued by a serpent, or a deer by a panther, like snake in the hands of a snake charmer, or a rat played with by a cat, or a devil charmed by an exorcist, like the moon when it is seized by Rahu, like a snake caught in a basket, or a bird in a cage, or a fish in a net, like a man who has lost his way in a dense forest haunted by wild beasts, etc.,"[249].

In this text the demon Rahu as the Moon's Node is related not only to eclipses but to the ancestral links with the past, frequently also implied or stated to be karmic inflictions or retribution. Another volume of texts recording the enquiries made of the Saint, Nagasena, in answering the questions of King Milinda, preserves in a section that defines the seven qualities of the Sun in a reply: "And again, O king, as the sun is terrified with fear of Rahu (the demon of the eclipses); just so, O king, should the strenuous Bhikshu (religious novice), earnest in effort, seeing how beings are entangled in the waste wilderness of evil life and rebirth in states of woe, caught in the net of the mournful results here of evil done in former births, or of punishment in purgatory, or of evil inclinations, terrify his mind with great anxiety and fear. This, O king, is the sixth quality of the sun he ought to have."[250].

Rahu is identified as one of the many "myriad demons" as one of the four chiefs[251] and emphasises his malevolent influence through the eclipses, for which he was thought responsible, to have upon life on Earth. However, the above texts notes, in comparison, that the eagle (Garuda) and the serpent are considered opponents as they are in Mexico and interesting also is the comparison, among others, between the eclipse demon Rahu and fish caught in a net since this is reminiscent of remarkable similar projected imagery to found on a stela found in Izapa (*3.051*), so important in an earlier work regarding cross-Pacific contacts[252]. In the second textual reference the association of the Moon's North Node with a serpent and the ills of the past, and past lives that might cloud the concentration of the novices is interesting since the shedding of the snakeskin has, in other areas of philosophy, been paralleled to the shedding of past lives.

Eclipses were almost invariably perceived as malevolent and inauspicious except during the Sraddha, or funeral, celebrations in India[253]. The most acceptable time was in fact during an eclipse of either the Sun or Moon and this appears to relate to the Eclipse being perceived as relating to the sacred belt or girdle identifying with the ecliptic of the zodiac and this in turn appears to have derived from Ancient Middle Eastern traditions. The belt or girdle was seen as separating the upper, spiritual world and the upper person and the lower person and the Earth and it appears to be this symbolic relationship that is behind the fact that the eclipse, separating two worlds is appropriate in the Sraddha. Those who wished to achieve maximum advantage at these times of the eclipse were those who bathed in the mornings during the months of Magha or Phalguna[254]. This appears to be the characteristic building of virtue to see through the dark periods believed to be imposed by eclipses.

Rahu - Variations on a Theme
In a very long myth, a parallel to the Rahu myth found in North India, a child from the seed of a great serpent called Samgraha, who had attempted to abduct the wife of the storm god Indra, had fallen into a pool and from this a serpent child was born. This serpent was called Jalodbhava ("Waterborn") and he obtained the right from Brahma to remain immortal while he remained in the water. Jalodbhava, however, was a true son of his father and began to eat the people in the surrounding land, always being careful to return to the water after. The king of the Nagas (serpent worshipping people), Nila, was visited by his father Kasyapa (Turtle), the Buddhist successor to the Buddha himself, after he had visited the four corners, North South, East and West. They crossed the Yamuna, a sacred River, flowing into the Ganges, the sacred Sarasvati River,

11.076 : Brow disks worn by youths decorated for the rurepo dance characteristic of those found in Melanesia but clearly related to those of South East Asia and Polynesia. WagaWaga tribe, New Guinea, Melanesia, Late 19th. - early 20th., century, A.D.

11.077 : Browmark on bridegroom 's forehead indicates a devote Vishnu the Sky God of India. This same browmark is found on the Enchique Disk (*7.101*) from Peru. The tall Caucasian bridegroom reflects Aryan descent while the child bride indicates some indigenc negrito descent. South India, early 20th., century, A.D.

11.078 : Brow marks with central red tika or tilak, a brow dot representing the Sun, and the three marks as its wings derived from traditions in the Ancient Middle East. South India, Early 20th., century, A.D.

and Kurushetra, a place of resort particularly associated with the eclipse demon Rahu. From there they went and crossed the River Satadhru and on to the land of Madra where the serpent was devouring the people of the surrounding land. Nila requested of his father that he should prevent the serpent from doing so, to which the father agreed and they went to Brahma to plea for assistance in dealing with Jalodbhava. In gaining the aid of the gods the waters of the lake began to drain away but the serpent divined their plan and by recourse of magic created "dense darkness" and the world became invisible. But then Siva seized the Sun and the Moon thereby causing the darkness to disappear and the light prevailed, and in that moment Vishnu took up battle with the serpent and a fierce encounter ensued with trees and mountaintops as their weapons. In the end, however, Vishnu, the Sky god prevailed and the serpent's head was cut off and this alone remained immortal and the gods rejoiced[255].

The myth is another version of the eclipse demon (Rahu) myth but here it is somewhat longer than some other versions and incorporates the use of the Sun and Moon in bringing light to destroy the serpent's body. It will be remembered that in the Tahaki myth the eyes of the father, Hema, were attached to the belt of the female demon Roi-matagotago and the hero was able to retrieve them, thereby restoring their sight when replaced in the sockets again. In Polynesian myths the eyes particularly relate to the Sun and Moon in their mythology, but where the belt is largely associated with the ecliptic, the Sun's yearly path reflecting their probable origin in the myths of India and the Ancient Middle East. In the myths of the Gilbertese Bue, the counterpart of Tahali, he was particularly associated with eclipses in the mythology surrounding him and later with the clan he represented.

In the Jain versions of the Rahu myths this deity is associated with five colours and it is recorded that there were 42 "eclipse month cycles of lunar eclipses" and 48 eclipse cycles of solar eclipses and these could be determined from the use of these colours[256]. The more myths of the Buddhists, Hindus and Jains are much more sophisticated versions of many preserved among the Aboriginal peoples in India. Many tribes hold the simplified version of the Rahu myth in the form of a serpent attempting to swallow the Sun or Moon, or of a giant who fell in love with the Moon and attempts to seize he. Other versions record that the Sun and Moon were in debt to moneylenders and that they were threatened with being devoured unless the debt was repaid. Some myths relate that these debts were accrued by the Sun or Moon to sweepers who attempted to regain their loans, or similar related versions and players[257]. The serpent belts representing the ecliptic have clear references to the Sun and Moon being attached in some form to the sacred belts reflects the iconography so widely illustrated in the serpent belts of the Moche on the North Peru Coast. Sweeping has been a common aspect noted of the shrine and temple enclosures in Ancient Peru suggesting another aspect transferred from the Ancient fire-religions of the Ancient Middle East and India.

The more extensive and interrelated philosophies of India and even more so those of the Ancient Middle and Near East could not be transferred by mariners who in many cases were not in any way privy or trained in the religious instruction of the temples. It is therefore only possible that they were able to relate the complexities of the Hindu, Buddhist and Jain religions as adherents and their descriptive fluency, or lack of it, would be critical in conveying any part, let alone the whole of these religions to those many hundreds, and thousands of miles away. For the most part the high rituals and texts of India are unlikely to be commonly broadcast but the simple myth of the eclipse demon as the great serpent is ideally suited for transfer to other regions where snakes are native to those islands or continents. Where serpents are few in the landscape or of little importance then the transfer may be projected onto other animals that the local peoples would have considered lethal or dangerous. The further from India, the greater the adaption would need to have been, the rule generally for any myths so transferred. The variation and gradual disintegration into separate elements such as is evident in the Tammui myth is therefore inevitable in dispersion from India or in any other long distance transfer.

Rahu the Eclipse Demon in South East Asia

In South East Asia, myths closely similar to those of the Rahu myths of the Hindus are frequent and have clearly been transferred by mariners, traders and pilgrims over the past couple of thousand years. Frequently the serpent is substituted with a great frog[258], or a large bird[259], but the myths are still recognisably the same as those from India, and these may have been a mutation of the Hindu and the Aboriginal myths of India before departure. The Khasi preserve an eclipse myth featuring a great toad and in some of these Aboriginal Indian myths the hare is also featured with the Moon, as it was among the Maya, and an extension related to it states that the harelip of a new-born child is believed to be the result of an eclipse[260].

Among the Assurs of Central India, early linked to the probable ironworkers of Hatti or

11.079 : Stone surfaced road in Polynesia virtually identical to those in Inca Peru. Marquesas Islands, Eastern Polynesia, 10-14th., century, A.D.

11.080 : Stone surfaced road still surviving in the Andes into the twentieth century identical to those found in the Marquesas Islands. Inca Dynasty, Phara region, Peru, 1350-1500 A.D.

Hittite from Anatolia, the equivalent of Rahu is known as Jwala Mukhi[261]. In the earliest texts of the Vedas the deities Indra, the storm-god, and Varuna, the sea god, are both called Asuras, originally a term of honour in these texts, and it is generally believed that the Assurs of India are their descendants[262]. In later texts the term becomes degraded and "Asuras" is an epithet for demon or anti-god where the deities of the Vedas are downgraded to secondary gods.

Rahu as Eclipse Demon of Nagas of Assam

The Lhota Nagas of Assam have myths similar to those of the Hindus except that the serpent attempting to swallow the Sun or Moon is a dog[263], and it was believed that the Moon at one time was as hot as the Sun and dung was smeared over its face to cool it power - the almost identical myth found in South America[264]. The Ao Nagas have already been already noted for their eclipse demon Tammui who was believed to cyclically swallow the Sun and Moon[265]. Among their traditions also is the belief that there were seven Suns in ancient times and six of these were shot down with arrows because it was too hot for humanity to survive[266].

In the cooler hills of Assam serpent symbolism was less prominent and the reptile fewer to preserve the lowland fear of them but this was replaced by the tiger as the major threat. It is not a surprise therefore that the eclipse myths are similar to India but with the tiger substituting for the serpent in being accused of attempting to swallow the Sun or Moon[267]. These are therefore very similar to the "night jaguar" eclipse myths of the Amazon Basin.

The Eclipse - Melanesia and Polynesia

In Melanesia the eclipse in the Solomon Islands was thought to be a ghost swallowing the Moon[268]. The eclipse in Polynesia was also observed and was noted by the first missionaries to have "filled them with dismay"[269]. It was believed that at this time the eclipse was caused by angry spirits and that they pinched and bit the Moon as well as trying to swallow it[270] - there being no reptiles onto which the demon Rahu as a serpent or other dangerous animal could be projected or retained.

Rahu - The Eclipse Demon in South America

The Chiriguanaos, who resided in the foothills of the Andes south east of Lake Titicaca, were a constant threat to the Inca Empire, and probably also the empire of Tiahuanaco before it. They were notoriously fierce and their reported customs were closely similar to those recorded of the Naga tribes of Assam in North East India and the Dyaks of Borneo. They took the heads of their enemies as trophies back in triumph to their villages after skirmishes and those taken as prisoners were usually fattened during a period of slavery and butchered and quartered, sometimes with the excision of the heart. Their deity was called Iya[271], and this is remarkably similar to the Polynesian deity Io, or perhaps Ira, the term for their ancestral land - probably Iran, and Io is clearly Deo from the Aboriginal supreme deity Maha Deo (literally Great God). During eclipses they believed that a "wild beast" was attempting to swallow the Sun and they made a great noise with their flutes and whistles, also pounding water jars and gourds, in an attempt to frighten the monster away and this follows the same reaction of the peoples of India as well as Assam on the other side of the world[272]. Other peoples of the Amazon and Gran Chaco considered that the eclipse demon was the jaguar of the dark forests, a night hunter that was the equivalent of Rahu[273].

In the Andean highlands Father Bernabe Cobo noted soon after the Conquest that the people considered an eclipse to be caused by a "lion" (that is Mountain Lion or Puma), or a great serpent to be attacking the Moon and attempting to tear her apart. The people were witnessed by the early Spanish to threaten the eclipse serpent by throwing spears and shooting arrows to frighten the demon away[274]. Arriaga notes that during the eclipse of the Moon the people "... whipped dogs, beating drums, and shouting through the town to bring the moon back to life", and this event they called "Quillamhuanum" meaning "the moon dies" or Quilla Tutyan[275]. Cobo notes celebrations that took place at the New Moon festival called the Citua Festival in the tenth month and these were celebrated immediately after the first eclipse of that month[276]. He also notes that both lunar and solar eclipses were interpreted as evil omens along with seeing a rainbow that was believed to presage death or serious injury[277]. Considering that the Incas chose the rainbow as one of their emblems, in these terms it would not seem to have been a propitious choice, but this may have been linked to the idea that for a commoner to look at the ruler was a crime and this applied in many regions of the Old World and was better-known for being the practise up until the end of World War 2 in Japan. It seems probable therefore that the dire consequences of looking at the rainbow was a rule that applied to all but the ruling clans.

The Eclipses and Associated Myths in Central America
In Central America the Moon's nodes, determined by the crossing of the Moon's path across the ecliptic, or Sun's orbit, occurs every 173.31 days and eclipses can only occur within an eighteen day period of the crossing of these orbits. Three of these "eclipse half-years" is very near to the 260 day sacred cycle of the Mayan calendar and it is believed that this may have been the origin of that particular calendar[278]. The number 17 or eighteen occurs frequently in the symbolism of the Americas as well as in the Old World and this number related to the eclipse may well have been the origin of this number associated in Mayan codices with the Chac, or long-nosed god, but a deity probably originating in the elephant god of India - Ganesa. The number twenty has been linked elsewhere with the conjunctions of Jupiter and Saturn. These conjunctions usually take place every twenty years, as an average of the more usual three (triple-) conjunctions occurring over a period of several months - being a forward conjunction, then one in retrograde before the final forward and final conjunction[279]. In the myths of the far North West of North America the use the symbolic day for a year - known as a secondary progression, in determining time cycles and the journeys of mythical heroes[280] is noted elsewhere. This form of predictive calculation is still utilised in the mythical and religious observances of India and in traditional Western astrology.

Sun and Moon Eyes and Rahu as the Eclipse
It has been earlier noted that Tahaki restored the eyes of his blind father, Hema, from the belt of Roi-matagotago[281], and it has been also recorded that Bue, Maui and Tahaki, local variants of the same heroes. In the Gilbert Islands (Kiribati), Bue is particularly associated with the eclipse cycle in their mythology. In the myths of these islands it is said that the creator as Na Areau te Moa-ni-bai ("Sir Spider, First-of-all-Things"), lay with the "Water" and from their union came a son and a daughter, Na Atibu and Nei Teakea. Ne Areau took the right eye of Na Atibu, and flung it into the eastern sky where it became the Sun, and then took the left eye and threw it into the western sky and it became the Moon[282]. The myth follows those of Ancient India and the Pan Kua myth of China where the body of the Creator is dismembered and these become elements in the creation of the world. Na Areau crushed Na Atibu's brain and scattered it over the heavens to become the stars, he dismembered the flesh and scattered it on the waters so that the pieces became the land, and the bones he planted in this land and from them grew the Tree of Samoa, the ancestral race of the Gilbertese. These myths have been paralleled with the myths in Ancient Egypt where the Sun and Moon were created from the eyes of Khepera (the divine Scarab)[283].

In another Gilbertese myth Na Areau the Younger is the " little man" who "sprang forth" from a swelling in the forehead of his father Na Areau the Older, and he is instructed to sit sometimes in the left eye of his father and sometimes in the right[284]. The association of little men identified with the Sun has been examined earlier but in the myths of Ancient India there are references from which the Polynesian variants must derive. In one Vedic text it is noted: "5) Now the person who is seen in the eye, he is Rik, he is ... Brahman. The form of that person (in the eye) is the same as the form of the other person (in the sun), ... Is the name of the other"[285].

The swelling in the brow so notable in the myths of the Gilbert Islands is also found in similar Creation myths of Aboriginal India where dirt from the forehead of Maha-purub is used to create a man[286]. In ancient symbolic imagery the waist was perceived as relating to the ecliptic where the upper half was the sky and spiritual part and the lower half below the belt to the Earth. As a parallel to this in a more localised form of symbolism the golden circlet placed on the brow of the ruler, king or victor was also seen to represent to the Sun and its orbital course in the sky and there appears to be many equivalent examples of this in the New World as in the Old. In the South American examples the brow-bands appear to reflect calendrical, or zodiacal divisions in the manner of those in Ancient India. Eclipses relate to the position of the Sun in relation to the Moon and the symbolic geocentrically perceived orbit of the sacred knot relating to Jupiter's path is described in the ancient texts of the Middle East. The sacred knot clearly relates to the sacred girdle reflecting the ecliptic and to the eclipses associated with it[287] and considered in an earlier work[288]. Since the Sun and Moon are both identified with the human eyes it is clear that the whole tradition relating eclipses to eyes has diffused from India and the Ancient Middle East into the Pacific and beyond into South America. In recent archaeological finds the remarkable find of the tomb of a ruler at Sipan on the North Coast of Peru revealed that a nearly pure gold foil disk had been placed over the right eye and one of a gold copper alloy over the left suggesting a deliberate differentiation in symbolic terms between the right and left[289] as representing the Sun and Moon. The same mummy had a gold plate attached to the nose and an elongated strip with impressed teeth marks and a slit deliberately cut between them seeming to imitate the ritual of opening the mouth so well known in Ancient Egypt and also in the contemporary Middle East.

11.081 :
Seated Cross-legged deity with a crown similar to gold crowns in Colombia and the Inca. The rope around the neck is found in the iconography and rituals of South Peru and Polynesia. Pachacamac, 300-1000 A.D.

11.082 :
Carved monolith of a figure with crossed arms and what appears to be a rope dangling from beneath suggesting that this probably represents a prisoner closely similar to depictions on the North Central Coast of Peru. Pacific Coast, Guatemala, 400-700 A.D.

Eyes - Biting the Eyeball in Polynesian Traditions

In the Gilbert Islands, along with many other islands in Polynesia, it was the custom during the many wars to extract and bight, or swallow the eyes of the enemy[290]. In Rarotonga, the main island of the Cook Islands, the oral traditions note that in defeat the eyeballs of Apopo were "scooped out"[291]. In so doing the eyeballs were first offered to the great Polynesian god Tangaroa with the saying: "Catch the eyeballs, offer them to Tangaroa in the skies, to Rongo and Tane; an evil pastime is war"[292]. In avenging the death of the son of a woman named Apakura, a hero named Te Ariki-taania went to the Apai group of islands and invited aboard his canoe the brothers of the woman who had committed the deed. In a ruse he managed to throw a rope around their necks and decapitated them, and in presenting their heads to Apakura he said "... let us swallow their eyeballs, as a token of what will be the fate of Orokeva-uru; so that

11.083 : A Dyak consulting the shaman for prognostication using traditional liver divination. Borneo, Indonesia, Early 20th., century, A.D.

11.084 : A clay model of a sheep's liver for divination purposes. This is probably the ancient centre for dispersion of this form of divination to India through to the Americas and so noted in Peru. Babylonia, c900 A.D.

11.085 : The depiction of the upside-down traditional birth with supporters is well-known in Ancient India and probably the prototype for similar depictions in Peru (*2.071*). This goddess is usually identified with the Earth Mother, Adya-Sakti, the Akimbo Goddess (*2.037*). South India, 18th., century, A.D.

he be crushed in my mouth"[293]. This tradition of crushing the eyeball is particularly associated with the Maori[294] and the similar tradition in Tahiti and Rarotonga confirms their own legends that these islands were stopovers in their ancestral journeys in the Pacific.

    Such a fate was not reserved exclusively for sacrifice after war but whenever human sacrifices were deemed necessary in the rites and ceremonies on the various islands. The chosen victim was not necessarily an enemy as Reverend William Ellis noted almost two centuries ago: "In general, the victim was unconscious of his doom, until suddenly stunned by a blow from a club or stone, sometimes from the hand of the very chief on whom he was depending as a guest for the rights of hospitality. He was usually murdered on the spot - his body placed in a long basket of cocoa-nut leaves, and carried to the temple. Here it was offered, not by consuming it with fire, but by placing it before the idol. The priest, in dedicating it, took out one of the eyes, placed it on a plantain leaf, and handed it to the king - who raised it to his mouth as if desirous to eat it, but passed it to one of the priests or attendants, stationed near him for the purpose of receiving it. At intervals during the prayers some of the hair was plucked off, and placed before the god, and when the ceremony was over, the body was wrapped in the basket of cocoa-nut leaves, and frequently deposited on the branches of an adjacent tree. After remaining a considerable time, it was taken down, and the bones were buried beneath the rude pavement of the marae. These horrid rites were not infrequent, and the number offered at their great festivals was truly appalling."[295]. These victims were called "fish" suggesting that they were originally mariners or had some connection with the tree on which fish were hung. A sacrificial rite of any fisherman or mariners arriving on the coast of the Solomon's, who were almost invariably killed were called Malahau[296]. It was also noted that when important persons were ill similar sacrifices were instituted and pigs and "a number of men, with ropes around their necks" were also led to the temple and presented before the idol. However in this circumstance the men were not always sacrificed[297]. This may have been a ritual reflecting numerous depictions of apparent victims or prisoners on the Peruvian coasts with ropes around their necks (*11.081/2*) but also had symbolic meaning in Central America earlier noted. This may also have been influenced by imported

11.086 : A typical mummy bundle for a foetus that corresponds to the respect for the unborn child shown also among the Maoris. Chimu, Chan Chan, 900-1450, A.D.

beliefs from Asia since it is noted elsewhere in this work that there are many elements of Tibetan iconography on the North Coast of Peru, and Ecuador. In the Tibetan Book of the Dead the following admonition is recorded for the less than perfect soul after the end of earthly life: "Then the Lord of Death will place round thy neck and drag thee along; he will cut off thy head, tear out they heart, pull out thy intestines, lick up thy brain, drink thy blood, eat they flesh, and gnaw thy bones; but thou wilt be incapable of dying. Even when they body is hacked to pieces, it will revive again. The repeated hacking will cause intense pain." This text appears to be refected in many examples of extreme tortures applied in Ancient Coastal Peru and Ecuador and religious references such as this from Evans-Wentz's translation (page xlvii; 1960) may have been assimilated into whatever social justice system applied at the time.

The Rev. William Ellis spent many years in Tahiti as a resident missionary where these sacrificial rites were witnessed and recorded by him but he also referred to the many similarities evident in cultural aspects that were known in South America. It has already been noted that the term for a shell trumpet in the Marquesas Islands was Putona and the Moari was Pu Tara, while in Peru it was pututu earlier noted. The stone carvings, roads and forts in Peru and Bolivia appear to be closely related to those in the Marquesas and other islands of Polynesia (*11.079*). Feather capes and wigs in the Polynesian Islands and the Marquesas in particular are virtually identical to those of Peru (*11.080*) and the poncho is found in both regions[298].

Ellis noted that there appeared to be a connection between the name of the First Man in Polynesia, Taata or Tangata, was the same as the deity Tangatanga in Peru[299], and this same name appears in Central America as Tamagastad[300] and Thomagata in Colombia[301]. A game similar in principle to hockey called apai or paipai in Tahiti was the identical game found in Ancient South America called there palican, and this same game was found all the way northwards into North America[302]. Ellis described the blackening of the legs from the foot to the knee by the highest class of the Areois priests and this appears to concur exactly with the warrior depictions of the Moche on North Central Peru[303] earlier noted.

In the Marquesas Islands the warrior sacrifices were sacred to the god Tu, and the enclosure, platforms and temples were the preserve of the men and the priests. The sacrificial victims as described by Ellis were hung up in the sacred tree beside the platforms or sacred precinct and the body wrapped in palm fronds and hung by a fishing hook through the mouth in the imitation of a fish catch. It was said that this custom was instituted when the deity Tohetika let down a hook from the sky with which to secure the victim. In this, and another versions of the myth featuring Tiki-tuao, the eyes of the victims were said to have been eaten with the sacred drink, kava, and from these traditions it is likely that the custom of the priest eating the eyes of the victim as he was sacrificing him appears to have originated.

Occasions requiring human sacrifice were many in the Marquesas and those associated with the excision of the human eyes is apparently only associated with male sacrifices and one example is recorded as follows: "Some bodies taken to the temple at these times appear to have been eaten. At certain points during the chanting, according to Pere Jean, the inspirational priest took out the eyes of the victim one at a time and ate them. He cut open the body and took out the heart, which he ate immediately. In the same way he devoured the breast, the bottoms of the feet, and insides of the hands. The body he cooked, cut up, and divided among the participants in the rite"[304].

The heart being cut out clearly has references to the similar practice in Mexico and South America, including among the Incas. The special portion noted here of the hands and feet is widely found throughout Polynesia and elsewhere as the king's or priest's portion earlier noted.

Eyes - Related Traditions and Myths in South America

Among the Cubeo and other Amazonian tribes it was said that the jaguar owned fire and passed it onto mankind. The Kayapo-Gorotire believed that even in the present day the light of the fire could be seen in its eyes, this being a symbol of his fertility and aggression, and it was thought that the jaguar ate the eyes of its prey. In perceiving this quality in the jaguar the human male warriors ate the eyes of the jaguar to assimilate this vigour and fertility[305]. It will also be remembered that the night jaguar in its predatory form was believed to be identified with the eclipse in attempting to swallow the Sun or the Moon both related to the eyes of the sacrificed deity in creation.

Among the Tukano Desana the Master of Animals, earlier noted, was usually conceived as a dwarf and as such shared the characteristic with the jaguar of having prominent eyes[306]. A particular demon, a "deer-jaguar", was said to have a human voice and to devour people who had become lost in the forest. In doing so it was said to eat the eyes first, because they represent the seminal principle, and therefore fertility[307]. This relation clearly has references to the Marquesan traditions where the eyes are important in initiating the sacrifice. In a Chorote myth from the Gran Chaco it was stated that a boy who carried the Star Woman around in a net was attacked later when he was not with her since he had given the bag to his sister to carry. He had been attacked when he had become lost and his attacker began to eat the eyes first. However, the Star Woman heard about it and came to his rescue, and revived him[308]. In a Cayapo myth the people known as the "Kube Pari Kam No" or "people-with-eyes-in-their-feet" (no = eyes; pari = feet), were said to have large penises and kill women after they had used them[309]. This appears to be in the same tradition of the giant myths and vagina dentata myths and it is not surprising that other myths among this tribe mentions giants who were aliens ("Kube").

Eyes - Myths and Traditions in North America

Among the Kwakiutl on the North Pacific Coast of North America it is recorded in their myths that Q'o'mogwa, the "Coppermaker", was said to have consumed the "eyes" of his enemies as his food[310]. Among many other myths this suggests close contacts with the Polynesians and these links in myth are explored in an earlier work[311]. In a Bella Bella myth, from the same region, a hero named Q!omq!omg.ila visited the chief of the East, West and South, sailing initially eastward and after passing four lakes he reached the hole from where the Sun emerged daily. Here a chief named Skin-maker is found and married his daughter. The chief is described as having a face in front and one behind. He eventually arrived at the house of the chief of the north, Coppermaker, where he is given human eyes to eat[312]. This again suggests contact with Polynesians, as many other aspects appear to do, and this confirms Thor Heyerdahl's assertion that these Indian tribes resident on the North West Coast of North America were culturally connected to the Pacific Islanders and the Maoris in particular[313].

CHAPTER 12

PACHACAMAC: ASPECTS of COSMOLOGY
and the ORIGINS of the CUMBI in PERU

Pachacamac and the Pacific

Pachacamac is located on the cast of Peru in the Lurin Valley[1] about 16 kilometres south of Lima. It was a prime target for the Conquistador's search for gold and in so doing raised it to a pile of mud brick ruins. It was, up until the Spanish Conquest, an "oracular" centre much revered and frequented even by widely distant peoples in the Andes and coastal regions of Peru and proba- bly also from Lake Titicaca region in what is now Bolivia. From the present state of archaeo- logical research it is deduced that Pachacamac was probably a Huari settlement in its final form[2] but built on over much older foundations dating back to at least the first millennium B.C. There is some suggestion that this site may in fact have had links with Chavin de Huantar in the Central Highlands[3]. However, Pachacamac iconography reflects that of Tiahuanaco[4] and this site may have been an early landing site on the coast for Pacific Ocean mariners as a staging post on the route into the highlands to Chavin in the Central Andes and Tiahuanaco further to the southeast in the Bolivian highlands.

The principal god at Pachacamac was represented by a carved wooden statue, probably gold covered with precious stone inlay, in the characteristic style of surviving images from the shrine. This was guarded in a windowless shrine chamber on top of the stepped pyramid and it was shrouded from profane eyes by a curtain drawn across the entrance. Only the oracular priest was allowed to see the image and not even the Incan prince Tupa, earlier noted for his voyage west across the Pacific Ocean, was allowed to see the image[5]. This description appears identical to shrines in Southern India where the image of the deity was usually screened in a similar win- dowless shrine by a curtain[6]. The rites and ceremonies associated with the Pachacamac shrine was confessional and oracular as it was with the Viracocha shrines[7]. Cieza de Leon recorded that the entrance "door is said to have been of gold plates, richly inlaid with coral and precious stones"[8]. De la Vega notes of the resident supreme deity, "... They call him Pachacamac, a word composed of pacha, which means the universal world, and camac, the present participle of the verb cama, to animate, whence is derived the word cama, the soul. Pachacamac therefore means He who gives animation to the universes ..."[9]. The term cama in interesting since the reincar- nating soul in India is said to be reborn because of its karma, or the accumulation of deeds in past lives, and is therefore a term specifically associated with the soul. De la Vega, descended from an Inca mother, also stipulates that Pachacama as a deity was considered greater than the Sun[10] and in some traditions the Sun was considered to be the son of Pachacama[11]. He further notes of Pachacamac that, "... Those who more particularly had adopted this belief before they were con- quered by the Yncas, were the ancestors of king Cuismancu, who built a temple to Pachacamac and gave the name to the valley where it stood" ... "The Yncas placed their idols in this temple, which were figures of fishes, and among them there was an image of a fox"[12].

This relation is of some importance since it notes the importance of fish gods, probably a reference to mariners and their deities. This would appear to confirm many record oral tradi- tion referring to mariners and migrants from the Pacific Ocean all along the coast to Ecuador and where some of these ancient gods were identified with Viracocha and, or Pachacamac. In anoth- er contribution De la Vega notes that there was a "traditional animosity" between the Chimu and the ceremonial priests of Pachacamac appearing to confirm the opposition between the Sun deity, Con, in the north, and Pachacamac in the south. This may also derive from two separate mariner traditions arriving on the distant parts of the Pacific coast to carve out rival trading empires, since both have traditions of dynasties or deities associated, and their arriving from the sea[13].

Pachacamac is the site mentioned in the Coniraya myth where the goddess Cavillaca, fleeing from Coniraya enters the sea with her child and then turned to stone. This is as earlier noted a myth motif found widely in the Pacific Islands and particularly in Melanesia through to India. Here it was after Coniraya had reached Pachacamac and discovered his beautiful Cavillaca had turned to stone, he walked along the beach and met the daughters of the priestess who attended the sacred serpent in the shrine located there[14]. This shrine housing a serpent suggests an oracular cult similar to that of the pythoness at Delphi in Greece but similarly dedicated temples of this type are found also in India.

Pachacamac, however, appears to have been a Creator deity in his own right from long before the Incas[15]. If Montesinos is to be believed the Ecuadorian giants at Manta, noted in an earlier chapter, and on the peninsula of Santa Elena, also built the shrines at Pachacamac[16]. It was considered that Pachacamac was the son of Con, and this deity was the god of the Skyris of Ecuador. Con is probably the same as Con-i-raya, but Con himself was said to be a spirit without corporeal form who created the mountains and landscape along the Andes from North to South[17]. Gutierrez, from his informants, records that the Creation was the work of two distinct beings, the first was called Cons and the other Pachacama. The myths he had knowledge of described Cons as having created the world while Pachacamac destroyed this creation and then remade it to his own plan[18].

In a myth, seeming to reflect a conflict between Pachacamac and the Sun, perhaps as Cons, it is said that Pachacamac created a man and a woman but omitted to provide them with food. The man died and the woman in her distress appealed to the Sun for help and in response he gave the woman a son and taught them to live on wild fruits growing around them. Pachacamac was enraged at this interference and killed the son, dismembered the body burying the parts in the earth, and from these the cultivatable plants arose. From the teeth arose the corn; from the bones, yucca, from the flesh, vegetables and fruits. This is clearly another version of the Chinese Pan Kua dismemberment myth earlier noted. The Sun, however, gave the woman another son who was named Wichama, but while the Sun was absent, Pachacama slew the woman who was by that time very old. Wichama in his anger pursued Pachacamac but he disappeared into the sea, and Wichama vented his anger upon the rest of mankind by scorching the earth and turning many of them to stone[19]. The association of the name "Con" with the Creator[20] suggests also the name of Con Ticci Viracocha, indicates that these versions have all probably originated from the same traditions. It may also have been that they were adopted and regaled with similar titles taken from other deities in the same way as had occurred in India. These tangled associations tend to be confirmed by the fact that in one tradition Viracocha, the "great white bearded man", whose beard was likened to the rays of the Sun[21], departed for his voyage west across the Pacific Ocean and not at Manta, far to the north in Ecuador, as other traditions state[22].

This Wichama myth has been perceived as symbolising the seasonal cycles since the scorching of the earth is a characteristic of the hot desert coastal regions of Peru, but overall the whole myth tends to relate to imported aspects from the Pacific to the West, where Pachacamac was said to have disappeared to, along with Viracocha and other heroes or deities. These myths appear to relate closely to the Con-iraya myths since there are separate myths relating to Iraya as the deity of Pachacamac[23] and this appears to have derived from those associated with Con-i-raya reflecting deities with similar names in Melanesia and India.

The fundamental basis of these South Coast Peruvian myths appears to derive from the old opposition between the Sun as eagle and Pachacamac associated with serpent worship and this opposition appears in India between the Garuda (eagle) and Nagas (serpents), and in Mexico reflected also in the Aztec heraldic device of the eagle with the serpent in its beak. The term Con-i-raya is also of interest since Con is known as the god of light in ancient Eurasia, and Iraya is clearly Aryia, the name for Ancient Iran, and in India, Raya, is the name for king or ruler earlier noted where it relates by extension to the Southern European Indo European term for king, Rei.

It is likely therefore that Con-Iraya was in fact introduced by an earlier Aryan migration from Ancient Iran direct or from South India where many influences originate in South America.

Interestingly, Coniraya is identified with one of the most important places in Inca history, Huarochiri, in the mountains not far from Cuzco. Here he is identified with Viracocha as Con-i-raya Viracocha, and Paraiacaca, earlier noted, said to have been Viracocha's son, and to have defeated the primordial god, Huallalla Carhuinchu. After this defeat the latter's supporters, the Huanca, retreated after this confrontation into the highlands[24]. Thomas Joyce a century ago noted that the deities from the coast at Pachacamac appear to be trickster figures, much more like those in the west of North America. In the works of the renown American scholar, Joseph Campbell, his map of myth distribution (*1.007*) shows clearly that the intrusive influences on the coasts of both North and South America originated in the Pacific. This distribution map clearly indicates that it was from the oceanic currents direct from Asia that mariners transported these myths and myth motifs into North and South Americas. Thomas Joyce writes as a conclusion when referring to the mythical heroes associated with Pachacamac: "One fact seems to result, namely, that many, if not most, of the Peruvian tribes worshipped each a supreme creator-god, and that the attributes of these creator-gods were sufficiently similar to admit of their identification when the cults came into contact"[25].

Joyce's observations tend to confirm the obvious conclusion that these deities were imported and diffused by successive intruders or culture-bearers from the Pacific Ocean. From the available evidence these religions, or simply a poor man's version of them, largely originated in India, each bringing their own god, or their own version of the same god, into Ecuador, Chile and Peru, at least in the period of the high cultures after about 3000 B.C. Earlier research indicates that the influences from Pachacamac were transferred to the North Coast of Peru and that the star shape-headed club so favoured by the Incas as their sceptre of rulership, appears first on the coast at Nazca and from Pachacamac northwards[26]. It is unlikely to be a coincidence that the identical star shape-headed club is found in Melanesia and New Guinea. Here they are concentrated on islands flanking the only viable sea route from South America back to India, and it is in this same region that panpipes and bark trumpets are found along with cranial deformation and trepanation identically with those in South America. It is undoubtedly significant that metallurgy is first found being utilised in the hills above Pachacamac near what is now Ayacucho and that copper pectorals and other ornaments and implements are so widespread in the cultures in Southern Bolivia and Northern Chile and Argentina extending from this section of the Pacific Coast.

The myth motifs of heroes or deities turning to stone; birth from a tree, bamboo, or the emergence of a tree from the body of a hero deity or other person buried, or from the skull, is widely found along the sea routes of the Pacific Ocean from India to South America. The appearance of the same motifs in this myth from Pachacamac should not, therefore, be a surprise. De la Vega noted in the 16th., century that pacha meant "heaven" and camac meant "soul", extending to associated variations of meaning. It has been noted above that camac appears to bear a close similarity to expressions in India, where karma means the soul's evolutionary pattern, and therefore Pacha might then hold a clue to another cross-Pacific importation, even if a little distorted by time and distance.

The Term *Pacha* in Peru and India

It is likely that Pacha actually derives from Pancha because the number five repeatedly occurs in the myths and legends of South America and among the Inca in particular. But other related aspects appear to indicate other associations that are of significance.

The Malayali are a widespread people in Southern India and in one of their tribal origin legends it is said that three brothers left their homelands from the sacred city of Kanchipuram, and the youngest settled in the Pachaimalais, the "Green Hills"[27]. This gave them their name of Pachaimalais whereas one of the other brothers went to the Kollamalais and this gave them their name. These people are considered to be related to the Tottiyans who call them brother-in-law (Macchan) indicating earlier marriage ties between them[28]. Some of the Malayali call themselves Kanchi-Mandalam referring to their descent from the revered ancient city not far from modern Madras (Chennai).

The Malayalis were settled into their own villages and over each group of ten villages was appointed a headman or Patta-Karan[29] and the headman is called Pattan[30]. The term Patta is a title identically used for the Brahman Batta and it is unlikely to be a coincidence that this highest caste name is found also among the Inca[31]. The Malayali house was a beehive shaped hut made of bamboo and thatched with palm leaves and grass, with smaller versions as granaries. Outside the village was located a sacred tree, usually old and lofty, beneath which was located a shrine. Inside this shrine was a small stone slab standing on stone blocks or supports and placed on the slab numerous ancient stone celts or axe-heads believed to be sent as thunderbolts to earth by the gods for due adoration[32]. These are many a similar traditions found widely distributed from India through the Pacific Islands and Aboriginal Australia to the Americas.

Throughout India it was a strictly applied injunction to enter the temples anciently, and to this present day, barefoot[33] and in many cases to approach the god or ruler in the palace bare-chested and the same regulation applied also in Incan Peru[34] (*7.089*). In Peru the Inca supplicant had, when being interviewed by the ruler, to carry a load and wear poor clothing. The Malayalis took this barefoot rule in the temple precincts further and insisted that nobody should go other than barefoot in their villages, and this included the highest status Brahman or ruler[35].

The village council, as with so many of the settlements in India, was governed by the Pancha-yat, a council made up of five elders (pancha = five). In the philosophical constructs of the Ancient Middle East and India the number five was sacred and identified with the five aspects or ganas. These five aspects were reflected in the highest Self, Being (Brahman) or God[36] and this religious structure was reflected in the council of the villages. There are references, however, that this model was in fact a reflection of an older system from ancient times where there were five recognised races relating to the evolution of the caste system and adopted generally as the cultural influences from Ancient Iran spread through into India from the North West[37].

The Malayali among others practised tattooing and the headmen claim a privileged right to use parasols denied some of the other castes[38]. The art of the tattoo is identified with the Polynesians more than any other people, even though it was unlikely to have been their invention. In India similar myths are found associated with tattooing as similarly occur in Indonesia, Melanesia, and in parts of South America, particularly those indicating that it was required to adorn the women to prevent the attack of "evils spirits". On the male face it was believed to enhance their identification with the vigorous attributes of their gods by imposing a likeness, called the moko by the Maoris.

In India a tribal caste called the Korava, known also as the Koracha and Yerukala, and who call themselves the Kurru, practised tattooing and among the Kunchu Korava where it is practised as a lively-hood and was called "pricking with green" - Pacchai Kutti[39]. The term Pacchai is attached to caste subdivisions who were in some way connected in occupation with the colour green and among the Kamma caste it is used by itself as a title of one subdivision and among the Devangas the caste employed in the tobacco trade are called Pacchi Powaku ("Green Tobacco")[40]. The Pacchai Botlu are tattooers among the Oddes in the Central East Coast of India and these people were better-known for their construction in earthworks and building.

The term "Pacchai" means "green" in India in these contexts but in earlier works it has been noted that there are many aspects of the various cultures of India that must have been transferred from their to India in the first millennium A.D. greatly influencing the Maya in Central America and Mexico. Among the Maya yax[41] and yaxchi means "green" or "fresh" tree[42]. This would seem, among other aspects, to derive from India and Miles Poindexter considered the Quiche-Maya the prime candidates to have been the ancestors of the Quichua of Peru. The fact that at least two of the Inca origin myths records migrations from the north suggests that he may be correct. It is likely therefore that Panch, "five" reflecting heaven or Brahman and pachai, "green" in India, was the origin of the Peruvian pacha also for heaven but as the Yaxcha for green tree, or the Ceiba of Central America, that is the Mayan Tree of Heaven, Wacah Chan, meaning "six sky" or "raised-up sky"[43]. The term chan has been related by Poindexter to an for town or settlement earlier noted in Central Asia, and probably denotes the ancestral home to which the Mayan ruler was destined after death depicted so famously on the sepulchral slab of Pacal at Palenque. The term wakah is less obvious in its original derivation but considering the many references to Polynesian terms absorbed into Mayan terminology then it is likely that the tree was a euphemism for the solar boat, constructed from the World Tree, where waka is the term for a canoe in Polynesian. Bone carvings found in Mayan tombs indicate that the canoe was in fact the means in at least one tradition centered on Tikal that the soul descended into the Underworld by that means[44]. Polynesian terms found among the Maya are; ahau = ruler or chief, tepeu - a ruling dynasty or tribe, and the use of barkcloth and bark beaters identically, indicates contact between the Polynesian and the Maya. The term for canoe in India derives from vaka the wind required for a sailing boat earlier noted. The same can be said of the South Americans where parallel influences and terminology is evident into the Inca Empire from Polynesia and all places west from India.

In considering whether the term pacha is derived from India it can been seen that it has ancient roots in its probable original from pancha = five = heaven but it should also in this respect be noted that Siva, the great phallic deity of India was also called Panchanana or "Five-faced", reflecting the five orders of creation[45] linking again to heaven and the gods, particularly where they lived in the heaven on the five peaks of the Himalayas. This number appears emulate to the contexts displayed in Peru too frequently not to be in some way connected with those in India, and it is probable that this influence derived for the most part from the great pilgrim city of Kanchi in South East India.

Tattoos were widely known and practiced in Central and South America and it can only be conjectured whether the term Pachacuti, as an elevated title applied to the Inca Pachacuti - Tupac's father, is in any way derived from Pacchai Kutti, since tattooing was a highly revered practice in Polynesia from where the influences from India would have transitted as a penultimate influence before entering Peru. Tattooing appears to have been common on the Peruvian Coast from at least early Moche times where examples are depicted on many ceramics and cult objects (*1.036*). Was the sudden expansion in Inca culture in his time from an incursion of new blood from Southern India via Polynesia that might indicate that Inca Pachacamac was influenced from abroad? Certainly there is a sudden reformation and rebuilding of Cuzco based on the principle of the four quarters of the cardinal points that remains unexplained, but usually attributed to older traditions inherited from Tiahuanaco. But there are several centuries gap between the fall of Tiahuanaco and the rebuilding of Cuzco and it may be that this ruler has usurped the credit and possibly the titles of newcomers bringing new ideas and impetus along with radical theories relating to ceremonial site planning to the cardinal points as occurred much earlier in the time of the Tiahuanaco Empire. These influences may have been introduced via Pachacamac through the Chinchas who were particularly noted for the fine stature and advanced culture and may have been descendants, at least in part, from the Huari. It has been noted that the giants of Ecuador were considered to have cast a malevolent influence but Montesinos noted that these giants were also associated with Pachacamac[46] and might have been the ancestors of these Chincha people. The Chinchas were said to have been a warrior race who entered the "fairest valley in the land" and found many inhabitants "... but all of small stature that the tallest was barely two cubits high" (about 3-3½ feet or a metre high)[47]. These people were a threat to the Incas and were believed to have introduced notable cultural advances.

It has been recorded that the Inca Tupa heard from mariners in Ecuador that there were lands with gold to be found across the sea to the west. Cieza de Leon notes a similar tradition that originating from south of Pachacamac (Arica in North Chile?) that, "... opposite Acari, but very far out to sea, there are some very large islands, and it is publicly reported that much gold is brought from them to trade with the natives of this coast"[48]. "Publically reported" clearly indicates that all knew of these traders, and that they probably visited the South Peruvian coast on more than one occasion, and on the strength of these reports and that of the Tupa voyage the Spanish sent out an expedition in 1550 A.D. under Mendana. However, in considering the location of these large islands and where gold might be readily available it is unlikely that these lands could have been anywhere else other than Asia since Polynesia and even the larger islands of Melanesia were not known for gold production. The mariners inevitably utilized knowledge of the prevailing winds and ocean currents to reach their destinations. Because of the strength of the Peruvian, or Humboldt Current flowing from the West Wind Drift Current directly under the roaring forties to Acari it would have been almost impossible to arrive on this south coast unless using this Southern Pacific Current from the Western Pacific. The only other likely approach is using this current but coming from the North by sailing far out into South Eastern Polynesia near or beyond Easter Island and then sail with the southern current to the North Chilean and Peruvian Coast. It may have been in utilising this sea route that Easter Island was discovered and settled.

Capacocha in Ancient South America and Polynesia - Arnavan and Child Sacrifice
In the middle to latter part of the twentieth century the reports in Spanish texts were repeatedly brought into question as to their veracity and it was declared by some that they were propaganda exercises instituted by the European colonialists to mask and justify their own brutality in suppressing the Amerindians throughout the Americas[49]. This attitude was augmented by the rise of political correctness using this theory to undermine the researches of earlier archaeologists, anthropologists, and interested parties among those such as Miles Poindexter, who supported cross-Pacific contacts from Asia to the Americas. The Native American cultures, as they were declared, were portrayed as advanced civilisations of ideal peacefulness and models for the highest aspirations of political and social development. Even where there were obviously less developed societies in the forests of the Amazon and Gran Chaco they were still eulogised as fine examples of the "noble savage". The prime target in this campaign against "contaminating" influences threatening this utopian vision of the Americas were the Spanish reports of human sacrifice and capacocha - the sacrifice of children.

In Mexico the eyewitness accounts of the sacrifice of humans warriors were difficult to counter, because archaeological evidence was readily available in the surviving depictions of tzompantli, or skull racks, and other frequent references in murals and ceramic designs, but there were attempts to questions the numbers that were sacrificed to deflect attention from these considered horrific practises. In the Coastal and Andean cultures of Peru, even though there was no lack of archaeological evidence for such practices, these reports of capacocha were used to undermine and debunk the post-Conquest reports of both the civil and religious Spaniards. The veracity of the early Spaniards was deemed questionable in all aspects because there was no readily available evidence for ritual child sacrifice and the whole of their reports were therefore considered questionable.

The Spanish priest Christoval de Molina described the capacocha system in 1574 A.D. and this appeared to be later confirmed by the Inquisitor Hernandez Principe in 1621 A.D. This dedicated Inquisitor priest recorded on the reports of the worship of a goddess called Tanta Carhau, a mountain deity, in the village of Ocros in Peru. He stated that the tradition went that Tanta Carhua was in fact a "beautiful daughter" of the local chief and because of this she was dedicated to the Sun and consequently sacrificed as a child to the mountain deities in about 1430 A.D. It was said that she had been sent to Cuzco for approval, and there dedicated to the Sun, and on her return was feted and then led to the high mountain locally named Mount Aixa and sacrificed by being walled in a tomb earlier constructed[50]. Through long exertions Principe located the tomb and dug the capacocha out of the 20 foot deep shaft tomb describing the small silver pins, ornaments pots and jars immured with her.

The description given by Hernandez Principe of the capacocha child sacrifice that occurred, reputedly, a century before the Spanish Conquest was important not only because it did confirm Molina's contention that such sacrifices has taken place but described the grave goods associated with it. In February, 1954, in Northern Chile, two miners searching for the fabled lost treasure of the Incas on Mount Plomo discovered a stone wall high up on a glacier slope. This peak is almost 18,000 feet high and, not far from the head of the glacier, under a heap of rocks on the wall, they discovered a large stone slab. Prying this loose they discovered the first Inca capacocha sacrifice excavated in modern times. The burial goods associated with the small boy appeared to be similar to those that Principe described accurately centuries earlier. The child himself appeared to be high born since he wore the silver arm bracelet and "H"-shaped pectoral hung around his neck, both known to indicate an elevated social status. One gold figurine of a llama was included, one of Ecuadorian Spondylus shell, a larger silver figurine dressed in the lavish attire of an Inca princess, and five pouches containing locks of hair, teeth and nail clippings, and a purse adorned with flamingo feathers containing sweet-smelling coca leaves. Less frequently mentioned is the fact that this child, as with so many other examples and depictions, had his long dark hair braided into ringlets typical of the Ancient Middle East, and the earlier peoples of Coastal South America. Among these latter, particularly those along the Peruvian Coast where interments have survived intact due to the barren conditions, red, blonde, fair and light brown are more frequent than dark hair. The hair type and texture is distinctly Caucasian as noted by the researches and archaeologists in the nineteenth and early twentieth centuries[51].

Since the discovery of the Inca boy on Mt. Plomo there have been several other discoveries of capacocha burials in Argentina and Peru and they all not only reflect Molina and Principe's accounts but also several earlier references recorded by Bernabe Cobo[52] and others. In one of the reports noted by Cobo a fourteen year old girl, in the selection process of being examined was found to have a small mole under her one of her breasts and was deemed therefore unworthy to be selected for a sacrifice to the Sun[53]. Cobo also notes that during the festival of Itu, after the children selected were sacrificed, the celebrants worn their hair braided down to their feet sometimes and wore long tunics made from cumbi as well as headdresses of feathers and other accessories[54]. The customs most in accord with those found in recent times he describes those for the capacochas on the "hill of Chuquichanca" where the children were strangled, common in these sacrifices, and "buried with gold and silver"[55]. This belief that any blemished person was unworthy to be a sacrifice was also held in both the early Vedic texts and in the Ancient Near and Middle East, from whence the custom almost certainly originated.

These discoveries have been instrumental in a re-examination of the Spanish chronicler's works from the post-Conquest period since the surviving descriptions proved not only their veracity but that their other references, not yet all proven or in doubt, might be given a second reading and receive validation by further research not previously undertaken. This has led to a much greater interest in the traditions and customs, particularly those of daily life and rituals, surviving from the time of the Incas into the present day, and are, or will be therefore more readily verifiable in the future.

Highly rated among the post-Conquest chroniclers is the work of Pachacuti-Yamqui Salcamayhua, not a Spaniard but a Christianised Peruvian, believed to be of Inca descent, and he too notes the custom of capacocha. He attributes, through his knowledge of Inca traditions, the first introduction of the custom of child sacrifice to the early part of the reign of the great Inca Pachacuti after the death of his father Inca Usca Mayta, or Mayta Ccapac[56]. In time it is said that Pachacuti challenged the practitioners of these rites and the degeneracy that had undermined the religion of the people and the Incas themselves and challenged them to a trial between their effectiveness and those of the traditional stricter Inca religion. The sorcerers lost the challenge and they were all banished but of interest is the fact that this duplicates the challenges issued by the Buddha to the Naga practitioners and found also in similar relations in the texts of the Hindus. This challenge is also reminiscent of the Biblical challenge of the Jesus Christ to Satan in the wilderness and suggests that the reforms instituted against the traditional worship of deities and ancestors resident in stones, lakes and rivers, so closely similar to those of Asia was instituted by Pachacuti with something appearing to be influenced or resembling traditional Christianity and Buddhism. This might be attributed to possible influence from India - either Buddhist or Hindu but more likely Syrian Christian (missionaries of St. Thomas or Tonapa). Interestingly Salcamayhua noted also that these child sacrifices were offered by the Collas (Aymaras) to the Sun and the Sky along with Cuis (guinea-pigs) and recorded that they stated that they received answers from Tayta, meaning God the Father and also minister of the huacas[57]. The name of Tayta is clearly the same variation on an Aryan name for "father" - Tata, found among the pre-Spanish Mexicans and preserved intact and found also in Melanesia, Indonesia and South East Asia.

In the capacocha sacrifices it has been noted that in post-Conquest records, and found in recent excavations, girls were among the capacochas. Salcamayhua, however, notes when it was first introduced in the time of Inca Pachacuti: "They say that, in his time, they invented the sacrifices of Capaucha-cocuy, burying virgin boys with silver and gold; and of the Arpac with human blood or with white lambs called Uracarpana, cuyes, and grease"[58]. This confirms the description of Cobo, Molina and Principe, but the original sacrifice specifically notes that it is that of the sacrifice of boys, and this, associated with the examination for blemishes clearly indicates a more likely influence from Asia where only the male sacrifice was considered acceptable for the ancient Aryan ancestral gods[59]. This same belief is found also in India and through into the Pacific Islands and therefore by extension logically to South America and the inclusion of the white llama is clearly the substitute the white lamb or ram in Christian tradition, and in that of the Aryan West and South Asia, referred to elsewhere in this work. But equally, if there had been contact from Asia with South America then inevitably there should be found to be traces of the Peruvian assimilation of the original boy sacrifice, and possibly including female children on the return journey from South America to Asia.

Capacocha or Child Sacrifice in Polynesia

Capacocha appears to have been a characteristic sacrifice in the annual cycles of fertility, rain-making propitiation, and in rituals associated with the various annual festivals celebrated with the adoration of the Sun and other deities. In the Polynesian Islands, reflecting so many aspects of Peruvian culture in the Marquesas Islands, early reports recorded that children were sometimes buried alive with the body of the inspirational priests during his burial rites[60]. The early writers in Polynesia were frequently missionaries who were sent from London missionary societies to convert and minister to the needs of the peoples of the many islands. Among these the well-known figure of the Reverend W. Wyatt Gill is important because of his writings recording the existing customs of the people before their conversion and their cosmology before being modified or compromised by contact with the Europeans. He notes the sacrifice of children for festivals to the deities but are of interest particularly when the health of one of their living relatives was under threat. Wyatt Gill sought out the most reliable informants who were known to have been involved in such practises not so much to incriminate them, but for the more worthy motive of attempting to understand the former beliefs, ceremonies and motivations initiating and preserving such rites for so long among these people. He describes from his informant, who was responsible for betraying his uncle, Ikakona, as a sacrifice to the god of war - Rongo, that not long after this event his brother Akapori had suffered the same fate and was lain on the altar of the god of the night, on Mangaia in supplication for success in a plot to seize the chieftainship[61].

The Reverend Wyatt Gill reported on the child sacrifices from those whom he considered to be able to provide an accurate account before the introduction of Christianity in Mangaia in 1824 A.D. making contact with those who had been intended victims or themselves participated in these rites. One of his informants, Paitiki, was not only reliable but had himself actively participated in some of the child sacrifices that occurred only a few years earlier[62]. One is worth repeating here verbatim as he recorded it: "Makimaki had a brother named Akaruke, who a few years previously had been laid upon the altar. But then the lad followed his father's tribe and god, Teipe. At the time of his death he was about eight or nine years old. A rope was tied around his little naked body for the convenience of those who led him to slaughter. The mother of Akaruke wished to die with her boy, but was detained by sheer violence. The child was led round the northeast part of the island in order to secure the approbation of certain powerful chiefs who lived there. On their way the victim-seekers killed a relative of the boy in revenge for some ancient grudge, not for the altar. Arrived at the residence of the chiefs, a feast was made for the murderers. This over, late in the afternoon, they started again. But little Akaruke was this time in the care of Katia (who recently died in the faith), who really had a tender heart under a most rugged exterior. He bade the child hide himself in the dense bush till nightfall. But it was in vain; for as soon as it was known that Akaruke was missing a careful search was instituted, and the rope revealed the hiding-place of the victim. They were now all on the watch, and led him on carefully until they reached Tuopapa, where the child was slain, and his body conveyed with shouts of joy to the bloody altar of Rongo. This occurred circa 1810. This boy, had he lived, would have been brother-in-law to the king of Mangaia[63].

This remarkable narrative records several aspects of the capacocha system of child sacrifice in Peru from where it is likely to have been adopted. The child is led around to the sacred houses of the chiefs and on a long tour of the shrines as other earlier, and later, child sacrifices had also followed. This appears to follow the same principle as those in Peru where children were led along the ceque lines radiating from Cuzco to the shrines and in some cases sacrificed at one of them. Others were taken to the high mountains where the bodies were preserved by the perpetual sub-zero temperatures. In Mangaia, strangling by a rope also repeats the capacocha system and such apparent sacrifices were recorded in figurines dating from before and during the Moche on the North Peruvian Coast from about 2000 years ago (*11.081/2*). The climatic conditions were very different in Mangaia since the tropical rain meant abundance in the Pacific Islands and rain gods were less revered unlike the war god. This deity was believed to require important sacrifices since conflict was ever present, whereas in Peru and Bolivia rain was of major importance and regular rains were meagre, and occasional catastrophic failure in the annual rains was of major importance in regions where agriculture was dependent on large-scale irrigation works. Modifications in the sacrificial requirements were therefore inevitable but the fundamental principle of child sacrifice in Polynesia appears to be too similar to that of Peru to be accidental.

Another remarkable record of capacocha, or child sacrifice, relating to the Polynesian peoples of Tonga is to be found in the biography of Edward Mariner. This young man, born in 1791 A.D., went to sea at the age of thirteen years, not unusual at that time, under the protection of Captain Duck in charge of the ship Port au Prince, a friend of, and arranged by his father. The ship was seized and scuttled for booty by the Tongans when it arrived in the Pacific and Mariner was one of only a few of the crew allowed to survive - Captain Duck, his father's friend having died earlier before it reached these islands. Mariner arrived back in London in June, 1811 A.D. having spent most of those formative teenage years among the Tongans. He was adopted by the ruling chief at that time, Finau (also Finow in the text), and therefore saw the whole of Tongan society at that time from a position of some privilege and while there he formed a close friendship with the chief's son. Having learnt the Tongan form of the Polynesian language he was able to understand and convey more accurately the traditions and customs as experienced in everyday life in Polynesia while having only a minimal external cultural influence in compromising their later interpretation with too jaundice an eye of daily life resulting no doubt from his youth and impotence in the face of an unexpected isolation among these warrior people.

In several references in his biography by John Martin M.D., Mariner records the frequent occasions when child sacrifice was resorted to and these were usually when some important person was suffering a serious illness[64]. He notes in particular the distress caused to a mother when a child was seized to be strangled as an offering for the recovery of an ill father. The mother was so distraught for so long after the event that she appeared to have become unbalanced to the point that the ruler, Finau, ordered her to be shot dead as she danced about the locale with little covering. In another case, when a man was killed while seeking sanctuary in the sacred ground where acts of violence were strictly forbidden and considered extremely sacrilegious, the inspirational priest was consulted as to a remedy for this heinous act of infringement of the sacred ground that had been committed. He deemed, after consulting the ancestral spirits, that a high born child should be sacrificed and one was seized on the agreement of the father, a local ruler, by one of his concubines. This reference in Mariner's biography is worth noting because the Tongan traditions probably derived from Peru, not Asia, since they allowed the sacrifice of female children as well as male.

In Asia the highest status male sacrifice was only considered acceptable but here a child of lesser status is agreed to as in Peru, and therefore a further degeneracy of the original Asian tradition as Mariner remembered: "The child was accordingly sought for; but its mother, thinking her child might be demanded, had concealed it: being, at length, found by one of the men who were in search of it, he took it up in his arms, smiling at delight at being taken notice of. Its poor mother wanted to follow, but was held back by those about her; on hearing its mother's voice it began to cry, but, when it arrived at the fatal place of its execution, it was pleased and delighted with the band of gnatoo (high quality barkcloth) that was put round its neck, and looking up in the face of the man who was about to destroy it, displayed in its beautiful countenance a smile of ineffable pleasure; such a sight inspired pity in the breast of every one: but veneration and fear of the gods was a sentiment superior to every other, and its destroyer could not help exclaiming, as he put on the fatal bandage, O yaooe chi vale (poor little innocent!) two men then tightened the cord by pulling at each end, and the guiltless and unsuspecting victim was soon relieved of its painful struggles. The body was then placed upon a sort of hand-barrow (litter), supported upon the shoulders of four men, and carried in a procession of priests, chiefs and matabooles (council leaders), clothed in mats, with wreaths of green leaves round their necks. In this manner it was conveyed to various houses consecrated to different gods, before each of which it was placed on the ground, all the company sitting behind it except one priest who sat beside it, and prayed aloud to the god that he would be pleased to accept this sacrifice as an atonement for the heinous sacrilege committed, and that punishment might accordingly be withheld from the people. After this was done the body was given up to its relations to be buried in the usual manner"[65].

This passage clearly suggests South American influence where the perambulation round the sacred temple and shrines in the Tongan Islands is clearly reminiscent of the children before their immolation if Peru being led along the sacred paths or ceques to the various shrines before being sacrificed. In Peru the most acceptable and highest sacrifice was that of a child of the highest status families and in Tonga, when Mariner was under the protection of the chief Finau, the latter fell ill and in this case one of his own children was deemed alone suitable to ransom his recovery from the gods[66]. Mariner confirms the kingly title was How (Hau)[67] in the Tonga Islands and is the same as the term ahau found among the Maya and in South America earlier noted. In an extraordinary parallel to Ancient Peru Mariner witnessed occasions where children actually vied for the right to be sacrificed, and in some rites 3 or 4 children were strangled[68].

In the area to the north of the great island of New Guinea known as Pilotu, clearly derived from the name of the Polynesian Underworld, Pulotu, a great sea monster was said to exist. Because the people in these smaller island archipelagos depended to a great degree on fishing and sea trading (the Kula), anything remotely fearful at sea, real or imaginary, loomed large in the imaginations of the people. It is said that a giant sea monster called a kwita, likened to a giant octopus, terrorised the local mariners and when it was said to grasp and hold fast the boats at sea, a boy was sacrificed by throwing him to the monster[69]. This account appears a crude form of propitiation but is still in the tradition of the more sophisticated child sacrifice in Ancient Peru, Bolivia and Chile through into Polynesia. More reminiscent of the capacocha sacrifices in the same islands is the belief to what were called "moving stones" at sea. Europeans have had these pointed out to them when at sea by natives who insist that they are real, but the Europeans have averred that they could detect nothing but the sea itself. Those who recorded these beliefs state that reefs could not have been intended since the navigational skills of the islanders clearly indicated that they knew exactly where they were located and their appearance. These stones were two types and called nuwakekepaki and vineylida and the latter were believed to be inhabited by witches. It was said by the islanders that these stones grasped the canoes while at sea and would not let go unless a sacrifice was given and this was reported as follows: "A folded mat would first be thrown, in an attempt to deceive it; if this were of no avail, a little boy would be anointed with coco-nut oil, adorned with arm-shells and bagi necklaces, and thrown over to the evil stones"[70].

It is interesting to note the anointing of the child and particularly shell armbands since these were considered evidence of status in their inclusion in the capacocha sacrifice of the Inca boy on Mount Plomo. The identification of these malevolent forces at sea is reminiscent of the heroes and deities turning to stone in the Peruvian myths already noted but more particularly with the shrines along the ceque lines radiating from Cuzco, many of these being sacred stones or shrines. It has been earlier noted that many of the rites associated with these ceque lines are also linked to rivers and streams precisely because they flow from the mountains to the sea. The major heroes surviving into the Inca periods are all noted as having some links, or disappearing into the west across the sea to the west, that is to Polynesia, Melanesia, Indonesia or Asia. This may account in principle for the diffusion of capaocha rites into the Pacific Islands.

In New Guinea, and Melanesia generally, child sacrifice appears to have been customary in some regions long before the advent of the Europeans. In Milne Bay reports of the sacrifice of babies was traditional in the ancient council meeting place at Tagorewa. The council area was defined by a number of stones placed in a circle and at the largest the two headmen sat while the lesser chiefs sat at the others. When the large stone was being erected it was said that a number of babies were killed and placed underneath it[71]. This does not sound as if it derived specifically from the capacocha system but there are many archaeologically substantiated reports of children and adults placed under pillars in Asia, Ancient Central and South America. In South America there are many reported cases of this tradition carried on into the present day and is clearly part of the capacocha custom there in the Andean region[72].

In other parts of Melanesia aspects of headhunting and child sacrifice were associated more with the burial of chiefs as it was in South America but in this part of the Pacific child sacrifice probably reflected as much of the traditions in Asia as those of South America and is noted as such in the Solomon Islands. On San Cristoval, one reference was recorded as follows: "When a chief dies, they bury him so that his head is near the surface, and over it they keep a fire burning, so that they may take up the skull for preservation in the house of the man who succeeds to power. An expedition then starts to procure heads in honour of the deceased, now become a tindalo to be worshipped. Any one not belonging to the place will be killed for the sake of his head, and the heads procured are arranged on the beach, and believed to be mana, spiritual power, to the new tindalo; until these are procured the people of the place do not move about. The grave is built up with stones, and sacrifices are offered upon it" ..."The dead man's wife and child were then dragged to the open grave and strangled there, and their bodies thrown in together with his possessions, ..."[73].

These reports, although not specifically related to capacocha do have a strong resonance in considering South America since these almost exact ceremonies are known there from the earliest times in the burials of chiefs and high status people. Headhunting in particular is widely depicted in South American art and especially so in the ceramics of the Nazca plain, this southern Peruvian region reflecting so many aspects of the cultures of the Indonesian Islands and the Nagas of Assam. The Solomon's are a halfway house between these distant regions and clearly absorbed imperfectly many of the customs of mariners to a lesser or greater degree as indicated in their myths and legends and these burial rites are clearly just one aspect of those influences.

In the rites associated with child sacrifice and headhunting the Indonesians were notable for the extent of these customs. In North Celebes over a century ago such ceremonials were common place and noted by one naturalist who visited the islands as follows: "....A human head, or the body of a child, specially obtained for the purpose, had to be placed beneath the principal pile of every new house, and when the house was finished a fresh head had to be obtained to hang up in the roof. Victory was celebrated by the drinking of the blood of the captured enemy, or cutting his body into fine pieces (tumuktok)"[74]. The close similarities between the customs of the Amazonian tribes, those of the outer islands of Indonesia and the Nagas of Assam have been noted from the earliest days of European research in these regions. The abundant iconographical references obtained from archaeological excavations from the Nazca plains in Southern Peru suggests that similar customs and rites originated there or the Amazon Basin, and then diffused back toward Asia into Assam in North East India.

In South India, the Madiga caste retained bull sacrifices into recent times suggesting that they were anciently associated with herding before their present impoverished existence. In the festival to their village goddess, usually female and wrathful on the perimeter of Hindu societies in South India, a young unmarried man was selected and fasted from the beginning of the festival. He was naked except for a few leaves around his waist and lead in a procession followed by the Madigas carrying baskets. He feigned a swoon and was carried to the temple in what appeared to be the religious trance of a shaman. After this a Poturazu, or priest, took up a young ram and carried it as he would a child[75].

The substitution of a child by a ram or goat, one of the five acceptable sacrifices under the ancient Vedic laws, appears here for an actual youth and resembles the rites of the capacocha where both white llamas and children were sacrificed. Among the Gonds the euphemism for the human sacrifice was the "two-legged goat" and among them it was believed that only clan-deities whose ritual objects were required to be made from gold demanded human sacrifices[76]; perhaps not unconnected to the abundance of gold ritual items among the Incas and capacocha burials. Other traditions in India include those of the Madigas in the Godavari District recording a belief that in crossing a river that is unsafe it will separate if a child sacrifice is offered[77]. It is clear therefore that such child sacrifices were in fact common in India, particularly among the peripheral and Aboriginal peoples in India before the colonial period.

The custom of capacocha appears to be traceable back to India from South America and leads directly to South India, as well as Assam, and appears to reflect to another aspect of the heroes and deities earlier considered. It has been shown that Aravan, the deity in South India was probably no other than Arnauan, the alternate name for Tonapa among the Aymara. It is unlikely that this identification is not accidental but imported since Tonapa is probably a reference to St. Thomas, also believed to be from the same region of South India. It is, however, more likely that it was the missionaries from the Syrian Christian Church in his name, who have long maintained a foothold in Southern India, who were identified with Tonapa and the boy hero Aravan from the same region. Aravan in South India is probably a confusion with the Aryan Fire priest of Iran, Arthavan, and Iravan, this being another variation of Aryan and his temples are attended to be the Pallis, including also the Draupadi Temple[78]. This confusion of the identity of Arnavan extends into the local beliefs in the legends of the Pandavas, the ancient Aryans from the Mahabharata, five of whom were said to have immigrated into South India from the North West. Edgar Thurston, the curator of the Madras Museum, noted more than two generations ago the legend of Aravan as follows: "Local tradition says that, when the great war which is described in the Mahabharata was about to begin, the Kauravas (Pauravas or Purus, earlier noted), the opponents of the Pandavas, sacrificed, to bring then success, a white elephant. The Pandavas were in despair of being able to find any such uncommon object with which to propitiate the gods, until Arjuna suggested that they should offer up his son Aravan. Aravan agreed to yield his life for the good of the cause, and, when eventually the Pandavas were victorious, he was deified for the self-abnegation that had thus brought his side success. Since he died in his youth, before he had been married, it is held to please him if men, even though grown up and already wedded, come now and offer to espouse him, and men who are afflicted with serious diseases take a vow to marry him at his annual festival in the hope thereby of being cured..."[79].

The headman of the Vallan caste is called the Aravan and this appears to derive from the regional term of Iravan or Aryan[80]. It has already been noted that the Vallans were the canoe rowers who had jealously guarded customary privileges for oaring the serpent boat of the Raja of Cochin. The Aravan stood in front of the Raja in his canoe that resembled the myths and legends of the serpent boat[81] of the Desana Tukano in Amazonian Colombia. It is likely therefore that the mariners who were associated with the long distance oceanic trade were rowers such as the Vallans and their passengers were probably the missionaries of St. Thomas, personified as Tonaca or Tonapa. Being from the same region of South India, the identification and confusion in distant Peru was therefore a natural, and an obvious one.

Canara, the Caras and Caribs of South America
Throughout this work it has been noted that many parallels to South American culture exists among the peoples of South India even extending to the caste system that originated in the north

of India before being imposed by the Brahmans and Hindus when achieving local supremacy. The coast of South West India and Sri Lanka was particularly noted for known contacts with the Ancient Middle East and later with Ancient Greece and Rome. One of the most interesting parallels between South India, Ecuador and Peru must be in the ancient name of what was Malabar in the British administration, now Kerala, and that was Canara (also Kanara). The language of Canara was originally Dravidian and this is related to that of the Gonds, Bhuiyas, and Munda tribes[82] so frequently noted in this work. There are traditionally considered to be five Dravidian languages - Tamil, Telugu, Malayalam, Canarese and Oriya[83].

Traditions recorded a century ago note that there was a Madiga dynasty, said to have descended from the sage Matanga Muni, that ruled in Canara. As noted, the original Canarese language in the region was Dravidian and two of the associated tribes to the Bhuiyas and Gonds were the Santals and Bhils. The major deity of the Santals was Marang Beru and it has earlier been noted that both elements of this name corresponding to the ancestral land of the Gilbertese in Polynesia. In Canara the paternal ancestor of the Madiga dynasty, the sage Matanga Muni, suggests that there is a corresponding connection in ancient times between them relating to South India and Polynesia. Matangi is the name of the elephant deity often associated with the smallpox goddess, Kali as Sitala, and Muni is a named associated with the Buddha, and perhaps the sage was in fact a Buddhist who converted to Hinduism or was later identified as such by Hindu descendants. Found also in the Southern parts of India are the lesser status Rajput caste known as the Marwaris[84], who migrated from their original homeland in the north Marwar, and it has been suggested that this caste may have been the origins of the Maoris and Morioris in Polynesia[85].

In Canara, the Nayars, a Dravidian caste only one level lower in the social scale than the Brahmans, were a warrior caste who divided their military and social organisations into groups of six hundred[86]. Each of the six hundred was governed by a leader called the Kara-navan, or elder, and their existence are known to have been documented from before the Syrian Christian copper plate inscription dated to 925 A.D.[87]. This is highly reminiscent of the Incas dividing their military and social organisations into groups of one hundred. The Pallis have been noted in an earlier chapter relating that during the marriage ceremony the bride and groom were conducted to the bridegroom's house together with one hundred, occasionally 110 cakes[88]. It has been suggested that the term for the female line of Incas, Pallas, may have derived from this caste.

In India some of the temples of the Hindus were famed for their temple women who were dancers, called deva-dasis, and who served the caste devotees of their own status or higher within the sacred precincts. There were several ways in which a daughter may be dedicated as a deva-dasi and in Canara some of the tribes among the Boyas and Bedarus dedicated a daughter to the temple if they had no male issue[89]. This resembles not only the institution of the vestal virgins in Rome but also that of the Incas where the ruler alone had access or delegation rights to the special women of the Sun.

Brief references have already been made in Chapter 4 to the descendants of Caran and his invasion on the coast of Ecuador in the review of archaeological evidence in this region of South America. One of the earliest reports in post-Conquest South America records briefly Cieza de Leon's visit among these people called the Canaris. It was reported by him when passing through Ecuador that the people wore their hair "very long and rolled up into a bun on top", in what would be known now as a topknot. It was noted that the women were particularly attractive in appearance but unlike other tribes the men remained at home and it was they who were the weavers[90].

Garcilasso de La Vega also wrote a description of the Canaris and that they were well-known for their long hair wound up into a topknot, and that the nobles and chiefs wore a "hoop like a sieve, three fingers in height, through which were passed skeins of different colours"[91]. Instead of the "sieve" some of the poorer Canaris wore almost no clothing and used a calabash on their heads around which they wound their heads earning them the name Mati-uma or "calabash head". Topknots were also a characteristic of the Polynesians and Rev. John Stair noted a century and a half ago the rituals of undoing and tying up the hair among the Samoans was similar to that of the Chinese[92]. The topknot described by de la Vega and Cieza de Leon both suggest that the "frames" placed on top of the head as headdresses or topknots were similar to those among the Nagas of Assam and the Tibetans who have been of critical interest throughout this work (*4.027-30*).

The lack of clothing scandalised the Spanish when they first landed at Manta since, although the men sometimes wore a small shirt, they wore nothing below leaving exposed "... that which should have been concealed"[93]. This report is an interesting one since so many aspects of Polynesian, Indonesian, and from India appear on this coast. This "shirt" was probably developed from the blanket of cloth, or animal skin used by mariners and thrown around the shoulders or wrapped around the waist when not required while at sea, the less worn meant that there was less likelihood of chill from cold and particularly damp clothing. This easily discarded type of clothing was noted also in Aboriginal Australia, in New Zealand, and the far south of South America, the North West Coast of North America, and throughout the Pacific Islands

The Canari Phase in the archaeology of Ecuador is of some importance, not least because of the face urns, typical of the culture and so similar to those found in the North West of Argentina, but also because they so resemble those in Western Asia. The Canari phase was noted also for their gold and copper work as well as the decorated pottery that featured thin walls of a high polish finish and fine decoration. The mountain of Curitaqui was the scene of the sacrifice of one hundred children annually in the belief that it would ensure a bountiful harvest[94]. The lance used by these Canaris was called the chasca-chuqui[95] and this was distinguished by the fringe hanging from under the spearhead closely similar to that of the Maya, Maori and Nagas of Assam suggesting among other things a common origin.

The Moon was the principal deity among the Canaris before the Incas and it was recorded that they also revered trees and were stone worshippers. Of particular interest in their province was that, along with the Manta region of Ecuador, gold beads were a feature of their craftsmanship[96] and tiny, finely wrought examples were inserted into their teeth as decoration, a custom known both among the No Su in Southern China and the Nagas of Assam[97]. A characteristic of their neighbours, the Palta Indians is that they traditionally applied cranial deformation to their children, a custom known further south in Peru[98].

It is likely that the Canaris were in fact the Caras, related to other tribes with similar name variants, and the first historical references given by Velasco record that the Caras arrived on the coast of Ecuador in balsa rafts, and settled there for about two hundred years. During this time they were ruled over by eight or ten chiefs called the Scyris (also Shyris; Skyris,etc). It was reported in the local traditions that the Canaris were lead by their leader Caran when they arrived and founded the city of Caraquez[99]. After that period they ascended the river Esmeraldas and conquered the Quitus in about 980 A.D. settling in the foothills of the Andes near modern Quito. The eleventh Skyri was not succeeded by any male heirs so he arranged that his daughter, Toa, should marry, Duchicela, the son of the Puruha king, and when they succeeded him the kingdoms were united[100]. It is significant that the Canari kingdom, named Caranqui, should be allied to the kingdom of the Puruha and suggests that there were long standing cultural contacts and probably origins shared by them. As noted in the previous chapter the terms puru and puruha are traceable through the Pacific Islands to India.

De la Vega wrote: "The religion of the Caran Scyris was that of the sun and moon. They built a temple of the sun on a height near Quito, now called Panecillo, the eastern door of which had two tall columns before it, for observing solstices. They also had twelve pillars on one side of the temple, as gnomons, to point out, by their order, the first day of each month. On an adjacent height, now called San Juan Evangelista, they built a temple to the moon. They interred their dead in a desert place, built over them a vault, and piled stones and earth over it till it formed a great heap called a tola"[101]. These tolas were pyramidal in form suggesting a tradition of building stepped mounds or pyramids[102].

The term tola is an interesting one since the term means a mound and this was a distinguishing feature of the coastal cultures of Coastal Ecuador. One most famous for its gold ornaments in South America was La Tolita on the coast, named after the many mounds found on the north coast of Ecuador. The term tola or tila is also found in India and means something similar and applied frequently to a mound, but in ruins, on which a stupa had been erected during the Buddhist period from about 2500 years ago[103]. Among the Munda peoples these mounds are associated with a long megalithic tradition and the burial sites of their ancestors and probably dating to a similar period[104]. Among these same people the name of the small hamlet or village in which they live was more specifically called a tola[105]. This identification between tila and tola probably derives from occupation sites being built over old mounds into which the ancestors had been interred, a custom known in South America. Interestingly also a measurement for the weighting of gold anciently in Orissa, in North East India, was called a tola[106] suggesting another connection with Ecuador.

The record of the Scyri (or Skyri) also notes that they were great "lapidaries" (craftsmen in precious stones) and their "distinguishing mark" was a "great emerald" worn in their headdress[107]. The Sun deity, Con, appears to be associated with the Scyris[108] and this appears to be another element indicating that the Canaris and the Scyris as their rulers originated in India or in the foothills of the Himalayas. Colombia, in South America, is the foremost producer of emeralds in the world and it is understandable therefore that this precious stone should be utilised as the symbol of kingship in that, and adjacent regions. Cieza de Leon recorded the reports in Manta on the Ecuadorian coast writing that, "... the Lord of Manta had an emerald of great size and value, which the people and their ancestors held in great veneration. On certain days it was publicly displayed, and worshipped as if it contained some deity. On these occasions if any man or woman was sick, they performed a sacrifice, and then came forward to pray to the stone. ... They also say that, although threats and menaces have been resorted to discover where this great and rich emerald is concealed, they have never been able to find it, nor will the natives betray the place if they are all killed, so great is the veneration in which it is held"[109].

The second most famous shrine in South America was that in Ecuador, after Pachacamac far to the south, and this was dedicated to the god of health, Umina. The worship of this god, sometimes goddess, was the focused on an idol, housed in the shrine, and this was said to be half human in form and carved from "... a great stone of very fine emerald"[110]. The so-called "grandmother" goddess, Umina, was offered small emeralds and this name appears to relate to that of the Mayan goddess Uminhah[111]. In Mexico the wife of Tlaloc, the rain god, was Emerald Lady, Chalchihuitlicue, and their children were said to be the clouds or Tlalocs[112]. Lady Emerald's symbol was that of the green frog that was supposed to dwell in the volcano. Among the Quiche-Maya the "master Totecat" was said to be the lapidarist of emeralds[113].

In India the emerald also had a reverential following. It is in fact associated with the mani jewel, and is usually termed marakata - literally emerald[114]. This gem is included among the five sacred gems (panka = 5; ratna = gem) each of which represents one of the five elements. It was also identified with the nine planets or graha in the cosmological system of India and the emerald was associated with the planet Mercury[115]. In the serpent mythology of India the emerald is associated with the Garuda, the eagle as the sky deity, and therefore the fierce opponent of the Nagas, or serpents, and this gem was credited with being able to alleviate the effects of poison[116].

An emerald deity in India named Vina-yaka, is worshipped among the Nattu-Kottia Chetti clan. Their origin myth states that in the ancient of days the Vaisyas of the luner race were worshippers daily of their emerald god, Vinayaka, in the country of Naga-nadu (Serpent-country) in Jambudvipa (India). They were traders in precious stones and led the lives of orthodox Saivites, worshippers of Siva, wore the sacred rudraksha beads, and smeared themselves with ashes, the sign of a Saivite sadhu to this day. In one period of their history they were oppressed by the ruler so they migrated south to Conjeeveram (Kanchipuram) near the south east coast of South India. Here they remained for a long time until they were again oppressed with "heavy taxes and fines" so they again migrated to the adjacent Chola ruled kingdom, said to be in the year 2312 of the Kaliyuga, placing them by certain calculations to about the 9th., century, B.C. considered unlikely by some. In their new estates they were said to be much appreciated by the ruler who regaled them with great privileges including the crowning of the ruler. The main town of Kaveripumpattanam was divided into caste streets with the Vaisyas occupying the north street, but the king did not wish to uproot them so the east, west and south streets were allocated to the Nattukottai Chettis as newcomers[117].

The Nattukottai Chettis are interesting in that they are placed in the two locations in the South of India so noted for their expansion across the sea into Indonesia as well as Burma. As proposed elsewhere in this work it is likely that these two dynasties of the Pallavas (Kanchipuram) and the Cholas are those that initiated more evident contacts also with the Americas and so noted in an earlier work[118]. The illustrations of rudraksha beads are identically found in India, in Cambodia, and at Palenque[119]. Because of their convenient location and association with the trade in precious gems it is likely that they are in part at least, responsible for the trade in emeralds on the Ecuadorian coast. The centre of the emerald trade being located on this coast and not in Colombia, where the raw emeralds were obtained, is probably of critical significance. It is likely also that the emerald goddess' name in Ecuador, Umina, is simply a common gender reversal and local abbreviation to Vina - where the more formal Nattukottia Chetti term is Vina-yaka.

Caras as Migrants in South America

The Caras are usually identified with the Canaras or Canaris in Ecuador and, consistent with their originating as a mariner people, or at least in the male line, they are found all around the coastal regions in North West South America. They are reported in Northern Peru, Ecuador and Colombia, where the coastal regions are washed by the Pacific Ocean currents but are also found on the Caribbean shores of Colombia and Venezuela as well as through into the Amazon Basin via the Orinoco River. The fierce Tainos, who migrated late from the Orinoco Delta into the Caribbean Islands, were probably, as the name suggests the followers of Tane, one of the great Polynesian gods. In Ecuador the Cara phase in Ecuador reflected elements of culture from Colombia[120].

Traditions of the Cara; Caran and Karan in India

The Karan was the writer caste among the Brahmans and this formed one of the most elevated status subdivisions among them[121] where the Brahmans were the highest of the four recognised castes in Vedic and Hindu India. Since the basic divisions and religious inheritance through the Vedas is from Iran and beyond in the Caucasus, it is from there that the term Karan, Karen or Karun can be traced. One of the sacred rivers in Ancient Iran, is the Karun and at one time it was a tributary, along with the Shaour River, of the Tigris[122] near Susa, one of the great twin rivers in Mesopotamia. This was at a time when the great stepped pyramids and platforms and terracotta cone bricks were being used in building construction. This river is located in the North West of Iran in the province of Khuzistan, and a centre for the Mandaeans into more recent times[123].

In South India the term Karan, used by itself or in conjunction with other terms of status, is found frequently particularly in association with other titles indicating status of elevated inheritance such as arya or ayya denoting Aryan descent. The members of the trading caste, the Agrawal, claimed the title of aiya or ayya and another caste title is Patnul-karan claiming Brahman status of the Tamil Pallans[124]. In South India also the Ambala-Karans were the palanquin-bearers to the Zamorin of Calicut[125] on the South West Coast and therefore regionally from the same districts associated with the rowing castes and serpent canoes of the Aravan and the Raja of Cochin. The Ambattans are a caste of barbers in Southern India and in their residential region was divided into four divisions, each of which was administered by a Perithanak-karan and he controlled family heads of, more usually, six hundred, occasionally a thousand families called Kudithalak-karans[126].

Karan is also the general title of some of the musicians called Melak-karens who performed as accompaniment for the temple dancers, the deva-dasis[127]. This group of musicians is very ancient and was considered several generations ago as the repository of traditional Indian music and probably the most ancient of its type in the world[128].

In other tribes and castes the term Karan, Karen or Karin is applied to a deity, often an ancestor, and among the Pulayan (also called Cheruman), one of their primary deities was named Karin-kutti[129]. It is said in the oral histories of South India that the Nayakkan kings of Madura were dissatisfied with the weaving skills of the Kaikolans so weavers from the north were sent for named the Patnul-Karans, who specialised in fine weaves particularly silk[130]. The term Kaikolan derives from kai = hand, and kol = shuttle[131] and shows the manner in which terms were constructed for the castes, these being work-related social divisions in India from Ancient times. The Kong-Vellalas divided their caste region or Nad into twenty-four nadus each comprising of a certain number of villages. The headman of each village was called the Kottu-Karan, each group of villages was under the control of the Nattu-Karan and each region under the Pattak-Karan. This highest of the headmen wore gold rings on his toes and was always saluted with clasped hands[132], a recognisably Middle Eastern form of address. The term for headman including both Patta and Karan appears frequently in South India[133] and this is also true of the Malayali where the headman was called Patta-Karan[134], the term Patta also being found among the Incas[135].

These terms, either as the prefix or suffix usually reflect some ancestral references to the title karan and this almost invariably can be traced to the Ancient Middle East. In ancient texts in India it was common in recording origins to indicate the region and since many successful empires were based around a prominent river, the Yakshas were described as originating from the Jaxartes River region and therefore the Caran or Karan from the Karun River region. It has been noted early in this work that the South of India reflects many sea-borne influences from the Ancient Middle East before the Brahmans imposed their control from the North of the Subcontinent. Those who were rulers in that southern region were eventually subjected to social relegation to the lowest status after the Brahmans had established their hold on that part of India. But many of these people retained into the twentieth century remnants of beliefs and social systems clearly derived from the Ancient Persian Gulf region reflecting a link with origins of the male line from around the Karun River. The Kurava in South India were a partially Hinduised caste of low status but they also retained the worship of the departed ancestors called the "Chavars". The most revered deities were, however, the mountain deities and these were called Katiyati-Kal. Kal is the ancient word derived from the Ancient Middle Eastern priest the Kallu who sacrificed at the stone altar, and among other tribes in India the term kal refers to a sacred stone or to the priest officiating at the stone altar noted earlier. Small shrines were maintained by the Koravas and attended by a priest named the Piniyali, and the equivalent of the shaman of this tribe, who became possessed in times of consultation with the mountain spirits, was called the Rarak-karan and the priest, Kaik-Karan[136].

Particularly notable in the retention of traditional ancestral links in tribal and caste titles are those of the Tottiyan, referred to earlier in this work. The headman in the Tinnevelly district was called the Mandai Periadanak-Karan and this includes not only the link of the term karan to the Ancient Middle East but also the Mandaean connection, as Manda, so frequently found throughout India[137]. A deity already noted among the Tottiyans is Vira-Karan and links two hero elements in the one term[138]. The Pattanavans means a dweller in a town (= pattanam), but as a caste of fishermen these people were called Karaiyan or "sea-shore people"[139] and have been noted elsewhere. In this expression the Kara or Karan were identified as sea people in India as they were on the North West Coast of South America and in both cases the regional name of Canara was preserved into the present day. The Kuruba are a large tribe in India and in some of their divisions a temple at Bellary dedicated to their deity Siva is known for the "cryptic" utterances of the priest called the Karan-ika containing a prophecy regarding the coming agricultural season[140]. Karen tribes in the south of Burma follow similar agricultural practices as those of the Sema Nagas[141].

Some of the people in India retain the title of karan in their tribal or caste name, although its significance, apart from ancestral, is long forgotten. A Marathi-speaking caste called the Kuru-Vik-Karans[142] retain two illustrious names, that of the Kurus, an Aryan people entering India from the North two millennia earlier and Karans, both originally having Ancient Middle Eastern connections.

In South India, merchants of part-Arab descent, were called Labbai and also Koddikal-Karans or "betel-vine people"[143] giving a direct influence from the Middle East, even though not as ancient as some others. Arab sea traders in contact with South India goes back millennia and the Muslim boat pilots and mariners in the Laccadine Islands were known as Uruk-Karan clearly indicating their Ancient Middle Eastern origin[144]. The term karan here as "people" has the same connotations that many other people dwelling among less developed races give themselves by an appellation that often translates as "men", to separate their identity from the other people who were considered "less than men". The Lambadi were a people who migrated as traders from Gujarat in the North West of India to the south, and were also called Vanjari, Banjari Sukali, etc. It was believed the term Banjari derived from the Sanskrit, Vanijya and as merchants they were called Vanijya-Karakas"[145]. The term Karaka probably developed from Karan particularly as the term Van, Ban and other similar ones probably indicates their origin around Lake Van, in Ancient Armenia, or Anatolia, in what is now Eastern Turkey. This is all the more likely since so many other aspects of Vedic religion, such as the gods, Indra and Varuna are first found in Hittite inscriptions in Anatolia in the second half of the second millennium B.C. Not only do the terms Karan, Caran, Cara and Canara from South India appear in Peru but so does the term Kanaka, and Curaca. The Malaialis also called themselves, when earlier living at the great temple city of Kanchipuram, Karalan and Malak-kara[146].

In Colombia among the Tukano Desana and others there were dwarf deities of importance and in India the round-eyed dwarf with big ears born from the "burning" eye of Siva was called Karin-Kali - described as the "primeval black dwarf"[147]. Near Mysore in South India the Sholaga worship a deity called Kara-iyya, clearly indicating a derivation from Karan and Aiyya or Aryan[148]. Among the Uralis exogamous septs or clans were called "karais"[149]. In Central North East India the Bhuiyas call their god Karo Byro[150] indicating a probable origin from contact with mariners along the coast from South India.

In the Andaman and Nicobar Islands demons called Kareau were probably memories of incursive mariners from India in centuries past[151]. The Tungkhul Nagas' deity is named Kajing Karei[152], and there is evidence that there is Naga influence in the Nicobar Islands. The deity variously known as Karei, Karo or Kari, is found widely among the indigenous negrito and pygmoid tribes of Malaya[153]. This deity is often associated with thunder and lightning[154] and seems to have been an import or an elevation of the status of mariners who came from the Ancient Middle East or India. Even earlier researchers noted that these deities were similar to ancestral heroes in India and to those of the Australian Aborigines[155]. In a gender reversal on the Indonesian island of Celebes (Sulawesi) among the Minahassers, a major goddess was called Kareima, probably originally Kare-ima[156] where Ima = the Polynesian Hima relating to the Moon. Among the Toradja of Central Celebes the term for "silent lord" was Karaen ma'loko-loko[157].

In Aboriginal Australia the term Kari applied among the Narang-ga tribe of South Australia to one of the four classes or marriage divisions, Kari the emu[158]. Around the Macquarie River region of Central Eastern Australia the term for a medicine man was Karakeel[159]. In this South East region of Australia it has been shown that there are many references to the cultures of India, including the Tamil, along with the Munda and Bhuiya tribes. The people of Orissa were noted in an earlier work for their log gods known also among the Nagas of Assam and in the Marquesas Islands gods were housed in shrines and where banyan trees were planted next to the sacred platforms as they are in India[160]. In Tahiti, among the most eastern of the Polynesian Islands nearest the Americas an important deity was called Karei-Pahoa[161]. This record dates from century and a half ago and no explanation is given but the prefix appears to derive from the Karei of India and Malaya and Pahoa is the Polynesian wind deity also recorded as Paoa and this is another form of the wind deity of India Pawan. The principal deity on part of the Peruvian coast was known as Inkarri, almost certainly a version of Karei or Karan, in the region of Puquio, a term related to the wells and underground irrigation channels in the Nazca Plain so similar to those of the Ancient Middle East called qanats[162].

Origins of the Terms Tambu, Tampu in Peru from Tambun and Tamburan in India

In Peru there are many anomalies in the Incan traditions, and one is the name, recorded for the father of the first Inca ruler Mano Capac. Only a few of the Inca Origins myths records the name of Manco Capac's father, or other connection, and this is given as Apu Tampu (also Apo and Tampo) and recorded in this work in Version 1, or as related to Tambo lineage in Versions 2,10 and 11. One of the most reliable chroniclers, Pachacuti-Yampqui Salcamayhua, a Christianised native and believed to be an Inca, recorded that the name Apu-Tampu, as the father, and also that the mother of Manco Capac was Apachamama-Achi[163]. His version is one of the few, along with Sarmiento's, actually noting that there were believed to have been three windows or portals through which the first Inca brothers, and sisters, emerged from the cave into their chosen land. The first of these windows was called Tampu-Toco and the locations from where the first Indians emerged were usually called Pacarai-Tampu[164] whereas Sarmiento calls the cave Tambotoco. The term toco meant window but tampu is usually identified as the term for an "inn" - a place of rest and recuperation, and in Sarmiento's version the opening to the cave may have been the mouth or toco. The name apu[165] was the form of reverential address to a learned elder or the spirit of an ancestor. The ancestral spirits were believed to reside in the mountains and as a group were referred to as the apus[166].

The most interesting references to Apo Tampu, as Salcamayhua recorded it, is where Tonapa, already of great interest in an earlier chapter, arrived at the village of the headman Apo Tampu[167]. Because Apo-Tampu received him hospitably, in contrast to his countrymen around

Lake Titicaca, Tonapa gave him his staff in appreciation. It was this staff that was said to have later turned to gold to become the Tupac-Yauri[168] and that Manco Capac used to determine the place of settlement for his dynasty of Incas. This meeting between Tonapa and Apo-Tampu reputedly took place southeast of Cuzco near Lake Titicaca in the traditional lands of the Aymara in the Colla-suyu suggesting that the paternal line, in part at least, derived from the Aymara, and other references identify the origins of the Inca with Tiahuanaco in that region. In other references the term tambo refers to chieftains or clan leaders who were knights and appeared to be paralleled by the Apu-Curacas and Auquis of Inca tradition[169].

In the organisation of clans original divisions of Tambo, Maras and Sutic, have been detected by one modern researcher as the foundation upon which the Inca created their own social organisation in Cuzco[170]. This group also included Pinahua in some references (see Origin Myths, Versions 1; 2B and 8), and is associated with Tiahuanaco[171]. Tom Zuidema notes that the references to tambo are used to designate certain of the clans in early Cuzco while in other references it actually refers to certain of the lines of royal lineage, namely those of Apu Mayta panaca and Usca Mayta panaca. Early translators noted that Apu meant "great lord" or "high judge" while Capay Apu meant "king"[172]. Interestingly usca meant "beg" as an Inca term and in many of the castes of India had attached to it a begging or mendicant caste to which was attached no opprobrium and Edgar Thurston noted several castes where the lower status divisions were beggars only upon those of their higher status divisions and did not solicit outside their caste.

Tambo was therefore seen as a clan and Zuidema notes that, it is to this division that Apu-Tampo, Manco Capac's father, belonged, but more intriguingly there is another unexplained term - uacan associated with the clan title[173]. Miles Poindexter recorded many references to support his belief that the Quichua, the main tribal element in the Inca Empire, were in fact of Quiche-Mayan descent. The term uacan, thought to be a reference to a great grandfather figure in the Inca Origin myth, may be another element added to those Poindexter recorded possibly referring to, and derived from their main deity Huracan noted in their sacred book, the Popol Vuh.

In other references it has been considered that the location of Tambotoco may have been Ollantay-Tambo and de la Vega uses the alternative spelling of tampu[174]. In pre-post-Conquest Peru, and into the present day, lodges or inns were called tampus[175], but this may simply be a misidentification of similar sounding words noted earlier under the term "otiose". The term tampu or tambo cannot be so simply explained and especially since it is associated with kingship and regal descent as the foregoing references clearly indicate and its derivation must be found elsewhere.

It is unlikely to be a coincidence that tambo or tampu in Ancient Peru and Bolivia was a term associated with kingship where, in South India, the term tampan was anciently a name indicative of kingship. In some of the oldest surviving Sanskrit verse it is noted that eight divisions of Kshatryas, (warrior caste) occupied Kerala in coastal South West India and one of these was known as tampan. This was considered to be derived from Tampiran and was a title associated with the Rajas of that region[176]. The Nambidis are a section of the Amabalavasi caste and were addressed with the term Tampuran - "Lord"[177]. Similarly the Nambutiri Brahman was addressed as Tampu-rakkal and refers to both temporal and secular sovereignty[178]. In Travancore in Southern India the Rajas were addressed as Tambu-ran[179] as their high-born Kshatriya warrior servants took the title of Tambiran.

The term Tampi-ran was used for the ruler of the Samantan caste of Malayali Rajas[180]. Associated with the sacred sites and temples the Pandarams in Southern India were the garland-makers serving in the Siva temples to decorate the lingam. This is the sophisticated, formalised carved stone phallus so long developed in an linear tradition from the megalithic religions of Asia and identical to those found at San Agustin in Southern Colombia. The temple managers recruit-

12.001: Guardian flanking pillars with central deity in principle similar to those in San Agustin in Southern Colombia. New Caledonia, Melanesia, Pre-20th., century, A.D.

12.002: Carved timber figure of a deity in characteristic form found similar to those of Colombia and other parts of the Americas. New Caledonia, Melanesia, Pre-20th., century, A.D.

12.003: Carved monoliths depicting guardian deities flanking the central god usually fanged as shown here capped with a large stone slab and overall about 2.5 metres high. These are clearly related to those in New Caledonia. San Agustin, Southern Colombia, Early mid-first millennium, A.D.

12.004: Vast carved arrangements of monoliths and stone carvings spread over several square kilometres in the Northern Andes. The fanged head in the foreground is reminiscent of many illustrations of fanged carvings throughout Central and South America but also in India and South East Asia. Note also the owl or eagle carving to the right with a serpent in its mouth also found in the same cultural regions. San Agustin, Southern Colombia, Early-mid first millennium, B.C.

12.005: Central carved cone with flanking guardian deities apparently depicted with bib-like beards similar to those art San Agustin in Southern Colombia. New Caledonia, Pre-20th., century, A.D.

ed from these people are reverentially saluted as Tambiran, the same term for the Samantans. But even more telling was that when the Pandarams sang the hymns to the gods they were addressed as Meikaval. This term almost certainly derived from melka, another title for (earthly)"lord"[181] and a title known in Ancient Peru noted earlier as malki or malqui.

The Supreme deity among the Pulayans, once rulers centuries ago in Southern India, was the Sun. The most important aspect of this deity was as the rising Sun and the term they gave to this deity was Utaya Tampu-ran[182]. In ancient times the five deities were, as a principal of cosmologies, associated with the five sacred elements and these deities became identified with the five Pandava brothers in Southern India. These original five deities were called Anchu Tampu-rak-kal and their association with the Pandavas is found widely among the tribes and castes of South India including the now lowly Pulayas.

Tambu-ran was a title of respect used by lesser status peoples in addressing the warrior caste, the Nayars[183]. Tambi on the other hand was used as a term of affection in the Tamil country and meant "younger brother" when used in address to another person, not necessarily related[184]. Of particular interest however, must be the use of the term among the Tottiyans, again, for their ancestral spirits - Malai Tambiran[185], where Tambu referred to the ancestors of the Inca. Tambi appears to be a Tamil term and is preserved among them as a caste name[186].

In Ancient Burma in the myths and legends of the Buddhist religion it was believed that

12.007 : Siva linga or phallus with the face of Siva carved on its side, almost identical to those found in San Agustin in Southern Colombia. Cave 4, Udaigiri Caves, Vidisha, West Central India, 415-425 A.D.

12.009 : Stone monoliths representing phalli and face images identical to those so widely identified with the Hindu god Siva found in India. San Agustin, Southern Colombia, 50 B.C.-800 A.D.

12.008 : Double faced carved monolith, called a "rain-stone", almost certainly intended to be the local representation of the Hindu Siva. New Hebrides, Melanesia, Pre-19th., century, A.D.

12.006 : One of several phallic monoliths found at the megalithic ceremonial site of San Agustin. Southern Colombia, 50 B.C. - 800 A.D.
the world was divided into four quarters and these were represented by four islands floating on the cosmic sea. The southern of the four was called Zabu-dipa, where Dipa = Dvipa in India the name for an island and the whole imagery was equated and encapsulated by the term Tambo - the centre of this cosmic diagram that was a giant fig tree or World Tree[187].

It has been noted that in Borneo and other Indonesian islands there are many traditions corresponding to those of South America. The association of the term Tambo with an inn or resting place in Peru is an interesting one since in Borneo there was a tradition of people plucking the leaves of a tree or bush and throwing them on a heap beside the path where a legendary Dusan man was struck down. This appears to resemble the tradition of placing a stone in a heap, called a cairn, in a land where in many places the alluvial or silt of the river plains left few loose stones on the surface. This heap so formed was called a tambunan[188], probably derived from a more ancient term, and suggests that the original place of rest in Peru was derived from a cairn beside which people rested or dwelt a while to pay their respects. This became confused in time with the South Indian term for kingship, Tampu, Tampuran or Tambiran, but not entirely reconciled in the Andean traditions.

The Chiefly Titles of Apu, Apo and Aphu

In India the term apu, or apo, occurs rarely in this form in the titles of the tribes and castes and this suggests that these either derived from another part of Asia or as an abbreviated expression from South America or some country between from another similar title in India. The term Appan is used by some castes in India when addressing a father in the tribe and interestingly these people also use the term Achchan when addressing the maternal uncle[189], an important figure in peoples who retain cross-cousin marriages. This latter term is identical to Uchhan and is probably the origin of the term Ucha in South America earlier noted. The title Appu-ppan occurs as the name of a deity of the Kurava[190] and similar other examples are to be found there.

The title from which Apu or Apo is probably derived is that of Appa, almost invariably associated with the tribes and castes claiming Aryan descent, and its relationship or derivation from Ayya, Ayar, Arya, Anna and the other Aryan titles is obvious. A Telugu-speaking caste of temple priests in South India were the Tambalas and they were particularly centred around the ancient region of the Godavari and Kistna Deltas in South Central East India. Their titles were Aiya and Appa and such titles usually designated not only tribal or caste rank but racial origins[191]. The Idiga are a caste of palm-wine makers in South Coastal India and their titles are also Aiya and Appa[192]. The Kannadiyan were also from South India and among their titles was Appa and

758

Anna[193]. In the province of Mysore around Madura, well-known for its blanket-making, were a tribe known as the Kurubas located in the town of Kolar where the women spin the wool and not the men. The names of the Kurubas are derived from their gods, and some of these reflect their probable Ancient Middle Eastern origin, and their affixes frequently include ayya, appa and anna[194]. Interestingly their patron saint is called Bir-appa combining the name of the monkey god Hanuman as Bir earlier noted as a form of Vir or Vira. This term is itself traceable itself to Ancient Iran relating to the wind deity, and the traditional variation of its origin among the Aryans of the Ancient Middle East - appa. These people will be of more interest when considering weaving and the loom.

These Aryan titles clearly derive from Ancient Iran and apart from indicating status they were attached to names, usually as a affix, indicating tribe or caste descent above noted but also relationships, such as appa = father; anna = brother; and amma = mother[195]. Amma is undoubtedly derived from am or ama in the Ancient Middle East where it was originally a male title - gender reversals being common when transferred from one country, or one religion, to another. This was true also for other prominent castes in Canara and the Telugu-speaking peoples such as Idiga, Kannadigan and Linga Balija[196]. The Tiyans of South India worshipped among their chief deities one named Appan[197], widely revered in that part of the Subcontinent.

There are traces of the term Apo or Apu in the Pacific before reaching South America and manifested as Aku or Ako relating to ancestral spirits but in South America it appears that these titles or prefixes are entirely derived from India. This is evident since they are used in the same, or similar ways and are associated with the term Ayya, Aiya or Ayar relating to Aryan origins as they do in Ancient Peru and Bolivia. The title Apu meaning "lord" in South America and is frequently used in conjunction with other terms to indicate an elevated meaning and, apart from those already noted earlier, it is used in other religiously orientated expressions indicating aspects relating to a higher plane. Apu Saqro meant the "sacred mountain of the devil" or the "sacred mountain of the cat"[198], and these expressions were related to the compass points or "four quarters". Apu Saqro was female and her husband, Apu Wanumarka were said to have two children, Apu K'otin and Apu Quisqamoko, known together as the four Apus[199]. The Sun god Inti was also referred to as Apu Inti[200] particularly when in the triadic form with Punchao and Inti-Guauqui201 and is also identified with Viracocha[202] - all of these terms finding their parallel in terms in Ancient India and Iran. The wildcat deity, the Ccoa or K'owa, identified with the hail as the "tears of the Staff God" in an earlier chapter, was also called the "cat of Apu"[203] - Apu referring to the mountain deity(s)[204]. In other sacred aspects, huacas or shrines to ancestors or deities were denoted by the term Apu such as Apu Yurac and Apu Xillan[205]. In more mundane terms Garcilasso de la Vega noted that the term Hatun Apu meant "king", probably an Inca title, while Apu Tambo was that of the Colla.

It has been noted that there appears to have been contacts between the Nazca plain in particular and the islands of Celebes and Borneo through to the Nagas of Assam and also South China. This appears to be further confirmed by the transfer of the term Apu in the South American form to those distant regions only possible by the means of sea voyages. Among the Kayan people of Central Borneo, Apu Lagan was the sky-world[206]. The cultural connections between Malaysia and Indonesia and Polynesia have long been recognised and Lagan is clearly Langi, the sky deity of Central and Eastern Polynesia while Rangi is a variation of the same name. Clearly the transfer must have been by mariners over thousands of miles of ocean and the same must be true in local assimilations of the title Apu. Among the Toradja of Central Celebes the term for "lord" was Ampu[207] and Puya - the "land of souls"[208] and these appear to have been derived from Ampu or Apu. Among these same people, the Toradjas, the term for a seer or shaman is Paita[209] and this appears to have common origins with the Tukano-Desana name for

12.010 : Classic bronze figurine of Siva as Kankalamurti showing a genital disk. Madras, Chola, South India, 8th.,-12th., century, A.D.

12.012 : An Eastern Rengma Naga warrior in ceremonial dress showing a genital disk horned headdress and cross braces all of which are found in the Americas. Eastern Rengma Nagas, Assam, North East India, early 20th., century, A.D.

12.013 : Stela showing a priest or ruler displaying a genital disk similar to that of India and Mexico. Guatemala, 600-900 A.D.

12.014: Deities with a surmounting spirit head are common in Buddhist and later Hindu iconography in India and found also in Central America and San Agustin in Colombia. Sadasivamurti, 700-900 A.D.

12.011 : Genital cov sibly incorporating pha symbolism and associa Aztec, Valley of Mexic c1450 A.D.

12.015 : Carved bas monolith re ing Colomb influence, b playing a g cover or sp similar to th found amon Mexicans, I Nagas of A and in India spirit guard carved abov ilar to India (12.015). Chontales, Nicaragua, 1200 A.D.

12.016 : Mayan stone disk showing the rain deity Tlaloc with a genital disk identical to that found in Ancient India. Tuxtla Gutierrez, Late classic period, 600-900 A.D.

their shaman Paye[210]. This would appear to correspond with the term Paya meaning grandmother[211] and probably also grandfather as Zuidema notes in Peru, where these terms correspond to ancestral deities. It is likely, therefore, that this Peruvian term Paya equates to that of Pawa - referring to the "Old Gods" found among the Maya and therefore links directly to Pawan, the wind deities and Pawabans of India, and Pauahtuns among the Maya in Central America. In Borneo, the giant island adjacent to Celebes, the term Api meant fire[212] and is clearly a derivation from Agni, the Fire God of India. It is probable that this term is a confusion between the identification of Apu and the Sun as occurred in Peru, and the name of the Fire God of India, particularly as there are so many other references to Agni that had been transferred by the Ayar Incas to Peru.

In Southern China the form of the term Apu appears to be closely similar to that of the Peruvians and Bolivians. The Na Khi or No Su, commonly known as the Lolos, retained a deity called Uncle Apu, and he was a wind deity - half bird and half human[213]. It is interesting to note that these people preserved many aspects of culture with apparent close links to Central America considered in an earlier work[214] and in this work their term for priest is identical to that of the Desana in Colombia. It is not surprising therefore that there are other elements corresponding to those of South America. These same people and the region they occupy in South China, has been associated with the people of the Sepik and Purari Rivers in New Guinea and the Maori of New Zealand. For more than two centuries naturalists have been searching the world for new species of plants and particularly flowering shrubs and trees. A century ago one of the best known was Ernest H. Wilson whose forays into the Chinese landscape were legendary. He noted that there was a distribution of certain tree types that suggested transfer by human hand rather than natural ecological distribution[215]. This reference is quoted from his work in Chapter 2 in this work.

The implications of Wilson's deliberations are of great interest since they concur not with the natural distribution propounded by so many modern theories. This is usually left as an unexplained distribution of flora by natural phenomena such as seeds being carried by sea, birds and wind currents - mostly by the former means. The prevailing winds and sea currents, however, cannot apply here since in the last case in particular the sea and wind currents do not extend from the southern Hemisphere to the north to carry the seeds as proposed. What is clearly evident is that the distribution recorded by Wilson is that of the known sea migrations by the Maori. This southern route directly to, and from Chile, Peru and Ecuador from Maori New Zealand is also the route via the Cook Islands in Central Polynesia that the sweet potato, a South American native tuber, took, or was taken from Peru. The known and authenticated distribution of ornamental design and related techniques from Southern China to New Guinea and onward to New Zealand is attributed to the Maori and this follows the route of some of the plant species noted by Wilson. This must also be true of the Libocedrus since the distribution of the species is far from its native habitat across in the Americas on the California coast but, more telling, in Chile connected to New Zealand by direct sea currents but not to California. The cultural connections have been shown to be abundant between the Pacific, West coast of South America and the Maori and their textile designs are in many cases identical to those of the Moche through to and including the Incas and weaving will be of more interest in due course.

Apu - A Title among the Nagas of Assam

The Southern Chinese share many cultural elements with the Nagas of Assam and have done so since at least the time of the great emperor of India, Asoka, in the 3rd., century, B.C. Apu was the term for father[216] among the Sema Nagas but apu is a term also used for boys not related to the addressee, whereas ichu is used for a brother-in-law[217]. On the coast of Peru there was a special class of shaman called Ichuri (grass men) who originated from Collao or the Colla region of highland South Peru and Bolivia. They specialised in confessions where the supplicant divulged their sins into a bunch of grass and this was then thrown into running water for cleansing[218]. Grass (darbha) was sacred to the Brahmans and after cleansing rituals they scattered this around their ritual huts and on the sacred fire altars[219].

Among the Angamai Nagas Apo meant father and Pot-sa meant father's side of the clan[220]. The Lhota Nagas also used the term Aaphu or Apo for addressing the father[221], and interestingly they used a special miniature Khasi hoe for tending and harvesting sweet potatoes[222]. The date when the sweet potato entered Asia is not known from South America and has always been considered to have been transferred from there by the Spaniards after the 16th., century, although there is no record of them doing so. Since there is now evidence that the sweet potato was cultivated at least as early as the 10th., century, A.D. in the Cook Islands[223] and probably long before that in the highlands of New Guinea, it is possible and even probable, that the Nagas brought the sweet potato with them on their journey from South America through Indonesia into Assam. This can be conjectured since the term Apo or Apu is preserved among the Nagas of Assam along with many other aspects of culture more similar than almost anywhere in Asia to that of South America. This appears to indicate that the Nagas were the result of the return leg of cultural influences originating in India or the Ancient Middle East, that were transferred to South America. These traders, crewmen and their descendants then returned with, and as mariners over many generations to the Ganges Delta and thence migrated gradually into the Himalayan foothills towards the Chumbi Valley and Tibet following a long used well-beaten path.

Curacas or Karakas of Peru and India

In the Inca Empire, a term often associated with Apo or Apu was Curaca, so that Apo Curaca was a term frequently recorded by the Spanish Chroniclers. The term curaca was given to a clan leader or tribal chief so that Apu Curaca is interpreted as "Great Lord"[224]. It was these "lords", or the tribal chiefs of the local clans and tribes around Lake Titicaca named Asillu and Hucuru, who were said to have informed the Inca Ypanqui that in "ancient times, a poor thin old man with a beard and long hair, had come to them in a long shirt, and that he was a wise councillor in affairs of state, and that his name was Tonapa Vihinquira"[225]. In the submission of some of these tribes, where peaceful surrender was obtained to the Inca demands for their incorporation into the Empire, that they were often granted the title of Apo besides being allowed to retain Curaca status[226]. In some cases this included the right to be carried in litters[227] and is a privilege also noted related to high status in India. The Curaca controlled the ayllu, or clan lands, allocated to it and there was rarely any other distinction in levels of status within the clan, and his family therefore formed the only nobility as such[228].

When Pizarro's Conquistadors arrived in Peru it was the local Karakas (Curacas) who addressed these unexpected guests, and there were usually two representing each of the dual divisions of the clan organisations common throughout Peru and Bolivia[229]. The Curacas were appointed by the Inca[230], and they in turn supplied the Inca with the necessary goldsmiths and craftsmen to adorn the court and person of the Inca[231]. The Curacas also arranged the affairs of the ayllu to accord with the agriculture calendar and this knowledge was passed from one generation to another within the family line[232]. The much discussed group of servants called Yanaconas were taken from the sons of the Curacas and these were the servants and bodyguards of the Incas at court[233]. The Yanaconas appear to have been considered of low status but they would possibly have been more realistically used as hostages to ensure the loyalty of the non-Inca Curacas and their tribes.

The social division of the Incas was based on the decimal and every 10 taxpayers formed a basic unit overseen by a foreman. For every ten units of 10 taxpayers a Pachaka Karaka was appointed as supervisor. These supervisors were appointed in multiplies of 10 until a Hona Karaka who was designated to supervise 1000 units of 10 - or lord over 10,000 taxpayers[234]. Inca governors ruled their appointed regions through these local hierarchies of Curacas[235].

In India a caste of merchants called the Vanijya, also called Balijas from Gujarat, a maritime province for over five thousand years of history in North West India, had the title of Karaka[236]. These people have already been noted earlier in this chapter and the term Karaka probably derives from the term Karan, earlier considered, spread from the Ancient Middle East by mariners. In South India the Ambalak-karans, claimed descent from one of the sixty-three

Saivite saints named Kannapa Nayanar. The headman of the caste was called kariyak-karan and his office was hereditary in the ruling clan families[237] and this combination also tends confirms the derivation of the term Karaka from Karan.

In Ecuador and the Amazonian region the term karaka was found also and among some of the tribes the term was modified to Kuki[238]. The Nagas of Assam again appear to have trans-ferred this South American form where one of the major tribes was named Kuki. Earlier researchers have noted the close resemblance of the Gond culture in Central India to that of the Nagas including Meriah Sacrifice or human sacrifice undertaken so that the blood and pieces of flesh could be interred with the seed in early spring[239]. The Kuki tribes included the Garos, Mikirs and Kacharis but their traditions are a little at variance with the other Nagas tribes and they retained traditions of securing the skulls of the deceased headman in the clefts and recesses in the mountains[240]. The fringed spears of the Kukis are similar to the types used by the other Nagas tribes and almost identical to those of the Igorot of the Philippines[241]. These are closely similar to those of the Maya and the taiaha of the Maori and also similar to the fringed examples found in Peru.

The Apparent Mystery of the Title Pata, Patta or Pataca

In the records left by the Spanish Chroniclers soon after the Spanish Conquest the term pata, or patta, is found occasionally but their association or derivation are not elicited. Salcamayhua notes it a few times and then only as an suffix when referring to a location known as Huacay-pata[242]. The term appears to be used more specifically as the term for an agricultural terrace[243] and as a title retained by at least a few people close to the Inca ruler. The term pata as an agri-cultural terrace suggests the term in India for a foot, pata, and probably derives from the foot of the workers on the ground where the cultivated food-plants were cultivated. This would appear to have been extended to apply to any level area such as a meeting place, a level area, since they were also called pata recorded in the name of the small flat plateau on top of the sacred moun-tain Apu Wanumarka[244]. Here ceremonials to the ancestral spirit of the mountain were under-taken. Pata as a title occurs in that of Pata Yupanqui, a personal servant of Pachacuti Inca Ypanqui, Tupac's father, and the name of Chima Chaui Pata Yypanqui[245], both of whom were from high status families. The name pata appears therefore to have associations with status and sacred rites in Ancient Peru as it did in India.

The term pata is significant in South India since the term of status associated with Brahmans in their courtly duties was Patta or Batta. In the north of India, where the Vedic Aryans first entered India, the Brahmans were considered the highest caste, theirs being the priestly caste. In South India they were in a tiny minority to begin with and after migrating from the north over several centuries and ingratiated themselves with the local rulers who were often of Dravidian descent, they were allowed to settle but were designated a lesser status than the king as their court servants. The Brahmans, although the priestly caste in the Hindu social strata, were certainly not all priests and engaged in trading throughout the Subcontinent and often they opened the way for the conversion of the Southerners to Hinduism. The term Bhatta is Sanskrit form of Patta and is usually applied in its translation as "teacher" and in the South, in imitation, the term became patta or Pattar adopted by the Tamil Brahmans meaning the same thing[246].

The terms ayya, aiya, anna and appa were all used as titles by tribes and castes in India who claimed Aryan descent and the term patta was also used in the same way[247]. This term is applied both as a prefix to the case name such as Patta-navans[248] or as a suffix, e.g. Komara-patta[249]. The title of the headman in the important tribe of the Devangas was Pattarar[250] and this was also true of the Holeyas[251]. One of the council who assisted the headman in decisions among the Sholagas in South India was the Pattagara[252] and this is also known from other tribes and castes.

The headman of the Kaikolan, a weaving caste, already noted, is the Patta-Karan[253], as it was among the Konga-Vellelas[254] and this title of Pata also appears to integrate with the ancient Iranian name Karan earlier noted. The term Patta-Karan was also used by the Malayali[255] where the contraction of Pattan was also used as a substitute. The title Pata also appears in the names of clan subdivisions, Patta-pu among the Korava[256] and other tribes and castes. Pattavans was the name of the ancestral spirits of the Malayalis and these are considered those who suffered violent deaths while others considered them to have been great sportsman who hunted wild game, particularly tigers in the forests[257].

To be of some interest in the following section the term for the sacred silk waist cords or threads was pata and the Oriya caste who manufactured these were called the Patra[258]. However, from these examples in India it is clear that the term pata or patta in Ancient Peru was another term transferred along with the many already noted from India, and from the South of India in particular, but it is this later mentioned connection with the ancient weaving industry that is of special note.

The Royal Inca Title of Coya or Colla - Looms and the Weaving Pallas

One of the most interesting aspects of Andean research, so easily missed, in the early Spanish chronicles is that the Inca woman are only occasionally mentioned in their, and later works. The title of the Inca queen was Coya[259], and because many of the Coya's names appear to relate to the villages near the sacred sites around the mountains near Cuzco it is suggested that these were not their true names[260]. The ruling Inca was said to be the incarnation of the Sun so the Coya as queen reflected the Moon[261]. The Coya was particularly identified with the Moon as Mama Quilla - "Mother Month" or called Coya Capac - "Noble Queen" and it is indicated by some researchers that the term Coya is in fact a modification of Colla[262]. The Coya was also identified with the Earth as Pachamama and the breasts rising from her body symbolised the mountain and the rivers and streams flowing from the mountaintops were her milk[263]. In these terms it is interesting to note that the sacred mountain, indicated by the suffix tabu, in the Amphlett Islands to the east of New Guinea was named Koya-tabu[264]. This occurs in a region of Melanesia where many aspects of Peruvian culture are found particularly in implements such as star clubs and musical instruments such as panpipes.

The Coya, as Inca queen, is perceived in the surviving records and scholarship to be the highest reflection of women in the arts of weaving in Ancient Peru but it is recorded by Salcamayhua that it was the son and successor of Manco Capac, Sinchi Ruca (Rocca) Ynca who was the great patron of weaving greatly encouraging its development[265]. Perhaps the most interesting, and telling depictions, of the Coya and the female children of the Incas are those showing her dressed in a mantle with a Phrygian Cap a well-known Eurasian headdress usually associated with mariners from the earliest times in the Mediterranean. It is particularly associated with the headdresses of the Tibetans where it is found with earflaps identically to those of Ancient Peru and Bolivia, and still worn into the present day in both disparate regions (*9.075-89*). The mantles worn by the Inca women, including the children, show them held with the traditional tupu, silver or gold pins[266], and others of lower status are found in copper and bronze and identical to those found in Tiahuanaco centuries before that in turn were identical to those found in Luristan in South East Iran.

It is contended in this work that the Inca males were from abroad, and from the Aryans in India in particular and if this is so, then it would be logical that the women chosen for their wives would be from the ruling families of Aymaras, Collas, or Kollas in and around the long established Lake Titicaca region. The terms Colla or Kolla may have given rise to the name of

Coya already considered by other researchers. However, also contended in this work is that the earlier peoples from India settled the coastal and highland regions of Peru and Bolivia and that these were also as a result of early migrations from India and the Ancient Middle East. The name of the expansionist South Indian dynasties in the early, middle and late first millennium A.D. were the Chol or Cholas, a Tamil dynasty, at least in their later reign[267]. They were prominent in the first half of that millennium but were forced to give way to the Pallavas, noted for their cultural expansion into Sumatra and Java in the second half of that millennium, and were renown for the fine stonework reflected in the enormity of their ceremonial complexes and prodigious carvings. The Cholas regained control in the latter centuries and retained the reigns of power until the 9th. - 14th., century A.D.[268]. The Cholas were also known as the Collas (Kollas) and it has long been debated whether they were a high status branch of the Dravidian Kols who were largely represented by the lower caste groups in South India, some of whom moved northwards over the centuries, or were an independent local tribe. As this work nears its end it hardly seems necessary to draw comparisons between India and Peru since the vast number of connective cultural strands must have long since indicated that coincidence can no longer be considered and only the extent of the contacts is left to be further researched.

Beside the obvious connections between the name of Chol, Chola Col and Colla with Collas as the Aymara in Bolivia, there are also elements of particularly important tribal groups to be considered. Because of being referred to so many times in this work, the Gonds are inevitably to be of noted once again and among them there is a sub-group called the Koya[269]. It is among the Gonds that the term Kawachi is found, the probable origin of the name given to the capital, Cahuachi, on the Nazca Plain in Southern Peru noted earlier. In some regions the ancient name of the Gonds was in fact Koi, and in more recent researches dating from early last century the six major divisions of the Koi was recorded as Bhattra, Gond, Maria, Muria, Koya and Darja, where Bhattra clearly derives from the Brahmanic status title of Bhatta, Batta or Patta[270]. It should also be noted that in Sanskrit, the ancient Vedic language of India, a cow was termed gava, its milk gorasa and the five sacred fluids, panka-gavya (panka = five)[271]. The Sanskrit terms were mispronounced even in India, since literacy was reserved for the higher Aryan castes, and it may be that the term Koya derives from the mother's milk from the Divine Cow, Kalpa-Dhenu, where Kalpa represents the Great Age of a World Cycle. This would parallel the imagery of the Coya in Inca tradition noted in the above. It is worth noting also that along the path from South India to Peru, in Burma, foreigners were called kollahs and the probable origin of this term being the Cholas of South India and transferred as such as the progenitors of the Collas of Bolivia[272].

The Lineage of the Inca Queens - Palla and the South India Pallis or Pallavas
Only Garcillasso de la Vega notes to any degree the occupation of the Inca queen, the Coya, but of special interest is that he records the name for Inca women collectively as Palla. He notes that she was expected to set an example at whichever social function her husband had been delegated by the Inca. The Palla was expected to show exemplary industry by weaving and working at appropriate tasks even when she was receiving visitors or official delegations. When those of equal or lower status visited her they would be expected to ask for weaving work to assist their host for the length of the stay[273].

In social divisions it was stated that the clan divisions, relating so directly to acceptable marriage classes, was noted by Bertonio in 1612 A.D. to be divided into Inaca, Palla, Nusta, Auqui, and Hanan/Hurin. Here Inaca was described by him[274] as an alternate name for Hatun Ayllu and Palla appears to derive from a group specifically related to the female Incas, or perhaps originally from which marriage partners of the male Aryan Incas contracted their wives. Nusta is said to be the term for princess, but in other references it appears related specifically to carved step altars such as at Nusta Issapana, suggesting that nusta had another meaning or derivation. The term nusta appears as an early term for an island in Indonesia and it may be that Nusta Issapana may have been intended to reflect this imagery as a rock appearing as an island in its lush tropical vegetation surrounding it (*8.080-2*).

When a child was expected to leave the cradle it was nursed and suckled by her own mother, regardless of status, and when occupied with other tasks in the house the child was contained within a specially made hole in the floor, but when outside, while tending to the fields, the child was placed in a hole in the ground[275]. Child pits were not exclusive to Ancient Peru but, perhaps no longer unexpectedly, they were a feature of some castes in India. In South India among the tribal Irulas children were placed in pits in the cooler season near a fire to keep them warm[276]. This is true also among the Nanga Porojas for the same reasons, but in an extension to this custom in the spring, all the girls were placed in a pit in the ground and a young man, who was ready to select a bride under parental consent came and proposed to the one he preferred. If the girl refused him he approached another with the same intent until accepted[277]. Child marriage was common in South India into the twentieth century.

In South India the Tamil name for the extensive farming caste of South India was Vellalan. The term has been researched to its origins and it is believed to derive from Pallan or Palli and corresponded to the title of Valli, Pallan or Palli that meant "lord" as a reverential address. In colonial South India the Tamils addressed the European as Vella Karan[278] and this had the same connotations as Palla Karan. Palli also means a temple, town or caste or the dwellings of ascetics, and particularly has been used to denote Jain temples[279]. Palli Terus is the name given to the caste streets in which the Pallis resided in the characteristic town divisions separated from the other castes and corresponded to their appropriate perceived status according to the Hindu system[280].

In some of the researches into the historical records and oral traditions surviving over the last two or three thousand years it has been considered that the Vanniyans are the descendants of the warrior tribes of North India, the Kshatriyas. These claims are based on the records relating that the ancient fire races from Iran, named the Agni-Kula, were the Vahni-Kula who became the Vanniya many centuries later[281]. It is no surprise therefore that it is among these people that the record of the sacrificed youth Aravan[282] was preserved and therefore possibly child sacrifice, being in this work identified with Tonapa as Arnauan in Bolivia. It is probably not a coincidence, by extension also, that the Vedic fire god Agni can be traced in the origins of the rites and ceremonies in Ancient Peru and Bolivia.

In Canara, in South India, the Tamil peoples were generally known as Pallis and this term, although originally applied by the Tamil themselves referring to a more elevated status, it became a general, or colloquial term used by the non-Tamil people to describe the Tamils as a whole in more recent times[283]. The Amabalavasi were members of the Nambutiri caste and Palli was the term used by them to denote anything sacred. The four castes forming the Ambalavasi group were called unnis, and the names of these divisions were in order from the highest status, Pushpakans, Brahmanis, Tiyattunis and Nattu Pattars. The name given to members of the Pushpakans as the highest caste among them was Pushpalli, since palli denoted the sacred duty of making the garlands to regale the images of the gods. The Ti-yattunis were also employed in the shrines hence the prefix, identical to that of the Americas, ti for god. Interestingly it is also known that in former times the Pushpakans (probably originally Push-Karans) were also identified with the Nambi-yassans, or Nambis and these people were known to have kept gymnasia and military training schools called Kalari[284].

The Pallis as part of the broader indigenous Dravidian people of South India were also connected to the sea since only the centre of that region occupied by them was any distance from the coast. They were represented in all the occupations of a once independent people where fishing castes and coastal occupations such as mariner and sea traders were represented among them. Occupying such a critically located peninsula as a mid point between the Ancient Middle East, South East Asia and the Pacific the Tamils must, and were involved in many ways in the long distance oceanic trade. This extended, and must have been undertaken, by them also from the Ancient Middle East to Java and Sumatra and into the Pacific for at least a period of three thousand years and almost certainly much longer.

Palla has been noted as deriving from Vella, and the Vellalas are considered deriving from Pallan, Palla or Palli meaning or "Lord" and their traditions include a more complete series of myths relating to Siva and his mountain paradise of Kailasa already considered in an earlier chapter. Their clan divisions are called kulams and this means "descendant", and one of these is called Ganga Kulam meaning "descendant of the Ganges"[285]. Located in Malabar, and in the Nilgiri Hills where the Todas are located, both sections of Canara in South India, the Wyanad caste were divided into a dual organisation, one of which was named Manda-dan Chettis. These people wore topknots, usually a sign of elevated status, and their bridegrooms wore turbans of red cloth and wore a silver girdle[286]. The red turban is reminiscent of the red haired, and turbanned heroes in the Solomon Islands known as Sina Kwao and Sina Gweo[287], and the red turbans carved in red scoria for the moai (platform statues) on Easter Island. The headman of the Wyanad was named Kolla-Palli, and in death a gold coin as obolos was placed in the mouths of the deceased males, a custom found also in Ancient South America.

It can be seen that there are numerous parallels between the Pallas, or Pallis of South India and Ancient South America where the term occurs as the Palla, the Inca term for the women of their own caste. In the last given example from the Wyanad caste the name Manda, occurring frequently in South India derived from the Mandaean incursions from the Ancient Middle East and this term is found also on the coast of Ecuador where the sea currents deliver directly from Asia, and reveals connections in names, terms and customs occur repeatedly in Canara in South India as in South America. These are just some of the many connections all of which appear interrelated, in both India and Andean Peru.

Origins of Inca Weaving and the Loom

The women of the Incas, the Pallas, were recorded as being required to be examples for other women in the diligence and industry in state service to others and were also noted as being teachers of this art to those of women of lesser status. De la Vega wrote that women were taught the skill of weaving by the Coya, or queen, Mama Occlo Huaca, the wife of Manco Capac, but this was probably a piece of myth-making and does not actually indicate that it was an industry created by, and the preserve of women[288]. The exceptional achievement, not only of the Incas but in the earlier high cultures of the South American coast and Andean Ecuador, but particularly in Peru and Bolivia, has long been recognised and in some elements was unsurpassed. In more recent decades any attempt to compare and trace the origins of the techniques and design styles of the Ancient Peruvians and Bolivians to the Old World has been avoided, and indeed castigated. In the second half of the twentieth century the more strident formulation of the indigenous origins of the cultures of the Americas, more broadly considered the Americanist theories of isolated development, has been vigorously promoted with the resultant marginalisation of those with less extreme views. Earlier researchers in the late nineteenth century and the first half of the twentieth century saw many parallels, not only in the designs and techniques, but also in the social systems and origins of the peoples who instituted and maintained the weaving arts. The same researchers also provided cogent theories of the origins and means by which this influence reaching South America from Asia and one of these was Miles Poindexter whose writings sought origins of the Inca among the Aryans of Ancient India.

Early Weaving Traditions in South America

The simplest form of weaving - twinning, has been found as string and basketry dating in South America from about 8600-8000 B.C. having been introduced, it is believed, from North and Central America. By about 3000 B.C. twinning of cotton used in fabrics is found on the Peruvian coast and these soon become elaborate and decorated using the simplest of twinning technique. By a later date the heddle loom appears on the coast in the late pre-ceramic and this allows the development of fabrics to be utilised more comprehensively not only in daily life but in the more elaborate shrouded burials evident in those recovered preserved from this period. Of particular note from the very early period are the "stockinged" caps preserved in these burials[289] and these appear to be derived from the mariner's cap known as the Phrygian cap more typical in earlier times in Eurasia, the Mediterranean in particular, through to South and South East Asia (*9.075-89*).

The Spanish priest Bernabe Cobo wrote that in Peru the Indians had more clothing than in any other region of the New World. He noted that cotton was abundant in the Inca Empire and that they also had a plentiful supply of wool from the native llamas and vicunas. He was complimentary regarding their wide range of dyes in "excellent colours" of blue, yellow, red, scarlet, black, and many others. He reported that the women were always spinning and when they had no other pressing duties they carried on with spinning even when they were walking in the street. Cobo did mention that, although women did most of the spinning, men were the spinners in some places and that they considered the process "their own"[290]. This tends to confirm Cieza de Leon's report from the Canari district that it was the men who were the weavers and this was also the case in many districts of India. Cobo noticed that most of the looms in Peru were in fact very crude consisting only of a few sticks stuck into the ground and he describes their construction and set-up ready for weaving.

Most of the traditional examples of looms used by the Indians today are identical to those surviving in illustrations from ceramics long before the Inca Empire and these concur with Cobo's description of their construction and use. They were, for the most part, belt looms, that is the body of the fabric is extended from these stakes as Cobo describes by means of a belt extending around the waist of the weaver[291] (*12.017-30*). As he further describes, the structure of the loom was extremely crude and has its parallel only in the widespread looms of poorer villages throughout Asia suggesting again, through lack of development of the loom itself in South America, that it was an imported item. This introduction was not part of a continuous development in its Peruvian environment and therefore in the same spirit developed no further. This tends to be confirmed by the fact that Cobo noted that the fundamental structure of the cloth also remained basic and they never evolved techniques such as raising the knap that gave the cloth added qualities of warmth in a cold climate. Although he recognised this lack of development in the fundamental techniques of weaving and the structure of the loom he was filled with admiration for the final product considering it as beautiful, and in some cases more so than similar items in the Old World[292].

Weaving techniques were to be found throughout many tribes in the whole of South America and including the Amazonian tribes where the Omaguas and Cocamas were particularly noted in the seventeenth century for their traded woven fabrics[293]. Balls of yarn in some districts acted as a form of currency and were traded by one tribe for finished cloth from another and this form of trade was recorded between the Arecuna and the Chibcha in Colombia[294]. Among the high culture Colombian Indians the god of weaving was called Neucatocoa and his interest was seen as extending to those who painted fabrics[295]. Among some of the Amazonian

12.017 : Loom of a type found in Ancient Chile surviving into the twentieth century. Mapuche, Auracania, Chile, Early 20th., century, A.D.

12.018 : Aymara woman working at a simple traditional ground fixed loom. Lake Titicaca, Bolivia, Early 20th., century, A.D.

12.019 : Belt loom of the type found in Central and South America as well as in South and South East Asia. Palakau, Bismark Archipelago, Papua-New Guinea, Early 20th., century, A.D.

12.020 : A Kachari frame loom long traditional in North East India and Assam among other types such as the belt loom. Early 20th., century, A.D.

12.021 : Simple back-strap loom shown on the Codex Borbonicus, Mexico, Pre-post Conquest.

12.022 : A Mayan belt loom of the type similar to those found in South America, in Melanesia and through into Asia. Guatemala, Late 19th., century, A.D.

tribes, as among the Andean peoples, weaving was largely in the hands of women, as it was exclusively among the Lengua of the Gran Chaco whose traditions appear to indicate they may have been a remnant of the Incas who migrated into the lowland forests[296]. There are many books and articles covering the weaving techniques and the fine art of the finished results as well as the construction and use of the looms and need not be considered further here except to illustrate the exact parallels in their construction in Asia through illustrations included.

In Peru along the much warmer coastal plains the clothing was made from cotton but in the highlands it was largely from wool. Cobo describes the various elements of clothing but of particular interest is the general form known as the poncho, also called cuzma, and the cumbi, a shirt of finer material not unlike the poncho, and in some places the Incas employed cumbi camayos who wove only these garments[297]. The poncho is of interest because it extends in the identical form to Eastern Polynesia through Indonesia to Burma and into the Himalayan foothills among the Nagas of Assam. But it is the cumbi of Peru that is the more important since this is found traditionally in Celebes in Indonesia and widely in India from early times and bears the same name.

Weaving and the Kambli or Kumbli in India

Examples of ancient weaving are found in abundance from the graves of coastal Peru and the dryer regions away from the seaboard. Unfortunately the climate in India, because of the sum-

12.023 : Back-strap loom of a type found anciently in Mexico and Peru. Shan, Burma, Early 20th., century, A.D.

12.024 : Simple belt loom characteristic of those found illustrated by the Moche between 200 B.C. to 600 A.D.. Lhota Naga, Assam, North East India, Early 20th., century, A.D.

12.026 : Simple framed loom here being used by a Kuruba man to weave a Kumbli (Peruvian Cumbi) - an ancient blanket often considered sacred in India. Kuruba or Kurumba, South India, Early 20th., century, A.D.

12.025 : Typical ground fixed frame loom here worked by an Inkar weaver caste man associated with the Gond tribes in India. South Central India, Early 20th., century, A.D.

mer monsoons, is unsuitable for the long-term preservation of fabrics and few have survived more than a few centuries. There are however, more permanent records of ancient pattern textile designs in the many ancient carvings surviving over the last two millennia and some times from earlier epochs. Many villages in India preserve the most ancient forms of looms including those identical to those in Ancient South America. One of the more positive aspects of the caste system is that the weaving castes retained their means of occupation and the technology, no matter how primitive, over many centuries and the terms and traditions related to them were often jealously guarded. Being largely occupationally orientated, maintained in a hereditary line from father to son, many of these weaving related castes, even the smallest item was eventually devolved to a specialist section, or subdivision of a caste and these often eventually expanded to become a recognised separate caste.

The Acchu-Varu were a section attached to the Devanga weavers, and they received their name from the fact that they threaded the long comb of the loom, an occupation called accupani. They corresponded to other castes who had the same occupation such as the Jati-Pillais attached to the Kaikolan weavers in South India[298]. Achan is also a name meaning "lord" or "father" in the social sense and this appears to correspond with the term Uchu among the Incas earlier noted. The gradual subdivision of duties was in time extended to the type of cloth woven, some higher castes specialising in fine cloth while lower castes in coarser types such as the Gadabas who wove from vegetable fibres and cotton[299]. Some of the castes specialised in coloured cloth while others were restricted to white cloth, these latter being represented by castes such as the Bilimaggas of South Canara[300].

The Chaliyans were a cast of Malayali weavers who migrated from the East Coast of India to the West in about the 11th., century A.D. and they lived in caste streets called Teruvan. These were streets occupied by the caste and these Teruvan among the Malayali were divided into left and right - those lived in the left-hand section worshipped Bhagavati and those who lived

12.027 : Traditional Ainu loom pegged out onto the ground in a simple form. Hokkaido, North Japan, Late 19th., century, A.D.

12.028 : Looms were known in forms similar to those found among the Maya, and as belt looms known also in South America, that must have been imported technically from Asia similar to those of New Guinea. Bismark Archipelago, Papau-New Guinea, Early 20th., century, A.D.

12.029 : Ground fixed simple loom here worked by a man of the Oraon tribe. Note the leg pit with extended cords. Central India, Early 20th., century, A.D.

12.030 : Simple belt loom similar to those in Asia and South America in the Western Pacific. Nitendi, Melanesia, Early 20th., century, A.D.

in the right were considered of lesser status and worshipped Ganesa, the elephant god[301]. These caste streets appear to have been related to similar clan and caste divisions in the towns and villages of Ancient Peru earlier noted.

The Devangas were a weaving caste and were also called Jada or Jadaru[302]. They were known for carrying metal tweezers attached to a metal chain extended from their waistbands used for removing thorns of the Acacia arabica common around the home district of Bellary in South Central India from their feet[303]. Similar tweezers, used for this purpose no doubt but also by other tribes to remove hair from their faces, are found in Central and South America.

In many cases the names given to the castes is directly derived from their occupation rather than their tribes and the name given to the Kaikolan was said to derive from the term kai = hand, and kol = shuttle earlier noted. Other derivations, perhaps another example of the transfer of meaning to something unrelated earlier noted in the Americas or otiose, is found in the belief by the Kaikolans themselves that it refers to the precious dagger, or Ratnavel, of the deity Subramanya. The loom of the Kaikolans was the focus of many mythical attributions and its various parts were attributed to the various devatas (angels) and Rishis (ancestral gods identified with the Great Bear constellation)[304]. It has been noted earlier that the headman of the Kaikolan weaving caste was called the Patta-Karan and this in both its elements has apparent cultural transfers into the terms utilised by the Incas. The Kaikolans preserved for themselves a traditional role in the annual festival for the goddess Gangamma. Ganga is the female goddess of the River Ganges and Gangamma is a related goddess of water and this festival dedicated to her was held at Tirupati in the far south of India. In this celebration disguise is an important element in the morning and evening sections of the festival and these are associated with the vehicle called Matangi, the elephant, more usually the vehicle of the smallpox goddess Sitala, an aspect of Kali[305]. The special Sunday Matangi vesham, or rite, in this festival is performed only by a Kaikolan who had cross-dressed as a woman, and is performed in the house of a high status Brahman or Mahant whose wife has pre-deceased him. In the performance of this rite the

Kaikolan drives himself into a trance and while in this state a wire is forced through his tongue resembling the long traditional rites of infibulation known in South India. The cross-dressed Kaikolan then rides through the streets of the town and distributes to worthy persons saffron paste and flowers special to the goddess[306].

In the sacred temple city of Conjeeveram (Kanchipuram) another ceremony called Punta (flower car) was witnessed a century ago focused on a lightly built deity cart with four wheels on which an image of Kali, the wrathful goddess of India, was placed. This cart was dragged by about thirty men using cords inserted through the skin of their backs. This festival was organised by weavers called Sankunram Mudaliars who were the inhabitants of a part of the city known as Pillaipalyam, considered very ancient, and instituted as a propitiation to elicit for protection from the goddess from the greatly feared disease of smallpox[307]. These festivals are interesting and were in fact common in principle to many throughout India from the most ancient times before the intrusion of the Aryans from Iran. Cross-dressing was frequent in these rituals and associated with many rites of Kali in India and it is notable that cross-dressing and the homosexual rites associated with them were common throughout Americas and particularly notable of the Yauyos in Peru who were "persuaded into their Empire by the Incas"[308]. Such practices scandalised the Spanish Conquistadors and they justified their brutal suppression of the Indian religion and ceremonial and social practices or the universal acceptance and practise of these perceived perversions among the Central and South Amerindians. It is notable in India also that the Kaikolans in Kanchipuram were designated Palla or Pillai by their residential district indicating another aspects of transference and identity with the Inca term Palla in Peru.

The Kaikolans were a lesser status section of the Kammalans, a powerful military caste first recorded around about the beginning of the 11th., century A.D. It was said that Kaikolan deva-dasis (temple-dancers) betrayed the Kammalans and they lost power and social standing but they still retained their claim to high status using the equivalent of the Brahman titles, Avharya and Bhatta, as Achari and Paththa[309]. Their personal titles were Ayya, Appa and Anna all advertised their claim to Aryan descent, earlier noted[310], reflecting the related titles claimed in the antipodes in South America by the Incas.

The Kurubas were especially noted for their aptitude for physical sports and wrestling in particular. Many of the men wore wristbands as amulets made of black sheep's wool, and often with a thread band tied around the arm or neck

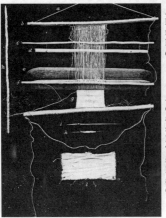

12.031 : Typical Mayan loom similar to that from Peru found in the Yucatan and Belize. Mayan, Late 19th., century, A.D.

12.032 : Some of the evidence for weaving techniques and looms have been preserved on fine ceramics from North Central Coastal Peru. These graphic depictions show that the simple belt looms was the most common at that time. Moche, North Central Peru, 200-600 A.D.

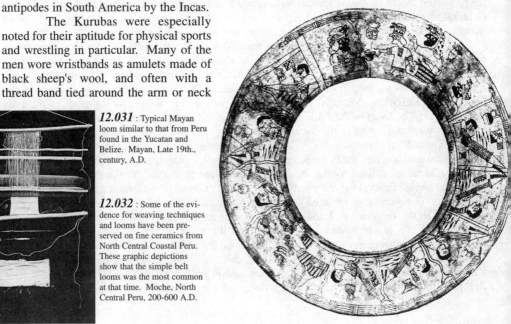

with sacred ashes wrapped inside. The Kurubas were occupied in many trades and in agriculture but were also known as weavers for the fine quality blanket speciality made from lamb's wool known in former times as a cumbli (kumbli,or kambli)[311]. In more recent times this becomes the name of a much coarser product and usually produced by the men except in the Madura and Kolar region in far south of South India and here it is the Kuruba women who weave the cumbli[312]. It can hardly be considered coincidental that not only the basic loom but the name of the "dress" blanket used for wrapping around the shoulders is virtually identical to that of the Incas - cumbli corresponding to cumbi. The techniques from shearing and the use of several colours direct from the sheep's back through the weaving process to the final finishing is described elsewhere and need not be included here[313].

Those Kurubas who are most usually, and best known, for the cumbli are those in the Bellary District in South Central India and reside in the locale of the Ancient Chalukyan kingdom centred at Aihole and Patta-dakal. The Chalukyans have been shown in a previous work to be prominent in the transfer of iconography from India to the Maya of Central America and this is evident at Palenque in particular[314]. Their influence at some of the South American sites, particularly Tiahuanaco, is referred to in this work also.

Among the wealthiest of the castes in South India were the traders and moneylenders known as the Nattu-Kottai Chettis. Their name is said to derive from that of a country fort - Nattukottai, and their power and influence allows them to enter the innermost temples to the door of the inner shrine[315]. They live in caste streets, called Ilayaththukudi, and they maintained reverence for an emerald god named Vinayaka[316]. It is conceivable that the Ancient Ecuadorian Emerald goddess Umina and that of Uminahah of the Maya was in fact derived from this deity in its abbreviated form, Vina - the name only slightly deviating from the south Indian original. Nattukottai men have their ears bored and extended but only occasionally in recent times wore ornaments in the dilated aperture. Their wives are largely closeted in the caste street area and were noted for their dressing down in lesser quality cloth used for clothing and their virtuous attention to even the most menial housework that is reminiscent of the reports of Inca women. They plaited baskets as well as spun cloth in their home compounds[317].

Another caste claiming high status in India are the silk-thread weavers known as the Patnul-Karans. These people are a caste found in the Tamil region of South India but originated in the North West in Gujarat. In Gujarat they are referred to as Patta-Vayaka and are recorded as such in the Kumara Gupta inscriptions dated 473 A.D. These weavers were induced by this king to immigrate to Mandasor in the Centre West of India because of their silk weaving skills and in time they migrated further South to the Tamil country[318]. The name Patta indicates their high status and perhaps a few may have migrated even further from their original home - to Indonesia and on to Peru.

The term Pattu, silk, may also derive from the fact that it could only be afforded by the very wealthy, or those entitled Patta. The largest section of weavers among the Telugu tribe of India were called the Sales, from the Sanskrit, salika - a weaver. They are divided into two main endogamous divisions, the padma - a lotus, and Pattu - silk. The Pattu Sales wear the sacred thread, whereas the Padma do not, and considered themselves of the highest status. The Pattu Sales wove superfine cloth and silk while the Padma Sales wove coarser cloth[319] reflecting another aspect of a dual social organisation reflected through occupational castes.

The fine textiles of Peru were noted for their design, colour and enormous width woven on up to three shuttle widths on the looms. Not considered, because no serious comparisons have been undertake, is the fact that the traditional looms in India also extended to these three shuttle widths that were known in Ancient Peru. Observations on the traditional weaving capability in India is noted by A. Chatterton in the first part of the twentieth century before the destruction of the hand-loom industry by those of the modern powered industry and his observations were as follows: "The hand-weavers may be divided into two great classes - (1) plain weavers, whom weave fabrics with a single shuttle, which carries the weft from selvage to selvage; (2) bordered cloth weavers, who weave cloths in which the threads of the weft of the portion of the fabric forming the borders are distinct from the threads of the weft of the main body of the cloth. To manufacture these cloths, three shuttles are employed, and as yet no successful attempt has been made to imitate them on the power loom ..."[320].

The traditional weaving skill in India was second to none and in technique and development of several looms were some way in advance of Peru. As Cobo noted the Peruvians sense of design and quality of finish was exceptional particularly considering the looms they used were so basic. But perhaps the most startling conclusion of any comparisons between the finished designs in Peru with those of India is that in principle they are so similar but adapted to local iconography, social demands and availability of coloured dyes and basic materials of cotton and wool. This can be extended to the fact that the highest status garment in Peru, the cumbi, is the exact equivalent of the cumbli or kambli of India. This is clearly shown when illustrations from the vastly disparate regions are juxtaposed and a more valid comparison can be made, together with techniques, that indicates that these influences must have been transferred originally the Ancient Middle East to India, and from both of these regions to Peru.

The Cumbi - the Mantle of Status in Ancient Peru

The term cumpi in Ancient South America is that recorded for the finer quality garment worn by the Peruvian Indians in the Inca period but is also recorded as cumbli in India along with similar terms. Salcamayhua states that it was not only the weaving process that Manco Capac's son and successor, Ynca Sinchi Ruca, was the patron but declares that it was he who "understood" the making of the cloth for the cumpis[321]. It was said that in the reign of the Inca Pachacuti, when he was very old, a mission arrived from across the sea and from this vessel a youth arrived at court and gave the Inca a "great book" and then disappeared. Not long after this he was succeeded by his second son, Tupac who had undertaken the great voyage to the west and on his accession he distributed headdresses of plumes called Paurcahuas, and cumpis[322]. Clearly the cumpis had some degree of high status attached to them from at least that time (early 15th., century), and at the Conquest among the treasures recorded as being secreted away from the invading Spanish the Incas cumpis are specifically mentioned[323].

Bernabe Cobo notes that cumbis were among the offerings made during the sacrifices to the hill ancestors and spirits[324], and to the statues of the Sun in the main squares at the appropriate festivals[325]. Father Pablo Joseph de Arriaga wrote after the Conquest that the idols of the gods were dressed in cumbis draped around the statue itself[326], identical to the same tradition found anciently into the present day in India, and he admonished missionaries in Peru to ensure that they were burnt because of their association with the idolatry of the Indians. He also notes that the cumbis were worn during the performances of religious mystery plays as follows: "For these performances they wear their best clothes, made of cumbi, and on their heads they wear something like a half moons of silver called chacrahinca, or other objects called huama, and little round medals called tincurpa, or clasps"[327].

The Cumbli or Kambli in Ritual and Belief in India

In India Western clothing has largely supplanted traditional male dress in the urban cities and towns, but several generations ago the wearing of the native clothing was described by several writers. One includes the description of the typical Tamil apparel worn by the Muduvar tribe in the south of India where the "... cumbly, or blanket is invariably carried".... "The cloth, after being brought around the waist, and tucked in there, is carried over the body, and two corners are knotted on the right shoulder"[328]. This appears to be a rare reference to the customary blanket or animal skin cape found depicted reflecting this exact same way of tying this garment among the Nagas of Assam (*3.028*), the Tasmanians (*3.026/7*), and the Peruvians (*3.029*) transferred by mariner peoples. The cumbli, or kambli, in India was also associated with rituals and propitiation to deities and ancestors. Among the Nayadis in South India, when a person was ill, a "... kambli ..., with a quantity gingelly (Seasamun), mustard, turmeric, and coconut tied up in the four corners, is passed three times over the patient and presented to a Nayardi, together with a palm umbrella, a stick and a cucumber. This is called Kala-Dhanam, or offering to Yama, the god of death, whose attack has to be warded off by propitiatory offerings"[329]. It is clear that the cumbli, or kambli, had equal ritual significance in India as the cumbi or cumpi had in Ancient Peru, and when worn was tied in the same way.

The Malayalis, already mentioned relating to other cultural reference of transference, are a Tamil people who migrated from the plains of South India and they also adopted the kambli, and this was a "... luxury denied to the females, but does duty for the males, young and old, in the triple capacity of great coat, waterproof, and blanket"[330]. Among many of the tribes and castes of India there are close parallels with Polynesian culture and finger amputation was one of these. The Morasu Kapulu were a tribe in India practising this act, mostly by women, but one of their customs is reminiscent of the association of the cumbi in Peru with sacred rites. Edgar Thurston reported that the "... Morasu Kapulu women never touch the new grain of the year without worshipping the sun (Surya), and may not eat food prepared from this grain before this act of worship is performed. They wrap themselves in a kambli" ... "after a purificatory bath, prostate themselves on the ground, raise their hands to the forehead in salutation, and make the usual offering of coconuts, etc...."[331].

In Borneo, capes of status, worn only by those who have succeeded in capturing and returning with a trophy head from headhunting forays in the dark forest life of this large tropical island were called klambis, clearly derived in name and function from those in India[332]. In Indonesia there are numerous indicators that the term for the Indian cumbli or kambli extended far from the shores of South India and the term for the sacred textile cloth in Sarawak in Northwest Borneo is pua kumbu among the Iban (Dyak) people[333]. In Sumba, a central island in the Indonesian Straits, noted for its megalithic architecture and ceremonial dress so similar to that of the Nagas of Assam, the men's wraps or sacred cloth was called hinggi kombu, and one was worn around the waist and another over his shoulder. Clearly both klambi and kombu are the cumbi or cumpi of Peru and the cumbli, or kambli of India.

Large numbers of finely designed and woven textiles are associated with the burial rites of Bolivia and Peru but this is largely because the extremely arid coastal climate allowed the textiles to survive from the first millennium B.C. In other regions of the world cloth has long been associated with rituals, as well as utilised for their practical value, in India and in Asia generally. Into the twentieth century ritual burials in the Philippines and Indonesia involved surrounding the body of the deceased with fine textiles while in it sat in state before the burial and others added while in the coffin itself[334]. It is significant that these are the island regions where closely similar aspects of rituals and myths have been transferred from India to South America and receive the influences from that distant continent on the return journey back to South and South East Asia.

It must be clear at this point that the Peruvian term cumbi must derive from India where a similar garment with its many uses, both mundane and religious, and termed the cumbli. For a term to have survived so exactly in pronunciation and meaning, along with so many other terms, indicates that it must have been transferred within a generation directly from India to Peru so that

12.033 : Traditional turbans and and worn with shirts identical to the cushmas and ponchos of ancient Peru. Karen tribe, Burma, Early 20th., century, A.D.

12.034 : Fine poncho with typical abstracted geometric design characteristic of the Inca period. 1350-1500 A.D.

12.035 : Fine poncho with designs reminiscent of Chinese characters. South or Central, Peru, c1300-1532 A.D.

12.036 : Typical traditional Karen costume showing the close similarities with the Inca poncho. Bwe Karen, Burma, Early 20th., century, A.D.

12.038 : Traditional bark-cloth poncho showing the basic form of the head-hole in the centre of a large cloth. Indonesia, Pre-20th., century, A.D.

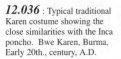

12.037 : A Conibo cushma or poncho. The patterns utilised by these Amazonian forest people have a close parallel in Ainu designs. Eastern Peru, Early 20th., century, A.D.

12.039 : Typical ponchos of the traditional Pacific Islands type closely similar to those of Peru. Ruk Archipelago, Micronesia, Early 20th., century, A.D.

it was not compromised by time and distance.

The Importance of Textile in Ritual Exchange and Ceremonial

The vast numbers of textiles discovered in the sands of Peru, their extraordinary length and width, and the beautiful colours and apparently unique designs has been the subject of many well-illustrated books. It is clear that textiles, particularly those described as cumbis, were of great ritual significance and an indicator of wealth and status[335]. Arriaga is one of the first to describe cloth as being of significance in burial rites[336] and his reports, along with others such as those from Bernabe Cobo[337] foreshadows the greater interest taken by researchers over the last two centuries. It is less known that in India textiles and cloth were also of great importance anciently and into recent times in a similar manner and that is it not only the name of cumbli that derives from the Sub-continent but also the customs surrounding textiles. Textile techniques such as tie-dye (plangi)[338] and batik are more usually associated with Indonesia, but "suddenly" appear in Central Peru in the mid-first millennium, B.C., but were originally transferred from India into Indonesia.

12.041 : A traditional star pattern identically found in India as it was in Ancient Peru. Kathiawar, North West India, 19th., century, A.D.

12.040 : A traditional star pattern identically found in India as it was in Ancient Peru. Kathiawar, North West India, 19th., century, A.D.

12.042 : Tapestry depicting abstract geometric pattern including the Inca Morning Star pattern identical to those found also in Ancient India. South Coast Peru, 1300-1525 A.D.

The Nayars, an important military caste of high status in South India, exchanged cloths for the rituals services provided by priests, officiants and participants at marriages and funerals typical of many tribes and castes in India[339] and these were given also at puberty rites, religious celebrations and funerals. The Nayar marriage pandal, or hut, was surfaced with mats, carpets and the best quality white cloths. Of particular note in this marriage ceremony was that the father of the girl presented new cloths tied in a kambli (cumbli, cumbi) to the marital couple and these cloths they change into as part of ritual exchange and the symbol of marriage. The bridegroom is called pillai, and is a name associated in South India with elevated status but also identifies with the god Ganesa, the elephant god, and for wealthier Nayars elephants are traditionally part of the marriage procession[340]. At the completion of the ceremony high quality cloths are sent from the bridegroom's house to that of the bride suggesting an earlier form of bride purchase[341]. Should there be a divorce at a later date a ritual is performed where a cloth is ritually torn in half indicating the symbolic and perhaps legal importance of cloth and textiles generally in India[342].

At the funeral rites the shroud cloth of the Nayar is taken from the body after the rites and torn into two[343], reflecting that of divorce, and cloths to provide for the deceased in the afterlife were also included in a similar way by most tribes in India. In some tribes the sitting posture the deceased is placed in is similar to the sitting posture found in South America. The Irulas of South India dug a circular pit and the deceased was placed in a sitting posture with his legs crossed "tailorwise", and clad in his own clothes with a new cloth and with a lamp and grain[344]. Many of the Saivite burials are seated and interred while the Vaishnavite supporters usually resort to cremation. In the simplest tribal burials in the villages of rural India cloth and food is provided for the deceased for the believed survival of the soul in the afterlife[345] while others are orientated with the feet to the south and the head to the north with a new cloth wrapped around the corpse of the deceased[346].

The ancient rituals of India closely follow those of the Ancient Middle East and typical are the washing of the body before wrapping in a new shroud[347], similar to the rites recorded in Ancient Peru. The evolution of many of these ancient rituals have been obscured by the adoption of cremation rites for the dead thought to have been introduced by the Vedic Aryans. Some tribes maintained both inhumation and cremation where associated rituals survive similarly for both. One of these tribes is the Maravans of South India where the burial tradition where a pit that is dug, and salt, powdered brick and sacred ashes are scattered over the floor. For a cremation the deceased is carried to the grave on a palanquin or litter, and new cloths are placed on the ground to the pit where the deceased is set down in it in a sitting posture[348].

A less usual use for the textile shroud was found among the Nagatha tribe of South India

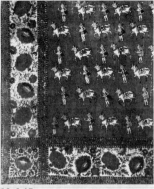

12.043 : Embroidered stem stitch textile with winged pattern where the overall design style and bordering is identical to that found in India. Late Paracas, South Coastal Peru, 300 B.C.-100 A.D.

12.044 : Embroidered stem stitch textile with winged pattern where the overall pattern style and bordering is identical to that found in India. Late Paracas, South Coastal Peru, 300 B.C.-100 A.D.

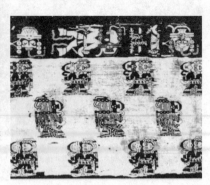

12.045 : A cotton canopy cloth with an even distributed pattern across the body that is block-printed including the border. Gujarat, North West India, 19th., century, A.D.

12.046 : A sinhasana - a painted and printed cotton cloth with an even distributed motif across the main body of the cloth and a more complicated border design similar in principle to many of the Ancient Peruvian textiles. Rajasthan, North West India, 19th., century, A.D.

where instead of a litter or palanquin to carry the deceased on the last journey he was wrapped in his new blanket (kambli or cumbli) and carried in this by the bearers[349]. This method is a characteristic also of the Ode or Wodde in Central India[350]. This tradition suggests that the blanket was a substitute for the cattle skin shroud known among cattle-herding people such as the ancestors of the early Vedic Aryans in Iran. Cloth was a characteristic presentation for the last journey whether cremation or interment was the current mode of disposal. Even for the cremations cloths were laid on the corpse suspended over the pyre and these were also reduced to ashes[351].

Palanquins or litters were a characteristic of burials to convey the dead to their last resting place. Among the Valluvans, Tamil caste priests, the body was conveyed on a litter made out of a palm leaf mat and bamboo frame and the corpse wrapped in a new cotton cloth[352]. It is interesting to note that palanquins and mats were a feature in Ancient Peruvian burials, noted and illustrated elsewhere in this work (*1.027-33*).

There can be little doubt that textiles, in both name and technique, were transferred direct from India through Indonesia anciently and that this included later techniques such as plangi (tie-dyeing) and batik better known in Indonesia. Undoubtedly the developments in the Indonesian Islands were also a major contributory factor and provided other related influences from time to time into Peru. From the traditions of burial, textiles presentation both into the grave and those officiating and the wider use and status associated with textiles there can be little doubt that much of the initiating impetus in Ancient Peru derived from India and its long history of development and cultural assimilation from the Ancient Middle East.

The Flood Myth as Evidence of Cultural Transfer by Mariners

One of the first reports by Spanish chroniclers in Latin America noted that the Indians "... knew of the flood of Noah, and they said that he escaped in a canoe with his wife and sons; and that the world afterwards been peopled by them"[353]. In these versions of the myth the name of the flood hero or survivor is not the Biblical Noah but the myth as a whole in structure and motif is so similar as to appear to have derived from the Ancient Near and Middle East. In some cases however, the Flood Survivor appears to have been directly derived since in Mexico the Aztec Flood hero, Nata[354], appears too similar to the Biblical Noah not to have derived from it[355].

In Ancient Peru Bernabe Cobo records that the Flood resulted from a deliberate act by Viracocha and that this was as a result of his displeasure of the wilfulness of mankind. This reason so given for catastrophe is almost identical to some of the most ancient Flood references in

12.047 : A complex textile design depicting a ruler or deity with an expansive feather headdress with the central crown illustrating the lozenge design similar to that found traditionally in India. Inca Dynasty, 10th.,-15th., century, A.D.

12.048 : A typical sacred lozenge textile design decorating this coverlet found widely in India anciently but also in Central and South America. The pattern is a traditional block-print on cotton. North India, 19th., century, A.D.

12.049 : A dancing figure representing Garuda, or Hindu eagle god, wearing typical sarongs with the sacred lozenge pattern found in South and South East Asia anciently but identical to those found in Central and South America. Sketches of 13-15th., century figures, Burma.

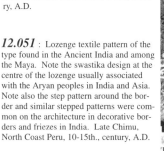

12.050 : Characteristic lozenge pattern sacred to Hindu and translated into textiles designs. This pattern is frequently based on a lotus within a square as it is shown here and is found as such on the Peruvian Coast. Brahman Cave Shrine, Aihole, Central South India, 6-7th., century, A.D.

12.051 : Lozenge textile pattern of the type found in the Ancient India and among the Maya. Note the swastika design at the centre of the lozenge usually associated with the Aryan peoples in India and Asia. Note also the step pattern around the border and similar stepped patterns were common on the architecture in decorative borders and friezes in India. Late Chimu, North Coast Peru, 10-15th., century, A.D.

12.052 : The lozenge design is characteristic of patterns found in Peru but more so typical of Ancient India and into the present day. Coastal Peru, c100-1400 A.D.

Sumerian myth in the Ancient Middle East where the gods tired of man's infidelity shown towards their creators[356]. In another myth Cobo notes that the Incas retained a myth that in the early days of their dynasty they worshipped the cave at Pacaritampu, considered by them their Cave of Origin, from which they emerged into the World. Others, however, claimed that the first Incas went into the cave when the waters of the Great Flood rose and sealed up the entrance until the waters had subsided and then re-emerged into the World to establish their dynastic control over the highlands of Bolivia and Peru[357]. This relation bears similarities to the versions found among the Indians on the North West Coast of North America where some survivors were said to have sealed themselves into huts by caulking their 'dwellings submerged during the Great Flood[358]. Others such as the Bella Bella in the same region refer to mountains extending upwards to stay above the rising floodwaters[359], a motif found also in Peru among the people of Ancasmarca near. Mountains or plateaus myths being the last retreat of flood survivors are found among the Melanesians[361] and in Polynesia[362].

Some accounts incorporate not only recognisable Biblical motifs such as survivors

12.053 : A rollout from a Mayan vase depicting the typical lozenge design of the ritual ceramic or basket centrally placed considered sacred in the ancient symbolism of India. Guatemala, Late Classic Period, 600-900 A.D.

12.054 : A section of a ceremonial cloth, called a pua kumba, showing designs reminiscent of Ancient Peru said to represent swimming serpents in water. Iban (Dyak), Sarawak, Borneo, Indonesia, Early 20th., century, A.D.

being saved by an ark substitute - a boat or canoe, but by birds sent out to seek for land over many days of drifting on the flood waters. However some motifs are so unusual that they are unlikely to have been found in a wider context since they appear as to have been invented locally, adapted to the flood myth and then carried abroad by mariners who visited that locale.

Bernabe Cobo gives a similar account of the Great Flood to that of Christoval de Molina except that it appears to have been influenced by Inca or Quechua adaptations. Cobo's account notes that this myth follows that of Molina in structure, recording that two young brothers alone were saved from the Flood by climbing Mount Huacayan (Huracan is a deity associated with the Flood in Quiche-Mayan myths). When they were running low on food, they returned one day to find that there was a lavish meal prepared for them with chichi - the maize beer of South America. After ten or twelve days following the same pattern they wished to know who their benefactor was so one remained hidden in the hut while the other went out to work. After a time two guacamayas, macaws - a native parrot-like birds, flew into the hut and they transformed themselves into two beautiful Canari pallas, or aristocratically dressed young women of noble lineage. They took off their llicllas, or fine mantles, and began to prepare the meal. The young man who was hidden then emerged and greeting the young women, attempting to talk to them, but they became flustered and hurriedly transformed themselves who their bird forms and flew off. Having reported the outcome of the confrontation to his brother when he returned and they decided they both should hide in the hut to see if the guacamayas would return. Three days later the birds returned and again changed into the two young pallas, or noble-women, the young men waited until they had began to prepare the meal and then rushed out, blocking the door. The brothers embraced the young ladies holding them firmly as they attempted to scream and break loose. Calming them with soothing words, eventually the young men were able to ask them where they had come from and from which families they were descended. The macaw-women told them in response that god Viracocha had sent them to assist the brothers so that they would not die of hunger. The two young men took the young ladies as their wives and their descendants repopulated the world, and it was believed by the Indians that all the native peoples of South America were descended from them[363]. The Molina version states that the brothers captured only the youngest guacamayos and that they both had "carnal knowledge" of her - these unions resulted in six son and daughters and from these all Canaris were said to have descended[364].

In reference to this myth Cobo recorded that he had seen in Lima, the capital of Peru, a small copper pillar with the images of two guacamayas birds perched on top also made of copper. He discovered that this pillar and its birds had been brought from Ecuador, from the province of Canaribamba, the land of the Canares Indians already noted and that these were worshipped by them in memory of their descent from the Great Flood and their ancestors being saved by the guacamayas sent by Viracocha. It is probably not a coincidence that this fable was preserved particularly by these Indians since their connections as mariners arriving on the Ecuadorian coast

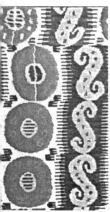

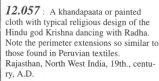

12.057 : A khandapaata or painted cloth with typical religious design of the Hindu god Krishna dancing with Radha. Note the perimeter extensions so similar to those found in Peruvian textiles. Rajasthan, North West India, 19th., century, A.D.

12.059 : A textile design depicting an image of a griffon-like figure of anthropoid puma similar to those found in early Bolivia, North America and the Ancient Middle East. The leaf designs in the border are characteristic of the pre and post Inca Dynasty. Pachacamac, 1200-1500 A.D.

.055 : Patterns cread from circles and egalithic S" designs re commonly known Asia and South nerica. Turkestan, ntral Asia, Early 20th., ntury, A.D.

12.056 : The body of a young man surrounded by textiles in a traditional manner similar to the traditions known in Peru. Luzon, Philippines, Early twentieth century, A.D.

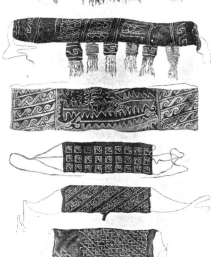

12.058 : Painted textile found on the coast of Peru but with circular patterns identical to similar painted textiles in India into Central Asia. Coastal Peru, 1000-1500 A.D.

and the links to Viracocha, identified with his departure from Manta, tends to confirm that they were probably from Canara in South India. Throughout the Pacific regions there are many carvings of birds atop pillars (*9.001-8*), probably revering the eagle or hawk or other bird used in navigation on long sea voyages and in Ancient India it was common to elevate carved birds, animals, heroes and deities in the same way as found also in Ancient Pacific Coast South America.

12.060 : Inca textile pouches with decorative fringed extensions identical to those anciently known in Ancient India (*12.057*). Inca Dynasty, Peru, 1350-1500 A.D.

    In a more recent study of Flood Myths from around the world Professor Alan Dundes compares the South American version by Molina to that of the Tlapanecs version in Mexico and notes that there are close similarities except it is a dog-woman who assists the Flood Hero[365]. Another myth from the Totonac traditions on the East Coast of Mexico states that the bitch's skin was burnt by the Flood survivor so that she could remain in the human state and assist the hero to repopulate the world[366]. Similar myth versions of the dog, who was discovered as the same type of mysterious housekeeper, occurs among the Indians of Vancouver Island and in the Amazon Basin[367]. It is in these same distant region that it has been shown earlier to have been in contact through other myths such as those of Si'wit and Kixwet earlier noted. Other versions of the Flood myths in the Americas are so similar to the Biblical version that they must be considered evidence of some pre-Conquest contact since other pictorial records in the codices, and textual references in chronicles, appear to indicate similar myths long before the arrival of the Spanish. However, as a study of myth motifs in the Americas will show, particularly in the Amazon Basin, motifs utilised in various versions are interchangeable and appear in other flood myths as well as being utilised separately from them in other contexts. This indicates the great age and the variability of memory in their descent from one generation to another and in their re-telling - but does not necessarily invalidate them in terms of cross-cultural transfers.

12.061 : A Indian fakir, a Harivyasa Vaishnavite, wearing a large mantle-like robe made from many patches in the manner of a quilt, a technique also found in Ancient South America. North West India, Late 19th., century, A.D.

In principle this is true in all regions of the world and in a myth from the Admiralty Islands in Melanesia, not actually related to a Flood myth, it was said that ten fruits were hanging in a tree protected by their husks, but at nightfall the husks opened and they fell out onto the ground below. The fruit changed into women and bathed into the sea. A man who was passing at that time saw them and was greatly attracted by their pale skins - "like that of albinos" - and he persuaded them to talk to him and he proposed marriage to all of them. Nine agreed but the tenth refused and she fled back to the branches of the tree and slipped back into her husk to become a fruit again[368]. This myth appears to have common origin with birds changing into humans and becoming the progenitors of the race. This reflects aspects in other clan origin myths in this region that have been frequently recorded and these are focused on the exploits ten hero brothers as culture bearers. Fruit, earlier noted, have been described in myths as the ancestors of clans and tribes in the New Hebrides and other islands in the same region and these have merged with common motifs in some myths and dissociated in others.

In a myth from the west of the island of New Guinea, more similar to the South American records, it is recorded that a tradition from the Numfor people stated that a man saw a sky-women who had come down to Earth to bathe. She had taken off her wings before entering the water so he hid them as she bathed herself so that she could not return to the sky. They married and their children were the ancestors of their clans. The woman later found her wings and she, her husband and children flew up to the sky but later returned to earth to form the ruling clans of Gilolo[369] - an island identified with South China and the Ancient Middle East in an earlier chapter. A more extensive and elaborate myth is recorded of the Murut people in Borneo where there are a number of similar myths describing human heroes marrying sky women where the clothes, or their bird disguise, were laid aside for a time, these being hidden by the hero in the same manner as those in New Guinea[370].

The motif of an animal becoming human and them returning to the animal state again is illustrated in the ancient texts of India. In the Panchatanta it is record-

12.062 : Painted textile characteristic of many produced in India with the traditional "Megalithic S", also known in Peru, before the 16th., century, A.D. North India.

12.063 : Textiles in India were associated with specific occupational castes and in this illustration a family from a Chhipa caste who specialised in stamp printing calico are shown with their designs and the stamps utilised to impress the patterns. Gujarat, North West India, Early 20th., century, A.D.

12.064 : Cross-legged figure with a fez-like cap characteristic of early Java and Sumatra. Sican or Chimu, North Central Peru, 7-15th., century, A.D.

12.065 : Carved stela showing the exact form found of the seated "lotus" position in Peru originating in India but also found in Indonesia. Pasemah, Sumatra, Indonesia, 6-7th., century, A.D.

12.066 : Seated Buddha crudely carved, possibly by non-professional masons and closely similar to the so-called pot-bellies known on the Pacific Coast of Guatemala and in Sumatra in Indonesia. Burma, 7-10th., century, A.D.

ed that human parents had a serpent son who was later married to a human girl. On his wedding night he assumed his human form, by shedding his snakes skin, and his father, awaiting this act, promptly prevented him from returning to his serpent form by burning the skin. The first researchers recording these myths noted the close parallels of the myths of India with those of the far north of Europe and concluded that one must have had a common origin with the other. This particular myth is paralleled with the Norse myth in the Volsungasaga where the were-wolves, Sigmundr and Sifjotli, were saved from their damnation, to repeatedly become were wolves, when their wolf's hides were burnt when they assumed their human form[371]. A similar snake myth is told of a Brahman who was informed by a spirit that he would have a son unsurpassed by all others but his wife gave birth to a snake. The father betrothed the daughter of a cousin to his son, and on the wedding night, as with the above myth, the Brahman waited until his son had shed his skin to assume his human form and burnt it so that he could not return to it[372].

In India, the Gonds, so frequently a fundamental factor in the transfer of traditions into the Pacific and to South America, preserve long myth cycles regarding the traditions of their origins and heroes. Among these traditions the Seven Panior Brothers feature large since they were considered the heroes from whom the Gonds descended after they dispersed from their legendary home at Dhanegaon. It is said that they made their way to a place called Bourmachua, carrying their Sale, or sacred rod, where they decided to settle and built their first cattle pen and houses. Before they reached their settlement they had encountered the Tsakati Raja and they frightened the Raja's people by their "violent reproaches". The daughter of this Raja, however, could not rid her mind of thoughts about these brothers so secretly she sought out the house of the Panior brothers and entered it undetected. While the brothers slept she did the housework, prepared the food and fetched the water, and all before dawn, and before the brothers awoke she left to return to her parents without them knowing. The brothers each thought one of the others had arisen early and completed all the domestic chores, but none would admit to it. This occurred for the next five nights and the eldest brother decided to stay awake to find out why this was happening but fell asleep and awoke to find all the domestic work had been done including the preparation of their food. But soon after this the youngest brother cut his finger and the pain kept him wake all night and later in the night he saw the Tsakati Raja's daughter enter the house and undetected he watched her from a hiding place. When she had finished the work he caught hold of her and awoke his brothers. When questioned she told them she was their mother's brother's daughter and because of this the eldest brother decided to marry her (cross-cousin marriage tradition). In a latter part of the myth the youngest brother converts himself into a mango fruit to avoid being attacked by a tiger, and this was plucked by a crow that carried it away but dropped in into a water tank where it was swallowed by a fish. She was caught by a poor woman who went fishing and the youngest brother called to her to open the fish carefully so as not to hurt him and when she did he stepped out from the belly as a boy child and within two years was fully grown bringing wealth and luck to his adopted family[373].

The myth carries on at great length and includes many of the myth motifs found in the Pacific and familiar in South America and includes references to one of the goddesses who was revered by the Gonds named Manko[374]. The basic motif of a woman, or women, assisting heroes is this Gond and other myths recorded here from India is closely similar to that of South America. Allowing for the adaptions and assimilation of motifs to other myths the Gond version is recognisable as the same across the various culture regions through which it was transferred and appears to have finally become embedded in the myths of South America. The many aspects of Gond culture appearing in South America suggests that they are among the peoples from India who reached South America before the Aryans who formed the Ayar Inca. As Carl Lumholtz noted among the Huichol in Western Mexico many aspects assimilated from other cultures and particularly from the Spanish after the Conquest were subjected to gender reversal to depotentiate them so as not to conflict in their own mind to assimilation among their existing traditions.

This principal is found throughout the world and is possibly the principle that applies to the Gond god named Manko, a female deity who appears to have reached the Peruvian coast after being transferred there from India and was adapted and assimilated from the Aymara or coastal Indians in South America. In a role reversal this name became associated from the beginning of the Inca ascendancy with leadership. It then appears, in the Incas' attempts to legitimise their own claim to inherited descent from the people in Tiahuanaco, that the term Manko had become sanctified with leadership but were still retained along with the assimilated Aryan titles of India. It has been earlier noted that the Vedic Aryan Brahmans into more recent times paid some deferment to the Gonds perhaps recognising in them so traces of their own people who had arrived earlier in India and therefore assimilated to a greater degree among the indigenous people in the Subcontinent.

12.067 : Seated statue of the Buddha as teacher, the possible prototype of similar imagery in the Pacific and Central America. Ratnagiri, Orissa, North East India, 8th., century, A.D.

12.068 : Seated deity probably derived in origin from Buddhist intrusive influences in Central America. East Antilles, West Indies, c800-1400 A.D.

12.069 : Seated female ancestress or deity with a child seated on a bench that almost certainly derives from ancient Buddhist influence. Ruviana, Solomon Islands, Melanesia, Pre-20th., century, A.D.

12.070 : Seated deity, priest or ruler similar to many known of the Buddha in Orissa in India. Rio Sumpul, Honduras/El Salvador border, 200 B.C. - 200 A.D.

Flood Hero with Female Counterpart Saved in a Box or Gourd

From the eastern forests of Peru, a western region of the Amazon Basin, a myth has been pre-served stating that the Flood hero was saved by climbing into gourd or calabash - a motif found in India and South East Asia. This Amazonian myth is recorded by Farrabee as follows: "A great feast was to be held, and two boys were sent away into the forest to get game. They made a camp under a tree, and went out to hunt. They secured much game, dressed it, and hung it up at the camp. The second day when they returned heavily laden with game, they were surprised to find that their first day's catch had been stolen. Then they returned on the third day, they again found the meat had been stolen. On the next day, one remained in hiding to discover the thief. He found it was a great snake that lived in the hollow of the tree under which they camped. To destroy the snake they built a fire in the tree, and the snake fell into the fire. The boys were hun-gry, and one of them ate some of the roasted flesh of the snake. He soon became thirsty, drank all of the water they had at the camp, then went to the spring, and from there to the lake. He was soon transformed into a frog, next into a lizard, and finally into a snake, which began to grow rapidly. His brother was frightened, and tried to pull him out of the water, but the lake began to overflow. The snake then told his brother that the lake would continue to grow until the whole world would be covered, and that the people would perish unless he returned and told them to make their escape."

"He told his brother to put a calabash in his pocket, to go on top of the highest mountain, and when the water came, climb the highest palm. The brother returned, and told his people what had happened, but they refused to believe him, accusing him of destroying his brother; so he fled to the mountain, and when the water came, climbed the palm tree. After many days the water began to subside, and he came down to the ground. From the top of the mountain he could see the vultures eating the dead people in the valley, so he went back to the lake where he found his brother, and carried him away in his calabash"[375].

This myth appears to follow those of the Cuna in Panama and those where either a ser-pent or tree bursts to cause the Flood, but includes a calabash as the container in which one of the survivors is installed. However, other versions note that the Flood Survivors are saved in it instead of an ark or canoe and this closely follows those found in Asia[376]. The calabash appears in closely paralleled versions where a box or coffin is the ark or gourd substitute. Several ver-sions of the Flood myth current immediately after the Conquest were recorded by Christoval de Molina and one Incan account of the Flood he notes as follows: "They say that all people and all created things perished in it, insomuch that the water rose above all the highest mountains of the world. No living things survived except a man and a woman who remained in a box, and when the waters subsided, the wind carried them to Huanaco (Tiahuanaco), which will be over seventy leagues (210 miles approx.) from Cuzco, a little more or less. The Creator of all things commanded them to remain there as mitimas; and there, in Tiahuanaco, the Creator began to raise up the people of all nations that are in the regions, making one of each nation of clay, and paint-ing the dresses that each one was to wear. ..."[377].

The term mitimas, or mitimaes, is an interesting term since it refers to settlers who were moved from one place another, often if they were considered antagonistic to the Incas and their imperialistic ambitions[378]. The term for an obligatory service among the Aymara was ayni, and in Quechua the equivalent was mit'a[379]. This form of service was imposed by the Inca and refers to the system in principle of obligatory requisition of labour for Public works in return for equal exchange of work or other payment. This appears to be related by extension to the term miti-maes since forced labour was termed mita[380] where whole settlements were established to under-take labour for either agriculture or civil works. Work was often paid for in cloth and this is exactly the same as the long established system in India. The heavier services such as construction and soldiering in term of military operations was entirely devolved upon the men and millions were drawn upon by the Incas in the establishment and construction of their Empire[381].

In Assam, the Apa Tanis call their deities ui a term probably at the root of the Polynesian term Maui, suggesting an early connection with them, and the term apa appears to be identical to the use of the term Apu among the Ancient Peruvians. The term for their dual organisation were mura and mite (mitay), a section of a migrant people, suggesting that these people may have been a group of mariners and or traders who travelled from Peru through the Pacific Islands to Assam. Perhaps an explanation of this term may derive from nearby Bengal where it was noted in the nineteenth century that domestic servants were usually called mehtar, a Persian (Iranian) word for "... a great personage, a prince, and has been applied to a class in question out of irony, or rather consolation. But the name has so completely adhered in this application, that all sense of either irony or consolation has perished"[382].

In returning to the Flood myths of South America Christoval de Molina recorded another account that has been utilised in more recent researchers as indicating a foreboding of doom in the history of Peru dating back about the 7th-8th., century, A.D.[383]. This version of the Flood myth was preserved from the province of Ancasmarca about fifteen miles from Cuzco: "They say that a month before the flood, came, their sheep (llamas) displayed much sadness, eating no food in the day-time, and watching the stars at night. At last the shepherd, who had charge of them, asked what ailed them, and they said that the conjunction of stars showed that the world would be destroyed by water. When he heard this, the shepherd consulted his six children, and went to go to the top of a very high mountain, called Ancasmarca. They say that as the waters rose, the hill grew higher, so that it was never covered by the flood; and when the waters subsided, the hill grew smaller. Thus, the six children of that shepherd returned to people the province"[384].

Dark Cloud Cosmology - Deities and Myth

In more recent decades the cosmology of the Incas and their forebears has gradually been of growing interest to scholars. There are a number of learned publications now available recording the sophisticated system of belief reconstructed from the available records, archaeology and the preserved remnants of the system still adhered to in the more isolated villages of Peru.

It is not necessary to repeat this research here but it is worthy of note that the fundamental aspects of the Inca's cosmological system have their parallels far beyond the South American shores. It is of particular interest that even some of the most conservative researchers have recorded that the most similar aspects of the so-called dark cloud constellation cosmology, fundamental to the Peruvian system, are found in Polynesia[385], Melanesia[386], Indonesia[387] and Aboriginal Australia[388]. This corresponds to other aspects of cultural and religious practices known on both side of the Pacific Ocean such as the mystical use and belief in crystals and general and specific practices in shamanism[389]. No attempt to go further than to mention such parallels is attempted or to show that one originated from the other or from a common origin, and this is true for other aspects of South America culture.

In Western cosmology the study of the night sky has developed toward a philosophical construct based on the disposition of the stars and their clusters in the darkened sky. This has been at the expense of considering the dark areas between those stars and their cluster forms, many of which have been linked together to form constellations, and from these star clusters imagery forming that of the Western zodiac has developed. Although the constellations known to the West appear to have been important in the considerations of Ancient Peru under different names and forming differently shaped constellations it was the "dark cloud" constellations, Yana Phuyu[390], that appear to have considerable equity in the system. It is these that will be considered briefly here. Yana is the term for dark or black in Ancient Peru and this term appears to be identical to that of the God of Death in India Yama, whose colour was black and identified with the South.

In the researches recorded by Gary Urton he notes that the dark cloud constellations, alongside star clusters, were noted equally by his Peruvian informant. Urton records that it was often difficult to determine whether it was the "dark cloud" itself, apparently empty to the naked eye, or the "dark cloud" and the adjacent stars, or the dark area and the surrounding stars defining its shape that constituted the native Peruvian constellation[391]. Urton also notes that definition in the Western sense is not entirely perceived in the same way as the Westerner, and that there was a "general disinclination" to point to any object that was considered sacred, including not only the stars and associated "dark clouds" but mountains and rainbows.

The dark cloud constellations described by the Peruvians, appear too similar to those recorded a century ago, and longer, in Aboriginal Australia, Africa and Java but also in the Ancient Near and Middle East not to be derived from the same origin. In terms of star clusters the Milky Way was named as Mayu in Peru[392], the serpent, identifying this star trail with the Amazon River. Similar references in the Amazon Basin and Gran Chaco identifying the Milky Way, the rainbow, and the giant serpent of the Amazon River[393] are found in Asia and Melanesia[394]. The Milky Way was perceived as a giant starry serpent, Mayu, probably developed from Amaru, the Amazon River and as the giant mythical serpent in the night sky that was believed to form an oceanic girdle around the Earth[395]. This same concept is to be found in the West Pacific Islands[396], Aboriginal Australia[397] and in India[398].

The stars generally were referred to as Papa or "father", but it was also common for them to be considered female or androgynous. The term papa is the name the Polynesians used throughout their islands for the Earth Mother. This is probably a role reversal common in cosmological aspects transferred from one culture to another and where Rangi was the sky father derived from India as an incarnation of the Sky god, Vishnu[399], from Indonesia also[400] and found among the Nagas of Assam[401]. The constellation of the Pleiades was of great importance in the agricultural calendar throughout South America, known as Qutu or pile[402], and also Central and North America. This agricultural identification with the Pleiades appears to reflect the same related focus by the Polynesians, where their name for the constellation, Matahiki[403] clearly derives from the Ancient Middle East where it was known as Makha-ili[404].

The earliest account of the Inca constellations is that recorded in 1571 A.D. by the Spanish Licenciate in Peru, Polo de Ondegardo. He describes several including llamas, a serpent, birds and felines[405] that have long puzzled those interested in the night sky. It was only when it was realised that the dark patches in the night sky were actually being included in the imagery that more recent investigations could progress. Because of the rotation of the Earth through the annual solar cycle the night sky appears to move in relation to the horizon and zenith in observation. These variations in the tilt of the Earth's axis revealed dark, and star constellations as they rose across the Andes differently and these appeared to correspond with the two major seasons in Peru - wet and dry. This meant that constellations in one part of the sky and their apparent specific relation to known points on the horizon, in this case the peaks of the Andes mountains, indicated rain so important for agricultural cycle commencing in the spring corresponding to the time for sowing in the soil. Humboldt, in the records of his famous journey to South America in the early 19th., century, also noted this determination from the night sky by the Indians for the appropriate time for sowing[406] and the Pleiades particularly was seen as important in this respect[407].

It is extraordinary, recorded through recent research, that the Ancient Peruvian belief was that the dark cloud constellations were caused by pieces of earth taken up by the Milky Way

12.071 : The so-called "elephant" stela at Copan showing two elephant heads and trunks at each corner in the Buddhist manner found at Sanchi. In this earliest photo the two mahouts are shown above the elephant heads. The ruler depicted is 18-rabbit and he wears a false beard typical of Ancient China. Stela B, Copan, Honduras, Early 8th., century, A.D.

12.073 : A finely carved relief scene of Buddhist city life in the late first millennium, B.C. Eleephants were prominent in symbolic display both in war and religious and state processions and were identified with the Aryan homeland of Airavata. Sanchi Torana, North Central India, 100 B.C. - 100 A.D.

12.074 : An elephant retained as a sacred symbol of the Hindu religion here adorned on it trunk with the symbol of the firepan and a flame in it - the sign of the Aryan Sky God, Vishnu. Kanchipuram, South India, 2001 A.D.

12.072 : The Hindu deity Gajamurti who tamed the elephant demon on whose head and trunk he dances - a reference to convey Hindu triumph over Buddhism. The Hindus also retained the Aryan imagery of their homeland Airavata as the elephant earlier recorded by the Buddhists. Dharasuram, South India, 8-11th., century, A.D.

at the place where it touched the horizon into the sky[408]. This appears to converge with recent astronomical research into dark matter in the universe and the disintegration of stars after the super-nova stage that provided the fuel for new stars to be. In the Peruvian concepts these dark patches appear to be regions that allow deities and heroes from beyond the star constellations to access the Earth and conversely for heroes and priests to gain access past what appear to be largely malevolent star deities to the world beyond and that forms part of the references in underlying the theme of Douglas Sharon's and Gary Urton's researches. A dark cloud constellation was also considered related to a specific clan or Ayllu[409].

In the Amazonian tribes in South America there are many references to holes in the sky through which deities descend, and often ascend later to their "homes" beyond the starry canopy. The sky vault is often perceived as a solid roof-like structure onto which are attached, or through which, the stars penetrate and glow as viewed from Earth. Many myths indicate that humankind at one time lived above this vault where this was one of several inhabited layers, levels, or spheres extending upward away from the Earth. These myths usually state that a hero dug a hole through this vault and saw the Earth below and descended by a rope to become the first person on the Earth and reference ino similar myths have been included earlier in this work. After this initial penetration it is usually indicated that other people also descended and the first people began to populate the Earth. However, this rope was later cut, or hauled up and mankind was isolated here since that time[410]. Virtually the identical myths occur in Central and North America

12.075 : The goddess Gadja-Laksmi - Gaja = elephant, Lakshmi = wife of Sky God Vishnu, being lustrated by two elephant deities with holy water flowing from the Kalasa, or bowl, with two upturned vessels that were used to convey the sacred Water-of-Life to the shrine of the goddess. The upturned bowls probably represent the sacred mountain of Siva, Kalaisa, from the which the Ganges was believed to flow and the four elephants represent that cardinal points. The Goddess is identified with the Earth Goddess, Adya-Sakti (2.037), also known as Padmamunda (Padma = lotus), and this Gadjalaksmi is shown with a poll of lotuses in the foreground. Note the parasol representing the World Axis above the bowl. Cave 16, Elora, West Central India, 8th., century, A.D.

12.076 : A clay bowl with two hemispherical objects modelled integrally into the upper surface. The shapes of the objects might suggest traditional maize bread called wah but ecause they are intended here to integrate with the plate surface it is more likely to represent smaller ritual upturned vessels. It has been noted earlier that the there is a vessel from the same region that appears to be intended as part of Soma rituals identical to Ancient India (*9.152*). It is likely therefore that this ritual platter is meant for lustration in the same manner as that depicted in the imagery shown in the cave at Elora (*12.075*) and that the objects in the vessel are intended to represent Mt. Kailas in a transferred and assimilated version in Central America. Chalchuapa, El Salvador, Late-Post Classic.

and through the Pacific Islands to Asia (*11.048*).

Reflections of many aspects of Peruvian culture are to be found in the Marquesas Islands. The basic principle of a cosmology, including the concept of holes in the sky, is also found here where the levels above the earth composing the sky were believed to be three. Each of these levels was designated under the control of a god who headed an order of gods associated with each level. Throughout Polynesia the sacred ceremonial hut or temple was constructed as a microcosm of the cosmological precepts of the sky vault and the deities who ruled them and these have been recorded in detail in the works or Sir Arthur Grimble and Kjell Akerblom.

Dark patches, or holes, were seen as apertures through which heroes or those of high status passed though after death or the inspirational priest could pass in trance in a spirit body during life to communicate with the ancestors and deities who dwelt above the sky vault. In the Marquesas Islands, the fundamental cosmological concept appears closely related to that of Peru, albeit simplified, and includes the symbols of pieces of wood representing the deities of the three sky levels in the temple that was called papa and the Creator name was Tiki[411]. In these myths trees are said to be the food of the dead and as the World Axis were common in South America. The name given for the Earth Mother was Pachamama, and the Inner World, or "heart of the earth" in Peru was also the Polynesian term for the Earth goddess, Papa, probably an abbreviation of the Peruvian term and may have derived from there.

The fundamental cosmological symbols within the Marquesan temple (fae'e takau), where there was a shrine (ananuu) to these deities were noted by Craighill Handy in the early twentieth century, recorded by him as follows: "There were no images of any kind. Three pieces of wood spoken of as papa (plank or board), one apparently resting on the ananuu, the second midway up in the interior, were suspended or attached to the sides, and a third was hung beneath the ridge of the roof. On each of these, after writing had been introduced, the following legend was inscribed with the burnt end of a fau stick: 'Te ani puta is Fau' (The sky hole of Fai). Before the introduction of writing had been introduced, a symbol standing for the same thing was used. It consisted of four designs (tiki) named tava enclosing an open space in the middle representing a cave - the sky hole of Fai - from which the sky god Fai was supposed to have brought fire"[412]. Other fragmentary myths record that Fai sought fire in a cave or hole on the top of the mountains.

The association of fire with the Sun has been noted repeatedly in this work and this reference of its association with the cave is reminiscent of the emergence of the four brothers or Sons of the Sun from the cave in the Inca myths and legends. It is interesting to note that when the sacred house for the inspirational priest and a new shrine had been constructed a rite was followed which included a group of warriors approaching and hurling their spears at the crests and religious ornamentation said to test the strength of the construction and when it was the house of the priest he sat at the front of the building while this rite was being enacted. It is thought that this was a symbolic test of the priest's power and the chief of these warriors and sea captain was termed ariki. In the Gran Chaco the Toba Indians they feared a deity called Kalo-araik[413], and this appears to derive from the terms Kal for deity or stone in India, and Arik meaning a hero leader or headman or ancestral deity in Polynesia. The Toba terms for deities and demons along with other Indians in the region was Aittah[414], clearly derived from the Aitu or lesser deities in Polynesia. Tattooing was common among the Toda men[415], but women included face tattoos as in South East Asia, and the Toba maintained professional warriors unlike other tribes of the region[416].

The concept of fire being obtained from a cave accessed through a hole in the sky has its parallel among the Maori where the Sun is described as whanga-matata or "heaven-opening"[417] and their concept also reflects the idea of a series of planes above the sky vault where in the lowest level the Sun moved across the sky. In the red centre of Australia, the Aboriginal tribe known as the Wingara retained a myth centred on the mythical snake known as Bolibi-Bolibi and in an excerpt it is said in an oral tradition that two boys using the rib of a snake as a boomerang that created a hole in the sky[418]. Spencer and Gillan who recorded this myth notes the similarity to those in the Pelew Islands in Micronesia. The Kaitish tribe preserve in their oral traditions that their sky deity Atnatu went up to the sky a very long time ago in the Alcheringa, or the mythical times. It is said that he has another sky and another Sun beyond the place where he now lives. Even before the Alcheringa, the far distant past, he had many sons and daughters, but because they did not treat him with due respect he created a hole in the sky and threw then down onto the Earth. He gave them everything they needed to live on the Earth including boomerangs, spears, clubs, etc.[419]. The term Alcheringa, the "dreamtime" of the ancestral spirits, is interesting since the term for the ancestral spirits in Peru was Achachilas and suggests that there may be a common origin and notable along with other possible cross-cultural transfers earlier in this work.

The Australian Aboriginal Kamilaroi believed that the spirit of a man after death ascended to Maianba, a dark patch in the Magellanic Clouds clearly seen in the night sky in Australia[420]. Maianba have been seen in an earlier chapter to have a common origin with Baiame, and in turn this name of a culture-bearing hero appears to derive from Buddha according to some, or Brahma, or a confusion of both. In South Australia the Yerkal-Mining people adhered to strict circumcision rites during a boy's initiation and contemporary accounts were recorded as follows: "If a boy is of the Wenung division (Yerkla-Mining) he is circumcised in the morning. Boys of the other classes are not, and they are left tied on the ground till the Milky Way is seen in the sky. Then the lad is asked, 'Can you see the black spots?' When he has seen them, he is allowed to go to his camp; and then the medicine men tell him the following legend. A very long time ago a great bird came and devoured all the people, excepting three men and one woman. The men fought the bird and killed it; but after it was dead, only two spears were found in the body, one belonging to the Kura, and one belonging to the Wenung man. Then they went up to the Milky Way, and the name given to the two black spots, to which they went, is Nug-Jil-Bidai-Tukuba, or the 'far-away-men'. ..."[421]. Other tribes believe that it is through a hole in the sky that Bunjil, a deity earlier noted, was reached by ghosts or medicine men from whom they received their magical powers[422].

It appears that these black spots derived from some contact with more complete cosmologies from Asia in contact with Aboriginal Australia without transference of the whole of the related philosophic constructs. Some of these aspects lack the dark patches or "spots" but are similar in reflecting the holes as the burrow of an armadillo or those of the roots of the tree in the sky as so frequently noted in the Amazonian Myths. Among the Punans of Borneo it was recorded that they believed the stars were seen from below as small holes in the floor of another, brighter world. These holes were said to have been the result of roots of plants that had penetrated the ground of that world[423]. This concept is virtually identical with the motifs in many myths in the Amazon Basin and Gran Chaco in South America[424].

In Ancient China the symbol of heaven was the lie-chhiu, a circular plate with a hole on the centre through which the lightning flashed[425]. The hole in the Sky, in some myths singular and in others plural, is universal in the myths of Melanesia and in many of them a hole allows those from the world above either to look down or to descend by a rope from above, or a tree that had grown up from the Earth, so closely similar to those of South America[426]. These motifs appear to be reflected in the myths of the Nagas of Assam[427] and in some of the Aboriginal myths in Australia and India. Similar related myths are also found in Tibet[428] but these appear to have originated in the myth cycles of Ancient Iran[429] and then disseminated into India and through into the Pacific to South America.

As with so many other aspects of transference of culture into India and the Pacific it is in the references from the early fire religions of Iran that holes in the sky are found. It was believed, and recorded in the contemporary texts, that the demons associated with Ahriman, the dark twin of the god of light Orhmazd, attempted to "swallow" the agents and angels of the lighter twin[430]. The gaping mouth of the demon Az, was said to be that of a hole in the sky and it is probably from this myth that many of the dispersed versions, albeit largely misunderstood, derive. The narrative, preserved in its later corrupted versions, is remarkable for its symbolic references that can be read as being remarkably similar to the present day, scientifically based cosmological theories indicating that one constellation can collide and "swallow" another.

The abundance on myths related to sky heroes and demons characteristically involving ropes descending from a hole in the sky, or other motifs, are found from Asia through the Pacific Islands and throughout the Americas are so common to all that it is impossible to include more than the few already noted here. It is clear, however, that many of these are so specific that these must have had a common origin in Asia and that, although these are in some places only fragments of a much more complete religious and myth cycles, they could only have been disseminated by mariners, traders and missionaries from the Ancient cultures of India, the Ancient West of Asia and China.

Clearing Up Some of the Loose Ends in Myth, Imagery and Iconography

The mariners as an occupational group have long been considered the most superstitious of men. Undoubtedly this is as a result of so large a part of their lives being subject to the threat of annihilation through storms, hurricanes and high winds that constantly threaten their lives and frequently for extended periods of time. These ever present threats, along with the constant danger of shipwreck and being cast upon the shores, if they survive, from hostile peoples undoubtedly exacerbated their perceived dependence upon their gods on who they believed their survival depended. The elephant as a deity would not appear to be the first totemic or icon that might come to mind to be associated with mariners and ocean travel. Although an elephant that is well able to swim, in its own way, it is usually associated with land-based symbolism, unlike crocodiles, dolphins, sharks, turtles, and fish in general, and birds that are perceived as assisting with the winds to fill the sails of ocean-going sailors. When reaching a distant foreign land an elephant, therefore, would seem an unlikely deity to be held up in veneration and gratitude by the mariners on stepping onto that foreign shore.

Mariners and the Elephant Gods, from Ganesa to Vighnesvara

It is in the iconography of the land of origin of these mariners, in whole or part, that the answer lays. The elephant appears clearly, even the casual observer, to have been the subject in part carved on one of the surviving Mayan stela of Copan, illustrated in a previous work[431]. Other elephant iconography is found at Palenque, but now lost (*11.029*) and also in a vase from Yalloch in Guatemala (*6.109*). The so-called "Long Nosed God" - God N[432], is also a representation of an elephant of a form found more frequently in Indonesia but also in the Chalukyan Empire in Southern India[433]. It is clear that the elephant as a deity must have been of considerable importance in the belief system of those who preserved their memory so far from home and in a land that had no comparable animal to utilise as an iconographical substitute. To include the imagery of an elephant in the temples built or influenced in their new homes in the Americas by mariner peoples, traders or missionaries must therefore indicate its importance as a mariner god.

Indra, noted above, is the Vedic deity par excellence that the Aryans brought with them from Anatolia and eventually, perhaps over centuries, through Iran into India. When they reached India the horse was considered the finest mount of the gods and related imagery still survives in the iconography of the Sun god Surya usually seen astride, or carried by horse (*9.158*). However, in time, the horse was superseded by the elephant for the greatest deities, Indra among

12.077 : Back views are found characteristically from the earliest Buddhist period in North West India. Gandhara, Kushan, 100-300 A.D.

12.078 : Finely carved rear view of a deity showing Hellenistc influence from Bactria. Amaravati, Godavari Delta, South East India, 3rd., century, A.D.

12.079 : Remarkable and very rare rear-view depiction of the lower of the two ballplayers on a Mayan ceramic vase. Both figures appear to emulate the characteristic Buddhist depictions so widely found in India. The rear view of the lower figure appears to be closely followed in the Yalloch vase (*6.109*). Maya, Guatemala, Late Classic, 600-900 A.D.

them. Indra is most frequently said, and depicted, seated on his elephant mount named Airavata (*7.087*). Airavata is the name given to the former ancestral homeland of the Aryas, or Aryans, reflected in the name. The elephant as Airavata is said to be the chief of the Suras - "gods", and Indra was their master[434]. In the early Iranian derived imagery the divine cow was seen as the body of the universe, perhaps influenced from Ancient Egypt, or from a common origin with it, and although this mythical element was still retained in later Hinduism in India in the elephant became more identified with that concept, especially so in Buddhism.

In the conventional and more popular interpretation of the Vedas through later Hinduism that developed from Brahmanism the elephant was identified with Siva that was reflected in the anthropomorphic symbolism of Ganesa, Ganapati or Gajadhipa. In the most famous myth associated with this elephant god it is said that Siva's wife, Parvati, concerned that she had no guard for her door rubbed the "scurf" from her skin and from this her son named Ganapai was born who she installed as her door guardian. Siva required entrance to Parvati's bedroom but was denied access by Ganapati and Siva retaliated by having his head cut off. Parvati was consumed with grief, so much so that Siva relented and ordered that the head of the first living being to approach should be cut off and placed on the body of Ganapati to bring him back to life and this first being was an elephant[435]. Siva and Parvati resided in the great, and sacred "pleasure palace" of Kailasa of note in an earlier chapter. Beside this intimate association of the elephant with Kailasa located in the Himalayas Indra is also believed to reside there and both these elements have their close parallels with the Kalasaya and Akapana and the myths surrounding and associated with Tiahuanaco that have been of note in this work.

For the Hindus the name for the elephant deity is gaja, and Ganapati meaning "lord-of-categories" referring to all distinctions in the elements of creation[436] and this is usually also the interpretation given to the more usual term for this deity, Ganesh or Ganesa. He is also called Gajanana, "elephant-faced"; Gajadhipa, "Lord-of-Elephants"; Vinayaka, "Great Leader" - earlier noted as possibly connected to the emerald trade, and of particular interest, Vighnesvara, "Lord-of-Obstacles"[437].

In several of the ancient texts Ganapati is elevated above the trinity, or trimurti, and it is of interest to note that there appeared to be trinities relating the high gods in both the religious beliefs systems of the Aymaras and the Incas. Ganapati is especially associated with the higher attributes of the scribe, usually identified with the monkey god Hanuman as among the Maya, and was said to have written down the sacred texts and he is identified therefore with the great teacher of the gods - Brihaspati, Great-Lord. Ganapati or Ganesa was above all considered a god of good luck and would therefore have been associated with any undertaking where this was necessary such as sea trade or travel.

In this, it is believed in Hinduism that before any undertaking is initiated it is Ganesa that should first be worshipped. He is associated in this aspect with the identification of microcosm and macrocosm, and therefore with the steps of the venture planned and where each stage should be regaled with luck and spiritual approval, that is the fundamental principle of sympathetic magic is unfolded in ritualised steps at the altar or shrine[438]. Over doors and at the entrances to towns and city his images are to be found, and frequently in the present day on the dashboard of buses and cars or any vehicle undertaking long journeys.

As Vighnesvara, Lord of Obstacles, he is perceived as the deity who is to be invoked to remove obstacles and difficulties that might be known or reputed to lie ahead on a journey. It will be recalled that in the Kula in Melanesia special rituals and propitiations were undertaken before and during the voyage including those relating to Beauty Magic before reaching the destination. In the surrounding islands there are many references to "big-eared" gods and these appear to have derived from the elephant of India earlier noted, and it is likely that, originally the those relating these rituals and ceremonials of the Kula in the early 20th., century, were referring to dim memories of rites imported anciently from India.

In removing obstacles, and this would most certainly have applied to the Kula, it is specifically stated in the Ganapati Upanishad that he was the "... embodiment of the giver of gifts who destroys obstacles"[439]. Taken literally it is clear that this presentation of gifts was anciently, as it has been in more recent times in establishing links with remote tribes in New Guinea and the Amazon Basin, the means to ally fears and to deflect possible hostile reaction and is no doubt the intent that has been perverted illustrated in the Chama vases of the Maya (*1.025/6; 6.116*).

In Tantric Buddhism the fierce deity Mahakala, whose reflective image appears on the coast of Ecuador and Peru (*9.064*), is depicted trampling the elephant-headed demon as Vinataku (*9.044*). It is of special note that in his cosmic aspect Ganesa is associated with the Milky Way[440] and therefore not only the luck necessary to undertake voyages but the necessary mariner skills. This would be seen as a particular reason to have held this elephant deity in the greatest esteem and to be given precedence for due reverence. Clearly these references to Ganesa or Gapanapti must have been transferred by mariners from India to the New World but must have soon abated in importance since there were no animals with which his imagery and associated myths could be identified, unlike that of the lion or tiger that could be transferred to the Jaguar.

In Mayan iconography, particularly at Copan, incorporating the elephant are clearly seen to this day, but only because the site declined rapidly and fell into ruins not long after this imagery was imported, and therefore remained unaltered into the present day decaying only through natural exposure. The Meriah Sacrifice rites, earlier noted, included elephant images where the tusks were an essential element in securing the sacrificial victim, and this sacrifice finds echoes in the Antisuyu division of the Inca Empire.

It is interesting to note that there are carvings and, or myths in Melanesia and South America depicting a single tooth, or one only in the upper and lower jaws, and in the myths associated with Ganapati one of his curious aspects was that he was said to be single tusked[441]. Although less often depicted as such this may also have some reference to such images in South America (*4.086-8*) and possible linked in origin with the mountain deity among the Mapuche called Pillan, who was said in some myths to be large-eared. The Tamils of South India anciently named the elephant deity, Pillai or Pillaiyar[442], and it has already been noted that this elephant-headed deity as Ganesa was associated with the Himalayas, therefore possibly preserving elements of this deity from early Peru when they had otherwise disappeared and been assimilated. The great popularity of this god from early Hinduism to the present day and his attributes as the "hand allaying fear" that indicates that Ganapati was "beyond the realm of time, of death, to which all fear pertains" indicates that this god and his associations with the mariner's prime navigation map, the Milky Way, were of great importance for mariners setting out from India for their destination the Americas.

The Silent Witness of the Elephant Vase from Yalloch in Guatemala

In the researches published by the Smithsonian Institute, Bulletin 64, resulting from an expedition into the forests of Belize and Guatemala at the beginning of the 20th., century, many interesting objects (*11.018*) that appear to relate to South America (*11.019*), Indonesian (*11.020*) and Asian figurines (*11.021*) and iconography were illustrated. Among the few colour illustrations were the two opposite sides of a cylindrical vase from Yalloch in Guatemala. The figures represented are two aspects of the same god, deity, or demon that are described as the "Long-nosed God", or God B in the Schellhas classification of Central American figure representations. Schellhas also identifies this god with Quetzalcoatl of the Ancient Mexicans or Kulkulcan of the Mayans. In earlier works by the present author Quetzalcoatl has been identified with the mariner gods of the Pacific[443].

The less perfect manufacture and technical skill of the ceramicist and artist indicates a late date from the highly prized Classic to Late Classic vessels dating this vase to the 9-10th., century, A.D. But of special importance are the depictions elevating this vase in historical importance above many of those more perfectly finished from the earlier periods. Both figures are clearly of the same animal or mythical figure but there are important differences that are also crucial to their relevance to the present work.

The snout of the Long-nosed God, or God B, depicted here is clearly far longer than others so depicted and is clearly a trunk in both figures on either side of this same vessel. The left hand figure (*6.109*) clearly depicts the legs and feet of an elephant, and not badly so considering the artist was probably recording a verbal description by an eyewitness who had voyaged from South or South East Asia. The front legs are treated indistinctly as arms repeating those of the back legs, and this is true also for the other representation on the other side of the vessel. Projecting from behind these leg-shaped arms in both illustrations is a crook-like instrument, coloured white at the extremity, and this appears to be the near identical form of the hook-shaped elephant goad used anciently through into the present day in India and South East Asia. Both correctly record the dark grey colouring of the elephant and a good representation of the body generally, albeit a little longer than in life is the depiction of the tail. Characteristic of Mayan figurative illustrations the artist has attempted to include all the elements of the elephant as described to him and this has ended in distortion but clearly it was conveyed to him that the god was both an animal, and an animal-headed deity and he has attempted to depict both aspects on either side of this vessel.

The left hand illustration attempts to show the elephant as the animal while the right hand depicts him as the anthropomorphic god since the lower half provides him with the necessary human legs. Of special interest, however, is the fact that these legs are not only meant to be human but are seem from the rear as if taken from the human figure viewed from the back. Virtually all Mayan figurative art depicts the human form from the front, occasionally from the side, and in depicting the rear legs of this animal figure on the Yalloch vase from the rear indicates that there was a special reason for varying from the norm. Rear figurative views are almost non-existent in Mayan illustrations and one of a very few known is that depicted on a Late Classic vase depicting ball-players (*12.077*) in a less conventional manner suggesting outside influence from a tradition that had a long figurative art in the round - that is from all sides. There are only two almost identical of the figures shown on this ballplayer vase that are viewed from the rear view and, although somewhat awkward, clearly indicate their disposition as depicted imparting that this aspect to be intentionally important. The lower figure illustrated shows his left arm bent in a way that is clearly meant to indicate a rear view and this is coupled with the line of the underscoring of the right buttock centrally covered by his ceremonial kilt of this lower figure. Of particular interest is the rear view of the legs and feet since they are clearly indicated to be the rear view with the calf below the knee, the Achilles tendon, heel and foot depicted naturally and almost so completely identical to that of the elephant that it might almost be said that the earlier Classic vase was used as a model for the latter elephantine form.

It has been attested in an earlier work, and in this volume, that there had been cultural and iconographic transfer to Central America, the Maya in particular, at Palenque and Copan from India and that this was particularly so in references to Buddhist imagery. Buddhist imagery is singularly rich in figurative carvings in groups, large and small, and often occurs in supporting panels to the focal point of a roundel or frieze. Many of the finest and most numerous examples of rear view figurative art are found from the East Coast site of Amaravati in India and it is known that the Buddhists in this region and along the coast both north and South of this delta were long involved in the sea trade with China, South East Asian and Indonesia in particular. The tradition of the rear figurative aspects were then, and still remained a feature in India after the decline of Buddhism and is frequently found in the depictions of Ravanna. This demon king of Sri Lanka was said in myths to hold up the sacred mountain of Kailasa after his submission to Siva (*7.092*), but not in the illustration included in this work since other rear views from India are shown (*12.078/9*), an appropriate reference considering the earlier chapters in this work. It is clear therefore that the imagery on the Yalloch vase represents the elephant, probably in its own terms; as the demon mount, Matangi, of the fierce goddesses of India - Durga and the smallpox goddess, Sitala; and as the anthropomorphic elephant-headed god Ganesa of such note in the foregoing in this chapter; all aspects that must have been imported, with the remarkably accurate iconography under the circumstances, from India.

The Indi Bird of the Incas and the Ark of the Covenant
In the final consideration of aspects recorded in the Inca Origin myths there is an item recorded as a "fetish" that Manco Capac and his descendant, Mayta Capac, retained, consulted and was especially associated, it seems, with the Inca's own perceived right to rule. Significantly this is recorded only in the version in Sarmiento de Gamboa's record that he obtained through his privileged access to Inca tradition since, as earlier noted, he married a first rank Inca princess. Sarmiento's version is noted as follows in Sir Clement Markam's translation; "This Mayta Ccapac was warlike, and the Inca who first distinguished himself in arms after the time of Mama Huaco and Manco Ccapac. They relate of him that he dared to open the hamper containing the bird - Indi. This bird, brought by Manco Ccapac from Tampu-toco, had been inherited by his successors, the predecessors of Mayta Ccapac, who had always kept it shut up in a hamper or box of straw, such was the fear they had of it. But Mayta Ccapac was bolder than any of them. Desirous of seeing what his predecessors had guarded so carefully, he opened the hamper, saw the bird Indi, and had some conversation with it. They say that it gave him oracles, and after the interview with the bird he was wiser, and knew better what he should do, and what would happen."[444].

Miles Poindexter drew parallels between this bird in a hamper with the Ark of the Covenant[445], and extended these to parallels between Asian and South American traditions. In this he may be right, but the image is perhaps equally reminiscent of the Henu boat of Memphis in Ancient Egypt that was dragged around the temple before the rising of the morning Sun. This was a sled representing the solar boat that had a miniature shrine constructed on it, and surmounting this shrine was the image of the hawk god, Horus, a symbol of the Sun at dawn. There are many images of this sledge or "boat" that have survived in the papyri that make up the Egyptian Book of the Dead. It must also be remembered that in an earlier chapter it was noted that the Morioris, the first Polynesians in New Zealand predating the Maoris by some centuries, considered themselves Tchaps, "sacred chaps"[446], or the descendants of the revered ancestors known as the Tchakat Hennu[447]. The Sun and the idea of the solar boat was strong among all the Polynesian peoples and led to speculation a century ago that the "Solar" religions of Egypt and the Ancient Middle East had diffused into the Pacific. This was supported by the fact that the Polynesian terms anciently for the Sun and Moon was Ra and Sin respectively, identical to the name of the Sun in Egypt and the Moon in Mesopotamia and Coastal Peru. It was recorded by Victorian researchers who settled among the last of the Morioris in the Chatham Islands, east off New Zealand's main islands that the reed boats used by them were identical to those found on Lake Titicaca in Bolivia[448], and it might be said those further west in Tasmania also. It was also noted that another racial type completely different in physical stature and appearance was evident among them and was termed "Aztec" by the Victorians[449]. In fact, due to the many aspects of

12.080 : Incised head with disgorging motif believed to be blood after decapitation, possibly reflected in other cultures by the projecting tongue. Cerro Sechin, Casma Valley, Central Coast Peru, Late second millennium, B.C.

12.081 : Fine, four-times natural size "Caucasian" heads with characteristic gaping mouth. Santa Lucia Cotzumalguapa, West Coast Guatemala, 400-700 A.D.

12.082 : Characteristic votive head with gaping mouth found widely in Peru, Mexico and Central America. Sipan, Moche Culture, North Coast Peru, 200-300 A.D.

12.083 : Incised graffiti showing an anthropomorphic figure with protruding tongue - an element of iconography found throughout the Americas, the Pacific Islands and Asia. Tikal, Mid-Classic Period, 400-700 A.D.

culture that connect the Polynesians, and the Morioris and Maoris in particular with South America it is more likely that this section of Moriori people were from Bolivia or Peru since there is a direct ocean current connecting the Peruvian Coast with New Zealand. Common also among the Morioris and Maoris were burial boxes known as hakana[450], more similar to reliquaries and this may have been the type referred to as "hamper" in the Inca myth.

It must also be remembered that birds' migration routes were an essential prognostic tool in their ocean-going voyages and the elevated image of this vital aspect for survival led to the deification of such migrating species of bird and of the eagle or hawk in particular. If the Morioris were the very distant Egyptian venturers into the Pacific then their identification with the eastern Sun would be understandable since this was the direction they used in sailing for the Pacific, that is into the sunrise. The Egyptians would not have missed such synchronistic symbolism and therefore a bird shrine pulled by a boat, the Henu sledge, is likely to have been appropriated to their cause. It may have been through their sea-going enterprises, probably as traders, that cocaine was transferred back from South America to Egypt where this plant is only known in that part of the world, and found in mummy bindings from the early first millennium B.C. If the Morioris were in fact early Egyptian traders, as the Tchakat Hennu, then this would correspond with the sudden radical, social, cultural and metallurgical changes that took place in Peru at that time and ultimately the foundation of Tiahuanaco from whom the Inca's claimed direct descent and assumed their right to rule. It would also explain why a bird image was of such importance since the original Sun deity was identified with the canoe, the direction the mariners sailed to reach South America, but also that bird migration routes were used to safely navigate to the shores of Ecuador, Peru or Bolivia.

In considering the possible Moriori's associations with Egypt it might be mentioned that the term Tchatcha meant "chief" or "head"[451] and was specifically used in Egypt to refer to the four aspects of Osiris (the dying Sun), usually identified with the canopus jars, or shawabtis. It is unlikely that the Morioris could have accidentally retained for themselves names or titles that

12.084 : Seated fanged deity with protruding tongue typical of Polynesian imagery. Remojadas Culture, Veracruz, East Coast Mexico, Mid- first century, A.D.

12.085 : Traditional greeting from two Tibetans by protruding the tongue as a sign of respect. Tibet, Early 20th., century, A.D.

have an identical interpretation in Ancient Egypt such as Tchakat Hennu that can literally be translated as the "Four Chiefs of the Hennu Sun Boat". It is likely that this had some allusion relating to these Moriori mariners as those who following the rising Sun to the four corners of the Earth. It is also recorded that the Morioris constructed miniature boats and set them sailing into the rising Sun[452] and earlier in this work it is noted that the Chinchorros on the North Chilean coast also placed miniature boats with sails in the graves of their ancestors.

There is a long period of development between the possibility of Egyptian traders reaching South America, most likely in the first millennium B.C., and the Incas and in this intermediate period there can be little doubt that it was from the Ancient Middle East and India that the majority of advanced foreign influences originated. There are several aspects that are of interest in this Indi bird "fetish", as reported by Sarmiento, so worthy of consideration, that were probably introduced during one of these periods of major change. These extend beyond revering a mariner origin in the obvious symbol of the Sun eagle, or hawk, and these are indicated particularly through the term Indi and other associations.

Indi is unlikely to actually derive from India since there was no such place by that name until the British Colonial period but there are several references that indicate that the contemporary culture of India was involved. In Maori myth, and also in the Moriori myths, it is from the ancestral lands of Irihia (Maori) and Irea that they claim their calendar was derived and that the year was calculated from the rising of a star[453]. This is a well known aspect in the early Vedic, Hindu, Buddhist and Jain calendars but also noted more famously in the rising of Sirius in the constructs of the Egyptians. Irea, as for Iriha is almost certainly India or the ancient land of the Aryans, Iran, the near identical terms being found in both of these regions in Asia and the probable origin of the Inca title - Ayar. It may also be that Inca is itself a corruption of Irihia or Irea. In Ancient Peru it has been noted that the three chief gods of the Incas are all Sun deities but also encompass the storm and lightning gods so well- known as well as in Bolivia among the Aymara. The serpent has also been seen to be identified with lightning because of the serpentine form of its strike corresponding to representations in Ancient South America, India and West Asia. Among the Moriories, in supporting the common origin of their Moriroi myths and those of the Maori from India, is has been seen by Victorian researchers that the eel-form of gods among the Moriori were particularly of the type associated with the Vedic storm god in India - Indra[454]. It is most likely that the Indi bird derives its origin and name from this deity.

However, in later myths in India, in Hinduism developed from Vedic Brahmanism, Indra deity faded from the first rank of gods but the importance of the bird in Inca myth appears to have some associations with this deity in India and particularly with especially sacred aspects of the fire-altar, that are of such importance in India and Ancient Peru. In the oldest of the Vedic texts, the Satapatha Brahmana, Indra is described as the "... talon-slaying eagle, the king of the birds"[455]. It is of particular note in this text that his "vital power" is described as Virya (virile power), an abbreviation of Indriya (virile power identified specifically with Indra)[456], and from this phallic reference the Indi bird of the Incas may have derived its name. This would be particularly appropriate for a warrior Inca such as Mayta Ccapac so that the name is likely to be remembered in these terms. Few other references occur in the myths and legends of the Incas to the Indi bird except in the legend associated with the reign of Viracocha Inca and his son, the great Pachacuti, where it again figures but there is little to indicate its exact nature.

In certain of the Inca origin myths Viracocha is termed Imay Viracocha, linking to Iamy Pachacamac on the Peruvian coast[457], and this might also be a derivation from Indra and relating to the storm god in the Andes considered with other Viracocha references in an earlier chapter. Viracocha's son, Imaymana Viracocha[458] appears also to carry something of this title as an extension to a highland origin.

In early Wankarani carvings the puma type griffon, so similar to that of the Ancient Assyrians, is found on the Bolivian Plateau near Lake Titicaca (*7.012*). This griffon form is also repeated in the Spiro Mounds iconography dating to a millennia later in North Eastern United States. The griffon is adapted in later iconography from the Mesopotamian Zu bird in Iran to become the Simburgh, and from this the Garutman, later the Garuda evolved. Interestingly, in some of the ancient Vedic texts, the griffon-bird is described as a bat, and this was a favoured symbol among the Mayans and Mexicans of Central America[459], but in others it is separate and probably is represented as a type of lion-bird[460]. The lion-bird is the Saena that became the Sinamru, Simburgh or prototype Garutman or Garuda and is particularly associated with the tree of seeds called the Jad-besh. Here he is identified with Rashnu Razista, the "Genius of Truth" that dwells in a tree in the "middle of the sea" called Vouru-Kasha[461]. It so often occurs, as here, that many sacred or revered places are reached only by mariners in some isolated place over the sea, suggesting sea-borne ventures from the earliest times.

In other texts there are two falcons identified with the griffon bird called Amru and Kamru[462] appearing to parallel similar myths noted earlier among the Gonds in India. Another Pahlevi textual reference from Iran notes that the griffon bird builds its nest in the many-seeded tree to guard it and the Kinamros bird alights in the tree after the griffon birds has broken off the twigs to release the seed. This bird then collects the seed to scatter it across the land and this is followed by the Tistar (Sirius) that collects the seed to water it. The Kinamros bird is second highest in rank of the birds and was said to defend the land of the Aryas from invasion by picking up hostile regions and disposing of them like grains of corn[463]. In Buddhist myths, and also absorbed into Hindu and Jain myths, the Kinnara, clearly derived from the Kinamros, were bird deities closely similar to the Garuda and this Iranian deity would seem to bring the appropriate military qualities to identify and merge with Indra's eagle as the Indi bird of the Inca.

In Peru, if there were several suitable models for a totemistic icon that could readily be adopted by a clan - the harpy eagle and the condor must have been considered worthy contenders. In Iran also the vulture was an important deity and that called Verethraghna was said to have been revered, having been created by Ahura[464], a deity, or group of deities who became demonised in Vedic India hence not transferred in their original form by the Aryans. The deity is said to have worn a golden collar and is likely to have had its qualities absorbed in the imagery of Garuda in India. In the same Pahlevi book there are references to the same golden vulture but in a section associated with him it is stated that Zarathustra's wife, the sage of Zoroastrianism, begs for the "good narcotic", bang, or marihuana, so that the soul may ascend to heaven[465]. This episode is reminiscent of the use of narcotics by the mariners of the Ancient Middle East, India and others in suppressing hunger and thirst on long sea voyages and frequently depicted as quids in the

12.086: Gold dish with a central image of Simburgh - the lion-eagle, that appears to have been the prototype for the Vedic and Hindu Garuda. Late Sassanid, Iran, 6-7th., century, A.D.

12.087 : A finely crafted beaten gold plaque in the form of an eagle similar to others that have been retrieved from excavations. They appear to reflect closely the winged deities known in the Ancient Middle East for millennia. Late Huari, Chancay, Central Peru, c1100 A.D.

12.088 : Silver vase dedicated to the deity Nin-girsu depicting the eagle in flight - a potent symbol for all Mesopotamian and Iranain peoples and transferred by the Aryans into India and probably later identified with the Indi bird of the Incas. Babylonia, c2nd., millennium, B.C.

12.089 : The eagle mascot adopted by the Ancient Iranians is shown accompanying the warrior chariot to war. This became the Simburgh (*12.082*) and was later assimilated into Vedic India as the Garuda. This is the likely origin of the Indi bird in Inca Peru. Nimrud, Assyrian Period, 900-700 B.C.

cheeks of many South American ceramic figures.

It has been noted elsewhere in this work that the earliest forms of sacrificial fire altar in Central Asia were modelled on the finest of the five acceptable sacrificial animals - the male human warrior, and textual references were still retained in the Vedas after the Aryans entered India. In other references the eagle as Garutman, later Garuda, was the model for one of the fire altars and in the Artharva-Veda the associated ritual involved eating "milk-porridge" made on the fire built up of bird's nests[466].

The bird shaped fire altar derives from an ancient myth that states that the first Creator, Prajapati, dismembered his own body to create the world and all the flora and fauna in it. To restore the body of Creator, Agni, the god of fire, gave up his own body, the fire altar itself, so that this could be achieved, and in so doing his own fiery spirit entered the recreated Prajapati. The altar was bird-shaped and was believed to have been that of an eagle or falcon, so that it could fly up to the gate of Heaven. It is also said that the altar was bird-shaped as a means to ensure that the priest of sacrificial performer, or his spirit, could fly up to heaven on the wings of the altar-bird so created[467]. This may be the origin of the claim of many Australian Aboriginal medicine-men to be able to "fly" up to the Sun, stars or holes in the Sky.

The description of the construction of the fire altar in the shape of a bird is given in the Satapatha Brahmana and notes that the body was constructed of bricks in a square shape. Significantly after the altar had been completed a gold disk representing the Sun was placed on it and a small gold figure of a man representing Agni-Prajapati[468]. The rituals relating to the various elements performed at the fire altar are described throughout the same text and confirm that it is the eagle that is most frequently associated with the bird form of the altar[469].

Garuda - the Indi Bird Prototype?

In the Vedic texts Garuda is noted the king of the birds and in later Hindu mythology he is the vahana or vehicle of the Sky god Vishnu[470]. It is recognised that he developed from the bird deity known as Garutman in Ancient Iran and is found widely depicted in India from the earliest times in iconic art and correspondingly in the regions of South East Asia influenced from the Subcontinent. In a Jain text Sakra (Indra) and Isana (holder of the thunderbolt - Ilapa?) fan the god as the first great saint, or Thirthankara, and his palanquin was said to be carried by Garuda on the western side and Nagas on the north undoubtedly relating this mode of transport to the cardinal points[471]. In the myths of India the Garuda as the eagle was perhaps best known as the enemy of snakes[472].

After the lion-bird entered North India from Iran in the first millennium, B.C. it was adapted as a lesser deity into Buddhism, but because of the association of the eagle with mountain ranges, and certainly with the increasing influence of Hinduism, this deity became a favourite in the iconography of the Himalayan kingdoms and in Tibet. It is in the form in these regions, particularly around the Ganges and Brahmaputra Deltas northward, that the Garuda imagery was transferred to the coast of Northern Peru. The form of the bird deity in Sipan (*5.132*) is clearly that of the Himalayan form of Garuda (*5.129*) and this appears to correspond with other elements of iconography from the same region of North East India and Tibet on the Ecuadorian coast at Jama-Coaque and Manteno. It is likely therefore that associated symbolism, myths, legends and rituals also were transferred but modified, merged or discarded over generations and centuries away from their original environment and the nurture of their former living cultural traditions. The Inca Origin myths that note that they migrated from the north and in these they may have had the assimilated the Sipan form of the Garuda as the Indi and the name of Indi itself may have derived from the Vedic storm deity, Indra, derived from the Caucasus region through Mitanni and Ancient Iran, as noted above.

Indra has many aspects that accreted over several thousand years of worship from the Hittite kingdom and his final, but less illustrious incarnation in Hindu India. As a storm god Indra was particularly associated with the mountainous regions of the Himalayas, but in many aspects he is a parallel to Viracocha in Bolivia who may in fact have developed from the Vedic/Hindu model. Viracocha appears to have been a creator deity, encompassing all the attributes of a storm deity including that of thunder and lightning, and identifying also with the Sun including Punchao, although separated as such in Inca cosmology and ceremonial precinct allocation in Cuzco. In several references this Andean High God was referred to as Illa Ticce Viracocha where Illa appears to be the storm god Il or El or Bel in West Asia and transferred as the god Indra in India. Viracocha is also referred to as Imay Viracocha and Imay may be another inflection on Indra, and related to one of his sons named by Molina as Imaymana[473].

Viracocha has already been noted as having been associated with the four quarters and with the previous world cycles[474], and his five sons are equated with the five "Suns" of previous ages or epochs[475] and this would appear to correspond exactly to Indra's attributes in India. In Vedic India, before the rise of Hinduism, Indra was considered the highest of the gods[476], very much in the same way as Viracocha was for the Aymara and Quechuas in the Andes and was likewise considered in his original form as a rain god. As the rain god, Indra was perceived to rain upon his people for 4 months of the year and was perceived to correspond to great benefits being showered by their god, and for the other 8 months drew water up to himself[477] in a manner not unlike that in Andean belief. In other references it is stated in a religious myth that Indra became a bird and in this he is associated with the Sun as a vehicle and the wind god Vayu[478], of some note elsewhere in this book.

Birds have often been perceived as the messengers of the gods or as special deities and in the myths related to Indra it is said that he was brought to submission by a parrot who undertook austerities related to food restrictions[479]. This could be a perfect model, at least merging with the eagle or condor, for the Inca's Indi bird since all Andean peoples would have been aware of the brilliantly coloured parrots, macaws, so widespread in the forests of the nearby Amazon Basin but considered to have malevolent attributes. But it is the bird as a symbol of the sky that appears to be fundamental to both mythical traditions. In this, both Viracocha, noted in an earlier chapter, and Indra are closely identified with the wind as the other important personification of the atmosphere that supports the bird in flight that has prominence between heaven and earth. In the Vedic texts, Indra is identified as the lord of the winds[480] and in others he is identified with the wind god, Vayu. Vayu, in one of these texts is associated with the distribution of the nectar of the gods, the ambrosia - the Soma, the male generative fluid, and the sacred vessels apportioned to each god are called vayavya - Vayu's vessels[481]. In this section of text Indra and Vayu are closely identified as a pair and in describing the vessel in which the Soma is served it is said to be a wooden vessel with a "belt" around it and that it was reserved for the Asvins, the horse deities associated with the wind earlier noted. This vessel had the shape of a head and is described as "lip-shaped"[482]. This is highly reminiscent, and is possibly the prototype for, many ritual vessels, or censers, found in Central and South America that are "face-urns", or are ceramic heads with gaping mouths and prominent lips (*12.081/2*).

In the oldest of the Vedic texts, the Satapatha Brahmana, Indra and Vayu are identified as each other. The text is interestingly expressed, lyrically in an expansive, commanding manner, intonated during the Agni fire god rituals at the fire altar. Several of these sequential verses are as follows:

2)   "'To the wind Ocean (I offer) thee, hail!' - the (aerial) ocean (samudra) indeed is he who blows here, for from out of that ocean all the gods and all the beings issue forth (samudru-dru): it is to him (Vayu, the wind) he thus offers it, and therefore he says, 'To the wind Ocean (I consecrtae) thee, hail!'"

3)   "'To the wind Flood - thee, hail!' - the flood (sarira) indeed is he who blows here, for from out of that flood all the gods and all the creatures come forth together (saha irate): it is to him he thus offers it, and therefore he says, 'To the wind Flood - thee, hail!'."

4)   "'To the wind Unassailable - thee, hail! To the wind Irresistible - thee, hail! - unassailable and irresistible indeed is he who blows here: it is to him he thus offers it, and therefore he says, 'To the wind Unassailable - thee, hail! To the wind irresistible - thee, hail!'"

5)   "'To the wind Favourable - thee, hail! To the wind Ogress-ridder - thee, hail" - favourable and an ogress-ridder indeed is he who blows here: it is to him he thus offers it, and therefore he says, 'To the wind Favourable - thee, hail! To the Ogress-ridder - thee, hail!'"

6)   "'To Indra, accompanied by the Vasus and Ruidras, (I offer) thee, hail!' - Indra is he who blows here: ..." etc.[483].

This text is remarkable for a supposedly land-based Aryan people in India and the whole tone suggest that it was written from the annals of sea-going peoples who were well experienced in the vagaries of the wind during Ocean voyages. In South America flood myths occur throughout both the Andean regions and the Amazon forests and here the Vedic record notes that close similarities with the gods emerging after a great Flood that are recorded similarly among the South Americans. In this text Indra and Vayu are identified as one and reflects the traditions among the Andean people preserved for Viracocha and or Tonapa.

In many sections of Vedic text the principle of fire, the essence of the god Agni, and Agni in this sense is specifically stated as being owned by Indra and Agni jointly[484], and these deities are said to be responsible for the construction of the fire-altar[485]. They are likewise represented on the fire-altar as a gold disk and a small male figure[486]. It is stated also that all the gods were believed to have emerged from their substance jointly[487] and from them seed pours forth to bring all things into existence. In this same section of text there are references to Indra's thunderbolt providing another element in common with Viracocha-Tonapa in the Andes.

Indra is said to have the Sun as a vehicle, that is the horse is the Sun[488] and on the sixth day of the fire-rituals where the Soma cups are distributed to the gods the two are identified as the same being[489]. This follows similar identifications of the storm god and the Creator Viracocha in the Andes with the Sun and this is the subject of several scholarly works in an attempt to unravel their attributes in the last few decades (see Arthur Demarest and Douglas Sharon). In further textual references Indra is considered to be the Sun[490], and to burn "bright" as the Sun[491] and where he is identified with the Rik or Rishis the ancient sages - the Great Bear constellation[492], in a similar, apparent confusion to the similar Andean dilemma.

In a further interesting parallel in the Andean myths, perhaps the most famous, was that the Sun disappeared for a long period of time and the Creator, Viracocha ordered the world in its present incarnation to come forth initiated by the Sun then rose over Lake Titicaca in great splendour, noted earlier. In a parallel, perhaps the original Indra retrieved the Sun after the demon Svarbhanu "smote" him causing the great darkness that is probably a reference originally to an eclipse[493]. It is interesting to note that to appease and "expiate" the demon of darkness the gods in the forms of sacrifices of various coloured ewes, one black, another red, a third white[494] and this appears to be the origin of the selection of various coloured "sheep", or llamas, noted in Andean sacrifices. This reference to eclipses appears to have its further parallel in Indra performing the New and Full Moon sacrifices in the Vedic texts associated with the cardinal points of the compass[495].

12.090 : Fanged monster mask with the fangs spirally downwards and outwards in the identical fashion found in many images in the Americas (*9.080*). Temple 2, Nalanda, 5/6th., century, A.D.

12.091 : Tenoned head of a makara or mythical crocodile-fish of the Ganges River in India. The makara head is sometimes depicted as a lion and note the fangs and similarity to tenon heads in the Americas (*7.018/9*). Bihar, North India, 11th., century, A.D.

12.092 : A griffon or composite mythical creature that is probably the model for those in the Americas (*7.012; 7.017*). Assyria, Mesopotamia, 900-600 A.D.

12.093 : A characteristic smiling figurine displaying a mouth tattoo of the type found anciently among the Ainu of Japan and in the Amazon and Gran Chaco in South America. Note the dual projections with a central raised section that may have its reflections in the dual feathers and combs used in the Pacific Islands to Assam and India. Note also the cross-legged posture characteristic also of India. Remojadas, Veracruz, East Coast Mexico, 600-900 A.D.

The relationship of the storm god Indra with the Sun is clearly seen as paralleling that of Viracocha-Tonapa with "Lord Sun", or Apu-Inti and Punchau in the Andes. Also similar to these Andean gods is the relation between Indra and Pushan, or Pun-shan in Vedic India. Pushan was earlier paralleled with Punchau as the prototype of the Inca deity, and in India there are references to the "all-coloured goat" sacrifices being shared equally between Indra and Pushan indicating originally that they were of a related parity in status and association[496]. At the end of the calendrical year a sacrifice was made jointly for Indra and Pushan and this was again shared equally indicating the same status and ancient cyclical association[497].

As a vehicle for Indra the Sun is, as noted, one where he is, in the earliest texts, probably imported originally with the deity from Ancient Iran, but more usually Indra is depicted astride his great elephant Airavata[498] (*7.087*). In lavish descriptions Indra, in the Jain texts, is said to be regaled with gold ornaments and as lord of the southern half of the sky as he sits astride his elephant mount as Maghavan surrounded with the many lesser rulers of the world[499]. The fact that Indra is identified in this aspect with the southern half of the world appears to correspond with the textual excerpts in the paragraphs recorded above relating to mariners and sea voyagers - the southern hemisphere being largely water. The bow is also called the Ajagava or the southern Sun-path[500]. The name of the elephant immediately indicates its origin as identifying with the homeland of the Aryans regaled with the same name. The elephant is a well-known motif for the cosmos in Buddhist myth and found widely, inevitably, in Hindu myths and legends. The dispersal of the Indra myths and his assimilation into the Americas under adapted, localised names and titles appears to be supported by elephant iconography associated with him being found so identifiably in Mexico and Guatemala (*12.071*). In India, Indra as a deity was identified particularly as the high god of the Aryans and was specifically associated with the nobility[501] and this probably had a special attraction for the Incan forebears when in their ascendancy in Peru relating to their claimed.

Indra's Bow - the Pinaka and Pirrhua in Andean Myth

Indra was most famous for his thunderbolt in the shape of the Vajra (*7.087*) or lightning bolt, a highly stylised form of that found earlier in the Ancient Middle East (*6.077*; *7.005*). However, he is anciently associated with the bow, the Indrahanus[502], and its allusion in form to the rainbow. In a textual reference relating to the Sky god, Vishnu, who supplanted the Vedic Indra as Supreme God in the succeeding Hindu religion, Lakshmi, his wife, in one address states in one section:
"9) I reside in the sun, in the moon, and in the cloudless atmosphere in which the flock of the stars is spread out. (I reside) in that cloud, from which the waters of the rain pour down, in that cloud which is adorned with Indra's bow, and in that cloud from which the rays of lightning flash forth."[503].

Interestingly, this belief in India that such phenomena as the Sun Moon, planets, stars and the rainbow were aspects of a manifested god in India this belief finds its exact parallel in Peru where recent researchers record the similar beliefs including the prohibition of pointing at them[504]. To point at the rainbow as a manifestation of Indra was expressly forbidden in the Vedic texts[505] and in the same text it is also forbidden to look at the Sun when it rises and sets. However, as always, the sadhus or holy men or priests, do not need to abide by the same strictures imposed by religious prescription and it is noted that a sadhu should always carry a staff (as was true of Tonapa in Bolivia) and if he pointed at the rainbow should address it as "the jewelled bow" (manidhanu) and exclaim "There is Indra's bow" (Indra-dhanu)[506]. Some oriental scholars consider that the association with the many coloured jewels with the seven colours of the rainbow derives from earlier origins in Ancient Iran and is preserved in essence in one of the Pahlavi texts[507].

However, for this study and the possible associations of Indra with Viracocha-Tonapa in the Andes it is of particular note that in the aspect of bowman Indra is called Pinakin and the bow itself Pinaka. Rudra, "The Lord of Tears", of such note earlier in this work so reminiscent of the Staff God at Tiahuanco, is identified with Pinakin in Hindu myth, and in this association he is further identified with Siva who holds a bow in his hand "... made of a powerful serpent with seven heads and poisonous teeth"[508]. Here the parallels between Andean myth and that of Ancient India turn full circle since the staff god is also depicted with serpents as rods held in his hand and the whole of the Ancient traditions of India associated with Indra, Rudra and Siva are seen to be virtually mirrored in the Andes.

The native Peruvian chronicler, Pachacuti Yamqui Salcamayhua is considered one of the most reliable of the historians from the 16th. century producing his work on Inca traditions in 1613 A.D. In this history of the Inca he notes that Manco Capac was hostile to the huacas or stone and fetish shrines and destroyed those of Pinahua (Pinao) Capac and another chief named Tocay whom he called a great idolator and overthrew[509] - Inca Origin Version 1.

In Version 8 of the Inca Origin myths, recorded by Garcilasso de la Vega descended through his mother to the Incas, that when a culture hero emerged in the Colla country after the great Flood, near Lake Titicaca, identified with Tiahuanaco, and divided the country among four lords or kings. It is noted that he delegated the northern section to Manco Capac, the South to Colla, the east to Tocay and the west to Pinahua[510]. Zuidema notes the probable reality of this subdivision identifying several regions with traditions of tribes that inhabited them[511].

It may be that these were all related tribes that had originated in Tiahuanaco and dispersed with the expansion of the empire to rule certain region, but after the collapse of Tiahuanco in about the 10-11th., century, A.D. became independent kingdoms. This might have also occurred at the earlier collapse in the 6th., century, A.D. However, it cannot be missed that three or four of these names may have their origins in India, Manco has been considered as a role reversal of a Gond goddess, a people of such import in cross-Pacific transfers; Colla is probably originally the Chol or Cola of South India, who rules as a dynasty from before the first millennium, A.D. to about the 13th., century, A.D. with a couple of centuries break when the Pallavas replaced them. Tocay will be of more interest while Pinahua must surely represent the deity Indra as Pinaka noted in the foregoing. Characteristically the Ancient Americas followed a similar practise to that in Eurasia and named their children after heroes, saints or the particular deity associated with the day on which a child was born. It is likely that all four of the hero names associated with the quartering of the four regions of this pre-Inca Andean kingdom, centred on Tiahuanco, represented cultural heroes or deities from the original Ayar, or Aryan kingdoms in their distant homeland.

In a record preserved in Montesinos it states that Manco Capac is the son of Pirua Pacari Manco, called more officially Tupac Ayar Uchu, and that it was he who first entered Cuzco and his son succeeded him[512]. It is probable therefore that this Pinhua represented the "nobility" just as it was believed so of Indra in Ancient India and in the Inca myths the ruler Pinahua is antecedent and therefore part of the noble line of earlier Ayar kings in Bolivia that expanded into highland Peru as the Inca. Just as Pinahua is associated with the four cardinal points, so also Indra, Pinakin, and his bow Panaka is the Sky. The other ruler of interest is Tocay[513], and this name as Toco is probably identified with the term denoting the revered window(s) in the mythical emergence of the first Incas from the cave of origin.

In Tierradento in Southern Colombia, the ridge of a mountain range anciently levelled in a remarkable feat of engineering by the ancient inhabitants of the region and not far distant to San Agustin where phallic carvings so resemble those of Ancient India. Having removed the tops of the mountains the long flat extended platforms so created were excavated into the rock for large subterranean tombs with steps down to their entrances similar to those in the adjacent valley. To have undertaken such feats implies a very great faith in their deities and the afterlife that appears to have formed part of their belief system. It is interesting to note that Indra was said to have cut of the mountaintops in Vedic myths[514] and as the cloud god it would appear to be appropriate that the Tierradentro mountaintop tombs would have disappeared into the clouds in the rainy season. Anyone processing on the levelled mountain platform would have been over-whelmed by the feeling of being on a level completely separated and above the Earth since these mountains are young and the side fall precipitously away from the artificially created platform. It might be conjectured therefore that the founders of this culture were Aryan worshippers of Indra, and where San Agustin was that dedicated to Siva worshippers as their phallic monuments indicate (*12.006-9*).

It has been noted that the Indi bird may have been the equivalent of the Garuda in India, identical iconographically to that found in Sican iconography. Indra is also associated with the Garuda and the parrot, but in the very long history in the evolution of iconography and symbol-ic imagery in India these have been confused and identified with other icons of importance but others that have long lost their original associations. In most of the texts in India certain birds have some consistency in identification, such as the falcon with the eagle and both of these with the vulture. In other Vedic texts the bird associated with Indra is the goose, or Hamsa, more usu-ally identified with Brahma the Creator, but more significantly the flamingo. The Brahman goose resembles closely the myths surrounding the "Great Cackler" of Ancient Egypt, however, in some texts the goose, or Hamsa, is identified with the flamingo[515], something of a rarity in more recent times in India. The flamingo as the Hamsa is in aspect that associated particularly with the Sun, no doubt because of its reddish colour representing the dawn and sunset. Because of this solar association this bird is especially related to the cardinal points as the texts that record and are spoken as if by the Hamsa as the flamingo in this case record:
"3) ..."'Fire is one quarter, the sun is one quarter, the moon is one quarter, lightning is one quar-ter. This is the foot of Brahman (his imprint on the World), consisting of four quarters, and called Gyotishmat (full of light)."
"4) 'He who knows this and meditates on the foot of Brahman, consisting of four quarters, by the name of Gyotishmat, becomes full of light in this world. He conquers the worlds which are full of light, whoever knows this and meditates on the foot of Brahman, consisting of the four quarters, by the name of Gyotishmat."[516].

In the world of the Aryan Vedas it was believed that all animals created on earth went to sleep at night except the Hamsa[517] and in this sense it identifies entirely with the Sun itself[518]. In this sense also the Hamsa is completely the "firebird" - the flamingo. It is unlikely to be coin-cidence that the bird most noted in Andean sky over Bolivia after the Condor, is the flamingo, found here more concentrated on Lake Popoo than anywhere else outside of lakes of tropical East Africa. It is possible therefore that the cosmology surrounding and arrogated early to the Vedic storm god Indra was transferred and identified, at least in part, with the totemic Indi bird, as the falcon but possibly the flamingo, adopted by the Incas or inherited by them from Tiahuanaco.

However, another possibility, related to the flamingo as the Indi bird, exists and that is in the name of Tocay, found as noted, in the ruler of the cardinal region, or suyu, of the West in the Inca Origin myths. In India the term Tocay or Tokei, or Tukki-im, is the Tamil (Dravidian South India) for the peacock[519], associated in West and South Asian thought from the earliest times with royalty and the Sky - the eyes of its tail being identified as the many eyes of Indra. The Sanskrit name for this bird is the Mayura[520], or Mayur, and is widely depicted in the art of Ancient India, particularly as the vehicle, vahana, of the Son of the Sun in India, Skanda[521] (*7.065*), and who in this form the peacock is known as Paravani[522]. This flamboyant bird was the badge of the

Maurya Dynasty, its most famous son being the last great emperor, Asoka, and their badge was the Mayura, probably because of the pun in the names[523] since it is also called Mora[524], and Sikhin referring to its attributes relating to fire[525]. It was considered to be a "Sun-bird" and also identified with Garuda as the pre-eminent Sky bird, and was regarded as the bird of immortality, and like Garuda was a killer of snakes[526]. The Mayura-Pattra (-piccha or - puccha) was the bundle of peacock tail-feathers[527] so beloved of the Gonds but also among most of the peoples of India, and this was used as a headdress and as "rays" descending from the sun disk (moghi) worn on the backs of Gond dancers into last century and identical to those found in depictions in Mexico and Central America (*7.062*). Indra is also shown with his peacocks in the lowest register in *7.087*.

It has been noted earlier that in the predominantly South India country of the Tamils the Syrian Christians ministered since about the 6th., or 7th., century, A.D. Here St. Thomas was also identified with the peacock or Tokei in the local language[528], and it is likely therefore that, just as the Maurya dynasty identified with the peacock as the Mora or Mayura, so the Christians also identified with the peacock (*7.023*) and transferred it to South America along with other aspects and religious beliefs in South Indian culture under the aegis of the Cholas or Pallavas after the 7th., century, A.D. It is of particular interest that the finest mantle associated with South Indian status was that of the peacock feather cape and this may well be the origin and prototype of the feather capes associated with rulership throughout the Pacific Islands and Central and South America[529]. It is likely therefore that because there was no bird similar to the peacock in the Americas that this became identified in the Andes with the flamingo in particular, and possibly the Condor, merging in a way that is consistent with similar identifications long known in India. The name Tocay then became dissociated from its original intent and meaning as Tokei, or peacock, but retained as a name identifying with the Sun, particularly Son of the Sun. This may then have been inherited or seized in the rise of the Incas under Manco Capac along with the image known as the Indi bird that relates to Indra regardless of which of these the image of the India bird itself actually resembled.

However, there is no bird in South America that would suitably substitute for the peacock and it is likely that if the Tokei, or Tocay, was the origin for the Indi bird then it is likely that the flamingo or falcon would have been the vehicle for a redirection of the associated mythology after entering the Andes. One further reference might be considered and that is from the authority of Arriaga who recorded that red ochre, so widely used in interments in Peru and Asia, was called paria in Peru, and that the flamingo was named pariana or parihuana[530]. It must be significant that the deified hero named Paria-caca is associated with the eastern mountains of the dawn and therefore particularly associated with the red glow of dawn and dusk as the flamingo is in India. The flamingo is largely confined to Lake Poopo in Bolivia and it is likely therefore that in time this identifications merged with that of the falcon as a general identification for the Indi bird that is more widely notable throughout the Andes.

In these last few elements or "loose ends" it is clear that the Indi bird and its probable origin in the form of a totemic fetish, was preserved in the transfer as a form of an Ark of the Covenant. This suitably acts as an encapsulation for all influences assimilated into the cultures in the various epochs up until the Spanish Conquest. There are too many parallels that clearly survive in Inca and Aymara myths to invoke the spectre of coincidence although many researchers imposing personal ideologies and political preconceptions would dearly wish to consign them to oblivion.

CONCLUSION

In considering the available evidence assembled through archaeological investigation it is clear that Pre-Colombian South America presents unexplained aspects of cultural advances that are abrupt and lack evidence of the normal internal, evolutionary development that could account for such cultural leaps. This is so in technology and metallurgy but is especially notable in weaving with the introduction of the loom. Such occurrences are evident from at least the fourth millennium, B.C. and so much so that some prominent historians have resorted to the suggestion that different evolutionary forces are responsible that are not found elsewhere[1]. The iconography and constructional techniques from the earliest epochs, and particularly evident at these epochs of marked or "sudden" advances, suggest otherwise since they appear clearly to relate in parallel to contemporary developments in the Ancient Middle East and later in Ancient India.

In the Ancient Middle East and India the fire-worshipping belief system developed over millennia closely parallels that in the Andes and Coastal Peru where it appears to have retained the iconography and even terms that are evidently derived from cross-Pacific contacts. It is clear from records of the Inca Dynasty that their myths and legends include specific terms written down by the first Spanish chroniclers that indicate that they were more than just the direct descendants, as they claim and perhaps correct in part, from Tiahuanaco but were probably also descendants from the Colhua and Quiche from Ancient Mexico and Guatemala. It is also clear that to retain many of the references, so well preserved, in relation to those of India in their myths and legends there must have been periodic infusions of peoples from India into these earlier lines of hereditary reinforcing their original Aryan descent, hence the variations in their origin myths and the resultant differing versions.

The languages of India are largely traceable from the Indo-Aryan groups that penetrated through the Hindu Kush in the northwest of the Sub-continent. However, in the Himalayas forming the northern boundary of India, there is a marked linguistic incompatibility in the confrontation between the Aryan groups and those from China and Mongolia further north and northeast. These are so very marked that in the foothills the Aryan Sanskrit terms for deities and gods deriving from the India and Ganges areas are retained for those in the Himalayan interface and Tibet since they are easier for the later researchers and peoples of India themselves to pronounce. These terms are, among the Tibetan speakers clearly discernable since the Mongoloid language groups are so much more difficult for Indo-Aryan speakers more directly to pronounce and remain identifiable without appreciable assimilation even after many centuries from the time of their introduction.

The Amerindian peoples are known to have descended almost entirely from the Mongoloid migrants from Siberia who travelled across the land bridge of Alaska and the Aleutian Islands into the continents of the Americas. Their languages therefore should have been more or less entirely an evolutionary development and adaptions from divergent Mongoloid groups. However, in Mexico and among the Mayans peoples there have been many studies indicating that there are many words in the Pre-Colombian languages, particularly deity and associated names, that appear too closely similar to those of the Ancient Middle East not to be related. This has resulted in a burgeoning of theories, among others, that the Mexicans and Mayans were the Biblical lost tribes of Israel. In South America it has been shown in this work that there are many terms that are too closely similar to those of their Aryan counterparts in Ancient Peru and Bolivia, such as Intihuatana and Agni-kayana - the sacred Inca Hitching Place of the Sun, as well as many aspects of ritual and belief, to be coincidental and indicate that they were imported and preserved long enough for them to be recorded by the Spanish at the Conquest. This repeats the same principle of intrusions that occurred for millennia, and still evident to this day, in the

Himalayan regions of India and the Mongoloid territories to the north.

The near indigestibility of one set of completely different words and expressions by another, here the Mongoloid, is evident in Ancient South America where they are retained in their original semblance for centuries. For these many terms to have been so faithfully retained similar to or near identical to the Indo-Aryan originals in South Asia it would have been likely for them to have been refreshed and revitalised not just by one major cross-Pacific transfer but by several over a number of centuries. The extended evidence for this route with the tracing of myth types from Asia across the Pacific to the Americas is included also in the works of the American scholar Joseph Campbell. The same is also true for innovations and techniques where the notoriously conservative indigenous Amerindians show little progressive evolution in material culture but where archaeological research indicates abrupt advances without a convincing period of initiative and innovation resulting in an evolutionary development to produce those advances. As the Amerindians myths and legends have for the most part averred that these advances were introduced by great culture-bearers and when the peoples themselves clearly indicated that their deified heroes were similar in appearance and culture to the Spanish themselves. It cannot be an accident that all of the most important advances and developments took place on the Pacific Coast of South America where the ocean currents of the Pacific wash onto the shores of Ecuador, Peru and Chile providing a direct conveyor for mariners from Asia and no where else in South America apart from those from Central America on the North Coast of Colombia. This is confirmed by the fact that many mummy bundles retrieved in excavations along the arid Pacific coast dating from the mid-first century B.C. onwards are red- or fair-haired with hair texture clearly of the Caucasian type and these are readily to be seen as Peruvian museum exhibits.

The arrival of those transferring cultural achievements from Asia is evidenced by the fact that all the high cultures of the Americas, except those much later in Ohio established by Mexican migrations, can be traced to the Pacific (or Atlantic) shores at those stretches where the oceanic currents convey and deliver mariners directly from Asia to both Central and South America. Why was it that the indigenous Mongoloid derived Siberians entering the Americas, who formed almost the entire ancesty of Amerindians, ignored some of the most productive regions of North America before establishing themselves in the less envitronmentally attractive lands far to the south in Central America? The demogaphy of the distribution and dispersion of high culture in both Cemtral and South America clearly indicates that it is at the points of confrontation of these Siberian peoples, or Amerindians, in both these regions with mariners arrving on the incoming currents washing the Pacific shores that these cultures effloresced.

Underlying so much of the myth, legend, belief system and rituals recorded of the Incas are the references to the great god-hero, Viracocha, and the connection with the sea. It is clear that this deity is certainly likely to have arrived by sea and then departed across the Pacific to the West, undoubtedly returning to Asia, from where he originated. This emulated, or is identical with the Syrian Christian missionary intrusions associated with Tonapa. It is likely also that the great Inca ruler, Tupac, was inspired to follow in this deity's, and probably his ancestors' footsteps. The treasure and other items he returned with to Peru were clearly Asian and in fact these items could only have been derived from there if the record is correct.

It should be clear that there is an irresistible consistency of logic of cultural transfer, by shear weight of numbers of the parallels, from Asia to South America over the millennia. This consistency is particularly illustrated, among many others, by the identification of Andean hero-deity Tonaca as Arnauan with St. Thomas (or missionaries in his name) from South India and therefore the Syrian Christians where the local deified, unmarried youth was Arnavan was probably the prototype. Because of the very numerous parallels with the Aryan heritage, caste system, looms and weaving and many others cultural aspects from South India is so evident in Peru, it is inevitable that the trading ventures from this same part of India, so long linked with sea voyages, would have been utilised to facilitate Christian missions and influence into contemporary Andean Peru. This is also true for all religious and trading missions in the epochs before and after in the Ganges region of North India through to Tibet and in the Ancient Middle East.

Perhaps most contentiously are the probable influences from the Ancient Middle East detectable in South America. It cannot be other than very clear that the surviving iconography from the Assyrians, particularly illustrated in their extensive relief's illustrating their triumphs in wars, that the treatment of prisoners and the cruelties inflicted were from what appears a delight in torture are replicated by the Moche in the first millennium, B.C. extending into the first millennium, A.D. The "pegging-out" of prisoners, illustrated in flaying scenes, are reflected in many Moche ceramic illustrations along with prisoners racked or tied to frames among other recognisable tortures and executions that were such a feature of the Pre-Colombian cultures in the Americas. Trophy heads and the accumulation of these severed heads in Assyria reflects the Aztec tzompalli, or skull racks that appears to be so similar to those in Ancient Mexico and beyond in South America that it would indeed appear that this part of the Peruvian Coast was heavily influenced from the Ancient Near East if not directly from Assyria itself.

It has been argued, incorrectly, that the South Americans never left their shores by boat to venture into the Pacific away from the coast, but modern research into West Mexican history shows clearly that cultural transfer took place from the sea and reflects South American iconography in particular. The first Spanish, part of Pizarro's expeditionary force before the Conquest, record that they met large, loaded, trading sea-going rafts out to sea far from the sight of land off Ecuador. In the Ancient Middle East, in China and Japan, and later in India, long distance sea traders were operating from at least the 5th., millennium, B.C. and no doubt before, and it is likely that they extended their routes far across the Pacific to the Americas where similar ceramic types are found.

In considering the vast amount of evidence available - archaeological, recorded accounts, legendary and from myths, there can be no justification for sweeping statements, referred to in the Introduction to this work that interest into cross-Pacific contacts can be filed under "fanciful notions". Genuine scholarship undertakes research not necessarily to prove predetermined conclusions, although it is often the case, and frequently that research may result in disproving one theory while confirming another. To adhere or impose deregatory or prejudicial references or jibes and impose themwithout comprehensive investigation and analysis of all available evidence cannot be justified. This is particularly important where those who hold such opinions can stifle genuine research in their appointments in major institutions and in education

From the extensive references - textual, iconographic and artefactual, included in this work there can be little doubt that cultural transfer took place from Asia across the Pacific Ocean to the Americas. Mariners and traders over several thousand years were responsible for this diffusion of ideas and technology from the contemporary developments in Asia to South America and along the Pacific coast in particular. There can be little doubt also that these adventurous peoples would have soon found out about the great navigable riverine highways of the Amazon. The headwaters of the major rivers in South America all rise near to the Pacific Coast with access via several reasonably easy routes through the Andes and these would have allowed mariners to extend their explorations and trading into the Amazon Basin and Gran Chaco. In extending their range, and having a lifetime to achieve it, they undoubtedly reached the Atlantic Ocean and discovered their route back to Asia via the eastern route - this theme, however, will have to remain for the future and be the subject for the next, projected book.

SUPERSCRIPT NOTES

Introduction

[1] McEwan; C. – Antiquity, Vol.70, No.270, Dec. 1996

[2] Sharp; A. – 93

[3] Sharp; A. – 103/4

[4] Sharp; A. – 97

Chapter 1

[1] Kearsley; G.R. [M.G.] – 842-5

[2] Vogel; J.Ph. – 57

[3] Hather; J.G. – 75/6

[4] Hather; J.G. – 75

[5] Buck; P. – 15

[6] Buck; P. – 33

[7] Buck; P. – 61

[8] Rawson; J. – 14/5

[9] Wharton; W.J.L. – 103

[10] Wharton; W.J.L. - 105

[11] Rawson; J. – 14/5

[12] Furer-Haimendorf; C. [R.G.A.] – 114/5

[13] Kramer; S.N. – 63; Dalley; S. – 184

[14] Kramer; S.N. – 37/8

[15] Dalley; S. – 184/5

[16] Dalley; S. – 107

[17] Kramer; S.N. – 65-8

[18] Jacobsen; T. – 87

[19] Clay; A.T. – 95

[20] Clay; A.T. – 96

[21] Clay; A.T. – 97

[22] Clay; A.T. – 82/3

[23] Gurney; O.R. – 31;35

[24] Gurney; O.R. – 86

[25] Gurney; O.R. – 115

[26] Gurney; O.R. – 159/60

[27] (Harden; D. – 78)

[28] Bibby; G. – 34/5

[29] Bibby; G. – 29

[30] Bibby; G. – xi

[31] Cleuziou; S. & Tosi; M.

[S.I.A.S.] – 41/2

[32] Kearsley; G.R. [M.G.] – 31-4

[33] Kearsley; G.R. [M.G.] – 984-1035

[34] Kearsley; G.R. [M.G.] – 522-4

[35] Kearsley; G.R. [M.G.] – 805-56; 901-38

[36] Fabri; C.L. – 28;67

[37] Mukherjee; P. – 29

[38] Mukherjee; P. – 12;28

[39] Fabri; C.L. – 28;72

[40] Fabri; C.L. – 4;168

[41] Fabri; C.L. – 113; 160; 168

[42] Fabri; C.L. – 67

[43] Thurston; E. [C.T.S.I.] – v4-44

[44] Thurston; E. [C.T.S.I.] – v4-62

[45] Furer-Haimendorf; C. [R.G.A.] – 226/7

[46] Furer-Haimendorf; C. [R.G.A.] – 372/3

[47] Vogel; J.Ph. – 34

[48] Drower; E.S. [B.Z.] – 89

[49] Drower; E.S. [M.I.I.] – xviii

[50] Drower; E.S. [M.I.I.] – 118

[51] Thurston; E. [C.T.S.I.] – 279

[52] Thurston; E. [C.T.S.I.] – v7-214/5

[53] Seligmann, C.G. – 43

[54] Fabri; C.L. – 28

[55] Tilburg; J-A. – 41

[56] Tilburg; J-A. – 40

[57] Tilburg; J-A. – 42/3

[58] Thurston; E. [C.T.S.I. – v1-75

[59] Drower; E.S. [M.I.I.] - 143

[60] Thurston; E. [C.T.S.I. – v5-439

[61] Thurston; E. [C.T.S.I. – v6-298

[62] Thurston; E. [C.T.S.I. – v6-394-6

[63] Thurston; E. [C.T.S.I. – v3-397

[64] Thurston; E. [C.T.S.I. – v3-47

[65] Bhattacharya; G. [S.I.A.S.] – 351

[66] Thurston; E. [C.T.S.I. – v5-57

[67] Thurston; E. [C.T.S.I. – v6-1

[68] Thurston; E. [C.T.S.I. – v6-4/5

[69] Thurston; E. [C.T.S.I. – v7-258/9

[70] Furer-Haimendorf; C. [R.G.A.] – 404

[71] Malinowski; B. – 2

[72] Malinowski; B. – 82

[73] Malinowski; B. – 83

[74] Malinowski; B. – 81

[75] Malinowski; B. – 93

[76] Malinowski; B.   81; 83

[77] Malinowski; B. – 95

[78] Malinowski; B. – 96

[79] Malinowski; B. – 91

[80] Malinowski; B. – 113

[81] Malinowski; B. – 114

[82] Brewster; A.B. - 75

[83] Malinowski; B. – 126/7

[84] Malinowski; B. – 125

[85] Malinowski; B. – 126

[86] Malinowski; B. – 134

[87] Malinowski; B. – 299

[88] Malinowski; B. – 142

[89] Malinowski; B. – 147

[90] Malinowski; B. – 197

[91] Malinowski; B. – 199

[92] Malinowski; B. – 214

[93] Malinowski; B. – 309

[94] Malinowski; B. – 202

[95] Malinowski; B. – 203

[96] Malinowski; B. – 204

[97] Malinowski; B. – 334/5

[98] Malinowski; B. – 335

[99] Batchelor; J. - 22

[100] Brewster; A.B. - 26-30

[101] Brewster; A.B. - 78

[102] Malinowski; B. – 336

[103] Handy; E.S.C. - 242

[104] Kearsley; G.R. [M.G.] – 363/4; 555; 840/1

[105] Howitt; A.E. – 126; 133

[106] Cobo; B. – 30-2;197

[107] Hutton; J.H. [A.N.] – 45

[108] Hutton; J.H. [A.N.] – 48; 188/9

[109] Seligmann; C.G. – 18

[110] Handy; E.S.C. – 43; 46

[111] Kearsley; G.R. [M.G.] – 804-9; 918-23

[112] Dalton; E.T. - 140

[113] Grimble; A.F. – 2;37

[114] Cavallo Sforza et al – 68/9; 71

[115] Karsten; R. [I.T.A.B.C.] – 88

[116] Hutton; J.H. [A.N.] – 279

[117] Karsten; R. [I.T.A.B.C] – 106

[118] Karsten; R. [I.T.A.B.C] – 84; 89/90

[119] Allchin; R. & B. - 92

[120] Elwin; V. [M.M.I.] - 413

[121] Roy; S.C. – 20/1;22

[122] Howitt; A.W. – 4/5; 31

[123] Grigson; W.V. – 235

[124] Grigson; W.V. – 260

[125] Thurston; E. - 146

[126] Thurston; E. - v4-130

[127] Thurston; E. - v7-315

[128] Thurston; E. - v6-296

[129] Thurston; E. - v5-414

[130] Thurston; E. - v5-413; 414

[131] Thurston; E. - v6-388

[132] Thurston; E. - v4-131

[133] Thurston; E. - v4-130

[134] Thurston; E. - v4-131

[135] Howitt; A.W. - 40

[136] Howitt; A.W. - 71

[137] Howitt; A.W. - 149

[138] Howitt; A.W. - 276/7

[139] Howitt; A.W. - 630

[140] Howitt; A.W. - 632

141 Howitt; A.W. - 490/1

142 Mountford; C.P. [R.A.A.S.E.A.L.] - 256

143 Mountford; C.P [R.A.A.S.E.A.L.] - 208

144 Howitt; A.W. - 430

145 Spencer; B. & Gillan; F.J. [T.N.T.C.A.] - 621

146 Liebert; G. - 185

147 Thurston; E. [O.S.] - 295

148 Howitt; A.W. - 553

149 Danielou; A. - 298

150 Howitt; A.W. - 89

151 Howitt; A.W. - 405

152 Howitt; A.W. - 431

153 Howitt; A.W. - 493

154 Howitt; A.W. - 388/9

155 Kearsley; G.R. [M.G.] – 653-6

156 Howitt; A.W. - 389/90

157 Howitt; A.W. - 390

158 Howitt; A.W. - 546

159 Howitt; A.W. - 559

160 Boas; F. - Vol.xxvii-2

161 Howitt; A.W. - 494

162 Howitt; A.V. - 494

163 Howitt; A.W. - 494

164 Howitt; A.W. - 490/1

165 Howitt; A.W. - 315

166 Howitt; A.W. - 314

167 Howitt; A.W. - 407/8

168 Howitt; A. - 501/2

169 Reichard; G.A. –18/9; 484/5

170 Kearsley; G.R. [M.G.] – 666-8; Howitt; A.W. – 502

171 Howitt; A. - 502

172 Mathew; J. - 147

173 Howitt; A. - 585

174 Harle; J.C. – 161/2

175 Thurston; E. - v4-226

176 Haddon; A.C. - 46

177 Riesenfeld; A. - 320

178 Riesenfeld; A. - 522/3

179 Riesenfeld; A. - 321

180 Riesenfeld; A. - 530/1

181 Riesenfeld; A. - 322

182 Handy; E.S.C. - 206

183 Haddon; A.C. - 143

184 Haddon; A.C. - 146

185 Haddon; A.C. - 144

186 Haddon; A.C. - 144

187 Riesenfeld; A. - 417

188 Handy; E.S.C. – 43;46; Riesenfeld; A. - 420

189 Riesenfeld; A. - 489

190 Reisenfeld; A. – 494/5

191 Reisenfeld; A. - 529

192 Howitt; A.W. - 431

193 Howitt; A.W. - 496/7

194 Bonwick; J. - 190

195 Howitt; A.W. - 498

196 Howitt; A.W. - 499

197 Howitt; A.W. - 499/500

198 Bonwick; J. - 202/3

199 Howitt; A.W. - 134

200 Howitt; A.W. - 485

201 Howitt; A.W. - 390/1

202 Howitt; A.W. - 444

203 Skeat; W.W. - v2-165

204 Giles; H.A. - 18

205 Giles; H.A. - 53

206 Howitt; A.W. - 73

207 Howitt; A.W. - 89

208 Howitt; A.W. - 128

209 Howitt; A.W. - 361

210 Howitt; A.W. - 377

211 Howitt; A.W. – 422

212 Howitt; A.W. - 433

213 Stair; J. - 24

214 Howitt; A.W. - 489

215 Howitt; A.W. - 491

216 Howitt; A.W. - 430

217 Howitt; A.W. - 429

218 Howitt; A.W. - 433

219 Howitt; A.W. - 405

220 Howitt; A.W. - 489

221 Howitt; A.W. - 489/90

222 Mathew; J. - 20

223 Howitt; A.W. – 578

224 Kearsley; G.R. [M.G.] – 80/1; 701-6

225 Dundes; A. - 129

226 Grimble; A.F. – 54;56

227 Berndt; R.M. & C.H. - 325

228 Rutter; O. - 250

229 Snellgrove; D. - 127

230 Snellgrove; D. - 127

231 Snellgrove; D. - 129

232 Snellgrove; D. - 128

233 Howitt; A.W. - 407/8

234 Snellgrove; D. - 131

235 Snellgrove; D. - 130

236 Kearsley; G.R. [M.G.] – 475-7; 483/4; 634-6

237 Mathew; J. - 147

238 Mathew; J. - 15

239 Howitt; A.W. - 485

240 Howitt; A.W. - 486

241 Gomes; E.H. - 185-91

242 Kearsley; G.R. [M.G.] – 901-37

243 Dalton; E.T. - 141

244 Dalton; E.T. - 147

245 Kearsley; G.R. [M.G.] – 918-21

246 Roy; S.C. [H.B.O.] - 196

247 Roy; [H.B.O.] - 221

248 Roy; S.C. [H.B.O.] - 264

249 Roy; S.C. [H.B.O.] - 262/3

250 Hutton; J.H. [S.N.] - 172

251 Gurdon; P.R.T. – 164-6

252 Dundes; A. - 129

253 Reichel-Dolmatoff; G. [S.R.S.T.I.] - 195

254 Grey; G. - 340/1

255 Grey; G. - 341/2

256 Grey; G. - 342

257 Kempers; A.J.B. – 5

258 Gomes; E.H. - 164

259 Gomes; E.H. - 185-91

260 Hose; C. & McDougall; W. - v2-2

261 Hose; C. & McDougall, W. - v2-15

262 Gomes; E.H. - 196;215

263 Gomes; E.H.- -205

264 Gomes; E.H. - 215

265 Kearsley; G.R. [M.G.] – 441

266 Morley; S.G. & Goetz; D. [P.V.] - 131-6

267 Rutter; O. - 250

268 Rutter; O. - 253

269 Furness; W.H. - 55

270 Perry; W.J. - 59

271 d'Almeida; W.B. - v1-175/6

272 Alpers; A. - 387

273 Loeb; E. & Heine-Geldern; R. - 157

274 Layard; J. - 18

275 Grimble; A. - 43;104

276 Morley; S.G. & Goetz; D. [P.V.] – 118

277 Riesenfeld; A. - 354/5

278 Riesenfeld; A. - 198

279 Keeler; C.E. [L.M.E.] – 28; 30; 68

280 Riesenfeld; A. - 306

281 Riesenfeld; A. - 420

282 Malinowski; B. - 132

283 Malinowski; B. - 216

284 Malinowski; B. - 504

285 Deacon; A.B. - 646

286 Fornander; A. - 49

287 Fornander; A. - 50

288 Thurston; E. - v3-251

289 Covarrubias; M. [I.B.] - 20

290 Hickson; S.J. - 56

291 Hickson; S.J. - 239

292 Hickson; S.J. - 246

293 Hickson; S.J. - 308

294 Hickson; S.J. - 318

295 Roy; S.C. [H.B.O.] - 121

296 Kaudern; W. - 124

297 Blackwood; B. - 228-39

298 Riesenfeld; A. - 455

299 Riesenfeld; A. - 453

[300] Williamson; R.W. - 159

[301] Osborne; H. – 117

[302] Gifford; E.W. [T.M.T.] – 192-4

[303] Roy; S.C. [M.] – 52/3; Bradley-Birt; F.B. – 119; 122

[304] Kearsley; G.R. [M.G.] – 170-80

[305] Grigson; W.V. - 57

[306] Grigson; W.V. - 52

[307] Kearsley; G.R. [M.G.] – 408-11

[308] Grigson; W.V. - 104/5

[309] Elwin; V. [M.T.G.] – 195/6

[310] Elwin; V. [M.T.G.] - 194

[311] Grigson; W.V. - 135

[312] Grigson; W.V. - 158

[313] Grigson; W.V. - 200

[314] Grigson; W.V. - 200;233

[315] Deacon; A.B. – 559;563

[316] Deacon; A.B. – 336; Layard; J. – 440/1

[317] Elwin; V. [M.T.G.] - 36

[318] Grigson; W.V. - 228

[319] Grigson; W.V. - 227;228

[320] Grigson; W.V. - 281

[321] Grigson; W.V. - 283

[322] Grigson; W.V. - 283

[323] Grigson; W.V. - 283

[324] Kearsley; G.R. [M.G.] – 922

[325] Thurston; E. [C.T.S.I.] - 290

[326] Thurston; E. [C.T.S.I.] - v2-292

[327] Thurston; E. [C.T.S.I.] - v2-317

[328] Thurston; E. [C.T.S.I.] - v3-440

[329] Thurston; E. [C.T.S.I.] - v3-451

[330] Thurston; E. [C.T.S.I.] - v3-456

[331] Thurston; E. [C.T.S.I.] - v4-41

[332] Thurston; E. [C.T.S.I.] - v4-260

[333] Thurston; E. [C.T.S.I.] - v4-455

[334] Fornander; A. - 8/9

[335] Daum; W. - 13

[336] Daum; W. - 88

[337] Daum; W. - 107

[338] Daum; W. - 78

[339] Doe; B. - 233

[340] Sharon; D. - 84/5

[341] Berndt; R.M. & C.H. - 130/1

[342] Berndt; R.M. & C.H.- 221-3

[343] Berndt; R.M. & C.H. - 237

[344] Berndt; R.M. & C.H. - 272- 4

[345] Berndt; R.M. + C.H.- -309

[346] Best; E. [M.R.M.] - 60

[347] Howitt; A.W. - 432/3

[348] Howitt; A.W. - 433

[349] Howitt; A.W. - 433

[350] Howitt; A.W. - 56

[351] Howitt; A.W. - 120/1

[352] Howitt; A.W. - 393

[353] Howitt; A.W. - 770

[354] Howitt; A.W. - 402/3

[355] Howitt; A.W. - 429/30

[356] Howitt; A.W. - 443

[357] Howitt; A.W. - 443

[358] Howitt; A.W. - 444

[359] Howitt; A.W. - 443

[360] Howitt; A.W. - 467/8

[361] Muller; M. & Eggeling;J. - 97

[362] Crooke; W. - v1-273

[363] Marshall; H.I. - 195

[364] Hutton; J.H. [S.N.] - 208; 211

[365] Hutton; J.H. [S.N.] - 214

[366] Kearsley; G.R. [M.G.] – 192; 439

[367] Mills; J.P. [L.N.] - 22

[368] Wilson; E.H. - 181

[369] Wilson; E.H. - 183

[370] Wilson; E.H. - 219

[371] Spencer; B. & Gillan; F.J. [T.N.T.C.A.] - v1-424

[372] Spencer; B. & Gillan; F.J. [T.N.T.C.A.] - v1-425

[373] Spencer; B. & Gillan; F.J. [T.N.T.C.A.] - v1-445

[374] Spencer; B. & Gillan; F.J. [T.N.T.C.A.] - v2-428

[375] Spencer; B. & Gillan; F.J. [T.N.T.C.A.] - v2-344/5

[376] Mountford; C.P. [W.M.J.] - 13

[377] Howitt; A.W. - 399/400

[378] Spencer; B. & Gillan; F.J. [T.N.T.C.A.) - v2-312

[379] Grigson; W.V. - 130

[380] Russell; R.V. - v1-126/7

[381] Spencer; B. & Gillan; F.J. [T.N.T.C.A.] - v2-289

[382] Spencer; B. & Gillan; F.J. [N.T.N.C.A.] - v1-154

[383] Spencer; B. & Gillan; F.J. [N.T.N.C.A.] - v1-132

[384] Spencer; B. & Gillan; F.J. [T.N.T.C.A.] - v1-135

[385] Spencer; B. & Gillan; F.J. [N.T.N.C.A.] - v1-143

[386] Spencer; B. & Gillan; F.J. [N.T.C.A.] - v2-280

[387] Riesenfeld; A. - 539;541

[388] Riesenfeld; A. - 562

[389] Riesenfeld; A. - 371

[390] Arriaga; P.J. de - 30

[391] Howitt; A.W. - 25

[392] Bonwick; J. - 157

[393] Bonwick; J. - 157/8

[394] Kearsley; G.R. [M.G.] – 1008/9

[395] Howitt; A.W. - 2/3

[396] Bonwick; J. - 159/60

[397] Mathew; J. - 62

[398] Howitt; A.W. - 31

[399] Howitt; A.W. - 27

[400] Howitt; A.W. - 24

[401] Mathew; J. - 3

[402] Mathew; J. - 4

[403] Mathew; J. - 7

Chapter 2

[1] Buck; P. – 46-9; Smith; S.P. – 26/7; 57-63

[2] MacMillan Brown; J. - v1-188

[3] MacMillan Brown; J. - v1-183

[4] Ivens; W.G. [I.B.P.] – 143/4

[5] Skinner; H.D. - 3

[6] Skinner; H.D. - 3

[7] Skinner; H.D. - 17

[8] Skinner; H.D. - 18

[9] Heseltine; N. – 51

[10] Heseltine; N. – 57

[11] Wharton; W.J.L. – 87

[12] Spencer; B. & Gillan; F.J. [N.T.N.C.A.] - v2-145

[13] Spencer; B. & Gillan; F.J. [N.T.N.C.A.] - v2-145

[14] Howitt; A.W. - 484/5

[15] McBryde; I. - 267-9

[16] Bonwick; J. - 19

[17] Bonwick; J. - 19

[18] Bonwick; J. - 20

[19] Bonwick; J. - 24

[19] Bonwick; J. - 24

[21] Howitt; A.W. - 313

[22] Howitt; A.W. - 381/2

[23] Skinner; H.D. - 383

[24] Howitt; A.W. - 440

[25] Skinner; H.D. - 18

[26] Skinner; H.D. - 38

[27] Skinner; H.D. - 35

[28] Skinner; H.D. - 37

[29] Skinner; H.D. - 357

[30] Skinner; H.D. - 37

[31] Skinner; H.D. - 38

[32] Skinner; H.D. - 17

[33] Skinner; H.D. - 24

[34] Howitt; A.W. - 122

[35] Buck; P. [C.M.] - 18/9

[36] Skinner; H.D. - 55

[37] Kearsley; G.R. [M.G.] – 198-205

[38] Skinner; H.D. - 55

[39] Skinner; H.D. - 24

[40] Skinner; H.D. - 372

[41] Skinner; H.D. - 383

[42] Budge; E.A.W. - xxxvi

[43] Budge; E.A.W. - 43

[44] Budge; E.A.W. - 210

[45] Budge; E.A.W. [B.D.] - 25; 150

[46] Budge; E.A.W. - 29

[47] Budge; A.E.W. - 19

[48] Skinner; H.D. - 62

[49] Budge; E.A.W. - 244/5

[50] Buck; P. - 18

[51] Tilburg; J.-A. - 112

[52] Skinner; H.D. - 74

[53] Kearsley; G.R. [M.G.] – 921-3

[54] Skinner; H.D. - 344

[55] Heyerdahl; T. [A.A.] – 145; Kearsley; G.R. [M.G.] – 92

[56] Russell; R.V. – v2-111

[57] Eggeling; J. in Muller; F.M. – 440

[58] Skinner; D.H. - 344

[59] Skinner; H.D. - 48

[60] Skinner; H.D. - 49

[61] Skinner; H.D. - 46/7

[62] Skinner; H.D. - 49

[63] Furer-Haimendorf; C. [R.G.A.] – 188/9; 277

[64] Skinner; H.D. - 119

[65] Skinner; H.D. - 52

[66] Skinner; H.D. - 52

[67] Loeb; E. & Heine-Geldern; R. - 140

[68] Skinner; H.D. - 51

[69] Skinner; H.D. - 8

[70] Skinner; H.D. - 101

[71] Morgan; W.N. – 12

[72] Morgan; W.N. – 10;12

[73] Hutton; J.H. [A.N.] - 47

[74] Loeb; E. & Heine-Geldern; R. - 99

[75] Buck; P. - 4

[76] Buck; P. - 4

[77] Heyerdahl; T. [A.I.P.] – 245

[78] Smith; P. - 109

[79] Buck; P. - 5

[80] Buck; P. - 5

[81] Buck; P. - 15

[82] Kearsley; G.R. [M.G.] – 305/6

[83] Kerry-Nichols; J. - 190/1

[84] Buck; P. - 65

[85] Buck; P. - 65

[86] Buck; P. - 66/7

[87] Buck; P. - 61

[88] Buck; P - 71

[89] Smith; P. - 52/3

[90] Smith; P. - 47

[91] Smith; P. - 47/8

[92] Danielou; A. - 221

[93] Danielou; A. - 298

[94] Danielou; A. - 299

[95] Danielou; A. - 237

[96] Danielou; A. - 98/9

[97] Danielou; A. - 99

[98] Kearsley; G.R. [M.G.] – 632-7

[99] Buck; P. - 62

[100] Hather; J.G. - 71

[101] Hather; J.G. - 72/3

[102] Heyerdahl; T. – [A.I.P.] - 433

[103] Buck; P. - 89

[104] Buck; P. - 25/6

[105] Buck; P. - 25/6

[106] Buck; P. - 26

[107] Buck; P. - 271

[108] Buck; P. - 278

[109] Smith; P. - 75/6

[110] Smith; P. - 75/6

[111] Buck; P. - 515

[112] Buck; P. - v1-439

[113] Buck; P. - v1-440

[114] MacMillan Brown; J. - v2-110/1

[115] Hose; C. & McDougall; W. - v2-142

[116] Perry; W.J. - 167/8

[117] Handy; E.S.C. - 245

[118] Handy; E.S.C. - 244/5

[119] Handy; E.S.C. - 245

[120] Kramer; S.N. - 52

[121] Buck; P. - v1-443

[122] Elwin; V. [M.M.I.] - 78/9

[123] Elwin; V. [M.M.I.] - 79

[124] Elwin; V. [M.M.I.] - 79

[125] Riesenfeld; A. - 295

[126] Kearsley; G.R. [M.G.] – 913/4; 927-30; 1006-16

[127] Riesenfeld; A. - 294/5

[128] Howitt; A.W. - 427

[129] Miller; M. & Taube; K. - 85

[130] Buck; P. – 429; Handy; E.S.C. – 248-53

[131] Hutton; J.H. [S.N.] - 214

[132] Bridges; E.L. - 433

[133] Morley; S.G. & Goetz; D. [P.V.] – 205/6

[134] Buck; P. - 455

[135] Kearsley; G.R. [M.G.] – 206-11; 436-43

[136] Stair; J.B. – 273-5

[137] Seligmann; C.G. – 402-4

[138] Keeler; C.E. [L.M.C.] - 30

[139] Gurdon; P.R.T. – 164-6

[140] Buck; P. - 441

[141] Buck; P. – 508

[142] Skeat; W.W. - v2-319/20

[143] Kearsley; G.R. [M.G.] – 209-11

[144] Buck; P. - 510

[145] Buck; P. - 510

[146] Kearsley; G.R. [M.G.] – 195; 305

[147] Buck; P. - 514/5

[148] Budge; E.A. Wallis – 146-51

[149] Howitt; A.W. - 488

[150] Cobo; B. – 130-41; Zuidema; R.T. [C.S.C.] - 260

[151] Buck; P. - 514/5

[152] Ellis; W. – v1-311; Fornander; A. – v1-51; 89; Salcamayhua; P.-Y. – 88; 108

[153] Buck; P. - 473

[154] Buck; P. - 476

[155] Buck; P. - 462

[156] Heyerdahl; T. [A.I.P.] – 244-9

[157] Buck; P. – 462

[158] Buck; P. – 515

[159] Elwin; V. [M.M.I.] – 349

[160] Black; J. – 146

[161] Buck; P. - 429

[162] Buck; P. - 429

[163] Hutton; [S.N.] – 214

[164] Macpherson; S.C. – 18

[165] Brewster; A.B. – 84; Brown; G. – 209;242

[166] Handy; E.S.C. – 248-53

[167] Bridges; E.L. – 433

[168] Morley; S.G. & Goetz; G. [P.V.] – 205/6

[169] Gurney; O.R. – 86;107

[170] Buck; P. - 430

[171] Buck; P. - 430

[172] Haddon; A.C. - 41

[173] Best; E. – v1-271

[174] Riesenfeld; A. - 97

[175] Riesenfeld; A. - 98

[176] Riesenfeld; A. - 106-8

[177] Riesenfeld; A. - 412

[178] Riesenfeld; A. - 129

[179] Thurston; E. [C.T.S.I.] – v7-241

[180] MacMillan Brown; J. - v1-64

[181] MacMillan Brown; J. - v1-164

[182] MacMillan Brown; J. - v1-164

[183] MacMillan Brown; J. - v2-68

[185] Hutton; J.H. [A.N.] - 50/1

[186] Hosie; A. - 214

[187] Kearsley; G.R. [M.G.] – 195; 545-9

[188] Wilson; E.H. - 149

[189] Wilson; E.H. - 160/1;182

[190] Wilson; E.H. - v2-10

[191] MacMillan Brown; J. - v2-133

[192] Heine-Geldern; R. [T.S.A.P.] – 45-65

[193] Bruhns; K.O. - 351

[194] Wilbert; J. [F.L.G.I.] – v2-369

[195] Kearsley; G.R. [M.G.] – 134-43

[196] Russell; R.V. - v1-128

[197] Russell; R.V. - v1-388

[198] Thurston; E. [C.T.S.I.] - v7-122

[199] Grimble; A. - 53

[200] Smith; P. - 190

[201] Smith; P. - 148

[202] Smith; P. - 148

[203] Smith; P. - 149

[204] Smith; P. - 150

[205] Smith; P. - 151

[206] Smith; P. - 163

[207] Smith; P. - 162

[208] Smith; P. - 174

[209] Graves; M.W. et al - W.A., Vol. 26, no. 3, Feb. 1995, p381-95

[210] Smith; P. - 161

[211] Heyerdahl; T. [A.I.P.] - 93;675/6

[212] Heyerdahl; T. [A.I.P.] - 82

[213] Heyerdahl; T. [A.I.P.] - 676)

[214] Heyerdahl; T. [A.I.P.] - 677

[215] Heyerdahl; T. [A.I.P.] - 677

[216] Ellis; W. - v2-337

[217] Smith; P. - 171/2

[218] Smith; P. - 183

[219] Smith; P. – 174

[220] Smith; P. - 174

[221] Buck; P. – 27;66-72

[222] Smith; P. - 178

[223] Boas; F. [K.T.] - 85

[224] Smith; P. - 184

[225] Smith; P. - 185

[226] Smith; P. - 179

[227] Kearsley; G.R. [M.G.] – 1016/7

[228] Smith; P. - 179

[229] Smith; P. - 182

[230] Smith; P. - 183

[231] Bahn; P. - 66

[232] Tilburg; Van; J-A. - 90

[234] Routledge; K.S. – 241; 278-80

[235] Kerry-Nicholls; J. - 123

[236] Kerry-Nichols; J. - 195

[237] Kerry-Nicholls; J. - 195

[238] Kerry-Nicholls; J. 191

[239] Ellis; W. - v1-84

[240] Ellis; W. - v2-67

[241] Ellis; W. - v2-197

[242] Ellis; W. - v4-23

[243] Falkner; T. - 148

[244] Falkner; T. - 148

[244] Falkner; T. - 148

[246] Falkner; T. - 54/5

[247] Falkner; T. - 112

[248] Falkner; T. - 118

[249] Falkner; T. - 117

[250] Bridges; E.L. - 62

[251] Bridges; E.L. - 262/3

[252] Bridges; E.L. - 443

[253] Bridges; E.L. - 66

[254] Bridges; E.L. - 375

[255] Bridges; E.L. – 402/3

[256] Bridges; E.L. - 404/5

[257] Bridges; E.L. - 409

[258] Bridges; E.L. - 415

[259] Bridges; E.L. - 412/3

[260] Bridges; E.L. - 414

[261] Bridges; E.L. - 415

[262] Bridges; E.L. -112

[263] Lumholtz; C. [U.M.] - v2-165

[264] Kearsley; G.R. [M.G.] – 191

[265] Lumholtz; C. - v2-167

[266] Lumholtz; C. - v2-166

[267] Kearsley; G.R. [M.G.] – 190; 192

[268] MacMillan Brown; J. - v2-133

[269] Lumholtz; C. - v2-169

[270] Lumholtz; C. - v2-171

[271] Campbell; J. - 262

[272] Pranavananda; S. – 17/8

[273] Lumholtz; C. - v2-198

[274] Lumholtz; C. [U.M.] - v2-198

[275] Falkner; T. - 115

[276] Kearsley; G.R. [M.G.] – 191

[277] Heyerdahl; T. [A.P.] - 151

[278] Bridges; E.L. - 230

[279] Bridges; E.L. - 364/5

[280] Campbell; J. - 160

[281] Campbell; J. - 256

[282] Campbell; J. - 254

[283] Elwin; V. [M.M.I.] – 253-99

[284] Campbell; J. - 255

[285] Kearsley; G.R. [M.G.] - 147

[286] Reisenfeld; A. – 371

[287] Kearsley; G.R. [M.G.] – 613-8

[287] Hose; C. & McDougall; W. – v2-142

[289] Batchelor; J. – 73/4

[290] Boas; F. [F.C.S.] – 156/7

[291] Bridges; E.L. - 427

[292] Bridges; E.L. - 413

[293] Kearsley; G.R. [M.G.] - 192

[294] Bridges; E.L. - 417

[295] Bridges; E.L. - 419

[296] Bridges; E.L. - 413

[297] Bridges; E.L. - 414

[298] Bridges; E.L. - 414

[299] Bridges; E.L. - 302

[300] Bridges; E.L. - 435

[301] Hadingham; E. - 278

[302] Dillehay; T.D. - 225

[303] Dillehay; T.D. - 226

[304] Dillehay; T.D. - 226

[305] Dillehay; T.D. - 226

[306] Dillehay; T.D. - 228

[307] Dillehay; T.D. - 228

[308] Dillehay; T.D. - 231

[309] Dillehay; T.D. - 230

[310] Dillehay; T.D. - 231

[311] Speiser; F. [T.Y.N.W.P.] – 98; Layard; J. - 565

[312] Hose; C. & McDougall; W. – v2-10

[313] Thurston; E. [C.T.S.I.] – v6-356

[314] Tierney; P. - 98

[315] Tierney; P. - 24

[316] Dillehay; T.D. - 226; Tierney; P. - 98

[317] Thurston; E. - v2-330

[318] Layard; J. – 293-305

[319] Moseley; M.E. - 92/3

[320] Moseley; M.E. - 94

[321] Bruhns; K.O. - 110

[322] Lynch; T.F. - 9

[323] Lynch; T.F. - 9

[324] Kolata; A.L. - 76

[325] Kolata; A.L. - 76

[326] Kolata; A.L. - 250

[327] Kolata; A.L. - 272/3

[328] Salmorel; M.L. - 28

[329] Pachacuti; Y.S. - 109

[330] Karsten; R. [I.T.A.A.C.] - 7

[331] Pelleschi; G. - 31/2

[332] Karsten; R. - [C.S.A.I.] - 110/1

[333] Karsten; R. [C.S.A.I.] - 112

[334] Batchelor; J. - 32

[335] Pelleschi; G. - 32

[336] Salmorel; M.L. - 107

[337] Metraux; A. -[H.S.A.I.] - 225

[338] Meggers; B.J. – 50-2

339 O'Neale; L.M. [H.S.A.I.] - 116

340 O'Neale; L.M. [H.S.A.I.] - 74

341 O'Neale; L.M. [H.S.A.I.] - 116

342 Metraux; A. [H.S.A.I.] - 252/3

343 Metraux; A. [H.S.A.I.] - 255

344 Metraux; A. [H.S.A.I.] - 246/7

345 Metraux; A. [H.S.A.I.] - 247

346 Bandelier; A.F. - 110

347 Church; G.E. - 206/7

348 Wiley; G.R. [H.S.A.I.] - 172

349 Bennett; W.C. [H.S.A.I.] - 32

350 Bennett; W.C. [H.S.A.I.] - 54/5

351 Wilbert; J. [F.L.T.I.] - 70

352 Wilbert; J. [F.L.T.I] - 193

353 Pelleschi; G. - 34

354 Osborne; H. - 129

355 Kearsley; G.T. [M.G.] – 635

356 Kearsley; G.R. [M.G.] – 632/3

357 Metraux; A. [H.S.A.I.] - 244

358 Pelleschi; G. - 99/100

359 Karsten; R. [C.S.A.I.] - 417

360 Karsten; R. [C.S.A.I.] - 425

Chapter 3

1 Karsten; R. [I.T.A.B.C.] - 6/7

2 Karsten; R. [I.T.A.B.C.] - 23

3 Karsten; R. [I.T.A.B.C.] - 24

4 Karsten; R. [I.T.A.B.C.] - 28

5 Karsten; R. [I.T.A.B.C.] - 28

6 Karsten; R. [I.T.A.B.C.] - 32

7 Kartsen; R. [I.T.A.B.C.] - 33

8 Karsten; R. [I.T.A.B.C.] - 40

9 Karsten; R. [I.T.A.B.C.] - 45

10 Karsten; R. [I.T.A.B.C.] - 45/6

11 Karsten; R. [I.T.A.B.C.] - 46

12 Kearsley; G.R. [M.G.] – 159; 528; 651; 933

13 Karsten; R. [I.T.A.B.C.] - 49

14 Karsten; R. [I.T.A.B.C.] - 38

15 Karsten; R. [I.T.A.B.C.] - 1

16 Karsten; R. [I.T.A.B.C.] - 28

17 Karsten; R. [I.T.A.B.C.] - 7

18 Karsten; R. [I.T.A.B.C.] - 109/10

19 Karsten; R. [I.T.A.B.C.] - 44

20 Karsten; R. [I.T.A.B.C.] - 111/2

21 Karsten; R. [I.T.A.B.C.] - 44

22 Karsten; R. [I.T.A.B.C.] - 111

23 Karsten; R. [I.T.A.B.C.] - 112

24 Karsten; R. [I.T.A.B.C.] - 113

25 Karsten; R. [I.T.A.B.C.] - 118

26 Karsten; R. [I.T.A.B.C.] - 115

27 Karsten; R. [I.T.A.B.C.] - 116

28 Karsten; R. [I.T.A.B.C.] - 116/7

29 Kearsley; G.R. [M.G.] – 632-7; Kearsley; G.R. [P.P.P.] – 50/1; 30-2

30 Kearsley; G.R. [M.G.] – 192; 625

31 Vogel; J.Ph. – 198

32 Kearsley; G.R. [P.P.P.] – 25; 32/3; 35; 40

33 Riesenfeld; A. – 352/3

34 Roy; S.C. [M.] – App.1x/x; xxiii

35 Handy; E.S.C. – 106

36 Drower; E.S. [M.I.I.] – 300-5

37 Heyerdahl; T. [A.I.P.] – 151

38 Karsten; R. [I.T.A.B.C.] - 101

39 Riesenfeld; A. - 371

40 Rivers; W.H.R. – 26/7

41 Karsten; R. [I.T.A.B.C.] - 101

42 Karsten; R. [I.T.A.B.C.] - 54

43 Karsten; R. [I.T.A.B.C.] - 87

44 Kearsley; G.R. [M.G.] – 209-11

45 Rutter; O. – 119

46 Haddon; A.C. – 199; Speiser; F. [E.N.M.H.] - 324

47 Seligmann; C.G. – 74; 493

48 Thurston; E. [C.T.S.I.] – v3-364; v4-430; Rivers; W.H.R. – 576-9

49 Handy; E.S.C. – 106-9; 206

50 Buck; P. – 443; Smith; S.P. – 100/1

51 Karsten; R. [I.T.A.B.C.] - 90/1

52 Karsten; R. [I.T.A.B.C.] - 103;107

53 Luckert; K.W. – 144/5

54 Karsten; R. [I.T.A.B.C.] - 106

55 Karsten; R. [I.T.A.B.C.] - 88

56 Hutton; J.H. [A.N.] - 279/80

57 Grubb; E.B. - 49

58 Grubb; E.B. - 50

59 Grubb; E.B. - 51

60 Grubb; E.B. - 51

61 Grubb; E.B. - 52/3

62 Grubb; E.B. - 52/3

63 Grubb; E.B. - 20/1

64 Grubb; E.B. - 139/40

65 Grubb; E.B. - 114

66 Covarrubias; M. [I.A.M.C.A.] – 6

67 Grubb; E.B. - 114

68 Grubb; E.B. - 120

69 Grubb; E.B. - 120

70 Grubb; E.B. - 118/9

71 Grubb; E.B. - 119

72 Grubb; E.B. - 135

73 Grubb; E.B. - 135

74 Grubb; E.B. - 139

75 Grubb; E.B. - 162

76 Spencer; B. & Gillan; F.J. [T.N.T.C.A.] - 525

77 Burger; R.L. – 72

78 Lumholtz; C. [A.M.] – v2-198

79 Kearsley; G.R. [M.G.] – 555; Leon-Portilla; M. - 32

80 Grubb; E.B. - 139/40

81 Grubb; E.B. - 177/8

82 E.L. Bridges - 415

83 Wilbert; J. [F.L.S.I.] - 12

84 Grubb; E.B. - 177

85 Grubb; E.B. - 177

86 Grubb; E.B. - 319

87 Grubb; E.B. - 233/4

88 Grubb; E.B. - 143

89 Karsten; R. [C.S.A.I.] - 4/5

90 Karsten; R. [C.S.A.I.] - 30/1

91 Karsten; R. [C.S.A.I.) - 37)

92 Karsten; R. [C.S.A.I.] - 279

93 Karsten; R. [C.S.A.I.] - 41

94 Karsten; R. [C.S.A.I.] - 4/5

95 Karsten; R. [C.S.A.I.] - 41

96 Karsten; R. [C.S.A.I.] - 161

97 Karsten; R. [C.S.A.I.] - 32

98 Karsten; R. [C.S.A.I.] - 6/7

99 Karsten; R. [C.S.A.I.] - 47

100 Karsten; R. [C.S.A.I.] - 50

101 Karsten; R. [C.S.A.I.] - 55

102 Karsten; R. [C.S.A.I.] - 59

103 Karsten; R. [C.S.A.I.] - 47

104 Karsten; R. [C.S.A.I.] - 188/9

105 Karsten; R. [C.S.A.I.] - 158/9

106 Karsten; R. [C.S.A.I.] - 156-8

107 Haddon; A.C. – 222/3; Williamson; R.W. – 225/6

108 Karsten; R. [C.S.A.I.] - 159

109 Karsten; R. [C.S.A.I.] - 176

110 Layard; J. – 500

111 Karsten; R. [C.S.A.I.] – 55

112 Karsten; R. [C.S.A.I.] - 145

113 Karsten; R. [C.S.A.I.] - 71

114 Karsten; R. [C.S.A.I.] - 131/2; 135; 139/40

115 Karsten; R. [C.S.A.I.] - 186

116 Karsten; R. [C.S.A.I.] - 121

117 Karsten; R. [I.T.A.B.C.] - 57

118 Karsten; R. [C.S.A.I.] - 122

119 Karsten; R. [C.S.A.I.] - 112

120 Karsten; R. [C.S.A.I.] - 111

121 Karsten; R. [C.S.A.I.] - 252

122 Karsten; R. [S.R.S.A.I.E.A.] - 135

123 Bruhns; K.O. – 228

124 Andagoya; P. de – ii

125 Moseley; M.E. – 29

126 Wafer; L. – 210-3

127 Moseley; M.E. – 27

128 Moseley; M.E. – 81

129 Moseley; M.E. – 81

130 Moseley; M.E. – 82

131 Burger; R.L. – 11

132 Moseley; M.E. – 86

133 Moseley; M.E. – 87/8

134 Moseley; M.E. – 91

135 Moseley; M.E. – 92/3

136 Maier; V. -205

137 Moseley; M.E. – 94

138 Burger; R.L. – 11

139 Burger; R.L. – 27

140 Burger; R.L. – 12

141 Moseley; M.E. – 99

142 Burger; R.L. – 31

143 Moseley; M.E. – 99

144 Burger; R.L. – 60/1

145 Burger; R.L. – 61 – photo caption

146 Potts; D.T. – 6

147 Potts; D.T. – 49

148 Potts; D.T. – 47

149 Potts; D.T. – 47

150 Potts; D.T. – 46

151 Potts; D.T. – 47/8

152 Potts; D.T. – 46

153 Potts; D.T. – 49/50; 51

154 Potts; D.T. – 81

155 Potts; D.T. – 95; 97/8

156 Potts; D.T. – 100/1

157 Potts; D.T. – 58/9

158 Harden; D. – 33/4; 59; 156

159 Burger; R.L. – 62

160 Burger; R.L. – 27

161 Burger; R.L. – 28

162 Moseley; M.E. – 115

163 Moseley; M.E. – 116

164 Moseley; M.E. – 118/9

165 Burger; R.L. – 28

166 Burger; R.L. - 29

167 Burger; R.L. – 31

168 Burger; R.L. – 36

169 Burger; R.L. – 32

170 Burger; R.L. – 38

171 Burger; R.L. – 32

172 Burger; R.L. – 29

173 Burger; R.L. – 34/5

174 Burger; R.L. – 37

175 Burger; R.L. – 36/7

176 Burger; R.L. – 39

177 Burger; R.L. - 40

178 Burger; R.L. – 41

179 Moseley; M.E. – 120

180 Moseley; M.E. – 119

181 Moseley; M.E. – 120

182 Moseley; M.E. – 119

183 Moseley; M.E. – 121

184 Moseley; M.E. - 113

185 Moseley; M.E. – 113/4

186 Moseley; M.E. – 114/5

187 Moseley; M.E. - 114

188 Burger; R.L. – 46

189 Moseley; M.E. – 100/1

190 Burger; R.L. – 45

191 Moseley; M.E. – 112/3

192 Burger; R.L. – 45

193 Burger; R.L. – 45/6

194 Burger; R.L. – 47/8

195 Eggeling in Muller; F.M. [S.B.E.] – v44-119

196 Julius Eggeling in Muller; F.M. [S.B.E.] – v12-50; v41-162; 166; v44-xxxiii; 403-20

197 Burger; R.L. – 50

198 Burger; R.L. – 42

199 Burger; R.L. – 50

200 Moseley; M.E. – 100/1

201 Moseley; M.E. – 102

202 Burger; R.L. – 42/3

203 Burger; R.L. – 44/5

204 Burger; R.L. – 53/4

205 Burger; R.L. – 53

206 Burger; R.L. – 52/3

207 Bruhns; K.O. - 360

208 Burger; R.L. – 57

209 Burger; R.L. – 57/8

210 Moseley; M.E. – 102/3

211 Moseley; M.E. – 103

212 Moseley; M.E. – 103

213 Moseley; M.E. – 104

214 Moseley; M.E. - 106

215 Burger; R.L. – 63

216 Burger; R.L. – 64

217 Burger; R.L. – 64

218 Burger; R.L. – 65

219 Handy; E.S.C. – 241/2

220 Handy; E.S.C. - 170

221 Handy; E.S.C. – 253

222 Handy; E.S.C. – 239-44

223 Handy; E.S.C. – 240

224 Handy; E.S.C. – 169

225 Burger; R.L. – 65/6

226 Burger; R.L. – 67/8

227 Burger; R.L. – 71

228 Burger; R.L. – 70

229 Burger; R.L. – 72/3

230 Enock; C.R. 226; 234; 243; 299; 303/4

231 Burger; R.L. – 73

232 Weaver; M.P. – 85

233 Burger; R.L. – 73/4

234 Burger; R.L. – 74

235 Burger; R.L. – 58

236 Moseley; M.E. – 106

237 Burger; R.L. – 75/6

238 Moseley; M.E. – 107

239 Moseley; M.E. – 107

240 Moseley; M.E. – 108

241 Moseley; M.E. – 110

242 Black; J. – 158/9

243 Thurston; E. [C.T.S.I.] – v2-310; v7-322; 355

244 Moseley; M.E. – 110

245 Moseley; M.E. – 110

246 King; L.W. – 124/5

247 Langdon; S. – 30

248 Moseley; M.E. – 110/1

249 Moseley; M.E. – 112

250 Mills; .L.H. in Muller; F.M. [S.B.E.] – v4-210/1

251 Mills; L.H. in Muller; F.M. [S.B.E.] – v31-313-6

252 Eggeling; J. in Muller; F.M. [S.B.E.] – v-43-341-56

253 Moseley; M.E. – 112/3

254 Moseley; M.E. – 113

255 Eggeling; J. in Muller; F.M. [S.B.E.] – v41-325-417

256 Drower; E.S. [M.I.I.] – 30-6; 9

257 Moseley; M.E. – 113

258 Moseley; M.E. – 113

259 Moseley; M.E. – 144

260 Burger; R.L. – 59

261 Burger; R.L. – 59

262 Burger; R.L. – 59/60

263 Moseley; M.E. – 144

264 Moseley; M.E. – 145

265 Moseley; M.E. – 145

266 Moseley; M.E. – 148

267 Moseley; M.E. – 125

268 Burger; R.L. – 77

269 Moseley; M.E. – 125

270 Moseley; M.E. – 143

271 Burger; R.L. – 77

272 Bollaert; W. – 137

273 Burger; R.L. – 77

274 Burger; R.L. – 78

275 Burger; R.L. – 79

276 Burger; R.L. – 78/9

277 Burger; R.L. – 79

278 Burger; R.L. – 79

279 Burger; R.L. – 80/1

280 Moseley; M.E. – 141

281 Burger; R.L. – 83

282 Burger; R.L. – 84

283 Burger; R.L. – 82

284 Burger; R.L. – 83

285 Burger; R.L. – 88

286 Burger; R.L. – 83

287 Tylor; E.B. – 86

288 Tylor; E.B. – 86

289 Burger; R.L. – 85

290 Burger; R.L. – 86

291 Burger; R.L. – 88/9

292 Burger; R.L. – 89

293 Burger; R.L. – 90

294 Burger; R.L. – 105

295 Burger; R.L. – 106

296 Burger; R.L. – 84

297 Burger; R.L. – 106

298 Burger; R.L. – 107/8

299 Burger; R.L. – 108

300 Burger; R.L. – 109

301 Burger; R.L. – 109/10

302 Burger; R.L. – 110

303 Burger; R.L. – 111/2

304 Burger; R.L. – 112/3

305 Burger; R.L. – 207

306 Burger; R.L. – 207

307 Burger; R.L. – 113

308 Burger; R.L. – 114/5

309 Burger; R.L. – 115

310 Burger; R.L. – 116/7

Chapter 4

1 Burger; R.L. – 119/20

2 Weaver; M.P. - 94

3 Liebert; G. - 125

4 Burger; R.L. – 118/9

5 Burger; R.L. – 120

6 Burger; R.L. – 121

7 Burger; R.L. – 122

8 Burger; R.L. – 127

9 Moseley; M.E. – 146/7

10 Moseley; M.E. – 147

11 Moseley; M.E. – 147

12 Moseley; M.E. – 149

13 Moseley; M.E. – 150

14 Moseley; M.E. – 149/50

15 Buck; P. – 423

16 Speiser; F. [E.N.M.H.] – 308

17 Wollaston; A.F.R. – 139

18 Moseley; M.E. – 151

19 Anton; F. – 48; 65; 141

20 Burger; R.L. – 128

21 Burger; R.L. in Townsend; R.L. – 265

22 Burger; R.L. in Townsend; R.F. – 266

23 Burger; R.L. – 128/9

24 Burger; R.L. – 130

25 Moseley; M.E. – 125

26 Moseley; M.E. – 156/7

27 Anton; F. – 215

28 Anton; F. – 20

29 Burger; R.L. – 130/1

30 Burger; R.L. – 132

31 Burger; R.L. – 134

32 Burger; R.L. – 135

33 Kearsley; G.R. [M.G.] – 205; 449; 734; 213/4; 974

34 Burger; R.L. – 130/1

35 Burger; R.L. – 132

36 Burger; R.L. – 136

37 Thurston; E. [C.T.S.I.] – v6-134

38 Burger; R.L. – 142

39 Burger; R.L. – 143
Moseley; M.E. – 154/5

40 Burger; R.L. – 144

41 Burger; R.L. – 149

42 Burger; R.L. – 145

43 Burger; R.L. – 164

44 Burger; R.L. – 146

45 Buck; P – 4

46 Haddon; A.C. – 46/7;

Seligmann; C.G. – 558/9; 726

47 Batchelor; J. – 525-7

48 Vogel; J.Ph. – 8/9

49 Burger; R.L. – 147

50 Burger; R.L. – 152

51 Burger; R.L. – 154

52 Roe; P.G. – 282/3

53 Kearsley; G.R. [M.G.] – 688; 764; 816

54 Roe; P.G. – 293/4

55 Roe; P.G. – 296

56 Kearsley; G.R. [M.G.] – 105-13

57 Anton; F. – 19

58 Burger; R.L. – 154/5

59 Gartelmann; K.D. – 30

60 Burger; R.L. – 157

61 Burger; R.L. – 159

62 Burger; R.L. – 157

63 Burger; R.L. – 160

64 Burger; R.L. – 162/3

65 Poindexter; M. [A.I.] – 34

66 Burger; R.L. – 166

67 Burger; R.L. – 166

68 Burger; R.L. – 168/9

69 Burger; R.L. – 169

70 Burger; R.L. – 168/9

71 Burger; R.L. – 171

72 Burger; R.L. – 173

73 Burger; R.L. – 179

74 Burger; R.L. – 173

75 Burger; R.L. – 178/9

76 Burger; R.L. – 174

77 Gartelmann; K.D. – 30/1

78 Gartelmann; K.D. – 44/5

79 Burger; R.L. – 174/5

80 Burger; R.L. – 176

81 Kearsley; G.R. [M.G.] – 623; 626; 827

82 Burger; R.L. – 179

83 Moseley; M.E. – 156

84 Moseley; M.E. – 157

85 Burger; R.L. – 183

86 Burger; R.L. – 184

87 Burger; R.L. – 185

88 Burger; R.L. – 185/6

89 Burger; R.L. – 186

90 Burger; R.L. – 188)

91 Burger; R.L. – 187

92 Burger; R.L. – 188

93 Burger; R.L. – 191

94 Burger; R.L. – 196

95 Burger; R.L. – 197

96 Kearsley; G.R. [M.G.] – 209-11

97 Burger; R.L. – 198)

98 Burger; R.L. – 198/9

99 Burger; R.L. – 199/200

100 Arriaga; P.J. de – 69; Burger; R.L. - 135

101 Handy; E.S.C. – 313

102 Mills; J.P. [L.N.] – 85

103 Burger; R.L. – 201

104 Lishkt; S.S. – 52;81; 165

105 Burger; R.L. – 201

106 Burger; R.L. – 201/2

107 Burger; R.L. – 203

108 Burger; R.L. – 207

109 Burger; R.L. – 210

110 Burger; R.L. – 204/5

111 Burger; R.L. – 213-5

112 Burger; R.L. – 212; 214/5

113 Burger; R.L. – 215/6

114 Burger; R.L. - 218

115 Burger; R.L. – 219

116 Burger; R.L. – 220

117 Bruhns; K.O. – 251

118 Demarest; A.A. – 67

119 Demarest; A.A. – 68; Donnan; C.B. - 2

120 Demarest; A.A. – 68

121 Burger; R.L. – 217

122 Burger; R.L. – 217

123 Bruhns; K.O. – 141

124 Kearsley; G.R. [P.P.P.P.] – 83; 113; 131; 140/1

125 Burger; R.L. – 217

126 Bruhns; K.O. – 189/90

127 Bruhns; K.O. – 191

128 Townsend; R.F. – 42

129 Kolata; A. – 101

130 Moseley; M.E. – 192

131 Roe; P.G. – 296

132 Urton; G. – 10

133 Moseley; M.E. – 125

134 Moseley; M.E. – 137/8

135 Moseley; M.E. – 138/9

136 Moseley; M.E. – 139

137 Moseley; M.E. – 140

138 Bruhns; K.O. - 360

139 Burger; R.L. – 213

140 Donnan; C.B. – 4

141 Shimada; I. et al – 255

142 Bruhns; K.O. – 254

143 Bruhns; K.O. – 251

144 Demarest; A.A. – 63

145 Anton; F. – 20

146 Demarest; A.A. – 7

147 Poznansky; A. – 117; Zuidema; R.T. – 211

148 Arriaga; P.J. de – 24

149 Farrabee; W.C. – 147

150 Bruhns; K.O. – 5

151 Bruhns; K.O. – 260

152 Bruhns; K.O. – 261

153 Bruhns; K.O. – 314

154 Bruhns; K.O. – 359

155 Bruhns; K.O. – 262/3

156 Stahl; P.W. – 141

157 Stahl; P.W. – 140

158 Bruhns; K.O. – 82

159 Bruhns; K.O. – 142

160 Bruhns; K.O. – 142

161 Bruhns; K.O. – 143

162 Bruhns; K.O. – 148

163 Bennett; W.C. [H.S.A.I.] – 50

164 Metraux; A [H.S.A.I.] – 245

165 Gartelmann; K.D. – 198

166 Bray; T.L. – 219

167 Mukherjee; P. –31; Roy; S.C. [M.] – 385

168 Bray; T.L. – 220

169 Bruhns; K.O. – 82

170 Bruhns; K.O. – 48

171 Bruhns; K.O. – 201

172 Bruhns; K.O. – 201

173 Bruhns; K.O. – 269/70

174 Bruhns; K.O. – 267

175 Bruhns; K.O. – 270

176 Liebert; G. – 202

177 Liebert; G. – 110

178 Gartelmann; K.D. – 307

179 Vega; G. de la – v2-347

180 Kearsley; G.R. [M.G.] – 508-63

181 Poindexter; M. [A.I.] – 28

182 Vega; G. de la – v2-334

183 Poindexter; M. [A.I.] –x-xiv

184 Meggers; B.L. – 36

185 Meggers; B.J. – 37

186 Meggers; B.J. – 38

187 Meggers; B.J. – 38/9

188 Meggers; B.J. – 42

189 Nelson; S.M. – 63;98

190 Meggers; B.J. – 48;50

191 Gartelmann; K.D. – 379

192 Meggers; B.J. – 55

193 Meggers; B.J. – 56;59

194 Meggers; B.J. – 59/60

195 Meggers; B.J. – 61/2

196 Meggers; B.J. – 94

197 Meggers; B.J. – 95

198 Meggers; B.J. – 117

199 Meggers; B.J. – 94

200 Rawson; J. – 14/5

201 Townsend; R.F. [A.W.M.] – 233-43

202 Anawalt; P.R. – 233

203 Anawalt; P.R. – 236

204 Anawalt; P.R. in Townsend; R.F. [A.W.M.] – 243/4

205 Meggers; B.J. – 84

206 Meggers; B.J. – 97/8

207 Meggers; B.J. – 86

208 Meggers; B.J. - 88/9

209 Meggers; B.J. – 93

210 Meggers; B.J. – 87

211 Meggers; B.J. – 90/1

212 Meggers; B.J. – 94

213 Meggers; B.J. – 86

214 Poindexter; M. [A.I.] – xiii;156

215 Poindexter; M. [A.I.] – ix;x

216 Meggers; B.J. – 86

217 Stair; J.B. – 285/6

218 Meggers; B.J. – 94; Gartelmann; K.D. – 256

219 Kearsley; G.R. [M.G.] – 358-67

220 Valdez; F. in Townsend; R.F. – 230

221 Meggers; B.J. – 103

222 Valdez; F. in Townsend; R.F. – 230

223 Meggers; B.J. – 116

224 Valdez; F. in Townsend; R.F. – 231

225 Valdez; F. in Townsend; R.F. – 232

226 Meggers; B.J. – 104

227 Valdez; F. in Townsend; R.F. – 231

228 Meggers; B.J. – 105/6

229 Meggers; B.J. – 141/2

230 Kearsley; G.R. [M.G.] – 548/9

231 Meggers; B.J. – 108-112

232 Meggers; B.J. – 120

233 Meggers; B.J. – 121

234 Meggers; B.J. – 120

235 Meggers; B.J. – 119

236 Meggers; B.J. – 124

237 Meggers; B.J. – 125

238 Roe; P.G. – 236

239 Niles; S.A. in Townsend; R.F. – 351

240 Markham; C.R. [T.P.C.L.] – 101

241 Markham; C.R. [T.P.C.L.] – 101

242 Schnitger; F.M. – 191

243 Vogel; J. Ph. – 14

244 Martynov; A.I. – 86/7

245 Martynov; A.I. – 86

246 Mair; V. – 205/6

247 Martynov; A.I. – 100

248 Gartelmann; K.D. – 256

249 Gartelmann; K.D. – 254

250 Meggers; B.J. – 130/1

251 Kirchhoff; P. [H.S.A.I.] – 310

252 Cobo; B. – 172-4

253 Kearsley; G.R. [M.G.] - 197/8; 304

254 Thurston; E. [C.T.S.I.] – v2-249-51

255 Sinha; I. – 43/4

256 Thurston; E. [C.T.S.I.] – v2-329

257 Thurston; E. [C.T.S.I.] – v3-288-92

258 Crooke; W. – v1-36

259 Kearsley; G.R. [M.G.] – 995-8; 1024

260 Kearsley; G.R. [M.G.] – 641; 655/6; 928-31

261 Crooke; W. – v2-173/4

262 Crooke; W. – v2-176/7

263 Thurston; E. [C.T.S.I.] – v4-214

264 Thurston; E. [C.T.S.I.] – v3-463

265 Thurston; E. [O.S.S.I.] – 202

266 Thurston; E. [O.S.S.I.] - 202

267 Thurston; E. [C.T.S.I.] – v5-62

268 Elwin; V. [M.M.I.] – 40

269 Thurston; E. [O.S.S.I.] - 206

270 Thurston; E. [C.T.S.I.] - v6-330/1; Thurston; E. [O.S.S.I.] - 206

271 Roy; S.C. [H.B.O.] – 121

272 Hutton; J.H. [A.N.] – 12

273 Hutton; J.H. [A.N.] – 158/9

274 Furness; W.H. – 140

275 Hose; C. & McDougall; W. – v2-104/5

276 Loeb; E. & Heine-Geldern; R. – 35

277 Loeb; E. & Heine-Geldern; R. – 36

278 Blackwood; B. – 504

279 Ivens; W.G. [I.B.P.] – 23

280 Russell; v1-171/2

281 Arriaga; P.J. de – 42

282 Arriaga; P.J. de – 44

283 Vega; G. de la – v1–51/2

284 Vega; G. de la – v2-293/4

285 Tierney; P. – 306

286 Luckert; K.W. - 27/8

287 Luckert; K.W. – 145

288 Luckert; K.W. – 7

289 Handy; E.C.S. – 253

290 Riesenfeld; A. – 238

291 Donnan; C.B. – 6;8;27

293 Grigson; W.V. – 114

293 Mills; J.P. [L.N.] – 25

294 Holmes; J.H. – 194; Riesenfeld; A. – 368

295 Akerblom; K. – 134-6; Tilberg; J.-A. – 69;72

296 Reichel-Dolmatoff; G. [A.C.] – 106;108

297 Furer-Haimendorf; C. [R.G.A.] – 170;182

298 Hutton; J.H. [S.N.] – 48

299 Mills; J.P. [L.N.] – xxvii

300 Mills; J.P. [L.N.] – xxix

301 Mills; J.P. [L.N.] – xxx

302 Blackwood, B. – 540

303 Eggeling; J. in Muller; F.M. [S.B.E.] – v44-xvii/xviii

304 Eggeling; J. in Muller; F.M. [S.B.E.] – v44-419-20

305 Eggeling; J. in Muller; F.M. [S.B.E.] – v44-404

306 Eggeling; J. in Muller; F.M. [S.B.E.] – v44-405/6

307 Drower; E.S. [M.I.I.] – 30

308 Liebert; G. – 67 Thurston; E. [C.T.S.I.] – v6-398

309 Eggeling; J. in Muller; F.M. [S.B.E.] – v44-407/8

310 Eggeling; J. in Muller; F.M. [S.B.E.] – v12-160

311 Kearsley; G.R. [M.G.] – 461/2

312 Crooke; W. – v2-107

313 Russell; R.V. & Hira Lal; - v1-19

314 Kearsley; G.R. [M.G.] – 471-4; 898/900

315 Miller; A.G. – 54

316 Thurston; E. [C.T.S.I.] – v2-270

317 Langdon; S. – 154/5; Buhler; G. in Muller; F.M. [S.B.E.] – v25-192 Eggeling; J. in Muller; F.M. [S.B.E.] – v41-267

318 Thurston; E. [C.T.S.I.] – v2-272

319 Bruhns; K.O. – 48

320 Bruhns; K.O. – 168

321 Bruhns; K.O. – 169

322 Bruhns; K.O. – 150

323 Bruhns; K.O. – 150

324 Bruhns; K.O. – 150

325 Meggers; B.J. – 18

326 Meggers; B.J. – 22

327 Bruhns; K.O. – 150

328 Bruhns; K.O. – 314

329 Bruhns; K.O. – 316

330 Bruhns; K.O. – 316/7

331 Bruhns; K.O. – 317

332 Meggers; B.J. – 136-8

333 Allchin; B. + R. – 277

334 Meggers; B.J. – 142/3

335 Bellwood; P. – 74

336 Meggers; B.J. – 144

337 Meggers; B.J. – 151-3

338 Meggers; B.J. – 157

339 Bruhns; K.O. – 207

340 Allchin; B. + R. - 331

341 Bruhns; K.O. – 207

342 Bruhns; K.O. – 210

343 Bruhns; K.O. – 212

344 Bruhns; K.O. – 213/4

345 Bruhns; K.O. – 214

346 Bruhns; K.O. – 271

347 Bruhns; K.O. – 287

348 Bruhns; K.O. 343

349 Bruhns; K.O. – 343

350 Bruhns; K.O . – 349

351 Bruhns; K.O. – 348

352 Bruhns; K.O. – 349

353 Bruhns; K.O. – 152

354 Bruhns; K.O. – 153

355 Bruhns; K.O. – 153

356 Bruhns; K.O. – 266

Chapter 5

1 Roe; P.G. – 273

2 Burger; R.L. – 90

3 Burger; R.L. – 91

4 Moseley; M.E. – 161

5 Moseley; M.E. – 163

6 Moseley; M.E. – 163

7 Moseley; M.E. – 164

8 Moseley; M.E. – 162

9 Kearsley; G.R. [M.G.] – 28-50

10 Moseley; M.E. – 165

11 Moseley; M.E. – 166

12 Moseley; M.E. - 166/7

13 Parpola; A. – 399-415

14 Boltz; W.G. – W.A., v17; No.3, 430

15 Moseley; M.E. – 166/7

16 Moseley; M.E. – 182

17 Moseley; M.E. – 179

18 Moseley; M.E. – 181

19 Lehmann; W. – 17

20 Moseley; M.E. – 184/5

21 Bruhns; K.O. – 252/3

22 Rienhard; J. – 291

23 Hadingham; E. – 68/9

24 Hadingham; E. – 121

25 Hadingham; E. – 133

26 Hadingham; E. – 127

27 Reinhard; J. – 294

28 Reinhard; J. – 298/9

29 Hadingham; E. – 80

30 Hadingham; E. - 82

31 Hadingham; E. – 87

32 Urton; G. – 3;114

33 Hadingham; E. – 112

34 Hadingham; E. – 117

35 Hadingham; E. – 117

36 Reinhard; J. – 291

37 Bruhns; K.O. – 200

38 Moseley; M.E. – 185

39 Poindexter; M. – 117/8

40 Anton; F. – 62

41 Anton; F. – 63

42 Anton; F. – 62/3

43 Anton; F. – 63

44 Anton; F. – 65/6; 72/3

45 Anton; F. – 76

46 Kearsley; G.R. [M.G.] – 594

47 Metraux; A. [H.S.A.I.] – 244/5

48 Verrill; A.H. – 64

49 Metraux; A. [H.S.A.I.] – 255/6

50 Moseley; M.E. – 186

51 Shimada; I. – 254

52 Handy; E.S.C. – 346

53 Moseley; M.E. – 187

54 Anton; F. – 71

55 Moseley; M.E. - 191

56 Moseley; M.E. – 192

57 Moseley; M.E. – 201/2

58 Moseley; M.E. – 202

59 Burger; R.L. – 127

60 Moseley; M.E. – 203

61 Kearsley; G.R. [P.P.P.P.] – 118; 129; 131; 140

62 Kolata; A. – 111

63 Moseley; M.E. – 205

64 Moseley; M.E. – 204/5

65 Moseley; M.E. – 106/7

66 Moseley; M.E. – 208

67 Moseley; M.E. – 217

68 Moseley; M.E. – 219

69 Moseley; M.E. – 217/8

70 Moseley; M.E. – 218

71 Moseley; M.E. – 219/20

72 Moseley; M.E. – 220

73 Moseley; M.E. – 221

74 Moseley; M.E. – 221

75 Moseley; M.E. – 221/2

76 Moseley; M.E. – 225/6

77 Moseley; M.E. – 227

78 Moseley; M.E. – 228

79 Moseley; M.E. – 228/9

80 Potts; D.T. – 18

81 Potts; D.T. 22

82 Potts; D.T. – 155

83 Potts; D.T. – 396

84 Moseley; M.E. – 229

85 Moseley; M.E. – 209

86 Alva; W. & Donnan; C.B. – 24

87 Markham; C.R. [T.P.C.L.] – 154

88 Donnan, C.B. – 2

89 Roe; P.G. – 273; 296

90 Donnan; C.B. – 10/1

91 Gartelmann; K.D. – 121

92 Moseley; M.E. – 211

93 Moseley; M.E. – 212

94 Bruhns; K.O. – 193

95 Bruhns; K.O. – 195

96 Alva; W. + Donnan; C.B. – 126

97 Ellis; W. – v1-238

98 Demarest; A.A. – 68

99 Shimada; I. – 253

100 Shimada; I. – 255

101 Benson; E.P. in Townsend; R.F. [T.A.A.] – 303

102 Benson; E.P. in Townsend; R.F. [T.A.A.] – 305/6

103 Pranavananda; S. - 9; 17/8

104 Danielou; A. – 210/1

105 Moseley; M.E. – 216

106 Bruhns; K.O. – 290-3

107 Moseley; M.E. – 231/2

108 Moseley; M.E. – 232

109 Moseley; M.E. – 241/2

110 Moseley; M.E. – 243

111 Moseley; M.E. – 243

112 Moseley; M.E. – 245

113 Moseley; M.E. – 245

114 Vega; G. de la – v2-195/6

115 Salcaymahua; P.-Y. – 108

116 Moseley; M.E. – 246

117 Moseley; M.E. – 247

118 Moseley; M.E. – 247

119 Moseley; M.E. – 249/50

120 Fornander; A.F. – v1-4 1/2

121 Fornander; A. F. – v1-39

122 Poindexter; M. – v1-155-7; v2-111

123 Fornander; A.F. – 40

124 Moseley; M.E. – 250

125 Mariner; E. – 289

126 Gurney; O.R. – 29

127 Donnan; C.B. – 88

128 Anton; F. – 151

129 Bollaert; W. – 202

130 Kearsley; G.R. [P.P.P.P.] – 82; Kearsley; G.R. [M.G.] 46

131 Demarest; A.A. – 45

132 Moseley; M.E. – 251

133 Kearsley; G.R. [M.G.] – 632-7;1024/5

134 Moseley; M.ER. – 251

135 Moseley; M.E. – 253

136 Moseley; M.E. – 254

137 Moseley; M.E. – 254

138 Moseley; M.E. – 260

139 Moseley; M.E. – 254

140 Moseley; M.E. – 255

141 Moseley; M.E. – 256

142 Moseley; M.E. – 256

143 O'Neale; L.M. [H.S.A.I.] – 94-6

144 Zuidema; R.T. – 206; 214

145 Moseley; M.E. – 252

146 Moseley; M.E. – 260

147 Hadingham; E. – 46/7

148 Salcamayhua; P.-Y. - 74-6

149 Osborne; H. – 45-7

150 Bandelier; A.F. – 303-5

151 Cotterell; A. – 218

152 Graves; R. – 443

153 Bandelier; A.F. – 295

154 Bandelier; A.F. – 325

154 Bandelier; A.F. – 325

156 Bollaert; W. – 123

157 Markham; C.R. in de la Vega; G. – v1-73

158 Bandelier; A.F. – 305/6

159 Vega; G. de la – v1-71/2

160 Vega; de la – v1-73/4

161 Ondegardo; P. de –153/4

162 Bandelier; A. – 316/7

163 Bandelier; A.F. – 294

164 Bandelier; A.F. – 294

165 Telang; K.T. in Muller; F.M. [S.B.E.] – v8-37-131

166 Telang; K.T. in Muller; F.M. [S.B.E.] – v8-2/3;37/8

167 Sastri; H.K. – 226/7

168 Rivers; W.H.R. – 695

169 Rivers; W.H.R. – 699

170 Furer-Haimendorf; C. [R.G.A.] – 105

171 Thurston; E. [C.T.S.I.] – v1-19

172 Mills; L.H. in Muller; F.M. [S.B.E.] – v31-379

173 Eggeling; J. in Muller; F.M. [S.B.E.] – v31-69

174 Eggeling; J. in Muller; F.M. [S.B.E.] – v31-76

175 Eggeling; J. in Muller; F.M. [S.B.E.] – v26-118

176 Thurston; E. [C.T.S.I.] – v1-19

177 Kearsley; G.R. [M.G.] – 936-8

178 Whitehead; H. [V.G.S.I.] – 19; 96

179 Whitehead; H. [V.G.S.I.] – 33

180 Thurston; E. [C.T.S.I.] – v2-332

181 Thurston; E. [C.T.S.I.] – v2-330

182 Boning; E. – 30

184 Thurston; E. [C.T.S.I.] – v1-19

185 Thurston; E. [C.T.S.I.] – v1-20

186 Arriaga; P.J. de – 24

187 Moseley; M.E. – 250

188 Mariner; E. – 289

189 Gurney; O.R. – 29

190 Thurston; E. [C.T.S.I.] – v2-277

191 Thurston; E. [C.T.S.I.] – v2-279

192 Thurston; E. [C.T.S.I.] – v5-415

193 Thurston; E. [C.T.S.I.] – v5-106

194 Thurston; E. [C.T.S.I.] – v5-108

195 Thurston; E. [C.T.S.I.] – v5-108

196 Thurston; E. [C.T.S.I.] – v2-285

192 Verrill; A.H. – 297; Poindexter; M. [A.I.] – v2-69/70

198 Thurston; E. [C.T.S.I.] – v2-36

199 Thurston; E. [C.T.S.I.] – v2-365

200 Thurston; E. [C.T.S.I.] – v6-192

201 Thurston; E. [C.T.S.I.] – v6-245

202 Thurston; E. [C.T.S.I.] – v2-366

203 Thurston; E. [C.T.S.I.] – v5-63/4

204 Thurston; E. [C.T.S.I.] – v2-498

205 Thurston; E. [C.T.S.I.] – v3-21

206 Thurston; E. [C.T.S.I.] – v3-251

207 Thurston; E. [C.T.S.I.] – v4-74

208 Thurston; E. [C.T.S.I.] – v4-116

209 Thurston; E. [C.T.S.I.] – v4-120

210 Thurston; E. [C.T.S.I.] – v4-450

211 Thurston; E. [C.T.S.I.] – v4-137

212 Thurston; E. [C.T.S.I.] – v4-383

213 Thurston; E. [C.T.S.I.] – v4-389

214 Thurston; E. [C.T.S.I.] – v5-455

215 Thurston; E. [C.T.S.I.] – v5-472

216 Thurston; E. [C.T.S.I.] – v5-476

217 Thurston; E. [C.T.S.I.] – v5-483

218 Thurston; E. [C.T.S.I.] – v4-362

219 Thurston; E. [C.T.S.I.] – v4-383

220 Thurston; E. [C.T.S.I.] – v7-241

221 Thurston; E. [C.T.S.I.] – v5-52/3

222 Thurston; E. [C.T.S.I.] – v5-52

223 Thurston; E. [C.T.S.I.] – v5-56

224 Thurston; E. [C.T.S.I.] – v7-5

225 Buck; P. – 510

226 Thurston; E. [C.T.S.I.] – v6-280

227 Thurston; E. [C.T.S.I.] – v6-108

228 (Thurston; E. [C.T.S.I.] – v6-370

229 Thurston; E. [C.T.S.I.] – v7-339/40

Chapter 6

1 Zuidema; R.T. – 23

2 Poindexter; M. [A.I.] – xi; 195

3 Zuidema; R.T. – 1

4 Cobo; B. – 51-83

5 Zuidema; R.T. – 10

6 Zuidema; R.T. – 14/5

7 Zuidema; R.T. – 10

8 Layard; J. – 11;22;85-163

9 Zuidema; R.T. – 23

10 Zuidema; R.T. – 25

11 Zuidema; R.T. – 26

12 Zuidema; R.T. – 26/7

13 Zuidema; R.T. – 43/4

14 Zuidema; R.T. – 81

15 Zuidema; R.T. – 46/7;49

16 Zuidema; R.T. – 44;52/3

17 Zuidema; R.T. – 53/4;78

18 Crooke; W. – v1-98

19 Zuidema; R.T. – 99

20 Betanzos; Juan Diaz de; cap. xvi, p112; Zuidema; R.T. – 83

21 Zuidema; R.T. – 98/9

22 Salcamayhua; P.-Y. – 76

23 Russell; R.V. & Hira Lal – v1-16

24 Zuidema; R.T. – 119

25 Thurston; E. [C.T.S.I.] – v5-301

26 Zuidema; R.T. – 276

27 Rivers; W.H.R. – 582/3; Thurston; E. [C.T.S.I.] – v1-71; 309-13; 375; 380; v3-420; v4-124

28 Grigson; W.V. – 223

29 Clay; A.T. – 45; Loeb; E. & Heine-Geldern; R. – 157/8

30 Brundage; B.C. – 194

31 Poindexter; M. – 195

32 Poindexter; M. – 198

33 Russell; R.V. & Hira Lal – v1-8

34 Allchin; B. & R. – 240/1

35 Allchin; R. & B. – 99; 107; 133; 217

36 Zaehner; R.C. – 124/5

37 Zaehner; R.C. – 229/30

38 Russell; R.V. & Hira Lal – v1-80

39 Russell; R.V. & Hira Lal – v1-86

40 Russell; R.V. & Hira Lal – v1-30

41 Russell; R.V. & Hira Lal – v1-73/4

42 Thurston; E. [C.T.S.I.] – v6-86

43 Thurston; E. [C.T.S.I.] – v7-274

44 Thurston; E. [C.T.S.I.] – v7-18

45 Thurston; E. [C.T.S.I.] – v5-243

46 Thurston; E. [C.T.S.I.] – v5-408

47 Thurston; E. [C.T.S.I.] – v6-16

48 Kolata; A. – 104;106

49 Urton; G. – 40/1

50 Russell; R.V. & Hira Lal – v1-16

51 Russell; R. & Hira Lal - v1-17

52 Russell; R.V. & Hira Lal – v1-17

53 Zuidema; R.YT. – 58;87

54 Zuidema; R.T. –157

55 Zuidema; R.T. – 189;196

56 Kolata; A. – 218

57 Urton; G. – 40/1

57 Urton; G. – 40/1

59 Kolata; A. – 100

60 Kolata; A. – 100/1

61 Kolata; A. – 277

62 Kolata; A. – 101

63 Muller; F.M. [S.B.E.] – v1-131

64 Drower; E.S. [M.I.I.] – 11

65 Muller; F.M. [S.B.E.] – v10-13/4

66 Urton; G. – 40/1

67 Muller; F.M. [S.B.E.] – v10 (Pt.2)-30; 44/5; 95; 141

68 Roe; P.G. – 146; Dundes; A. – 140

69 Thurston; E. [C.T.S.I.] – v1-134

70 Thurston; E. [C.T.S.I.] – v2-393/4

71 Thurston; E. [C.T.S.I.] – v2-394

72 Thurston; E. [C.T.S.I.] – v3-351

73 Thurston; E. [C.T.S.I.] – v3-369/70

74 Thurston; E. [C.T.S.I.] – v3-417

75 Thurston; E. [C.T.S.I.] – v3-450/1

76 Thurston; E. [C.T.S.I.] – v4-5

77 Thurston; E. [C.T.S.I.] – v4-10

78 Thurston; E. [C.T.S.I.] – v4-116

79 Thurston; E. [C.T.S.I.] – v4-119/20

80 Thurston; C. [C.T.S.I.] – v4-121/3

81 Thurston; E. [C.T.S.I.] – v4-130/1

82 Thurston; E. [C.T.S.I.] – v5-104

83 Thurston; E. [C.T.S.I.] – v4-345/6

84 Thurston; E. [C.T.S.I.] – v4-407

85 Thurston; E. [C.T.S.I.] – v4-450

86 Thurston; E. [C.T.S.I.] – v5-443

87 Thurston; E. [C.T.S.I.] – v5-428

88 Thurston; E. [C.T.S.I.] – v6-176/7

89 Thurston; E. [C.T.S.I.] – v6-189

90 Thurston; E. [C.T.S.I.] – v6-265

91 Thurston; E. [C.T.S.I.] – v6-360

92 Thurston; E. [C.T.S.I.] – v6-396

93 Thurston; E. [C.T.S.I.] – v7-18

94 Thurston; E. [C.T.S.I.] – v7-19

95 Cobo; B. – 115

96 Black; J. – 153/4

97 Thurston; E. [C.T.S.I.] – v3-40

98 Thurston; E. [C.T.S.I.] – v2-66

99 Thurston; E. [C.T.S.I.] – v5-28

100 Thurston; E. [C.T.S.I.] – v5-449/50

101 Thurston; E. [C.T.S.I.] – v6-361

102 Thurston; E. [C.T.S.I.] – v4-294/

103 Vega; G. de la – v2-128; Salcamayhua; Y.-P. – 112; Karsten; S.R. [C.S.A.I.] – 71

104 Thurston; E. [C.T.S.I.] – v6-15

105 Howitt; A.W. – 149

106 Thurston; E. [C.T.S.I.] – v4-345/6

107 Thurston; E. [C.T.S.I.] – v4-340

108 Thurston; E. [C.T.S.I.] – v3-463

109 Thurston; E. [C.T.S.I.] – v4-214

110 Thurston; E. [C.T.S.I.] – v7-145

111 Vega; G. de la – v1-317

112 Howitt; A.W. – 473

113 Arriaga; P.J. de – 51

114 Arriaga; P.J. de – 36

115 Arriaga; P.J. de – 55/6

116 Thurston; E. [C.T.S.I.] – v1-236/7

117 Thurston; E. [C.T.S.I.] – v2-316/7

118 Thurston; E. [C.T.S.I.] – v4-67

119 Sharon; D. – 40

120 Roy; S.C. [H.B.O.] – 202/3

121 Hutton; J.H. [S.N.] – 211

122 Mills; J.P. [L.N.] – 119

123 Brown; G. – 170/1

124 Stair; J.B. – 184

125 Bastien; J.W. – 137

126 Hadingham; E. – 181

127 Hadingham; E. – 187

128 Kolata; A. – 99/100

129 Sharon; D. – 86/7

130 Kirchhoff; P. [H.S.A.I.] – 302

131 Kirchhoff; P. [H.S.A.I.] – 302

132 Cobo; D. – 51-84

133 Kirchhoff; P. [H.S.A.I.] – 304

134 Kirchhoff; P. [C.T.S.I.] – 303

135 Urton; G. – 10

136 Drower; E.S. – [M.I.I.] – 6)

137 Drower; E.S. – [M.I.I.] – 10

138 Drower; E.S. – [M.I.I.] – 16

139 Kearsley; G.R. [M.G.] – 1016/7

140 Drower; E.S. [M.I.I.] – 11

141 Drower; E.S. [M.I.I.] – 12

142 Drower; E.S. – [M.I.I.] – 83/4

143 Kearsley; G.R. [M.G.] – 988

144 Drower; E.S. – [T.T.Q.] – 116

145 Drower; E.S. – [M.I.I.] – 86

146 Kearsley; G.R. [M.G.] – 1006-16

147 Drower; E.S. – [M.I.I.] – 122

148 Drower; E.S. – [M.I.I.] – 128

149 Drower; E.S. – [M.I.I.] –

150 Drower; E.S. [M.I.I.] – 8-1

151 Drower; E.S. [M.I.I.] – 28

152 Gurney; O.R. – 86;107

153 Allchin; R. + B. – 99-103

154 Gurney; O.R. – 111

155 Gurney; O.R. – 127

156 Gurney; O.R. – 127;150

157 Gurney; O.R. – 152

158 Gurney; O.R. – 124;127

159 Gurney; O.R. – 20-32

160 Gurney; O.R. – 23-5

161 Allchin; B.R. – 240/1

162 Allchin; B. & R. – 219-22

163 Ellis; W. – v1-389-91; Kearsley; G.R. [M.G.] – 121/2

164 Kearsley; G.R. [M.G.] – 215/6

165 Dalton; E.T. – 139

166 Dalton; E.T. – 139/40

167 Roys; S.C. [M.] – 112

168 Roys; S.C. [M.] – 122; Kearsley; G.R. [M.G.] – 914

169 Dalton; E.T. – 140

170 Dalton; E.T. – 140

171 Dalton; E.T. – 147

172 Drower; E.S. – 5-7

173 Drower; E.S. – 142/3

174 Dalton; E.T. – 148

175 Dalton; E.T. – 144

176 Dalton; E.T. – 147

177 Dalton; E.T. – 141

178 Howitt; A.W. – 129

179 Drower; E.S. [M.I.I.] – 1, 2

180 Kearsley; G.R. [M.G.] – 909-38

181 Pravananda; S. – 10

182 Elwin; V. – xxvii

183 Elwin; V. – 1

184 Elwin; V. – 2

185 Elwin; V. – ½

186 Elwin; V. – 3;5/6

187 Allchin; R. + B. – 242;337-212

188 Elwin; V. – 10

189 Elwin; V. – 11

190 Elwin; V. – 11

191 Elwin; V. [A.] – 21

192 Elwin; V. [A.] – 20

193 Elwin; V. [A.] – 22

194 Elwin; V. [A.] – 21/2

195 Elwin; V. [A.] – 22

196 Kearsley; G.R. [M.G.] – 1032-5

197 Elwin; V. [A.] – 23

198 Elwin; V. [A.] – 24

199 Elwin; V. [A.] – 2

200 Elwin; V. [A.] – 99/100

201 Elwin; V. [A.] – 61/2

202 Elwin; V. – 336

203 Thurston; E. [C.T.S.I.] – v4-13; v5-133; 476; v6-301; Rivers; W.H.R. – ; 690; Elwin; V. – 90/1

204 Elwin; V. [A.] – 66

205 Elwin; V. [A.] – 62

206 Liebert; G. – 219

207 Thurston; E. [C.T.S.I.] – v1-386

208 Thurston; E. [C.T.S.I.] – v6-182

209 Roy; S.C. [H.B.O.] – 146

210 Roy; S.C. [H.B.O.] – 30

211 Dundes; A. – 286

212 Ka; Maung Po – 3

213 Kearsley; G.R. [M.G.] – 918-23

214 Crooke; W. – v1-87/8

215 Rutter; O. – 148

216 Rutter; O. – 227

217 Tilburg; J.-A. – 90/1

218 Orbell; M. – 67

219 Orbell; M. – 210

220 Orbell; M. – 136/7

221 Orbell; M. – 67

222 Handy; E.S.C. – 282/

223 Handy; E.S.C. – 293

224 Landa; D. de – 60/1

225 Roys; R.L. – xvii/xviii

226 Roys; R.L. – 10;13;14

227 Danielou; A. – 32

228 Roys; R.L. – 14

229 Sastri; H.K. – 77

230 Kearsley; G.R. [M.G.] – 759-67

231 Roys; R.L. – 157

232 Kelley; D.H. – 72/3

233 Kelley; D.H. – 72/3; 73; 122

234 Sharon; D. - 62-72;142

235 Zuidema; R.T. – 258

236 Salcamayhua; P.-Y. – 70

238 Arriaga; P.J. de – 1

239 Arriaga; P.J. de – 68

240 Arriaga; P.J. de – 47;49

241 Arriaga; P.J. de – 50

242 Arriaga; P.J. de – 54

243 Arriaga; P.J. de – 72

244 Arriaga; P.J. de – 76

245 Arriaga; P.J. de – 84

246 Arriaga; P.J. de – 121

247 Bollaert; W. – 122

248 Tierney; P. – 221

249 Tierney; P. – 344

250 Hadingham; E. – 62

251 Hadingham; E. – 245

252 Kearsley; G.R. [M.G.] – 125-34

253 Kolata; A. – 41

254 Kolata; A. – 93

255 Kolata; A. – 80/1

256 Kearsley; G.R. [M.G.] – 721; 1007; Drower; E.S. [T.T.Q.] – 212

257 Sharon; D. – 95/6

258 Kearsley; G.R. [M.G.] – 1032-4

259 Drower; E.S. [M.I.I.] – 8/9

260 Drower; E.S. [M.I.I.] – 73

261 Drower; E.S. [M.I.I.] – 319

262 Drower; E.S. [M.I.I.] – 269

263 Kearsley; G.R. [M.G.] –

989; 997; 1002; 1006-17

264 Drower; E.S. [M.I.I.] – 269/70

265 Thurston; E. [C.T.S.I.] – v4-53

266 Thurston; E. [C.T.S.I.] – v6-47

267 Furer-Haimendorf; C. [R.G.A.] – 253

268 Howitt; A.W. – 447

269 Howitt; A.W. – 803

270 Gurney; O.R. – 2

271 Gurney; O.R. – 13/4

272 Gurney; O.R. – 20

273 Gurney; O.R. – 36

274 Thurston; E. [C.T.S.I.] – v1-111

275 Thurston; E. [C.T.S.I.] – v2-355

276 Thurston; E. [C.T.S.I.] – v3-216

277 Thurston; E. [C.T.S.I.] – v3-368

278 Thurston; E. [C.T.S.I.] – v3-374/5

279 Thurston; E. [C.T.S.I.] – v4-141

280 Thurston; E. [C.T.S.I.] – v5-439

281 Rutter; O. – 242

282 Roy; S.C. [M.] – App. xix-xxxvii

283 Furer-Haimendorf; C. [R.G.A.] – 188/9; 242/3; 259/60; Thurston; E. [C.T.S.I.] – v7-260

284 Malinowski; B. – 467

286 Roy; S.C. [H.B.O.] – 57

287 Roy; S.C. [H.B.O.] – 214/5

288 Roy; S.C. [H.B.O.] – 26

289 Roy; S.C. [M.] – 56

290 Roy; S.C. [M.] – 471

291 Gurney; O.R. – 86;107

292 Roy; S.C. [M.] – 115

293 Sandar; N..K. – 39;140

294 Roy; S.C. [M.] – 444

295 Roy; S.C. [M.] – 120/1

296 Bradley-Birt; F.B. - 122/3

297 Roy; S.C. [M.] – xxiv/xxv

298 Roy; S.C. [M.] – xxv

299 Roy; S.C. [M.] – 120/1

300 Roy; S.C. [M.] – 146

301 Roy; S.C. [M.] – 388

303 Roy; S.C. [M.] – 409

304 Furer-Haimendorf; C. [R.G.A.] – 177

305 Furer-Haimendorf; C. [R.G.A.] – 236

306 Thurston; E. [C.T.S.I.] – v1-170

307 Dothan; M. & T. – 82; 117; 216-8

308 Dothan; M. & T. – 82; 117; 216-8

309 Thurston; E. [C.T.S.I.] – v2-355

310 Thurston; E. [C.T.S.I.] – v5-38

311 Thurston; E. [C.T.S.I.] – v3-84

312 Thurston; E. [C.T.S.I.] – v3-92

313 Thurston; E. [C.T.S.I.] – v5-43

314 Rivers; W.H.R. – 79

315 Thurston; E. [C.T.S.I.] – v3-262

316 (Thurston; E. [C.T.S.I.] – v6-69

317 Thurston; E. [C.T.S.I.] – v6-294

318 Thurston; E. [C.T.S.I.] – v7-183; 306/7

319 Buck; P. – 509/10

Chapter 7

1 Demarest; A.A. – 3;4

2 Demarest; A.A. – 9

3 Demarest; A.A. – 8

4 Demarest; A.A. – 9

5 Zuidema; R.T. – 238

6 Poindexter; M. [P.P.] – 25/6

7 Burger; R.L. – 150

8 Demarest; A.A. – 53

9 Kolata; A. – 5

10 Kolata; A. – 6/7

11 Kolata; A. – 7

12 Hadingham; E. – 35/6

13 Hadingham; E. – 62

14 Hadingham; E. – 246

15 Hadingham; E. – 246

16 Bastien; J.W. – 74

17 Bollaert; W. – 122

18 Vega; de la – v2-66

19 Arriaga; P.J. de – 43/4

20 Arriaga; P.J. de – 72

21 Bandelier; A. – 97

22 Bandelier; A. – 294

23 Bandelier; A. – 297/8

24 Bandelier; A. – 298

25 Bandelier; A. – 294; 336

26 Markham; C.R. [T.P.C.L.] – 367

27 Markham; C.R. [T.P.C.L.] – 310

28 Markham C.R. [T.P.C.L.] – 343

29 Vega; G. de la – v2-50

30 Vega; G. de la – v2-65

31 Vega; G. de la – v2-69-71

32 Sharon; D. – 94

33 Lumholtz; C. [U.M.] – v1-134

34 Cobo; B. – xv

35 Cobo; B. – 12

36 Cobo; B. – 12

37 Elwin; V. [M.M.I.] – 16

38 Eggerling; J. in Muller; F.M. [S.B.E.] – 173

39 Moseley; M.E. – 15/6

40 Sharon; D. – 94

41 Cobo; B. – 13

42 Cobo; B. – 13

43 Cobo; B. – 20

44 Cobo; B. – 22

45 Cobo; B. – 23

46 Cobo; B. – 109/10

47 Cobo; B. – 111

[48] Cobo; B. – 23

[49] Eggeling; J. in Muller; F.M. [S.B.E.] – v26-62

[50] Eggeling; J. in Muller; F.M. [S.B.E.] – v41-406

[51] Eggeling; J. in Muller; F.M. [S.B.E.] – v44-xxv

[52] Rivers; W.H.R. – 277/8

[53] Rivers; W.H.R. – 355

[54] Cobo; B. – 113

[55] Cobo; B. – 123

[56] Drower; E.S. [M.I.I.] – xxi; 101; 118-20; 125

[57] Cobo; B. – 124

[58] Cobo; B. – 137

[59] Sharon; D. – 88/9

[60] Urton; G. – 26

[61] Kolata, A. – 267

[62] Eggeling; J. in Muller; F.M. [S.B.E.] – v41-130

[63] Eggeling; J. in Muller; F.M. [S.B.E.] – v41-225

[64] Eggeling; J. in Muller; F.M. [S.B.E.] – v48-365/6

[65] Eggeling; J. in Muller; F.M. [S.B.E.] – v48-367

[66] Eggeling; J. in Muller; F.M. [S.B.E.] – v48-370) Eggeling; J. in Muller; F.M. [S.B.E.] – v15-250

[67] Eggeling; J. in Muller; F.M. [S.B.E.] – v34-xxxix;252-7

[68] Eggeling; J. in Muller; F.M. [S.B.E.] – v42-208; 625

[69] Eggeling; J. in Muller; F.M. [S.B.E.] – v42-664

[70] Eggeling; J. in Muller; F.M. [S.B.E.] – v7-101

[71] Eggeling; J. in Muller; F.M. [S.B.E.] – v46-61

[72] Bandelier; A.F. – 96;97

[73] Arriaga; P.J. de – 44

[74] Thurston; E. [C.T.S.I.] – v6-124

[75] Thurston; E. [C.T.S.I.] – v6-125

[76] Crooke; W. – v2-176/7

[77] Howitt; A.W. – 367/8

[78] Fergusson; J. – 68

[79] Buck; P. – 462

[80] Cobo; B. – 16

[81] Cobo; B. – 167

[82] Zuidema; R.T. – 164/5

[83] McEwan; C. & Guchte; M. van der – 369; Zuidema; R.T. – 165; 166

[84] Zuidema; R.T. – 167

[85] Zuidema; R.T. – 258

[86] Osborne; H. – 76

[87] Osborne; H. – 76;78/9

[88] Osborne; H. – 83

[89] Danielou; A. – 91/2

[90] Demarest; A.A. – 71

[91] Vega; G. de la – v2-178/9

[92] Reichel-Dolmatoff; G. [A.C.] – 10

[93] Reichel-Dolmatoff; G. [A.C.] – 43

[94] Reichel-Dolmatoff; G. [A.C.] – 65

[95] Reichel-Dolmatoff; G. [A.C.] – 16

[96] Reichel-Dolmatoff; G. [A.C.] – 16

[97] Alva; W. & Donnan; C.B. – 55; 143; 164/5

[98] Mariner; W. – v1-327/8; Loeb; E. & Heine-Geldern; R. – 36

[99] Malinowski; B. – 307

[100] Reichel-Dolmatoff; G. [A.C.] – 79

[101] Grimble; A.F. – 39

[102] Dalton; E.T. – 139

[103] Dalton; E.T. – 140

[104] Dalton; E.T. – 147

[105] Dalton; E.T. – 144

[106] Thurston; E. [C.T.S.I.] – v1-267

[107] Whitehead; H. – 95

[108] Thurston; E. [C.T.S.I.] – v3-35

[109] Thurston; E. [C.T.S.I.] – v5-21

[110] Thurston; E. [C.T.S.I.] – v3-101;102/3

[111] Thurston; E. [C.T.S.I.] – v3-218

[112] Thurston; E. [C.T.S.I.] – v4-150

[113] Thurston; E. [C.T.S.I.] – v4-151

[114] Thurston; E. [C.T.S.I.] – v4-153/4

[114] Thurston; E. [C.T.S.I.] – v4-153/4

[115] Thurston; E. [C.T.S.I.] – v4-154

[116] Thurston; E. [C.T.S.I.] – v6-4

[117] Thurston; E. [C.T.S.I.] – v6-5

[118] Thurston; E. [C.T.S.I.] – v6-5/6

[119] Thurston; E. [C.T.S.I.] – v6-245

[120] Avila; F. de – 124-31

[121] Thurston; E. [C.T.S.I.] – v6-182

[122] Thurston; E. [C.T.S.I.] – v7-410

[123] Sastri; H.K. – 79

[124] Cobo; B. – 128

[125] Thurston; E. [C.T.S.I.] – v7-192

[126] Thurston; E. [C.T.S.I.] – v7-196

[127] Thurston; E. [C.T.S.I.] – v1-110/1

[128] Thurston; E. [C.T.S.I.] – v1-111

[129] Liebert; G. – 340

[130] Lumholtz; C. [U.M.] – v2-9

[131] Thurston; E. [C.T.S.I.] – v6-6/7

[132] Thurston; E. [C.T.S.I.] – v6-10

[133] Danielou; A. – 176)

[134] Danielou; A. – 180

[135] Danielou; A. – 315

[136] Kearsley; G.R. [M.G.] –

[137] Thurston; E. [C.T.S.I.] – 493-5

[137] Thurston; E. [C.T.S.I.] – v6-10/1

[138] Thurston; E. [C.T.S.I.] – v6-11/2

[139] Bandelier; A.F. – 11

[140] Thurston; E. [C.T.S.I.] – v6-85

[141] Dalton. E.T. – 147

[142] Kearsley; G.R. [P.P.P.P.] – 25; 32/3; 35

[143] Zaehner; R.C. – 58

[144] Zaehner; R.C. – 82

[145] Zaehner; R.C. – 82

[146] Zaehner; R.C. – 83

[147] Zaehner; R.C. – 84/5

[148] Danielou; A. – 91

[149] Zaehner; R.C. – 85

[150] Zaehner; R.C. 338; 378

[151] Zaehner; R.C. – 338

[152] Liebert; G. – 219

[153] Liebert; G. – 317

[154] Muller; M. – 241

[155] Liebert; G. – 334

[156] Kearsley; G.R. [P.P.P.P.] - 25; 32/3; 35; 49

[157] Drower; E.S. [M.I.I.] – 58

[158] Kearsley; G.R. [M.G.] – 1006-17

[159] Muller; M. [S.B.E.] – 275

[160] Bandelier; A.F. – 318

[161] Bandelier; A.F. – 318

[162] Bandelier; A.F. – 327

[163] Bandelier; A.F. – 328

[164] Pachacuti-Yamqui Salcamayhua – 72

[165] Salcamayhua; P.-Y. – 71

[166] Salcamayhua; P. -Y. – 71

[167] Salcamayhua; P. -Y. – 73

[168] Salcamayhua; P.- Y. – 79

[169] Salcamayhua; P. -Y. – 87

[170] Salcamayhua; P.-Y. – 87

[171] Osborne; H. – 86

[172] Osborne; H. – 87

[173] Osborne; H. – 87

[174] Demarest; A.A. – 3;8/9

[175] Demarest; A.A. – ¾

[176] Arriaga; P.J. de – 51

[177] Demarest; A.A. – 31

[178] Demarest; A.A. – 35/6

[179] Demarest; A.A. – 37

[180] Demarest; A.A. – 41

[181] Demarest; A.A. – 50

[182] Demarest; A.A. – 51

[183] Demarest; A.A. – 51/2

[184] Demarest; A.A. – 52; Bandelier, A.F. – 93;107

[185] Demarest; A.A. – 55

[186] Demarest; A.A. – 52

[187] Demarest; A.A. – 56

[188] Demarest; A.A. – 57/8

[189] Demarest; A.A. – 58

[190] Demarest; A.A. – 59

[191] Demarest; A.A. – 63

[192] Demarest; A.A. – 63

[193] Bollaert; W. – 35

[194] Brinton; D.G. – 90/1

[195] Brinton; D.G. – 95

[196] Brinton; D.G. – 22

[197] Demarest; A.A. – 2;16

[198] Brinton; D.G. – 225

[199] Rivers; W.H.R. – 719/20

[200] Rae; G. Milne – 15/6

[201] Rae; G. Milne – 22

[202] Rae; G. Milne – 39

[203] Rae; G. Milne – 24

[204] Rae; G. Milne – 57

[205] Rae; G. Milne – 25

[206] Rae; G. Milne – 97

[207] Rae; G. Milne – 96

[208] Rae; G. Milne – 105/6

[209] Rae; G. Milne – 109

[210] Rae; G. Milne – 117

[211] Rae; G. Milne – 128

[212] Rae; G. Milne – 135

[213] Rae; G. Milne – 136

[214] Richards; W.J. – 110

[215] Thurston; E. – v5-411/2

[216] Thurston; E. – v5-409

[217] Thurston; E. – v6-410

[218] Rae; G. Milne – 169

[219] Rae; G. Milne – 156

[220] Rae; G. Milne – 159

[221] Thurston; E. [C.T.S.I.] - v5-407

[222] Rae; G. Milne – 154/5

[223] Rae; G. Milne – 162

[224] Maier; V. – 114)

[225] Maier; V. – 114

[226] Thurston; E. – v6-413

[227] Thurston; E. – v6-420

[228] Thurston; E. – v6-420

[229] Thurston; E. – v6-426/7

[230] Rae; G. Milne – 124

[231] Rae; G. Milne – 125

[232] Rae; G. Milne – 266/7

[233] Thurston; E. – v2-393

[234] Thurston; E. – v5-241/2

[235] Vega; G. de la – v1-110/1

[236] Arriaga; P.J. de – 23; 54

[237] Demarest; A.A. – 13

[238] Vega; G. de la – v1-105

[239] Zuidema; R.T. – 155;164

[240] Demarest; A.A. – 14;50

[241] Sharon; D. – 135

[242] Demarest; A.A. – 32/3

[243] Demarest; A.A. – 50

[244] Hadingham, E. – 249

[245] Hadingham; E. – 248

[246] Sharon; D. – 93

[247] Anton; F. – 192

[248] Urton; G. – 51

[249] Gurney; O.R. – 150/1

[250] Cotterell; A. – 24

[251] Graves; R. – 75

[255] Cotterell; A. – 24

[253] Cotterell; A. – 25

[254] Driver; G.R. – 55

[255] Graves; R. – 7

[256] Black; J. – 106

[257] Driver; G.R. – 83

[258] Driver; G.R. – 29

[259] Vogel; J.Ph. – 106

[260] Clay; A.T. – 164/5

[261] Gomes; E. – 185

[262] Brewster; A.B. – 88

[263] Robertson; H.A. – 447

[264] Fornander; A. – v1-49;50

[265] Miller; M.E. – 60/1;98;169

[266] Miller; M.E. – 167;169

[267] Miller; M.E. – 60/1

[268] Wilbert; J. – [F.L.Tel.I.] – 9/10

[269] Wilbert; J. – [F.L.Tel.I.] – 21

[270] Bandelier; A.F. – 107

[271] Bandelier; A.F. – 120

[272] Bandelier; A.F. – 151

[273] Bandelier; A.F. – 107

[274] Joyce; T.A. – [S.A.A.] – 158

[275] Arriaga; P.J. de – 53

[276] Muller; M. [S.B.E.] – v5-16/7

[277] Muller; M. [S.B.E.] – v44-249

[278] Muller; M. [S.B.E.] – v44-251

[279] Joyce; T.A. [S.A.A.] – 244

[280] Arriaga; P.J. de – 23

[281] Burger; R.L. – 149/50

[282] Arriaga; P.J. de – 36

[283] Arriaga; P.J. de – 51

[284] Arriaga; P.J. de – 85

[285] Arriaga; P.J. de – 119

[286] Roe; P.G. – 185/6

[287] Vega; G. de la – v1-104

[288] Roosevelt; A.C. – 412

[289] Hadingham; E. – 110

[290] Black; J. – 54

[291] Vega; G. de la – v1-105

[292] Sharon; D. – 76/7

[293] Sharon; D. – 135

[294] Miller; M.E. & Taube; K. – 59/60

[295] Miller; M.E. & Taube; K. – 106/7

[296] Miller; M.E. & Taube; K. – 165

[297] Miller; M.E. & Taube; K. – 59/60

[298] Miller; A.G. – 12

[299] Miller; M.E. & Taube; K. – 116/7

[300] Miller; M.E. & Taube; K. – 191

[301] Miller; M.E. & Taube; K. – 166

[302] Lothrop; S.K. [P.C.R.N.] – 75/6

[303] Lothrop; S.K. [P.C.R.N.] – 66/7

[304] Miller; M.E. – 40/1

[305] Fornander; A. – v1-76

[306] Morley; S.G. & Goetz; D. [P.V.] – 82

[307] Morley; S.G. & Goetz; D. [P.V.] – 82/3

[308] Perry; W.J. – 133/4

[309] Keeler; C.E. [L.M.C.] – 191

[310] Hoop; A.N.J.A.T van der – 94

[311] Schnitger; F.M. – 48

[312] Schnitger; F.M. – 125

[313] Kearsley; G.R. [M.G.] – 353; 355

[314] Tobing; Ph. L. – 163-9

[315] Vega; G. de la – v2-178/9

[316] Riesenfeld; A. – 290; Malinowski; B. – 475

[317] Riesenfeld; A. – 389

[318] Malinowski; B. – 342

[319] Skinner; H.D. – 57

[320] Grimble; A. – 183

[321] Howitt; A.W. – 498/9

[322] Berndt; R.M. + C.H. – 346

[323] Mountford; C.P. [T.A.M.C.] – 44

[324] Elwin; V. [M.I.I.] – 88

[325] Elwin; V. [M.T.G.] – 261

[326] Kloss; C.B. – 287

[328] Christie; A. – 46

[329] Christie; A. – 49

[330] Christie; A. – 56

331 Munro; N.G. – 13

332 Batchelor; J. – 355

333 Batchelor; J. – 355

334 Roy; S.C. [H.B.O.] – 279

325 Roy; S.C. [H.B.O.] – 280

336 Vogel; J.Ph. – 3

337 Drower; E.S. [B.Z.] – 153/4

338 Black; J. – 40;47

339 Black; J. – 85; 110; 111; 118; 142;

340 Hutton; J.H. [S.N.] – 252/3

341 Cobo; B. – 54

342 Cobo; B. – 69

343 Cobo; B. – 175

344 Bandelier; A.F. – 93

345 Osborne; H. – 89

346 Beuchler; H.C. – 96

347 Beuchler; H.C. – 101

348 Hadingham; E. – 249

349 Hadingham; E. – 254

350 Mills; J.H. [L.N.] – 172

351 Demarest; A.A. – 59

352 Hadingham; E. – 62

353 Hadingham; E. – 246/7

354 Bollaert; W. – 47

355 Wilbert; J. [F.L.Tel.I.] – 8

356 Heyerdahl; T. [A.A.] – 168

357 Riesenfeld; A. – 377

358 Kearsley; G.R. [M.G.] – 453-5

359 Fison; L. – 14-31

360 Elwin; V. [M.M.I.] – 7

361 Kearsley; G.R. [M.I.] – 408-11

362 Elwin; V. [M.M.I.] – 183

363 Elwin; V. [M.M.I.] – 182/3

364 Macpherson; S.C. – 48/9

365 Risley; Herbert H., "The People of India", 1908; Thurston; E. [O.S.S.I.] – 202

366 Vogel; J.Ph. – 17

367 Drower; E.S. [M.I.I.] – 180

368 Danielou; A. – 12;206

369 Danielou; A. – 103

370 Danielou; A. – 23

371 Danielou; A. – 192

372 Danielou; A. – 87

373 Danielou; A. – 194

374 Kearsley; G.R. [M.G.] – 662/3

375 Danielou; A. – 124

376 Danielou; A. – 178

377 Danielou; A. – 192

378 Danielou; A. – 193

379 Danielou; A. – 194/5

380 Danielou; A. – 195/6

381 Danielou; A. – 200;202

382 Danielou; A. – 311

383 Danielou; A. – 205

384 Muller; M. [S.B.E.] – v1-Upanishads; IV Khanda, 4 – 151

385 Muller; M. [S.B.E.] – v15-Upanishads; III Adhyaya, 9 - 245

386 Muller; M. [S.B.E.] – v32-Vedic Hymns, Mandala I, Hymn 43 –419

387 Muller; M. [S.B.E.] – v32-Vedic Hymns, Mandala II, Hymn 33 – 426/7

388 Muller; M. [S.B.E.] – v32-Vedic Hymns, Mandala VII, Hymn 46 – 436

389 Muller; M. [S.B.E.] – v42-Vedic Hymns, Stanza 23, Commentary – 637

390 Danielou; A. – 217

391 Avila; F. de – 130

392 Avila; F. de – 140

393 Sastri; H.K. – 77

394 Sastri; H.K. – 16

395 Sastri; H.K. – 194

396 Sastri; H.K. – 197

397 Danielou; A. – 216

398 Liebert; G. – 134

399 Liebert; G. – 173

400 Thurston; E. [C.T.S.I.] – v2-255

401 Danielou; A. – 215

402 Thurston; E. [C.T.S.I.] – v2-255

403 Danielou; A. – 215

404 Banerjea; J.N. – 447

405 Banerjea; J.N. – 447/8

406 Howitt; A.W. – 404

407 Ellis; W. – 235

408 Ellis; W. – v1-243/4

409 Ellis; W. – 235

410 Ellis; W. – 234

411 Ellis; W. – v1-238

412 Ellis; W. – v1-229-33

413 Miller; M.E. & Taube; K. – 40

414 Arriaga; P.J. de – 37

415 Arriaga; P.J. de – 37

416 Sharon; D. – 92/3

417 Sastri, H.K. – 97; 100; 102/3

418 Riesenfeld; A. – 181

419 Riesenfeld; A. – 326

420 Telang; K.T. in Muller; M. [S.B.E.] – v8-Bhagavad Gita, Ch. XXX, 1– 354

421 Jacobi in Muller; M. [S.B.E.] – v45-Sutrakritanga, Book, 1, 6 – 288/9

422 Eggeling; J. in Muller; M. [S.B.E.] – v12-Satapatha Brahamana, 1 Kanda, 4 Adhyaya, 1 Brahmana, 36– 110

423 Cowell; E.B. in Muller; M. [S.B.E.] – v8-Bhuddha-Karita of Asvaghosha, Book, XIII, 34-48 – 142/3

424 Danielou; A. – 109

425 Cotterell; A. – 225

426 Brown; J.M. – v2-130; Handy; E.S.C. – 247

427 Thurston; E. [C.T.S.I.] – v4-234

428 Crooke; W. – v1-115/6

429 Thurston; E. [C.T.S.I.] – v2-285/6

430 Thurston; E. [C.T.S.I.] – v7-240

431 Furer-Haimendorf; C. [R.G.A.] – 156

432 Harle; J.C. – 180/1

433 Pranavananda; Sri – xix

434 Pranavananda; S. – 14-6

435 Danielou; A. – 220/1

436 Pranavananda; S – 6

437 Pranavananda; S – 10

438 Pranavananda; S – 22

439 Pranavananda; S – 8

440 Pranavananda; S – 9

441 Pranavananda; S – 9/10

442 Pranavananda; S. – 14

443 Pranavananda; S – 16

444 Pranavananda; S – 17

445 Pranavananda; S – 19/20

446 Pranavananda; S – 55

447 Drower; E.S. [M.I.I.] – 9/10

448 Thurston; E. [C.T.S.I.] – v2-136

449 Thurston; E. [C.T.S.I.] – v1-164

450 Thurston; E. [C.T.S.I.] – v1-382

451 Thurston; E. [C.T.S.I.] – v4-383

452 Kirchhoff; P. [H.S.A.I.] – 301

453 Moseley; M.E. – 56

454 Kirchhoff; P. [H.S.A.I.] – 302/3

455 Urton; G. – 136;142; 159

456 Kolata; A. – 8

457 Kolata; A. – 8

458 Kolata; A. – 9

459 Salcamayahua; P.-Y. - 106

460 Sharon; D. – 87

461 Black; J. – 179

462 Zuidema; R.T. – 150

463 Zuidema; R.T. – 160

464 Bastien; J.W. – 139

465 Thurston; E. [C.T.S.I.] – v1-56

466 Liebert; G. – 312

467 Danielou; A. – 285

468 Liebert; G. – 310

469 Liebert; G. – 312

470 Liebert; G. – 312

471 Danielou; 106; 226

472 Bridges; E.L. – 302

473 Donnan; C.B. – 110

474 Donnan; C.B. - 112/2

475 Seligmann; C.G. – 325

476 Kramer; S.N. – 41

Chapter 8

1 Kolata; A. – 8

2 Zuidema; R.T. – 42

3 Zuidema; R.T. – 84;254

4 Cobo; B. – 100

5 Urton; G. – 140;150

6 Handy; E.S.C. – 18

7 Kearsley; G.R. [M.G.] – 545-9

8 Kearsley; G.R. [M.G.] - 70/1; 94-7

9 Burger; R.L. – 135

10 Handy; E.S.C. – 313

11 Legge; J. in Muller; M. [S.B.E.] – v16-376

12 Legge; J. in Muller; M. [S.B.E.] – v16-377

13 Legge; J. in Muller; M. [S.B.E.] – v40-96

14 Legge; J. in Muller; M. [S.B.E.] – v40-250

15 Legge; J. in Muller; M. [S.B.E.] – v39-16/7

16 Legge; J. in Muller; M. [S.B.E.] – v39-18/9

17 Legge; J. – v1-242

18 Legge; J. 315/6

19 Marshall; H.I. – 262/3

20 Liebert; G. – 116

21 Liebert; G. – 119

22 Danielou; A. – 279

23 Liebert; G. – 119

24 Zuidema; R.T. – 119; 281

25 Danielou; A. – 132

26 Danielou; A. – 133

27 Danielou; A. – 202

28 Liebert; G. – 118

29 Kearsley; G.R. [M.G.] – 358-96

30 Kolata; A. – 89; 91

31 Cobo; B. – 102

32 Moseley; M.E. – 203

33 Kolata; A. – 98

34 Kolata; A. – 99

35 Kolata; A. – 109

36 Kolata; A. – 109/10

37 Kolata; A. – 111

38 Kolata; A. – 129

39 Kolata; A. – 97

40 Kolata; A. – 104

41 Potts; D.T. – 46

42 Harle; J.C. – 176; 204/5

43 Potts; D.T. - 46;49

44 Black; J. – 27

45 Eggeling; J. in Muller; F.M. [S.B.E.] – v43-15

46 Eggeling; J. in Muller; F.M. [S.B.E.] – v43-17/8

47 Eggeling; J. in Muller; F.M. [S.B.E.] – v43-18/9

48 Eggeling; J. in Muller; F.M. [S.B.E.] – v43-19/20

49 Moseley; M.E. – 15

50 Gartelmann; K.D. – 133; 211/2

51 Eggeling; J. in Muller; F.M. [S.B.E.] – v43-36; 44; 190

52 Eggeling; J. in Muller; F.M. [S.B.E.] – v8-270

53 Muller; F.M. [S.B.E.] – v15-27/8; 293

54 Eggeling; J. in Muller; F.M. [S.B.E.] – v12-343

55 Eggeling; J. in Muller; F.M. [S.B.E.] – v26-298;432

56 Eggeling; J. in Muller; F.M. [S.B.E.] – v26-298

57 Eggeling; J. in Muller; F.M. [S.B.E.] – v43-60

58 Danielou; A. – 266

59 Liebert; G. – 20

60 Liebert; G. – 289

61 Liebert; G. – 9

62 Liebert; G. – 9

63 Kolata; A. – 118

64 Kolata; A. – 148;162

65 Kolata; A. – 97

66 Bibby; G. – 36

67 Bandelier; A. – 237/8

68 Bandelier; A.F. – 327

69 Bandelier; A.F. – 239

70 Arriaga; P.J. de – 51

71 Avila; F. de – 127

72 Bollaert; W. – 220

73 Bollaert; W. – 220

74 Demarest; A.A. – 26/7

75 Demarest; A.A. – 32/3

76 Demarest; A.A. – 23

77 Urton; G. – 6

78 Urton; G. – 77

79 Urton; G. – 68

80 Zuidema; R.T. – 161/2

81 Bollaert; W. – 185

82 Thurston; E. [C.T.S.I.] – v1-315

83 Thurston; E. [C.T.S.I.] – v2-88

84 Thurston; E. [C.T.S.I.] – v7-23

85 Thurston; E. [C.T.S.I.] – v5-104

86 Thurston; E. [C.T.S.I.] – v5-370

87 Thurston; E. [C.T.S.I.] – v6-257

88 Thurston; E. [C.T.S.I.] – v5-322

89 Thurston; E. [C.T.S.I.] – v6-202

90 Thurston; E. [C.T.S.I.] – v7-11

91 Thurston; E. [C.T.S.I.] – v6-132

92 Elwin; V. [M.M.I.] – 52

93 Crooke; W. – v1-5

94 Crooke; W. – v1-6/7

95 Thurston; E. [C.T.S.I.] – v6-333

96 Elwin; V. [M.M.I.] – 41; 55; 64

97 Danielou; A. – 94/5

98 Danielou; A. – 96

99 Eggeling; J. in Muller; M. [S.B.E.] – v44-498

100 Eggeling; J. in Muller; M. [S.B.E.] – v41-265-7

101 Eggeling; J. in Muller; M. [S.B.E.] – v41-265

102 Eggeling; J. in Muller; M. [S.B.E.] – v41-272

103 West; E.W. in Muller; M. [S.B.E.] – v5-22-4

104 Eggeling; J. in Muller; M. [S.B.E.] – v43-333

105 Muller; M. [S.B.E.] – v15-192

106 Muller; M. [S.B.E.] – v15-311/2

107 Muller; M. [S.B.E.] – v15-337

108 Eggeling; J. in Muller; M. [S.B.E.] – v44-125

109 Eggeling; J. in Muller; M. [S.B.E.] – v44-484

110 Oldenberg; H. in Muller; M. [S.B.E.] – v29-328

111 Kearsley; G.R. [M.G.] – 632-7

112 Muller; M. [S.B.E.] – v1-143

113 Eggeling; J. in Muller; M. [S.B.E.] – v44-472

114 Danielou; A. – 92

115 Danielou; A. – 93

116 Danielou; A. – 93

117 Danielou; A. – 94

118 Black; J. – 94

119 Ellis; W. – v3-170/1

120 Black; J. – 112

121 Zaehner; R.C. – 101

122 Zaehner; R.C. – 147/8

123 Zaehner; R.C. – 159

124 Zaehner; R.C. – 186

125 Perry; W.J. – 150

126 Boas; F. – v27-2

127 Zaehner; R.C. – 334

128 Joyce; T.A. [S.A.A.] – 154

129 Kearsley; G.R. [M.G.] – 363; 381; 1008

130 Cobo; B. – 26

131 Arriaga; P.J de – 22

132 Cobo; B. – 57

133 Cobo; B. – 57

134 Demarest; A.A. – 16;21;23

135 Demarest; A.A. – 39

136 Demarest; A.A. - 14

137 Cobo; B. – 26

138 Zuidema; R.T. – 258

139 Demarest; A.A. – 39

140 Demarest; A.A. – 44/5

141 Demarest; A.A. – 53

142 Demarest; A.A. – 50-61

143 Reisenfeld; A. – 59-61; 496/7

144 Cobo; B. – 197;250-2

145 Hutton; J.H. [A.N.] – 45; 47

146 Hutton; J.H. [A.N.] – 49; 188/9; 206/7

147 Mathew; J. – 20

148 Dundes; A. – 129/30

149 Rutter; O. – 249/50

150 Rivers; W.H.R. – 443/4

151 Rivers; W.H.R. – 444

152 Rivers; W.H.R. – 445

153 Elwin; V. [A.] – 25

154 Muller; M. [S.B.E.] – v1-313

155 Muller; M. [S.B.E.] – v15-199

156 Poindexter; M. – v1-154-7

157 Thurston; E. [C.T.S.I.] – v6-206

158 Eggeling; J. in Muller; M. [S.B.E.] – v12-16

159 Eggeling; J. in Muller; M. [S.B.E.] – v12-37

160 Eggeling; J. in Muller; M. [S.B.E.] – v12-267

161 Eggeling; J. in Muller; M. [S.B.E.] – v12-270/1

162 Eggeling; J. in Muller; M. [S.B.E.] – v12- 53

163 Eggeling; J. in Muller; M. [S.B.E.] – v26-136

164 Eggeling; J. in Muller; M. [S.B.E.] – v12-213

165 Oldenberg; H. in Muller; M. [S.B.E.] – v46-154

166 Kearsley; G.R. [M.G.] – 662/3

167 Danielou; A. – 124

168 Muller; M. [S.B.E.] – v15-89

169 Muller; M. [S.B.E.] – v15-335

170 Alva; W. + Donnan; C.B. – 90/1

171 Eggeling; J. in Muller; M. [S.B.E.] – v26-57

172 Bloomfield; M. in Muller; M. [S.B.E.] – v42-135

173 Eggeling; J. in Muller; M. [S.B.E.] – v44-352/3

174 Eggeling; E. in Muller; M. [S.B.E.] – v44-293

175 Muller; M. [S.B.E.] – v30-61

176 Muller; M. [S.B.E.] – v30-216-8

177 Muller; M. [S.B.E.] – v32-424

178 Bloomfield; M. in Muller; M. [S.B.E.] – v42-99

179 Danielou; A. – 116/7

180 Danielou; A. – 124

181 Liebert; G. – 296

182 Liebert; G. – 316/7

183 Kearsley; G.R. [M.G.] – 509-18

184 Roy; S.C. [M.] – 121

185 Kearsley; G.R. [M.G.] – 901-38; Bradley-Birt; F.B. –36/7

186 Cotterell; A. – 225

187 Rivers; W.H.R. – 436

188 Rivers; W.H.R. – 447

189 Rivers; W.H.R. – 207;592

190 Vogel; J.Ph. – 35

191 Cobo; B. – 48-50

192 Telang; K.T. in Muller; M. [S.B.E.] – v8-189

193 Mills; J.P. – 25

194 Hutton; J.H. in Mills; J.P. – 25

195 Mills; J.P. – 25

196 Crooke; W. – v1-69

197 Crooke; W. – v1-105

198 Lumholtz; C. [U.M.] – v2-334

199 Hutton; J.H. [S.N.] – 250

200 Bandelier; A.F. – 315/6

201 Howitt; A.E. – 122

202 Howitt; A.E. – 428

203 Howitt; A.W. – 427

204 Mountford; C.P. [A.L.] – 230; Seligmann; C.G. – 381

205 Spencer. B & Gillan; F.W. [T.T.C.A.] – 561

206 Spencer. B & Gillan; F.W. [T.T.C.A.] – v2-471

207 Mountford; C.P. [R.A.A.S.E.A.L.] – 479/80

208 Mountford; C.P. [R.A.A.S.E.A.L.] – 493

209 Mountford; C.P. [R.A.A.S.E.A.L.] – 502

210 Muller; M. [S.B.E.] – v12-342; Callait; C. – 181

211 Mills; J.P. [L.N.] – 172/3

212 Ereira; A. – 63

213 Bonwick; J. – 190/1

214 Fornander; A. – v1-49-53

215 Riesenfeld; A. – 182

216 Danielou; A. – 110

217 Riesenfeld; A. – 182

218 Fox; C.E. – 16

219 Ivens; W.G. [I.B.P.] – 292

220 Haddon; A.C. – 188

221 Akerblom; K. – 15;137

222 Grimble; A. – 183

223 Bollaert; W. – 12

224 Bollaert; W. – 14

225 Bollaert; W. – 47

226 Bollaert; W. – 48

227 Bollaert; W. – 48

228 Wilbert; J. [F.T.B.I.] – 6

229 Wilbert; J. [F.T.G.I.] – 17

230 Wilbert; J. [F.T.G.I.] – 17/8

231 Wilbert; J. [F.T.G.I.] – 78

232 Arriaga; P.J. de – 42

233 Lehmann; W. – 3

234 Handy; E.S.C. – 320/1

235 Ellis; W. – v3-170/1

236 Fox; C.E. – 360

237 Buck; P. – 508

238 Elwin; V. [M.M.I.] – 56

239 Rivers; W.H.R. – 206/7

240 Rivers; W.H.R. – 287

241 Zaehner; R.C. – 159

242 Riesenfeld; A. – 265

243 Zaehner; R.C. – 159

244 Drower; E.S. [M.I.I.] – 289

245 Roy; E.S.C. [H.B.O.] – 285-92

246 Kearsley; G.R. [M.G.] – 1009-15

247 Elwin; V. [M.M.I.] – 52

248 Danielou; A. – 96

249 Howitt; A.W. – 432

250 Mills; J.P. [L.N.] – 172

251 Elwin; V. [M.M.I.] – 53/4

252 Mills; J.P. [L.N.] – 173

253 Hutton; J.H. [S.N.] – 250

254 Mills; J.P. [A.O.] – 301

255 Elwin; V. [M.M.I.] – 41

256 Elwin; V. [M.M.I.] – 53-5

257 Mountford; C.P. [R.A.A.S.E.A.L.] – v1-502

258 Fox; C.E. – 338

259 Grimble; A. – 83

260 Lumholtz; C. [U.M.] – v1-511

261 Cobo; B. – 26

262 Markham; C.R. [T.P.C.L.] – 298/9

263 Miller; M.E. – 69/70

264 Zuidema; R.T. – 212

265 Kearsley; G.R. [M.G.] – 186-9

266 Urton; G. – 38

267 Rivers; W.H.R. – 397;592

268 Black; J. – 137

269 Batchelor; J. – 58

270 Roe; P. G. – 227/8

271 Bingham; H. [E.H.P.] –306

272 Bingham; H. [Calancha's Chronicle] – 157

273 Bingham; H. – 157

274 Danielou; A. – 227

275 Landa; D. de – 8;25

276 Hammond; N. – 5

277 Avila; P.J. de – 131-47

278 Thurston; E. [C.T.S.I.] – v6-85

279 Gurney; O.R. – 153/4

280 Davidson; H.R.E. – 21;96; 123

281 Danielou; A. – 248

282 Danielou; A. – 228

283 Danielou; A. – 43

284 Danielou; A. – 275

285 Danielou; A. – 275

286 Handy; E.S.C. – 111; Skinner; H.D. – 112

287 Muller; M. [S.B.E.] – v12-327/8

288 Avila; P.J. de – 124-130

289 Lumholtz; C. – v1-511-3

290 Wilbert; J. [F.T.B.I.] – 198

291 Rivers; W.H.R. – 207

292 Rutter; O. – 259-61

293 Malinowski; B. – 308/9

294 Danielou; A. – 298;299

295 Kearsley; G.R. [M.G.] – 436-43

296 Lumholtz; C. [U.M.] – v2-159/60; 161; 163

297 Lumholtz; C. [U.M.] – v2-191

298 Wilbert; J. [F.T.G.I.] – 226

299 Wilbert; J. [F.T.L.I.] – v2-201-16

300 Wilbert; J. [F.L.G.I.] – 217

301 Robertson; H.A. – 389

302 Robertson; H.A. – 403

Chapter 9

1 Kearsley; G.R. [M.G.] – 52-61

2 Boas; F. [K.T.] – 177

3 Boas; F. [K.T.] – v26-179/80

4 Boas; F. [K.T.] – v26-181

5 Vogel; J. Ph. – 25;29

6 Kearsley; G.R. [M.G.] – 111

7 Mills; J.H. [L.N.] – 164

8 Bandelier; A.F. – 102

9 Boas; F. [K.T.] – v26-187

10 Boas; F. [K.T.] – v26-182

11 Wilbert; J. [F.T.C.I.] – 234

12 Goetz; S. & Morley; S.G. [P.V.] – 153/4

13 Wilbert; J. [F.T.C.I.] – 76;80

14 Wilbert; J. [F.T.C.I.] – 67/8; 76

15 Roe; P.G. – 105

16 Grimble; A. – 104

17 Spencer; B. + Gillan; F.W. [N.T.C.A.] – 415

18 Kearsley; G.R. [M.G.] – 440/1

19 Seligmann; C.G. – 402-4

20 Kearsley; G.R. [M.G.] – 206-11; 436-43

21 Riesenfeld; A. – 318

22 Riesenfeld; A. – 318;496/7

23 Layard; J. – 36

24 Kearsley; G.R. [M.G.] – 453/4

25 Riesenfeld; A. – 515/6

26 Elwin; V. [M.M.I.] – 158

27 Elwin; V. – 292

28 Roe; P.G. – 63-6

29 Zuidema; R.T. – 161; 237

30 Bandelier; A.F. – 298

31 Salcamayhua; P.-Y. – 72

32 Salcamayhua; P.-Y. – 87

33 Cobo; B. – 35

34 Cobo; B. – 79

35 Cobo; B. – 61

36 Avila; F. de – 127

37 Avila; F. de – 141

38 Avila; F. de – 146/7

39 Osborne; H. – 64

40 Moseley; M.E. – 53

41 McEwan; C. & Guchte; M. van – 368

42 Karsten; R. – [C.S.A.I.] – 337/8

43 Wilbert; J. [F.T.Teheu.I.] – 65/6

44 Verrill; A.H. – 98

45 Lumholtz; C. [U.M.] – v2-132

46 Riesenfeld; A. – 524

47 Riesenfeld; A – 501

48 Seligmann; C.G. – 388/9

49 Malinowski; B. – 44

50 Malinowski; B. – 45

51 Malinowski; B. – 315

52 Malinowski; B. – 331-3

53 Malinowski; B. – 235; 374; 375

54 Gomes; E. – 205/6

55 Rutter; O. – 258/9

56 Hoop; A.N.J.T. A. T. van der – 60/1

57 Kaudern; W. – 124/5

58 Howitt; A.W. – 431

59 Howitt; A.W. – 802/3

60 Mountford; C.P. [R.A.A.S.E.A.L.] – 22

61 Mountford; C.P. [R.A.A.S.E.A.L.] – 33

62 Mountford; C.F. [W.M.J.] – 12

63 Roy; S.C. [M.} – 388

64 Elwin; V. – 484/5

65 Rivers; W.H.R. – 187

66 Rivers; W.H.R. – 439/40

67 Avila; F. de – 123

68 Cobo; B. – 6-8

69 Arriaga; P.J. de – 25

70 Arriaga; P.J. de – 24

71 Avila; F. de – 119

72 Arriaga; P.J. de – 11

73 Arriaga; P.J. de – 20

74 Arriaga; P.J. de – 25

75 Arriaga; P.J. de – 119/20

76 Arriaga; P.J. de – 29/30

77 Arriaga; P.J. de – 44

78 Sharon; D. – 59

79 Arriaga; P.J. de 52/3

80 Arriaga; P.J. de – 68

81 Sharon; D. – 7/8

82 Avila; P.J. de – 82

83 Arriaga; P.J. de – 119

84 Arriaga; P.J. – 85

85 Arriaga; P.J. de – 86

86 Arriaga; P.J. de – 47

87 Arriaga; P.J. de – 48

88 Rivers; W.H.R. – 133

89 Rivers; W.H.R. – 135

90 Rivers; W.H.R. – 382/3

91 Thurston; E. [C.T.S.I.] – v1-323

92 Thurston; E. [C.T.S.I.] – v2-82

93 Thurston; E. [C.T.S.I.] – v2-374/5; 378

94 Thurston; E. [C.T.S.I.] – v5-143

95 Thurston; E. [C.T.S.I.] – v6-403/4

96 Thurston; E. [C.T.S.I.] – v7-25

97 Thurston; E. [C.T.S.I.] – v4-169

98 Thurston; E. [C.T.S.I.] – v4-388

99 Thurston; E. [C.T.S.I.] – v4-422

100 Thurston; E. [C.T.S.I.] – v3-157/8

101 Thurston; E. [C.T.S.I.] –

v4-14

[102] Thurston; E. [C.T.S.I.] – v2-340

[103] Sturrock; J. – 2

[104] Furer-Haimendorf; C. [R.G.I.] – 70

[105] Furer-Haimendorf; C. [R.G.I.] – 315

[106] Furer-Haimendorf; C. [R.G.I.] – 317

[107] Furer-Haimendorf; C. [R.G.I.] – 333

[108] Furer-Haimendorf; C. [R.G.I.] – 355

[109] Furer-Haimendorf; C. [R.G.A.] – 242

[110] Furer-Haimendorf; C. [R.G.A.] – 294

[111] Cobo; B. – 116

[112] Cobo; B. – 176

[113] Bruhns; K.O. – 62

[114] Alva; W. & Donnan; C. – 91

[115] Alva; W. & Donnan, C. – 215

[116] Arriaga; P.J. de – 129

[117] Furer-Haimendorf; C. [R.G.A.] – 363

[118] Whitehead; J. [V.G.S.I.] – 101/2

[119] Spencer; B. & Gillan; F.J. [N.T.C.A.] – 185

[120] Liebert; G. – 355

[121] Kearsley; G.R. [M.G.] – 304; 463

[122] Mills; J.P. [L.N.] – 6

[123] Mills; J.P. [L.N.] – 28/

[124] Mills; J.P. [L.N.] – 166

[125] Thurston; E. [C.T.S.I.] – v6-388

[126] Hutton; J.H. [A.N.] – 179/80; Hutton; J.H. [S.N.] – 255

[127] Hutton; J.H. [A.N.] – 232

[128] Mills; J.P. – xxxi

[129] Riesenfeld; A. – 120

[130] Riesenfeld; A. – 433

[131] Salmorel; M.L. – 139

[132] Bandelier; A.F. – 107; Demarest; A.A. – 58

[133] Cobo; B. – 26

[134] Cobo; B. – 97

[135] Osborne; H. – 78

[136] Bollaert; W. – 13

[137] Bollaert; W. – 13

[138] Bollaert; W. – 13

[139] Bollaert; W. – 20

[140] Kearsley; G.R. [M.G.] – 809-14

[141] Roys; R.L. – 25

[142] Bhattacharya; V-C. – 535

[143] Moseley; M.E. – 219

[144] Hadingham; E. – 39

[145] Furer-Haimendorf; C. – 117/8

[146] Furer-Haimendorf; C. [R.G.A.] – 223

[147] Thurston; E. [C.T.S.I.] – v6-189/90

[148] Grimble; A.F. – 134

[149] Schnitger; F.M. - 114; 125

[150] Tobing; Ph.L. – 163

[151] Tobing; Ph.L. – 170/1

[152] Drower; E.S. [M.I.I.] – 321

[153] Drower; E.S. [M.I.I.] – 34

[154] Zaehner; R.C. – 68/9

[155] Rivers; W.H.R. – 89

[156] Rivers; W.H.R. – 190-2

[157] Ka; Maung Po – 15

[158] Spencer; B. & Gillan; F.J. [N.T.C.A.] – 122

[159] Spencer; B. & Gillan; F.J. [N.T.C.A.] – 283/4

[160] Spencer; B. & Gillan; F.J. [N.T.C.A.] – 362

[161] Spencer; B. & Gillan; F.J. [N.T.C.A.] – 360

[162] Thurston; E. [C.T.S.I.] – v1-10-5; 108; 143; v7-180

[163] Riesenfeld; A. – 147/8

[164] Handy; E.S.C. – 49

[165] Skinner; H.D. – 53

[167] Wilbert; J. [F.T.B.I.] – 77

[168] Wilbert; J. [F.T.C.I.] – 76

[169] Sarmiento; P. de Gamboa [H.I.] – 135

[170] Sarmiento; P. de Gamboa [H.I.] – 136, see also Markham; C.R. Pedro Sarmiento de Gamboa, "To the Straights of Magellan",

[171] Sarmiento; P. de Gamboa [H.I.] – 137

[172] Meggers; B. – 160-5

[173] Sarmiento; P. de Gamboa – 134/5

[174] Sarmiento; P. de Gamboa [H.I.] – 137

[175] Sarmiento; P. de Gamboa – xiii

[176] Salcamayhua, P. – 76/7

[177] Oldenburg; H. in Muller; M. [S.B.E.] – v46-8

[178] Oldenburg; H. in Muller; M. [S.B.E.] – v46-153

[179] Oldenburg; H. in Muller; M. [S.B.E.] – v46-179

[180] Oldenburg; H. in Muller; M. [S.B.E.] – v46-198

[181] Oldenburg; H. in Muller; M. [S.B.E.] – v46-330

[182] Muller; M. [S.B.E.] – v8-330/1

[183] Eggeling; J. in Muller; M. [S.B.E.] – v41-21

[184] Telang; K.T. in Muller; M. [S.B.E.] – v8- 89

[185] Eggeling; J. in Muller; M. [S.B.E.] – v44-24

[186] Eggeling; J. in Muller; M. [S.B.E.] – v44-424/5

[187] Buhler; G. in Muller; M. [S.B.E.] – v14-268

[188] Bloomfield; M. in Muller; M. [S.B.E.] – v42-183

[189] Bloomfield; M. in Muller; M. [S.B.E.] – v42-214

[190] Eggeling; J. in Muller; M. [S.B.E.] – v44-465

[191] Wales; H.G.Q. – 1

[192] Wheatley; P. – 250/1

[193] Wheatley; P. – 250

[194] Wheatley; P. – 250

[195] Kearsley; G.R. [M.G.] – 457/8, 460

[196] Wales; H.G.Q. – 3

[197] Fabri; C.L. – 28; 67; 72

[198] Wales; H.G.Q. – 1;6

[199] Maier; V. – 78/9

[200] Fabri; C.L. – 125

[201] Higham; C. – 252/3

[202] Higham; C. – 251/2

[203] Higham; C. – 252

[204] Bibby; G. – 23

[205] Dayton; J.E. [S.I.A.S.] – 225

[206] Fabri; C.L. – 28; 67; 72; Mukherjee; P. – 12; 29; Harle; J.C. – 201

[207] Wales; H.G.Q. – 16

[208] Kearsley; G.R. [M.G.] – 514; 515

[209] Wales; H.G.Q. – 24

[210] Wales; H.G.Q. – 25

[211] Nebesky-Wojkowitz; R. de – vii

[212] Sastri; H.K. – 6

[213] Waddell; L.A. – 15

[214] Maier; - 76/7

[215] Maier; V. – 78/9

[216] Nebesky-Wojkowitz; R. de – 345

[217] Kearsley; G.R. [M.G.] – 680; 682; Kearsley; G.R. [P.P.P.P.] – 158/9

[218] Weaver; M.P. – 96

[219] Nebesky-Wojkowitz; R. de – 19

[220] Rawson; J. – 43

[221] Rock; J.F. – 5-10

[222] Kearsley; G.R. [M.G.] – 545-9

[223] Waddell; L.A. – vii

[224] Waddell; L.A. – ix

[225] Waddell; L.A. – xxvi

[226] Waddell; L.A. – xxvi

[227] Waddell; L.A. – xxvii

228 Waddell; L.A. – 30

229 Thurston; E. [C.T.S.I.] – v7-192; Grigson; W.V. – 225

230 Hadingham; E. – 246/7; Sharon; D. – 7/8

231 Nebesky-Wojkowitz; R. de – 223

232 Nebesky-Wojkowitz; R. de – 241

233 Nebesky-Wojkowitz; R. de – 243

234 Waddell; L.A. – 62

235 Grigson; W.V. – 225

236 Thurston; E. [C.T.S.I.] – v7-192

237 Nebesky-Wojkowitz; R. de – 243/4

238 Nebesky-Wojkowitz; R. de – 345

239 Nebesky-Wojkowitz; R. de – 552

240 Nebesky-Wojkowitz; R. de – 552

241 Nebesky-Wojkowitz; R. de – 553

242 Pranavananda; S – 41

243 Pranavananda; S. – 6

244 Nebesky-Wojkowitz; R. de – 223

245 Vogel; J.Ph. – 13

246 Davis; F. H. – 71-3

247 Boas; F. – v28-28;181

248 Bandelier; A.F. – 102

249 Vogel; J.Ph. – 25;29; Mills; J.H. [L.N.] – 164

250 Thurston; E. – v6-180/1

251 Crooke; W. – v2-123/4

252 Allchin; R. & B. – 240/1; 242

253 Harle; J.C. – 496

254 Loeb; E. & Heine-Geldern; R. – 215

255 Bruhns; K.O. – 159

256 Verrill; A.H. – 304

257 Osborne; H. – 14

258 Eggeling; J. in Muller; M. [S.B.E.] – v41-227

259 Eggeling; J. in Muller; M. [S.B.E.] – v12 - 12; v43 - 23-30

260 Muller; M. [S.B.E.] – v30-199

261 Muller; M. [S.B.E.] – v30-199

262 Muller; M. [S.B.E.] – v32-26

263 Miller; M.E. & Taube; K. – 124/5

264 Eggeling; J. in Muller; M. [S.B.E.] – v41-274

265 Eggeling; J. in Muller; M. [S.B.E.] – v44-435

266 Eggeling; J. in Muller; F.M. [S.B.E.] – v12 - 59-67; Kearsley; G.R. [M.G.] – 227/8

267 Eggeling; J. in Muller; M. [S.B.E.] – v41- 334

268 Oldenberg; H. in Muller; M. [S.B.E.] – v46-302

269 Oldenberg; H. in Muller; M. [S.B.E.] – v46-363/4

270 Oldenberg; H. in Muller; M. [S.B.E.] – v46-105; 109; 114-6

271 Buck; P. – 442; 443-5; 437; 531

272 Oldenberg; H. in Muller; M. [S.B.E.] – v46-103

273 Muller; M. [S.B.E.] – 29-328

274 Oldenberg; H. in Muller; M. [S.B.E.] – v46-331

275 Muller; M. [S.B.E.] – v46-96; 99

276 Muller; M. [S.B.E.] – v46-308

277 Muller; M. [S.B.E.] – v46-312 (Verse 9)

278 Eggeling; J. in Muller; M. [S.B.E.] – v41-287/8

279 Eggeling; J. in Muller; M. [S.B.E.] – v41- 288/9

280 Muller; M. [S.B.E.] – v41-290

281 Kearsley; G.R. [M.G.] – 343; 345

282 Eggeling; J. in Muller; M. [S.B.E.] – v41- 292/3

283 Muller; M. [S.B.E.] – v41-291

284 Eggerling; J. in Muller; F.M. [S.B.E.] – v41-208

285 Eggeling; J. in Muller; M. [S.B.E.] - v41- 206/7

286 Eggeling; J. in Muller; M. [S.B.E.] - v41-208

287 Thibaut; G. in Muller; F.M. [S.B.E.] – v38-260/1

288 Eggeling; J. in Muller; M. [S.B.E.] - v41-207-12

289 Eggeling; J. in Muller; M. [S.B.E.] - v41-217

290 Bandelier; A.F. – 11

291 Oldenberg; H. in Muller; M. [S.B.E.] – v46-45

292 Oldenberg; H. in Muller; M. [S.B.E.] – v46-52

293 Oldenberg; H. in Muller; M. [S.B.E.] – v46-119

294 Muller; M. [S.B.E.] – v46-122/3

295 Oldenberg; H. in Muller; M. [S.B.E.] – v46-194

296 Oldenberg; H. in Muller; M. [S.B.E.] – v46-170

297 Oldenberg; H. Muller; M. [S.B.E.] – v46-171

298 Muller; M. [S.B.E.] – v46-382

299 Zuidema; R.T. – 259

300 Zuidema; R.T. –160/1

301 Zuidema; R.T. – 97

302 Zuidema; R.T. – 101

303 Zuidema; R.T. – 189

304 Zuidema; R.T. – 198

305 Morley; S.G. & Goetz; D. [P.V.] – 227

306 Keeler; C.E. [L.M.C.] – 55

307 Sharon; D. – 93; Urton; G. – 63

308 Sharon; D. – 76/7;80/1

309 Urton; G. – 38;42/3

310 Beuchler; H.C. – 93

311 Liebert; G. – 81

312 Mills; J.P. [A.N.] – 164

313 Sastri; H.K. – 176

314 Thurston; E. [C.T.S.I.] – v6-35

315 Thurston; E. [C.T.S.I.] – v2-86

316 Thurston; E. [C.T.S.I.] – v4-437

317 Thurston; E. [C.T.S.I.] – v7-304

318 Muller; M. [S.B.E.] – v32-20-3

319 Muller; M. [S.B.I.] - v32-31

320 Eggeling; J. in Muller; M. [S.B.I.] – v26-229

321 Eggeling; J. in Muller; M. [S.B.E.] – v41-409; v42-402

322 Oldenberg; H. in Muller; M. [S.B.E.] – v46-104

323 Bloomfield; M. in Muller; M. [S.B.E.] – v46-137

324 Eggeling; J. in Muller; M. [S.B.E.] – v41-409; v46-23; 29

325 Oldenberg; H. - Muller; M. [S.B.E.] – v46-57; 59

Chapter 10

1 Reichel-Dolmatoff; G. – 4;5

2 Reichel-Dolmatoff; G. [A.C.] – 30

3 Reichel-Dolmatoff; G. [A.C.] – 24/5

4 Reichel-Dolmatoff; G. [A.C.] – 32

5 Reichel-Dolmatoff; G. [A.C.] – 32/3

6 Reichel-Dolmatoff; G. [A.C.] – 3

7 Reichel-Dolmatoff; G. [A.C.] – 34

8 Reichel-Dolmatoff; G. [A.C.] – 55

9 Reichel-Dolmatoff; G. [A.C.]

[−] – 57

[10] Reichel-Dolmatoff; G. [A.C.] – 27

[11] Reichel-Dolmatoff; G. [A.C.] – 208

[12] Reichel-Dolmatoff; G. [A.C.] – 203

[13] Reichel-Dolmatoff; G. [A.C.] – 107

[14] Reichel-Dolmatoff; G. [A.C.] – 108

[15] Reichel-Dolmatoff; G. [A.C.] – 113

[16] Bollaert; W. – 12;13; 21/2

[17] Broomhall; A.J. – 19

[18] Reichel-Dolmatoff; G. [A.C.] – 45

[19] Stair; J.B. – 24

[20] Howitt; A.E. – 426

[21] Reichel-Dolmatoff; G. [A.C.] – 46

[22] Reichel-Dolmatoff; G. [A.C.] – 128/9

[23] Reichel-Dolmatoff; G. [A.C.] – 65/6

[24] (Reichel-Dolmatoff; G. [A.C.] – 122/3

[25] Reichel-Dolmatoff; G. [A.C.] – 135

[26] Hutton; J.H. [S.N.] – 262

[27] Hutton; J.H. [S.N.] – 14

[28] Gomes; E.H. – 166/7

[29] Fornander; A. – v1-35

[30] Fornander; A. – v1-38

[31] Fornander; A. – v1-40

[32] Fornander; A. – v1-60

[33] Buck; P. – 513

[34] Smith; S.P. – 183

[35] Smith; S.P. – 84;86

[36] Buck; P. – 530

[37] Tilburg; J.A. van – 86

[38] Ivens; W.G. [M.S.E.S.I.] – 61

[39] Kearsley; G.R. [M.G.] – 545-9

[39] Broomhall; A.J. – 19

[40] Munro; N.G. – 15

[41] Brown; J.M. – v2-134/5

[42] Reichel-Dolmatoff; G. [A.C.] – 15;101

[43] Reichel-Dolmatoff; G. [A.C.] – 198;214

[44] Reichel-Dolmatoff; G. [A.C.] – 253

[45] Reichel-Dolmatoff; G. [A.C.] – 27/8; 36/7

[46] Reichel-Dolmatoff; G. [A.C.] – 29/30

[47] Reichel-Dolmatoff; G. [A.C.] – 19/20

[48] Reichel-Dolmatoff; G. [A.C.] – 27/8

[49] Kearsley; G.R. [M.G.] – 887/8; 972/3

[50] Reichel-Dolmatoff; G. [A.C.] – 35/6

[51] Reichel-Dolmatoff; G. [A.C.] – 44/5

[52] Reichel-Dolmatoff; G. [A.C.] – 59

[53] Reichel-Dolmatoff; G. [A.C.] – 118

[54] Reichel-Dolmatoff; G. [A.C.] – 139

[55] Reichel-Dolmatoff; G. [A.C.] – 148/9

[56] Reichel-Dolmatoff; G. [A.C.] – 122/3

[57] Reichel-Dolmatoff; G. [A.C.] – 190

[58] Salzano; F.M. – 133

[59] Salzano; F.M. – 138;153

[60] Reichel-Dolmatoff; G. [A.C.] – 195

[61] Reichel-Dolmatoff; G. [A.C.] – 136; 196/7; Keeler; C.E. [L.M.C.] – 28-30; 33/4; 67/8

[62] Mills; J.P. [L.N.] – 106/7

[63] Fornander; A. – 45; 66; Stair; J.B. – 273/4; Smith; P. – 26- 8; 216

[64] Reichel-Dolmatoff; G. [A.C.] – 166/7

[65] Wilkins; H.T. – 92/3

[66] Church; G.E. - 119/20

[67] Wallace; A.R. – 500

[68] Karsten; R. – 309

[69] Reisenfeld; A. – 102/3;106-8; 126; 358; 572

[70] Kearsley; G.R. [M.G.] – 719-21; 736-9

[71] Kearsley; G.R. [M.G.] – 84/5

[72] Howitt; A.W. – 783-5; 783/4; 785; 786; 791

[73] Lumholtz; C. [U.M.] – v1-353

[74] Reichel-Dolmatoff; G. [A.C.] – 87-9

[75] Reichel-Dolmatoff; G. [A.C.] – 80

[76] Roe; P.G. – 231

[77] Roe; P.G. – 238

[78] Roe; P.G. – 234

[79] Roe; P.G. – 221

[80] Danielou; A. – 196

[81] Danielou; A. – 274

[82] Sastri; H.K. – 151

[83] Sharon; D. – 92

[84] Grubb; W.B. – 119

[85] Grubb; W.B. – 119

[86] Loeb; E. & Heine-Geldern; R. – 216

[87] Aston; W.G. – 103

[88] Aston; W.G. – 111

[89] Skeet; W.W. & Blagden; C.O. – v2-301

[90] Skeet; W.W. & Blagden; C.O. – v2-301

[91] Sastri; H.K. – 194

[92] Crooke; W. – v2-227

[93] Riesenfeld; A. – 86

[94] Riesenfeld; A. – 86/7

[95] Seligmann; C.G. – 733

[96] Seligmann; C.G. – 679

[97] Malinowski; B. – 512

[98] Skeet; W.W. & Blagden; C.O. – v2-284/5

[99] Mills; J.P. [A.O.} – 308

[100] Mills; J.P. [A.O.] – 309

[101] Roth; W.E. – 153

[102] Crooke; W. – v1-133

[103] Thurston; E. [C.T.S.I.] – v3-368

[104] Thurston; E. [C.T.S.I.] – v7-351

[105] Elwin; V. [M.T.G.] – 170

[106] Reichel-Dolmatoff; G. [A.C.] – 64

[107] Reichel-Dolmatoff; G. [A.C.] – 65

[108] Bollaert; W. – 49-56

[109] Reichel-Dolmatoff; G. [A.C.] – 65/6

[110] Bonwick; J. – 157

[111] Thurston; E. [C.T.S.I.] – v5-95; 418

[112] Buhler; G. in Muller; F.M. [S.B.E.] – v1-131; 132

[113] Reichel-Dolmatoff; G. [A.C.] – 125

[114] Reichel-Dolmatoff; G. [A.C.] – 65/6

[115] Reichel-Dolmatoff; G. [A.C.] – 122/3

[116] Reichel-Dolmatoff; G. [A.C.] – 135

[117] Reichel-Dolmatoff; G. [A.C.] – 126

[118] Thurston; E. [C.T.S.I.] – v5-364

[119] Reichel-Dolmatoff; G. [A.C.] – 126

[120] Reichel-Dolmatoff; G. [A.C.] – 180;186

[121] Roys; R.L. – xv; 55; 56/7; P.V. – 97

[122] Williamson; R.W. – 241

[123] King; L.W. – 126

[124] Reichel-Dolmatoff; G. [A.C.] – 48/9

[125] Reichel-Dolmatoff; G. [A.C.] – 49

[126] Reichel-Dolmatoff; G. [A.C.] – 45

[127] (Reichel-Dolmatoff; G. [A.C.] – 27/8; 36/7

[128] Reichel-Dolmatoff; G.

[A.C.] – 47/8

129 Reichel-Dolmatoff; G. [A.C.] – 48

130 Reichel-Dolmatoff; G. [A.C.] – 49

131 Reichel-Dolmatoff; G. [A.C.] – 71

132 Reichel-Dolmatoff; G. [A.C.] – 71/2

133 Reichel-Dolmatoff; G. [A.C.] – 73

134 Loeb; E. & Heine-Geldern; R. – 165; D'Almeida; W.B. – v2-108

135 Reichel-Dolmatoff; G. [A.C.] – 74/5

136 Reichel-Dolmatoff; G. [A.C.] – 79

137 Reichel-Dolmatoff; G. [A.C.] – 79

138 Muller; M. [S.B.E.] – v25-138

139 Muller; M. [S.B.E.] – v40-244

140 Grimble; A.F. – 39

141 Grimble; A.F. – 53

142 Grimble; A.F. – 40/1

143 Reichel-Dolmatoff; G. – 79

144 Reichel-Dolmatoff; G. – 215

145 Roy; S.C. [H.B.O.] – 229; 265

146 Roy; S.C. [H.B.O.] – 20;30

147 Roy; S.C. [H.B.O.] – 32

148 Roy; S.C. [M.] – 135-9

149 Vogel; J.Ph. - 245/6; Bradley-Birt; F.B. - 9-11

150 Roy; S.C. [M.] – 135-8

151 Fox; C.E. – 83

152 Reichel-Dolmatoff; G. [S.M.C.] – 10

153 Fox; C.E. – 88-93

154 Reichel-Dolmatoff; G. – 106

155 Reichel-Dolmatoff; G. [A.C.] – 79

156 Reichel-Dolmatoff; G. [A.C.] – 149/50

157 Kearsley; G.R. [M.G.] – 637

158 Kearsley; G.R. [M.G.] – 661

159 Grimble; A.F. – 136

160 Grimble; A.F. – 21

161 Grimble; A.F. – 134

162 Kearsley; G.R. [M.G.] – 135-7; 141

163 Grimble; A.F. – 208

164 Grimble; A.F. – 199

165 Grimble; A.F. – 199

166 Grimble; A.F. – 207

167 Grimble; A.F. – 210

168 Grimble; A.F. – 211/2

169 Grimble; A.F. – 13

170 Suggs; R.C. – 165

171 Kearsley; G.R. [M.G.] – 231; 466; 928-31

172 Elwin; V. [M.T.G.] – 12

173 Elwin; V. [M.T.G.] – 194

174 Elwin; V. [M.T.G.] – 196

175 Elwin; V. [M.T.G.] – 243

176 Elwin; V. [M.T.G.] – 204

177 Reichel-Dolmatoff; G. [A.C.] – 107

178 Elwin; V. [M.T.G.] – 205

179 Reichel-Dolmatoff; G. – 146; 211

180 Elwin; V. [M.T.G.] – 651

181 Brewster; A.B. – 94-7;101-4

182 Fison; L. – 14-31

183 Speiser; F. [T.Y.N.W.P.] – 100, 242; Layard; J. [P.O.] – 331-53

184 Speiser; F. [T.Y.N.W.P.] – 100

185 Speiser; F. [T.Y.N.W.P.] – 242

186 Layard; J. [P.O.] – 332

187 Riesenfeld; A. – 32/3

188 Riesenfeld; A. – 149

189 Layard; J. [P.O.] – 334

190 Mills; J.P. [L.N.] – 25

191 Mills; J.P. [L.N.] – xxvi

192 Hodson; T.C. [N.T.M.] – 11/2

193 Hodson; T.C. [N.T.M.] – 13/4

194 Hodson; T.C. [N.T.M.] – 15

195 Hodson; T.C. [N.T.M.] – 15

196 Hodson; T.C. [N.T.M.] – 16/7

197 Hodson; T.C. [N.T.M.] – 102

198 Kearsley; G.R. [M.G.] – 1033/4

199 Hodson; T.C. [N.T.M.] – 164

200 Hutton; J. H. [S.N.] – 14

201 Hutton; J. H. [S.N.] – 44

202 Hutton; J. H. [S.N.] – 48

203 Hutton; J. H. [S.N.] – 73

204 Hutton; J. H. [S.N.] – 174

205 Hutton; J. H. [A.N.] – 241

206 Hutton; J. H. [A.N.] – 242

207 Hutton; J. H. [S.N.] – 175

208 Hutton; J. H. [A.N.] – 232

209 Mills; J.P. [L.N.] – 139;141

210 Mills; J.P. [L.N.] – 136

211 Mills; J.P. [L.N.] – 143

212 Grigson; W.V. – 277

213 Luckert; K.W. – 27

214 Donnan; C.B. – 27;72/3

215 Mills; J.P. [L.N.] – 144

216 Mills; J.P. [A.O.] – 255

217 Mills; J.P. [A.N.] – 221

218 Mills; J.P. [A.N.] – 279

219 Mills; J.P. [A.N.] – 280

220 Loeb; E. & Heine-Geldern; R. – 173

221 Loeb; E. & Heine-Geldern; R. – 174

222 Leon; C. de – 414

223 Reichel-Dolmatoff; G. [A.C.] – 136

224 Gomes; E. H. – 88

225 Gomes; E.H. – 216/7

226 Elwin; V. – [M.T.G.] –

11/2; Russell; R.V. & Hira Lal – v1-368

227 Riesenfeld; A. – 293

228 Riesenfeld; A. – 313

229 Seligmann; C.G. – 464

230 Mills; J.P. [A.N.] – 279

231 Fox; C.E. – 225;362

232 Ivens; W.G. [I.B.P.] – 302

233 Grimble; A.F. – 86

234 Stair; J.B. – 184/5

235 Wharton; W.J.L. – 65/6

236 Joyce; T.A. [C.A.W.I.A.] – 48/9

237 Kirchoff; P. [H.S.A.I.] – 295

238 Mills; J.P. [A.N.] – 215

239 Mills; J.P. [A.N.] – 206

240 Mills; J.P. [A.N.] – 215

241 Hutton; J.H. [A.N.] – 48

242 Hutton; J.H. [A.N.] – 45

243 Hutton; J., H. – 48

244 Hutton; J.H. – 206/7

245 Hutton; J.H. – 206/7

246 Gomes; E.H. – 214

247 Cobo; B. – 115;124

247 Cobo; B. – 115;124

248 Sharon; D. – 8

249 Black; J. – 68

250 Saggs; R.C. – 162

251 Bahn; P. – 147

252 Handy; E.S.C. – 43

253 Handy; E.S.C. – 46

254 Handy; E.S.C. – 205

255 Handy; E.C.S. – 205

256 Handy; E.S.C. – 92

257 Handy; E.S.C. – 135

258 Karsten; R. [C.S.A.I.] – 62-7

259 Karsten; R. [C.S.A.I.] – 67-9

260 Handy; E.S.C. – 6

261 Buck; P. – 484

262 Buck; P. – 479

263 Buck; P. - 484

264 Skinner; H.D. – 3-383;

Buck; P. – 13; 15; 161

265 Riesenfeld; A. – 419

266 Riesenfeld; A. – 417

267 Kearsley; G.R. [M.G.] – 453-5

268 Riesenfeld; A. – 417

269 Riesenfeld; A. – 419

270 Riesenfeld; A. – 420

271 Hather; J.G. – 72/3

272 Hather; J.G. – 75

273 Seligmann; C.G. – 233

274 Seligmann; C.G. – 18

275 Seligmann; C.G. – 56

276 Seligmann; C.G. – 62

277 Seligmann; C.G. – 19/20; 49

278 Seligmann; C.G. – 22

279 Seligmann; C.G. – 65

280 Riesenfeld; C.G. – 480

281 Seligmann; C.G. – 62

282 Seligmann; C.G. – 61

283 Zuidema; R.T. – 258

284 Cobo; B. – 197

285 Cobo; B. – 251

286 Reichel-Dolmatoff; G. [A.C.] – 110/1

287 Reichel-Dolmatoff; G. [A.C.] – 135/6

288 Karsten; S.R. [C.S.A.I.] – 238

289 Markham; C.R. [C.V.A.] – 190

290 Bandelier; A. – 140/1

291 Vega; G. de la – v2-100

292 Andagoya; P. de – 3

293 Joyce; T.A. [C.A.W.I.A.] – 93

294 Ellis; W. – v1-189

295 Linton in Heyerdahl; T. [A.I.P.] – 687

296 Murray; A.W. – 407/8

297 Reisenfeld; A. – 416

298 Loeb; E. & Heine-Geldern; R. – 139

299 Perry; W.J. – 48

300 Schnitger; F.M. – 197/8

301 Kempers; A.J.B. – 5

302 Perry; W.J. – 36

303 Thurston; E. [C.T.S.I.] – v5-317

304 Thurston; E. [C.T.S.I.] – v7-51; Thurston; E. [C.T.S.I.] – v7-63; 88/9

305 Rivers; W.H.R. – 29/30

306 Rivers; W.H.R. – 102

307 Grigson; W.V. – 64

308 Grigson; W.V. – 223

309 Hutton; J.H. [S.N.] – 243

310 Kearsley; G.R. [M.G.] – 186-9

311 Grimble; A. – 83

312 Grimble; A. – 234/5

313 Grimble; A.F. – 132-6

314 Grimble; A.F. – 83

315 (Kearsley; G.R. [M.G.] – 186-9

316 Grimble; A.F. – 104

317 Heine-Geldern; R. [T.S.A.P.] – 45-65

318 Bradley-Birt; F.B. – 119; Elwin; V. [M.M.I.] – 285; 445; 479

319 Danielou; A. – 283; Crooke; W. –v1-132/3

320 Grimble; A.F. – 137-49

321 Grimble; A.F. – 60

322 Grimble; A.F. – 37

323 Grimble; A.F. – 95

324 Kearsley; G.R. [M.G.] – 139; 446; 489

325 Grimble; A.F. – 149-51

326 Stimson; J.F. – 53-75

327 Meggers; B.J. – 160

328 Heyerdahl; T. [A.A.] – 304

329 Heseletine; N. – 57

330 Kearsley; G.R. [M.G.] – 121/2; 739

331 Skinner; H.D. – 52

332 Perry; W.J. – 92

333 Haddon; A.C. – 166

334 Haddon; A.C. – 167/8

335 Dalton; E.T. – 139-47

336 Dalton; E.T. – 139; Roy; S.C. [H.B.O.] – 19

337 Roy; S.C. [M.] – 111

338 Russell; R.V. – v2-306-7

339 Dalton; E.T. – 139

340 Dalton; E.T. – 140

341 Dalton; E.T. – 141

342 Reichel-Dolmatoff; R. [A.C.] – 10

343 Mathews; J. – 147

344 Stair; J. – 285/6

345 Kearsley; G.R. [M.G.] – 632-7

346 Thurston; E. [C.T.S.I.] – v42 -291

347 Mills; L.N. in Muller; M. [S.B.E.] – v23 - 27

348 Mills; L.N. in Muller; M. [S.B.E.] – v23- 228

349 Vogel; J.Ph. – 134

350 Eggeling; J. in Muller; M. [S.B.E.] – v26- 3/4

351 Eggeling; J. in Muller; M. [S.B.E.] – v26- 3

352 Gartelmann; K.D. – 44; Moseley; M.E. – 110

353 Hutton; J.H. [S.N.] – 37; 46; Roy; S.C. [H.B.O.] – 57

354 Deacon; A.B. – 26; Layard; J. – 270/440

355 Elwin; V. [M.T.G.] – 242/3

356 Akerblom; K. - 1-153

357 Bloomfield; M. in Muller; M. [S.B.E.] – v42 - 192/3

358 Vogel; J.Ph. – 9

359 Davids; T.W. Rhys in Muller; M. [S.B.E.] – v20-76

360 Legge; L. in Muller; M. [S.B.E.] – v16 - 57; 59

361 Legge; J. in Muller; M. [S.B.E.] – v16- 409-14

362 Eggeling; J. in Muller; M. [S.B.E.] – v44- 389/90

363 Kearsley; G.R. [M.G.] – 264

364 Danielou; A. – 215;221

365 Harle; J.C. – 14

366 West; E.W. in Muller; M. [S.B.E.] – v18- 110

367 Mills; L.N. in Muller; M. [S.B.E.] – v23 - 60; 75

368 Bloomfield; M. in Muller; M. [S.B.E.] – v42 -146

369 Bloomfield; M. in Muller; M. [S.B.E.] – v42-349

370 Zaehner; R.C. – 159

371 Zaehner; R.C. – 164

372 Kearsley; G.R. [M.G.] – 632-7

373 Muller; M. [S.B.E.] – v20-143

374 Muller; M. [S.B.E.] – v20-233

375 Langdon; S. – 87

376 Black; J. – 128

377 Langdon; S. – 202

378 Clay; A.T. – 68

379 Clay; A.T. – 69/70

380 Verrill; A.H. – 309-5

381 Clay; A.T. – 69/70

Chapter 11

1 Vogel; J.Ph. – 34/5

2 Vogel; J. Ph. – 13

3 Sharon; D. – 82

4 Riesenfeld; A. – 225

5 Berndt; R.M. & C.H. – 123

6 Hyde; T. – 4

7 Riesenfeld; A. – 232/3

8 Riesenfeld; A. – 396

9 Zaehner; R.C. – 66

10 Zaehner; R.C. – 66

11 Drower; E.S. [P.A.] – 133

12 Rivers; W.H.R. – 49; 77

13 Elwin; V. [M.M.I.] – 104/5

14 Elwin; V. [M.M.I.] – 296; 350

15 Elwin; V. [M.M.I.] – 318

16 Elwin; V. [M.M.I.] – 460

17 Thurston; E. [C.T.S.I.] – v3-82

[18] Thurston; E. [C.T.S.I.] – v3-218

[19] Marshall; H.I. – 168

[20] Fox; C.E. – 17

[21] Blackwood; B. – 126

[22] Mountford; C.P. [A.R.] – 40

[23] Ivens; W.G. [I.B.P.] – 214

[24] Codrington; R.H. – 399-402

[25] Riesenfeld; A. – 128/9

[26] Leon; P. Cieza de – 73

[27] Roe; P.G. – 194

[28] Roosevelt; A.C. – 88

[29] Saville; M.H. – 9

[30] Saville; M.H. – v1-10

[31] Saville; M.H. – 105

[32] Boas; F. [K.M.] – v28-151

[33] Boas; F. [F.T.C.S.] – v27-334/5

[34] Riesenfeld; A. – 196/7

[35] Riesenfeld; A. – 181/2

[36] Landtmann; G. – 74

[37] Riesenfeld; A. – 570

[38] Roe; P.G. – 173/4

[39] Elwin; V. [M.M.I.] – 170

[40] Davis; E. H. – 367

[41] Wilbert; J. [F.T.Teuh.I.] – 69/70

[42] Wilbert; J. [F.T.Teuh.I.] – 69/70

[43] Bloomfield; M. in Muller; M. [S.B.E.] – v42-103

[44] Bloomfield; M. in Muller; M. [S.B.E.] – v42-540

[45] Furer-Haimendorf; C. [R.G.A.] – 372-83

[46] Riesenfeld; A. – 294/5

[47] Avila; F. de – 129

[48] Fox; C.E. – 88/9

[49] Fox; C.E. – 93

[50] Fox; C.E. – 93-7

[51] Tierney; P. – 270

[52] Williams; F.E. - 151-3

[53] Keeler; C.E. [L.M.C.] – 31/2; 63

[54] Deacon; A.B. – 554/5;

Layard; J. – 225/6; 238/9

[55] Muller; M. [S.B.E.] – v29-330

[56] Muller; M. [S.B.E.] – v44-92

[57] Zaehner; R.C. – 164

[58] Schele; L. & Miller; M.E. – 109

[59] Alva; W. & Donnan; C.B. – 177

[60] Hadingham; E. – 110

[61] Howitt; A.W. – 431

[62] Mountford; C.F. – [T.A.M.C.] – 154-9

[63] Mountford; C.F. – [T.A.M.C.] – 107-9

[64] Mountford; C.F. – [R.A.A.S.E.A.L.] – 208

[65] Mountford; C.F. – [R.A.A.S.E.A.L.] – 212

[66] Mountford; C.F. – [A.R.] – 152-4

[67] Karsten; R. [C.S.A.I.] – 361

[68] Roe; P.G. – 181

[69] Roe; P.G. – 219

[70] Kearsley; G.R. [M.G.] – 632-7; 1020-5

[71] Roe; P.G. – 301/2

[72] Crooke; W. – v2-137

[73] Roe; P.G. – 302

[74] Kearsley; G.R. [M.G.] – 585

[75] Moseley; M.E. – 251/2

[76] Boas; F. v28-146/7

[77] Kearsley; G.R. [M.G.] – 50-61; 102-25

[78] Donnan; C.B. – 22

[79] Danielou; A. – 180

[80] Muller; M. [S.B.E.] – v29-143

[81] Kearsley; G.R. [M.G.] – 161; 163

[82] Riesenfeld; A. – 306

[83] Karsten; R. [C.S.A.I.] – 145

[84] Karsten; R. [C.S.A.I.] – 188/9

[85] Karsten; R. [C.S.A.I.] – 186

[86] Kearsley; G.R. [M.G.] –

209-11

[87] Karsten; R. [C.S.A.I.] – 179-82

[88] Elwin; V. [M.M.I.] – 354-94

[89] Elwin; V. [M.M.I.] – 360

[90] Mountford; C.P. [R.A.A.S.E.A.L.] – 29; Mountford; C.P. [A.R.] – 25; 62; Mountford; C.P. [W.M.J.] – 4/5

[91] Mountford; C.P. [R.A.A.S.E.A.L.] – 39

[92] Mountford; C.P. [A.R.] – 132; Mountford; C.P. [T.A.M.C.] – 124

[93] Elwin; V. [M.M.I.] – 375

[94] Zingg; R.W. – 255; 319; 538

[95] Roe; P.G. – 244

[96] Roe; P.G. – 158

[97] Roe; P.G. – 158/9

[98] Spencer; B. & Gillan; F.J. [T.N.T.C.A.] – 152/3; 156/7

[99] Elwin; [M.M.I.] – 253-60

[100] Zingg; R.W. – 362

[101] Roe; P.G. – 186/7;244

[102] Mukherjee; P. – 2;11

[103] Handy; E.S.C. – 235; 239

[104] Thurston; E. [C.T.S.I.] – v5-106; Rivers; W.H.R. – 433/4; Grigson; W.V. – 51; 52

[105] Grigson; W.V. – 138

[106] Kearsley; G.R. [M.G.] – 408-10

[107] Grigson; M.V. – 5/6

[108] Kearsley; G.R. [M.G.] – 809-14

[109] Grigson; M.V. – 235

[110] Grigson; M.V. – 236

[111] Grigson; M.V. – 241

[112] Elwin; V. [M.T.G.] – 21

[113] Elwin; V. [M.T.G.] – 61

[114] Thurston; E. [C.T.S.I.] – v7-305

[115] Russell; R.V. & Hira Lal – v1-370

[116] Roy; R.S. [H.B.O.] – 146

[117] Thurston; E. [C.T.S.I.] – v5-436

[118] Thurston; E. [C.T.S.I.] – v5-443

[119] Elwin; V. [A.] – 11

[120] Davis; F.H. – 350/1

[121] Legge J. in Muller; M. [S.B.E.] – v3-50; 104; 112; 120

[122] Legge; J. in Muller; M. [S.B.E.] – v3-138

[123] Legge; J. in Muller; M. [S.B.E.] – v3-140; 145

[124] Legge; J. in Muller; M. [S.B.E.] – v3-152-4

[125] Eggeling; J. in Muller; M. [S.B.E.] – v41-146/7

[126] Stair; J.B. – 24

[127] Eggeling; J. in Muller; M. [S.B.E.] – v41-389-91

[128] Bloomfield; M. in Muller; M. [S.B.E.] – v42-403

[129] Kearsley; G.R. [M.G.] – 223-30

[130] Eggeling; J. in Muller; M. [S.E.] – v43-1/2

[131] Eggeling; J. in Muller; M. [S.E.] – v43-358/9

[132] Eggeling; J. in Muller; F.M. [S.B.E.] – v44 - xxxvii; 403-20

[133] Kearsley; G.R. [M.G.] – 560

[134] Kearsley; G.R. [M.G.] – 901-38

[135] Hutton; J.H. [A.N.] – 7/8

[136] Anton; F. – 64; 71

[137] Hadingham; E. – 141/2

[138] Hadingham; E. – 158/9

[139] Moseley; M.E. – 187

[140] Hadingham; E. – 191

[141] Drower; E.S. [M.I.I.] – 258/9

[142] Friedel; D. & Schele; L. – 78

[143] Dalton; E.T. – 140; Kearsley; G.R. [M.G.] – 999; 1009

[144] Roy; S.C. [M.] – 409

[145] Roy; S.C. [M.] – v/vi

[146] Kearsley; G.R. [M.] – 809-14

[147] Fox; C.E. – 132/3;327

[148] d'Almeida; W.B. – v2-108; Scheltema; J.F. – 126; 218

[149] Ivens; W.G. – 117;169

[150] Saville; M.H. – v2-85

[151] Saville; M.H. – v1-114

[152] Friedel; D. - Schele; L. – 66

[153] Poindexter; M. – v1-155-7

[154] Roosevelt; A.C. – 88

[155] Black; J. – 175

[156] Miller; M.E. & Taube; K. – 132; 175

[157] Reisenfeld; A. – 179

[158] Kearsley; G.R. [M.G.] – 202; 740/1; 849

[159] Reisenfeld; A. – 179

[160] Riesenfeld; A. – 156/7

[161] Handy; E.S.C. – 173

[162] Endle; S. – xiii

[163] Endle; S. – 3

[164] Endle; S. – 34

[165] Riesenfeld; A. – 362/3

[166] Riesenfeld; A. – 362

[167] Giles; H.A. – 7/8

[168] Wheatley; P. – 11

[169] Riesenfeld; A. – 364

[170] Hose; C. & MacDougall; W. – 142

[171] Roy; S.C. [M.] – 390

[172] Roy; S.C. [M.] – 388

[173] Mountford; C.P. [W.M.J.] – 1-194

[174] Danielou; A. – 271;273

[175] Liebert; G. – 110

[176] Leibert; G. – 189

[177] Meggars; B. – 78-82

[178] Grimble; A.F. – 199

[179] Furer-Haimendorf; C. [R.G.A.] – 380

[180] Gurney; O. – 55/6

[181] Wallace; A.F. – 513

[182] Wallace; A.F. – 517/8

[183] Poznansky; A. – 25

[184] Church; G.E. – 138

[185] Mills; J.P. [A.O.] – 184

[186] Rapson; E.J. – 384

[187] Rapson; E.J. – 55

[188] Herodotus – 3

[189] Rapson; E.J. – 61

[190] Rapson; E.J. – 472-5

[191] Mukherjee; P. – 29

[192] Thurston; E. [C.T.S.I.] – v2-179

[193] Thurston; E. [C.T.S.I.] – v7-94

[194] Thurston; E. [C.T.S.I.] – v5-120

[195] Thurston; E. [C.T.S.I.] – v7-34

[196] Kulke; H. & Rothermund; D. – 35

[197] Roy; S.C. (H.B.O.] – 64

[198] Dalton; E.T. – 144

[199] Roy; S.C. [H.B.O.] – 47; 221; 151

[200] Roy; S.C. [H.B.O.] – 221

[201] Liebert; G. – 57

[202] Roy; S.C. [H.B.O.] – 221

[203] Roy; S.C. [H.B.O.] – 25

[204] Roy; S.C. [M.] – 84-6; 88/9

[205] Muller; M. [S.B.E.] – v46-49

[206] Riesenfeld; A. – 362/3

[207] Riesenfeld; A. – 366

[208] Holmes; J.H. – 13

[209] Holmes; J.H. – 182

[210] Thurston; E. [C.T.S.I.] – v1-10-15

[211] Ivens; W.G. [M.S.E.S.I.] – 2

[212] Ivens; W.G. [M.S.E.S.I.] – 50

[213] Ivens; W.G. [M.S.E.S.I.] – 56

[214] Ivens; W.G. [M.S.E.S.I.] – 55

[215] Lumholtz; C. [U.M.] – v1-350; 360;v 2-27; 296/7; 299/300

[216] Ivens; W.G. [M.S.E.S.I.] – 61

[217] Hather; J.G. – W.A., Vol. 24, No.1, June, 1992

[218] Ivens; W.G. [M.S.E.S.I.] – 109

[219] Ivens; W.G. [M.S.E.S.I.] – 112/3

[220] Ivens; W.G. [M.S.E.S.I.] – 196

[221] Ivens; W.G. [M.S.E.S.I.] – 242

[222] Ivens; W.G. [M.S.E.S.I.] – 481

[223] Buck; P. – 514/5

[224] Bollaert; W. – 96

[225] Wallace; A.R. – 511; 513

[226] Pachacuti; Y.S. – 70

[227] Urton; G. – 43

[228] Furer-Haimendorf; C. [R.G.A.] – 122/3; 230/1

[229] Cobo; B. – 35/6

[230] Bruhns; K.O. - 60

[231] Kearsley; G.R. [M.G.] – 307/8

[232] Kearsley; G.R. [M.G.] – 632-7

[233] Mills; J.P. [A.O.] – 299

[234] Mills; J.P. [A.O.] – 301;314

[235] Kloss; C.B. – 51

[236] Kloss; C.B. – 296

[237] Thurston; E. [C.T.S.I.] – 292

[238] Riesenfeld; A. – 398/90

[239] Riesenfeld; A. – 361/2

[240] Riesenfeld; A. – 316

[241] Riesenfeld; A. – 299/300; 330

[242] Church; G.E. – 60

[243] Church; G.E. – 116

[244] Covarrubias; M. – 200

[245] Kearsley; G.R. [M.G.] – 298-300

[246] Kearsley; G.R. [M.G.] – 632-7; Kearsley; G.R. [P.P.P.P.] – 132-9

[247] Muller; M. [S.B.E.] – v1-143

[248] Muller; M. [S.B.E.] – v8-224

[249] Davids; T.W. Rhys in Muller; M. [S.B.E.] – v35-37/8

[250] Davids; T.W. Rhys in Muller; M. [S.B.E.] – v36-321

[251] Kern; H. in Muller; M. [S.B.E.] – v21-6

[252] Kearsley; G.R. [M.G.] – 359/60; 815/6

[253] Jolly; J. in Muller; M. [S.B.E.] – v7- 241

[254] Jolly; J. in Muller; M [S.B.E.] – v7- 270

[255] Vogel; J.Ph. – 235-7

[256] Lishk; S.C. – xx

[257] Elwin; V. [M.M.I.] – 68/9

[258] Schebesta; P. – 195

[259] Schebesta; P. – 237

[260] Elwin; V. [M.M.I.] – 70-3

[261] Elwin; V. [A.] – 3;24

[262] Elwin; V. [A.] – 19

[263] Mills; [L.N.] – 172/3

[264] Bandelier; A.F. – 315/6

[265] Mills; J.P. [A.O.] – 299

[266] Mills; J.P. [A.N.] – 301

[267] Hutton; J.H. [S.N.] – 250

[268] Ivens; W.G. [I.B.P.] – 263

[269] Ellis; W. [P.R.] – v1-331

[270] Ellis; W. [P.R.] – v3-170/1

[271] Church; G.E. – 234/5

[272] Church; G.E. – 237

[273] Osborne; H. – 129

[274] Cobo; B. – 29

[275] Arriaga; P.J. de – 60

[276] Cobo; B. – 145

[277] Cobo; B. – 175-7

[278] Aveni; A.F. [A.P.A.] – 18

[279] Kearsley; G.R. [M.G.] –

641-7

[280] Kearsley; G.R. [M.G.] – 59; 61

[281] Stimson; J.F. – 53

[282] Grimble; A.F. – 41

[283] Grimble; A.F. – 214

[284] Grimble; A.F. – 53

[285] Muller; M. [S.B.E.] – v1-14/5

[286] Elwin; V. [M.M.I.] – 47

[287] Langdon; S. – 162/3

[288] Kearsley; G.R. [M.G.] – 1024/5

[289] Alva; W. & Donnan; C.B. – 90/1

[290] Grimble; A.F. – 246

[291] Smith; S.P. – 172

[292] Smith; S.P. – 174

[293] Smith; S.P. – 153/4

[294] Smith; S.P. – 154

[295] Ellis; W. [P.R.] – v1-348

[296] Ivens; W.G. [M.S.E.S.I.] – 45

[297] Ellis; W. [P.R.] – v1-349

[298] Ellis; W. [P.R.] – v2-394

[299] Ellis; W. [P.R.] – v1-334

[300] Lothrop; S.K. [P.C.R.N.] – v1-65/6

[301] Bollaert; W. – 11

[302] Ellis; W. [P.R.] – v1-213

[303] Ellis; W. [P.R.] – v1-238

[304] Handy; E.S.C. – 243

[305] Roe; P.G. – 207

[306] Roe; P.G. – 231

[307] Dolmatoff; G. R. [A.C.] – 212

[308] Wilbert; J. [F.L.C.I.] – 254

[309] Wilbert; J. [F.T.G.I.] – 392-4

[310] Boas; F. [K.C.] – v28-130

[311] Kearsley; G.R. [M.G.] – 51-61; 103-16

[312] Boas; F. [B.B.T.] – v25-112

[313] Heyerdahl; T. [A.I.P.] – 80; 82; 4; 12; 114; 122; 126

Chapter 12

[1] Anton; F. – 144

[2] Bruhns; K.O. – 253/4

[3] Burger; R.L. – 192

[4] Demarest; A.A. – 66; Anton; F. – 144

[5] Burger; R.L. – 144

[6] Whitehead; H. [V.G.S.I.] – 18/9; 95

[7] Demarest; A.A. – 18

[8] Markham; C.R. [T.P.C.L.] – 251

[9] Vega; G. de la – v1-106

[10] Vega; G. de la – v1-114

[11] Sharon; D. – 90

[12] Vega; G. de la – v2-186

[13] Vega; G. de la – v2-195/6

[14] Avila; F. de – 127;129

[15] Bollaert; W. – 12

[16] Bollaert; W. – 208/9

[17] Bollaert; W. – 219

[18] Bandelier; A.F. – 302

[19] Joyce; T.A. [S.A.A.] – 151

[20] Demarest; A.A. – 31

[21] Demarest; A.A.- 32;33

[22] Demarest; A.A. – 53

[23] Anton; F. – 112

[24] Zuidema; R.T. – 165/6;238

[25] Joyce; T.A. [S.A.A,] – 152

[26] Metraux; A. [H.S.A.I.] – 255/6

[27] Thurston; E. [C.T.S.I.] – v4-407

[28] Thurston; E. [C.T.S.I.] – v4-408

[29] Thurston; E. [C.T.S.I.] – v4-407

[30] Thurston; E. [C.T.S.I.] – v4-424/5

[31] Thurston; E. [M.G.] – v6-186

[32] Thurston; E. [C.T.S.I.] – v4-420/1

[33] Thurston; E. [C.T.S.I.] – v2-388; Rivers; W.H.R. – 694

[34] Anton; F. – 186; Arriaga; P.J. de 51; Cobo; B. – 93; Vega; G. de la – v2-279

[35] Thurston; E. [C.T.S.I.] – v4-428

[36] Muller; M. [S.B.E.] – v15-178; Thibaut; G. (S.B.E.) - v34-257

[37] Muller; M. [S.B.E.] – v42-92; Oldenberg; H. (S.B.E.) - v46-194

[38] Thurston; E. [C.T.S.I.] – v4-431

[39] Thurston; E. [C.T.S.I.] – v3-456

[40] Thurston; E. [C.T.S.I.] – v5-447

[41] Roys; R.L. [R.B.] – xvi

[42] Roys; R.L. [R.B.] – 69

[43] Friedel; D. – 66

[44] Schele; L. + Miller; M.E. – 270

[45] Danielou; A. – 210

[46] Bollaert; W. – 208/9

[47] Markham; C.R. [T.P.C.L.] – 260

[48] Markham; C.R. [T.P.C.L.] – 268

[49] Bruhns; K.O. – 360

[50] Tierney; P. - 33/4

[51] Werthmann; A. in Poindexter; M. [A.I.] – v1-116-8

[52] Cobo; B. – 8; 54; 58; 67; 71; 81; 99

[53] Cobo; B. – 99

[54] Cobo; B. – 151

[55] Cobo; B. – 156

[56] Salcamayhua; P.-Y. – 85

[57] Salcamayhua; Y.-P. – 100

[58] Salcamayhua; P.-Y. – 85

[59] Eggeling; J. in Muller; F.M. [S.B.E.] – v44- xxxvii; Thibaut; G. in Muller; F.M. [S.B.E.] – v38-220-2; v44-xvii; xviii

[60] Handy; E.S.C. – 106/7

[61] Gill; W. W. – 42/3

[62] Gill; W.G – 40/1

[63] Gill; W.W. – 40/1

[64] Mariner; E. – v1-91

[65] Mariner; E. – v1-230

[66] Mariner; E. – v1-379

[67] Mariner; E. – v1-359

[68] Mariner; E. – v1-453/4

[69] Malinowski; B. – 234

[70] Malinowski; B. – 235

[71] Riesenfeld; A. – 314

[72] Tierney; P. – 26/7; 30/1; 133/4; 201/2; 383/4; 394/5

[73] Codrington; R.H. - 256/7

[74] Hickson; S.J. – 216

[75] Thurston; E. [C.T.S.I.] – v4-312

[76] Furer-Haimendorf; C. [R.G.A.] – 252

[77] Thurston; E. [C.T.S.I.] – v4-341/2

[78] Thurston; E. [C.T.S.I.] – v6-10

[79] Thurston; E. [C.T.S.I.] – v6-10/1

[80] Thurston; E. [C.T.S.I.] – v7-286

[81] Thurston; E. [C.T.S.I.] – 291

[82] Russell; R.V. & Hira Lala – v1-71

[83] Thurston; E. [C.T.S.I.] – v1-liv

[84] Russell; R.V. & Hira Lal – v1-388

[85] Kearsley; G.R. [M.G.] – 923

[86] Thurston; E. [C.T.S.I.] – v1-147/8

[87] Thurston; E. [C.T.S.I.] – v1-407

[88] Thurston; E., [C.T.S.I.] – v6-21

[89] Thurston; E. [C.T.S.I.] – v2-129

[90] Markham; C.R. [T.P.C.L.] – 167

[91] Vega; de la G. – v2-334

[92] Stair; J.B. – 120

[93] Meggers; B.J. – 127

[94] Meggers; B.J. – 151-3

[95] Vega; G. de la – v1-176

[96] Vega; G. de la – v2-336;338

[97] Kearsley; G.R. [M.G.] – 548/9

[98] Vega; G. de la – v2-335

[99] Gartelmann; K.D. – 307

[100] Gartelmann; K.D. – 308

[101] Vega; G. de la – 347

[102] Joyce; T.A. [S.A.A.] – 64

[103] Harle; J.C. – 59

[104] Roy; S.C. [M.] – 78/9

[105] Roy; S.C. [M.] –385

[106] Mukherjee; P. – 31

[107] Vega; G. de la – v2-348

[108] Bollaert; W. – 219

[109] Markham; C.R. [T.P.C.L.] – v1-183

[110] Saville; M.H. – v1-14

[111] Saville; M.H. – v1-114

[112] Verrill; A.H. – 66

[113] Morley; S.G. & Goetz; D. [P.V.] – 87/8

[114] Liebert; G. – 173

[115] Liebert; G. – 194

[116] Vogel; J.Ph. – 18

[117] Thurston; E. [C.T.S.I.] – v5-258/9

[118] Kearsley; G.R. [M.G.] – 520-8; 905/6; 919/20

[119] Kearsley; G.R. [M.G.] – 781/2

[120] Meggers; B.J. – 157

[121] Russell; R.V. & Hira Lal – v1-31

[122] Loftus; W.K. – 428

[123] Drower; E.S. [M.I.I.] – 1;2

[124] Thurston; E. [C.T.S.I.] – v1-19

[125] Thurston; E. [C.T.S.I.] – v2-127

[126] Thurston; E. [C.T.S.I.] – v1-35/6

[127] Thurston; E. [C.T.S.I.] – v2-83

[128] Thurston; E. [C.T.S.I.] –

[129] Thurston; E. [C.T.S.I.] – v2-83

[130] Thurston; E. [C.T.S.I.] – v3-31

[131] Thurston; E. [C.T.S.I.] – v3-33

[132] Thurston; E. [C.T.S.I.] – v3-418

[133] Thurston; E. [C.T.S.I.] – v7-241

[134] Thurston; E. [C.T.S.I.] – v4-420

[135] Urton; G. – 51; Sharon; D. – 96/7; Salcamayhua; P.-Y. – 87; Zuidema; R.T. – 108

[136] Thurston; E. [C.T.S.I.] – v4-124/5

[137] Thurston; E. [C.T.S.I.] – v7-183

[138] Thurston; E. [C.T.S.I.] – v7-196

[139] Thurston; E. [C.T.S.I.] – v6-177/8

[140] Thurston; E. [C.T.S.I.] – v4-154

[141] Hutton; J.H. [S.N.] – 63/4

[142] Thurston; E. [C.T.S.I.] – v4-181-7

[143] Thurston; E. [C.T.S.I.] – v4-198

[144] Thurston; E. [C.T.S.I.] – v7-257

[145] Thurston; E. [C.T.S.I.] – v4-207

[146] Thurston; E. [C.T.S.I.] – v4-410

[147] Thurston; E. [C.T.S.I.] – v7-351/2

[148] Thurston; E. [C.T.S.I.] – v6-385

[149] Thurston; E. [C.T.S.I.] – v7-244

[150] Dalton; E.T. – 147

[151] Kloss; C.B. – 85

[152] Hodson; T.C. – 110

[153] Schebesta; P. – 67

[154] Schebesta; P. – 185

[155] Skeat; W.W. + Blagden; C.O. – v1-54

[156] Hickson; S.J. – 241

[157] Ween; H. van der – 192

[158] Howitt; E.A. – 129

[159] Bonwick; J. – 176

[160] Kearsley; G.R. [M.G.] – 466; 934/5

[161] Ellis; W. – v4-91

[162] Zuidema; R.T. – 139

[163] Salcamayhua; P.-Y. – 77

[164] Salcamayhua; P.-Y. – 78

[165] Sharon; D. – 136

[166] Sharon; D. – 76;77

[167] Salcamayhua; P.-Y. – 71

[168] Salcamayhua; P.-Y. – 74

[169] Salcamayhua; P.-Y. – 115/6

[170] Zuidema; R.T. – 62; 87/8

[171] Zuidema; R.T. – 73

[172] Zuidema; R.T. – 88

[173] Zuidema; R.T. – 89/90

[174] Zuidema; R.T. – 234

[175] Hadingham; E. – 225

[176] Thurston; E. [C.T.S.I.] – v4-80

[177] Thurston; E. [C.T.S.I.] – v5-149/50

[178] Thurston; E. [C.T.S.I.] – v5-164

[179] Thurston; E. [C.T.S.I.] – v7-6/7

[180] Thurston; E. [C.T.S.I.] – 285

[181] Thurston; E. [C.T.S.I.] – v6-46

[182] Thurston; E. [C.T.S.I.] – v1-87/8

[183] Thurston; E. [C.T.S.I.] – v6-129

[184] Thurston; E. [C.T.S.I.] – v7-6

[185] Thurston; E. [C.T.S.I.] – v7-196

[186] Thurston; E. [C.T.S.I.] – v2-366

[187] Ka; M.P. – 1

[188] Rutter; O. – 247

[189] Thurston; E. [C.T.S.I.] – v7-249

[190] Thurston; E. [C.T.S.I.] – v4-124

[191] Thurston; E. [C.T.S.I.] – v7-5

[192] Thurston; E. [C.T.S.I.] – v2-366

[193] Thurston; E. [C.T.S.I.] – 207

[194] Thurston; E. [C.T.S.I.] – v4-137

[195] Thurston; E. [C.T.S.I.] – v2-199

[196] Thurston; E. [C.T.S.I.] – v1-50

[197] Thurston; E. [C.T.S.I.] – v7-99

[198] Urton; G. – 51

[199] Urton; G. – 51/2

[200] Cobo; B. – 25

[201] Demarest; A.A. – 14; 23/4; 25

[202] Demarest; A.A. – 34

[203] Urton; G. – 90

[204] Sharon; D. – 77-9

[205] Arriaga; P.J. de – 86;89

[206] Perry; W.J. – 118

[207] Ween; H. van der- 38

[208] Ween; H. van der- 194

[209] Ween; H. van der – 193

[210] Reichel-Dolmatoff; G. [A.C.] – 65

[211] Zuidema; R.T. – 252

[212] Skeat; W.W. & Blagden; C.O. – v1-111

[213] Graham; D.C. – 84

[214] Kearsley; G.R. [M.G.] – 545-9

[215] Wilson; E.H. – v2-10

[216] Hutton; J.N. [S.N.] – 138

[217] Hutton; J.N. [S.N.] – 237/8

[218] Sharon; D. – 92

[219] Eggeling; J. in Muller; F.M. – 6; 10/11; 19/20; 55/6; 84-7

220 Hutton; J.N. – [A.N.] – 115

221 Mills; J.P. [L.N.] – xxxi

222 Mills; J.P. [L.N.] – xxvi

223 Hather; J.G. – W.A., Vol.24, No.1, June, 1992

224 Salcamayhua; P.-Y. – 82/3

225 Salcamayhua; P.-Y. – 87

226 Salcamayhua; P.-Y. – 94

227 Salcamayhua; P.-Y. – 112

228 Cooper; J.M. [H.S.A.I.] – 307

229 Moseley; M.E. – 52

230 Vega; G. de la – v1-82

231 Root; W.C. [H.S.A.I.] – 209/10

232 Moseley; M.E. – 65

233 Cooper; J.M. [H.S.A.I.] – 299

234 Moseley; M.E. – 65

235 Moseley; M.E. – 261

236 Thurston; E. [C.T.S.I.] – v4-207

237 Thurston; E. [C.T.S.I.] – v1-260

238 Gartelmann; K.D. – 195

239 Grigson; W.V. – xv

240 Mills; J.P. [L.N.] – xvi; xxiv

241 Mills; J.P. [L.N.] – xxvi

242 Salcamayhua; P.-Y. – 87

243 Sharon; D. – 96/7

244 Urton; G. – 51

245 Zuidema; R.T. – 108

246 Thurston; E. [C.T.S.I.] – v6-186

247 Thurston; E. [C.T.S.I.] – v1-60

248 Thurston; E. [C.T.S.I.] – v1-60

249 Thurston; E. [C.T.S.I.] – 55

250 Thurston; E. [C.T.S.I.] – v2-163

251 Thurston; E. [C.T.S.I.] – v2-349

252 Thurston; E. [C.T.S.I.] – v6-382

253 Thurston; E. [C.T.S.I.] – v3-33

254 Thurston; E. [C.T.S.I.] – v3-418

255 Thurston; E. [C.T.S.I.] – v4-420

256 Thurston; E. [C.T.S.I.] – v3-451

257 Thurston; E. [C.T.S.I.] – v4-432

258 Thurston; E. [C.T.S.I.] – v6-176

259 Zuidema; R.T. – 131

260 Zuidema; R.T. – 136

261 Sharon; D. – 93

262 Urton; G. – 79/80

263 Sharon; D. – 135

264 Malinowski; B. – 46

265 Salcamayhua; P.-Y. – 78

266 Anton; F. – 195

267 Harle; J.C. – 292/3

268 Liebert; G. – 63

269 Grigson; W.V. – 4

270 Grigson; W.V. – 35

271 Buhler; G. in Muller; F.M. [S.B.E.] – v2-276; Jolly; J. in Muller; A.F. [S.B.E.] – v7-89

272 Marshall; H.I. – 12/3

273 Vega; G. de la – v1-317/8; 320

274 Zuidema; R.T. – 91

275 Vega; G. de la – v1-317

276 Thurston; E. [C.T.S.I.] – v2-385

277 Thurston; E. [C.T.S.I.] – v6-214

278 Thurston; E. [C.T.S.I.] – v7-361

279 Liebert; G. – 207

280 Thurston; E. [C.T.S.I.] – v76-16

281 Thurston; E. [C.T.S.I.] – v6-1-3

282 Thurston; E. [C.T.S.I.] – v6-10/1

283 Thurston; E. [C.T.S.I.] – v7-29

284 Thurston; E. [C.T.S.I.] – v7-221-3

285 Thurston; E. [C.T.S.I.] – v7-361-3

286 Thurston; E. [C.T.S.I.] – v7-413

287 Ivens; W.G. [I.B.P.] – 65; 96; 141-4; Riesenfeld; A. – 79/80; 297

288 Vega; G. de la – v1-81/2

289 Bruhns; K.O. – 159

290 Cobo; B. – 223

291 Cobo; B. – 224

292 Cobo; B. – 224

293 O'Neale; L. [H.S.A.I.] – 9

294 O'Neale; L. (H.S.A.I.] – 102

295 Bollaert; W. – 11

296 Grubb; W. B. – 68

297 Cobo; B. – 225

298 Thurston; E. [C.T.S.I.] – v1-1

299 Thurston; E. [C.T.S.I.] – v2-244/5

300 Thurston; E. [C.T.S.I.] – v1-239

301 Thurston; E. [C.T.S.I.] – v2-11

302 Thurston; E. [C.T.S.I.] – v2-154

303 Thurston; E. [C.T.S.I.] – v2-165

304 Thurston; E. [C.T.S.I.] – v3-32/3

305 Crooke; W. – v1-132/3

306 Thurston; E. [C.T.S.I.] – v3-42

307 Thurston; E. [C.T.S.I.] – v3-43

308 Vega; G. de la – v2-143-6)

309 Thurston; E. [C.T.S.I.] – v3-116

310 Thurston; E. [C.T.S.I.] – v4-137

311 Thurston; E. [C.T.S.I.] – v4-134

312 Thurston; E. [C.T.S.I.] – v4-137

313 Thurston; E. [C.T.S.I.] – v4-135-7

314 Kearsley; G.R. [P.P.P.P.] – 118; 129; 131; 140

315 Thurston; E. [C.T.S.I.] – v5-249-53

316 Thurston; E. [C.T.S.I.] – v5-258/9

317 Thurston; E. [C.T.S.I.] – v5-270

318 Thurston; E. [C.T.S.I.] – v6-160/1

319 Thurston; E. [C.T.S.I.] – v6-265

320 Thurston; E. [C.T.S.I.] – v6-267

321 Pachacuti; R.-Y. – 88

322 Salcamayhua; P.-Y. – 97

323 Salcamayhua; P.-Y. – 118

324 Cobo; B. – 142

325 Cobo; B. – 154

326 Arriaga; P.J. de – 68;87

327 Arriaga; P.J. de – 50

328 Thurston; E. [C.T.S.I.] – v5-97

329 Thurston; E. [C.T.S.I.] – v5-276

330 Thurston; E. [C.T.S.I.] – v4-406

331 Thurston; E. [C.T.S.I.] – v5-80

332 Gomes; E.H. – 37

333 Maxwell; R. – 124

334 Maxwell; R. – 108

335 Anton; F. – 7-2

336 Arriaga; P.J. de – 55;75

337 Cobo; B. – 215-9

338 Anton; F. – 76;146/7

339 Thurston; E. [C.T.S.I.] – v6-328/9

340 Thurston; E. [C.T.S.I.] – v5-314/5

341 Thurston; E. [C.T.S.I.] – v5-334

342 Thurston; E. [C.T.S.I.] – v5-315

343 Thurston; E. [C.T.S.I.] – v5-351

344 Thurston; E. [C.T.S.I.] – v2-380

345 Thurston; E. [C.T.S.I.] – v3-5

346 Thurston; E. [C.T.S.I.] – v3-497

347 Thurston; E. [C.T.S.I.] – v4-372

348 Thurston; E. [C.T.S.I.] – v5-40/1

349 Thurston; E. [C.T.S.I.] – v5-137

350 Thurston; E. [C.T.S.I.] – v5-432

351 Thurston; E. [C.T.S.I.] – v5-350

352 Thurston; E. [C.T.S.I.] – v6-108

353 Andagoya; P. de – 14/5

354 Spence; L. – 122/3

355 Kearsley; G.R. [M.G.] – 999-1002

356 Kramer; S.N. – 97/8

357 Cobo; B. – 16

358 Boas; F. – v28-136

359 Boas; F. – v25-1-5

360 Cobo; B. – 16

361 Fox; C.E. – 9

362 Ellis; W. – v1-386-93

363 Cobo; B. – 14/5

364 Molina; C. de – 8/9

365 Dundes; A. – 185/6

366 Dundes; A. – 205/6

367 Dundes; A. – 209-12

368 Riesenfeld; A. – 400/1

369 Riesenfeld; A. – 516

370 Rutter; O. – 259-61

371 Vogel; J.Ph. – 166

372 Vogel; J.Ph. – 174/5

373 Furer-Haimendorf; C. [R.G.A.] – 223/4

374 Furer-Haimendorf; C. [R.G.A.] – 222

375 Farrabee; W.C. – 124

376 Dundes; A. – 269;273-8

377 Molina; C. de – 4

378 Salcamayhua; P.-Y. – 97

379 Moseley; M.E. – 51

380 Sharon; D. – 23

381 Moseley; M.E. – 67

382 Thurston; E. [C.T.S.I.] – v5-58/9

383 Sullivan; W.F. – 15

384 Molina; C. de – 9/10

385 Handy; E.S.C. – 233; Skinner; S.P. – 55

386 Reisenfeld; A. – 405

387 Hose; C. & MacDougall; W. – v2-214

388 Spencer; B. & Gillan; F.J. [T.N.T.C.A.] – 435

389 Sharon; D. – 153

390 Urton; G. – 109

391 Urton; G. – 95

392 Urton; G. – 109

393 Urton; G. – 177;184

394 Crooke; W. – v1-25/6

395 Urton; G. – 59;172

396 Hickson; S.J. – 246/7

397 Howitt; A.W. – 426

398 Eggeling; J. in Muller; F.M. – xiv; Furer-Haimendorf; C. [R.G.A.] – 122/3

399 Thurston; E. [C.T.S.I.] – v1-96; v2-372; 374; v6-385

400 Leob; E. & Heine-Geldern; R. – 192; 246/7

401 Hutton; J.H. 237; Mills; J.P. [L.N.] – 193

402 Urton; G. – 114

403 Kearsley; G.R. [M.G.] – 118; Fornander; A. – 118

404 Lishk; S.S. – 206

405 Urton; G. – 169

406 Urton; G. – 173

407 Urton; G. – 174

408 Urton; G. – 174

409 Urton; G. – 10

410 Wilbert; J. [F.L.G.I.] – 8; v2-46

411 Handy; E.S.C. – 233

412 Handy; E.S.C. – 233

413 Karsten; R. [I.T.A.B.C.] – 109

414 Karsten; R. [I.T.A.B.C.] – 78; 115

415 Karsten; R. [I.T.A.B.C.] – 90/1

416 Karsten; R. [I.T.A.B.C.] – 105

417 Skinner; H.D. – 55

418 Spencer; B. & F.J. Gillan; [T.N.T.C.A.] – 435

419 Spencer; B. + Gillan; F.W. [T.N.T.C.A.] – 498/9

420 Howitt; A.W. – 439

421 Howitt; A.W. – 665/6

422 Howitt; A.W. – 405

423 Hose; C. & McDougall; W. – v2-214

424 Wilbert; J. – [F.L.G.I.] – v1-106; 107/8; 110/1; v2-18; 47

425 Christie; A – 56

426 Wilbert; J. [F.T.G.I.] – v6-8; 106; v2-46

427 Hutton; J.H. [S.N.] – 329; Mills; J.P. [L.N.] – 194

428 Majumdar; D.N. – 127/8; 129; 132; 134

429 Zaehner; R.C. – 107;183

429 Zaehner; R.C. – 107;183

431 Kearsley; G.R. [M.G.] - 171/2

432 Kearsley; G.R. [M.G.] – 174/5

433 Kearsley; G.R. [P.P.P.P.] – 156, *5.10*

434 Jacobi; H. in Muller; F.M. [S.B.E.] – v22-222

435 Danielou; A. – 292

436 Danielou; A. – 291

437 Danilou; A – 292

438 Danielou; A. – 292/3

439 Danielou; A. – 294

440 Liebert; G. – 337

441 Danielou; A. – 295/6

442 Sastri; H.K. – 176

443 Kearsley; G.R. [M.G.] – 297-300; 553-8

444 Sarmiento; P. de Gamboa – 68

445 Poindexter; M. [A.I.] – v2-132

446 Skinner; H.D. – 372

447 Skinner; H.D. – 383

448 Skinner; H.D. – 119

449 Skinner; H.D. – 357

450 Skinner; H.D. – 344

451 Budge; E.A. [B.D.] – 25; 150

452 Shand; A. – 254

453 Skinner; H.D. – 52

454 Skinner; H.D. – 57

455 Eggeling; J. in Muller; F.M. [S.B.E.] – v44-215

456 Eggeling; J. in Muller; F.M. [S.B.E.] – v44-214; 217

457 Joyce; T.A. [S.A.A.] – 152

458 Osborne; H. – 64

459 West; E.W. in Muller; F.M. [S.B.E.] – v5-71

460 West; E.W. in Muller; F.M. [S.B.E.] – v5-182

461 (Mills; L.N. in Muller; F.M. [S.B.E.] – v23-173

462 Mills; L.N. in Muller; F.M. [S.B.E.] – v23-210

463 West; B.W. in Muller; F.M. [S.B.E.] – v24-112

464 Mills; L.N. in Muller; F.M. [S.B.E.] – v23-240

465 Mills; L.N. in Muller; F.M. [S.B.E.] – v23-267

466 Bloomfield; M. in Muller; F.M. [S.B.E.] – v42-458

467 Eggeling; J. in Muller; F.M. [S.B.E.] – v43-xxi; 111/2; 114-6; 135/6; 285/6

468 Eggeling; J. in Muller; F.M. [S.B.E.] – v43-1;18-22

469 Eggeling; J. in Muller; F.M. [S.B.E.] – v43-4

470 Telang; K.T. in Muller; F.M. [S.B.E.] – v8-90; Muller; F.M. [S.B.E.] – v49-57

471 Jacobi; H. in Muller; F.M. [S.B.E.] – v22-198

472 Davids; T.W. Rhys in Muller; F.M. [S.B.E.] – v35-38

473 Osborne; H. – 64

474 Zuidema; R.T. – 211

475 Zuidema; R.T. – 212/3

476 Eggeling; J in. Muller; F.M. [S.B.E.] – v44-249

477 Buhler; G. in Muller; F.M. – v25– 398

478 Muller; F.M. [S.B.E.] – v15-128

479 Davids; T.W. Rhys in Muller; F.M. [S.B.E.] – v36-6

480 Cowell; E.B. in Muller; F.M. [S.B.E.] – 110

481 Eggeling; J. in Muller; F.M. [S.B.E.] – v26-265-9; 362; 418-21

482 Eggeling; J. in Muller; F.M. [S.B.E.] – v26-277/8

483 Eggeling; J. in Muller; F.M. [S.B.E.] – v44-479

484 Eggeling; J. in Muller; F.M. [S.B.E.] – v41-212; 253; 285

485 Eggeling; J. in Muller; F.M. [S.B.E.] – v41-375

486 Eggeling; J. in Muller; F.M. [S.B.E.] – v43-342

487 Eggeling; J. in Muller; F.M. [S.B.E.] – v41-212

488 Muller; F.M. [S.B.E.] – v32-16

489 Eggeling; J. in Muller; F.M. [S.B.E.] – v26-419

490 Eggeling; J. in Muller; F.M. [S.B.E.] – v26-96

491 Eggeling; J. in Muller; F.M. [S.B.E.] – v26-407

492 Eggeling; J. in Muller; F.M. [S.B.E.] – v26-438

493 Eggeling; J. in Muller; F.M. [S.B.E.] – v41-65/6; 406; v42-294

494 Eggeling; J. in Muller; F.M. [S.B.E.] – v41-406

495 Eggeling; J. in Muller; F.M. [S.B.E.] – v44-15-20

496 Eggeling; J. in Muller; F.M. [S.B.E.] – v44-xxv

497 Eggeling; J. in Muller; F.M. [S.B.E.] – v44-xliv

498 Telang; E.T. in Muller; F.M. [S.B.E.] – v8-89

499 Jacobi; H. in Muller; F.M. [S.B.E.] – v22-212; v45-290

500 Danielou; A. – 217

501 Eggeling; J. in Muller; F.M. [S.B.E.] – v43-74

502 Buhler; G. in Muller; F.M. [S.B.E.] – v2-221

503 Jolly; J. in Muller; F.M. [S.B.E.] – v7-298/9

504 Urton; G. – 96-111, 169

505 Buhler; G. in Muller; F.M. [S.B.E.] – v2-96

506 Jolly; J. in Muller; F.M. [S.B.E.] – v14-242; Oldenburg; G. in Muller; F.M. [S.B.E.] – v29-318

507 West; E.W. in Muller; F.M. [S.B.E.] – v18-210

508 Danielou; A. – 217

509 Salcamayhua; P.-Y. – 76

510 Zuidema; R.T. – 81/2

511 Zuidema; R.T. – 82

512 Montesinos; F. de – 5

513 Salcamayhua; P.-Y. – 77

514 Muller; F.M. (S.B.E.) – v32-101

515 Muller; F.M. [S.B.E.] – v1 – 56

516 Muller; F.M. [S.B.E.] – v1 – 62

517 Muller; F.M. [S.B.E.] – v42 – 28

518 Muller; F.M. [S.B.E.] – v42 – 462

519 Milne Rae; G – 136

520 Liebert; G. – 35

521 Sastri; H.K. – 77-89

522 Danielou; A. – 298

523 Liebert; G. – 177

524 Liebert; G. – 180

525 Liebert; G. – 269

526 Liebert; G. – 177/8

527 Liebert; G. – 178

528 Milne Rae; G. – 124-30

529 Milne Rae; G. – 125

530 Arriaga; P.J. de – 45

Conclusion
1 Bruhns; K.O. – 360-9

BIBLIOGRAPHY

AMERICAS:

ADAMSON; T - "Folktales of the Coast Salish"; Vol. xxvii; American Folk-Lore Society,

ALVA; W. & DONNAN; C.B. - "Royal Tombs of Sipan", University of California Press, 1993/4.

ANDAGOYA: P. de - "Narrative of the Proceeding of Pedrarias Davila, etc.", Translated by Clements R. Markham, Hakluyt Society, 1865.

ANTON; F. - "Ancient Peruvian Textiles", Thames & Hudson, 1987.

ARRIAGA; P.J. de - "The Extirpation of Idolatry in Peru", University of Kentucky Press, 1968.

AVENI; A.F. - "Archaeoastronomy in Pre-Colombian America"; Texas University Press; 1975.

AVILA; Dr. F. de - "Of the Errors, False Gods and other superstitions .... In which the Indians of Huarochiri, Mama, and Chaclla lived in ancient times" (1608), Hakluyt Society, 1873.

BANDELIER; A.F. - "Titicaca and Koati", Hispanic Society of America, 1910.

BASTIEN; J.W. - "Healers of the Andes", University of Utah Press, 1987.

BASTIEN; J.W. - "Quechua Religions: Andean Cultures", Encyclopaedia of Religion, Vol. 12, Collier MacMillan Publishers, 1987.

BENNETT; W.C. - "Handbook of South American Indians" Vol. 5, Ed. Julian H. Steward, Smithsonian Institute, 1949.

BEUCHLER; H.C. - "The Bolivian Aymara", Holt, Rinehart & Winston, 1971.

BLANTON; R.E. et al. - "Ancient Mesoamerica", Cambridge University Press, 1981.

BOAS; F. - "Bella Bella Tales"; Vol. xxv; American Folk-Lore Society, 1932.

BOAS; F. - "Kwakiutl Tales"; Vol. xxvi; Columbia University Press, 1935.

BOAS; F. - "Kwakiutl Culture"; Vol. xxviii; American Folk-Lore Society, 1935.

BOAS; F. - The Social Organization and Secret Societies of the Kwakiutl Indians, Smithsonian Institution, 1897.

BOLLAERT: W. - "Antiquarian, Ethnological and Other Researches in New Granada", Trubner & Co., 1860.

BOYD; M. - "Tarascan Myths and Legends"; Texas Christian University Press, 1969.

BRIDGES; E. Lucas - "Uttermost Part of the Earth", Hodder & Stoughton, 1948.

BRINTON; D.G. - "American Hero Myths", Watts & Co., 1882.

BROTHERSTON; G. - "Painted Books from Mexico", British Museum Press, 1995.

BROWMAN; D.L. - "Titicaca Basin archaeolinquistics: Uru, Pukina and Aymara A.D. 750-1450", Vol. 26, No. 2, Oct. 1994.

BRUHNS; K.O. - "Ancient South America", Cambridge University Press, 1994.

BRUNDAGE; B.C. - "Empire of the Inca", University of Oklahoma Press, 1951/63.

BURGER; R.L. - "Chavin and the Origins of Andean Civilisation", Thames and Hudson, 1992.

BURGER; R.L. - "The Ancient Americas - Art From Sacred Landscapes", The Art Institute of Chicago/Prestel Verlag, 1992.

CHURCH; G.E. - "Aborigines of South America", Chapman and Hall, 1912.

COBO; B. - "Inca Religion and Customs", University of Texas Press, 1990.

COE; M.D. - "The Maya", Thames & Hudson, 5th., Edition, 1993.

COE; M.D. - "Mexico - From Olmec to Aztec", Thames & Hudson, (1962) 1994.

COE; M.D. - "Native Astronomy in Mesoamerica", in Aveni, A.F. (see above).

COE; M.D. & DIEHL; R.A. - "In the Land of the Olmec", University of Texas Press, 1980.

COOKE; R. & RANERE; J.R. - "Prehistoric human adaptions to the seasonally dry forests of Panama", World Archaeology, Vol. 24, No.1, June, 1992.

COOPER; J.M. - "Handbook of South American Indians" Vol. 5, Ed. Julian H. Steward, Smithsonian Institute, 1949.

COUCH; N.C.C. - "The Festival Cycle of the Aztec Codex Borbonicus"; B.A.R. International Series 270, 1985.

COVARRUBIAS; M. - "Indian Art of Mexico and Central America"; Alfred A. Knoff (N.Y.), 1957.

DEMAREST; A.A. - "Viracocha - The Nature and Antiquity of the Andean High God", Peabody Museum Monographs No. 6, Harvard University Press, 1981.

DILLEHAY; T.D. - "Mapuche ceremonial landscape, social recruitment and resource rights", World Archaeology, Vol. 22, No. 2, Oct. 1990.

DONNAN; C.B. - "Moche Art and Iconography", University of California Press, 1976.

DRANSART: P. - "Llamas, herders and the exploitation of raw materials in the Atacama Desert", World Archaeology, Vol. 22, No. 3, Feb. 1991.

EDMUNDSON; Rev. G. - "Journal of the Travels of Father Samuel Fritz", Hakluyt Society. 1922.

EKHOLM; G.F. & WILLEY; G.R. - "Archaeological Frontiers and External Connections" -
(Heine-Geldern; R.) Handbook of Middle American Indians - Vol. 4, 1966.

ENOCK; C.R. - "The Secret of the Pacific", T. Fisher Unwin, 1912.

FALKNER; T. - "A Description of Patagonia", Armann & Armann, 1935,

FARABEE; W.C. - "Indian Tribes of Eastern Peru", Cambridge, Mass., 1922.

FARON; L.C. - "The Mapuche Indians of Chile", Holt, Rinehart & Winston, 1968.

FASH; W.L. - "Scribes, Warriors and Kings"; Thames & Hudson, 1991.

FLANNERY; K.V. - "The Early Mesoamerican Village", Academic Press, 1976.

FLANNERY; K.V. & MARCUS; J. - "The Cloud People", Academic Press, 1983.

FLANNERY; K.V. & MARCUS. J. - "Zapotec Civilisation"; Thames & Hudson, 1996.

FOLAN; W.J. - "Calakmul, Campeche: a centralized urban administrative center in the Northern Peten", World
Archaeology, Vol.24, no.1, June, 1992.

FREIDEL; D. & SCHELE; L. - "A Forest of Kings"; William Morrow & Co. (N.Y.), 1990.

FURST; P.T. - "The Parching of the Maize", Acta Ethnologica et Linguista, No. 14, 1968.

GARTELMANN; K.D. - "Digging Up Prehistory", Editiones Libri Mundi, 1986.

GRIJALVA; J. de, - "The Discovery of New Spain in 1518", The Cortes Society, 1942.

GRUBB; W.B. - "An Unknown People in an Unknown Land", Seeley & Co., 1911.

HADINGHAM; E. - "Lines to the Mountain Gods", Harrap, 1987.

HAMMOND; N. - "Ancient Maya Civilization"; Cambridge University Press, 1982.

HAMMOND; N. & GERHARDT; J.C. - World Archaeology, Vol. 21, no.3, Feb. 1990.

HEALAN; D.M. - "Local versus non-local obsidian change at Tula and its implications for post-Formative Meso-
America", World Archaeology, Vol. 24, No.3, Feb. 1993.

HABEL; S. - "The Sculptures of Santa Lucia Cosumalwhuapa in Guatemala", Smithsonian Institute, 1878.

HEINE-GELDERN; R. - "The Problem of Transpacific Influences in Mesoamerica" in Handbook of Middle American
Indians, Vol. 4; see Ekholm; G.F.

HESTER; R. T.& SHAFER; H.J. - "Exploration of chert resources by the ancient Maya of northern Belize, Central
America", World Archaeology; Vol. 16, no.2, Oct. 1984.

HOSTLER; D. & LECHMAN; H.+HOLM; O. - "Ax-monies and their Relatives", 1990

JONES; J. - "Explorations of the Aboriginal Remains of Tennessee"; Smithsonian Institution - Contributions to
Knowledge, Vol. 22, 1876.

JOYCE; T.A. - "Central American and West Indian Archaeology", Handbooks of Ancient Civilizations Series, 1916.

JOYCE; T.A. - "South American Archaeology", Handbooks to Ancient Civilization Series, 1912.

KARSTEN; R. - " The Civilizations of the South American Indians", Kegan Paul & Co., 1926.

KARSTEN; R. - "Indian Tribes of the Argentinean and Bolivian Chaco", Helsinki, 1932.

KARSTEN; R. - "Studies in the Religion of the South American Indians East of the Andes", Helsinki, 1964.

KEELER; C.E. - "Land of the Moon Children", University of Georgia Press, 1956.

KEELER; C.E. - "Secret of the Cuna Earthmother", Exposition Press, 1960.

KEHOE; A.B. - Personal Communication, Nov., 1997.

KELLEY; D.H. - "Deciphering the Maya Script", University of Texas Press, 1976.

KIRCHHOFF; P. - "Handbook of South American Indians" Vol. 5, Ed. Julian H. Steward, Smithsonian Institute, 1949.

KOLATA; A.L. - "The Ancient Americas - Art From Sacred Landscapes", The Art Institute of Chicago/Prestel Verlag,
1992.

KOLATA; A.L. - "The Tiwanaku - Portrait of an Andean Civilization", Blackwell/Oxford, 1993.

KRAMER; F.W. - "Literature Among the Cuna Indians", Etnologiska Studier no. 30, 1970.

LANDA; D. de - "Yucatan Before and After the Conquest", The Maya Society-Baltimore, 1937.

LEHMANN; W. - "The Art of Old Peru", Ernest Benn, 1924.

LEON-PORTILLA; M. - "Pre-Colombian Literature of Mexico"; University of Oklahoma Press; 1969/86.

LOTHROP; S.K. - "Cocle- An Archaeological Study of Central America", Memoirs of the Peabody Museum of
Archaeology and Ethnology, Harvard University, Vol. 7 and 8, 1937.

LOTHROP; S.K. - "Pottery of Costa Rica and Nicaragua", Contributions from the Museum of the American Indian,
Heye Foundation, Vol. 8, 1926.

LUCKERT; K.W. - "Olmec Religion - A Key to Middle America and Beyond", University of Oklahoma Press, 1976.

LUMHOLTZ; C. - "Unknown Mexico", 2 Vols., MacMillan and Co.,1903.

MARKHAM; C.R. - "Expeditions into the Valley of the Amazons", Hakluyt Society, 1859.

MARKHAM; C.R. - "The Incas of the Peru", Smith., Elder & Co., 1910.
MARKHAM; C.R. - "The Travels of Pedro de Cieza de Leon 132-50", Hakluyt Society, 1864.
MARKHAM; C.R. - "The Voyages of Pedro Fennandez de Quiros 1595-1606", 2 vols., Hakluyt Society, 1904.
MAUDSLAY; A.P. & A.C. - "A Glimpse at Guatemala", John Murray, 1899.
MEGGERS; B.J. - "Ecuador", Thames and Hudson, 1966.
METRAUX; A. - "Handbook of South American Indians" Vol. 5, Ed. Julian H. Steward, Smithsonian Institute, 1949.
MILLER; A.G. - "The Painted Tombs of Oaxaca, Mexico", Cambridge University Press, 1995.
MILLER; M. & TAUBE; K. - "The Gods and Symbols of Ancient Mexico and the Maya", Thames & Hudson, 1993.
MOLINA; C. de - "An Account of the Fables and Rites of the Yncas", Hakluyt Society, 1873.
MONTESINOS; F. - "Memorias Antiguas Historiales del Peru", Translator - Means, P.A., Hakluyt Society, 1920.
MORLEY; S.G; & RECINOS; D. - "Popol Vuh", University of Oklahoma Press, 1950/69.
MOSELEY; M.E. - "The Incas and their Ancestors", Thames and Hudson, 1992.
NEEDHAM; J. & LU; G.-D. - "Trans-Pacific Echoes and Resonances; Listening Once Again", Singapore World
    Scientific, 1985.
O'BRIEN; M.J. & LEWARCH; D.E. - "Regional analysis of the Zapotec empire, Valley of Oaxaca, Mexico", World
    Archaeology, Vol.23, No.3, Feb. 1992.
O'NEALE; L.M. - "Handbook of South American Indians" Vol. 5, Ed. Julian H. Steward, Smithsonian Institute, 1949.
OSBORNE; H. - "South American Mythology", Paul Hamlyn Publishing, 1968.
PARSONS; L.A. - "Bilbao, Guatemala", 2 Vols., Milwaukee Public Museum Press, 1967.
PAUL; A. - "The Ancient Americas - Art From Sacred Landscapes", The Art Institute of Chicago/Prestel Verlag, 1992.
PELLESCHI; G. - "Eight Months on the Gran Chaco of the Argentine Republic", Sampson Low & Co., 1886.
PENNANT; T. - "Of the Patagonians", Darlington, 1788.
POINDEXTER; M. - "Peruvian Pharaohs", Christopher Publishing House, 1938.
POINDEXTER; M. - "The Ayar-Incas", Horace Liveright Publishers, N.Y., 1930.
POPOL VUH (P.V.) - see Morley; S.G.
REED; A. - "The Ancient Past of Mexico", Hamlyn, 1966.
REICHEL-DOLMATOFF; G. - "The Sacred Mountains of Colombia's Kogi Indians", E. J. Brill, 1990.
REICHEL-DOLMATOFF; G. - "Amazonian Cosmos - The Sexual and Religious Symbolism of the Tukano Indians",
    University of Chicago Press, 1971.
RIVERO: M.E. & TSHUDI; J.J. von - "Peruvian Antiquities", George P. Putnam & Co., London, 1857.
ROE; P.G. - "The Cosmic Zygote", Rutgers University Press, 1982.
ROOSEVELT; A.C. - "Moundbuilders of the Amazon", Academic Press, 1991.
ROYS; R.L. - "Ritual of the Bacabs", Uni. of Oklahoma Press, 1965.
SALZANO: F.M. - "South American Indians", Oxford/Clarendon, 1988.
SALCAMAYHUA; P.-Y. - "An Account of the Antiquities of Peru", Translator: Clements R. Markham, Hakluyt
    Society, 1873.
SALMORAL; M.L. - "America 1492", Facts on File, 1990.
SARMIENTO; P., de Gamboa - "History of the Incas", Hakluyt Society, 1907.
SAVILLE; M.H. - "Antiquities of Manabi Ecuador", Contributions to South American Archaeology, 2 vols., G.G. Heye
    Foundation, Contributions to South American Archaeology, Vol. 1,2, 1907.
SANCHEZ; C.S. - In "Teotihuacan", ed. by Berrin; K. & Pasztory; E., Thames & Hudson, 1993.
SCHELE; L. & MILLER; M. - "The Blood of Kings", Sotherbys Pub. 1986.
SHARER; R.J. - "The Ancient Maya", Stanford University Press, 1994.
SHARER; R.J. & DANIEN; E.C. - "New Theories on the Ancient Maya", Vol. 3, University Pennsylvania Press, 1992.
SHARON; D. - "Wizard of the Four Winds", The Free Press/Collier MacMillan, 1978.
SHIMADA; I. et al - "Cultural impacts of severe droughts in the prehistoric Andes application of a 1,500 year ice core
    precipitation record", World Archaeology, Vol. 22, No. 3, Feb. 1991.
SPENCE; L. - "North American Indians - Myths and Legends", George G. Harrap and Co., Ltd., 1914.
SPENCE; L. - "Mexico and Peru - Myths and Legends", Thomas Y. Cromwell and Co., 1920.
SQUIER; E.G. - "Nicaragua, its People, Scenery, Monuments, etc.", 2 vols., New York, 1852.
STIERLIN; H. - "The Art of the Maya", MacMillan, 1981.
SULLIVAN; W.F. - "The Secret of the Incas", Crown Publishers, Inc, N.Y., 1996.
TAUBE; K.A. - "The Major Gods of Ancient Yucatan", Dumbarton Oaks Research Library and Collection, 1992.
TAYLOR; C. - "Myths From the North American Indians", Laurence King Publishing, 1995.

THOMAS; C. - "The Maya Year", Smithsonian Institute, Bureau of Ethnology, Bulletin no. 18., 1894.
TIERNEY; P. - "The Highest Altar", Bloomsbury Publishing Ltd., 1989.
TOMPKINS; P. - "Mysteries of the Mexican Pyramids", Thames & Hudson, 1976.
TOWNSEND; R.F. - "The Ancient Americas", Prestel, 1992.
TYLOR; E.B. - "Anahuac or Mexico and the Mexicans Ancient and Modern", Longmans, 1861.
URTON; G. - "At the Crossroads of the Earth and the Sky", University of Texas Press, 1981.
VEGA; G. de la - "The Royal Commentaries of the Incas", 2 Vols., Hakluyt Society, 1869.
VERRILL; A.H. - "America's Ancient Civilizations", G. P. Putnam's Sons, 1953.
WAFER; L. - "The New Voyage and Description of the Isthmus of America", London, 1699.
WALLACE; A.R. - "A Narrative of Travels on the Amazon and Rio Negro", London, 1853.
WASSEN; S.H. - "The Complete Mu-Igala in Picture Writing", Etnotogiska Studier - Goteborg - No 21.
WASSEN; S.H. - "New Cuna Myths", Etnologiska Studier, no. 20, 1952.
WAYMAN; M.L. - "Aspects of Early North American Metallurgy", British Museum Occasional Paper 79, 1992.
WEAVER; M.P. - "The Aztecs, Maya, and their Predecessors", 3rd., Ed., Academic Press, 1993.
WILBERT; J. - Folk Literature of the Bororo Indians", UCLA Latin American Center Publication, 1983.
WILBERT; J & SIMONEAU - "Folk Literature of the Chorote Indians", UCLA Latin American Center Publication, 1985.
WILBERT; J & SIMONEAU - "Folk Literature of the Ge Indians", UCLA Latin American Center Publication, 1978.
WILBERT; J & SIMONEAU - "Folk Literature of the Selknam Indians", UCLA Latin American Center Publications, 1975.
WILBERT; J & SIMONEAU - "Folk Literature of the Teheulche Indians", UCLA Latin American Center Publication, 1984.
WILBERT; J & SIMONEAU - "Folk Literature of the Toba Indians", UCLA Latin American Center Publication, 1982.
WILEY; G.R. - "Handbook of South American Indians" Vol. 5, Ed. Julian H. Steward, Smithsonian Institute, 1949.
ZINGG; R.M. - "The Huichols - Primitive Artists", Millwood Kraus, University of Denver Contributions to Ethnography, 1938.
ZUIDEMA; R.T. - "The Ancient Americas - Art From Sacred Landscapes", The Art Institute of Chicago/Prestel Verlag, 1992.
ZUIDEMA; R.T. - "The Ceque System of Cuzco - The Social Organization of the Capital of the Inca". E. J. Brill, 1964.

CHINA/JAPAN:

ASTON; W.G. - "Shinto (The Way of the Gods)", Longman, Green, and Co., 1905.
BATCHELOR; J. - "The Ainu and their Folk-lore", R.T.S., London, 1901.
BOLTZ; W.G. - "Early Chinese Writing", World Archaeology, Vol. 17, No.3, Feb. 1986.
CHRISTIE; A. - "Chinese Mythology", Paul Hamlyn, 1968.
DAVIS; F. Hadland, - "Myths and Legends of Japan", George Harrap and Co., 1913.
FITZGERALD; C.P. - "The Tower of Five Glories", Cresset Press, London, 1941.
GILES; H.A. - "Religions of Ancient China", Archibald Constable, 1905.
GRAHAM; D.C. - "Folk Religion in South-West China", Smithsonian Miscellaneous Collections, Vol. 142, no. 2, 1961.
HACKIN; H. et al - "Asiatic Mythology", G. and G. Harrap and Co., 1932.
HO; Chui-mei; - "Pottery in South China: River Xijiang and Upper Red River Basins", World Archaeology, Vol. 15, No. 3, Feb. 1984.
HOSIE; A. - "Three Years in Western China", MacMillan and Co., 1890.
HUDSPETH; W.H. - "Stone-Gateway and the Flowery Miao", Cargate Press, 1937.
KIDDER; J.E. - "Ancient Japan", Weidenfeld and Nicolson, 1965.
LAUFER; B. - "Notes on Turquois in the East", Field Museum of Natural History, Vol. xiii, No. 1, 1913.
MUNRO; G. - "Ainu Creed and Cult", Routledge and Kegan Paul, 1962.
NELSON; S.M. - "The Archaeology of Korea", Cambridge University Press, 1993.
POLLARD; A.J. - "In Unknown China", Seeley, Service and Co., 1921.
BROOMHALL; A.J. - "Strong Tower", China Inland Mission, 1947.

RAWSON: J. - "Ancient China", Trustees of the British Museum (B.M.P.), 1980.
ROCK; J.F. - "The Ancient Na-Khi Kingdom of Southwest China", Harvard/Yenching Institute, 1947.
ROCK; J.F.C. - "The Na-Khi Naga Cult and Related Ceremonies", M.E.O. Serie orientale Roma, no. 4, 1952.
ROWLEY-CONWY: P. - World Archaeology, Vol.16, No.1, June, 1984.
SMITH; A.H. - "Chinese Characteristics", Kegan Paul and Co., 1892.
SMITH; A.H. - "Village Life in China", Kegan Paul and Co., 1892.
WATSON; W. - "Archaeology in China", Max Parrish, London, 1960.
WERNER; E.T.C. - "Myths and Legends of China", Harrap and Co., 1922.
WHEATLEY; P. - "The Pivot of the Four Quarters", Edinburgh University Press, 1971.
WILSON; E.H. - "A Naturalist in Western China", Methuen and Co., 1913.
UNDERHILL; A.P. - "Pottery production in Chiefdoms: the Longshan Period in Northern China", World Archaeology, Vol. 23, No. 1, June 1991.
ZHIMIN; A. - "Radiocarbon Dating and the Prehistoric Archaeology in China", World Archaeology, Vol. 23, No. 2, Oct. 1991.

INDIA:

ALLCHIN: R. & B. - "The Rise of Civilisation in India and Pakistan", Cambridge University Press, 1993.
ASHER; F.M. - "The Art of Eastern India", Uni. Minnesota Press, 1980.
BANERJEA; J. N. - "The Development of Hindu Iconography", University of Calcutta Press, 1956.
BHATTACHARYA; B.C. - "The Jaina Iconography", Thacker, Spink & Co , Calcutta, 1939/1974.
BHATTACHARYA; G. - "Buddha Sakyamuni and Panca-Tathagatas: dilemma in Bihar-Bengal", South Asian Archaeology, Scandinavian Institute of Asian Studies, Occasional Papers No. 4, Curzon Press, 1985.
BHULER; G. in MULLER; F.M. - "The Sacred Laws of the Aryas", Sacred Books of the East, Vol. 2, Motilal Banarsidass Publishers Private Ltd., 1897/1992.
BHULER; G. in MULLER; F.M. - "The Laws of Manu", Sacred Books of the East, Vol. 14, Part 2, Motilal Banarsidass Publishers Private Ltd., 1882/1991.
BHULER; G. in MULLER; F.M. - "The Laws of Manu", Sacred Books of the East, Vol. 25, Motilal Banarsidass Publishers Private Ltd., 1886/1993.
BLOOMFIELD; M. in MULLER; F.M. - "Hymns of the Atharva-Veda", Sacred Book of the East, Vol. 42, Motilal Banarsidass Publishers Private Ltd., 1897/1992.
BRADLEY-BIRT; F.B. - "Chota Nagpore", Smith, Elder & Co., 1903; 1910;
CAILLAT; C. & KUMAR; R. - "The Jain Cosmology", Harmony Books, 1981.
CAIN; J. - "The Koi - A Southern Tribe of the Gonds", 1881.
CAMPBELL; J. - "Wild Tribes of Khondistan", Hurst & Blackett Publishers, 1864.
CLEUZIOU; P. & TOSI; M. - "The Southeastern Frontier of the Ancient Near East", South Asian Archaeology, Scandinavian Institute of Asian Studies, Occasional Papers No. 4, Curzon Press, 1985.
COWELL; E.B. in MULLER; F.M. - "Buddhist Mahayana Texts", Sacred Books of the East, Vol. 49, Motilal Banarsidass Publishers Private Ltd., 1894/1997.
CRADDOCK; P.T., WILLIS; L., et al. - "Ancient lead and zinc mining in Rajasthan, India, World Archeology, Vol.16, Oct. 1984.
CRAVEN; R.C. - "A Concise History of Indian Art", Thames & Hudson, 1976.
CROOKE; W. - "Folk-lore of Northern India"; 2 vols., Archibald Constable and Co., 1896.
CUNNINGHAM; A. - "The Stupa of Bharhut", London, 1879.
DALTON; E.T. - "Descriptive Ethnology of Bengal", Government of Bengal, 1872.
DANIELOU; A. - "The Myths and Gods of India", Princeton University Press, 1985/91.
DAVIDS; T.W, in MULLER; F.M. - "Vinaya Texts", Part 3, Sacred Books of the East, Vol. 20, Motilal Banarsidass Publishers Private Ltd., 1885/1998.
DAVIDS; T.W, in MULLER; F.M. - "The Questions of King Milinda", Part 1, Sacred Books of the East, Vol. 35, Motilal Banarsidass Publishers Private Ltd., 1890/1997.
DAVIDS; T.W, in MULLER; F.M. - "The Questions of King Milinda", Part 2, Sacred Books of the East, Vol. 36, Motilal Banarsidass Publishers Private Ltd., 1894/1999.
DEVENDRA; D.T. - "Classical Sinhalese Sculpture- c300 B.C. to A.D. 1000", Alex Tiranti, London, 1958.

EGGELING; J. in MULLER; F.M. - "The Satapatha Brahmana", Part 1, Sacred Book of the East, Vol. 12; Motilal
    Banarsidass Publishers Private Ltd., 1882/1993.
EGGELING; J. in MULLER; F.M. - "The Satapatha Brahmana", Part 2 - Books 1 & 2, Sacred Book of the East, Vol.
    15, Motilal Banarsidass Publishers Private Ltd., 1884/1995.
EGGELING; J. in MULLER; F.M. - "The Satapatha Brahmana", Part 2 - Books 3 & 4, Sacred Book of the East, Vol.
    26, Motilal Banarsidass Publishers Private Ltd., 1885/1994.
EGGELING; J. in MULLER; F.M. - "The Satapatha Brahmana", Part 5 - Books 11-14, Sacred Book of the East, Vol.
    41, Motilal Banarsidass Publishers Private Ltd., 1900/1994.
EGGELING; J. in MULLER; F.M. - "The Satapatha Brahmana", Part 4 - Books 8-10, Sacred Book of the East, Vol.
    43, Motilal Banarsidass Publishers Private Ltd., 1894/1996.
EGGELING; J. in MULLER; F.M. - "The Satapatha Brahmana", Part 3 - Books 5-7, Sacred Book of the East, Vol. 44,
    Motilal Banarsidass Publishers Private Ltd., 1894/1996.
ELWIN; V. - "The Agaria", Oxford University Press, 1942.
ELWIN; V. - "Myths of Middle India", Oxford/Vanya, 1949/91.
ELWIN; V. - "The Muria and Their Ghotul", Oxford University Press, 1947.
ELWIN; V. - "Tribal Myths of Orissa", Oxford Uni. Press, 1954.
EVANS-WENTZ; W.Y. - "The Tibetan Book of the Dead", Oxford University Press, 1960.
FABRI; C.L. - "History of the Art of Orissa", Orient Longman Ltd., 1974.
FERGUSSON; J. - "Tree and Serpent Worship", London, 1873.
FRANCIS; P. - "Beadmaking at Arikamedu and Beyond", World Archaeology, Vol.23, no.,1, June, 1991.
FURER-HAIMNEDORF; C. - "The Raj Gonds of Adilabad", MacMillan & Co., 1948.
FURER-HAIMNEDORF; C. - "The Reddis of the Bison Hills", MacMillan & Co., 1945.
GILES; H.A. - "The Travels of Fa-Hsien", Cambridge University Press, 1923.
GRIGSON; W.V. - "The Maria Gonds of Bastar"; Oxford University Press, 1938.
GURDON; P.R.T. - "The Khasis", MacMillan & Co., 1914.
HAEKEL; J. - "Baba Golio, etc.", Intiv fur Volkerkunde der Universitat Wien, 1968.
HAEKEL; J. & WEISINGER; R. - "Contributions to the Swinging Festival in Western Central India", Intiv fur
    Volkerkunde der Universitat Wien, 1968.
HARLE; J.C. - "The Art and Architecture of the Indian Subcontinent", Yale Uni. Press, 1994.
HASTINGS; J. - Ed. Encyclopaedia of Religion and Ethics", Vol. 7, T. & T. Clark, Edinburgh, 1914.
HODSON; T.C. - "The Naga Tribes of Manipur", MacMillan & Co., 1911.
HOJLUND; F. - "Some new Evidence of Harappan Influence in the Arabian Gulf", South Asian Archaeology,
    Scandinavian Institute of Asian Studies, Occasional Papers No. 4, Curzon Press, 1985.
HUTTON; J.H. (A.N.) - "The Angami Nagas", MacMillan & Co., 1921.
HUTTON; J.H. (S.N.) - "The Sema Nagas", MacMillan, 1921.
JACOBI; H. in MULLER; F.M. - "Jaina Sutras", Sacred Book of the East, Vol. 22, Part 1, Motilal Banarsidass
    Publishers Private Ltd., 1884/1994.
JACOBI; H. in MULLER; F.M. - "Jaina Sutras", Sacred Book of the East, Vol. 45, Part 2, Motilal Banarsidass
    Publishers Private Ltd., 1895/1995.
JANSEN; M. - "Water and Sewage Disposal at Mohenjo-Daro", World Archaeology, Vol. 21, No., 2, Oct. 1989.
JOLLY; J. in MULLER; F.M. - "The Institutes of Vishnu", Sacred Book of the East, Vol. 7, Motilal Banarsidass
    Publishers Private Ltd., 1880/1992.
JONES; J. - "Explorations of the Aboriginal Remains of Tennessee", Smithsonian Institution, 1876.
KA; M.P. - "Legends of the Seven Greatest Pagoda of Burma", Vol. 1, Rangoon, British Burma Press, 1911.
KNOX; R. - "Amaravati - Buddhist Sculpture from the Great Stupa", British Museum Press, 1992.
KULKE; H. & ROTHERMUND; D. - "A History of India", Croom Helm, 1986.
    Sacred Book of the East, Vol. 10, Motilal Banarsidass Publishers Private Ltd., 1881/1998.
LEGGE; J. in MULLER; F.M. - "The Sacred Books of China", Part 1, Sacred Book of the East, Vol. 3, Motilal
    Banarsidass Publishers Private Ltd., 1879/1996.
LEGGE; J. in MULLER; F.M. - "The Sacred Books of China", Part 2, Sacred Book of the East, Vol. 16, Motilal
    Banarsidass Publishers Private Ltd., 1882/1994.
LEGGE; J. in MULLER; F.M. - "The Sacred Books of China", Part 5, Sacred Book of the East, Vol. 39, Motilal
    Banarsidass Publishers Private Ltd., 1891/1993.
LEGGE; J. in MULLER; F.M. - "The Sacred Books of China", Part 2, Sacred Book of the East, Vol. 40, Motilal

Banarsidass Publishers Private Ltd., 1891/1994.

LIEBERT; G. - "Iconographic Dictionary of the Indian Religions", E.J. Brill, Leiden, 1976.

LISHK; S.S. & SAJJAN SINGH; - "Jaina Astronomy", Vidya Sagara Pub., Delhi, 1987.

MACPHERSON; S. C. - "Religion of the Khonds in Orissa", London, 1852.

MAN; E.H. - "The Andaman Islanders", Anthropological Institute of Great Britain and Ireland, 1885.

MARSHALL; J. - "Mohenjodaro", Arthur Probsthain, 1931.

MARSHALL; W.E. - "A Phrenologist Amongst the Todas", London, 1873.

MILLS: J.P. (A.N.) - "The Ao Nagas", MacMillan & Co., 1926.

MILLS: J.P. (L.N.) - "The Lhota Nagas", MacMillan & Co., 1922.

MILLS; L.H. in MULLER; F.M. - "The Zend Avesta", Part 1, Sacred Book of the East, Vol. 4, Motilal Banarsidass Publishers Private Ltd., 1887/1998.

MILLS; L.H. in MULLER; F.M. - "The Zend Avesta", Part 2, Sacred Book of the East, Vol. 23, Motilal Banarsidass Publishers Private Ltd., 1882/2000.

MILLS; L.H. in MULLER; F.M. - "The Zend Avesta", Part 3, Sacred Book of the East, Vol. 31, Motilal Banarsidass Publishers Private Ltd., 1887/2000.

MUKHERJEE; P. - "The History of Medieval Vaishnavism in Orissa", Chatterjee, Calcutta, 1940.

MULLER; F.M. - "Ancient Hindu Astronomy", Oxford, 1862.

MULLER; F.M. - "The Upanishads", Part 1, Sacred Book of the East, Vol. 1, Motilal Banarsidass Publishers Private Ltd., 1900/1993.

MULLER; F.M. - "The Dhammapada", Sacred Book of the East, Vol. 10, Motilal Banarsidass Publishers Private Ltd., 1881/1998.

MULLER; F.M. - "The Upanishads", Sacred Book of the East, Vol 15, Part 2, Motilal Banarsidass Publishers Private Ltd., 1891/1994.

MULLER; F.M. - "Vedic Hymns", Sacred Book of the East, Vol. 32, Part 1, Motilal Banarsidass Publishers Private Ltd., 1881/1998.

MULLER; F.M. - "Buddhist Mahayana Texts", Sacred Book of the East, Vol. 49, Motilal Banarsidass Publishers Private Ltd., 1894/1997.

OJHA; G.K. - "The Upanishads", Sacred Book of the East, Vol. 1, Part 1, Motilal Banarsidass Publishers Private Ltd., 1900/1993.

OLDENBERG: H. in MULLER; F.M. - "The Grihya-Sutras", Sacred Book of the East, Vol. 29, Part 1, Motilal Banarsidass Publishers Private Ltd., 1886/1997.

OLDENBERG: H. with MULLER; F.M. - "The Grihya-Sutras", Sacred Book of the East, Vol. 30, Part 2, Motilal Banarsidass Publishers Private Ltd., 1892/1998.

OLDENBERG: H. with MULLER; F.M. - "Vedic Hymns", Part 2, Sacred Book of the East, Vol. 46, Motilal Banarsidass Publishers Private Ltd., 1897/1994.

PARPOLA: A. - "The Indus Script: A Challenging Puzzle", World Archaeology, Vol.17, No.3, 1986.

PRANAVANANDA; S. - "Kailas-Manasarovar", S.P. League Ltd., Calcutta, India, 1949.

RAE; G. Milne - "The Syrian Church in India", William Blackwood & Sons, 1892.

RAPSON; E.J. - "Ancient India", The Cambridge History of India, 1922.

RHIE; M.M. & THURMAN; R.A.F. - "The Sacred Art of Tibet", Thames & Hudson, 1996.

RICHARDS; W.J. - "The Indian Christians of St. Thomas", Bemrose & Sons, Ltd., 1908.

RISSMAN; P. - "Public displays and private values: a guide to buried wealth in Harappan archaeology", World Archaeology, Vol. 20, no. 2, Oct., 1988.

RIVERS; W.H.R. - "The Todas", MacMillan & Co., 1906.

ROY; S.C. - "The Hill Bhuiyas of Orissa", Man in India Office, Ranchi/India, 1935.

ROY; S.C. (M.) - "The Mundas", Jogendra Nath Sarkar, Calcutta, 1912.

RUSSELL; R.V. & HIRA LAL - "Tribes and Castes of the Central Provinces", MacMillan & Co., 4 vols., 1916.

SAHAI: B. - "Iconography of Minor Hindu and Buddhist Deities", Abhinav Publishers, 1975.

SASTRI; H. - "Nalanda and its Epigraphic Material", Memoirs of the Archaeological Survey of India, No. 66, 1942.

SINHA; I. - "Tantra", Hamlyn Pub., 1993.

SNELLGROVE; D. - "Buddhist Himalaya", Faber & Faber, 1957.

TELANG; K.T. in MULLER; F.M. - "The Bhagavadgita", Sacred Book of the East, Vol. 8, Motilal Banarsidass Publishers Private Ltd., 1882/1998.

THIBAUT; G. in MULLER; F.M. - "The Vedanta-Sutras", Part 1, Sacred Book of the East, Vol. 34, Motilal

Banarsidass Publishers Private Ltd., 1904/1998.

THIBAUT; G. in MULLER; F.M. - "The Vedanta-Sutras", Part 2, Sacred Book of the East, Vol. 38, Motilal Banarsidass Publishers Private Ltd., 1962/2000.

THIBAUT; G. in MULLER; F.M. - "The Vedanta-Sutras", Part 3, Sacred Book of the East, Vol. 48, Motilal Banarsidass Publishers Private Ltd., 1904/1996.

THURSTON; E. - "Castes and Tribes of Southern India", Government of Madras Printers, 1909.

THURSTON; E. - "Omens and Superstitions of Southern India", T. Fisher Unwin, 1912.

VOGEL; J.Ph. - "Indian Serpent Lore", Arthur Probsthain, 1926.

WEST; E.W. in MULLER; F.M. - "Pahlevi Texts", Part 1, Sacred Book of the East, Vol. 5, Motilal Banarsidass Publishers Private Ltd., 1880/1993.

WEST; E.W. in MULLER; F.M. - "Pahlevi Texts", Part 1, Sacred Book of the East, Vol. 5, Part 2, Motilal Banarsidass Publishers Private Ltd., 1882/1994.

WEST; E.W. in MULLER; F.M. - "Pahlevi Texts", Part 2, Sacred Book of the East, Vol. 18, Part 2, Motilal Banarsidass Publishers Private Ltd., 1882/1994.

WEST; E.W. in MULLER; F.M. - "Pahlevi Texts", Part 3, Sacred Book of the East, Vol. 24, Part 2, Motilal Banarsidass Publishers Private Ltd., 1885/1994.

WHEELER; M. - "India and Pakistan", Thames & Hudson, 1959.

WHITEHEAD; H. - "The Village Gods of South India", Humphrey Milford/Oxford University Press, 1916.

TIBET and SOUTH-EAST ASIA:

BAUDESSON; H. - "Indo-China and its Primitive People", Hutchinson & Co., 1919.

BENNETT: A. - "The contribution of metallurgical studies to South-East Asian archaeology", World Archaeology, Vol.20, No.3, Feb., 1989.

BRODERICK; A.H. - "Little China: The Annamese Lands", Oxford University Press, 1942.

EVANS-WENTZ; W.Y. - "The Tibetan Book of the Dead", Oxford University Press, 1960.

HACKIN; J. et al. - "Asiatic Mythology"; G.G. Harrap & Co., 1932.

HIGHAM; C. - "The Archaeology of Mainland Southeast Asia", Cambridge University Press, 1989.

HIGHAM; C. - Human biology, environment and ritual at Khok Phanom Di", World Archaeology, Vol. 24, No. 1, June, 1992.

MALONEY; B.K. - "Late Holocene climatic change in South East Asia: the palynological evidence and its implica tions for archaeology", World Archaeology, Vol. 24, No.1, June, 1992.

MARSHALL; H.I. - "The Karen People of Burma - A Study in Anthropology and Ethnology", University of Colombia Press, 1922.

QUARITCH WALES; H.G. - "Towards Angkor", G.G. Harrap & Co., 1937.

SCHEBESTA; P. - "Among the Forest Dwarfs of Malaya", Hutchinson & Co., 1929.

SKEAT; W.W. & BLAGDEN; C.O. - "Pagan Races of the Malay Peninsula", 2 vols., MacMillan and Co., 1906.

STENCIL; R. et al. - Science, Vol. 193, 23.07.1976.

TAYLES; M. & N. - World Archaeology, Vol.24, No.1, June 1992.

WERNER; E.T.C. - "Myths and Legends of China", G.G. Harrap & Co., 1922.

INDONESIA:

d'ALMEIDA; W.B. - "Life in Java", 2 vols., Hurst & Blackett, 1864.

COVARRUBIAS; M. - "Island of Bali", Alfred A. Knopf, 1937.

FURNESS; W.H. - "The Home-Life of Borneo Head-Hunters", J.B. Lippincott 6, Philadelphia, U.S.A.1902.

GOMES; E.H. - "Seventeen Years Among the Sea Dyaks of Borneo", Seeley & Co., 1911.

HEINE-GELDERN; R. & LOEB; E. - "Sumatra: Its History and People", Wiener Beitrage zur Kulturgeschichte und Linguisti, Austria, 1935.

HICKSON; S.J. - "A Naturalist in North Celebes", John Murray, 1889.

HOOP; A.N.J.T.T. van der, - "Megalithische Oudheden in Zuid-Sumatra", Vol. 3, W.H. Thieme & CIE, Zutphen, Netherlands, 1932.

HOSE; C. & McDOUGALL; W. - "The Pagan Tribes of Borneo", 2 vols., MacMillan & Co., 1912.
HYDE; T. - "An Account of the Famous Prince of Gilolo", England, 1692.
KAUDERN; W. - "Megalithic Finds in Celebes" - Ethnographic Studies of Celebes V, 1938.
KEMPERS; A.J.B. - "Ancient Indonesian Art", Harvard Uni. Press, 1959.
LUMHOLTZ; C. - "Through Central Borneo", T. Fisher Unwin, 1920.
PERRY; W.J. - "The Megalithic Culture of Indonesia", Victoria University Publications, Ethnological Series No. 3., Manchester, 1918.
REED; W.A. - "Negritoes of Zambales", Bureau of Science, Ethnological Survey Publications Vol. 2 Pt. 1, Division of Ethnology, Philippine Islands, 1903/4.
RUTTER; O. - "The Pagans of North Borneo", Hutchinson & Co. (Pub.) Ltd., 1929.
SCHELTEMA; J.F. - "Monumental Java", MacMillan & Co., 1912.
SCHNITGER; F.M. - "Forgotten Kingdoms in Sumatra", E.J. Brill, Leiden, 1939.
VEEN; H. van der - "The Merok Feast of the Sa'dan Toradja", Martinusnijhoff, s'Gravenhage, 1965.

OCEANIA (Melanesia, Micronesia and Polynesia):

AKERBLOM; K. - "Astronomy and Navigation in Polynesia and Micronesia", Ethnographical Museum, Monograph Series, Publication No. 14, Stockholm, 1968.
BELLWOOD; P. - "Man's Conquest of the Pacific", Collins, 1978.
BAHN; P. & FLENLEY; J. - "Easter Island, Earth Island", Thames & Hudson, 1992.
BELLWOOD; P. - "The Polynesians - Prehistory of an Island People", Thames & Hudson, 1978/87.
BELLWOOD; P. - "Prehistory of the Indo-Malaysian Archipelago", Academic Press, 1985.
BERNDT; R.M. & C.H. - "The Speaking Land", Penguin Books, 1989.
BEST; E. - "The Maori", 2 Vols., Harry H. Tombs Ltd. (N.Z.), 1924.
BLACKWOOD; B.M. - "Both Sides of Buka Passage", Clarendon Press, 1935.
BONWICK; J. - "Daily Life and Origin of the Tasmanians", Sampson Low & Co., 1870.
BREWSTER; A.B. - "The Hill Tribes of Fiji", Seeley, Service & Co., 1922.
BROWN; G. - "Melanesians and Polynesians", Hutchinson & Co., 1910.
BROWN; J. MacMillan - "Peoples and Problems of the Pacific", 2 vols., ????, 1927.
BUCK; P. (TE RANGI HIROA) - "The Coming of the Maori", Maori Purposes Fund Board, 1950.
CAYLEY-WEBSTER; H. - "Through New Guinea: and Other Cannibal Countries", Unwin, 1898.
CHRISTIAN; F.W. - "Tahiti and the Marquesas Islands", Robert Scott Pub.. 1910.
CODRINGTON; R.H. - "Melanesian Anthropology and Folk-Lore", Clarendon Press, 1891.
CONNOLLY; R. & ANDERSON; R. - "First Contact", Viking Books Ltd., 1897.
DEACON; A.B. - "Malekula - A Vanishing People in the New Hebrides", George Routledge & Kegan Paul, 1934.
ELLIS; W. - "Polynesian Researches", 4 Volumes, London, 1832.
FISON; L. - "The Nanga", Journal of the Anthropological Institute of Great Britain, Vol. XIV, Trubner & Co., 1885.
FORNANDER; A. - "An Account of the Polynesian Race", 3 vols., English and Foreign Philosophical Society, 1878.
FOX; C.E. - "The Threshold of the Pacific", Kegan Paul & Alfred A. Knopf, 1924.
GIFFORD; E.W. - "Tongan Myths and Tales", Bernice Bishop Bulletin No. 8, 1924.
GOSDEN; C. - "Production systems and the colonization of the Western Pacific", World Archaeology, Vol. 24, No. 1, June, 1992.
GRAVES; M.W. & ADDISON; D.J. - "The Polynesian settlement of the Hawaiian Archipelago: integrating models and methods in archaeological interpretation", World Archaeology, Vol. 26, No. 3, Feb., 1995
GREY; G. - "Journals of Two Expeditions of Discovery in North-West and Western Australia 1837-9", 2 Vols., London, 1841.
GRIMBLE; A. - "Migrations, Myth and Magic from the Gilbert Islands", R.K.P., 1972.
HADDON; A.C. - "Headhunters, Black, White, and Brown", Methuen & Co., 1901.
HANDY; E.S. Craighill. - "The Native Culture in the Marquesas", Bernice P. Bishop Museum Bulletin 9, 1923.
HATHER; J.G. - "The Archaeobotany of subsistence in the Pacific", World Archaeology, Vol.24, No.1, June, 1992.
HEYERDAHL; T. - "Aku-Aku", Penguin Books, 1960.
HEYERDAHL; T. - "American Indians in the Pacific", George Allen & Unwin, 1952.
HOLMES; J.H. - "In Primitive New Guinea", Seeley, Service & Co., 1924.

HOWITT; A.W. - "The Native Tribes of South-East Australia", MacMillan & Co., 1904.

IVENS; W.G. - "Melanesians of the South-East Solomon Islands", Kegan Paul Trench Trubner, 1927.

IVENS; W.G. - "The Island Builders of the Pacific", Seeley, Service & Co., 1930.

LAYARD; J. - "Stone Men of Malekula", Chatto & Windus, 1942.

MALINOWSKI; B. - "Argonauts of the Western Pacific", Routledge, & Kegan Paul, 1922.

MATHEW: J. - "Eaglehawk and Crow", D. Nutt, London, 1899.

MCBRYDE; I. - "Kulin greenstone quarries: the social contexts of production and distribution for the Mt. William site", World Archaeology, Vol. 16, No. 2, Oct. 1984.

MOUNTFORD; C.P. - "Ayers Rock - Its People, Their Beliefs and Their Art", Angus & Robertson, 1965.

MOUNTFORD; C.P. - "Records of the American-Australian Scientific Expedition to Arnhem Land", Vol. 1, Melbourne University Press, 1956.

MOUNTFORD; C.P. - "The Tiwi - Their Art, Myth and Ceremony", Phoenix House, London, 1958.

MOUNTFORD: C.P. - "Winbaraku and the Myth of Jarapiri", Rigby Ltd., Publishers, 1968.

RIESENFELD; A. - "The Megalithic Culture of Melanesia", E.J. Brill, Leiden, 1950.

ROBERTSON; H.A. - "Erromanga - The Martyr Isle", Hodder & Stoughton, 1902.

ROTH; W.E. - "Ethnological Studies Among the North-West-Central Queensland Aborigines", Government Printer, Brisbane, 1897.

ROUTLEDGE; K. Scoresby. - "The Mystery of Easter Island", Sifton, Praed & Co., 1919.

RUTTER; O. - "The Pagans of North Borneo", Hutchinson & Co., 1929.

SELIGMANN; C.G. - "The Melanesians of British New Guinea", Cambridge University Press, 1910.

SHARP; A. - "The Journal of Jacob Roggeveen", Oxford/Clarendon Press, 1970.

SKINNER; H.D. - "The Morioris of Chatham Islands", Memoirs of the Bernice P. Bishop Museum, Vol. 9, No. 1, 1923.

SMITH; S.P. - "Hawaiiki", Whitcombe & Tombs, New Zealand, 1904.

SPEISER; F. - "Ethnographische Materialien Aus Den Neuen Hebriden", Berlin, 1923.

SPEISER; F. - "Two Years with the Natives in the Western Pacific", Mills & Boon, 1913.

SPENCER; B. & GILLAN; F.J. (N.T.C.A.) - "The Native Tribes of Central Australia", MacMillan & Co., 1899.

SPENCER; B. & GILLAN; F.J. (T.N.T.C.A.) - "The Northern Tribes of Central Australia", MacMillan & Co., 1904.

STAIR; J.B. - "Old Samoa", Religious Tract Society, 1897.

STIMSON; J.F. - "Legends of Maui and Tahaki", Bernice P. Bishop Museum Bulletin 127, 1934.

SUGGS; R.C. - "Archaeology of Nuka Hiva", Anthropological Papers of the American Museum of Natural History, N.Y., 1961.

THOMSEN; B. H. - "The Fijians", William Heinemann, 1908.

TILBURG; J.-A. van, - "Easter Island", British Museum Press, 1994.

TILBURG; J.-A. van & Lee; G. - "Symbolic stratigraphy: Rock Art and the Monolithic Statues of Easter Island", World Archaeology, Vol. 19, No. 2, Oct. 1987.

WHARTON; W.J.L. - "Captain Cook's Journal", Ellis Stock, London, 1893.

WILLIAMSON; R.W. - "The Mafulu Mountain People of British New Guinea", MacMillan & Co., 1912.

WOLLASTON; A.F.R. - "Pygmies and Papuans", Smith, Elder & Co., 1912.

GENERAL:

BAILLIE; M.G.L. - "Marking in marker dates: towards an archaeology with historical precision", World Archaeology, Vol. 23, No. 2, Oct., 1991.

BIBBY; G. - "Looking for Dilmun", Stacey International Publishers, 1970/96.

BLACK; J. & GREEN; A. - "Gods, Demons and Symbols of Ancient Mesopotamia", British Museum Publications, 1992.

CAVALLI-SFORZA; L.L. et al. - "The History and Geography of Human Genes", Princeton University Press, 1994.

CAMPBELL; J. - "The Way of the Animal Powers", Times Books, 1983.

CHAMBERLAIN; A.T. - "Chronologies", World Archaeology, Vol. 23, No. 2, Oct., 1991.

CLAY; A.T. - "The Empire of the Amorites", Yale Oriental Series, Researches, vol. 6, 1919.

CULICAN; W. - "The First Merchant Venturers: The Ancient Levant", Thames & Hudson, 1966.

DALLEY; S. - "Myths from Mesopotamia", Oxford University Press, 1989.

DRIVER; G.R. - "Canaanite Myths and Legends", T. & T. Clark, 1956.

DOTHAN; M. & T. - "The People of the Sea", Maxwell MacMillan International, 1992.

DROWER; F.S./STEVENS; E.S. (B.Z.) - "The Book of the Zodiac", Royal Asiatic Society, London, 1949.

DROWER; E.S./STEVENS; E.S. (P.A.) - "Peacock Angel", John Murray, 1941.

DROWER; E.S./STEVENS; E.S. (M.I.I.) - "The Mandaeans of Iraq and Iran", Clarendon Press, 1937,

DROWER; E.S./STEVENS; E.S. (T.T.Q.) - "The Thousand and Twelve Questions", Deutsche Akademie Der Wissenschaften Zu Berlin, Institut fur Orientforschung, V Ekoffentliching No. 32, 1960.

DUNDES; A. - "The Flood Myth", University of California Press, 1988.

EIDEM; J. & HOJLUND; F. - "Trade or Diplomacy? Assyria and Dilmun in the Eighteenth Century B.C.", World Archaeology, Vol. 24, No., 3, Feb., 1993.

ELIADE; M. - "The Encyclopeadia of Religion", MacMillan & Co., Vol. 9., 1987.

GURNEY; O.R. - "The Hittites", Penquin Books, 1952/1990.

HARDEN; D. - "The Phoenicians", Thames & Harden, 1962.

HASTINGS; J. - Encyclopeadia of Religion and Ethics", Vol. viii, 1915.

HAUG; M. - "Sacred Language, Writings, and Religion of the Parsees", Bombay, 1862.

HEINE-Geldern; R. von - "Die Asiatische Herfunnft Der Sudamerikanischen Metalltechnik", in Paedeima, Volume 5, pp347-423, (Frobenius Institut), Bamberg, 1954.

KING; L.W. - "Legends of Babylon and Egypt in Relation to Hebrew Tradition", British Academy, London, 1918.

KRAMER; S.N. - "Sumerian Mythology", Harper & Row, 1961.

LANGDON; S. - "The Babylonian Epic of Creation", Clarendon Press, 1923.

MARTYNOV; A.I. - "The Ancient Art of Northern Asia", University of Illinois Press, 1991.

MELLAART; J. - "Earliest Civilisations of the Near East", Thames & Hudson, 1965.

OATES; J. - "Babylon", Thames & Hudson, 1979.

OATES; J. - "Trade and power in the Fifth and Fourth Millennia B.C.: New Evidence from Northern Mesopotamia", World Archaeology, Vol. 24, No. 3, Feb., 1993.

PHILLIPS; W. - "Qataban and Sheba", Victor Gollanz, 1955.

POTTS; T.F. - World Archaeology, Vol. 24, No. 3, Feb., 1993. (2 articles).

POTTS; D.T. - "The Archaeology Of Elam", Cambridge University Press, 1999.

SANDARS; N.K. - "The Sea Peoples", Thames & Hudson, 1978/85.

TRIGGER; B.G. - "Prospects for a World Archaeology", World Archaeology, Vol.18, No. 1, 1986.

DAUM; W. - "Yemen: 3000 Years of Art and Civilization in Arabia Felix", Pinguin-Verlag, Umschau-Verlag, 1987.

ZAEHNER; R.C. - "Zurvan, a Zoroastrian Dilemma", Clarendon Press/Oxford University Press, 1955.

INDEX

Ababou: 633-5; 653; 655;

Abba/Abe: 617; 721;

Abe Mango: 619;

Achacallas/Achachilas: 427; 455; 790;

Achchan/Acchu (see Ucchu).

Adya-bija/Adya-Sakti/ Kali-Bija/Padmamunda: 242;

Agni: 68; 169; 174; 334; 384; 490/1; 505/6; 516/7; 573; 574; 597; 601-3; 605; 614; 649; 671; 704; 705; 708; 720; 800;

Agni-Eyes: 609/10;

Agni-Kayana (see also Inti-Hautana): 603-7;

Agni-Kula: 418; 422; 766;

Agriculture: 176; 180; 181; 183; 197/8; 202/3; 206; 211; 220/1; 252; 285/6; 295; 299/300; 399;

Aguada: 239;

Ahau/Ao/Hau/Sau/Chau: 105; 431; 506; 510; 513; 569; 637; 740; 746;

Ahpikondia: 416; 613; 621; 628; 651;

Ahriman: 424; 449; 678;

Ahuena: 142;

Ahuia-teteo: 466;

Ai Apaec: 514;

Ainu: 35; 48; 67; 92; 130; 136; 146; 454; 525;

Airavata: 575; 608; 792; 803;

Aitu: 105; 790;

Aiyu/Aiya-appa (see Ayya; Aiya).

Akapana: 289-95; 468-77; 483; 486-94; 495; 589;

Akimbo Imagery: 88; 89;

Akkad: 16; 17; 19; 165-7; 325; 454; 522;

Alasaya: 356/7;

Alcauiza: 325; 328; 414; 608;

Alcheringa/Ularaka: 71; 80/1; 561; 568; 790;

Alexander: 19;

Alinga/alluna: 517;

A-mautas: 714;

Ama/An/Anna: 335;

Amaru: 281; 450; 674; 787;

Ambats (see also Kabats): 358; 456; 649;

Anatolia: 351; 364; 379-81; 380; 659; 673; 678; 700; 702; 716; 717/8; 730; 754; 792;

Ancon: 184;

Andaman Islands: 117;

Andean Corridors: 148;

Anga: 61: 635; 636;

Angkor Wat: 294; 580; 581;

Animal Headdress: 229; 230;

Animal Sacrifices: 409; 410/1; 491; 510;

Animal Tallow (see Llama Fat).

Anti-suyu: 342; 375; 406; 414; 455; 477;

Ao/Aoba/Au: 636/8; 642;

Ao-marau: 569;

Apadana/Apana: 488-94; 580;

Apinaye: 344; 520;

Apo/Apu: 506; 507; 554; 555; 571; 755/6; 758-62;

Apu-Inti: 409; 496;

Apu-Saqro: 445;

Apu-Tampu: 322; 427; 755/6;

Ara: 426;

Arabia: 79:

Araucanians: 138; 144; 239; 449; 497;

Aravan/Iravan/Arrnuan: 423; 606; 669; 707; 748; 766;

Architecture: 111; 222; 226/7;

Areca Nut: 91; 722;

Areois/Areoi/Aeroi: 42; 465-8; 624; 734;

Ari: 520;

Ariki: 11; 12; 31; 87; 134; 145; 148; 244; 390; 394; 422; 430; 515; 741; 790;

Arnauan/Arnavan (see Aravan).

Arrows-into-Sky: 112;

Arundati: 568;

Aryaman: 513

Aryavarrta (see Airavata.

Asoka: 19; 578; 583; 761;

Aspero: 164; 167; 171;

Assyria: 19; 285; 300; 305; 325; 709;

Asuras/Assurs/Agaria: 384-6; 396; 510; 627; 659/60; 700; 701; 717; 730;

Asvins: 597; 598; 599; 601-3; 609;

Atahualpa: 158; 244; 570;

Atea: 614;

Athavan (see Aravan)

Atua/Aittah: 72; 107; 142; 326/7; 331; 412;

Auquis: 756; 765;

Ava (see Chiriguanos)

Ava Chumbi: 562; 570-3; 664;

Axe Money: 268/9; 316; 318;

Axis Mundae (see World Tree)

Ayar: 145; 158; 244; 342; 350; 468; 574; 576; 583; 590; 605;

Ayar Cachi: 322; 324; 325; 328; 329; 548; 607;

Ayar Manco (see Manco Capac)

Ayar Ucho: 322; 324; 325; 328; 329; 477; 515; 548; 805;

Ayar Ziwa: 425;

Ayavas: 333; 334;

Aya-viri: 576;

Ayllu (see also Ayu): 348; 351; 356; 373-6; 788;

Aymara: 234; 238; 244;